# GLOBAL BUSINESS REGULATION

Across an amazing sweep of the critical areas of business regulation – from contract, intellectual property and corporations law, to trade, telecommunications, labour standards, drugs, food, transport and environment – this book confronts the question of how the regulation of business has shifted from national to global institutions. Based on interviews with 500 international leaders in business and government, *Global Business Regulation* examines the role played by global institutions such as the WTO, the OECD, IMF, Moodys and the World Bank, as well as various NGOs and significant individuals. The authors argue that effective and decent global regulation depends on the determination of individuals to engage with powerful agendas and decision-making bodies that would otherwise be dominated by concentrated economic interests. This book will become a standard reference for readers in business, law, politics and international relations.

**John Braithwaite** is Professor in the Research School of Social Sciences at the Australian National University. His previous publications include *Crime, Shame and Reintegration* (Cambridge University Press, 1989), *Corporations, Crime and Accountability* (with B. Fisse, Cambridge University Press, 1993) and *Responsive Regulation* (with I. Ayres, 1992). He has been active for three decades in social movement politics.

**Peter Drahos** is the Herchel Smith Senior Fellow in the Centre for Commercial Law Studies at Queen Mary and Westfield College, University of London. He is the author of *A Philosophy of Intellectual Property* (1996).

# GLOBAL BUSINESS REGULATION

*John*
**BRAITHWAITE**
*Australian National University*

*Peter*
**DRAHOS**
*Queen Mary and Westfield College,
University of London*

CAMBRIDGE
UNIVERSITY PRESS

PUBLISHED BY THE PRESS SYNDICATE OF THE UNIVERSITY OF CAMBRIDGE
The Pitt Building, Trumpington Street, Cambridge, United Kingdom

CAMBRIDGE UNIVERSITY PRESS
The Edinburgh Building, Cambridge CB2 2RU, UK
40 West 20th Street, New York, NY 10011–4211, USA
10 Stamford Road, Oakleigh, 3166, Australia
Ruiz de Alarcón 13, 28014, Madrid, Spain
Dock House, The Waterfront, Cape Town 8001, South Africa

http://www.cambridge.org

First published 2000
Reprinted 2001

Printed in China by Everbest Printing Co. Ltd.

*Typeface* Giovanni (*Adobe*) 9.5/12.5 pt.    *System* QuarkXPress®   [PK]

*A catalogue record for this book is available from the British Library*

*National Library of Australia Cataloguing in Publication data*
Braithwaite, John, 1951–.
Global business regulation.
Bibliography.
Includes index.
ISBN 0 521 78033 0.
ISBN 0 521 78499 9 (pbk.).
1. Foreign trade regulation. 2. Industrial policy –
International cooperation. 3. Consumer protection –
International cooperation. I. Drahos, Peter, 1955–.
II. Title
381.34

ISBN 0 521 78033 0 hardback
ISBN 0 521 78499 9 paperback

Esther Peterson, 9 December 1906 – 20 December 1997

# Dedication

We decided to dedicate this book to one of the many interview informants who touched our spirits. Esther Peterson was chosen because she shaped our ideas in the final chapter of this book and because she was a key player in not one but three great social movements – the labour, women's and consumer movements. Our method of an anthropology of global cultures was only possible because during the 1990s there were people still alive who, like Esther, were players in the crucial globalizations of regulation, most of which have occurred since the Great Depression. Esther died, aged ninety-one, in 1997.

Esther Peterson first organized and won a Boston strike in the 1930s among women who sewed dresses at home. She was arrested several times fighting for the first wages and working hours Act in the US (1938) and fought on for women's rights to the same conditions of employment as men. Esther Peterson worked for the International Ladies Garment Workers Union, the American Federation of Teachers and the Amalgamated Clothing Workers of America. In the 1940s and 1950s she raised her family of four children overseas, when her husband had diplomatic postings to Europe. There Esther internationalized her engagement with the labour and women's movements. Later she served on the Women's Commission of the International Confederation of Free Trade Unions. In Brussels in 1952 she founded an international school for women in the trade union movement.

This kind of work exemplified her philosophy: 'She always worked according to the pattern: first educate and then organize people – teach them that with knowledge and united strength they can influence the politics that govern their lives' (*Consuming Interest* 1985: 14). Eleanor Roosevelt was a friend and mentor. Esther was Executive Director of the President's Commission on the Status of Women, chaired by Eleanor Roosevelt, that led to the Equal Pay Bill. Esther was a great compromiser. A piece of advice she endlessly gave to those of us she mentored was one given to her by Eleanor Roosevelt: 'always be ready to compromise…but compromise upwards!' Discussions with Esther on this theme informed the ratcheting-up analysis of Chapter 26. It is significant that this analysis was passed down from Eleanor Roosevelt, who our empirical work has shown to be the quiet entrepreneur of events now seen as beginning the birth of regulatory globalization.

John F. Kennedy appointed Esther Peterson as an Assistant Secretary of Labor and Director of the Women's Bureau of the Labor Department: 'During the Kennedy years she belonged to his "little Cabinet" of special advisers' (*Consuming Interest* 1985: 14). Lyndon Johnson also appointed Esther to the White House, as his special adviser on consumer issues, a capacity in which Jimmy Carter later also appointed her. Later still, she worked for the Clinton administration in a largely honorary role with the US delegation to the UN.

During the Nixon and Ford administrations she was vilified by some in the consumer movement for doing something unprecedented: she took a job as Vice-President for Consumer Affairs at Giant Food Inc. Effective compromiser that she was, she persuaded Giant Food to begin many supermarket policies that we now take for granted. One was label-unit pricing, so a calculator is not needed to work out whether 1 kg for $2.29 is better value than 1.2 kg for $2.79. She persuaded Giant Food into trying nutritional labelling before it was required by law, and date-marking that consumers could read (previously, dates on perishables were in letter-numeric codes that only the store could read). Discussing this experience with Esther shaped our thinking about individual entrepreneurship and Latour's theory of power as translation, as developed in several of our later chapters.

Esther Peterson's greatest disappointment came in her eighties, when her leadership as the Consumers International representative to the UN repeatedly failed to secure the UN Code of Conduct for Transnational Corporations. Here, as in the campaign for the UN Guidelines for Consumer Protection and the Kennedy consumer rights campaigns of the 1960s, she was an ally of the environment movement, fighting for language about regulating the environmental impact of production and consumption. Yet there were successes late in life too. Rhoda Karpartkin, President of Consumers Union, on whose board Esther served, said in the *New York Times* of 23 December 1997:

> **Peterson, Esther**...a great woman, and a great consumer leader and activist...you couldn't fool her...you couldn't stop her when she was fighting for what she believed in. As Consumers International's representative to the UN, she lobbied the UN successfully to adopt the UN Guidelines for Consumer Protection. They've become the basis for many consumer protection laws around the world, especially in Third World countries.

Esther Peterson helped us to see that international agreements did not need to be enforceable to count: 'Once a nation puts its name to an international document, there can be enormous moral pressure exerted to honor it. No nation enjoys being condemned as hypocritical'. From this, Esther, during her last decade of life, acquired the seemingly implausible belief that a green global consumer movement could become the force in the twenty-first century that her beloved labour and women's movements had been in the twentieth century. In our final chapter, we conclude that this belief is not beyond the bounds of plausibility.

# Contents

# Abbreviations

| | |
|---|---|
| ACTN | Advisory Committee for Trade Negotiations |
| AIPPI | International Association for the Protection of Industrial Property |
| APEC | Asia-Pacific Economic Cooperation Forum |
| ASEAN | Association of South-East Asian Nations |
| Basle Committee | Basle Committee on Banking Supervision |
| BAT | Best Available Technology |
| BCSD | Business Council of Sustainable Development |
| BEUC | Bureau of European Consumer Unions |
| BIAC | Business and Industry Advisory Committee to the OECD |
| BIRPI | United International Bureaux for the Protection of Intellectual Property |
| BIS | Bank for International Settlements |
| BSA | Business Software Alliance |
| CIA | Central Intelligence Agency (US) |
| CPMP | Committee for Proprietary Medicinal Products |
| CSD | Commission on Sustainable Development (UN) |
| EC | European Commission |
| ECE | Economic Commission for Europe (UN) |
| ECIS | European Committee for Interoperable Systems |
| ECOSOC | Economic and Social Council (UN) |
| EFPIA | European Federation of Pharmaceutical Manufacturers Association |
| EFTA | European Free Trade Association |
| EMAS | Eco-Management and Audit Scheme |
| EMEA | European Agency for the Evaluation of Medicinal Products |
| EMS | European Monetary System |
| EPA | Environment Protection Agency (US) |
| EPO | European Patent Office |
| EU | European Union (the term 'European Union' came into conventional use after the Treaty on European Union came into force on 1 November 1993. Prior to that the term 'European Community' was used) |
| FAA | Federal Aviation Administration (US) |
| FAO | Food and Agriculture Organization |
| FATF | Financial Action Task Force |
| FCC | Federal Communications Commission (US) |
| FDA | Food and Drug Administration (US) |
| FDI | Foreign Direct Investment |
| FIA | International Automobile Federation |

| | |
|---|---|
| Final Act | Final Act Embodying the Results of the Uruguay Round of Multilateral Trade Negotiations, Marrakesh, 15 April 1994 |
| FTC | Federal Trade Commission (US) |
| G-5 | France Germany, Japan, UK and US (the currencies of these countries constitute the basket of currencies for the Special Drawing Right of the IMF) |
| G-7 | Canada, France, Italy, Germany, Japan, UK and US (held annually to discuss international economic policy) |
| G-8 | G-7 plus Russia |
| G-10 | Belgium, Canada, France, Germany, Italy, Japan, Netherlands, Sweden, Switzerland, UK and US (the ten principal creditor nations of the IMF. Switzerland became the eleventh member of G-10 when it became a full member of IMF in 1992) |
| G-77 | Group of developing nations (more than seventy-seven) |
| GATS | General Agreement on Trade in Services (part of the Final Act) |
| GATT | General Agreement on Tariffs and Trade 1947, as revised. The Final Act (see above) contains the General Agreement on Tariffs and Trade 1994 which is defined to include the GATT 1947 as revised. GATT 1947 never became an official international organization, although the contracting parties to it were assisted by a GATT secretariat. The WTO is formally established by the Agreement Establishing the World Trade Organization, which forms part of the Final Act. We use 'GATT' primarily to refer to the GATT regime as it stood before the Final Act |
| GEF | Global Environmental Facility |
| GSP | Generalized System of Preferences |
| HACCP | Hazard Analysis Critical Control Points |
| HAI | Health Action International |
| IACS | International Association of Classification Societies |
| IAEA | International Atomic Energy Agency |
| IAIS | International Association of Insurance Supervisors |
| IAPI | International Airline Passengers Association |
| IASC | International Accounting Standards Committee |
| IATA | International Air Transport Association |
| ICAO | International Civil Aviation Organization |
| ICC | International Chamber of Commerce |
| ICFTU | International Confederation of Free Trade Unions |
| ICH | International Conference on Harmonizationof Technical Requirements for Registration of Pharmaceuticals for Human Use |
| ICOLP | Industry Cooperative for Ozone Layer Protection |
| ICSID | Interntional Centre for the Settlement of Investment Disputes |
| IFALPA | International Federation of Airline Pilots Associations |
| IFPMA | International Federation of Pharmaceutical Manufacturers Associations |
| IIPA | International Intellectual Property Alliance |
| ILO | International Labour Organization |
| ILSI | International Life Sciences Institute |

| | |
|---|---|
| IMF | International Monetary Fund |
| IMO | International Maritime Organization |
| INPO | Institute of Nuclear Power Operators |
| INTELSAT | International Telecommunications Satellite Organization |
| INTUG | International Telecommunications Users Group |
| IOCU | International Organization of Consumers Unions |
| IOSCO | International Organization of Securities Commissions |
| IPC | Intellectual Property Committee |
| ISO | International Organization for Standardization |
| ITO | International Trade Organization |
| ITU | International Telecommunication Union |
| JAA | Joint Aviation Authority (Europe) |
| MAI | Multilateral Agreement on Investment (OECD) |
| MaLAM | Medical Lobby for Appropriate Marketing |
| MFN | Most Favoured Nation |
| MITI | Ministry for International Trade and Industry (Japan) |
| MOU | Memorandum of Understanding |
| MPA | Motion Picture Association of America |
| NAFTA | North American Free Trade Agreement |
| NATO | North Atlantic Treaty Organization |
| NGBT | Negotiating Group on Basic Telecommunications |
| NGO | Non-government Organization |
| NHTSA | National Highway Traffic Safety Administration (US) |
| NPT | Nuclear Non-Proliferation Treaty |
| NRC | Nuclear Regulatory Commission (US) |
| NYSE | New York Stock Exchange |
| OECD | Organization for Economic Cooperation and Development |
| OFTEL | Office of Telecommunications (UK) |
| OICA | International Organization of Motor Vehicle Manufacturers |
| OSHA | Occupational Safety and Health Administration (US) |
| PTT | Post, Telephone and Telegraph |
| Quad | Canada, EU, Japan and US |
| RAPS | Regulatory Affairs Professionals Society |
| SEC | Securities and Exchange Commission (US) |
| SPS | Agreement on the Application of Sanitary and Phytosanitary Measures of the GATT |
| TMI | Three Mile Island |
| TNC | Transnational Corporation |
| TRIMS | Agreement on Trade Related Investment Measures (part of the Final Act) |
| TRIPS | Agreement on Trade Related Aspects of Intellectual Property Rights (part of the Final Act) |
| UN | United Nations |
| UNCED | UN Conference on Environment and Development |
| UNCITRAL | UN Commission on International Trade Law |
| UNCTAD | UN Conference on Trade and Development |

| | |
|---|---|
| UNDP | UN Development Program |
| UNEP | UN Environment Program |
| UNESCO | UN Educational, Scientific and Cultural Organization |
| UNICE | Union of Industries of the European Community |
| UNIDROIT | International Institute for the Unification of Private Law |
| Uruguay Round | Uruguay Round of Multilateral Trade Negotiations |
| USTR | Office of the US Trade Representative |
| WANO | World Association of Nuclear Operators |
| WCTU | Women's Christian Temperance Union |
| WHO | World Health Organization |
| WIPO | World Intellectual Property Organization |
| WTO | World Trade Organization |

# Figures and Tables

# Part I
## INTRODUCTION

## CHAPTER 1

The Historical Canvas

Most of the significant globalization of rules occurred in the twentieth century, particularly since 1970. This globalization has proceeded furthest with business regulation because of imperatives such as those of international trade, saving the planet from environmental collapse and regulating nuclear and chemical weapons. Still, most of the rules that have the greatest effect on our lives are extremely local – the rules that regulate our family lives, workplaces and neighbourhoods. The globalization of business regulation has been a historically uneven process. While the globalization of business rules has been mostly partial and recent, the globalization of many of the foundation concepts in the laws that regulate business has been total and existed for centuries. For example, all states have elaborate written laws enforceable by institutions called courts, where outcomes can be tested under the guidance of rules of evidence. Once those laws were carved in stone; now they are universally printed on paper; soon they will be universally accessible electronically. We know of no contemporary national legal system that does not confer powers on a central bank, that does not tax centrally, that does not have a concept of a legally enforceable contract or of crime. Legal systems do vary (though decreasingly so) according to whether business corporations can be conceived as having committed a crime, but they all enforce sanctions against corporations collectively (as distinct from only against their individual owners). So we need to be careful, in detecting differences in the world, not to lose sight of the fact that many of the fundamentals of business regulation are utterly global.

Outside Europe and the US, even at the level of rules, the extent to which states have become rule-takers rather than rule-makers is greater than most citizens think, largely because when governments announce new regulatory laws they are somewhat embarrassed to disclose that the national legislature voted for those laws without having any say in shaping them. As Australian authors, we note, for example, that for years some of Australia's air safety standards have been written by the Boeing Corporation in Seattle, or if not by that corporation, by the US Federal Aviation Administration in Washington. Australia's ship safety laws have been written by the International Maritime Organization in London, its motor vehicle safety standards by Working Party 29 of the Economic Commission for Europe and its food standards by the Codex Alimentarius Commission in Rome. Many of Australia's pharmaceuticals standards have been set by a joint collaboration of the Japanese, European and US industries and their regulators, called the International Conference on Harmonization. Its telecommunications standards have been substantially set in Geneva by the International Telecommunication Union. The Chair (and often the Vice-Chair) of most of the expert committees that effectively set those standards in Geneva are

Americans. The Motorola Corporation has been particularly effective in setting telecommunications standards through its chairmanship of those committees. As a consequence, Motorola patents have been written into many of the ITU standards that we all must follow. This global privatization of public law seems benign to some, though not to the person who asked how many Microsoft engineers it took to change a lightbulb. 'None', was the answer. Bill Gates simply declared darkness the industry standard.

Many chapters show the importance of the Roman empire to the globalization of foundation concepts. The ancient Greek, Chinese, Indian and pre- and post-Islamic Arab empires have left some quite significant traces in various chapters, as indeed have smaller maritime powers such as Rhodes. Diasporas of Italians, Chinese, Jews and Armenians across the globe after the heyday of the empires that had encompassed them are important to global modelling of fundamental concepts like bookkeeping rules and the very idea of the business corporation. Some of the great early modern empires, such as the Habsburg empire, however, have left much less significant globalized legacies, though there are some minor Habsburg traces in the regulation of telecommunications (Chapter 14), food standards (Chapter 16) and even competition law (Chapter 10).

When we say the history of business regulation has been uneven, we refer to the fact that after the sacking of Rome the legacy of Roman law was lost to Europe for almost a millennium. We refer to the reversal of the liberalization of trade rules under the British hegemony of the nineteenth century, the resulting collapse of international trade, the beggar-thy-neighbour policies of early US hegemony and the unravelling of the global financial system in the early 1930s. We see the US Federal Reserve and the Bank of England leading the world down to financial deregulation in the early 1980s, then leading global prudential standards back up through the G-10 after the banking crises of the mid 1980s. In reverse, the US Federal Communications Commission led the world into an international regime to control communications in space in the 1960s, then dismantled it piece by piece in the 1980s.

It is a mistake to see history in terms of the rise of powerful states like Russia and Germany unifying regulatory laws across a large swathe of national territory, then later working with European states toward European harmonization/mutual recognition and ultimately with all states toward global convergence. Not only was this cumulative story interrupted by Russia in 1917 and East Germany in 1945 changing to a radically oppositional regulatory order, but harmonization within states as a building-block of harmonization across states is not what happened. Considerable inter-state harmonization of weights and measures, for example, was negotiated in the ancient world to facilitate trade, particularly between North Africa, the Middle East and southern Europe. Across the Indus Valley of the Indian subcontinent in 2300–2000 BC, there was a 'wealth of standardized weights and measures' (Mann 1986: 106). No *nation* had unified weights and measures laws until the nineteenth century (Mann 1986: 423); the International Bureau of Weights and Measures was established in 1875. In the second millennium, when Egypt was the leading gold producer, gold appears to have operated in the manner of an international currency. The vast ancient Chinese civilization probably has the longest history of coinage and, through the invention of paper money, helped unify what remains today more than a fifth of the world's people. In contrast, the English nation-state did not possess a uniform coinage until the 1160s, nor France until 1262.

We think Michael Mann (1986) is right that the building of capitalist regulatory institutions in medieval Europe is generally underestimated, just as the significance of the northern Italian

Renaissance is somewhat overplayed. The shared identity of Christendom was the important element in the pan-European medieval harmonization of so many of the fundamentals of business law (see the discussion of the law merchant in Chapter 7). There was northern Mediterranean leadership toward 'general recognition of norms regarding property rights and free exchange. These were guaranteed by a mixture of local customs and privileges, some judicial regulation by weak states, but above all by the common social identity provided by Christian Europe' (Mann 1986: 504). Honouring contracts was a Christian thing to do, and it obtained specificity of meaning in the informal context of this shared merchant identity rather than as a result of canon or state law, which followed business custom more than led it.

A summary might be that the most important conceptual legal foundations of globalized business regulation were laid in ancient Rome and medieval Western Europe. The most important institutional organizational foundations were laid in the three decades after Bretton Woods (1944–74). Most of the limited actual harmonization and mutual recognition of rules has been accomplished since 1974.

Since that date we find that regulation of the environment, safety and financial security have ratcheted up more than they have been driven down by globalization. Normatively, one can have the view, as we do, that the environment, consumer product safety, occupational health and safety and transport safety are appallingly underregulated in most of the world. But globalization cannot be blamed for this state of affairs.

While ratcheting-up is more common than races-to-the-bottom in the regulation of safety and environment, the opposite is true of economic regulation. In domains of economic regulation beyond those that anchor financial security (e.g. capital adequacy standards for banks), we find that ratcheting-down has been the dominant dynamic – globalizing deregulation. The striking exception to this dynamic in economic regulation has been intellectual property, which has been ratcheted-up.

Among the environmental, safety and financial security domains that have been ratcheted-up are chemicals regulation, oil spills at sea, ozone-depleting substances, whaling, acid rain, nuclear safeguards and safety, occupational health and safety, discrimination in employment, freedom of association, child labour and slavery, the regulation of prescription drugs, illicit drugs and tobacco, food standards, safety at sea, motor vehicle standards, air safety, prudential regulation, accounting standards, regulation of corruption, securities and money-laundering.

Among the other domains of economic regulation where the dominant dynamic of the past quarter-century has been more one of deregulation are licensing restrictions on financial institutions, exchange rate controls, tax competition driving rates down and eliminating taxes, some (limited) driving-down of corporate law standards through corporate law havens and competition toward limited liability, reduction and elimination of tariffs, technical barriers to trade, restrictions on the free movement of investment, labour markets and professional services (beyond the domain of core security standards), breaking up of cartels and restrictive business practices, telecommunications and the economic regulation of air transport.

While the globalization of business regulation has been non-linear, in this book we have been able to reach some conclusions of general import about the process. In struggling with our data to reach these conclusions we realised an ethical dilemma lurked within them. We concluded that a basis for the strong dominating the weak, the rich defeating the poor in the world system, was their superior capacity to control and use knowledge. We hoped that we were enhancing knowledge of what makes global business regulatory systems tick. So we decided to pursue knowledge that would be illuminating to social scientists, and to place that knowledge in a framework that would be most useful to the weaker players of global regulatory games – citizen groups and developing countries. Hence, after listing (Chapter 5) the forty-four empirical conclusions that we regard as the most important, Chapter 6 foreshadows the strategic thinking of the final chapter about how our insights might be deployed to enhance the sovereignty of ordinary people, particularly those in poor, undemocratic nations. Before doing that, Chapters 2–4 outline the objectives, concepts and method of our inquiry. Part II applies this method to thirteen cases that we regard as the most important domains of business regulation. Part III analyzes the lessons from the large sweep of empirical materials discussed in Part II.

## How to Read this Book

This is undeniably a big book. One way to read it is to begin with Part I, paying particular attention to the conclusions in Chapters 5 and 6. Then the summary Tables 20.1 (p. 476), 21.1 (p. 508) and 22.1 (p. 532) are worth a look. Next, readers could skim the early, more foundational chapters of Part II (e.g. Chapters 7–12), then pay attention to those parts of Chapters 13–19 of special interest to them. Alternatively, they could read the opening section on the history of the globalization of regulation in Chapters 7–19 and the conclusion in each chapter. Chapters 20–26 (Part III) are important for all readers.

| # Globalization and Regulation

## *Overview*

Chapter 1 showed that the globalization of business regulation is a process with a long history. Roman legal principles continue to be transmitted through our regulatory traditions even though Roman armies have long ceased marching. In this process both state and non-state actors strive to establish principles of their choosing using the mechanisms at their disposal. In each of our case studies (Chapters 7–19) we present globalization as a contest of principles – a contest, for example, between the principle of harmonization and the principle of national sovereignty. Our study identifies a number of recurrently important principles (summarized in Chapter 21) and mechanisms (summarized in Chapter 22) in global business regulation. The contest among actors (summarized in Chapter 20) is unequal. Actors like the US can mobilize coercion mechanisms that are not available to weaker actors like community groups. Actors with large markets can impose trade sanctions. When staring at defeat in one international forum, they can shift the contest to a more favourable forum (Chapter 24). Yet there is one mechanism that weaker actors can use to shape regulatory outcomes – the mechanism of modelling (Chapter 25). Through devising and proliferating alternative models of regulation, the weak create opportunities for themselves to change existing regulatory orders.

In the thirteen case studies in this book no one actor appears as master of the world. Similarly, there is no master mechanism of globalization. Instead, there are webs of influence (Chapter 23). We divide these webs of influence into webs of coercion and dialogic webs. We find that actors prefer to work through webs of dialogue rather than webs of coercion. Understanding the different strands that make up these webs is fundamental to accomplishing global regulatory change. With this understanding, strategies can be developed for intervening in the webs. Successful interventions are not, as our case studies demonstrate, confined to powerful actors. Dialogic webs offer individuals the possibility of micro action to secure macro change. We do not claim that possibilities for micro action pervade dialogic webs, merely that these webs sometimes allow individuals to bring about globalization sequences that culminate in global regulatory change. There are no simple logics or manuals on how to do this. Much as chess players have to learn to choose fruitful lines of attack from a potentially overwhelming range of complex sequences of moves, so actors faced with the complexity of globalization must learn to identify the web strands that will allow them to influence the process of globalization.

Developing strategies to enhance citizen sovereignty is the subject of the final chapter of this study (Chapter 26). Global regulation does not necessarily rob citizens of their sovereignty and can, under conditions that we discuss, increase it.

## Globalization

Three distinct kinds of globalization are relevant:

1   the globalization of firms;

2   the globalization of markets;

3   the globalization of regulation.

Each type of globalization involves, at base, a comprehensive spread of a phenomenon. Global firms are firms which, originating in a specific territory, spread their operations through corporate groups and structures to other territories. Markets are where buyers and sellers meet. In the case of global markets, buyers or sellers from any one territory can meet (physically, through agents or electronically) with buyers and sellers from any other territory to conduct transactions. Financial markets are the standard example of genuinely global markets. The globalization of regulation involves the spread of some set of regulatory norms. The globalization of regulation does not mean that regulation has necessarily harmonized. Most states now have patent law (globalization), but there are many differences in the level of rules between those systems, for example in the scope of what can be patented.

Globalization is a process of degrees. Holm and Sorensen's (1995: 1) definition of globalization as the 'intensification of economic, political, social and cultural relations across borders' nicely epitomizes this claim. A phenomenon does not have to traverse the entire globe before it can be conceived as part of globalization. We can add that the more convergent the phenomenon in question, the stronger the globalization. For example, patent systems that move toward the same set of rules are more globalized than those that simply recognize the same basic principles of patentability.

Despite its length, this book is narrow in its focus upon the globalization of business regulation. The role of transnational corporations (TNCs) in the international economy is an established field of study. Perhaps the most popular topic in the globalization literature is the globalization of markets. This literature has provoked scepticism. The evidence to which sceptics point is economic evidence relating to lower than expected levels of market integration for a genuinely global economy (Held et al. 1999: 5). It is important to understand that the connections among processes of globalization of markets, regulation and firms are contingent. Even if a particular market turns out not to be globalized, it does not follow that the regulation of that market is not global regulation or that the firms active in that market are not global firms. The examples below reveal the contingent nature of the relationship between the three types of globalization and why scepticism about the existence of one does not warrant scepticism about the existence of the other two.

*Market globalization without regulatory globalization.* The market for gambling has substantially globalized, with Internet gambling and high-rollers being flown to casinos under special deals to attract their custom. But at the time of writing the regulation of gambling has not global-ized: different states regulate it in completely different ways.

*Regulatory globalization without market globalization.* In Chapter 15 we see that standards of Good Manufacturing Practices and many other requirements for prescription drugs have substan-tially globalized in recent years. Yet markets here are not global. In many of the biggest markets, the state is a monopsonistic buyer of most prescription drugs. The state then supplies the drugs to citizens as a welfare benefit. In these regimes states dictate the prices they pay; as a result there is no global price for a product. The product can sell in one market for many times the price it sells in another. There are also cases where regulatory globalization in fact prevents market globaliza-tion. For example, if global intellectual property laws allow the prohibition of parallel imports, it follows that intellectual property right holders can price-discriminate between markets by grant-ing the right of importation to an exclusive agent (Walker 1998). The price, for example, that a person pays for books in Australia is nothing like the price that a person pays for the same books in the US, even allowing for transport costs.

*Globalization of firms without market globalization.* The preceding example reveals how there can be globalization of firms without globalization of markets. In no industry sector are the largest corporations more globalized than in pharmaceuticals. The top twenty firms are quintessential transnationals that have subsidiaries in all the largest markets and many of the smaller ones.

*Globalization of firms without regulatory globalization.* There are global media companies, such as Rupert Murdoch's News Corporation. There is also a global trade in audio-visual services such as film and TV programs. With some qualifications, the regulation of media remains a national affair. States have different laws on matters such as the allowable concentration of media owner-ship, the kind of pornography or politics they tolerate in the media and the amount of domestic content they require.

## Principles, Mechanisms and Actors

These three concepts are foundational to the theories that we develop. Chapter 4 offers a detailed analysis of them. Each case study is structured around the idea that regulatory globalization is a process in which different types of actors use various mechanisms to push for or against principles. Principles serve as the infrastructure of global regulation – they pattern the complex regulatory superstructures that follow them. Principles are abstract prescriptions that guide conduct. Their relationship to other kinds of norms are discussed in Chapter 4. Mechanisms are tools that actors use to achieve their goals. In this study we limit ourselves to examining the mechanisms that are closely linked to the intentions and goals of actors – the devices that bring about their desires, we might say. Coercion and the giving of rewards are two examples of mechanisms that we analyze. More abstract mechanisms such as evolution or rationality are not part of this study. Our list of actors, as an examination of Table 20.1 (p. 476) will show, is reasonably self-explanatory.

## Regulation and Enforcement

Modernity cannot be comprehended without understanding regulation. This is most vividly illus-trated in the final two sections of Chapter 15, where we show that the wave of mass addiction to different drugs is a distinctively twentieth-century phenomenon. We conceive mass drug use in Weberian terms as a calculated attempt by individuals to regulate their bodies[1] – to control pain, lose weight, stimulate, calm, energize, instill confidence, work harder, run faster. National drug control regimes reinforce states' capacities to regulate this bodily self-regulation. Then, since 1909, global regimes appear to regulate national regulatory regimes. Regulation of regulation of regulation. Our objective is to show, in a distinctive way, that there are few projects more central to the social sciences than the study of regulation. Michel Foucault can be read as sharing this objective, though our method is very different from his. It is the regulation of scholarship by the mainstream disciplines of the social sciences that has obscured the centrality of regulation as a topic. The global perspective on regulation we promote not only reframes individuals as subjects as well as objects of regulation (as in the drug case) and states as subjects and objects of regulation (by Moody's, the IMF, the Rothschilds and Greenpeace). Understanding modernity, we find, demands the study of plural webs of many kinds of actors which regulate while being regulated themselves.

We have conceived the globalization of business regulation broadly as the globalization of the norms, standards, principles and rules that govern commerce and the globalization of their enforcement. Our starting assumption was that a globalization of rules without a globalization of enforcement would not be a process of great consequence. Empirically, we found this assumption to be false in the course of our research. Globalized rules and principles can be of consequence even if utterly detached from enforcement mechanisms. Rules or principles do not have to be incorporated into state law or international law to have significance. Modelling of self-regulatory principles and the rules of the private justice systems of corporations are crucial to understanding how the globalization of regulation happens. Chapter 23 shows the importance of one globalization sequence that starts with a globalization of business practice, an instance being the way the law merchant in the Middle Ages began to globalize ideas of contract and property (Chapter 7).

The chapter on property and contract covers terrain that Western lawyers would call private law, while the remaining chapters predominantly discuss public regulatory laws. The private/public law divide is not important in our analysis. Our object of study was the modes of regulation of business that our informants said were most fundamental to constraining and enabling business transactions. There are other private law concepts, such as tort, and public law concepts, such as crime, that are relevant in most chapters as tools for enforcing the globalization of rules. Given the way our webs of control analysis evolved, we found it better to include discussion of these recurrently important strands in all chapters.

---

1  Drug use is simply the most widely used and consequential technology for the regulation of bodies. Others are contraception, exercise, psychotherapy, diet, bulimia, alarm clocks, sex-change operations, ECT, brassieres, meditation, perfume, anger management courses, cosmetic surgery, pacemakers, straitjackets, seat-belts, prisons, workstations, education, electronic bracelets, acupuncture, aphrodisiacs, tanning studios, spectacles, tampons, hypnosis, massage, orthodontics, muzak, corrective running/walking shoes, drill, virtual reality devices, toothpaste, castration and prayer. Perhaps only castration and prayer, from this list, have not become globalized and regulated by institutions such as churches, corporations, professions and states. Even so, we cannot understand why there are fewer eunuchs now than there were formerly without understanding national and global regulation of slavery (Chapter 6) and we cannot understand why there has been deregulation of prayer by churches, schools and states without understanding constitutional change to separate church and state and the globalization of human rights to regulate freedom of religion. More generally, we show that where deregulation occurs, it is usually associated with the deployment of regulatory technologies for securing deregulation.

| Method

## Interviews and Informants

The domains of regulation chosen were those that a previous national study (Grabosky & Braithwaite 1986) had identified as the domains covered by the most important 101 business regulatory agencies in Australia. That study warranted some claim to being systematic in its coverage of the most consequential fields of regulation. As the most comprehensive study of the business regulatory agencies of a single nation, it laid a foundation for the sweep of this global study of regulation. Second, sticking with the same domains meant that one of the authors began this study with knowledge from having interviewed top regulators in ninety-six regulatory agencies and read all acts and key policy documents, for at least one country. Third, we could ask those national regulators who were the crucial players at the global level for us to interview.

As our interviews and reading proceeded, new types of actors emerged as important in shaping the globalization of different forms of regulation. Similarly, it became clear that the actors recurrently mentioned some principles in explaining what the globalizers were pursuing or the resisters were resisting. Our interviews therefore made sense of a view that globalization might be understood as a contest of principles. We are not the only scholars to reach this conclusion: for example, Meyer (1994: 128ff) and Teubner (1997) describe the resilient softness of the *Lex Mercatoria* as 'more a law of values and principles than a law of structures and rules' (Teubner 1997: 21). Finally, our informants spoke of what we came to call 'mechanisms of globalization'. The research was able to identify recurrently important mechanisms.

A deficiency in selecting what contemporaries regard as the most important domains of regulation for study today is that we neglect forms of regulation that were more important in an earlier era. For example, the regulation of postal services is not included, yet it was probably the first elaborate form of business regulation to develop. Globalization of this industry's regulation works so smoothly today that we take it for granted. The Persian empire 2500 years ago set up a sophisticated system for regulating mail deliveries (Luard 1977: 11). Roman, Arab and Habsburg (under the entrepreneurship of Franz von Taxis) international regimes followed. In 1670 there was a postal treaty between England and France. In 1863 there was the Paris Conference, which ultimately led to the establishment of the Universal Postal Union, the first intergovernmental organization with a permanent secretariat, in which most of the world participated by the late nineteenth century (Codding 1964).

In this study, our most important sources of data are the 500 people (see Acknowledgments, pp. 630–9) we interviewed as we followed the webs of influence around the globe (plus what we learnt as we hung around the corridors of organizations like the WTO). The method was just as anthropological as the methods of fieldworkers who sip tea around a campfire. We sipped Beaujolais around the bistros of Paris, New York and Geneva.

The 500 key informants were neither randomly sampled nor sampled by an atheoretical snowball technique. Rather, we began our fieldwork at what the existing literature and Australian insiders told us were the key sites of global regulatory power in places like Washington (e.g. IMF) and Vienna (e.g. IAEA). From these early interviews, we deduced that there were webs of influence whose strands we should follow until we found who was controlling them. 'You say the US Trade Representative's Office is the prime mover behind the idea of a new global investment regime. Can you recommend who the right person would be in the USTR to give us, from the horse's mouth, how they are going about this?' Once we locked onto some well-networked players in the web, they were generous in allowing us to use their names to gain entree to other key players, especially after we shared insights from our research that were valuable to them. In this way the sampling was not atheoretical snowballing, but based on fieldwork at strategic sites followed by a theoretically grounded strategy of tracing the strands of webs of control. Thus we were able to gather data from the most micro source possible – the perceptions of individuals – individuals, however, chosen to give the most macro perspective possible because they were part of a global web.

Almost half the 500 interviews were done by both authors, gaining the methodological benefits that arise from having two interviewers (Braithwaite 1985). We never used research assistants to do interviews. Most of the people interviewed are listed in the Acknowledgments at the back of the book, though many are not because they asked for anonymity. Where we have quoted a person from a particular organization as saying something controversial or damaging about their organization, we have played it safe by not listing their name in the Acknowledgments. Some people on the list assisted by sending written comments on a draft section of the book. Part of our method was to send our text, for comment, to key informants and to others who we did not manage to interview. Hence, the Acknowledgments list everyone who gave information useful to this research through some form of direct communication. We thank both them and the many people who gave us interviews and are not listed. The Acknowledgments show the diversity of the spheres our informants traversed – international organizations, states, NGOs and business organizations. There was considerable success in getting access to a large number of key players; we had very few refusals.

Not shown in the Acknowledgments are informants from previous studies whose insights have been regularly imported into this work. First, there are the officials of the ninety-six Australian regulatory agencies where Peter Grabosky and John Braithwaite conducted interviews together. Second, interviews at transnational corporations that had been through adverse publicity crises, conducted jointly by Brent Fisse and John Braithwaite, were relied upon from time to time (Fisse & Braithwaite 1983, 1993). Third, the interviews with 131 executives of pharmaceutical companies conducted by John Braithwaite (1984) were particularly useful because they enabled a comprehensive understanding of one globalized industry's reactions to the entire gamut of issues in this book – intellectual property, tax, companies and securities, trade and competition, corruption, labour standards, environment and safety regulation.

An attractive feature of studying the globalization of business regulation is that, while it has a long history that can only be studied with the methods of a historian, in most domains the critical moments in the history of globalization have occurred since the Great Depression of the twentieth century. Consequently, it is possible to interview people who have lived through many of these moments. We added two dimensions in rewriting their narratives. First, we usually read the history more widely than they, so we could take their story back further. Second, we wove many narratives of different regulatory domains together into a wider narrative. Each informant made some connections with other domains. Our job was to assemble the interconnections into a broader fabric. This process led us into the development of the micro–macro method, the topic of the next section.

## Micro–Macro Method for the Anthropology of Global Cultures

A conclusion of this book is that globalization of regulation never occurs on the basis of a single mechanism, no matter how powerful. Attempts at globalization based on a small range of mechanisms are not found to succeed, in this study. Dense webs of influence are needed to pull off an accomplishment as difficult as establishing a global regulatory regime that secures the compliance of relevant actors in business and the state. Such webs are dense in the sense of involving many types of actors mobilizing many types of mechanisms. With the globalization of pharmaceuticals (Chapter 15), for example, we see pharmaceutical companies as enmeshed in webs of global controls in which important strands include the WHO, the EU, the European Free Trade Association, the International Conference on Harmonization, the self-regulation of the International Federation of Pharmaceutical Manufacturers Associations, global law firms running tort cases, Health Action International, the Medical Lobby for Appropriate Marketing, health professions and the Regulatory Affairs Professionals Society, among others.

Quantitative studies of single mechanisms, such as discussed in systematic studies of economic sanctions in international relations (Hufbauer, Schott & Elliott 1990), show that these generally fail. More importantly, we conclude that such single-factor quantitative studies miss the point. The point is how one strand in a web of controls works to strengthen the mesh of the web (or to unravel it). In the case of apartheid in South Africa, for example, economic sanctions can be understood as an important strand in a web of controls that delivered convergence on a universal human rights regime.

In this book, we think we can lay claim to diligence in studying a large a number of cases of globalization. Yet the number of cases is still so small (thirteen substantive chapters) and the number of types of strands involved in webs of control so large that quantitative methods like multiple regression analysis, favoured by economists, are out of the question, as are the even more rigorous experimental methods favoured by psychologists. A combination of the qualitative methods of anthropologists and historians is required. In a study with such scope, we have attempted to be anthropologists and historians of global regulatory communities/cultures which have sufficiently finite numbers of living key actors and sufficiently limited numbers of documentary sources, many of them carefully recorded because they are laws and usually relatively recent, for us to be thorough enough to be persuasive. On the other hand, the many available people we have not been able to interview and the countless documents we have not read will mean that well-informed readers are sure to pick up errors in a study so ambitious. Doubtless some will be howlers; we apologise for them, yet ask whether they are sufficient in number to invalidate the conclusions in Chapters 20–26.

Embedded in our research experience on this challenging topic is another methodological conclusion. A way of describing the kind of grounded theory (Glaser & Strauss 1967) we attempt is that it is micro–macro theory. Much theory in the social sciences is of limited use because it is macro–macro theory which turns out to be wrong when its implicit micro foundations are false in a specific context. Macroeconomics and grand theory in sociology are replete with illustrations. Psychological theory, on the other hand, tends to be micro–micro (informing a science which studies individuals with macro context held experimentally constant). As a consequence it tends to be irrelevant to understanding the major structural forces that shape human lives. Micro–macro theory attempts to remedy these defects by comprehending micro processes that constitute structural change, just as those micro processes are constituted and constrained by the structural. A rational-choice analysis of the globalization of equal employment opportunity would only get us so far when it takes the rational subject as given. A suitable micro–macro theory specific to the arena, in contrast, seeks to conceive gendered subjects as constituted by global institutions such as transnational business, Hollywood and institutions such as families and states that are intermediate between the subject and global regimes. In the contemporary world, some of the important constitutive structures of the micro are global.

We believe this study shows that a method for generating a micro–macro theory of full sweep and power is for researchers to be anthropologists of global communities and cultures. The methodological prescription is to gather data on the most macro phenomenon possible from the most micro source possible – individuals, especially individuals who act as agents for larger collectivities. The individuals we found worth interviewing were those with a capacity to enrol others to pull one of the significant strands in a web of global influences. Ideally, we wanted to interview them within their institutional context. So there was virtue, where we could manage it, in interviewing trade diplomats within the walls of the WTO as they moved from room to room in Geneva negotiating the deals that constitute the world trading system. From the people inside that building, we could better understand which documents matter, which are given life by the institutional oxygen of the WTO, and which are public relations documents, intended to breathe life into the institutional oxygen of the world's media organizations rather than within the WTO itself.

| Concepts: Mechanisms, Principles and Actors

The principal thesis of this chapter is that the process of globalization is best conceptualized in terms of the relationships between actors, mechanisms and principles. This thesis is not intended to rival or eclipse other more abstract explanations for globalization since, as our discussion of mechanisms makes clear, we allow for the possibility that the mechanisms we identify as important to globalization can be linked to theories that are more reductive or structural in orientation. Our categories of analysis allow for an interoperability of theory. In brief, this chapter argues that actors use relatively simple or lower-order mechanisms to support those principles that best serve their interests and goals. Principles are presented as abstract prescriptions that precede rule complexity. Other norms, such as guidelines and standards, also feature in global regulation, but understanding conflicts of principles is key, we argue, to understanding regulatory globalization. In the final section we suggest how the analysis of principles and mechanisms helps support our claim (in Chapter 2) that processes of globalization have non-linear dynamics.

## Mechanisms

Emphasizing explanation by mechanisms is an approach Jon Elster advocates. Roughly, his argument is that events (which are logically prior to facts) of interest to the social sciences are best explained in terms of causal mechanisms that link those events (Elster 1989). Why do elephants become more endangered after the passage of legislation designed to protect them? A mechanisms explanation might target the rational adaptive behaviour of ivory-hunters. For Elster, a mechanism is not a general law. A general law is conventionally articulated in the form of 'all As are Bs'. It is general laws that physicists seek and, on one view of the social sciences, what social scientists also seek (Ryan 1973: 4). A knowledge of general laws grounds both explanation and prediction. But in Elster's account the quest for general laws in the social sciences seems one that has only a remote, if any, chance of success. Rarely will social scientists be able 'to state necessary and sufficient conditions under which the various mechanisms are switched on' (Elster 1989: 9). What they are more likely to be able to do is identify a causal mechanism that led to an event and thus shed light on why something happened – but why that mechanism rather than another was triggered is likely to remain under a veil. Speaking somewhat loosely, we can say that mechanisms in Elster's sense are shortish causal chains which are not generalizable as laws.

Like Elster, we found that explaining events (in our case the different degrees of globalization of business regulation) in terms of mechanisms was the right direction in which to set out. For one thing, many of our knowledgeable interview informants spoke a language of mechanisms that shaped globalization. But we want to distinguish their and our mechanisms approach from Elster's. In order to do this we have to introduce some distinctions. The first is between higher- and lower-order mechanisms. For the most part the mechanisms which occupy Elster's attention are what we would call higher-order mechanisms. These include mechanisms of individual choice such as those made by rational people, selfish people or altruistic people as well as mechanisms that involve interaction, such as the market mechanism. Higher-order mechanisms are characterized by their abstractness, the fact that they can accommodate a large number of different cases. Rational choice and social norms are both examples of the higher-order category of mechanisms.

Our focus is not on higher-order mechanisms, but on lower-order mechanisms. Lower-order mechanisms are concrete specifications of higher-order mechanisms. Reinforcement, for instance, is, in terms of our distinction, a higher-order mechanism. Reinforcement, as laboratory rats know, can be positive or negative. One important mechanism we have found to operate in the context of our study of business regulation is coercion, or the threat of it. States, for example, coerce other states either militarily or economically. An example of economic coercion which we discuss is the system of trade retaliation that the US employs under its Trade Act in order to achieve its agenda. Military coercion was important in the globalization documented in seven of our thirteen case studies, and was of minor significance in four others. Clearly, coercion can be accommodated as a higher-order mechanism of reinforcement, as can systems of reward, another mechanism on our list. But we prefer to concentrate on these as lower-order mechanisms. Most of the mechanisms we identify are lower-order mechanisms. We stay at the lower order of mechanisms in our analysis because in the histories of globalization which we offer it is those mechanisms that have been the salient ones, the ones which have recurrently and concretely been important in the globalization of business regulation.

Working with lower-order mechanisms is also part of our inductivist method. The data we have collected instantiates, we show, a set of lower-order mechanisms. These mechanisms, as a matter of theory, can be aggregated under higher-order mechanisms, which in turn may be related to patterns and general laws. A full-blooded explanation of global business regulation would travel from events and lower-order mechanisms to underlying patterns and their associated laws. Elster may be right that social science will have to be content with explanations that rely on something less than general laws. We remain open to the possibility that more might be achieved. But in this book we largely focus on the lower rungs of an explanatory ladder, a ladder in which a historical understanding of lower-order mechanisms at work in the globalization of business regulation represents the first step.

A second feature of the mechanisms we discuss is that they are largely ones of actor design. This simply means that they are mechanisms used by actors either unilaterally or in cooperation with others in order to achieve their goals and plans. Not all mechanisms have this element of contrivance. Reinforcement may operate on an actor to produce a habit in that actor without that actor being aware of the process. Lack of agent knowledge about the operation of a mechanism may also be true of mechanisms of natural selection. But in the histories of regulation we present actors have, for the most part, sought to consciously utilize mechanisms like coercion, capacity-building and modelling to achieve their goals. This is not to say that the goals have always been clearly defined or that uses of the mechanisms have not resulted in unintended and negative consequences. US regulatory hegemony over the illicit drugs trade has been affected by such consequences (Chapter 15).

After these preliminary remarks, we can define the mechanisms which operate in the context of the globalization of business regulation in the following way: these mechanisms of globalization are processes that increase the extent to which patterns of regulation in one part of the world are similar, or linked, to patterns of regulation in other parts. Inductively, we find the key processes to be coercion, systems of reward, modelling, reciprocal adjustment, non-reciprocal coordination and capacity-building. These processes involve one or more actors (state and non-state) in a series of actions (and reactions) that are linked to the goals and desires of the actors. These processes are lower-order processes in the sense specified. They can be simple or complex.

One final observation before we discuss principles. Focusing on explanation by mechanisms could easily lead to an explanation of the globalization of business regulation in terms of social systems – a Parsonian functionalist explanation, in other words. Mechanisms, it might be said, imply systems. And in fact system theoreticians routinely talk about mechanisms of social control and mechanisms of socialization. One can say a lot or a little about a functionalist systems approach to globalization. We will say only a little. The crucial difference between a functionalist approach and ours is that the former would require an explanation of the globalization of business regulation in terms of a system need (perhaps a world system) or group of system needs. In a functionalist approach, international organizations like the WTO or IMF emerge because there is a fundamental need for such an organization (Mitrany 1948). This need is systemically defined in terms of the increased complexity of relations between states, or something of that sort. The important thing to note about this kind of explanation is that the consequences of creating the organization (reduction of complexity) becomes in some sense the 'explanation' for the emergence of the organization.

To us, explanation is not indissolubly linked to social systems. In fact, some of the business regulation mechanisms in our case studies help to constitute social systems. Modelling, for instance, helps to constitute epistemic communities with a world-wide membership in all our case studies. And these epistemic communities help to forge a partial value consensus, which for systems theorists is an essential prerequisite for the existence of a social system.[1] We are not, therefore, methodologically committed to uncovering 'system' needs. This also means that we accept the idea of individual actors being the originators of change rather than mere agents of change. In philosophical language, we can say that we take seriously the intentionality of agents and the ways in which their beliefs and desires can lead them to change their regulatory worlds. We will see, in our discussion of intellectual property (Chapter 7), that the entrepreneurship of some Washington lawyers achieves the link between trade and intellectual property. The consequences of this particular regulatory change are yet to be properly fathomed.

---

1  See, for example, Teubner's (1997: 7) analysis of global law as 'the proto-law of specialized, organizational and functional networks…The new living law of the world is nourished not from stores of tradition but from the ongoing self-reproduction of highly technical, highly specialized, often formally organized and rather narrowly defined, global networks of an economic, cultural, academic or technological nature'. We call these 'global epistemic communities'. While we agree with Teubner's analysis, we also think, unlike Teubner, that global law as 'inter-national' law remains important.

## Principles and Actors

From the perspective of a business actor, a given regulatory regime is often seen as a thicket of rules. Rule complexity is one feature of business regulation. But standing behind regulatory regimes are principles, such as transparency, national treatment, Most Favoured Nation, reciprocity and thirty others that we discuss. The idea of principles standing behind rules and informing their application, or being used to create new rules, is found in the jurisprudential literature that deals with the theories of judicial decision-making and interpretation. The analytical lines of demarcation between rules and principles are drawn in different ways by different theorists. One way to draw such a line is to say that rules apply in an 'all-or-nothing fashion' to determine a decision (Dworkin 1967: 25). Principles have less specificity. Unlike rules, they can conflict. This conflict is settled by decision-makers assigning 'weights' to the relevant principles in order to reach a decision. Another way – perhaps a better way – in which to draw the distinction is to say that 'Rules prescribe relatively specific acts; principles prescribe highly unspecific actions' (Raz 1972: 838). There are probably many actions to which an environmental principle like the precautionary principle could apply; a rule preventing the dumping of chemical X relates only to that action.

For our purposes it is important to insist on a distinction between rules and principles. Probably the best way in which to do this is in the way Raz does – focusing on the degree of abstractness entailed by the action-guiding prescription in question. The distinction is important because we have found that actors involved in processes of globalization articulate, support and seek to entrench principles in regulatory systems in different ways. Different actors, we shall see, align themselves with different principles. Within the environmental arena, green groups seek to institutionalize principles such as sustainable development and the precautionary principle, while other actors such as TNCs will support principles of economic growth and lowest-cost location. Understanding the conflict of principles is integral to understanding the globalization of business regulation. The successful weighting of one principle over another has consequences at both the level of conduct and for regulatory change. To give a quick example, when the US manages to shift the principle of national treatment to a multilateral forum like the GATT and tie its application to a high-standard intellectual property agreement (such as TRIPS, see Chapter 7), intellectual property laws around the world take a significant step toward convergence on a similar set of standards. When TNCs endorse and act on a principle of lowest-cost location they find themselves in conflict with green groups which track and attempt to expose the TNCs' minimal compliance activities.

These examples should make it clear that the 'principles' we refer to do not mean exclusively legal principles. Some of the principles we discuss have a clear legal and juristic character. This is obviously true of principles like national treatment and sovereignty. But other principles we identify, like lowest-cost location, continuous improvement, rule compliance and world's best practice are not legal principles as such. They are principles in that they constitute an agreed standard of conduct. They propel action in a certain direction. Their source, however, is not the legal system although they may ultimately find a place there. They evolve from the values and practices of a given community of actors. The principle of continuous improvement and other total quality management (TQM) principles are rooted in the work of writers such as Deming (1986), Juran (1988) and Ishikawa (1985). The principles behind the TQM philosophy of these writers have found their way into corporate culture and practice. The process by which this happens leads us back to an explanation by mechanisms. In the case of TQM principles, the process of diffusion is best explained by the modelling mechanism. Principles, to us, may be legal or non-legal in character and may have different origins – in law, in the social practices of groups, in acts of individual knowledge entrepreneurship.

What role do principles play in the globalization of business regulation? A detailed answer is given in Chapters 21 and 24, but we provide here a brief outline of the tasks that principles perform. We have already said that actors articulate and ally themselves with certain principles. Why? A rough answer is that principles function to secure objectives and goals which are important to the actor. Principles, for us, function in a somewhat instrumental fashion. Actors seek, through principles, to incorporate into regulatory systems and social practices changes that are consistent with their general values, goals and desires. The abstract nature of principles means that the successful weighting of one principle or set of principles over another only means that the direction for action has been settled on. Once the direction has been set, processes for generating the detailed rules of conduct (or changing them) can take place. For example, the US, through the mechanism of coercion, manages to force states to take seriously the principle of national treatment (at the expense of principles like national sovereignty) in the context of intellectual property regulation. By so doing it secures its most basic objective – the preservation of its economic interests as an information economy and net intellectual property exporter. Other states now have to adopt intellectual property regimes or reform their existing ones. It is a good example of rule complexity following a change of principles.

One can present the globalization of business regulation as a two-tiered process. At the first tier the process occurs at the level of rules and at the second tier at the level of principles. It is this second, higher-order level that is the focus of our theoretical inquiries. This is necessary because millions of national or supranational rules are within the scope of our inquiry, an utterly unmanageable number. We have very briefly outlined the role of principles in global regulatory change, and sketched what we see as the relationship between actors and mechanisms and actors and principles. Implicit in these remarks is an account of the relationship between principles and mechanisms. Briefly, we propose that in the contest of principles actors use mechanisms to give weight to some principles over others. Military and economic coercion are two obvious ways in which state actors can ensure the triumph of some principles, but these are mechanisms available only to powerful actors. Other actors have to weight their chosen principles in more subtle ways.

Norms, standards, principles and rules are all elements that can be conceptualized or assembled in different ways to build theories of regulation. Here we want to give our definitions of these elements and the relations among them. Our simple conceptual scheme starts with an actor language approach. During the course of our interviews the actors we spoke to would refer to principles, standards, rules or guidelines. Similarly, much of the organizational literature they gave us used these concepts. To us, it is these elements that are important conceptual building-blocks in a theory of the globalization of regulatory norms. We have given these elements a conceptual 'tweak' by placing them into a set of relations and specifying a meaning for each element. Figure 4.1 gives a schematic illustration of the way the elements are related.

'Norms' is a generic category which includes rules, principles, standards and guidelines. We have already distinguished rules from principles in terms of the degree of abstractness. Rules are specific, principles have a high degree of generality. Principles, we said, are settled agreements on conduct, recognized by a group. 'Principles' and 'standards' are sometimes used interchangeably. To us there is a difference. A central feature of standards is that they are used as measures of conduct. Principles bring about mutual orientations between actors. Standards are norms that

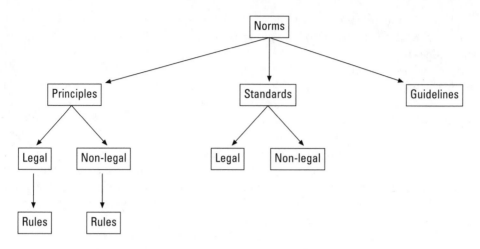

FIGURE 4.1    From norms to rules

can be applied to measure their performance. So, for example, committees like the Basle Committee on Banking Supervision or the International Accounting Standards Committee can support principles such as those of transparency and consolidation, as well as setting standards by which the performance of other actors (banks, business enterprises) can be judged. Standards, unlike principles, can have a high degree of specificity – accounting standards and capital adequacy standards are good examples. 'Guidelines' are used to suggest a direction for conduct in conditions of uncertainty. If actors find themselves in strange or rapidly changing circumstances they often resort to guidelines. Guidelines do not have the degree of 'settledness' which principles possess and are very often issued as a provisional measure until more is known about the relevant problem. The 'Risk management guidelines for derivatives' put out by the Basle Committee in July 1994 are an example. Guidelines often arise when there is agreement that 'something needs to be done', there is no agreement on the principles that should guide it but there is some possibility of practical agreement on guides to some of the actions that need to be taken. Sunstein's (1996) discussion of the use and virtues of 'incompletely specified agreements' in the law is relevant to the distinctive contribution of guidelines.

In the regulatory histories we have examined we see that norms belonging to one species can undergo a process of transmutation. Norms put out by the Basle Committee started as guidelines. Progressively they have become standards accepted by banking regulators around the world. Similarly, some of the non-legal accounting standards developed by the IASC have become part of the legal systems of the EU. Guidelines can become standards or legal rules. Non-legal standards can become legal ones. Non-legal principles can become legal ones.

## The Principle of Reciprocity and Reciprocity-based Mechanisms

One of the principles that we discuss – the principle of reciprocity – merits special discussion, because it leads directly to the concept of reciprocity. 'Reciprocity' is a foundational concept or idea that is said to lie at the root of many social institutions and practices. It has been claimed, for instance, that it is reciprocity which forms the basis of Roman, Germanic and Anglo-Saxon contract law, treaty law and international law generally (Lenhoff 1954/55; Atiyah 1979; Grieg 1994). Reciprocity is an equally pervasive idea outside law. Reciprocity has featured in theories of international relations, trade and the emergence of cooperation (Axelrod 1984; Keohane 1986; Rhodes 1989).

Reciprocity in some abstract form could turn out to be a universal underlying principle, a principle to which other principles can be reduced (the principle of national treatment, for instance, might be reduced to a variant of reciprocity). And because reciprocity is also a social process, it can plausibly be characterized as a mechanism with sweeping application. But developing reciprocity in this way is something we have avoided. The reason is connected to our methodology. The key idea behind our micro–macro method is gathering data on the most macro phenomenon possible from the most micro source possible. This method is also inductive in nature. It seeks data from individuals in a specific regulatory domain, over a number of regulatory domains. In formulating instances of mechanisms and principles we have been guided by the idea of fidelity to the relevant domain. This simply means that in identifying and articulating principles we have used, where possible, those principles that the actors in the relevant domain have identified as important and active. In trade-related contexts this means focusing on the principles of Most Favoured Nation and national treatment; in the area of environment we focus on the principle of sustainable development and the principle of lowest-cost location. When formulating principles we have, wherever possible, cast them in narrower rather than broader language. We have deliberately avoided trying to reduce the number of principles by mapping different patterns of conduct onto a small set of principles in abstract form. (The principle of national treatment, the principle of Most Favoured Nation and perhaps even the principle of reciprocity might be argued to represent different dimensions of the principle of equality.) This would push our investigation in the direction of macro–macro theory. Such a theory would be more universal in the sense that it would claim to cover a larger range of phenomena, but it would also be more detached from the micro foundations of the phenomena it was purporting to explain and therefore more likely to run into problems of verification. Our goal is micro–macro theory. Our idea is to generate a descriptively rich set of principles on which to build our theory. Although we have kept our categories of explanation to a minimum (mechanisms, principles, actors) we have inductively sought to enrich those categories with specific instances and types. In contrast, macro–macro theory tends to use abstract categories of explanation which appear to be more universal and seemingly allow theories to sweep across a larger range of phenomena (examples are mode of production, relations of production in Marx's theory and rationality in economic theorizing generally). The principles we put forward are more proximate to the action of the individuals from whom we obtained our data. They are the principles that actors in business regulation fight for or against. And yet, as principles, they have a sufficient degree of abstractness to promote the structural change that lies at the heart of the global regulatory stories we tell. Similarly, we have chosen to work with lower-order mechanisms rather than higher-order ones. One advantage we claim for this method is that generalizations across domains that are built on concrete principles and lower-order mechanisms are more likely to be robust (less likely to be false in a specific context).

In what specific ways do we employ the idea of reciprocity? In its abstract form, reciprocity could be said to be the contingent exchange of action between two actors. For reasons that will be clearer in a moment, we can tie this definition to interests by saying that each actor has an interest in having the action performed by the other. X performs an action on a contingent basis when he expects that Y will, by way of repayment, also perform an action. This expectation of repayment of action lies at the heart of reciprocity. The expectation of X and Y can be characterized as a kind of double expectation. When X performs an action he expects that Y will also, by way of repayment, perform an action; X also expects that Y will be reading X's expectation as that.

We are interested in two concrete manifestations of reciprocity. First, reciprocity is evident as a juridical principle in statutes and treaties. Typically, such laws involve an exchange and recognition of rights and obligations between two sovereigns. Sovereign 1 agrees to recognize the rights and obligations of citizens of Sovereign 2, if Sovereign 2 agrees to do the same for citizens of Sovereign 1. Reciprocity statutes and treaties have existed for a long time. Lenhoff observes that 'since the thirteenth century treaties between various territorial rulers frequently contained the reciprocity clause which was intended to ensure equal treatment of their subjects' (Lenhoff 1954/55: 766). The principle is commonly found in tax and investment treaties. The US used the principle of reciprocity in its *Semiconductor Chip Act 1984*, whose purpose was to globalize protection for the US semiconductor chip industry. We are centrally interested in the principle of reciprocity as a juridical principle. In this form, the principle formally commits actors to a course of action. Moreover, once the principle is embedded in a treaty it becomes part of positive law. There can be little argument over its existence or the fact that an actor who is engaging the principle is pursuing a reciprocity-based strategy. Clearly, reciprocity in the abstract form described earlier is potentially relevant to an inquiry such as ours. Reciprocity may well explain the evolution of international law doctrines like comity, as well as much of private and public international law. But using abstract reciprocity in this way is something we eschew, for the reasons given. It is the site-specific manifestations of reciprocity that interest us rather than its more abstract and therefore more distant form.

The second form of reciprocity which matters for present purposes is the role it plays in two mechanisms, those of reciprocal adjustment and non-reciprocal coordination. In order to explain these mechanisms we must explain their relationship to their higher-order relative, the mechanism of cooperation. Rather than defining cooperation in terms of reciprocity, we will say that cooperation involves one actor helping another actor to satisfy an interest or goal which one or both actors possess. Cooperation can be reciprocally or non-reciprocally based. One actor may decide to help another, without holding the double expectation that marks the presence of reciprocity.

'Reciprocal adjustment' is a form of cooperation that is triggered by the presence of reciprocal interests. The interests of two actors can be said to be reciprocal when those interests drive those actors towards an agreement on the same rule or convergence upon some set of rules. Reciprocal adjustment is a mechanism that produces a rules outcome. This outcome can be the adoption of a new set of rules, the harmonization of existing rules, or mutual recognition. A good example of reciprocal adjustment in action is given in Chapter 12, when we discuss states' adoption of the Montreal Protocol on ozone-depleting substances. In summary: when the interests of actors are targeted on the same rule or rules they can be said to have reciprocal interests. We call the process of bringing these adjusted rules into existence, the mechanism of reciprocal adjustment.

Reciprocal cooperation can also take place on the basis of non-reciprocal interests. This mechanism we call 'non-reciprocal coordination'. It operates when the parties do not have interests in achieving a rules outcome, but have interests in achieving a particular alliance that will benefit both. A good example of non-reciprocal coordination appears in Chapter 7, the intellectual property case study. In the Uruguay Round of trade negotiations Australia was a strong supporter of the US in the negotiations over trade-related aspects of intellectual property rights. Australia, as a net intellectual property importer, had strong economic reasons not to support an agreement that would strengthen intellectual property protection internationally. Yet, as one US trade negotiator remarked to us, Australia was a member of the Friends of Intellectual Property, a group that was formed during the intellectual property negotiations, and faithfully attended the group's meetings. Why did this happen when, for example, an Australian government report in the 1980s observed that there was little or no economic reason for Australia to continue to participate in the international patent system (*Patents, Innovation and Competition in Australia* 1984: 17)? The answer lies in the fact that Australia thought that, by cooperating with the US on something that mattered dearly to the US, it might secure US cooperation on agriculture, something that mattered dearly to Australia and that had led it to form the Cairns Group, a group of countries with a comparative advantage in agriculture. The cooperation between Australia and the US on intellectual property could not be characterized as an example of reciprocal interests leading to reciprocal adjustment. Nothing could have been further from Australia's economic interests than the globalization of stronger intellectual property rights. It is an example of non-reciprocal interests leading to a process of non-reciprocal coordination. The US and Australia, and other states, coordinated on intellectual property and the alliance was one factor that contributed to the globalization of intellectual property.

The mechanism of non-reciprocal coordination is an indirect mechanism of globalization. It leads to alliance structures that explain why a particular regulatory event occurred or did not occur – non-reciprocal coordination may lead to the formation of a veto coalition. Non-reciprocal coordination is a mechanism of alliance creation. Reciprocal adjustment is a simpler mechanism of rule creation.

## A Non-linear Dynamic

In the chapters that follow we will see that there is a basic 'messiness' about the globalization of regulation. Each regulatory domain has a distinct range of actors contending for victory at different sites, actors with different principles who are using different mechanisms. A principle such as the common heritage of mankind, which is a completely defeated principle in the domain of intellectual property, re-emerges in the context of debates over access to genetic resources in the Food and Agriculture Organization. The International Telecommunication Union, an organization that was once the global sovereign of telecommunications standard-setting, finds itself competing with regional standard-setting bodies, business consortia and individual companies. It desperately seeks to reorganize itself in its new environment. The US scores crushing victories such as TRIPS but also suffers losses, as in the case of the regulation of prescription drugs (Chapter 15).

One truth about this messy process is that the interaction between mechanisms, principles and actors in each domain constitutes a distinctive dynamic for each domain. Principles bring order to a domain, but that order can be destabilized by other actors contending for victory with different principles. Rule structures of formidable complexity are ultimately fragile because they can be contested at the level of principles. Principles do not have set 'weights' in a domain. Actors continually invent new principles, such as sustainable development or farmers' rights, or borrow existing principles from other domains. The conflicts of principles are not simple tug-of-war affairs. We could predict much more about globalization if they were. Actors find themselves connected through a web of influences to a range of other actors. The multiple connections and different circumstances of each and every actor make it difficult to predict where the web of influences will next take the process of globalization. The facts that defeated principles can make comebacks, that there are different actor coalitions in different domains and that there is no all-conquering mechanism of globalization mean that regulatory globalization does not proceed like a tide that never ebbs. Like the real tide it ebbs and flows. Unlike the real tide, the control of these ebbs and flows is found not in celestial law but in the intricate struggles of actors as they seek to influence the tide.

## Definitions

We are now in a position to offer definitions of the kinds of actors, principles and mechanisms that we found recurrently useful in research during our interviews. Throughout this book are quotes revealing how our informants spoke about these actors, principles and mechanisms so readers can make their own judgments, based on at least a smattering of data, about how these definitions fit with the conceptualizations used by strategic actors.

### Actors

- *Organizations of states:* Organizations formed by groups of states that meet and employ staff to explore common agendas (e.g. the World Bank, the OECD, treaty secretariats).
- *States:* Organized political communities with governments and geographical boundaries recognized by international law (e.g. France). For many analytic purposes in this book, it is more useful to disaggregate the state into component parts, such as the Ministry of Trade.
- *Business organizations:* Organizations formed by firms and/or business organizations that meet and employ staff to explore common agendas. They can be national (e.g. US Chamber of Commerce) or linked to international organizations (e.g. International Chamber of Commerce).
- *Corporations:* Organizations formed by actors who invest in them as commercial vehicles (e.g. General Motors, US Postal Service).
- *NGOs:* Organizations formed by citizens and NGOs (excluding business organizations) that meet and employ staff to explore common agendas. They can be international (e.g. Consumers International) or national (e.g. British Standards Institute).
- *Mass publics:* Large audiences of citizens who, although they might not meet or employ staff, can express together a common concern about a regulatory question.
- *Epistemic communities of actors:* Large audiences of state, business and NGO actors who meet sporadically and share a common regulatory discourse based on shared knowledge, sometimes technical knowledge requiring professional training.

### Key Principles

- *Lowest-cost location:* The prescription of economic activity being located wherever and under whatever regulatory rules it can be transacted most cheaply.
- *World's best practice:* The prescription of economic activity being conducted under rules that substantially exceed the requirements set by present practice or regulation.
- *Liberalization–deregulation:* The prescription of reducing the number, stringency or enforcement of rules.

- *Strategic trade:* The prescription of designing the content and stringency of regulation so as to advantage national exporters or importers over foreign exporters or importers.
- *Rule compliance:* The prescription that companies ought to consider that legality exhausts their obligations; to go as far as the rules require (e.g. in reducing pollution) but no further.
- *Continuous improvement:* The prescription of doing better every year than the previous year in terms of a regulatory objective such as protecting the environment, even if legal requirements were exceeded in the previous year.
- *National sovereignty:* The prescription that the nation-state should be supreme over any other source of power on matters affecting its citizens or territory.
- *Harmonization:* The prescription that different levels of government and different governments should set the same rules.
- *Mutual recognition:* The prescription that different levels of government and different governments should recognize one another's rules and permit economic activity performed under one another's rules, even if the rules are different.
- *Transparency:* The prescription that any person should be able to observe regulatory deliberation or easily discover the outcomes (and their justifications) of the deliberation.
- *National treatment:* The prescription that a state should regulate foreign corporations according to the same rules as national corporations.
- *Most Favoured Nation:* The prescription that any regulatory benefit accorded to importers or exporters from one nation should be accorded to importers or exporters from other nations.
- *Reciprocity:* The prescription that if one nation grants a regulatory benefit to importers or exporters from a second nation, the second nation should grant the same regulatory benefit to the first nation regardless of the regulatory benefits it accords third nations.

## Mechanisms

- *Military coercion:* Globalization of regulation achieved by the threat, fear or use of military force.
- *Economic coercion:* Globalization of regulation achieved by the threat, fear or use of economic sanctions.
- *Systems of reward:* Globalization of regulation achieved by systematic means of raising the expected value of compliance with a globalizing order (as distinct from coercion, which reduces the expected value of non-compliance).
- *Modelling:* Globalization of regulation achieved by observational learning with a symbolic content; learning based on conceptions of action portrayed in words and images. The latter cognitive content makes modelling more than mere imitation; imitation means one actor matching the actions of another, usually close in time.
- *Reciprocal adjustment:* Globalization of regulation achieved by non-coerced negotiation where parties agree to adjust the rules they follow. This is conceived as cooperative adjustment where reciprocation occurs without coercion, for example all parties agreeing to drive on the left side of the road to avoid crashes.
- *Non-reciprocal coordination:* Occurs when movement toward common rules happens without all parties believing they have a common interest in that movement. One party believes the new rule is in their interest, but this belief is not reciprocated. Non-reciprocal coordination often

involves non-reciprocity within an overall reciprocity of issue linkage: X wins on this and loses on that, Y loses on this and wins on that.

- *Capacity-building:* Globalization of regulation achieved by helping actors get the technical competence to satisfy global standards, when they wish to meet them but lack the capacity to do so.

## Other Concepts Frequently Used in the Analysis

- *Hegemony:* Hegemony achieves globalization of regulation by actors following the lead of the dominant power because those other actors define their interests in terms of those of the dominant power (without need of threat or offer of reward by the hegemonic power).
- *Regime:* 'Principles, norms, rules, and decision-making procedures around which actor expectations converge in a given issue-area' (Krasner 1982: 185).

## CHAPTER 5

Conclusions

There are important contextual conclusions in each chapter about the globalization of each specific domain of regulation. Clearly, what is true of the regulation of finance (Chapter 8, which covers monetary policy, banking, tax and insurance), is very different from what is true of drugs (Chapter 15, which covers prescription drugs, over-the-counter drugs, illicit drugs, alcohol and tobacco). Indeed, it follows from our 'webs of influence' model that each web is contextually complex and paradoxical and therefore requires less a law-like understanding and more a clinical diagnosis of when a particular web tightens or unravels. Although contextual understanding is ultimately the most useful, we have forty-four things of general import to say.

## The Process of Globalization

### Powerful Actors

1   The US state has been by far the most influential actor in accomplishing the globalization of regulation. Today the European Commission (EC) is beginning to approach US influence. When the US and EC can agree on which direction global regulatory change should take, that is usually the direction it does take. Japan's influence is remarkably weak.

2   States have always been objects as well as subjects of regulation, regulators and regulatees. States were regulated by the Fuggers in the sixteenth century, the British East India Company in the eighteenth century, the Rothschilds until the 1930s, and today by business organizations like the Big Five accounting firms, IATA, the Société Générale de Surveillance, Moody's and Standard & Poor's plus international organizations like the IMF and World Bank. In 1999, British mercenary corporation Sandline International, in a dispute over its involvement in the war in Bougainville, took legal action to freeze various overseas funds of the Papua New Guinea government in order to chill its capacity for overseas borrowing.

3   The most recurrently effective actors in enrolling the power of states and the power of the most potent international organizations (e.g. the WTO and IMF) are large US corporations.

4   The ICC is an important actor in the globalization of regulation because, in addition to having an interest-group strategy for shaping regulation, for seventy years it has had a private

ordering strategy based on recording its members' customary practices and releasing them in the form of model rules and agreements.

5   Individual legal entrepreneurs sometimes exert enormous power by selling a regulatory idea to the CEO of a large company and persuading the CEO to enrol the power of a pivotal state actor, such as the US president. Many individuals listed in the Acknowledgments do not see themselves as passive puppets of inexorable global forces but as deft puppeteers, capable of pulling strings to move the big players who remain passive until activated by someone with the imagination to inspire them with a vision of where their interests lie.

6   Most influence to shape regulation globally is accumulated in thousands of obscure technical committees of international organizations like the ITU and private standard-setting bodies like the ISO.

7   The last two decades of the twentieth century saw the rise of a 'new regulatory state', where states do not so much run things as regulate them or monitor self-regulation. Self-regulatory organizations frequently become more important than states in the epistemic communities where debates over regulatory design are framed.

## The Role of Coercion

8   Until the end of the Second World War, military coercion was a surprisingly important mechanism in the globalization of business regulation.

9   Since the Second World War, economic coercion has been much more important. However, it is effectively available only to the strong. Even the US is extremely reluctant to achieve regulatory objectives by imposing trade sanctions, and rarely does so. Actors other than the US do not apply trade sanctions except in extraordinary cases, like South Africa, because they consider sanctions ineffective and fear retaliation. 'Watch-listing' seems to work for the US as a 'sword of Damocles' that is rarely lowered. A routine where the US Congress is a 'hard cop' threatening trade sanctions and the executive branch is a 'soft cop' resisting them has served US objectives well. Economic coercion is much more widely used in the form of strong states cutting off foreign aid to weak states, the IMF and development banks imposing conditions on loans to struggling economies and insurers refusing coverage or imposing punitive premiums.

10  The more profound the hegemony of a state, the less it has to resort to the threat or use of economic sanctions, yet the more the compliance it secures is grounded in the fear of that possibility.

11  Coercion is more widely used and generally more cost-effective than reward for actors who want to enlist compliance with a global regulatory regime. The main reason is that threatening and withdrawing coercion can work well, but promising and reneging on rewards does not. Contextual diplomatic wisdom is especially important to understanding what works.

## Forum-shifting

12  When the post-Second World War US has not been able to get multilateral agreement on what it wants, it either attempts to shift decision-making to an alternative multilateral forum

or shifts to a sequence of bilateral deals with other key states. These accumulated bilaterals often later set the framework for a new attempt at multilateral agreement.

13 There are three basic strategies of forum-shifting around international organizations: (a) moving a regulatory agenda from one organization to another; (b) abandoning an organization; and (c) pursuing the same agenda in more than one organization. The first two strategies are widely used only by the US, and have been practically available only to the US, the EC and (formerly) the USSR. Forum-blocking (preventing an international organization from acting as a forum for regulatory development in the first place) is a fourth strategy used by major players.

14 Strong states forum-shift to fora that embed the principles most valued by them for the relevant regulatory problems. For example, the principle that knowledge is the 'common heritage of mankind' was defeated by shifting intellectual property issues from UNESCO and UNCTAD to the World Intellectual Property Organization and the GATT, where knowledge was treated as property subject to trade principles.

## The Role of Epistemic Communities

15 To enrol the support of strategic actors for regulatory change, it is usually necessary to work epistemic communities. The OECD is the single most important builder of business regulatory epistemic communities. Epistemic communities are more than transgovernmental elite networks. They include technically competent regulatory experts from science, professions, business and NGOs.

## The Role of Principles

16 The globalization of business regulation proceeds through contests of principles. Negotiation occurs mostly at the level of principles because it is too complex for each nation to put its national rules on the table as a negotiating position.

17 Transparency is the principle that has most consistently strengthened in importance in regulatory debates. It is an emergent property of globalization, a meta-principle in the sense of revealing the operation of all other principles.

18 Although the principle of national sovereignty retains enormous bite, it has been the principle that retreats most in the face of advancing harmonization and its allied principle, mutual recognition.

19 The entrenchment of national treatment and Most Favoured Nation in the trade agreements of the Uruguay Round of the GATT has inched these non-discrimination principles toward a formal juridical triumph in the world system.

20 Often the more dominant a principle becomes in a regime, the more viable a niche market is created in opposition to it. For example, the influence of the principle of world's best practice in shipping creates a niche market for 'flags of convenience' with low standards; transparency's dominance on the New York Stock Exchange creates a niche for lowest-cost listing on Asian exchanges (and a compromise niche at the Australian Stock Exchange, with middling transparency).

21 Principles are often used symbolically in global regulatory regimes as part of a rhetorical strategy to engender quiescence. This can backfire when mass publics are stirred out of quiescence by a disaster the regime fails to prevent; the principles may then form an expansive framework for instrumental rules. Indeed, sequences of disasters have ratcheted up a number of symbolic framework agreements.

22 Mechanisms of globalization are more potent influences on action if they are linked to principles which give symbolic meaning to the direction of influence. Conversely, principles depend on mechanisms such as economic coercion to push-start them to the point where they gain their own momentum.

23 Empirically, the rule of law is not as influential in global regulatory regimes as it is in liberal nations; indeed, it is endlessly trumped by the principles of reciprocity and conditionality at institutions like the WTO and the IMF respectively. International regulation is not characterized by a rule of laws which constrain but by a rule of principles. Under the rule of principles, principles are weighed and balanced.

24 Because it is normally too complex to negotiate a new regulatory regime as a contest of rules, regimes mostly start as a framework of principles. Framework agreements to enshrine principles disadvantage poorly resourced parties less than do interminable and complex negotiations over rules. Paradoxically, contests of principles make conflicts sharper, clearer and more accessible than conflicts at the level of systems of rules.

**The Role of Mechanisms**

25 Military coercion, economic coercion, systems of reward, reciprocal adjustment, non-reciprocal coordination, capacity-building and modelling have all been mechanisms of some importance to the globalization of regulation. There is no master mechanism and little prospect of a parsimonious rational choice account that explains all.

26 Modelling, a mechanism that may relate more to identity than to rational choice, has been the most consistently important mechanism. Histories of globalization involve complex networked actions which means that few, if any, actors have the synoptic capacity to be rational in the way rational choice theory would have it. They dither in a confusion of complexity they cannot grasp, which is why they can be led by entrepreneurs who encourage them onto a plausibly interest-enhancing path.

27 Reciprocal adjustment is a more important mechanism of globalization of regulation when the externalities imposed by the firms of one state on other states are reciprocated by externalities imposed by the other states on the first state (e.g. the US and Canada polluting the Great Lakes). Where externalities are non-reciprocal, issue linkage can constitute a contract zone and the mechanism of non-reciprocal coordination can deliver globalization.

**Regulation and the Nature of Capitalism**

28 The issuance of government bonds in the eighteenth century began processes of world securitization and corporatization which, combined with its progressive contractualization, have given global capitalism its regulatory character.

29  Contemporary capitalism has shifted from industrial to information capitalism. Information capitalism was constituted by regulated transparency and a legal commodification of knowledge. Abstract objects such as patents were thus the most important kind of property in the new capitalism. Hegemony in the world system shifted from the control of territory, to industrialization (and the control of capital and labour it implied), to the control of abstract objects.

30  WTO enforcement of a positive set of harmonized intellectual property standards is unique. A crucial question for the future is whether other domains of regulation, such as the environment, will be accorded the same positive linkage to the trade sanctions of WTO panels.

## Webs of Influence and Citizen Sovereignty

### Weak Actors and Webs of Influence

31  There are paradoxes of sovereignty in the growth of global regulation. When national sovereignty and the sovereignty of elected parliaments are eroded, the sovereignty of ordinary citizens is sometimes enhanced.

32  Realist international relations theory gives a poor account of our data. State power is best understood as constituted by and helping to constitute webs of regulatory influences comprised of many actors wielding many mechanisms.

33  Histories of globalization are complex. They cannot be understood in terms of the agency of single actors using single mechanisms. Something as hard to achieve as the globalization of regulation seems to require a web of influences – many actors deploying many mechanisms. Weak single strands in webs of influence often become strong by being tied to other weak strands.

34  International agreement sometimes arises when united minority factions from many states (working with NGOs) defeat majority factions. While majority factions 'control' states, if they fail to work with majority factions from other states they can be defeated by minorities joined in cross-national alliance. Often power is not a matter of imposing a sovereign will, but of enrolling the cooperation of chains of actors.

35  Attempts by developing countries and NGOs to exercise influence by organizing independently of the business-dominated epistemic communities have failed. For example, the influence of the G-77 has declined and the forum it captured, UNCTAD, has been substantially neutralized.

36  NGO influence has been greatest when it has captured the imagination of mass publics in powerful states. The most important instances have been the temperance, anti-slavery, labour, women's and environment movements. We found Ralph Nader to have had a wider influence across a range of regimes than any other individual in the history of the globalization of business regulation.

### Countering Forum-shifting

37  Weaker players should rely on the insight of the 'nested game' to increase complexity for a stronger player who forum-shifts. This is accomplished by linking the game played in an

abandoned or ignored forum that embeds an opposed principle, to the game in the forum the strong player has chosen. For example, players like Ralph Nader link the intellectual property game of extending pharmaceutical patents to the public health game of affordable health-care and the competition policy game of minimizing monopoly. Principles can be used strategically by weaker actors to increase levels of nested complexity for stronger actors. This can reduce the returns gained from forum-shifting.

38  The history of failed attempts to forum-shift from the ILO reveals that forum-shifting may be more difficult from an organization with a more tripartite constitution.

## The Role of Dialogue

39  Webs of coercion can be used by the strong but not by the weak (which allows the strong to exercise domination or hegemony without even hinting at coercion). Webs of dialogue are available to both (though access and domination are still easier for the strong). A consolation for the weak is that webs of dialogue are both more commonly used and more often effective than webs of coercion. Our informants prefer to rely on webs of dialogue because they believe that coercion disrupts relationships in regulatory diplomacy.

40  In addition to the facilitation of modelling, dialogue builds regimes through defining issues as a concern, creating contracting spaces where complex interdependency can induce cooperation, constituting normative commitments, nurturing habits of compliance that are then institutionalized into bureaucratic routines, communicating informal praise and shame that are then institutionalized, and building capacity. When many different types of actors use many dialogic mechanisms of this sort, both impressive regime-building and impressive compliance have been repeatedly demonstrated.

41  Webs of dialogue build both top-down and bottom-up globalization sequences. 'Top-down' means defining a problem, agreeing on principles to solve it, agreeing on rules and enforcing rules. 'Bottom-up' means defining a problem, some firms changing practice to solve the problem, others modelling the new practice, globalizing the new custom and globalizing law in the shadow of custom.

## The Role of Modelling

42  Model mongers float a variety of models until they find one that catches opponents off-balance by forming a resonant appeal to a people's sense of identity. Because a model touted by an NGO can frame a debate, clever model mongering can give the weak a decisive advantage over the strong.

43  Theoretically, the possibility of the weak prevailing over the strong in the world system is illuminated by marrying Latour's theory of power and enrolment and Putnam's theory of global politics as a two-level game (or as an even more nested game). Marrying these with a sociological theory of modelling in the world system reveals surprisingly potent mechanisms for the weak prevailing over the strong.

44  There are recurrent proactive and reactive sequences of strategic micro action to secure global regulatory change (see Figure 5.1).

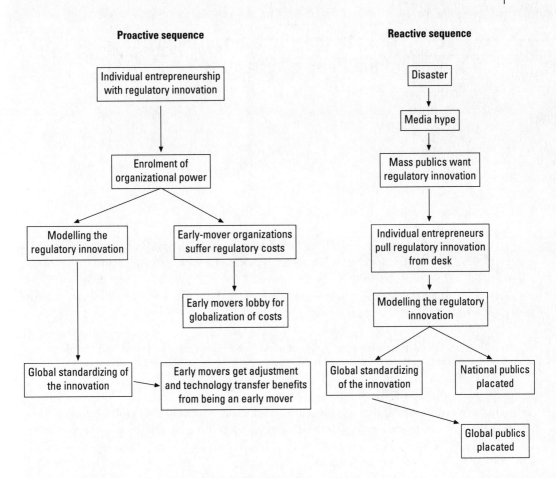

FIGURE 5.1    Proactive and reactive sequences of strategic micro action

## CHAPTER 6

# The Struggle for a Sovereignty of the People

Forty-four is a long list of empirical conclusions for readers to remember. Yet the richness of the inductions about the thicket of actors, principles and mechanisms summarized in Tables 20.1 (pp. 476–7), 21.1 (p. 508) and 22.1 (p. 532) sets up a normative conclusion of considerable power and focus. This particularly follows from empirical conclusion number 31 in Chapter 5:

> 31 There are paradoxes of sovereignty in the growth of global regulation. When national sovereignty and the sovereignty of elected parliaments are eroded, the sovereignty of ordinary citizens is sometimes enhanced.

The very complexity of the webs of actors mobilizing mechanisms of global business regulation enables citizen groups, even individual citizens, to exert genuine influence over globalization. Our data document how entrepreneurship by the weak can prise open conflicts among stronger players, enrolling big business or strategic states in the cause of citizen groups. Modelling, which we find to be the most consistently important mechanism of globalization, is shown in some compelling ways (Chapter 25) to be more useful to the weak than to the powerful. For citizens to assert their sovereignty in the world system, they must understand the formidable array of strategies much more available to big players – from forum-shifting to military coercion to capacity-building. Part III of this book shows that the weapons of the weak are different from those of the strong. When NGOs touch the identities of mass publics and communicate with them through the mass media and the Internet, our data show that they often win. When they turn the strength of the strong against itself (political ju-jitsu) by deft working of epistemic communities, our data show that they often win.

While large corporations and their home governments usually dominate agendas through the formidable set of strategies at their disposal, the significance of epistemic communities in our analysis is that global regulation is surprisingly deliberative. It has to be, because coercion is so often counterproductive. At the end of the twentieth century, for example, political power more effectively comes from the barrel of a gun within states than between them. Although we find that national sovereignty over business regulation is in decline and will continue to decline, Chapter 26 concludes that there is no certainty that globalization will erode the sovereignty of the people conceived in a republican way.

Some citizen sovereignty might be recovered by a cautiously crafted role for an elected Second Assembly of the UN, a citizens' Constitutional Convention for the UN, a treaty on treaties that secures greater tripartism in global business regulatory institutions, transparency guarantees and funding of NGO participation in debates (see Chapter 26). But that is not the main game.

There are always business players who fight hard to lessen regulations that protect citizens and to strengthen regulation that confers monopoly power. Ordinary citizens more often support increased regulation to protect citizens and deregulation of monopoly power. Asserting the sovereignty of citizens against the effective sovereignty of big business therefore requires a new kind of political program in the new millennium. This program would aim to change lowest common denominator regulation into global ratcheting-up of both protective regulation and competition law to effect deregulation of monopoly power.

To this end, Chapter 26 considers five strategies for NGOs to intervene in webs of regulation to ratchet-up standards in the world system:

1   exploiting strategic trade thinking to divide and conquer business;

2   harnessing the management philosophy of continuous improvement;

3   linking Porter's 'competitive advantage of nations' analysis (1990) to best available technology and best available practice standards;

4   targeting enforcement on 'gatekeepers' within a web of controls (actors with limited self-interest in rule-breaking, but on whom rule-breakers depend);

5   taking framework agreements seriously.

Chapter 26 also considers four strategies for intervening in global webs of regulation to counter monopoly:

1   using competition policy to divide and conquer business;

2   harnessing continuous improvement in competition law compliance;

3   building global epistemic community in competition enforcement;

4   transforming the consumer movement into a watchdog of monopoly.

This is an egalitarian agenda because citizens of the poorest nations suffer most from abuse of monopoly power, from crises in the world financial system caused by inadequate financial regulation, from unsafe workplaces and consumer products, from chemicals in the environment, from soil erosion and desertification. A joint program to deregulate monopolies and to increase regulation that prevents the foisting of these externalities onto the world's poor can bolster economic growth in developing countries. To a lesser degree, a package of invigorated antitrust that enhances competition, regulation that increases financial system security and incorporates externalities into prices, can help deliver more efficient economies in the developed world. Capitalism has not flourished best when it has been centrally planned by the state, nor when it has been unregulated. Plural good governance of capitalism by states, international organizations, business self-regulation, professions and NGOs is needed for secure, egalitarian and efficient capitalism.

International NGOs tend to be European-dominated and, to a lesser extent, US-dominated (Boli, Loya & Loftin 1999) and this is not very egalitarian. The optimistic fact, however, is that breadth of participation in international NGOs has grown fastest in poorer nations since 1960 (Boli, Loya & Loftin 1999), even though the growth of participation in the North has also been formidable.

Our conclusion is that NGOs are the key to invigorating global good governance. A political program to strengthen civil society is the practical path to embedding in cultures the trust that enables economic efficiency (Putnam 1993, 1995) and simultaneously institutionalizing the distrust (the regulation) that prevents abuse of power (Braithwaite 1998). Transparency International is an early version of this new kind of NGO. It has a global agenda of simultaneously ending corruption (the abuse of power) and improving economic efficiency through good governance reforms.

Ours is not an argument for weakening national governments. They must remain strong to perform their part in credible global webs of regulation. Nor do we argue that NGOs ought to abandon traditional Greenpeace-style guerrilla campaigns that mobilize mass publics, opting instead for besuited engagement with epistemic communities. Rather, we argue that the best way for NGOs to add value to what they already do is to use citizen volunteers to engage more systematically with the thousands of global epistemic communities of regulation, and to do this simultaneously with engaging the global competition policy epistemic community. Because this way of adding value to the objectives of global NGOs will contribute to prosperity and security, it is an initiative that a visionary foundation might consider funding one day.

Yet the promise of our political program lies more in its democratic appeal than in its economic appeal. It is a practical response to recover some citizen sovereignty in the face of eroding national sovereignty. It is a way of moving toward the republican ideal of the separation of powers (Pettit 1997) in the context of a global polity where, at the end of the millennium, the big concentrations of power are in corporations rather than states (Braithwaite 1997). A global separation of powers. One where NGOs with direct citizen input are the emerging check and balance, adding value to the existing checks and balances of national and international courts, UN institutions and national legislatures.

The basis of a political program for sovereignty of the people over global regulation can be identified. Our motif is that individual readers can engage in a way that makes a difference. That engagement can be through an internationalizing women's movement, an environment group, an ad hoc coalition on the Multilateral Agreement on Investment that can be joined via the Internet, or by being a businessperson, scientist, lawyer, economist or state official who joins the great global debates with these groups. We hope that some readers will use this book to help them pick an important arena, begin to understand its history, and seek the contextual wisdom to be an active world citizen. More effective and decent global regulation depends on ordinary citizens doing this. Without citizen action, regulatory agendas are dominated by concentrated economic interests and decision-making is impoverished by an insufficient plurality of perspectives on the interests at stake.

# Part II
## CASES

CHAPTER 7 | Property and Contract

This chapter outlines the history of the globalization of the law of property and contract. These two are treated together because, arguably, together they form the foundation of a private law-based system of commerce. Property law constitutes the objects of property; contract enables the exchange of those objects. Through contract the objects of property become capital. The focus is on the way the principles of property and contract have harmonized, or not, as the case may be. The influence of Rome, through its jurists and their writings, has been crucial.

First, we must place some boundaries for the chapter. Early in their studies law students are disabused of the notion that property is a thing. Modern jurisprudential wisdom holds that property is a set of relations between individuals, those relations being constituted in terms of rights and duties. This is true. It is also true that these rights and duties relate to things. A's duty not to trespass on B's land is a duty A owes to B in relation to a thing. It is a mistake to uncouple what Pollock calls the 'thinglikeness' of property from the rights and duty relations of property. They are what make property comprehensible as an institution. It is property that determines who may have access to things and under what conditions – who, in other words, may use what resources.

Property can be divided into real property (basically land) and personal property. We say little about real property and a lot about personal property. The regulation of land has not been subject to the same pressures for international harmonization that we will see in the case of personal property forms and contract.[1] Money, goods, shares, negotiable instruments of various

---

1 Even in the case of land there are examples of regulatory harmonization across borders. The best example is seen in systems of land law that operate on the basis of registered title. Central to such a system is the maintenance of a written record of all transactions relating to the land, thereby providing users with complete information about title to land. The alternative to such a system is often a costly hunt to establish a chain of title. The Torrens system of registration, named after its creator Robert Torrens, was first enacted in South Australia in 1858. Torrens is said to have drawn some of his ideas from the English *Merchant Shipping Act 1854* (Whalan 1982: 6). The Torrens legislative scheme was copied by a number of countries including Uganda, Kenya and Brunei (Meek 1968: 278). Land regulation is one of the few areas covered in this book where it remains possible to speak of a genuine state sovereignty. Activities carried out on land (e.g. air pollution) are, through international environmental regulation, being affected by processes of globalization, but the regulation of land use and planning (e.g. zoning) remains firmly in the grip of states, often at the level of local government.

One last point concerning the regulation of land, although it is rather a large one. Land lay at the heart of feudalism. Feudalism was not just a system of land law based on tenure. It was also a form of government. In feudal times land was the meeting-place of what we now call public and private law. It is unclear to what extent we can speak of harmonized systems of feudalism operating in Europe from the tenth to the thirteenth centuries. Clearly, before any system might be called feudal it must have certain basic characteristics including the relationship of lord and tenant. After that, one can talk of different kinds of feudalism. The extent to which one can say that feudalism represented a harmonized system for the regulation of land remains unclear and in any case is a question for others to answer.

kinds, copyright and patents are all examples of personal property. Roman private law drew a distinction between corporeal things and incorporeal things. In the *Institutes* of Gaius and the *Institutes* of Justinian, which simply follow Gaius in this respect, the distinction is between what can be touched and what cannot, the tangible and the intangible (Justinian's *Institutes*, 533 AD: 2.2). This distinction is still found in modern common law and civil systems. This chapter's main focus is on intangible property forms or, putting it another way, property rights in abstract objects.

Another boundary needs to be set, so that this chapter does not encroach too much on following chapters. Personal property forms such as money and shares, as well as contract, might easily lead to a discussion of financial regulation and the regulation of securities markets. A discussion of the regulation of the circulation and trade of these personal property forms appears in Chapters 8 and 9. Before an intangible property form or a contract can be traded it has to be constituted by a set of legal norms. For example, a patent is an entity of law; an invention is not. Without patent law there is no patent to assign. It is true that trade in physical goods like inventions is facilitated by rules of property and contract. But basically physical goods can be bartered between individuals even without a common system of property and contract rules. This chapter examines the extent to which property and contract have been globalized as constituent legal norms. We are interested in the role that property and contract play in the instantiation of the objects and relations of commerce. More specifically, we are interested in the degree to which this constitutive task of property and contract proceeds under conditions of global harmonization of property and contract norms.

Finally, a historical discussion of the globalization of personal property should include a discussion of the institution of slavery – people as property. The regulation of this institution of empires represents one of the earliest and most lasting forms of regulatory and market globalization. The regulation of slavery is discussed in Chapter 11, which deals with labour.

## History of Globalization

### Before Rome

The history of the globalization of property and contract is linked to the rise and fall of the Roman empire. Property and contract have a history before the Roman empire, but it seems to be a history that is largely locked up in the custom and religion of a people or a tribe (Maine 1861). Property and contract are also the subject of other great legal systems that have ancient, non-Roman origins, Hindu law being an example (Nanda & Sinha 1996). But in terms of its regulatory impact and influence on the institutions and laws of other countries, Roman law has been the most important. More than any other legal system, it has exercised an influence beyond its time. The principles and rules of Roman private law are embedded in the common law and civil systems of many states.

### The Harmonization of Property and Contract Under Rome

Gaius, in the *Institutes* (commonly dated 161 AD), divides law into the law of persons, of things and of actions. This simple three-fold classification is also found in the *Institutes* (533 AD) of the Roman emperor Justinian. Justinian's *Institutes* are largely modelled on those of Gaius. Property and contract in the modern common law senses do not have exact equivalents in either of the *Institutes*. The 'thing' in the law of things (*res*) refers to the idea of an economically valuable asset (Buckland 1963: 182). Obligations fall under this broader meaning of thing, so the law of things includes obligations. Contractual obligations were included in the classificatory structure for obligations. Under this scheme it can be seen that property is broadly conceived and that contract forms a distinct part of it.

The content of the law of things, including contractual obligations, to which Gaius' *Institutes* are only an introduction, is not our concern. Our interest is in the extent to which Roman private law applied throughout the Roman empire.

In terms of territorial reach, the empire attained its zenith in the period of the Principate (27 BC–284 AD) (Tellegen-Couperus 1993: 66–7). It stretched into central and western Europe and included parts of Germany as well as England and Wales (Scotland was conquered, but not occupied for any length of time). In the east, Armenia, Assyria and Mesopotamia became territories. By the second century AD Rome formed the centre of a global trading system. It depended upon its rich provinces in Spain, Africa and Asia to supply it raw materials, labour and revenue. These provinces also supplied the frontiers of the empire. In addition to its complex intra-empire trade Rome also traded with the 'barbarian periphery' from which it obtained labour and the raw materials and luxury goods it could not get within its borders (Cunliffe 1988: 4). The trade networks that sustained the lifestyles of conspicuous consumption of Rome's wealthier inhabitants reached into Africa, China and India.

Running parallel to Rome's territorial and commercial expansion was the creation and expansion of its private law. Private law, says Justinian's *Institutes*, 'is about the well-being of individuals' (1.1). The development of Roman private law was largely undertaken by a body of men commonly called jurists. It is the jurists from the classical period (the Principate) who 'are the real builders of the great fabric of Roman Law' (Buckland 1963: 20). Jurists were private individuals who, through their writings and opinions, developed the principles and rules of private law. Often belonging to influential families, they were writers who 'dirtied their hands'. Advocates sought their views on points of law arising in lawsuits and they were called on to draft legal documents. Their interpretations became authoritative for judges, although the formal binding effect of their interpretations remains a difficult question of Roman law scholarship (Nicholas 1962, 31; Watson 1995, 4). Using the Greek dialectical method, they turned Roman jurisprudence into a legal science (Schulz 1946: 67–8). This scientific jurisprudence was of a distinctive technical kind. It was not primarily concerned with the abstract questions such as the nature of justice, which had preoccupied the Greeks. Instead, it sought to systematize and classify different parts of law according to genus and species and to identify principles that might be used to solve new problems. It was a secular jurisprudence of legal praxis, not a philosophy of law. By the end of the classical period Roman private law was a system of enormous technical detail, governed by a complex set of legal principles. The system was complemented by a scientific jurisprudence that was aimed at solving legal problems and maintaining the internal coherence of the system. Viewed in this way Roman private law was a powerful regulatory model, powerful because of its conceptual depth, technical detail and its capacity to solve new problems. More states, as we will see, fell under its influence than ever fell to Rome's armies.

To what extent did Roman private law apply throughout the empire? Basically, it progressively extended throughout the empire as more and more of its inhabitants acquired citizenship. Roman private law applied to Roman citizens. The grant of citizenship was used to integrate cities into the empire and to reward individuals. In 212 AD the emperor Antonine, by edict, gave citizenship to all free subjects in the Roman empire (Buckland 1963: 98). Prior to that the application of Roman law was more complex. Legal relations between non-citizens (*peregrini*) and citizens were regulated by a law for foreigners that was developed by a special magistrate with jurisdiction over foreigners, the *praetor peregrinus* (Stein 1988: 19). This law (known as *ius honorarium*) was based on Roman private law and much of it related to matters of property and contract. *Ius honorarium* was innovative and less formal than *ius civile,* and because of its advantages it became available to citizens. It also began to merge with the *ius civile,* which it came to complement in the manner that equity complements common law. In this way Roman private law diffused throughout the territories and frontiers of the empire. Clearly the existence of a body of contract and property rules applicable to citizens and non-citizens would have helped to facilitate commerce within the empire.

The next key event in this brief history is the systematization of Roman law during the reign of the emperor Justinian (527–65 AD). By the time Justinian came to the throne of the eastern Roman empire in Constantinople, Rome was no longer part of the empire. It had fallen to the Ostrogoths in 476 AD. The barbarian periphery had taken over much of the empire's territory. Justinian managed to recapture significant parts of the western empire, including Italy, but this was something of a last flurry before the empire headed toward extinction. Much more important than Justinian could ever have foreseen was his initiative to systematize Roman classical law, for it was through the spirit of its law that Rome continued to influence institutions and thinking in Europe.

Before Justinian's reign Roman private law had been steadily undergoing a transformation. The refinements and distinctions of the classical period were being abandoned, and classical law became increasingly mixed with the local law and custom of the various territories. The harmonized system of Roman private law of the classical period was fragmenting. A supranational model of law was disintegrating, displaced by local variants. This process is generally referred to as the vulgarization of Roman law (Kaser 1965: 4–5).

Justinian desired to bring certainty and coherence to the legal system of the empire. To this end he directed his minister Tribonian to initiate a series of law-reform projects. These culminated in the publication of what is referred to as the *Corpus Iuris Civilis*. The *Corpus* is comprised of four works; the *Institutes*, the *Digest*, the *Codex* and the *Novels*. The scale of the project was vast. The *Digest*, a work of 150 000 lines, embodies the labours of the classical jurists and involved reading 2000 scrolls (3 million lines) (Tellegen-Couperus 1993: 142). The result was a body of learning that presented a classificatory structure and conceptual scheme of law as well as a vast array of detailed technical statements on all the topics of private law.

After the publication of its main parts in 533 and 534 AD the *Corpus,* like the empire, began to fade, particularly in the west, where the process of vulgarization was more profound than in the east. Much of the western empire soon fell into non-Roman hands. In 568 AD most of Italy was under the rule of the Lombards, who were of Germanic origin. Unlike the empire, however, the *Corpus* was destined for revival and a second journey of conquest. This journey began in the eleventh century in Bologna, where the scholar Irnerius was principally responsible for beginning a study of the *Corpus Iuris.*

## The Second Journey of Roman Law

During the eleventh century western Europe, especially the northern cities of Italy, began to experience greater economic prosperity, based on trade. There was also greater interest in learning, based on the recovery of ancient cultural achievements. In the study of law this interest in past learning was dramatically stimulated when a copy of the complete text of the *Digest* was found in Pisa. This discovery sparked a quiet revolution. Prior to that university academics had been studying fragments of classical texts and, through the scholastic method, trying to make sense of them. It was a process of work in which 'lawyers had more than their fair share' (Vinogradoff 1929: 32). The discovery of the *Digest* led to the recovery of the *Corpus Iuris*, which was akin to a library of information, on occasions poorly organized. This turned out to be an advantage, as it meant that the *Corpus* could be interpreted in a way that suited medieval needs (Nicholas 1962: 47). Led by Irnerius, groups of scholars in Bologna began to work on the *Corpus* with the aim of producing a version that represented a comprehensible and usable system. Their method of work – writing short marginal notes on the texts – led to them being known as 'Glossators'. The *Corpus Iuris* became more or less the sole object of legal study. Bologna became the centre of Roman law studies in Europe and maintained its dominance into the thirteenth century. Thousands of students came to Bologna to be instructed in the methods and interpretations of the Glossators.

The reception of Roman law into Europe travelled, at first, along academic routes. University after university began to develop the study of Roman law. The teaching of Roman law spread throughout western and eastern Europe. One of the crucial factors in this diffusion was that the Glossators had, in effect, constructed a useful resource:

> the law of the *Corpus Iuris* was a highly developed system providing solutions for many difficult legal questions and was conveniently assembled in one great codification. In contrast with this, the local laws were undeveloped and differed from region to region, and often from community to community. Many had never been put to writing and were thus inaccessible to scientific treatment and academic teaching (Wolff 1951: 191).

The agents of the reception of Roman law were university teachers and those trained by them who entered the legal system – the administrators, judges and advocates (Watson 1991: 90). Throughout Europe the legal communities of different territories began to gravitate towards Roman law. The details of this reception would form a work of many volumes. No country in Europe escaped the process. In Germany the process of reception was helped by the gradual replacement of lay-judges (*Schöffen*) who administered customary law, with lawyers who at university had been trained in Roman law (Ryan 1962: 21). In France, Justinian's *Institutes* had been kept alive through the work of academicians; it was the *Institutes* to which Napoleon's codifying commission of 1800 turned for a structure for France's legal code. The march of Roman law did not halt at the English Channel. The structure of Blackstone's *Commentaries* (1765–69) is essentially that of Justinian's *Institutes* (Birks & McLeod 1987: 24). Scottish law, more overtly and consciously than the common law, borrowed from Roman law. Again the universities were central in the process of transmission. Scots were studying Roman law at the University of Bologna in the second part of the thirteenth century (Stein 1988: 327).

The reception of Roman law throughout Europe did not entail the reception of one model legal system in all localities and states. The Glossators and the school that succeeded them, the Commentators, through their study of Roman law created a storehouse of principles, rules, techniques and ideas about law. Roman law functioned as a kind of legal treasury for Europe from the time of Irnerius onwards. All states in Europe borrowed from this treasury, but what they borrowed remained at the more abstract level of principles and structure rather than detailed regulatory models. Roman law (along with canon law, particularly in the areas of matrimony and wills) worked as a centripetal harmonizer. It became the handmaiden of different western medieval legal systems – canon law, imperial law, the systems of positive law of emerging secular states (Berman 1983: 204–5). But there were also centrifugal forces at work. Customary law, especially that of the Germanic kings, spread through their invasions of the Roman empire, remained important in various parts of medieval Europe. The common law borrowed from but did not become a civil law system. A more important and fundamental centrifugal influence was a new form of social organization – the nation-state. The growth of nation-states brought deep change to patterns of legal regulation, change that can be presented as a shift from a principle of personality to a principle of territoriality. During the time of the Roman empire, the acquisition of new territory by Rome did not mean that Roman law applied to all within that newly acquired territory. Legal relations between the inhabitants of such territories continued to be governed by their customary law. Roman law applied only to relations between citizens; relations between citizens and non-citizens were governed by the law developed by the *Peregrine Praetor* (the civil magistrate for foreigners). Roman law thus recognized that some law followed individuals by virtue of their belonging to a tribe or a people – what we will call the principle of personality. This principle of personality was recognized by the barbarian conquerors of the empire. Whether under the rule of the Lombards, the Franks or other barbarian government, Romans were allowed to follow Roman law. The principle of personality allowed for the coexistence of the different laws of different peoples. It thereby produced great complexity and uncertainty, particularly in trade.

> In all these and in many other respects the legal rights of the Roman would be at variance with those of his German neighbours. These, again, would act differently, each according to his peculiar nationality, as Salian Franks or Ripuarians, Bavarians or Burgundians, &c. The position became very intricate when members of different nationalities, living under different laws, were brought together to transact business with each other. As Bishop Agobard of Lyons tells us about 850, it happened constantly that of five people meeting in one room, each followed a law of his own (Vinogradoff 1929: 25–6).

Nation-states over time developed an alternative to the principle of personality. The sovereign of a nation-state, it came to be accepted, had the right to enact laws for a particular territory. Sovereignty came to mean a right of command over the inhabitants of a territory rather than simply a people. Territorial sovereignty, which through the work of Grotius came to underpin the law of nations, was born of a complex intermingling of ideas. It was largely a fusion of Roman property concepts (sovereignty as *dominium*) and feudalistic doctrines that defined a person's powers, rights and duties in terms of their relationship to land (Maine 1861: 110, 114). Sovereignty, which for a long time had been bound up with ideas about the responsibility of an individual sovereign for the custody and welfare of a people, came to be linked to control over a territory with defined borders. Territorial sovereignty was complemented by the development of an important legal principle, the principle of territoriality – the principle that the laws of a sovereign applied absolutely within the territory that constituted the sovereign's state but did not apply in the territories of other sovereigns. This principle, like the principle of personality, worked against the harmonizing influence of Roman law. The principle of territoriality brought unity of law within a state. It enabled the intrastate harmonization of law. But the principle also left scope for national systems of law to develop. It was not a principle that worked in favour of the cross-border harmonization of a given set of rules because, under the principle, the sovereign's commands stopped at the borders of their nation-state.

The spread of Roman law, which had begun so forcefully in the eleventh century, began to lose its impetus in the sixteenth. The work of Renaissance legal humanists was crucial in this

(Hazeltine 1926: 155). It was they who, through their attacks on medievalist interpretations of Roman law paved the way for renewed interest in the study of customary law. Beginning in the sixteenth century, customary law throughout Europe underwent a process of redaction. Jurists and legal historians reclaimed and reconstituted in systematic form the native origins of law. The rise of legal orders based on the principle of territoriality left open the possibility of nation-states having distinctive national legal orders. The study of customary law by schools of national jurists throughout Europe was crucial to the development of national legal systems each with its own indigenous jurisprudence. Roman law, which through its reception into Europe had offered the elements of a universal legal system, had to be content with casting its shadow upon the legal systems of nation-states. Roman private law, particularly contract and property, was still studied and it provided the emerging national legal orders of Europe with a common conceptual vocabulary, but not a universal legal system. The common law, which was the least influenced by Roman contract law, developed its own distinctive theory of contract based on the doctrine of consideration (Holdsworth 1937: vol. 3: 413). Civil-code countries also developed the principles governing matters such as remedies for breach of contract in different ways. The differences among secular legal systems, however, developed later. In the thirteenth and fourteenth centuries there were remarkable degrees of harmonization at the level of principle between, for example, the law of the king's courts of France and the king's courts of England (Berman 1983: 477–81). The unity of canon law in the thirteenth and fourteenth centuries was, to a slightly lesser extent, shadowed by the unity of secular systems. Canon law and secular law systems interacted and cross-pollinated in various ways, both drawing on Roman law principles (especially in contract and property law).

The rise of nation-states brought a decline in the supranational potential of Roman law. The resistance to the total Romanization of law had been made possible by groups of national jurists interested in the recovery of customary law. Customary law turned out to be crucial in giving legal systems a national identity. Pope Gregory VII (1073–85), in *Dictatus Papae*, declared the Pope's supreme legislative and judicial power across all Christendom; the moments when canon law actually had such influence were few. Property and contracts were regulated by both canon law and secular systems of law. Canon law generally was 'more highly developed' and therefore 'available for imitation', but the extent of its imitation by secular authorities was limited by fear of expanding ecclesiastical power, as well as by the existence of customary sources of law that secular systems could draw upon (Berman 1983: 274). Islam was more potently transnationally integrative in the Middle Ages, but contemporary legal systems owe even less to it than canon law, as most Islamic states emerged from nineteenth-century colonialism with overwhelmingly European laws of property and contract.

Elsewhere another group of men – merchant traders – had a very practical interest in having their affairs regulated by one set of rules. While customary norms generally formed the basis, in Europe, of counter-movements to the Romanization of law, the commercial customs of merchant traders provided one form of agency for harmonization.

### The Medieval Law Merchant: *Lex Mercatoria*

Feudal society was not simply a static world of obligations, bonds and tenure based on relations to land. It was also a trading society. Trade grew in the eleventh and twelfth centuries, which led to the professionalization of trade. Increasingly, trade was carried out by merchants whose livelihood was based upon the pursuit and exchange of goods and who, through charters of privilege, managed to escape the restrictions of feudal law that bound many lowly peasant producers

(Postan 1973: 138–42). Trade acquired an international and exotic character in southern Europe where the quest for goods led merchants, especially those from northern Italy, to the Middle East, Africa and China.

The principle of personality which allowed each merchant to bring the law of their people to any trade deal did not serve the interests of merchants as a class. When merchants from different ethnic groups met and traded, there were complex problems of conflicting law. Merchants saw clearly that if trade, particularly international trade, was to flourish they needed clear and certain rules as well as speedy dispute resolution mechanisms. Through the application of commercial practical reason merchants evolved a set of customary norms that applied to them as a professional class. The origins of Law Merchant (*Lex Mercatoria*) lie in the customary practices of merchants that transcended local custom or law and which came to be recognized by national courts. The core of these practices was the principle of good faith in the making of agreements, a principle policed by merchants' need to maintain trading relations so that the growing international commerce could continue (Trakman 1983: 7). The creation and reinforcement of this body of merchant custom was aided by the evolution of codes of conduct in important trading centres, codes that had an influence across state boundaries. In the case of maritime trade the most important were the Amalphitan Table (1095, from the republic of Amalphi in Italy), the Rolls of Oléron from the island of Oléron (c. 1150), the Consulato del Mare from Barcelona in 1340 and the Laws of Wisby (c. 1350) from the Baltic (Berman & Kaufman 1978: 224–5). The Rolls of Oléron entered English commercial law through their adoption into the Black Book of the Admiralty. It was to the Rolls of Oléron and other parts of the Law Merchant that the Admiralty Court, the Courts of Fairs and Boroughs and the Staple Courts in medieval England looked in mercantile disputes. The common law was held at bay for a time.

Regular meetings between merchants, essential in founding a body of common custom, took place throughout Europe at the great trade fairs of Champagne, Lyons, Anvers, Genoa and others. These fairs became the hubs of international medieval commerce. The most important of these were the fairs of Champagne which took place under the protection of the counts of Champagne. The amount of trade conducted at the Champagne fairs was so great that they became 'the clearing-house of medieval Europe' (Baldwin 1968: 92–3). The fairs also became places for the resolution of disputes between merchants. Merchants' tribunals and courts were set up and administered by merchants themselves. At the Champagne fairs the counts appointed 'Guards of the Fair', who came to operate as an independent force (Abu-Lughod 1989: 59). Through specialist and independent decision-making procedures merchants were able to create and reinforce the Law Merchant. Specialized merchant courts meant that the Law Merchant did not become cluttered by technicality and formality on matters of evidence and procedure. And because merchant courts based themselves on merchant custom they remained sensitive to changes in that custom.

The emerging nation-states helped to promote a unified body of commercial law for traders, because they did not want to be bypassed by the growing international trade. In England, for example, special statutes like the *Carta Mercatoria 1303* and the *Statute of Staple 1353* were passed so that local and foreign merchants were guaranteed quick dispute resolution and the application of their own rules (Goode 1995: 4). Mercantile matters were heard by the prerogative courts such as the Court of Admiralty, before judges who had been educated in Roman law and who had become familiar with negotiable instruments and insurance well before their common-law counterparts (Stein 1988: 218–19). European rulers also aided the growth of the Law Merchant by issuing its customs in code form, the *Book of Customs* of Milan of 1216 being one such example (Berman 1983: 355).

The pressures that pushed the Law Merchant in the direction of a unified system met countervailing pressures. Some fairs, like those of Champagne, kept their own distinctive merchant usages. The discrimination by some local merchant courts against foreigners led Italian cities to treat foreigners in Italy as their own citizens were treated in foreign lands (Trakman 1983: 19). Such pressures led to the Law Merchant being pulled back into the orbit of the legal orders of nation-states, thus it progressively lost the transnational unity that had characterized its emergence. But the guiding principle of merchant law – that the law regulating merchants should be based on their customs – remained an immanent norm within national legal orders. So, for example, when Lord Mansfield, the eighteenth-century founder of English commercial law, heard commercial matters he did so with a jury of merchants drawn from the City of London so that he could more accurately determine the actual practice of merchants (Wright 1939: xii).

## The Intangible Instruments of Trade

Trading beyond one's borders or even beyond one's village brings the problem of how to effect payment. Clearly, carrying bags of gold or coin on horseback for long distances is both inconvenient and dangerous. As international and intra-regional trade in medieval Europe grew, the problem of how to arrange the payment of goods became more pressing. Solutions came in the creation of financial instruments, documents that were easier and safer to transport than gold or coin. These instruments, such as the bill of exchange, became part of the landscape of personal property and, with the rise of negotiability, tradable entities in their own right. More importantly, from the point of view of this chapter, their use came to be regulated by rules that were harmonized across borders. The origins of these rules lay in the customs of merchants.

These instruments of trade (bills of exchange, letters of credit, promissory notes) have very ancient origins. The merchants of medieval Europe were not the first international traders. Letters of credit, for instance, existed in Ancient Egypt, Ancient Greece and Ancient Rome (Mugasha 1988: 4–13). There is a Babylonian clay promissory note dating back to about 3000 BC, and there is evidence that Phoenician merchants used bills of exchange in their trade in the Mediterranean (Trimble 1948: 982, 984). Various theories suggest that the bill of exchange was borrowed from the Orient and Arabia (Postan 1973: 57). In fact, it seems that most financial instruments had been invented by Islamic countries well before European traders began to experience a need for them (Abu-Lughod 1989: 224). Once societies had developed the means for symbolically representing (through writing) their money (physical objects) their traders began to develop symbolic forms of transferring rights and obligations to money (Braudel 1975: 358–9) (money itself evolves from concrete commodity to currency: Geva 1987). The use of these forms grew and spread along international trading routes.

Ancient systems of law made it difficult to transfer rights to debt because conceptually such systems required the transfer of a physical thing. In the case of a debt there was no physical thing, only an intangible in the form of a right. It was also a problem that debtor-based relationships were seen as personal to the original parties, and incapable of being switched to involve other parties. In the eighth and ninth centuries the Lombardian lawyers of northern Italy began to invent documents that contained clauses in which debtors promised performance to nominees of the creditor or simply to producers of the documents (Holdsworth 1937: 115). In other words, they began to introduce into Europe the idea of a documentary transfer of an intangible (the right to a debt). Because of their high commercial convenience, these types of documents were used widely in Europe by the thirteenth century. Italian merchants were among the earliest and most sophisticated users of these documents. They had learnt of the documents' advantages through their trading links and connections with eastern merchants (Abu-Lughod 1989: 67).

These financial instruments were used to settle debts between merchants engaged in international trade. Of particular importance was the bill of exchange, the *tratta*, or letter of payment as it was known. By the fifteenth century a standard version was used everywhere in Europe (Postan 1973: 54). A merchant in Italy might owe money for goods bought from a merchant in London. Rather than arrange for coins to be transported to London, the Italian merchant would agree to pay the debt, perhaps at one of the major trade fairs. An Italian money-exchanger, who had been given funds by the Italian merchant, would draw a document ordering payment in favour of the London merchant; this order would be accepted by a London money-exchanger representing the London merchant at the fair (Holdsworth 1937: 128–30). It became part of merchant routine to make bills of exchange payable at trade fairs – from the thirteenth to the fifteenth century most European trade and business was transacted at fairs. The documents became progressively more sophisticated, as did the practices that surrounded them. Money-exchangers became banks. Because they represented many merchants and multiple transactions from many places, banks began to aggregate the debts they owed to each other and set them off in order to simplify their dealings with each other. The modern categories of the bill of exchange (the drawer, drawee, payee and holder) became formalized. Merchants with large sums of money used bills of exchange to arrange credit. Postan has argued that the widespread imitation of the Italian *tratta* in all countries, including England, was due to the emergence of a new type of commercial actor in Europe: 'the rise and development of that type of commercial organization of which the Italian banking-houses were a specimen: we mean the appearance of firms with permanent connections abroad' (1973: 63). Growing international trade meant that such firms had increasing funds in the hands of their partners and agents abroad; bills of exchange were a safe and convenient means by which those funds could be shifted to meet obligations.

The financial instruments that were an indispensable part of medieval commercial expansion were part of a complex bootstraps process. Trade usage and acceptance brought these instruments into being. Because they were used by groups with transnational memberships, the instruments existed in a surprisingly harmonized form. States not wishing to be bypassed by trade allowed use of the instruments, with courts in particular taking the view that as a general rule they should declare the law relating to instrument use in ways that were consistent with merchants' practices. States allowed the proliferation of merchant tribunals throughout Europe that placed the emphasis on informality, merchant practice and speed of adjudication (Trakman 1983: 13). Growth in the use of financial instruments helped to create, preserve and expand trading relationships. One reason for this was that these instruments became central to the development of a credit system. Essentially, they allowed debts to be detached from the original transactions so that they could be re-used in further financial transactions (Atiyah 1979: 135). The evolution of a credit system in each state partly depended on how quickly its legal system moved to allow the negotiability of financial instruments.

The history of bills of exchange and other negotiable instruments is specific to each state and beyond the scope of our present project. The important feature, for this book, is that the paper contracts that form the basis of these instruments came to form personal property, special forms of chattel which embody obligations (Barak 1983). The evolution of full ownership rights in these instruments took time, as the exploitation of such rights ran into the prohibition of usury

(Holdsworth 1937: 100–13). Once again, the practices of merchants were the basis upon which these instruments gained the attributes of ownership. Merchants needed to be able to shift debt between themselves as a form of payment. On the Continent methods for the transfer of these documents began to be developed. Promissory notes, for instance, were drafted so that they were payable to the original creditor or to the bearer of the note (Holden 1955: 68).

However, transferability by itself was not enough. There would be no incentive for a merchant to accept a financial instrument if they might lose the benefit of it to another trader who could show a prior interest in it by virtue of an earlier transaction. In order to promote certainty and stability in commerce, merchants began to accept the practice that a trader who purchased an instrument in good faith did so free of any prior interests that might have become attached to the instrument. With the recognition of this rule the principle of negotiability became fully fledged in the Law Merchant. The rate of acceptance of this principle into general commercial law varied from jurisdiction to jurisdiction, as it did for other types of financial instruments. In England the principle of negotiability was eventually recognized by the common-law courts. Under the aggressive leadership of Lord Justice Coke the common-law courts took over the lucrative work of the Admiralty Court and began a long slow process of reinventing the principles of the Law Merchant. Through the judgments of Holt CJ and Lord Mansfield (Chief Justice 1756–88) the common law absorbed and adapted the Law Merchant, including recognition of the principle of negotiability. Over time negotiability spread over all European jurisdictions. The recognition of this principle, along with the transferability of commercial paper, meant that the holder of such paper also acquired some of the incidents of ownership which Honoré (1961) has suggested feature in a mature legal system, incidents such as the rights of use, possession, security and transmissibility.

## Financial Instruments Meet Legislative Instruments

Merchants' travels over Europe helped create a mercantile world which recognized principles such as good faith in dealings and which cultivated the use of commercial paper to pay debts and fund new enterprises. It was also a world of increased complexity. The ease with which commercial paper moved meant that merchants became part of ever longer chains of dependency. It was also a world in which there were broken promises, dishonesty and business deals that had gone bad. All going well, a bill of exchange was a good way to move money around, but what if, to take a simple case, the drawee in a bill of exchange failed to pay the holder of the bill? In a world of increasingly complex transactions between merchants, custom alone could not provide all the details needed to cover the various contingencies (the destruction of goods, the liability of partners in a firm, the effects of unauthorized signatures and so on) that might arise during a trade deal involving the use of commercial paper. Increasingly, merchants looked to the state to supplement the operation of custom with legal norms.

The basic pattern of response was to codify mercantile law. France followed this path in 1673 in the form of the 'Ordonnance de Commerce' and reworked it in the 'Code de Commerce' of 1807 (Cowen & Gering 1966: 15–16). The French Code became the basis of codes in the Netherlands, Spain, Greece, Egypt and parts of South America. The German states, led by Prussia, developed a regional model, which was enacted by the National Assembly in 1848 as the *Allgemeine Deutsche Wechselordnung* (Hudson & Feller 1931: 335). The *Wechselordnung* became the basis of codes in Denmark, Sweden, Norway, Switzerland, Italy, Peru, Portugal, Bulgaria, Hungary, Rumania, Russia, Japan, Brazil, El Salvador, Uruguay and Venezuela (Hudson & Feller 1931: 336; Cowen & Gering

1966: 16). Even the common-law stronghold of England followed the path of codification with the passage of the *Bills of Exchange Act 1882*, England's first codifying Act. Like Germany's, it was an example of a regionally unified model which was then modelled by many other states. The Act applied to the entire UK and was subsequently adopted, usually with very little change, by colonies or former colonies of the British empire. For example, it was adopted by all the Australian colonies and when the Australian parliament enacted the *Bills of Exchange Act 1909* it was 'in the main a transcript of the English Act of 1882'.[2] The law on bills of exchange in countries that had been linked to the British empire remained remarkably uniform because courts in those countries maintained English modes of interpretation in relation to the English Act and continued to look towards English precedents. This was especially true of countries which retained the right of appeal to the Privy Council (Barak 1968: 9).

In the US the codification of important parts of commercial law was also begun. The work of the National Conference of Commissioners on Uniform State Laws saw the emergence, in 1896, of a draft model for negotiable instruments. Known as the Negotiable Instruments Law (NIL), it drew on the English Bills of Exchange Act, but it was not a faithful transcription. The influence of New York law in particular produced discrepancies (Hudson & Feller 1931, 337). By 1924 all US states had adopted NIL. The drafter of the Bills of Exchange Act, Sir Mackenzie Chalmers, also drafted the *Sale of Goods Act 1893*, which explicitly preserved the operation of *Lex Mercatoria* in relation to contracts for the sale of goods. Like the Bills of Exchange Act, the Sale of Goods Act was adopted in many countries, usually verbatim. In the US it became the model for the *Uniform Sales Act 1906*, an Act adopted by more than two-thirds of US state legislatures. Other parts of commercial law in the US continued to be codified (*Uniform Warehouse Receipts Act 1906* and *Uniform Bills of Lading Act 1909*). Rather than allowing US commercial law to have many codes, the idea of having a single commercial code incorporating all the others began to be discussed in the 1940s. Under the sponsorship of the National Conference of Commissioners and the American Law Institute, the Uniform Commercial Code emerged in 1951. Pennsylvania was the first state to enact the Code, in 1953. By 1968 all states bar one had it on their legislative books.

This period in the history of basic financial instruments like bills of exchange, promissory notes and cheques can best be represented as a period of national code-building. Two basic types of code emerged: the English code, which drew heavily on its common law but which was also influenced by the writings of major Continental jurists, and a civil-law model which had French and German variants. Countries like Belgium, Spain and Puerto Rico produced a hybrid based on the French and German models. The common-law model was faithfully followed by countries in the British empire or with close connections to it. US law, while it belonged to the common-law model, tended to adhere less to its English origins, primarily because many US states continued to tamper with the law of negotiable instruments (Barak 1968: 11).

### Commercial Codes Meet International Conventions and International Organizations

Financial instruments and ducks have at least this in common – they are migratory. Bills (of exchange) are part of international transactions and routinely cross state boundaries. A good

---

2  *Stock Motor Ploughs Ltd v. Forsyth* (1932) 48 CLR 128, 137.

example is the nineteenth-century case of *Horne v. Rouquette,* involving an English drawer of a bill of exchange, a Spanish payee and a series of transactions culminating in the bill being dishonoured when it was presented for acceptance by the final Spanish holder.[3] Cases like these led to complex problems of private international law in which courts had to work out which law applied to a chain of transactions involving foreign parties. Medieval merchant law had dealt with the problem of coordination between foreign parties by developing a set of customary norms which applied to all merchants. With the absorption of the Law Merchant into the jurisdictions of nation-states, that law inevitably became less harmonized as the national courts applied the Law Merchant in different ways. Courts set about solving the conflicts between national systems of law by having recourse to the principles found in international private law. None of this was particularly conducive to ease of commerce.

The movement to unify negotiable instruments internationally began in the second half of the nineteenth century. It was primarily driven by proposals from jurists either individually or through organizations of jurists like the International Law Association. Results came in the form of two conferences at the Hague in 1910 and 1912 and a Convention on the Unification of the Law Relating to Bills of Exchange and Promissory Notes, in which states agreed to introduce the Uniform Regulation on such instruments into their jurisdiction. For various reasons, including the First World War, no state ever ratified the Convention (Hudson & Feller 1931: 343). In the 1920s the International Chamber of Commerce (ICC) became the champion of the unification cause and, through its pressure on the Economic Committee of the League of Nations, conferences on the unification of negotiable instruments were held in Geneva in 1930 and 1931. The two conferences produced six conventions, two dealing with the substantive law relating to negotiable instruments, two dealing with private international law (conflict of laws) issues and two with stamp laws in connection with negotiable instruments. The two conventions dealing with substantive law, the Uniform Law for Bills of Exchange and Promissory Notes and the Uniform Law for Cheques, did more to unite civil-law countries than the common-law world. Neither the US nor the UK became members of these conventions because of technical differences between their laws and the model laws proposed in the conventions.

The use of international conventions to provide uniformity for the sale and carriage of goods also began to proceed; for example, the Hague Rules of 1921 for the carriage of goods by sea, the Warsaw Convention of 1929 for the carriage of goods by air and the Hague Conventions of 1964 dealing with a Uniform Law on the International Sale of Goods and a Uniform Law on the Formation of Contracts for the International Sale of Goods (Goode 1995: 17–18). The Hague Conventions were replaced by the UN Convention on Contracts for the International Sale of Goods of 11 April 1980, a convention which goes some way towards establishing general principles of contract law (Lando 1992: 575).

Running parallel to the emergence of international conventions on commercial law was the establishment of specialist international organizations dedicated to the task of providing a commercial law for the world. One such organization was UNIDROIT (the International Institute for the Unification of Private Law), established in 1926 in Rome under the aegis of the League of Nations and reconstituted through a multilateral treaty in 1940 after the League had ceased to function. All major trading nations are now members. UNIDROIT is not an arm of the UN. It is

---

3  [1878] 3 QBD 514.

very much a forum of juridical experts. For example, the UNIDROIT General Principles for International Commercial Contracts were developed by experts appointed by the organization's Governing Council rather than by state delegates. In the words of one of the members of the working group, 'this made it strikingly more possible to conduct a realistic search for the "best" solution' (Furmston 1996: 11).

In 1966 the UN General Assembly established the UN Commission on International Trade Law (UNCITRAL), whose purpose was to work towards a unified system of international trade law. This mission has taken it into contract and commercial law generally. In the field of negotiable instruments, it produced in 1988 the UN Convention on International Bills of Exchange and International Promissory Notes. The main aim of this Convention was to unify the Anglo-American and Geneva systems on negotiable instruments. UNCITRAL has a huge work program in the area of private law, aimed at producing either a model law (e.g. the 1976 Model Rules on Arbitration) or an international convention (e.g. Vienna Sales Convention 1980). Before UNIDROIT and UNCITRAL there was the Hague Conference on Private International Law, an idea first proposed by the Italian jurist Pasquale Mancini in 1874 (UNCITRAL 1971: 24). The Hague Conference on Private International Law was held in 1893, and in 1955 the Conference took the form of a multilateral treaty. Essentially the Conference has remained a European affair, its most successful convention being the Convention on the Law Applicable to International Sales of Goods. Other international organizations, such as the UN Conference on Trade and Development (UNCTAD) and the UN Educational, Scientific and Cultural Organization (UNESCO) have also been involved in developing an international commercial contract law, but the three organizations mentioned above can probably claim to be the most important.

The presence of international organizations in the private law field meant that the project of unifying contract and commercial law generally became an enduring one. It no longer depended on the temporary effort of a given jurist or state.

The Cold War divide did not dramatically change the Soviet Union's approach to international trade contracts; in fact the Soviet Union operated within the framework of the Law Merchant (Berman & Bustin 1975: 1014). It also developed organizational equivalents of free-market organizations (e.g. the USSR Chamber of Commerce and Industry) which participated in international meetings on international trade law and retained lines of communication on the development of international trade law (Berman & Bustin 1975: 998). Socialist states did achieve a high level of regional unification of contract law, governing trade among themselves, through the Council for Mutual Economic Assistance's 1968 adoption of the General Conditions for the Delivery of Goods (Hoya 1970). The more significant Cold War divide over the possibility of an internationally unified commercial contract law was between common-law and civil-code countries. The US in particular tended to stay out of various Conventions. The following lengthy quote from a US observer at the 1956 Hague Conference on Private International Law reveals some of the differences of jurisprudential attitude between common-law lawyers and civil lawyers, differences that have made the journey towards a world commercial law a long one:

> We Americans, in company with our other common-law brethren, are suspicious of attempts to regulate by statute broad areas of any so undeveloped a subject as conflict of laws. Generally, we prefer to proceed on a case-to-case basis and to decide problems only as they arise. This method may lack the virtues of certainty and predictability of result, but it does avoid the danger of laying down binding rules that may subsequently turn out to have been badly conceived. The drafting techniques of the civilians likewise differ markedly from our own. They are inclined to frame broad rules and to trust

that the individual judge will avoid the harsh results to which a literal application of these rules would occasionally lead by application of the public policy (*ordre public*) doctrine. We, on the other hand, are accustomed to draft a statute in terms sufficiently detailed and complex to care for what we hope will prove to be all possible situations and then to expect literal application of the statute by the judge (Reese 1956: 613).

## The Private Ordering of Private Law

Medieval *Lex Mercatoria* was a spectacular example of transnational private ordering. It was merchants who devised and cultivated the rules that regulated the commercial relations between them. Courts, for the most part, were content to operate in a declaratory mode in this area of commercial life. Custom remained for centuries a source of the Law Merchant despite the fact that national courts gained jurisdiction over it. The influence of private ordering on the Law Merchant never disappeared, but its character changed as merchants began to develop new forms of organization. The rise of trade associations, such as the London Corn Trade Association and the UK Timber Trade Federation, in the main European trading centres in the nineteenth century brought a proliferation of standard contracts. The problem was that the contracts were drawn on the basis of the legal system with which the relevant trade association was familiar (UNCITRAL 1971: 27). It was not only trade associations that engaged in this form of unilateral ordering. Lloyd's of London achieved such dominance in marine insurance that the understandings and activities that surrounded its Ships and Good Form became the basis of common-law marine insurance and found legislative expression in the *Marine Insurance Act 1906* (the Ships and Good Form was put in the Schedule to that Act) (Muchlinski 1997: 86–7). It is still true today, for example, that a large manufacturer can impose on its business partners the contract law of its choice (normally its domestic law) (Bortolotti 1993: 1). Thus, private unilateral ordering gave international trading merchants an array of standard contracts to choose from and the suspicion that a trade association contract might not be to the advantage of an outsider (more formally, a problem of informational asymmetry). This phenomenon of powerful private actors ordering markets through a capacity to set standards is one that we shall see repeated in later chapters (e.g. Chapter 14, on telecommunications). International governmental organizations in the twentieth century began to attempt to bring uniformity to the diversity of contract law created by the decentralized form of private ordering. The Economic Commission for Europe, for example, began to issue its own conditions of sale and standard contract, which were drafted by representatives from trade associations and business (UNCITRAL 1971: 27).

Merchants also began to organize their own means of international coordination. The single most important international business organization in the field of private law unification became the ICC. Founded in 1919, the ICC operates through an elaborate structure of national committees and working parties which, in the case of international trade, is utilized to ascertain the actual business practice of merchants. Drawing on this database of custom, the ICC began to formulate standard codes for the regulation of financial instruments. Its code on Uniform Customs and Practice for Documentary Credits, first adopted in 1933, by 1966 had been applied in 173 countries and had transcended Cold War differences. The ICC also formulated a set of interpretive rules for frequently used terms in international trade. These 'Incoterms' are now used by most trading nations. The formulation of model contracts has been another means by which the ICC has worked towards achieving a uniform international commercial law. Again, in drafting such models the ICC draws on and in effect partly codifies the customary base of its members. The ICC Agency Model Contract, for example, is based on a *Lex Mercatoria* approach to formulating its terms because, in the words of the working party responsible for the model, such an approach would be 'capable of offering a common and neutral ground between parties from different countries' (Bortolotti 1993: 2).

It can be seen from this and the preceding section that, in the twentieth century, unification of commercial law is a crowded field. Private ordering through codes of practice, model contracts, guidelines helped by public coordination and public ordering through codification and conventions helped by private input has produced what some scholars have seen as an evolution towards a new or revitalized *Lex Mercatoria* (Goode 1995: 1210–12; Berman & Kaufman 1978: 273). The existence and applicability of this new *Lex Mercatoria* is hotly debated among scholars (Mertens 1997). The chief feature of *Lex Mercatoria* (old and new) is that its regulatory norms travel from the bottom to the top (Cooter 1996). Organizational actors further up in the hierarchy attempt to systematize these norms in order to bring clarity and certainty to the norms being produced from below.

## Secure, Negotiable, Efficient Property and Global Capitalism

We have seen that secure property rights gained through citizenship status had Roman origins, but were transformed under the new territorial citizenship of national sovereigns. Though the specificities of rights to land and other property were highly variable under the new world system of state sovereignty that evolved during the Middle Ages, there are three generalizations we can make. First, states made increasing use of property rules, both civil and criminal, for a variety of social purposes. The law of theft, for example, expanded to cover a far greater range of activities. Second, property rights became progressively more secure, progressively more immune from arbitrary confiscation by the ruling power. Third, the law of contract made it more possible to negotiate transfers of property with certainty of effect. Prudential regulation, as we will see in Chapter 8, provided another important kind of certainty – increased certainty that the banks that stood behind negotiable instruments would not collapse before the negotiation was completed.

These trends towards the expansion, security and negotiability of property were more or less universal. Property rights emerged in response to changing externalities (Demsetz 1967). States which did not guarantee property and contract did not flourish economically compared to states that did. States that failed to pursue the goal of efficient property rights paid the price in terms of reduced economic growth and loss of hegemony (North 1990: 139). Property and contract law were basic in enabling capitalism to take off. The economic base of Marx's capitalism turned out to *need* legally defined, complex personal property rights to fully constitute itself as a mode of production. Some states were slow to learn this, but today there is no national regime that has not accepted it as a lesson of history. At this level, the globalization is total. Of course, although state law stands behind secure property rights and the enforcement of contracts by courts that are independent of the state, in many parts of the world the independence of the judiciary is a fiction – when the executive unlawfully seizes property or dishonours contracts, the courts are mute.

At the level of formal law, there has also been a total globalization of the notion that property ought to be secure from theft or fraud at the hands of other private citizens. Prescriptions against theft long pre-date capitalism (e.g. the Twelve Tables of Rome and the Covenant Code in Exodus). But ancient laws against theft placed the remedy of execution in private hands, at least in relation to thieves who had been caught in the act (Fletcher 1976: 477). Larceny in its ancient form was more concerned with the maintenance of community relations than with the protection of property. Rules of property existed, but in a diffuse form in the local and tribal customs of the European peoples (Berman 1983: 50–1). The state system, however, globally transformed property norms. Property law became part of the secular legal order of states. Peasants, serfs and vassals became citizens, and citizens gained property rights created by the sovereign of the state. Women stopped being the property of their husbands and became property-owners. The strengthening of property rights was partly helped by the emergence of the idea of individuals having natural rights, including natural rights of property. Theft changed from being a breach of faith with a feudal lord (felony) to a crime punishable by the state. Larceny became conceptualized as a 'crime against property' (Fletcher 1976: 503). This move was important to securing property rights in a way that made it possible for capitalism to flourish. Until the territorial sovereign took responsibility for creating a pacified space within their kingdom, valuable property could not be moved between towns without constant fear of robbers. Until the sovereign's navy secured the safety of their sea-lanes, the crime of piracy was a profound threat to trade. Security of property rights combined with more complex, richly defined property rights allowed the emergence of more trades as well as different kinds of trading.

There are still weak states such as Colombia (Goldsmith 2000) and Papua New Guinea (Dinnen 1996) which can offer little semblance of a guarantee that they will deploy their legal monopoly of the use of force to make their roads safe to travel with property. Consequently, as the development banks keep advising Papua New Guinea, the investment and free flow of trade needed for economic development is chilled. The problem remains in unpacified spaces of even the strongest states, however, as shown by the flight of capital from many unsafe central cities to the Sunbelt in the US. Again, although implementation of the legal ideal is uneven, there is globalization of the formal legal doctrine that theft and fraud are crimes which are the responsibility of the state. The doctrine that the protection of property afforded by the criminal law extends not only to the property of individual citizens but to the property of non-citizens and that of corporations, domestic or foreign, is also global. This is not to deny that there are other important protections to the security of property, for example in land law and the law of tort, that have experienced only very limited globalization.

Outside criminal law, however, security of property rights, to no expropriation other than under a law that applies universally to all citizens, remains a citizenship right. And citizenship remains a territorial concept. It is for this reason that states negotiate bilateral investment treaties to protect the real and personal property which their investors hold in foreign states. Property rights have been least secure when the property is off-shore from the territory that defines the citizenship of its owners. In fact, the mid twentieth century saw massive arbitrary appropriations of off-shore property – Nazi appropriations in Europe, US appropriations of German companies in the US, appropriations of the savings of Jews by Swiss banks, Japanese appropriations in Asia, Soviet appropriations in Eastern and Central Europe. Socialists tended to believe that although the property of individuals should be secure (other than to equitable taxation), corporate property should be vulnerable to nationalization, especially if it were foreign-controlled corporate property.

Chapter 10 shows that the next phase in the globalization of the security of property is under way. This is a movement toward the global regulation of the security of investment that would not have been possible during the heyday of Soviet power. An objective of these emerging regimes is to extend security of property rights to non-citizens, especially to transnational corporations. In a sense, the Multilateral Agreement on Investment and the Trade Related Investment Measures agreement discussed in Chapter 10 jeopardizes the feasibility of socialism under international law. Any future socialist regime would have to have fantastic fiscal riches to be able to legally compensate expropriated capitalists.

Hence, secure property and contracts have been vital in allowing capitalism to flourish; once it has flourished, the political and economic power of capitalists has been mobilized to expand the sphere of security and the sphere of what can be 'propertized' and contracted (see Chapter 11 on labour as property that can be contracted). Capitalist legal systems have been characterized by their capacity to innovate property forms. The most important expansion of the concept of property has been the creation of the notion of intellectual property. This has ancient origins, but only in the 1990s did intellectual property regimes move to the centre of trade regulation and global markets. Capitalist economies in the second half of the twentieth century, led by the US, have progressively become information economies (Machlup 1962; Baumol, Blackman & Wolff 1991: Ch. 7). Drucker argues that the basic economic resource is now knowledge (Drucker 1993: 8). We prefer to say that capitalism's relentless commodity production is now expressed in the pursuit of abstract objects, the objects of intellectual property laws (Drahos 1996). The old capitalism was a capitalism of goods, factories and labour. These days factories and labour, even skilled labour, are in abundant supply. The new capitalism focuses on the control of abstract objects. What matters to a multinational corporation is a trademark which is globally recognized by consumers, a trademark that allows the corporation to set up shop in those states that offer the most favourable investment conditions, a trademark which the corporation can attach to anything it chooses to manufacture, a trademark that can be licensed. Similarly, if one can patent a genetically engineered cow that produces twice as much milk as an ordinary cow, one has an asset equal in value to all the dairy herds of all farmers. It is also a more liquid asset than all that milk, all those cows and farm labourers! The new capitalism centres on proprietorial control over algorithms, genes, formulae and other abstract objects. This is why it is difficult to overestimate the importance of intellectual property globalization to the foundations of a future world capitalism and its systems of regulation. This is why the US negotiating position for the Uruguay Round of the General Agreement on Tariffs and Trade (GATT) was 'No intellectual property, no round'. We now look at the new property of the new capitalism.

### Intellectual Property: Back to Rome Again

Intellectual property is one important form of personal property. It is normally divided into industrial property rights (patents, designs, trademarks) and rights in artistic and literary works (copyright). It is an expanding area of law. New forms of intellectual property are minted by legislatures: plant variety rights, semiconductor chip protection and database protection are all examples of rights which have gained legislative currency in the twentieth century – in many countries only in the last decade or two.

Intellectual property rights in legal parlance are often referred to as incorporeal rights or intangibles. Taxonomically they are classified within English law as choses in action. Behind this specialist language lies the philosophical idea that the world can be divided into physical and non-physical things. In terms of legal history, the distinction between physical and non-physical things can be found in the *Institutes* of Gaius. The recognition that incorporeal things could be the subject of ownership was a profound conceptual innovation, received by both common-law and civil-law systems as part of the general reception of Roman law into Europe. It should be said that neither ancient Rome nor Greece had intellectual property law as we know it. Trademarks which did exist in those times apparently had no developed basis of protection (Ladas 1930: 6–7).

Lying at the heart of intellectual property law is the idea that one owns an intangible object, something which is abstract and not to be equated with any one physical object. A good example of how one can own an abstract object without owning the physical is the letter written to a friend. The friend owns the physical letter, but the writer owns the copyright in the letter (the right of reproduction and publication). The ownership of an abstract object is not an end in itself, since by definition one cannot see it or touch it. Rather, people seek the ownership of intangibles as a means to an end, as a way of controlling important material resources. So, for instance, the ownership of a patent on a chemical compound is the ownership of an intangible, but it also allows one to control the production and distribution of the drug based on the compound. Through the ownership of abstract objects intellectual property owners can reach into the material world and control vital resources. With these rights comes, potentially, great power.

The following sections outline the evolution of the regulation of abstract objects. The protection of intellectual property at an international level can roughly be divided into three periods. The first period – the territorial period – is characterized by an absence of international protection. The second period – the international period – began in Europe towards the end of the nineteenth century, with some countries agreeing to the Paris Convention for the Protection of Industrial Property 1883 (the Paris Convention) and a similar group agreeing to the Berne Convention for the Protection of Literary and Artistic Works 1886 (the Berne Convention). The third period – the global period – began with the US link in the 1980s between trade and intellectual property, a link which emerged at a multilateral level in the form of the Agreement on Trade Related Aspects of Intellectual Property Rights 1994 (TRIPS).[4] The dates of the various conventions do not represent a sharp divide. They do, however, mark a significant change in the evolutionary direction of intellectual property protection.

### The Territorial Period

The different subject areas of intellectual property originate in different places and at different times. Very probably all these laws can be traced back to the system of royal privilege giving which seems to have operated in most of medieval Europe. The Venetians are credited with the first properly developed patent law, in 1474. In England, the *Statute of Monopolies of 1623* swept away all monopolies except those made by the 'true and first inventor' of a 'method of manufacture'. Revolutionary France recognized the rights of inventors in 1791 and the US enacted a patent law in 1790. These patent laws were nothing like today's complex systems. They were short, simply recognizing the rights of the inventor. After these beginnings, patent law spread throughout Europe in the first half of the nineteenth century (Machlup & Penrose 1950: 3). Statutory forms of trademark law appeared late in the second half of the nineteenth century, even though trademarks had been in use for much longer. Trademark law is based on the marks used by merchants to identify their goods and the guilds' use of marks to identify works by their craftsmen

---

4 TRIPS is binding on all members of the WTO. See Article II, 2 of the Agreement Establishing the World Trade Organization (WTO Agreement). Both TRIPS and the WTO Agreement are part of the Final Act Embodying the Results of the Uruguay Round of Multilateral Trade Negotiations, Marrakesh, 15 April 1994.

(Schechter 1927: 814). The English courts developed protection for trademarks through the action of passing-off (Ricketson 1984: 599). For a variety of reasons this proved unsatisfactory, and statutory systems of trademark registration began to appear in Europe: in England in 1862 and 1875, in France in 1857, in Germany in 1874 and in the US in 1870 and 1876 (Ladas 1975a: 8). Copyright follows a similar kind of pattern, modern copyright law beginning in England with the *Statute of Anne of 1709*.

The second part of the nineteenth century saw the European proliferation of national intellectual property regimes. It was a period of somewhat chaotic growth, with much borrowing and cross-pollination of intellectual property law between states. The principles of patent law to be found in the English *Statute of Monopolies* were gradually recognized in other states. The English devised the first law on designs in 1787 but were influenced by the French design law of 1806 when they reformulated their law in 1839. Outside Europe, intellectual property grew along colonial pathways. So, for example, the self-governing colonies of Australia enacted copyright and patent statutes that were essentially faithful copies of English models.

The territorial period was dominated by the principle of territoriality, the principle that intellectual property rights do not extend beyond the territory of the sovereign which granted the rights. The principle is the product of the intimate connections between sovereignty, property rights and territory. It was a principle which courts recognized in the interests of international comity.[5] A world in which states regularly claimed jurisdiction over the property rights established by other nations would be a world in which the principle of negative comity would have largely vanished. The principle of territoriality meant that an intellectual property law passed by country A did not apply in country B. Intellectual property owners faced a classic free-riding problem, or, putting it another way, some countries were the beneficiaries of positive externalities. Dealing with free-riding and positive externalities led states into the next phase of intellectual property protection, the international period.

## The International Period

In the nineteenth century, copying foreign works without the author's permission was (to all intents and purposes) a customary norm of international commerce in Europe and the US. Later it would be thought of as piracy, but the fact is that many within Europe saw it not as piracy but as an honourable activity (Briggs 1906: 37).

During the nineteenth century states began to take an increasing interest in the possibility of international cooperation on intellectual property. At first this interest was manifested in the form of bilateral agreements (Ricketson 1987: 25–38). In copyright, a French decree of 1852 granting copyright protection to foreign works and foreign authors without the requirement of reciprocity did much to keep bilateral treaty-making in copyright alive (Henn 1953: 45). States which were worried about the free-riding problem began to negotiate bilateral treaties with other states, while states which saw themselves as recipients of a positive externality remained isolationist. The UK and the US provide an example of each response. The UK found in the eighteenth century that many of its authors' works were reproduced abroad without permission and without royalties being paid. Much of the 'piracy' was taking place in the US, where authors like Dickens were very

---

5  *British South Africa Co. v. Companhia de Moçambique* [1893] AC 602, 622–4.

popular with the public and therefore with US publishers. The US was not the only culprit, as the following passage from *Hansard* (1837) makes clear (Sherman 1995: 7):

> Every work written by a popular author is almost co-instantaneously reprinted in large numbers both in France, Germany and in America and this is done now with much rapidity, and at little expense…All the works of Sir Walter Scott, Lord Byron, Messrs Robert Southey, Thomas Moore…and indeed most popular authors are so reprinted and resold by Galignani and Bardens at Paris.

The UK response to this problem was to pass Acts in 1838 and 1844 that protected works first published outside the UK. These Acts grounded a strategy of reciprocity. Foreign works would only gain protection in the UK if the relevant state agreed to protect UK works. The 1844 Act saw a considerable number of bilateral agreements concluded between the UK and other European states (Sherman 1995: 10). International copyright policy in the US took a different turn. The US *Copyright Act 1790* granted copyright protection only to citizens and residents of the US. This form of national protectionism prevailed in US copyright policy for a surprisingly long period: 'For over a hundred years, this nation not only denied copyright protection to published works by foreigners, applying the "nationality-of-the-author" principle, but appeared to encourage the piracy of such works' (Henn 1953: 52). It was not until after the Second World War that the US began to exercise real leadership in international copyright (Ringer 1968). As shown in the next section, it did so with a boldness few could have foreseen.

Like copyright, the different parts of industrial property also became the subject of bilateral treaty-making, mainly between European states. By 1883 there were sixty-nine international agreements, most dealing with trademarks (Ladas 1975a: 43, 54–5). They operated on the basis of the national treatment principle, itself the outcome of reciprocal adjustment between states. States had come to accept that if they did not discriminate between nationals and foreigners when it came to the regulation of intellectual property rights, neither would other states.

Bilateralism in intellectual property in the nineteenth century was important in that it contributed to the recognition that an international framework for the regulation of intellectual property had to be devised, and it suggested a content in terms of principles for that framework. But this bilateralism was a prelude. The main movement towards serious international cooperation on intellectual property arrived in the form of two multilateral pillars, the Paris Convention of 1883 and the Berne Convention of 1886. The Berne Convention formed a union for the protection of literary and artistic works and the Paris Convention formed a union for the protection of industrial property.

The Paris Convention began with US disgruntlement over a world fair for inventions, planned for Vienna in 1873. These world fairs, like the trade fairs of medieval Europe, were important meeting-places. The US, echoing the fears of other countries, suggested that many inventions at the fair would end up benefiting the Austrian public without foreign inventors gaining any returns. The idea of a unified international patent system had been circulating for some time, Prince Albert having raised the possibility of a harmonized patent system at the London World Exposition in 1851 (Beier 1984: 2). It was German engineer, Karl Pieper, who managed to persuade the Austrians to hold in 1873 a Congress for Patent Reform. After another Congress in 1880, the Paris Convention of 1883 was opened for signature. Within twenty-five years most major trading nations had joined the Convention.

The Berne Convention was also a product of meeting-places in Europe. The framework of bilateral copyright treaties was more often than not only a 'paper' reality. It also produced great complexity. Authors wanting to know the extent of their protection in other countries would have had to consult a series of treaties and domestic laws. Influential authors including Victor Hugo, whose reputation and works crossed boundaries, formed the International Literary Association in Paris in 1878 (Kampelman 1947: 410–11). This Association began to hold regular meetings in Europe; at its 1883 meeting in Berne it produced a draft international copyright agreement. The Swiss government was persuaded to organize an international conference using the draft as a starting-point for a multilateral convention on copyright. Berne became the site of intergovernmental conferences in 1884, 1885 and 1886, the year in which the Berne Convention was completed and opened for signature and ratification to the world at large. Like the Paris Convention, the Berne Convention was based on the principle of national treatment and a set of minimum rights.

The Paris and Berne Conventions ushered in the multilateral era of international cooperation in intellectual property. The twentieth century saw the proliferation of intellectual property regimes. Areas that have become the subject of international agreements include trademarks (Madrid Agreement (Marks) 1891 and Madrid Agreement (Indication of Source) 1891), designs (Hague Agreement 1925), performance (Rome Convention 1961), plant varieties (International Convention for the Protection of New Varieties of Plants 1961), patents (Patent Cooperation Treaty 1970) and semiconductor chips (Treaty on Intellectual Property in Respect of Integrated Circuits 1989). The Paris and Berne Conventions underwent numerous revisions. Regional agreements also begin to appear in larger numbers in the twentieth century. The North American Free Trade Agreement (NAFTA) contains extensive provisions on intellectual property and there are a number of European treaties and many directives dealing with intellectual property. Regional agreements have quite a long history in intellectual property. An example is the Montevideo Conventions of 1889 which dealt with patents and trademarks, involving Argentina, Bolivia, Brazil, Chile, Paraguay, Peru and Uruguay (Ladas 1975a: 1745–6).

Treaty-making in intellectual property was accompanied by the rise of international organizational forms. The Paris and Berne Conventions saw the creation of international bureaux (secretariats) which were merged in 1893 to form the United International Bureaux for the Protection of Intellectual Property (known by the French acronym of BIRPI) (Bogsch 1992: 7–8). BIRPI was superseded by a new organization called the World Intellectual Property Organization (WIPO), which was established by treaty in 1967. WIPO became a specialized agency of the UN in 1974.

The international world of intellectual property over which BIRPI and then WIPO presided was one in which sovereign states had agreed to certain basic principles, the most important being the principle of national treatment. By no means was it a world in which there was a harmonization of technical rules. States retained enormous sovereign discretion over intellectual property standard-setting. The US continued with its first-to-invent patent system, other countries operated with a first-to-file system. Civil-code countries recognized the doctrine of moral rights for authors, common-law countries did not. Developing countries (and for a long time many developed countries) did not recognize the patenting of chemical compounds. Standards of trademark registration varied dramatically, even between countries within the same legal family. The law of unfair competition was a projection of local instinct even though the Paris Convention required all member states to protect against it.

Although by 1992 WIPO administered twenty-four multilateral treaties, it presided over an intellectual property world of enormous rule diversity. By 1992 the organization also sensed, perhaps more strongly than anyone, the change that was about to take place in the regulation of intellectual property. The 'trade barbarians' in Geneva, the GATT, were about to see to that. WIPO stood by as brutish trade lawyers pushed the world of intellectual property into the global era.

## The Global Period

During the international period the harmonization of intellectual property was painstakingly slow. After the Second World War more and more developing countries joined the Paris and Berne Conventions. These Conventions ceased to be Western clubs and, under the principle of one-state–one-vote, Western states could be outvoted by a coalition of developing countries. Developing countries were not content to be only a veto coalition. They wanted an international system which catered to their stage of economic development and so, in the eyes of the West, they began to throw their weight around. Led by India, in the area of copyright developing countries succeeded in obtaining the adoption of the Stockholm Protocol of 1967. The Protocol aimed to give developing countries greater access to copyright materials. Its adoption provoked something of a crisis in international copyright (Sacks 1969). The Paris Convention also became the subject of Diplomatic Conferences of Revision in 1980, 1981, 1982 and 1984, with developing countries pushing for more liberal provisions on compulsory licensing.

During the 1960s India's drug prices were among the highest in the world, so it designed its patent law in a way which would help to lower drug prices. Indian law granted patents for processes relating to the production of pharmaceuticals, but not for chemical compounds themselves. When it came to reforming the Paris Convention, countries like India pushed for provisions that would give developing countries more access to technology that had been locked up through patents. To India, this was rational social policy for the educational and health-care needs of its citizens. To the US, it was a case of free-riding. The US became increasingly isolated at meetings relating to the Paris Convention.

The international period was one in which a lot of free-riding was tolerated. The only enforcement mechanisms under the various intellectual property treaties were appeals to the International Court of Justice and most states made reservations on such clauses. No state was in a position to cast the first stone when it came to free-riding. The US was not a member of the Berne Convention, but US publishers took advantage of its higher standards of protection 'through the back door' method of arranging simultaneous publication in a Berne country like Canada (Henn 1953: 65).

Not everybody in the US was happy with this *laissez-faire* attitude toward the enforcement of intellectual property rights. For US film and pharmaceutical industries in particular, intellectual property (copyright for the former, patents for the latter) was the backbone of their industries. For pharmaceutical companies like Pfizer, intellectual property was an investment issue. They wanted to be able to locate production anywhere in the world, safe in the knowledge that their intellectual property would be protected. Within the lobbying networks that had been organized by these global business entities, an idea began to be bounced between a small group of consultants, lobbyists and lawyers (notably Eric Smith, Elery Simon and Jacques Gorlin) – that of linking intellectual property to trade. There were two obvious advantages to such a move. First, if a set of intellectual property standards were part of a multilateral trade agreement it would give those standards fairly global coverage. Second, use could be made of the enforcement mechanisms that states had developed for settling trade disputes.

Crucial in the evolution of the US trade-based strategy for intellectual property was the work of the Advisory Committee for Trade Negotiations (ACTN). This committee was designed to give the US business sector direct input into US trade policy. ACTN was a direct line of communication between business and the bureaucratic centre of trade policy.

From 1981 ACTN was chaired by Edmund Pratt, the CEO of Pfizer. Senior executives of Pfizer had done a great deal of thinking about the problem of intellectual property protection, partly because Pfizer had made a strategic long-term commitment to doing business in developing countries. Pratt became a leading advocate of a trade-based approach to intellectual property protection, and his speeches did much to alert other US business leaders to the possibilities of such an approach.

ACTN established a Task Force on Intellectual Property. The recommendations of this Task Force were fundamental to the development of a US strategy for intellectual property. In essence, the strategy required the US to have a long-term goal of placing intellectual property in the GATT. Bilateral and unilateral efforts using trade tools would provide an interim strategy for improving intellectual property protection abroad. ACTN's basic idea was to link intellectual property protection to as many levers as the US could pull, particularly using problem countries' dependency on the US market. A key lever was the Generalized System of Preferences (GSP) which allowed beneficiary countries duty-free trading privileges in the US market. Favourable treatment under the GSP program, ACTN suggested, should be made conditional upon countries setting the right level of intellectual property protection. ACTN suggested other ways of using conditionality. It recommended that US Executive Directors to the International Monetary Fund (IMF), the World Bank and regional development banks should, in exercising their voting power, examine a country's record on intellectual property protection.

During the 1980s the US reshaped its trade law to give it a series of bilateral enforcement strategies against countries it considered had inadequate levels of intellectual property enforcement or which only weakly enforced such rights. Links between intellectual property and trade had appeared earlier in US legislation, in particular the legislation which implemented the Caribbean Basin initiative. The US copyright industry was worried about piracy of its films in the Caribbean, and as a condition of US assistance to Caribbean states it required that those states protect intellectual property rights. As one of the lobbyists we spoke to pointed out, the success of the Caribbean Basin initiative for the US copyright industry marked the beginning of a change in intellectual property. The significance of the event was, hardly surprisingly, not widely appreciated. The link between trade and intellectual property was really the proposal of a few individuals with experience of the Washington political scene. Most of them were lawyers. It was they who alerted US industry to the potential of the link and it was they who led industry down the trade path. It was a classic case of legal entrepreneurship.

In 1984 the US amended its *Trade Act 1974* to include intellectual property in the section 301 trade process. Like a successful Hollywood movie, the 1984 amendment had a sequel in the form of the *Omnibus Trade and Competitiveness Act 1988* (see Chapter 10). This latter Act strengthened the 301 process by adding more processes called 'Regular 301', 'Special 301' and 'Super 301' (Getlan 1995: 179). Essentially these provisions, when put together, required the Office of the US Trade Representative (USTR) to identify problem countries, assess the level of abuse of US intellectual property interests, enter into negotiations to remedy the problems and ultimately, if this proved futile, to impose trade sanctions by either withdrawing the trade benefits those countries were being given by the US or to impose trade restrictions on the goods of the other country (Getlan 1995: 178–84). The 301 processes are procedurally complex, but countries involved in them know that behind them lies a simple truth. If countries fail to act on intellectual property they will, sooner or later, face retaliatory action by the US.

The 301 process played a crucial role in US strategy on intellectual property in the Uruguay Round of trade talks. Once the US had persuaded a sufficient number of countries to act on the intellectual property issue at a bilateral level, it could expect little resistance to the TRIPS proposal (in fact resistance to US negotiating objectives at a multilateral forum could and did trigger the 301 process). This strategy proved so effective that disputes over intellectual property issues during the Uruguay Round became disputes between the intellectual property triumvirate, the US, Europe and Japan. By the final stages of the negotiations, developing countries had long given up resisting the TRIPS proposal.

At the Ministerial Meeting at Punta del Este in September 1986, the meeting which launched the Uruguay Round of trade talks, intellectual property was included as a negotiating issue. The US had the support of Europe, Canada and Japan for including intellectual property in the Round, but basically it was a US initiative. It was the US, more specifically the US business community, which had made all the running on the matter of intellectual property.

On 15 April 1994 the Uruguay Round concluded with the signing, in Marrakesh, of the Final Act Embodying the Results of the Uruguay Round of Multilateral Trade Negotiations. More than a hundred countries signed the Final Act, which contained a number of agreements including the Agreement Establishing the World Trade Organization and TRIPS. TRIPS was made binding on all members of the WTO. There was no way for a state which wished to become or remain a member of the multilateral trading regime to sidestep TRIPS.

## Post-TRIPS

TRIPS marks the beginning of the global property epoch. It is based on the principles of territoriality and national treatment, but it also represents the beginning of property globalization. Via the trade linkage, TRIPS reaches all states which are members of the multilateral trading system or which, like China, wish to become members. One of the key objectives of the regional commercial unions that have developed recently is the implementation of TRIPS. Cooperation and convergence on intellectual property law is taking place among the states of the Central European Free Trade Agreement, the Association of South-East Asian Nations, the Mekong River Basin Countries and the Asia-Pacific Economic Cooperation Forum (Blakeney 1998).

In the past, states have been able to steer their way through the international intellectual property framework by taking reservations on clauses in treaties or by not ratifying certain protocols or conventions. All of TRIPS is binding on all members of the WTO. TRIPS incorporates various other intellectual property conventions by reference. States therefore have to implement a common and enlarged set of intellectual property standards, standards that become common to more states by virtue of their participation in regional and multilateral trade regimes. More and more standards are becoming mandatory rather than permissive. States, for example, have less discretion to determine what can be patentable and what cannot.

The post-TRIPS era has been one in which countries have had to engage in national implementation of their obligations under TRIPS. Least-developed countries have the advantage of a ten-year transitional period under the agreement, but they have been pressured by developed countries, particularly the US, to move sooner rather than later on its implementation. Even for countries like Australia, with highly developed systems of intellectual property, TRIPS has meant a significant degree of legislative activity. TRIPS also operates under an institutional arrangement designed to promote compliance. The WTO Agreement establishes a Council for TRIPS and TRIPS requires this Council to monitor members' compliance with their obligations under the agreement. The practice which seems to be developing is that states like the US and Europe are asking other states to explain their intellectual property law and whether it complies with TRIPS. For example, in 1996 the US asked Australia a number of questions including the following (Commonwealth Attorney-General's Department 1996):

> Q4. Please explain whether and how Australia provides full retroactive protection to works, phono-grams and performances from other WTO members, as required by TRIPS Articles 9.1, 14.6 and 70.2, each of which incorporate by reference or rely upon Berne Article 18. Please give the date back to which such protection extends in respect to each category of subject matter.

The Council for TRIPS monitoring and periodic reviews of compliance, along with the active interest of the US and Europe in the enforcement of rights and the fact that disputes under TRIPS can be made the subject of dispute resolution proceedings under the dispute resolution mechanism of the Final Act, mean that TRIPS obligations will become a living legal reality rather than suffering the fate of so many conventions, that of remaining paper rules.

In the post-TRIPS period multilateral treaty-making in intellectual property has continued. The draft text for a Multilateral Agreement on Investment has gone through a number of changes, but all versions have defined investment to include every kind of asset including intellectual property rights. On 20 December 1996, under the auspices of WIPO, the WIPO Performances and Phonograms Treaty and the WIPO Copyright Treaty were concluded. The US was one of the main agitators for a new international instrument to deal with copyright in the digital age. When abstract objects become digital they become much easier to copy and distribute. As part of its National Information Infrastructure Initiative in 1993, the US had established a working group on intellectual property rights. This working group recommended in a 1995 report that the distri-bution right of copyright owners be clarified to include transmission and that the law prohibit the circumvention of copyright protection systems. The US sought to globalize this copyright owners' agenda by pushing for the inclusion of some new form of communication right in an inter-national instrument. The negotiating history of these two treaties is significant in that copyright owners met with organized resistance from copyright users. The US consumer movement, for instance, was particularly active in successfully opposing the proposed database treaty. Copyright owners had both wins and losses at these negotiations. The Copyright Treaty grants copyright owners a right of communication to the public, but recognizes the right of states to determine the extent of the copyright owner's right of distribution.

All this suggests that treaty-making in intellectual property will be a complex game fought between user and owner groups that transcend national boundaries. Library groups, educational institutions, Internet service providers and developers of software applications are likely to unite in opposition to large software companies and publishers on matters of copyright reform. Indige-nous people's NGOs and environmental NGOs are likely to unite to fight the extension of the patent system to higher-order life-forms. The 1999 review of Article 27(3)(b) of TRIPS, which deals with the scope of patentability in the biotechnology area, saw indigenous and environmen-tal NGOs opposing proposals to redraft the text of the Article in a way that obliges states to increase the scope of biotechnology patenting. The position of companies in the life sciences business (e.g. Monsanto, DuPont and Novartis) is essentially that restrictions and discretions on the scope of patentability in biotechnology should be eliminated. Triumphs on the scale of TRIPS may be much harder to secure in the future.

Intellectual property norms are also becoming a part of the emerging *Lex Cybertoria* – the trade norms of cyberspace. The ICC stated in a recent discussion paper that 'In cyberspace, all assets are intangible and can be classified as intellectual property' (ICC 1998: 11). More generally, governments and business NGOs have agreed that the intellectual property issues raised by e-commerce have to be clearly settled. So far, norm-setting on the intellectual property issues has proceeded largely through model laws generated by international organizations of states (e.g. the UNCITRAL Model Law on Electronic Commerce), national law reform bodies (e.g. the work of the National Conference of Commissioners on Uniform State Laws on Article 2B, which deals with the licensing of intellectual property rights) or business organizations (e.g. the ICC).

## *Actors*

### States

The Roman empire dwarfs all others in terms of its importance in spreading the principles of contract and property law, because Roman law survived as a codified resource after the collapse of the western empire. Within the Roman state itself, both Justinian's codification and the work of the jurists of the classical period were crucial to the emergence of a system of Roman contract and property law. (The jurists can probably be considered to be part of the Roman state, at least during the time of Augustus when he gave some jurists the right to make replies on his behalf (Watson 1995: 4)). France and Germany were the most important states in developing and spreading competing modernized versions of Roman principles during the nineteenth century. Napoleon, who played a major personal role in drafting his Code Civil, said, perhaps rightly, during his exile on St Helena: 'It is not in winning forty battles that my real glory lies, for all those victories will be eclipsed by Waterloo. But my Code Civil will not be forgotten, it will live forever' (Zweigert & Kötz 1987: vol. 1, 86).

Courts and individual judges have been significant state actors in the process of creating a harmonized international commercial law. The early specialist commercial courts like the Staple Courts and the Court of Admiralty in England bound themselves to the principle of recognizing the customary practices of merchants, which in turn helped to produce and reinforce the Law Merchant. Innovative judges were also important to the diffusion of the Law Merchant. A good example was the work of the Chief Justice of the King's Bench, Lord Mansfield. Judges like Mansfield were innovators of principle, but they usually sought those principles in the jurisprudence of other jurisdictions. A spectacular example of Mansfield LCJ's abilities to synthesize principles based on transnational sources is *Luke v. Lyde*.[6]

In the nineteenth century there was not a great deal of state activity on the harmonization of contract. Contract was the subject of law-making, but it was the law-making of states interested in the codification and systematization of contract as part of a national legal order. It was

---

6  [1759] 2 Burr 882.

a different matter for intellectual property. States like the UK, which saw trade gains in parts of intellectual property, took an interest in the negotiation of bilateral treaties dealing with copyright or patents. There was increasing state activity in the twentieth century in both contract and intellectual property. Many states became members of various intellectual property conventions but no one state led the development of a world intellectual property regime. European states, for instance, led the way on the development of international copyright, but the US (until the beginning of its TRIPS campaign in the 1980s) stayed out of the main multilateral copyright treaty, the Berne Convention. Developing countries joined the Paris and Berne Conventions in droves and were able to secure concessions in some areas, such as compulsory licensing. At the same time they made the US realize the futility of trying to achieve its own reform agenda in an international forum like WIPO, where one-state–one-vote meant that the US was always likely to be outvoted. This, we will see in Chapter 24, led the US to develop a strategy of forum-shifting.

During the 1980s the US became the single most powerful state in the determination and enforcement of a world set of intellectual property standards. Within the US bureaucracy the influence and importance of the USTR grew, and today the position of USTR is one of the most sought-after. The US is the most important member of an intellectual property triumvirate, the other two members being Europe and Japan. It was primarily responsible for bringing about the new intellectual property/trade paradigm and it continues to be the strongest agitator both bilaterally and multilaterally for the global spread of intellectual property rights. Europe is also a strong supporter of intellectual property harmonization, particularly through the European Commission (EC) and the European Patent Office (EPO). But the Europeans went into GATT negotiations on intellectual property, in the words of one Brussels lobbyist, 'accepting the premises given to them by the US government'. Japan's role was and is essentially that of polite cooperator. And it remains so, even though it was one of the first states to suffer US enforcement action under TRIPS for backpayment of royalties on sound recordings.

Developing states are no longer the powerful veto coalition that they once were in the area of intellectual property. Countries like Singapore and South Korea have become powerful economies in their own right and accept intellectual property as a necessary part of a legal infrastructure for a modern economy. The lessening of resistance to intellectual property has much to do with the perception that weak intellectual property protection may result in a state being bypassed by global investment flows. Even India, which provided much of the leadership against intellectual property in the 1960s and against the TRIPS initiative, has adopted a differentiated approach to the harmonization of intellectual property. The Indians remain fierce critics of the patent provisions of the TRIPS Agreement, arguing that its implementation in India will destroy the generic pharmaceutical industry and consequently increase the price of drugs for Indian consumers. But India also has a strong software industry and is the world's largest producer of films ('Bollywood'), and so is a supporter of copyright.

The harmonization of contract law, like intellectual property, is dominated by Western states. Our interviews suggested that the most influential states at UNCITRAL were the US, the UK, Canada, Australia, France, Spain and Germany, with the Nordics also important on some issues. Italy is more influential in UNIDROIT (because the group is based in Rome). Within this Western grouping there is a clear division between common-law countries and civil-law countries, resulting from differences of legal culture. They are also differences that usually relate to technical matters of law. There is no hegemonic actor within this group in the way that there has been for intellectual property. Developing states have not played a great role in the harmonization of contract law because for a state to be influential in this game it must possess very high levels of technical expertise. Not many developing states can put together a group of legal experts on the esoteric aspects of, for example, the international leasing of equipment. For that matter, neither can many developed countries. A state like the US, which has the benefit of a well-developed legal system and tradition as well as a large legal market, can find such specialists and send them to the relevant treaty negotiations, where they usually make a difference. This is one reason why the US is likely to remain the most significant player in determining the rules of contract for electronic commerce.

At the regional level, the EU has been active in trying to harmonize the principles of contract law among its member states. The aspiration to harmonize contract law has been driven by the desire to create a strong internal market and the realization that the progressive harmonization of commercial law in the US through instruments like the Uniform Commercial Code have been an important factor in the growth of domestic trade between US states. Using directives to achieve this purpose has not proved particularly successful because such directives have to bridge differences of language as well as differences of tradition (common law and civil) (Lando 1992: 574–6). The goal of harmonization remains real, however, with the European Parliament passing a resolution in 1989 asking that work be carried out on the unification of private law including contract law (Lando 1992: 577).

Developing countries have had little to do with the formulation of the new Law Merchant, which has led to scepticism about claims that it represents universal norms:

> The so-called *Lex Mercatoria* is a creation of a coterie of Western scholars and arbitrators who have loaded it with norms entirely favourable to international business (Sornarajah 1989: 17, footnote omitted).

> The new *Lex Mercatoria* can hardly be said to bear the imprint of universality. Is it seriously suggested that the trade usage of the highly sophisticated international conglomerates in the Western world are to be found or accepted in less developed commercial societies? (Rogers 1989: 159).

The problem for developing countries is two-fold. In order to influence treaty-making processes relating to contract they must have the relevant technical expertise. Private ordering and harmonization of contract law may be a spontaneous process but it is also one dominated by large corporate actors who are willing to cooperate on the development of rules that protect their international trading interests. It is a process beyond the capacity of developing countries' governments to influence.

## Organizations of States

Within intellectual property, the single most important international organization is WTO. The head of WIPO observed in 1992 that if the draft proposals for an agreement on intellectual property were to become reality 'the question will arise in which of the two organizations – WIPO or GATT…the international norms of the protection of intellectual property will be further developed' (Bogsch 1992: 21). With the creation of WTO and the inclusion of TRIPS in the Final Act, WIPO lost its pre-eminence as the lead organization in the field of intellectual property. Probably the single most important factor in WIPO's loss of pre-eminence was the fact that even if it could deliver a treaty on intellectual property that treaty would not be tied to an effective enforcement mechanism. As one WIPO official observed somewhat ruefully, 'WIPO does not have a big stick or any stick'. In the post-TRIPS era WIPO remains an important organization simply because of its vast specialist expertise and the fact that it can draw on the specialist knowledge and experience of the hundreds of international and national NGOs to which it has granted observer status. The WTO trade cycle of negotiations is probably more suited to controversial matters of policy, like the extension of the patent term, to which developing countries would never have agreed in the context of WIPO. WIPO will remain important on the technical matters raised by the process of intellectual property harmonization. To states that lead on matters of intellectual property, such as the US, the presence of both WIPO and WTO in the field of intellectual property standard-setting means that there are two fora in which to play for a win on intellectual property.

The international organization which has been most marginalized by the shift of the intellectual property forum to WTO has been UNCTAD. Since its creation in 1964 UNCTAD served as a forum for developing countries' initiatives. These initiatives had two broad thrusts. One was to gain access to developed countries' markets through duty-free trading privileges, and to encourage the transfer of resources from North to South. The second broad initiative saw UNCTAD develop analytical work which showed that existing intellectual property regimes were unfavourable to developing countries. UNCTAD supported principles that favoured the transfer of technological resources from North to South, the most important being the principle that technology was the common heritage of humanity. It also pushed for codes of conduct on technology transfer and the activities of transnational corporations. More than any other international organization, UNCTAD had a legitimate claim to jurisdiction over the development of a trade-related agreement covering intellectual property rights, but because UNCTAD was an organization representing the interests of developing countries the US would never have recognized or supported that claim. Thus the one UN organ with high levels of analytical expertise on trade and intellectual property has largely become irrelevant in affecting intellectual property standard-making.

Much the same might be said of UNESCO, which began as a potentially important forum for developing countries to develop copyright in a way which was consistent with the needs of educational and scientific users of information. When UNESCO was formed in 1946 one of its stated purposes was to 'recommend such international agreements as may be necessary to promote the free flow of ideas by word and image…maintain, increase and diffuse knowledge…by initiating methods of international cooperation calculated to give the people of all countries access to the printed and published materials produced by any of them' (Article 1, cited in Kampelman 1947: 428). But, as one UNESCO official pointed out to us, these days copyright is not a priority and budgetary constraints mean that only a token staff are maintained in the area. UNESCO is a marginal player in the international copyright game.

The International Labour Organization (ILO) has taken an interest in intellectual property as it has affected the livelihood of musicians, singers, actors and other performers. At the request of the International Union of Musicians in 1926, the ILO began to examine the impact of technology on the livelihood of performers (Thompson 1973: 303). The ILO was one of the main actors responsible for the International Convention for the Protection of Performers, Producers of Phonograms and Broadcasting Organizations 1961.

The organizations which have been most important in constructing international contract law have been UNCITRAL, UNIDROIT and the oldest organization of the three, the Hague Conference of Private International Law (1893). The members of the Hague Conference are mainly European states. Its method of harmonization has been to prepare draft conventions which generally have only small numbers of states acceding to them. UNCITRAL has become 'the leading international agency for the harmonization of private commercial law' (Goode 1995: 18, fn 64). Like the Hague Conference, UNCITRAL has used conventions and model laws to promote the goal of harmonization, the Convention on Contracts for the International Sales of Goods 1980 being its most successful convention. Its work on bills of exchange and promissory notes harmonization is also significant; it is currently focusing on bank guarantees, letters of credit and replacing commercial paper with electronic funds transfer. UNCITRAL is the most representative of the three organizations working in the field of private law harmonization.

Since its creation in 1926, UNIDROIT has been a key player in efforts to harmonize private law. With a majority of European members, its original preferred tool of harmonization was the production of draft conventions, such as the Convention Relating to a Uniform Law on the International Sale of Goods (Corporeal Movables) 1964. Recently, however, it has signalled a different approach to the goal of harmonization, through its production of the UNIDROIT Principles of International Commercial Contracts 1994. Rather than attempting to draft a uniform law for the world, UNIDROIT has concentrated on a set of general and flexible principles, which it says can be amended in much the same way that the ICC amends its own rules (Farnsworth 1992: 700).

Aside from these three main players, other organizations which have dealt with aspects of contract law harmonization are UNCTAD and the regional commissions of the UN, such as the Economic Commission for Europe. At a regional level there have been a number of quiet initiatives towards the harmonization of commercial law, including contract law, examples being the work of the EU, the Bustamante Code (dealing with conflict of laws issues on matters relating to international commercial law) signed by many South and Central American countries, the Benelux Commission for the Unification of Private Law and the work of the Nordic Council (formed by Denmark, Norway, Iceland and Sweden in 1952) on uniform laws for the bills of exchange and sale of goods (UNCITRAL 1971: 32–5). The League of Nations produced conventions on bills of exchange and cheques in 1930 and 1931, but these were supported only by civil-law countries.

## Companies

Lloyd's of London is an example of a company that played a strategic role in the globalization of the law of contract, specifically in the domain of marine insurance contracts. Business organizations have been centrally important in the globalization of intellectual property. These days US multinationals have influential business NGOs like the Intellectual Property Committee (IPC), the International Intellectual Property Alliance (IIPA) and the Business Software Alliance (BSA) to represent their interests. Because of the technical nature of intellectual property, large business tends to rely on such organizations to do the analytical work and the lobbying. It was not always so. The pharmaceutical corporation Pfizer was a key player in developing the links between intellectual property and trade. In 1981 ACTN, the business committee advising on US trade policy, was chaired by Edmund Pratt, the CEO of Pfizer. Other key companies in the early days of the TRIPS negotiations were IBM and DuPont. IBM was more active than most multinationals on a number of intellectual property issues including copyright and computer software. Keen to maintain the dominance of its Systems Network Architecture in the world of mainframes, IBM wanted a model of copyright law that made it difficult for competitors to engage in reverse engineering so that they could produce compatible products. IBM, Apple, Lotus and Microsoft began a campaign to ensure that copyright laws around the world did not allow the reverse engineering of computer programs. These and other companies, largely led by IBM formed the Software Action Group for Europe. Their opponents (including Bull, Fujitsu and Olivetti) formed a counter-organization, the European Committee for Interoperable Systems (Band & Katoh 1995: 229). In the ensuing 'softwars' most countries ended up recognizing that some limited form of reverse engineering of software was allowable under copyright.

Throughout the TRIPS negotiations US companies took an interest in those parts of intellectual property that represented the backbone of their industry. Intel Corporation worried about protection for semiconductor chips and compulsory licensing and a number of high-technology companies including Motorola, Texas Instruments, Intel Corporation, Eastman Kodak and Advanced Micro Services showed leadership in evolving the TRIPS border enforcement procedures.

**International Business Organizations**

Merchants' families, which in essence were business enterprises, were key actors in spreading the standards of professional conduct that became the basis of *Lex Mercatoria*. Merchant norms based on trust and symbolic action are found throughout antiquity (Silver 1995). Merchant associations, guilds and colleges were widespread in the time of the Roman empire (Toutain 1930: 316). Medieval trade was dominated by the merchants of Italian city-states, and they helped to spread commercial innovations throughout western Europe. It was they who became the merchant bankers at the Champagne trade fairs and introduced the commercial instruments and techniques that made banking, credit and bookkeeping possible (Abu-Lughod 1989: 67). The Lombardian Guild of Merchants and guilds from the republics of Genoa, Lucca, Florence and Venice spread throughout Europe. The pivotal role of northern Italian merchants lies in the fact that these merchants had kept their links with the East and had learnt from the commercial customs of their Eastern counterparts. The Venetian merchant Marco Polo reported with great excitement upon the use and convenience of 'pieces of paper' in China for settling payments in China, pieces of paper which were similar to bills of exchange and cheques (de Rooy 1984: 6). Abu-Lughod (1989: 67) argues that the Italian merchants 'were subsidiary to the Middle East', pointing out that Venetian and Genoese merchants used the gold coins of Constantinople and Egypt 'up until the second half of the thirteenth century'.

During the late nineteenth and early twentieth centuries the mercantile community began to develop more international and bureaucratic structures to deal with the complexities of doing business in a world of many states and many national legal orders. The most important of these is the ICC, which has been one of the lead organizations in the unification of international commercial law. The ICC has employed two kinds of strategy, an interest group strategy and a private ordering strategy. As an influential interest group it has pushed governments and international organizations to hold international meetings of states for the purpose of developing model laws in convention form. For example, during the 1920s the ICC kept the issue of the unification of the law of financial instruments before governments. It has always been more influential than most states at UNCITRAL. Its 1927 adoption, at its fourth Congress, of a set of uniform rules for negotiable instruments was crucial in stimulating international actions by states and the League of Nations on the issue (Hudson & Feller 1931: 344–5). The ICC's private ordering strategy has been based on recording its members' customary practices and releasing them in the form of model rules and agreements. ICC Incoterms and the ICC

Uniform Rules on Letters of Credit enjoy widespread recognition around the world. The ICC has also been an important and long-term player in the globalization of industrial property. From its beginning in 1919, the ICC established a permanent Commission for International Protection of Industrial Property (Ladas 1975a: 188).

Intellectual property is populated by hundreds of business organizations, both national and international. Some, like the European Committee for Interoperable Systems (ECIS), are of recent origin and have been formed to contest a single issue, such as the reverse engineering of software under copyright. Other business organizations, like the International Federation of the Phonographic Industry, are devoted to the interests of a single industry and have existed for a long time. They understand the international game of copyright extremely well and push the interests of their members in all possible fora. Yet others, like the ICC, work on all aspects of intellectual property standard-setting.

A feature of intellectual property globalization is the formation of international business organizations dedicated exclusively to the cause of globalizing enforceable intellectual property standards. Among the most important are the IPC, the IIPA and the BSA. The IPC grew out of the work of ACTN. US business leaders on ACTN realized that nothing would come of their idea to link intellectual property and trade unless the US had the agreement of the other Quad states (the Quad being composed of the US, the EU, Canada and Japan). This meant that Japanese, Canadian and European large business all had to support the proposal. The IPC was formed to build that consensus among the international business community. Its membership consisted of Bristol-Myers, DuPont, FMC Corporation, General Electric, General Motors, Hewlett-Packard, IBM, Johnson & Johnson, Merck, Monsanto, Pfizer, Rockwell International and Warner Communications.

The IIPA is probably the single most important copyright lobbyist in the world and is a regular user of the US 301 process. It is an umbrella organization consisting of eight trade associations: the American Film Marketing Association, the Association of American Publishers, the Business Software Alliance, the Computer and Business Equipment Manufacturers Association, the Information Technology Association of America, the Motion Picture Association of America, the National Music Publishers Association and the Recording Industry Association of America. The BSA represents the elite of the US software industry and, like the IIPA, is a major user of the 301 process.

Without the work of these business organizations the intellectual property/trade paradigm might never have happened. The work of the IPC was particularly important. It coordinated with the Keidandren and UNICE – the peak industry bodies for Japan and Europe respectively – to produce a draft text on intellectual property that was given to states as a 'Statement of Views of the European, Japanese and United States Business Communities' (Intellectual Property Committee 1988). The IPC also established close working relations with the US administration and Congress; in the words of the IPC this allowed it 'to shape the US proposals and negotiating positions during the course of the negotiations' (IPC Release 14 June 1988).

We obtained a glimpse of the power of these business NGOs and their role in intellectual property harmonization in an interview with Jack Valenti, head of the Motion Picture Association of America (MPA). In 1985 the MPA brought a 301 action against South Korea. Valenti told us that a South Korean minister travelled to Washington and spent several days negotiating in Valenti's office to sort out a deal on the showing of US films in South Korea so that the MPA would drop its action. And, as Valenti explained to us, during the GATT negotiations the official trade negotiators were not the only players – there was a parallel process of 'backroom bargaining' between key players like himself and the French film producers.

## International and National NGOs

The International Law Association, formed in 1873, has been an important force for the international unification of negotiable instruments. It formed a working committee on bills of exchange as early as 1875. Through its international membership and accumulated juristic expertise it has been able to formulate proposals that have made unification an ongoing project. Other international NGOs with a long presence in the field of contract harmonization are the International Association of Legal Science and the Institute of International Law. At the national level, the American Law Institute and the Commissioners on Uniform State Laws, through instruments like the Restatements (contract being one of the first Restatements), model and uniform laws, have been crucial to the harmonization of US contract law (Rosett 1992: 689). Contract harmonization has historically been very much a bottom-up process in which the epistemic community of contract has worked to convince local bars and the national profession of the merits of harmonization. The work of national NGOs like the American Law Institute on national harmonization in large jurisdictions like the US is fundamental to global contract harmonization. Moreover, the synthesizing work of these US NGOs in complex areas like the licensing of intellectual property means that it is US standards of contract that have the best chance of globalizing. The EC's comparative lack of success in the area of contract harmonization (directives being a top-down process) has led to the formation of the Commission on European Contract Law, 'a non-governmental body of lawyers from the 12 EC countries', most members being academics not appointed by any government (Lando 1992: 580).

Intellectual property, unlike contract, has hundreds of international and national NGOs. Aside from the international and national business NGOs mentioned above there are NGOs comprised of professionals, which mainly represent intellectual property holders. Two important ones are the Licensing Executives Society International and the International Association for the Protection of Industrial Property (AIPPI). During an interview with a member of the latter we were told that AIPPI tends to identify with the right holder, taking the attitude that 'what is good for the customer is good for me'. Creators' interests are also represented through NGOs. The International Literary Association, for instance, formed in 1878 to help authors establish an international framework for protection of their works. Similarly, the International Federation of Musicians has been important in developing performers' rights.

Consumer organizations have not been players in the globalization of intellectual property. By the time consumer organizations understood the import of TRIPS, the ink on it had largely dried. Realization of the social and economic implications of property rights in abstract objects has seen consumer NGOs and Third World NGOs begin to mobilize against parts of the global intellectual property paradigm. The work of Indian feminist Dr Vandana Shiva has been important in alerting indigenous peoples to the 'biopiracy' which occurs when TNCs acquire patents in genetic material developed using indigenous knowledge (Shiva 1996). Similarly, the Indian National Working Group on Patent Laws, led by B.K. Keayla, has become a focal point in India and other developing countries for resistance to the patent provisions of TRIPS (Keayla 1996). In the US the Ralph Nader-led organization, the Centre for the Study of Responsive Law, has criticized TRIPS, arguing that it is inconsistent with good health-care policy.

### Epistemic Communities of Actors and their Key Individuals

The epistemic community for contract and property is very old. Justinian's court at Constantinople, the University of Bologna, medieval trade fairs and modern law schools all played roles. Probably the single most important group is the Roman jurists. Roman private law exerts such a harmonizing influence in the history of legal systems because, in the classical period, it reached a high degree of conceptual refinement and organization. It was a system that was rich in interpretive detail. With this depth of detail there was a simplicity and economy of structure probably first fully developed by Gaius in his *Institutes* and repeated later in Justinian's *Institutes*. The construction of this resource, which became so important over the centuries, would not have been possible without the work of the jurists of the classical age. Watson puts it thus:

> The jurists were primarily interested in interpretation according to rules they devised for themselves, and they neglected other parts of legal work. It was the conceptualization resulting from their interpretation, coupled with the *Institutes*, that made Roman law the supreme law force for succeeding centuries (Watson 1995: 205).

Writers of textbooks were also important in the spread of *Lex Mercatoria*. In England, Gerard Malynes' *Lex Mercatoria* became a major source of the Law Merchant. It was published in 1622 and reissued throughout the century (Stein 1988: 219). The spread of mercantile principles through the textbook tradition was also important in America, where a new nation was seeking to develop a commercial law. Classic European texts made their way to America, where they became regularly cited. The *Treatise on Obligations* (1761) by French jurist Pothier was translated and published in America in 1802 and a translation of Azuni's *The Maritime Law of Europe* (1795) was published in New York in 1806 (Stein 1988: 421). Pothier's work exercised a long-term influence on English courts and jurists: 'Sir Mackenzie Chalmers, the draftsman of the Sale of Goods Act, was profoundly influenced by Pothier's *Traité du Contrat de Vente*, as is evident from the frequent references to Pothier in his own work, notably in the Introduction to the first edition (1894)' (Goode 1995: 7, fn 15).

Chalmers himself was the author of two of the most internationally modelled Acts in history, the *Bills of Exchange Act 1882* and the *Sale of Goods Act 1883*. His description of the drafting process for the former Act reveals the influence that a jurist model-builder can have when they synthesize usable principles from overwhelming complexity. Chalmers read 2500 cases and seventeen statutory enactments to produce a Digest of the law of negotiable instruments, which then became the basis of an Act with 100 sections (Chalmers 1886). The convenience of accessible principles was readily apparent to the merchant and banking community and so they supported the codification process. Chalmers also travelled to the US, where he spoke to the American Bar Association in favour of the codification of mercantile law (Chalmers 1903).

The importance of textbooks in the constitution of epistemic communities of commercial lawyers is perhaps more important than we realize. Legal texts did not just report the law. They were also important in the production of legal doctrine and subject matter because their authors sought to organize legal rules and principles in a coherent and logical form. Writers of texts were engaged in a creative as well as a descriptive enterprise. Textbooks were important in the subject matter of contract and property. The Roman jurists of the classical period, it must be remembered, were great writers of books (Watson 1995: 4). Textbooks were probably the most important form of communication among members of an epistemic community living in different states.

They became part of library systems and court systems as well as the collections of private individuals. Through this process of transmission, merchants in different countries, and their advisers, could draw upon a common stock of specific information about documents and rules to facilitate their international trade deals.

It would be a mistake, however, to cast jurists in the role of faithful harmonizers. They have also led intellectual insurgencies against processes of harmonization. The attack on the universalizing influence of the 'Italianised Roman law of the Bartolists' by French jurists in the sixteenth century is one striking example, and there are others such as the work of Spanish legal historians in the sixteenth and seventeenth centuries on native law, the codification of customary law by French jurist Guillaume de Lamoignon in the seventeenth century and the development of Roman Dutch law which, through the hands of figures such as Grotius, was synthesized from elements of Roman law with customary legal norms of Germanic source (Hazeltine 1926: 156, 157–63).

This particular epistemic community has been dominated by jurists. They, more than any other group, have been able to synthesize usable norms from domains of particular complexity, domains such as international business practice, the decisions of courts and the comparative legal practices of states. Some further examples of their work can be mentioned. The comparative work of jurist Felix Meyer on bills of exchange was crucial to the convening of an international conference on the unification of the law relating to bills of exchange and promissory notes at the Hague in 1910 (Hudson & Feller 1931: 341). In the US, legal academics have been centrally involved in the drafting of restatements of laws, model laws and uniform laws. The best example of this is the drafting of a Uniform Commercial Code, a process which was headed by the American Realist and scholar Karl Llewellyn and which involved leading US contracts scholars (Symposium 1982: 535–84). In Europe, a group of jurists who believed that Europe must work towards a uniform contract law formed in 1980 the Commission of European Contract Law (Lando 1992: 576). The Commission is essentially an NGO of jurists. Influenced somewhat by the success of the US Restatement of Contract Law, the Commission has used comparative methods to attempt to distil principles of contract law that will serve private parties and act as a model for European states seeking to harmonize their law of contract.

The epistemic community for contract is much broader than lawyers. It comprises 'merchants, shipowners, insurance underwriters, bankers and others' who 'form a transnational community which has had a more or less continuous history, despite countless vicissitudes, for some nine centuries' (Berman & Kaufman 1978: 222). For contract at least, the epistemic community is the mercantile community. Critical agents of the globalization of its creation were ethnic diasporas of Armenians, Jews, Genoans and Venetians, among others (Braudel 1979). Trust within the merchant cultures they forged as geographical enclaves in all the great medieval trading centres built confidence in the new rules of business, not so much rules that regulated business (though partly that) as rules that constituted business. Natives learnt from the constitutive regulation in the enclaves of the ethnic diasporas within their cities. Slowly, painfully, a rule-governed capitalism globalized out of this process of learning.

The community for intellectual property is somewhat narrower. The perception of common problems that helped to constitute a mercantile community with a broad membership, in the case of contract, has been largely absent in the case of intellectual property. To take but one example, merchants wishing to import legitimate copies of works subject to copyright or trademarks are hardly likely to consider that the absence of a restriction on parallel importation is a problem. And only merchants who are confident that they will benefit more as creators of abstract objects than as users of them are likely to be ardent supporters of intellectual property. The dominant core of the epistemic community of intellectual property is comprised of transnational elites with important intellectual property portfolios to protect – and their lawyers. Lawyers, by virtue of their technical knowledge, are a driving force in this epistemic community. Their crucible is Geneva – developing countries' lawyers are inducted into the intellectual property community via the mystique of Geneva meetings, not to mention the charm of field trips to Switzerland!

## Contest of Principles

### Sovereignty, National Treatment v. Harmonization, National Treatment, Most Favoured Nation

We argued in Chapter 4 that actors involved in global regulatory processes push for the recognition or weighting of particular principles. The development of global regulation can be analyzed in terms of a contest or opposition between two or more principles (see Chapter 21). The clash of principles with which we begin occurs in the context of intellectual property. National treatment appears on both sides of the contest. During the nineteenth century the principle of national treatment (also called the principle of assimilation) served the principle of sovereignty because, although it mandates the equal treatment of foreigners, it does not require a state to adopt specific standards of intellectual property protection. A state can adopt the principle of national treatment and still remain sovereign over standard-setting in intellectual property. It can choose, for example, not to grant patents for pharmaceutical compounds or grant rental rights to copyright owners. During the global period of intellectual property, when states begin to harmonize their national standards of intellectual property protection, the effect of the principle is that the citizens of different states possess the same set of rights and obligations. The citizens of Rwanda, for example, have the same right as the teams of genetic engineers working for Pfizer to apply for a patent on a genetically engineered micro-organism in the US. The Pfizer teams have the same right to apply for a patent in Rwanda. Both US and Rwandan patent law must recognize the patentability of micro-organisms (Article 27 of TRIPS) and both states must extend that right to non-nationals. When the principle of national treatment is combined with national laws that have been harmonized, nationals of states are in a position of formal reciprocity, each possessing the same set of rights and obligations in each other's territory. Obviously the capacity of citizens of different countries to exploit a globalized set of duties and rights in intellectual property will vary dramatically. TRIPS also adds the Most Favoured Nation (MFN) principle to intellectual property, so that any right granted by one state to the nationals of another must be granted to the nationals of all other member states (Article 4).

The impact of a globally harmonized set of property rights on the principle of state sovereignty is spectacular. For example, the way that rights of copyright are defined has important consequences for the build-up and diffusion of human capital and the way that patent rights are defined has important implications for a state's innovation system. Whether there will be global welfare gains from a global set of property rights is not well understood (Subramanian 1991; Lyons 1987). What is clear is that global property rights set strong limits on a state's capacity to define territorial property rights in ways that enhance national welfare.

## Reciprocity v. National Treatment

The principle of reciprocity was the dominant principle in international copyright protection until the Berne Convention in 1886. The French were the first, in 1793, to extend copyright protection to both foreign and domestic works, and did so again in 1852, but other European states usually operated on the basis of reciprocity (Kampelman 1947: 410). The principle of reciprocity remains important in the context of intellectual property. The US, for example, used the principle of reciprocity in its *Semiconductor Chip Protection Act 1984*. Worried about its declining share of the computer chip market and Japanese competition in this vital industry, the US defined its Act on the basis of strict reciprocity (Correa 1990: 196). It would only protect the computer chip designs of other countries if they extended protection based on US standards to US chip-makers. The upshot was that many Western countries adopted a semiconductor chip regime based on the US Act. The size of the US market meant that the US was able, through the principle of reciprocity combined with the mechanism of economic coercion, to globalize semiconductor chip protection.

## Free Flow of Information, Common Heritage of Mankind, Deregulation v. Harmonization

This particular cluster of principles has interacted in complex ways. Chapter 14 (telecommunications) shows that US corporate actors have supported the principle of free flow of information on the basis that there should be no restrictions on the trade in information. Developing countries have resisted this trade version of the free flow principle. In the context of intellectual property, developing countries have argued that technological and cultural information ought to flow as freely as possible throughout the world. They have seen the free flow principle, in other words, as a principle of access to information. The claim that technology is the common heritage of mankind is also a principle of access which has been supported by developing countries and rejected by developed countries. Both the principle of free flow of information and the common heritage principle, when articulated as principles of access, are supported by the principle of deregulation in the context of intellectual property. The reason is that intellectual property rights are administratively costly and complex forms of government intervention in the marketplace. Governments which act to reduce or halt the level of propertization of information are, in effect, following the principle of deregulation. Governments which seek to harmonize intellectual property protection are regulating in ways that cut across the principles of free flow of information, common heritage and deregulation. In this clash of principles the principle of harmonization has been the victor. The other principles are principles which, these days, are in search of a forum.

## Sovereignty (Personality and Territoriality) v. Harmonization

The clash between sovereignty and harmonization has been the main event in the harmonization of contract law. The presence of the principle of harmonization in contract has ebbed and flowed. The medieval Law Merchant was not a harmonized system of contract, but it was closer to being such a system than the nationalized Law Merchant which began to emerge in the sixteenth and seventeenth centuries in Europe. Local domestic courts which did not have the international outlook of the medieval merchant tribunals acquired jurisdiction over the Law Merchant. They, like their medieval predecessors, understood the importance of allowing merchant practice to constitute the Law Merchant, but domestic courts began to look to local merchant norms to decide cases. Perceptions of national interest in the regulation of commerce (the principle of sovereignty) and the desires of domestic tribunals to shape 'their' commercial law (the principle of territoriality) led to national variants and fragmentation of the international Law Merchant. Trakman puts it thus: 'Under these pressures, the Law Merchant was indeed translated into a nationalized form, adapted in nature and in content to the socio-political demands of each forum' (Trakman 1983: 24).

During the nineteenth and twentieth centuries the principle of harmonization gained some ascendancy. Codes and models emerged in both civil-law and common-law countries, the codification of bills of exchange in the *Bills of Exchange Act 1882* (UK) and the subsequent spread of that Act throughout the British empire being a good example of this ascendancy. The principle of harmonization has advanced in other ways. The demand among merchants for a standardized contract law to govern international trade has remained high and so they have continued to be active supporters of the principle of harmonization. It may be that a 'new Law Merchant' or a 'revitalized Law Merchant' is developing (Trakman 1983: Ch. 3). Merchant-led harmonization has shown in organizations like the ICC developing standard rules and meanings to apply to trade transactions and merchants using those standardized rules and meanings, for example incorporating them by reference into their contracts. The ICC's Incoterms is a good example of the process of harmonization. This process of harmonization contrasts sharply with that of intellectual property, where positive law is being used to harmonize divergent national systems.

### Strategic Trade, Lowest-cost Location v. Harmonization, Rule Compliance, World's Best Practice

When states refuse to extend intellectual property protection to a particular area it is sometimes because they wish to lower production costs in their jurisdiction. Refusing to recognize another country's patents is an example. One of Australia's fears about recognizing the moral rights doctrine in copyright was that it would raise the cost of cultural production too much (Copyright Law Review Committee 1988: 23). The principle of lowest-cost location seems to have been largely pushed out by the progressive harmonization of intellectual property law – the belief that a nation and its firms will become more competitive when intellectual property standards are high. In a world where different parts of a product or service are often contributed by different places, an argument in terms of world's best practice is that a state or firm will not attract investment unless it adheres to the world standard of intellectual property protection. More simply, investors will not risk their fund of abstract objects in markets where they believe it can be pirated. The belief that has been sold by the intellectual property epistemic community is that harmonized regulation of piracy by states and rule compliance by firms enhances the competitiveness of both. This belief, however, does not appear to be backed by the empirical evidence (see Abbot 1997:44).

The principle of strategic trade was important in intellectual property in the nineteenth century. States would routinely design their patent or copyright laws in a way that advantaged domestic producers over foreign ones. So, for example, states would often not recognize the copyright of foreign authors or would do so only on a reciprocal basis. The US did not recognize foreign copyright until 1891 and then only if the foreign work was published and printed in the US simultaneously with publication in the country of origin. The London *Times* saw this as an attempt to make New York the centre of world publishing (Briggs 1906: 93). Similarly, the states of the German *Zollervein*, despite forming a customs union in 1833, maintained the right to prevent the importation of goods on which they had issued patents (thereby protecting the domestic market of their patentees) (Penrose 1951: 14). As shown in the historical discussion, the principles of national treatment and harmonization have progressively become dominant in intellectual property. The trade impulse, however, just as in the nineteenth century, continues to drive states' selection of principles. In royalty terms, the US enjoys a 4:1 ratio in its favour when it comes to the licensing of technology (Degan 1998: 145). The principles of national treatment, harmonization and world's best practice serve the US well in the case of intellectual property. It has largely abandoned the principle of strategic trade for intellectual property and, as our discussion of the mechanism of economic coercion makes clear, forced developing states to do the same.

### Continuous Improvement

Nowhere in our data collection or our interviews did we find continuous improvement invoked as a principle that guided strategic action. Rule compliance with obligations to respect property or honour contract was often invoked, but there was no commitment to continuous improvement in relation to such matters. Officials from some countries would tell us that they were committed to a high standard of intellectual property protection, meaning the standards set by the US rather than improving upon those standards.

### Transparency

Transparency is a principle explicitly institutionalized in Article 63 of TRIPS. This Article requires members to publish information relevant to the Agreement, to provide information to other members upon written request and to provide relevant information to the Council for TRIPS so that it can carry out its monitoring duties. The globalization of the legal device of the patent is partly a globalization of a form of transparency, as patent law requires a public record of how the patented product is engineered. This is not a necessary feature of globalized property and contract laws. For example, the globalization of trade secret law (see, for example, Article 39 of TRIPS) globalizes an intellectual property regime that makes knowledge less transparent to others.

## Mechanisms

### Military Coercion

Military coercion has been one of the dominant mechanisms in the harmonization of contract and property law. Conquerors have often imposed their legal culture and rules. Roman armies brought Roman law, although conquered foreigners could not take advantage of Roman private law unless they were granted citizenship. After most of Europe was conquered between 1790 and 1812 by the French revolutionary and then Napoleon's armies, the Roman-influenced Code Civil came into force transnationally. After Waterloo these states recovered their sovereignty, 'but their private law retained the impress of the ideas of the French Code' (Zweigert & Kötz 1987: vol. 1, 103). Spanish colonial domination over nearly three hundred years in Latin America brought a measure of unification of private law including contract law (Garro 1992: 604). As a Spanish colony, the Philippines were extended Spanish intellectual property law in 1887, but after the

Spanish-American War, when the Philippines became part of US territory, the US *Patent Act 1913* applied (Jimenez 1997: 268). Similarly, Indonesian patent law was until 1953 based on Dutch colonial law (Kardono & Johnson 1997: 157). The intellectual property law of Hong Kong, Malaysia and Singapore is based on English models. English property law has had an important influence on the Hindu law of personal property (although not the law of real property ) (Gled-hill 1954). A developing country might have a civil-law or common-law system because that was the legal system of a conqueror.

### Economic Coercion

Intellectual property is perhaps our most spectacular example of economic coercion. The US *Trade Act 1984* amended the 301 process so that it expressly allowed the President to impose trade sanctions against countries that did not adequately protect intellectual property. A further reshaping of the 301 process to protect US intellectual property interests took place in the *Omnibus Trade and Competitiveness Act 1988*. That Act stated that the:

> principal negotiating objectives of the United States regarding intellectual property are...to seek the enactment and effective enforcement by foreign countries of laws which recognize and adequately protect intellectual property...to establish in the GATT obligations to implement adequate substantive standards based on the standards in existing international agreements that provide adequate protection, and the *standards in national laws if international agreement standards are inadequate or do not exist* (section 1101, emphasis added).

The US, in other words, was signalling in the clearest terms that it wanted the rest of the world to match US domestic standards.

The US 301 process drove countries to the bilateral negotiating table and in many cases countries improved their protection of intellectual property and concluded a bilateral treaty with the US on intellectual property (e.g. South Korea and the US concluded an agreement on intellectual property in 1986 and China and the US concluded agreements on improving the enforcement of intellectual property in 1995 and 1996). The US approach to the use of 301-based trade sanctions was highly focused. For example, in 1962 Brazil, which for a long time had criticized the international patent system, attempted to turn the UN into a forum for the study and reform of the international patent system, an initiative which ultimately failed (Anderfelt 1971: 198–9). In 1987, the US Pharmaceutical Manufacturers Association initiated a 301 action against Brazil for failing to protect pharmaceutical products and processes. The action ultimately resulted in President Reagan authorizing the imposition of trade duties to the tune of $US39 million on Brazilian products imported into the US (products not related to pharmaceuticals) (Getlan 1995: 189). Eventually Brazil reformed its patent law. As one lawyer from a US multinational explained to us, the 301 process was highly effective because once tariffs were imposed on a developing country's imports into the US those tariffs 'killed their markets' and in many cases the developing country would never recover its previous market share. In the face of such coercion, the value of non-compliance with US demands on intellectual property by developing countries plummeted dramatically. At the same time the cost of US non-compliance with the GATT rules as they then were (many US 301 actions were probably illegal under GATT) was negligible, since the US could often block the formation of a GATT dispute panel while, in the words of one informant, 'the tariffs did the job for you'. It is probably this calculus of threat and coercion that explains Hudec's observation that:

Today, it is the United States more than any other GATT country that imposes conditions on others before agreeing to panels, that blocks panels' adoption of adverse reports, that blocks requests for authority to retaliate, and, for good measure, that takes its time about complying with adopted panel rulings (Hudec 1990: 203–4).

Countries also became more ready to contemplate a multilateral agreement within the GATT negotiations on intellectual property, thinking that this would save them from having to deal with US trade negotiators on a bilateral basis, which by all accounts was not a relaxed business. One South Korean negotiator we spoke to said 'they [the US] start threatening early'. (This seems to be a cross-cultural truth: Australian officials also remarked on the heavy-handed approach of US trade officials. The US trade negotiators we spoke to mentioned their frustration with the slowness of officials from other countries to respond to the issue of better intellectual property protection.)

By contrast, coercion seems to have been absent from the globalization of contract. A possible explanation lies in the fact that property rights determine the direction of wealth flows while the creation of common rules of contract helps to smooth the act of exchange. The temptation for any hegemonic power within a global trading environment is to define property rights in a way that produces wealth transfers even if the definition of those rights is not efficient. (It cannot, for example, be efficient to retrospectively increase, as TRIPS does, the patent term for patents already in existence.) The incentive to use coercion in relation to property rights may sometimes be quite high, in a way that it is not for contract.

### Modelling

The complex process of the reception of Roman law (including contract law) throughout medieval Europe is best explained by the mechanism of modelling. The agents of modelling were jurists or courts, like the Great Council of Mechlin established in 1473. With jurisdiction over the provinces of Netherlands, the Great Council brought Roman law to these provinces (Lee 1961: 4).

Legal culture extended into another country by military means has often formed an invisible tie that continues to bind even in post-colonial or post-empire periods of a country's history – the modelling mechanism serves to maintain a hold that was established militarily. For instance, in the complex history of legal systems in Latin America, European private law models have had strong influence, particularly the Spanish and French Codes which were often closely copied (Garro 1992: 604–7). The Dutch carried their Roman Dutch law to South Africa in the seventeenth century, including the Law Merchant. In 1887 Natal passed a bill of exchange law that 'was very closely modelled on the English codifying Act' (Cowen & Gering 1966: 21). As we have seen, the English *Bills of Exchange Act 1882* has been faithfully modelled by most Commonwealth countries. In the twentieth century, intergovernmental organizations like UNIDROIT and UNCITRAL have generated model laws, although these have not usually been widely adopted.

Modelling has been important throughout the history of the spread of intellectual property law. The following examples illustrate the point. The historical evidence suggests that the Venetian *Patent Act 1474* (thought to be the first patent statute) provided the basis for the spread of the patent system from Italy to Germany, Holland, Belgium, France and England (Anderfelt 1971: 6). Massachusetts (1641) and Connecticut (1672) were influenced in their adoption of a patent law by the English *Statute of Monopolies 1623* (Anderfelt 1971: 11). US colonies tended to base their copyright law on the English *Statute of Anne 1709*, and the Australian government in 1912 adopted the British *Copyright Act 1911*.

WIPO has been responsible for developing model laws in the field of intellectual property, but these have been largely developed for developing countries (Bogsch 1992: 59–60). WIPO has also been an important source of model laws for countries in Central and Eastern Europe undergoing the transition to market economies.

The dramatic use of coercion by the US with respect to intellectual property in the 1980s has obscured the fact that the modelling mechanism had been quietly at work even in countries that ended up on various US watchlists for intellectual property. Many former East Asian colonies, after they gained independence, followed the models of intellectual protection imposed upon them by their colonizers (Sharpe 1989; Gutterman & Brown 1997). The extensive provisions on intellectual property contained in NAFTA served as a model for TRIPS. Now that economic coercion has established the trade-led paradigm for intellectual property, modelling will probably become the dominant mechanism. It is undoubtedly true, however, that the modelling mechanism, because it works on a needs basis, could not have achieved the speed of harmonization that the US has achieved through economic coercion. Countries such as the Philippines and Indonesia did not place a high priority on strong intellectual property protection.

Contract law harmonization has been dominated by developed countries, which have had the resources and the institutional and scholarly capacities needed to conduct comparative analyses of technical subject matter. Intellectual property is a more complex story. For a long time Western countries were the only source of intellectual property models. During the twentieth century, particularly in the 1960s, this began to change. Developing countries began to adjust their intellectual property laws in ways that met their economic and social development objectives. For instance, with the aid of BIRPI (WIPO's predecessor organization), developing countries formulated in 1963 a draft model law on patents that met their economic interests as technology-importing countries (Anderfelt 1971: 200–3). They insisted, for example, that foreign patents be locally worked. Another example of modelling by developing countries was the 1960s initiative of African countries to develop a copyright law that protected folklore. These initiatives by countries of the periphery or semi-periphery helped to produce regional harmonization of some intellectual property law, but much of it was swept aside by TRIPS. Coercion operated in this case as a trumping mechanism.

## Reciprocal Adjustment

The mechanism of reciprocal adjustment has had different outcomes depending on whether it has operated in a bilateral or multilateral setting. Reciprocal adjustment can produce either rule or principle harmonization. During the nineteenth century most of the bilateral treaties and multilateral treaties dealing with intellectual property operated on the basis of national treatment, but only in bilateral treaties did national treatment produce anything remotely resembling rule harmonization. In the multilateral context the principle entrenched rule diversity. The reason for this is that in the bilateral situation a state could use its bargaining power to obtain a set of standards of intellectual property protection from another state. Those standards, when tied to the principle of national treatment, would push the two states in the direction of bilateral harmonization. A good example is the copyright treaty negotiations between Prussia and Britain in the 1830s and 1840s. The Prussians broke off negotiations in 1840 because Prussian law gave greater protection to Prussian copyright owners than British law gave to British copyright owners (Sherman 1995: 11). Under the principle of national treatment British authors would have been better off in Prussia than Prussian authors would have been in Britain. When Britain changed its domestic law to accommodate Prussian concerns, a treaty between the two states was concluded in 1846.

National treatment in the multilateral setting produced a different effect. Reciprocal adjustment led to the adoption of the principle of national treatment, but states could not agree on a set of standards. The negotiations leading up to the Paris Convention illustrate the point. In relation to standards of protection for industrial property, 'The French members of the Congress [of 1878]…wished that the uniform universal rules should be taken from French law, while foreign delegates stood by their own laws' (Ladas 1975a: 62). The upshot was that states agreed to a minimal set of rules all would have to recognize. National treatment remained but it promoted rule diversity, as states retained massive sovereign discretion over the setting of intellectual property standards. A further aspect of this analysis will be discussed in Chapter 21. Mechanisms operate to spread principles, but it is principles that pattern regulatory growth.

Reciprocal adjustment has been the most important mechanism in the evolution of a harmonized contract law. Merchants wishing to do business across borders in medieval Europe had a great incentive to develop one set of rules to govern their relations. Pollock, exaggerating a little, described the Law Merchant as a type of natural law (Pollock cited in Wright 1939: xi). He was simply drawing attention to the fact that reason and convenience had driven merchants to recognize their reciprocal interests and to establish rules common to all merchants to serve those interests. Reciprocal adjustment was also, for a long time, the dominant mechanism in the globalization of intellectual property. But because it was the dominant mechanism it also set limits on the extent of that globalization. States which were net intellectual property importers had no rational reason to increase intellectual property protection in the short term, but taking a longer-term view might be persuaded to agree to a minimal set of international obligations that did not unduly interfere with their sovereignty over the setting of property standards. This is more or less what happened in the nineteenth century and for a large part of the twentieth. During the 1980s economic coercion became the dominant mechanism of international intellectual property standard-setting. US corporations pushed the intellectual property issue to the forefront of the US trade agenda and the US began to use trade sanctions to back its demands for better intellectual property protection. This has produced a higher level of harmonization of intellectual property than would have been possible during the same period under the mechanism of reciprocal adjustment.

### Non-reciprocal Coordination

Contract harmonization is not, by international standards, a fiercely contested site, and it is fights that lead to the strongest presence of non-reciprocal coordination. States have simply not thought it worthwhile to make concessions in areas like agriculture or trade in services to build an alliance for an agenda of contract harmonization. UNIDROIT and UNCITRAL are specialist fora, so issue linkage has not promoted alliances between states. Contract harmonization has mostly been a quiet evolutionary process. Non-reciprocal coordination began to feature in intellectual property when it entered the deal-trading environment of GATT. The US, for example, created a Friends of Intellectual Property Group during the Uruguay Round negotiations. Australia, despite being a massive technology importer, joined the Group because it thought that doing so it would help its cause in agriculture. Other countries, such as some South American countries, also thought that showing support for TRIPS would improve their chances of getting more open agricultural markets in the US and Europe. The fact that the GATT agenda allowed states to make deals across a vast range of subject matter (e.g. tariffs, agriculture, sanitary and phytosanitary measures, textiles, investment, subsidies, services, government procurement and intellectual property) and the fact that the intellectual property issue was at first deeply divisive meant that the US had both a reason and an opportunity to use non-reciprocal coordination.

### Systems of Reward

Systems of reward seem to have been little used to promote the globalization of contract or property.

### Capacity-building

WIPO has a significant program of assistance for developing and least-developed countries. There are two permanent committees dedicated to development cooperation, one for industrial property and the other for copyright. Development assistance takes a variety of forms including the drafting and provision of model laws, and training in the administration of intellectual property. Such assistance is crucial since setting up and running a patent or trademark office is not for novices. WIPO also cooperates with national (e.g. US Copyright Office) and regional industrial property offices (e.g. European Patent Office) in delivering assistance. The UN Development Program funds some of this work. The major patent offices around the world (the US, European and Japanese Patent Offices) also carry out training in developing countries. Interviews with officials from each of these offices made it clear to us that the hope behind providing technical assistance is that the developing country will adopt the laws and administrative procedures of the office providing the assistance. Capacity-building in the case of patent law is driven by an agenda being played out between the three main patent states, the US, Japan and Europe. The more converts there are to a particular system the more likely it is that that system will become the basis of a model for a world patent system. The UN Industrial Development Organization has been important in providing services on technology transfer issues to developing countries. UNCTAD has been an important source of advice and training to developing countries on intellectual property issues. Under its new Director-General, Dr Kamal Idris, WIPO embarked in 1998 on a set of initiatives to increase WIPO's capacity-building role in relation to developing countries. The demand by developing countries for services to improve their capacity to administer intellectual property regimes is very high because of their obligations under TRIPS. A market is rapidly developing that model mercenaries (see Chapter 25) will undoubtedly fill.

Capacity-building has not been a priority in the field of contract law harmonization. UNCITRAL has had increasing requests for technical assistance from developing countries, but budgetary constraints have meant only very limited efforts in this area (UNCITRAL 1994: 397). At the time of our interview in 1994, UNCITRAL had only seven lawyers on staff.

Both intellectual property and, to a lesser extent, contract are characterized by consciousness-raising exercises, usually in the form of seminars. These are very minor forms of capacity-building since more is needed for a developing country to gain the relevant regulatory capability. The assistance delivered by international organizations in intellectual property is not always appropriate. One former WIPO official, for example, pointed out that although WIPO had helped to establish an Industrial Property Office in Hanoi, it had filled it with Swedish patent documents. Not many people in Hanoi read Swedish, he said.

## Conclusion

For much of the history of their globalization, contract and property have been affected by the same two mechanisms – reciprocal adjustment and modelling. The TRIPS era has seen a sharp departure from the centuries of globalization driven by these two mechanisms. Actors within the US form an alliance to achieve a new global *dominium* over abstract objects, a *dominium* that has important implications for the US *imperium*. At one level one might see TRIPS as a story about continuing US hegemony. Hegemonic powers must have control over raw materials, the sources of capital, markets and competitive advantages in the production of highly valued goods (Keohane 1984: 32–3). Algorithms implemented in software, the genetic information of plants and animals, chemical compounds and structures are all examples of abstract objects that form an important kind of capital in the global economy. TRIPS, one might say, helps to institutionalize proprietorial powers over the kinds of abstract objects in which the US has a human capital advantage.

The effects on state sovereignty of a global property regime are potentially dramatic. Historically, property rights have been used by states to solve externality problems. New externalities arise within a society as a result of changes in technology and knowledge (Demsetz 1967). In the past individual states or social groups have decided on the use of the property instrument to solve their particular externality problem. Under a globally harmonized and enforceable set of property rights, individual sovereigns have a restricted capacity to use property rights to solve new externality problems. A state, for instance, may have sound economic reasons for not providing protection for databases, but if that is what the global regime obliges it to do then it must comply or face the enforcement consequences. One sovereign cost of a global intellectual property regime, then, relates to a sovereign's loss of capacity to steer its economy using property rights in information and knowledge.

The sovereignty cost to nations of a global property regime is not simply a matter of economic adaptability. Property rights are not just economic tools, they are the product of broader social, cultural and philosophical traditions and ideas. The rights of UK citizens to wander about in their countryside tell us as much about the social and political history of that country as they do about externality problems. Local property arrangements are the products of moral and cultural traditions, traditions which are living traditions and which people do not necessarily want changed. The crucial issue is not the loss of tradition but the loss of autonomy over institutions that carry and implement the moral values a society holds important. When governments exercise legislative power over property arrangements they have to do so in ways that are consistent with the trust granted to them by the community they represent. This is a fundamental tenet of liberal democratic traditions. Its best defender is probably still John Locke in his *Second Treatise of Government* (1690). He argues that citizens enter into society for the preservation of their property and that governments are under an obligation to exercise the power given to them in ways consistent with the property interests of all. Property is broadly construed by Locke. Property for a citizen includes life and liberty. To Locke, property is an institution that is rich in moral content. It is not just a legal notion.

The potential 'moral sovereignty' cost of a global property regime can be illustrated by the debate over the patenting of higher-order life-forms (Hoffmaster 1988). In relation to animals, it is clear that different communities have very different attitudes and practices (compare bull-fighting, whale-hunting and kangaroo-shooting). The genetic engineering of animals is a comparatively recent phenomenon. Attitudes to this practice are still evolving, especially since scientific evidence about its hazards remains inconclusive. The problem is that when decision-making in relation to intellectual property standards shifts to the supranational level, local or indigenous solutions to the issue of biotechnology patents may never be given an opportunity to develop. The shift to the supranational level turns problems of decision-making into a classic collective action problem. The pharmaceutical companies who have most to gain from uniform world patent standards, including uniform standards for biotechnologies, are more likely to be organized and present a unanimous view than the many world communities. Concentrated private interests, in other words, are far more likely to drive a globalized intellectual property system than are diffuse public interests. And while one property standard sometimes fits all the players in the pharmaceutical game it is unlikely, in moral terms, to fit all communities.

Animal patents provide one example of the moral sovereignty cost of a global property system. There are other examples of this cost, a cost which affects both state and citizen sovereignty. The criminalization of conduct is generally a matter of national criminal justice policy, as are the levels of penalties. One of the striking features of the evolution of intellectual property law is the increased involvement of criminal law. There has been no serious discussion of why the state should mete out criminal penalties in an area that has traditionally been a civil matter. In the evolving global regime states are increasingly using criminal enforcement resources on behalf of intellectual property owners. The fact that US law enforcement agencies are choosing to make copyright infringement a priority is a matter for the US. However, its criminal law enforcement ethos is not necessarily that of other countries. The danger under a globalized property regime is that it will become so. The fact that Australia is required to devote resources to criminalize and enforce intellectual property rights will no doubt please US copyright owners, but one wonders whether Australian citizens would be equally pleased, if they knew.[7]

The globalization of intellectual property rights is fraught with dangers for citizen and state sovereignty. The explanation for this lies ultimately in the fact that property is much less a neutral institution than is contract. Buyers and sellers, importers and exporters have common interests in a set of enforceable contract rules that define a set of mutually understood rights and obligations. Property rights share this role, but they also define who has the right to exclude others from certain resources and who can claim rights to the economic value of those resources. In a world of no transaction costs the distribution of property rights does not stand in the way of maximizing welfare gains (Coase 1960). But as North (1990) has argued, the real world is full of positive transaction costs. It is also a world where capabilities and power are unequally distributed. In such a world the definition and distribution of property rights turns out to shape the economic destiny of all concerned. Property rights become things to play for and win at all costs, including the costs of coercion. US intellectual property exporting firms called on the coercive power of the US state to play for and win an expanded frontier in the property of knowledge in 1994.

---

7  The figures are startling. The Annual Reports of the Australian Federal Police for the period 1992–95 show that the number of reported copyright offences increased from 763 to 1924. This has significant resource implications, particularly since copyright enforcement is an area full of evidentiary problems.

Contract law harmonization has been led by the epistemic community of jurists, which forms an important subset of the mercantile community. It is jurists who have carried the idea of harmonization and drafted the restatements, the models and the conventions. The extent to which they have succeeded in the task of harmonization has been very much affected by the extent to which they have produced rules based on actual business practice and business morality. The drafters of successful codes have remarked on the need to stay close to existing norms (Chalmers 1886, 1903). The Uniform Civil Code was written with an audience of merchants in mind and the expectations of that audience formed an important check on the directions of the Code (Danzig 1975). While the epistemic community of jurists has led in terms of synthesis and organization of norms, it in turn has been led by the custom and trade usage of business. Where jurists have ignored that lead their codes and conventions have become monuments rather than embodiments of living principle.

Conventions as a tool of harmonization of private law have not been particularly successful. The proliferation of conventions in the twentieth century dealing with the unification of contract law imply more progress than has actually occurred. Ratification rates of many of these conventions have been low. In the words of Joachim Bonell, chairman of the working group that prepared the UNIDROIT Principles of International Commercial Contracts, many of 'these instruments often remain little more than a dead letter' (Bonell 1992: 617). Generally, only relatively small numbers of states have become members of any one convention (UNCITRAL 1971: 41). States have found it difficult to overcome attachment to their own legal order, perhaps because at the micro level of negotiations their legal experts have had great faith in the virtues of their own legal systems. The following passage illustrates the point:

> Any lawyer has a mental ballast. He may have studied foreign legal systems and the aims and methods of comparative law. Nevertheless, he cannot forget what he learned in the law school at home. Each member of the Commission [on European Contract Law] has faced drafts which have inverted his legal conception of contract law (Lando 1992: 583–4).

Law as a culture and belief system has tended to weaken the perception of reciprocal interests and strengthen the perceived importance of the principle of sovereignty. Another problem seems to lie in the fact that conventions impose legal obligations upon states and this leads to problems of implementation (e.g. the problems of jurisdiction in a federal system, objections from the domestic legal profession and so on). The requirement of positive law to implement a model creates costs that states have been reluctant to pick up in the area of contract law. For this reason jurists have turned their attention to 'obligation-free' methods of unification. One such method can be seen in the UNIDROIT Principles of International Commercial Contracts, which elaborates a set of basic principles for international commercial contracts, principles which are meant to persuade and guide rather than command (Bonell 1994: 15, 107).

The mechanism of reciprocal adjustment has been much more effective in the context of the private ordering of contract law. In this process Western players have been dominant. Transnational business actors, not burdened by fidelity to a given territorial system of law, have seen the need to achieve a greater harmony of contract law and so, working mainly through the ICC, have codified in a general and flexible fashion their trade customs. Reciprocal adjustment operates with a double effect. It produces the transnational customs in the first place and, when those customs are given some general form of codification, it works to spread the relevant codified form (the widespread use of Incoterms is an example of this double effect). The custom-based nature of the codes ensures that they gain acceptance. Global convergence occurs because nations cannot be economically competitive if they resist and deviate too much from international business custom.

The contrast between intellectual property and contract is a contrast between a mechanism which operates in a top-down fashion (coercion) and two mechanisms (reciprocal adjustment and modelling) that have operated with contract in a bottom-up fashion. The mechanism of economic coercion is one that only the powerful can use to achieve their global agendas. But the case of intellectual property also reveals the multiplier effects of networks on economic power – an important lesson for all players in the global regulatory system. US business needed the rest of the international business community to agree to the TRIPS proposal for it to have a chance of success. Without the support of the Japanese and European business communities TRIPS would never have made it onto the ministerial agenda at Punta del Este. TRIPS might have become a dead letter, like so many international agreements, were it not for the fact that the US has built a web of surveillance around it. US multinationals continue to feed information to organizations like the IIPA about piracy problems in various countries. The USTR continues to maintain the 301 process and can also pursue actions against countries using dialogue at the WTO and the WTO dispute settlement procedures. The Council for TRIPS is obliged to monitor the Agreement (Article 68). Some Articles of TRIPS, such as Article 27(3)(b), commit states to a specific review of its provisions. The provisions of TRIPS, in other words, are surrounded by internal and external networks of relentless surveillance. These networks in effect generate power externalities for a hegemonic actor like the US, and mean that the threat of economic coercion can be much more effectively deployed. Although weaker actors cannot use the mechanism of economic coercion, the strategy of generating power externalities through networks is something that weaker players in the global regulatory system can utilize.

## CHAPTER 8

Financial Regulation

## History of Globalization

### Money: The Root of All Financial Regulation

Financial regulation begins with money. In a barter economy the wants of the parties have to coincide. Nothing more needs to happen for a transaction to take place. When trade or exchange takes place via the medium of money the transaction becomes more normatively complex. If money is to carry out its functions – payment and a standard of value – it must be accepted by the parties to the transaction. This role of promoting the acceptance of money by credibly stabilizing its functions has generally been carried out by some third party, a party who through regulatory devices creates money so that desires can be satisfied.

Money has a long, long history. Exactly when money originated nobody knows. As Keynes puts it, 'Its origins are lost in the mists when the ice was melting' (Keynes in G. Davies 1994: 48). We do know that lots of different objects have served the role of money, including dogs' and whales' teeth. Rings appear to have been used as money in Egypt in the fourth millennium BC. Babylon had a legally regulated money economy by the third millennium BC. The Code of Hammurabi (c. 2123–2081 BC) contains provisions regulating the use of grain and silver as money and dealing with the supply of credit (Einzig 1949: 212–14). Gold appears to have functioned as an international currency in the second millennium when Egypt was the leading gold producer (Einzig 1949: 207). China probably has the longest history of coinage of any civilization, and invented paper money. After money come accounting records, which date at least from 2300 BC in Egypt (Carruthers & Espeland 1991) and in 1999 are globally harmonized.

Money crossed borders well before its regulation did so. The cowrie, for instance, has been used as a currency among the peoples of Africa, China and the Pacific. This phenomenon of money crossing borders and constituting markets is repeated throughout history – Eurocurrencies (the money of a state deposited in a bank outside that state) are another example. A history of monetary regulation in Europe can perhaps begin when issuing metallic coins became a practice. This practice is said to have originated with the Lydians in the seventh century BC. From Lydia the practice of coining was quickly diffused to Asia Minor, Greece, Italy, Sicily and Carthage (Burns 1965: 52). For a time in the ancient world, bankers, merchants and money-changers issued their own coin in competition with the king. By about the sixth century BC the private issue of coinage had largely disappeared. The right to coin became the hallmark of sovereign power. It also became the symbol of tyranny. The development of currency in the seventh and sixth centuries

BC in Greece was also the age of tyrants, when people used power over coinage as a means to political supremacy (Burns 1965: 81–2). Throughout ancient times one of the first things a city-state or region did, once it had regained autonomy, was to recommence a local currency. Most coins circulated in the territory in which they were minted. Some coins, like the silver coins of sixth-century Aegina, gained a reputation for reliability. As trade expanded they became an international currency.

Monetary harmonization in the ancient world was mainly the work of empires. The Persian and Roman empires, for example, assumed control over coinage and issued an imperial currency. The Roman empire guarded its right of gold coinage carefully. Coins circulating in a territory were seen as a symbol of Roman power. A currency for the empire also made tax collection easier. A less common means of monetary harmonization was through the formation of a monetary union based on a treaty. Such unions, which aimed to increase trade, were formed among some of the independent city republics of Greece from the end of the fifth century (Burns 1965: 111). The financial regulation of the ancient world converged in other ways. For example, the weight standard of 130 grains for a gold unit remained the standard for almost all gold currencies (Burns 1965: 219).

## Taxes and the Warfare State

Taxes may be even older than money. Egyptian squiggles on fragments of clay and ivory 5300 years old challenged the view that writing was invented by the Sumerians. They are being interpreted as receipts for tax payments on quantities of linen and oil, to a king called Scorpion. The globalization of tax in the ancient world was primarily linked to the growth of empires. Empires were built by armies. Those armies had to be paid for. As empires grew so did the need for tax collection to fund military expenditures. The Roman empire had a vast array of different kinds of taxes and an equally vast bureaucracy to administer and collect them (Levi 1988: 71–94). Their main purpose was to pay Rome's armies.

The European origins of national taxation lay in the thirteenth and fourteenth centuries when the system of feudal dues became slowly displaced by the idea of public taxes consented to by a community and administered on its behalf (Harriss 1975: 3–4). The most important driving force behind the evolution of national tax systems was war. From the thirteenth century onwards war became an increasingly investment-intensive activity (Pounds 1994: 434). Armies were becoming professional. The building of castles and forts was costly. The rulers of emerging nation-states made increasing use of their powers to tax so that their armies could kill each other on a larger scale and more systematically.

European rulers did not develop tax policy as part of some overall plan of economic development. Rather, tax policy was driven by the exigencies of military conflict or its possibility. Taxes, unlike merchant law, were deeply embedded in the socio-political and cultural matrix of states. They were the product of royal desires and needs, power struggles, bargaining, what populations would tolerate, what rulers thought they could get away with before the taxpayers revolted (on the last point there was a lot of misjudgment). Taxes had a deeply national character. This remained a feature of taxation into the twentieth century, and one which would cost states dearly in terms of their capacity to coordinate management of the business cycle.

Out of the non-system of taxes states began to design and implement systems of taxation. This was part of a process in which states began to develop techniques for the management of public finance. National debt, as we shall see in the next chapter, was consolidated, securitized and sold. The creation of markets in government debt meant that the savings of citizens could be uplifted through the issue of new government stock. The states that did this best had more financial resources available for war. In this way the 'British government borrowed 31 per cent of expenditure in the War of the Spanish Succession, 37 per cent in the Seven Years' War, and 40 per cent in the American War of Independence' (Kindleberger 1984: 165). Earlier, the Dutch state had also had remarkable success in extracting money from its citizenry to pay for its armies. By 1648 the Dutch army of 55 000 represented 3 per cent of the population and by 1695 one-third of the income of an average Dutch household was disappearing in tax (Dudley 1991: 165, 318).

The national tax systems which evolved were complex amalgams of direct and indirect taxes, at times somewhat idiosyncratic in nature. Misogyny was thought to lie behind the British tax of 1785 on female servants. No one was quite sure what lay behind the tax on hair powder, but it hastened the move to shorter hairstyles and hair oil (Sabine 1966: 20). Tax systems continued to march to the beat of war drums. The purpose of the *Income Tax Act 1799* was to help England to prepare for the coming conflict with Napoleon (Sabine 1966: 42).

## Where the Money Is: Banks

Babylonian temples, because they were places where people took valuables, were probably the first banks. Certainly there is evidence that banks were operating in the second millennium in Babylon. The history of European banking is more recent. The island of Delos became in the third and second centuries BC a centre of international banking for Mediterranean trade and commerce. Later the great trade fairs of Champagne in the twelfth and thirteenth centuries became the place where merchants began to carry on the services of changing money, extending credit and settling debts between traders. The provision of these services was dominated by the Lombards of Italy, but Jews, Cahorsiens and the Knights Templar were also involved (Baldwin 1968: 96). These services were regulated by customs that developed at these international fairs. The Italian money-changers (*campsores*) of city-states like Venice and Genoa played a pivotal role in institutionalizing banking services throughout Europe. Banks as public organizations of the state came later. It was the *campsores* who, meeting at the fairs of Champagne, Lyons, Anvers and Genoa, adjusted accounts among the traders of Europe (Holdsworth 1937: 128–9). The work of the *campsores* extended in other ways. Traders began to leave money with them for future transactions and so a practice of making deposits began. These deposits became the source of loans to other merchants and to the kings and queens of Europe. By the fourteenth century something akin to the modern banking practice of taking deposits and making loans was being regularly undertaken by the *campsores*. Italian banking families like the Bardi, the Peruzzi and the Medici spread their practices and business by establishing representative commercial organizations in the main cities of Europe. The result was that banking practice evolved in a surprisingly harmonized form between the thirteenth and sixteenth centuries in Europe. The customs of Italian bankers contributed to the creation of the Law Merchant.

Banking and trade grew together. Trade meant that merchants acquired capital. The practice of banking allowed that capital to be pooled; the use of instruments like the bill of exchange and the promissory note turned that capital into a system of credit. A promise to repay capital could be moved from transaction to transaction. From the merchant groups that gathered in the trade-centre cities grew the insider merchant networks that transformed those cities into international markets for the supply of credit. The kings and queens of Europe depended upon these private credit markets, allowing financiers like the House of Fugger in the sixteenth century considerable influence in the politics of the emerging states of Europe. Antwerp in the sixteenth century, Amsterdam in the eighteenth century and London in the nineteenth century were centres in which the international system of credit was created and maintained (Germain 1997: 34–44). A law of bankruptcy based on a blend of Justinian and Germanic principles accompanied the growth of this credit system (Berman 1983: 352).

Proposals for public banks had been put forward in the fourteenth century, but it was in the fifteenth century that such banks came to be formed. The first state bank of deposit was established in Genoa in 1407 (Kindleberger 1984: 47). One of the most successful and widely imitated state banks was the Bank of Amsterdam. Created as a bank of deposit and exchange in 1609, its purpose was to ensure the supply of a valid standardized currency throughout the United Provinces. The rise of nation-states exercised a pull upon the regulation of banking in Europe. National banks were formed, and these banks became central banks. The Bank of England was established in 1694 (and nationalized in 1946), the Bank of France was established in 1880 (although there had been a number of public banks in France before then, beginning with the Banque Générale in 1716), and the Reichsbank (successor to the Bank of Prussia) was created in 1875 to provide for the financial needs of the German empire. The history of the Bank of England and the broader London financial community is the most important in the globalization of financial markets and their regulation. The reason for this lies in the early and widespread imitation of English financial models (Cameron 1967: 15).

## The Bank of England

The establishment of the Bank of England in 1694 was motivated by the government's desire to fund a war against France (Holden 1955: 87–8). It became much more than just a war chest for the British government. Over time it assumed the four functions of a central bank: the government's lender, currency regulation, a bankers' bank and a lender of last resort (Morgan 1965: 1). With the benefit of economic history's hindsight, it seems that the Bank of England probably did not do much to contribute to England's economic growth between 1750 and 1844. Cameron, for instance, claims that at 'almost every point at which banking and monetary policy might have been used constructively to promote economic growth, the authorities either made the wrong decision or took no action at all' (1967: 58). This ineptitude is not surprising. The newly emergent states of Europe had little to guide them in the regulation of banking except some economic theory. Monetary theory did not emerge as a distinct part of economics until the end of the eighteenth century (Morgan 1965: 49). The nineteenth was the century in which the Bank of England acquired more power and gained regulatory experience. It was the century in which it took on the role of a central bank. The Bank became the lender of last resort. The *Bank Charter Act 1844* brought the Bank much closer to being the only issuer of banknotes. Through open market operations (the sale of government securities), the use of the bank rate (the rate at which it lent to other banks) and the discounting of commercial paper it learned about the possibilities of leading financial markets. The use of the bank rate was particularly crucial in this respect. The directors of the Bank came to appreciate that rises in the bank rate could be used to attract money and to defend the Bank's gold reserves. They also saw that rises in the Bank's rate were frequently followed by rises in the rates of other central banks. During this time the Bank was at the centre of vigorous debates on the financial practices it should follow. When in 1797 the Bank suspended the convertibility of the pound, a debate ensued between the bullionists, who wanted a return to convertibility, and the anti-bullionists (G. Davies 1994: 300). By the end of the century monetary policy had been fashioned from the debates between economists and the practical actions of bankers into 'an orthodox body of doctrine commanding general acceptance' (Morgan 1965: 243).

The Bank of England was at the centre of a financial system which itself had become the centre of the international financial world. London's growth as a financial market had been aided by the extensive use of commercial paper by British banks and merchants. Bills of exchange were the principal means by which international trade was financed. More and more bills circulated in the London financial system. Merchants trading internationally found that London was a place where they could readily get their bills discounted, as well as obtain credit. London offered convenience and political stability. Increasingly, commercial paper was denominated in pounds sterling. Foreign banks found London a convenient place to deposit money and settle transactions. All this meant that more foreigners could place demands upon deposits of pound sterling. It also meant that the Bank of England's regulatory decisions had ramifications for financial groups beyond England's shores.

### The Rise of National Systems: The Regulation of Banking, Tax and Insurance

Within Europe, after the era of banking under the Law Merchant, banking became more formally organized through the corporate and partnership laws of nation-states. Nation-states began to develop their own financial systems and institutions. In this process the Italians, the Germans and the Dutch were leaders in the sixteenth and seventeenth centuries. They, for example, internationalized understanding and use of double-entry bookkeeping. But it was in England, spurred by the dramatic growth in the number and kinds of banks, that a sophisticated banking system first emerged. The number of banks in England went from around a dozen in 1750 to between 100 and 150 by 1775, and over 800 banks by 1810 (G. Davies 1994: 286). England did not remain a country of many banks. Bank amalgamations during the second part of the nineteenth century reduced the number. By the 1930s most of British banking was dominated by five banks – Barclays, Lloyds, Midland, National Provincial and Westminster.

The evolution of banking took a different path in the US. Banks were chartered either nationally or at state level. A restriction on branch banking at state and federal level meant that thousands of banks at the state level continued to be formed. The US developed in 1913 a unique central monetary authority, a federation of twelve Federal Reserve Banks over which presided a Federal Reserve Board. It had to. In the absence of a central banking system, private bankers had taken on the role of regulators. In 1907 the interventions of J.P. Morgan and James Stillwell saved the US financial system from systemic disaster (Germain 1997: 50). In addition to its responsibility for monetary policy the Board was given regulatory authority over Federal Reserve Banks and banks which, by owning stock in Federal Reserve Banks, became members of the Federal Reserve system (de Saint Phalle 1985: 6). Banking regulation in the US took the form of a dual regulatory structure in which federal and state agencies carried out a mixture of unique and joint functions. This decentralized, strongly local banking structure which allowed the birth of many banks also experienced a high mortality rate. During the 1920s and 1930s hundreds and then thousands of banks a year went bust.[1] Franklin Roosevelt's presidency was key in the reform of

---

1 For example, 168 in 1920, 505 in 1921, 367 in 1922, 976 in 1926, 1352 in 1930, 2294 in 1931, 1456 in 1932 and 4004 in 1933. See the table of banking suspensions in Cooper and Fraser (1993: 56).

the US bank system. The *Glass–Steagall Act 1933* prevented banks from entering the securities business, created the Federal Deposit Insurance Corporation and rules about capital requirements and gave more powers to bank regulators. The reforms to the banking system under the New Deal saw bank failures drop from an average of 2200 per year between 1931 and 1934 to an average of forty-five for the remainder of the 1930s (G. Davies 1994: 511).

When it came to the constitution of central banks and their powers, by the end of the 1930s there were two dominant models, the American Federal Reserve system and the system presided over by the Bank of England. The UK model consisted of a highly concentrated market structure in which there was one powerful regulator, a regulator that operated in a close-knit, exclusive community and relied upon understandings, convention, trust and tradition in doing its job. The US model consisted of a highly decentralized market structure. There were a number of regulators (the Federal Reserve, the Comptroller of the Currency, the Federal Deposit Insurance Corporation, the Treasury and state agencies). Regulation was more rule-bound, formal and bureaucratic. One of these two systems was generally used by other states as they began to develop national systems of banking supervision. While there were considerable differences between the two systems both were committed to one key idea – the relative independence of central banks from government.

Until the 1970s regulation of interest rates was widespread but by the 1980s the approach had become more outcome-oriented: 'I don't care who you lend to for how long at what rates. But you've got to make a profit so that you can improve your capital base. If you don't, I'm going to jump on you, threaten your licence. You've got six months to get your capital base' (1991 OECD interview).

Insurance, like banking, was first regulated by the customary norms of merchants. Sea transportation of goods involved the greatest risks; in fact, insurance did not diversify much beyond shipping until the twentieth century. Merchants began to spread the risks of carrying sea cargo in the fourteenth century, Italian merchants being the first to make a practice of insuring cargo (Pounds 1994: 424). The practice of insurance spread slowly to the rest of Europe. The regulation and supervision of insurance has remained in the grip of different national regulatory models. In the eighteenth and nineteenth centuries one regulatory model was all-important – that of Lloyd's of London – which traded insurance to cover a majority of the world's shipping. But it was a peculiarly City of London gentlemen's club model of self-regulation watched over by the Bank of England, that could never be transplanted. Nothing like the international convergence of regulation that has occurred in banking and tax regulation has occurred in the regulation of insurance. In the US, for example, insurance regulation remains essentially a state rather than federal matter. Generally, in all countries insurance companies are regulated under legislation specifically dedicated to that purpose (European Commission 1992). Unlike banking, insurance does not have supranational entities working on the harmonization of insurance regulation. Bank regulators, in a sense, have been big brothers to the insurance regulators. The principles for the prudential and consumer protection regulation of insurance have derived from those in the banking arena.

By the 1930s many Western states had also modernized their tax systems although in many cases this had happened only recently. England had introduced a general income tax in 1799. Other states took far longer. The French introduced one in 1909. The Reichstag in 1920 passed an income tax law and a corporate tax law. The First World War had taught it that this was a preferable way to pay for the cost of war (Holtfrerich 1987). The US enacted an income tax law in 1913 after first amending its Constitution to ensure the legislation's constitutionality (an income tax law had been held unconstitutional by the Supreme Court in 1895).

At the same time as states were striving to extend and consolidate the fiscal reach of their tax systems through periods of war and depression, a new species of actor – the large corporation – appeared on the scene. The rise of dominant corporations was most prominent in the US, but such entities also formed part of the market structures of all Western economies, especially Germany and the UK. These corporations were not simple unitary entities. Company law permitted corporations to hold shares in other corporations. The details varied from jurisdiction to jurisdiction but this basic rule allowing intercompany shareholding meant that corporations could organize as groups. By the beginning of the twentieth century complex corporate groups consisting of parent corporations, holding companies and subsidiaries had been organized in the US (Blumberg 1993: 307). The corporate group eventually became the dominant form of business life in all jurisdictions.

When in 1909 the US enacted a corporation tax of 1 per cent on corporate profits, business leaders organized a litigation campaign in the Supreme Court to test the constitutionality of the legislation (Ratner 1967: 294–5). They failed to get the legislation struck down, but they had staked out the taxation of corporations as a battleground. In the decades that followed the US increased its taxation of corporations. Roosevelt's New Deal principles found their way into tax policy. Worried by the concentration of economic power that corporations represented, their tax avoidance schemes and the effect of this on the fiscal base, Roosevelt took initiatives in the revenue legislation of the 1930s, including measures to prevent tax avoidance through corporate group strategies, the introduction of progressive taxation for corporate income and a tax on undistributed profits. No state has done more than the US to develop corporate taxation in the twentieth century.

Tax policy and law remained in the US and elsewhere deeply rooted in national life and culture. The endless differences in the way that states treated income and capital for tax purposes, the kinds of taxes they imposed, the thousands of exceptions and qualifications they allowed to the basic principles of tax law reflected their different interest group politics, as well as their perception of how equality and justice were to be achieved through the tax system. Culture, lobbying and the politics of populism pervaded the tax policies of nation-states. The lack of harmonization did not matter so much in the case of individual citizens. Most of them transacted their affairs within the jurisdictional enclosure of one nation-state. They had neither the know-how nor the money to shift transactions between jurisdictions in order to achieve the best possible tax outcome. It was a different matter for corporate groups. Some groups, especially those based in the US, had grown into international businesses. They were thus able to take advantage of the jurisdictional and regulatory differences between states in ordering their tax affairs. For example, if an Australian company wants to invest in Brazil, it can buy a computer program that shows the best route through the bilateral tax treaties to minimize tax. States' response to this is discussed next.

## The Golden Era of Sterling: 1880–1914

Gold, silver, and copper coins all circulated in medieval Europe, but silver predominated. Gradually, the many distinctive coinages of towns, city-states and regions were replaced by standardized currencies, a process facilitated by the rise of nation-states. Within Europe, nation-states for a long time used different metals by which to set the standard of values for their respective currencies. Ultimately, they settled on one – gold. England went down the path of gold first. The adoption of the gold standard for the pound sterling is sometimes said to be from 1717 when Isaac Newton (then Master of the Mint) fixed the price of gold at £3 17s 10d (Kindleberger 1984: 59). Gold was made the official standard of value in England by the *Currency Act 1816*. The French took a different line, favouring bimetallism. Monetary bimetallism advocates the use of two metals to act as the standard of value. In France gold and silver were chosen for the purpose; Sweden chose copper and silver. The French, the main supporters of bimetallism in Europe, lost the fight for the bimetallic standard. In the Latin Monetary Union of 1865, formed between France, Belgium, Switzerland and Italy, the French successfully insisted on bimetallism. Other countries in Europe did not toe the line, however. Germany, after the formation of the Reichsbank, went to the gold standard and began dumping its stocks of silver. By 1880 the gold standard had become universal in Europe (Kindleberger 1984: 68). By then the US had also adopted the gold standard.

The emergence of an international gold standard coincided with the arrival of sterling as the world currency. International trade deals were financed by means of the paper instruments discussed in Chapter 7. The most important of these was the bill of exchange. During the nineteenth century London discount houses developed expertise in buying and selling international bills of exchange, so much so that the London discount market came to dominate the trade in these bills. On one view it was London's possession of a specialized discount market that gave it international financial supremacy (King 1936). Bills of exchange were in use throughout Europe in other financial centres like Paris and Berlin, where the bills were used to finance the trade of those countries (Cassis 1991: 54). Bills drawn on London were used to finance world trade. With more and more of the world's trade deals being written in sterling and more and more sterling being moved around by means of these London bills, the banks of other countries established offices in London. Another kind of actor arrived on the scene – the merchant family, soon to be the merchant financiers of the world of international trade. From Germany came the Barings, the Brandts, the Rothschilds and others, from Holland the Raphaels and from the US the Seligmans and the Morgans (G. Davies 1994: 344). These families formed the hub of a London financial aristocracy that dominated world finance.

Sterling was no longer just a national currency. It formed part of a system and financed 60 per cent of world trade and the investment in £4000 million worth of foreign securities between 1860 and 1913 (Williams 1968: 268). Sterling was the principal currency of capital export. For example, in 1913 Britain exported roughly £4 billion, more than Germany and France put together (Cassis 1991: 54).

It is exaggerating only a little to say that up to the First World War there was one international financial centre in the world (London), one central bank that led the rest (the Bank of England) and one world currency (sterling). One view says that this system was a sterling system managed by the Bank of England (Kindleberger 1984: 68). Just how much world central banks cooperated in maintaining this international monetary system is a moot point (Bloomfield 1968). It is not clear to what extent there was a set of 'rules of the game', tacitly understood, that enabled central banks to coordinate their actions to maintain the system. What is clear is that the international regulation of the monetary system did not take the form of a positive legal regime of the kind that was to emerge at Bretton Woods. Rather, international coordination, to the extent that it occurred, was governed by the 'clubbish' cultural norms of central bankers.

## World Wars and Depression: 1914–45

During the First World War and until 1923 most currencies underwent dramatic fluctuations, with a trend towards depreciation. The relative stabilization of foreign exchange that occurred from 1923 was largely destroyed by the Wall Street crash of 1929. During the interwar period international monetary regulation was drawn into the vortex of nationalist politics. Until 1914 foreign exchange regulation was characterized by a *laissez faire* approach. Government interventions were the exception, taking the indirect route of changes in bank rates (Einzig 1970: 280). International monetary cooperation might have formed the basis of a supranational strategy for dealing with national problems – German hyperinflation, war debts, reparations, mass unemployment. Instead, states began to see their sovereign power over currency as a means of solving their national problems at the expense of their neighbours. In all states the voices for the creation of an international monetary system were drowned out by the voices of nationalism, protectionism and, in some cases, fascism and militarism. There were attempts at international cooperation, in the form of the Brussels Conference of 1920 and the Genoa Conference of 1922, but these produced little real action.

The first half of the 1930s featured currency depreciation races as first the UK then the US devalued their currencies in order to revive their economies. The French, still on the gold standard, saw that they would also have to devalue. But unilateral devaluation on their part, they realized, could bring further retaliatory devaluations from others. The French were in one of the many dilemmas that lurk in financial regulatory systems. The solution lay in opening communication channels with the other two principal currency states, the UK and the US. 'For the first time, international negotiations came into play in arranging an exchange depreciation' (Clarke 1977: 5).

The attempt to come to some agreement on exchange rate stabilization at the World Economic Conference of 1933 in London failed. Roosevelt, worried by the possibility of a stronger dollar emerging from the conference and the adverse impact of this on US commodity and stock prices, rejected the possibility of stabilizing the dollar. This destroyed the conference. An agreement did emerge between the three currency powers in 1936, the Tripartite Monetary Agreement. The main importance of this Agreement was that it marked the beginnings of cooperation on exchange rate management. Clarke describes it as a 'gentlemen's agreement' (Clarke 1977: 52). But it was too little cooperation and far too late. The Agreement did nothing to slow the forces that were pushing for militaristic answers to national problems of unemployment, recession and instability.

There was one example of cooperation in this period that bore fruit after the end of the Second World War. This came in the form of the creation of the Bank for International Settlements in 1930. Located in Basle, Switzerland, its main purpose was to handle the payment of First World War reparations by Germany. After the Second World War it became a meeting-place for European central bankers, the central bankers' bank (Howell 1993: 376).

There was more cooperation between states on international business taxation in the first few decades of the twentieth century. As states turned to the direct taxation of corporations, those corporations with presences in more than one state began to face the problem of double taxation: 'the imposition of comparable taxes in two (or more) states on the same taxpayer in respect of the same subject matter and for identical periods' (OECD Committee on Fiscal Affairs 1996: 7). The position of business was simple. If corporate income had to be taxed, tax should only be paid once on the same income, not twice.

Working through the ICC, international business began to put pressure on states to devise a solution to the problem of double taxation. Germany and Austria had a treaty to avoid double taxation as early as 1890. The ICC worked with the Fiscal Committee of the League of Nations during the 1920s. The work of this Committee did not lead to a multilateral treaty. The Committee thought that such a treaty would be desirable, but pointed out that 'the extreme diversity of existing fiscal systems made it impossible at the present time to recommend a convention which could be unanimously accepted (Fiscal Committee of the League of Nations, cited in UN 1950: 40).

The work of the Fiscal Committee did, however, establish some broad principles which were given expression in model tax conventions drafted by the Committee. The principle of permanent establishment required that taxing a foreign company at source could only occur if that company operated through a permanent establishment; the principle of residence stipulated that the state in which the entity was resident could tax the foreign income of that entity provided it offered some kind of relief for foreign tax already paid on that income (Picciotto 1989: 25). When a company had a number of permanent establishments, the Fiscal Committee suggested that the permanent establishments be treated as separate accounting units with price dealings between them being determined as if they were independent persons operating at arm's length (Picciotto 1989: 26).

Between the wars the number of bilateral tax treaties grew slowly. They were mainly negotiated among the US, European states and British empire countries. Areas of disagreement also appeared. Countries which were importers of capital supported the principle that the right of taxation should be exercised by the state in which the income was generated. Capital-exporting countries favoured retaining the power of taxation over the foreign income of their residents. All states carefully guarded their taxing power. The US developed the tax credit system, under which it gave a tax credit to its nationals for taxes paid by them to a foreign government. The US retained the power to tax its nationals wherever they resided. The work of the Fiscal Committee of the League of Nations produced two model tax conventions. The Mexico model (1943) provided for taxation at source (favoured by capital-importing states) and the London model (1946) recognized states' taxing power over the foreign income of their residents (favoured by capital-exporting states) (UN 1950: 44). Differences also began to emerge between the Anglo-American and European agreements. By far the most important of these bilateral treaties was the one agreed in 1945 between the US and UK, the two major financial powers of the twentieth century. It was used by each as the basis for tax treaty negotiations with other states. This treaty, more than any other, underpinned the development of the postwar bilateral tax regime (Picciotto 1992: 39).

After the Second World War the number of agreements began to increase. The work of the League of Nations was taken over by the Fiscal Committee of the Organization for Economic Cooperation and Development (OECD). The model conventions it produced further stimulated the use of bilateral tax treaties. The regulation of international taxation became locked into bilateralism, something for which states would pay a heavy price. The ICC, in contrast, had served its members well. Poorly designed and enforced double-tax treaties often meant that tax was paid in neither state.

## Bretton Woods: Birth and Breakdown

Toward the end of the Second World War it was realized that more than just a gentlemen's agreement would be needed to achieve meaningful economic coordination between states. An international monetary system administered by an international organization was required if states were to renew their economies and live in peace. With this in mind, delegates from forty-four countries met in July 1944 at a place called Bretton Woods.

Bretton Woods is just a little beyond Mt Washington in New Hampshire. In this tiny place plans were laid for three big global institutions – the International Monetary Fund (IMF), the

World Bank and the International Trade Organization (ITO). At the closing Plenary Session of the Conference, John Maynard Keynes, one of the principal architects of the Agreement, opened with these words (22 July 1944, 101):[2]

> We, the Delegates of this Conference, Mr President, have been trying to accomplish something very difficult to accomplish. We have not been trying, each one to please himself, and to find the solution most acceptable in our own particular situation. That would have been easy. It has been our task to find a common measure, a common standard, a common rule applicable to each and not irksome to any.

He concluded on an optimistic note (22 July 1944, 103):

> Finally, we have perhaps accomplished here in Bretton Woods something more significant than what is embodied in this Final Act. We have shown that a concourse of forty-four nations are actually able to work together at a constructive task in amity and unbroken concord. Few believed it possible. If we can continue in a larger task as we have begun in this limited task, there is hope for the world.

Thirty years after Keynes had delivered these words, analysts were producing tracts describing the breakdown of the Bretton Woods system. Keynes was right to think of the Final Act at Bretton Woods as a magnificent achievement. For the first time there was a codified form of rules and principles that imposed some obligations on states in the conduct of their monetary affairs. Given that money had always been a symbol of political power, the incursion of Bretton Woods into state sovereignty was considerable. Moreover, the institutions of Bretton Woods were part of a planned global regulatory system for trade and finance. Financial regulatory cooperation among states in the past had been bilateral. It had been based on the need to deal with a crisis, as in the case of cooperation between the central banks of England and France during the nineteenth century, or it had been cooperation based on following the Bank of England's lead. Bretton Woods represented a different kind of cooperation. It was a shift away from the tacit, convention-based cooperation of central bankers to a sweeping, rule-based, multilateral cooperation of states.

During the 1930s states had experienced a series of connected problems: shortage of gold, exchange rate instabilities, the movement of 'hot' money in and out of their realms, and the lack of a mechanism to adjust balance of payments problems (Johnson 1968: 114–15). The IMF was designed to deal with these difficulties by putting in place an international monetary system that contained a stable exchange rates regime with some scope for revaluation ('pegged but adjustable'), provided for the convertibility of currency, provided a mechanism for overcoming short-term liquidity crises and an organizational actor for managing the system (Williamson 1977: 2–28). The World Bank was designed to help the economic and industrial reconstruction of Europe and to help developing countries achieve industrialization. The purpose of the ITO was to propel states down the path of free trade, to stop them from defecting to protectionism as a way of responding to balance of payments problems (e.g. by imposing import quotas as an alternative to devaluing their currency). The ITO never emerged, because of US concerns. Instead, a weaker agreement known as the General Agreement on Tariffs and Trade took its place (see Chapter 10). In this grand plan for international institutions in the postwar era tax, as an object of regulation, was absent. Keynes' letters and reports around the time of Bretton Woods do not dis-

---

2  The dates which appear hereafter in relation to Keynes refer to the dates of Keynes' speeches or letters. All references are to Donald Moggridge (ed.) 1980, *The Collected Writings of John Maynard Keynes*, vol. 26, *Activities 1941–1946: Shaping the Postwar World: Bretton Woods and Reparations*. London: Macmillan.

cuss the coordination of tax policy between states. Tax policy, the implication seems to be, would be retained by the nation-state.

It is an exaggeration to say that the whole Bretton Woods system broke down. What did break down was the rules of cooperation for the convertibility of the dollar into gold and the exchange rates regime. After the war, the US dollar became the international reserve currency. The US also went from being in surplus to running trade deficits. States at first wanted US dollars to meet their trade obligations. They were also happy to let the US run deficits since this provided liquidity in the international monetary system. This situation led, however, to a crisis first anticipated by the economist Triffin in 1960 (Triffin 1960). The problem was that if the US attempted to correct its balance of payments deficit it would cause a liquidity crisis. If it allowed its deficit to continue, other states would lose confidence in the dollar as a reserve currency and seek to convert their dollars into gold. US deficits continued to increase, partly because the US had to pay for its war in Vietnam. Confidence in the dollar started to slide. States began to seek, as the gold standard allowed them to, the conversion of their dollars into gold. The US reacted by announcing in August 1971 that it was going to abandon the convertibility of the dollar.

This unilateral action ended the exchange rates regime that had been negotiated by states at Bretton Woods. Other states were more or less forced to float their own currencies. There was the minor matter that the US and other states were in breach of the IMF agreement. The real problem lay in deciding on a new form of cooperation for exchange rates. Between 1971 and 1974 there was a series of international meetings aimed at solving this problem. The US found that its action in suspending convertibility had led to its isolation at the G-10 (the IMF's main creditor nations). It went forum-shopping, a strategy it has repeated with success in other regulatory domains. The forum which eventually emerged was an ad hoc forum within the IMF, officially called the Committee of the Board of Governors on Reform of the International Monetary System and generally referred to as C-20. The membership of C-20 was drawn from countries that had control over executive positions at the IMF (Williamson 1977: 61). The C-20 negotiations allowed states very considerable sovereign discretion over the setting of exchange rates. Williamson (1977: 73) put it thus: 'The outcome of the C-20 was, in effect, a decision to learn to live with the non-system that had evolved out of a mixture of custom and crisis over the preceding years'.

The era of flexible and floating exchange rates that followed the breakdown of the Bretton Woods exchange regime was not really a victory for the principle of national sovereignty as much as a triumph of US financial hegemony. Keynes had always thought that in the postwar era the only hope for peace and economic growth lay in the creation of an international monetary system. He saw that sterling's lustre was fading and so the UK had to cooperate with the US in this enterprise. In his briefing notes to the UK Chancellor on 15 February 1945 he writes:

> The idea that there is some bilateral system which would weld the empire more closely together is a pure delusion. Nothing would be more likely to break up the economic relations within the empire and destroy the primacy of London in the sterling area system than a wanton rupture with the currency and commercial systems of North America before there was any proof that the alternative system, so much better for all concerned if it would work, must necessarily break down (Keynes 1945: 191).

Keynes wanted a genuinely independent international monetary system, one that disciplined deficit and surplus nations alike. The IMF Agreement that came out of Bretton Woods contained a scarce currency clause, which, as Keynes pointed out, 'commits the US to finding a way out in the event of the balance of trade turning obstinately in its favour' (Keynes, 15 February 1945, 189). This clause was never invoked against the US. European states wanted US dollars. When the US also became a deficit country it was able to avoid disciplinary adjustment by suspending the convertibility of its currency into gold. In fact the suspension of convertibility in 1971 'was accompanied by bellicose demands that other countries should revalue their currencies so as to eliminate "unfair exchange rates", backed up by the imposition of a 10 per cent import surcharge until such time as they complied' (Williamson 1977: 43). The US was, in other words, seeking to pass on the cost of adjustment to other states.

International monetary regulation had led to a particular kind of structural problem. Basically the problem arises when the dominant currency in world monetary relations is also the currency of a hegemon. The convenience of a dominant currency in trade terms is undoubted. It is this convenience that drove the formation of monetary unions in Ancient Greece and it was through trade that sterling achieved much of its ascendancy at the end of the nineteenth century. If at the same time this dominant currency is the currency of a hegemon (hegemonic dominant currency), the temptation facing the hegemon is to use it to run its own agenda and solve its domestic, economic and political problems (e.g. the deficit financing of a war). Moreover, the hegemon may use its power to evade the discipline that an international monetary order must impose on surplus and deficit nations alike in order to achieve a stable equilibrium. Hegemonic dominant currencies are, in other words, a fragile basis on which to build an international monetary order. Other states are left without any real disciplinary recourse when the hegemon defects from the order.

Keynes had been a strong advocate of the idea of an international monetary authority administering a new international monetary unit. His plan was for a central bank for the world, an 'International Clearing Union' that could issue a new unit to be called the 'bancor, unitas, dolphin, bezant, daric and heavens knows what' (Keynes, 23 May 1944, 10). This plan for a more powerful international monetary authority was never discussed seriously at Bretton Woods. Support for it in the UK was lukewarm. Nor did the US support it. The IMF that was born at Bretton Woods was probably as much as Keynes could have hoped for. In a report to the Chancellor in 1946 about Bretton Woods, he writes:

> The Fund can scarcely be, at any rate in the early years, the nucleus of a super-central bank, such as we hoped. It will be a different kind of body, much more closely linked in its activities to the Treasury and other Whitehall Departments, and much less to the Bank of England, than we had been anticipating. But it may prove none the less important (Keynes, 27 March 1946, 232).

In the years that followed the events of 1971, international monetary cooperation again changed its nature. Keynes' vision of an international monetary system capable of disciplining both deficit and surplus nations, thereby bringing equilibrium to the economies of the world, faded. Instead states looked to fora like the G-7 and the G-5 to coordinate international monetary policy. In a world of floating exchange rates the level of cooperation also floated. The meetings of G-7 finance ministers became a centre of monetary cooperation, but from that centre came a different kind of cooperation to the institutionalized, rule-based, multilaterally binding cooperation of Bretton Woods. G-7 meetings were more about information exchange and consultation, conditional policy understandings, than about rule-based guarantees. Industrialized countries kept lines of communication open with each other and used the IMF to bring monetary and fiscal discipline to developing debtor nations. At the Bonn G-7 summit of 1978 the US, Germany and

Japan agreed to restart the world's economy, but this cooperation dissipated in the face of inflationary fears. Cooperation was rekindled with some success with the Plaza Accord of 1985 (an agreement to let the value of the dollar decline) and the Louvre Accord of 1987 (an agreement to stabilize the value of the dollar). Generally, the G-7 has a mixed record in delivering the kind of public goods from monetary cooperation that the IMF was initially designed for (Kahler 1995: 58–9). Similarly, central banks have coordinated their operations in foreign exchange markets, but the success of this has become increasingly problematic in the face of ever more powerful currency speculators (Gunter 1996: 116–17).

Another consequence of the breakdown of Bretton Woods was that it speeded up EC planning for monetary union. By the 1970s the Bundesbank was the most powerful central bank in Europe. After the suspension of dollar convertibility and the ensuing currency storms of the early 1970s, it realized that defending fixed exchange rates was futile. More important was the establishment of the European Monetary System (EMS) in 1979. This system was intended to bring exchange rate stability to Europe by setting up an exchange rates regime in which the currencies of participating European states would adjust against one another within a fixed range rather than simply floating. This was an initiative taken by Chancellor Helmut Schmidt and President Valéry Giscard d'Estaing. Schmidt's role was crucial, as he made a passionate speech to the Council of the Bundesbank persuading it to support the EMS when the Council was worried about the implications of the EMS for German monetary independence and power (Marsh 1993: 194). The logic of European monetary union had been talked about since the early 1960s. After the creation of the EMS that logic drew increasing support, particularly from the influential French policymakers who saw monetary union as a way of breaking free of the hegemony of the Bundesbank. Under the leadership of Jacques Delors, President of the EC, the EC devised a three-stage plan for European monetary union. Bundesbank leadership underwrote Delors' leadership:

> If there is no stability there can be no monetary union. We as the anchor state need to solve our inflation first. Then dialogue is important and learning. That means you have to defend your case within the union. But against the shared objective of non-inflationary growth. They want union and the price is price stability policies (Bundesbank interview 1994).

At a meeting in Maastricht in 1991, European states entrenched in treaty form a timetable and set of conditions for monetary union. Essentially, states wishing to be part of the union had to commit themselves to the prevailing principles of macroeconomic orthodoxy; a low inflation rate, reduced government deficits and the stabilization of their currency. Monetary union would involve the introduction of a single currency (the euro, introduced on 1 January 1999) and the creation of a single monetary authority for Europe (the European Central Bank). On 1 January 1999 Germany, France, Italy, Spain, Netherlands, Belgium, Austria, Portugal, Finland, Ireland and Luxembourg participated in stage 3 of economic and monetary union by adopting the euro as their currency. The UK, Sweden and Denmark opted to stay out of the single currency for the time being, while Greece did not achieve the required economic targets to be able to adopt the euro.

## International Capital Markets

Running roughly parallel to the breakdown of Bretton Woods was the expansion of capital markets and the growth in multinational banking. After the Second World War US corporations progressively expanded their operations into other countries. They needed financial services (and telecommunications services) to facilitate this. US banks were the first to realize the scale of demand. Led by Citicorp, US banks began a drive for the corporate customers. They were stunningly successful. In 1960 less than ten banks in the US had overseas branches and foreign assets were less than $US4 billion. By 1977 more than 100 US banks had overseas branches, with a total of $US230 billion in foreign assets (Channon 1988: 4).

Circles of causality began to operate in complex and reflexive ways to produce larger and more integrated capital markets. Banks and financial markets were locked into a bootstraps enterprise in which banks, by going international, had helped to create international markets and in turn had to devise organizational strategies for survival in those markets. US domestic regulation, because it restricted trading in different states, had forced US banks to go off-shore looking for opportunities. Once US banks had built overseas branches and offices, developments in telecommunications and information technology allowed them to integrate their operations in various ways. Client demand and the fact that banks from other countries, most notably the UK and Japan, had entered the corporate market aggressively forced all banks to be inventive about their services. Financial services and instruments underwent an extraordinary period of innovation. Since this innovation was endogenous in nature it was fast, both in terms of rate and spread. The floating exchange rates environment that followed the breakdown of Bretton Woods presented banks and others with further opportunities in the foreign exchange markets. More opportunities also meant more risks. Banks began to devise hedging instruments and so, for example, markets for futures contracts, swaps and currency options developed (OECD 1985a: 16).

Other opportunities occurred through the growth of off-shore currency markets. For a variety of reasons US dollar deposits abroad grew. One reason was that US banks with overseas branches were not bound by US restrictions (in the form of Regulation Q imposed by the US Treasury) on the amount of interest they could pay on deposits in those branches. As the US went into deficit to pay for the Vietnam War more dollars found their way into the Eurodollar market. Other currencies like the yen and deutschmark also began to make up the Euromarket. From small beginnings in the 1950s, the Eurocurrency market grew into the world's largest capital market. International banks became key players in this market, both as lenders and borrowers. The markets became a crucial source of credit to multinationals. Governments and corporations with large borrowing requirements also created the Eurobond market (bonds sold in a country which uses currency other than the currency in which the bond is denominated). The combination of floating currencies and the sheer size of these markets brought new risks. Currency speculators had a ready source of credit to fund their attacks. Those involved in old-fashioned commodity capitalism – the sale of tangibles – realized that their gains from trade could be wiped out by currency fluctuations. Their fears and desires for risk protection fuelled a new form of service, that of risk protection through the creation of derivative financial instruments – contracts that derive their value from another instrument (e.g. a share) or commodity (e.g. wool), their purpose being to protect the parties from a risk of some kind (the risk of a currency fluctuation, share market fall, a price rise).[3] Some forms of derivatives became the subject of trade on exchanges. In

---

3 Financial derivatives may be broadly defined as financial instruments which derive their value from the performance of assets, interest or currency exchange rates, or indexes. Derivative transactions include a wide assortment of financial contracts, including structured debt obligations and deposits, swaps, futures, options, caps, floors, collars and forwards, and various combinations thereof. See Banking Circular 277, Comptroller of the Currency, Administrator of National Banks, 'Risk Management of Financial Derivatives', 27 October 1993, p. 4.

just the same way that securitization (discussed in the next chapter) created tradable markets in loans of various kinds, the 'contractualization' of risk (identifying, separating and transferring risk to those in the best position to bear it) created tradable markets in risk – the markets in derivatives. Australian farmers who entered into foreign currency loans because the rates were cheaper could at the same time enter into a second contract to protect (called hedging) against the risk that the value of the Australian dollar would fall, driving up the cost of the foreign loan. Because there was so much risk in deregulated markets, the trade in derivatives grew astronomically. Interest rate futures (one form of tradable derivative) went from $US588 billion in 1986 to $US4783 billion in 1992 (OECD Financial Market Trends, cited in Hirst & Thompson 1996: 41).

Banks also found that their position as financial intermediaries was no longer sacrosanct. The invention of securitization for loans, mortgage loans, car loans and credit card loans meant that borrowers and investors had less need for banks. Corporations began to issue more commercial paper as a way of directly financing their activities. Banks found themselves being bypassed by large borrowers, a process known as disintermediation. Declining profitability made them look to providing other kinds of services. Under the banner of deregulation they began to push into the securities and insurance markets. Where they were allowed to, banks and securities firms became part of the same corporate group. The sharp organizational lines between financial actors, upon which much prudential regulation in English-speaking countries had been built since the New Deal, began to blur.

Exogenous factors also affected the process of the internationalization of markets. After the oil shock of 1973 international banks found themselves holding the deposits of oil-exporting countries. The Eurocurrency market increased by an estimated $US30 billion (Channon 1988: 160). Banks keen to lend these funds entered into loan agreements with developing countries, the governments of which were equally keen to borrow as a way of financing their deficits. Banks thought that the risk of these loans was low because it was sovereign risk. 'Countries never go bankrupt', observed Walter Wriston, head of Citicorp, one of the most powerful leaders of international banking in the 1970s (cited in Sachs 1989: 8). Billions of dollars began to flow to countries in Africa, Asia and Latin America. There is no need to tell here the history of the 1980s debt crisis. The important feature is that bank regulators stood by and watched as multinational banks lent billions of dollars to developing countries. Poland was the first to default on these loans, in 1981, followed by Mexico and Brazil in 1982. Most Latin American countries had to reschedule payment on loans. All invoked the help of the IMF. It became clear that banking regulation had not worked at all well. In the US, the Bank of America, Citicorp, Chase Manhattan, Manufacturers Hanover, Bankers Trust, Chemical Bank, First Chicago, Continental Illinois and Morgan Guaranty had lent more than their total capital worth to just two countries, Mexico and Brazil (de Saint Phalle 1985: 221). Low-level sovereign risk, everybody now realized, had become international systemic risk of unprecedented magnitude.

### The Basle Committee: The Beginnings of Global Banking Regulation

The globalization of banking and financial markets was not accompanied by a globalization of prudential regulation. The regulation of banking practices remained the province of national regulators. Those regulators faced a capacity problem and an information problem. No single national regulator had powers over the international banking system. Regulators found that because of the complex cross-border lending and borrowing activities of multinational banks they had to base their prudential oversight on poor information. There was another problem. Financial crises which had begun in one country in the eighteenth and nineteenth centuries were usually transmitted to other national economies. In the integrated financial markets of the 1960s and 1970s the problem of systemic risk posed by financial crises grew greater. Regulators and bankers slowly began to realize that the integrated financial system that self-interest had built now demanded a more communal and cooperative response if it were to be maintained. Financial engineering, just like nuclear engineering could lead to meltdown. Both vocations are 'communities of shared fate' against meltdown (see Chapter 13).

The first strong signal of this possibility came with the 1974 failure of the Herstaat Bank in Germany because of foreign exchange dealings. In that same year a US wholesale bank, the Franklin National Bank, also failed. The response of the custodians of financial systems, the central bankers, was swift. Under the auspices of the G-10, the central bank governors of that group of countries established at the end of 1974 the Standing Committee on Banking Regulations and Supervisory Practices (now called the Basle Committee on Banking Supervision – the Basle Committee). The initiative for the formation of such a committee had come from London. The first two Chairs of the Committee came from the Bank of England (Sir George Bluden 1974–76, Peter Cooke 1977–88). London's financial system had been colonized by international banks, particularly US banks, and British regulators had good reason to be worried about systemic risk. It was clear that any unilateral regulatory attempt to deal with international banks might rob London of its reputation as a good place to locate if one were in the banking business (Kapstein 1989: 329). Two apparently irreconcilable objectives had to be achieved – the maintenance of London's reputation for regulatory flexibility and the competitive advantages that flowed from that, as well as the reduction of systemic risk. The solution lay in a multilaterally coordinated approach that could produce a set of standards all could live with.

The Basle Committee's first accomplishment was the production of a set of principles aimed at working out supervisory lines of responsibility for a bank established in more than one jurisdiction. Known as the Basle Concordat of 1975, its key principle was that no part of an international bank should escape adequate supervision. Other principles flowed from this. Since the solvency of bank branches depended upon the health of the parent bank, primary responsibility for supervision of solvency fell to the parent authority of the parent bank. In 1983 the Basle Committee issued a revision of the 1975 Concordat (Basle Committee 1983). In 1990 a supplementary document dealing with the practical aspects of implementing the Concordat (authorization, information flows, bank secrecy and external audit) was issued by the Committee (Basle Committee 1990). In 1992 the Committee issued another document further refining the supervision of banks' cross-border establishments (Basle Committee 1992). A process had been set in place whereby broad principles, once articulated and accepted, were revisited and reformulated, often in more detail, with a view to practical implementation to meet the agreed goal of adequate supervision.

The Basle Committee continued to learn from crises. In 1983 an Italian bank, Banco Ambrosiano SpA, failed. Somehow the Luxembourg branch of Italy's largest private bank was relieved of $US1.3 billion. It was a crime drama in the finest Italian tradition, involving the Vatican (owner of the bank), Panamanian companies belonging to the Vatican and the death of Italian banker Roberto Calvi (de Saint Phalle 1985: 229–30). The supervisory net that the Basle Committee had put into place applied only to banks. The Banco Ambrosiano, however, had a financial holding company called Banco Ambrosiano Holdings which was incorporated in Luxembourg. Even though the holding company carried on the business of banking it was beyond the reach of Luxembourg's banking laws since it was not a bank (Herring & Litan 1995: 101). Moreover, Luxembourg's secrecy laws veiled Banco Ambrosiano Holdings' operations from the Bank of Italy. The Basle Committee in its 1983 revision of the Concordat recommended that 'where host authority supervision [Luxembourg] is inadequate the parent authority [Bank of Italy] should either extend its supervision...or it should be prepared to discourage the parent bank [Banco Ambrosiano SpA] from continuing to operate the establishment [Banco Ambrosiano Holdings] in question' (Basle Committee 1983: 3).

The BCCI disaster is also sometimes presented as an example of the failure of the Basle Committee's international supervisory net. BCCI was a big and dirty bank, a 'banker to the world's biggest criminals' (Fisse & Braithwaite 1993: 222). Referred to by the CIA as the 'Bank of Crooks and Criminals International' (known to the investing public as Bank of Credit and Commerce International), BCCI was able to evade the net because its lawyers and accountants devised a complex corporate structure that pivoted on a holding company in Luxembourg and which made use of the secrecy laws of that state and the Cayman Islands (Herring & Litan 1995: 104). Under the Basle Committee's guidelines no one supervisory authority was able to put BCCI under the lens of consolidated supervision. The BCCI story also shows that the very existence of the Basle Committee serves as a warning system for those who move in elite financial circles. Through its evasion of consolidated supervision BCCI came to the notice of the Basle Committee during the early 1980s (Herring & Litan 1995: 103). The Basle Committee, we must remember, is comprised of the central bankers and regulators of the G-10. The financial elites of those states were well wired into the work and concerns of the Basle Committee. By the time BCCI went under, the smart money had long left it. Those who lost were thousands of poorly informed investors from developing countries. One of BCCI's legacies was to wipe out the social security fund of Gabon (Fisse & Braithwaite 1993: 222). BCCI was a tragedy for Gabon, but it never posed the systemic danger to the financial centres of industrialized countries which under other conditions it might have done. The financial elites of the West continued to be players in expanding global capital markets. The people of Gabon were left to ponder the fact that after a lifetime of work they had nothing.

### Regulating Money-laundering

In pushing for the globalization of financial regulation, the US highest priority has not been uniform accountancy standards, harmonizing tax, macroeconomic policy coordination, nor even capital adequacy for banks. It has been money-laundering. 'Money-laundering is the process through which the existence, illegal source and unlawful application of illicit gains is concealed or disguised to make the gains appear legitimate' (General Accounting Office 1991: 8). Dirty money must be laundered because it comes from the international trade in child prostitution, major corporate frauds and, most importantly from a US perspective, the drug trade. The domestic priority of tackling the drug trade and the political attractions of blaming foreigners (see Chapter 15) has made money-laundering the top US priority. Coincidentally, as we will see in Chapter 15, national security objectives are bundled into the issue: the war on drugs has been a useful weapon against the likes of General Noriega, and the CIA has an interest in being a major launderer of dirty money itself, while making it harder for the competition to do it.

By 1990 only six states had modelled the US approach of making money-laundering a specific criminal offence (Financial Action Task Force 1990: 11). The US drafted the Basle Statement of Principles on Money Laundering, which was approved by the Basle Committee in 1988. Later in 1988, eighty countries signed the UN Vienna Convention against Illicit Traffic in Narcotic Drugs and Psychotropic Substances. The Convention created obligations, upon ratification, to criminalize and extradite money-laundering and to cooperate on international enforcement.

The most important initiative was taken at a 1990 G-7 Economic Summit meeting with the President of the Commission for the European Communities. The summit invited eight non-Summit participants to join a Financial Action Task Force (FATF). By 1994, this club had expanded to more than thirty invitees. The FATF has crafted forty recommendations for cracking down on money-laundering. States join the FATF when they are ready to be subjected to peer review on implementation of the forty recommendations by two other FATF members. The peer review assesses the global consolidated compliance of home country financial institutions. Peer review reports are discussed at meetings of the FATF – shades of the dialogic approach to compliance of the Council of TRIPS (Chapter 7), the Trade Policy Review Mechanism (Chapter 10) and the ILO's Committee on Freedom of Association (Chapter 11). Compliance with global money-laundering standards is therefore more intensively monitored than other financial standards. Contrast the Basle Committee's approach to capital adequacy standards for banks. It has no database on compliance with the standards and thus no peer review of implementation.

The 1991 meeting of the FATF made a conscious decision not to create a black-list of states who were refusing to act on its plan, but to build an expanding white-list of complying states. Members check FATF peer review reports before renewing or granting a bank a new licence to enter their market. It is now impossible for a bank to become a player in major economies unless it has a money-laundering compliance officer reporting suspicious cash transactions to the police, promoting a know-your-customer culture in the bank and moving the bank toward compliance with the forty-point FATF plan. The global strategy has been to build, from the G-7, a wider epistemic community of money-laundering compliance based on peer review from within the white-list of participating states. It may not have worked in eliminating money-laundering, but it has worked as a strategy for globalizing an extremely expensive new regulatory order.

### The Bilateralism of Tax

By 1991 the number of bilateral treaties covering international taxation had grown into a dense web. More than 1000 treaties had been signed. Despite this, for reasons which we will come to in a moment, states had less control over their fiscal base than ever before. The proliferation of bilateral tax treaties had been aided by the work of the Fiscal Committee of the OECD. This Committee produced in 1963 the Draft Double Taxation Convention on Income and Capital and in 1977 a revision called the Model Double Taxation Convention on Income and on Capital. After the 1977 Convention the Committee on Fiscal Affairs (successor to the Fiscal Committee) adopted the strategy of amending the model Convention on a regular basis. It turned the Convention into an 'ambulatory Model Convention' (OECD Committee on Fiscal Affairs 1996: 9). The OECD model became widely used in agreements between OECD members as well as between OECD and non-OECD members.

The main purpose of these bilateral treaties was to address the problem of double taxation. Over the decades states had expended hundreds of thousands of hours negotiating to establish in treaty form a set of principles to deal with this problem. But how much of a problem it was in economic terms, how much disruption it caused to trade and investment flows, was something that had never been quantified. Non-tax factors in investment abroad were probably just as important, if not more important – something the ICC readily agreed with. Closer analysis also suggested that the economic problems of double taxation might be overstated (Bloch & Heile-mann 1946). Nevertheless, international business kept pushing states into doing something about double taxation.

States had turned to the bilateral model for the purposes of regulating international taxa-tion because they saw it as consistent with retaining their fiscal sovereignty. It turned out to work in exactly the opposite way. The fact that tax policy remained so interlinked with national life meant that there was a wide diversity of types and rates of taxes. The web of bilateral treaties rep-resented a set of principles for the allocation of taxable income between states. States had gener-ated an international tax structure of polycentric, regulatory diversity. Corporate actors had, through the law of corporate groups, created their own complex organizational structures. Impor-tantly, though, their complexity was of a monocentric kind – there was one seat of decision and one seat only when it came to strategic decision-making for tax purposes. In the contest between states and corporations over the payment of taxes, the objective of corporations was to shift prof-its to low-tax jurisdictions and losses to high-tax jurisdictions. Regulatory diversity had generated tax arbitrage opportunities. The framework of bilateral treaties provided a set of rules for this tax arbitrage game. The monocentric complexity of corporations meant that a coordinated strategy could be developed against states which were locked into polycentric diversity. Some states became tax havens – places with no taxes or very low taxes. They encouraged the establishment of subsidiaries and the movement of profits into their jurisdiction. They effectively turned the tax game into a game of one-way transparency. Corporations knew the rules by which states oper-ated, but the secrecy laws of these rogue fiscal kings meant that corporations operating in their domain did so under the cloak of law, their affairs hidden from the scrutiny of taxing states.

News Corporation is perhaps the best exemplar of monocentric complexity in the world of transnational corporations. In 1995 it paid tax at around 7 per cent, which is low even by the standards of TNCs. Interviews with former executives provide examples of what we have been describing.

On monocentrism (one seat of strategic decision-making):

> Even senior executives of News International in London admit they have no idea how the group's finances are structured.

One former executive said:

> 'We weren't privy to the structure because it wasn't seen as important to our job. The structure of the business was managed at corporate level in New York where DeVoe pulled all the best legal and finance minds', the former executive said (*Sydney Morning Herald*, 20 July 1996, p. 60).

On corporate group complexity:

> The group has forty-nine subsidiaries in the British Virgin Islands, another twenty-five based in the Cayman Islands, five more in the US Virgin Islands and four in the Netherlands Antilles (*Sydney Morn-ing Herald*, 20 July 1996, p. 60).

On shifting profits around, a former director of News Corporation states:

> I just send up the figures, they get spun around a bit and out they come. There's no way of reconciling them once they've been treated for tax (*Sydney Morning Herald*, 20 July 1996, p. 60).

The problems of the bilateral model of international tax regulation continue to worsen. The OECD model says nothing of substance on the tax issues raised by foreign exchange dealings (Vann 1991a: 108). The rapid rate of innovation in financial markets will continue to place more stress on the model. In an interview at the US Treasury we were told that complex derivative transactions were being used to shift money out of the reach of Treasuries. Transfer pricing has remained a perennial problem under the OECD model. Transfer pricing is a generic term for strategies that involve two or more members of a corporate group in a transaction for goods or services. One member of the group transfers the good or service to another member at a price that produces a favourable tax outcome for the group overall. For instance, a US firm might be able to sell its tennis racquets in Europe for $300, but rather than selling direct it sells the racquets to a subsidiary in Taiwan for much less. The Taiwanese subsidiary then sells the racquets to European consumers. The purpose of the transfer is to minimize the tax of the US parent company and locate the profit from selling the racquets in a low-tax jurisdiction. Setting a price for tax purposes for such transactions is the single most important factor in dividing the tax base between two states, since the possible tax liability of a corporate group is often in the millions (Owens 1993: 36). The OECD model, following the League of Nations model, has entrenched the principle that prices for such transactions are to be determined as if the two members of the group were dealing at arm's length. But finding an arm's-length price is very difficult in a world where the norm is increasingly trade within corporate groups and what is being traded are property rights in intangibles that are difficult to value (Vann 1991a: 105).

For these and other reasons a consensus is emerging that an alternative to the bilateral approach has to be developed (Owens 1993; Picciotto 1993; Vann 1991b). One possibility being discussed is a general agreement on taxes to be administered by the World Trade Organization (WTO) or some body like it. The creation of a new multilateral system for tax seems politically unsaleable to the world fiscal sovereigns. A more likely possibility is that the present bilateral model will be replaced by a system that evolves from specific regulatory solutions to the present problems of the bilateral system. The transfer prices issue might eventually be dealt with through some version of unitary taxation. Under unitary taxation a corporate group would be treated as one and its finances, for the purposes of tax, consolidated. The resulting tax base would then be divided between the relevant states on the basis of an agreed formula. Some states within the US, notably California, have used the method. The unitary method runs into problems when one state uses it to reach for a share of the global profits of a company. Other treasuries take the view that their tax base is being poached. California's unitary tax has brought it into conflict with big business and other treasuries as well as US federal tax officials (Picciotto 1993: 396). California's experience shows that introducing unitary methods of taxation on a unilateral basis is likely to fail. But as states find that the arm's-length principle becomes less workable they may be readier to implement alternative methods of taxation. A sense of fiscal jeopardy is also likely to see states remain receptive to regulatory innovation in the tax area. The US and Australian tax authorities, for instance, have been entering into advanced pricing agreements, agreements that specify transfer prices acceptable to tax officials and the company concerned. Since transfer pricing involves other jurisdictions, national authorities have had to involve other tax authorities in these agreements (Picciotto 1993: 403–4). A kind of covert harmonization of administrative method led by experienced tax bureaucrats may have more success with the transfer prices problem, a problem that is likely to remain intractable at the level of multilateral negotiations among fiscal sovereigns.

More generally, there has been a considerable growth in cooperation between national tax administrators in the taxation of international business. But arrangements of mutual assistance and information exchange have followed the pathways laid down by bilateral treaties. It has been a cooperation largely between developed countries, characterized by a 'reciprocal bargaining of national interest' (Picciotto 1992: 306). Regulatory complementarities in the accounting field may also help to bring about the reform of the bilateral model. For the purposes of financial reporting the accounting profession has had to develop techniques of consolidated accounting, techniques which can be used for tax accounting under a unitary method of taxation. More generally, the Big Five accounting firms have themselves become agents for the development of harmonized accounting standards. The interest of international accounting firms in the problems generated by different accounting standards for international business dates back to the beginning of the twentieth century, when they met at International Accounting Congresses in St Louis, Paris and Brussels to discuss the issues (Samuels & Piper 1985: 59). It is true that the accounting profession is involved in the tax arbitrage games described earlier. But large accounting firms like PricewaterhouseCoopers have to help their multinational clientele make investment decisions. They need the kind of transparency that comes with harmonized standards, the kind of standards that allow an accounting firm in London to say to its European client that the foreign exchange exposure of a South Korean company makes that company a bad bet. The accounting standards that generate the information that investors need to reduce uncertainty in global markets may in time replace the tax accounting standards that mask the true investment and profit picture. We shall see later in this chapter that many actors, both state and non-state, agree on the need for harmonized accounting standards. Such standards will make a system of world unitary taxation more feasible.

At the time of writing in 1999, the OECD Committee on Fiscal Affairs and the G-8 seem to have more momentum than ever before toward securing an international agreement on defining and limiting unacceptable forms of tax competition. The OECD is laying an analytical base from which to tackle the problem of harmful tax competition[4] (see its *Harmful Tax Competition: An Emerging Global Issue* OECD 1998). In December 1997 the EU Council of Economic and Finance Ministers agreed to a Code of Conduct for Business Taxation as a first step in combatting harmful tax competition (the code can be found in OJ No. C2, 6 January 1998, p. 1). It includes requirements for reporting and transnational peer review of compliance with the code.

## Financial Regulation: The Uruguay Connection

Financial regulation, like other regulatory domains we examine in this book, has been importantly affected by the multilateral trade agreements concluded at the Uruguay Round in 1994 (see Chapter 10). The agreement most relevant to financial regulation is the General Agreement on Trade in Services (GATS). Trade in services during the 1970s and 1980s continued to grow. The US was the largest services exporter, followed by the EC and Japan. Financial services formed a crucial

---

4  The detailed definition of what constitutes harmful tax competition is one of the key issues to be resolved by states. At its core lie measures designed by a state to attract foreign direct investment (FDI). Examples include reduced tax rates on income earned by foreign investors, tax holidays for foreign investors, investment allowances and the creation of tax-free zones (Pinto 1998). Such measures are harmful because they have a lose–lose outcome for states. The state enacting the measures to attract the FDI gains little extra revenue, and the state losing the FDI gains none. When repeated among many states this lose–lose game degrades the fiscal base of all states.

part of the US strength in the global services market. For example, a US Technology Office assessment put US direct services exports in 1983 between $US67 000 million and $US84 000 million and sales of services in the same year by overseas affiliates of US companies between $US87 000 million and $US97 000 million (Veale, Spiegelman & Ronkainen 1988: 53). Many of the sales related to financial services like insurance and accounting.

In the lead-up to the Uruguay Round the US pushed for services to be included as part of the negotiations over GATT. The developing countries, led by India and Brazil, were afraid of including services under the auspices of GATT, essentially because they thought that the US would use the strategy of linkage to fulfil its goals for trade in services (by making concessions on goods) (Bhagwati 1988: 58). Thus the fear of services in GATT gave birth to GATS. A compromise between the US and the G-10 countries saw the US agree to a separate negotiation on services.

GATS is crucially important to financial regulation for two reasons. First, it introduces to financial regulation the trade principles of Most Favoured Nation (MFN) and national treatment. Second, it is a framework agreement that commits members of the WTO to 'successive rounds of negotiations...with a view to achieving a progressively higher level of liberalization' (see Article XIX of GATS). This, as we shall see, contrasts with framework agreements in other areas like the environment which, historically, have mostly not committed states to ongoing processes of negotiation. Institutionalizing processes of negotiation is crucial to understanding the globalization of regulation because it allows states with negotiating power to drive globalization agendas.

GATS can be divided into three parts. The first part deals with the general obligations of members, of which the most important is unconditional MFN (Article II). The second significant component of GATS is the Annexes dealing with specific service areas. In the case of financial regulation there are two. Finally, there are the schedules of specific commitments. These are the opening offers (which can be qualified in all sorts of ways) that states make concerning the service areas they are prepared to open to the multilateral trade regime. Essentially, what occurs under GATS is a sectoral negotiation for an area such as financial services that consists of bilateral deals between states. These bilateral agreements are then aggregated and become a protocol to GATS. GATS creates bilateral negotiating within a compulsory multilateral framework, a framework that obliges states to enter into successive rounds of negotiations (see Article XIX).

GATS has the potential to bring a massive liberalization of trade in services. Trade in services is defined to include service supply through commercial presence in a territory. GATS is aimed at an outcome that would allow the insurers and banks of one state to establish themselves in the banking and insurance markets of another. However, the speed at which GATS has brought liberalization to the financial services sector has been affected by the fact that the operation of the principles of MFN, national treatment and market access can be qualified. States, for example, had the option of not embracing unconditional MFN; they could use conditional MFN, which is reciprocity in poor disguise. During the financial services negotiations that followed the signing of the Final Act of the Uruguay Round the US blanketed its entire offer on financial services with conditional MFN. The US argued that other countries' offers were inadequate. This tactic spurred Europe into finding ways in which the talks could produce better offers on financial services. The US tactic was not particularly directed at Japan or Europe, which were both committed to liberalizing their financial sectors (Wang 1996: 118). Rather, its resort to reciprocity was directed at the major developing countries which the US felt were free-riding on US offers made under the MFN principle. The US tactic worked. December 1997 saw the conclusion of the financial services negotiations. The Agreement, according to the WTO website, covers 'more than 95 per cent of trade in banking, insurance, securities and financial information' (http://www.wto.org). At the time of writing 102 countries, including many developing countries, had made commitments on financial services.

The Final Act of the Uruguay Round also contained the Agreement on Trade-Related Investment Measures (TRIMS). This is a comparatively modest Agreement doing little more than imposing national treatment obligations on states in respect of trade-related investment measures. Our 1994 interviews with US companies and US business NGOs revealed that a small number of US business actors had set their sights on a more comprehensive investment regime than the Uruguay Round delivered. As the CEOs on the Advisory Committee on Trade Negotiations (see Chapter 7) tossed ideas around for the coming Uruguay trade round, they concluded that a multilateral investment regime should form the backbone of the agreements being negotiated at the round. Since Europe, the US and Japan were not united on the issue of investment TRIMS turned out to be a relatively low-key part of the Final Act of the Uruguay Round. During our 1994 interviews we were also told that investment represented unfinished business. A high-standard investment agreement from the perspective of business would hopefully be concluded at the OECD and perhaps find its way into the WTO. During 1997 and 1998, after a draft of the Multilateral Agreement on Investment (MAI) being negotiated at the OECD was leaked to a Canadian NGO, opposition to the MAI from consumer groups, unions and the environmental movement spread rapidly. Developing countries which had always opposed TRIMS were critical of the MAI. At the Ministerial Conference of the World Trade Organization in December 1996 at Singapore, India led the resistance to the proposal that the WTO take up work on the MAI. At the time of writing the MAI is far from dead, but it is firmly in the OECD too-hard basket.

The MAI, if it does eventuate, may not prove to be a decisive influence on global investment flows. The progressive removal of capital controls by states since the 1970s, combined with floating exchange markets, has seen a large increase in short-term capital flows (Hirst & Thompson 1996: 51). It is also clear that long-term capital flows in the form of foreign direct investment (FDI) have increased dramatically under the existing bilateral regime of investment treaties. FDI flows increased by 19 per cent in 1997, climbing for the seventh year in a row (UNCTAD 1998: 1). Hirst and Thompson argue that FDI, rather than trade, has been the main source of economic growth since the 1980s. Most FDI is carried on by multinationals (with the largest 100 accounting for a third of the world's FDI stock). Japan, North America and Europe at the beginning of the 1990s accounted for 75 per cent of total FDI stock and 60 per cent of the flow (Hirst & Thompson 1996: 63). Finally, GATS makes its quiet contribution to the loosening of investment flows. Under Article XI, subject to some limited exceptions, states must not restrict the payments and transfers that accompany their market access agreements.

### There's Nothing New Under the Sun: Digital Cash and Ancient Greece

Private coining, for a while at least, was common practice in the ancient world (Burns 1965: 75–7). Eventually it became a state monopoly. For most of the twentieth century the issue of currency has been a state monopoly. Technology in the late twentieth century has enabled a return to the private coining practices of ancient times. Computers and sophisticated encryption techniques enable customers to create their own digital coins, which are then validated by banks acting as issuers (Tyree 1997). In theory at least, anyone can become the issuer of digital coins. Digital technology is beginning to cause the currency system to differentiate into complex subsystems. In addition to digital cash there are smart cards (cards that contain a processor allowing the card to perform debit and credit functions without having to be linked to a central database). In Australia Mondex/Mastercard have launched a smart cards scheme, as have Telstra/Visa. Smart cards and other digitally based systems of payment represent a form of private coining. Digital cash does not constitute legal tender, but its acceptance by banks, merchants and their customers turns 'digicash' into a medium of exchange – a global medium, in fact. And just as in ancient times, the acceptance of these modern forms of private coinage depends on the reputation of those behind the system. The regulation of these systems, which are sometimes international, remains uncertain, primarily because phenomena like digicash do not fall neatly into existing categories of banking law. National regulators have adopted a wait-and-see approach to these systems. The globalization of regulation for these systems may take the form of a matrix of industry codes of practice devised by global players, for themselves.

The idea of consumers and traders participating in global markets by means of digital technologies has led, in the last few years, to a wide variety of initiatives on electronic commerce. International organizations like the OECD, the WTO, the UN Commission on International Trade Law (UNCITRAL) (UNCITRAL has a Model Law on Electronic Commerce), business NGOs, and regulators like the Basle Committee and the EC, as well as many others, are all writing reports, discussion papers and policy papers in response to an ideas agenda for electronic commerce and the information society developed by key US individuals. The ICC told us in a 1998 interview that it was so concerned about the proliferation of potential global regulators of e-commerce that it was developing a 'Global Action Plan' to sell a business perspective on which international organizations should do what. This ideas agenda is based on the US National Information Infrastructure Initiative of 1993, the Global Information Infrastructure Initiative of 1995 and the report entitled 'A Framework for Global Electronic Commerce' released by the White House in 1997. Lying at the heart of the US initiative on global electronic commerce is a notion of facilitation. Governments and regulators round the world should help to facilitate private sector electronic commerce. Unlike the medieval *Lex Mercatoria*, the *Lex Cybertoria* will require massive and detailed coordination between governments and supranational regulators in many areas including customs, taxation, electronic payment systems and model contracts for electronic commerce. For the time being, it is US policy initiatives which are driving the development of a regulatory framework for global electronic commerce.

## Actors

### States

Throughout the ancient period, the Middle Ages and the early medieval period, city-states, sovereigns and then emerging nation-states were variable forces in the globalization of financial regulation. The empires of Rome and Persia were important in monetary harmonization. But in international financial regulation it was merchant money-changers, operating in ports and market places, who through customary norms spread other financial institutions like the foreign exchange market (Einzig 1970: Ch. 3). Financial merchants, whether in the guise of money-changer, banker, trader or broker, remained important in the spread of customary financial norms, reaching the zenith of their harmonizing influence in the period of the Law Merchant (discussed in Chapter 7).

After this period states become more important actors in the globalization of financial regulation, but only after they had constructed their own national systems of regulation.

The UK can, with some justification, claim to be the most important actor in the globalization of financial regulation, at least until the beginning of the twentieth century. Both within and outside the empire, Britain's banking system was widely copied. The Bank of England led the international monetary system in the nineteenth century. It also watches over the self-regulation of Lloyd's of London, which dominated the world insurance market. Actually it more than dominated it: Lloyd's self-regulation constituted the market. Even today, Lloyd's reinsurance arrangements enable capitalism's most risky activities – satellites, off-shore oil rigs, supertankers, professional liability insurance for the Big Five accounting firms – all dominated by Lloyd's throughout the twentieth century. Yet during the twentieth century the UK began to share and then lose its influence over financial regulation. After the First World War it became clear that states would not return to a gold standard administered by the Bank of England. Bretton Woods saw international monetary cooperation reach new heights in the form of a regime for exchange rates. The US and the UK were the principal architects of the Bretton Woods institutions. Progressively, the Bank of England became less important in international monetary affairs as the US dollar became the currency of international trade and the US state the supplier of liquidity to the world. Regionally, the rise of the Bundesbank further eroded the Bank of England's influence in Europe. After the move to floating exchange rates in the 1970s, the G-7 states became the states which could best initiate monetary cooperation, with the US the most important of these. As Germain (1997: 163) has argued, the sheer size of the international markets that are coordinated in New York, Tokyo, Frankfurt and London 'empower their respective state authorities' to be regulatory leaders. Of these public authorities, those of the US have the most power. A decision, for example, by the US Federal Open Market Investment Committee to purchase government bonds on secondary markets adds to the liquidity of the entire world financial system (Germain 1997: 153). Other states cannot exert this kind of influence.

The role of states in the globalization of banking regulation has been a comparatively recent one. In the period of the Law Merchant, banking regulation was in the hands of the merchant community. States absorbed the customary Law Merchant into their national systems. By doing so they robbed it of much of its harmonized nature. British banking models became models for other states in the nineteenth and early twentieth centuries. These days no one state really leads the globalization of banking regulation. A start has been made on international prudential regulation of banks in the form of the Basle Committee, a UK initiative which has been supported by G-10 states. However, the hegemony of the US in international monetary relations has no counterpart in banking regulation.

Tax regulation has been more a case of policy convergence between states than a case of rule harmonization. In bringing about this policy convergence two states have been important. The British income tax of 1799 showed other states the advantage of a secure and direct tax base for the purpose of funding war. It was, as Sabine (1996: 26) puts it, the 'tax that beat Napoleon'. In the twentieth century the US more than any other state has brought about policy convergence in taxation matters between states. The world-wide taxation reforms of the 1980s, based on the ideas of lower rates and stricter enforcement combined with tax base broadening, were ideas most strongly pushed by the US state. Both the UK and the US have been important in entrenching the bilateral model of taxation to deal with the problem of double taxation. After the Second World War each signed a large number of these Agreements. Transfer pricing is of concern to all states, but the US has been most active in dealing with this problem. The US established advance pricing agreements (APA) as part of its tax regime to deal with this problem in 1991. Unlike Japan, which was the first state to have a unilateral APA procedure, the US has pushed the APA program both bilaterally and multilaterally (Conference on Transfer Pricing 1993: 917).

The US is a dominant state in tax regulation, but its dominance does not extend to the level we saw in intellectual property. It can and regularly does override its bilateral tax treaty obligations (usually through enacting contrary domestic legislation). But so can New Zealand breach its tax treaty obligations with the US and, provided it does it through 'surreptitious means', nothing much happens (Vann 1991a: 109). The US capacity to bring about policy convergence is limited. States might follow the US in a competition over the tax base (e.g. reducing corporate taxes), but persuading states not to engage in tax competition is much harder. Moreover, in a competition to reduce taxes a small state which decides to become a tax haven can always do better than the US. The US has only limited powers to discipline tax havens. When we asked senior US Treasury officials about the tax haven problem, we were told that it was possible to exclude such states from the bilateral treaty process (US Treasury interview 1994). Beginning in 1983, the US Treasury began to terminate its tax treaties with places like Anguilla, Barbados and the British Virgin Islands on the basis that the treaties did not impose sufficient information exchange obligations (Caccamise 1988: 559). However, the US Treasury ran into problems with this strategy when it cancelled its treaty with the Netherlands Antilles in 1987. The end of the treaty meant the end of the withholding tax exemption on income derived from bonds. The bonds became less desirable both for holders and issuers since the latter now had to factor in the tax cost to the lender. For US issuers this meant paying more for the cost of capital. The market in these bonds fell. In that same year the US Treasury reinstated tax exemption for interest earned from the bonds. To add insult to injury, some tax havens terminated their treaties with the US before the US did. This provides an example of the US not being particularly successful bilaterally (in contrast to other areas like intellectual property and telecommunications), one of the reasons being that bilateralism in this particular context cannot really be backed by economic coercion. The threat of loss of trading privileges in the US market is hardly likely to matter much to the Netherlands Antilles or any other small tax haven state. Of course, where such economic dependence does exist the US can and has been successful in changing the financial laws of other states. Economic pressure was successfully brought to bear on Swiss banks to modify their position on secrecy.

Finally, groups of states have also been important in the globalization of financial regulation. The G-5 and G-7 have been important in international monetary cooperation, the G-10 in banking regulation. The G-22 (the G-7 plus fifteen emerging market economies) is a forum where ideas for a new financial architecture in response to the global financial crisis of 1997–98 have been mooted.

## Organizations of States

At Bretton Woods the IMF was created to preside over a pegged but adjustable exchange rates regime. The functions of the World Bank were to provide finance for reconstruction of war-torn economies and 'the development of the less developed areas of the world in the general interests of the standard of life, of conditions of labour, and the expanse of trade everywhere' (Keynes, 22 July 1944, 103–4). Things have not gone exactly to plan.

In the original Bretton Woods concept the IMF would not interfere in matters of financial regulation. Keynes made this plain in a speech to the House of Lords which explains the consequences of the IMF. He describes three principles for which he has fought (Keynes, 23 May 1944, 16). First, that 'the external value of sterling shall conform to its internal value as set by our own domestic policies, and not the other way round'. Second, that the UK control its domestic interest rate 'without interference from the ebb and flow of international capital movements or flights of hot money'. Third, that while inflation was to be a target, deflation was not to come 'at the dictates of influences from outside'.

For a while the IMF fulfilled the role of monitoring the agreed international rules for the regulation of exchange rate relationships. After the breakdown of the system in the early 1970s, in 1978 states amended the Articles of Agreement to create a new role for the IMF. States would have more freedom to set exchange rates, but they would also be subjected to surveillance by the IMF according to a code of conduct established for the guidance of all members (Guitián 1992: 6). The effect of this, which would only become apparent later, was to establish a much closer nexus between the IMF's function of surveillance and national economic policies. In taking back discretion over exchange rates, states left it open for the IMF to monitor the exercise of that discretion including the aspects of domestic financial policy and regulation that matter to exchange rates. The IMF, through surveillance and the use of the principle of conditionality (discussed later), has become much more enmeshed in issues of institutional and microeconomic reform at the national level – precisely those areas in which Keynes had planned no part for the IMF.

The IMF and the World Bank have become important in bringing about regulatory convergence between states on matters of financial regulation. Somewhat paradoxically, the IMF has become less important in international monetary relations. For reasons we shall give in the Conclusion it seems less likely than ever to become a super central bank. Nor does it seem likely that the system of Special Drawing Rights (SDR) administered by the IMF will become the world's reserve currency to the exclusion of other currencies, particularly the dollar. As of April 1997 only two states had pegged their currencies to the SDR (IMF Survey 1997: 20) The US pushed the idea of a specially created international reserve asset in the form of a SDR in the mid 1960s to head off a French initiative to strengthen the role of gold in the monetary system (Walter 1991: 174). The SDR is a supplementary currency at best. The bulk of international financial transactions are based on the dollar.

The IMF will continue to be important in the re-engineering of the regulatory systems of states, particularly those which seek financial assistance packages from it (as of the end of 1996–97, sixty Stand-By, Extended and Enhanced Structural Adjustment Facility Arrangements were in place with members of the IMF (IMF Survey 1997: 2)). In this role it will at least be an agent of regulatory convergence and perhaps even harmonization. Tax provides an example of our claims. Over the years the IMF has become increasingly involved in dispensing detailed advice to states concerning their tax regimes. Generally, the IMF has pushed tax policy in the direction of indirect taxes, lower income taxes and lower rates of corporate taxation. However, IMF officials deny that there is a uniform IMF approach to tax reform (Tanzi 1990: 19). In our interviews at the IMF and the World Bank, officials stressed that there was no standard set of policy prescriptions that were applied by the IMF or World Bank. However, in 1994 they also told us that while twenty years earlier they had been recommending 50–55 per cent corporate tax rates, by 1994 their confidential advice to states was usually for rates of around 30 per cent. We questioned this by conceding that individual states might be able to attract more investment with lower rates, but if all states are getting the same advice in aggregate aren't all African states that compete for the same investment going to have worse problems of fiscal imbalance? The reply was that individual countries are the clients for IMF advice. IMF advice seems to be a factor in globalizing lower rates of corporate taxation and thereby worsening fiscal imbalances, that other parts of IMF advice redress by budget cuts.

Even if the special needs of client states temper the extent to which the IMF will be a force for regulatory harmonization, it will become a stronger force for bringing about regulatory convergence between states. One reason for thinking this is that as the new institutionalism of economics develops its ideas about the links between economic growth, and social, political and cultural institutions those ideas (which represent the beginnings of a synthesis between micro and macroeconomic theory) will, through the medium of epistemic communities, draw the IMF further down the path of analysis, review and finally policy prescription for the institutions of individual nation-states. In 1997 the IMF signalled that in carrying out its function of surveillance of exchange rate policies it would focus more on the banking regulation and practices of members and governance issues generally (IMF Survey 1997: 8–9). Under the label of 'good governance' it will probe more into the governance systems of states. One mechanism for this dialogue beyond conditionality with structural adjustment packages is an annual consultation with member governments. An IMF staff team goes to the country and writes a report which is discussed at the IMF Board. It then conveys further comments to the member, in writing.

The Bank for International Settlements (BIS) is a much lower-profile organization than either the IMF or the World Bank. Yet since the end of the Second World War it has become a forum in which central bankers from the US, Germany, Switzerland, the UK, France and other countries hold meetings. The BIS was formed in 1930 to coordinate Germany's payments of reparations after the First World War. For a long time the US did not assume its seat on the BIS Board of Directors (among other things, it saw the BIS as a competitor to the IMF and was worried by its connections with states in the Eastern bloc). The Chairman of the Board of Governors of the Federal Reserve System filled that seat in 1994 (Siegman 1994: 900). He did so because the BIS had become an international financial organization from which the US could no longer afford to stay away. By the time the US assumed its seat at the BIS, the BIS had become the secretariat backbone to the world's most important financial standard-setting committees. The BIS had become the financial world's most strategically networked regulator. It plays host to and services (see Howell 1993: 375–6; Siegman 1994: 900–1):

- meetings of G-10 central bank governors;
- the Basle Committee;
- the Committee on Payment and Settlement Systems;
- the Eurocurrency Standing Committee;
- the Committee of the Group of Experts on Gold and Foreign Exchange;
- the Group of Computer Experts;
- the Group of Experts on Monetary and Economic Databank Questions;
- the Committee of Governors of the Central Banks of the Member States of the EC;
- the Board of the Governors of the European Monetary Cooperation Fund.

It also acts as a research centre for the G-10 and the OECD.

It is the more informal, less politicized nature of BIS, combined with the persistent need for cooperation in international financial regulation, that explains why BIS has managed to foster so much cooperation between central banks. The BIS has been selective in the way that it has expanded membership of its Board of Directors (the central bank governors of Canada and Japan were not elected until 1994), but it has striven to involve the global community of central bankers in its activities. It has been an assiduous networker, building links with regional central banking organizations like the Executive Meeting of East Asian and Pacific Central Banks, the Central Banks of South-East Asia, New Zealand and Australia and the South-East Asian Central Banks. Cooperation has been its hallmark. During the 1960s, working through the BIS, central bankers devised a currency swap network, formed a gold pool and encouraged the use of US Treasury bonds (known as Roosa Bonds), all in an attempt to stabilize the exchange rates regime under Bretton Woods (Howell 1993).

The Basle Committee on Banking Supervision is the pre-eminent organization in the globalization of banking regulation, even though it is not a legal body but 'just a club of gentlemen who get together' (1991 OECD interview). Represented on the Basle Committee are the supervisory authorities of the G-10 states as well as the authorities of Luxembourg and Switzerland. This is a small group of states but, as Peter Cooke, a former Chair of the Committee, pointed out, most of the 'world's banking business is conducted in banks with their headquarters in G-10 nations' (cited in Shah 1996: 374). Formally, the Basle Committee has an advisory function for G-10 nations. But it has had a regulatory impact well beyond advice. A good example of its standard-setting role is the 1983 revision of the Basle Concordat that was accepted by banking supervisors from seventy-five non-G-10 countries at the 1984 Rome conference of banking supervisors. Similarly, a review by the Basle Committee of the Basle Capital Accord of 1988, which recommended capital adequacy ratios for banks, found that the most important banks in non-G-10 countries had introduced or were introducing the capital standards recommended by the Committee (Basle Committee, press statement, 13 September 1993). Since then, with some pushing from development banks and the IMF demanding compliance,[5] the G-10 capital adequacy standards have globalized remarkably for banks trading internationally. Purely local financial institutions (which are said to pose no systemic risk) do not have to meet them:

> Initially, our objective was narrow – to get Japanese banks into the system. Then getting all internationally active banks in the G-10 countries to adopt sound risk-management practices was the priority and if we accomplish that we think we have done well. In fact, many international banks beyond the G-10 now have come on board. Now we have a Liaison Group with major non-G-10 economies to encourage that and a wider still Coordination Group (1998 Basle Committee interview).

In a 1993 interview, the Secretary-General of the Basle Committee saw it as 'amazing' that the capital adequacy standards had been so universally adopted, given the competition in laxity that had been the reality of the 1980s and the wide differences in negotiating positions before the Agreement. He saw the keys to effective harmonization as '1. Working on good relationships; and 2. Precommitting to make a decision'.

There are several factors that explain the acceptance of the Basle Committee's standard-setting work. It is a small committee of highly experienced and senior technocrats. 'We don't have a staff; we have a network.' This, combined with its more informal organizational nature, makes cooperation and the attainment of consensus among members easier. Together the Committee's

---

5 'The IMF is spreading our gospel. They take our rules and give out booklets derived from our work' (Basle Committee interview 1993).

members preside over those banking systems where most of the world's banking is done. This means that there is a vast pool of experiential knowledge upon which to draw. Like the BIS, the Basle Committee is strategically linked and networked. It has worked on issues with the International Accounting Standards Committee, the International Auditing Practices Committee of the International Federation of Accountants and the ICC. It has links with the EC, the European Banking Federation and securities regulators in key states. The guidelines that emerge from the Committee's work can be genuinely said to represent 'best practice'. Once the most important banking nations in the world accept these guidelines, they effectively constitute a regime of practice which most other supervisory authorities see little point in staying away from. So, for example, both the Off-shore Group of Banking Supervisors and the Commission of Latin American and Caribbean Banking Supervisory and Inspection Authorities have begun to follow the Basle Committee's guidelines (Hackney & Shafer 1986: 490–1). Most regions now have some form of supervisory grouping. For example, there is the Caribbean Supervisors Group (regular meetings since 1983) and supervisory groups from the Arab Gulf states, the SEANZA countries of the Indian subcontinent, South-East Asia and Australasia, Eastern Europe and Africa. Generally, national and regional groups of banking supervisors follow the lead of the Basle Committee, slowly turning guidelines into practice. The pace at which these regional supervisory groupings work is perhaps influenced by crises in their region. Regional meetings of supervisors may just be talk-shops. When a crisis hits, the Basle standards assume a different kind of salience for supervisors desperate to build better systems of bank supervision. At this point they become seriously interested in world's best practice. The recent banking crisis in Asia, for instance, will perhaps see the meetings of East Asia and Pacific central banks (regular meetings since 1991) become a stronger forum for the implementation of Basle best practice standards.

The way in which the Basle Committee reaches its best practice standards is nicely described by former Chairman Peter Cooke (cited in Shah 1996: 375):

> We tried very hard in the [Basle] Committee to learn from each other's experience. We sat around the room very conscious of the mistakes that each of us had made in the events that led to failures in banks and the banking system, and we all tried to learn from them. The great advantage of such a forum is that people talk very frankly about their particular experiences, and then we had a much better chance of putting in place sensible, practical and well-judged regulations to prevent further regulatory failures. Out of this process arose a corpus of best practice, which has enormously advanced the professionalism of the regulator in exercising his/her functions over the last 20 years. This has been a real benefit for every national regulator.

During the 1980s and 1990s the Basle Committee continued to extend its influence. Its approach has been to tackle specific problems, issue general guidelines and then do follow-up work on those guidelines. For example, since the 1988 Basle Accord dealing with minimum capital standards, the Basle Committee has generated 'consultative proposals' on the Prudential Supervision of Netting, Market Risks and Interest Rate Risk (April 1993), Measurement of Banks' Exposure to Interest Rate Risk (April 1993), the Supervisory Treatment of Market Risks (April 1993), the Supervisory Recognition of Netting for Capital Adequacy Purposes (April 1993) and Risk Management Guidelines for Derivatives (July 1994). Through this process the Basle Committee pushes the broader banking community towards higher levels of internalization of its standards. Its norms begin life as guidelines of best practice and become minimum standards that all must comply with. During its consultations the Committee reminds those in international banking circles that cooperating to avoid the dangers of systemic risk has an inescapable logic. It helps to build personal links between supervisors, bringing them together as part of a global village community of banking supervisors. Slowly, quietly, step by step the Basle Committee moves towards coordinating the supervision of banks around one set of standards. Progress is slow because powerful banks sometimes argue that the Basle Committee does not create the level playing field it claims, and financial experts disagree on fundamental financial concepts such as the definition of capital. Eventually a consensus does emerge, a standard is set and the Committee moves on to the next problem.

Insurance, like international banking, has acquired its own standard-setting committee in the form of the International Association of Insurance Supervisors (IAIS). Formed in 1994, the IAIS is dedicated to the task of developing standards for the supervision of the insurance industry. Like the Basle Committee, the IAIA uses the BIS infrastructure. Unlike the Basle Committee, the IAIA, being a much younger committee, has made only a few ventures into the field of standard-setting. The infrastructure of BIS is now being used for a joint forum of banking, securities and insurance harmonizers.

The OECD has been an important analyst and chronicler of financial regulatory trends (see, e.g., *Trends in International Taxation*, OECD, Paris 1985; *Trends in Banking in OECD Countries*, OECD, Paris 1985). It has also been the progenitor of important ideas in international financial regulation (e.g. the link between financial services and the international trade regime). Its Model Tax Convention on Income and Capital (which built on the work of the League of Nations) has been widely implemented by states in bilateral double-taxation treaties. One reason that the OECD's work on taxation has been so influential is that tax, unlike many other areas of international regulation, does not have a dedicated international institution. The OECD, through its Committee on Fiscal Affairs, fills this vacuum by bringing together senior tax officials from OECD countries and using them in working parties on particular issues like transfer pricing and environmental taxes. In many respects the OECD has been a remarkably successful harmonizer in the tax field. It can claim to have globalized a model of double taxation and produced a high degree of policy convergence on at least some areas of tax policy (e.g. the use of indirect taxes). The ICC is keen to maintain the OECD as the pre-eminent forum on tax policy (1998 ICC interview).

The EC has been the key player in bringing about the financial integration of the EU. It has generated many directives on different aspects of financial regulation since the 1960s. These have covered the harmonization of banking and insurance (Powell 1990) standards and some harmonization of value added taxation, but not other forms of tax. Its White Paper of 1985 on the completion of the internal market process has been a key policy document in achieving financial integration. Similarly, its Second Banking Directive of 1989 has been foundational in the creation of a single banking market in the EU. The convergence and harmonization work of the Commission is not just important to the EU, but to international monetary relations in general. In a speech in 1997, Yves-Thibault de Silguy, the member of the EC responsible for economic, monetary and financial affairs, observed that the US dollar dominated the international monetary scene, being used in 50 per cent of commercial transactions and 80 per cent of financial market operations.[6] The fact that the dollar is the hegemonic currency means that, if it chooses, the US

---

6  Yves-Thibault de Silguy, speech delivered at the Euro and Asian Financial Markets Conference, Hong Kong, 23 September 1997, Speech/97/187.

can more easily evade the 'consequences of its abuses of sound monetary policy' (de Saint Phalle 1985: 277). The European international monetary agenda is to break the hold of the US dollar over financial markets and commerce, as de Silguy's speech makes plain:

> Europe is the world's number one economic and commercial power, but has no presence on the international monetary scene. The arrival of the euro will correct this paradox, opening the way to a more balanced multi-polar international monetary system. It also opens the opportunity for the yen to develop alongside the euro. Instead of one dominant currency, there will be three – the dollar, the yen and the euro.

Japan has been far less active than Europe in promoting the idea of a regional yen bloc. The idea of a yen bloc remains precisely that – an idea. Asia's financial and trade deals remain under the currency hegemony of the US. The possible consequences of a tripolar monetary regime is explored in the Conclusion of this chapter.

### Business Actors

The ICC, as shown in other chapters, has had some degree of involvement in most areas of international regulation that affect business. Financial regulation is no exception. The ICC worked with the League of Nations and then the OECD on the issue of double taxation. The role of business NGOs in tax has gone through two distinct phases. Both the ICC and later BIAC (Business and Industry Advisory Committee to the OECD) worked hard to globalize a model of double taxation that was favourable to large business. When that model had sufficiently diffused throughout the international community, their role changed to that of the vigilant keeper of the regime. Both the ICC and BIAC carefully monitor the OECD's work on tax, reiterating their support for the arm's-length principle and downplaying the usefulness of advance transfer pricing agreements. They want the unitary method of taxation to be an optional extra (since sometimes it can lead to a lower tax assessment for a company), all the time seeking to avoid dramatic change to the existing regime. Multinational companies also carefully watch developments in tax policy. Multinational banks have been central players in the deregulation of financial services markets. They, along with the large accounting firms, were strong supporters of GATS. In the field of international banking regulation banks have supported initiatives which are essentially information exchange systems. An example is the Institute of International Finance, which was formed in 1982. Most significant commercial banks are members. The main purpose of the Institute is to collate and analyze information on the financial and economic status of debtor states (Hackney & Shafer 1986: 484–5). In this way commercial banks increase the financial transparency of states as borrowers.

The International Fiscal Association formed in 1938 is not strictly a business organization since it is comprised of individual tax experts. It has had a strong influence because of its technical expertise in comparative tax reform. It is a forum where the strengths and weaknesses of different models of tax are discussed.

Tax and international banking regulation are both areas where business activism has recently been absent, so the speed of globalization has been slow. The international business community is happy, in relation to tax, to maintain the status quo after having helped to create the bilateral model of tax. In the case of banking regulation, international banks support the building of transparency through best practice guidelines and information exchange systems. They are not prepared to go beyond coordination through guidelines.

Of profound importance to the globalization of financial regulation is the work of the International Accounting Standards Committee (IASC). The issue of international accounting standards was talked about within the accountancy profession for most of the twentieth century, but it was after the Second World War that some members of the profession, particularly those involved in servicing the needs of international business, realized that harmonized accounting standards would serve the interests of both the profession and business investors. Individuals such as Sir Henry Benson were key players in pushing the profession towards international coop-eration. The Accountants International Study Group was established in 1966 to examine the problems. The IASC was the product of the Tenth International Congress of Accountants, held in 1972. It was proposed that an international body to write accounting standards for world use be established (Samuels & Piper 1985: 70). The IASC held its first meeting in 1973.

Those individuals closely involved in the formation of IASC thought that its contribution would be evolutionary rather than revolutionary: 'I have never thought that the impact of IASC will be revolutionary or immediate…the impact will be important in the next ten years and of dominating importance in the presentation of financial statements by about the year 2000' (Benson, cited in Samuels & Piper 1985: 70).

This prediction is not far off track. The IASC is a private-sector business organization which is committed to a process of continuous improvement in the development of international accounting standards for financial reporting by business. Its accounting standards, however, are not norms of law, but non-legal norms of good practice. The IASC has to persuade business enter-prises and national accounting professions to use its international standards. Like the Basle Com-mittee, the IASC has become a strategic networker, seeking to entrench its standards in the operations of other key actors, operations which, like those of securities regulators, can some-times give obligatory force to a voluntary standard. Securities regulators have been targeted by IASC because they can insist that domestic companies and foreign issuers comply with the inter-national accounting standards developed by IASC. There are examples of Italian, US and Japanese securities regulators using international accounting standards in this way (Cairns 1996: 53). The IASC's standards have also been mandated by stock exchanges from 1999 as a condition of listing (see Chapter 9).

In addition to links with national securities regulators, IASC has links with the International Organization of Securities Commissions (where it works on international accounting standards related to multinational securities offerings), the EC (IASC standards influenced the Seventh Direc-tive on Consolidated Accounts), the World Bank and other development banks (the World Bank requires that financial reporting from borrowers comply with IASC standards), the International Federation of Accountants and national accounting standard-setting bodies (e.g. the Canadian Accounting Standards Board) (Cairns 1996). The IASC, by building cooperative links with strategic agencies, in effect creates a global network of proliferation for its standards. Moreover, since it is committed to the continuous improvement of its standards, international accounting standards are not only harmonized, but are harmonized to progressively higher standards. The globalization of accounting standards offers an example of a global regulatory ratchet, a phenomenon we theo-rize in Chapters 21 and 26. All the actors involved in the globalization of these standards (IASC, the World Bank, the SEC, the NYSE, the Financial Accounting Standards Board, the G-7) recognize the need for high standards of financial reporting. The argument over the globalization of stan-dards is not an argument about whether there ought to be global standards, but rather which stan-dards constitute world's best practice and therefore should be global. The SEC continues to prefer

US accounting standards because it believes they are higher. Since all parties are publicly committed to the principle of world's best practice none can afford to be seen as lowering accounting standards. Under these circumstances, the content if not the practice of accounting standards cannot sink to a deregulatory bottom. The question becomes, rather, who is to lead?

## Individuals

Naming some individuals important in the globalization of financial regulation means leaving out many who have played a part. Yet there is one individual in the twentieth century who strides across the financial landscape – John Maynard Keynes. Two supraregulatory institutions of world finance, the IMF and the World Bank, bear his stamp. It is hard to capture in a few words the ways in which his ideas, theories, books, articles, speeches, talks, letters, media appearances, lobbying and negotiating shaped the outcome at Bretton Woods. The following passage from a letter written to Lord Catto from Bretton Woods on 4 July 1944 reveals something of Keynes' personal involvement:

> My dear Governor,
>
> Today is the first breathing space I have had in which to write you a gossipy letter…We have reached now a point where much spadework has been done behind the scenes and the material is being consigned to small committees…and for the time being at least I am sending the other boys to the meetings and staying away myself.
> Hitherto we have been spending most of our time trying to get, so far as possible, a version agreed with the Americans behind the scenes. Over a very broad front this has been successful. Harry White is fighting various battles in his own camp and in his own press and is most disinclined to take on any issue with us if he can possibly help it – which, of course, makes it very much more easy for us to obtain satisfaction (Keynes, 4 July 1944, 77–8).

Harry Dexter White, to whom Keynes refers, was the other key individual at Bretton Woods. There were three Commissions of the Conference at Bretton Woods. Keynes was Chair of the Commission on the Bank and White chaired the Commission on the Fund.

The idea of regular high-level consultation on international monetary affairs between the states of the G-7 was, in the words of one present at the birth, the product of 'an informal Sunday afternoon chat in the White House Library' between three key Western Ministers of Finance in May 1973, Valéry Giscard d'Estaing, Helmut Schmidt and George Shultz (Karl Otto Pöhl, former President of the Bundesbank: Pöhl 1994: 9). Schmidt was also important in pressing the Bundesbank to accept the idea of the European Monetary System. The idea of a single currency for Europe had been discussed by the EC and others in the 1960s. However, it was Jacques Delors, the Chairman of the Commission from 1985 to 1994, who underpinned this goal with a concrete legislative plan of action by placing monetary union in the *Single European Act 1986* and in 1989 producing a report that outlined a three-stage process for achieving that union (Marsh 1993: 235).

## Mass Publics

Panicked mass publics have been prime movers in the regulation of banking. When bad things happen to lots of people's money, governments have to respond. Moreover, these mass publics have been international. Panic crosses borders just as easily as money. The crash of Wall Street in

1929 is a spectacular example, but there are many financial crises that have gone international and generated mass publics, to be followed by national regulatory responses. The South Sea Bubble and Mississippi Bubbles fall into this category. As part of John Laws' plan for bringing order to French fiscal affairs he created the Mississippi Company to exploit opportunities in the Mississippi basin. In 1719, 30 000 foreigners charged into Paris seeking shares in the company (Kindleberger 1978: 120). French investors scrambled to buy shares in the South Sea Company. All over Europe people were bound in a speculative frenzy. When the bubbles burst and frenzy turned to panic the UK, US and French governments learnt from the experience. A little over 100 years later, when President Jackson vetoed the extension of the charter of the Bank of the United States, he is reported to have said: 'Ever since I read the history of the South Sea Bubble I have been afraid of banks' (G. Davies 1994: 268). International concern over Herstaat, BCCI and Barings collapses all produced significant changes in global regulatory coordination.

## Epistemic Communities of Actors

> There's the OECD, the European Commission, the BIS, the G-7, the IMF – networks at different levels. It's the whole network that matters, not the forum. You've got several hundred people in the Western world in constant dialogue. The IMF is particularly important, but they all are. And it's not just the top people (Bundesbank interview 1994).

The epistemic community that steers financial regulation is a community of the North. Its most influential members are largely English-speaking. The ideas of this community now dominate the financial regulation of all states. Countries from the South are progressively converting to the key ideas of this community concerning the need for independent central banks, inflation-first policies, monetary control, fiscal restraint and open markets. It is these ideas that have formed the building-blocks of financial transformation in former communist states. In a 1998 European central bank interview we were told that these amounted to 'a paradigm of stability requirements that were imposing themselves'; we think the imposition is actually by an epistemic community of finance.

The intellectual icons of this community have been economists – Keynes and Friedman in the twentieth century, Ricardo in the nineteenth and Smith in the eighteenth century. Economists have not only contributed ideas, they have helped to develop orthodoxies of practice. Walter Bagehot, editor of the *Economist*, published *Lombard Street* in 1873. This was a highly influential synthesis of central banking practice. Before the domination of this community by economists, merchants exercised an important influence upon the ideology of financial regulation. In the seventeenth century the ideas of bullionism and mercantilism were developed by merchants like Gerard Malynes, Thomas Mun (1571–1641) and Edward Misselden (1608–54). Earlier still, in fourteenth- and fifteenth-century northern Italy, merchants established *scuole d'abbac* – schools of the abacus – along European trade routes (Nuremburg had forty-eight such commercial secondary schools by 1613), diffusing bookkeeping and auditing norms (Carruthers & Espeland 1991: 48–9).

The other arm of this community is practitioners of finance, including bankers, financiers, dealers in commercial paper, money-market players and speculators. In the nineteenth century no group exercised more influence on the world's markets and banking practices than the practitioners based in the City of London. Foreign banks like the Chartered Banks of India, Australia and China and the Standard Bank of South Africa, all doing business in the colonies, former colonies and dominions of the empire, established their headquarters in London. Directors of these banks formed interlocking patterns of influence and control with the directors of UK banks and the Bank of England (G. Davies 1994: 359). Within this group the dynastic families of merchant financiers like the Rothschilds and the Barings played the key role in developing international capital markets. These families, with their long traditions and understanding of trading and finance, came to London where through their networks they serviced states' needs for capital and investment. They understood the essential liquidity of capital, how it might be turned from one asset into another and relocated, across continents if necessary, to where the demand was. In the twentieth century this epistemic community has broadened its base. The elite families of finance have been swamped by the many professionals that have come with managerial capitalism. Yet even with mass professionalization the epistemic community of finance has retained its inner circles: 'If I want to talk to the representatives of the British banks, or indeed of the whole financial community, we can usually get together in one room in about half-an-hour' (Governor of the Bank of England in 1957, cited in Moran 1986: 15).

The IMF has an explicit policy of fostering a public finance epistemic community:

> The idea is to develop a 'club spirit' among neighbours to encourage one another to pursue sound policies. Such a tradition is most firmly established in Europe, where regional surveillance and peer pressure have produced an impressive degree of macroeconomic convergence. The G-7 also practise mutual surveillance. In Asia, there are signs of growing regional cooperation (IMF Managing Director Camdessus, IMF Survey, 6 October 1997, 294).

The Bundesbank has defined the heartland of ideas toward which this epistemic community is converging, notwithstanding the pessimism of one of its senior people in a 1994 interview:

> On microeconomics there is a consensus on objectives but disagreement on technical questions. On macroeconomics, there's no consensus on objectives, not even agreement on a diagnosis of the problem. Well, the Plaza Agreement did at least come to a common diagnosis. Germany was one out for so long on inflation discipline.

Finance is broken into epistemic communities which are interlinked – the community of central bankers, the community of treasury officials and so on. The deregulation of financial services and international trade in such services has led states to place more reliance on national competition regulators. We have seen with the global money-laundering issue that a new epistemic community can be created by one state which moves from bilaterals to constituting a core group of committed states and their financial compliance communities (the FATF) which continually adds new members who pass peer review.

## Contest of Principles

### Deregulation, Liberalization v. National Sovereignty

The logic of a liberal free-trade order is that capital, goods and labour should be free to move to those economies where profit opportunities exist. The principles of deregulation have gone a long way to implementing this logic for capital. Broadly speaking, capital has freedom of movement. States have progressively dismantled controls over capital movements. In 1997 the IMF announced that it would be seeking an amendment to its Articles so that it could become a more active proponent for the removal of members' restrictions on capital account mobility. Movement of unskilled labour remains chained by national capitalism. Global financial capitalism requires that those highly skilled in the financial arts be allowed the freedom to follow capital. Goods, through multilateral trade agreements, are progressively achieving freedom of movement.

### Conditionality v. National Sovereignty

Conditionality is the principle that access to and use of a lender's funds is linked to the borrower agreeing to meet certain requirements set out by the lender. Both the IMF and the World Bank employ conditionality. The World Bank uses conditionality in its structural adjustment lending. The IMF recognizes high and low conditionality, high conditionality requiring compliance with a specifically designed program to overcome a budget deficit. High conditionality was introduced at the insistence of the US in 1953 (Williamson 1983b: 607). During the early part of its history the IMF had made little or no use of the principle. Lending was largely automatic. 'Conditionalities' now form a central part of the IMF's lending policies. In 1968 the practice of conditionality was formally incorporated into the IMF's Articles of Agreement. Initially the increasing use of conditionality was justified on the basis of preserving the IMF's resources, and later on the basis that it was part of its task as manager of the international monetary order (Dell 1983: 28). The countries most subject to conditionality have been the poorer developing countries which have been classified as a bad risk by the world banking system. Nigeria, Uganda, Mozambique and Nicaragua are all countries that have signed adjustment deals with the IMF and the World Bank (Ghai 1991).

States borrowing money under high conditionality arrangements are subject to performance criteria which involve them agreeing to eliminate budget deficits, raise interest rates, eliminate government subsidies and devalue their currencies (David 1985: 22). Increasingly the IMF has, especially in the case of post-communist states, become involved in institution-building. Confining oneself to macroeconomic policy prescriptions in such an exercise is difficult and so, in the words of one IMF publication, 'it may be necessary now more than it was in the past for IMF conditionality to broaden its scope' (Guitián 1992: 32). The increasing involvement of the IMF in blueprinting institutions for some states appeared in our interviews at the IMF. A senior IMF official who had played a role in the loan negotiations with the Czech government told us how the IMF team found that their policy advice went well beyond macroeconomic prescriptions concerning central banking and inflation-first policies into details of banking law, contract law, company law, the role of the judiciary and so on (IMF interview, October 1993).

Conditionality is an enabling principle. It involves other principles and policies – deregulation, liberalization, privatization and monetary orthodoxy. Conditionality is a means of enforcing what one IMF official described as the 'iron laws of economics', laws which countries ignore at their peril (IMF interview, October 1993). Roughly speaking, conditionality has been linked with a monetarist approach, at first a demand-side approach (deficit reduction, devaluation, control of money supply, price deregulation, free trade) and later a complementary focus on the supply side (reduction of public sector, creation of financial deregulation, promotion of savings) (Sidell 1988: 5–6). Conditionality may also be a welfare-maximizing principle, if IMF or World

Bank policy advice is a success.[7] Through conditionality an organization like the World Bank can create welfare gains where the private lending market cannot because the market has no means of enforcing policy prescriptions, even if it could generate them in some systematic way (Vines 1996: 21). The expansion of conditionality clearly comes at the expense of national sovereignty over financial regulation. This need not necessarily be a bad thing. Some states which lack a financial plan or which have political masters with a partiality for personal financial extravaganzas may benefit from conditionality.

### Reciprocity (and Conditional MFN) v. MFN, National Treatment

Reciprocity has been a dominant principle in the regulation of trade in financial services, with many states (e.g. Denmark, France, Greece, Ireland, Italy, the Netherlands, Spain and the UK) having required, as a matter of positive law, reciprocal concessions from other states before making concessions of their own (Wang 1996: 121–2). Some regional agreements, such as NAFTA, have fully implemented the principle of MFN for financial services. GATS represents an attempt to bring unconditional MFN to trade in financial services but, as shown in the history section of this chapter, the option of conditional MFN has allowed the US with its large domestic market to use reciprocity in order to persuade other states to improve their position on trade in financial services. This particular contest involves the principle of reciprocity being used to nudge some states towards accepting unconditional MFN as the basis for trade in financial services. In the case of banking the US has traditionally followed the principle of national treatment. But US banking regulation has also been highly regulated. US banks, for instance, cannot generally enter the business of securities, a regulatory legacy of the Great Depression. Under national treatment this restriction on securities activities also applies to foreign banks. European banks, which under domestic law may engage in securities activities, are worse off in the US market than in their own. At the same time, US banks are better off in the European market than in their own. The European response has been to leave the way open, under the Second Banking Directive, for the possible operation of the principle of reciprocity (Shaw & Rowlett 1993: 115–16). This would, for example, allow Europe the option of preventing US banks from pursuing securities activities unless European banks could do the same in the US market. Since banking, insurance and securities regulation vary so much, the principle of national treatment does not necessarily produce satisfactory economic outcomes for outsiders wishing to enter the financial markets of a state because national treatment does not oblige the lifting of restrictions, merely their equalization. At a bilateral level one common solution has been to apply the principle of reciprocity. GATS is an attempt to deal with the problem multilaterally.

There is little doubt that the principle of national treatment is gradually strengthening in financial regulation. Reciprocity is only a means by which one state attempts to persuade another that national treatment on matters like the establishment of banking is the right principle to

---

7  On the difficult issue of how to define and measure success see Williamson (1983a: 129). On the question of whether IMF conditionality serves to destabilize Third World countries see Sidell (1988). Even if IMF operations are a success in terms of economic criteria, the patients in these operations, particularly Third World patients, must wonder whether the cost of structural adjustment in terms of price increases for basic food items, public sector cuts (especially to hospitals) and increased unemployment really mean these operations are successful. For a survey of some the social and political consequences of policies of structural adjustment in Third World countries see Ghai (1991).

follow. As part of the Europe Agreements signed in 1991 between the EC and Czechoslovakia, Hungary and Poland, the EC entrenched the principle of national treatment in relation to banking and other financial services.

The principle of reciprocity has been the dominant principle in international tax regulation. The MFN principle has not been widely used. In fact states have sometimes, in a bilateral negotiation, avoided agreeing to a beneficial provision for fear of being pressured to grant it to other states with which its operation would not be so beneficial (Picciotto 1992: 59). States have carefully avoided giving tax regulation to an international organization. Tax was never on the agenda at Bretton Woods or in the creation of the WTO. The OECD has served merely to advise and assist states on matters of international tax; it has created a negotiating space where the trade principles of MFN and non-discrimination are beginning to be imported into tax discussion. The dominance of the principle of reciprocity is probably best explained by the belief that it serves sovereign fiscal interests. Moreover, the operation of reciprocity in the development of international tax has been chilled by self-interested unilateralism. States that override their treaty obligations by means of domestic legislation are far more common in the international tax regime than in any other area of regulation we discuss. The intricacies of tax treaties have been shaped by the interests of capital-exporting states (linked to the taxing of residents) and capital-importing states (linked to taxing at source of income), as well as the strength of need for capital investment (linked to the grant of tax concessions by states). The present bilateral tax regime resembles the bilateral intellectual property regime of the mid nineteenth century. It, like tax, was based on reciprocity. In the case of intellectual property, the US and international business combined to place the principles of harmonization, national treatment and MFN in an international agreement (TRIPS) administered by an international organization (the WTO) with powers of enforcement. As we have seen, international business shows no signs of supporting these principles in the context of tax. States, believing that reciprocity best serves their sovereignty, continue to cling to reciprocity in tax as thirteenth-century rulers did in their tax agreements (see Chapter 7).

### Harmonization, Mutual Recognition v. Deregulation, Strategic Trade

Opposition to harmonization in banking regulation arises when the harmonized standards are considered too high. Then the principles of deregulation or strategic trade are invoked to maintain the advantage of national regulation. For example, countries which allow banks to operate with low capital ratios advantage their banks over countries that demand higher standards. Japanese banks were thought to be advantaged in this way over US and European banks. The principles of harmonization, deregulation and strategic trade behave in financial standard-setting in a way similar to the way they behave in telecommunications standard-setting (see Chapter 14). States support harmonization provided that it is their standard that will be harmonized. Sometimes the impasse between standards is resolved, in other cases the world has to learn to live with competing standards. On other occasions a group of states can force the adoption of a standard. For example, when the discussions at the Basle Committee on international capital adequacy standards became bogged down by technical disagreement, the US Federal Reserve Board and other US authorities began private discussions with the Bank of England on appropriate standards. The upshot was a document called 'Agreed proposal of the United States federal banking supervisory authorities and the Bank of England on primary capital and capital adequacy assessment'. Released on 8 January 1987, it had no legal status (Norton 1991: 89).

It was essentially announcing a 'zone of cooperation' between the US and the UK (Kapstein 1989: 340). The implicit threat was that foreign banks (especially Japanese banks, at which it was largely aimed) might not be able to do business in the US or UK unless they complied with the new standard. This was enough to move discussion of the issue back to the Basle Committee, where states eventually agreed on a set of standards.

The principle of harmonization, like the principle of national treatment, is one which is becoming stronger in financial regulation. The EC is the best example of the use of positive legal norms to implement harmonization of financial regulation. The *Single European Act 1986* made the goal of an internal market part of the Treaty Establishing the European Economic Community (Treaty of Rome 1957). The goal of an internal market is part of the continuation of the concept of a common market. The principle of harmonization (along with the principle of mutual recognition) is the principle that has to be followed if, in the words of the Treaty, there is to be 'free movement of goods, persons, services and capital' in the internal market. (Harmonization requires that the same standards be set for matters like prudential regulation, mutual recognition requires that state authorities recognize each other's application of the standards.) Directives are the means by which the principle has been given form. Directives on aspects of financial regulation can be found well before 1986 (e.g. the directives of 1960 and 1962 on the liberalization of capital movements, a directive on banking in 1977 and a directive on insurance in 1964). One of the key Directives since 1986 in financial regulation has been the second Banking Coordination Directive of 1989, which allows a member to grant a banking licence according to a common set of standards. The licence is valid in all member states, allowing the licence holder to provide services in those states. The Directive also contains a list of banking activities which all member states must recognize.

The principle of harmonization is also being extended through treaties. For instance, those states which have signed the Agreement establishing the European Free Trade Area have agreed to follow EC law on financial services, thereby extending the ambit of the principle of harmonization.[8]

### Deregulation v. National Sovereignty, Consolidation, Transparency

Given the vast changes in financial markets, the innovation in financial instruments and the growth in different kinds of financial organizations, it would be easy to conclude that the principle of deregulation is victorious. This needs some qualification. The boundaries between different kinds of depository institutions have blurred, as have the boundaries between depository and non-depository institutions. Organizations like American Express are financial supermarkets which offer a wide range of services including insurance, securities, financing, credit cards, investment advisory services and data-processing services. Global manufacturers like General Motors run finance companies and credit card systems. Banks offer brokerage, insurance, credit and debit card services.

Historically, prudential regulation has been focused on banks because banks create money. Because of changes in the nature of financial markets and organizations, the trend in OECD countries has been to extend supervisory coverage to organizations based on the nature of the financial functions they perform rather than whether they are a bank (OECD 1987b: 27).

---

8 The states which have signed are Austria, Finland, Iceland, Liechtenstein, Norway, Sweden and Switzerland.

Function-centred regulation is slowly replacing organization-centred regulation.[9] The real success of the principle of deregulation lies in the fact that its application in financial regulation is progressively removing restrictions on what different kinds of actors may do in a given market. Under deregulation, banks can offer a range of different services such as securities and insurance. Actors can enter other geographical markets (US banks in Europe, European banks in the US). Deregulation has not, however, resulted in certain kinds of activities or functions becoming free of regulation. In fact the reverse seems to have happened. No one seriously suggests that there should be less supervisory coverage of the banking function. Supervisory authorities operating in deregulated markets have in fact been successful in pushing for an extension of their supervisory powers. A good example is the secondary bank crisis in the UK in the mid 1970s. Banks not supervised by the Bank of England extended vast amounts of credit to property companies. This property boom ended in the loss of hundreds of millions of pounds and necessitated a rescue package by the Bank of England (Moran 1986: Ch. 5). It also produced the *Banking Act 1979*, which created a Deposit Protection Fund and increased the supervisory reach of the Bank of England.

The principle of deregulation has an important counterweight – the principle of consolidation. Banking and other financial services are, in modern markets, provided by entities with complex corporate structures consisting of holding companies, subsidiaries and affiliates. Prudential supervision of a banking group based on information about one part of the structure may go awry since the supervisor does not know all the bank's business. Prudential supervision is increasingly based on the principle of consolidation. The Basle Committee, which has been one of the most active supporters of the principle, defines it in this way:

> The principle of consolidated supervision is that parent banks and parent supervisory authorities monitor the risk exposure – including a perspective of concentrations of risk and of the quality of assets – of the banks or banking groups for which they are responsible, as well as the adequacy of their capital, on the basis of the totality of their business wherever conducted (Basle Committee, May 1983: 5).

Conceived in this way, the principle of consolidation implies home-country supervision that covers the globe rather than relying on host-country supervision. The principle of consolidation is also emerging in the area of tax regulation, where states led by the US are using it to counter abuses to their fiscal base. Using what is called 'controlled foreign corporations' legislation, OECD states have taxed the earnings of foreign companies which are in effect controlled by their residents. The effect of this legislation is to treat the relevant corporation as a consolidated entity for taxation purposes (Vann 1991a: 108). The principle of consolidation is co-active with transparency. Transparency requires corporate groups to make information about their balance sheet items (and increasingly their off-balance sheet items) and related data available to supervisors,[10] while the principle of consolidation requires supervisors to aggregate that information and data in ways that reveal the corporate entity's overall condition.

---

9   There is also a functional analysis of financial regulation which argues that the task of regulation should be to preserve basic financial functions within a system rather than preserve specific institutions. For a discussion see Nicholls (1998).

10  At the time of our 1998 Basle Committee interviews, the Committee's Working Group on Disclosure released six principles on bank disclosure to inform its future work on transparency.

The operating strength of the principles of consolidation and transparency in financial regulation depends on the actors' perception of systemic risk in a given area of financial regulation. In the case of banking regulation all the actors, including banks, see the need for an early warning system so that they can find out about a BCCI. The Basle Committee can develop regulatory guidelines around these principles, knowing that the perception of shared risk will help drive their implementation. More recently the IMF, as part of its response to the Asian financial crisis, has developed a Code of Good Practices on Fiscal Transparency (IMF Survey 1998: 122–4). The principles of consolidation and transparency gain state support because they are a way of states retaining and perhaps even recapturing sovereignty over their financial systems. In the case of tax regulation the perception of systemic risk is, if present, a long-run possibility which perhaps only state treasuries worry about. 'Save the tax base' simply does not elicit the same reaction as 'save the whale'. Perceptions of shared risk in tax regulation do not constitute cooperation in a regulatory community in the way that they do in banking regulation. Further, states compound the problem by failing to cooperate with each other. They believe that they can remain fiscal sovereigns by cashing in on principles that depend on them acting unilaterally, an example being the principle of lowest-cost location as manifest in tax havens. Even in the EC, where member states have adopted the idea of a qualified majority for decisions concerning the internal market, tax has been carefully dealt with. On some matters it requires a unanimous vote. As a result the harmonization of direct taxes has rarely moved beyond the stage of a draft proposal. Any one state can play the role of a veto coalition.

## Lowest-cost Location v. Harmonization, Rule Compliance, World's Best Practice, Transparency

The principle of lowest-cost location is certainly visible in financial regulation. Business leaders and business NGOs frequently parade the principle in the tax field, saying that states must remain competitive on tax. In a world of high capital mobility this suggestion has some force. The principle gives rise to a number of issues in the tax field. The first is the extent to which the principle has been responsible for competing on taxation incentives to attract foreign investment or the corporate location of services and financial activities. Evidence of the existence of competition on tax incentives seems strong, particularly in developing economies and former communist states (Owens 1993: 26). Further, it is clear that no state wishes to be perceived as tax-unfriendly to business. A related issue is the extent to which tax incentives actually affect decisions concerning foreign direct investment (FDI). There is a considerable amount of empirical literature that suggests tax incentives are not of central consequence in corporate FDI decision-making processes (Yelpaala 1984). There may be less combat over tax incentives than states believe. There is also the complex economic issue over whether competition among states over the taxation of capital is a desirable form of competition. States caught between tax competition and market disapproval of government borrowing to fund deficits may withdraw from providing public good infrastructure, to the point where economic growth suffers.

Tax is the area of financial regulation in which the principle of lowest-cost location is strongest, though Vanuatu, St Lucia and the Cayman Islands have also been important as havens from banking laws. Companies make constant use of the principle at a rhetorical level even if a state's tax regime is not the sole basis upon which they make locational and investment plans. It is a low-cost principle for them to mobilize and a high-cost principle for states to resist. Some states base their entire economies on the principle and become tax havens. Most states play a double game when it comes to tax havens and tax evasion. To help maintain the legitimacy of their domestic system in the eyes of their citizens, from time to time they talk up the need to be tough on wealthy individuals and the need for more aggressive enforcement of the rules. Covertly, they play the tax haven game. Most states end up being a tax haven *vis-à-vis* some other state's taxation system. The decision of US and UK authorities not to tax income from bonds held by non-residents proceeds on the hope of 'enforcement of their own taxes and to provide inducements for international financial markets to locate in London and New York, where they may be more effectively supervised, while in effect offering arrangements facilitating the evasion of the laws of other countries' (Picciotto 1993: 393). Developments in the field of taxes on bank interest payments (where many states have abolished withholding taxes for non-residents) mean that for the rich these taxes have become 'almost a voluntary tax' (Owens 1993: 31). One of the reasons capital is so mobile is that states, through their tax system, regularly offer inducements to relocate capital from the realms of one treasury to another. All this is leading to a quiet but deep crisis. The OECD has begun to look at the problem of 'fiscal degradation' (the use of tax incentives by one state that erodes the tax base of another state). Similarly complex derivative transactions which have had an adverse effect around the world have become a focal point of discussion at the OECD.

Outside tax, the principle is less dominant. Companies list with the New York Stock Exchange because it has the highest standards, not the lowest. In interviews at the US Federal Reserve we were told: 'It's a competitive advantage for our banks that they come from a solidly regulated home base…Regulation instills confidence though you can have a niche market based on secrecy like the Cayman Islands where confidence does not matter'. Bankers worry more about systemic risk and loss of reputation. Following the principle of lowest-cost location increases the risks of both. Lowest-cost location has not prevented cooperation on the prudential regulation of banks. The dominance of the principle of lowest-cost location in the tax field is atypical in the field of financial regulation. States and regions are realizing that financial regulatory systems designed around the principles of world's best practice and harmonization are more likely to bring economic growth and investment. 'Competition in market integrity', we were told in a Bank of England interview, was the main game. Growth of compliance staffs within financial institutions has been rapid. Merrill Lynch had a compliance staff in 1996 of about 500 (McCaffery & Hart 1998). Large institutional investors want a variety of investment options, safety, predictable returns or investments where the risks are transparent. Being able to offer this to investors means that states will increasingly take seriously the idea of following world's best practice on matters of financial regulation. For many states world's best practice will become a national objective. Even if states do not enforce the Basle capital adequacy standard, to take a key example, banks that do not meet it will be dealt with on less favourable terms by other banks – money will cost them more. States also have the stimulus of constant crises to remind them that their existing financial systems remain weak (e.g. see the survey of banking crises in Finland, Norway, Sweden, Japan and the US by the IMF in *International Capital Markets: Part II: Systemic Issues in International Finance*, IMF, Washington DC 1993).

## Mechanisms

### Military Coercion, Economic Coercion

Military coercion was a dominant mechanism of monetary harmonization in the ancient world. Once an imperial currency was introduced into a conquered territory its convenience in trade helped to promote its acceptance. The Persian gold daric and the silver shekel became the currency of Persian dominions in Asia. Philip of Macedon and his son Alexander the Great turned the stater into an imperial currency, one that was used as far away as India. Roman currency went everywhere Roman roads did.

There are also twentieth-century examples of military coercion as an instrument of globalization. When the US occupied Japan one of the first things it did was to pass laws that separated the corporate and partnership ties between Japanese banks and industry (G. Davies 1994: 587–8), changes that were only partially sustained. Generally the use of military coercion to dictate conditions of financial regulation has declined.

Economic coercion by states has been surprisingly unimportant in the globalization of financial regulation. There are some examples of its use. The veiled threat in 1987 by the US and UK that foreign banks would not be able to operate in their respective jurisdictions if they did not meet US/UK capital adequacy standards is an example. Generally, though, states have not globalized financial regulation by saying 'accept regime X or we will impose sanction Y'. The US has engaged in bilateral negotiations with states on the opening of financial markets, but these negotiations have not culminated in the use of trade sanctions. We do not mean to downplay the importance of threat. By 1991 one senior OECD official could praise the effectiveness of drumbeating about the possibility of capital flight in the context of negotiating bilateral investment agreements as 'substantially eliminating controls on direct foreign investment'.

A similar kind of economic coercion has been important in putting pressure, backed by the spectre of loss of business, on inefficient financial regulatory systems:

> If settling checks was slow in the old days you could live with it. But now the effectiveness of your system depends on the effectiveness of other systems. For example Italy was slow on settling shares, so the other links in the chain put pressure on them – the securities houses and governments from other countries (OECD interview 1991).

Many in developing countries view IMF and World Bank conditionality as economic coercion. There seems reason for this:

> They can ignore our advice on the independence of the central bank. Then we say you're foolish. You're making it hard on yourself. We say you will have to be responsible for the inflation yourself. And we'll set them down an inflation target. If they don't achieve it, they'll get no more money (IMF interview 1993).

The World Bank and the IMF use a mix of structural adjustment sticks and carrots to regulate for global deregulation of the financial sector.

## Reciprocal Adjustment

The monetary unions of Ancient Greece are early examples of how reciprocal adjustment drove monetary harmonization. City-states agreed to a common currency because it made trade among themselves easier. Once harmonization was achieved and a common currency accepted, its usefulness made the rationality of change questionable. For example, the electrum coins agreed to by the cities of Asia Minor in 500 BC were allowed to circulate as a common currency in the region under the Athenian and Persian empires because of their convenience for merchants (Burns 1965: 91–2).

**TABLE 8.1**   History of monetary and exchange rate regimes

| REGIME | PERIOD |
|---|---|
| 1  International gold standard | 1879–1914 |
| 2  Interwar instability | 1918–1939 |
|     Floating | 1918–1925 |
|     Return to gold | 1925–1931 |
|     Return to floating | 1931–1939 |
| 3  Semi-fixed rate dollar standard | 1945–1971 |
|     Establishing convertibility | 1945–1958 |
|     Bretton Woods system proper | 1958–1971 |
| 4  Floating rate dollar standard | 1971–1984 |
|     Failure to agree | 1971–1974 |
|     Return to floating | 1974–1984 |
| 5  EMS and greater deutschmark zone | 1979–1993 |
| 6  Plaza–Louvre intervention Accords | 1985–1993 |
| 7  Drift towards renewed global floating | 1993– |

*Source:* Reprinted from Hirst and Thompson (1996: 32)

Reciprocal adjustment has fluctuated in intensity in international monetary regulation. This is because reciprocal adjustment works best when actors view their long- and short-term interests in the same way. That is to say, they believe that they have a strong reason to engage in international cooperation today, tomorrow and next week as well as for years. When actors in the international system believe that their reciprocally linked short-term interests are part of a continuum with their reciprocally linked long-term interests, reciprocal adjustment is most robust. Regimes produced under this set of conditions are more likely to have a period of continuous evolution (international telecommunications regulation is one such area). Financial regulation is a domain in which the perception of a continuum between short-term and long-term interests continually breaks up. Reciprocal adjustment does not operate continually. The pattern is one of crisis causing short-term and long-term interests to rejoin, thereby allowing the formation of a regime, followed by a period of stability in which long-term and short-term interests gradually separate, with the next crisis pushing them back together to form yet another regime. Table 8.1, which summarizes international monetary cooperation in the twentieth century, reveals how the operation of reciprocal adjustment has fluctuated.

All states recognize that they have a long-term interest in an international monetary system that equilibrates imbalances of payments between states. The universal gold standard that operated in the early twentieth century was, it was thought for a while, one means by which imbalances in international payments could be adjusted. The Bretton Woods system was another. International monetary crises remind states of their long-term interests in finding a means of adjustment. They allow leading economic minds to travel to places like Bretton Woods and devise a set of regulatory institutions for the world. But the recognition of this long-term interest is undermined by the fact that adjustment costs. A government may find it easier not to impose policies of inflation control on its voting citizens. Restraining the supply of credit is not an easy policy to sell, especially if powerful cronies are demanding credit. On the other hand, savvy politicians sometimes like to be forced to do this by the IMF, then blame Washington for the unpopular measures.

It is international crises, both financial and non-financial, that remind actors within the international monetary system that the long-run fate of the system in which they participate is the responsibility of all. Central banks probably appreciate this best. Examples of central bank cooperation go back a long way. In 1825 the Bank of France shipped gold to the Bank of England, which was experiencing a crisis, and in 1847 the Bank of England returned the favour (Kindleberger 1984: 64). The Cuban missile crisis, the assassination of President Kennedy and the sterling crisis of 1963 brought about very high levels of central bank cooperation (Whittlesey 1968: 261). There are also examples of cooperation between states on exchange rates before central banking. Einzig (1970: 165) documents examples of treaties between European states since 1523. Crises invigorate the mechanism of reciprocal adjustment. They stimulate the defence of an existing system or promote the search for a new one. They allow those charged with the duty of preventing the danger of systemic risk to make strides in cooperation among a broader community caught in the race for short-term profits.

Reciprocal adjustment is a mechanism to which actors persistently return in financial regulation. But they also regularly abandon it in favour of an important short-term interest. For example, both the US and West Germany (as it then was) had reason to cooperate on the international regulation of Eurocurrency markets, since both were worried about the effects of those markets on their capacity to control monetary policy. The US proposal for coordinated reserve requirements to apply to Euromarkets was initially supported by the Bundesbank. That support was subsequently withdrawn, for entirely domestic reasons. With the Bundesbank's counter-proposal not gaining US support, the negotiations on the regulation of the markets broke down (Dale 1984: 27, 42). On the defining issue of inflation-first, Bundesbank leadership has not really been based on mutual adjustment but on one-way adjustment, not on cooperation through international deals but on national responsibility:

> If the deal is interest rate stability, fine. Cooperation can work then in a common framework. It's dialogue really, not deals. Our position is each country must put its own house in order – achieve domestic price stability. There is an accountability argument against international coordination (Bundesbank interview 1994).

One could make the same point about a public sector deficit no higher than 3 per cent of GDP as a condition for European monetary union in the Maastricht Treaty.

Tax offers a third example of the way in which the operation of reciprocal adjustment fluctuates in intensity. When states introduce beggar-thy-neighbour tax measures they generate negative externalities for other states. States have reciprocal interests in avoiding these externalities. Reciprocal adjustment has produced a system of international treaties based on bilateral treaties. But at the same time states have retained tight sovereign control over the details of the bilateral treaties they negotiate, as well as which states they negotiate treaties with. In Picciotto's words, the bilateral system has been 'a rather crude method for achieving harmony between tax systems' (Picciotto 1992: 62). It has been an imperfect harmony based on the desires of individual states to retain a maximum slice of the fiscal cake, thereby seeking to preserve their sovereignty rather than give it up in order to achieve a better global tax system. When the degradation of their respective fiscal bases becomes a clear long-term crisis, states will be forced to return to reciprocal adjustment in a more serious and committed way.

**TABLE 8.2** International monetary, securities and banking crises

### INTERNATIONAL MONETARY AND SECURITIES CRISES

| | |
|---|---|
| 1971 | Breakdown of Bretton Woods |
| 1970s | OPEC inflation shock |
| 1980s | International debt crises (Polish crisis, Mexican crisis, Brazilian crisis etc.) |
| 1985–1986 | Fall of the overvalued dollar |
| 1987 | World-wide stock market crash (followed by the aftershock of 1989) |
| 1994–1995 | Mexican crisis |
| 1998 | Russian crisis |

### BANKING CRISES

| | |
|---|---|
| 1973–1975 | UK secondary banking crisis |
| 1989 | US savings and loans crisis |
| 1987–1992 | Banking crises in Finland, Norway and Sweden |
| 1990 on | Japanese banking crisis over real estate loans |
| 1997 on | Asian banking crisis |

### SIGNIFICANT INDIVIDUAL FAILURES

| | |
|---|---|
| 1974 | Herstaat Bank, Franklin National Bank |
| 1983 | Continental Illinois Bank, Banco Ambrosiano SpA |
| 1991 | BCCI |
| 1995 | Barings |
| 1996 | Sumitomo |
| 1998 | Long-term Capital Management |

The analytical work being done on this problem at the OECD suggests that reciprocal adjustment is working at least weakly in this field. International banking regulation is also a good example of the complex interplay between short-term and long-term interests that gives reciprocal adjustment a cyclical operation. Despite the debt crisis, the failure of countless banks in numerous Western countries and regular warnings from institutions like the IMF about weaknesses in national banking systems, the best that Western states have been able to devise for international banking regulation is a loose form of coordination based on the work of an informal committee working with guidelines. Adjustment in international monetary relations since 1972 has perhaps focused more on adjusting to the consequences of a US policy of unilateralism concerning the dollar (Germain 1997: 144) than on adjustment based on a reciprocity of interests.

This said, reciprocal adjustment will probably become a stronger mechanism of globalization in financial regulation for the simple reason that the world's financial system has been in fairly constant crisis with the occasional outbreak of stability (see Table 8.2, which sets out some highlights). Reciprocal adjustment drives the global harmonization of financial regulation and crises drive actors to use reciprocal adjustment. When one form of coordination breaks down, another kind emerges to take its place. Webb (1991: 309–42), for instance, argues that the coordination of the 1960s on balance-of-payments financing and exchange rate coordination was replaced by coordination on monetary and fiscal policies. In February 1999, G-7 Finance Ministers approved the creation of a new committee to watch over the global financial system. The membership of this committee includes G-7 central bankers, finance officials, IMF members, the BIS and the World Bank.

## Non-reciprocal Coordination

'I can't see any practical policy for trading monetary policy for say free trade' (Bundesbank interview 1994). More than this, the new orthodoxy of independent central banks that pursue their inflation targets with resolute unwillingness to bend to other political objectives has made non-reciprocal coordination structurally impossible for central bankers. Policy horse-trading is a game the 1990s central banker cannot play. They would not be taking seriously their chartered norm of independence if they did. Moreover, 'at the G-7, heads of central banks are not there and heads of state cannot commit heads of central banks' (US Federal Reserve interview). Heads of central banks, in turn, can't trade other political benefits.

This mechanism has not been significant, with the important exception of the Uruguay Round where states with interests in agriculture agreed to support the US initiative on trade in services in exchange for concessions on agriculture. In the post-Uruguay GATS negotiations non-reciprocal coordination is often a fact of bilaterals: 'I'll give you deregulation of foreign bank licensing if you give my national airline access to your protected air services market'.

## Modelling

Modelling has been one of the key mechanisms in the globalization of financial regulation. Two kinds of modelling have dominated – modelling from core to periphery and modelling among core states. An obvious example of core periphery modelling is the use of London banking models throughout the British empire (Sayers 1952). British banking followed colonial trade routes. One of the reasons that the British banking model was so widely followed in the nine-teenth century was that it exported not only capital, but personnel (G. Davies 1994: 360). Institutes of Bankers were set up in England, Wales and Scotland. Bankers trained by these institutes found employment and promotion in overseas banks, where they followed British methods and practices. Immigrant Scots were particularly important in bringing British banking practices to dominion banks (Sayers 1952: 3).

Another illustration of core to periphery modelling is the Japanese financial system, which is the product of a number of Western regulatory models. Beginning with the Meiji Restoration, using Western advisers like the English banking adviser Alexander Shand, Japan reconstructed its financial system from an eclectic mix of Western regulatory models (Patrick 1967: Ch. 8). The Bank of Japan established in 1882 was modelled on the Belgian Central Bank. One of the early specialist banks of Japan, the Hypothec Bank, was based on the French Crédit Foncier and the Japanese *National Banking Act 1872* was modelled on the US system.

Fear drives the second kind of modelling – fear of volatile markets, systemic collapse, the political fallout of institutional collapse, the pace of financial innovation and its unknown consequences and so on. These fears form an incentive to regulatory learning. Regulators operating in core states with sophisticated financial markets spend a lot of time talking to and learning from regulators in other such markets, studying their models about how to manage risk and protect the financial system. The widespread introduction of deposit protection schemes in OECD countries is an example of this. Core to core modelling has been important in tax. For example, most OECD states have controlled foreign corporations (CFC) legislation. The aim of CFC legislation is to impose a tax liability on residents who are attempting to avoid tax liability through the holding of shares in tax haven companies. The US CFC legislation enacted in 1962 served as a model for West Germany's legislation (Picciotto 1992: 144). Other OECD states have also moved towards using this legislation to combat tax avoidance, with the OECD playing a role in helping to harmonize CFC provisions.

In recent decades the Bundesbank has been an important model of political independence in an anti-inflationary monetary policy. The IMF has been the leading missionary for this central bank independence model: 'History teaches us that governments that have monetary policy in the hands of politicians have not been as effective in fighting inflation. Because the politicians take a short-term view at election time they create inflationary expectations' (IMF interview 1993).

Financial regulation is deeply intertwined with technology. When technological systems are modelled regulatory practices also change. For example digital technology has meant that transfer and settlement can take place without the need for people to meet. Electronic systems for securities transfer and settlement that have proved successful in major financial markets have been copied in smaller markets. For example, the Australian company Austraclear Ltd offers an electronic securities and settlement service that draws on two European systems, Euro-clear and CEDEL. The Group of Thirty has considered the possibility of a single global clearing system.

Money could not have globalized as a standardized medium without metallurgy, credit without paper, derivatives without digital technology.

Financial regulation also reveals how modelling, a mechanism of individual agency, can fail to work when structural systems remain closed to the voice of the model missionary. In the inter-war years of monetary regulation, innovative ideas along the lines of a Bretton Woods system were put forward by individuals like Keynes (Clarke 1977: 58). But mass unemployment, social instability and increasingly intense nationalistic politics – a politics of distrust – saw citizens engulfed by ideologies that cost many of them their lives. Confronted with oppositional forces of this magnitude, individual modellers stood little chance of their models being followed.

### Systems of Reward

Systems of reward have not been strong in the globalization of financial regulation. An example where it has been used was the Baker plan proposed by the US Secretary of the Treasury, James A Baker, in 1985 in response to the debt crisis of international banks. Baker's proposal was that commercial banks and the World Bank would continue lending (to the tune of $US20 billion) to developing countries with severe debt problems. The idea was that it would encourage states which became part of the program to adopt more market-oriented policies in order to recover economic growth. The Marshall Plan under which the US agreed to provide economic aid to Europe after the Second World War is another example of this mechanism. The US saw the aid as a means of allowing Europe to move sooner rather than later on compliance with Bretton Woods rules, to the extent that it attempted to use Marshall aid as the basis for increased scrutiny of European exchange rate policies (Walter 1991: 160–1). It was also a $US350 million contribution under the Marshall Plan that shifted European states away from a bilateral to a multilateral clearing system (called the European Payments Union) to deal with the settlement of international trade payments (Germain 1997: 84).

### Capacity-building

The OECD, IMF and World Bank are all involved in providing assistance to states on aspects of financial regulation. This takes the form of technical assistance, training and education. An example of coordinated assistance is the field of tax for states making the transition to market economies. This assistance operates through regional tax centres (International Fiscal Association 1994: 160). The Basle Committee has held annual seminars since 1987 for up-and-coming bank supervisors, including those from non-G-10 countries. The BIS gives technical assistance to the central banks in Eastern European states. With other international organizations, it participates in running the Joint Vienna Institute, an institute devoted to training in central banking and financial regulatory practices.

When states hit a financial crisis the IMF sends in a team, sometimes of dozens of economists, sometimes a joint team with the World Bank and other institutions, to help design a plan to deal with the crisis and prevent another. After the diagnosis is completed, the client state prepares a letter of intent for a macroeconomic and microeconomic reform program. This becomes the basis for a structural adjustment package. The World Bank is more bottom-up and microeconomic in its capacity-building, the IMF more top-down, crisis-driven and macroeconomic.

Capacity-building in the field of financial regulation relates strongly to the capacity of states to transplant a regulatory model from one system to another. A tax expert hired by the IMF travels to Lesotho, where he or she meets a drafting expert sent there under another country's foreign aid program. The two of them blueprint and draft a new tax system for Lesotho in a week or two. The draft is handed to the local politicians to enact and the two experts move onto the next job, the next developing state. The capacity to administer the new tax system is another kind of capacity. This requires trained tax officials, a tax-literate judiciary, an accounting profession and so on. The kind of capacity needed to run a financial regulatory system is much harder to build. More resources are devoted to the first kind of capacity-building, the capacity to acquire rather than the capacity to manage.

## Conclusion

Financial markets are often thought to be the prime example of the way in which globalization has cost states their sovereignty. The conclusions we are about to draw from our discussion of financial regulation do not all travel in this direction. We want to suggest that the globalization of financial regulation may deliver better outcomes for states in terms of sovereignty than has been their historical experience to date.

Persons engaged in the international trade of tangibles and intangibles (apart from currency) find it convenient to have a stable exchange regime, preferably with fewer rather than more kinds of currency. The desire for one stable money goes back to ancient times. Even those trading in currencies with a view to profiting from the devaluation of one currency in relation to another try to pass on, by means of derivatives, as much of their risk as they can. The financial history we have examined shows that exchange rate stability, when it occurs, has usually been linked to a hegemonic dominant currency. The problem with such a currency is that the hegemon has a shield that allows it to escape the full costs of breaking agreed monetary discipline. State sovereignty under these conditions is a fragile sovereignty, perhaps genuine for only a few states. This is true whether the regime is one of floating exchange rates or a rule-based one. Under a floating arrangement the holder of the hegemonic currency has possibly even more power. The US is in a stronger position now to influence the dollar than under the Bretton Woods regime, where it could only influence the dollar exchange rate within set margins (Williamson 1977: 200). Nor have macro regulatory systems based on a hegemonic currency necessarily delivered efficient capital flows. Under the classical gold standard of the twentieth century, capital tended to have an Anglo-American orbit – the Bretton Woods system did not have a genuinely global membership (Held et al. 1999: 198, 221).

One possible solution to the problem of a hegemonic dominant currency is that suggested by Keynes and others – a world central bank. This is an intellectually defensible option. Of course, the US, Europe and Japan would have to be persuaded to agree to it. For this reason it seems infeasible (see Chapter 20). The link between tyranny and the control of money, established in Ancient Greece, lives on in nationalist, federalist and regional memory. Another regulatory solution is the one which may yet evolve, a tripolar monetary regime which operates in highly liquid and deep capital markets. Whether this will occur is open to question. Since the historical path of monetary regulation begins with single hegemonic currencies, it may not lead to a tripolar regime. There is some evidence that a tripolar regime is developing in relation to interest rates, with the power of the US Federal Reserve Board to influence interest rates globally partially circumscribed in the last few years by the regional powers of the Bundesbank and Tokyo (Germain 1997: 159). There are some influential supporters in the US, Japan and Europe for such a 'new Bretton Woods'. Our description of actors showed that the EC explicitly saw European monetary union as an opportunity for a more balanced international monetary system. The euro and yen would form a counterweight to the dollar. A Director of the European Central Bank we interviewed in 1998 viewed talk of a tripolar 'new Bretton Woods' as going too far, especially in relation to the yen. However, he did feel the arrival of the euro would cause a 'competition to be good. By good I mean achieving price stability. Also a good settlement system, a smoothly functioning payment system, etc. But good mainly means price stability attached to a healthy economy'.

A tripolar monetary regime has the potential to overcome the problems associated with a hegemonic dominant currency. The capacity of any one member of the triad to defect from agreed monetary discipline and goals is reduced, because there are two other dominant currencies that can be tapped for investment, as a reserve currency and for use in commercial transactions. There is an added danger for a state in defecting. Speculators, using the resources of highly liquid global markets, may launch a speculative attack on the defector's currency. Such an attack could be successfully resisted, but it would weaken the defector. A successful defence might require cooperation from the other members of the currency triad, which might not be forthcoming if the defector was reneging on agreed goals of world monetary policy. Under conditions of tripolar monetarism speculators might play a more constructive role than they presently do. As an independent force they could weaken or coerce a defector, but would never be able to launch a successful attack on one member of the triad when two or more combined against the attack. Two or more members of the triad would always have a rational reason to combine if the member being attacked was sticking to agreed monetary discipline. Speculators, under this set of conditions, would be more likely to be the enforcers of that set of economic ideas constituting the prevailing monetary orthodoxy to which states had for the time being bound themselves.

The essential idea behind tripolar monetarism is that of a separation of monetary power between three key states and the global foreign exchange markets. The power of global foreign markets to dominate the currencies of states might further be reduced by implementing a proposal put forward by the Nobel laureate James Tobin in 1972, for a currency transactions tax. The size of global capital flows means that those who can direct the flows can make enormous profits by betting on or bringing about very small changes in currency exchange and interest rate movements. The bulk of transactions in these markets is short-term, with 80 per cent of all transactions making a round trip in a week or less (Haq-ul, Kaul & Grunberg 1996b: 3). Tobin's original proposal was for a tax of 1 per cent on 'all spot conversions of one currency into another' (Tobin in Haq-ul, Kaul & Grunberg 1996b: 1). Since then he has suggested that the tax would have to be lower, between 0.25 per cent and 0.1 per cent. The key feature of the tax is that it 'would automatically penalize short-horizon round trips, while negligibly affecting incentives for commodity trade and long-term capital investments' (Tobin 1996: xi). If states agreed on it, it would raise a huge amount of revenue, enough to reverse the fiscal crisis states face from the race to the bottom in tax rates.[11]

Another feature of tripolar monetarism is that it does not depend on the cooperation of one key state. At the same time it does not invite the kind of competition without cooperation that featured in the beggar-thy-neighbour rate policies of states in the 1930s. The economic case for monetary coordination is mixed (Cohen 1993: xv). Economic analysis has identified cases where monetary coordination between two central banks is not welfare-enhancing (e.g. Rogoff 1985). The basic case, however, for some form of international monetary coordination remains unanswerable. The real question relates to the optimal form of this cooperation. One reason that states may become more interested in tripolar monetarism is that it is less dependent on the cooperation of many for its institutionalization than is the option of a world central bank. It is also less vulnerable to collapse when one key member defects. Finally, tripolar monetarism may not require high levels of cooperation to sustain it. All that might be required between the three dominant currency states would be a contract of understanding concerning exchange rates, with currency speculators acting as monetary watchdogs over that agreement. Interestingly, George Soros, writing about the possibility of coordination between the dollar and the euro, observes that such coordination would not necessarily involve the complete integration of the two currencies (which would be cooperation-intensive). There could be, he suggests, 'almost unlimited swap agreements in which each side would guarantee the other against a change in the rate of exchange' (Soros 1998: 186). We saw earlier that the BIS had played a role in devising a currency swap network in the 1960s, which contributed to exchange rate stability at that time. Under tripolar monetarism there could be a much more limited, but much more powerful, network of swap agreements. We may be better off, in other words, to encourage monetary collusion between key players rather than attempting to devise cooperation-intensive monetary regimes. Weak states may get less protection from a vote on a world central bank board than from a tripolar system where the strong check each other's worst abuses.

Banking and its regulation begins with the customs of merchants, as does the international provision of credit. Actors other than merchants became enmeshed in this system. Merchant financiers regulated by customary norms of banking came to regulate states, or rather the sixteenth-century rulers who needed credit to turn territories into states. Their need for credit entangled international financiers in court intrigues. The practice of individual bankers regulating states in various ways continued in the twentieth century, with J.P. Morgan and James Stillwell saving the US financial system in 1907. Banking regulation is in an era in which states for perhaps the first time are in a position to establish a meaningful sovereignty over their banking systems. It is only states that can provide the kind of international coordination on prudential supervision that modern transparency capitalism requires. The shift to transparency capitalism is discussed in the next chapter.

---

11 On the issues of the feasibility and enforceability of the Tobin Tax see Haq-ul, Kaul and Grunberg (1996a: Chs 4, 5 and 6).

Integrated capital markets are hardly a twentieth-century phenomenon. The capital markets of Amsterdam and London were highly integrated in the first quarter of the eighteenth century (Neal 1990: Ch. 7). Similarly financial crises, as Kindleberger (1978) shows, have tended to be international. Nation-states have for a long time, in other words, been exposed to volatilities and crashes in foreign financial markets. What is different now is that there are many more entry-points into these markets than there were in the eighteenth century, many more points on the globe where a crisis can begin. Finally, in the case of regulating their own banking systems, nation-states have been faced with the problem of ignorance. Much of the history of banking regulation in the eighteenth and nineteenth century is the history of central banks learning to understand the operations of emerging banking systems under conditions of crisis and integrated financial markets. The Bank of England was well ahead of other central banks, but it did not reach the zenith of its influence till the end of the nineteenth century. The truth about national supervisory power over banking is that for the most part it has been based on uncertainties about how to exercise that power, imperfect information flows between national regulators concerning international crises, and a lack of early warning systems to detect the development of those crises. The existence of multinational banking offers states the opportunity to develop international supervisory standards which will make the exercise of their national supervisory power much more effective than it has been in the past. The need for detailed international standards work on banking supervision was realized in the 1970s, leading to the creation of the Basle Committee in 1974. Equally important was the death of an idea – the idea that moral suasion could form the basis of a system of prudential regulation. The secondary banking crises in England in the 1970s, the Johnson Matthey Bankers crisis of 1984 and the international debt crisis made the Bank of England quietly bury this idea, although occasionally its office-bearers still refer to the importance of 'customary powers of persuasion' (Quinn (Executive Director of the Bank of England) 1991: 6).

The international reality which is emerging through the work of the Basle Committee, BIS and the EC is that of internationally coordinated standard-setting for international banking. Admittedly the standards take the form of guidelines rather than norms of positive law. Increasingly, they are likely to discuss disclosure of consolidated corporate risk management systems and the outcomes they are guaranteeing (Dale 1996: 164–8) – enforced self-regulation (Ayres & Braithwaite 1992), an issue we discuss further in the next chapter. But these reflexive standards represent best practice. No regulator wants to face the uncertainties of globalized banking without best practice standards. In any case, these standards will find their way into the legal systems of the key states such as the US and Germany (Norton 1991: 94). The process of convergence that the Basle Committee has begun will take time. Experts will continue to have technical disagreements about what constitutes risk, how to measure it and what standard represents best practice. But the process of devising an internationally accepted set of supervisory standards is irreversible. Lead states support the process, as do the banks. Bank deaths in global financial markets remind all banks that these markets may be their graveyard. Banks have responded by creating risk management systems and stress-testing their books for possible disaster scenarios. The Basle Committee and banks exchange information about these systems and how they might be used to improve supervision (Hayward 1991: 77). Fear of risk inclines them to share information about risk technology (see Chapter 9).

Small committees with senior membership and high levels of technocratic expertise along the lines of the Basle Committee may end up leading an organic process of norm-building in global financial regulation. Such committees and their networks, linked to other committees and their networks, constitute the dialogic webs of global financial regulation, webs which we argue (in Chapter 23) are fundamental to understanding the accomplishment of globalization. Reciprocal adjustment may no longer take the form of mega-institution-building that led to the institutions of Bretton Woods. The WTO represents the fulfilment of a Bretton Woods plan that included a global institutional trade pillar. Adjustment in the future may come more through an accretion of committees, for example the IASC working with IOSCO, IOSCO with the Basle Committee, BIS working with a committee set up by the G-7 to oversee global financial regulation and so on – small regulatory groups with strategic networks working towards better systems of banking governance, more transparency, more common standards and allowing banks the flexibility to exceed those standards through their own risk management systems. Rewiring rather than building a 'new financial architecture' is the way that global financial regulation may go.

Even so, it is somewhat shocking that international regulatory monitoring to catch money-laundering by drug dealers is more rigorous than the monitoring and peer review of capital adequacy and risk management by banks. Major banks mostly comply, but considering that the simultaneous collapse of a few minor ones could cause a systemic crisis, the monitoring and enforcement failure in this area is of concern.

The principles of transparency and consolidation which lie at the core of emerging international supervisory standards for banking will also apply to other basic areas of finance, such as insurance. Insurance regulation remains locked into diverse models of national regulation. But as the boundaries between insurance and banking functions blur and banks and insurance companies become part of the same corporate group structure, insurance activities will succumb to internationalizing supervisory principles negotiated at Basle.

The globalization of financial regulation has not been about the loss of state sovereignty. Lack of cooperation between states on international monetary policy has at times cost states and their citizens dearly. The sovereignty which states have exercised over their banking systems has not been particularly effective. Taxation is perhaps the one area of financial regulation where there has been a genuine erosion of state sovereignty that has also affected individual citizens. There is little doubt that tax competition between states and the bilateral model of international taxation has not served the economic and social development interests of states or their citizens. The problem does not lie in a shortage of ideas about what to do. There are regulatory proposals and technologies to deal with these problems, in the form of accounting techniques of consolidation, unitary methods of taxing multinationals and the suggestion of a General Agreement on Tax to solve the coordination problem among states. The real problem lies elsewhere. However, the issue of international taxation lacks the systemic crises that would help to realize solutions. Perhaps indirect tax avoidance through shopping on the Internet will fuel that crisis. When banking failures and the debt crisis threatened the entire world's bank system in the 1970s and 1980s, banking regulators were left in no doubt that something had to be done. Likewise, international environmental regulation (see Chapter 12) progresses much faster in an atmosphere of crisis. At a 1994 interview with the EPA we asked about the prospects of a carbon tax. Tellingly, our interviewee replied that the prospects for a carbon tax would improve 'if we have a couple of hot summers'. Carbon taxes need hot summers, international tax regulation needs visible crises of fiscal degradation. An Internet tax, a carbon tax, a Tobin tax, MFN in corporate tax (no tax cuts to attract foreign investment that are not also given to domestic firms) are all possible elements for a future General Agreement on Tax.

| Corporations and Securities

## History of Globalization

### Corporatization and Securitization

Corporations and securities are institutions which were generally unknown until the nineteenth century. Even in Europe during the nineteenth century, corporations were few in number and few people understood what securities were. Today these institutions are ubiquitous and influential everywhere. They are creations of law, abstract objects quite different from physical objects like ships and food (which are the subject of later chapters). Ships and food were known before maritime law and food law. In contrast, it is the globalization of companies and securities law that constitutes the corporatization and securitization of the world.

Corporations existed for more than a millennium before securities. For our purposes, a security is a transferable instrument evidencing ownership or creditorship, as a stock or bond.[1] The legal invention of the security in the seventeenth century was the most transformative movement in the history of corporations. It enabled the replacement of family firms with very large corporations based on pooled contributions of capital from thousands of shareholders and bondholders. These in turn enabled the great technological projects of eighteenth- and nineteenth-century capitalism – the railroads, the canals, the mines.

When it was first invented, however, the historical importance of the security had nothing to do with the corporatization of the world. Rather, it transformed state finances through bonds that created long-term national debts. Still today, some of the most important securitization involves a transformation of banking and finance, not the creation of new corporations. An example is mortgage-backed securities – securities backed by bundles of loans on real estate, automobiles or credit cards issued by banks (Cooper & Fraser 1993: 222). Even FIFA's insurance cover against soccer's World Cup being cancelled has been securitized. These securities may not create or be issued by corporations (e.g. when they are issued by a government home-loan insurance organization). Other forms of securitization, such as the privatization of fractions of the state by selling them to shareholders, continue to accelerate the corporatization of the world. Securitization has therefore been a great historical force in its own right as well as the major cause of an even greater historical force – corporatization.

---

1 There are more formal and legally technical definitions in other jurisdictions. For a discussion see Sykes (1986: 12–13).

While the idea of dividing the national debt into bonds was invented in Naples in the seventeenth century, it was England that, by the eighteenth century, used the idea in a financial revolution that helped it gain an upper hand over its principal rival, France (Dickson 1993). England seized full national control of public finance: formerly private tax- and customs-collecting were nationalized in the seventeenth century, a Treasury Board was established in the eighteenth century, and finally the Bank of England was given national regulatory functions. The Treasury Board realized that the national debt could be made in effect self-liquidating and long-term, protecting the realm from extortionate interest rates during war and from the kind of vulnerability that had brought the Spanish empire down when short-term loans had to be fully repaid after protracted war. Instead of making England hostage to a Continental banker, the national debt was divided into thousands of bonds, with new bond issues placed on the market to pay for old bonds that were due to be paid.

> The long-term debt converted itself almost spontaneously into a perpetual debt. From now on, it did not have to be repaid by the state which, by converting its floating debt into a consolidated debt, did not have to exhaust its credit or cash reserves. As for the subscriber, he could now transfer his title to a third party – this was allowed after 1692 – and thus recover his initial payment at any time. This was a miracle: the state never repaid the loan, but the lender could recover his money whenever he wanted it (Braudel 1979: 526–7).

Securitization paid for the warships that allowed Britannia to rule the waves, to trade and colonize. A good investment for British bondholders and its state and a transformative one.

## Globalizing Regulatory Innovation Enables Globalizing of the Corporate Form

A transformation of even greater importance has been the rise of the corporation. Its sweep has been utterly global; there is no nation where corporations do not dominate economic and social life. The largest transnational corporations have incomes higher than the GDPs of most states. In fact, for the first time, in the mid 1990s, the majority of the 100 largest 'economies' in the world were corporations (Anderson & Cavanagh 1996).

Yet in the US, where incorporation began earlier and more vigorously than elsewhere, there had been only 335 incorporations by 1800 (Davis 1961: vii). Today, in contrast, when important things are done, whether for good or ill, they are more likely to be the actions of corporations than of individuals. Ronald Burt has shown (in Coleman 1982: 12) that during the century from the 1870s to the 1970s the percentage of front-page space in the *New York Times* devoted to individual persons fell continuously and the proportion devoted to corporate actors rose continuously. By the end of the Second World War three times more of the front page was devoted to corporate actors than to persons. In the middle of the nineteenth century, fewer than 20 per cent of participants in New York State Court of Appeals cases were corporations; in 1923, for the first time, the number of corporate participants exceeded the number of individuals (Grossman, cited in Coleman 1982: 11).

Two inventions of northern Italian merchants were primarily responsible for the initial rise of the business corporation. One was double-entry bookkeeping, developed in Italy during the fifteenth century (which was enabled by replacing the Roman with the Arabic number system). Double-entry bookkeeping enabled the creation of the business as a financial entity, a fund separate from the affairs of the merchants who invested in it, yet linked to them through entries of debits and credits. The metaphysics of the firm as an independent financial entity was complemented by the Italian lawyers' invention of the corporation as a *persona ficta*. The corporation was given a legal personality distinct from that of its members, yet linked to them through rights and duties.

These are the features that define a corporation: it is a group of individuals who create a financial entity separate from their personal finances that is granted a legal identity by the state as a corporate person. By definition, regulation therefore creates corporations (as well as shapes their form) because state law is necessary for the authoritative designation of a group of individuals as a corporate person. Once that recognition had been granted, the corporation could own land, enter into contracts, sue and be sued and ultimately be held criminally responsible.

The need to accommodate such a legal personality to collective entities predates the rise of the business corporation. In the Middle Ages, the most important corporations were the ecclesiastical owners of land and accumulators of wealth in perpetuity, municipal corporations responsible for the governance of the emerging towns and cities, universities, schools, charitable hospitals and, most importantly, guilds. The medieval rise of corporate power which was independent of state power had been foreseen by Roman emperors, who for this reason did not encourage the institution. For example, emperor Trajan writes to Pliny the Younger:

> **Pliny:** A great fire has devastated Nicomedia. Would it be in order to establish a society of 150 firemen?
>
> **Trajan:** No. Corporations, whatever they're called, are sure to become political associations (Davies 1997: 191).

Despite these political fears, Roman law by Justinian's time accorded the status of corporation to many groups including religious cults, burial clubs, guilds, churches, hospitals, asylums and orphanages (Berman 1983: 216). The principles of Roman corporate law were part of the reception of Roman law into medieval Europe that we described in Chapter 7. Drawing on these principles, as well as on German and Christian concepts, canonists fashioned a corporations law that gave the Church a distinctive corporate personality and provided later Western corporate law systems with their conceptual foundations. Canon law made its own contributions to Anglo-American company law; these were at odds with the Roman tradition, such as the Christian notion of 'the legal absorption of the group in its headship' (Davis 1961: 238). It was the canonists of the thirteenth century, not the earlier Roman lawyers or the later English lawyers, who developed the idea of the corporation as a *persona ficta*.

## The Globalization and Decline of Guilds

Medieval guilds had many purposes, including 'the preservation of the peace, the promotion of social fellowship, the performance of religious worship or some other phase of social activity of common interest to its members' (Davis 1961: 148). They were the corporate organizers of entertainment such as plays, pageants and fairs in medieval towns. They funded and ran almshouses, schools and hospitals. The most consequential guilds were the merchant and craft guilds, some restricted to merchants as employers, some to craftsmen who were employees. Many guilds incorporated both merchants and journeymen. Some merchant guilds effectively governed and organized the military defence of medieval cities. Many accumulated economic power because the sovereign granted them a monopoly in a certain sphere of commerce. The grant of such monopolies made guilds the principal business regulators (of ethics, price, interest rates, professional qualifications, weights and measures and other trade standards) in the Middle Ages – much more significant regulators than states and rulers.

In the end nation-states crushed the guilds for precisely that reason. States acquired sufficient control over their territories to take over regulatory responsibility from guilds. In doing so they were able to bestow political favours on those who wished to compete against the old guild monopolies, disperse threatening accumulations of economic and political power and increase national wealth by enabling the greater efficiency of freer commerce.

We do not know whether the European guilds of the Middle Ages were modelled (through the Levant and Rome) on the guilds of ancient India. Indian guilds have been traced as far back as 800 BC, though they became firmly established only around the third century BC (Rungta 1970: 272). Even if they did, we cannot trace a line from ancient Indian to medieval European guilds to nineteenth-century business corporations because by the seventeenth century the guilds had been destroyed as centres of economic power almost everywhere. The modern corporation came from a different corporate lineage.

### *Commenda* and the Globalization of Limited Liability

Between the fifteenth and eighteenth centuries the biggest fortunes were accumulated not by people who made things but by those who traded them. Fortunes were especially made by Genoan, Venetian and Florentine traders and by diasporas of Jews and Armenians. Their success was based on ethnic communication networks across long distances. Trusted informants of the same ethnicity living in different trading centres wrote to one another with information on prices for different commodities. Their surviving letters record emerging surpluses and shortages. Superior market intelligence acquired through such networks allowed them to dispatch ships to buy in the ports where prices were low then sail to the ports where the goods could be sold at the highest prices. The profits were fantastic, because few others were organized into trusted communication networks (Braudel 1979: 400).

But there were great risks of ships sinking, piracy, erroneous or dated market intelligence, or predatory pricing by a competitor acting with intent to crush the monopoly on a particular trading circuit. Italian investors were more likely to survive if they spread their risks from owning one ship to being the part-owner of many. The institution that was used to solve this problem was the *commenda*. Under the *commenda*, the organizers of a voyage would collect funds from a number of investors. The liability of those investors would be limited to the funds they invested, whereas the liability of the promoter would be unlimited. Hence if catastrophe ensued, the principal of the *commenda* could be bankrupted to pay debts, while the other investors could not be called upon for more than the amount they put in.

Risk spreading through limited liability for investors was not the only appeal of the *commenda*. It was also a way around the laws of usury for investors with spare cash who did not want to run a business themselves. Instead of illegally lending money for interest, a rich individual could reap a legal capital gain in a *commenda*. This was also the *commenda*'s appeal to its inventors in the Islamic world: 'the Prophet himself and his wife who was a rich widow had set up a *commenda*' (Braudel 1979: 556). Whether copied from the Arabs or reinvented, the Italian traders spread the institution from city to city in Europe, variations modified by local traditions being evident across the Hanseatic ports by the fourteenth century. A Florentine statute of 1408 codified the conditions of public responsibility attached to a *commenda*: 'capitalists were freed of all liability beyond their contributions, while the management contracted in their own names and were responsible for the debts of the business' (Cooke 1950: 46). So-called *commandite* or limited partnerships, where directors had unlimited liability and investors limited liability, slowly replaced family firms throughout Europe, though not in England. *Commandite* organizations were the dominant style of firm in France in the nineteenth century until it acquired a modern law for the free incorporation of limited liability companies in 1867 (Freedeman 1993: 2–5).

### Joint-stock Companies Colonize the Western and Southern Hemispheres

England was a laggard in all these developments. It was late to convert from Roman to Arabic numerals for recording business transactions, late to adopt double-entry bookkeeping, and clung to the partnership form of business organization in preference to the *commenda* (Cooke 1950: 46). However, England (along with the Dutch) did charter the most significant joint-stock companies of the early modern era. The trouble with both the *commenda* and partnerships was that they collapsed or had to be reorganized on the death of the principals. Joint-stock companies created a permanent fund from shares in the stock of the company, invested by capitalists and managed by a select body drawn from the members (a board of directors). When members died their shares could be sold to a new member. The crucial contribution of the joint-stock company to the development of the corporate form was perpetuity: a corporation that 'marches on in its elephantine way almost indifferent to its succession of riders' (Boulding 1953: 139).

Some of the most important joint-stock companies started out as regulated companies – corporate charters for particular international trading activities granted to a number of specified individuals by the rulers of north-west European states. These developments begin with the Muscovy Company (chartered in 1555 for trade into Russia), the Levant Company (chartered in 1581 as a regulated company and re-chartered as a joint-stock company in 1605) and the Morocco Company (1588). The most important joint-stock company – the East India Company – seems to have been an off-shoot of the Levant Company. By 1617 the company's 954 shareholders owned thirty-six vessels, among other assets (Davis 1961: 119).

Corporations like the East India Company, the Hudson's Bay Company, the Massachusetts Bay Company, the African Company and the British South Africa Company were given charters which made them prime agents of colonial expansion for the British empire. They were given the power to govern colonies, to make laws for them (consistent with the laws of England), to tax locals and to wage war within the territories where they held sway. Significant as it was as a commercial trader, the British East India Company was more significant as the private government of the Indian subcontinent in the eighteenth century. The Virginia Company was quite insignificant and short-lived commercially, but it did settle the first English colony in America and wrote a Constitution for Virginia that provided for the first representative legislature in America (Davis 1961: 168). It was private corporate governance that first tilled the soil of democracy in Virginia, which later produced Jefferson and Madison.

Similarly, the Massachusetts Bay Company developed a democratic Constitution of Massachusetts with checks and balances and a separation of legislative and judicial powers. It and the Virginian Constitution became a model for other colonies aspiring to governance by elected representatives constrained by a rule of law. 'The constitution of the colonial trading company was therefore perpetuated to a large extent in the state and federal constitutions of the United States'

(Davis 1961: 201). In America, governmental institutions 'largely derived from corporations' (Davis 1961: 205) had a democratic vitality that was lacking elsewhere, because they took root in American soil clear of feudal institutions. In the 1980s a new wave of colonization of the state by the corporation commenced: corporatization within government – the division of monolithic state bureaucracies into separately managed corporatized operating units (Hood et al. 1999: Ch. 9).

There is not only a historical discontinuity between the guild, monastery or municipality as corporations and the joint-stock company, there is also a sharp conceptual divide between the corporation as a division of society and the corporation as an association of individuals. Corporations 'were now enlarged individuals, not reduced societies' (Davis 1961: 246–7). Their growth into the modern liberal corporate form was far from continuous. By 1688 there were still only sixteen joint-stock companies in England, but by 1695 there were 140 (Morgan & Thomas 1962: 16–17).

The English, French and Dutch stock markets crashed massively around 1720, at the end of an extraordinarily unrealistic bull market. The Board of the South Sea Company in England had been responsible for scandalous stock manipulation. It was established to trade African slaves to Spanish America, touted as a company that would do for the (vaguely defined) South Seas what the East India Company had done in Asia. The hope was that with the peace following the War of the Spanish Succession, the company might get direct access to the Spanish colonies.

So great was the outrage in Britain when the bubble burst (and so great were the losses by members of parliament, many of whom had been bribed with shares on favourable terms) that the *South Sea Bubble Act 1720* flatly prohibited the formation of new joint-stock companies. In 1711 unfunded national debt had been compulsorily converted into shares of the South Sea Company. After 1720, Britain was convinced that it was better to rely on business development through partnerships where the partners took a personal interest in the business. But shareholder capitalism was too resilient to be legislated out of existence. A principal method of circumventing the spirit of the Bubble Act was for property to be held in a trust for an unincorporated group of investors. A body of trustees acting under a trust deed thus became the functional equivalent of the Board of Directors of a group of shareholders.

### Liberalization of Incorporation and the Globalization of the Institution of the Stock Exchange

In the nineteenth century the policy of the Bubble Act was reversed as it became clear that progressively more liberal corporations law was needed to enable the grand capital-raising required for railways and ships, for mining and large-scale industrial enterprises. The view developed that banks should also be creatures of limited liability, to encourage deposits. By 1870 most Western nations had adopted laws permitting free incorporation (without need for government authorization of the corporation's purposes) with limited liability. Even developing economies such as India had liberalized by 1870 and the Bombay share market was formally organized in 1875 (Rungta 1970: 257). Liberalization of the law had a dramatic effect on capital formation and the proliferation of the corporate form of human organization: following liberalization in France, incorporations increased from an average of fifteen a year (1852–67) to 362 a year (1868–82) (Freedeman 1993: 6). The limited liability corporation became a means of enticing investors to form large pools of capital in exchange for reducing their risks. This was the historical pattern in all industrializing societies.

In the second half of the nineteenth century, stock exchanges were established in most major cities in regions where capitalism flourished – approximately 250 in the US, for example

(Michie 1987: 167). Everywhere, the demand from investors was basically similar – a law that recognized simple procedures for the transfer of shares, shares of conveniently small denominations and a banking system that provided simple means of payment. By the end of the seventeenth century, these conditions had been fulfilled only in Holland and England (Morgan & Thomas 1962: 11). The first major stock exchange emerged in Amsterdam: by 1585 lists of stocks being traded existed in Amsterdam (Windcott 1946: 2). The London Stock Exchange surpassed Amsterdam as the premier market when French troops arrived in Amsterdam in 1795. It consolidated its global dominance, against intermittent competition from the Paris Bourse, until 1914 when the New York Stock Exchange assumed its mantle. The influence of Dutch financial institutions on London in an era when William of Orange successfully invaded England and took its throne, had resonances when New York took over on financial foundations forged when it was New Amsterdam.

Stockbroking as a profession seems to have evolved from the tally-brokers who dealt in short-term government debt (Morgan & Thomas 1962: 19). The idea of partitioning a permanent national debt into divisible bonds that could be sold to many wealthy individuals both within and outside the state was originally proposed by the Neapolitan Lorenzo Ponti in 1653. The brokers of Amsterdam and then of London were consummate practitioners of this idea, not only selling parcels in the British national debt but parcelling out the national debts of many nations, making international markets in their bonds. In turn British government loans and stock in the Bank of England and the East India Company were actively traded on the Amsterdam Stock Exchange both before and after the South Sea Bubble burst (Morgan & Thomas 1962: 52). Only in the last decade of the seventeenth century was there enough corporate stock available for brokers to begin specializing in stockbroking (Morgan & Thomas 1962: 20) and it was only in the second half of the nineteenth century that the London Stock Exchange ceased being totally dominated by the trade in government securities.

When an Act of the British parliament of 1673 regulated all forms of broking, it made no specific mention of stockbroking. This licensing of brokers was the only form of regulation that affected stockbrokers. Their trade was a creation of spontaneous ordering forged in a number of coffee-houses in the City of London and in Exchange Alley 'between the salters, the Italian merchants and the Canary merchants' (Morgan & Thomas 1962: 27) in the Royal Exchange building. In 1697, however, an Act 'To Restrain the Number and Ill Practice of Brokers and Stockjobbers' was passed. Its preamble states:

> Whereas for the Convenience of Trade Sworn Brokers have been Anciently Admitted and Allowed of within the City of LONDON, and Liberties thereof, for the making and concluding of Bargains and Contracts between Merchant and Merchant, and other Tradesmen, concerning their Goods, Wares and Merchandizes, and Money taken up by Exchange, and for negotiating Bills of Exchange between Merchant and Merchant: And whereas divers Brokers and Stock-Jobbers, or pretended Brokers, have lately set up and carried on most unjust Practices and Designs, in Selling and Discounting of Talleys, Bank Stock, and Bank Bills, as may be most Convenient for their own private Interest and Advantage; which is a very great abuse of the said Ancient Trade and Employment, and is extremely prejudicial to the Public Credit of this Kingdom and to the Trade and Commerce thereof, and if not timely prevented, may Ruin the Credit of the Nation, and endanger the Government itself.

But it was only for a decade that stockbrokers were licensed as such by the City of London, the Act not being renewed (Morgan & Thomas 1962: 23–6). Thereafter brokers' self-regulation set the regulatory framework for the securities and bond markets. A building was described as the Stock Exchange in Threadneedle Street in 1773, still without a restricted broker membership.

The Stock Exchange building on its present site, with a committee restricting membership was not opened until 1802.

It was not until 1812 that the first rule-book of the London Stock Exchange was collated (Morgan & Thomas 1962: 60). Five years later these rules were a resource when the New York Stock Exchange was formally organized. Long before this codification, the London Stock Exchange had refined customary rules through its committee structure. As Clarke (1986) has shown, regulation in the City of London largely worked informally, based on trust and shame among men who shared a code of honour they had learnt at the same schools. In the 1802 structure, 'At the south end under the clock was a board on which the names of defaulters were exhibited' (Morgan & Thomas 1962: 71). Weber attributed the orderly trading on the nineteenth-century Hamburg exchange, compared to the instability of the Berlin market, to the Hanseatic tradition of honour and consensus on business ethics among the Hamburg merchant class (Bendix 1977: 27).

In the evolution of capitalism, there is a long period before trust becomes generalized in a culture (Fukuyama 1995), allowing trading in shops and in commerce with people one has never met, with a certain degree of trust (Krygier 1997). During this painful gestation of generalized trust, trust worked in culturally homogenous networks, including global ones of Jewish, Venetian, Genoese, Armenian and Chinese diasporas. Competitive advantage was secured when culturally homogenous, trusting communities of traders self-regulated their affairs to enable complex and sophisticated forms of quick and clean trading that other societies could not manage. This was the accomplishment of the City of London from the late eighteenth century. Earlier in the century there had been a pragmatic recognition of the kind of homogenous networks that worked in financing markets. For example, while brokers ordinarily had to be freemen of the City of London, early in the eighteenth century an exception was made to provide twelve seats at the exchange for Jews (Morgan & Thomas 1962: 65).

Prior to the gentlemen's-club era of self-regulation, female stockbrokers seemed not to be uncommon (Morgan & Thomas 1962: 53). They traded in an unregulated informal market open to the general public, along with others excluded from membership of the London Stock Exchange. This happened in and around the Rotunda of the Bank of England from 1765 until the Bank excluded them from the precinct in 1838. By then all the reputable money was going to the London Stock Exchange. Even modern writers have questioned the repute of the female stockbrokers in the most chauvinist way possible: 'The presence of the "female jobbers" is vouched for in contemporary illustrations though there is some doubt as to how far they were dealing in stock and how far plying an even older trade' (Morgan & Thomas 1962: 53).

### Technological Change and the Hegemony of London and New York

There is a sense in which the New York Stock Exchange 'made' New York, rather than vice versa. The financing of the Erie Canal, which made New York the commanding port of the continent, came from the New York Stock Exchange (McCraw 1984: 162). The communications revolution of the mid nineteenth century – first the telegraph, then the telephone, then the tickertape machine – caused an enormous centralization of trading in the London and New York Stock Exchanges which, until then, had substantial competition from provincial markets within their own states. The Dow index of NYSE stock averages, which started in 1897, was destined to become something not only New Yorkers would hear daily on the evening news. A century later, moves from localized open-outcry trading to screen-based trading at large distances from the metropoles reinforced the grip of the major markets while 'glocalizing' the stockbroking industry away from the site of the exchange, glocalizating to where the investors live.

By 1910, approximately two-thirds of trading in stocks in the US occurred on the New York Stock Exchange (Michie 1987: 169). Progressively, the market-making in major stocks happened in London for the UK and in New York for the US. The biggest markets became the hubs from which the new communications wires ran. This allowed London and New York brokers to dominate international securities arbitrage – buying stock cheaply on one international market while simultaneously selling the same amount of stock at the highest price prevailing in any of the world's markets. Since arbitrage is simply market-making in one exchange writ large as market-making across all the world's exchanges, London and then New York progressively made the world's markets in securities important enough to be internationally traded. Once rapid communication allowed this to happen, the culture of trading changed so that provincials watched what was happening at the metropole and adjusted accordingly.

This also limited how far other markets could diverge from the regulatory framework for securities trading set in London and New York. Other exchanges could, did and still do compete for the listing of lesser companies by setting lower regulatory standards than New York. They can list a new Chinese stock that could have been listed on the New York Stock Exchange – except the company preferred the weaker disclosure requirements of a lesser exchange. This international regulatory competition had, until recently, only limited impact on New York. Domestically, the New York Stock Exchange had always been content to concentrate on blue chips that play by their rules, allowing the second board and provincial exchanges to pick up the rest.

However, just as a fast, efficient, high-disclosure market like New York has been important to encouraging Western investors to put their money into equities, less open and efficient markets in Shanghai, Hong Kong and elsewhere have been important to the formation of large private corporations in China. In all this, however, stock markets are only fundamental as a secondary market. This secondary market entices investors to buy new securities with the confidence that they will be able to sell some or all of them whenever they want, with low transaction costs. Stockbrokers are responsible for only a small proportion of new share issues – the primary market in equities. In the nineteenth century, the merchant bankers who had dominated the international issuance of new government bonds – Barings and Rothschilds in Europe, J.P. Morgan in New York – also dominated new share issues for private corporations (Michie 1987: 116). The emergence of a vibrant finance capitalism (as discussed in Chapter 8) was essential to the emergence of strong corporate capitalism and securities markets.

### The Rise of State Regulation Around the World

The licensing of brokers during the early centuries of the London Stock Exchange was the regulatory responsibility of the Lord Mayor of London rather than of the nation-state. Even this public regulation was of little consequence compared to the self-regulation of the Exchange. This was the global pattern of securities regulation in Europe, Asia and the Pacific, Africa and the Americas. The most important state intervention during the nineteenth century was Britain's *Directors Liability Act 1890*. But this established modest rights in private law rather than public-law regulation. It subjected directors and promoters to civil liability for false statements in prospectuses (the information released with a new share issue to attract investors).

It was not until the *Companies Act 1929* that a somewhat systematic regime of state regulation was instituted; prospectuses had to be publicly registered and certain information to be disclosed in them was prescribed. The regulation of corporations was therefore not part of MacDonagh's (1961, 1977) pattern of nineteenth-century government growth. Nineteenth-century England is best characterized by the liberalization of state limitations on the issuance of corporate charters, and the growth and refinement of self-regulatory institutions dependent on traders' honour. The period of government regulatory growth dates from the onset of the Great Depression and was rejuvenated by the crash of 1987.

Both the 1890 and 1929 British legislative initiatives were widely modelled throughout the British empire (Jordan 1996) and beyond. Even China acquired a *Stock Exchange Law* in 1929 (Hsu & Liu 1988: 169). Most critically, after Wall Street crashed in 1929, the British *Companies Act 1929* was the model that shaped the rise of US state regulation (Wood 1995: 260; Seligman 1982: 57). But UK company law provided no more than a framework into which the US injected details of prescription and state enforcement that remained foreign to the UK until it had to deal with outsiders, with the internationalization of securities trading in the 1980s (Clarke 1986).

The dramatic US development was the establishment in 1934 of the Securities and Exchange Commission. This was only one of a number of New Deal independent regulatory commissions, but it was one which has remained consistently powerful and effective. It was also the decisive move in the takeover of corporations and securities regulation from state governments by the national government, a move that ultimately occurred in other federal states such as Germany, Australia and Canada. As will be discussed in more detail below, under the principle of transparency, the securities laws of 1933 and 1934 were revolutionary in the 'thirty-two categories of information that must be disclosed in the registration statements of corporations issuing new securities' (McCraw 1984: 173).

Japan was persuaded to adopt US-style securities regulation before reopening its markets after the Second World War. Much later, other Asian states such as South Korea modelled Japanese regulation while Latin American states modelled the US (Wood 1995: 261). The pattern of government growth did not spread throughout Western Europe until the first EEC Company Law Directive of 1968, and in Eastern Europe until the fall of communism in 1989. In Germany, Switzerland and the Netherlands, state regulation of securities markets remained thin to non-existent until late in the twentieth century; liberalism was tempered by self-policing clubs of securities dealers, stock exchanges and banks (Wood 1995: 262). The Francophone states experienced the pattern of government growth earlier, setting up institutions that modelled the SEC. In 1967, the French Commission des Operations de Bourse was very considerably modelled on the SEC (Bordeaux-Groult 1987: 453).

It is perhaps surprising that national regulation of this early modern institution – the business corporation – with its ancient history should come so much later than the national regulation of late modern institutions such as telecommunications (Chapter 14), intellectual property (Chapter 7) and air transport (Chapter 19). This lateness is also a feature of the globalization of companies and securities regulation, notwithstanding the early emergence of international arbitrage, described above. While the International Telegraphic Union (now the ITU) was established in 1865, the International Organization of Securities Commissions was fully established only in 1986.

### Cross-border Trading and US Resistance to the Impetus to Globalization of Regulation

We have seen that international regulatory competition initially had limited impact on the New York Stock Exchange, which had been content to concentrate on the US blue chips that in the decades immediately after the Second World War were the big players of global capitalism. Rest-

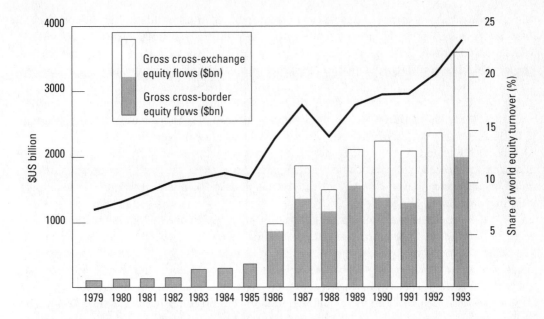

FIGURE 9.1　Changes in cross-border equity flows, 1979–1993
*Source:* **Barings Securities, from Dale (1996: 2)**

lessness about international regulatory competition only sharpened in New York during the bull market between 1982 and 1987. Those five years saw a remarkably sudden globalization of securities markets; in the US, foreign securities transactions increased ten-fold (US Treasury 1983, 1988). Globally, Figure 9.1 shows, if we can trust data collected by Barings Securities, the big jumps in cross-border equity flows occurred in 1986 and 1987 and have not fallen since. Even so, more than three-quarters of equity transactions in 1993 were totally domestic.

London fought back during the 1980s against the domination New York had enjoyed since the First World War, more so after the deregulation of securities trading in London with the Big Bang of 1986. At the end of 1986, only fifty-nine foreign companies were listed on the New York Stock Exchange (a third of them Canadian) and the London Stock Exchange had 512 foreign listings (Longstreth 1988: 183).

But the US of the late 1980s and early 1990s was torn between the imperatives of global regulatory competition that was seeing business go to London, and domestic imperatives to crack down on the excesses of the 1980s. The domestic imperatives were at first more important. US voters were more moved by Hollywood's portrayal of Gordon Gecko in the movie *Wall Street* than by the need for its securities industry to be internationally competitive. Rudolf Giuliani could build a national political profile as a prosecutor of insider traders, a potential presidential candidate and mayor of New York. In this, the US mass public was by no means economically irrational or short-sighted: the sums people lost to shady market manipulators in the late 1980s were massive in comparison to the economic benefits from US domination of global share-trading.

How did the US negotiate this tension? It supported the formation of the Inter-American Association of Securities Commissions in 1974, which became the International Organization of Securities Commissions (IOSCO) in 1983, and it supported the dialogue within IOSCO toward upgrading the disclosure and other requirements of laggard securities regulators. Yet when it came to reaching agreement on global harmonization of securities standards, for the first decade of IOSCO's existence the SEC usually refused to come to the party, steadfastly refusing any easing of its requirements to meet the regulatory laggards halfway. Instead, the US campaigned within the laggard states for tougher regulation, pointing out that US capital would be wary of markets that lacked credible regulation. This strategy met with modest success. The US was the only state that proscribed insider trading after the Great Depression (from 1934). France followed in 1970, the UK in 1980, Sweden in 1985, the Netherlands in 1986 and Switzerland in 1987 (Peters & Feldman 1988: 33–4), then a host of countries including Japan, New Zealand, Italy, Belgium, Denmark and Ireland. In 1989 the EC adopted a directive on insider trading in an attempt to harmonize the enforcement approach of member states. Most of these states rarely or never imprisoned insider traders as the US did, but substantial global movement toward the US regulatory posture was certainly accomplished.

At the same time, the SEC position was supportive of 'flexibility...looking behind the reasons for our rules so, for example, we can assist British Telecom to be sold in the US...accommodation is more important than harmonization' (SEC interview 1992). To the US, international agreement on internal auditing standards, for example, should not mean that 'we have to use them for domestic purposes, but that we find them acceptable for foreign offerers' (SEC interview 1992). This approach, of an effective double standard – fending off competition from London by lower standards for foreign firms listing in New York than for domestic firms – is hard to sustain for the long haul and frowned upon in a US Congress afraid of foreign Gordon Geckos. The attitude reflected the long-standing US view that it was still able to dictate regulatory terms: 'You have to come here and convince us. Issuers will come to this big market' (SEC interview 1992). The SEC was critical even in the early 1990s of 'EC compromises that accommodate everyone. You can't have it where you're giving something to everyone where your core concern is prudential rigour. The EC has settled for a lowest common denominator to reach agreement. The US position is that agreement is not the be all and end all' (SEC interview 1992).

### Financial Innovation, Disasters and Progress with Globalization of Regulation

The expansion of cross-border trading was not the only impetus to global convergence in regulatory standards. The pace of financial innovation since the 1980s has been such that states did not have the luxury of retaining regulatory standards that had stood them in good stead in the past. New standards had to be written for new technologies like screen-based trading, engineering of new products to reduce risk, indeed innovation into completely new types of markets (such as the futures exchanges now institutionalized in all major economies). Wall Street merchant banker Michael Milkin invented the junk bond and eventually went to prison for insider trading on a scale previously unimagined. Wall Street lawyer Michael Lipton invented the poison pill, which was used by hundreds of major companies to fend off the takeover frenzy of the 1980s, along with other innovations such as golden parachutes, pac-man defences, scorched-earth retreats, shark repellents and lock-ups (Powell 1993). Global regulatory convergence became somewhat easier when everyone was forced to go back to the drawing-board, especially when a disaster of global visibility, such as the Barings collapse, prompted rethinking. On some key issues they decided to sit around a common drawing-board.

Although the G-10 managed to agree on capital adequacy standards for banks that globalized almost instantly in the 1980s (see Chapter 8), IOSCO found it impossible to settle capital adequacy standards for securities firms. The nub of the problem was the difficulty of inventing a way of assessing capital adequacy suited to both the banks that dominate securities business in some countries and the non-bank securities firms that dominate in others. Deregulation and product innovation have blurred this divide, however. European agreement on capital adequacy became somewhat easier when the British desire to attract business saw it allow the bank acquisition of member firms of its exchanges. Increasingly, in most of the world, banking and securities business is combined in financial conglomerates. The regulatory separation of banking and securities business has long since collapsed in Japan and is crumbling even in the US, so the different levels of functional integration that in the past have left states with divergent interests on capital adequacy standards are beginning to dissolve.

Advances in computing power have driven innovation in engineering financial products. New financial products could be invented as a result of the new ease, speed and cheapness of collecting, processing and disseminating data. An example is securitization itself – the conversion of cash flows from specific assets into marketable securities. Securitization is based on the simple insight that assets are worth more if they are converted from lumpy assets to parcels of securities that can be easily traded, becoming little pieces of many investors' diversified portfolios (Edmunds 1996). A single home-loan mortgage is a messy investment that is not of interest on Wall Street because investors do not want to 'poke around suburbs to find out whether the home-owner to whom he had just lent money is creditworthy' (Lewis 1989: 85). But if a corporation pools a large number of mortgages and sells shares in the combined debt, investors can play the law of averages in their valuation of default risks. Another change is innovation in derivative products – futures, options, swaps and various hedging instruments – and associated specialized markets. The collapse of Barings, the UK's oldest merchant bank, as a result of derivatives trading by a single employee in Singapore, increased global regulatory impetus for IOSCO's Working Party on Derivatives to devise, with the Basle Commission on Banking Supervision, a common framework for evaluating the risks of derivatives business among banks and securities firms. Their joint report on derivatives, written just before Barings, has been widely accepted as a framework for convergence by key players including the SEC and the US Commodity Futures Trading Commission (Cheek 1996: 250). IOSCO reports on 'Contract Design of Derivative Products on Stock Indices' and 'Mechanisms to Enhance Open and Timely Communication Between Market Authorities of Related Cash and Derivative Markets during Periods of Market Disruption' have also fostered convergence (IOSCO 1993: 4).

After years of impasse, in 1995 IOSCO and the International Accounting Standards Committee (IASC) reached agreement on international accounting standards, with the objective of allowing companies that meet IASC accounting standards to list on any capital market by 1999 (Asher 1996: 6).

Major privatizations have been important sources of regulatory innovation on which cross-border regulatory cooperation has been required. The British Petroleum and British Gas privatizations, the latter being the largest equity underwriting ever, started a new era of equity offerings occurring simultaneously on the US and European markets (Becker 1988: 243). The difficulties Qantas encountered in keeping its foreign shareholdings within prescribed limits motivated the Macquarie Bank in Australia to tailor-make QanMac: 'an innovative security which had the characteristics of a Qantas share, in terms of price and yield, but which was not subject to the same regulatory restrictions, since it was not considered to give foreign investors a direct shareholding in Qantas' (Sackman & Coltman 1996: 28). A more standardized product innovation is the global depository receipt. Banks that act as depositories for foreign shares issue global depository receipts in units that represent the underlying value of those shares. Foreign investors can effectively trade the shares without having to deal with labyrinthine local registration and transfer procedures, confident that settlement will occur and that all transactions will reach them in US dollars or the currency of their choice (Sackman & Coltman 1996: 22). De facto stockholders who use GDRs find it difficult or impossible to cast votes as shareholders, complicating the principled basis of corporate governance and its regulation.

The latter illustrates how innovation generates new kinds of regulatory challenges that confront all states simultaneously with the need for regulatory redesign. Commonality and simultaneity of financial innovation and global financial crises are more conducive to convergence than is 'grandfathered' regulation that has established entrenched habits of industry practice, training, accounting, culture and structure. While these realities are the basis for expecting faster progress toward global convergence of securities regulation, until now there has been only limited accomplishment and weak institutional infrastructure for globalization.

## Actors

### International Organizations

Political will for globalization of corporations and securities regulation has been limited, particularly on the part of the US, as testified by the late arrival, limited accomplishment and minimal resourcing of the most important international organization, IOSCO. At the time of writing IOSCO has only four staff, most of the work being done by the chairs of working groups of representatives of member commissions. 'The philosophy is to let the agencies write the solutions. Then they won't throw them in the bin' (IOSCO interview 1994).

IOSCO began as a regional coordinator for the Americas. Following an initiative by UK regulators who wished to discuss cross-border insider trading, IOSCO opened its membership to all states in 1986 (Davidson 1994: 716).

When it finally got underway IOSCO struggled for some years without Germany and Japan as members. Now, however, IOSCO's 110 members account for 99 per cent of global capitalization. The history of a Pan-American organization evolving into a global body parallels Working Party 29 of the Economic Commission for Europe becoming the de facto global standard-setting body for motor vehicles (see Chapter 18).

During its first decade IOSCO's accomplishments were minimal assessed in terms of settled harmonizations. IOSCO compared unfavourably with the Basle Committee's accomplishments on the harmonization of banking standards during the same period. As one senior regulator who had been active in both IOSCO and the Basle Committee portrayed the difference: 'Basle is an example of leadership; IOSCO is an example of democracy. IOSCO had democracy with no leadership'. In particular, US leadership was limited. Yet during its first decade IOSCO did facilitate the evolution of a common language among securities regulators.

It is not impossible that the structural conditions within which IOSCO now operates – expanding cross-border trading, regulatory competition, innovation in financial products and exchanges to deliver them, continuous screen-based trading, crises that demand a global rather than a national response – will enable it to convert its history of impotence into rapid and substantial accomplishment of regulatory convergence. For the time being at least, IOSCO will remain a supranational coordinator of securities markets rather than a regulator. An example of where IOSCO has helped to facilitate a culture of cooperation in securities markets regulation was the formulation in 1991 of principles for Memoranda of Understanding (MOU). MOUs are legally non-binding statements of cooperation between regulatory authorities. In the longer term the IOSCO principles will help to standardize cooperation between securities regulators.

Compared to other domains of business regulation discussed in this book, the OECD has played an extremely modest role as an incubus of ideas for convergence in companies and securities regulation. The International Federation of Stock Exchanges and the International Council of Securities Dealers and Self-Regulatory Organizations have also been minor forces for regulatory globalization.

The EC has edged Europe toward convergence of companies and securities law through a number of key directives including the Listing Particulars Directive, the Interim Reports Directive, the Prospectus Directive, the Major Shareholders Directive, the Insider Trading Directive, the Investment Services Directive and a variety of directives on the formation, structure, governance, accounts, audit, disclosure requirements and merger of companies (Wymeersch 1994: 251–9). The Investment Services Directive guarantees securities firms free access to all EC markets (the European passport) as long as the regulatory authority of their home state certifies that they have met harmonized minimum requirements.

During the 1990s, the EC played more of a leadership role at IOSCO, organizing European Commissions to take more unified positions to the international forum, prompting the US to caucus defensively among the Western hemisphere members.

## States

Since the New Deal the US, through the agency of the SEC, has usually been the state that has dictated terms. IOSCO's weakness as an institution indicates that this leadership has not been directed to sustained institution-building in the way shown in other chapters. Although there has been activism in the 1980s and 1990s in negotiating bilateral MOUs, US leadership, like the UK, Dutch and Italian leadership before it, was more passive than active, more a result of creating domestic institutions that others copied than of regulatory diplomacy.

The influence of the SEC, thus understood, is not just about the fact that US market capitalization remains considerably higher than that of Europe combined, it is also about the SEC's depth of expertise – legal, economic and in terms of market experience – compared with that of any other securities regulator. It is also about respect for the SEC as a regulatory success story that, for example, the US Federal Trade Commission does not enjoy, as it was put to us immodestly, but nevertheless accurately, in one SEC interview:

> It's not just the capitalization of the US that gives it weight. Still close to 40 per cent of the world's capitalization is in the US. Who are the success stories? The SEC has respect. Also it's the sheer size of the SEC as a regulator. The investor confidence that has come of its competence. Japan has 20 per cent of the world's market capitalization but no one holds it up as a model of securities regulation. That's about scandals, the insider mentality begetting no international respect.

The US also has the most innovative market: innovations hit Wall Street first, so the SEC has to deal with them first. As Powell (1993) has shown, Wall Street legal entrepreneurs do not wait for clients to ask for their latest tactics – they proactively sell them to boards, first domestically, then internationally. Foreign regulators know that whatever is troubling the SEC now is likely to be giving them grief soon.

## Business Actors

The colonies of northern Italian merchants who could be found in every major commercial centre of Europe in the fifteenth century – Geneva, Lyon, Barcelona, Seville, London, Bruges and especially Antwerp – diffused double-entry bookkeeping and other forms of business knowhow, particularly the use of credit, that laid foundations for the corporatization of the world in later centuries (Cameron 1989: 122).

One might have expected that major individual corporations which are issuers of shares, with their interest in being able to list globally, would have been major forces for the global harmonization of companies and securities law. We have seen no evidence of this. 'The accounting firms try to get them [US TNCs] interested in harmonization but they don't care' (IOSCO interview 1994). Corporations that struggle to raise capital lack the clout to shape debates; blue chips that have little difficulty in doing so have more important fish to fry, as do the industry associations they dominate. In the nineteenth century the house of Rothschild was more powerful than most states. By the end of the century J.P. Morgan had become more powerful, an influence it retained for the first few decades of the twentieth century. But the twenty-first century will have no Rothschild or Morgan (or Fugger) who can dictate terms to heads of major states (Chernow 1990: xvii). Merchant banking today is an extremely competitive industry with power diffused among many firms that are tiny compared to the industrial TNCs. In short, the height of merchant banker power preceded not only the globalization of regulation, but the rise of state regulation from 1934.

The City of London aside, in no other economy does the securities industry account for a notable proportion of GDP. National and international associations representing stockbrokers have certainly been active players in international debates, but the major changes we have discussed cannot be attributed to their lobbying – they have been reactive rather than proactive.

The stock exchanges, particularly those of New York and London, have been preeminently important actors. But their influence on events has been rather in the same mould as that of the US state – more a passive one internationally than one of active diplomacy. When the New York Stock Exchange sets its domestic rules, it also sets global rules simply because other actors choose to model its policies. The three major exchanges – New York, London and Tokyo – are all active participants in IOSCO deliberation, Tokyo less than the other two. IOSCO, in the words of one official from the New York Stock Exchange, has changed from a 'social organization to actually getting things done' (NYSE interview 1994). Tokyo dominates trading in Japanese securities but is not a major trader of international securities. 'Not many international companies want to list in Tokyo. They do want to list in the US' (IOSCO interview 1994). This seems related to the respect and insider mentality concerns about Tokyo discussed above. Tokyo seems too embedded in the Japanese governmental matrix. Global investors are wary of it. There are really only three major markets and two major competitors for international listings. The next largest market, the Paris Bourse, is much smaller than the big three and much less influential in global policy discussions. 'Any agreement requires the US, the UK and Japan, though if Japan doesn't agree it doesn't matter much. Then the others will follow' (interview with key insider). In futures trading London is the second market, after Chicago.

Some stock exchanges, with the Investment Bankers Association, took a proactive role in the US after the Great Crash of 1929 (McCraw 1984: 167) in pushing for what we will argue has been the paradigmatic shift of the twentieth century from insider capitalism to transparency capitalism. However, the President of the New York Stock Exchange, Richard Whitney, told Senate staff investigators in 1933: 'You gentlemen are making a great mistake. The Exchange is a perfect institution' (McCraw 1984: 194).

The most influential actors in the proactive diplomacy sense have been the major accounting firms:

> The big accounting firms have been putting tremendous pressure on all the players for globalization of accounting standards. Peat Marwick and Price Waterhouse have been the most active. They have also been very active at the GATT on their associated agenda to free up the trade in accounting services. They also lobby the SEC who lobby our Working Groups (IOSCO interview 1994).

In the terms we will discuss in Chapter 25, the major accounting firms are the model mercenaries in the globalization of US regulatory and corporate governance practice.

**NGOs and Mass Publics**

After many years of impotence, the IASC, which represents some 100 professional accounting bodies in fifty countries, has reached an agreement with IOSCO that seems to lay down a framework for harmonized accounting rules. One would have to say, however, that the role of professional bodies here has been much less significant than that of the leading firms. Prior to the New Deal the American Institute of Accountants advanced the cause of uniform accounting rules. Although the profession were advocates of transparency they were largely a feeble force then, dominated by their corporate clients.

National NGOs like the Australian Shareholders Association do exist, but they have limited influence on national debates and none on global debates.

We have seen that mass publics, more precisely the new mass of middle-class equity owners, have had enormous influence in recent decades, particularly in the US market, which has shaped so much of the global regulatory change.[2] They bayed for blood following the excesses of the 1980s and got a level of criminalization of insider trading which, while it might have been feeble measured as law in action (Tomasic & Pentony 1991), transformed the law on the books in many countries and led to the only period in the history of securities enforcement where the criminal law has become of major importance (Shapiro 1984). It has been the demands of middle-class investors transmitted through pension funds, mutual funds and investment advisers that has transformed capitalism more structurally from localized insider investment networks to global risk-spreading based on aggressive demands for performance and transparency by those who make the investments on behalf of the new middle-class equity owners. In the era of networked insider capitalism, mass publics were 'a befuddled chorus of common people, alternately fascinated and horrified by the doings of the major players' (McCraw 1984: 162).

Under transparency capitalism (see below under the 'transparency' heading) befuddled impotence is no longer an accurate way of describing the relevance of mass publics. The workings

---

2 According to a survey by the New York Stock Exchange in 1990, roughly 51 million Americans owned equities (about one in four adults, in other words). See NYSE Fact Book 1991.

of firms are not transparent to individual investors, but they are increasingly so to those empowered by investor demands for vigilance, such as stockbrokers, investment advisers, mutual funds and pension funds. None of these watchdogs has become more powerful than the pre-eminent US rating agencies – Standard and Poor's Corporation and Moody's Investors Service. No issuer of securities in the world – corporate or state – is beyond the power that transparency capitalism delivers to the New York ratings agencies. They all shudder at the effect on investing publics of even a hint that one of these agencies might qualify their credit rating.

## Individuals

In tune with the conclusion we will reach later that modelling is by far the most important mechanism of globalization, it is the individuals whose innovations were modelled who have been the most decisive actors in the globalization of companies and securities regulation. It is beyond our historical reach to know who were the individuals responsible for the idea of the corporation as a *persona ficta*, the *commenda*, double-entry bookkeeping, stockbroking and market-making and the Amsterdam Stock Exchange. Securitization seems to been invented by the Neapolitan Lorenzo Ponti in 1653, when he proposed partitioning national debts into divisible bonds. In terms of building primary markets for securities through developing the institution of the merchant bank, perhaps the Rothschild family should be mentioned, for its pre-eminence not only in England and France but in all the major centres of early capitalist Europe.

In the twentieth century, James Landis was a pre-eminent architect of transparency capitalism: 'In the history of American liberalism, Landis embodies the generational links from Brandeis [he clerked for Brandeis], the old progressive, through Roosevelt and the New Deal, down to John F. Kennedy and the New Frontier. He served all three men' (McCraw 1984: 153).

Early in 1933, President Roosevelt asked his friend Felix Frankfurter to help with writing new securities legislation that might prevent another Great Crash. Frankfurter turned to, among others, his brilliant young co-author at Harvard Law School, James Landis. To Landis fell the task of leadership in drafting the *Securities Act 1933* and the *Securities Exchange Act 1934*, the latter 'among the most harshly contested pieces of legislation in the twentieth century' (McCraw 1984: 171). Landis and his colleagues were described as, among other things, 'a bunch of Jews out to get J.P. Morgan' (Seligman 1982: 96). Wall Street came to hate FDR and Landis was FDR's front line, first as principal drafter, then as FTC and SEC Commissioner, then as SEC Chairman from 1935 to 1937.

Landis (1931, 1938), before and after, was a seminal scholar of regulatory strategy, a critic of legislative enactment uncoupled from a theory of administrative design (Ritchie 1980). His regulatory genius was in seeing the need for an institutional design that gave all gatekeepers – executives, accountants, brokers, bankers, lawyers – a stake in enforcing the law. Part of the disclosure regime in the 1933 Act, for example, was the provision of the names and addresses of lawyers who passed on the legality of a security issue. This was a radical innovation in giving lawyers a reputational stake in enforcing the law. His ideas, subsequently modelled globally not only in securities regulation, were for regulation that was self-enforcing, that engaged industry participants in self-regulation monitored by a federal agency. He envisaged participatory regulation within a regulatory community, to use a term later deployed by Meidinger (1987). Landis was severely attacked both by business leaders who detested transparency and by liberal New Dealers, including some within the SEC itself, who wanted dirigiste, punitive control rather than cooperative regulation with the business community as partners. The Landis vision prevailed in the practice of the SEC and many other agencies that admired its accomplishments. Landis himself slipped into obscurity after 1937 as an undistinguished Dean of Harvard Law School who let alcohol get the better of him. He also had an undistinguished stint as Chairman of the Civil Aeronautics Board under Truman. But Landis' 1961 *Report to the President-Elect*, John F. Kennedy, highlighted the problems of regulatory decay and the need for periodic rejuvenation of regulatory agencies, which began under Kennedy.

Many stood beside Landis, including two colleagues, Joseph Kennedy and William Douglas, who possibly administered the SEC with greater finesse than Landis (Seligman 1982). He also stood on the shoulders of his mentors, Brandeis and Frankfurter. But no shoulders were sturdier than those of the man who appointed him, as Landis wrote to Roosevelt when he resigned as SEC Chairman: 'Our Commission and our work sprang from your mind, your utterances, your ideals' (Seligman 1982: 155).

## Epistemic Communities of Actors

How does one describe Wall Street and the City of London? Not as markets. Both encompass a number of markets for money, stocks, bonds, credit, insurance, reinsurance, accounting services, legal services, indeed regulation. Both Wall Street and the City of London are involved in all those markets. One does not have to do much fieldwork in the City and on Wall Street to realize that these are communities in quite a serious sense.

It is disappointing that only economists seem to deploy their methods to analyze Wall Street, that we do not see more anthropologists studying the rituals and customs of the natives. Gunningham (1990, 1993) has completed revealing ethnographic work on the Chicago Futures Exchange and the Hong Kong Stock Exchange that demonstrates some of the ways 'community' is a relevant variable at those sites. Tomasic and Pentony (1989, 1991) have undertaken interview-based research in Australia on the culture of insider trading that reveals more the character of a casino than of a community. Yet they still find some professional community among lawyers, accountants and older-established brokers, and plead for renewal of ethical community. Clarke (1986) is doubtless right that the City of London is not the tight-knit and homogenous community of decent chaps it once was. There are women in it now. Yet the common observation in the business culture literature, that the City of London is more communitarian than Wall Street, is still probably true (e.g. Wechsberg 1966: 41; Coleman 1990: 109).

Perhaps the richest ethnography of Wall Street is the intricate account by two journalists from the *Wall Street Journal* (Burrough & Helyar 1991) of the titanic takeover battle for RJR Nabisco. The following passage illustrates, through the agency of Henry Kravis, the investment banker who won the takeover battle, that communitarian values like healing and forgiveness are important in enabling Wall Street to work. Perhaps community is transacted in a mode that seems vulgar to non-natives, especially in the way money ceaselessly colonizes the lifeworld. But we would say that those who can only read market and cannot find community in the following illustration have not learnt how to read human drama:

> Wall Street is a small place, and in the interests of harmony Kravis wasted no time healing wounds inflicted during the fight. He made peace with Peter Cohen at a summit in February and actually hired Tom Hill to investigate the possible takeover of Northwest Airlines...Kravis also moved to smooth relations with Linda Robinson. Soon after the Gerstner episode, Linda took a message that Kravis had called. She ignored it. Within days she received a small ceramic doghouse with a cute note from

Kravis, suggesting he was in the Robinsons' [her husband Jim Robinson, the CEO of American Express, was also involved] doghouse. Linda Robinson waited a few days, then sent Kravis a twenty-pound bag of dog food. All was forgiven. She and Kravis still own 'Trillion'.

Fees, of course, went infinitely further toward soothing Wall Street's wounds…Kravis even spread the largesse to those whose feelings he might have bruised. Geoff Boisi's Goldman Sachs got the job of auctioning Del Monte, while Felix Rohatyn's Lazard Freres did the same for the company's stake in ESPN (Burrough & Helyar 1991: 508).

In a 1993 London interview at the Securities and Futures Authority, the following diagnosis was given of the seemingly insurmountable problem of getting equity markets working in former communist states:

You need public spirit in practitioners. In Eastern Europe they lack this. Where do you get market-makers from? People who will buy because they reckon they can sell on. Probably the black-market operator who used to operate from the corner of Stalin Avenue and Lenin Boulevard. But idealistic academics like Havel somehow think they can find Western-style ethical market-makers.

In retrospect, given the corruption of many post-communist privatizations by the Russian mafia and others, perhaps it was Havel who was the hard-headed one. Specific laments were made during this interview over the difficulties of making a market in shares of the Bolshevik Biscuit Factory, a challenge that would perhaps have been beyond the good Lord himself. But the basic thrust of the SFA official's account remains perceptive: You can't make markets without some depth of intimate relationships that work in a locally meaningful sense in a financial community.

Wall Street and the City of London are meccas of a global epistemic community that constitutes a culture. It is this culture that makes stock exchanges and futures exchanges work in many places. In many other parts of the world such exchanges cannot be made to work. One reason is that the civil societies of those nations do not share the culture of the global securities epistemic community. Hence there are good reasons for a senior US diplomat to suggest during our interview:

If you have on your resumé that you have worked with a reputable firm in the City [of London] or on Wall Street, that will stand you in good stead in seeking any position of power in any society. I don't care what kind of power or what kind of society.

## Contest of Principles

### Transparency

Transparency is emerging as the triumphant principle in the globalization of companies and securities regulation. Transparency was decidedly not a dominant principle during British hegemony of finance capitalism. The dominance of London bankers and brokers over world financial markets in the nineteenth and early twentieth centuries was based on networks of experts with insider knowledge, in whom people with money put their personal trust. Risk was managed by relying on a combination of the knowledge advisers had as members of an inner financial circle and their honour as members of an inner social circle – a club, a group of Eton chums (Clarke 1986). But even in this opaque world of inner circles the principle of transparency began to emerge for banking regulation through the medium of the British state. Stability in a monetary system is not feasible without it.

US capitalism was also networked insider capitalism. Many major companies did not release annual reports until they were forced to in 1934. Corporate affairs were regarded as private and privileged, as revealed in this interrogation of Henry O. Havemeyer, head of the gigantic American Sugar Refining Company, by Thomas Phillips, member of an ad hoc Industrial Commission set up by the US Congress in 1899:

> **Phillips:** You think, then, that when a corporation is chartered by the state, offers stock to the public, and is one in which the public is interested, that the public has no right to know what its earning power is or subject them to any inspection whatever, that the people may not buy stock blindly?
>
> **Havemeyer:** Yes; that is my theory. Let the buyer beware…They have got to wade in and get stuck and that is the way men are educated and cultivated (McCraw 1984: 166).

In contemporary capitalism investors manage risk very differently. They ask their friends and unfamiliar people in their bank or the accountancy firm that does their tax or the superannuation officer at work to recommend an investment adviser. That investment adviser is a complete stranger and essentially does not rely on insider knowledge in telling us where to put our money. What they rely on is comparative analysis of the risks of many kinds of investments in many countries that they might never have visited. If the investment adviser suggests we invest in a mutual fund, that advice is based on quantitative data on the comparative performance of dozens of mutual funds over a number of years, the national and international diversification of the risks and the size and quality of the group of analysts they have poring over their computers.

In short, today we rely for investment advice on a more impersonal kind of (sometimes accredited) trust than on personal trust; we rely on transparency more than on insiders. We make transparency work for us by nesting our advice. We end up investing a small fraction of our savings in a Chinese manufacturer because a Hong Kong bank and a Shanghai analyst have both given our pension fund or mutual fund managers a lot of promising data (audited by its US accounting firm) on the financial performance of that manufacturer, because our investment advisers have had publicly disclosed to them data on the comparative performance of this mutual fund compared to others and because we have had advice from acquaintances on which investment adviser has a good track record. Moreover, we continue to test the investment advice against the daily prognostications in the investment advice columns of the popular media and we would really jump if we read that Moody's were downgrading its credit rating. Advice on the advice on the advice of advisers where the credibility of each layer of advice depends on audited public disclosure of financial information. Global transparency capitalism has succeeded local insider network capitalism.

Even if you have a network as good as George Soros' (1994), local insider network capitalism will no longer work as well as global nesting of critical analysis. However good the oil of the insider, if the local currency plummets, interest rates shift, confidence collapses in the local share market or derivatives trading spirals unpredictably, our money is unlikely to perform as well as it would if prudently hedged across investment in stocks of different markets in different currencies, across stocks, bonds and property.

The investing public in the 1990s is a mass public in the developed economies. Insider traders – compromisers of transparency – epitomize evil to the new shareholding mass public.

That is why democratic forces in the most advanced shareholder democracy – the US – have caused it to resist global harmonization of corporate disclosure rules that water down transparency. The Landis–FDR transparency-based regulatory policy that is responsive to US shareholder democracy is the great attraction of the financial universe that is sucking, has sucked, the rest of us into its vortex.

The decisive historical moment in the shift from insider network capitalism to global transparency capitalism was the New Deal. While other economies responded to the Depression by tightening the in-house rules of their financial clubs, FDR's New Dealers were not all old boys; many like Landis were new boys. Their credo was Brandeisian fervour about sunlight as the best disinfectant. At first, Americans limited the globalizing of their investment pretty much to putting their money in US transnationals that established subsidiaries around the globe. In time, however, foreign firms realized that they could attract US capital if they played the game in compliance with US rules. That meant disclosure of a lot of financial data, checking of that data by outside directors who sit on a Board Audit committee and, most importantly, external audit by a major US accounting firm. Foreign firms who do that to a satisfactory level may attract investment from US mutual fund managers or takeover bids from US TNCs and, if they do it to an exemplary level, listing on the New York Stock Exchange.

These US fund managers have been the knights on white chargers of transparent capitalism, Brandeisian crusaders who have invaded the temples of infidel money-changers, publicizing their secrets. Rather than overturning the money-tables, they have hung an American Express logo on them and put Peat Marwick on their prospectus. The potential of US capital investment caused them to securitize their money-changing business, incorporating in compliance with US standards as well as local ones. If US fund managers and the New York Stock Exchange started as the great attractions for the securitization and corporatization[3] of the world, European and Asian fund managers soon realized the benefits of focusing their attention on transparent foreign firms audited to US standards rather than to their own national standards.

The securitization and corporatization of the world was not limited to foreign private firms. In the 1990s foreign states with airlines, health-care systems and telecommunications systems that needed capital, securitized and corporatized major slabs of the state itself. In doing so, foreign states had to submit that part of their activities to US regulatory standards, especially in respect of transparency. The most recent development has been the securitization of stock exchanges themselves, so that they are traded on their own markets, and in future potentially on the NYSE. At the time of writing only the Stockholm and Australian Stock Exchanges have demutualized, submitting to reflexive securitization.

The final collapse of the UK gentlemen's-club model of capitalism was symbolized by Nick Leeson, a boy from Watford, who was trusted enough that he could secretly trade into bankruptcy

---

3 Neither all nor most securitization involves corporatization – the formation of new corporations. For example, the securitization of banking creates new classes of bondholders rather than new corporations. These bondholders acquire tradable securities in illiquid bank assets, such as mortgages. The bank pools, unbundles, repackages and refinances the mortgages into securities that investors can buy on capital markets. What they buy is a share in the value of the income flow due to the bank from the pooled set of mortgages. In this process something which is basically untradable (an individual loan backed by a bit of dirt) is pooled with millions of others to become a mortgage bond, itself an abstract object represented by a piece of paper that can now be bought and sold by large institutional investors in world bond markets. The globalization of intellectual property has enabled other forms of securitization. For example, the rock star David Bowie in 1997 issued bonds in the New York market backed by a royalty stream from his albums.

the merchant bank rivalled only by Rothschilds in building UK capitalism, a house so powerful that in the nineteenth century the Baring Brothers were often referred to as the 'sixth great power' in Europe (Ziegler 1988). Barings had collapsed in 1890, but then it had been saved by the City, led by Lord Lidderdale, Governor of the Bank of England, and the Rothschilds (G. Davies 1994: 348). This time Barings went under because global transparency capitalism was resilient enough to withstand the shock of its departure (which turned out only to be temporary), a departure the City could not have withstood a century earlier. In a television interview after the Barings collapse, Nick Leeson said that the house of Morgan and its auditors would never have allowed him to get away with the kind of massive covert trading in derivatives he managed at Barings.

In fact, it was the US merchant bank J.P. Morgan who, in October 1994, did something extraordinarily significant. J.P. Morgan released for general use its own proprietary risk management model, RiskMetrics, accompanied by the dataset on the volatilities of different types of financial products used with the model (Dale 1996: 165). As a big player, J.P. Morgan realised that it was in a community of fate with smaller players (like Barings) which used less sophisticated risk-management techniques than RiskMetrics. A major financial collapse that would affect all might occur, unless the risks of derivatives trading became more transparent. Trading in derivatives does not generate new kinds of risks; it generates risks that can get out of hand with a rapidity obscured by the complexity of secondary markets. Primary markets in shares, in contrast, are transparent and move slowly enough to be observed, as it were, with the naked eye.

Transparency capitalism depends on the value and risks of tradable assets being visible to the internal management of traders, their auditors, regulators, analysts, fund managers, rating agencies and investment advisers, if not ordinary shareholders. In the case of Barings, the risks of Nick Leeson's billion-dollar losses were visible to none of these players. At the very moment of the total triumph of global transparency capitalism, the complexity of the financial products that screen-based investment has spawned seems to beckon investors back to the security of local insider network investment. J.P. Morgan has put its systemic interest ahead of its proprietary interest. There is a direct analogue in Chapter 13, where the nuclear industry shared its proprietary risk-management systems when it realized, after Three Mile Island and Chernobyl, that another disaster would cause the demise of the entire industry. Ironically, global market collapses these days are referred to as market 'meltdowns'. Nuclear technology and the risk-engineering technology of derivatives trading both create a community of shared fate among industry participants, when misuse of the technology risks systemic collapse.

In Chapter 7, we concluded that contemporary capitalism is an information capitalism wherein market dominance arises from the control of abstract objects such as intellectual property, rather than from the control of tangible property. J.P. Morgan is a classic example of information capitalism – a major economic force that owns no factories and little land, its wealth based on knowhow in trading on financial markets. This is why it is so extraordinary that J.P. Morgan should give away a significant part of the information on which it flourishes. It did this because we live not only in an information society but in a risk society (Beck 1992) where the wealth born of more sophisticated analyses of information is also vulnerable to systemic risk.

IOSCO, the Basle Committee and all securities and banking regulators realize that they must reach global agreement on how to mandate risk-monitoring and risk-reporting of derivatives trading through regulation. The industry realizes that up to a point it must share risk control technology globally. Risk-spreading and global growth via diversification into off-shore investment can be facilitated by mandating off-shore compliance with international accounting standards. But it will backfire if foreign firms cultivate their own Nick Leesons who lose money they do not own through derivatives trading between audits. The regulatory challenge is enormous, as Susan Phillips of the US Federal Reserve Board has pointed out: 'with derivatives and highly liquid securities, risk profiles can change drastically not only day to day, but hour to hour and minute to minute' (cited in Dale 1996: 171).

Regulators also must acquire great wisdom in choosing when to abandon a presumption in favour of requiring transparency of risk. If a securities trader linked to a bank (a bigger one than Barings) suddenly got into trouble through risky derivatives trading the regulator may decide to keep it quiet, to prevent a run while the bank is given a chance to trade its way out of difficulty. Often there is a strong case against doing so. There is a place for both crisis prevention through a transparency that scares investment away from unacceptable risk, and for crisis management that brings down the shutters when transparency has failed. Crisis prevention through transparency is the more important side of this coin. Alan Greenspan, Chairman of the US Federal Reserve Board, has outlined what confronting it might mean for regulators:

> regulators would specify the magnitude of the market shocks that they expect banks to be able to withstand. The banks would then use their internal models to simulate the effects of such shocks on the market value of their trading portfolio. Banks would then be expected to maintain adequate capital to withstand the declines in market value produced by the specified market stresses. Examiners would assess the adequacy of the models and related internal controls and allow this approach only if the models and internal controls met or exceeded specified standards (cited in Dale 1996: 167).

A working group of the Euro-currency Standing Committee of the G-10 (the Fisher Report) has recommended that financial institutions should be required to disclose publicly their internal risk management system and the information generated by it (Dale 1996: 170–1). This amounts to mandating regulation of the step J.P. Morgan took voluntarily.

The attraction of this proposal is that it would not only improve the dynamic assessment of risk by the market and create a market incentive to have the best risk-management systems, but it would foster learning from those with the best systems. It would be a step to seize the intellectual property rights of financial risk managers that perhaps could only be taken globally: nations could not be expected to force their traders to disclose knowhow to foreign competitors unless the competition were required to do the same.

All IOSCO working groups are in some important sense concerned with an international convergence of standards that assures transparency. There is also a working group on disclosure which in 1998 promulgated 'Disclosure Standards to Facilitate Cross-border Offerings and Listings by Multinational Issuers'.

## Mutual Recognition, National Sovereignty, Harmonization

To some extent, mutual recognition of corporations chartered in other countries has always been a fact of life. Whenever a ship owned by a foreign corporation sails into a port and an officer of the corporation goes ashore and buys something on behalf of the corporation, the actor has been constituted as an actor under another nation's law. Domestic law for many purposes can hold individuals liable when they act for a foreign corporation; domestic registration can be required before certain activities are undertaken. But nations realized early that it was not necessarily practical to require a visiting pope to reincorporate the Catholic church domestically before he was allowed to act on its behalf. We could not begin to survey the differences among national laws between the extent and circumstances in which foreign incorporation is recognized. But to our knowledge there is no state without some degree of mutual recognition of incorporation elsewhere.

Mutual recognition has been an important principle in North American securities regulations and between Australia and New Zealand. In 1987 the latter two countries agreed that a prospectus prepared under the law of one jurisdiction could be accepted in the other. The EC has, through its system of directives, been the main exponent of harmonization of securities regulation.

At the same time, states have been jealous of their sovereignty to incorporate on their own terms domestically and to demand that firms incorporated elsewhere at least register locally before they trade to locals. Efforts to harmonize companies and securities law have been very recent and, except within the EC, have so far amounted to little. In short, harmonization has been a late and limp ideal.

Many stock exchanges have been fairly relaxed about recognizing one set of standards for domestic listings and different standards for foreign listings. This does not mean they have been attracted to 'anything goes' for foreign listings, but that they judge how much elasticity of mutual recognition is justified in a particular case.

## Lowest-cost Location v. World's Best Practice, Deregulation

Lowest-cost location is seen as a major issue in the corporate law literature because of the Delaware phenomenon in the US. Delaware attracts a lot of out-of-state incorporation because of lower costs in doing so. There is, however, little evidence of this happening in other federal states and the EC (Romano 1996). Internationally, if firms incorporated and listed on exchanges where costs, particularly demands for disclosure, were lowest, they would all do so in developing countries. However, what most do is incorporate and list domestically. When they want to list internationally in order to get access to foreign investors, they pursue that objective by listing on exchanges that give them maximum credibility in the eyes of foreign investors. Listing in New York brings most credibility. Passing the test of the most stringent listing requirements constitutes maximum competitiveness in pursuit of foreign investment. Hence, the principle of world's best practice clearly dominates that of lowest-cost location. In an interview at the New York Stock Exchange a senior official told us that the NYSE takes the view that 'higher standard regulation draws a lot of business'. When we pressed him on this, suggesting that competition among stock exchanges might drive down standards, he disagreed, pointing out that the US initiative on insider trading had not resulted in trading moving off-shore.

That said, New York Stock Exchange rules, particularly on disclosure, are far too demanding for most German or Chinese companies. Many German companies are comfortable with disclosure to the standards required by the London Stock Exchange, however. If the costs and openness demanded in London are too high for most large Chinese companies, competition for their listing might occur between the Hong Kong and Singapore exchanges. That competition is not a lowest-cost race to the bottom. It is niche competition for a middling level of market credibility – lower than New York, higher than Shanghai.

There are corporate law havens where incorporation can be bought off the shelf for a pittance with no questions asked, no taxes to pay and limited transparency (e.g. see Kenny 1993). This is a different niche market. Its market is to serve those who seek to avoid domestic taxes by locating off-shore, to obscure movements of assets, to create a complex round-robin of holding companies to conceal a fraud from shareholders or creditors, or some other form of law evasion.

In the words of one interviewee, there are always some activities that people 'will want to do in the dark' (interview at NYSE 1994).

The world system thus has niche competition, essentially between New York and London for high-credibility, high-cost international listing; niche competition between exchanges with middling credibility (e.g. Singapore v. Hong Kong); and niche competition at the bottom of the market for lowest-cost off-shore incorporation of non-listed companies.

The highwater-mark of deregulation in companies and securities law was the nineteenth century. By then most monarchs had liberalized their prerogatives to dictate the terms of corporate charters. Incorporation took off when firms were free to incorporate for any business purpose. The Great Depression saw a triumph of state regulation over the principle of deregulation. This triumph was never really reversed in the supposed heyday of Reagan–Thatcher deregulation of the 1980s. Ronald Reagan's transition team found the SEC in 1980 to have a 'deserved reputation for integrity and efficiency...appears to be a model government agency'. Indeed it was during the 1980s that the handcuffs were out on Wall Street more than during any other period of regulatory history (Ayres & Braithwaite 1992: Ch. 1; see also OECD 1995). After the crash of 1987, although there was some deregulation, there was more tightening of standards globally to some degree.

### Strategic Trade, National Treatment, Most Favoured Nation, Reciprocity

Strategic trade has never been an important principle in companies and securities law. This is the prescription of designing the content and stringency of regulation so as to advantage national over foreign firms. Sometimes this principle arises faintly, as in the content of simultaneous multinational securities offerings. The fear in the US is that foreign issues of multinational stock will divert business from US issuers in US capital markets. The solution is sometimes argued to be that national regulation should not encourage the emergence of such offerings. To some extent, as we have seen, exchanges have given domestic investors ready access to certain foreign firms by being less demanding of foreign offerors. The content of corporations and securities law has not been contested in trade policy.

For this reason, the trade policy principles of national treatment, Most Favoured Nation and reciprocity have never played a significant part in the contest of principles fought over the companies and securities law-making of any nation.

### Rule Compliance v. Continuous Improvement

We have not encountered a company law text which discusses the principle of continuous improvement – the prescription of doing better every year than the previous year in terms of a regulatory objective, even if legal requirements were exceeded in the previous year. The job of company lawyers is mostly seen as advising clients in what we have defined as the principle of rule compliance: the prescription that companies ought to see legality as exhausting their obligations; to go as far as the rules require, but no further. The contest with environmental law is between rule compliance and continuous improvement; in company law the contest is really between the notion that lawyers should advise clients how to comply or advise how to avoid or evade. One exception in the literature is Wheeler and Sillanpää's (1997: 340) *The Stakeholder Corporation*, which argues for continuous improvement in transparency and public reporting and says that empirically there has been a global shift toward increased accountability (1997: 82).

## Mechanisms

### Military Coercion, Economic Coercion, Systems of Reward

While some US companies and securities law concepts were put in place during the occupation of Japan after the Second World War, these were not dictated as terms of postwar reconstruction in the way that a competition law that would break up the *zaibatsu* was dictated. British companies and securities law was usually chosen by the colonial legislatures later in the colonial experience rather than imposed as laws that displaced indigenous law at the time of conquest. Military coercion was therefore not an important mechanism of globalization.

Given that corporations and securities law has not been an important focus of contest in trade diplomacy, states have not sought to globalize such law through threat or use of economic sanctions or systems of reward.

### Modelling

Double-entry bookkeeping and limited liability ultimately acquired legislative vindication, but their global spread was more a result of modelling custom than modelling law, at least with the former. We have seen that the London Stock Exchange was the crucial model during the nineteenth century when hundreds of stock exchanges opened around the world. Rarely was the setting up of a stock exchange the result of a state legislative enactment. Nor is it quite right to describe it in Hayekian terms as spontaneous ordering. A stock exchange is an elaborate self-regulatory regime that most of the world copied or adapted from London. It globalized because business people in all centres where capitalism flourished – from Charters Towers to Bombay – wanted to organize themselves to raise capital and invest it.

The modelling of the SEC as a regulatory institution, shifting company law back into the public-law domain from the domain of private law where it languished during the centuries of liberalization of corporate chartering, was a modelling of law rather than a modelling of custom (that was later codified). More than just law was modelled from the SEC; there was also modelling of the enforcement strategy and administrative practice initiated by James Landis. An explicit mechanism for this modelling is the bilateral MOUs the SEC has signed with many other national regulatory authorities since the 1980s. The SEC has been the initiator of these MOUs. IOSCO has helped facilitate their spread. The MOUs oblige but do not legally bind national regulators to share intelligence, conduct surveillance in global markets at the request of their partners and conduct investigations for the foreign partner where their powers allow.

In the case of insider trading, US diplomatic pressure was deployed, quite determinedly in cases such as Japan, for the modelling of a law which only the US had for many years. But most of the concepts in the UK and US companies and securities laws of the 1929–34 period were widely modelled without any diplomatic pressure to do so. Although companies and securities laws differ in very important ways, a striking fact is that comparative surveys of the law such as those of Robinson (1985) and Euromoney Publications (1992) include a comparative index covering a common set of basic concepts. Boards have different structures in different legal systems, but they all have them, and there is much in common in directors' legal duties. The voting rights of shareholders vary a lot, but there is less variation in how to elect company directors than in the way citizens of the same countries elect their governments. Universally there is a concept of annual reporting based on a European calendar, something that was not even universal within the US before 1934. There is a surprising globalization of technical concepts such as incorporation itself, debentures, takeover announcements, prospectuses.

The main divides found by Wood (1997) in a global survey of financial law, heavily weighted to the consideration of corporate bankruptcy, were:

• a common-law group of states that includes a surprisingly high 33 per cent of the world's population (subdivided into a traditional English group of the nineteenth-century British empire and an American common-law group that includes Liberia and ten small Pacific states);
• a traditional Franco-Latin legal framework (about 20 per cent of the world's population, including France, Spain, Portugal and their former empires covering nearly all of Central and South America, most of Africa and some of the Middle East and the Pacific, Belgium, Bulgaria, Romania and Greece);
• a Germanic and Scandinavian group that accounts for 7 per cent of the world, including Germany, Indonesia, Switzerland, Poland, Taiwan and Scandinavia;
• a mixed Franco-Latin/Germanic group that includes Italy, Denmark, Thailand, Louisiana, the Philippines, Turkey, Austria (Hungary) and much of its former Central European empire (6 per cent);
• a mixed Roman and common-law group that includes Japan, South Korea, Quebec, Scotland, Sri Lanka, South Africa and a number of other African states (5 per cent);
• an Islamic group of seven Middle Eastern jurisdictions (1 per cent).

Almost 30 per cent of the world's population lived in 'emerging' or unclassified jurisdictions, mostly former communist states, the most important being China and Russia: 'It is probably too early to say which of the other groups they will join, but most appear to be leaning towards the Germanic and Scandinavian group (especially China)' (Wood 1997: 8). What is noteworthy about this interesting global map of financial law is that 99 per cent of the modelling is of a Western European model. The exception is the small Islamic group, but even there it is noteworthy that Egypt, Iran, Iraq, Jordan, Lebanon, Syria, the United Arab Emirates, Algeria, Morocco and Libya are members of the traditional Franco-Latin group rather than the Islamic group.

Western European modelling of securities law was assisted by the fact that most non-Western exchanges were run by European brokers. For example, all ninety-five stockbrokers operating in China in 1914 were European, seventy-two of them British (Michie 1988: 49). Exceptions where the membership of exchanges was mainly native were Bombay and the Japanese exchanges, but even there the self-regulatory framework of the exchanges was European/North American (Sarna 1990).

There are significant elements of regional modelling as well. For example, the Singapore Companies Code is partly based on Australian company law and there have been some Australian influences on Malaysian, Melanesian and Indonesian corporate law, the education of key drafters in Australian law schools being a factor.

Since the New Deal, modelling has predominantly emanated from concepts forged in Washington and New York. Consider the important instance of Board Audit Committees. The innovation began in 1940 when the SEC recommended a Board Audit Committee of Outside Directors at an administrative hearing where it found that audited financial statements prepared by Price Waterhouse for the pharmaceutical company McKesson and Robbins were false and misleading (Samet & Sherman 1984: 43). For the next three decades the SEC only very sporadi-cally and informally encouraged companies to have Board Audit Committees. In 1967 the American Institute of Certified Accountants responded to a wave of concern over the question of director liability by recommending Audit Committees. A special committee went further in 1978, recommending Audit Committees as a condition of audit, a recommendation not accepted by the membership.

From 1974 the SEC began more formally to encourage the use of Audit Committees by requiring disclosure under the *Securities Exchange Act 1934* of the existence or lack thereof of a standing Audit Committee. In 1978 the New York Stock Exchange took the stronger step of requir-ing an Audit Committee as a condition of listing. Non-members of the exchange in the US also complied with the requirement, because they assumed the courts would interpret the NYSE policy as establishing a new standard of responsible behaviour (Samet & Sherman 1984: 46). More sig-nificantly, major accounting and law firms recommended it to their clients: it became part of the standard of responsible professional conduct that protected them from negligence suits if they rec-ommended, indeed urged it. US accounting and law firms applied this policy not only within the US but globally to their large corporate client base. In many if not most countries, whatever the Big Five accounting firms define as responsible professional behaviour in the accounting industry becomes so defined by the domestic industry. Certainly this was true in respect of the globalization of Audit Committees of outside directors during the 1980s and 1990s.

In sum, the mechanism of modelling shows the principle of transparency; it helps to forge a US-style transparency capitalism based on the idea that 'more information is better for most people' (NYSE interview 1994).

### Reciprocal Adjustment, Non-reciprocal Coordination

Finally, there is substantial evidence of reciprocal adjustment occurring, at least in respect of internationally agreed accounting standards, after centuries of indifference to that principle. IOSCO is a comparatively recent institution for fostering reciprocal adjustment. Because the hege-monic states have basically not cared whether other states modelled their companies and securi-ties laws (except within the EC), because they have never loomed as significant in GATT negotiations, there is no evidence of the mechanism of non-reciprocal coordination being used. We know of no case where one state has changed its corporations law in response to a trade or other benefit offered by another state in an unrelated policy domain.

### Capacity-building

Capacity-building is a mechanism of globalization of only small significance. IOSCO has a Development Committee to assist emerging markets. It puts a dozen or so developing country regulators through an on-the-job training program each year. The 1993 IOSCO budget for this work was a meagre $US20 000. France, the UK, US and EC also contribute to training developing country regulators, but only modestly. The SEC effort is not trivial, however. It runs an annual two-week training program for about thirty regulators from developing securities markets. Most of the investment in these programs in recent years has gone to post-communist societies.

## Conclusion

The globalizations of several regulatory innovations have been responsible for the rise and rise of the corporation as a twentieth-century transformation rivalling in importance the rise of the nation-state in the Middle Ages. By the end of the twentieth century many of the things once monopolies of family or state are now done by corporations: child-care, cooking, policing, imprisonment, rail transport, telecommunications, entertainment, water supply, electricity, even the very regulation of incorporation that has been constitutive of this takeover.

An Italian legal innovation was required to facilitate this growth – the idea of a corporation as a *persona ficta* that could own land, for example. An Italian accounting innovation – double-entry bookkeeping – was essential to the separation of ownership and control, of moneys due to investors and managers, that was vital to the globalization of the business corporation. Limited liability (probably Arab), securitization (Neapolitan) and the stock exchange (Dutch) were institutional innovations which globalized in a way that enabled the business corporation to spread.

Technological innovation – telegraph, telephone, tickertape and computer – centralized efficient market-making for securities in dominant metropolitan exchanges. Communication and processing of financial information became so efficient that an incredible variety of new assets were securitized. The retail stores where we shopped were formerly owned by families, now they are corporations that build shopping centres with money supplied in small parcels by shareholders. Owners of large assets like shopping malls learnt that they were worth more if they were securitized, because there was more demand for a piece of a high-quality asset than for buying it in one big lump. Investors wanted to spread risks and have a liquid asset that could be traded on a day's notice. Just as the private individual who owned a large asset found it was worth more to 10 000 shareholders than to a single buyer of the lump asset, so states learned that tradable fractions of the state were worth more to shareholders than they were to the state. As a consequence large slabs of states have been securitized, expanding the dominion of corporations and markets. This lesson was the obverse of the lesson of three centuries earlier, that national debt could be sold at lower interest rates by breaking it up into bonds than by selling it in one lump to family bankers like the Fuggers and Welsers, as had previously been done.

As a result of these changes, the state itself became subject to the regulatory imperatives of a corporatized, marketized world. States were no different from other borrowers and issuers of securities in requiring a credit rating from corporate risk-assessors – rating agencies such as Standard and Poor's and Moody's. It follows that we cannot view the globalization of the regulation of corporations and securities as public or state regulation. Our understanding must be more reflexive than that because the state is object as well as subject of the global regulatory transformation. Moreover, our analysis suggests that the self-regulatory activities of the New York Stock Exchange may have more profound effects on the regulation of major foreign corporations than their own states will. The expectations for financial disclosure it transmits through the agency of large US accounting firms with branches everywhere are important even for stock offerors with no interest in listing on the New York Stock Exchange. Wall Street not only makes the most important markets, it also makes the regulatory framework for many of the less important ones.

Through their reflexive operation, the processes of corporatization and securitization ratchet-up levels of transparency. Privatization around the world builds listings. The New York Stock Exchange gets the cream, but the total pool also increases. Other stock exchanges also pick up listings. Emerging stock exchanges expand, and this changes the nature of their market operation. Their growth forces them to reassess their practices. They move closer to New York's standards because they are growing and want to keep growing. And the New York Stock Exchange cannot lower its standards.

Our story has shown the triumph of the US model of regulated transparency, the progressive securitization of the world on terms that will attract US purchasers of securities. A Big Five accountancy firm audits the privatized Chinese widget manufacturer not because that is what the Chinese state wants, nor because that is what the US state wants (though the SEC applauds). It happens because US investors want the auditor to be an agent of the US regulatory standards that they long since forced upon US companies through the US Congress, the SEC and the New York Stock Exchange. US investor demand for US regulatory standards applies whether the US investors are institutional or retail and whether the investment occurs inside or outside the US. European and Japanese institutional investors, in contrast, do not like US disclosure requirements for their domestic investment; at home they have a comparative advantage over US capital because they have insider understanding of local risks and opportunities (Soskice 1999). When they spread their risks into off-shore investment, they too quite like US-style investor protection before they put their toe in the water.

The big picture of the history of the twentieth century is that every nation is corporatized and securitized, some more completely than others. But all have a credit rating set in New York. The decisive historical moment in this process is the New Deal. The decisive regulatory idea is transparency, demanded of US securities markets by the SEC, transmitted by the New York Stock Exchange and US accounting firms as a global regulatory ideal when investment globalizes. Neither IOSCO nor any other international institution is a central actor in this process, though IOSCO became more important after the Barings fiasco dramatized the risks of insufficiently transparent derivatives trading. Modelling by actors who want to flourish in the face of global market imperatives – states, corporations, self-regulated exchanges, IOSCO itself – is the key mechanism of globalization.

Of course, economists would say that the market is the key mechanism. And it is true that one reason why the institution of the stock exchange has globalized is that it satisfies actors' economic interests. Yet the evidence suggests it to be a false theory that stock exchanges will spontaneously organize wherever they are functional for capital formation. Many places are quite incapable of market-making; at some point in history all places were incapable of doing so. Securitized, corporatized capitalism might have taken off in Italy, Spain or Poland centuries earlier than it did.[4] The knowhow, starting capital, banking infrastructure and economic interest were no less accessible in such places than in England. Indeed, why not go back further and ask the same question about China, given its greater economic development than England until the last few

---

4  'Paul Grousset...claimed that "contemporary capitalism has invented nothing". Sapori is even more explicit: "Even today, it is impossible to find anything – income tax for instance – which did not have some precedent in the genius of one of the Italian republics". It is true that everything seems to have been there in embryo: bills of exchange, credit, minted coins, banks, forward selling, public finance, loans, capitalism, colonialism – as well as social disturbances, a sophisticated labour force, class struggles, social oppression, political atrocities' (Braudel 1979: 91). We might add holding companies, that were invented in Florence (Braudel 1979:128) and patents, in Venice. Flourishing capitalism is based less on original invention than on appropriating and institutionalizing the inventions of others. Witness Japan. Even blast furnaces and mining techniques fundamental to UK industrialization were appropriated from more technically advanced Germany by importing Germans with the knowhow (Braudel 1979: 552).

centuries, its invention of paper money and letters of credit, or the Arab world which invented the numeration system, the *commenda*, bills of exchange, even the steam-powered turbine (Braudel 1984: 543) a millennium or more before England made so much of these innovations?

Our argument is that to understand the corporatization and securitization of the world by the modelling of London and New York we need to understand the way specific entrepreneurial actors kept innovating, building one institution on another (a futures (secondary) market on top of a primary market), taking non-tradable assets and turning them into tradable ones (e.g. the mortgage bond market) and so on. This requires more than a market. It requires more than a market to allow David Bowie to turn his personality and music into a tradable security on the New York market (the 'personality bond'). Without the globalization of intellectual property that we described in Chapter 7 these intangible assets cannot be securitized. The market is constituted by an epistemic community hospitable to entrepreneurship and by institutions which are constitutive of more elaborated institutions. These institutions are created by purposive action, not just because they are functional. Most importantly, under the framework adopted in this book, regulatory institutions, not just laws, but the customs of the London Stock Exchange or the *Lex Mercatoria* (see Chapters 8 and 10) are constitutive of abstract objects such as corporations and securities that transform the whole world. Entrepreneurial lawyers in this story are not passive agents waiting on instructions from the powerful, nor are they superstructural dupes in the vulgar Marxian sense. They forge structures actively by selling ideas like the *persona ficta*, the securitization of the national debt, intellectual property protections and poison pills to popes, potentates, princes, parliamentarians and moneyed principals (see Powell 1993; Cain 1994; McBarnet 1994).

Understanding purposive entrepreneurship at the centre to pick up ideas like limited liability from the periphery is not enough for understanding the corporatization and securitization of the world. To understand that, we also need a theory of modelling from centre back to periphery – the topic of Chapter 25.

*History of Globalization*

### Tolls, Tariffs and the Mercantilist State System

Winham (1992: 10) is surely wrong when he says 'regulation and taxing of trade are almost as old as trade itself. Cuneiform tablets found at Tell el-Amarna certainly show that a commercial treaty between the kings of Egypt and Babylon involved duties on imports; Kautilya's *Arthasastra*, a manual of Indian statecraft written at least two millennia ago, contains a tariff schedule (Winham 1992: 14–16); Carthage had a trade treaty with Rome in 509 BC (the first extant document from Rome (Mann 1986: 251) and is believed to have had earlier treaties with the Etruscans (Law 1990: 124). Yet the movement of obsidian used in blades indicates trading from boats around the Mediterranean by 7000 BC (Curtin 1984: 71) and we assume from ethnographic work among pre-urban civilizations in places such as Africa that rich trading relationships go back millennia before tariff schedules were conceived.

As we saw in Chapter 7, the spread of the Law Merchant in the Middle Ages, modelled by diasporas of Venetian, Genoan, Jewish and other merchants across Europe and the Levant and into Asia, was critical to the growth in trade between cities. Bills of exchange, sale of goods rules and dispute resolution practices, along with standard forms of contract and ways of interpreting them in a partially globalized form, were taken from the *Lex Mercatoria* into national laws as states progressively nationalized law from the twelfth century. Unlike other areas of law, therefore, those derived from the *Lex Mercatoria* started existence as national laws in a partially harmonized shape.

The most important feature of the history of the past millennium, compared with previous millennia, has been the rise of the nation-state. One reason this form of human organization globalized from Western European origins is that the parts of the world that formed nation-states earliest flourished and dominated regions where the nation-state rose later. A major reason why the early nation-states flourished is that they created pacified spaces where trade could flow more freely. It became more possible to travel with goods from one town to another without fear of robbers. Equally importantly, tolls and entry restrictions on the flow of goods between cities were progressively dismantled. Technical standards became more standardized, avoiding many technical barriers to free intranational trade. By the nineteenth century nation-states controlled almost all of the world's territory and trade was mostly free within states. Yet it had not been until 1671 in England that the state had taken control of customs (Braudel 1979: 525).

States persisted with the same barriers to trade between states as they had dismantled within their borders. In fact, they expanded them. Tariffs – taxes on imports – grew ever higher and became a major source of revenue for states. They were in the grip of mercantilism – the principle of selling more to foreigners than they sell domestically lest a balance of payments deficit leave the state with an inadequate supply of circulating gold or silver.

## Unilateral and Bilateral Free Trade

Adam Smith's (1776) *The Wealth of Nations* and David Ricardo's (1817) *The Principles of Political Economy* knocked the intellectual props from under mercantilism, yet two centuries later many of its institutional props remain. Ricardo's principle of comparative advantage – import goods produced more efficiently than by local producers, export where one has the greatest comparative advantage over other nations – did not gain widespread intellectual currency until the mid nineteenth century. At that point, however, the British government became so convinced that it unilaterally dismantled protectionism and set out to persuade the rest of the world to be free traders.

Free-trading agreements had an early history among the counts of Champagne (from 1180), the Northern European Hanseatic League and the northern Italian city-states in the era before most nation-states had been created. At some time, two hundred cities belonged to the Hanseatic free-trade network. There was no centre, though from 1373 Lubeck was confirmed as the home of a Court of Appeal that consolidated legal rights of anchorage, storage, residence and local immunity. 'To be Hanseatic was to belong to an inimitable, international civilization based on shared values...In European history [the Hanseatic tradition] shines as a beacon for all who seek a future based on sturdy local autonomy, international co-operation, and mutual prosperity' (Davies 1997: 341).

These limited free-trading agreements were vital to the rise and spread of capitalism. But it was Victorian England, first pursuing a unilateral free-trade policy then later in the nineteenth century negotiating bilateral trade treaties with other European powers, that set out to spread the Most Favoured Nation (MFN) principle (which a century later became the cornerstone of the GATT). European wealth expanded on the back of decisions such as the 1868 declaration of the Rhine as a free route for ships of all nations and the expansion of the German customs union from 1818. But recessions later in the nineteenth century, combined with US mercantilism grounded in the principle of protecting infant industries, later reversed much of the mid-century liberalization (Trebilcock & Howse 1995: 19). After the decline of UK hegemony with the First World War, its leadership toward MFN treaties totally collapsed into an era of beggar-thy-neighbour policies that ultimately contributed to the Great Depression from 1929.

The Roosevelt administration in the US saw this and negotiated thirty-two bilateral liberalizing trade agreements based on a principle of reciprocity during the 1930s. Many 'had clauses that foreshadowed those that are currently in the GATT' (Jackson 1989: 31), just as the nineteenth-century British bilaterals foreshadowed MFN. The other important development between the wars was an International Convention Relating to the Simplification of Customs Formalities, negotiated by the League of Nations. As the end of the Second World War approached, the Roosevelt administration was convinced that beggar-thy-neighbour policies had been a cause of both the Depression and the war. So at Bretton Woods in 1944 the US showed leadership toward new global institutions that would impose a cooperative order on postwar reconstruction, currency markets and liberal trade. The Bretton Woods institutions were the IMF, the World Bank and ultimately the GATT.

The US administration opened its campaign for the adoption of an international trade organization under the slogan 'if goods can't cross the borders, soldiers will' (Marceau 1994: 61). At its first meeting in 1946 the UN Economic and Social Council adopted a resolution calling for a conference to draft a charter for an International Trade Organization (ITO) and the US tabled a draft of the proposed ITO Charter (with the full support of the UK, with which the US had penned the text). Four meetings were held to rework this draft into the Havana Charter of 1948. But by 1948, although the presidency remained in Democrat hands, the US Congress had fallen to the Republicans. When the President submitted the ITO Charter to the Congress for approval, it refused. The rest of the world saw no point in a global trade organization without the US, so the ITO never came into being.

## The GATT

The President had pre-existing congressional approval to negotiate a multilateral tariff-reduction treaty, however, so the General Agreement on Tariffs and Trade (GATT) came into existence as a treaty without a secretariat but with a Protocol of Provisional Application. From this point the history of the global regulation of trade is largely the history of the GATT. For half a century the GATT remained the provisional protocol for a treaty that had never come into force. It evolved as an elaborate system of side agreements to flesh out the rules of the world trading system: by 1990 the GATT consisted of more than 180 treaties, many of which were not mutually consistent and not entirely consistent with the original GATT Provisional Protocol (Jackson 1990: 26). At the 1955 Review Session of the GATT, an organizational protocol was drafted to establish an Organization for Trade Cooperation, a bare institutional framework for the treaty stripped of the original ambitions for the ITO. But the US Congress stood by its insistence that it had approved a multilateral treaty, not a multilateral organization, and refused again. So how did the GATT emerge as arguably the most powerful economic institution in the world?

Against the forcefully reiterated will of the US Congress, Sir Eric Wyndham White, the British chief administrative officer of the UN group that assisted at the drafting conferences for the ITO and the GATT, built a highly competent GATT secretariat which circumvented the fiction that the GATT was not an 'organization'. After the collapse of US ratification for the Havana Charter:

> an Interim Commission for the ITO (ICITO) was set up, in the typical pattern of preparing the way for a new international organization. A small staff was assembled to prepare the ground for the ITO, and this staff serviced the needs of the GATT. As years passed and it became clear that the ITO was never to come into being, this staff found that all of its time was devoted to the GATT, and it became de facto the GATT secretariat (Jackson 1989: 37).

By the time he retired in 1968, with the title of Director-General of the GATT, Sir Eric Wyndham White had forged an unconstitutional, temporary GATT into the most powerful, entrenched non-organization the world had seen. At least the Provisional Protocol provided virtually no Constitution. White, like subsequent Directors-General, was hands-on, drafting text for the first six GATT rounds, brokering deals behind the scenes to break stalemates between nations in order to reach final agreement. To this day, much symbolic effort goes into sustaining the fiction that the GATT is little more than an agreement which creates a space for multilateral contracting. For example, mysterious parchments headed 'Non-Paper of the Chair' of such-and-such a GATT committee are widely circulated.

The GATT secretariat finally became a fully legal personality when the Uruguay Round Final Act of 1994 created the World Trade Organization. Interestingly, the proposal to set up the WTO as an international organization came not from the US, which was seen as guarded about supporting it publicly, but from its Quad and NAFTA allies, Canada, the EU and Mexico.

GATT rounds work by contracting parties making offers to liberalize trade. The major players – the US, the EC and Japan in the Tokyo Round (1973–79), the Quad of these three plus Canada in the Uruguay Round – define the industry sectors and types of trade barriers that should be the subject of offers. Iterated negotiation of these offers bilaterally ultimately puts the Director-General in a position where he or she can draft a text of the final agreement that meets the approval of the major players.[1] Negotiation then proceeds more multilaterally around that text.

In the seven rounds to the end of the Tokyo Round, the GATT accomplished huge reductions in tariffs on industrial production. The Tokyo Round alone accomplished approximately a 35 per cent reduction in the industrial tariffs of major economies (Jackson, Louis and Matsushita 1982: 272–3). Notwithstanding real progress in the Tokyo Round Agreement on Technical Barriers to Trade toward dismantling technical barriers to trade, these remain considerable. For example, national technical standards are still written so as to favour the production specifications of domestic firms over those of foreign competitors. Managed trade may well be worse than it was before tariffs were reduced – for example, 'we will voluntarily restrain our exports of X if you undertake to increase your imports of Y by a certain percentage'.

### The 1980s: Aggressive US Unilateralism

A worsening trade deficit of the US with a number of other countries in the 1980s fomented a mood of protectionism among the US people and Congress. Trade unions and certain sections of industry played important roles in fanning this discontent. Bhagwati (1990: 12) likened it to the 'diminished giant' syndrome in late nineteenth-century Britain that saw the rise of the National Fair Trade League, the National Society for the Defence of British Industry and the Reciprocity Fair Trade Association. While the decline in the proportion of the world's wealth in the hands of the US at the end of the century has not been as sharp as the UK decline in the early part of the twentieth century, massive deficits with trading partners were not something to which the American people were accustomed. Their response in the 1980s was xenophobic.

In the mid 1980s the Congress was awash with protectionist Bills. The Omnibus Trade and Competitiveness Act which finally passed in 1988 was moderate compared with some of the retaliatory trade legislation being touted. The Republican administration argued consistently for moderation, though in the end it seemed pleased enough with a trade policy which involved it being the soft cop and Congress being the hard cop. The bottom line was a rise of 'aggressive unilateralism' (Bhagwati & Patrick 1990) by the US. Its vehicles were 1988 amendments to section 301 of the *Trade and Tariff Act 1974*. Super 301 and Special 301 provisions were enacted. Super 301 requires the US Trade Representative to prepare a priority list of countries imposing trade barriers to US exports, set deadlines for their removal and make decisions on trade retaliation should they fail to comply. Special 301 applies a similar regime to a priority list of countries which fail to respect US intellectual property rights.

While the legislatively preferred route for section 301 concerns is that they be pursued through GATT dispute resolution first and dropped if a GATT panel finds against the US, in six

---

1 For the perspective of a former Director-General on the role of the Director-General, see Long (1987: 52–3).

'Regular 301' cases pursued between 1975 and 1989 retaliation had not been authorized by the GATT (Bhagwati 1990: 2). The unrealistic deadlines of Super and Special 301 made the 1988 law even more likely to cause future US aggressive unilateralism to be GATT-illegal. It marked a decisive move away from a rule-based toward a power-based approach to trade negotiation.

The risk was that other nations would retaliate by enacting their own Super 301 laws and that the rule of international trade law would collapse. Worse, the whole trading system might have fallen apart. Commenting on the wisdom of the US in holding back on GATT-inconsistent 301 sanctions and specifically on finally settling with Brazil rather than ignoring a likely Panel Finding that its 301 action against Brazil was illegal, a GATT official said: 'The alternative is the US not caring about panels. GATT is not something important to us. Then ripples of non-credibility move out. It would not take long with loss of trust and confidence for the whole system to fall apart.'

The threats from abroad were clear: 'What if the EC was to assert that the US patent system is discriminatory and should be repealed since it takes "first inventing, first served" as its premise for Americans and "first applying, first served" as its basis for dealing with foreigners?' (Kuroda 1990: 220–1). But the threats largely remained in the realm of the possible. Most states did not have the large domestic markets needed to give their equivalent of a Super 301 the necessary coercive backing. Without that backing it was a difficult matter to get US trade negotiators to listen. Europe created a New Trade Instrument with similar capabilities to Section 301. But, as one EC official told us, the problem was that in Europe getting a 'clear mandate to hit somebody over the head is impossible. There are too many conflicting interests. France wants to sell a fast train to Korea, so it goes soft on IPR'. The same official observed that Europe had no real equivalent to the 301 process: 'It has no gun to shoot'.

In the case of Japan, retaliation did not occur because, in the words of a former Vice-Minister of the Ministry of International Trade and Industy (MITI), Japan put its trust in 'perspicacious individuals' in the US administration like US Trade Representative (USTR) Carla Hills who saw the danger and 'seem[s] to be seeking to deflect attention away from Super 301 while taking pains to ensure that the provision is applied to its minimum extent' (Kuroda 1990: 221). Australian trade officials were less optimistic about such 'perspicacious individuals', but Australia was in no position to respond in kind to the US: 'On 301, Congress says: "Either you use the weapon you've got or we'll give you a bigger one and make you use it". So they [the administration] can't listen to voices like ours saying "Put your gun away now"' (Australian trade official). The Australian perception seems realistic even though there are grounds for short-term, but only short-term, optimism, given the following kind of statement from a senior USTR official: 'It's clear to US decision-makers that after Uruguay, the US will have to be more circumspect on bilateral enforcement. We sign an agreement and abide by it. The US will abide by the spirit at least for a couple of years!' (USTR interview 1993). Later he explained that if an issue is important enough the US will break ranks with an international agreement. International norms, he claimed, could always be resisted by the US through relying on the idea of civil disobedience: 'A legitimate violation of rules for a high purpose' is okay.

### The Hard Cop and Soft Cop within the US State

Ultimately, a simple calculus of threat and coercion lay behind the US use of the 301 process. Despite the GATT-inconsistent use of its 301 process, the costs to other countries of the US acting on its threat (clearly articulated) to scotch trade multilateralism by abandoning the Uruguay Round were much higher than the costs of the threats (not clearly articulated) by other countries to engage in their own brand of unilateralism. The US knew, in other words, that it could bank on its own threats (coupled with occasional action) being taken seriously by other states so that it would probably not have to wear the costs of a protectionist war. To use Ayres and Braithwaite's (1992) terminology, the US effectively deployed an enforcement pyramid: 'Watchlists got us out of retaliation exercises while keeping the spotlight on important areas. India was a failure but there was a lot of success from sabre-rattling and occasionally taking it out of the scabbard' (US Chamber of Commerce interview).

At the same time, the US could assume that states would be reluctant to back any threats they made because those states did not want to risk bearing the costs of a protectionist war. The US figured, rightly, that it would not have to suffer the full costs of its threats and that other states would be deterred from resistance by the prospect of having to bear the costs of their own threats. Finally, the US was helped by the fact that other states (e.g. the EU and Australia) would free-ride on its 301 process by seeking to obtain bilateral agreements with those states with which the US had concluded a bilateral agreement using the 301 process.

Hence, the US hard-cop–soft-cop policy worked. The unravelling of the Uruguay Round and the entire rule-based system of international trade that might have occurred had the administration been faithful to the wishes of the congressional majority did not occur. In fact, Special and Super 301 helped bring the Uruguay Round closer to the conclusion the US wanted. The administration used the new weapons to select Brazil and India for trade sanctions as they were the countries most strongly resisting the US Uruguay Round agenda (particularly on TRIPS (Trade-Related Intellectual Property)), TRIMS (Trade Related Investment Measures) and GATS (General Agreement on Trade in Services). A top USTR official was prepared to admit as much in print (Feketekuty 1996). Brazil and India were also strategic targets because each was 'too small as a market for US products to wield any counterretaliatory power, but large enough as a country of continental dimension to be noticed and to be credible as the target of exemplary deterrence' (Moreira 1990: 259; Moreira is a former Brazilian Ambassador to the US).

There was a third, even more strategically important, sense in which the restrained yet ominous use of 301 worked well for the US. It targeted its Section 301 action on forms of conduct that it was seeking to control through the Uruguay Round, such as disrespect for US intellectual property laws and restrictions on US foreign investment. Other states became more amenable to the TRIPS and TRIMS Agreements being promoted by the US as multilateral agreements when they realized the alternative was aggressive unilateral US enforcement of its demands in those areas. US strategists were explicit in articulating the objective of threatening destabilizing bilateralism to accomplish multilateral agreement. For example, one senior USTR official said:

> In addition to establishing the Uruguay Round as the top US trade policy priority, the administration listed five categories of trade barriers as areas of priority concern. Within each of these categories, the administration identified a specific country practice that the administration intended to pursue within the Super 301 context. The five categories, and the country practices identified under each category, were: quantitative restrictions (Brazilian balance of payments restrictions); exclusionary government procurement restrictions (Japanese procurement restrictions on supercomputers and satellites); technical barriers to trade (Japanese standards on forest products); trade-related investment measures (trade performance requirements imposed by India on foreign investors); and barriers to trade in services (Indian prohibition on foreign insurance)…The five categories of barriers identified under Super 301, along with intellectual property, subsidy and agricultural policy issues, constitute the major US objectives for the Uruguay Round (Feketekuty 1990: 100).

There were major victories beyond those listed. Brazil was also targeted under Special 301 on intellectual property issues related to pharmaceuticals, and caved in. Korea responded to 301 listing by committing itself, among other things, to 'terminating the performance requirements on foreign investment as a term or condition of permitting an investment, or as a condition of receipt of any incentive' (Kim 1990: 255; Kim is a former principal trade negotiator for the Korean government). Indeed, from the early days of the Reagan administration, its policy had been to use 'Regular 301' to target both intellectual property and the trade in services (Feketekuty 1990: 93). Priorities of the Democratic Congress, not shared by the administration, were labour rights abuses and anticompetitive practices, which were listed in the 1988 Section 301 amendments as abuses about which private parties such as unions could complain, and trigger USTR investigation and possible trade sanctions. Labour standards and competition policy later became priorities of the Clinton administration.

Many US opinion-leaders on trade policy responded to critics by crowing about the successes achieved by the threat of 301 and painting their country as a white knight standing up to more protectionist economies, even citing the authority of Adam Smith:

> The US Congress did not invent this technique of trade policy. In the seventeenth century it was used by the government of Flanders, which retaliated against England's prohibition of imports of its lace by prohibiting the importation of English woollens. This forerunner to Section 301 was successful: England removed the offending trade barrier. Section 301 is often labelled a tool of the managed traders; but Adam Smith, the supreme antimercantilist, approved of Flanders' action: 'There may be good policy in retaliations of this kind, when there is a probability that they will procure the repeal of the high duties or prohibitions complained of' (McMillan 1990: 203).

Critics among the leaders of the US economics profession said that this was humbug:

> While greater US openness *vis a vis* Japan is open to doubt, Hong Kong's greater openness *vis a vis* the United States is not. In fact, Hong Kong, aside from nineteenth-century Britain, is a textbook example of (substantially) free trade. Yet US high-handedness in dealing with its legal service sector was a matter of public dispute in early 1989 as the legal profession of Hong Kong was threatened by punitive tariff retaliation for the colony, unless it opened up Hong Kong to American lawyers (Bhagwati 1990: 28).

Moreover, if relative US economic power declines further in comparison to an expanding EU, China and other powers, to the point where aggressive untilateralism will no longer work, the US can be assured that foreign trade bureaucrats will have a long memory. They will not remember aggressive US unilateralism as having saved the GATT, shown in the following comment by the deputy head of the EC delegation in Washington:

> As to GATT's weaknesses, let us not forget that it was Congress that voted down the International Trade Organization. It is Congress that has included in the trade act aspects that other GATT partners consider GATT-illegal. And it is Congress that has difficulties agreeing to act on GATT determinations that US laws are discriminatory (e.g. super import quotas, Superfund, customs user fees, Section 337). So Congress, wanting a weak GATT in order to preserve its margin of manoeuvre, now believes that GATT weaknesses force it to take unilateral measures (Pirzio-Biroli 1990: 262).

So one rather important byproduct of trade unilateralism for the US may have been that it has, as one Taiwanese bureaucrat put it, 'taught people to be its effective enemies'.

### The 1990s and Beyond: Shifts Between Multilateralism and Bilateralism

As to the future, trade and competition policy is an agenda item that is likely to become more important, as we will see in the next section. Trade and environment is developing as a future work program. The US hopes it will deliver clear agreement on when trade measures can and cannot be used to enforce environmental agreements (currently at least seventeen international environmental treaties provide for enforcement by trade measures (Colley 1994: 6)) and when states can require importers to meet their environment standards not only on the content of the product but how it was produced (process and production methods). Environmental groups sometimes succeed in pushing the idea of environmental countervailing duties onto this agenda (see Chapter 12). No national trade ministries support this, unless it is to put it on the research agenda so it can be dismissed as a viable policy. The US would also like to tidy up animal rights process and production issues as part of the environment agenda. It worries about the potential for the liberal trading system to be disrupted by non-tariff barriers against cosmetics tested on animals, leg-hold traps, clubbing baby seals, dolphin-catching and other such issues that can tap the concerns of mass publics.

Since the 1996 ministerial meeting in Singapore, labour standards are largely off the agenda, though the US and France like to be seen as keeping it on. India pushes the free movement of labour as a factor of production as part of its long-term agenda, with an eye to allowing more of its people to acquire skills in the West, to ship in workers to undertake major construction projects such as bridges, even perhaps to take some pressure off domestic population problems. Indian NGOs also invoke the principle of national treatment in this debate: why should European states be allowed to permit freer migration of US workers than of Indian workers? At first it seemed so implausible as to be little more than a negotiating chip to embarrass Western economists who believe in free trade in all factors of production other than labour. Yet if labour shortages become acute enough in ageing European populations, the shape of this debate could change.

A global agreement on the free movement of investment dominated the trade policy debate in the 1990s. It was central to the aspirations of US business in the Uruguay Round. US business pushed for the inclusion of a strong multilateral agreement on investment, but ended up with the comparatively modest (from its perspective) TRIMS Agreement. This was disappointing, because US companies, led by Pfizer, had come to visualize TRIMS as an 'overarching piece' for the entire GATT Round, as one business interviewee told us. For US multinationals the new world trading order was being increasingly conceptualized in terms of investment flows rather than the movement of goods. Former USTR Carla Hills put the aspiration clearly: 'We want new rules governing investment. We want corporations to be able to make investments overseas without being required to take a local partner, or export a given percentage of their output, to use local parts, or to meet any of a dozen other restrictions.' Research and development is underway on this at both the OECD and the WTO. A draft Multilateral Agreement on Investment (MAI) was tabled at the OECD. One MAI negotiator boasted that 'we are writing the constitution of a single global economy' (*Guardian*, 15 April 1997). The MAI's proponents say 'let the investing nations agree on a framework for the multilateral regulation of the free flow of investment at the OECD. Then let non-OECD nations join it if they want to signal clearly that they desire the benefits of our investment.' The aspirations of many business leaders were for a lessening of investment controls through incorporating 'standstill' (no new regulations) and 'roll-back' reviews on a periodic cycle.

The draft MAI in effect allows foreign investors to get greater benefits than domestic investors, but forbids giving domestic investors benefits that are denied to foreign investors.

Developing countries see a dangerous uncertainty in the MAI. They are desperate for investment but argue that a managed liberal investment regime would best serve developing countries' interests (Panchamukhi 1996). As one Indian member of parliament told us in 1996, 'we would not like the subterfuge of global investment laws to intrude on our judgment of what is right for the economy'. Many developing countries have consequently opposed investment vigorously as a WTO agenda item, though some would prefer to see it negotiated at the WTO where they have some voice rather than at the OECD where they have none. For developing countries 'preparedness [on the MAI] is the problem', as one Indian official said to us. They do not have the resources of an OECD member state and fear being swamped by the analytic work the MAI would require. Many wanted UNCTAD to do the R&D on an investment agreement, something the US and Europe would not tolerate, though UNCTAD has done some analytic work on investment. The US vacillates between being the chief advocate of an MAI and saying that because the negotiations on the Agreement are not proceeding to its liking, it would prefer to stick with investment agreements which are negotiated bilaterally. There are now some 700 bilateral agreements operative in the world system; the first was negotiated in 1959 (Seid 1999). Many of these treaties routinely provide for disputes to be settled by the International Center for the Settlement of Investment Disputes under the Convention on the Settlement of Investment Disputes, thereby incrementally globalizing international investment law through a degree of institutional centralization of the case law.

When the previously secret draft MAI Agreement was leaked to NGOs in 1997, a virtual coalition of anti-MAI activists appeared through the Internet almost overnight. Many old faces, such as Ralph Nader, were prominent in this grassroots campaign. But the interesting phenomenon was the tens of thousands of new faces. For the moment, this coalition seems to have been successful in putting the MAI on ice. Meanwhile, the big players return to insinuating their terms into bilateral treaties.

The US has played the same game with various aspects of the GATS. For example, in telecommunications and financial services it pulled out of negotiations until the parameters of the Agreement returned to its liking. The immediate and most major items on the WTO agenda are expansion of the reach of GATS and TRIPS (intellectual property). New areas of GATS that are likely to attract attention are professional services and business services (such as consulting and advertising). A new telecommunications round is likely in 2000. Some transport issues such as shipping conferences and aviation are likely to become important.

**How the WTO Works**

The WTO was set up in 1995 with a Ministerial Conference and General Council on top and specialist Councils for Trade in Goods, Trade in Services and TRIPS at the next level, along with Trade Policy Review and Dispute Settlement Bodies and various more specific committees (e.g. agriculture) at the third level.

The real work does not fit these formal structures, however. The WTO represents a 'hierarchy of negotiating processes' (WTO official). Ad hoc meetings are where the action is. There are informal meetings of states and, as shown in Chapter 7 on contract and property, informal meetings among the large business players with a stake in the outcome of the negotiations. Strategy meetings are held by the Quad, the Cairns Group, EC members, the 'Boeuf Rouge Group' of like-minded states who meet at a Geneva restaurant of that name, bilateral and multilateral offers and counteroffers are made among the trade negotiators of states, members of the secretariat draft text then invite one or two or six key states with different views on the text to thrash out a compromise, then widen this to the ten most consequential states for that particular issue or a ten-plus-ten meeting (ten developed and ten developing states). 'Once you've got relative representativeness right, you don't need everyone there' (WTO official). Issues move between narrower and wider groupings until there is a consensus that the secretariat, consulting with the strong states, can make the weaker states agree to.

The least developed countries do not get a seat at any of the meetings that matter, so they are often opponents to the end: 'They have nothing to offer. So they can just complain until the end and ask for special treatment through being an irritant...If the stakes are high enough, only certain states have a veto because everyone wants the agreement. Australia can't veto. But the Cairns Group can; the US and EC can' (WTO official). One way to be an irritant is to 'hint in the lobbies that they might ask for a vote' (Long 1987: 55) in a system where every state formally has one vote, but dominated 'consensus' decision-making rarely succumbs to a vote that might put some states on the spot domestically.

Informal dispute resolution is also more important than the formal dispute resolution body. As one GATT old-timer recounted a GATT saying: 'More conflicts are settled over cups of coffee in the cafeteria than before panels.' There have been over 400 GATT dispute resolution cases, but most have been settled. Even so, the formal Dispute Resolution Process of the GATT has handled three or four times as many cases as the World Court across all its domains of jurisdiction, some of them, according to Jackson (1993: 1033), 'significant indeed, such that they have caused, and could cause, governments to fall'. As one member of the WTO secretariat argued: 'GATT disputes work. Other organizations like WIPO don't have dispute mechanisms that work'. They work better for stronger states, especially the US. The EC and its members were complained against about twice as frequently between 1948 and 1989 as the US, but the US was the most frequent complainant in an analysis of 207 cases. Moreover, it was more often successful than other states both when it complained and when it was complained against (Hudec, Kennedy & Sgarbossa 1993). Weaker states lose most often. More importantly, with the exception of Japan, which persistently avoids conflict by settling before cases go to a Panel, it is the weakest states that settle most often and the US that settles least. When the US does lose, it is more likely than other states to ignore the ruling. Overall, however, this is rare; compliance with rulings is the overwhelming norm, even for the US. This picture holds true under the WTO process for the 100 complaints occurring in the first two and half years of the WTO: thirty-four were lodged by the US and twenty-one by the EC. No other complainant reached double figures.

'Moral pressure' of a sort seems to work, as one former Director-General put it (Long 1987: 66). For example, when the US at the height of its power in 1971 introduced a temporary 10 per cent surcharge on imports, a GATT Working Party sternly warned that the measure was 'a trade-restrictive measure' and 'inappropriate'. No formal censure or legal finding. Just a moral pressure which, if ignored, would legitimate retaliatory surcharges. A US that did not want to be held responsible for a major setback to trade liberalization withdrew the surcharge; the upshot of the confrontation was the Tokyo Round.

While compliance is generally obtained by such non-legal means when a significant dispute arises, there is so much flexibility in deciding what matters that the GATT is hardly a rule-of-law regime. Least developed countries can often breach the GATT without any consequences because the amount of trade involved is so small as to make it hardly worth the while of other states to suffer the costs of a diplomatic dispute. While the analysis we will develop of 'negotiating fatigue' means that least developed states are losers, a concomitant 'disputing fatigue' leaves them winners. As J.H. Jackson put it in 1969: 'a spirit seems to pervade the GATT that allows the less-developed country to deviate substantially from the GATT without great fear of consequences' (cited in Long 1987: 95). Or as Oliver Long, a former Director-General, put it: 'Reform has usually been preceded by an intermediate phase during which there is flexible, pragmatic application of the rules' (Long 1987: 95). Rules might be laid down, but not a rule of law until a period of 'flexible' application of the rules convinces the powerful contracting parties that the rules are sound enogh to be interpreted as legally binding.

## The Globalization of Competition Policy

The national regulation of trade by customs duties has a much longer history than the national regulation of monopolies. In 483, emperor Zeno issued an edict to the Praetorian Prefect of Constantinople:

> We command that no one may presume to exercise a monopoly of any kind of clothing, fish, or of any other thing serving for food or for any other use...nor may any persons combine or agree in unlawful meetings, that different kinds of merchandise may not be sold at a less price than they have agreed upon among themselves.

We saw in Chapter 7 that the statutory regulation of patent monopolies began in Venice in 1474 and spread throughout Europe. The regulation of medieval monopolies was deeply influenced by just-price theory which, along with the prohibition on usury, formed the basis of Church authority over the medieval economy (Tawney 1938). As early as 1525, the Nuremberg Reichstag pronounced against giant firms (the Fuggers, Welsers and others) which were monopolizing trade in various commodities. On that occasion, edicts in favour of the monopolists by emperor Charles V saved them from state regulation (Braudel 1979: 418). Early decisions of the English courts from the end of the sixteenth century limiting the granting of monopoly powers by the Crown were important steps in the separation of powers between the judiciary and the executive, between the Crown and commerce.

The greatest European monopolists of the seventeenth and eighteenth centuries, the Indies Companies, were also legally sanctioned because they were such important sources of the rulers' wealth. The comment of Dutch East Indies lawyer Pieter Van Damm might have been said of other Indies Companies: 'The state ought to rejoice at the existence of an association which pays it so much money every year that the country derives three times as much profit from trade and navigation in the Indies as the shareholders' (Braudel 1979: 445).

States negotiated hard for more profits each time these legal monopolies came up for renewal. This produced the first stirrings of regulatory competition, as Dutch capitalists, irritated by exclusion from the East Indies trade under the legal monopoly, supplied capital to create or attempt to create Indies Companies in France, Denmark, Sweden and Tuscany (Braudel 1979: 452) and indeed the English East India Company (Chase-Dunn 1989: 72). The monopoly of the French Indies Company was withdrawn in 1769 after a campaign organized by the 'economists' (Braudel 1979: 454–5).

After the French Revolution, the law of 2 March 1791 'proclaimed freedom of industry and commerce from state restrictions' (Keller 1991: 15). During the nineteenth century, English common law and French and German commercial law became more liberal and less corporatist, occasionally striking down restrictive business practices of trade associations. The Prussian *Trade Regulation Act 1811*, for example, restricted the powers of guilds and abolished the price-fixing authority of police (Keller 1991: 16). Yet the main story of 'freedom of industry' in the nineteenth century was a logic of industrialization toward ever-larger firms, the use of dominant market positions to form cartels and secure monopoly prices. While the English common law played an important role after 1598 in declaring monopolistic guild bylaws void (Magwood 1981: 5–6), successful uses of the common law to tackle the new industrial cartels of the nineteenth century could be counted on the fingers of one hand. Simpson (1925) found only eleven court actions against cartels in the UK between 1829 and 1925. Most were unsuccessful.

Citizens became extremely concerned in the late nineteenth century about these new concentrations of power. Austria was the seedbed of the European administrative-law approach of using bureaucratic deliberation and publicizing abuses of power to regulate cartels rather than the US criminal/civil-law model (Gerber 1992). Its influence was largely mediated by Europe's first competition law proper, the German regulatory law of 1923, which established the administrative law of the Cartel Court. The Austrian influence was not a result of its laws, but rather of published analyses by the Austrian bureaucracy and Austrian economists on why its long-standing anti-cartel laws had not worked. After 1803, in response to profiteering caused by the Napoleonic wars, Austria had criminal prohibitions against price-fixing. In 1870 these were moved out of criminal law and into a statute that permitted the formation of workers' associations but prohibited abuse of their power by agreements to strike, while at the same time invalidating 'agreements between business people for the purpose of increasing the price of a good to the disadvantage of the public' (Gerber 1992: 420). The law proved totally ineffective against both the rising worker and business cartels of the 1870s.

By 1890 at least ten US states had passed antitrust laws, at which point the Sherman Act was passed by a virtually unanimous vote of the US Congress. A year earlier Canada had passed its *Act for the Prevention and Suppression of Combinations Formed in Restraint of Trade 1889*.

The effect of enforcement of the *Sherman Act* by US courts was not exactly as intended by the progressive social movement against the railroad, oil, steel and tobacco trusts. Alfred Chandler Jr noted that 'after 1899 lawyers were advising their corporate clients to abandon all agreements or alliances carried out through cartels or trade associations and to consolidate into single, legally defined enterprises' (Chandler 1977: 333–4).[2] US antitrust laws thus actually encouraged mergers instead of inhibiting them because they 'tolerated that path to monopoly power while they more effectively outlawed the alternative pathway via cartels and restrictive practices' (Hannah 1991: 8). The US found that there were organizational efficiencies in managerially centralized, big corporations that made what Chandler called a 'three-pronged investment':

---

2  The same crucible that shaped US and ultimately global corporate capitalism also created many of the large US law firms which now dominate transnational markets for legal services.

1  'an investment in production facilities large enough to exploit a technology's potential economies of scale or scope';

2  'an investment in a national and international marketing and distribution network, so that the volume of sales might keep pace with the new volume of production';

3  'to benefit fully from these two kinds of investment the entrepreneurs also had to invest in management' (Chandler 1990: 8).

According to Tony Freyer's (1992) revealing study in the Chandler tradition, the turn-of-century merger wave fostered by the Sherman Act thrust US long-term organization for economic efficiency ahead of the UK's for the next half-century, until the UK acquired its *Monopolies Act 1948* and *Restrictive Trade Practices Act 1956*. Until the 1960s the UK economy continued to be dominated by family companies which did not fully mobilize Chandler's three-pronged investment. Non-existent antitrust enforcement in the UK for the first half of the twentieth century also left new small business entrepreneurs more vulnerable to restrictive business practices of old money than they were in the US. UK commitment to freedom of contract was an inferior industrial policy to both the visible hand of UK law-makers' rule of reason and the administrative guidance of the German Cartel Courts. For the era of managerial capitalism, liberal deregulation of state monopolies formerly granted to Indies Companies, guilds and other corporations was not enough. What was required was a special kind of regulation for deregulation of restrictive business practices which tolerated bigness.

Ultimately, this US model of competitive mega-corporate capitalism globalized under four influences:
- extension of the model throughout Europe after the Second World War under the leadership of the German anti-cartel authority, the Bundeskartelamt, a creation of the US occupation;
- cycles of mergers and acquisition (M&A) mania in Europe catalyzed partly by M&A missionaries from US law firms;
- extension of the model to the dynamic Asian economies in the 1980s and 1990s, partly under pressure from bilateral trade negotiations with the US and Europe (who demanded breaking the restrictive practices of Korean *chaebol*, for example);
- extension of the model to some developing countries with technical assistance from UNCTAD.

International agreements helped only a little to consolidate these modelling effects.

The first attempt at global regulation of restrictive business practices occurred at the League of Nations Economic Conference of 1927. The possibility of international regulation of monopolies collapsed utterly, as the chasm was so wide between the Americans who wanted a dismantling of cartels and the European powers who rather supported the cartels' rational systematizing of orderly production (Marceau 1994: 59). The ILO also made an abortive attempt in 1944 to build consensus for the international regulation of monopolies (Marceau 1994: 60).

Next was the attempt by Roosevelt and Truman, for which they ultimately got no support from the US Congress, to set up an International Trade Organization (ITO). Under the Havana Charter (which was never ratified), the ITO would have become an international regulator of restrictive business practices in the same way that the GATT was to become an international regulator of industry protection. Article 46 of the Havana Charter required states to act against monopolies and restrictive business practices that had harmful effects on the expansion of trade. Restrictive business practices which signatories would have been required to regulate included price-fixing, dumping, exclusionary practices, export cartels, partitioning markets into territorial monopolies, discrimination, voluntary export restraints and abuse of patents to restrict commerce. The ITO would have received complaints in relation to these matters, performed an investigatory and dispute resolution role and ultimately acquired the capacity to refer disputes to the International Court of Justice for an advisory opinion or to the executive board of the ITO for resolution.

If the ITO had been created as the third Bretton Woods institution, history may have been very different. Would the OPEC oil cartel have survived it? Would we have seen the voluntary export restraints which have been the cornerstone of trade negotiations between Japan and the US? Could the TRIPS Agreement at GATT have passed muster in an ITO, when its Article 46(e) prohibited the 'preventing by agreement the development or application of technology or invention whether patented or unpatented' and Article 46(f) prohibited 'extending the use of rights under patents, trademarks or copyrights granted by any member to matters which are not within the scope of such grants, or to products or conditions of production, use or sale of which are likewise not the subjects of such grants'? Such uncertainties about these major economic turning-points in the second half of the twentieth century make it easy to understand why the ITO made US big business nervous, a nervousness reflected in congressional unwillingness to grant that level of regulatory control over monopoly power to Geneva.

In 1951, the UN Economic and Social Council set up an Ad Hoc Committee to prepare proposals to achieve 'the objectives laid down in Article 46 of the Havana Charter. When the proposals came back to ECOSOC in 1953, the US delegation would not support them. Another attempt to inject restrictive business practices into GATT failed between 1958 and 1960' (Marceau 1994: 63–4). However, dumping, one of the restrictive business practices targeted in the Havana Charter, was subjected to global regulation under the GATT 1967 Anti-Dumping Code.

Although the US did not want to submit itself to discipline from Geneva on restrictive business practices, it did want to submit other states to discipline from Washington. During the US occupation of Japan and Germany after the Second World War, it forced the partial breakup of German monopolists like IG Farben and Japanese *zaibatsu*, insisting on the enactment of antitrust laws modelled on those of the US.

Since the Alcoa decision of the Supreme Court (*US v. Aluminium Co. of America* 148 F2d 416 (1945)), the US has been willing to enforce its antitrust laws extraterritorially against actions in other states that have an adverse effect on competition and prices in the US economy (Marceau 1994: 72–3). This effects doctrine is also favoured by the EC, but the European Court of Justice has systematically refused to rely on it. Weaker states tend to be opposed to the effects doctrine and some have introduced legislation to block the extraterritorial jurisdiction of US antitrust law against their firms. They have not reciprocated with attempts to enforce their own competition laws extraterritorially against US firms.

While antitrust has been the main battleground of the postwar extraterritorial reach of US law, it has not been the only one: trade, technology export and tax laws are also becoming particularly important (Picciotto 1996: 163), as are banking, securities and foreign exchange regulation. It would be a mistake, however, to see extraterritorial application of any national law as a major impetus to globalization of regulation. As Picciotto (1996: 103) points out, a 'developing legal doctrine of "moderation and restraint" in the exercise of concurrent jurisdiction' originally developed in US case law is a principle that has received 'some international endorsement' through the OECD (1987a). With heavyweight actors in global politics such as the G-7 and the ICC (1986) also active in warning of the dangers to the certainty of all investment, not least future US investment, from eroding rule of law based on a state system of territorial sovereignty, 'moderation and restraint' has indeed generally been exercised (see ICC 1986: 78–81) on the 'emerging jurisdictional rule of reason').

## OECD Leadership on Competition Laws

In 1967, the OECD became the key player in attempts to globalize competition policy when its Council adopted a Recommendation concerning Cooperation between Member Countries on Restrictive Business Practices Affecting International Trade. Its call was for:

(1) notification of investigation if another country's important interests are at risk;
(2) cooperation when two or more countries proceed against the same RBP in international trade;
(3) transmission of information; and
(4) use of mutually beneficial methods of dealing with an RBP (Marceau 1994: 77).

Subsequent OECD work set a framework of 'positive comity' (a proactive commitment to act for the benefit of both states) on antitrust enforcement actions affecting more than one state, under which a number of bilateral MOUs for cooperation on restrictive business practices have been negotiated, mainly between the US and other major states.

At the conclusion of the Uruguay Round, Trade and Competition was established as a crucial work program for the WTO. The OECD is rising to the intellectual challenge through joint meetings of its Trade and Competition Committees. The US agenda is not to require signatories to have a competition law. It is not to harmonize competition law. It is not to abolish anti-dumping laws by requiring their incorporation into competition laws that treat predatory pricing from imports and domestic production equally. It is simply a code that sets out certain competition rules as applicable when trade is affected, some general principles of competitive conduct to which states can appeal under the GATT. 'To harmonize would be dumb, counterproductive. Yet perhaps there could be a minimum core element of everyone's competition law. But then we could bog down on even that' (USTR official). The USTR is responding in part to the Federal Trade Commission and the Antitrust Division of the Justice Department, who basically want the trade bureaucrats in Geneva to leave them alone: 'we don't want to change anything we do'. At the same time, many states are keen to reach an agreement which would strike down exemptions in the antitrust laws of other states (including those of the US) for export cartels.

US strategists are patient and cautious about any general agreement for the convergence of competition law. They realize that competition law can be read to include different objectives such as the prevention of unfair competition, protection of the individual competitor or the process of competition, market access and the dispersal of market power. Only some of these objectives suit US interests – hence the strategy of negotiating new competition rules, industry by industry, at the WTO. There is more certainty in designing industry-by-industry rules to suit US interests – cross-sectoral commitment to general principles might adversely affect US interests in some industries. The Europeans likewise have said to the US: 'Don't bring services and competition together. They say: "We'll be there when you want to deal with post, telecoms, etc. one by one to increase competition. So I said okay"' (senior USTR official).

The US and the EC are certainly keen to force nations like Japan and Korea to more vigorously enforce their competition laws, leading to less consideration of harmonization of laws than of a performance-indicators approach to competition law enforcement. US–Japan and EC–Japan negotiations such as the Strategic Impediments Initiative in the 1990s have looked at products that are highly internationally competitive but are not getting into the Japanese market, and are asking why not.

Today all OECD economies have competition laws. Many acquired them only in the past decade or two. Most of the post-communist societies (and China) have acquired them since 1989 and a growing list of developing economies have also done so, including India (1969), Pakistan (1970), Thailand (1979), South Korea (1980), Sri Lanka (1987), Brazil (1962), Chile (1973), Argentina (1980), Venezuela (1991), Colombia (1992), Jamaica (1993), Mexico (1993), Kenya (1988), Gabon (1989) and Cote d'Ivoire (1993). Some developing countries have taken the competition-law path because they see a link between it and trade policy, a link which is still evolving. A national competition law is something that they are still in a position to shape. Some also hope that competition law will eventually subsume anti-dumping laws, laws which are often used against developing country exports.[3] One regulator at the Fair Trade Commission of Taiwan told us that competition law 'is a way of saying to your locals, "we can protect you to some extent"'. While prohibiting restrictive business practices with varying effectiveness, all have followed the US path of tolerance of bigness, contrary to many earlier aspirations to break up concentrations of power. In our interviews at the Fair Trade Commission of South Korea, the attitude seemed to be that more could be done to open up this *chaebol*-dominated economy through liberalization of the national economy than through domestic competition policy. In the US itself in 1985 17000 mergers were screened and nine challenged; 700 were screened in West Germany and seven challenged; 1000 in Japan and none challenged; 200 in the UK and none challenged; 100 were screened in Australia in 1985 and one challenged (Davidow 1990: 617). On the other hand, although private antitrust suits are common in the US they are virtually nonexistent anywhere else, because nowhere else has modelled the US incentive of multiple damages (Davidow 1990: 620–1).

Most states still do not have antitrust laws. In many countries, where certain conservative families control political elites to guarantee their business ventures have monopoly status, those elites will not abide antitrust. These societies are kept poor by the same kind of royal patronage of business monopolies that held back the economic growth of Europe for centuries.

## Competition in Regulation Itself

Much contemporary analysis of competition policy holds that competition among different sets of national rules increases economic efficiency. According to this analysis, investment flows to the jurisdictions where regulation is most efficient. Economists have long advanced this analysis with respect to taxation – low-tax states increase efficiency by attracting business from states with inefficiently high taxation. The analysis has been advanced at least since the 1920s debates in the League of Nations on double taxation (Einaudi 1928; Picciotto 1996: 108). Tiebout (1956)

---

3 Australia and New Zealand have replaced their anti-dumping laws with provisions of their competition laws. See section 46A of the *Trade Practices Act 1974* (misuse of market power in the trans-Tasman market). As from 1 July 1990 anti-dumping provisions ceased to apply to goods originating from Australia or New Zealand.

developed a formal economic model of regulatory competition which became widely applied to discussions of US federalism. What gave vitality to the US debate about regulatory competition was the way business-friendly incorporation laws in the tiny state of Delaware attracted many of the largest US firms to incorporate there. It seems, however, that the US is rather exceptional in this respect, as regulatory competition over company law seems to feature neither in other federal states nor in the EU (Romano 1996). In the nineteenth century, however, regulatory competition was important in the spread of innovations such as limited liability in company law. At the international level, it may be, as Picciotto (1996) argues, that regulatory competition and coordination are not mutually opposed but are symbiotic or, at most, mutually constraining. He uses the example that the Basle Committee's capital adequacy standards for financial institutions (see Chapter 8) 'are by no means precise rules which can automatically be applied to the diverse circumstances of all banks, but rather provide a new framework of broadly defined common rules within which regulatory competition takes place' (Picciotto 1996: 121).

Regulatory competition can run deeper than simply competition in rules. As the work of Dezalay (1996) and Dezalay and Garth (1996) shows, there can be competition between whole regulatory fields and entire forms of lawyering (and alternatives to lawyering) such as the competition they document between the US Cravath model of lawyering and the French model of *grands corps* of elites trained in *grandes écoles* to be intermediaries between state and market, or competition between nationally legitimated modalities of commercial arbitration. Potentially, regulatory competition as a principle renders competition policy a meta-regulator of all the other forms of regulation in this book. 'Bring your disputes to our commercial arbitration industry, to jurisdictions and firms with our kind of lawyering', these competitors say. 'Foster such competition among forms of law/arbitration/mediation', the advocates of regulatory competition urge.

It is premature to pronounce on the global significance of competition policy in this respect. In each chapter, we include a discussion of this issue when we consider the contests among the principles of lowest-cost location, world's best practice, harmonization and liberalization-deregulation. The significance of these collected empirical findings will be summarized in Chapters 20, 21 and 23.

## Globalization of Anti-corruption Law and the Code of Conduct Era

All nations have laws preventing bribery. It is a matter of dispute whether Hammurabi's Code for Babylon should be interpreted as prohibiting judges from taking bribes (Noonan 1984: 9). Certainly by the time of the Law of Moses in the ninth century BC, accepting bribes was proscribed; there is also an Egyptian hieroglyph for the concept of a gift that perverts judgment (Noonan 1984: 12–13). Over two and a half millennia all states learnt that laws against bribery were just and promoted the efficiency of trade. But of course not all states enforce them assiduously. In the aftermath of Watergate a US Congressional Committee, the Church Committee, investigated bribery by US aerospace firms among other scandals (most notably ITT's role in overthrowing the Allende government in Chile, which stirred mass concern in developing countries about abuse of power by TNCs). The most spectacular revelations concerned bribes by the Lockheed corporation to heads of state, defence ministers and others in many countries, including the Prime Minister of Japan (Fisse & Braithwaite 1983).

In response, the US Securities and Exchange Commission instituted a 'voluntary disclosure program' whereby as long as major companies voluntarily disclosed all their foreign bribes (so the SEC and equity markets could judge whether these posed a material risk to a firm's financial position) no prosecution would be launched. Prosecutions were launched against a number of major corporations that failed to disclose. The US public was shocked by the sheer magnitude of the bribery of their business elite. As a result, the *Foreign Corrupt Practices Act 1977* was passed. It provided for extraterritorial reach of US anti-corruption law and required firms to have corruption prevention programs. Because the large US accounting firms who serviced most big non-US firms standardly required the corruption prevention measures introduced through the Foreign Corrupt Practices Act, these programs partially globalized, at least among the TNCs.

This climate of public concern also led the OECD Committee of Experts on Restrictive Business Practices to draft in 1974 what was to be promulgated in 1976 as the OECD Guidelines for Multinationals (Marceau 1994: 87). Abuse of market power, predatory pricing and other restrictive business practices were ultimately lumped in with bribery and a variety of labour rights, disclosure and consumer protection concerns which were defined as undesirable and in need of voluntary restraint. At the same time, UNCTAD set up a group of eminent persons to study the effects of multinational corporations on world trade. This ultimately led to the establishment of a UN Commission and UN Centre on Transnational Corporations, in New York. From 1975 until its abolition in the mid 1990s under US pressure, the UN Centre on Transnational Corporations failed to build consensus for a UN Code of Conduct for Transnational Corporations covering a broad range of abuses of power concerning labour, consumers, women, the environment, corruption and restrictive business practices (or for a draft International Agreement on Illicit Payments to regulate bribery). Implacable US and business opposition to the Code was always the major problem.

In the 1980s and 1990s there were various fall-back proposals from the consumer movement for 'Guidelines' rather than a Code of Conduct for Transnational Corporations. These were also defeated, though UN Guidelines for Consumer Protection were passed by the General Assembly in 1985. These were mainly guidelines for governments, however; they established no mechanism for complaints against abuse of power by TNCs. One exception was WHO's International Code of Marketing of Breast-milk Substitutes, adopted by the World Health Assembly in 1981. In that case, mass publics had been outraged by revelations in books such as Andy Chetley's *Nestlés Kills Babies* about the devastating effect TNCs were having on Third World health by discouraging breastfeeding. States were required under the Breast-milk Substitutes Code to have monitoring and complaint-handling procedures which were monitored by WHO. Many did, with some positive effects in encouraging a return to breastfeeding and exposing TNCs' unethical trading practices.

A rather vague UNCTAD Set of Multilaterally Agreed Equitable Principles and Rules for the Control of Restrictive Business Practices was passed in the form of a non-binding recommendation by the UN General Assembly in 1980. It has had some impact in globalizing competition law among developing countries. UNCTAD continues to provide useful technical assistance to developing countries that want to establish a competition regulator. Today the OECD competition policy agenda has supplanted UNCTAD's restrictive business practices agenda in the key forum of the WTO. Similarly, UNCTAD's Draft Code of Conduct on Transfer of Technology was never even passed, that agenda shifting to the Western intellectual property axis of WIPO and later the TRIPS agenda at GATT. As one senior OECD official told us, 'UNCTAD's RBP Code came from the wrong perspective'. The correct perspective, he explained, was to think about competition policy in terms of trade policy, where competition translates into market access. Worse, the 700 bilateral investment Agreements now in place regularly forbid developing countries from demanding transfer of technology as a condition of foreign investment.

The mid 1970s codes era did see the ILO promulgate the Tripartite Declaration of Principles Concerning Multinational Enterprises and Social Policy. As we will see in Chapter 11 on labour standards, this Code has been ineffective. The ILO has not followed through with serious mechanisms for hearing and acting on complaints against TNCs for breaching the wide-ranging abuses covered in the Tripartite Declaration.

In sum, the mid 1970s saw a frenzy of code and guideline development on various abuses of power by TNCs in the climate created by the revelations of the Church Committee and UNCTAD ambitions for a new international economic order (rubber-stamped by the General Assembly in 1974). Development NGOs, unions, consumer groups and other NGOs did stir mass publics around these issues. But in the end it was a classic case of Edelman's (1964) thesis of diffuse interests such as consumers getting symbolic rewards (like a platitudinous set of guidelines) and concentrated interests (TNCs) getting tangible rewards (non-enforcement, business as usual, Pinochet replacing Allende). Some of the codes were radical in their ambitions; in retrospect, it was remarkable that they were voted through. For example, the Andean Pact's (Bolivia, Chile, Colombia, Ecuador, Peru) Foreign Investment Code of the 1970s required the fading-out of foreign ownership – TNCs would 'relinquish at least majority control of the enterprise over a fifteen- to twenty-year period' (Kline 1985: 36).

From the late 1940s, the ICC had been pushing for a very different kind of investment code, when it issued its International Code of Fair Treatment for Foreign Investment, which in 1972 became the ICC's Guidelines for International Investment. It included some investor obligations, for example in relation to restrictive business practices. The ICC's agenda of free trade in investment and protection against expropriation was what the US insisted on putting in the UN Code of Conduct for Transnational Corporations, against the opposition of the Soviets and the G-77. With the collapse of the Soviet Union and the decline of a G-77 that drew strength from playing the superpowers against each other, the shoe is now on the other foot. The ICC free trade in investment agenda is being developed through the WTO and the OECD's Multilateral Agreement on Investment (MAI). Unions (ICFTU), consumer (CI) and environment groups demanded the addition of clauses on TNCs meeting obligations to balance the proposed new rights to free investment. These demands had so little success that NGOs turned completely against the MAI.

The constant contest of linkage between international Agreements on free investment and international codes on responsible investment and trading practices by TNCs was well illustrated in 1994 by the final defeat of the Guidelines for Global Business at the UN Commission for Transnational Corporations. US lobbying against the Guidelines, in the words of one delegate, amounted to them 'moving around the hall saying "I thought we had an agreement with your country on foreign direct investment"'. In the post-Cold War era, developing countries value the free flow of investment into their economies more than they value international agreement to ensure that trade and investment is ethical. A US Mission to the UN Demarche Request of 26 March 1991, sent to all US foreign embassies to lobby to kill the UN Code of Conduct for Transnational Corporations, said:

> We believe that the Code is a relic of another era, when foreign direct investment was looked upon with considerable concern. The Code does not reflect the current investment policies of many developing countries which have improved their investment regimes in recent years. In light of the above, Washington agencies have decided to seek the support of host government officials responsible for foreign investment and quietly build a consensus against further negotiations...We stress that the Demarche should be given to officials responsible for investment not/not those responsible for UN affairs.

NGOs did have minor victories in the APEC development of a non-binding Asia–Pacific Investment Code. Article 3 of this Agreement forbids the relaxation of health, safety and environment regulations as an incentive to investment. In the North American arena, NAFTA was only passed by the US Congress after negotiation of side Agreements to upgrade environmental and labour standards in Mexico (see Chapters 11 and 12). In 1993, the formation of a new NGO, Transparency International, returned the regulation of bribery and corruption in world trade to the limelight in a new way. Transparency International published on the Internet a corruption index for many nations. It also lobbied aid organizations to prioritize and require progress on 'good governance' to ensure that aid was not wasted because of corruption. World Bank and IMF conditionality has responded to this campaign by giving more emphasis to good governance demands when governments are given assistance. In July 1997 the IMF suspended a $US220 million loan package to Kenya on grounds of governmental failure to fight corruption. A recent review of the WTO's Trade Policy Review Mechanism has also recommended that it 'systematically' review bribery and corruption countermeasures and performance (Keesing 1997). The USTR also publicly advocated a WTO Agreement on illicit payments to, in effect, globalize the US Foreign Corrupt Practices Act, ending the competitive disadvantages US business considered that it suffered under the Act. The OECD is supporting this push. In 1997 all OECD members and five non-members signed a Convention on Combating Bribery of Foreign Public Officials in International Business Transactions (www.org/PRESS/PRESRELS/new97104.htm). This took effect in 1999, and at the time of writing had been ratified by eleven states. It prohibits bribery of foreign officials and 'off-the-books' accounts, among other things – in effect, the provisions of the US Foreign Corrupt Practices Act. Corruption has never been a high US priority at GATT, however, largely because when they need to US companies can pay bribes without any difficulty, although the Foreign Corrupt Practices Act makes it illegal to do so.

The MAI campaign is putting business at risk of a new Code of Conduct era. In 1999 the European Parliament approved the first reading of a Bill to enable a legally binding code for European TNCs operating in developing countries. The Code would set minimum standards for human rights, indigenous rights, labour, environment, animal welfare, public health, anti-corruption measures and all the topics covered in the ILO Tripartite Declaration on Multinational Enterprises. Pursuant to the Bill, discussions are underway on setting up a European Monitoring Platform of independent experts who would hear complaints on violations of the Code, receive reports from TNCs on compliance with it, and name and shame breaches. The Bill also foreshadows a new development: linking the Code standards to the new EC directive on a European-incorporated company, rendering them enforceable company law.

## Actors

### Organizations of States

Until the collapse of the Soviet Union in the late 1980s, UNCTAD was a competing organization to the GATT and the OECD, though always of much less practical consequence. UNCTAD was a forum where the interplay between the G-77 developing economies and the communist bloc held centre stage. In the 1970s it developed a framework for a New International Economic Order. This had some modest impact on the GATT through institutionalizing a Generalized System of

Preferences (GSP) that granted preferential tariffs to developing countries (Carlson 1985: 1189). Yet once GATT had pulled down tariffs for all states, with non-tariff barriers still the deeper problem, the advantages the GSP delivered to developing countries were modest. As one Indian former GATT official said to us, the 'GSP is only a tariff preference but where is the trade preference' that developing countries needed? He further observed that when the GSP was incorporated into the GATT it meant that countries could use the GSP and not be subject to the MFN principle. The unintended byproduct of incorporating the GSP into the GATT was to give developed countries another lever that they could lawfully use to achieve their strategic objectives. That lever was routinely pulled by the US in pursuit of its intellectual property agenda. The G-77 faded in importance as a grouping of states when it and its members could no longer play the Soviet bloc off against the West on trade and development questions. Moreover, some of its most powerful members, such as South Korea and Mexico, defected to the OECD.

One of UNCTAD's more important achievements, referred to earlier, was its preparation of the Set of Multilaterally Agreed Equitable Principles and Rules for the Control of Restrictive Business Practice (the RBP set) under the UN New International Economic Order initiative of 1974. The RBP set established an Intergovernmental Group of Experts (IGP). The IGP and the UNCTAD secretariat have played a major role in facilitating the spread of the RBP set among developing countries. This has included help with drafting competition legislation, training officials and being a gathering-point for the growing epistemic community of developing and Central European country competition policy regulators. Sell summarizes this UNCTAD success story in the following way:

> By actively approaching UNCTAD both for help in the design of these policies [RBP] and for consultations to improve their functioning, developing countries have been volunteers rather than coerced targets of manipulation by the powerful...Furthermore, UNCTAD has provided an arena in which developing countries can choose from an array of approaches to RBPs, design and adopt RBP control policies for their own reasons, learn from each other as well as industrialized countries' experts, and do so in such a way that does not compromise domestic legitimacy (1995: 345).

Despite this success UNCTAD is not the active forum it once was. The competition policy agenda is firmly in the grip of the OECD and the WTO, with UNCTAD on the outer. Speaking in the context of competition, one UNCTAD official told us in a 1993 interview that although the OECD participates in UNCTAD meetings, UNCTAD was not invited to participate in OECD meetings. The OECD has also taken over leadership from UNCTAD on the corruption question through its success in the late 1990s in persuading members and non-members to model the key provisions of the US Foreign Corrupt Practices Act. UNCTAD has a considerably larger secretariat than that of the WTO, but functions as little more than a thinktank, an OECD for developing countries.

The WTO secretariat and the GATT secretariat before it do not dominate agendas in the way the secretariats of some international organizations do. In a sense, the WTO is more a contracting institution than a regulatory institution. That is, a more important feature at the WTO is meetings between two or more states, making offers of trade liberalization in an area if the other states will make better offers in that area. Rather, the WTO offers an aggregation of such bilateral and progressively more multilateral contracting processes. In terms of the enforcement of GATT Agreements, the secretariat has virtually no role; detection and enforcement of breaches is bilateral. The WTO is very different from, say, the ILO in this respect; the ILO has a central mission or policy to advance (in a way the WTO does not) and the ILO enforces the International Labour Code multi-laterally (see Chapter 11).

One of the key US players in accomplishing the intellectual-property–WTO linkage perhaps exaggerated the contrast somewhat when he said: 'At the GATT traders decide what they want and tell the secretariat to write it down. At WIPO it's the other way. The secretariat writes it and we have to go cap in hand to them'. The TRIPS Agreement illustrates the point well. The GATT secretariat did not want to take intellectual property over from WIPO. They did not even think it was sensible to force intellectual property into an Agreement to liberalize trade. As a senior GATT official put it: 'Greatness was thrust upon us with IP by the US'.

This contrast also ignores the fact that individuals in the secretariat have considerable draft-ing power when the US and the EC cannot agree. Very often in that circumstance, a compromise drafted by a member of the secretariat will prevail. This is particularly true at the level of draft texts of Agreements for entire rounds drafted by the Director-General. The Director-General has the role of forging consensus by taking something from one major player in one part of the Agree-ment and giving a compensatory concession in another part. The power of the drafter's pen can also be used to favour the major players, particularly during a period of crisis. During the Uruguay Round, when negotiations were stalled, Director-General Dunkel was instructed to produce a compromise draft. That draft, we were told by one Indian bureaucrat involved in the TRIPS nego-tiations, eliminated the proposals made by a number of developing countries led by India: 'All our efforts were wiped in one second by Dunkel'.

This considerable power of the Director-General is symbiotically linked to the power of the US and EC. One senior US trade official pointed out, for example, that in the later stages of the Uruguay Round the Director-General (Sutherland) 'conspiring with us' made it almost impos-sible to change texts. He said the onus was on a country proposing change to build consensus: 'That meant effectively that only us and possibly the EU could do it.' India, we were told, could not do it, much as it might have liked to, 'because it really only had two people in Geneva. We have the capacity to get around to everyone and project a consensus'.

The WTO still has a small secretariat of about 200 professionals who service some forty committees, an amazingly lean operation. Many senior WTO personnel see the WTO as 'suffering negotiating fatigue'. Expanding the secretariat would not solve the problem, however, because states want a private-law model, they want the WTO to be a nexus of contracts where they have control over their own contracts:

> We set up a Subcommittee with a Chair and a Secretary who turned up for their first meeting on trade needs of LDCs [least developed countries]. No LDCs came. No developed countries came. No one came. Not one country showed up. If it had been telecoms, the chamber would have been packed [with special interests and states pushed by telecom interests] (WTO official).

A situation of negotiating fatigue 'suits the US and Europe' with their large infrastructure for trade negotiation in Geneva. They want the WTO to take on 'more and more good things' that will liberalize trade, knowing that only they can resource the committees properly. 'Big players can afford to play cat and mouse (like the US are currently doing on telecoms and finance nego-tiations) when they are suffering less negotiating fatigue than others' (WTO official). In contrast, the developing countries, and even middling trading powers like Australia, have an interest in lobbying with the beleaguered WTO secretariat to rationalize the work program, trim the number of 'good things' to a level they can service adequately with competent trade bureaucrats. Directors-General, however, are wont to leave their mark with accomplishments like a millennium round that encompasses competition policy, liberalization of government purchasing and investment, with further progress on services, as well as settling the trade status of environment and labour standards. Hence Directors-General, who owe their incumbency to the US and EC, are their ally against the weaker nations and their own secretariat in supporting negotiating fatigue. As one US trade negotiator described the position of top management at the WTO: 'Their success is measured by successful agreement. Bigger rather than smaller. Quicker rather than slower. Smoother rather than acrimonious.'

Negotiating fatigue among weaker states is one explanation, for example, of why 100 states signed the TRIPS Agreement of the Uruguay Round when they were net importers of intellectual property rights. According to a key US negotiator, 'only about ten countries sent experts from their capitals on IP' to the crucial TRIPS negotiations. 'Information is everything in trade negotiation', according to one senior WTO official, and on TRIPS most states did not have it.

Most developing countries want to keep investment, competition policy and labour standards off the WTO agenda, preferring educative measures to improve performance in these domains.

The Tokyo Round Agreement on Technical Barriers to Trade established a kind of symbiotic relationship between the GATT and the ISO. The ISO would be responsible for what the internationally accepted standards would be; how they would be used would be the GATT responsibility. The same model was adopted with the symbiotic relationship between Codex standards for food and the WTO established from the Uruguay Round (see Chapter 16).

In trade policy, the EC is more fragmented than in other areas of policy. DG-3 of the Commission has a division for each major industry that formulates trade negotiating positions affecting that industry in a way that captures the interests of the industry. In other words, the EC bureaucracy, like the trade bureaucracies of most nation-states, is structurally mercantilist rather than consumerist. But this is decidedly not true of the EC Directorate-General for Competition, which aggressively promotes competition law enforcement to liberalize trade. We were surprised at the level of political independence it enjoys compared with competition authorities in other states which are supposedly independent regulatory commissions. For example, in a discussion with the Directorate-General for Competition in 1993 on forcing European states to open voice telephony to competition, one official said: 'If Council doesn't do it [by regulation or directive] then we will [by enforcing the Treaty of Rome in the European Court]. We reckon we're right and we'll get public support. We're saying to them, "Here's your chance to do something, but we'll do it if you don't"'. The same officer then made the same point about deregulating air transport if European ministers failed to act: 'It will be popular once the vested interests have been resisted.' This international executive has demonstrated an effective capacity to usurp the traditional role not only of legislatures and elected officials, but also, in limited ways, that of the judiciary. This is because fines for competition offences are recommended administratively, can be massive, and are open to negotiation in response to undertakings by the offending organization.

The EC (rather than member state competition authorities) runs all the major competition cases that have implications beyond one member. In states where competition authorities have weak enforcement capabilities, the EC still runs some cases that only have implications for that state. The European Economic Area Agreement has seen non-EU EFTA (European Free Trade Agreement) countries adopt carbon copies of EU competition rules as part of a wider Agreement to allow EFTA countries to join the single market without joining the EU (Council of the European Communities 1992), as have 'Europe Agreements' with Central European states.

The rise of the EC has strengthened liberalization more than frustrated it through thrusting the world into a new era of trading blocs. This is because the EC deregulated trade internally among some of the world's largest trading nations and its general stance (agriculture and intellectual property being major exceptions) has been to support deregulation of trade.

Similarly NAFTA and APEC (Asia–Pacific Economic Cooperation) are feared by some as next steps toward an era of trading blocs, but there is little evidence of these groups doing much beyond liberalizing trade somewhat among themselves. The same might be said of MERCOSUR, the Agreement between Argentina, Brazil, Paraguay and Uruguay. This said, the rest of the world watches with interest moves to link NAFTA to groups like MERCOSUR to establish a free trade area for the Americas by 2005.

## States

Throughout the postwar period the US has obviously been the key actor; prior to that the UK was. The most fundamental US strategy has been to act tough on bilateral negotiations to set frameworks for subsequent multilateral negotiation. It almost never goes directly to seeking a multilateral agreement in the way weaker states regularly do. For example, in the lead-up to the TRIPS Agreement, the US negotiated forty bilaterals on intellectual property, 'each time getting them closer to the ultimate TRIPS Agreement' (US negotiator). The 1986 Agreement with Korea following 301 action against that state was a particularly important crucible of what would be demanded in later bilaterals. The strategy of opening with bilaterals allows the US to assess the desirability of a multilateral treaty. So, for example, while the US has moved towards a multilateral approach for intellectual property, in the area of competition policy it has been content to enter into non-treaty bilateral arrangements of cooperation with other states.

Most of the insiders we interviewed saw the Cairns Group of agricultural exporting nations as a more important third force after the US and the EU than Japan. At the GATT secretariat we were told that 40 per cent of the text for the Sanitary and Phytosanitary Standards Agreement to make Codex standards for food GATT-enforceable (see Chapter 16) was written out of the Cairns Group. The Cairns Group was a 'constructive bridge-builder and consensus-seeker' among both the major players and between them and developing countries. Former USTR Clayton Yeutter has claimed, in a television interview, that he suggested to Australia that it set up the Cairns Group for this reason. Various Australian officials who wish to share credit for what is generally regarded as a 'brilliant' move by trade negotiators deny this. There is no doubt that the Cairns Group changed the reality of the GATT from that of the Tokyo Round where only the US, the EC and, to a lesser extent, Japan mattered.

The membership of Australia and Canada was critical as these were among the 'few countries, other than the major players in the Uruguay Round, with a sufficiently substantial and skilled multilateral trade bureaucracy capable of understanding the complexities of the GATT negotiating process not only in the specific negotiating panel on agriculture but also *in toto*' (Higgott & Cooper 1990: 616). Another important aspect of the innovation was joining middling developed economies and major developing ones in the same coalition. The developing members of the Cairns Group kept agriculture high on the agenda of the G-77, UNCTAD and the FAO, while Canada could keep it seriously on the agenda of the G-7 and the Quad.

In these senses the Cairns Group was a bridge rather than a strong new current or a significant threat to the Quad. It should be seen as simply the most important of a number of complex coalitions that emerged in the Uruguay Round:

many states are members of a variety of informal groups, such as the De la Paix Group, with its interests in GATT dispute settlement, safeguards, anti-dumping, tariff and non-tariff measures, and the functioning of the GATT system; the Morges group on agriculture; the Pacific Group on safeguards; the 'Victims' Group on anti-dumping; the 'Friends' Group on trade-related aspects of intellectual property and trade-related investment measures; and the Rolle Group on negotiations about services (Higgott & Cooper 1990: 591).

Japan's philosophy is exemplified by its approach to TRIMS and the MAI at the OECD. A senior official of the Ministry of International Trade and Industry explained:

> Japan takes the situation as given. It [Japanese business] is good at getting over hurdles. They don't feel strongly about abolishing investment barriers because they have learnt how to get over them and many competitors from other countries have not. US companies want to take the world to US rules. Japan thinks, when in Rome, do as Romans. The US view is when in Rome, do as Americans do.

Japan is sometimes paralyzed by a failure to reach consensus nationally and an unwillingness to articulate any clear view until there is such a consensus. At the time of our MITI interviews in 1994 there was no consensus between MITI and the Environment Ministry on the GATT trade and environment agenda. The relevant officials were meeting in an attempt to reach consensus in Paris at gatherings of the OECD Trade and Environment Committee. We could not get any of the MITI officials interviewed to nominate any area of trade policy where Japan was seeking to show a lead.

> **USTR official:** 'If the US and EC agree on a major trade matter it's only a matter of time before it happens.'
> **JB:** 'Any cases where Japan has held up agreement when the US and EC have agreed?'
> **USTR official:** 'No.'

This official agreed with our summary that the US basically sets the trade agenda, the EC constrains it and, to a much lesser extent, Japan constrains it when the Quad settles the direction. WTO officials, who see more of the hard work of rounding up the lesser states, have a slightly different perspective: 'Without consensus among the Quad countries, you can't move. It's a precondition, but it's not enough.'

In the early stages of negotiating multilateral trade Agreements, states are highly fragmented actors. For example, when we visited Germany in 1994, the Ministry of Economics was firmly against incorporating labour standards into the GATT but the Ministry of Labour firmly for, a situation mirrored in many states. But by the time texts start being passed around, trade ministries are firmly in control.[4] A clause on labour is available to be traded against clauses on agriculture, environment and many other items, by which point labour, agriculture and environment ministries are minor players, never in the room when the final deal is done.

The fact that most states are delighted to have even one individual in the room when a critical trade-off is negotiated at the WTO is only one reason why trade ministries normally prevail to

---

4  This can include control over legislatures. For example, in US Structural Impediments Initiative bilateral negotiations with Japan over toughening the enforcement of Japanese antitrust, 'business resistance was mediated through the Liberal Democratic Party in the Diet. There was not heavy MITI resistance. Many in MITI support open markets and see it as in Japan's interests to open up competition. The Fair Trading Commission had to be seen to be opposed' (US Justice Department official). In the formal outcome, the MITI–US negotiated position prevails over those of other fragments of the Japanese state, but of course what prevails during the detail of implementation is a much more complex matter.

become the voice of a unitary state. There is also the fact that long before then, in most states, they can manipulate more marginal ministries. The Chair of the OECD Trade Committee explained that when it set up a joint OECD Trade and Environment Committee it caused trade ministries to actually listen to their own environment ministries in Paris, something they did not normally bother with at home. 'At first, the environment and trade people would express two different views. Then, at the next stage the trade people, who were more powerful, would crush the environmental people. Then we had to say to them, "Coordinate but don't suppress"'. Of course, the extent to which trade bureaucrats suppressed the voices of their own environment ministries varied from country to country.

The weaker developing countries 'need a rule-based system more than anyone; everyone loses if it collapses, but the US lose least' (Indonesian trade negotiator). While the US can pick and choose among bilateralism, regionalism and multiterism to suit its long-term interests, developing countries have no bilateral clout and can only take multilateral deals skewed to Quad interests, which they believe still leave them better off (because of improved market access or reduced agricultural subsidies, for example). Some improvement there may have been, but the broad picture is one where the exports developing countries rely on most – textiles, clothing, food, oils and fats, beverages, sugar, rice – have experienced below-average reduction in protection. Even this picture of developing countries gaining, but gaining less, is not universally true. The Uruguay Round Agreement left some sub-Saharan African states clearly worse off (Mehta & Davison 1993: 18).

The US has also been the key state in instigating liberal cooperation on competition matters. More recently Europe has been moving down this path, but it has made far fewer bilateral arrangements than the US. Japan is a party to such Agreements rather than an instigator of them. Europe more than the US seems to push the idea of an international competition authority, but no one, not even the Europeans, seriously expects a world antitrust agency to emerge in the short or medium term. Rather, the picture that is developing is bilateral Agreements and cooperation between the US and the countries it considers important, combined with including some competition policy objectives (notably market access) into the trade regime – globalization through bilateral accretion and managed policy convergence.

Finally, it should be noted that the decisions of US courts in the competition law field and the competition jurisprudence developed by the European Court of Justice has had an important influence in other jurisdictions. The High Court of Australia, for example, routinely looks at the work of these courts when deciding competition cases (e.g. *Queensland Wire Industries Pty Ltd v. BHP* (1989) 167 CLR 177).

## Business Actors

With the intellectual property trade agenda, Pfizer and IBM have been the key actors; with services, American Express and Citicorp; leading the AMEX coalition with telecommunications are the US and UK telecommunications giants; with professional accounting services, Arthur Andersen; with audio-visual services, Jack Valenti representing Hollywood.

Although it is coalitions of small numbers of US companies that have been the most influential business actors since the Second World War, the ICC sometimes plays an important coordinating role, for example in producing discussion papers on issues like trade and environment and extraterritoriality of regulatory laws. In the 1940s, the ICC played an important role in business' successful campaign to scuttle the ITO and the Havana Charter (Kline 1985: 11).

Among the leading US trade and competition policy-makers we interviewed, CEOs of large companies such as those mentioned above also commanded more respect than the industry associations, especially the US Chamber of Commerce, referred to by more than one senior econocrat as the US Chamber of Compromisers.

Business actors have been advocates of forum-shifting to suit their trading interests. For example, the above companies lobbied for the shifting of the intellectual property action from WIPO to the GATT when WIPO was insufficiently aggressive in forcing the globalization of their favoured intellectual property order. There is no shortage of hypocrisy in how they do this: for example, in Sherif Seid's (1999) research, business interests argued that it was better for the MAI to be negotiated at the OECD rather than the WTO because the OECD was more transparent! Of course, it also excluded developing countries. In the new frontier of a global investment Agreement, TNCs consistently argue for the freedom of foreign investors to choose the arbitral rules and fora which should apply to disputes involving their investment – be they International Centre for the Settlement of Investment Dispute rules, UNCITRAL rules, the ICC Court of Arbitration or indeed the option of going to local courts without forfeiting the right to international arbitration. Developed states in a sense play for rules that systematically privilege fora accommodating to their domestic firms; when it comes to specific disputes firms seek to choose from all available fora without systematically favouring any.

US merger and acquisitions (M&A) lawyers are important actors in the picture portrayed in this chapter. In the merger mania of the late 1980s, cross-border M&As rose to 84 per cent of foreign direct investment (FDI) in 1988, falling back to 61 per cent by 1993 (P. Evans 1995: 13). Just as Wall Street lawyers were critical in shaping global capitalism at the end of the nineteenth century by advising US captains of industry to merge and compete rather than cartelize, in the latter part of the twentieth century M&A missionaries from Wall Street crossed the Atlantic to cultivate European grandees. These legal entrepreneurs changed the technology of the M&A market with innovations such as the leveraged buy-out, the 'poison pill', junk bonds, proxy battles, judicial 'guerrilla warfare', tax and financial engineering (Dezalay 1991). In the 1980s, there was no such thing as a blue-chip company invulnerable to a hostile takeover orchestrated by the wizards of Wall Street M&A, who attracted foreign clones in London, Paris, Frankfurt and Sydney.

> Like gunpowder in ancient China, all these techniques were known, but their use was strictly limited and controlled by the hierarchical structures of the different professions. Only their joining together could create an explosive mixture, capable of threatening even the best established enterprises. The power of the technology used in hostile takeovers derives from the fact that these legal-financial battles are fought out simultaneously on several levels and they create a reconstruction of technical knowhow (Dezalay 1991: 6).

Another kind of legal entrepreneur was the Washington lawyer/economist, for example Eric Smith, Elery Simon and Jacques Gorlin (see Chapter 7), who forged the ideas for linking the global trade regime to the intellectual property regime.

The American Bar Association was cited in many of our interviews as an important player not only in influencing US antitrust policy, but in lobbying for the international standards its antitrust bar favours at the OECD and the EC.

## NGOs and Mass Publics

Actors at the level of states, regional organizations like the EU and global organizations like the WTO did not see trade unions as critical actors. They never shaped trade or competition policy agendas at the international level, though at the national level they could be important in resisting liberalization in areas such as textiles and steel, where job losses were prospectively large. The consumer movement has not played an important role in shaping the globalization of trade regulation through the GATT or any other institution; it has been largely reactive and ineffectual, in the eyes of the key players. For example, the GATT secretariat told us that, incredibly, the consumer movement never demanded any specific changes to the TRIPS Agreement, yet the International Organization of Consumers Unions lobbied for the Dunkel text of which it was a part. It is hard for NGOs to be more influential: 'I have my work cut out trading off views held by member governments without taking account of views that some of those governments hold. So they know, like all other lobbies, it's best to lobby governments' (GATT official). The environment movement has succeeded in getting the trade–environment linkage on the GATT agenda, but at the time of writing there are as many potential dangers as benefits for the environment movement.

Having failed in lobbying for a Code of Conduct for Transnational Corporations, the environment, trade union and consumer movements lobbied at the OECD for inclusion of some of its provisions (largely through reference to the OECD Guidelines for Multinationals) in the MAI. In addition, Consumers International appealed directly to TNCs to voluntarily adopt its Consumer Charter for Global Business, as a fallback to international agreement on a Code of Conduct enforced by states.

Mass publics began to engage with global trade policy in the mid 1990s (at the time of the signing of NAFTA and the Uruguay Round) to an unprecedented extent. On many occasions during the past 150 years there have been swellings of national concern about losing jobs to markets where labour costs are lower, with resultant popular appeals for higher tariffs. The mid 1990s concern was different in that it began to focus on global institutions. 'GATTZILLA' advertisements in US newspapers pictured the monster of a world trade organization swiping at the US from the Empire State Building. India saw mass demonstrations against the GATT in the mid 1990s, with 200 000 farmers rallying against the TRIPS Agreement in March 1993 and 500 000 in October 1993 (Sutherland 1998: 3). The GATT made it through the US Congress (only because President Clinton invoked fast-track procedures) but key elements of the Uruguay Round could not make it through the Indian parliament because of mass unrest over questions like intellectual property. NAFTA barely scraped through Congress. One senior US trade official saw GATT as 'too abstract' to create major problems of opposition among the US public and Congress: 'The image of jobs and pollution going across the Mexican border was much more concrete with NAFTA'.

Global trade policy is a remote issue for most individuals and not a central issue for most NGOs. Lori Wallach of Ralph Nader's Public Citizen was a key player in coordinating a US Citizen Trade Watch Campaign, with participation from many unions, consumer groups, environmental groups and some farm groups. From Wallach's wider public interest movement perspective, it was a struggle to persuade NGOs that GATT would affect them domestically: 'It will undermine all your work of the past thirty years'. Now that the Uruguay Agreement has passed, it is doubtful that many NGOs consider that the predictions of the early to mid 1990s have come true. Our interview with Ralph Nader revealed a fear and our interviews with US trade officials a hope that there would be an 'exhaustion factor' – tht the public would lose interest in an issue as abstract as trade treaties. Yet after that interview Nader managed to be a lead player in another global coalition, forged on the Internet, to halt the MAI.

An exotic case of strategic NGO action that should be noted as an interesting precedent is the way the Hong Kong Consumer Council, in a state which until merger with China had no competition authority at all, 'acts as the competition law watchdog in the absence of any such law' (P. Evans 1995: 2). Its *modus operandi* has been to produce reports on competition in industry sectors then lead public agitation for administrative guidance to secure voluntary cessation of the anti-competitive practices revealed.

## Individuals

> What I want to know if I negotiate with someone is: What ministry are you from and what it takes for you to get promoted (US trade negotiator).

We have seen that many of the most crucial trade negotiations are made in a room where one person represents a TNC, like American Express, or a nation. These individuals have only a partial understanding of the interests of the huge collectivity they represent. And we have seen that it makes a considerable difference whether a representative of an environment ministry or a trade ministry represents a nation on trade and environment negotiations. This is an important aspect of the theory of forum-shifting we develop in Chapter 24: one of the ways a powerful player in global regulation games can shape outcomes is to shift negotiation from an FAO forum dominated by representatives of agriculture ministries in Rome to one dominated by individuals from trade ministries in Geneva. An equally interesting question is the way commanding individuals with a respected grasp of a given topic can coopt powerful collectivities. For example, we encountered an UNCITRAL regular, a university professor, who had attended UNCITRAL meetings as a formal representative of two different nations (Monaco and France) and one industry association on different occasions. The most striking incidents of individuals coopting the power of collectivities we have seen involve entrepreneurial Washington and New York lawyer/business strategists selling their ideas for poison pills or linkage of intellectual property and trade regulation, to organizations at the commanding heights of global capitalism.

The push for services to become a central GATT agenda item came from a small number of US companies, led by James D. Robinson III, the CEO of American Express. Chapter 7, as well as this chapter, has shown that Edmund T. Pratt Jr, the CEO of US pharmaceutical company Pfizer, is another individual with an enormous impact on global trade regimes during the 1980s and beyond. The President of one US business organization we interviewed recalled 'a table-thumping speech' Pratt had delivered in 1985 at an annual dinner, in which he proposed that the solution to US losses on intellectual property was to make intellectual property a trade issue. It was a proposal that 'aroused a lot of interest' among his listeners. Pratt was on the Advisory Committee on Trade Negotiation (as it was then called) when the Special and Super 301 provisions came into force, along with the CEO of IBM, John R. Opel, and various other influentials. During 1984–85 they used the Advisory Committee on Trade Negotiation to argue for linking intellectual property regulation and the GATT regime of trade regulation, the most important change that came out of the Uruguay Round. It was an implausible accomplishment to persuade a trade liberalization regime to incorporate a major new form of trade regulation, to persuade a body concerned to increase competition in the world economy to extend the life of patent monopolies and other intellectual property monopoly rights. More, it was a remarkable accomplishment to persuade 100 countries who were net importers of intellectual property rights to sign an Agreement to dramatically increase the cost of intellectual property imports.

Behind Pratt and his colleagues on the Advisory Committee on Trade Negotiations there were a small number of other key individuals. Eric Smith, a lawyer (now Executive Director of the International Intellectual Property Alliance) and Jon Baumgarten, an influential copyright lawyer, developed the links between intellectual property and the 301 process. Smith's International Intellectual Property Alliance has become the most powerful copyright lobbying organization in the world. Jacques Gorlin, a Washington consultant economist, wrote a paper for IBM on the benefits to companies that own a lot of intellectual property (IP) rights of linking IP with trade regimes. Gorlin was the entrepreneur of legal ideas. IBM's CEO Opel, with Pratt, convinced the Advisory Committee on Trade Negotiation that the linkage was a good idea. In 1986 the USTR said 'I'm convinced on IP. But when I go to Quad meetings, they are under no pressure from their industry. Can you get it?' (Washington interview). Opel and Pratt responded by working with Gorlin to develop a Quad private-sector consensus for an IP–WTO linkage. They set up an Intellectual Property Committee of CEOs of twelve key US companies to lead the charge to persuade European and Japanese business. It is easier for Washington legal and idea entrepreneurs like Gorlin to work with ad hoc groups of individual companies with common interests, than to seek to conquer the consensus demands of industry associations. The CEOs of these twelve companies were in a position to make their case direct to the President and the USTR, and did so.

Gorlin worked with the Intellectual Property Committee to develop a written proposal for the IP–WTO linkage. The USTR sent it to all governments, saying 'This is what we want'. By this time, the peak European Employers Federation, UNICE, and the Japanese electronics industry were part of the global IP coalition. In June 1988 the IPC (US), UNICE (Europe) and the Keidanren (Japan) released a document called Basic Framework of GATT Provisions on Intellectual Property: Statement of Views of the European, Japanese and United States Business Communities. Faced with this trilateral expression of business will, it became clear to most players that a strong Agreement on intellectual property would form part of the final Uruguay package. The strategy was repeated with the IP–NAFTA linkage, which was even stronger than with the GATT.

Key individuals shape which powerful collective actors will be involved in particular deliberations. For example, in 1982, Bill Brock, the USTR, created the Quad. It was created to formulate the framework for the Uruguay Round. Later in the 1980s, the USTR created a group of nations called Friends of Intellectual Property, which added nations such as Switzerland, Sweden, Australia and Hong Kong to the Quad. The objective was to engage this group of states in promoting support for the IP–GATT linkage. But toward the end of the Uruguay Round, when the negotiation got tougher with only the hard issues left for resolution, the USTR contracted the consensus-building forum on IP back to the Quad.

Collectivities are more powerful than individuals. But collectivities, like individuals, can be captured. The individuals (such as Jacques Gorlin) whose ideas can capture the most powerful collectivities can thereby shape which collectivities are invited to participate in formulating a consensus that sets the agenda (before other collectivities can organize a competing agenda with clout).

### Epistemic Communities of Actors

The epistemic community of trade negotiators, Geneva trade institution-builders, Washington legal entrepreneurs and intellectuals from the disciplines of economics and law, is held together and torn apart by a dialectic between mercantilism and liberal trade theory. The economists dominate the latter side of the dialectic, trade negotiators the former. The great moments of synthesis have been the signings of new GATT rounds. The math of rational choice models have been the icons of the liberal trade theorists, win–win deals the icons of postwar mercantilists, win–lose deals of prewar beggar-thy-neighbour mercantilists. One side is historically driven by a logic of math, the other by a logic of reciprocity.

In the 1990s the dialectic changed significantly with the rise of strategic trade policy, which liberal trade theorists saw as 'protectionism wrapped in new, mathematical clothes' (van Bergeijk & Kabel 1993: 185). They see strategic trade theory as neo-mercantilist in its formal conclusions that trade restrictions can be used to deliver lasting national welfare gains. The shift in the mercantilism debate with the arrival of strategic trade policy simply underlines the unifying commitment to rational choice, economistic thinking (rather than rule-of-law thinking, for example) in the trade diplomacy epistemic community.

The rifts within the competition policy epistemic community are shallower than in the trade policy community, but they are real enough, between Chicago School and Harvard thinking on antitrust, for example. This epistemic community is in a sense in the business of developing a global customary case law on microeconomic analysis of merger and other kinds of competition cases. As different states deal with similar kinds of mergers, indeed even the same mergers, increasingly they read the microeconomic analyses and the court decisions of other states. Intellectuals who teach microeconomics in universities become the vanguard of reform debate in states which are yet to introduce competition laws.

The trade and competition policy epistemic communities come together at joint meetings of the Trade and Competition Committees of the OECD. As when trade and environment meet, trade dominates. Yet there are intriguing imperialist aspirations within the competition policy epistemic community. The belief is that trade liberalization will not work if restrictive trade practices are not fixed – there is no point reducing tariffs into Japan if Japanese retailers will not put imports on their shelves. Hence, in the words of the head of one national competition authority: 'Trade policy needs to be recharacterized as a subset of competition policy.' An emblem of this competition policy imperialism is the global push to abolish anti-dumping laws, treating dumped imports under competition law according to the rules that apply to domestic predatory pricing.

The competition policy community is quietly building global networks, a fact that is important to fulfilling the strategies that we identify in the final chapter for increasing competition. Korean and Japanese competition regulators meet regularly, and there are meetings between Korean and French and between Korean and German competition officials, we were told in an interview (1995) at the Fair Trade Commission of Korea. The emphasis is on an informal process of exchanging ideas and information. Much the same process of consultation and coordination revealed itself at interviews (1995) in the Fair Trade Commission of Taiwan. Our interviews in the Ministry for Economic Competition of the Czech Republic and in Poland (1993) also revealed regular networking between competition officials. US consultants had been used in the developmental stages of the Czech Republic's and Poland's competition laws. Links had been established with the German competition authority and there was close contact with the OECD. Contacts were also being developed with the competition authorities of other post-communist societies.

A multilateral code on competition continues to be quietly discussed in this community. The desirability of such a code is not much doubted, but competition officials are under no illusions about the difficulty of obtaining it. 'Not a matter decided at my level', as one senior Korean regulator observed (1995 interview). Thus the members of this community use dialogue in preference to treaties. They swap stories and experiences at meetings around the world, thereby building ties that unite them across borders, not formally, but as reflective members of an increasingly global community with a distinctive expertise. The future importance, to citizen sovereignty, of this particular community is discussed in Chapter 26.

Obversely, there is a libertarian wing of the trade policy epistemic community who believe that 'free trade...makes antitrust concerns largely irrelevant' (Godek 1991). They believe that import competition can make any domestic price-fixing hopelessly unstable and even the most powerful domestic monopoly vulnerable to competition. Adherents of this view argued against transfer of US antitrust to post-communist societies. Their fears have put a brake on the spread of competition laws. They fear that older, more populist and restrictive policies toward mergers and bigness might be modelled, rather than contemporary US policies that are permissive toward mergers. These analyses by the libertarian wing of the trade policy epistemic community have legitimated the policies of Hong Kong and Singapore in being strong free-traders while eschewing antitrust.

## Contest of Principles

### Liberalization/Deregulation v. Mercantilism/Strategic Trade

Clearly the most fundamental contest of principles within the trade and competition regimes has been between liberalization (deregulation) and mercantilism. The surges of institutional triumph of liberalization over mercantilism occurred in the second half of the nineteenth century (led by the UK) and the second half of the twentieth century (led by the Roosevelt administration and its successors, though frequently resisted in the US Congress). The period in between, from the late nineteenth to the mid twentieth centuries, saw a resurgence of mercantilism that had disastrous beggar-thy-neighbour consequences – depression and war. These consequences were so serious that even though mercantilism has usually triumphed over liberalization, the commitment to a WTO and regional trading arrangements that cage the tiger of mercantilism seems historically resilient today.

The liberalizations of Victorian hegemony and Roosevelt/Truman hegemony were institutionally quite different. In the mid nineteenth century, Britain pursued a unilateral free-trade policy without bothering much to use its hegemony to get other nations to reciprocate. After the Second World War, however, the US exerted enormous efforts in setting up multilateral, regional and bilateral institutions to enforce reciprocation of liberalization. Enforcement was needed in a world where the hegemon's trade and investment was more vulnerable. Mid-nineteenth century Britain did not have to worry about foreign states nationalizing its firms (something that happened to the US a lot during the 1960s) or creeping nationalization through imposing conditions on investment (as became common in the 1970s and 1980s). Purchasers of UK manufactures mostly could be told to take it or leave it, because there were few alternative suppliers and full production capacity. Obversely, raw material exporters to the UK had no clout in trade negotiations because there were many sources of supply. Contemporary investment is, as Yarbrough and Yarbrough (1992) explain, more relation-specific. A Japanese car-maker invests in a car production process designed to meet US standards and market preferences. This makes Japan vulnerable to US trade retaliation. A Dutch telecommunications equipment manufacturer is vulnerable to trade retaliation from another state when it invests millions in software peculiar to its telephone system. All intellectual property investment is relationally vulnerable. Because trade and investment today is more relation-specific, states want an institutional capacity for multilateral or bilateral enforcement.

The new challenge to liberalization is from strategic trade theory, which argues that regulated trade can deliver more national economic benefits than can deregulation. Liberal trade theorists, in contrast, believe that national economies benefit from dismantling protectionism even if they do so unilaterally. Economies benefit even more if protectionism is dismantled multilaterally. So the intellectual contest between liberal trade theory and strategic trade theory is over whether strategic protectionism is better or worse for national welfare. This leaves the high ground to the liberals, because they argue that, regardless of whether strategic trade measures enhance national welfare, a world where every state was captured by strategic trade theory or, worse, a world where the WTO, the EU, APEC and NAFTA as institutions abandoned liberalization in favour of managed trade, would leave everyone poorer. The most practical fear is that a world of hostile protectionist trading blocs would not only impoverish the world but would jeopardize the long peace among major powers.

Most of the trade negotiators we interviewed are sensitive to all these arguments. They think strategic trade theory is right in a lot of contexts and they want their state to act on it to advance national interests. But they want to advance the practice of strategic trade while mouthing the principles of liberal trade. They are thus committed to diplomatic hypocrisy. They fear that all states might strangle the goose that lays the golden egg by aggressively and openly pursuing their interests. So they prod furtively, mostly gently, at the goose, hoping that it will roll more of the eggs in their direction. They hope that their prodding will not be too visible, nor provocative, to other states. Even with the most dissembled trade diplomacy, those golden eggs are often all too visible. One reason is that part of every state's strategy for getting other states to be liberal traders (while they strategically deviate from liberalism) is to enforce transparency on everyone else (while making their own actions as opaque as possible). This strategy is obvious to all. So, as one South Korean negotiator told us, when the US negotiates with South Korea it says (hypocritically) 'we are interested in the rules [of free trade] and not in a managed trade outcome'. The trade game is basically a game about gains in which the rules of free trade are but one means to those gains.

While powerful states like the US can prod the goose in firm and obvious ways, we have seen that they dare not go so far with aggressive unilateralism as to jeopardize a rule-governed liberal trading regime. They have the power to thumb their noses at WTO Dispute Panel decisions, and occasionally they do. But mostly they want to be seen to comply by the rules of the liberal trading regime that has evolved around the GATT during the past half-century. They usually comply out of fear of unravelling the supranational rules that prohibit national regulation of trade.

Hence, at the level of the contest of principles, the victory of the principle of liberalization over the principle of strategic trade is decisive. At the level of practice, the reality is more complex, murky, shaped by covert deals to manage trade.

Liberal trade theory argues that domestic firms suffer in the long run from being located in states that are highly protectionist. They suffer because they are coddled, not forced to continuously improve to meet the competition, and thereby are left uncompetitive in export markets however well protected they are in the domestic market. They also suffer because their profits are reduced by the high cost of inputs from protected firms – steel is more expensive as a production input when its price is held up by high tariffs.

These factors attract investment to non-protectionist economies and sustain the value of such investments for shareholders. However, they are often trumped by the more concrete incentive of locating where states promise government procurement, tariff and non-tariff barriers that guarantee a lion's share of the domestic market. Firms are pragmatic in balancing whether they will do better by locating where they will be most competitive or where they will be most sheltered from competition.

### World's Best Practice, Lowest-cost Location

World's best practice is a principle that actors sometimes follow because they believe it will bring them trade gains. States will set best practice standards in environmental regulation in the hope that it will push firms into higher levels of innovation. States will adopt best practice standards of prudential regulation of the finance sector as part of a strategy to attract more investment. Other actors seek trade gains through the principle of lowest-cost location. States become tax havens, companies locate where labour is cheap.

With competition law, the contest between world's best practice in competition law compliance and lowest-cost location is not an important one. As one US Justice Department official said in an interview: 'There is not an antitrust Cayman Islands'. This is one reason why the US has been considerably less energetic in negotiating antitrust MOUs to exchange enforcement information with other states than it has in negotiating MOUs on companies and securities regulation or tax. US business does not move off-shore to avoid the costs the Sherman Act imposes on it.

### Continuous Improvement v. Rule Compliance

In terms of the rules of the trade regime, continuous improvement cannot be discerned as an objective of any company we know. Corporations might seek to continuously improve their environmental outcomes, their workplace health and safety or the opportunities they provide for female or minority employees, but not to dismantle the barriers they have erected to protect themselves from foreign or domestic competition. They often lobby for less protectionist policies nationwide when they believe it will aid national economic growth and reduce the cost of their own inputs. But when it comes to specific measures which protect their corporate outputs, they mostly do not seek to dismantle them and certainly do not seek to exceed legal requirements. At best they subscribe to the principle of rule compliance, though often this means being seen to comply with its letter while searching for new non-tariff barriers or new modes of tacit collusion to evade its spirit.

### Transparency

The officials we interviewed at the Japanese Ministry of International Trade and Industry believed that 'transparency is important, but negotiation should not be open to the public'. By this they mean they support greater openness among state officials, but 'the US is going too far' in its support for NGOs to be accorded official status at international meetings. NGOs, they said, 'should put opinions to their own governments'. During the closing phases of the Uruguay Round, the Clinton administration pushed for a public right to observe GATT dispute resolution proceedings and to provide for the possibility of *amicus curae* briefs to GATT Panels. The then US Ambassador to the GATT told us this attracted opposition from 'all other countries'.

Members of the GATT secretariat we interviewed in 1993 also viewed it as impractical: 'It's hard to negotiate when you have interest groups behind you. Farmers with agriculture. So keep them out. In the nature of things, they have to sell out some interest groups.' In other words, GATT professionals felt observation by interest groups would paralyze the GATT; it would prove impossible to negotiate an overall win–win situation because the domestic losers would make it politically impossible. None of this seems a reason, however, for the WTO to deny NGOs even the standard kind of consultative status that they have in the UN system.

Hence the transparency principle applies to transparency within the epistemic community of trade officials, but not to citizens. In the run-up to a trade negotiation, negotiators work out the likely links and trade-offs. Domestic constituencies are reassured but not given any real information. The position of the overwhelming majority of trade negotiators is clear. They want the actions of other trade negotiators to be maximally transparent to them, so they support such transparency in principle; their own actions to be minimally transparent, so they pursue the maximum secrecy possible in their own practice; and minimum transparency of trade negotiations to the citizens of all states including their own, indeed especially their own, so they oppose such transparency in principle. The upshot is that most WTO papers are restricted to contracting parties to the GATT. Submissions to WTO Dispute Panels are secret to the parties.

Some WTO work is almost entirely oriented to the hope of liberalizing trade simply by making regulatory barriers more transparent to foreign trade officials, who can then demand that they be dismantled in bilateral negotiations. For example, the WTO work on government procurement aspires to strengthen the Agreement on Government Procurement to require more transparent rules and processes for government purchases. Some of the standard ideas for increasing transparency in domestic administration have been translated to the world of trade negotiation. For example, the US persuaded Japan to establish the Office of the Trade Ombudsman in 1982 to receive complaints about trade barriers asserted by foreign exporters.

The most important initiative toward transparency under the GATT has been the Trade Policy Review Mechanism. A review staff of WTO economists produces a large report documenting the pace of liberalization and compliance with GATT obligations in the country under review. It covers all trade policies. The US, EU, Japan and Canada are on a two-year cycle of reviews, the next sixteen largest traders are on a four-year cycle and the rest every six years. The review is based on and bears some resemblance to the OECD economic survey and the ILO's Committee of Experts process for compliance with labour standards.

Domestic transparency is an important objective of the Trade Policy Review. The review is designed to help actors in the local economy see how their trade policies might be affecting national economic performance. But international transparency is a second objective – the reviews show other countries when they are being victimized by protectionist measures of the reviewed country. All reports are public.

After the secretariat and the contracting state have prepared reports, two half-day meetings are held in Geneva on the trade performance of the state before the Trade Policy Review Body. Two independent discussants are appointed for these meetings. Questions from the floor are directed at the reviewed state and at the reviewers. The US usually asks the best-prepared questions, having sent a questionnaire about the state under review to all relevant US government departments. Questions in writing, asked the first day, must be answered in writing, preferably on the second day. The faxes run hot overnight. For states which are not major traders, hardly anyone turns up to these review days. But for the major traders, up to three-quarters of contracting states will send observers. An average of about fifty sit in. Often ministers or deputy ministers of the reviewed state attend, with a delegation of four or five. The Trade Policy Review Body reacts to a report by raising concerns or complimenting a country where progress has been made.

Members of the WTO secretariat involved in the process see it as having an educative function, a transparency function and a function of bringing peer pressure to bear on states with incoherent or GATT-inconsistent policies from the community of trade diplomats. 'There is a competition to do well and pride at doing well'. Of course, if a protectionist practice revealed by the process is bad enough, it may trigger bilateral retaliation.

Unfortunately, the trade negotiators' club does not have a culture of transparency. The norm is to speak platitudes in public while brutally beating up other states in private meetings. The operant norm in this culture is reciprocity: trade diplomats fear frank talk in public because they believe those they talk frankly about will reciprocate when their turn comes. 'In public when they notice an itch on someone else's back, their urge is to scratch it and invite them in turn to scratch theirs' (WTO official).

Nevertheless, the educative part of the Trade Policy Review Process can work especially well with developing countries: 'You pick up simplified customs procedures from one country and say "Have a look at that" to other countries. Most voluntary change is not from a contest of analyses. It is more from educating them of things they have not seen or understood' (WTO official). Those in the Trade Policy Review Division of the WTO also see it as educating domestic publics. Often, domestic trade ministries will ask the reviewers to 'please recommend' and make the case for X, usually a liberalization they cannot sell domestically. Sometimes they even say: 'Please be critical of this. We'll get up and say the criticism is not balanced and in perspective. But it will help us in battles with other bureaucracies internally' (WTO official). Mexico and Iceland recently bought hundreds of copies of their reviews so they could disseminate them and foment change in their domestic policy climates. In Chapter 20, we discuss this phenomenon in terms of Putnam's (1988) model of international politics as a two-level game.

Beyond data supplied by the state under review, the US, which 'knows everything about every country it is dealing with', is an important source of information to the reviewers. In conclusion, transparency in the trade regime is not seen as something with a democratic rationale that need extend to citizen groups. Rather, transparency is conceived in the same way as verification in arms-control regimes. It is mainly believed to be important insofar as it enhances mutual understanding and trust among contracting states.

As Ralph Nader (1994: 5) has complained, the final text of the Uruguay Round Agreement was not made available to US citizens until about a month after it was signed, 'leaving the administration with a monopoly of describing the deal to news media'. This led to systematic distortion of the benefits of the Agreement and systematic suppression of costs for those states that had to bear their brunt. In Australia, for example, the press were told of the billions in benefits that would accrue to the Australian economy from the commitments Europe, Japan and the US had made on dismantling agricultural protectionism (commitments that were subsequently widely dishonoured), but no estimates were made and the newspapers made no reference to the costs Australia would bear as a result of TRIPS (compliance with which *was* vigorously enforced by the US). Since then, one economic study has suggested that the cost of retrospective protection for patents (required under TRIPS) alone will cost Australia almost $A4 billion (Gruen, Bruce & Prior 1996). Since most countries are patent importers, that kind of cost is likely to be suffered around the globe.

## National Sovereignty

> The whole point of the GATT is mutual exchange of national sovereignty (GATT official).

A former Director-General of the GATT considered that a central virtue of that position's power to broker compromises depended on the office being unconstrained by the sovereignty of any nation or people: 'Unlike governments, he has the advantage of not being submitted to the daily pressures of national political constraints. The expectation is, therefore, that he will be better placed to judge where the general interest lies and the best ways to promote it' (Long 1987: 53). NGO critics of the GATT/WTO such as Ralph Nader base their attack on the way the institution erodes national sovereignty and denies citizens a democratic voice in monumental decisions about their welfare. Indeed, as we have seen in the discussion of the transparency principle, citizens are denied even the knowledge of what their trade negotiators are arguing on their behalf.

For all of that, many ordinary citizens have been persuaded to subscribe to Roosevelt's analysis that unwillingness to compromise on national sovereignty, to build a cooperative world order based on free trade, was a cause of the Great Depression and the Second World War. The battle for the hearts and minds of mass publics and, most strategically, of the US Congress is a battle between the benefits of national sovereignty and the benefits of mutual exchange of national sovereignty. If the latter mutual exchange is to be freely agreed and democratically defensible, however, the problems of transparency and public participation in WTO processes must be resolved.

The principle of national sovereignty is a principle in retreat from the trade arena. The Final Act of the Uruguay Round required states to take Agreements like TRIPS and GATS as part of the total package. States were not given the choice of steering their way through these Agreements using a power of reservation.

## Harmonization, Mutual Recognition

When most readers were young, they probably noticed at ports all sorts and sizes of lumpy chunks of cargo being loaded onto ships. Today we see the same sized containers dominating the surrounds of every port in the world.

The GATT and the growth in world trade it has fostered does not directly require harmonization. However, as we will see in Chapter 16, the Sanitary and Phytosanitary Standards Agreement of 1995 effectively harmonizes global food standards to the Codex. The Tokyo Round Agreement on Technical Barriers to Trade strengthened the hand of the ISO in harmonizing standards for everything from cargo containers to bridge clearances and screws. TRIPS renders enforceable various global WIPO standards. The GATS agreement is forcing harmonization under certain ITU telecommunications standards and forcing the pace on the harmonization of accounting standards, as shown in Chapter 9.

The philosophy behind much of this work is that when nations have similar laws and policies for regulating international business, trade conflicts over the standards being used as non-tariff barriers are less likely to occur. Efforts at harmonization that fall short of full success also make mutual recognition easier. Mutual recognition of standards that are not subject to EC 'essential requirements' has been EC policy since the 1980s. Where the EC does have 'essential requirements', for example with health, safety, environment and consumer protection standards,

standards are presumed acceptable as long as they meet the requirements of international standardization bodies. The GATT/WTO has increasingly taken this European approach to mutual recognition in its work on technical barriers to trade. Article 2.7 of the Uruguay Round Agreement on Technical Barriers to Trade states: 'Members shall give positive consideration to accepting as equivalent technical regulations of other members, even if these regulations differ from their own, provided they are satisfied that these regulations adequately fulfil the objectives of their own regulations.'

There have not been concerted attempts to harmonize competition law since the collapse of ITO ratification. Partly this reflects a recognition that what is a sound antitrust standard varies greatly between a large economy with a lot of domestic competition and a tiny economy where domestic monopolies experience competition only from imports. Within the same economy, thinking and competitive circumstances can change considerably across time: 'if the US had succeeded in the mid 1970s in locking the world into the US antitrust model of that time [under the banner of the UNCTAD Restrictive Trade Practices Agreements of that era] we would have locked in a "Voss Grocery" standard. Modest efficient mergers would be stopped. In retrospect that would have been bad' (US Justice Department official). Soskice's (1999) comparative capitalisms project shows that an aggressive antitrust policy that is good for the firms that flourish in an ultra-liberal economy like the US may not be good for the industries that flourish in a collaborative economy like Germany or Japan (e.g. sophisticated engineering based on firms sharing technology).

Instead, what has been globalized through the competition policy epistemic community is not harmonized standards, but what that epistemic community regards as sound principles of microeconomic analysis of antitrust policy in its national and historical context. Within that epistemic community there is also the view that competition policy should be more responsive to the accumulation of empirical evidence about impacts on competition than to ossified standards in case or statute law. At the same time, there is considerable impetus for harmonization of notification requirements for cross-border mergers, so that different nations affected by a merger might become less likely to make different decisions with different timing based on different information which the merging companies are required to provide in different formats. 'It hasn't happened yet, but the day will come when the EC will say a US merger will be unacceptable in Europe' (US Chamber of Commerce interview).

### Most Favoured Nation, National Treatment, Reciprocity

MFN and national treatment are cornerstone principles of the GATT, APEC, NAFTA and the EU. MFN requires a country which offers a concession to one state to offer it to everyone else. MFN is often referred to as the principle of non-discrimination. The rigour of this principle is sometimes deflected at the stage of implementation in a trade Agreement as part of the dialectic between mercantilism and liberal trade theory. For example, even though Article II of the GATS Agreement establishes MFN for trade in services, the same Article allows a state to claim an MFN exemption in relation to sectors it so nominates (see the Annex on Article II Exemptions in the GATS). This, in effect, allows a state to pursue a strategy of reciprocity since an MFN exemption means that a state can negotiate access to a service market on a state-by-state, sector-by-sector basis. The principle does not concur with the reality of how much bilateral negotiation occurs in Geneva. When one state offers five banking licences for three landing slots for its aircraft, it is a liberalizing deal between two states only. However, other kinds of offers to liberalize services are tabled by states as liberalizing offers to all states, sometimes running to over 100 pages (which also provide a framework for the above kinds of bilaterals). And the ultimate multilateral agreement signed under the auspices of the GATT fundamentally enshrines the MFN principle (even if implementation and practice under the principle do not accord with the formal purity of the principle).

Pure MFN seems to be more a juridical ideal of trade law than a living reality of trade practice. Trebilcock and Howse (1995: 75–9) document eight major types of exceptions to MFN under the GATT. The most important are the authorization of customs unions and free-trade areas under Article XXIV and the institutionalizing of Conditional MFN under various non-tariff codes negotiated during the Tokyo Round. Conditional MFN means, in this context, that only states which sign the codes and accept their obligations can claim a right to be treated in the same way as the MFN.

A closely related principle is national treatment, which means that foreign products or foreigners should receive at least the same treatment under a state's domestic law as domestic producers or nationals are entitled to receive. The principle is found in the key agreements of the Uruguay Round (e.g. Article XVII of GATS, Article 3 of TRIPS). Again, the principle is nested in a complex language of implementation and cross-reference. There seems, for example, to be more scope for a state to gain an exemption from operating national treatment in the context of services than in the context of intellectual property. This perhaps reflects the fact that the main players in the services Agreement (the US and EU) were keener to maintain the option of reciprocity there than in intellectual property, where it was simply a case of the lead states requiring all states to grant protection to the nationals of all other states on the same terms. Article 2.1 of the Uruguay Round Agreement on Technical Barriers to Trade states:

> Members shall ensure that in respect of technical regulations, products imported from the territory of any member shall be accorded treatment no less favourable than that accorded to like products of national origin [national treatment] and to like products originating in any other country [MFN].

National treatment is required, unless an exception is obtained, under the Uruguay Round Agreement on Trade-related Investment Measures. The prospective dismantling of foreign investment review mechanisms is the brave new world of national treatment.

Until the Tokyo Round, GATT rounds were almost totally justified to national constituencies in terms of reciprocity:

> Each nation's negotiators wanted to be able to report home that they had obtained from the negotiation at least as much as they had given up. In negotiating tariffs, there were various quantitative and statistical ways to support such claims. For example, the percentage reduction in the tariff would be multiplied by the value of the goods imported in recent periods, and that would be designated as the 'value of the tariff concession' made in the negotiation (Jackson, Louis & Matsushita 1982: 270–1).

With the shift to dismantling non-tariff barriers in the Tokyo and Uruguay Rounds, such quantification became more difficult, which reduced reliance on the principle of reciprocity. Today, within the EU, France tends to be a supporter of reciprocity and retaliation in trade negotiation, Germany tends to be against it. The UK, Germany, the Netherlands and Denmark tend to be the EU states supportive of liberalizing trade multilaterally, the rest favour more regulated trade based on bilaterally negotiated reciprocity.

Unilateral liberalization and multilateral rules against protection under the sway of liberal trade theory have historically been vulnerable to calls for reciprocity whenever favourable trade balances turn into unfavourable ones. We saw this with the 'diminished giants', the US in the late twentieth century and the UK of the late nineteenth century that spawned the Reciprocity Fair Trade Association. Reciprocity is never far from the table at which trade negotiators sit. Its persistent presence regularly produces 'impure' versions of national treatment and MFN in trade Agreements.

This cluster of principles has been important in the bilateral spread of competition law. The US effects doctrine, first devised by US courts in 1911 (*Strassheim v. Daily*, 221 US 280) and applied in the competition context in 1945, probably helped contribute to a US belief that it did not need an international organization operating in the field of competition. The principle of extraterritoriality enabled the US to operate unilaterally in an economy that was slowly globalizing. The use of negative comity (taking into account the interests of another state when acting) in cooperative arrangements between states on competition, signalled a shift towards bilateralism. The growing use of positive comity (acting to assist another state) in such arrangements signals states' realization that there is no choice but to increase cooperation on the enforcement of competition policy. In a global economy of mega-mergers no competition authority, not even one as powerful as the US Justice Department, can do without the positive assistance of other authorities. The days of unilateralism and cool bilateralism are gone forever from the regulation of competition.

## Mechanisms

### Military Coercion

Military coercion was not important to shaping the trade regime. No state joined the GATT because of military force. However, the dominant view, to which we subscribe, is that the collapse of free trade into regulated protectionism can cause the outbreak of military coercion. Japan, after all, sold its 1935–45 military imperialism to Asia as the creation of a 'Greater East Asian Co-Prosperity Sphere' and successfully sold the war to its own people as its response to exclusion from the Western trading system.

Nevertheless, German trade officials told us that 'defending Berlin' and other military allusions were a constant of US trade negotiations with Germany during the Cold War. During the Second World War, the Potsdam Agreement of 1945 settled the ironic accord of Stalin with Roosevelt that: 'At the earliest practicable date, the German economy shall be decartelized for the purpose of eliminating the present excessive concentration of economic power as exemplified in particular by cartels, syndicates, trusts and other monopolistic arrangements' (P. Evans 1995: 9). Roosevelt rightly drew the conclusion, from the Nazi manipulation of cartels, that eliminating powerful cartels that could be controlled by states would eliminate 'weapons of economic warfare' (Martin 1987: 125). Military coercion has thus had a more decisive role in shaping competition laws than trade law.

As soon as the US occupation ended, Japan weakened its antitrust law and enforcement. But from the 1980s, the US replaced military with economic coercion by insisting on tougher Japanese antitrust in bilateral trade negotiations.

**Economic Coercion**

Economic coercion has always been fundamental to trade negotiation. Perhaps no mechanism is more fundamental. We see this with the explicit targeting of 301 sanctions on India and Brazil to punish them for resisting the US agenda on topics such as intellectual property. German trade negotiators told us they had asked the International Intellectual Property Alliance how countries like Mexico could be persuaded not to oppose TRIPS. '"Don't worry about Mexico", they said. "We've got them in our pocket." Reference was made to their aid dependence.'

The World Bank and IMF increasingly request the enactment of competition law as a condition of assistance to struggling economies. With Japan and Korea at least, the US has applied diplomatic pressure associated with threatened or actual use of section 301 to insist on strengthening of competition law enforcement to prevent domestic monopolies from excluding import competition. Economic coercion is the most important mechanism of trade policy globalization, but in regard to competition policy globalization modelling has been more important.

**Systems of Reward**

Systems of reward are not present in the competition policy regime. The national treatment and MFN principles in the trade regime are very much institutionalized as systems of reward, however. If a state joins the global regime and complies with it, it systematically gets the reward of equal regulatory treatment with all other members' domestic firms when the joining state exports into their markets. If a state joins and complies it gets the same benefit as any member extends to any other nation's importers for its imports into that member state. If a state doesn't join and comply with the regime, it is not assured of these benefits. Developing countries which have less to gain from the GATT, have been induced to support it through the Generalized System of Preferences for exports from developing countries to industrialized economies. Thus the GATT regime has globalized partly because its rewards for participation and compliance meet our definition of what is required for a 'system of reward' – that the reward be a *systematic* means of raising the expected value of compliance with a globalizing order (as opposed to coercion, which reduces the expected value of non-compliance). National treatment and MFN are institutionalized in the GATT and other regional trading Agreements as just such a systematic way of rewarding compliant participation in the regime.

**Modelling**

Modelling has been the most important mechanism of globalization of competition law: 'Hand in hand with the change in global politics has been the increasing pressure to both prove fealty to the new orthodoxy, and conform to the norms of behaviour expected in the main economic "clubs"' (P. Evans 1995: 11). Among the clubs to which Evans refers are NAFTA and the EU, which require effective competition laws as a condition of admission. The OECD is also important: 'We want to be in the OECD family', as an official of the Polish Antimonopoly Office put it.

The US antitrust bar and more recently the EC Directorate-General for Competition have been what we call (in Chapter 25) the 'model missionaries' for antitrust. A senior Justice Department official used this very language during an interview: 'The US has always had something of a missionary zeal about spreading antitrust'. Later he referred to an 'evangelistic zeal for spreading the word'. Sometimes this takes more the form of the 'model mercenary' rather than the 'model missionary', as when US law firms come in behind US trade negotiators to assist Japanese firms to implement antitrust compliance systems. The US M&A lawyers discussed above are another example of the legal model mercenary.

In most cases, nations have been persuaded to set up competition law authorities through a belief that this is something economies do when they want to become more efficient, internationally competitive and give better value to their consumers. Typically, they then look at the competition laws of other countries, modelling some elements of one country's law, other elements of a different nation's statutes. Our interview at the Czech Republic Ministry for Economic Competition nicely captured the modelling process in action. The 'impulse to entrench the law [competition] came from the outside, the World Bank'. The World Bank had suggested it as a necessary part of the privatization process. Much of the actual content of the new competition law had been taken from German law, but two US consultants were involved in various stages of its development. Finally, the new competition authority was maintaining close contacts with the OECD.

US power in trade regimes, and UK power before that, was considerably based on the fact that the process of trade liberalization in a particular industry or field took the form of a seminal bilateral Agreement (e.g. Korea on intellectual property). This Agreement becomes a model which can be spread by means of coercion or modelling. Other states with similar interests, in modelling the act of obtaining a bilateral Agreement, reinforce the model through seeking to use it as a precedent. A hegemonic actor like the US can trigger a sequence of modelling behaviour that results in the proliferation of a bilateral model. For example, once other states appreciated the deal that South Korea had given the US on intellectual property (the Agreement included retrospective protection for US patents) they also made a beeline to Seoul seeking an Agreement. An official from the EC explained to us that it became routine for the EC to follow the US into countries with which the US had concluded a bilateral arrangement on intellectual property. The EC official told us he obtains a copy of the Agreement, and then a mandate to negotiate from the European Council. He said that the EC 'never does better than the US and normally worse'. Australia is another country that makes a practice of following the US, at least in Asia where the US had softened up the 'pirate' states with its 301. A senior official of the German Ministry of Economics told us that the EU followed the US into Korea after its 1986 bilateral. However, 'the EU had a lot of trouble to get the same terms as the US. So much so that France favoured bilateral sanctions against Korea. Germany was against this'. The disagreement between France and Germany perhaps shows why the EU finds it harder to get the terms the US gets!

The point is that the bilaterally iterated model then becomes a natural option in a Director-General's text of a multilateral Agreement. The fact that the model is in a Director-General's text gives it, in the words of one US diplomat, 'an air of neutrality'. A powerful state supportive of regime-building can therefore acquire an early-mover advantage over a regime-resisting state by exploiting the power that flows from putting its bilateralized model on the table – it can shape custom bilaterally and then make the multilateral Agreement conform with custom.

The first-mover advantage also applies to new technical standards. Article 2.9 of the Uruguay Round Agreement on Technical Barriers to Trade attempts to deal with this by requiring states to publish new national standards where international standards do not already exist, and allowing time to receive submissions from other states before implementing the new standard. Mandated publication in advance not only has the virtue of restraining states pursuing a first-mover advantage from locking in an approach that suits their manufacturers more than importers, it also fosters international modelling of standards and therefore progressive harmonization – or at least convergence – in technical standards.

### Reciprocal Adjustment

Non-coerced negotiation, where the parties agree to adjust the rules they follow, is widespread in the trade regime and beginning to exist in the competition regime where MOUs are beginning to achieve some very modest reciprocal adjustment. Virtually no economic coercion and no military coercion whatsoever was applied to states to get them to agree to the harmonization of food standards settled in the Uruguay Round of the GATT. Almost all states are food exporters and worry occasionally that other states exclude their exports by using domestic food standards as non-tariff barriers. However difficult reciprocal adjustment of some standards would prove to be at the Codex Commission in Rome (see Chapter 16), states did not need to be coerced into agreeing that all would benefit from reciprocal coordination of food standards to remove non-tariff barriers.

### Non-reciprocal Coordination

A key difference between the WTO and a sectoral organization like the International Maritime Organization or the International Telecommunication Union is that negotiation in the following form takes place at the WTO: 'We'll offer you five more banking licences, but you'll have to give us three more landing slots for our aircraft'. This difference was deeply institutionalized during the Uruguay Round when it was decided states could not pick and choose sections of the final text. They could not sign the agriculture Agreement but refuse to sign the GATS Agreement on services, for example.

Key negotiating postures at the GATT were the US posture 'No TRIPS, no Round', which was more or less supported by the EU and the Cairns Group posture 'No agriculture, no Round'. Non-reciprocal coordination involved the US and EU yielding for the first time at the GATT to an Agreement on reduced agricultural protectionism, the Cairns Group bearing heavy costs from more expensive intellectual property imports.

The horse-trading orchestrated by the Director-General during the final stages of a GATT Round is an exercise in non-reciprocal coordination: 'They won't give you what you want in that industry sector. Can't you give in if they liberalize this other sector for your exports?' In other words, when negotiations bog down, the Director-General breaks the deadlock not by narrowing the agenda, but by broadening it. GATT Rounds take so many years because such a complex of non-reciprocal adjustment is being negotiated. Progressive broadening of the agenda makes it more possible for non-reciprocal coordination to put states in a win–win position on issues which are all win–lose when contested in isolation. The agenda-broadening also makes it too big to fail; the final stumbling-blocks to agreement are made to look small in comparison to the vast omnibus Agreement that has expanded horizontally and vertically through non-reciprocal coordination.

### Capacity-building

In the early 1990s the US committed $US7.5 million in foreign aid funds to assist former communist countries to set up competition authorities with the help of teams of lawyers and economists from the Justice Department and the FTC. Ad hoc programs of this type also exist in certain

developing countries, such as Venezuela. The American Bar Association has also organized significant volunteer efforts to assist with setting up antitrust law and practice in countries which do
not have them. Germany has provided considerable technical assistance to Central and Eastern
Europe on competition policy, as has the OECD Competition Policy Division. The EU PHARE
program also provided considerable assistance. For instance, when we visited the Polish Anti-
monopoly Office in 1993 it was using PHARE funds to hire UK and French law firms to provide
written analyses of difficult cases. At an interview with a minister of the Czech Cabinet in 1993 we
were told that the Czech Republic used PHARE funds to hire consultants 'who were specialized in
establishing supranational companies'. The minister also observed that to date there had only
been one concrete manifestation of aid under the PHARE scheme (the modernization of a border
control program); the rest of the money had been swallowed up by consultancies.

The OECD, in the terms we will outline in Chapter 25, are more model mongers than
model missionaries, like the US, in providing assistance:

> The Americans are in the forefront being entrepreneurial with their antitrust model. The FTC and Jus-
> tice are travelling all over Eastern Europe preaching the antitrust gospel. Wanting to change percep-
> tions about efficiency and markets. The OECD is taking care to offer alternative models for them to
> choose. The Eastern Europeans are interested in Spain and Portugal as countries that have moved out
> of command economies (interview with OECD official 1992).

Ultimately, the European models proved more influential and the European capacity-building
more helpful because the EU was the club the post-communist societies most wanted to join.

Capacities in market economics have been insufficient to transform command economies
at the speed hoped. An official of the Polish Antimonopoly Office offered the following analysis,
which a senior Polish legislator endorsed:

> State monopolies and their supporters in the Ministry of Industry have no experience in market econ-
> omy, but much experience and understanding of political influence. They successfully resist de-
> monopolization. Reformers have much understanding of the market economy but little
> understanding and experience of political influence.

Capacity-building has not been very important in inducing states to join and comply with
the liberal trading regime. As we have seen, at the GATT economically unimportant states tend to
be ignored rather than helped. A small secretariat struggling with negotiating fatigue certainly has
no capacity to help them. Most of the practical help comes from UNCTAD, though this has hardly
been a significant factor in the globalization of the GATT liberal trading regime. UNCTAD has
provided quite a lot of assistance to developing countries wishing to establish laws and authorities to regulate restrictive business practices. However, only a handful of developing countries
have used this technical assistance.

## Conclusion

Most of the important globalizations of trade regulation have occurred since 1950 under the auspices of the GATT. It is hard to escape the conclusion that the leadership of a small number of
major US companies has been the key to shaping the global trade agenda. The US state has been
more responsive to them than the EC to European business leaders. Moreover, the US has been

willing to use its unified economic, diplomatic and even military muscle to pursue the agenda handed to it by these business entrepreneurs. Aggressive unilateralism has been defused only when a multilateralism that institutionalized the comparative advantage of the corporate origina-tors of the strategy was put in place.

With considerable veracity, US trade negotiators have been able to portray themselves as holding off enormous pressure from Congress for even more aggressive unilateralism. 'Give us what we want or we, the soft cops, will succumb to this pressure from the hard cops' has been the message that has worked. It has worked because most trade negotiators believed during the Uruguay Round that 'the US Congress was the biggest danger to the Round, bigger than France' (GATT official).

Interestingly, though, when congressional pressure has not been backed primarily by cor-porate interests – for example, pressure to get tough on demanding a link between labour stan-dards and the GATT, pressure for transparency, allowing the public to observe GATT dispute resolution – the strategy of US trade negotiators has been less effective. They have blustered in as hard cops, talking tough with maximum media profile ('lead the parade', as one said), stirring up opposition from developing countries, which are then given victories. The USTR gives developing countries things it never wanted, or makes concessions in areas where there is only a soft domes-tic consensus (high-technology policy being an example in the Uruguay Round), in return for concessions in areas like services that it does want, on behalf of its corporate clients.

The same analysis applies where the US strategists are unsure whether they will do better bilaterally or multilaterally for corporate America. Investment is one area of such uncertainty. In the Uruguay Round the US settled for weak clauses of limited substance on TRIMS: 'Developing country governments could go back home and say they had a win. We beat the Americans' (senior USTR official). The USTR might be seen as weaker than Congress would like in an area such as services, but it is effective. It might be seen as tough in an area such as labour standards, but it is utterly ineffective. The beneficiaries of this configuration of success and failure have been the US TNCs who have been the primary ultimate shapers of the global trade agenda.

Symbolic politics is at the forefront of the US trade and environment agenda as well. One senior US trade official listed the number one objective as 'delivering hortatory language on the environment in the GATT'. As one senior USTR official said, 'you don't want any interest group biting you when you want congressional approval [for the GATT or NAFTA]'. But some of those interest groups (e.g. labour and consumer groups) are given symbolic rewards, while others (e.g. CEOs with a direct line to the President) are given tangible rewards (Edelman 1964). The Semi-conductor Industry Association, whose members are mainly based in California, had such excel-lent lines of communication with the White House that at the eleventh hour of the negotiations, with the whole Uruguay Round being decided, they were able to insist on US negotiators seeking a further concession on the protection of semiconductors as part of TRIPS, a concession which fatigued US negotiators dutifully obtained. An SIA representative told us that the US negotiator for TRIPS had rung him in the 'early hours' to tell him the good news. It is the kind of service that few other interest groups could expect to receive.

One USTR official was remarkably frank in saying that the US has no intellectual plan about the long-term national interest, no consistent commitment to any principle. Rather, the 'client state' is the model of the USTR: 'It's too socialist to plan…The businessman is the man who knows. So you respond to him.' And, we might add, the President likes it when business leaders get the trade agenda they want because they then reward him with support for his next campaign.

The USTR perhaps tempers business pressure and balances it with other interests at times, but fundamentally its search is not for an optimal policy – rather, it simply looks to the business community for the lead. That said, business leadership has led to a coherent analysis of how the US wants to transform the trading system to prioritize areas such as intellectual property and services, where it has a competitive advantage.

It would be a mistake to be overly cynical about the considerable hegemony over the trade regime the US has enjoyed for half a century (and now shares with the EC), a hegemony the UK and no other state held in any other century. It is, after all, a trade regime that leaves virtually every nation outside sub-Saharan Africa better off than it would otherwise be. Even sub-Saharan Africa might do worse under a return to beggar-thy-neighbour unilateralism and global contraction. Without the Roosevelt administration's vision in establishing the Bretton Woods institutions and the GATT, life would likely have been shorter, nastier and more brutish. Admittedly, prosperity might have been greater if the ITO had been allowed to globalize competition law.

Yet the whole edifice is made fragile by its US corporate domination, by its lack of transparency to citizens, by the threat it poses to mass publics' deep commitments to national sovereignty, by the hypocrisy of leaders who talk free trade for others while getting away with as much regulation as they can to benefit their own trade. This is why the trade regime hits trouble whenever it has to rally support from democratic legislatures in the US or India. Somehow the regime must be transformed to give it more integrity in the eyes of the world. Some initial steps might be sensible transparency reforms, observer status for NGOs, applying the lessons of the Cairns Group's agricultural accomplishments to giving ever-wider groups of disenfranchised states a voice[5] and building upon the educative potential of the Trade Policy Review Process. With competition policy, a Competition Policy Review Process based on a framework convention with broad competition performance indicators to be audited by review teams might similarly be a path to convergence, which brings citizens along with the way sovereignty can be preserved and shared globally. Such a process would strengthen that modelling of competition policy which has been the most influential mechanism in the slow globalization of competition law to date.

In Chapter 7 we saw how, with TRIPS, the world crossed the frontier into a globally regulated information capitalism surprisingly quiescently. The next frontier is a global investment Agreement. Notwithstanding the pull-back to bilateralism on investment at the time of writing, we suspect US business will get an Agreement close to what it wants by using essentially the same strategy it used with TRIPS and various services Agreements such as telecommunications: it will put in place the elements it wants through aggressive unilateralism and bilateralism, then will walk out on multilateral Agreements until the rest of the world will placate its destabilizing aggression with the multilateral Agreement it wants.

Domestically and globally, however, the US and EU could choose a more democratically palatable liberalization of investment by incorporating an enforceable Code of Conduct for TNCs

---

5 This means, among other things, developing countries, perhaps through the coordination provided by a revitalized G-77, learning to deal with negotiating fatigue by delegating states (and NGOs) with like interests to act as their agents: 'We'll develop the expertise to watch out for your interests on this committee if you develop the expertise to watch out for ours on that one. Then when the crunch comes on both committees we agree to support each other. We will learn to trust and audit the work we do at the WTO on each other's behalf'. Like the Cairns Group, such developing countries need to build an organizational infrastructure if they are to be a serious check and balance on the Quad.

with respect to environmental stewardship, consumer protection, labour standards, respect for human rights and transferring the technology of information capitalism to the poorer economies. These would be responsibilities that must be met to benefit from a right to freedom of invest- ment. The US and EU probably will not do this, though during 1998 the US became supportive of environmental, labour and consumer rights being incorporated into the (now dormant) MAI. In the long run, trade policy that serves only big corporate clients is democratically unsustainable. The NAFTA concession of side Agreements to placate environmental (Chapter 12), consumer and labour (Chapter 11) concerns shows that this holds even in the nation that benefits most from the liberal trading system. Citizen groups everywhere are catching up on how the secret deals in Geneva shape their lives without their having any voice in shaping them. Every victory for big business leaves these citizen groups more restless, even angry. The peace, prosperity and environ- mental sustainability of this planet in the twenty-first century requires a newly democratized vision of trade policy to rival the vision showed at Bretton Woods in the twentieth century.

Ironically, we might learn how to do this from the boldest trade policy victory US business has ever had – TRIPS. Picciotto (1998) points out that TRIPS is the only case of 'positive' linkage of non-trade regulatory standards to the GATT – where states are required to enforce specified minimum standards. All other linkages in the history of the GATT have been 'negative'. States are not required to meet minimum food standards by the SPS Agreement, for example. They are simply required to strike out national standards that cannot be justified by science or by reference to accepted international standards. Until TRIPS, every linkage of non-trade standards had been negative – subjugating regulatory standards to trade imperatives. TRIPS subjugated free trade to the regulatory standards, as is evident from the way China is being kept out of the WTO because its intellectual property standards fail to measure up.

Whatever we think of TRIPS, Picciotto (1998) says the TRIPS principle is right: positive link- age is sometimes justified. In the contest of law between the GATT and environmental treaties that are enforceable by trade sanctions, we must accept that some regulatory minimums are more important than free trade, for us to survive and flourish. Failure to honour them is an unfair trade advantage that responsible states should not have to accept. Picciotto (1998) sees the collapse of the MAI as a political opportunity. Among other things, the MAI broadly guarantees freedom to make financial transfers. But would it not be reasonable for states to have the right to withhold this privilege to banks and states that refuse to comply with the Basle Committee's Core Prin- ciples for Financial Supervision? These principles are currently unenforceable. Yet failure to comply with them next time may produce the systemic financial collapse that the Asian crisis of 1997–98 almost accomplished. Clearly, positive linkage is justified here: it would be utterly reasonable for the rest of the world to tell China that it cannot be admitted to the benefits of the WTO regime until it honours the Basle Committee's core principles. And China's individual banks cannot be guaranteed the right to freedom of financial transfer unless they meet the Basle Capital Adequacy Standards for Banks. For Picciotto (1999), fiscal crisis is reason enough for cooperation in tax matters to be subject to positive linkage to the MAI: if a state is a blatant tax haven, other states won't let it enforce MAI obligations, perhaps even GATT obligations, against them. The collapse of the MAI makes the millennium the right historical moment for a global democratic debate on whether intellectual property is the only matter important enough to jus- tify positive linkage to the trade regime. Agreement on which list of standards are of sufficient importance to justify positive linkage to the GATT would be difficult, but not impossible.

| Labour Standards

## History of Globalization

### The Regulation and Abolition of Slavery

The first globalizing movement in the regulation of labour culminated in rather detailed rules in Justinian's Code (issued progressively through the sixth century AD) and earlier in the Theodosian Code (438 AD). This regulation was of fundamental importance, as Engels pointed out in *Anti-Duhring*:

> It was slavery that first made possible the division of labour between agriculture and industry on a larger scale, and thereby also Hellenism, the flowering of the ancient world. Without slavery, no Greek state, no Greek art and science; without slavery, no Roman empire. But without the basis laid by Hellenism and the Roman empire, also no modern Europe (Marx & Engels 1987, Vol. 25: 168).

Perhaps even more Eurocentric than Engels, given the significance of both ancient Chinese slavery and politics, is Rihill's (1996: 111) extravagant claim:

> Ancient Greece was the first genuine slave society, and also the first political society. This was not coincidental. But slaves did not simply allow the classical Greeks the leisure time to participate in politics; rather, and much more significantly, the growth of slavery in the archaic period prompted the Greeks to invent politics.

Under Roman law even medicine did not attain the status of a 'liberal profession': Justinian's Code legislated medicine as unbefitting free men; the profession incubated under a regime of slave-physicians (Finley 1980: 106–7). Justinian's Code 'provided a finely worked instrument for Byzantine administration throughout the Middle Ages' (Phillips 1985: 38). When the Visigoths overran Spain in the early Middle Ages, 'they took over into their vulgar version of Roman law many provisions pertaining to slavery' (Finley 1980: 124). Slavery declined during the Middle Ages in Europe if not in the Islamic world (Phillips 1996: 78), though Justinian's systematization remained ready to be invoked, 'a sophisticated legal code with elaborate rules for operating [a slave system]' (Phillips 1985: 39). While feudal serfdom – an alternative form of legally enforceable unwaged part-time labour for a lord and master – more or less replaced the slave system (Bonnassie 1991), pockets remained. In England in 1086 still 9 per cent of the population were classified as slaves (Eltis 1993: 208). Yet this was a low number compared to the Italian peninsula during the first two centuries of the Roman empire, where perhaps three out of four residents were slaves (Fogel & Engerman 1974: 13).

The Church after the papal revolution of the eleventh century became the key actor in progressively eliminating peasant slavery from Europe by, for example, freeing slaves on its own vast landholdings and putting pressure on lords by offering peasants better working conditions on Church estates (Berman 1983: 320). Its conclusion that slavery was contrary to natural law became an important ideal for the anti-slavery movements of later centuries. Yet, at the same time, the logic of theology allowed the Church to conclude that slavery was permissible under positive law. Thus it expressly sanctioned the continuing relevance of the Roman law of slavery (Berman 1983: 617).

Moorish domination of Spain gave Europe the first experience of colonial slave labour (Solow 1987), experience implemented during the First Crusade. Venice and Genoa in the Levant (later in Crete and Cyprus) deployed black slave labour to supply sugar to all of Christian Europe (Solow 1987: 713). As the manorial system of labour obligations replaced the slave system in the rest of Europe, the Cornaro family 'were involved in an international agri-business', maximizing profits through transcontinental trade based on distant marketing networks and the combined inputs of capital and slave labour from different places (Solow 1987: 715). In the fifteenth century, Portugal ran an African slave trade into the Iberian peninsula and into Iberian-controlled islands off the coast of Africa (Fogel & Engelman 1974: 15). Slavery again became of major economic importance with the exploitation of African labour to develop the plantation economies of the New World. From the sixteenth to the nineteenth centuries, 9.5 million Africans were forcibly transported across the Atlantic (Fogel & Engelman 1974: 15). The principles of Roman slave law continued to influence nineteenth-century US slave labour (Cushing 1854: 129; Watson 1987: xvii–xix). The transatlantic slave trade began with the Spanish and Portuguese as early as 1502; English, Dutch and French traders later became important participants (Anstey 1975: 4).

This resurgence of slavery gave rise to the first of the great global social movements, the anti-slavery movement. The US and French revolutions gave impetus but not decisive victory to the anti-slavery movement. However, it was an anti-slave-trade movement which had the decisive victory of ending British and US participation in the international slave trade in 1807. In 1838 slavery was abolished throughout the British empire, later in increasing numbers of US states, and later still throughout the whole of Europe, the Americas and the Pacific. Evangelicals like William Wilberforce and John Wesley saw slavery as evil in Christian terms, were moved by the objections to slavery in the enlightenment political philosophy of Montesquieu and others, and in instrumental terms saw slavery as an obstacle to missionary work in Africa and the West Indies (Anstey 1975). Slavery was also seen as less economically instrumental to the kind of industrial economy emerging in Britain (Williams 1944). Adam Smith's arguments in *The Wealth of Nations* that slavery was not economically efficient were particularly influential. There were also advantages to British West Indies colonists in denying slaves to competitors.

The Quakers in North America and England were the most important early shapers of the social movement against slavery. In 1787 what had been a purely Christian, predominantly Quaker, social movement became a non-sectarian transatlantic movement with the establishment of the London Abolition Committee, which was linked with other committees throughout the British empire, in Philadelphia and New York and *Amis des Noirs* in Paris (Temperley 1972: 40). By 1838 there were 1350 local anti-slavery societies in the US (Keck & Sikkink 1998: 44). A World Anti-slavery Convention was held in London in 1840. Later, organizations like the Brazilian Society for the Suppression of the Slave Trade and the *Sociedad Abolicionista Espan-iola* joined the network.

The movement pioneered tactics now standard in social movement politics, such as using petitions, consumer boycotts (of sugar produced by slaves) and the courts, to highlight injustice. Granville Sharp in 1772 used the English courts to declare the freedom of James Somerset, an escaped Virginian slave, thereby conferring liberty on some 10 000 other British slaves (Temperley 1972: 10). In 1783 Sharp unsuccessfully attempted to prosecute, in the Admiralty Court, those responsible for throwing slaves overboard from the slave-boat *Zong* (Anstey 1975: 246). Although legislative change was more decisive, courts in both England and North America made important decisions on restricting and regulating, and then abolishing, slavery (Finkelman 1985, 1986).

After the British government announced in 1833 that it would emancipate slaves in the sugar colonies of the empire, the anti-slavery movement became even more internationally oriented. Organizations like the Society for the Universal Abolition of Slavery and the Slave Trade and the British and Foreign Anti-Slavery Society emerged. The social movement in Britain pressured it to apply diplomatic leverage against nations persisting in the slave trade. Britain had done this at the Congresses of Paris and Vienna, even offering territorial concessions (Trinidad to France) and financial rewards (£800 000 to Spain). British efforts to negotiate bilateral treaties with importing nations on eliminating or regulating the slave trade met with only limited success.

Britain then attempted to use its naval power to hound slavers off the seas, relying on right-of-search treaties which by 1838 had been negotiated with all slave-trading nations except the US and Portugal. British naval attacks right into Rio harbour effectively ended the Brazilian slave trade in 1853 (Temperley 1972: 183). Liberals in the new French government after the February revolution of 1848 moved immediately to emancipate slaves in all French colonies (Temperley 1972: 189–90). Sweden and Denmark abolished slavery at about the same time. But the Dutch anti-slavery movement did not obtain abolition in all Dutch colonies until 1863. The capitulation of the US Southern states following civil war with the North ended the era of slavery in the world's emerging great power. Mass publics had become imaginatively engaged with the ideals of the anti-slavery movement through Harriet Beecher Stowe's *Uncle Tom's Cabin* (1852), which sold over a million copies in Britain alone during its first eight months on the market, as well as being presented on stage and set to music (Temperley 1972: 224).

Yet, ironically, the biggest triumphs of a social movement driven by pacifist Quakers came from gun-barrels in Rio harbour, the streets of Paris and Gettysburg. With the substitution of European colonial rule for Arab rule in the Middle East and Northern Africa, the smaller Arab slave trade that predated the transatlantic trade by many centuries was crushed through cooperation by the European powers forged at the Berlin Conference of 1884–85 and the Brussels Conference of 1889–90 (which produced a comprehensive international agreement on combating the slave trade) (Temperley 1972: 264). This was reinforced in the twentieth century by ILO standards against forced labour.

The descendants of emancipated slaves in the twentieth century were less than free. They suffered deeply structured inequality of access to educational, training and employment opportunities. While nationalist revolutions in Latin America delivered substantial effective emancipation in the nineteenth century, it took the black civil rights movement under the inspirational leadership of Martin Luther King in the US during the 1960s to begin to inject some vitality into state regulation to end employment discrimination against former slaves and other disadvantaged minorities, and to install some (faltering) affirmative action measures. While anti-discrimination laws did globalize as laws on the books (if not as seriously enforced laws), affirmative action (positive measures to improve employment opportunities for disadvantaged groups) attracted legislative support in only a few Western states.

Illegal slavery continued on a large scale for many decades after it was outlawed by the major states (Emmer 1993: 108). Moreover, as we will see in the next two sections, slavery was replaced by other forms of coerced labour in the colonies of Britain, France, Portugal, Spain, Holland and Germany. Pockets of slavery still remain, particularly the enslavement of women and children as sex objects, as revealed by the World Congress on the Sexual Exploitation of Children in 1996, for example.

In summary, the demise of slavery proceeded through three stages: first, banning slavery in Europe; second, suppression of slave-trading; third, banning the owning of slaves in colonies. The same liberal forces that underwrote these three stages also underwrote the progressive abolition of serfdom in Europe. It was not until the early nineteenth century that earlier abortive attempts at liberating serfs, such as the English Peasants' Revolt of 1381 led by Wat Tyler, were widely interpreted in a sympathetic way. The French revolution and the second wave of liberal insurgency of 1848 were also important. Napoleon's conquests somewhat ironically continued the work of the revolution in this respect; the Code Napoleon totally abolished feudal servitudes,[1] conquered states adopted freedom of labour-contracting as law and often gave it more meaning as law in action after 1848. As we will now see, the effective abolition of servitude as labour law in action did not occur in the South until the twentieth century. With the emergence of capitalist labour relations, theory was always ahead of practice. This differed from finance, where practice led theory (for example, it was not until 1658 that Holland ruled that no banker could be denied communion for practising usury).

## Master and Servant Laws

The end of slavery was not the end of coerced labour. Colonial plantation economies were kept going by the transshipment of millions of Chinese coolies (Hu-Dehart 1993; Frings 1995), Indian (Jain 1988) and Melanesian (Munro and Firth 1990) labourers. There was also considerable transshipment of white indentured labour to the Americas (Beckles 1995). Many were involuntary immigrants, as many as 10 per cent dying during voyages under inhumane conditions (Hu-Dehart 1993: 69). Some were prisoners taken in clan fights. Colonial masters harnessed local dominating forces to coerce emigration – by the terror of Chinese secret societies, by the domination of Melanesian 'big men' who the British, Germans and French paid with guns.

The French in New Caledonia could keep indentured labour in virtual slavery by fining them for repeated petty offences such as 'being found in the town after 8 pm' (Shineberg 1991: 193), to the extent that labourers could never work off their debts to their masters. In this and other ways, eight-year 'free' contracts could extend for the entire useful working life of an indentured worker. Hu-Dehart (1993: 71) has shown that precisely when slave imports to Cuba ceased in the 1860s, coolie imports surged. 'As with slaves, the planters enjoyed "absolute power" over the coolies' (Hu-Dehart 1993: 76). Immigration of Indian indentured labour also started in 1834, the year in which slavery was abolished, with workers shipped to the British colonies of

---

1 The revolutionary cum Napoleonic bargain was not always such an attractive one: emancipation from serfdom combined with heavy taxation and merciless conscription.

Mauritius, Guyana, Trinidad, South Africa, Fiji and later Malaya, as well as to French and Dutch colonies (Jain 1988).

After the abolition of slavery throughout the British empire in the 1830s, 'free' labour in the colonies continued to be repressed by master and servant laws. These laws were modelled from those of the metropolitan powers in London (Craven & Hay 1994) and the Hague (Groenewoud 1995). However, the law of master and servant continued to limit freedom of labour for almost a century in the colonized world after it had ceased to be a dominant feature of labour law in the metropoles. As late as 1923 in British Tanganyika, new penal sanctions for offences such as 'Neglect or improper performance of work' and 'Wilfully neglecting property' were introduced and widely enforced under the *Master and Native Servants Ordinance 1923*. The British innovation to replace slavery in Tanganyika was to impose a poll tax that peasants could not possibly pay, then press defaulters into labour. A quarter of a million Tanganyikans were coerced into colonial labour between 1933 and 1942 by this method (Shivji 1982: 44).

In the Portuguese colony of Mozambique, penal laws of more direct kinds simply criminalized unemployment, sentencing 12 per cent of the entire registered urban workforce at some time between 1950 and 1962 to the institution of *chibalo*, a form of forced labour. Five per cent were also sentenced to at least one beating for violations of labour laws over matters sometimes as petty as breaking a cup (Penvenne 1995: 137–9). The Portuguese were also more perfunctory in how they implemented a pretence of abolishing slavery. In the cocoa settlements of Sao Tomé and Principe, 70 000 slaves were simply purchased for 'perpetual indenture' after abolition in 1875. These African slaves were technically freed after purchase, but were forced to agree to long contracts which were 'automatically renewed' on expiry (Clarence-Smith 1993).

Master and servant laws enabled employers to impose summary justice on workers for major breaches of contract such as absconding and minor breaches such as being late for work. Imprisonment and flogging were among the sanctions commonly provided by master and servant laws for breach of an employment contract. Corporal punishment and servitude were used least and abolished earliest in England itself. They were used more, but still at a comparatively low level, with somewhat later deregulation in predominantly white colonies like Ireland, Australia and Canada. Corporal punishment and servitude were used most and latest in non-white colonies (Craven & Hay 1994: 86). The major purpose of the laws was 'to compel work from workers who might be tempted to leave for higher wages' (Craven & Hay 1994: 82). In nineteenth-century Australia, for example, master and servant law was used much more widely than the law of conspiracy to break strikes: individual striking workers were prosecuted criminally for breach of contract (Creighton & Stewart 1994: 29).

Sanctions were progressively made available to workers against employers' breaches of contract, but these were rarely available in any practical sense. The most important penal sanctions against employers were for 'paying wages in excess of those set by justices or by statute' under the *Statute of Artificers 1720* (England) and the *Statute of Artificers 1771* (Ireland) (Craven & Hay 1994: 85).

Master and servant law existed in England at least since the *Statute of Labourers 1349*, which heavily regulated freedom of contract for labour. Among other things, the statute 'obliged all able-bodied men and women under the age of 60 who did not have the means to support themselves to work for anyone who required them to do so, and also fixed wages at the levels prevailing immediately before the outbreak of the plague' (the Black Death, which decimated the population and thus caused labour shortages) (Creighton & Stewart 1994: 22). The *Statute of*

*Labourers* was repealed in favour of the *Statute of Artificers* in 1563. It 'empowered the local justices of the peace to fix wages by reference to the price of bread and made it an offence for servants to leave their employment before the end of the agreed term other than with the permission of the master or for "good cause"' (Creighton & Stewart 1994: 23).

After being reconstituted by legislative changes many times until the nineteenth century, the law of master and servant was finally repealed in England in 1875 after one of the first coordinated trade union campaigns (Hay & Craven 1993: 175). In 1877 the Dutch parliament made the same move, declaring that 'the use of penal sanctions in a civil dispute was contrary to the classic-liberal legal principles it was eager to follow' (Groenewoud 1995).

Yet as late as 1907 in the British colony of Guyana, 20 per cent of indentured immigrants were convicted criminally for mostly minor infractions of laws based on the master and servant laws. Defendants were not allowed to give evidence in those proceedings (Jain 1988: 192).

A form of penal discipline of labour that existed in all European states except Britain was the workbook (*livret d'ouvrier*). It originated in eighteenth-century Italy, which required workers to possess a *benservito* (reference or testimonial) (Veneziani 1986). The French version of this institution was modelled in Belgium, the Netherlands, Prussia and Denmark. The institution of the workbook was central to keeping labour regulation within the realm of police rather than liberal contract until the second half of the nineteenth century for much of Europe. Employers and mayors could keep skilled workers by refusing to release their workbooks. Colonial regimes modelled the basic idea through the widespread practice of refusing labour mobility to coolies and other indentured labourers until they could get their master to release a testimonial.

In both common-law and Roman-law Europe, 'the employment relationship was originally governed by family law', involving the supremacy of the head of a household (Veneziani 1986). 'In Britain the judges were reluctant, even under the guise of contract, to interfere with the patriarchal authority of the master within his own household' (Veneziani 1986). Labour law became progressively more penal, until the penal-law era had been totally replaced with a civil law of contract, by the latter part of the nineteenth century. With the rise of trade unions the era of labour contracts as just another form of free liberal contracting was short-lived, replaced by labour law as a hybridized distinctive form of regulatory law. The dramatic oscillations of labour law were highly internationalized – from the private law of the family law era to the public features of the penal law era, back to the private law character of the deregulation of the remnants of the guilds and the nineteenth-century law of free labour contracts, back to public law in the regulatory era of twentieth-century welfare state ascendancy (in some states associated with specialized codification of labour law to unshackle it from the the general principles of private law) and finally the new liberalism of 1980s labour market deregulation. As we will now see, however, these internationalized sequential shifts were not mirrored in the South.

### Colonialism and the Globalization of Labour Law

Colonialism did not forge the globalization of labour law that we see in the world today, because colonialism pushed the South back to legal regimes that applied in earlier periods of Western history – to pre-feudal laws of a slave system during mercantilism, to pre-capitalist master and servant laws during the industrial revolution and into the twentieth century. Hence, just as labour law in the North was moving from penal to civil law, penal labour laws were being installed in the South. There was compatibility between English liberalism and English economic hegemony only as long as that liberty applied only on its land-intensive isle – and wealth could be built in other, land-abundant environments by the economic efficiency of the slave system. Fitzpatrick (1984) calls this phenomenon 'integral plurality': law 'depends integrally on what is contrary to it'. For example, liberal contract and labour law can only be sustained as liberal because more coercive legal orders, such as that of the patriarchal family, can be delegated responsibility for the unpaid work of housekeeping and disciplining children.

Integral plurality is constitutive of liberalism in Fitzpatrick's analysis: John Locke could own shares in the Africa Company and write a constitution for the Carolinas 'that incorporated a slave code, while at the same time laying out the theoretical basis for the Glorious Revolution in England' (Eltis 1993: 222). Such integral plurality – colonial law enabling metropolitan law that is contrary to it – is obviously the antithesis of global harmonization. At the same time, there were harmonizing counter-movements; ILO standards between the wars and immediately after were not without influence over African colonial labour laws (Cooper 1996: 30–56, 216–24).

Franz Neumann (1929) argued that state response to trade unions and labour standards has moved through four ideal types: repression, toleration, recognition and incorporation. A limit of that analysis is that it is a Western one; the Western unions that successfully worked through that succession sometimes supported opposite movements in the South in the direction of slavery and servitude, indeed even supported the repression of coolies within their own borders.

Another reason why colonialism was not a globalizing force in the domain of labour standards as it was in other regulatory domains was that the most efficient way for capitalists to dominate local labour forces was to coopt pre-colonial forms of domination. These were matters of considerable cultural particularity. For example, in Latin America the Spanish often simply removed the apex of the social pyramid – kings, royal houses, etc. – harnessing the infrastructure of rule by village chiefs and other lesser functionaries who were experienced in making their own coercive labour systems work (Bethell 1987: 316). This kind of infrastructure was used to manage slaves sent from Nicaragua to Peru in the sixteenth century, for example. African slavery built on these traditions of intracontinental slavery. The *ecomienda* was a grant to Spanish settlers, not of vassals but of income from a large group of Indians. It was widespread but varied enormously, depending on how local cultures worked. Debt peonage and the *repartimiento* (Lovell 1983) (which substantially succeeded the *ecomienda*) – a labour draft obliging a percentage of the healthy, male Indian population to travel away to work – were also widespread but culturally variable. Such colonial institutions might be viewed as instances of what globalization theorists now like to call glocalization – colonialism as a global force that exploits and accentuates distinctively local forms of labour regulation.

## The Labour Movement

Until recently, it was historical wisdom that labour resistance until the nineteenth century was resistance by a conservative crowd, occasionally rioting because of the disruption of customary reciprocities between the plebs and their masters. Now it is clear that from the thirteenth century and throughout the early modern era in France, Germany and the southern Netherlands, journeymen associations constituted themselves as free workers who asserted the liberty to work 'where, when, for which duration and, above all, with whom and at which rate of pay' (Lis & Soly 1994: 20). The fact that they were organized rather like nineteenth-century unions is reflected in their use of collective pressure on employers, defence of their skills as weavers, fullers, cordwainers, saddlers, bakers and the like, and their inclusion of strikes in their repertoire of industrial tactics to secure better wages and conditions. The likelihood that they were more republican radicals than traditional defenders of customary reciprocities is reflected in their nicknames for one another: 'Liberty', 'The Obstinate', 'Disrespectful', 'Victor' (Lis & Soly 1994: 21). The fact that they were not an ephemeral phenomenon is indicated by efforts throughout the Holy Roman empire and the English state from the sixteenth century to outlaw journeymen associations. It is clear that they were a globalizing phenomenon of the early modern era:

> To exert collective labour pressure, it was crucial to develop networks of association, which required strong cohesion and solidarity. It was necessary to bridge gaps in time and space, as members worked in various centres of production. This objective required transforming physical absence into mental presence, which meant creating a feeling of shared identity [across space] (Lis & Soly 1994: 51).

The modern labour movement rose and began its decline a century later than the anti-slavery movement. At its zenith, and even today, it engaged a level of participation from the ordinary working-class people who were its beneficiaries in a way that the anti-slavery movement never gained the participation of slaves. Not that slave strikes, riots and rebellions were absent; they were just less potent and not used so widely as these weapons in the hands of free workers. During the first half of the nineteenth century, it was organized white male skilled tradesmen in US cities who were at the vanguard of building on the progressive egalitarian agenda of the US republican revolution (Montgomery 1993; Tomlins 1993; Wilentz 1984). Between the mid nineteenth century and the First World War, however, there was a decisive victory of liberal individualism over redistributive republicanism. In the US, liberal individualist law was used to challenge workers' rights to collective bargaining with considerable success. Corporate capture of the liberal state was used to crush the labour movement; in the US labour never captured the state in the way it did, at least for short periods, in most industrialized economies. Brutal repression was also important: while seven workers were killed in labour disputes between 1872 and 1914 in Britain, sixteen in Germany and about thirty-five in France, 500–800 were killed in the US (Mann 1993: 635). Even so, in 1905 a slightly higher proportion of the US workforce was unionized than the British workforce and significantly more than in Germany, Sweden, France and Austria (Mann 1993: 631). Yet in the 1990s, with 15 per cent of US workers belonging to unions (the same level as 1905), the US had the weakest union movement in the West (Swepston 1994: 19).

By the time of the 1848 uprisings and the consequent shifts toward social democracy throughout Europe, Europe was the new cutting-edge of the politics of wealth redistribution. Karl Marx also made it the intellectual cutting-edge. The labour movement internationalized very early. By the 1860s, the London Trades Council had already experienced imported continental strike-breakers. This convinced them of the need to initiate the First International (1864–76). Marx was one of the speakers invited to a meeting to establish an International Working Men's Association headquartered in London. Marx became the chief drafter of the platform of the International – the economic emancipation of the working class. The International was not the major driving force behind the development of the labour movement in any nation. Each national labour movement went its own way, shaped largely by national political dynamics (Windmuller 1980: 17). The International was internally divided between Marxists, who wanted to conquer the state, and anarchists, who were bent on its destruction. Both sides were out of touch with the general direction of the pragmatists in national unions. In the Second International (1889–1914), both Marxists and anarchists were marginalized; Fabian socialism had supplanted Marxist aspirations for the revolutionary overthrow of the state. The German social democratic party, the British Trades Union Congress and the moderate French socialists became the dominant players.

Meanwhile, individual unions were forming International Trade Secretariats. Loose associations had been formed of the national unions of boot and shoe workers by 1889, miners (1890), printers (1893), clothing workers (1893), metal workers (1893), transport workers (1897) and many others. By 1914 there were thirty, mostly headquartered in Germany (Windmuller 1980: 23). Congresses of the Second International facilitated the formation of these International Trade Secretariats. While the secretariats supported nationalization of the means of production, they acted mostly as information exchanges on wages and working conditions and as coordination points for resistance of international strike-breaking strategies by employers. An International Secretariat of Trade Union Centres (1901–13) eventually became the International Federation of Trade Unions (1913–19). The International Federation of Trade Unions successfully lobbied for the establishment of the International Labour Organization (ILO) at the Versailles peace negotiations. The International Confederation of Free Trade Unions, albeit fragmented by competing communist and Christian international union federations, is the principal contemporary inheritor of the mantle of the International Federation of Trade Unions.

The Russian revolution of 1917 reinstalled Marxism as the dominant intellectual current in the labour movement until the 1980s. Soviet occupation of Eastern Europe after the Second World War, revolutions in China, Cuba and Indo-China and periods of elected Marxist rule in other nations put a third of the world's population under Marxist rule mid-century. This globalized a state socialist conception of labour standards. Unemployment was effectively abolished, though large numbers of the workforce were not fully or usefully employed. Great progress was made on equalizing employment opportunities for women, compared with the pitiful progress in the West. However, the communist regimes were totalitarian, consistently crushing basic labour rights such as freedom of association, until Solidarity in Poland successfully challenged that in the 1980s. It was hardly Marx's vision of communism. Yet the neglect of the fundamentals of the separation of powers that had been learnt from the republican transformations of the eighteenth century – rule of law enforced by a judiciary independent of the ruling party, rights and freedoms that can be enforced against the state – was a conscious neglect by Marx that naively sewed the seeds of worker oppression by communist states (Krygier 1990).

Most of the communist regimes collapsed in 1989, and the remaining communist states, such as China, moved away from state socialism and toward capitalism. The globalization of labour regulation under the Communist international, which had been so considerable, had ended. It ended at great cost to workers in these countries who suffered pandemic unemployment. A new politics of labour market deregulation was also externally enforced through conditions of lending imposed by the International Monetary Fund and the World Bank. Beyond the old communist states, Egypt, Senegal and Côte d'Ivoire, among other African states are amending or have amended their labour laws to make them more flexible pursuant to structural adjustment programs (Simpson 1994: 44).

In the West as well, the politics of labour market deregulation weakened unions. The battle to have labour viewed by state policy-makers as other than a commodity had been essentially lost. So much so that India and other developing countries are now pressing the WTO to liberalize labour movement as a factor of production. They want the General Agreement on Trade in Services (GATS) to allow companies to use their own low-wage skilled labour in foreign projects, for example by taking a shipload of workers to build a bridge. The attempt to use GATS to open the labour markets of Western states has had little success. GATS does define service to include the supply of service by means of the movement of natural persons from one territory to another (see Article 1). However, the Annex on Movement of Natural Persons Supplying Services under the Agreement makes it clear that states' capacity to regulate the movement of natural persons into their territories remains fundamentally untouched. Little wonder, then, that Indian commentators in describing GATS and the movement of natural persons have stated that 'the prospects of substantial gains in sector/subsectors of our export interest still appear to be a pie in the sky' (Iyer et al. 1996: 95).

More fundamentally, a weakening labour movement had already fallen victim to its own social democratic successes. The social-security safety nets created by the social democratic parties of the labour movement meant that workers no longer depended on unions to protect them from hunger and homelessness. In conditions of post-Fordist production, unions had persuaded employers that it was good for productivity to motivate workers by consulting, even empowering, them. Good employers held their best workers by granting them security and treating them decently, privileges productive workers were no longer dependent on unions to secure. In terms of our mechanisms, labour standards improved by a process of corporate modelling.

In African countries, where often less than 10 per cent of adults are in wage-earning employment, trade unions remain as irrelevant to the struggle for existence as they always were. The newly industrializing economies (NIEs) of Asia are moving so quickly from Fordist to post-Fordist conditions of production that they are missing the historical conditions for labour movement growth. Singaporean workers already enjoy higher wages and better job security than New Zealand workers.

## The Women's Movement

Feminist thought, as in the writing of Mary Wollstonecraft (1995), was an important intellectual current in the way it equated women's position with slavery in the terms of the eighteenth-century republican debate. However, the labour movements which were the inheritors of the republican and then the Marxist critiques of liberalism during the nineteenth century almost totally excluded women. The platform of the First International penned by Marx was the platform of the International Working Men's Association. There were always women who fought courageously to be heard in the labour movement. But in Australia, for example, it was not until the 1990s that enough men were listening, to appoint a woman to the top job in the national trade union movement.

This was one reason why the women's movement, that incubated during the same period as the First and Second Internationals, concentrated on social and political rights for women (mainly the franchise) rather than on economic rights. Nevertheless, when feminists gained a sprinkling of seats on national delegations to the Versailles peace conferences, they wrote some small victories into the ILO Constitution. Pre-eminently, women were required to be represented on ILO delegations whenever employment policies that involved women were to be discussed (Article 3). In practice, this requirement seems to have been ignored until the Roosevelt administration sent women to the ILO when the US joined in 1934. Eleanor Roosevelt was a driving force for women's rights. Her global influence continued after FDR's death; she was the first Chairman of the UN Commission on Human Rights and of the US Commission on the Status of Women in 1961.

Many of the paternal standards of the first two decades of the ILO protected women from jobs from which they might not have wished to be protected. Changing these standards has been an important task of feminists within the ILO and on national ILO delegations. Today, the ILO has more prominent and numerous feminist voices, as trade union representatives, than employer or government representatives. The ILO Special Adviser on Women Workers' Questions seeks to coordinate a 'coherent program of action for women across the ILO…and helps make women more visible by networking, mutual support and training among women from the governments, in the worker and employer organizations and in the Office'. She initiates studies of what unions are doing for the informal sector where women predominate, into unwaged agricultural work in developing countries. She seeks to 'go beyond the traditional constituents of the ILO to NGOs in developing countries where women are prominent. UNIFEM in New York is a useful ally here'. A Convention on Homework (No. 177) was adopted in 1996 and a Convention on Part-time Work (No. 175) in 1994. An important global step toward equality of work opportunities for women was the 1981 Convention on Workers with Family Responsibilities (No. 156) and an associated recommendation (No. 165), which provides a framework for the development of future obligations for work-based and community child-care, among other benefits. Preliminary work is underway towards an ILO convention on sexual harassment at work, but it has been dropped from the current agenda for standard-setting. Preliminary work means drawing positive attention in ILO reports (e.g. ILO 1988: 43–5) to the educative, legislative and enforcement work of states which have already moved on a problem like sexual harassment.

While ILO standards prohibiting employment discrimination against women have spread to most of the world, their effective enforcement has not. The Convention on Equal Pay for Men and Women 1950 (No. 100) is one of the most ratified (126 ratifications) and least adequately enforced, as is the Convention on Discrimination in Employment and Occupation 1958 (No. 111, 122 ratifications). An ILO convention on affirmative action or positive action for women is more a dream than a long-term aspiration. As of 1994 affirmative action received forceful national support at the ILO only from 'all the Nordics, the Netherlands, Australia and Canada, the US just going along and the European Community not being very supportive' (ILO interview). The energy of ILO feminists is therefore directed at reports to facilitate modelling by illustrating best practice on affirmative action.

The four UN World Conferences on Women culminating in Beijing (1995) were not 'conferences of commitments', notwithstanding partial success in Beijing, where sixty-five states made commitments which are not to be documented or monitored by the UN (Charlesworth 1996). They were, however, special moments in a growing dialogue that in 1979 settled the UN Convention on the Elimination of All Forms of Discrimination Against Women. Enforcement of the Convention consists of no more than a reporting procedure followed by 'constructive dialogue'. There is no complaint procedure, though an Optional Protocol is being negotiated for one. This means that the Convention on the Elimination of All Forms of Discrimination Against Women does not mark major progress in the domain of labour standards since (as we will see below) the ILO has more elaborate and better-resourced procedures for evaluating reports and complaints about the implementation of labour standards affecting women.

### The ILO

The creation of the ILO as part of the Versailles peace accord was both a pay-off to the labour movement for their cooperation with the Allied war effort and a conscious attempt by the Allied powers to defend capitalism from Bolshevism in the aftermath of the Russian revolution. Many conservatives shared with social democrats a belief that as capital became more internationally mobile, a race-to-the-bottom on labour standards would play into the hands of communist agitators. The pursuit of international minimum standards through an ILO seemed prudent.

Prior to the war, there had been only two treaties for the regulation of labour conditions, one on the use of white phosphorus in matches, the other on night work for women. An epistemic community of international labour legislation experts emerged from the late nineteenth century, especially with the formation of the International Association for Labour Legislation in 1897.

Edward Phelan and Harold Butler of the British Labour Ministry, both of whom would be future Directors of the ILO, drew up the proposal for the ILO. Phelan picked up from a Fabian Society of London pamphlet the idea of tripartism. A League of Nations institution was created, with the unique voting constituency of two votes for each state, one for the accredited worker organization of that state and one for the accredited employer association. The ILO is the only directly surviving League of Nations institution, largely because of this Constitution. The League foundered on unanimity as a prerequisite for action. At the ILO, in contrast, consensus decision-making emerged early and inevitably as a result of the tripartite structure (Osieke 1984). In practice, consensus means that no player or group of players with the clout to block a decision is so strongly opposed to the way the decision is formulated to block it. At the ILO, consensus in this sense is reached by groups of delegates (e.g. the G-77 and the employer group), then a general consensus is negotiated among the groups. The tripartite structure therefore forced a high degree of dialogue that brings out most of the good arguments for and against a proposition. And it has tended to avert the worst excesses of either the tyranny of the majority or the tyranny of the minority that can occur when states have a veto. Obversely, the demands of global tripartism have lent a lowest-common-denominator quality to many conventions and recommendations, and obsolescence in the face of social, economic and technological change (Creighton 1993).

This dialogue has settled 181 conventions (which have received more than 6400 ratifications) and 188 recommendations on standards ranging from social-security systems, occupational health and safety, regulation of working conditions and hours of work, and equal employment opportunities. In the first two decades of the ILO's existence the priority for standard-setting concerned hours of work, night work, holidays with pay, workers' compensation and weekly rest. The second priority was protective measures relating to women, youth and children. Today, some of these protective measures, such as preventing women from working underground in mines or from night work, are seen as having disadvantaged women. Discrimination against women has become a higher priority in ILO standard-setting, as has occupational health and safety (Dahl 1968: 320).

> In 1933, at the height of the Depression, US scholar and diplomat James T. Shotwell could write that most of labour's original goals for the ILO had been achieved. He was not being ironic. Laws then on the books in most industrialized countries mandated the eight-hour day, limited child labour, allowed unions to form, and required reasonable wages, weekly days for rest, equal treatment for foreign workers, equal pay for equal work and government safety inspection of workplaces. This record is impressive, especially when we consider that those labour goals of 1919 that had not been met by 1933 still have not been met today (Murphy 1994: 199).

During its first thirty years, a succession of ILO Directors to greater or lesser degrees saw a grander mission for the ILO, beyond standard-setting. They wanted the ILO to take a lead role in international macroeconomic coordination (Haas 1964). The ideology was social democratic, cooperatively tripartite, Keynesian welfare-statism. The very checks and balances of its tripartism

made it impossible for the ILO to get carried away with grand schemes of international unemployment reduction through coordinated public works programs and other global counter-
cyclical measures. Although it often talked of grand social democratic reform designs, it got on
with the practical work of consensus-building on global labour standards.

Consensus-building was easier until the 1950s, while the ILO remained a club of like-
minded states. Moreover, in the early years it concentrated on building commitment to the epistemic community by setting standards on which there was the greatest commonality of
viewpoint, then using that accomplishment of international community as a resource to weld
consensus on questions where differences were wider. The ILO epitomized a Western European
consensus on tripartite industrial relations. The US has ratified only twelve ILO conventions. It
was absent from the ILO in 1919–34, 1938–44 and 1977–80, as was the Soviet Union until 1954
(apart from a brief membership in 1934). In the late 1950s and 1960s the enlarged number of
Soviet bloc countries unsettled the Western European consensus, as did the huge surge of newly
independent developing nations that entered the ILO during that period. Great tensions arose. In
the 1970s they contributed to the withdrawal of the US for a period, over the lack of independence from government of many of the worker and employer delegates from new members.

A further problem with the growing membership (now 174) has been that standards that
made sense within the Western club were beyond the capacity of Second and Third World societies.
Most ILO members have not ratified most standards, leading many commentators to suggest that
minimum standards were often set at too aspirational a level by the original members of the Western European club. Indeed, Dahl (1968: 343) found that even by the 1960s revisions to ILO standards had lowered rather than raised them. This is perhaps an overly crude characterization of
what has been more a process of including flexibility in ILO standards by avoiding specificity in
favour of terms such as 'adequate measures', 'adequate protection' and 'appropriate measures'.
While many domains of standard-setting in this book underwent a ratcheting-up process during
the second half of the twentieth century, this was not the case with labour standards.

The ILO is one of the largest organizations in Geneva, once with over 3000 staff, today
with 2286.

## Linkage of Labour Standards and Trade Policy

There have been many, mostly unsuccessful, attempts to link trade privileges to compliance with
labour standards since 1919 (Hughes & Wilkinson 1998; Wilkinson 1999). Since the 1980s a few
commodity agreements, such as the 1981 Tin Agreement, the 1986 Cocoa Agreement, the 1987
Sugar Agreement and the 1987 Natural Rubber Agreement, have begun to require producers to
commit, rather vaguely, to improve labour standards (Servais 1989: 426). Much less vague was the
bilateral linkage of labour standards to US trade policy under section 301 of the *Trade Act 1974*, as
amended by the *Omnibus Trade and Competitiveness Act 1988*. The amended section 301 authorizes
the US Trade Representative (USTR) to withdraw or suspend trade benefits to a foreign country or
to impose duties or other restrictions on imports if it persists in a pattern of conduct that denies
certain key labour rights 'and burdens or restricts US commerce'. The rights concerned are those of
freedom of association and collective bargaining, prohibition of forced labour (slavery), child
labour and standards for minimum wages, hours of work and occupational safety and health. The
same standards apply under the General System of Preferences, and granting Most Favoured
Nation status to a developing country is subject to an investigation with regard to these rights.

Such investigations can be initiated on submission of a petition by an interested party, usually a union or human rights group. The USTR tends to be extremely reluctant to upset trade relationships by imposing bilateral trade sanctions over labour abuses. However, if the abuses are highly visible and a complaint is made, the USTR can be forced to act, as in the cases of Nicaragua, Romania, Paraguay, Chile, Burma and the Central African Republic in the 1990s. Under 1985 amendments to the law establishing the Overseas Private Investment Corporation, at least four countries have had insurance coverage withdrawn from US projects within their borders for failing to meet core labour standards (Charnovitz 1987: 574). In the case of Indonesia in the mid 1990s, when trade union officials were arrested, a US trade official told us they had said to the Indonesian government: 'We'll tilt the mirror if you'll just give the appearance of allowing a free trade union. But they had to shut it down even though it was a non-event. So now we are forced to threaten action because we told them we wouldn't so long as they allowed the appearance of a free trade union to exist.' The US sought to solve this problem by suggesting to Indonesia: 'You invite an ILO team in to audit what you're doing. Make it appear like that is their idea rather than yours'. An ILO team did go in, and an ILO official assured us how important it was to be seen to be invited by Indonesia rather than orchestrated by the US.

In other words, while linking intellectual property protection to the GATT was important enough for the US to force the issue by bilateral sanctions (see Chapters 7 and 10), such importance and such bilateral aggression has always been lacking in the case of labour standards. Hence, the US advocacy since 1992 of linking basic labour standards to the GATT has been met with accusations that the US was trying to get the WTO to do its 'dirty work'.

In 1995 the EU introduced a revised General System of Preferences to imports from developing countries, which allows temporary withdrawal of benefits for violation of core labour standards. At the time of writing, the first complaints under the scheme (allegations of forced labour in Burma and Pakistan) were being heard.

Advocacy in the US of GATT enforcement of minimum labour standards has been a 'Baptist–bootlegger' coalition. For some, the motivation has been to improve the condition of workers in developing countries and to redistribute wealth from capital to labour globally; for others, it has been to worsen the condition of workers in the developing world by pulling employment from them back to the US. Developing countries are almost universally opposed to linking labour standards and trade, as are the NIEs. They see it as an attempt to take away one of their few comparative advantages – cheap, competitive labour – over the rich countries.

This backlash has caused the key sponsors of the link – the US, France, Norway and the international trade union movement – to negate any suggestion that it would require an international minimum wage or even require nations to have a minimum wage set at a level suited to local development needs. The suggestion has been that only core ILO standards concerning freedom of association and the right to collective bargaining, child labour, discrimination, equal remuneration and forced labour should be enforceable by trade sanctions pursuant to the GATT. Trade sanctions would only occur after complaints were examined and upheld by a joint ILO/WTO Evaluation Committee of Experts, time was given to implement rectifying measures and technical assistance toward meeting the standards was offered. None of this convinced the overwhelming majority of states and business lobbies which opposed the linkage. It was rejected at the Singapore Ministerial Conference of the WTO in 1996.

In the meantime, a glimmer of a 'social clause' had been included in the North American Free Trade Agreement (NAFTA) 1992 between the US, Canada and Mexico. The NAFTA side agreement, the North American Agreement on Labor Cooperation, requires parties to enforce the minimum core standards listed above, plus their own minimum-wage law. A Commission for Labor Cooperation has been established to monitor compliance with the core standards and to receive complaints of non-compliance. Only after various stages of consultation between the parties and a Committee of Experts fail to induce compliance under a plan of action to remedy the dispute can trade sanctions be imposed (but only in respect of child labour, minimum wage and occupational health and safety standards) (ILO 1994).

While formal linkage of trade and labour standards has been an idea much discussed but rarely realized, the spectre of a US-backed incorporation of labour standards into the GATT has revitalized the ailing ILO regime. After the collapse of linkage at the Singapore Ministerial Conference, the ILO proposed a fallback. A committee of its Governing Body developed a procedure to monitor compliance of all ILO members (which includes all GATT members) with core labour standards. The monitoring will occur regardless of whether the relevant conventions had been ratified, being regarded as inherent in accepting the responsibilities of ILO membership. The 1998 International Labour Conference voted 273 in favour, none against (forty-three abstentions), to make four core labour standards binding on members even without ratification (freedom of association, forced labour, child labour and discrimination in employment). This novel development had considerable momentum because it was jointly proposed by workers and some employer delegates, and supported by some ILO member states. It is an example of forum-shifting from the WTO (Chapter 20), of consensus that can be accomplished in one forum when there is fear and loathing of something 'worse' happening at another.

### Globalizing Labour Standards by Targeting TNCs rather than States

Walter Reuther, President of the United Automobile, Aerospace and Agricultural Implement Workers in the US (1944–70), led the implementation of more effective international cooperation among trade unions in negotiations with global automobile manufacturers. Reuther had a different model of how to accomplish upward harmonization of labour standards from the ILO approach of getting nations to agree on standards in Geneva. It was transnational corporations (TNCs) that were in Reuther's sights, not states. The strategy was for national unions to cooperate to set up 'international trade secretariats' so that TNCs could not play off workers in one country against those in another. Instead of a race-to-the-bottom, where jobs would flow to where labour standards were weakest, workers in all countries would uniformly increase demands for a greater share of corporate profits and for safer workplaces.

Reuther's strategy was adopted by the setting-up of many company councils by international trade secretariats. The International Metalworkers Federation set up a World Auto Council in 1971, the year after Reuther's death in a plane crash. Multiple councils were established to negotiate with Ford, General Motors, Nissan, Volkswagen, Renault and others. The Agricultural Implement Council set up tricompany global negotiations in 1975 with Caterpillar and the other big tractor manufacturers. Electrical World Councils were established to negotiate with Westinghouse, General Electric, Siemens, Honeywell and other companies (Bendiner 1987: 82). The Chemical Industry Trade Secretariat formed world councils among unions in such TNCs as Michelin, Rhone-Poulenc, Dunlop-Pirelli and Ciba-Geigy. The International Union of Food and Allied Workers Association established world company councils for Nestlé, Unilever, W.R. Grace, British-American Tobacco, Coca-Cola, General Foods and others (Bendiner 1987: 86).

The conclusion of Bendiner's (1987) study of these attempts at coordination is that on occasion they have provided useful international assistance to weak links in the chain of national union claims against TNCs. However, transnational collective bargaining has never been attained. Indeed, even what Reuther regarded as a basic precondition – common expiration dates for union contracts in foreign subsidiaries and the parent company – has made little headway. International trade secretariats have therefore failed as vehicles for improving global labour standards, though in isolated cases they have helped prevent them being wound down. Effectively coordinated collective bargaining across one national border – the US and Canada, with steel and some other industries – is the maximum that has been secured.

A second strategy to ratchet-up labour standards targeted not individual TNCs but TNCs collectively (instead of states collectively). Trade unions were prominent in supporting the efforts of the G-77 from the early 1970s to gain a UN Code of Conduct for Transnational Corporations. For twenty years the US effectively vetoed this initiative, which was finally killed in the mid 1990s. In 1976 the OECD established Guidelines for Multinational Enterprises. The OECD guidelines have no enforcement mechanism, though there have been isolated instances of unions successfully resolving disputes through recourse to the OECD (Compa & Hinchcliffe-Darricarrere 1995). In 1977 the ILO adopted a Tripartite Declaration of Principles Concerning Multinational Enterprises and Social Policy. This provides for a more formal complaint procedure than the OECD guidelines, to a Standing Committee on Multinational Enterprises. Trade unions told us of great difficulties in getting the ILO to receive complaints against specific TNCs for violations of the Code.

In 1996 the Clinton administration established a tripartite Apparel Industry Task Force that has now issued a Workplace Code of Conduct, compliance with which will allow apparel to display a 'No Sweat' label. The Council on Economic Priorities (a US advocacy group) in 1998 established an Accreditation Agency for its auditable, continuous improvement SA8000 Social Accountability standard, which covers various fundamental labour standards. While companies have begun to apply for certification as complying with SA8000, it remains to be seen how many will do so.

## Actors

### Organizations of States

Obviously, the International Labour Organization (ILO) has been a key actor in our story. In particular, its Secretariat, the International Labour Office, has been influential during much of this history. Ernst Haas could go as far as to say: 'New conventions and recommendations, therefore, almost invariably originate in the Office itself, and rely for support on a portion of its staff' (Haas 1964: 179). Although the staff has shown leadership on writing an impressive web of conventions and recommendations which would comprise an invaluable safety-net for workers if most countries implemented them, most do not. Only a tiny fraction of ILO conventions have been ratified by enough states to cover most of the world's workers. But whoever thought it would be easy to build global consensus on matters of profound conflict between the interests of capital, labour and states? And there is systematic evidence that ratification significantly changes the behaviour of developed states, though not with less-developed countries (exceptions being Costa Rica, Cyprus and Malta) (Strang & Chang 1993; see also Chayes & Chayes 1995).

It is clear in terms of our webs of influence analysis (Chapter 23) that the ILO is a most important strand. Lech Walesa, the former Solidarity leader and President of Poland, says: 'The ILO played an important part in the process leading to the restoration of Polish trade union freedom'. Nelson Mandela, then President of South Africa, says: 'We thank you that you (ILO) refused to forget us. We thank you that you did not tire in your struggle'. Similar quotes can be found on the ILO's US homepage (http://us.ilo.org/).

What seems clear to most observers is that the ILO has done surprisingly well in gradually building consensus on inherently conflictual standards. And when states do ratify conventions, they overwhelmingly comply with their obligations to report progress on implementing the convention, something not accomplished with UN human rights, environment and transport safety regimes. Their reports are reviewed in detail by an ILO Committee of Experts, which passes its observations on reporting and implementation failures to the Conference Committee on the Application of Conventions and Recommendations. In relation to more serious violations of obligations, the Conference Committee holds discussions with the violating states. Recalcitrant states are subjected to various methods of naming and public entreaty to meet their obligations (see Chayes & Chayes 1995: 231–4; Samson 1979). An ILO team may visit the state. Evaluation research on this process suggests that often it works; in fact, about about two times out of three it at least partially works (Landy 1966: 198).[2] Today, ILO officials claim, three out of four questions raised by trade unions are either answered to their satisfaction or remedied in ways the union considers to be an improvement. The evidence from Landy (1966) and other studies is that the process works better with wealthy democracies than with developing countries.

The vigilance of worker and employer delegates to the ILO plays a role. They have an opportunity to comment on the reports of their own governments. This is especially valuable during discussions on whether national laws are actually put into practice. A tripartite Governing Body Committee on Freedom of Association receives and reports on complaints about freedom of association before each session of the ILO Governing Body. By November 1997, it had heard over 1900 cases (Kent 1997). Unlike the Committee of Experts, the Committee on Freedom of Association is not restricted to monitoring states that have ratified the relevant conventions. Kent (1997), for example, has documented the influence of the Committee over China, which has not ratified Conventions 87 and 98 on Freedom of Association. With regard to the Convention on Discrimination in Employment (No. 111), member states which have not ratified are nevertheless asked to report at four-yearly intervals on their position with respect to the Convention, obstacles to ratification and steps being considered to overcome them.

The Committee of Experts, led by advice from the International Labour Office, takes a global strategic view of how to raise standards. 'Based on a Committee of Experts decision, the Conference can have a special tripartite committee [the Conference Committee on the Application of Standards] decide to call up say 50 governments and target say two matters that we seek to change them on. We might wrap up the change process with a public session with published proceedings' (ILO official). The Australian Department of Industrial Relations (1994: 17) has described this process as follows:

> Member states are 'invited' to attend the Conference Committee to provide an explanation for their non-compliance. Debate can be extended and vigorous. The Conference Committee reports to the International Labour Conference in Plenary Session, and its Report often contains hard-hitting criticism of governments for their failure to honour their international obligations. In particularly serious cases these criticisms may be contained in a 'special paragraph' of the Committee's report.

---

2   ILO officials we interviewed claim that the Landy figures today are more positive: '35 per cent of changes suggested or questions raised by the Committee of Experts are resolved immediately either by the government answering the question in a satisfactory way or agreeing immediately to fix the problem; 25 per cent are resolved after three rounds of discussion; 20 per cent are never resolved'.

The ILO has the most sophisticated dialogic machinery for securing compliance of any international organization. Part of its genius is in separating the technical phase from a political phase of deliberation. During our interviews we were told about the head civil servant of one African Labour Ministry who was happy to talk with the Committee of Experts, but who found cross-examination before the large audience of the Conference Committee a gruelling experience – so much so that he told his Minister either to get the law changed to comply with the Convention or to face the Conference Committee himself at the next review! The Committee of Experts are distinguished people of impeccable political independence. Their allegiance is to a rights-based epistemic community. This builds trust. Only if the Committee has concerns does the conflict go to the more robust tripartite political discussion of the Conference Committee. The political discussion can be robust because, although states are reluctant to criticize other states when their own performance is not impeccable, NGOs are more able to be forthright. At the same time, as one ILO official expressed the policy: 'Every time we criticize, we offer help. Respect for standards is tied to technical assistance'.

> This mixture of firmness and realism has been found to be more effective than undue criticism and censure. The two Committees attempt to include in their observations concrete suggestions designed to assist a government in eliminating infractions. The experience gained by other countries in similar circumstances, the clarification of the bearing of a convention and the availability of technical aid are mentioned as incentives to secure more satisfactory implementation. This constructive promotional method is a useful tool in seeking a positive response from governments. It helps to improve the observance of standards far more than a mere recital of neglected obligations (Landy 1966: 201).

As in other domains of compliance, reintegrative shaming seems to work better than either tolerance or denunciation/stigma (Braithwaite 1989; see also Feitshans' (1995) plea for praise and positive sanctions (Grabosky 1995b)). Stigmatization is risked by polarized politicization; tolerance by you-scratch-my-back-and-I'll-scratch-yours politicization. The latter is well illustrated by the failure of the UN human rights regime to implement the institutional lessons of the ILO:

> The International Covenant on Economic, Social and Cultural Rights…provided only for a reporting system and those reports were to be examined, not by an independent expert committee, but by ECOSOC [the Economic and Social Council] as a whole…An additional, but unstated, reason was that most states preferred to entrust implementation to a political body over which they could exercise full control, rather than to a specialist body that might seek to develop either independence or expertise, or worse still, both (Alston & Bruno 1987: 748).

This is why Elizabeth Dole, President of the American Red Cross, can say that 'The International Labor Organization is the United Nations' most effective advocate of human rights'. The European human rights regime, as we will soon see, did better at learning these institutional lessons.

Beyond the ILO, the only organizations of states of major significance to the globalization of labour standards have been European, notwithstanding some regional NAFTA significance. In some areas of labour law of critical importance to business, such as occupational health and safety, the European Commission has settled directives which have accomplished a considerable degree of harmonization. With occupational health and safety, the general preference of European business has been for harmonized standards rather than regulatory competition. Non-binding recommendations, which allow disparate means of implementation (or none), rather than directives, have been the predominant approach to the status of women and other disadvantaged workers. For example, a proposal for a directive on positive action (affirmative action) was diluted to a non-binding recommendation (Meehan 1992: 60). In 1989 the heads of state of all European Community members except the UK signed a Charter on the Fundamental Social Rights for Workers (the Social Charter) which strengthens the enforceability of labour standards in the European Court of Justice.

According to Moravcsik (1995), the European human rights regime is the most effective set of international institutions for securing rights, though its success is more attributable to the Council on Europe (with thirty-two members) and the Conference on Security and Cooperation in Europe than to the EC. In 1949–50, before the birth of the EC, the Council on Europe settled the European convention for the Protection of Human Rights and Fundamental Freedoms, and in 1961 a Social Charter was signed, with a much heavier emphasis on labour rights and freedoms. Petitioning to the regime is active, with over 250 complaints having been resolved by court decisions. Beyond decisions of the European Court of Justice and the European Court of Human Rights, Europe has the capacity to sanction rights abuses by suspending trade preferences to developing countries, suspending aid and, in the case of European states wanting to join the EU, withholding membership. Moravcsik (1995) finds that these sanctions are rarely effectively used. Even in dramatic cases like Yugoslavia and South Africa, it was difficult to build and hold European consensus on sanctions that might 'bite'. Nevertheless, Moravcsik finds that the strength of the European human rights regime has been 'not in the transformation of undemocratic regimes, but in the improvement of democratic ones' (p. 159):

> The unique mechanisms of the European system, in particular its finely grained system of individual petition and supranational judicial review, function not by external sanctions and reciprocity, but by 'shaming' and 'coopting' domestic law-makers, judges and citizens, who then pressure governments for compliance. The decisive causal links lie in civil society: international pressure works when it can work through free and influential public opinion and an independent judiciary. The fundamental social, ideological and political conditions that give rise to active civil societies and representative political institutions, which in turn contribute decisively to the extraordinarily high rate of membership and compliance enjoyed by the European human rights regime, are distinctive to advanced industrial democracies (Moravcsik 1995: 158).

When Moravcsik says that the most important elements of the European rights regime are the most subtle, he refers to processes of periodic reporting and dialogue on compliance by committees of independent experts, and reporting and dialogue in response to petitions from citizens. Epistemic community has emerged strongly among these European human rights experts, epistemic community shared with European judges, who have benefited from a 'transjudicial dialogue' (Burley 1993) toward normative convergence among lawyers and judges in many nations. Legal challenges under the European rights regime have not shied away from the toughest and most pivotal disputes, such as challenging UK non-enforcement of gender equality in the workplace. With non-democratic regimes, where international judicial review and shaming do not work very well and where experience shows sanctions to be mostly out of political reach, Moravcsik prescribes capacity-building to strengthen domestic civil societies and democratic political institutions (see also Otto 1996). Europe, as we will see below, has attempted quite a lot of capacity-building.

## States

The UK was by far the most important state actor in the global demise of slavery; it was a party to every bilateral or multilateral anti-slavery treaty signed during the nineteenth century. Switzerland was an important state in the nineteenth-century epistemic community discussing the idea of international labour standards, and led institutional support to the forerunner of the ILO, hence ILO's location in Geneva (Ghebali 1989: 4). But in the actual institutional design of the ILO between the wars, the key ideas and actors were from the UK, as they had been in the previous century with the regulation of slavery. France and Germany were also key national players in the globalization of labour standards. The US was not always, though sometimes it was (Lindsay 1934). Under Roosevelt, the US was particularly influential. Although US administrations repeatedly disliked the ILO agenda, the kind of forum-shifting it used for other arenas of regulation was never really an option for labour standards. The ILO was always entrenched. If the US set up its own labour-standards forum on the other side of Geneva, it had to persuade not only states, but employer and labour organizations as well, to defect to the new forum. Tripartism hence inhibits forum-shifting (Chapter 24). The US might entice employers away to a new forum, but if workers vetoed it, it would always enjoy less legitimacy than the ILO.

The very fact that the ILO is the only League of Nations body alive today indicates the depth of entrenchment caused by its large Secretariat and tripartite structure. So when the rest of the world would not play ball with the US, it could not set up a new ball-game; the US could only take its bat home for a while and say that its domestic contest was the world series. The Soviet Union's approach was not dissimilar, though it did have its own formal grouping of Labour Ministers from behind the Iron Curtain, the Council of Mutual Economic Assistance. The Council coordinated a lot of block-voting at the ILO. Developing countries also tried to foster collective strength at the ILO through the G-77, though full G-77 meetings were always too large and amorphous for such purposes.

Where the US has always been more influential than any other state has been in the bilateral enforcement of labour standards – trilateral enforcement, in the case of NAFTA. This predates Section 301. In 1955 when concern about cheap and efficient Japanese factory labour was at its height, the US, during bilateral tariff negotiations, insisted that Japan put in place a new system of minimum wages (Charnovitz 1987: 579).

**Business Actors**

The structure and importance of the ILO meant that individual companies could never be dominant in the way they are in other international organizations. As business from each country has a vote that counterbalances the labour vote, it has to organize collectively at the international level. This it has done. Voting organized by meetings of the employers' group at the ILO has held together well (81 per cent cohesion, in a study by Kruglak (1989: 183)) whenever they have had to balance a block vote by the worker group (97 per cent cohesion in the Kruglak study). The ILO was something the trade union movement (except in the US) wanted and the employers agreed to, with varying degrees of reluctance. The regulatory models were set by trade union strategists and labour bureaucrats. The business role was a more defensive one. Thus the business lobbies were a bit like the US state – wishing they weren't there a lot of the time, wishing they could start another game but mostly seeing it as prudent to keep on eye on this game. There were many exceptions – leaders of employer organizations who believed in social peace and cooperation through fair international labour standards, others who believed international labour standards would reduce unfair competition from sweatshops. Of course, the business leaders who believed this more often nominated themselves for service in Geneva. Consequently, there have been moments in the history of the ILO where support from employer delegates was decisive in its survival.

At the ILO, the International Organization of Employers (which specializes in social matters) is more important than the International Chamber of Commerce (which specializes in economic matters) (Oechslin 1982). But the economic–social divide is fuzzy.

An unremarked part of NAFTA is the way the US Council for International Business and Mexico's Confederation of Chambers of Industry have launched a program of cooperation to foster exchanges of best practice in the fields of labour and environment (US Council on International Business 1992). Mexican business and labour officials are hosted at US corporate training programs. Bilingual US experts offer training programs in Mexico and funds are provided for seminars run by Mexican business. Technical assistance is provided with the development of industry self-regulatory codes and practices.

Individual companies like Levi-Strauss, Reebok and Starbucks Coffee have made modest contributions to the globalizing of labour standards by insisting on and enforcing compliance with a corporate labour code by their many international suppliers, as well as by their own subsidiaries (Compa & Hinchliffe-Darricarrere 1995).

## NGOs and Mass Publics

We have seen that human rights and development NGOs often organize publicity and lodge complaints against abuses of labour rights, particularly child labour. Historically, the anti-slavery NGOs were extremely important, as was the Church from which these movements drew their values and arguments. Today, the women's movement and the labour movement are the most important. No two social movements could be more different. The trade union movement is highly structured and hierarchical. National umbrella organizations such as the AFL-CIO in the US and the Trades Union Congress in the UK cover the overwhelming majority of unions; most of these national organizations in turn belong to the International Confederation of Free Trade Unions, which plays a major coordinating role on global labour standards. Hierarchical and umbrella organizations have been anathema to the women's movement. This has lent vitality and plurality to women's voices in global fora. It has also protected the women's movement from control by corrupt oligarchs, who have at times gained control of national union movements. On the other hand, the lack of electoral process for women's groups to designate peak representatives has sometimes allowed international organizations to select the women's voices that it suits them to privilege. Sometimes, these are groups without a wide base of support from women or groups with only a Western base.

The International Confederation of Free Trade Unions has the resources to provide a systematic overview of priorities through its *Annual Survey of Violations of Trade Union Rights* in every country. This is important, because it enables a check on whether the ILO Committee of Experts and the Committee on Freedom of Association are pursuing the worst abuses in the problems they select for more intensive monitoring and dialogue. The discipline of being globally systematic in documenting the worst abuses is a safeguard against disproportionate attention to the concerns of well-resourced Western groups or even unrepresentative Southern groups who have acquired a strong resource base through entrepreneurial flair at securing aid money.

Trade unions captured the ILO to a degree that no other NGOs have ever captured an international organization. Of course, establishing the ILO was, as Haas (1964) points out, an attempt by states that were terrified of Bolshevism to coopt unions to capitalist relations of production. The capture was reciprocal. The first Director of the ILO was a French trade-union leader and his successors were mostly labour bureaucrats strongly sympathetic to union aspirations.

'The masses' were more important to the labour movement during its early days than during its more oligarchic recent history. Perhaps this is one reason for the decline in union membership. The anti-slavery movement primarily sought to mobilize an elite mass public of educated gentlemen who would read pamphlets and sign petitions; it barely attempted to involve or communicate with slaves themselves. The women's movement, the civil rights movement, the disability, gay and lesbian rights and indigenous rights movements which have struggled against various kinds of discrimination in employment have all sought to achieve change by communicating with mass publics. Often this has involved taking outrageous cases of discrimination to the courts, or to anti-discrimination tribunals, with maximum publicity.

## Epistemic Communities of Actors

Epistemic communities of actors are interestingly and richly important to understanding how progress has been made with the globalization of labour standards. While mass participation has been encouraged by ILO standards themselves – workers all over the globe participate with management on safety committees pursuant to ILO standards, for example – this mass participation has not been the driving force for new standards. New global occupational health and safety standards do not bubble up from workers all over the world getting safety committees to take their concerns to ever-higher levels. They more commonly emerge at technical conferences of occupational health and safety professionals. When there is a sufficient consensus at such professional fora on the need for an international standard, then it appears on the ILO agenda. Of course, trade union health and safety representatives are at those conferences and are important members of the expert communities. Usually, technically unsophisticated workers are not.

Epistemic communities without a mass base, such as that based on the International Association for Labour Legislation at the end of the nineteenth century, were always important with labour standards. We have found the most important institutional embodiments of this epistemic community to be the Committee of Experts and the Committee on Freedom of Association at the ILO. They have built a remarkable degree of confidence in their impartiality and competence on matters of the most profound political divisiveness. The international human rights epistemic community is another important one, partly joined by a transjudicial dialogue across national systems in a discourse of universal human rights. The international human rights epistemic community enables the possibility of enforcement by international courts of a concept such as freedom of association, a concept that would have been politically inconceivable two centuries ago.

Under its first Director, Albert Thomas, the ILO aspired to an epistemic community of a much more radical sort. Haas (1964: 145) is worth quoting at length:

> Thomas, it seems, was not interested primarily in the legislative *output* of the ILO and gave little serious attention to the actual uniform standardization of labor conditions, though he paid it occasional lip-service. He thought of social democracy and worker rights as being introduced through the process of interaction generated at Geneva – 'the collaboration itself', the *act* of research, debate, and voting.
>
> This collaboration was conceived dialectically. Workers were the challengers seeking to penetrate the national environment and thereby transform the international scene. Employers opposed this trend, and governments tended to side with them, or at least to assess the process from a purely national vantage-point. Hence, it was the duty of a dynamic ILO – in the person of the Director and the Office – to provide the necessary synthesis as a result of which employers and governments would accommodate themselves to the new order and share in it constructively. The ILO would advance the synthesis by always going out of its way to seek the participation of voluntary groups, to strengthen and even create them. The Office would maintain direct and continuing contact with unions at the

*national* level through the system of ILO correspondents, and thus strengthen them against their dialectic opposites. Attachment to the kind of international competition in which labour cost factors were eliminated or held constant was merely a cover: the true aim of the ILO was to usher in universal social and industrial democracy. The ILO would act as the coordinator and unifier of national trade unions, compel employers to deal with labour as equals, produce impeccable research and advice that would eliminate the possibility of anti-labour criticism, and seek to convert everyone to the need for social justice. The ILO, in short, would be the medium for organizing a global consensus on justice as well as be the agent for realizing it.

Perhaps this all seems a little potty today. Yet we must remember that the global leadership accomplishments of the ILO were not trivial; at the end of the Second World War the ILO had 'the world's foremost collection of technical experts on social policy questions' (Haas 1964: 157). When the former US Assistant Secretary of Labor, David Morse, took over the ILO Directorship in 1948, the era of the ILO conceiving labour as the progressive challenger who must be helped to confront employers had passed. No longer a dialectic, but 'labour–management cooperation in ever-widening circles...discussion, education and demonstration' (Haas 1964: 176–7). Notwithstanding the shift from a confrontational posture and from grand schemes of Keynesian coordination of full employment, Thomas's emphasis of the importance of 'the collaboration itself' was central to Morse's 'promotional program' and is still central today. The commitment to the Fabian idea of a tripartite dialogic institution that would transform the world economy to a more just one, remains central. The ILO has built an epistemic community around that ideal; it is a model of epistemic community-building that other social movements, like the environment movement, the consumer movement and the animal rights movement might consider emulating. Thomas would be disappointed in the ILO today, with its acceptance of high unemployment and its retreat from fomenting counter-cyclical international public works, but he could not view 'the collaboration itself' as a total failure, irrelevant to a juster world.

## Contest of Principles

### Lowest-cost Location v. World's Best Practice

The principle of lowest-cost location was important in bringing Western employers to collaborate with the ILO. Thomas might not have taken it too seriously himself, but he pointed out to employers that they would lose business to low-wage, sweatshop economies unless labour standards were globalized. The principle of world's best practice has not been an important part of the labour standards debate except in relation to discrimination against women, education and training standards and some occupational health and safety standards. Here there has been some attempt to entrench the principle by pointing to its economic utility. Women's groups commonly say that nations and firms that do not accomplish equality of opportunity for women will be less competitive because they fail to fully develop half their human capital. The investments required for compliance with ILO standards on education and training are promoted as investments that will increase national competitiveness. Braithwaite's (1985) research on the coal-mining industry shows that many of the things required to run a mine more safely are also things that will run it more efficiently. There is nothing more inefficient than sealing dead workers in a mine that has exploded. At the same time, it is clear that world's best practice costs. Much safety investment involves a trade-off between safety and competitiveness. Minimum wage standards and most other basic labour standards are hard to defend in terms of the principle of world's best practice, and have not been defended in this way.

Nevertheless, there is a deeply neglected way in which the principle of world's best practice might have been used to argue for the costly ILO conventions concerning social security rights for workers. The traditional economic analysis is that generous welfare states lose investment and jobs because the strong welfare net pushes up the cost of labour and company taxes. Leibfried and Rieger (1995) reverse this argument. States with a weak safety-net find it politically and industrially impossible to restructure and lay off workers in response to rapid economic and technological change. States where retrenched workers will be protected by adequate social security and labour market retraining programs can adapt to global pressures earlier and with fewer strikes; they can find the political will to eliminate protection of inefficient industries which are a drain on national wealth. Strong social welfare is a precondition for a political capacity to cut corporate welfare. In this analysis, a strong welfare state – compliance with safety-net labour standards (best practice, in other words) – is a cause of global competitiveness, not a drag on competitiveness. This analysis explains the considerable accumulation of research evidence showing that foreign direct investment is not shifting to nations with the lowest labour standards, but is continuing to circulate among OECD states with comparatively high labour standards (Tripartite Working Party on Labour Standards 1996: 41; UN Conference on Trade and Development 1996). This analysis has not, however, been well received either by employers obsessed with tax and labour cost-cutting or by unions obsessed with defending jobs.

### Deregulation v. Strategic Trade, Labour not a Commodity

We have not discovered any mainstream labour standards where states have sought to achieve a strategic trade advantage by setting high standards.

Labour was massively regulated throughout the eras of slavery, the law of master and servant and the workbook.[3] In the UK, Holland, the US and other metropolitan powers, forces of liberalism made ironic alliances with emerging forces of organized labour to deliver a decisive blow to the deregulation of labour by striking out the law of master and servant from 1875. These curious alliances for deregulation were paradoxical, however, as liberals since the 1799 and 1800 Combination Acts in England had pushed for enforcement of penal provisions for conspiracy against workers who engaged in any kind of concerted action to advance their interests. The 1799 Act applied only to combinations of workers, while the 1800 Act prohibited concerted action by combinations of employers as well. No record exists of a prosecution against employers in England (Creighton & Stewart 1994: 24). However, such laws were commonly used against trade unions and helped permanently enfeeble the labour movement which in the early nineteenth century had been about the strongest in the world, that of the US (Tomlins 1993). Ultimately, the organized labour movement in all democratic societies struck down the law of conspiracy and combination against unions, a deregulatory move globalized in ILO freedom of association conventions (from 1921 for agricultural workers, universally from 1948). Part of the irony is that the

---

3 Private owners of slaves were empowered to write rules to control their property. The early nineteenth century saw some counter-regulation with the British Colonial Office despatching 'protectors of slaves', among the earliest government inspectors.

regulated liberalism of the *Combination Act 1800*'s prohibition of concerted actions by employers was revitalized in the twentieth century with the growing strength of antitrust law. It was not until the 1955 Conference of the ILO that the global deregulatory Convention for the Abolition of Penal Sanctions (Indigenous Workers) was adopted.

Hence, the *Statute of Labourers 1349* put in place 'a remarkably sophisticated system of labour market regulation' which, building on Roman slave law, continued an era of commitment to the principle of labour market regulation until the combined forces of social movement politics and liberal economic analysis struck down the law of slavery and the law of master and servant. These deregulatory moves occurred about a century earlier in the colonial powers than in their colonies. By the late nineteenth century, the labour movement throughout the West had shifted its agenda from a principally deregulatory one to a pro-regulatory agenda. Its affinity with liberal political parties disintegrated; it formed its own parties with a pro-regulatory agenda; in 1919 it succeeded in globalizing that agenda through establishing the ILO. In this process the principle of deregulation was used by labour to win basic freedoms, and regulation to preserve those freedoms. It was precisely the reverse for capital. Regulation was used to maintain power, deregulation to regain it.

The US stands as the powerful exception, consolidating the deregulatory shifts of the nineteenth century as a victory for liberalism rather than a victory for the labour movement, unenchanted with the ILO, determinedly resisting the change of the labour movement's agenda from deregulatory to pro-regulatory. In the 1980s two economically struggling Anglo-Saxon nations, the UK and New Zealand, interpreted their poor economic performance in comparison with the US as a result of excessive regulation, particularly of the labour market. When the UK and New Zealand, and the US, enjoyed greater employment growth than other OECD countries in the aftermath of their labour market deregulation, the principle of deregulation attracted growing support throughout the world. In the developing world this support was backed by IMF and World Bank conditionality. On the other hand, at the behest of the Clinton administration, the World Bank in 1998 decided to make assistance conditional on banning child labour.

The rediscovery of the principle of labour market deregulation in the 1980s (and even its embracing by political parties created by the labour movement for the purpose of strengthening labour market regulation) gave a new kind of contest – between decentralized and deregulated labour market institutions based on collective bargaining at local worksites, and centralized prices and incomes accords based on tripartite national negotiation by peak employer and union bodies with the state. Another influential view in the discipline of economics has been that both the highly deregulated labour markets of the US and the corporatist-collaborative highly regulated ones of northern and central Europe deliver the most satisfactory employment outcomes; the worst outcomes arise in hybrid systems that gain no benefits but the disadvantages of both systems (e.g. Calmfors & Driffill 1988). In the analysis of David Soskice (1999) and his 'comparative capitalisms' group, there are market niches best exploited by economies with high-security, high-training labour standards and other niches best exploited by economies with highly deregulated labour markets.

We will not seek to pronounce on any of these debates. The point is that the very differences in the ways different polities respond to them are undermining what had been, until the 1980s, a gradual and very partial convergence toward more global labour standards. Moreover, labour market deregulation undermines even national harmonization. Finally, the deregulation debate of the 1990s has obliterated one of the founding principles of the Socialist International and the ILO – that labour was no longer to be treated as a commodity.

## Rule Compliance v. Continuous Improvement

The ideology of labour market deregulation has also undermined employer commitment to the principle of rule compliance with regard to labour market standards. Labour standards are less likely to be viewed by employers as legal obligations set in concrete, more likely to be seen as open to negotiation on the shopfloor. For other employers, deregulation has given impetus to the principle of continuous improvement. For regressive employers, deregulation has given impetus to ruthless cost-cutting on worker rights. Labour market equality for women is an especially tragic casualty of deregulation in nations such as Australia, where centralized labour market regulation has substantially narrowed the gap between men's and women's incomes since the 1970s (Mitchell 1995; Whitehouse 1992).

Under the progressive analysis, employers compete to retain and recruit the highest-quality workforce and the highest-morale workforce possible by improving labour conditions. Continuous improvement has been particularly strongly embraced by progressive employers in two domains – employment and training opportunities for women and occupational health and safety. Some employers produce affirmative action plans that set more ambitious targets each year, actively trying to facilitate the recruitment of women, to promote women into higher management, to increase the number of places filled by women in training programs, to retain women by assisting with child-care, generous parental leave, job-sharing and flexible hours of work (Braithwaite 1992). It has become increasingly common for firms to integrate occupational health and safety standards into their ISO 9000 Quality Assurance Systems. Standards Australia and its Norwegian counterpart (NSF) are leading an international push for occupational health and safety management standards that may incorporate the notion of continuous improvement. As will be discussed in more detail in Chapter 26, the International Organization for Standardization Quality Assurance Systems requires companies to improve on their performance of the previous year in specified quality outcomes, in a continuous improvement plan. Improvement in outcomes must be audited.

From its inception, the ILO's tripartite collaboration in all areas of labour standards has involved the commitment of all three social partners to continuous improvement; injustice creeps back whenever the social partners become satisfied that justice has been secured. This continuous improvement philosophy is well illustrated by the 1988 report of the ILO Committee of Experts on Equality in Employment and Occupation:

> *The need for continuous action*...the Committee emphasizes once again the importance that it attaches to vigilance to ensure continuing action is taken in those areas where the national policy on equality of opportunity and treatment in employment or occupation is to be pursued. It is apparent that there will always be room for improvement. For that reason it is difficult to accept statements to the effect that the application of the convention gives rise to no difficulties or that the instrument is fully applied, especially when no other details are given on the contents and methods of implementing the national policy. The promotion of equality of opportunity and treatment does not aim at a stable situation that may be attained once and for all, but rather requires a permanent process so that policy may be adjusted to changes in society in order to eliminate the various forms of distinctions, exclusions and preferences based on grounds laid down in the 1958 instruments. The absence of a policy of this nature, far from signifying a lack of discrimination, would tend to imply the existence of discrimination. The observation made by the Committee in its General Survey of 1986 on equal remuneration applies equally to the present instruments: once rigorous action gets under way and new measures are adopted to implement the principle of equality of opportunity and treatment, the existence of problems will in practice be brought to the surface, thus requiring further progress (Committee of Experts 1988: 244–5).

### National Sovereignty v. Harmonization v. Mutual Recognition

Labour market deregulation involves a surrender of national sovereignty to global market forces. A key hope with deregulation is that workers, like managers, will want working conditions to be set in a way that secures their job by making their enterprise internationally competitive.

Until the 1980s, there had been some surrender of national sovereignty over labour market standards by the progressive ratification of more and more ILO standards by more and more nations, from 2900 ratifications in 1964 to 6400 in 1997. Mutual recognition has not been a powerful principle in the labour standards domain, though NAFTA does amount to a mutual recognition of the labour laws of Canada, the US and Mexico, with a commitment to technical cooperation to ensure those standards are enforced. With harmonization of occupational health and safety standards in Europe, national sovereignty has been surrendered to the principle of harmonization much more than to the principle of mutual recognition. As a representative of the peak European employer group, UNICE, put it: 'Since the 1989 framework directive on occupational health and safety, occupational health and safety is an area where there is not debate about harmonization versus mutual recognition. There is a Euro-consensus on the need to prevent unfair competition based on low occupational health and safety standards'.

Similarly, the US Occupational Safety and Health Administration (OSHA) has a strong commitment to harmonization. With regard to chemicals: 'The overall goal should be global hamonization of hazard classification criteria, labels, and material safety datasheets. No products or use categories should be exempted from consideration' (policy statement provided by Jennifer Silk, OSHA). Notwithstanding the difficulties, 'the long-term benefits in terms of trade and level of protection justify the short-term inconveniences'. According to OSHA, the principles of the global harmonization it should pursue include GATT consistency and 'The guiding principle should be to adopt the most risk-averse approach from the existing systems'. With regard to chemicals regulatory harmonization, as explained in Chapter 12, the OECD is the international institution that has played the crucial coordinating role.

### Transparency

The ILO has a strong commitment to the principle of transparency and a much more effective means of delivering it (within its tripartite structure) than can be done by the purely governmental clubs of other international organizations. For example, Kent (1997: 12–13 ) concludes from China's encounters with the Committee on Freedom of Association during the 1990s that:

> the very process of reporting brought a vital transparency to the administrative and judicial treatment of China's dissident workers which had hitherto been totally hidden from public and international scrutiny. In addition, by virtue of its tripartite worker/employer/government structure and long experience in objective standard-setting, the ILO was arguably less vulnerable to China's great power status than were other human rights bodies in the UN proper.

While bringing totalitarian regimes into the ILO caused deep problems in consensus-building over the level of worker rights that should be honoured, the conditions of membership forced those regimes to share various information with the world and, more importantly, with hand-picked worker and management representatives from their own countries. The transparency might have been fogged by misinformation and revealed to only a select few, but at least the regimes have been forced to accept the principle of transparency and be criticized when other members say that they are providing misinformation.

### National Treatment, Most Favoured Nation, Reciprocity

At times, there have been proposals for low wages and low labour standards to be reciprocated with tariff penalties of a value equal to the price advantage attributable to the cheap labour. These have never attracted support. Reciprocity has not been an important principle. In a world where the fruits of labour – but not labour itself – are traded across national boundaries, national treatment and the Most Favoured Nation principle are unimportant. This would change if developing countries' proposals to allow free movement of labour under the GATS were accepted. Then, if the US allowed an Indian contractor to bring a ship full of Indian labour to build a bridge, the Most Favoured Nation principle might require the US to allow in labour from other nations on the same terms. The principle of national treatment might require enforcement of the same working conditions for the imported labour as apply to domestic labour. For the moment, however, these are principles of no significance in the global debate over labour standards. Attempts by countries like India to make such principles operate under the GATS have largely failed. Commitments under GATS are first negotiated bilaterally between interested states (bilateral agreements become part of a multilateral package). States can choose to proceed cautiously on the movement of natural persons. The operation of the principle of national treatment can be qualified, as can market access commitments. Developing countries cannot force the pace of these bilateral negotiations in GATS as the US did in the context of the financial services negotiations (see Chapter 8). The upshot has been that the negotiations in GATS on the movement of natural persons have produced little in the way of commitments by states.

## Mechanisms

### Military Coercion

The ILO was established as part of a peace treaty, but no vanquished power was forced to join it. Military coercion has never been used to secure equal rights for women. However, military coercion was important in ending slavery, particularly where the numbers of slaves were largest: Brazil, where British naval power blasted the slavers out of the water, and the US, where the Union Army forced the South to give up slavery at a terrible cost in lives.

Most of the considerable expansion of the communist model of labour standards to a third of all workers in the mid twentieth century was accomplished through revolution and military conquest of Germany and Japan during the Second World War.

The most important use of military coercion to globalize labour market standards occurred between the beginning of the sixteenth and the early twentieth centuries, based on a global politics of race and colonialism. First, people from races that were regarded as inferior in many parts of the world, particularly in Africa, were subjected to a law of slavery systematized by Justinian. As slavery was progressively abolished, the law of master and servant which had become less important to regulating white workers became more important to regulating non-white colonial labour, replacing slavery with servitude (Craven & Hay 1994). In law, blacks were no longer slaves, but whites were still 'master'. We have seen, however, that colonialism was a localizing as well as a globalizing force, with labour standards that adapted traditional methods for enforcing servility. More structurally, colonialism pushed Southern labour law back to pre-capitalist forms that were not in harmony with capitalist labour standards.

## Economic Coercion

The predominantly pacifist UK anti-slavery movement unsuccessfully attempted to persuade the Victorian state to apply economic sanctions against slave-trading states. Instead the UK, believing many of the slavers to be virtual pirates beyond state control, used old-fashioned gunboat diplomacy.

Theoretically it would be possible under the ILO Constitution for the ILO Governing Body to impose sanctions pursuant to a judgment of the International Court of Justice. Such sanctions have never been applied. One state – the US – has been responsible for most of the bilateral economic sanctions, particularly their successful use. We have seen that the EU has recently acquired extensive powers under its trade laws and aid conventions to impose economic sanctions, though they have rarely been used, even in cases like South Africa where European consensus against apartheid was strong. Notwithstanding the reluctance of the US as well as Europe to use sanctions, insiders in the labour standards regime say that an effective way to put pressure on developing countries who flout labour standards is to say: 'our Congress would be concerned about this or that labour right. This vague threat backs up the more principled deliberations of the Committee of Experts and the Conference' (ILO official).

## Systems of Reward

We saw that there were unsystematic and unsuccessful attempts by Britain to offer rewards to France and Spain to give up the slave trade. In an 1815 Anglo-Portuguese treaty that restricted Portugal to the Brazilian slave trade, Britain forgave most of a £600 000 war loan (Eltis 1987: 109). The EU is putting in place a unique system of reward, applying to 145 countries and territories covered by its General System of Preferences, to grant preferential trade access to Europe for developing economies. A social incentive clause in the scheme allows, among other things, for supplementary duty preferences to be given to states that comply with specified core ILO conventions.

## Modelling

Modelling is extensive in this domain. 'When the ILO issues codes of practice, some countries virtually copy them into their mandatory national laws' (Chief, ILO Occupational Safety and Health Branch). Other states have self-executing statutes in regard to ILO convention ratifications: as soon as the government ratifies a convention, the convention is national law. At the ILO itself: 'We often use EC directives as a basis of discussion' (ILO official). In the other direction: 'The European Code of Social Security, adopted by the Council of Europe, is modelled on the ILO's Social Security (Minimum Standards) Convention 1952 (No. 102)' (Samson 1979: 581) (OSHA official).

In domains where the ILO cannot secure consensus for a new convention, for example affirmative (or positive) action, it proceeds by locating positive models – a corporation with an Equality for Quality program, a state such as Australia with an Affirmative Action Act sufficiently voluntaristic as not to scare the horses – and disseminates these examples for lagging companies and states to consider. States also do this. For example, the US Department of Labor publicly releases a 'Trendsetter' list of retailers and manufacturers who have taken responsibility for monitoring the labour standard compliance of their subcontractors and contractually obliging subcontractor compliance (in the manner of Reebok and Levi-Strauss, described earlier). In Eastern Europe, the US Department of Labor has 'assisted with setting up demonstration projects in workplaces that can act as a model of effective safety committee procedure or some other aspect of safety law'.

The EC set up three networks to promote positive action for women in its Second Action Program on Equal Opportunities: the Network for Positive Action in the Private Sector, the Working Group on Higher Levels of the Public Service and the Steering Committee on Equal Opportunities in Broadcasting and Television. These networks have fundamentally involved sharing models for change.

Modelling was as important as military coercion in understanding the globalization of master and servant law and of police, based on different variations on the workbook model from the seventeenth to the twentieth centuries, and the global use of laws against conspiracy to ban trade unions and journeyman associations. It was not all imposed immediately upon the conquest of colonized peoples. In the crucial example of the British empire:

> the nineteenth and the twentieth century saw the extension of the same kind of [master and servant] legislation, and the legal doctrines based on it, to almost every jurisdiction in the empire and subsequently the Commonwealth, as well as other parts of the common-law world...Its doctrines continue to be felt in some parts of modern employment law...In its wider imperial forms, the law of master and servant was re-enacted in virtually every British colonial jurisdiction between the seventeenth century and the twentieth, but with significant and distinctive amendments and additions (Hay & Craven 1993: 175, 177).

Craven and Hay (1994: 75) in their mammoth project on the diffusion of master and servant law, have collected around 1300 different master and servant statutes from a hundred different jurisdictions.

### Reciprocal Adjustment and Non-reciprocal Coordination

Reciprocal adjustment has been common with labour standards, in the early years on matters such as working hours and labour inspection and more recently on matters such as the European and global chemicals harmonization discussed above. Reciprocal adjustment from the old standards of many states has been needed to secure convergence. The ILO has never been like the WTO – one nation offering something on standard X in return for a second nation making an offer on standard Y. This is partly a result of tripartite deliberation – it is complex enough to deal with one convention at a time. Doubtless some non-reciprocal coordination goes on behind the scenes, but it is not very visible and therefore, we suspect, not a very prominent mechanism.

### Capacity-building

The distinctive thing about the ILO is the way resource allocation for capacity-building is tied to the process of monitoring and prodding compliance. This synergy is not a form of conditionality, but works as follows. When the Committee of Experts and the Conference (generally led by the Office) make observations that call upon a nation to meet its obligations, the Office asks whether there is any technical assistance that can be offered to assist compliance.

For example, the German government[4] funded an ILO International Program to Eliminate Child Labour in India, Indonesia, Thailand, Kenya, Turkey, the Philippines and Pakistan. The program consisted of setting up national non-governmental steering committees that (with government and ILO participation) established demonstration projects to provide schooling (in some cases with school meals) as an alternative to families sending children to work. State and corporate actors have been infected by the ILO philosophy of backing pleas for compliance with labour standards, with practical help. Hence, Levi-Strauss, when it discovered children under fourteen working in the plants of its Bangladeshi suppliers, engaged in dialogue with local officials which led to agreement that the children would return to school, they would receive some pay from the local contractors, Levi-Strauss would pay for their school tuition, books and uniforms, and the children would be offered jobs when they turned fourteen (Compa & Hinchliffe-Darricarrere 1995: 679). We have seen that the US Council for International Business does the same to assist Mexican firms to meet the labour standards expected under NAFTA.

Just as compliance and capacity-building are linked in an unusually strong way, so are modelling and capacity-building linked. The ILO Constitution is seen as requiring 'upward emulation' (ILO 1992: 3). The two founding documents, the Constitution and the Declaration of Philadelphia at the end of the Second World War, are interpreted as requiring the ILO to 'promote' or advance the aims and purposes in the Constitution. Similarly, members are seen as having these obligations: 'A state does not, as it were, passively acquire the rights and obligations specified in the Constitution, but agrees to take part in a collective endeavour whose objectives are defined in those texts [the Constitution and the Declaration of Philadelphia]' (ILO 1992: 3). Reading that kind of contemporary constitutional interpretation sensitizes us to the vision of the individual who had the greatest hand in writing both texts – the author of the ILO's tripartism, Edward Phelan.

In budgetary terms, until the 1950s, the funding of standard-setting meetings accounted for most of the ILO budget. Since the 1950s influx of developing countries into the ILO, the bulk of resources is spent on technical assistance. ILO technical cooperation expenditure in 1990 was $US152.2 million.

## Conclusion

Most of the great social movements of the past two centuries have been involved in the globalization of labour standards – the anti-slavery movement, the labour movement and the Socialist International, the women's movement, the black civil rights movement and the human rights movement generally. Discrimination in employment has also been a concern for groups representing the disabled, the aged, gays and lesbians, and racial, ethnic and religious minorities. Even the environment movement has been involved on questions like chemicals standards and nuclear

---

4 This kind of multi-bilateral funding is common at the ILO and is a tribute to the political advantages the ILO's tripartite structure offers state aid agencies in respect of certain politically sensitive matters where states might be wary of political paternalism (Ghebali 1989: 246).

safety. Once they came into existence, these social movement actors, particularly the trade union movement, have been more influential than business actors or any hegemonic state in framing the standard-setting agenda and in capturing the secretariats of international organizations.

For all this, labour standards is not an area where global standards have been ratcheted-up in recent decades. That did happen in the mid twentieth century. However, the combination of international competition in low-cost labour, and labour market deregulation to increase the flexibility of response to it, has undermined the labour standards in many places. Union membership and political clout has weakened. For different reasons, ILO standards have weakened more than strengthened. The nations from the Second and Third Worlds that joined the ILO from the 1950s found that they could not possibly meet many of the standards forged in what had been a wealthy-nations club. In making conventions and recommendations more flexible, more adaptive to disparate national conditions, they became less demanding. This must be qualified by pointing out that the newer elements of the International Labour Code are also more amenable to continuous improvement. That is, just as they allow for demanding less of a country with fewer resources to fund safety-nets than of European welfare states, they also allow for demanding more when economic conditions make it possible to do so. Given that the Constitution and Office culture of the ILO is about continuous improvement in its labour rights and social justice aims, there is the hope that continuous improvement within the context of the special conditions of each nation will return the world to an era where labour standards move up again. There can be little doubt that ILO standards have helped halt some of the excesses of contemporary deregulation and contributed to raising labour standards throughout the middle decades of the century.

Tripartism – the balancing of government representatives with worker and employer representatives – has had distinct advantages in securing high quality of deliberation. Block-voting by states and forum-shifting are more difficult when they cannot guarantee the votes of worker and employer delegates. States must be more honest in their reporting when either worker or employer delegates might dispute their claims. A dialogue that allows a plurality of perspectives is more likely; no perspective is likely to be slipped in without challenge from some quarter. Empirically, African states with tripartite industrial relations systems have higher rates of ILO convention ratifications (Cambridge 1984).

This is not to say that the plurality could not be richer, with more women's voices and more voices of non-union NGOs. Yet the degree of plurality that exists has been workable; it has produced 181 conventions and a lot of soft law in the International Labour Code, and has done so by consensus decision-making that has avoided the tyranny of the majority and of the minority (Osieke 1984: 408). It might be said that the diversity of views of three parties from 174 states gives enormous power to the secretariat. The ILO has always been an unusually dominating secretariat controlled by an unusually strong Director. While the plurality of global tripartism does deliver the office a kind of drafting freedom, it cannot exercise discretion in ways that might be vetoed by any block of delegates across states and constituencies. No one is ever satisfied with the compromises the secretariat forges, but the quality of the tripartite dialogue limits the degree of unacceptability any participant must suffer.

In short, the labour standards regime is a sophisticated one that has fallen on hard times. However, it has recovered from the debilitating effects of the Cold War politics that followed the mass entry of communist states from 1954; the US is back in the fold and paying its dues; it has begun to adapt to a world of labour market deregulation and weaker unions; it has even begun to adapt to substantial cuts in its operating budget. The enduring strengths of the regime even in these difficult circumstances are the greater quality and plurality of dialogue than can be found in other global regimes and its commitment to purposive continuous improvement of constitutional objectives, rather than maintaining the cosy job of administering a set of conventions. The ILO continues to countenance innovation, as evidenced by the suggestion in the 1997 Director-General's Report of a global social label to be awarded to states rather than specific products, with the ILO monitoring the code through an inspection system.

Ironically, there is much that healthier contemporary regimes can learn from this bruised and battered regime that has had glory days during its eighty years of existence. The impressive synergy among monitoring compliance, capacity-building and modelling is a direct result of the constitutional commitment to continuous improvement. We have seen that there is genius in the process of regular written reports on compliance with national obligations, evaluated by technical experts, open to critical assessment by the social partners, then (in the worst cases) exposing abuses to open dialogue in a tripartite conference. One ILO official said of this reporting and evaluation dialogue: 'The moral obligation and the moral strength of the ILO is there'. Even in the current adverse climate for progress in labour standards, there is strong evidence that this process works better than most methods of improving compliance in most of the global regimes in this book.

At the same time, the regime has failed to learn from newer regimes. The labour movement, which is the engine that drives the regime, has failed to learn from the tactics of NGOs like Greenpeace. In an era where so many governments are unresponsive to appeals for regulatory investment, especially in the East and South, the TNCs that are players in most of the big economic developments might have been targeted. Walter Reuther realized this long before Greenpeace. But national trade unions were never internationalist enough to give up sufficient power so that the international trade secretariats set up to pursue Reuther's vision would succeed.

In 1977 the ILO did promulgate the Tripartite Declaration of Principles Concerning Multinational Enterprises and Social Policy. It is a fine document. But unions have brought forward only a few complaints under the Declaration in twenty years. The ILO has adopted a highly restrictive approach to the 'receivability' of complaints under the Code and unions have not made it a priority to overturn this approach. Their philosophy has been that it makes more sense to complain to the Committee on Freedom of Association against governments responsible for regulating TNC conduct.

Similarly, the women's movement has not lodged complaints under the Code even though there are useful provisions relating to equality of opportunity and treatment (clauses 21–23). One might have thought that a response to the problem of Arab states denying labour rights to women and frustrating progress on a convention on positive action would be to go around them by targeting the TNCs that operate within their borders. Complaints against TNCs for denying Arab women equality of opportunity under the Tripartite Declaration might have been a way of making TNCs the vanguard of positive action in the Arab world. After all, voluntary compliance of US TNCs with the Sullivan Principles, voluntarily audited by Arthur D. Little, saw 150 US corporations operating in South Africa from 1977 formally end discrimination in their factories, promote 3000 blacks into management (to 30 per cent of managers), offer scholarships and adopt 150 schools (Perez-Lopez 1993: 43).

While even sympathetic states have little effective regulatory control over the informal sector where the worst labour abuses occur, mostly the informal sector supplies large corporations who have enormous leverage over them and know exactly what they are doing. The voluntary codes of companies like Levi-Strauss, and their seemingly successful efforts to end child and forced labour among their suppliers, show how public exposure[5] can strengthen the hand of socially responsible reformers within a corporation who want to clean up the businesses they deal with (on this point, see also the analysis of responsible care in the chemical industry, in Chapter 12). Levi-Strauss, Wal-Mart, Dayton-Hudson, Reebok and other firms have been pressured by media exposure and shareholder resolutions from ethical investment activists into auditing the compliance of their international subcontractors with labour standards (Clifford 1994). The RUGMARK campaign of the South Asian Coalition on Child Servitude shows how mass publics in countries like Germany and the US can be morally engaged with consumer as well as corporate enforcement against elements in the informal economy that abuse labour rights (Compa & Hinchliffe-Darricarrere 1995: 673–4). Parenthetically, it shows how unions might regain membership by taking corporate abuses to mass publics in the way Greenpeace and the South Asian Coalition of Child Servitude have done.

Hence, while the labour standards regime has lost its global vitality, the institutional infrastructure is there and exemplary – a comparatively well-resourced and professional secretariat, robust dialogic tripartite traditions that have forged many consensus global standards, high levels of voluntary compliance guaranteed by sophisticated linkage of capacity-building and modelling, a usable code of conduct for TNCs, and a background spectre of bilateral sanctions by the US and EC. The social movements are also there and concerned. Should the regime learn to use those institutions more imaginatively in an era of regulatory decentralization, labour standards that have begun to wind down might again be ratcheted-up across the globe.

The labour movement has already flipped its global regulatory strategy once – from being allies of liberal political parties in deregulating oppressive uses of the laws of servitude, contract and conspiracy against labour, to being opponents of liberals as labour parties ratcheted-up new sets of regulatory laws to protect labour on the foundations of the deregulatory accomplishments. The interesting question is whether we will see a new flipping of the labour movement's global strategy in response to a new era of deregulation.

---

5  Levi-Strauss's development of a global labour code predated its media scandal, but was hurried along by it. A 1992 media exposé showed abusive labour practices in Saipan that supplied Levi-Strauss, Sears and other US retailers (Compa & Hinchcliffe-Darricarrere 1995: 677).

## History of Globalization

### The Long Nineteenth Century

Environmental regulation by states has a long, if limited, history, but its globalization is recent. Greece's Solon the Law-giver proposed in the sixth century BC that agriculture should be banned on steep slopes to prevent soil erosion; Pisistratus introduced a bounty for farmers who planted olive trees to counter deforestation and overgrazing (Davies 1997: 99). Most of the important events in the history of the globalization of environmental regulation, however, have occurred since 1970. Yet there were some significant beginnings to the globalization process in the nineteenth century. Most of the pre-1970 international initiatives were not about protecting the environment for its own sake but about instrumental human concerns. In 1868, the first international instrument to propose restrictions on chemicals, the St Petersburg Declaration, sought to prevent the use of incendiary or fulminating substances in war (Martens 1985). This was followed by the 1899 Hague Declaration and, in the twentieth century, by extensive global efforts to limit or ban chemical and then nuclear weapons (Schindler & Tornau 1985). Chapter 13 deals with those regimes in greater detail.

The year 1868 was not only the date when humanity began to respond to the most catastrophic threat to the environment – from weapons of war – it was also the date of an assembly of German farmers and foresters which after another thirty-five years of lobbying, largely through International Ornithological Congresses, led to the 1902 European treaty on the Conservation of Birds Useful to Agriculture (Caldwell 1988: 17). The fact that the International Ornithological Congresses of 1891, 1893 and 1900 were the lobbying platforms for the treaty calls into question any view that the initiative was purely about economic interests. Early efforts at globalizing environmental regulation may have been articulated in a discourse of economic development, but that does not mean that the activists behind the treaties were motivated only in these terms. The same is true of the 1900 Convention for the Preservation of Animals, Birds and Fish in Africa, signed by European colonial powers with the primarily (but not exclusively) economic motivation of limiting ivory exports (Brenton 1994: 16).

The 1911 convention between the US and other powers which accomplished the restoration of northern fur seal herds (Young & Osherenko 1993: 35) was narrowly economic in its motivation to protect a valuable economic resource from extinction (Caldwell 1988: 18), as were early bilateral and multilateral efforts to regulate overfishing and the Whaling Convention of 1931. International agreements on seals, fisheries, whaling, ivory and endangered species rewritten in the second half of the twentieth century saw the discourse of wealth preservation superseded by a discourse of environmental preservation. Similarly, nineteenth-century economic agreements on the regulation of international waterways such as the Rhine and Danube were later appropriated by environmental epistemic communities (Springer 1988: 47). A significant historical transition was the 1909 Boundary Waters Treaty between the US and Canada, which included from the outset an instrumental-environmental injunction that boundary waters 'shall not be polluted on either side to the injury of health and property on the other' (Springer 1988: 47).

## Silent Spring

A key event in the transition from primarily economic to conservationist motivation for environmental regulation was the publication in 1962 of Rachel Carson's *Silent Spring*, whose central concern was agrochemical threats to fauna and flora. Carson's ideas were not only important in the history of English-speaking countries. Key regulators we interviewed in Germany, Poland and Japan testified to the book's impact on local debates. Certain catastrophic events contributed to the shift from economics to ideas as the driving force toward globalization. One was the outbreaks of Minamata disease from mercury poisoning in Japan in 1953–56 and in 1965. It seriously affected at least 1600 people, causing sixty-nine known deaths (Lonngren 1992: 94). In quick succession, the Japanese catastrophe led to the realization that Canada, Sweden, the US and other countries had serious problems with mercury in game and fish. Soon after *Silent Spring*, new science demonstrated the widespread environmental risks of polychlorinated biphenyls (PCBs) (Lonngren 1992: 97).

Once scientists revealed the evidence that built global concern, the UN decided in 1968 to convene the 1972 Stockholm Conference on the Human Environment. Most of the developed countries and some developing ones established national environment agencies between 1971 and 1972 (Janicke 1991: 19), some motivated by the wish to show how seriously they took the issue at Stockholm. After Stockholm, the number of states with national environmental agencies increased from twenty-six in 1972 to 144 a decade later (Dauvergne 1996). National regulatory growth was more a consequence than a cause of international regulatory dialogue. National regulatory development can now be seen in a more general way as an effect of international meetings: 'North Sea Ministerial Conferences were not a forum for pillorying states for "brown" policies (a deterrent strategy). Rather, they were "a convenient forum for ministers to play to the home audience[and]...provide a public demonstration of their green credentials" that produced a process of constant upgrading of industrial pollution standards' (Haas 1993: 173). 'The spikes in listings of World Heritage and Ramsar sites just prior to annual Conferences of the Parties suggest a similar dynamic in which socially desirable behaviour is driven by the regime's provision of positive political consequences not its imposition of negative ones' (Mitchell 1995: 17).

Communist countries stayed away from Stockholm and for more than a decade longer remained aloof from global environmental initiatives, the line being that pollution was a problem of capitalism and therefore not their responsibility. The Stockholm Conference decided to establish the UN Environment Program and a UN International Register on Potentially Toxic Chemicals, among other initiatives, in a 109-recommendation global action plan. On chemicals, however, the OECD had preceded the UN.

### OECD Leadership on Chemicals

Soon after *Silent Spring* (in June 1966), the OECD organized an Expert Meeting on Research on the Unintended Occurrence of Pesticides in the Environment. At the first meeting of the OECD Environment Committee in 1971, the US delegation proposed that the OECD establish a notification and consultation procedure for research on problem chemicals. From then, the OECD rather than the UN dominated the globalization of chemicals regulation. All the major chemical-exporting nations were in the OECD and it suited them that global coordination of chemicals was in the hands of an organization where they ruled. The most important aspect of this work became the Chemicals Testing Program (under US chairmanship), which involved years of work by 300 experts from government, industry and academia in a variety of working groups. In 1981 the OECD Council published fifty-one Guidelines for chemicals testing. These became de facto global rules of chemicals testing. Later the OECD Code on Good Laboratory Practice for chemicals testing (again prepared under US leadership) also became the global standard via a regime of mutual recognition. Nations had to comply if they wanted other nations to recognize data generated by their scientists. The OECD became the clearing-house for Good Laboratory Practice compliance procedures.

The OECD Test Guidelines implement a national treatment principle (identical treatment for imported and domestic goods and services) and a non-discrimination principle (identical treatment of imports regardless of origin): data from other countries must be accepted as long as they were collected in accordance with the Guidelines' methodologies. For example, the chemicals regulator of an importing OECD nation cannot require that new tests be done by the exporter in the importing country. In this, the OECD agenda is as much about removing non-tariff barriers to trade and guaranteeing the secrecy of proprietary information on chemicals as it is about promulgating state-of-the-art chemicals testing. The OECD has a dispute resolution procedure within its chemicals program which allows members to lodge complaints against other members, in effect making the OECD a supranational enforcement agency in this area. During interviews for this research, the OECD's Chemicals Division claimed that by the early 1990s over 80 per cent of the world was following OECD testing methods. One senior US government official we interviewed was more qualified: 'OECD Chemicals. It is a success story, on the surface a *total* success story. But underneath, individual companies will say, "Does Japan really accept OECD test guidelines? Or does it say yes, but then much more use their own standards?"'

OECD domination of this agenda has been achieved by working closely with the world's forty or fifty largest chemical manufacturers and the key manufacturing states. Small business, developing countries and consumer and environmental groups have had minimal input. This has been more the result of limited interest and expertise by these smaller players than of determined exclusion by the OECD Chemicals Program. Limited interest has been shown because the OECD work resulted in improvements from the perspective of NGOs, partly because the OECD has tended to capture the more concerned elements in the chemical industry. As one OECD bureaucrat put it: 'There are two types of business people who work with chemicals: responsible business and the cavemen. We listen most to responsible business'. Moreover, from a green perspective the US leadership of the OECD Chemicals Program has tended to be benevolent. Generally, the US has higher standards on chemicals than the rest of the world, and through the OECD it has attempted to raise other countries to its standards so that it does not suffer competitive disadvantage.

### Proliferating Interest in the Environment by International Organizations

Since the Second World War a number of UN agencies have become interested in environmental regulation. The International Labour Organization (ILO) gets involved where worker health and safety and environmental concerns overlap (e.g. PCBs, asbestos), the World Health Organization (WHO) where human health overlaps with environmental protection, the Food and Agriculture Organization (FAO) with problems such as pesticides, fertilizers and soil erosion, and the UN Educational, Scientific and Cultural Organization (UNESCO) with protection of cultural heritage. The European Commission (EC) is a most important supranational enforcer of standards across these domains, enforcing over 200 pieces of environmental legislation. Then there is the UN Environmental Program (UNEP), which plays a particularly important role in diffusing environmental regulatory technologies to developing countries, sponsoring negotiations on new treaties and supporting a growing band of regional environmental organizations (Boer 1995).

Finally, the UN Commission on Sustainable Development was convened following the Rio Summit of 1992 (UN Conference on Environment and Development, UNCED). It is pushing the Conventions on climate change and biological diversity which were opened for signature at UNCED, the so-called 'Forest Principles', and international action on desertification, among other environmental issues.

The sheer number of specialist international organizations and treaty secretariats dealing with environmental matters has fuelled repeated calls, starting with UN Secretary-General U Thant in 1970, for an International Environmental Organization that could adopt a more holistic approach to the challenges and better exploit opportunities for linking issues (Ayling 1997). A more recent rationale for such calls has been the perceived threat of the World Trade Organization (WTO) to the environment.

For the future, the central debate is whether the WTO will become a key environmental player (see Chapter 10). At the time of writing, analytic work on trade and environment is proceeding at both the WTO and through joint meetings of the Trade and Environment Committees of the OECD. When the Uruguay Round of the GATT was finalized in 1995, all signatories agreed to 'identify the relationship between trade measures and environmental measures in order to promote sustainable development' and 'to make appropriate recommendations on whether any modifications of the provisions of the multilateral trading system are required, compatible with the open, equitable and non-discriminatory nature of the system'. Environmental standards have rarely been used as a trade barrier; it is not green but dirty-brown protectionism that is the big threat to liberal trade regimes (Repetto 1993). However, environmental protectionism became an issue after Mexico successfully used the GATT to challenge a US ban on Mexican tuna because of excessive dolphin-netting in the process of Mexican tuna-fishing (Thomas & Tereposky 1993: 30–1). A subsequent successful challenge was made to a WTO Panel by a number of states over a US ban of shrimp imports netted in a way that endangers turtles (Wynter 1998).

Many green groups fear that the WTO might be used to 'pull back' nations that set the highest standards on matters like recycling, packaging and green labelling, with the argument that these standards are being used as non-tariff barriers to free trade. There is also a concern that provisions for trade sanctions in international environmental agreements will be considered WTO-illegal. The principle of deregulated trade is seen by thinkers such as Herman Daly as a threat to the 'polluter-pays' principle. According to this view, the best policy is for all countries to internalize the environmental costs of production into the price of their products, and then to have free trade. The second-best policy, when some countries refuse to internalize environmental costs, is for green economies to impose a compensating tariff on nations which refuse to make polluters pay. 'This is not "protectionism" in the usual sense of protecting an inefficient industry, but rather the protection of an efficient national policy of internalization of environmental costs' (Daly & Goodland 1994: 78). Indeed, duties on imports from a nation with environmental standards which fall below a baseline could be collected and returned to the exporting nation (at least if it is a developing country) for use in the development and enforcement of adequate environmental standards (Housman & Zaelke 1993: 558). In this view, the WTO is a regime which prevents economic efficiency by preventing the compensatory tariffs needed to create incentives for the globalization of an efficient polluter-pays principle. No GATT signatory has actually imposed environmental countervailing duties on imports.

Environmental and consumer groups therefore tend to be wary of the WTO as a threat to the globalization of tougher environmental standards. Most of them resist a link between environmental standards and the WTO; they would rather see global environmental issues deliberated within international environmental agencies and under environmental treaties which include trade sanctions that take precedence over the WTO. At the same time, consumer groups and some environmental organizations support WTO action against spurious environmental standards which lack a compelling environmental rationale, erected by states as non-tariff barriers to import competition. Six major environmental groups also supported the North American Free Trade Agreement (NAFTA) because of its side agreement. In return for improved access to US and Canadian markets, the side agreement provided for Mexico to upgrade its environmental standards. The environmental groups that supported NAFTA viewed it as a precedent-setting linkage of higher environmental standards, increased investment in clean-up and a forum to hear citizen complaints on lax environmental enforcement (and to impose trade sanctions for failure to implement action plans settled as a result of those complaints) – all as a condition for trade and economic integration. An equally large coalition of green groups, however, opposed the signing of NAFTA on the grounds that it would lower standards, for example by encouraging environmentally sensitive production to move to regions of Mexico where there was minimal enforcement.

Given the dissensus and powerful cross-cutting pressures both within and between sectors of influence on the issue of trade–environment linkage, it seems likely that trade policy, notwithstanding the current political ferment, will continue to not be a central factor in shaping the globalization of environmental regulation. Neither is it likely to become a major impediment to that globalization. No important actor wants the WTO to take over environmental policy. Environmentalists want to end the hesitancy about putting trade measures into environmental treaties from fear that they might be GATT-illegal. This may ultimately be accomplished in return for some reassuring words in the GATT that such trade sanctions must be robustly defensible in environmental terms rather than amount to green protectionism.

David Vogel (1995) argues that the GATT has not, to date, had any significant inhibiting effects on the global ratcheting-up of environmental standards. The response to the tuna–dolphin furore was a variety of negotiated settlements outside the GATT (including between the US and Mexico) to change fishing practices: 'As a result of all these initiatives, less than 5000 dolphin deaths were associated with tuna fishing in the ETP [Eastern tropical Pacific] in 1993 – a hundredfold decline in the space of two decades' (Vogel 1995: 117). At the same time, the GATT Panel ruling was of wider significance in that it called into question the GATT-legality of the Convention on International Trade in Endangered Species (CITES), the Basle Convention on Hazardous

Wastes and the Montreal Protocol on ozone. These treaties 'violate the GATT's Most Favoured Nation clause by imposing more restrictive provisions on GATT signatories who do not comply with their decisions than on those that do' (Vogel 1995: 138). The Montreal Protocol requires signatories to ban not only the import of controlled substances (generally permitted under the GATT), but also to ban the import of products produced with controlled substances (generally GATT-impermissible). These legal questions need to be clarified so that the WTO trade liberalization and environmental treaties can co-exist and prosper. To date, although the WTO has not had practical adverse effects on the environment and green protectionism has not significantly inhibited the liberalization of markets, the environment and trade regimes each threaten the legitimacy of the other. But the two regimes are profoundly compatible: environmental countervailing duties could increase the efficiency of free markets, and the empirical evidence is that the more closed economies are, the more they nurture 'dirty' industries (Birdsall & Wheeler 1992).

## Proliferating Framework Conventions

There may be 500 international agreements that affect national environmental regulation (Johnston 1988); Boer (1995: 114) suggests there are 900 multilateral or bilateral international legal instruments concerning the environment. Among the most important of these are the International Convention for the Regulation of Whaling (1946), the Convention on International Trade in Endangered Species (CITES) (1973), which bans trade in no fewer than 600 species and imposes control on trade in over 26 000 others (Brenton 1994: 101), the Convention for the Prevention of Pollution from Ships (1973), known as the MARPOL Convention, and the Convention on the Prevention of Marine Pollution by Dumping of Wastes and Other Matter (the London Dumping Convention) (1972). Other important conventions are the Convention on Long-Range Transboundary Air Pollution (1979), which is about acid rain, the Vienna Convention for the Protection of the Ozone Layer (1985), the Basle Convention on the Control of Transboundary Movements of Hazardous Wastes and Their Disposal (1989), the Framework Convention on Climate Change (1992), the Convention on Biological Diversity (1992) and the International Convention to Combat Desertification (1994).

Increasingly, framework conventions occurred in response to early resistance to a new regime; framework conventions allowed increasing acceptance over time. In the case of the Forest Principles negotiated at Rio, even a framework convention posed impossible demands upon consensus-building. A framework convention accomplishes little more than allowing nations to accept that there is an environmental concern that requires a global response. In the face of resistance, acceptance can be a major accomplishment, demanding years of expensive scientific research. It is important because, as a convention (rather than an arrangement or agreement), it has a high degree of formality in international law. While the content of a framework convention is generally minimal, its formality means that the obligation on states to continue dealing with the issues is more solidly entrenched than if a less formal style of treaty were used. With time, a more detailed instrument can be negotiated to give binding specific content to the framework convention. Often this is called a protocol.

In the words of Chairman Ripert of the Intergovernmental Negotiating Committee on Climate Change, 'constructive ambiguities' (Brenton 1994: 192) in a convention have their uses. They can be a resource for NGOs in progressive countries who wish to interpret the ambiguities in progressive ways to move their nation ahead of the pack. They can be a resource for those in resistant countries who want to persuade conservative politicians to sign an ambiguous commitment that arguably amounts to very little. They can be the basis for a process of 'pledge and review', where countries which interpret the demands of the treaty differently make different pledges to implement them and subject themselves to review in terms of those pledges.

The Convention on Biological Diversity (CBD) provides a good example of the way in which framework conventions create 'soft' diffuse obligations that can, over time, be made more detailed through rule-making. Article 15 of the CBD prescribes general principles that are to govern access to genetic resources, including a principle of benefit-sharing and a principle of prior informed consent. Article 8(j) recognizes the existence of indigenous intellectual property. Since the signing of the CBD a global dialogue involving states, international organizations and hundreds of NGO actors has developed on the key issues of control, access and benefit-sharing with respect to the use of genetic resources. This dialogue has led to different legislative and administrative initiatives, both national and regional (e.g. the Andean Pact Common System on Access to Genetic Resources) on implementation of the principles contained in the CBD. Regular meetings of the Conference of the Parties to the CBD, a structured work program, and the participation of a networked NGO community, have been key factors in the creation of an international regulatory community that is giving life to the principles contained in the CBD.

### The Club Within a Club: Acid Rain

The acid rain convention is a good example of a proposal that faced considerable resistance, notably from the US. But as scientific evidence on the effects of acid rain increased, more nations were willing to join the convention. Even so, it remains a convention that has no effect outside Europe. Acid rain was a classic case of the solution to national problems causing international problems. In the 1960s, industrialized countries increased the heights of smokestacks as much as sixfold to disperse sulfur dioxide and nitrogen oxide emissions, only for the emissions to fall on other nations as acid rain. The Nordics led lobbying for the convention. West Germany and the UK led the opposition, joined by other net exporters of acid rain – the US, Belgium and Denmark (Porter & Brown 1991: 72). But when German science showed how acid rain was destroying the Black Forest, even though the nation was a net exporter, West Germany switched from the veto coalition it had led to join the supporters. Even so, only thirty-five nations signed the toothless convention of 1979.

In 1983, Norway and Sweden proposed that signatories agree to the target of 30 per cent reduction in emissions by 1993. Initially only ten nations joined the 30 per cent club, in 1984. This jumped to twenty-one nations in 1985. Twelve countries achieved more than a 40 per cent reduction in sulfur dioxide emissions during the 1980s (Levy 1993: 114). While this remained a weak regime, excluding the three biggest exporters of acid rain – the US, the UK and Poland – the strategy of a framework convention followed by leadership and a gradual increase in nations willing to commit to a specific Protocol is a practical one for making progress against a powerful veto coalition. Then other strategies for dealing with key resisters to the regime can be sought. In the case of Poland, for example, the post-1989 fiscal crisis gave Germany, the Nordic countries and Switzerland an opportunity through a debt-for-environment swap. Some of the Polish national debt to Germany and other Paris Club members was forgiven, provided the money was dedicated to clean-up. This was a good deal for Germany, which did not want Poland to collapse under an impossible debt burden. Better for the Polish economy to revive in a way that reduced pollution into Germany and left Poland able to purchase German imports.

### Changing the Rules of the Club: Whales, Elephants, Hazardous Wastes

The International Convention for the Regulation of Whaling was a regime where the US, instead of being the key veto state, was the leading 'Save the Whale' state after the 1972 Stockholm Conference. Until then the International Whaling Commission had been in effect a club of whaling nations, with the purpose of dividing a stock that they allowed to deplete nearly to extinction. The US mobilized non-whaling nations to join the Commission, using its one-nation–one-vote Constitution to push through a complete moratorium on whaling. Then the US sought to enforce it, by threatening states who defied the regime with bilateral trade sanctions – a ban on imports of fish products and denial of fishing permits within the US 200 mile zone. Opponent states, notably Japan, formally complied with the regime, but got around it by conducting 'scientific' whaling on a considerable scale. Greenpeace exposed this tactic, swinging world public opinion against Japanese and other whalers who exploited it. In combination, the moratorium, the threat of US trade sanctions and Greenpeace shaming wove a web of controls that reduced whale kills massively, even though non-compliance is still a very serious problem.

Another market in which Japan was a potential pariah state was the market for ivory. Japan imports more than 80 per cent of all African ivory products for seal-stamps and an indigenous stringed instrument, the *samisen*. In 1988 the World Wildlife Fund and Conservation International defined the banning of trade in African ivory as an issue, by sponsoring a scientific study that concluded with the need to list the African elephant in Appendix 1 of CITES, a cause that was taken up by the US, a group of African states, Austria and Hungary. Botswana, South Africa and Zimbabwe were opposed because they were having success with the alternative of increasing their elephant herds by giving incentives to local communities for conservation via a quota system. Eventually the total ban went through; Japan supported it.

Why did Japan support a ban from which it had most to lose? Apparently Japan had decided to change its 'villain' image in species conservation. It had decided to host the 1992 CITES meeting and was worried that a Japanese veto of the ivory ban would have caused CITES members to withdraw the decision to have the meeting in Japan. This is a rather vivid illustration of reputation and subtle diplomatic pressure trumping clear economic interest. The regime seems to have had an effect, with prices for ivory dropping by as much as 90 per cent by 1990, undercutting economic incentives for poaching (Porter & Brown 1991:85).

Although the US took the lead on many global environmental initiatives during the 1970s, through the 1980s and up to its resistance to a biodiversity convention at Rio in 1992, it acted more frequently as leader of a veto coalition. Its resistance to the Basle Convention on the Control of Transboundary Movements of Hazardous Wastes (1989) is an example. The US effectively led rejection of a total ban, arguing instead for the principle of informed consent (PIC): a rich country should be able to pay a poor government to dump hazardous waste on its citizens as long as that government was fully informed of the hazardous nature of the waste. The US-led veto coalition won, with a position of either a PIC convention or no convention at all. As in the acid rain convention, however, thirty states and the EU made commitments within the framework of the convention that went beyond its requirements. They pledged to dispose of wastes at home and to ban export to nations without the technological capacity to deal with them (Porter & Brown 1991: 87). For a great many environmental regimes negotiated during the Republican administrations between 1980 and 1992, US resistance left them rather weak. There were exceptions, such as the Australian and French-led agreement for a fifty-year ban on mining in Antarctica, which was resisted alone and to the very end by the US without winning major concessions.

At least it must be said that the large number of environmental regimes put in place against US resistance since 1980 demonstrates that a hegemonic power (Kindleberger 1973) is not necessarily required to force global convergence (Porter & Brown 1991: 23; Young 1989: 353–4).

## A Genuine Success: Ozone

The most interesting 1980s case study where the US returned to being a leader not a blocker of environmental conventions, was the ozone-depletion case. The ozone layer in the stratosphere protects life on earth by absorbing ultraviolet-B radiation from the sun. In 1973 it was suggested that a class of industrial chemicals called chlorofluorocarbons (CFCs) might be destroying the ozone layer. In August 1977 a stratospheric ozone Amendment was passed to the US Clean Air Act in response to mobilization of public concern by green groups (especially the Natural Resources Defence Council) that had been continuing since 1974. As a consequence, the US became the first state to ban the use of CFCs in aerosol propellants for nonessential applications. US production of CFCs for aerosols quickly fell by 95 per cent and substitutes were soon on the market (Benedick 1991: 24). Green groups in Europe, which were more focused on acid rain, other chemicals issues and nuclear power, did not have the quick and decisive victory on CFCs of the US, though Sweden and Norway legislated in the late 1970s to restrict nonessential uses of CFCs. European business opposition, led by the UK company ICI, was strong; all the green groups accomplished was a 1980 EC decision for a 30 per cent cut-back in CFC aerosol use. The US had been the largest producer of CFCs (44 per cent of the world market in 1976 compared with the EU's 33 percent), so European producers enjoyed the opportunity to take over market leadership (Rowlands 1995: 105).

For two years after the appointment of the Reagan administration's new Environmental Protection Agency (EPA) Administrator Anne Gorsuch Burford, an anti-regulatory anti-UN Administrator, the US gave comfort to European resistance by downplaying the risk of ozone depletion. By 1983 the period of deregulatory ideology was over for the environment, William Ruckelshaus had replaced Gorsuch Burford, and the US joined with the UNEP, the Nordic countries, Switzerland, Canada and environment NGOs to pressure Europe to join a CFC ban. US business was in a curious de facto alliance with environment groups to persuade the Reagan administration to abandon its resistance to UN multilateral regulation and to push for a protocol under the Vienna Convention toward a total ban of CFCs. If US business had had to play by this tough set of rules since 1978, it wanted to work with environmentalists to demand that European and Asian business play by the same rules. In the words of De Sombre (1995), CFCs saw the equivalent of a coalition of 'Baptists and bootleggers', supporting prohibition for contrasting reasons.

Domestically, a green–business consensus in the US was unassailable. Sixty US embassies were ordered to lobby for a strong ozone Protocol, in the first instance by disseminating information to build international consensus on the science and the risks (Benedick 1991: 55). Mostly the embassies relied on persuasion rather than coercion, though we were told in Taiwan and the US that Taiwan was threatened with being placed on the US trade-retaliation list unless it moved toward removing CFCs from its products. At the 1987 G-7 Summit in Venice, President Reagan successfully persuaded the meeting to make protection of the ozone layer the top priority among environmental issues requiring common action. Notwithstanding this leadership, the US did not favour as fast a phaseout as some industrialized countries and was resistant to a large aid package to help developing countries with CFC-substitute technology. Throughout, a ferocious struggle raged between the Chemical Manufacturers Association and the 500-company Alliance for Responsible CFC Policy on one side (who switched from opposition to wanting a level playing field with the Europeans) and, on the other side, deregulatory, anti-UN ideologues within the administration. As the chief US negotiator of the Montreal Protocol explained: 'Although US initiatives were instrumental in first reducing CFC emissions in the 1970s, in achieving the Montreal Protocol in 1987, and in strengthening it in 1990, on four occasions during the ozone negotiations the US government either reversed or went close to reversing its position. It is noteworthy that on the three occasions since 1985, pragmatically oriented American industry forces intervened *in favour of* the international regulatory regime' (Benedick 1991: 202; see also Rowlands 1995: 113).

The combined forces of the US governmental and business establishment, other national allies such as the Nordic countries, the UNEP and the global environmental movement prevailed over the UK and industry-led European resistance in securing a strong Protocol for reductions of ozone-depleting substances at Montreal in 1987. Powerful early defectors from CFCs within European business, such as Hoechst, also helped. The Montreal Protocol was hailed as a major accomplishment. What followed as more scientific evidence poured in was growing commitment that caused the 1987 protocol targets to be handsomely exceeded, to the point where CFC production and consumption in the developed world has virtually ceased. The protocol was extended to new chemicals and $US200 million in assistance was given to developing countries to move away from CFCs. Although this is a rare case of a global agreement that has actually reduced the level of a type of environmental degradation, not just slowed its growth, it is possible that it is too late to avoid serious consequences from increased uv-B radiation. Moreover, ozone piracy, a thriving black market for CFCs, is now a problem in developing countries.

For environmental groups, ozone diplomacy had important implications. Many tactics were used in the ozone campaign that we have not discussed. Friends of the Earth (FOE) launched consumer boycotts of three UK manufacturers of aerosol cans, while in many countries FOE organized campaigns against styrofoam packaging. These had minor impacts compared to the change effected by global diplomacy. One of us was involved in the campaign, which seemed a major victory at the time, to get McDonald's to remove CFCs from its packaging. But these were little more than a helpful backdrop to the game of divide-and-conquer among global producers of the chemicals. Cynics and structural determinists sometimes espouse simple assumptions that business is strong and green groups are weak, so the victory of the latter is always extremely unlikely. Ozone diplomacy showed that an environmental victory in one major economy could divide and conquer business globally.

While unified global business will almost always defeat a unified green movement, an alliance of a unified green movement and US business can defeat European business. Also, an alliance of united greens and European business can defeat US business. An example of European business supporting the global environment movement against US business has been on certain aspects of the debate over environmental management standards in the International Organization for Standardization. European business, already stuck with Europe's demanding EMAS (Eco-Management and Auditing Scheme) standards on public disclosure of the results of policies to achieve continuous improvement, sought to force US and Asian business to live by the same rules. Environmental management standards will be discussed in more detail later.

The lesson is that green strategists should campaign in both Europe and the US. If there is only a one in four chance of victory in each place, there is a fifty-fifty chance of victory in one place or the other. And a unified global movement can do better than that by shifting its resources to the side of the Atlantic where it is making most progress. Once it has had a victory, it can often cause business on that side of the Atlantic to support it, as in the ozone and environmental management standards cases. An alliance between a unified green movement and that large fraction of business (and its associated governmental supporters) is then in a strong position to win the global battle. The other tactical consideration in favour of a pre-emptive regulatory standard in one major jurisdiction is, in the words of the chief US ozone negotiator: 'When influential governments (and, we might add, companies) make such a commitment, they legitimate change and thereby undercut the arguments of those who insist that change is impossible' (Benedick 1991: 206).

In the ozone case, one reason why the US was a softer target for the greens than Europe was that the US's biggest CFC manufacturer, DuPont, was ahead of its European competitors in developing cheap substitutes for ozone-depleting chemicals. DuPont could see that if regulatory demands for CFC substitutes globalized, it might enjoy an even bigger advantage over its competitors in the market for substitutes. Hence, DuPont led US business cooperation in the same way that ICI led European business's hardline opposition. Similarly, in the case of the acid rain regime within Europe, Germany was a supporter of substantial nitrogen oxide reductions in the late 1980s and the UK, France and Italy were opposed – under 1983 legislation German cars were already required to have catalytic converters, so German manufacturers, who also led in other relevant technologies such as fuel injection, looked forward to pan-European regulation that would deliver them a comparative advantage over the UK, French and Italian car-makers (Levy 1993: 95). To pragmatic environmentalists, the world is full of delicious ironies, available to be exploited. France might be a target for green groups because over 70 per cent of its energy comes from nuclear power (Dussol 1990: 10–11), yet it is this same fact that makes France one of the strongest possible allies in the campaign for a global carbon tax. Of course, windy countries or those with good aerospace or solar technologies might also be good carbon-tax targets.

Smart NGOs with a global strategy can in fact target individual firms and nations with a view to causing the global dominos to fall, as they did in the Montreal Protocol case. An ironic story based on this kind of strategic analysis is Greenpeace's advocacy of the 'green fridge' from 1992. This ozone- and greenhouse-friendly refrigerator uses a radical coolant mix of propane and butane. Greenpeace targeted an East German fridge manufacturer that was facing bankruptcy. It persuaded the German government to plough DM5 million into the new technology and to change German (and later European) law to mandate the new ozone- and greenhouse-friendly standard. Now firms from other European countries, China and Japan are picking up the new technology and the World Bank has accepted the technology as worth funding for developing countries. The irony is that the Greenpeace fridge is supplanting the HFC134a CFC-substitute refrigerants on which DuPont, Dow and Hoechst had patents. Although that substitute was ozone-friendly, it had very high global-warming potential which created the greener niche for the Greenpeace fridge.

NGOs can also push for open and inclusive scientific assessment procedures. DuPont began its assessment of the CFC problem in 'a state of denial', as one informant from the company told us. When it began to participate in international scientific assessment of the problem it began to change its position. It was the scientific evidence that eventually convinced DuPont scientists that something had to be done. DuPont managers we spoke to emphasized the transformative effect of the open scientific procedure for assessing the CFC problem. Through the UNEP assessment process environmental NGOs, governments and DuPont had access to the same data and were eventually able to agree on an interpretation of that data. Put another way, without the public-regarding dialogue within the epistemic community, DuPont may never have reassessed its underlying private interests – which were to support global regulation.

Although green NGOs suffer many more defeats than victories, to the point where we must despair about saving the planet, at least it is now possible to discern strategies where citizen groups can occasionally prevail against private interests. An aid to green groups has been some change in the thinking of global business itself.

## Business Thinking Begins to Change

Until the 1980s, the dominant way of thinking about globalization and environmental regulation within business was that the globalization of business provided opportunities to shift high-impact activities from nations with tough regulatory standards to 'pollution havens' (Braithwaite 1980: 1138; Castleman 1979, 1981). Today, this is a deeply contested way of thinking in the business community, indeed it is contested by considerable empirical evidence (Leonard 1988; Wheeler & Mody 1992; Repetto 1995; Jaffe et al. 1995; Levinson 1996; references cited by Vogel 1995: 305, fn. 19–28). The most influential proponent of the view that it no longer makes sense for international business to rush to pollution havens or to lower regulatory standards at home in order to be competitive abroad is the Harvard Business School's Michael Porter. He concludes, from a sweeping empirical analysis, in *The Competitive Advantage of Nations*:

> Establish norms exceeding the toughest regulatory hurdles or product standards. Some localities (or user industries) will lead in terms of the stringency of product standards, pollution limits, noise guidelines, and the like. Tough regulatory standards are not a hindrance but an opportunity to move early to upgrade products and processes.
>
> Find the localities whose regulations foreshadow those elsewhere. Some regions and cities will typically lead others in terms of their concern with social problems such as safety, environmental quality, and the like. Instead of avoiding such areas, as some companies do, they should be sought out. A firm should define its internal goals as meeting, or exceeding, their standards. An advantage will result as other regions, and ultimately other nations, modify regulations to follow suit.
>
> Firms, like governments, are often prone to see the short-term cost of dealing with tough standards and not their longer-term benefits in terms of innovation. Firms point to foreign rivals without such standards as having a cost advantage. Such thinking is based on an incomplete view of how competitive advantage is created and sustained. Selling poorly performing, unsafe, or environmentally damaging products is not a route to real competitive advantage in sophisticated industry and industry segments, especially in a world where environmental sensitivity and concern for social welfare are rising in all advanced nations. Sophisticated buyers will usually appreciate safer, cleaner, quieter products before governments do. Firms with the skills to produce such products will have an important lever to enter foreign markets, and can often accelerate the process by which foreign regulations are toughened.

Here we have an intriguing emerging international dynamic. Firms that have upgraded their safety standards early because of their location in states that are early movers to higher standards, have an interest in getting other states to follow that lead. There is thus a connected strategy for those who are active in international environmental or consumer movements. They must persuade targeted national governments to move first to upgrade regulatory standards, through the argument that they can actually benefit their national economy by doing so. Porter supplies many examples of nations that constructed important competitive advantages by being first to establish tougher health and safety standards. Home-base transnationals from those nations can be recruited to support upgrading of standards in other nations, through their subsidiaries in those nations, thus setting back their competitors from laggard nations.

The kind of evidence Porter adduces for his conclusions is the way the Japanese *Energy Conservation Law 1979* set demanding standards for refrigerators, air-conditioners and automobiles, stimulating product improvements that improved the international position of Japanese firms in these markets (Porter 1990: 648). Porter found that until the 1970s the US led the world in the export of pollution-control technology. But during the 1980s higher standards in nations such as Germany, Sweden and Denmark enabled them to seize much of the US export leadership. The German Environment Ministry has produced analyses concluding that its tougher environmental standards have been an economic asset, not just an environmental asset, to Germany (Blazejczak & Lubbe 1993; see also Feketekuty 1993: 188–9; Rowlands 1995: 130–1). It is estimated that pollution control accounts for 700 000 jobs in the German economy. These kinds of analyses encourage governments to offer export credits for clean technologies and pollution-control technology (OECD 1993), which further increases their incentives. In 1993, the US Secretaries of Commerce and Energy, together with the EPA Administrator, produced a *Strategic Framework for US Leadership* in environmental exports which concedes that, compared with their foreign competitors, US companies 'have operated in a *laissez-faire* climate which did not recognize the positive connection between environmental stewardship and economic competitiveness'. The report continues:

> Environmental technologies play a central role in our drive to move beyond the outdated notion that jobs must be traded off against sound environmental policies. Indeed, environmental technologies are a powerful engine for the creation of national wealth and high-paying jobs (Brown, O'Leary & Browner 1993: 7).

More recent work by Porter and van der Linde (1995a: 122) shows, moreover, that because pollution-prevention innovation allows firms to use various inputs more efficiently – from raw materials to energy to labour – the resultant enhanced resource productivity can increase rather than reduce competitiveness. 'When scrap, harmful substances or energy forms are discharged into the environment as pollution, it is a sign that resources have been used incompletely, inefficiently, or ineffectively' (Porter & van der Linde 1995a: 122). For example, Porter and van der Linde (1995a: 125) report from their program of empirical work that of 181 waste prevention activities in twenty-nine chemical plants, only one resulted in a net cost increase and, where specific data were available, the average increase in product yield was 7 per cent. Thus, companies like Dow initiate programs called 'Waste Reduction Always Pays'.[1] It does not always pay, as Porter's critics point out (see Palmer, Oates & Portney 1995; replies by Porter & van der Linde 1995b, 1995c). Yet the change in business leaders' attitudes on this issue is unmistakable. Many more now believe that green is lean and profitable. They are regularly plied with stories in the financial press like: 'Companies which "green" their corporate practices can make their shareholders up to 5 per cent richer, according to a study by ICF Kaiser, one of the US's largest engineering consulting groups' (*Financial Times*, 28 January 1997, p. 4). Indeed Weale (1992) sees a shift in the thinking of policy elites generally (in government, NGOs and business) to 'ecological modernization':

---

1 However, see Frank Popoff's (Dow Chairman) qualifications to the Porter and van der Linde analysis along with those of other CEOs in *Harvard Business Review*, November–December 1995, pp. 194–208.

Instead of seeing environmental protection as a burden upon the economy the ecological modernist sees it as a potential source for future growth. Since environmental amenity is a superior good, the demand for pollution control is likely to increase and there is therefore a considerable advantage to an economy to have the technical and production capacity to produce low-polluting goods or pollution-control technology (Weale 1992: 76).

### The Dynamics of Best Available Technology

In US writing on environmental regulation, Best Available Technology (BAT) is regarded as inefficient regulation that forces a technological solution on business. It is contrasted with setting an outcome and allowing business to work out how to meet it cost-effectively (Sunstein 1990: 87–8; Stewart 1985: 1334–7). This critique is right if BAT means a law that mandates a particular technology because it is the best available. But it is the German conception of BAT, not the US one, that is most influential in the world system. It does not involve mandating specific technologies. German law does require firms to implement BAT, but this does not necessarily mean that the actual environmental technology which is the best available is what must be put in place.[2] Under the German BAT model, firms are free to invent and apply technologies that are cheaper for them as long as they are as good or better than the BAT. This creates strong incentives for German firms to be inventive and at the cutting-edge of cost-effective environmental technologies.[3] In theory, in this BAT model, whenever a new and better environmental technology is invented anywhere, German industry is expected to meet the environmental protection standard that can be achieved by that technology. Of course, regulatory practice is more flexible, ambiguous and much less instantaneous. However, the correspondence of practice with the theory of BAT is sufficient to create incentives for German firms to invent new technologies that will be cheaper for them to meet the competition from the BAT. It is sufficient to create considerable German leadership in many environmental technologies. As it was put during a 1994 interview at the German Ministry for the Environment, Nature Protection and Nuclear Safety: 'We look worldwide for the Best Available Technology. Then we set standards that can be met with this technology. Industry can meet it with this technology or any other one. This forces innovation. It is becoming a more general view that BAT can force constant harmonization upwards'.

This has energized German leadership of other countries toward BAT and against the fixed-outcome standards approach that dominates in English-speaking countries. Western Europe, then Central and Eastern Europe have now followed Germany toward BAT in their law if not in practice. Note that if BAT continues to dominate fixed-outcome standards as the preferred national model,

---

2  The following analysis of how the German approach to BAT pushes forward environmental innovation would not be true under a BAT model that simply forced a particular technology on industry. It is also true in theory that an outcome standards approach which continually moved expected outcomes upwards beyond the reach of known technology would encourage innovation as well as or better than German BAT. However, the political appeal of BAT for environmentalists is that it is new technology that constantly raises standards; it does not require constant lobbying campaigns to push outcome standards upwards.

3  Of course, most firms will not rise to the challenge of this incentive. Our colleague, Neil Gunningham, points out that the experience of BAT and BAP in occupational health and safety has been of firms slavishly following codes of practice that the state accepts as meeting BAP, rather than innovating. From a global perspective, however, it only requires that the innovative few explore paths to better and cheaper technologies. When their invention sets a high standard, the innovative laggards are required by BAT to follow them up. With environmental auditing of continuous improvement of outcomes, the innovative firms have evidence of the advantage of their innovation over the BAP or BAT.

this has profound implications for the direction of global change. If outcomes remain fixed, pollution rapidly gets worse as more nations develop to the point where they are polluting up to the outcome limits. In contrast, over time, nations that adopt BAT are pushed to increasingly higher standards by the global competition for new environmental benchmarks that BAT nations are required to match. Globalization of BAT is a ratcheting-up mechanism for environmental standards, just as fixed-outcome standards are a prescription for guaranteed environmental decline.

### Pyrrhic Victories?

While pro-regulation groups can now see that a race-to-the-bottom is not inevitable in a global economy, the many successes of environmentalists in getting such a huge proliferation of international Agreements is engendering a kind of convention fatigue. So many Agreements and so little in the way of public, UN or NGO resources to breathe life into them. Most are frameworks with little substance, frameworks for saving a planet that is already substantially lost.

## Actors

### States

Most of the short history of the globalizing of environmental regulation tells the story in the traditional way of assuming that nation-states are the key actors. Indeed, they often have been. The US has consistently been the most important single actor in the globalization of environmental regulation. Until 1980, it was the actor that did most to raise global standards. Since 1981, it has rather been a resister than a promoter of attempts to elevate global standards, with important exceptions such as the ozone case and the WTO debate on trade and environment. However, Europe, particularly Germany, shifted during the 1970s from being more often laggards to being more often the most important leaders of efforts to raise global environmental standards. The other national actors most consistently showing leadership within international environmental regimes have been Sweden, Norway, Denmark and the Netherlands, fairly consistently toward higher standards (an important exception being Norway's resistance to the global whaling regime). When a regulatory lead country like Sweden enters the EU, two things happen. Sweden has a new forum in which it can show leadership, and it does. Other countries have a new forum in which they can work together to pull Sweden back to the pack, and they do. The latter is obvious in the OECD's Chemicals Program, as one OECD bureaucrat explained to us: 'Sweden is a pace-setter, out ahead of others on banning some chemicals and chemicals regulation overall. Other countries get together and try to pull them back. "You're undermining uniformity", they say. Now EC membership will make this easier'.

For most global environmental agreements, there is a group of states whose cooperation is so vital for a regime to work that they can form a veto coalition. The US, Germany and Japan are a coalition that can veto virtually anything through market power. But it is a coalition that actors have to form if they wish to veto effective international environmental action. Successful individual resistance is increasingly becoming difficult, even for powerful actors. Because of its insecurities about the impact of the Convention on Biological Diversity regime on intellectual property rights the US has not supported it, but this has not prevented its growth. Japan and a few other countries still interested in whaling can be (have been) a worrying veto coalition for any whaling agreement. The big fast-developing countries with fossil-fuel resources that will cause major future growth in carbon emissions (China, India, Brazil) to date are an effective veto coalition for a global carbon or energy tax, as is OPEC. Young and Osherenko's (1993) research on polar regimes shows that the support of a single hegemonic power is most critical for regime formation. This research shows that it can be important to have all effective veto states actively involved in negotiations. On the other hand, there are regimes that have got started by excluding intransigent states from the early stages of negotiations, with a view to bringing them into the regime later (Young & Osherenko 1993: 241).

Japan has been the site of some important crises of environmental management, and the Japanese response has not been one of international leadership. In some respects, however, it has led by domestic example, changing some of its environmental problems with strong governmental intervention of an effectiveness that Western nations at times have envied (Vogel 1979: 82–3). An important instance of Japan's leadership by example was its 1973 legislation on industrial chemicals in the aftermath of the Minamata catastrophe. Nations of the developing world are much more often resisters than supporters of higher global environmental standards. They have not been persuaded by Porter's message; they tend to believe that they give their firms a competitive advantage by demanding lower environmental standards; they doubt their capacity to innovate in the way Germans do. Their response to environmental initiatives from rich countries has increasingly been to ask for resources to effect shifts to greener technologies (a reverse polluter-pays principle – the polluter *gets* paid – that causes some economists to worry about 'moral hazard'). However, these pleas are articulated in the context of a post-Cold War world wherein securing aid by playing one major power against another is less possible. Hence, the South's ability to secure environmental aid from the North has been extremely modest.

### NGOs and Green Civil Society

National action in showing leadership toward global environmental regimes usually results from domestic environmentalist pressure. Keohane, Haas and Levy (1993: 14) conclude in their study, *Institutions of the Earth*, that 'If there is one key variable accounting for policy change, it is the degree of domestic environmentalist pressure in major industrialized democracies, not the decision-making rules of the relevant international institution'. Similarly, Caldwell (1988: 17) concluded from his study that 'Initiatives for international cooperation on environmental issues have almost invariably arisen outside governmental bureaucracies. They have seldom originated within the hierarchy of major political parties'. The ideas for international environmental regimes usually come from globalizing movements of concerned citizens and scientists, from actors who we describe as model mongers in Chapter 25, hawking models of environmental change from one bureaucracy to another, from one state to another, until they capture a powerful bureaucracy which will champion their model. Environment is not typical of how global business regulatory initiatives originate, as none of the other areas of business regulation discussed in this book have the broad popular base of environmental groups. In Australia for example, few other NGO sectors can boast the 300 000 voters (plus tens of thousands of young people who are ineligible to vote) who are members of conservation groups (Papadakis 1993: 9), just as few other NGO sectors in the US can boast the 13 million members of national environmental organizations there (Porter & Brown 1991: 57). Few regional peak organizations could boast the combined 20 million membership of the 120 national-level environmental organizations that comprise the European Environmental Bureau (Porter & Brown 1991: 57). The growing political clout of environmental groups is historically recent and not limited to industrialized nations. The Environmental Liaison Centre in Nairobi, established by NGOs to facilitate cooperation with UNEP, estimated in 1982 that there were then 2230 environmental NGOs in developing countries, of which 60 per cent were formed during the preceding decade, plus 13 000 developed-country NGOs, 30 per cent established during the preceding decade (Caldwell 1988: 19). Both Greenpeace and the World Wildlife Fund had bigger budgets than UNEP during the 1990s. Yet even before the growth of the modern environment movement, lobbying for the regulatory regimes of lead states that ultimately became global was often done by conservation groups. Global oil-pollution regimes were based on the regulation of the lead maritime states, the UK and US (Mitchell 1993). In the 1920s it was the Royal Society for the Protection of Birds that lobbied for UK regulation of pollution from ships and in the US it was the National Coast Anti-Pollution League (Mitchell 1993: 194).

Domestic political concern is not always mediated primarily through the actions of NGOs. Often concern is manifested by mass publics and directly acted upon by states concerned to visibly respond. The International Maritime Organization's regime for oceanic oil spills is a good example. Although NGOs played an important role in establishing that regime, few NGOs are still involved in it and those that are, such as Friends of the Earth International, have not been very influential (Mitchell 1993: 223).[4] However, major disasters such as the *Torrey Canyon* grounding of 1967 and the *Amoco Cadiz* of 1978 aroused such mass concern that mediation of this concern by the mass media was sufficient to stir states to action. Television reporters were gripped by the international nature of the problem and therefore communicated in their stories the need for global action. When the *Torrey Canyon* was wrecked, causing coastal damage to both the UK and France, it was carrying 117 000 tons of oil from Kuwait, was Liberian-registered, US-owned and chartered, sailed by an Italian captain and crew, grounded in international waters, contracted to a Dutch company for salvage, and destroyed by rockets of the UK navy and airforce. Dramatic cases such as this had an importance beyond oil-spill regimes; they helped forge what we might call a global regulatory imagination among mass publics, an effective political demand not only for national but for global action to deal with certain classes of problems. The globalization of the media obviously helps form political demand, by global publics prodding for global rather than only national action.

The globalization dynamic at work in a case like the oil-spill regime, as documented by Mitchell (1993), is therefore interesting and instructive for NGO actors interested in being effective model mongers. Initially, NGO concern in a couple of key states (the US and UK in this case) is not backed up by concern from global mass publics. But the confined NGO concern is sufficient to mobilize these lead states to put in place the framework for a (very weak) global regulatory regime. When a disaster strikes which does mobilize concern among a global public, a framework is ready and waiting to receive content as a response to the concern. Figure 12.1 shows the model epitomized by the oil-spill regime. Young (1989) makes the point that some environ-

---

4 Perhaps Mitchell's judgment was premature, however. Chayes and Chayes (1995: 259) point out how Greenpeace whistle-blowing on Russian nuclear waste-dumping brought about an IMO ban on all dumping of low-level nuclear waste in November 1993. Chayes and Chayes (1995: 260) also show how a Friends of the Earth study of non-reporting by nations of compliance with IMO rules seemed to cause improved reporting and improved compliance.

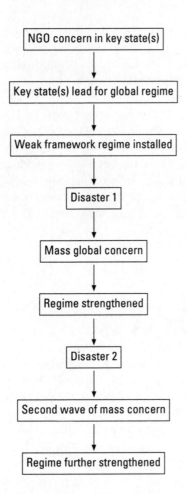

**FIGURE 12.1    Model of a globalization dynamic for regulatory regimes**

mental problems that have failed to produce credible regimes, such as greenhouse-gas emissions, have failed because of the want of a visible disaster (see also Young & Osherenko 1993: 239). Although global warming is a larger worry than ozone depletion, because there has been no sudden appearance of an ozone hole, no Chernobyl, mass global concern has been more difficult to mobilize. However, it began to occur in 1997 at the Kyoto Climate Change Conference on the basis of new evidence of global warming.

Another case which fits the model in Figure 12.1 moderately well is the global pesticide regime for which the FAO is primarily responsible (Paarlberg 1993). But here the disasters were smaller, more diffuse and less visible, with the odd tragic exception such as the Bhopal pesticide plant disaster that killed 2500 people in India in 1984. Here a more critical role is played by an intellectual who manages to draw together the small disasters so they can be redefined by mass publics as major, similar to the way Carson's *Silent Spring* highlighted a creeping crisis. The NGO involvement in Rome (FAO headquarters) and in all the major national capitals is much more concerted and continuous than in the oil-spill case. The key reason is international organization by a peak body which made a conscious decision to adopt a networking model – coordinating the work of many NGOs in many places toward a global strategy. The network was the Pesticides Action Network (PAN) established by the International Organization of Consumers Unions (now Consumers International). PAN mobilizing to exploit the Bhopal disaster at the 1984 meeting of IOCU in Bangkok was a moving spectacle of the practical possibilities for global democratic citizenship. The world's media watched as the people organized and the FAO responded with an (admittedly extremely weak) Code of Conduct on the Distribution and Use of Pesticides in 1985 (Paarlberg (1993: 332–3) and the chemical industry responded with 'Responsible Care'. Yet according to the strategy in Figure 12.1, the fact that only weak and voluntary codes were accomplished is not reason for utter despair. Today's voluntary code secretariat provides a contractual environment and a framework that can become tomorrow's treaty when the right kind of disaster supplies the catalyst. Levy, Keohane and Haas (1993: 412–13) make the point thus:

> None of the institutions we studied began life as successes, though some have become so. In fact, most international environmental institutions were first considered deep disappointments by those who had worked to create them. Our studies show that there is cause for optimism even following inauspicious starts, and that effective institutions seize opportunities to expand the consequences of their activity.

There are two basic models of NGO action with global environmental regimes – the network model (e.g. PAN and pesticides, Climate Action Network, Antarctic and South Ocean Coalition, World Rainforest Network) and the one rich global lead NGO model (e.g. Greenpeace with its 3.3 million members and whaling) – and various hybrids. Obviously, the big lead NGO model is best suited to lobbying that requires concentrated resources (e.g. ships to monitor and publicize whaling or nuclear testing), while the network model is best for problems (like pesticides) that are diffuse and variable across different locales. The network model has become increasingly attractive thanks to the Internet and as more powerful non-environment NGOs adopt selected green policies. Some even signal these explicitly so they can be picked up for green networking. For example, the International Confederation of Free Trade Unions has published *Environment and Development: The Trade Union Agenda* (ICFTU 1992).

## Business Actors

Business leadership, interestingly, follows the same basic two models as NGO leadership. There is leadership by a big company acting directly on its own behalf and networking among business groups. Small business has no choice but to push its agenda through industry associations. Big business makes a strategic choice whether to lobby directly through its own corporate public affairs staff or to work through industry associations. US big business is more individualist, regularly opting to lobby directly for a global regime as an individual company; European business is much more corporatist, generally preferring to work through trade associations. Hybrids are very common. Hence, in the case of ozone diplomacy, DuPont lobbied both directly and through the Chemical Manufacturers Association. When business networks, it is often a layered networking, both vertical and horizontal. There will be networking among members of a national sectoral association (e.g. for chemicals), networking among national sectoral associations within an international sectoral association, networking among national sectoral associations within a national peak association (like the US Chamber of Commerce) and networking among national peak associations within an international peak association (like the International Chamber of Commerce). In Europe, regional business associations (like UNICE) are especially important loci of networking. Business networking routinely brings key governmental actors into the network. Hence, the Chair of the [US] Chemical Manufacturers' Association Task Force on Harmonization explained to us that key people from the EPA, the Consumer Product Safety Commission, OSHA and other agencies are invited to their meetings when appropriate.

The ICC sent a 100 member delegation to the Kyoto Climate Change Convention in 1997. At the Rio Earth Summit, the ICC played hard-cop to the soft-cop of the Business Council on Sustainable Development (BCSD). BCSD laid out a global corporate vision of free-market environmentalism. It championed world's best practice, Porteresque ratcheting-up of environmental standards. ICC in contrast adopted a lowest-cost approach to regulation, ensuring that any bonhomie between environmentalists and BCSD did not lead to costly regulatory change. About half the BCSD companies were on the ICC Board.

With the climate change issue insurers have become important business actors (see generally Gunningham & Grabosky 1998: 106–21). Greenpeace ran a concerted campaign to persuade insurers to break ranks with manufacturing and energy interests on the issue. At the Kyoto Climate Change negotiations, insurers, which are also major institutional investors (owning about a third of the value of global stockmarkets), warned that they would unload the shares of companies that did not modify environmentally destructive practices. Some segments of the insurance industry are increasingly concerned that natural disasters associated with uncontrolled climate change could wipe them out. We will also see that insurers have been central actors in securing the effectiveness of the IMO's global regime for regulating oil spills.

Business networking is also like NGO networking in that it is often the work of individual entrepreneurs. In places like New York, Washington, Brussels and Geneva, individual lobbyists can make a lot of money by persuading a network of companies and industry associations to back a global regulatory reform or resistance idea. They create a network in the image of their idea, then get the network to pay them to represent the idea. It can be illuminating to conceive many of the actors discussed in this section, business firms, NGOs, international organizations or states, as loci of legitimacy and power waiting to be captured, networked and used as vehicles for the regulatory models of individual model mongers. Latour's (1986) translation theory of power as enrolment of other actors provides a relevant understanding of this process (see Chapter 20). The image of individuals as passive puppets of the forces of global corporate and state power is not the image of many of the informants listed in our Acknowledgments – they see themselves as the deft puppeteers, pulling strings and moving massive concentrations of power that remain passive until someone comes along to show them where their interest lies. Their view is that large bureaucracies tend to dither, baffled by the complexity of the world non-system, craving guidance by someone who can see a clear path of interest-enhancing action. Young and Osherenko's (1993) study of polar regimes is the most systematic empirical demonstration of the importance of independent leadership, particularly entrepreneurial leadership such as that shown by Tolba of the UNEP in the ozone case and others (Chayes & Chayes 1995: 275), in regime formation.

## International Organizations

Obviously, international organizations have also been important actors. The UNEP showed important leadership in a number of regimes. In their areas of expertise – the WHO with health, the ILO with occupational health, the FAO with agriculture, the IMO with pollution from ships – other UN agencies have at times been important leaders, though with pesticides, for example, there have been times when the FAO has attempted to hold back UNEP leadership. The UN Commission on Sustainable Development has responsibility for follow-up treaty development from the Rio Summit, adopting a coordinating role among different UN agencies which act as task managers for specific domains. The UN Economic Commission for Europe was the critical agency for globalization of the regulation of acid rain (Levy 1993).

The OECD has dominated the UN agencies in the trade and environment debate and in specific domains, notably chemicals, where intellectual leadership was needed to forge an international regime that was of critical importance to trade. The OECD is also interesting because of the way it has conducted peer reviews of member states' entire environment programs since 1993. The OECD Environmental Performance Review team conducts site visits during which it consults with NGOs as well as government and business. Compliance with international commitments is assessed. Once the report and recommendations are tabled, representatives of the ministries under review have an opportunity to defend or agree to modify their policies (Chayes & Chayes 1995: 244). Chayes and Chayes (1995: 274) believe such dialogic accountability can work:

> Despite a reservoir of professional sympathy, it remains difficult to explain before an audience of sophisticated and informed colleagues with whom you are engaged in trying to promote and enhance a regulatory regime that your government has found it impossible to comply with one or another of its undertakings. Delivering the message during the negotiations of the Montreal Protocol that the US had revoked its earlier commitment to contribute ozone fund resources 'additional' to existing foreign aid flows was, according to Ambassador Richard J. Smith, the hardest thing he had ever had to do.

In more recent times, environmental regulation has become important enough to be pushed at G-7 Summits, as President Reagan did with the ozone regime. Before the 1995 G-7 Summit in Halifax, environment ministers of the seven richest industrial nations met for the first time before the meeting in a effort to settle an environmental agenda that they could uniformly offer to their leaders for the summit (*Montreal Gazette*, 29 April 1995). As in so many areas of regulation, we may see the G-7 assume an increasingly important role. In addition to international governmental organizations, international non-governmental organizations, such as the International Organization for Standardization, have become increasingly important players in the globalization of environmental standards.

Treaty secretariats are particularly important collective actors with global environmental regimes (Sandford 1992, 1994). They have an interesting character because they tend to be composed of a staff designed to represent the various major stakeholders – business, government and non-government. They therefore have a capacity to broker trust, to advance a consensus position and to catalyze a negotiation environment (for bilateral and regional as well as global contracting) that other actors lack. They tend to be small, mostly fewer than twenty people. They build their own legitimacy as well as global commitment by networking – getting stakeholders to do most of the technical analysis and other work, rather than doing it themselves. Building global regimes requires tireless communication over decades rather than years – 'talking, talking and more talking' (Sandford 1994: 24). Secretariats are not the key talkers but the key actors for facilitating the talk.

## Capture of Nations by Other Actors

Many of the national actors that have played influential roles have done so at the behest of their business communities. This was well illustrated in the ozone case by the responsiveness of the US government to the Chemical Manufacturers Association and of the UK government to ICI. More recently, we have seen cases of both national governments and UN agencies being temporarily captured by environmental groups. We have seen cases of international environmental agreements being drafted in the offices of environmental NGOs then successfully sold to UN agencies (e.g. drafting of the Bamako Convention on Transboundary Movement and Management of Hazardous Wastes that occurred in the Greenpeace office). We have seen Greenpeace briefing and dragging delegates from the embassies of sympathetic developing countries to take their seats for critical votes at international meetings (Stairs & Taylor 1992: 130). An important case is the way the Centre for International Environmental Law helped form the Association of Small Island States as a key player in the global-warming debate (Chayes & Chayes 1995: 260-2). At times, Greenpeace manages to get its experts into meetings (that would otherwise be closed to them) as representatives of national governments. They cannot do this as often or as brazenly as their adversaries, however. The Japanese Commissioner to the International Whaling Commission has usually been the president of the Japanese Whaling Association (Porter & Brown 1991: 38). We have seen the Japanese whaling industry buy the votes of delegates from obscure developing countries at meetings of the International Whaling Commission, just as we have seen Saudi Arabia and Kuwait, working with energy TNCs, buying opposition to any UNCED energy-efficiency regime.

We must keep this juxtaposition in perspective. The capture of nation-states by business groups with an interest in resisting or promoting a particular regulatory regime is very common. Nation-states as captives of an environmental group is rare, in comparison. Yet that simplifies too much. The environment ministries of nation-states are often significantly under the influence of domestic environmental groups; economic ministries never are (at least not directly). Therefore what happens in an international regime often depends on whether the critical national actors are from environment or economic ministries, or whether they are neutralizing each other's leadership, leaving the leadership roles to states with a unified position. In the crucial US case, pro-environment bureaucracies and NGOs sometimes work through Congress to neutralize the brown values of economic bureaucracies. For example, the US Treasury is under instructions from Congress to give more emphasis to environmental reform agendas through its directorships of the World Bank and regional banks (which tend to track World Bank Guidelines on environmental issues). The effect has been US leadership, subject to grudging acquiescence by finance bureaucrats from other states, to institute much-improved environment assessment procedures and to develop World Bank Guidelines on specific concerns such as tropical forests. The US Executive-Director of the World Bank during the early 1990s sometimes became in effect a court of appeal for green groups concerned about brown financing proposals. Even non-US NGOs could get a hearing, through a US NGO. At the time of writing, however, the US Executive-Director of the World Bank is less active on environmental matters than formerly. A limited and transient green capture of the economic ministries in this (admittedly partial) way is a peculiarly US phenomenon. We cannot identify examples of finance ministries of any other state showing leadership on a global green agenda. We do not think that this is because US Treasury officials are more green or that the US is more green than other democracies. It is not a greener democracy, but it is a more interpenetrated democracy (Holtzman 1966: 62). And it cuts both ways; Western US coal interests can always get the forty senators they need to block energy taxes. Finance ministries elsewhere are more effectively segregated from the leverage of green NGOs. Persuading Congress to instruct Treasury to play a green hand in global negotiations is a uniquely Washington lobbying accomplishment. There are signs, however, that the European Parliament may in future be capable of this.

### Epistemic Communities of Actors

It is equally important not to consider business and NGO actors as simply capturing nation-states and international organizations to pursue their interests. An important part of their function is building international communities which share concerns, policy ideas, science and technologies relevant to solving specific problems. Reading daily newspapers is enough to show how environmental NGOs are no longer national organizations. Their international networking is prodigious, as is their infiltration into key international organizations, even conservative ones like the World Bank. The international community-building of business is less visible. One upshot of the ozone regime process was the Industry Cooperative for Ozone Layer Protection (ICOLP). Members included major US TNCs such as Ford, AT&T, Texas Instruments, Boeing, General Electric, Honeywell and Motorola. ICOLP members agreed to:

> (1) coordinate open, worldwide exchange of non-proprietary information on alternative technologies for ODS [ozone-depleting substance] solvents in the electronics industry; (2) sponsor seminars and workshops on technology transfer; (3) publish and distribute technical manuals; (4) distribute OZONET, a globally accessible database for technological solvents information; and (5) manage a multi-partner project to eliminate CFC solvents in Mexico's electronics industry by the year 2000. In turn, ICOLP joined other groups that then created a partnership between the government of Thailand, the US EPA, MITI of Japan, and JICOP [industry associations of Japan] to encourage multinational companies to stop use of CFC solvents in their Thai operations and to transfer new technologies to Thai-owned companies...A committee of world-class suppliers, purchasers and factory experts in developed countries with experience in ODS phase-out was brought together to implement the project (Canan & Reichman 1993: 65).

The major US and UK chemical companies have sponsored global Responsible Care initiatives for the chemical industry, through regional programs for Europe, South America, Asia–Pacific and the US and Canada (Gunningham 1995). According to Rees (1998), there are programs in thirty-seven countries. This amounts to an attempt at a progressive globalization of self-regulation in this industry through a number of voluntary codes which include an environmental stewardship code. While they are voluntary, in the US for example, participation in Responsible Care is an obligation of membership of the Chemical Manufacturers Association, which covers 90 per cent of US productive capacity for basic industrial chemicals. In both Canada (McChesney 1996) and the US (Gunningham 1998) there have been industry claims of 50 per cent reductions in releases of toxic chemicals to the environment by Responsible Care members.

Business schools, particularly those that teach through the Harvard case-study approach, have become important media for disseminating models of excellence in environmental management for continuous improvement (*Financial Times*, 19 July 1995, p.12). More important than the greening of MBAs, however, has been the professionalization of environmental auditing and environmental management as specialties which create their own epistemic communities (communities of shared knowledge) (Australian Accounting Research Foundation 1995).

Haas (1989) has developed the concept of epistemic communities and undertaken the most influential analysis of the role of epistemic communities in enabling international regulatory cooperation. Haas has used the Mediterranean Action Plan, a regime for the control of marine pollution, to show how an international regime can empower a group of experts, who then foster convergent state policies in compliance with the regime. The countries where these experts (ecologists and marine scientists) most dominated the channels of national decision-making became the strongest supporters of the regime and achieved the strongest compliance with it. While most member states initially opposed the Mediterranean Action Plan, it became a successful instance of international cooperation, with water quality and the safety of Mediterranean beaches improving significantly (Haas 1989: 383; for a more pessimistic view, see Downs, Rocke & Barsoom 1995: 25). External support for the epistemic community of marine experts from the UNEP was, according to Haas, important in sustaining the experts' authority to push through this accomplishment in their home governments. Change did not arise from the regional community of experts directly persuading governments; it came from the way the regime empowered domestic experts to seize the policy agenda within their home governments (Haas 1989: 398).

In summary, we have seen many different kinds of actors playing crucial roles in the globalization of environmental regulation – states, regional organizations of states, veto coalitions of states, NGOs, networks of NGOs, TNCs, national and international industry associations, business networks, international organizations, treaty secretariats and mass publics interpreted by mass media.

## Contest of Principles

### Lowest-cost Location, Deregulation v. World's Best Practice

The most important contest of principles with the globalization of environmental regulation is the contest within TNCs between the principle of lowest-cost location (which includes regulatory costs) and the principle of world's best practice (choice of the latter principle is best explained by Porter's theory of competitive advantage). This is the most important contest, because whereas the principle of lowest-cost location leads to a race-to-the-bottom for regulatory standards globally, we have seen how the principle of world's best practice can lead to a race-to-the-top in strategic cases. When the principle of lowest-cost location is in play, citizen groups have no choice but to play the global game with maximum adversariness, exposing corporate decisions that threaten the planet by shifting activities to the places where they will be least regulated. When the principle of world's best practice is in play, green NGOs can be strategically cooperative with the business actors and states best placed to raise global standards.

Adding to these two competing principles of corporate action are two competing principles of state action. Where TNCs adopt the principle of lowest-cost location, realist states will adopt the principle of deregulation so they can attract the investment of cost-cutters. Where TNCs adopt the principle of world's best practice, states can reject deregulation. We have seen how ozone diplomacy was a good example of a contest within the Reagan administration between the principle of deregulation (allied to a principle of national sovereignty and resistance to global standards) and a principle of world's best practice (allied to a principle of international harmonization).

### Rule Compliance v. Continuous Improvement

Another contest of principles which is less visible than some others, because the primary site of the contest is the intracorporate arena rather than the political arena, is the contest between the principle of rule compliance and the principle of continuous improvement. This is also a particularly important contest because the principle of rule compliance means that a company subscribing to it accepts an obligation to meet a formal legal standard, but no more. In a world where the principle of lowest-cost location is dominant, the effect of corporate adherence to the principle of rule compliance is pressure toward a race-to-the-bottom. Regulatory stasis is the finishing line for this particular race. In contrast, to the extent that TNCs voluntarily adopt the principle of continuous improvement in product stewardship and environmental protection, standards will be raised globally. National environmental standards have always been set in response to corporate practice; when spontaneous ordering by a principle such as continuous improvement leads corporate practices up, environmental standards follow them up. In a sense this race does not end. The gains come in the form of dynamic benefits (higher standards, more innovation).

During the past decade, the Trojan horse for a substantial voluntary shift from standard compliance to continuous improvement has been the way the ideology of total quality management has spread among TNCs (Talley 1991). Perhaps the central tenet of this corporate ideology is continuous improvement. When TQM is applied to environmental management, the firm is required to cause less environmental harm this year than it did last year, even if it complied with legal standards last year. Whether this annual improvement is achieved must be measured and reported to the Board of Directors. In the most effective schemes, improvement is audited independently. Initially, this voluntary ratcheting-up of environmental standards was simply a change in the principles of environmental management to which companies subscribed. But self-regulatory bodies (pre-eminently the British Standards Institute) then state regulators were quick to grasp that a voluntary shift in corporate philosophy could be harnessed and generalized. The British Standards Institute wrote an Environmental Management Standard (BS 7750) in 1994, which applied the principle of continuous improvement, including monitoring and reporting of improvement, under the leadership of corporate pacesetters like IBM (which had an economic interest in getting other companies to join in raising environmental standards)[5] (Cascio 1994).

Crucially, both the EC and the International Organization for Standardization, as well as many state environmental regulators, saw the virtue of generalizing this trend. Some states did so by requiring companies above a specified size to develop management plans for continuous improvement, to measure and report their success through environmental audit; the EU also legislated for voluntary participation (through CEN, the European Standards body) in a pan-European regime of environmental management certification (the EMAS).

The ISO sought to generalize the trend through a global voluntary standard, knowing that many corporations would pay for ISO's intellectual property right in the standard because some states and large corporations would decide not to purchase from firms which did not meet the standard. ISO believed this because of its experience of large purchasers (particularly states) requiring certification of compliance with the TQM standards of ISO 9000 (on product quality).[6] It is easy for a large purchaser concerned about either legal liability or public criticism for using

---

5 From a rational choice perspective, if Porter is right that firms can be leaner by being greener, then firms do not have an interest in dragging other firms up to higher standards so that the competitors will also reap the benefits of being leaner. On the other hand, a second part of Porter's analysis is that if community demand for cleaner production produces a long-term upward trend in environmental standards, firms do better to reap the competitive advantage of adjusting early to new demands rather than having to catch up. In this part of the analysis, the competitive advantage is being ahead, but not too far ahead, and ahead of firms that see survival as depending on catching up.

6 Here the ISO is therefore a model mercenary, in the sense described in Chapter 25, generating income through the global promulgation of a model.

defective or environmentally destructive products to protect itself by saying that it has a policy of purchasing only from ISO-certified producers. In this way, voluntary standards have a cascading effect throughout industry. Producers in the US may adopt environmental management standards so that they can mitigate penalties for environmental crimes under US sentencing guidelines (*Boston University Law Review* 1991).

Big corporate players and industry associations see the strategic importance of the ISO environmental management standards very clearly, though at first many 'saw them as just adding more useless bureaucracy'. That is why there are no fewer than a thousand people (mostly business experts) working on numerous committees under the ISO umbrella on environmental standards, at the time of writing. That is why European business, which has already been forced to accept strong continuous environmental improvement and auditing standards under EU Regulation 1836/93, is working with green constituencies within the ISO for a tougher global voluntary standard that will drag the US and Asia up toward EMAS standards. It is an example of where the desire for a level playing field in time produces a higher-quality field. TNCs such as IBM saw that a proliferation of different environmental management standards at the national level would make life difficult. Global businesses began to get involved in standard-setting in order to ensure that there was some harmonization. Once major companies like IBM began to get involved in the ISO process, they realized that it offered an opportunity for modifying their internal management techniques for global application. British Standard 7750, for example, modelled a number of IBM internal management practices. Once US and Japanese industry (which thought their standards high enough already) saw the impact of the ISO 9000 standard on the marketplace, they realized that standard-setting could not be ignored. US business experts now participate with European experts in the standard-setting game because in a global economy no country can afford to leave the table for fear that its opponents will set standards that advantage them. Already Asian business is moving to adopt ISO 14001 because TNCs like IBM say that they will 'favour ISO 14001-certified suppliers' (Kumarasivam 1996).

Many actors in the NGO sector consider ISO standards to be voluntary, toothless and therefore unimportant. Admittedly, there are worries about how genuinely transparent and accountable the various schemes are, and whether paper compliance rather than genuine improvement is all they will require. Yet strategic business actors are not so naive as to fail to grasp the way an ISO standard can lead global practice up or down. With the ISO 14001 standards on environmental management, European business wanted to lead the US and Asia up towards EMAS, while US business effectively resisted certain key elements of EMAS. One of the important ways ISO 14001 seems to undermine EMAS is through not requiring public reporting of the outcomes from implementing publicly announced environmental policies and objectives (Gunningham & Grabosky 1998: 172–87). Most important of all, while the standard of continuous improvement under EMAS is continuous improvement in environmental outcomes, ISO 14001 is being interpreted in the US as requiring continuous improvement in environmental management only (regardless of whether the managerial improvement actually affects environmental outcomes). This is not how ISO 14001 is being interpreted in Australia and Europe. One participant in the crucial drafting sessions said the standard was drafted to allow the dual interpretations – to allow European and Australian accreditation to interpret it as requiring continuous improvement in environmental outcomes and North America to interpret it as requiring only continuous improvement in environmental management. Had environmental groups earlier realized the importance of ISO 14001 and worked with European business in support of a standard closer to

EMAS, a rare opportunity to substantially raise global environmental standards might have been grasped. Instead, only a modest global movement upwards may have been achieved, with some actual undercutting of EMAS (Gunningham 1996).

What is distinctive about using the principle of continuous improvement to guide international standard-setting is that once that principle is enshrined in a standard, it structurally induces upward rather than downward movement in the global norm. Even ISO 14001 standards as interpreted in North America, for all their limitations, create a platform below which standards cannot fall, by mandating compliance with local law and on top of that requiring continuous improvement in environmental management.

Ratcheting-up standards by securing a platform in existing law then requiring continuous improvement beyond it can become more profound if ratchets are linked in series. For example, the Forest Stewardship Council (a novel coalition of the World Wide Fund for Nature, Greenpeace, the Environmental Defense Fund, Friends of the Earth, other NGOs, major retailers of wood products and other economic interests) requires a chain of custody and lifecycle thinking generally beyond the requirements of EMAS or ISO 14001 before its audits of sustainable forests will approve certification of wood products (a certification beginning to attract impressive consumer acceptance in Europe). But the Forest Stewardship Council (fscoax@antequera.com) also requires compliance with local laws as a minimum and consultation with local stakeholders on how these minimums ought to be exceeded for a particular forest. Consideration is also being given to requiring audits to meet ISO 14001 minimums. This kind of arrangement illustrates the possibility of a series of ratchets in the world system. Local law sets a platform; ISO 14001 requires the honouring and exceeding of that platform; plural coalitions like the Forest Stewardship Council may certify only if there is honouring and improving upon the ISO 14001 platform. The effect of serial ratchets is that whenever the demands of state law or ISO 14001 or local agreements pursuant to FSC-style audits go up, the standards for sustainable foresting are driven up. Any one of the three ratchets can drive the system up; all three define a platform which protects regulation from being driven down. It would be fanciful to see such smoothly working ratchets as a reality, but it would be unperceptive to fail to see them as a possibility.

Concern about the quality of environmental auditing under ISO 14001 from environmentalists, but also from free traders concerned about unequal audits being used for green protectionism, has seen mutual recognition of national accreditation of ISO 14001. To the extent that ISO 14001 leads the world regulatory system up or down, the kind of mutual recognition system in Figure 12.2 solidifies and generalizes the upwards or downwards movement.

NGOs need to fully appreciate the strategic opportunities of global standard-setting. Global business takes standard-setting very seriously because of its experience with the ISO 9000 standard. Major companies like DuPont and IBM saw the effects of ISO 9000 in the marketplace. Customers demanded compliance with the standard. Hence, companies like these are now heavily involved in the global standards-setting process. They are motivated by a desire to have one international standard rather than various national ones, and by the trade implications of standards. They recognize that ISO standards will have to be tough in order to be credible. Environmental NGOs, by participating in standard-setting, can help add the elements of toughness and credibility. The motivation for companies to comply with such voluntary standards is twofold. It adds to the company's reputation and, according to the Porter thesis, to its competitiveness. Making the standard work, some companies reason, may also help to reduce government reliance on a command-and-control style of environmental regulation. From the perspective of business, green

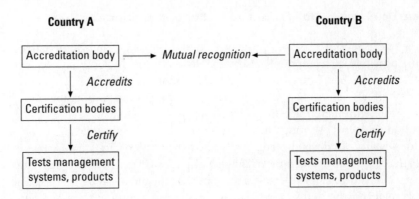

FIGURE 12.2    The evolution of mutual recognition of ISO 14001 auditing in different nations
Source: Adapted from a summary by John Hulbert (1996) at an ANU workshop

groups have often played the role of 'barking dogs'. But it is clear from our interviews that international business in particular is looking to some parts of the environmental movement for cooperation and help in the standards-setting game. The motivation is partly self-interest. But there is another dynamic at work, one that involves moral suasion of business by environmentalists. In the words of one of our interviewees, environmental concerns represents a 'new ethical standard we [business] are beginning to internalize'. In some cases the commitment to greener production by specific companies is worthy of being taken very seriously. For example, in 1996 ICI – the same ICI that led the 1980s opposition to the Montreal Protocol – committed to 'halve the environmental burden of our operations worldwide across a range of specific environmental parameters using 1995 as the baseline' (Knight 1996).

Earlier in this chapter, we saw how German leadership toward the globalization of BAT standards or best available practice standards[7] has the effect of ratcheting-up environmental standards. As new technologies offer improved environmental performance, firms in BAT states are required by law to meet that improved performance. In itself, this pushes standards up. But more importantly, these firms are given incentives to invent new technology that will meet the BAT, to avoid the competitive disadvantage of having to buy technology from an inventor who has designed the BAT to be most efficient for their (and not someone else's) manufacturing environment. Innovative firms attempt to seize the competitive advantage from the BAT inventor by themselves inventing a new and better BAT that is more cost-efficient (for them). So the international contest between BAT and fixed-outcome standards is a contest between a global ratcheting-up of standards and a global dead-hand on environmental progress. Of course, fixed-input standards (fixed specifications of technological inputs) are even worse than fixed outcomes, because at least fixed outcomes allow for continuous improvement in the efficiency with which the outcomes are achieved.

In the debates about the content of ISO 14000, Germany actually sought to require continuous improvement in outcomes and BAT. If it had succeeded, this would have created a synergy between the two ratcheting-up mechanisms.

---

7  The UK has adopted compromises in European fora that include 'best practicable environmental option' and 'best available technology not entailing excessive cost' (Haas 1993: 156).

### Sustainable Development, the Precautionary Principle v. Economic Growth

Perhaps the most central clash of principles in debates over environmental regulation is between the principle of (ecologically) sustainable development (popularized by the Brundt-land Report, *Our Common Future*, in 1987) versus economic growth (Esty 1994: 181–92). Sustainable development is one of a set of cognate principles about reconciling the environment and economic development, including the polluter-pays principle and eco-efficiency (Schmid-heiny & Zorraquin 1996). Although this is the key rhetorical divide, it is hard to see where clear victories for sustainable development over growth have been given a concrete institutional form. It might be no more than a new discourse though, as Dryzek (1996) says, discourses are the software of institutions (with rules as the hardware) – and software matters. The most that could be claimed is some shift in the balance of policy deliberation, toward sustainability. On the other hand, we have seen publications by the Asian Development Bank and the Inter-American Development Bank impugn mistaken unsustainable growth strategies in favour of sustainable development alternatives (Porter & Brown 1991: 31).

One way of giving concrete institutional meaning to global regulation toward sustainable development would be for the International Monetary Fund to demand environmentally adjusted national accounts of members. The IMF is doing technical development work on this possibility, though it is hardly advanced. The World Bank in 1995 published a new league table of national wealth that included natural resources in the calculation of per capita endowments. Until a nation-state does show a lead by solving the technical problems and putting a persuasive model of environ-mentally adjusted national accounts on the table, sustainable development will probably remain a rhetorical rather than an institutional principle. The same can be said of the precautionary princi-ple, which means that when there are threats of serious or irreversible environmental damage, lack of scientific certainty should not be used as a reason for stalling action which, on the balance of probabilities, might prevent the damage. The precautionary principle tends to lose in rhetorical battles with the principle of deregulation unless it is institutionalized through a legal commitment to BAT and best available practice. Interestingly, it was in Germany during the 1980s that the polit-ical influence of the greens gave birth to the precautionary principle.

We regularly see a contest over venues for global regimes which maps onto the contest over principles. For example, the UNEP (which is more supportive of the precautionary principle) has been supported by green groups as a more appropriate venue for decision-making in pesticide regimes, while the OECD and the FAO (which are less supportive of the precautionary principle and more supportive of deregulation) have been the venues more supported by agricultural inter-ests (Paarlberg 1993).

### Transparency, Harmonization, Mutual Recognition, National Treatment, Most Favoured Nation

The principle of transparency is increasingly institutionalized through the globalization of right-to-know regulatory reforms both by states and self-regulatory schemes such as Responsible Care. A variety of UN agencies have coordinated registers of toxic substances and research evidence on environmental impacts, reporting and inspection by representatives of treaty secretariats or other states. The Convention for the Regulation of Whaling was amended in 1977 to establish an Inter-national Observer Scheme. This provides for voluntary bilateral exchanges of observers on whaling vessels and at land stations. The observers increase transparency, thereby hopefully increasing assurance and reducing cheating, by making reports to the International Whaling Commission. Public reporting of environmental audit results for specific companies has been a central issue in the debate on environmental management standards within the International Organization for Standardization, national and European standard-setting authorities. In these senses, the transparency principle has been a major resource for environmental NGOs and one of the principles US and Asian business succeeded in watering down in the move from EMAS to ISO 14000 globally.

Both harmonization and mutual recognition are principles which have prevailed in different environmental regulatory contexts. Even within the same regime, such as the OECD chemicals regime, both principles operate, depending on the context. The choice partly depends on the interests of the large chemical manufacturers. They have pushed for harmonization upwards when their home-base government has already pushed them to a higher standard. Yet they support mutual recognition for an area such as monitoring good laboratory practice for chemicals testing, to gain maximum flexibility in where they do their research and in using data from one country to persuade regulators in another. Within Europe, mutual recognition has much less support as a principle of environmental regulation than in other areas of regulation: 'Mutual recognition of national standards is generally not appropriate in environment. Generally the view throughout the community is support for harmonization rather than mutual recognition' (1994 interview, German Environment Ministry).

National treatment (identical treatment for imports and similar domestic products) is a principle that has been dear to major chemicals producers. They want a liberal trading regime that does not require higher standards of them than of their domestic competitors in other nations in which they trade. Environmental NGOs support the principle, in insisting that foreign products imported into their state should meet domestic standards of environmental regulation. Reciprocity becomes a more important operative principle than national treatment or Most Favoured Nation when two countries discharge effluent into the same ecosystem. Effluent standards for each country will depend less on what is being expected of other polluters in other places within that country than on the controls offered by the other nation(s) polluting the same basin. For example, standards for Spanish polluters of the Mediterranean will depend less on what is expected of Spanish polluters into the Atlantic, than on what is settled reciprocally with other Mediterranean states under the Mediterranean Action Plan. Because of the principle of reciprocity, what Bilbao does on sewage treatment is less important to what Barcelona does, than what Egypt does.

Principles are mutually reinforcing. We have seen that companies that accept the principle of world's best practice are also likely to commit to the principle of continuous improvement, for example. In commenting on this chapter, Dr Robyn Eckersley provided a rather interesting reading (Table 12.1) of the relationships we have suggested among principles and the way different actors put them into play.

## Mechanisms

### Coercion

Coercion, either military or economic, has been relatively unimportant in constituting global environmental regimes in comparison with the other regimes in this book. Young and Osherenko's (1993) study of five polar regimes showed this systematically. In the future, wars may be

**TABLE 12.1**  Robyn Eckersley's summary of the appropriation of principles by different actors that can lead to races-to-the-bottom or top

| RACE-TO-THE-BOTTOM | RACE-TO-THE-TOP |
| --- | --- |
| Principle of lowest-cost location | Principle of world's best practice |
| **State response**<br>deregulatory strategy<br>delegitimates environmental NGOs<br>'no [economic] regrets'<br>resister of international regimes | **State response**<br>strategic trade strategy<br>legitimates moderate environmental NGOs<br>precautionary principle<br>progressive broker of international regimes |
| **Corporate sector**<br>reluctant rule compliance<br><br><br><br>threat of capital strike/flight<br><br>job blackmail, divide-and-rule | **Corporate sector**<br>energetic continuous improvement (BAT, world's best practice)<br>environmental management certification regimes, strategic modelling<br>close attention to green PR, generous environmental donor<br>strategic communication or alliance with leading environmental NGOs |
| **National environmental NGOs**<br>oppositional/radical<br>mass mobilization and public demonstrations<br>few links with industry or ministries/bureaucracies<br>symbolic use of media | **National environmental NGOs**<br>cooperative<br>behind-the-scenes negotiation or cooperation<br>close links with some industries and ministries/bureaucracy<br>'normal' use of media |

fought over environmental catastrophes (Homer-Dixon 1994; Levy 1995) and then perhaps environmental regulation may be imposed as part of peace settlements.

In regard to using coercion to enforce regimes, rather than constituting them, many environmental treaties do contain provisions for trade sanctions. But actual use has been virtually non-existent, both bilaterally and multilaterally. Very occasionally, the US threatens trade retaliation over an environmental matter, as it did in persuading Taiwan to phase out CFCs[8] and dissuading Norway from resuming whaling, but it has never actually imposed trade sanctions over an environmental issue. NGOs like Greenpeace and the World Wide Fund for Nature are slightly more willing than states to seek to mobilize enforcement action against states for failure to comply with international regimes (e.g. Sands & Bedcarre 1990: 819–21). This is facilitated when international agreements, such as the 1974 Nordic Convention on the Protection of the Environment, permit nationals of one state to bring proceedings in the courts and administrative tribunals of another state (in the case of the Nordic Convention, in the country from which transboundary pollution emanates) or when local courts can deal with off-shore actions of nationals, as in the Antarctic Environment Protocol (Hurrell & Kingsbury 1992: 29).

---

8  The chief US ozone negotiator also predicted that unless cuts in the CFCs happened at Montreal, Congress would unilaterally legislate to ban imports with CFCs, a prediction that seemed to affect Japan's thinking (Young & Osherenko 1993: 161; see also De Sombre 1995).

What is more common is national enforcement, where the national enforcement procedures are subject to mutual recognition. For example, the OECD good laboratory practice regime for chemicals control is subject to mutual recognition of compliance procedures based on laboratory inspection by national governments and self-audit by laboratories (Lonngren 1992: 303). The OECD acts as a clearing-house for these compliance procedures. In some states, criminal sanctions can be used for non-compliance; in others, civil penalties only apply. The Convention on International Trade in Endangered Species of Wild Fauna and Flora (CITES) has a global system of trade controls based on mandatory uniform export permits enforced by the 106 member governments (Sand 1991a). Increasingly, international environmental regimes rely on states requiring private certification of compliance within other states with whom they trade. For example, the Geneva company, Société Générale de Surveillance (SGS), through its subsidiaries in 140 nations, provides inspection services for various kinds of environmental quality certification. As discussed in Chapter 20, this privatized enforcement can have the major advantage (compared with state enforcement) of being more likely to be free of corruption. Corruption to circumvent implementation of global regimes has been a problem in domains like the international trade in hazardous wastes (Porter & Brown 1991: 85).

The significance of the use of third parties for securing compliance has been increasingly recognized in studies of domestic and international regulation (Heimer 1985; Grabosky 1995, Gunningham & Grabosky 1998). Mitchell has documented how national imposition of penalties for intentional oil spills (pursuant to the International Convention for the Prevention of Pollution from Ships (MARPOL)) has been rare and ineffective (Mitchell 1993, 1994a) What has been effective has been an equipment MARPOL subregime which enforces the installation of segregated ballast tanks and crude oil washing. The data suggest 98 per cent compliance with this subregime (Mitchell 1994a: 437), contrary to predictions of minimal compliance that were grounded in an economic analysis of regulation (Okidi 1978: 34). One reason why the equipment subregime achieved compliance, but the discharge subregime didn't, was transparency (Mitchell 1994a: 445). It is easy to check whether a tanker has segregated ballast tanks but hard to catch it actually discharging at sea.

The second critical factor is the role of third-party enforcers on whom the operators are dependent, and who have no economic interest in avoiding the considerable costs of the regulation. These third-party enforcers are builders, classification societies and insurance companies. Builders have no interest in building cheaper ships if those ships will not get certification by international classification societies nominated by national governments, for failing to meet the standards enforced by those societies. Classification societies have no interest in corrupting the standards they enforce, which are the whole reason for the generation of their income. Insurers will not insure ships which have not been accepted by a classification society, because they have an interest in reducing the liabilities that might arise from oil spills. Even if an operator can find a builder who will build an illegal ship, a classification society which will certify it and an insurer who will insure it, it will be at risk whenever its transparently non-compliant ship enters a port with inspectors from a state that takes the regime seriously. The discharge subregime did not work because most states, particularly oil-exporting states, had little interest in enforcing it (Mitchell 1994a: 447). The few developed oil-importing states who took the regime seriously had limited opportunities to catch offenders in their own waters. With the equipment subregime, however, the small number of states who take the regime seriously can eventually catch a violator of the equipment standards when an offending ship enters one of their ports. When standards are designed so that compliance is transparent and subject to enforcement opportunities by all nations, a few nations who take enforcement seriously may be enough to do the job. If compliance is opaque, even if all states are serious about enforcement it may not be enough. More fundamentally, as Mitchell (1994a: 449) expresses it, the lesson is that compliance with rules with high compliance costs can be achieved 'by ensuring that those actors with incentives to monitor compliance also had the practical ability and legal authority to do so'. Put another way, what we have is a regulatory strategy that changes the behaviour of soft targets such as insurers (who are soft because they have no interest in resisting the regulation). The regulated actors (tanker operators) are so dependent on these soft targets that they do not resist their regulatory demands. Finally, a key difference between the equipment subregime and the discharge regime is that while the latter is based on a thin line of deterrence after the event, the equipment subregime is based on redundant prevention (by builders, classification agencies, insurers and states).

To summarize this long story on the use of coercion to enforce compliance with regimes, supranational enforcement is virtually non-existent in environmental regimes; the most common enforcement strategy is some kind of mutual recognition of national or even private enforcement (as the critical roles of classification societies, insurers and ship-builders with MARPOL illustrates) (Sand 1991a). Moreover, most environmental regimes do not even allow for compulsory jurisdiction for dispute settlement. Multilateral agreements typically give each party a veto against reference to arbitration or to the International Court of Justice, 'usually by stipulating that third-party adjudication requires common agreement' (Sand 1991b: 257), though newer UNEP conventions provide for states to waive this veto right upon signature of the treaty. Notwithstanding the irrelevance of the International Court of Justice to environmental enforcement, in the international relations community there is a degree of optimism that Morgenthau may have been right when he said: 'the great majority of the rules of international law are generally observed by all nations' (Morgenthau 1978: 299). To understand how this optimism might not be totally misplaced, we need to consider other mechanisms of globalization.

### Systems of Reward

Carrots, for example subsidies to assist developing countries shift to ozone-friendly technology, have been used a little more often than sticks. But in no regime have systems of reward been substantial and in few have they been central to making the regime work. The most substantial investment in carrots has been the Global Environmental Facility (GEF), funded by the rich nations pursuant to Agenda 21 of the Rio Summit and administered under the auspices of the World Bank, UNEP and UNDP. One purpose of the GEF is to identify and fund projects in developing countries and Eastern Europe that reduce environmental destruction, but that are not profitable from a national point of view if the environmental effects are ignored. In addition, countries tend not to get GEF money unless they promise to do something for the environment. The EU's Cohesion Fund has to some extent been used as a 'financial carrot for backward regions to upgrade on environment and transport infrastructure' (EC interview).

Another important carrot has been debt-for-environment swaps that have allowed countries like Poland to make massive investments in environmental protection with debt money forgiven by the Paris Club of creditor nations. Indeed, Poland became so well-resourced for environmental innovation that it offers a number of new frontiers in regulatory models for the environment. Poland has been an exception among debtor nations in benefiting from debt-for-environment swaps, and even in its case most of its creditors, including big ones like Japan, are uninterested in forgiving debt for environmental progress.

Although expenditures on rewards for environmental responsibility in developing countries by rich countries has been very modest, within UN agencies major research and epistemic community-building projects are underway which provide incentives for green production. We have already mentioned the IMF's analytical work on environmentally adjusted national accounts (see also Schneider 1994). The most important consensus-building work, however, has been on models for global carbon taxes or carbon trading, particularly UNCTAD's (1992) *Combating Global Warming: Study on a Global System of Tradable Carbon Emission Entitlements*. Because carbon dioxide emissions, mainly from fossil-fuel consumption, have been responsible for more than half the enhancement of the greenhouse effect, global-warming research focuses on the idea of systems of reward for reducing fossil-fuel consumption.

In an effort to discover the lowest-cost means of reducing emissions while giving developing countries a chance to experience higher living standards, one option is adapting the off-sets idea (from national regulation) to cross-border trading of pollution abatement. This means allowing nations to earn credits toward pollution-abatement obligations under a global regime by paying for abatement in another country. For example, a rich country with sophisticated pollution-control technology, such as Germany, will find it much more expensive to reduce its own emissions by a given amount than to pay another country to deliver the same reduction to global emissions, at lower cost. Alternatively, poor countries could sell tradable pollution entitlements they do not yet require to rich countries who pay for investment in abatement within the poor country. This might require a new international agency to monitor emissions, record transfers of credits arising from off-sets and enforce compliance (UNCTAD 1992: IV), perhaps even a Global Environmental Organization rather like the WTO (Esty 1994: 78–83; Ayling 1997). The technical problems in making this work are a major challenge. Nevertheless, against bitter opposition, the US succeeded in including a clause in the 1997 Kyoto Protocol on greenhouse-gas emissions to allow emissions trading – one state buying reductions accomplished by other states, to apply them against the purchaser's quota.

An additional option would be international agreement for all nations to introduce carbon taxes, set them at a minimum level and increase them at an agreed rate. But the resistance of coal-producing TNCs in states like the US, Australia, Colombia and South Africa, of oil producers in the OPEC states, and of the large developing states whose growth of greenhouse-gas production is booming (China, India, Brazil), combined with the demonstrated willingness of some TNCs to threaten capital flight in response to national moves for a carbon tax, makes progress extraordinarily difficult (Rowlands 1995). New Zealand has developed the interesting compromise of committing in advance to a carbon tax if its industry fails to achieve emission reduction targets by other means.

Overall, the reward mechanism is not shaping up as very important for global environmental regimes. However, it is a crucial mechanism for the future and the decision at Kyoto to allow states to be paid for reducing greenhouse-gas emissions below their targets, by states which fail to do so, is a significant first step.

## Modelling

Modelling has been a much more important mechanism in the globalization of environmental regulation than coercion or economic incentives. The biggest changes had small beginnings. Innovative companies that were environmental leaders began in the 1970s to develop models of environmental auditing and reporting on stewardship for the entire lifecycle of products. For example, the Responsible Care Program began in Canada (Gunningham 1995, Gunningham & Grabosky 1998). This was picked up by the US Chemical Manufacturers Association and eventually spread throughout the world by global companies. These intracorporate self-regulatory models were picked up by some lead states, such as the Netherlands (Aalders 1991), which started programs to encourage companies to voluntarily commit to higher environmental management standards through transparency and a spirit of dialogue with green groups. The Business Council on Sustainable Development (an initiative of the ICC) has joined the bandwagon, producing guidelines on environmental auditing, entitled *Coming Clean*, that were commended to us by Greenpeace. The British Standards Institute developed an environmental management standard (BS 7750) in 1994. This ultimately led to the EC producing regulations on environmental management and eco-labelling standards, and the ISO adopting much from these models in its environmental management standard-setting described earlier (Cascio 1994). As we argued there, the potential for these processes of self-regulatory modelling to ratchet-up environmental standards through continuous improvement is considerable. If firms are under public pressure to report improvements annually, they will be continually on the lookout for new self-regulatory models that can raise their environmental performance. The modelling mechanism works through private networks as well as public. A procedure carried out by DuPont in relation to groundwater assessment can become a regulation in Singapore. Through global private networks significant environmental knowhow can be transferred to developing countries.

A common belief among senior bureaucrats in international agencies is that environmental progress most often comes from international cooperation to expose the best practices of innovators to other leading companies, who then become models for the diffusion of the innovation in their own countries. When we challenged them during interviews with the assertion that it was naive to think that industry will voluntarily move to higher international standards, without being forced to do so by regulation, they replied with statements like the following from an OECD chemicals division official: 'You get the risk reduction data and strategies out to industry and they'll get moving. That's my experience. The alternative is to wait for consensus of all twenty-three [OECD] governments. But by the time you get it, industry usually have moved already'. A shift to a somewhat parallel way of thinking was evident in interviews with some environment movement leaders. For example, Greenpeace's policy director told us that Greenpeace was shifting its energies to pressure on business firms rather than pressure on governments, in the belief that it was a quicker way to make progress. The key to the spread of a particular program like Responsible Care may be that global companies are usually in leadership positions in national associations of companies. Once such companies have become convinced of the validity of a program, they can spread it rapidly through their global networks.

The importance to NGOs of being able to influence at least one major private player is nicely captured in the following statements from a DuPont manager. Speaking of DuPont's announcement that it would move out of CFC production, he said it was like a '500 lb gorilla saying what he was gonna do'. To some effect, environmental NGOs can prod and follow in the path of 500 lb gorillas.

Our colleague, Neil Gunningham, has long despaired about the way hazardous chemicals regulation succeeds in changing the practices of the top twenty chemicals transnationals, but barely touches thousands of little chemical companies who are too many, too unsophisticated and too dispersed to be effectively supervised by state inspectors (see, e.g., Gunningham 1995). More recently, however, Gunningham has realized that most of these little chemical companies are vitally dependent on the TNCs as suppliers, distributors or customers, or all three. This has led him to the insight that a private or public regulatory regime which requires major companies to ensure not only that its own employees comply with the regulations, but also that upstream and downstream users and suppliers of its products comply, may massively increase the effectiveness of a regime.[9] A TNC that supplies a little chemical company has much more regular contact with it than any government inspector, more intimate and technically sophisticated knowledge of 'where their bodies are buried', greater technical capacity to help it fix the problems, and has more leverage than the state. Simply, weak players have the sensible habit of modelling strong players when they want to keep doing business with them.

Modelling is the mechanism that places less-powerful actors in the world system on a more equal footing with the powerful, just as coercion is the mechanism that puts them on the least equal footing. The International Union for the Conservation of Nature effectively set the agenda in the negotiations that led to the signing of CITES in 1973, by earlier tabling a draft convention on the trade in endangered species. The weak party to some extent dictated the terms of the debate by deciding the model that was the starting-point for debate. Powerful resisters of change are reluctant to do this because they do not want to bring on a debate about change. The IUCN attempted to capture the same strength-from-weakness in the biodiversity debate by tabling a draft biological diversity Convention in 1988 (Porter & Brown 1991: 62). Young and Osherenko (1993) found empirically that, to be influential, such models must be simple. Salient models can constitute international regimes by breaking through blockages in negotiation processes, but only if they are uncomplicated formulae that advocates and journalists can encapsulate for political and public consumption.

We have found modelling to be important not only at the level of firms modelling improved self-regulatory technology, but also at the level of national laws. A good example of a law that has been modelled in at least thirty nations is the Environmental Impact Assessment procedure first introduced by the US *National Environmental Policy Act 1969*. While attempts to globalize this EIA model by way of a treaty failed in the 1970s, the failure seems of little moment given the amount of voluntary national modelling that has occurred (Sand 1991b: 262). Some models lay dormant for decades without many nations being interested, until model mongers promoted the model aggressively. For example, the epidemic of modelling effluent fees/emission charges/pollution taxes picks up a regulatory model first instituted in the Ruhr River Basin in 1904 (Sand 1991b: 263). In all the countries we visited for this research, substantial parts of national environmental protection laws were modelled from other nations' laws. Eastern Europe seemed particularly rife with environmental model mongers during the mid 1990s – a French expert touting the French model of water law, Americans touting effluent-fee models and setting up centres for environmental economics in Polish universities, Germans with best available technology models, and so on. Many of these model missionaries are funded by governments of developed countries, the EU and other international organizations to help developing and Eastern European governments adapt Western environmental protection models to their circumstances.

## Reciprocal Adjustment and Non-reciprocal Coordination

The most important mechanisms for the internationalization of environmental regulation are the simple ones of reciprocal adjustment (as in the Mediterranean Action Plan) and modelling (as in

---

9  We rely here on personal communications with Gunningham at ANU seminars. But see also Gunningham and Grabosky (1998: e.g. at 223–4).

environmental auditing). People often feel cynical about international meetings which are just talk-shops, yet it is such talk that constitutes the epistemic communities which enable reciprocal adjustment and modelling to happen. The talk within epistemic communities constitutes and transmits knowledge and thereby enables action.

Reciprocal adjustment enabled by such deliberative fora is not only about enabling win–win solutions when the interests at stake are obvious (cleaner Mediterranean beaches). International deliberation is also about discovering mutual advantages that were not obvious before. Hence, institutions of global environmental deliberation have enabled Pacific Island states to discover that it is in their interests to be active in persuading rich nations to reduce greenhouse-gas emissions, lest the islands disappear under the Pacific. Global deliberative fora have enabled nations to learn that there are economic as well as environmental costs to deforestation, such as losing the resource of genetic diversity and the kind of soil degradation that threatens the Australian and Chinese agricultural economies. Exchange of knowledge that leads to the discovery of enlightened mutual self-interest is an increasingly important mechanism of globalization.

Majone (1994) has made an important distinction between reciprocal and non-reciprocal externalities. Externalities arise when one firm or state imposes uncompensated costs on another firm or state. International externalities are reciprocal in a case such as Italians and Greeks both pouring pollutants into the Mediterranean. Both nations benefit from this pollution and both are victims of it. In circumstances of such reciprocal benefits and costs, prospects for reciprocal adjustment can be good. However, if the externalities are non-reciprocal – winds blow Italian air pollution into Greece but Greek pollution is not blown into Italy – then the nature of the externality creates no incentive for Italy to be cooperative.

Non-reciprocal coordination is still possible when externalities are non-reciprocal, by linking two non-reciprocal externalities (where the direction of damage is reversed and counterbalanced). Issue linkage can transform non-reciprocal into reciprocal externalities. Hence the wider political irony: 'Where agreement is impossible, broaden the agenda'. For example, the Italian foreign minister can say to her Greek counterpart that she will see what she can do about the air pollution concern if the Greeks will address a Greek–Italian impasse over Common Agricultural Policy concerns (e.g. olive markets). A regional institution like the EU can 'enhance the contractual environment' (Levy, Keohane & Haas 1993: 406) wherein non-reciprocal externalities can be traded. In game theoretic terms, issue linkage can create a contract zone where one formerly did not exist. A contract zone defines a set of outcomes which all parties would prefer to non-agreement. Within a contract zone, there are a set of positive sum outcomes to a negotiation game. In the Greek–Italian air pollution negotiation above there is no contract zone; in the air–olives negotiation, there is.

Creative bargaining to constitute contract zones is often more possible in the international system than in smaller systems like universities or national markets, because the number of players in the latter systems is effectively much larger than in the states system (even if we include major NGOs as players). This is more true of an agreement on whaling or seals, which affects only a small number of countries, than an agreement on greenhouse-gas emissions, that affects all.

The most ambitious attempt to link issues was probably the 1992 UN Conference on Environment and Development. The rich and poor nations had non-reciprocal interests in environment and development. The idea, weakly realized in practice, was that poor countries which were not motivated to cooperate with environmental regulation would be motivated by development assistance, and rich nations not motivated by development assistance would be motivated by the challenge of securing the global commons.

Levy, Keohane and Haas (1993) and Chayes and Chayes (1995) find that international environmental institutions do not normally improve the global situation by mobilizing sanctions against those who defy international regimes. 'Enhancing the contractual environment', as in the Mediterranean Action Plan example, is a more important effect. This is accomplished by providing bargaining fora that reduce transaction costs for reciprocal adjustment and that create an iterated decision-making process that enables progressive commitment to higher standards and to improving monitoring of environmental quality, performance and policies. In addition to enhancing the contractual environment, regimes also increase governmental concern (as in the deforestation and biodiversity case) and build national capacity (as in the modelling of Western regulatory technologies in Eastern Europe). In their empirical investigation of seven international environmental regimes, Haas, Keohane and Levy (1993) find these to be the three paths to effectiveness for international regimes. In our analysis, we conceive these as establishing the conditions where the mechanisms of reciprocal adjustment, non-reciprocal coordination and modelling can work. Across their seven environmental domains, Haas, Keohane and Levy show that their paths to regime effectiveness are not relevant to enabling the mechanism of coercion to work.

## Capacity-building

Reciprocal adjustment and regulatory modelling are restricted by the limited willingness of wealthy nations to tolerate transfer of resources to poorer countries to allow capacity-building. Many of the deepest problems, such as agricultural chemical use (Paarlberg 1993: 347) and water-resource use by farmers, have a very local character that is unlikely to be touched by spontaneous modelling without substantial investment in capacity-building, building the capacity to follow models of environmental practice. This is not to deny the various kinds of capacity-building in the South and East, with resources from the North and West, that we have discussed in this chapter. Indeed, enough of it goes on for Haas, Keohane and Levy (1993) to conclude that building national capacity is one of the three key ways to restore the environment. The costs of making a big difference through capacity-building are high, however, so it remains largely unused.

We have seen that getting maximum agreement for a broad, vague framework convention, then injecting more substance into it over time, has become a fairly general strategy with environmental agreements since the difficulties encountered with the more comprehensive Law of the Sea Treaty (Sebenius 1991). This strategy is in tune with the lessons from research such as the *Institutions for the Earth* work of Haas, Keohane and Levy (1993). Debate over a platitudinous framework convention is often the best way to hold all nations in a debate that builds concern and shares regulatory models for reducing the problem at the firm and national levels. The increasing tendency of UN agencies to give NGOs and scientific experts a prominent role in discussions gives model mongers a forum for spreading their models internationally. At the same time, the framework convention enhances the contractual environment for moving toward an agreement of substance, once national concern has increased enough and the voluntary spread of control models has reached a level where feasibility can no longer be doubted. If necessary, the onerous consensus-building demands of ratification can be bypassed by formally delegating authority for periodic amendment of standards to an international technical body.

The framework convention process at the Commission on Sustainable Development is usually associated with a process where the Commission asks signatories to analyse the problem in their own country, prepare a report on what their nation has done about the problem, and open themselves to examination by other governments. This process is also calculated to build concern and to open nations up to examining each other's regulatory models. However, capacity-building remains the sticking-point because it requires more than dialogue; it requires movement of money from rich to poor nations. Consequently, in environment, as in financial regulation (Chapter 8), we see international agreements negotiated at fora such as the OECD among like-minded wealthy countries who wish to avoid the political difficulties of building a wider consensus and funding capacity-building.

## Conclusion

Crucial developments in the globalization of environmental regulation began 140 years ago, but most major initiatives have occurred since 1970. The key actors have been nation-states, with the US by far the most important force for pushing and blocking globalization initiatives – pushing being more common than blocking. Sometimes nation-states act as agents for domestic business interests when they veto environmental regimes; sometimes they act as agents for domestic environmental movements when they support them; more often they balance the political strength of both constituencies in deciding their national position in global fora. This might lead us to expect that because environmental regulation is a cost to business and because business is usually a more powerful domestic constituency than the environmental movement, there will always be a majority of states wanting to block regimes to upgrade environmental regulation. One reason why this is false is that business power in influential nation-states such as Germany is frequently directed at persuading their state to lead others toward implementing environmental technologies in which their business has a comparative advantage. More broadly, many of the most influential concentrations of business power in all nations have become persuaded that it is better business to be a leader than a laggard on environmental standards. When domestic environmental movements do succeed in upgrading regulation in a minority of nations, the business communities in those nations can become supporters of global upgrading to the same standard in order to level the playing field with their competitors.

More simply, if the green markets are very large, other nation-states must upgrade to the new standards if they wish to do business there. We are persuaded by Vogel's (1995) empirical findings with respect to global environmental regulation, that the Delaware effect is less powerful than the California effect – there is more ratcheting-up than racing down (but compare Swire's (1996) analysis). Vogel's (1995: 263) analysis also shows empirically that the trade treaties that have done most to reduce the use of regulation as a trade barrier have also done most to ratchet-up the stringency of regulation (e.g. the Single European Act).

This does not change the fact that ratcheting-up is from a low base of environmental protection. Business power continues to prevent the kinds of global regulatory regimes which might give the planet a sustainable future. For many in business, the principles of lowest-cost location and deregulation are more tangible, easier to understand, than the principle of world's best practice. New treaties have been added to the stock each year, to the point where their cumulation has led to a kind of treaty fatigue – in a domain where treaties tend to lead most national laws, where globalization is substantially treaty-driven in contrast with the substantially custom-driven globalization of the law of property and contract (Chapter 7). The treaties typically offer only symbolic victories to environmentalists – they are vague statements of intention with infrequent provision for enforcement of specific commitments. However, international NGOs find increasing appeal in these framework conventions because they have found that if they bide their time, the opportunity might come to include specificity. Often the upgrading of the commitments and enforceability of international environmental agreements does not even need the agency of NGOs. Direct pressure on states from mass publics communicated through the mass media, often in response to crises, do the trick. Both mass publics and organized social movements have been more influential on global environmental regimes than on the other types of regimes discussed in this book.

As the Harvard Institutions of the Earth research group concluded, global regulatory regimes that are strategically vague allow nations to move at differing paces toward a stronger commitment to environmental improvement:

> The studies at Harvard reveal four types of national policy responses. Some countries simply avoid international obligations by failing to sign treaty commitments. Others accept commitments but fail to live up to them. A third group accepts commitments and achieves compliance. Finally, a fourth group surpasses the explicitly required obligations. Effective institutions nudge countries further along this continuum of commitment and compliance (Levy, Keohane & Haas 1992: 14).

Effective institutions also nudge TNCs to surpass the commitments of the states in which they operate. They do this through the way global institutions directly affect firms' practices, via mechanisms such as modelling. The Institutions for the Earth project also concluded that with global environmental institutions, 'promoting re-evaluations of state [we might add TNC] interests was more important than forcing behaviour against a state's interest' (Levy, Keohane & Haas 1992: 398).

Many environmental regimes at first achieve no more than facilitation of a dialogue which increases governmental concern and thereby allows states to re-evaluate their interests. Until states recognize that they have an interest in, for example, preventing global warming, there is no possibility of considering any further coordinated action. But once that has been accomplished, work can begin on dialogue toward settling international norms, then national capacity-building toward satisfying those norms (e.g. transfer of technology and management knowhow), then moving from norms to rules, then to actual enforcement of the rules. What global environmental regimes accomplish is an 'enhanced contractual environment' (Levy, Keohane & Haas 1992: 406), bargaining fora for iterated decision-making, wherein this kind of dynamic can unfold. There is political necessity about a dynamic that moves from dialogue to build concern, to norms and capacity-building, to rules, to enforced rules. There can be no enforcement until there are rules, no rules until global consensus-building has generated norms, no norms until there is concern. Most commentators on international regimes assume that the geopolitics of such a dynamic are unfortunate, because regimes are only symbolic until the final enforceability stage is reached. On the contrary, the gradualism which is a geopolitical necessity with global regimes may also be a virtue, a virtue unavailable to domestic regulatory regimes which have the legitimacy to rush prematurely to rule-enforcement (Ayres & Braithwaite 1992: Ch. 2). The idea here, supported by research evidence, is that concern, norms and capacity build faster when they are not induced by threat (see generally Brehm & Brehm 1981). It is best to introduce threat only after the progress that can be made without it has been secured.

The globalization of the economy has increased opportunities to find the lowest-cost location for industry. In industries where environmental costs are unusually high, investment can be shifted to states with less-demanding environmental standards, encouraging a race-to-the-bottom of regulatory standards to attract investment. However, we have also seen that globalization introduces dynamics that push in the opposite direction. We have seen how a best available technology or a best available practice approach to environmental standards can ratchet standards up, just as fixed-outcome standards degrade the planet as producers increase their pollution to the fixed limit. We have seen how environmental management certification regimes which require audited demonstration of continuous improvement can also harness private actors to ratchet environmental performance upwards. It follows that a mindless structural determinism based on a static analysis of global power will not produce a useful understanding of whether the world will experience a race-to-the-bottom or a race-to-the-top. That is decided for any substantive problem through strategic action by actors with the capacity to enrol regulatory regimes to their projects. Threats of capital flight are a strategic resource for those wanting to drive global standards down; strategic modelling, insinuation of BAT, and the precautionary, strategic trade and continuous improvement principles are resources for those who want to drive them up.

## History of Globalization

### Eisenhower's Historic Bargain

The history of nuclear regulation is the shortest, but among the most intriguing, in this book. This is a study of business regulation, so the regulation of the military uses of nuclear power by states is beyond its scope. Nevertheless, the history of the regulation of commercial nuclear applications cannot be understood in a way that is divorced from the geopolitics of nuclear weapons. The story begins with the Manhattan Project sponsored by the US to develop atom-splitting technology during the Second World War (Hawkins 1983). After the atom bomb descended on Japan in 1945, the US pursued a policy of unilateralist control of nuclear technology, a policy which had an eye to both military hegemony and commercial monopoly. After the Soviet nuclear program detonated an atom bomb in 1949, the US continued to struggle for a Western monopoly of the technology, just as the Soviets monopolized the technology within the Soviet bloc. But in 1952, the UK detonated its first bomb and the genie seemed out of the bottle (Simpson 1983). In December 1953, President Eisenhower abandoned the policy of sole US control of nuclear technology by announcing in a speech to the UN the 'Atoms for Peace' program which laid the foundations for the establishment of the International Atomic Energy Agency (IAEA).

Atoms for Peace meant that the US would release a great amount of scientific and technical information on nuclear energy and supply enriched uranium, heavy water and other essential materials through the UN agency (IAEA) to nations who committed to controls to ensure the materials would be used for peaceful purposes (Scheinman 1987: 18). Following this announcement of intent, nuclear energy production was privatized in the US in 1954. After the *Atomic Energy Act 1954*, US companies in the electrical equipment engineering sector embarked on an era of world domination of nuclear power production. The Atomic Energy Commission (AEC) was transformed from a monopoly public producer of nuclear technology to a regulator of private production. The next step was for the US to enter bilateral agreements with cooperative countries for transfer of nuclear technology and materials in exchange for safeguards against diversion to non-peaceful use. These safeguards were guaranteed though inspections on foreign soil by US inspectors. The US strategy was one we see replicated in a number of our chapters – strategic bilateral agreements designed to set a framework for a subsequent multilateral agreement.

But the UK, then France, posed problems for this US strategy. UK scientists had contributed enormously to the Manhattan Project. The 1945–53 US policy of hegemonic control of nuclear technology had been in violation of the 1943 Quebec Agreement on postwar sharing of the technology. Finally the UK, but not France, was granted access to certain US military nuclear technology in exchange for US access to UK technology in 1955 (Simpson 1983: 114–16) and more fully with the signing of the Anglo-American Military Agreement for Cooperation in 1958 (Simpson 1983: 142–3). While France had not contributed as much as the UK to the Manhattan Project, nor had it gained the access to the inner sanctums of the project that UK scientists had, France acquired and developed sufficient technology to emerge as the major commercial rival to the US in the nuclear power industry, even though it did not detonate its first military device until 1960.

## EURATOM Helps Create Europe

French leadership was important in the establishment of EURATOM in 1957 (the UK did not become a member until 1973). While the establishment of IAEA was more important to the globalization of nuclear regulation, EURATOM was of greater importance to the globalization of business regulation more generally, because EURATOM was a major step toward the ultimate creation of the EU (Howlett 1990: 19–31). Without even considering its military significance, it is hard to understand today how nuclear power was seen in the 1950s as an economic issue. Cost-efficient nuclear power was perceived to be the path all nations would follow to competitive energy self-sufficiency. As the Chairman of the US AEC touted in 1954: 'It is not too much to expect that our children will enjoy in their homes electrical energy too cheap to meter' (Ford 1982: 50). The mistake is to see EURATOM as just another consequence of progressive European economic and political integration. Rather, the nuclear technology imperative was a cause of that process. In 1950 the European coal and steel community provided the first model for the integration of Europe. But by the mid 1950s, 'nuclear energy was gradually replacing coal and steel as the catalyst for cooperation in the region' (Howlett 1990: 20). When Belgium, the Netherlands and Luxembourg called for the 'Relaunch of Europe' in the Benelux Memorandum of 1955, nuclear power was cited as especially important in accomplishing European unity through economic integration. A reason the UK dropped out of the process of European integration in the 1950s was that, having a special bilateral nuclear relationship with the US, it did not want to become part of EURATOM, which became a 'Group of Six' institution – France, West Germany, Italy, Belgium, the Netherlands, Luxembourg (Howlett 1990: 22).

At a 1956 meeting of the pro-European integration group, the Action Committee for a United States of Europe, which was attended by the foreign ministers of the six, a group was established to study how integration could be advanced. This study group came to be known as the 'Three Wise Men' – Louis Armand (France), Franz Etzel (Germany) and Francesco Giordeni (Italy). The three wise men went to the US to persuade US Secretary of State Dulles and the US AEC that establishing EURATOM would be in US interests. This they did. The US agreed in principle to transfer technology and nuclear materials to EURATOM (Howlett 1990: 31). In many ways, however, the US remained suspicious of EURATOM as a third force that might unite Europe militarily and economically in a way it could not control. This suspicion was more deeply felt by the UK and the Soviet Union, who opposed the formation of EURATOM.

US suspicions were sufficient for it to refuse to support EURATOM's construction of a gaseous diffusion plant for the production of enriched uranium, support that was essential if the plant were to be built. Instead, EURATOM had to import enriched uranium from the US and then inspect the plants in member states in accordance with protocols set by the US. Needless to say, allowing inspectors from a regional agency to perpetrate 'legalized espionage' on the soil of sovereign states was a major step for Europe. Even so, allowing EURATOM inspection was viewed as a less complete sacrifice of sovereignty than welcoming US inspectors, as was required under the bilateral agreements signed until then. A France keen to compete with the US in the commercial exploitation of nuclear power wanted to get access to US technology without having US inspectors in its plants as potential agents of industrial espionage.

Raymond Aron considered the 1956 French National Assembly debate on the EURATOM Treaty 'the greatest ideological debate to have occurred in France since the time of the Dreyfus affair' (Howlett 1990: 61). This was understandable because a US objective was regional rather than national control of nuclear technology (constrained by US hegemony) that would exclude its NATO partners from independent nuclear production and thereby from 'equal strategic control of the [NATO] alliance' (Nieburg 1963: 130).[1] In one US view, EURATOM would prevent the creation of new nuclear weapons capabilities in Europe. In another view, if there were going to be a new nuclear weapon capability in Europe, better that it be EURATOM-controlled than nationally controlled (Howlett 1990: 46–8). At the same time, the US felt EURATOM would help strengthen Western Europe economically in a way that would bolster NATO. Three US policy goals with respect to EURATOM – non-proliferation, European integration and selling US nuclear technology – were all seen as enhancing a US-dominated and strong NATO.

EURATOM's centrality to the progress of European integration was short-lived. By 1957 a new institution, the EEC, formally created by treaty in Rome at the same time as EURATOM, was set to become more important and wider ranging in its integrative impact than EURATOM would ever be. Moreover, in the sphere of nuclear regulation, EURATOM was destined, when the Treaty on the Non-Proliferation of Nuclear Weapons (NPT) came into effect after 1970, to become a subsidiary agency to the UN organ which was the vehicle of US hegemony, IAEA. This was not so during the first decade of EURATOM and IAEA, which were established at the same time. During the decade to the mid 1960s, EURATOM managed to get a credible auditing and inspection system in place while IAEA struggled to do so. As a UN agency, IAEA had the massive problem of the Soviet Union to deal with. But by the mid 1960s international support for IAEA grew, particularly from the Soviet Union, which withdrew its previous opposition to the whole concept of the agency (Scheinman 1987: 267). This was a Soviet Union which (after the Cuban missile crisis) was exploring arms control agreement with the US and feared China becoming a nuclear weapons state, as happened in 1964. If the first decade of the IAEA was of US hegemony over it, the second decade was rather a cooperative US–Soviet hegemony, followed by a third decade in which 'Third World member states began to make their presence felt within the agency' (Scheinman 1987: 267). Since the collapse of the Soviet empire, there has been a return to the US hegemony which characterized IAEA during its first decade.

In the 1970s parallel EURATOM and IAEA regimes were replaced by a more integrated arrangement where most European inspection was done by EURATOM, but subject to oversight

---

1 The report of the Princeton University Conference on EURATOM and American Policy said that one of the 'advantages for the United States' of EURATOM inspections was that 'the US could depend on the French to watch the Germans, the Germans to watch the French, and the smaller nations to watch both the French and the Germans' (Knorr 1956: 13–14).

and independent inspections by IAEA to ensure that non-nuclear weapon states in the European Community were complying with IAEA regulations. This forced further convergence of EURATOM standards (which had already been substantially modelled on the requirements in bilateral agreements between the US and other states and on US law itself) with IAEA standards (which were substantially dictated by the US). The nuclear weapons states, France and the UK (which had joined the EC in 1973), were formally subject to the safeguards requirements of EURATOM but not IAEA. However, they reached voluntary agreements to submit their civil, not military, nuclear programs to both EURATOM and IAEA control. The safeguards regime in Europe is theoretically interesting in the way states are not directly involved: an international organization (IAEA) monitors the inspection program of a regional organization (EURATOM) which in turn exercises direct control within the territory of member states.

### Supplier Groups

The next major boost to the globalization of the safeguards regime to prevent the diversion of nuclear materials came with the shock of the detonation of an Indian bomb in 1974, just as IAEA had been a reaction to the disaster of the UK acquiring the bomb. In the 1950s a key part of the US strategy for getting all nations to submit to IAEA had been to secretly secure the commitment of all the uranium suppliers at the time – the UK, Canada, South Africa, France, Belgium, Australia and Portugal – to supply only to states participating in the IAEA regime (Simons 1994: 75–6). After the Indian debacle, the US saw a need to organize a more inclusive club of supplier states, not only suppliers of uranium but all the key suppliers of processed nuclear materials and nuclear technologies.

In 1975 the London Nuclear Suppliers Group was formed by the US, the USSR, the UK, West Germany, Japan, France and Canada, with Belgium, the Netherlands, Italy, Sweden, Switzerland, Czechoslovakia, East Germany and Poland joining later. The group submitted a trigger-list of material and facilities to IAEA (Hatch 1986: 122) which would be subject to the London Guidelines on the transfer of sensitive technologies. The key requirements involved assurances by the importing government to explicitly exclude uses which might result in a nuclear explosive (Jones et al. 1985). The London Suppliers Group agreed essentially to greater 'prudence' in its technology transfers and to clear them with IAEA for any technologies on the trigger-list.

The US backed this up with bilateral teeth through its *Nuclear Non-Proliferation Act 1978*. The Act provided for the immediate cessation of US exports to non-nuclear weapon states which violated IAEA safeguards or to states which violated any arrangement the US had entered into (such as the London Guidelines) on the transfer of nuclear technology. The Act created serious tensions within NATO when it was used by the US as a non-tariff barrier to favour US exports over West German transfers of nuclear technology in circumstances where the acquisition of nuclear weapons by the importer did not seem to be the issue (Hatch 1986: 124–34). The EURATOM states, led by France, resisted some of the provisions in the US Act. Notwithstanding these glitches, the work of the London Suppliers Group, backed by bilateral US sanctions, amounted to a significant strengthening of the regime for the regulation of nuclear technology.

### Two Regimes, One Set of Institutions

From the beginning, both EURATOM and IAEA were concerned with nuclear safety as well as safeguarding against the diversion of peaceful nuclear materials and technologies to weapons programs. Similarly with the US AEC (later the Nuclear Regulatory Commission, NRC) and most national regulatory agencies. From the beginning, Atoms for Peace had a capacity-building ethos. In return for playing the nuclear game by US rules, IAEA and EURATOM would help with transfer of technology, uranium, heavy water and other inputs. This meant primarily rules about weapons safeguards, but because the safety rules were part of the same IAEA package, nuclear safety globalized under the impetus of both the carrot of technology transfer and the stick of nuclear power politics backed by US trade sanctions (and indeed under the threat of US military might, witness Iraq). It is important to recognize the very secondary status of safety regulation compared to safeguards regulation. The NRC, commenting on a draft of this chapter, said: 'little or no IAEA attention was given to safety compliance until recent years and, even now, the "stick" which IAEA can wield is to withhold future assistance and to disclose information about poor safety practices to other governments and the public at large, actions which it is reluctant to exercise'.

The IAEA, AEC and EURATOM were all captured by the nuclear establishment of nuclear engineers, scientists and nuclear power producers. They all had an interest in the technology being rendered safer as well as in preventing it from falling into the hands of rogue states and terrorists. So safeguards against nuclear weapons proliferation and the industrial and environmental safety of nuclear production were both part of legitimating a future for nuclear technology. The one set of institutions – IAEA, AEC, EURATOM – administered two regimes, one we will call a safeguards regime, the other a safety regime. The safeguards regime protected against diversion of nuclear materials and technology to weapons programs by strict licensing and exporting controls and by assuring material accounts balance. This meant finely meshed accounting at the national, within-plant and within-room levels to ensure that every gram of nuclear material was accounted for as having been used for an inspectable peaceful purpose. The safety regime, in contrast, was primarily about assurance that the design and operating procedures of nuclear plants were redundantly secure against a major accident. They were also required to prevent radiation exposure and environmental harm.

## The Rise of Self-regulation in the Safety Regime

In 1975 the regulatory and industry development functions of the US AEC were split, industry development going to the Department of Energy, regulation going to a new Nuclear Regulatory Commission. After the Three Mile Island disaster discredited the hardware-oriented minimum-standards approach of the NRC, a nuclear industry self-regulatory association, INPO (the Institute of Nuclear Power Operations, established 1980) acquired a significance almost comparable to that of the NRC. This significance was limited to nuclear safety; it (and later the World Association of Nuclear Operators) was not involved with safeguards regulation. INPO's Board of Directors, elected by industry members of the Institute, consists largely of CEOs of companies which produce nuclear power. INPO is not an arm of a wider industry association which lobbies on behalf of the industry; it is an industry body whose function is the promotion of nuclear plant safety. It has about 370 staff and spends 'about equal to the budget of the Federal Trade Commission' (Rees 1994: 1). Its staff is supplemented by industry peer-reviewers who are temporarily assigned from their plant to inspect a similar one: 'On the typical INPO inspection that goes to a nuclear plant [for about two weeks on-site], as many as six peer evaluators are among its twenty or so members' (Rees 1994: 54).

In 1989, the INPO model globalized with the formation of the World Association of Nuclear Operators (WANO). Within four years globalization was total, with every nuclear power plant operator in the world becoming a member of WANO, submitting to its self-regulatory regime. WANO is still building legitimacy; it does not demand as much from its members as INPO does, since some of WANO's members are nuclear basket-cases. Its resources are meagre in comparison with INPO's; there were only about sixty WANO staff by 1996, with most work being done by peer reviewers and others from member plants.

INPO (and later WANO) became a major force in nuclear regulation after Three Mile Island 'not so much to stave off state intervention, but to accomplish what they [industry] believe the state cannot – a possibility that the corporatist and organization literatures have neglected' (Campbell 1988: 2). This may be overstated since at least some industry informants in Rees' study saw the avoidance of overly prescriptive regulation by the NRC as a motivation for INPO (Rees 1994: 44). Nevertheless, our interviews suggest that Campbell (1988: 2) may be right that an important motivation in forming INPO was 'to regulate the sector more effectively in areas where they felt the NRC's performance had been, and would probably continue to be, ineffective'.

Indicators of the safety performance of the US industry since INPO do suggest considerable improvement in nuclear safety (Rees 1994: 183–6). Scrams (automatic emergency shutdowns) per unit declined in the US from over seven per unit in 1980 to one by 1993 (data supplied by INPO). Foss (1999: 38–9) reports an even more dramatic decline in 'significant events per unit' between 1985 (2.38) and 1997 (0.10), based on NRC data. INPO's self-regulatory strategies have not only been modelled globally through WANO, but domestically within the US. Nuclear weapons manufacturing plants and their regulators in the Department of Energy are 'implementing the INPO standards just about verbatim' (Rees 1994: 4).

As Rees (1994) has shown, after Three Mile Island in the US (globally after Chernobyl) nuclear operators became 'hostages of each other', a community of shared fate (Heimer 1985). In the words of one US industry person, nuclear utility executives shifted from an 'attitude of "not my brother's keeper" to one of "everything my brother does is going to affect me"' (Rees 1994: 45). This, combined with the counterproductively prescriptive nature of an NRC driven by political imperatives to seem tough and tight, was the reason why self-regulation became such a serious, well-resourced and moderately effective force in the nuclear industry. Moreover, these self-regulatory influences globalized quickly, at first by non-US utilities from fifteen nations joining INPO as international members and other countries taking on nuclear performance monitoring activities similar to INPO's (Nuclear Energy Agency 1993: 85). This global modelling of INPO became more explicit during the 1990s under the guidance of WANO.

### In a Nutshell, US Hegemony

Equally, it is true that by the 1990s IAEA Codes and Guides had globalized impressively. While some nations regulate their nuclear plants in greater depth, detail and frequency than others, the convergence around IAEA Codes and Guides is considerable. Where US NRC standards require more, many other countries model those requirements in their laws (Nuclear Energy Agency 1993: 34). Some nations, such as Belgium, have their inspectors check compliance with US standards even where that is not required in their laws, so that operators can at least be advised if they are not meeting the US standards. The NPT has 184 parties, all but a handful of the members of the UN. The safeguards agreements negotiated by IAEA with each party have been greatly shaped by US demands.

In short, what globalized was predominantly US technology, US bilateral safeguards against its diversion to nuclear weapons, a US-sponsored treaty, US safety regulations and US self-regulatory strategies. The key international institutions – IAEA, EURATOM and WANO – were the principal vehicles for this US hegemony.

## Actors

### States

Obviously, the main actor in the globalization of nuclear regulation has been the US. Within the US, leadership has not come from technocrats at relatively low levels of specialized regulatory bureaucracies (as in other case studies), but often from the office of the President himself, starting with Albert Einstein, Eugene Wigner and Leo Szilard's letter to Franklin Roosevelt in 1939 which precipitated the Manhattan Project (Price 1989: 2). Since Chernobyl, nuclear safety has been an important issue at summits, such as the 1993 Vancouver Summit between Presidents Clinton and Yeltsin. Lower-level technocrats are also important, however. Whenever a nation declares an intention to start a nuclear power program for the first time, as Indonesia did in 1993, the US negotiates and signs a safety cooperation arrangement with it. This has happened twenty-eight times since 1974. Chairmen of the NRC have spent a remarkable proportion of their time visiting other nations to negotiate transfer of regulatory technology – a higher proportion, we suspect, than that of the head of any other domestic US regulatory agency.

When, in 1953, the US gave up on its unsustainable policy of unilateral control of the technology, the UK was its key ally. The Soviet Union also switched to being more a supporter than an opponent of the US-dominated regime once China became a nuclear player. France was a more irritating opponent to the US on many issues concerning the formation of EURATOM and its relationship to IAEA in particular. West Germany resisted the NPT until the Brandt government came to power in 1969. Until then, it saw in the NPT an equivalence to Versailles, an attempt by the US and the Soviet Union to close off Germany's future strategic options. The other key states were the remaining members of the initial core of the London Suppliers Group, Japan and Canada and, in the early days, the uranium-exporting states.

### Organizations of States

It is obvious that IAEA and EURATOM have been critical organizations of states in the process of globalizing nuclear regulation. EURATOM is growing in importance again with the negotiated accession of Eastern European states. The OECD Nuclear Energy Agency has also been important, and competes with the IAEA in some ways to build consensus on the globalizing of safety progress. Its 'attraction has been as a place for technical people to get together to learn from each other with less interference from politics than in other forums' (NRC interview). The OECD emphasis is on research and analysis of problems rather than on systematic incident reporting, technical assistance or regulation. More important, though, is the informal grouping of the Nuclear Suppliers Group, with a secretariat rotating among members' Vienna missions. The Nuclear Suppliers Group has its own guidelines to which (as of 1994) twenty-nine nations subscribed in whole or part.

The Nuclear Suppliers Group sets higher standards for supply of materials and technology than the NPT, as interpreted by the so-called Zangger Committee. The US wanted another forum where it could introduce these higher standards for suppliers without opposition from purchasers, a forum which it could use to pressure all suppliers to impose bilateral vetos on nuclear supply to states viewed by the US as rogue states. In other words, the US responded to the growing influence within IAEA of purchasing Third World states (from the mid 1970s) by shifting to a forum that de facto excluded them. As we have seen, this forum-switching strategy has been employed by the US in other contexts, notably intellectual property.

Consistent with nuclear regulation being an issue that engages the US President personally, the G-7 decided to establish a Nuclear Safety Working Group during preparations for the 1992 Munich Summit. The G-7 work focused on regulatory enhancement and risk-reduction for reactors of old Soviet design. At the 1993 Tokyo G-7 Summit, closure of high-risk plants in former communist societies in return for other kinds of assistance was an important issue. This work was followed by a G-7 plus 1 (Russia) summit of world leaders, the Moscow Nuclear Safety and Security Summit of 1996 (http://utl1.library.utoronto.ca/disk1/www/ documents/g7/96moscow.htm).

The G-24 is a group of nations – essentially those of the OECD – used as a platform to coordinate economic assistance programs to Central and Eastern Europe. It has established a Nuclear Safety Assistance Coordination Centre in Brussels, with an emphasis on targeting duplications and gaps in the assistance provided.

International voluntary standards organizations have committees working on a range of nuclear technology standardization issues. National regulators have representatives on these committees and regularly include the international voluntary standards in their mandatory national regulations.

Although these groups have important roles, IAEA is the organization of states of greatest contemporary importance. It has inherited the demanding historical task of Eisenhower's Atoms for Peace bargain – the US sharing peaceful nuclear technology as long as other nations forswear weapons technology. IAEA staff see themselves as 'guarantors of respect for that bargain', to quote from one of our interviews in Vienna, 'ensuring that we won't give a dangerous toy to those who can't use it prudently', to quote another. One-third of the $US260 million budget and 500 of the 2200 staff are dedicated to the safeguards regime, and much of the rest to nuclear safety. For a long time, the Soviet Union remained beyond the reach of IAEA inspection. Now the former Soviet empire is IAEA's top regulatory priority. The most important country still keeping IAEA inspectors out is India; Iraq and North Korea have been the most important non-compliant states who have been officially within the regime.

Even though there have been spectacular failures by IAEA to detect undeclared development of fissionable materials (Iraq, Pakistan), retrospectively, because IAEA's technological capabilities of detection are quite profound, the safeguards regime has been more effective than one might have expected in the 1960s. IAEA has access to fifty monitoring stations on the Tigris and Euphrates Rivers, which makes it more difficult for Iraq to again divert materials using clandestine plants. Nuclear materials leave traces in soil and water; the traces leave a signature; the signature can be analyzed to date it and to identify which of the finite number of nuclear activities produced the material. Satellite monitoring, images shared occasionally with the IAEA by the CIA, 'could allow us to read the brand name on the cigarette smoked by a guard at the entrance to a North Korean plant' (IAEA interview). In Iraq and North Korea, as elsewhere, IAEA has used continuous monitoring by tamperproof cameras on-site. Items restricted by treaty can be tagged by methods ranging 'from very sophisticated electronic devices to simple epoxy paint with mica flakes in it' (Chayes & Chayes 1995: 194). The task is difficult but much more technologically tractable than with the new Chemical Weapons Convention safeguards regime, where 'any fertil-izer plant can be a source', satellite monitoring or remote sensing on-site is no use, and the byproducts do not leave a signature that can be traced to a finite number of sources.

In addition to having more sophisticated detection technology and superior resources than other UN coordinators of global regulatory regimes, the IAEA has statutory enforcement powers. With the safeguards regime of the NPT, but not the nuclear power safety regime, IAEA has statu-tory rights; it can report non-compliance to the Security Council which can impose economic or military sanctions, if it chooses.

On the nuclear safety side, the IAEA has moved away from becoming a regulator enforcing NRC-like prescriptive standards globally. Its emphasis has shifted to 'creating an international safety culture' (IAEA interview) through a number of specific programs. These programs are all dialogic and capacity-building rather than coercive. 'States are okay about peer review because they don't want IAEA to be a super-cop. The super-cop option was debated and rejected' (IAEA interview). The Convention of Nuclear Safety 1994 is also devoid of specification standards and prescriptive procedures. 'We want to keep the weaker countries in rather than scare them off. So the Convention is little more than a framework for each country to report within and to open themselves up to peer review' (IAEA interview). The Convention requires signatories to submit regular reports on what they are doing to implement safety obligations under the Convention. The Convention also institutionalizes review meetings for the purpose of discussing the adequacy of the reports.

Peer review of another sort has been occurring since 1982 under the OSART (Operational Safety Review Team) program. On request to IAEA, plants can have a three-week in-depth review of safety practices by ten to fifteen experts, some seconded from the industry, some IAEA staff. Most, though not all, OSART reports are derestricted. In recent years the OSART philosophy in cases of serious problems has become to 'go back again and again', while remembering that 'the motivation and morale of people who work in the plant is important'. 'It's all about consensus-building', as one IAEA person put it. 'Our product is persuasion, getting them to continuously improve', said another. IAEA recommendations are not subject to mandatory public disclosure and when they are sensitive, for example a recommendation that it would be prudent to shut down a plant, efforts are made to keep the recommendation secure. 'Confidentiality is the price of being honest' is the IAEA view as expressed by one insider. Green and anti-nuclear NGOs are pub-licly critical of this lack of transparency, needless to say. Another peer review program is ASSET (Teams for the Analysis of Significant Safety Events). ASSET teams can be requested to help plants with diagnosis and prognosis following a serious safety problem. These reports are kept strictly confidential by IAEA.

The consensus-building point applies to both the safeguards and safety regimes: 'in the political field, we try to get people pointing in the same direction on non-proliferation. In the technical field, we try to get agreement on improving standards. In both fields we appeal to enlightened self-interest'. That includes an 'interest in getting together and talking to the big guys like the US, getting access to best practice'. In turn, the 'big guys prevent the small fry from en-dangering the security of the industry and strategic stability'. Not reciprocal externalities, as when the big guy and the small fry both suffer from the pollution in a shared sea; rather, non-reciprocal benefits that create a contract zone between the nuclear and non-nuclear states.

IAEA is an organization very much under the sway of US hegemony. Two intelligence analysts work at IAEA headquarters under the cover of more innocuous job descriptions, but their real job is receiving inputs from national security organizations and analyzing their intelligence. The IAEA Board has discussed and approved 'receiving intelligence in a brown envelope from any source and implicitly any nation's security service' (IAEA interview), though the CIA and the US state is the major source. US satellite pictures of undeclared, camouflaged North Korean nuclear facilities have been displayed openly at an IAEA Board meeting. With the North Korean showdown of 1993 over its refusal to grant access to suspected nuclear sites, the IAEA first attempted to deal confidentially with North Korean intelligence: 'Let us in quietly to check' (IAEA interview). North Korea's refusal first led to IAEA's threat of going public; its continued non-cooperation led to actually going public in a showdown that ultimately saw North Korea terminating its IAEA membership.

## Industry Associations

While individual companies like Westinghouse have played important roles in the history of sharing regulatory technologies, the regulatory problems have been so threatening that collective industry response has been much more profound than in other areas of regulation. The most interesting feature of this case study of the globalization of regulation is the role of the US national industry self-regulatory body (INPO) and the international equivalent that grew from it (WANO). These organizations have been of much greater significance to globalization of regulation than the industry trade associations, such as the Nuclear Energy Institute in the US or the Atomic Industrial Forum internationally (Price 1989: 34).

INPO was formed because of the Three Mile Island disaster in the US in 1979 (TMI). As a result of realizing certain facts about TMI, the principle of transparency triumphed decisively over the principle of trade secrecy. The investigations into TMI revealed that very similar accidents had happened in the US two other times during the previous five years, and that the power-operated relief valves whose failure was the major culprit in the accident had failed nine times before in reactors of similar design (Rees 1994: 22). Even the sequence of events that occurred at TMI had been postulated before and analyzed by the Tennessee Valley Authority and the NRC (Rees 1994: 22). But the TMI operators knew none of this. Hence, the first lesson from TMI was for the industry to abandon its traditional secrecy in favour of institutionalized information-sharing.

Second, TMI caused a triumph of the principle of continuous improvement over the principle of rule compliance. As with the triumph of transparency, INPO was instrumental in this transition. Rees' (1994) authoritative study found that, pre-TMI, there was a 'general industry mind-set of doing no more than what the NRC regulations require' (Rees 1994: 20). A 'pervasive formalism bred complacency', the complacency of believing that if one met the state's minimum standards all would be well. Rees (1994: 20) quoted one industry official: 'You had minimum NRC regulations that you could aspire to, which was just meeting the minimum regulatory needs. But standards of excellence were not available'. INPO constituted an institutional framework for continuous improvement. This was an important development because 'the pre-TMI normative system did not take institutions seriously' (Rees 1994: 21). It was hardware-focused regulation. After TMI, deliberation turned to the need for better institutions, which saw the rise of INPO and WANO. Those institutions in turn balanced the hardware focus with a software focus (literally computer software, in the case of risk analysis), a safety culture and focus on nuclear professionalism.

A critical catalyst was the Kemeny Commission into the TMI disaster. It excoriated the NRC for its emphasis on equipment to the neglect of the 'human beings' that 'constitute' safety systems (Kemeny 1979: 10, cited in Rees 1994: 21–2). We have seen how INPO was a serious self-regulatory push that even critics of the whole idea of a nuclear industry (in the Nader organization) concede has made a difference. This earnestness is grounded in the fact that after TMI, US operators were mutual hostages. After Chernobyl, worldwide operators were mutual hostages – so WANO was modelled on INPO.

WANO, like INPO, has no formal enforcement powers. Neither organization has withdrawn membership because a member failed to act on its safety recommendations. However, state regulators can and have moved in to shut plants when the legitimacy of a plant has been repeatedly challenged by INPO or WANO. The directors of one company were removed after INPO advised the NRC of the firm's recalcitrance. The industry-regulatory/state-regulatory link in the web of controls is important. Under the WANO umbrella, peer-review inspections are voluntary, whereas under INPO they are a requirement of membership. As one WANO official put it, 'INPO are police who send people out to check you, while WANO is a friendly neighbourhood watch – just an agreement to share, watch and help each other'. WANO copes with the backwardness of so many of its members by putting more emphasis on building their capacity to evaluate and improve themselves; the INPO emphasis is more on external regulation, though INPO is hardly a police-like regulator. Even so, WANO's principal programs correspond to the INPO priorities:

- nuclear plant event reporting and sharing;
- people to people exchange visits, workshops and seminars;
- exchange of good practices;
- publication of performance indicators;
- conduct of peer reviews.

The most important functions are to globalize good practice experience and mistake experience among those most likely to benefit from acting on the experience. Part of this is the simple accomplishment of a global computer network, where an operator in Korea can send out a global request, 'Has anyone written a procedure to do this?', and expect many answers. WANO coordinates some eighty pairing arrangements of weaker with stronger plants. Every German plant was paired with a plant in Russia. Pairing is coordinated to match plants with comparable designs or operating problems. WANO pilot peer-reviews started in 1991. Only fifteen were conducted in the first three years, thirty-eight by 1996. Fifteen to twenty engineers and other experts from various parts of the world are invited to audit a total plant system. The idea is not a list of subsystem technical solutions but a rich dialogue that occurs within the team each evening (and between the team and plant management). WANO reports are exercises in community-building diplomacy, balancing praise for strengths and improvements with helpful suggestions on weaknesses.

WANO has regional centres in Atlanta, Moscow, Paris and Tokyo and a Coordinating Centre in London. Liaison occurs with IAEA's OSART program to avoid duplication within a reasonable time period. Coordination is also assisted by US plants loaning employees to INPO, which in turn loans employees to WANO and IAEA.

WANO assists with the formation of users' groups of operators of plants of similar design. As one WANO officer put it during our interview: 'The users' group can speak with a common voice. For example, the owners of Soviet-designed reactors can say "Here's what we need to do to improve the safety of our design. If you are a supplier wanting to sell to us, work on solving these common problems"'. Such requests can link to INPO's coordination of supplier participants from the US, Europe and Japan through its Supplier Participant Advisory Committee.

WANO sees itself as very much in the business of community-building. Peer pressure in the culturally heterogenous community of WANO does not work as well as INPO meetings to compare performance indicators. It is not as 'candid and bloody' as INPO because on the global scene it has a harder job of keeping everyone in the community. And it believes that 'We're only as strong as our weakest link. We know who the weak links are and we must keep them engaged with us. Sometimes we'll chip in as a community and pay for the travel to and from plants who could not afford it [for peer review visits]'. All utilities operating civilian nuclear reactors are members of WANO, so WANO is succeeding in 'keeping them engaged'.

### Banks and the Insurance Industry

The World Bank will not lend developing nations money to build a nuclear plant, nor will most banks, and this has been important in limiting the spread of nuclear power in the developing world. The nuclear case is in some ways the most vivid illustration of the importance of the insurance industry as a regulator. Notwithstanding the global risk-sharing capabilities of the modern insurance industry, in the 1950s private insurers were only willing to insure nuclear plants to a maximum liability of $US60 million. The difficulty was that the US AEC had produced a study which envisaged a hypothetical accident in which 3400 people would be killed, 43 000 injured and $US7 billion damage caused to property (Walsh 1988: 21). A 1964 update of the study was suppressed by the AEC when it revealed that the larger reactors then planned could cause 45 000 deaths, 100 000 injuries and $US17 billion in property damage (Walsh 1988: 25).

Under these circumstances, the private sector was unwilling to invest in the technology. It is still true that a totally deregulated market for nuclear insurance could not function: 'If the extent of damage in all its forms was the basis for liability, then nuclear risks would be uninsurable' (Foss 1999: 52). The US Congress responded with the *Price-Anderson Act 1957*, which required the government to pay an additional $US500 million in compensation beyond the $US60 million in cover available privately for nuclear accidents. Beyond that $US560 million pool, the Act repealed citizens' common-law right to sue for damages. Without that law, a nuclear power industry would probably never have developed in the West and we can only speculate on whether one would have developed in the Soviet Union without the technology-sharing of the Atoms for Peace policy. It is an irony for anti-nuclear activists, who tend to be supportive of public regulation and suspicious of capitalism, that the unregulated invisible hand of the insurance market would have made the judgment that the risks of nuclear power generation did not justify the potential economic returns. Potentially, the international insurance industry had the power to stop what mass democracy could only wind back and state regulation could only risk-manage.

Contemporary insurance arrangements in the US and Europe reinforce the 'community of fate' quality of the nuclear industry. Under US law today, a consequence of a major nuclear power catastrophe would be that every reactor in the US would be required to pay $US75 million to fund compensation to victims (Nuclear Energy Agency 1994: 82). Reactors therefore are financially their brother's keeper and have an economic interest in helping each other to operate safely. The Brussels Convention (with fourteen European signatories) initiated by EURATOM members requires all signatory states (as opposed to reactors) to contribute compensation for a major catastrophe within another signatory state (Nuclear Energy Agency 1994: 52–5). This renders each state a hostage of every other state, with an incentive for mutual help to improve safety regulation.

The insurance industry realized the value of INPO; US insurance companies will not cover a nuclear power plant that is not a member of INPO. Anticipation that this would be the reaction of the global insurance industry to WANO may be one reason why every nuclear power plant operator in the world has joined WANO. In commenting on a draft of this chapter, WANO disagreed that that was a reason for the success of its recruitment.

### NGOs and Mass Publics

The most important regulation of nuclear power within states was not by technocratic regulatory agencies, but by high politics. Western political leaders, especially in Europe, feeling the anti-nuclear political winds blowing in the electorate, became reluctant to issue licences for new nuclear plants (Hatch 1986). In Germany, party politics was important – the rise of the greens in the 1980s (Joppke 1993: 169–76). But the deeper political reality was a global peace movement (Carter 1992) and an anti-nuclear movement (Price 1989; Flam 1994; Falk 1982) associated with a globalizing environmental movement (Joppke 1993).

When disasters happened, not only major ones like TMI and Chernobyl but also more minor ones, the media engendered mass political nervousness about nuclear energy, to which political leaders had little choice but to respond with licensing restraint. This social movement politics and mass politics created the environment where nuclear producers joined in a community of shared fate that has been reasonably effective in making self-regulation work. The high-water mark of political leaders learning to fear the mass politics of nuclear energy occurred in 1978, when Austrian Chancellor Kreisky threatened to resign if a referendum vote went against the commissioning of the Zwentendorf nuclear power station near Vienna. The people did vote against opening the plant and Kreisky did resign, albeit not immediately (OECD 1993: 136).

In Italy, a 1988 referendum following the Chernobyl accident effectively shut all nuclear power plants and halted further development of the technology (OECD 1993: 140–1). A 1979 Swedish referendum resulted in a government decision to phase out nuclear power by 2010; in Switzerland unsuccessful anti-nuclear referenda in 1979 and 1984 were followed by a post-Chernobyl referendum in 1990 which imposed a ten-year moratorium on issuing nuclear plant licences (OECD 1993: 142-3). US mass concern has been less profound, with only one of sixteen citizen-initiated referenda to shut a nuclear power plant succeeding (OECD 1993: 144). Yet even in the US, public resistance to nuclear plants – combined with high costs and demanding regulatory requirements – is such that no new plant has been ordered since the mid 1970s. This is one area where, in the battle between diffuse public interests and the concentrated interest of the industry association, the Nuclear Energy Institute, the latter is losing. Many states have been forced to implement front-end participation in wide-ranging public inquiries before new nuclear plant licences are issued. In no other area of regulation does the direct sovereignty of citizens have so much influence over specific regulatory decisions.

Since 1989, democratization in post-communist societies (Novak 1993) and in countries like South Korea clearly increased political resistance to the licensing of new facilities. Nevertheless, opinion polls in South Korea show most citizens support building more nuclear power plants and more are being built (Chung 1993), as they are in China, Taiwan, Romania and India. Thus the number of nuclear plants overall was still increasing in the late 1990s, despite the stagnation in the West.

The media, and the globalization of communication it enables, have been very important in mediating between democratic politics and resistance to nuclear power. The 1957 Soviet atomic waste dump explosion in the Ural Mountains that killed hundreds and left thirty towns uninhabitable was covered up for eighteen years by the Soviets and the CIA (Walsh 1988: xii), until Ralph Nader and others exposed the cover-up. This would be unlikely to happen today given the globalized tentacles of a media on the lookout for stories that build concern in every country over something that happens in one. The existence of freedom of information laws that Nader was able to exploit in 1976 to expose the cover-up is another factor.

In addition to the global social movement politics of the peace and environmental movements, specific national and local groups also prevent the start-up of new nuclear plants and lobby for shutting existing ones. In the US, the Nader organization's Critical Mass Energy Project has been important, as is the Nuclear Information and Resource Service and the Union of Concerned Scientists (which started with a group of MIT faculty concerned about AEC safety cover-ups). Other professional NGOs have been pro-nuclear lobbyists, perhaps the most important being the American Nuclear Society (Price 1989: 34). The suspicious death of Karen Silkwood, a worker at the Kerr-McGee plutonium reprocessing plant in Oklahoma, created a martyr that brought the National Organization of Women and the labour movement into the anti-nuclear movement (Price 1989: 12). Even behind the former Iron Curtain, groups like Klub Ekologiczny could maintain pressure on specific plants through more covert tactics such as 'Stop Zarnobyl!' graffiti campaigns (Latek 1993).

The self-regulatory activities of INPO and its equivalent outside the US have improved safety, and in time NGOs use this to raise legally mandated safety standards. As one former INPO person, who was working for WANO when we interviewed him in 1994, put it: 'Greenpeace, for example, picks up a gap between average industry practice and the government standard and urges narrowing of that gap in Congress. Some in the industry complain that through self-improvement we have been our own worst enemy'. As both Joe Rees and another WANO informant said in commenting on that quote, it is important not to exaggerate its significance. Neither Greenpeace nor other lead NGOs in the US like the Union of Concerned Scientists and Nader's Critical Mass Energy Project operate much by proposing (or even getting behind) specific technical reforms; they operate more as 'gadflies of the regulatory process'. It is nevertheless important to consider the role of NGOs in the context of a web of controls: INPO improves US practice as a result of the leadership of its most safety and environmentally conscious members; an NGO lobbies to raise national law to this new practice standard; through the mechanism of modelling and bilateral pressure by the US, US law and self-regulation have a global influence on practice. However, neither INPO nor WANO has direct dialogic relationships of any significance with anti-nuclear NGOs.

NGOs do work directly with sympathetic states, however. For example, Austria, where all parties are anti-nuclear, works with green NGOs to pressure the Czech and Slovak Republics to shut down plants.

## Individuals

President Eisenhower made the key decisions to privatize nuclear power and to instigate the Atoms for Peace program, which was global capacity-building through technology transfer in return for global commitment to a nuclear weapons safeguards regime and a nuclear safety regime at a new IAEA. The three wise men – Louis Armand, Franz Etzel and Francesco Giordeni – were instrumental in establishing the other key international institution, EURATOM, more important than IAEA in the 1950s and early 1960s. For the future, in the nuclear safety area, WANO may become more important than IAEA. The key initiators of WANO were Lord Marshall (the Chairman of the British Central Electricity Generating Board who became WANO's first Chairman), Duke Power (US) and Electricité de France. Duke Power's CEO Bill Lee was 'the principal industry force behind INPO's creation' (correspondence with Joe Rees). It could be argued that President Gorbachev of the Soviet Union was a key individual on the safeguards side because he gave independence and democracy to large areas of the Soviet Union on condition of decommissioning them as effective nuclear weapons sites (Potter 1995) (or at least withholding release codes, as in the Ukrainian case). On the safety side, Gorbachev insisted on dealing with Chernobyl with surprising openness. This ushered in a decade of nuclear safety technology transfer from the West. In the years before TMI and immediately after, the critical years when nuclear power slipped off its trajectory of rapid growth, Nader was a key opinion-leader and fomenter of oppositional NGOs (Price 1989)

## Epistemic Communities of Actors

Epistemic communities in nuclear regulation have been much more closed than those for drug regulation, for example. The nuclear regulatory epistemic community almost totally excludes the forces of opposition, which tend to oppose the very existence of the industry, quite a different situation from pharmaceuticals (Chapter 15). When nuclear safety standards are being set in the various international fora discussed in this chapter, it is exceedingly rare for NGO representatives to be at the table. This is partly due to the complexity of the technological issues and partly to the fact that NGOs are less interested in safety reform of the industry than in lobbying for its demise. NGOs do, however, participate in discussions on the legal liability regime and on the transport of nuclear materials by sea.

A seminal event in the construction of epistemic community was the 1955 Atoms for Peace Conference in Geneva, at which a great deal of information previously kept secret by nations (particularly the US and France) was shared with other specialists (Scheinman 1987: 69). The OECD Committee on the Safety of Nuclear Installations has been, with IAEA, the most important ongoing site for building a nuclear regulatory epistemic community. In 1980 the OECD set up an international incident-reporting scheme. By the mid 1980s the IAEA had extended this incident-reporting to all nations with operating nuclear power plants. About 200 incidents a year are entered on a computer database and ranked on a seven-point severity scale. This facilitates dialogue between facilities which are worried about experiencing a particular problem and facilities that have experienced it. Epistemic community is being built through experiential learning. Periodically, both the OECD Nuclear Energy Agency and the IAEA convene meetings of experts to discuss specific incident reports of special significance. Manufacturers of nuclear technology also facilitate epistemic community by establishing users' clubs to share practical experience with their technology (Nuclear Energy Agency 1993: 84).

Perhaps the most important fora for building epistemic community are IAEA-sponsored meetings of the world's top regulators to discuss a particular issue. The International Nuclear Safety Advisory Group – 'the wisest people the Director-General of IAEA can find' (NRC interview) – is particularly important.

The extensiveness and intensiveness of cooperation between nations on nuclear safety research is staggering, with US leadership being critical (NRC 1993). The end of the Cold War has seen important new collaborations between the NRC and the Russian Academy of Sciences, for example, on computer codes for probabilistic risk assessment.

## Contest of Principles

### Transparency v. Trade Secrecy v. Transparency of Secrets (Espionage)

Transparency may be the most-contested principle in nuclear regulation. Picking up on a question we asked about epistemic communities, one senior regulator described EURATOM as moving from 'espionage community to epistemic community'. Aspects of nuclear technology and its regulation are among the most secret things in the world. The desire and need to know the secrets of others made the nuclear technology community an 'espionage community'. At the same time, in many respects, the IAEA regime tries to increase security by enabling transparency in specific ways. Mostly this means transparency to the IAEA and/or to the states that are its members. It does not generally mean transparency to civil society. Most countries allow the reports of OSART missions to be public, but some ask that they remain restricted.

A major shift from a trade-secrets to a transparency approach to safety innovation has occurred since TMI, but it is a selective transparency revealed to some but not others. Prior to TMI safety innovations were conceived as a competitive advantage. Once TMI had created a community of shared fate, for most innovations it seemed pointless for one business to risk destroying the whole industry, including itself, by keeping secret an innovation that might prevent another TMI. Joe Rees points out that the regulated monopoly market structure of electric utilities muted the competitive pressures that might preclude such a community of fate in other industries. Deregulation of these monopolies is now opening up a discussion on whether the community of fate will surive it.

CoCom (Coordinating Committee) was an administrative mechanism set up in the late 1940s by Western powers to control the export of defence-sensitive technology to the Soviet bloc and China (Macdonald 1990). Membership of CoCom consisted of NATO states (excluding Iceland), Japan and Australia. The organization had no charter or public rules of procedure and no treaty states. It operated by circulating lists of embargoed goods, including the international lists which name goods that have a dual civilian and military application (Macdonald 1990: 13). Before an item on a CoCom list could be exported to an embargoed country, the consent of all CoCom members was required. The national export controls of members were used to stop exports of technology considered to be too dangerous to fall into wrong hands. CoCom was dominated by the US. It was the multilateral complement to US unilateral export controls. CoCom, in the words of one NRC official, 'probably did keep some safety technology from the Soviets (such as computers and reactor simulators). But the technology they needed for their reactors in many ways was different. So the importance of CoCom can be exaggerated. The Soviets were in their world and we were in ours. We assumed their technology was better than it was. We believed their bluff about their knowledgeability at international meetings'. CoCom has been disbanded and replaced by a much looser framework known as the Wasenaar Agreement.

A remarkable accomplishment in transparency is the publication by WANO of ten nuclear plant performance indicators. According to WANO, 99 per cent of operating nuclear power plants report at least seven indicators, and 77 per cent all ten (WANO Annual Review 1995). They show patterns of improvement and deterioration of the industry worldwide, providing individual plants with benchmarks to be exceeded. While the Plant Performance Indicator Program is a self-regulatory resource for individual operators, only aggregate statistics are published, not results for individual plants. Some of the performance indicators are efficiency rather than safety measures, such as the unit capability factor – the percentage of maximum energy generation a plant is capable of supplying to the grid. Even so, a plant with a lot of unplanned energy losses must be questioned on safety grounds when equipment is not being reliably operated and well-maintained. Other performance indicators focus on safety, such as 'Unplanned Automatic Scrams [automatic shutdowns of the plant in an emergency where control is taken out of operators' hands] per 7000 Hours Critical', 'Collective Radiation Exposure' and 'Industrial Safety Accident Rate'; while 'Volume of Low-Level Solid Radioactive Waste' is a product stewardship environmental indicator.

Notwithstanding the limited nature of the INPO-led, then WANO-led, increase in transparency, the increased transparency to Boards of Directors was singularly important. Pre-INPO and pre-WANO, CEOs could foil Board questions about the comparative safety performance of their plants with 'a lot of wiggle room'. Today, says a US nuclear utility vice-president, 'we're all sitting there looking at the INPO indicators which tell you where you stand with other plants of the same vintage and other plants of the same type' (Rees 1994: 99). As a result of this window of plant-level transparency (which admittedly only a few were allowed to look through), 'a hundred once-solitary joggers grouped into a single race' (Rees 1994: 99). In the US, comparative performance also becomes transparent at an annual gathering of nuclear CEOs:

> All the CEOs are gathered in a big room with Zack Pate [INPO's president], and he flashes up the most recent evaluation numbers for each of the utilities by name. That's the only time we learn how our peers are ranked, and it kind of hits you right between the eyeballs. The first slide has all the number ones, the best-rated utilities. Lots of praise from Zack, and all those CEOs kind of puff up and get a big smile on their face. [They also receive a plaque.] Then come out the number twos, and those guys also feel pretty good about it. And then come the number threes, and they just kind of sit there passive. Then you get down to the fours and the fives. And after some pretty frank discussion of their problems, those guys are feeling rather uneasy to say the least (quoted in Rees 1994: 104).

The 'unease' generally translates into improvement and reform because the shame the CEOs experience when their plants are rated five ('marginal') is not stigmatizing, but reintegrative (Braithwaite 1989; Rees 1994). It occurs not so much in a competitive, down-putting context, but within a respectful community of shared fate. In the words of another CEO, 'if the guy on the bottom of the list gets into trouble, the whole industry gets into trouble' (Rees 1994: 105). Hence transparency within but not outside the community of shared fate constitutes conditions for reintegrative shaming and 'communitarian regulation', to use Rees' (1994) term.

Secrecy and transparency are more complex here than in any other regime discussed in this book. The CIA is sharing with the IAEA Board some of the deepest secrets of its nation-state, secrets it would never share with US citizens. With both the safeguards and safety regimes, under both the industry self-regulation of INPO/WANO and state regulation, there is a kind of need-to-know transparency – sufficiently broad for complex interdependency and reintegrative shaming to deliver compliance, but cautious about keeping knowledge out of the hands of anti-nuclear NGOs.

### Harmonization v. National Sovereignty

The global reach of IAEA standards has been impressive. Most nuclear operators in the world claim to have adopted them and to be striving to meet them. At one level, this is harmonization. However, the IAEA safety standards are more in the nature of broad principles than rules, while the non-proliferation standards are much more stipulative. So while impressive harmonization is the right word to describe the accomplishment of the safeguards regime, it does not apply so well to the safety regime. With nuclear safety regulation, 'There is an underlying international consensus. Yet different countries have different regulations on frequency of inspection of this versus that. Internationally, what you have is a set of fundamental principles rather than a harmonized set of minimum standards. Though the Europeans are a little more for harmonized standards [within Europe]' (NRC interview). In contrast, with the safeguards regime, over a decade there was a total subjugation of the principle of national sovereignty to the principle of harmonization on US terms (in return for supply of fissionable materials and technology) covering most of the world.

Mutual recognition is also rather limited, given the level of harmonization that has been accomplished. Under the safety regime, nevertheless, there is acceptance that different states will deploy different means to move toward outcomes that are subject to global agreement.

National treatment, Most Favoured Nation and reciprocity have not been important as principles invoked in debates over the globalization of nuclear regulation because the trading of nuclear energy has been limited, with state monopolies and local national firms tending to be the only producers seeking and getting licences. In most Western countries no one has sought a new licence for two decades. The benefits obtained under the Non-Proliferation Treaty were shown to be non-reciprocal.

### Rule Compliance v. Continuous Improvement

The TMI disaster ushered in a decisive shift from the reign of the principle of rule compliance to one of continuous improvement. Institutional leadership for the shift came, as we have seen, from INPO in the US and then WANO globally. 'While the NRC 'stresses compliance with regulatory requirements', INPO 'stresses assistance in achieving excellence' (Rees 1994: 74). In Rees' path-breaking documentation of this shift, he also describes the shift in a more moral discourse as one from NRC's 'baseline morality' to INPO's 'morality of aspiration' (Rees 1994: 75). INPO institutionalized a 'quest for the best', as explained by one nuclear plant quality-control manager: 'INPO's standards continue to improve each year so that if you get an outstanding grade from INPO this year, and you don't make improvements in your processes or your programs, then you won't get that same high score next year from INPO because their standards have gone up in the meantime' (quoted in Rees 1994: 83).

### Lowest-cost Location v. World's Best Practice

This contest of principles, which is central in most contemporary areas of regulation, is irrelevant to nuclear safety and safeguards regulation. Both regimes are so effectively global that there are no regulatory havens. The industry is so capital-intensive that mobility is constrained. Location is determined by political rather than economic factors. However, vendors of nuclear power plants do have a competitive advantage if the plant design has been approved before in a country seen as having high regulatory standards, and better if it is viewed as having performed safely under that regime. Given that so much of the competition among vendors of nuclear plants is a competition in safety, Porter's theory of competitive advantage based on higher regulatory standards has some relevance here.

Concomitantly, the principle of deregulation has not been a mantra of the nuclear regulatory debates. Regulation has progressively become more demanding, happening later in some parts of the world (e.g. Eastern Europe) than others (e.g. Japan). While regulation has become more flexible in most places by no means has it amounted to deregulation, as the outcomes demanded have progressively escalated. There have been moments when the US has used demands for global standards to give its nuclear suppliers a strategic trade advantage, but this has not been a major distortion to the shape of either the safeguards or safety regimes, just an occasional sideshow.

## Mechanisms

### Military Coercion

Military coercion has been critical in persuading states to sign the Nuclear Non-Proliferation Treaty, with its associated safeguards and safety regulation baggage. Sweden opted to sign, after some hesitation, because it felt on balance the acquisition of nuclear weapons would make it a pre-emptive priority target for the Soviet Union (Reiss 1988: 252). South Korea did so, notwithstanding incentive and capability to acquire nuclear weapons, because it feared bilateral US action in the form of withdrawal of US military support if it did not sign (Reiss 1988: 253–4). The safeguards regime of the IAEA, but not the safety regime, has authority from the UN Security Council to react as it sees fit, even militarily in extreme circumstances, to non-compliance with the Treaty.

### Economic Coercion

Japan stuck with the Treaty partly out of fear that the US might cut off nuclear fuel supplies, crippling the Japanese nuclear industry (Reiss 1988: 255). India may have decided not to develop a weapons capability immediately after its 1974 detonation partly because it feared loss of the foreign aid it desperately needed (Reiss 1988: 257). Yet the withdrawal of foreign aid following Pakistan and India's competitive 1998 detonations of nuclear devices seemed of little consequence. In fact, the US cut off economic and military aid to Pakistan from 1990 because of its nuclear policies. The US made explicit its willingness to use economic coercion in the *Nuclear Non-Proliferation Act 1978*. The Act provided for the immediate cessation of US exports to non-nuclear weapon states violating IAEA safeguards or to states defying any arrangement the US had entered into on the transfer of nuclear technology. A totally deregulated market for nuclear insurance could not function, so the insurance industry mobilized limited economic coercion.

### Systems of Reward

After 1989 some US economic support for post-communist economies was conditional on decisions not to reopen some of their nuclear reactors that were most inadequate in terms of safety. Some were not reopened, though no operating plants were actually shut down as a result. The following strategy, articulated by a senior NRC official has not worked splendidly: 'We'll help you to complete those reactors but then you must get the riskiest reactors off-line'. A Nuclear Safety Account to be administered by an Assembly of Donors was established at the European Bank for Reconstruction and Development after the 1992 G-7 Summit discussion of the risks of old Soviet-designed reactors. The historic bargain of Atoms for Peace is the granting of economic rewards (in the form of transfer of technology) in return for scrupulous subscription to a global regulatory regime. At the time these rewards were offered, they seemed of fundamental economic significance. Reiss (1995) concludes that not only the US has used economic assistance to promote non-proliferation objectives; Japan, South Korea, Russia and Europe have also applied 'dollar non-proliferation diplomacy'. North Korea seems to have extracted no less than $US5 billion in return for accepting a number of non-proliferation measures.

## Modelling

The EURATOM and IAEA safeguards were modelled on previous bilateral agreements between the US and other nations and on the US *Atomic Energy Act 1954*. Curiously, the latter Act was itself modelled on the *Federal Communications Act 1934* (Walsh 1988: 21). While modelling of the US by IAEA has been almost total with the non-proliferation part of the regime, it has also been important with nuclear safety. IAEA's OSART missions, for example, were largely inspired by NRC team inspections. Much, perhaps most, of the modelling of US standards takes place without enacting them in the domestic law of second nations. This is also true of the implementation of IAEA standards. As a senior NRC official put it during our interview: 'When an operator is setting up say in China, they are told to "Get yourself a copy of all the IAEA standards and get yourself a copy of the NRC regs"'. European informants confirmed that this was the advice that industry peer-reviewers gave to newer and weaker plants. NRC regulations are more modelled than others partly because they are more thoroughly documented than any other country's regulations and are readily accessible. This accessibility has been assisted by the fact of countries such as Spain more or less adopting the whole NRC regulatory framework and regulations into their law.

The NRC has an extensive on-the-job training program for regulators from other countries. When we did our initial interviews at the NRC in 1993, there had been twenty-three staff members from nine other countries working at the NRC. The heads of both Finland's and the Czech Republic's regulatory bodies are former NRC 'assignees'.

Another factor in the globalization of US standards has been the practice of 'the country that sells a plant to another country offering technical assistance with regs as part of the sale', as one NRC official explained. 'Sometimes the purchasers of US plants say, "Give us an NRC licensing review as well", but the NRC says no, that's your sovereignty'. In the post-Chernobyl world, the competition between the vendors of nuclear plants is very much a competition in safety: 'Being able to say the plant design is approved by the NRC is important, for example'. This is a novel example of the principle of regulatory competition.

Finally, NRC regulations have been more influential than IAEA because IAEA standards are vague, while NRC standards have a specificity that provides more useful guidance to nations who need technical assistance with regulation. As one insider said: 'The US has been negative about global minimum standards because of the fear of a lowest common denominator. The least concerned countries would just settle for that. The US prefers principles that are the focus for constant upgrading'. Another reason is that uniform standards are difficult in a domain where most plants are considerably customized, built in different places at different phases in the development of nuclear technologies. So the US has prevailed with a principle of continuous improvement in regulation which in a sense is the antithesis of traditional US legalism. In part, this reflects US learning from the failures of its own legalism pre-TMI. That legalism, which was a product of domestic US adversarialism in regulatory politics,[2] resulted in a culture of settling for the minimum standard in the law (principle of rule compliance). At the same time, US global hegemonic politics, through the agency of NRC bureaucrats, insisted on a safety culture of continuous improvement in international fora – not so much modelling as 'Do what we say, not what we have done. But in the process use our standards as a resource to illuminate some of the things you must do'.

INPO and WANO peer-review and pairing programs are institutionalized modelling of unusual sweep, oriented to putting nuclear professionals from one plant into another (usually for two weeks) to swap safety ideas during an inspection. One INPO official said in Rees' (1994) study: 'One of INPO's basic principles is the concept of emulation. We want to identify those plants that are achieving a large measure of success in what they're doing so they can become a role model for everybody to emulate and to try to improve their performance'. Modelling is explicit in WANO's mission statement: 'To maximize the safety and reliability of the operation of nuclear power plants by exchanging information and encouraging communication, comparison and emulation among its members'. Much of the INPO methodology for reporting and sharing critical events was modelled on experience within a longer-standing community of shared fate – the international airline industry.

### Non-reciprocal Coordination, Capacity-building and Reciprocal Adjustment

Non-reciprocal coordination is an important mechanism because it was the foundation of the IAEA regime. The issue linkage was not reciprocal. The US offered the rest of the world access to fissionable material and nuclear technology for peaceful purposes. What it wanted in return was assurances of non-proliferation of nuclear weapons and of safe use of the technology.

One side of the linkage was a US commitment to capacity-building. This was not only building technological capacity; it involved transferring regulatory capacity to the rest of the world from the AEC (later the NRC and INPO). IAEA and EURATOM were explicitly set up as agencies with the mission of internationalizing capacity to handle nuclear technology wisely. The many means of capacity-building are impressive within this community of shared fate. There are INPO and WANO, IAEA, bilateral technical assistance from nations (especially from the US and Europe), bilateral pairing of plants under the auspices of WANO, EURATOM, assistance from suppliers of plants, and the Nuclear Energy Agency of the OECD. For someone starting a new plant, there is no shortage of high-level international help.

This non-reciprocal linkage of capacity-building and protection within an alliance to compliance with hegemonic US rules describes the key mechanism of the regime much more adequately than reciprocal adjustment. There is a more limited sense in which the hegemon adjusts

---

2 '[US] politicians want a piece of paper, "so we know what to shut down"' (NRC interview). 'Paperwork was the preoccupation of NRC inspectors in the 1970s and early 1980s, instead of watching the big picture' (NRC interview). Actually, in the immediate aftermath of TMI, the US moved to more prescriptive regulations, but since then the US has shifted to performance standards that emphasize whole systems – integrated systemic control rather than specifications for system components. This meant probabilistic risk analysis, known risk profiles for the whole system of a plant, computer analysis of event trees to discern risks of things going wrong at different points using models developed by the space program, and 'defence in depth' to allow some protections to fail with the assurance that redundancy from other systems would cover the gap.

its rules to accommodate the safeguards and safety rules of lesser states, and through significant mutual adjustment among non-hegemonic states, for example within Europe.

## Are We Safer from the Atom?

This book is about the regulation of business rather than the regulation of states. The prevention of nuclear war is primarily about the regulation of states, with business regulation to prevent diversion of nuclear materials within or to rogue states (also, increasingly, to terrorists) one of the means to that end. Yet it would be remiss not to say a little about whether the means (e.g. IAEA business regulation) does indeed contribute toward the end (non-proliferation among states).

IAEA has had some success in regulating diversion from declared nuclear activities. But if states decide not to declare clandestine programs, as the Iraq and North Korea examples show, IAEA inspection can reach the limits of its power (Harry 1995). In a sense, we might reach a conclusion rather similar to that of Chapter 15 in relation to, for example, the value of the Medical Lobby for Appropriate Marketing. Since the global regulatory rejuvenation that followed the thalidomide disaster, we have not had another drug disaster nearly as bad. The Medical Lobby for Appropriate Marketing is by no means the main reason why global regulation works better now than it did before. Yet we conclude in Chapter 15 that it is a useful part of a web of controls, wherein no single strand of the web is singularly important. Similarly with nuclear weapons, we have not had anything as bad as Hiroshima. The nuclear non-proliferation regime is one reason, and global business regulation to prevent the diversion of nuclear materials and technology from peaceful purposes is part of a web of controls that has been more effective in preventing proliferation than any reasonable person might have expected:

> President John F. Kennedy forecast a world of fifteen to twenty-five nuclear powers by the 1970s...Yet contrary to almost all predictions, the rampant proliferation of nuclear weapons among states has not occurred. Historically, as indicated by test explosions, the pace of nuclear weapons spread has actually declined. In the first ten years of the nuclear age three countries exploded their initial nuclear weapons. In the next decade two countries made their maiden nuclear tests. The third decade saw only one country detonate its first nuclear device. The fourth decade did not have any new members of the nuclear club (Reiss 1988: vii, xxii).

Since that was written, one country (Pakistan) that had not conducted a test explosion joined the club, drawing India into more public membership of the club. And South Africa (which had six bombs), North Korea, Argentina, Brazil and Iraq have all pulled back in some way from membership of the nuclear weapons club (Reiss 1995). In the study quoted above, Reiss concludes that the Nuclear Non-Proliferation Treaty was not the main reason Sweden, South Korea and Japan decided to resist the temptation to become nuclear weapon states. The Treaty was less important than bilateral pressures from the US and powerful neighbours. Yet, Reiss concludes, the Treaty was an important part of the web of controls, even though he does not use this language (see also B. Schneider 1994; Roberts 1995). In *Bridled Ambition*, Reiss (1995: 331) refers to the Treaty as 'the centrepiece of a network of interlocking overlapping and mutually reinforcing mechanisms and arrangements that are commonly referred to as the non-proliferation regime'. While the prevention of horizontal proliferation has been surprisingly successful, vertical non-proliferation has been a failure – the nuclear weapons states continued to develop new technologies of war. As soon as a treaty seemed to limit vertical proliferation, new technologies were being invented to beat it.

With nuclear safety, there were some disasters – the Ural Mountains explosion of 1957, TMI, Windscale and Chernobyl. There were almost certainly several serious disasters in the Soviet Union in the 1970s and early 1980s which were covered-up. Yet the disasters were not as many as we or the international insurance industry might have expected, and not as bad as those hypothesized by the US AEC. Perhaps the early disasters were bad enough, the pressure from democratic politics so withering, to create a community of fate among nuclear operators in the West. It became a decisively global community of fate after Chernobyl caused the creation of WANO. Worries have increased over what we now know to be the deplorable state of Eastern-bloc plants. None have been closed since the Soviet Union collapsed and many are struggling to pay wages and fund maintenance.

## Conclusion

The globalization of the regulation of the nuclear business is distinguished from the other cases in this book by its connection to high politics. One set of institutions runs two different regimes, one safeguarding against diversion of nuclear materials to weapons programs, the other on safety. The architecture of both regimes has periodically engaged the attention of US Presidents from Eisenhower to Clinton. While the legwork of globalization has been done by technocrats working on standards the public never hears about, linkage of the regimes to the high politics of G-7 summits and US–Soviet strategic interests has given the technocrats of IAEA, EURATOM and the NRC a mandate to push globalization a long way.

As in so many of the domains of globalization, the reactions of mass publics, NGOs and epistemic communities to disasters has been of enormous importance. The way the networked anti-nuclear, peace and environment movements exploited the fear and then the reality of disasters like TMI and Chernobyl was responsible for halting expansion of the nuclear industry in most Western nations. Figure 13.1 shows that support for nuclear power in the US after TMI withered dramatically, opposition to building more nuclear plants growing from 30 per cent to 80 per cent.

TMI was responsible for the creation of INPO, Chernobyl for INPO's globalization through WANO. In nations like the US and Germany, the evidence is that nuclear energy is no longer perceived as the imminent social problem that it was during the mid 1970s and immediately after TMI and Chernobyl (Joppke 1993: 130). As in Downs's (1972) concept of the 'issue–attention cycle', the novelty of the issue began to fade, or perhaps mass publics found its doomsday quality too anxiety-invoking to want it constantly in their political focus, or perhaps agitation about new social movement agendas such as global warming simply crowded nuclear energy out in a competition where not everything can grab the public imagination at the same time. The key question is whether the scarce resource of public attention is used by reformers to institutionalize change, the effects of which persist after the issue has slipped from public attention.[3] This did happen

---

3  Lawrence Sherman (1978) has shown this to be the case with the issue of police corruption. After corruption scandals, police forces duck for cover for a while, returning to their corrupt ways after the scandal blows over, except when reformers manage to institutionalize anti-corruption regulatory measures during the scandal. See further Fisse and Braithwaite (1993).

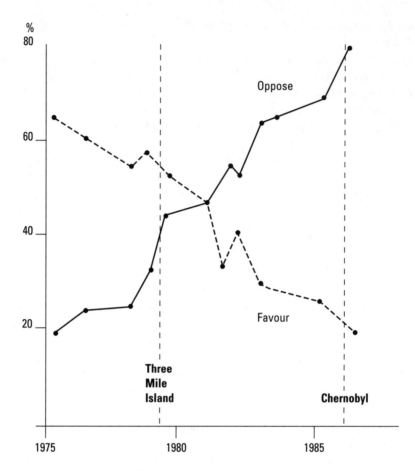

**FIGURE 13.1  US public opinion on building more nuclear power plants, 1975–1986**
Source: Adapted from Flavin (1986: 67). With permission from Worldwatch.

with the establishment of INPO and WANO for the institutionalization of continuous improvement in nuclear safety. It also happened on the safeguards front with the institutionalization of
the London Suppliers Group after India detonated its bomb.

INPO and WANO institutionalized a limited principle of transparency and marked a shift
away from the principle of national sovereignty toward a world where every nation's nuclear
industry would participate in a community of shared fate with every other nation's nuclear power
plants. Basically, in the nuclear case there is a thickening and globalizing of webs of control following crises that were effectively exploited by NGOs and reformers within states and the industry. We have seen that the big shift with INPO and WANO was away from rule compliance to a
principle of continuous improvement. Yet as Rees (1998) concluded in his study of the effectiveness of INPO compared to the comparative ineffectiveness of Responsible Care in the chemical
industry, the effectiveness of INPO as a strand in the web of controls depended on it being backed
by the NRC (INPO causing trouble for members with the NRC) – weak strands in a web of controls only acquire strength when tied to other strands with complementary strengths that can
cover the weaknesses. As the self-regulatory activities of INPO improved safety in the US, NGOs

like Greenpeace were able to lobby in Congress for higher safety standards to narrow the gap between legal standards and average industry standards in practice. As a result of modelling of the US in other countries, bilateral pressure by the US on other countries and US influence on IAEA standard-setting, US law has had a huge influence on global practice. This influence was also mediated by pairing US plants with plants in other nations, under the auspices of WANO.

If we consider NGOs as rather minor strands in the web of globalizing controls described here, anti-nuclear NGOs have no significant dialogic relationship with INPO, WANO or key firms in the industry. Yet an NGO, by lobbying for laws that consolidate self-regulatory gains, can in effect be pulling a number of interconnected strands in a web of controls – US bilateral pressure, multilateral pressure from IAEA and WANO, modelling of US law by other states. In network-theory terms, this is a case of 'the strength of weak ties' (Granovetter 1974). Greenpeace, as a small part of a global social movement to close nuclear power plants, exploits crises like TMI and Chernobyl that institutionalize new strands of control like INPO and WANO. The US insurance industry, a much more powerful strand than Greenpeace, refuses to insure plants that do not join INPO and meet its requirements. In such a world, strategic social movement actors can some-times tug weakly at a stronger strand, that in turn tugs strongly at a number of other strands to which it is connected in the web of controls.

In this case, the web of controls has netted the industry in a community of shared fate. Moreover, the transparency within this community (albeit not shared with outsiders) institution-alized by INPO and WANO has, in the words of Rees (1994: 99), grouped a hundred once-solitary joggers into a single race. Running last on safety evokes peer censure. Such an internally transparent and interdependent community of shared fate creates conditions where persuasion, praise and informal censure are extremely powerful. Informal processes of praise and shame then become the most important strands in the web of controls.

Most of the mechanisms of globalization listed in Table 22.1 are important in constituting and strengthening this web of controls – military and economic coercion, modelling, non-recipro-cal coordination and capacity-building, in particular. Upwards harmonization of both safety and safeguards standards has resulted. The limited regulatory competition (e.g. in the standards required by the host governments of vendors of nuclear technology) has tended to drive stan-dards up rather than down. Deregulation as a result of globalization is not even part of the vocab-ulary in the nuclear energy industry.

## CHAPTER 14

Telecommunications

Telecommunications, perhaps more than most of the domains in this book, raises issues about the impact of invention and innovation on regulatory change. It may be that technology, by changing the opportunity sets of individual actors has in a deeper sense 'determined' the course of telecommunications regulation. The Internet and associated technologies, for example, may turn out to be the primary cause of another Schumpeterian gale of creative destruction as business actors reorganize themselves around the new opportunities of the technology. But investigating whether technology is a macro determinant of change is not the concern of this chapter. Its focus is on the way that actors have used mechanisms and principles to determine the shape of international telecommunications regulation.

## History of Globalization

Telecommunications is a term that was coined in the 1930s (Snow 1986: 7). If we think of it in broad terms as communication over distance, then its history is a long one for it includes semaphore, smoke-signals and many other forms of signalling. It is more usual to think of telecommunications beginning with three nineteenth-century inventions: the telegraph (1837), telephone (1876) and radio (1899). This is where we will start.

Telecommunications regulation contains one of the earliest examples of international regulatory cooperation between states, with the creation of the International Telegraphic Union (ITgU) in 1865. But in other respects the regulation of telecommunications is a story of territorial containment. Much of the early regulatory development in the first half of the twentieth century was influenced by the economic view that telecommunications is a 'natural monopoly'. But no state thinks that there should be one world monopolist. Instead, the contours of this natural monopoly correspond with state boundaries. This national regulatory containment of telecommunications is in the process of breaking down, often in dramatic ways.

### Taxis, Taxes and the Post in Europe

Telecommunications regulation in Europe began with a state monopoly model. State bureaucracies were given the exclusive right to provide telephone and telegraph services. In many cases these bureaucracies had been providers of postal services (the European system is still referred to as the PTT: post, telephone and telegraph system). Postal services became the exclusive province of states because of the revenue needs of cash-hungry European monarchs. Towards the end of the fifteenth century the Habsburgs granted one family, the Taxis family, monopoly privileges over the carriage of post. What had been a courier service blossomed into a huge business that also generated much-needed revenue for the Habsburgs. No one thought that merchants' communications would reach the volumes they did. Naturally the size of the profits generated interest from cities and principalities and private players who wanted to establish their own postal systems. It was this struggle, the struggle for postal revenues between the sixteenth and eighteenth centuries, that shaped the emergence of the PTT system (Noam 1992: Ch. 2).

States like Prussia established postal monopoly systems which were carefully guarded against private competitors. In England the telegraphy network was by 1865 the subject of a cartel agreement between three companies. Users of the service, particularly newspapers, objected to the rates that the cartel charged and so began a campaign for the nationalization of the telegraph (Noam 1992: 18). The British Post Office took control of the telegraph in 1868. It was not only in England that newspapers pressed for better telegraph services. In far-flung New Zealand in the 1860s local newspapers campaigned for a better service – and received special rates on press telegrams (Wilson 1994: 28). This embryonic pattern of a business user-inspired change to telecommunications regulation was to reappear in Europe more forcefully in the 1980s.

## European Deregulation

Beginning with the UK in the 1980s, European states began to dismantle the public telecommunications monopolies which had been erected on the bureaucratic edifice of the postal monopolies. Like their medieval ancestors these states were still hungry for revenue, but other pressures pushed them along the deregulatory path. In 1979 Margaret Thatcher was elected to power. At the centre of her government's political philosophy lay confidence in markets and entrepreneurialism. It was naturally attracted to deregulatory agendas. It was just such an agenda that the Telecommunication Managers Association had been steadily pushing in the UK for a number of years. The Thatcher government was prepared to respond to ideas for change in UK telecommunications because it saw in US telecommunications deregulation a success story that could be replicated. No government wants to start with a failure. It also wanted to help revive the UK telecommunications equipment market. The Post Office monopoly over telecommunications became one of the first big targets. In 1981 British Telecom was established and in 1984 it was privatized. OFTEL (Office of Telecommunications) was formed as the regulatory body for the new telecommunications market. Earlier in 1981 the Thatcher government had privatized Cable & Wireless, its international carrier. Following the model of MCI in the US, Mecury was created to compete with British Telecom (Noam 1992: 110). A value-added telecommunications services industry was helped with the passage of the *Value-Added Network Service Licensing Act 1982*.

The shift to a more liberalized telecommunications sector occurred throughout Western Europe in the 1980s. Factors like the political strength of the local PTT, union resistance, the ideology of the elected government and, in the case of France, philosophy, all affected the speed of telecommunications deregulation. France has been something of a slow mover. There, telecommunications deregulation has been linked with loss of national sovereignty and US hegemony (Nora & Minc 1980). Although France Télécom has been restructured it remains close in spirit to the former PTT system. In 1981 the German Monopoly Commission issued a report that questioned the continuation of the Bundespost's monopoly. Drawing on the US experience, the report suggested that competition and deregulation were the right course (Weiss 1984: 141). There was also pressure from without. In 1982 the European Commission (EC) put pressure on the Bundespost to change its restrictive practices in the telecommunications equipment market and there was continuous pressure, particularly from the US, about procurement practices. In 1989 the Bundespost, one of the most dominant PTTs, was reorganized into three public corporations. Following this came a privatized Deutsche Telekom AG. An independent regulator along the lines of OFTEL in the UK has yet to appear.

European telecommunications regulation began to be progressively harmonized through the work of the EC. The EC's Green Paper (1987) outlined a number of objectives including the establishment of a European Telecommunications Standards Institute (ETSI), the development of Europe-wide services and a unified position on satellite communications. This policy work was followed by positive law in the form of Directives (e.g. the Commission Directive of 28 June 1990 on competition in the markets for telecommunication services) as well as Guidelines and Recommendations. There are now many of these reaching into all areas of telecommunications including competition rules in telecommunications, procurement, integrated services digital networks, protection of personal data and privacy, terminal equipment, cellular communications and trans-European networks (Scott 1996a).

The changes in telecommunications regulation have not been confined to Western Europe. Before the passing of communism the Soviet bloc was beginning to adopt a more open stance to foreign investment and joint ventures in the telecommunications sector (Borg & Emmert 1989). Eastern European countries, starting with Hungary, have begun restructuring telecommunications regulation by separating telecommunications and post and progressively introducing competition (Holcer 1995).

### The Rise and Fall of the Private Monopoly Model: The US

Beginning in 1876, the US telephone industry underwent cycles of economic concentration (A. Davies 1994: 33). The first cycle (1876–79) culminated in an agreement between the Bell Company and Western Union. Bell gained the local telephone market and Western Union the long-distance telegraphy market. During the second cycle (1880–94) Bell, relying on its patent monopolies, developed a long-distance voice network. During the final period Bell transferred its assets to its subsidiary, AT&T. This offspring-turned-parent became one of the greatest monopolies of the twentieth century:

> By 1930, the $US5 billion Bell system had become the world's biggest monopoly, a giant combination of financial and industrial power, with 454 000 employees, and the largest concentration of capital controlled by a single company in the history of private enterprise; all held together by centralized control (A. Davies 1994: 57).

The rise and rise of AT&T became a source of complaint from competitors and a matter of public concern. The Chairman of AT&T, Theodore Vail, saw the mounting criticism as an opportunity. Vail's vision was that of a private monopolist administering a system that was universal in the sense that it served the whole market. Universal service, to Vail, meant one telephone system that embraced all users rather than a series of independently competing systems (Mueller 1993:

13–14). This private monopolist would have to reach a regulatory accommodation with government, but that in itself would not necessarily hurt its profits and might even help it against competitors. This is more or less what happened. In a skilful public relations campaign Vail deflected much of the trust-busting sentiment of the beginning of the century (S. Douglas 1987: 248–9). Large corporations were things to be admired, not criticized. For various reasons public opinion began to swing in this direction. AT&T did reach a regulatory accommodation with state and federal levels of government. State utility commissions regulated telephone companies through a rate-base–rate-of-return method. The idea was that regulators and telephone companies would arrive at a calculation that reflected the company's expenses and allowed it a return on its rates base (Mueller 1993: 3). At the federal level the Interstate Commerce Commission and later the Federal Communications Commission (FCC) were given regulatory powers over telephone companies. AT&T was also subject to antitrust policing by the Justice Department.

AT&T had one of the longest monopoly runs in history, but after the Second World War US companies began to complain to US regulatory agencies about the level and price of the services they received from AT&T. The FCC came under pressure to open up the telecommunications market (Schiller 1982). In the decades that followed, the FCC (led by US courts) began to liberalize telecommunications. It broke AT&T's hold over the terminal equipment market and in the long-distance market it permitted the construction of private microwave systems (Baughcum 1986: 70–4). Through its First Computer Inquiry (1968) and its Second Computer Inquiry (1973) the FCC allowed business users to satisfy their data-processing needs by keeping regulation out of the domain of data-processing. Over time the rapid expansion of computer-based services drew the regulated telecommunications network into its deregulatory orbit. FCC decisions were central in this process.

The Department of Justice's oversight of AT&T led over the decades to a number of investigations and agreements between the two, which culminated on 8 January 1982 in an agreement (referred to as the Modified Final Judgment) by AT&T that it would divest itself of its local Bell Operating Companies (Snow 1995: 211). Before divestiture AT&T was a vertically integrated monolith. It had a monopoly in the provision of local telephone exchange services. Through Bell Labs AT&T was the main developer of telecommunications technology and through Western Electric the main supplier of equipment. After divestiture the local Bell companies were organized into seven regional companies. AT&T remained a long-distance carrier and was eventually allowed to enter the computer and information services market.

The divestiture of AT&T was a national event, and through it the US had signalled Europe and Japan about the strength of its commitment to competition and change in the telecommunications sector. The divestiture no doubt signalled European players that there were opportunities in the US market, but it also signalled – as time made clear – that the US was interested in European and Japanese markets.

The *Telecommunications Act 1996* continued the US federal policy of deregulation for telecommunications. 'Deregulation' is too simple a term to describe the US process. 'Regulatory experimentation' approximates the truth more closely. State public utility commissions continue to have regulatory powers over the local network. States, doubtless influenced by the importance of telecommunications in Atlanta's successful Olympic bid, have become sites of regulatory experimentation. Rate-base–rate-of-return regulation has in many cases been swept away and telematic projects of all kinds have been launched. Both at the federal level (led by the FCC) and the state level (led by desire for economic growth) there is intense pressure for regulatory innovation.

## Two Regulatory Models for Telecommunications

From about 1910 there were two clear regulatory models for telecommunications – the European PTT system and the US government-regulated private monopoly model. Both of these remained fairly stable until the 1970s, when deregulatory pressures become stronger. There was a third model of regulation, described by Davies as 'the decentralized alternative' (A. Davies 1994: 72). It consists of a state-owned long-distance carrier and numerous local telephone companies which are municipal enterprises or private ventures. Finland is perhaps the best exemplar of this model. And although by all accounts it is a very successful model, it has had few followers (Noam 1992: 212).

## The International Telecommunication Union

The International Telecommunication Union (ITU) grew from the cooperation between European states in the 1850s on the workings of the telegraph system. Austria, Bavaria, Prussia and Saxony had signed bilateral treaties to link their telegraph systems. In 1850 they formed the Austro-German Telegraph Union. Other European states began to follow the Austro-German initiative. The West European Telegraph Union was created in 1858. The French, seeing that telegraphic regionalism was counterproductive, organized a conference in Paris in 1865. Out of this conference came the Paris Telegraph Convention which formally established the ITgU.

The ITgU was an organization of states. States were obliged to apply the provisions of the Paris Telegraph Convention to companies within their jurisdiction. As Codding (1972: 42) observes, 'Nationalization or complete control over telegraph was always an unwritten prerequisite for membership'. A country like the UK, which at that time had a telegraph system under private control, could only participate through its colony India. The US never joined the ITgU, but US companies were active participants in the conferences of the ITgU for the simple reason that they sent telegrams to member states.

Through its early history the ITU was dominated by those European states which ran telegraphy as a public monopoly and gained large revenues by doing so. The ITU was at first only concerned with telegraphy, but over time it became involved with telephony and radio. The International Telegraph Union became the International Telecommunication Union in 1932 when states agreed at Madrid that it would be more administratively efficient to have one international organization and one international convention to deal with radio, telephone and telegraph. The modern structure of the ITU was created in Madrid. The new international instrument was attached to the Telegraph, Telephone, Radio Regulations and the Additional Radio Regulations. These Regulations dealt with the more technical aspects of telecommunications. It was a structure designed to maximize the possibility of cooperation among states. The International Telecommunication Convention consisted of general, non-controversial clauses. Matters like frequency allocation, which were likely to be the subject of dispute between states, were placed in the relevant Regulations and a state had only to sign one rather than all three main Regulations (Codding & Rutkowski 1982: 19).

The history of the ITU can be thought of as the rise of an international rational bureaucracy. There was no ignoring the fact that if states were to have viable national and international communications systems based on radio, cable and satellite they would have to coordinate the use and development of these technologies. This required the kind of rational, technocratic and rule-oriented organization at an international level that Weber saw would increasingly feature in modern social life (Albrow 1970: 45). Formally, states remained drivers of international telecommunications policy. It was only states acting through the Plenipotentiary Conference that could amend the ITU Convention and change the policy direction of the ITU. Over time a complex, rule-oriented decision-making process evolved. States became enmeshed in a detailed regulatory structure for telecommunications that was the product of the work of ITU study groups and committees, engineers, companies and scientific organizations. States still had the final say about adopting the multitude of recommendations put before them. At World Administrative Radio Conferences (WARC) or World Administrative Telegraph and Telephone Conferences (WATTC) they could agree not to adopt changes to the Radio Regulations (administered by WARC) or the International Telecommunications Regulations (administered by WATTC). More often than not they would adopt the recommendations before them. A good example of the way in which states were drawn into a de facto delegation of sovereignty occurred in 1973. States agreed that in order to facilitate the standard-setting process the Telegraph and Telephone Regulations should require telephone administrations or private operating agencies to comply with the recommendations of the International Telegraph and Telephone Consultative Committee (CCITT) (Codding & Rutkowski 1982: 218). In fact, in the whole area of standards states found it easier to allow the two committees of the ITU – the CCITT and the International Radio Consultative Committee (CCIR) – to make recommendations on appropriate standards for telecommunications networks, tariff matters, the use of the spectrum, performance standards for radio and so on.

The more recent history of the ITU has been characterized by pressure from outside for change. The US in particular has been critical of ITU efforts in areas such as satellite regulation and the accounting rates system. US companies like AT&T have also been critical of the ITU, describing its multilateral processes as 'plodding' and the organization itself as having a 'state-control mentality' (Tipson 1997: 256–7). In a series of conferences between 1989 and 1994, the ITU changed its organizational structure (Codding 1995). The justification offered was the need to adapt better to the rapidly changing nature of telecommunications.

## Regulating Radio Waves

The history of the internationalization of the regulation of radio (wireless telegraphy, as it was first known) begins with a fit of temper by Prince Henry, brother of the Kaiser. Prince Henry was returning to Germany on the *Deutschland*. The *Deutschland* was fitted with a non-Marconi radio apparatus. One of the rules of the Marconi Company was that Marconi operators would communicate only with other Marconi operators – the rule of non-intercommunication (S. Douglas 1987: 70). If the only issue had been the inconvenience to Prince Henry of radio isolation the incident might have remained a low-level diplomatic one. But the stakes were much higher. The Germans realized that the Marconi Company might one day have an international monopoly over communication using the ether (as the spectrum was then called). The military implications of this worried the Germans. The alliance between the UK and Marconi (Marconi's company was established in England) also affected the commercial interests of other countries. The Kaiser, in the name of world peace, issued invitations to the UK, France, Spain, Austria, Russia, Italy and the US to attend the Berlin International Wireless Conference of 1903 (S. Douglas 1987: 120). The Conference produced a set of principles in the form of a Final Protocol (Codding 1972: 86). These principles were aimed at facilitating communication between ship and shore, giving priority to requests for help from ships, and avoiding interference with other stations.

The meeting at Berlin also impressed upon the delegates the strategic military importance of government control over the ether. It was not a resource that could be left to market forces. As the 1904 war between Russia and Japan demonstrated, radio was too important a military tool. So at the second International Wireless Conference in Berlin in 1906 Germany, with strong support from the US, proposed 'that the ether be divided into regions by wave-lengths, with the military getting the largest and the best tracts' (S. Douglas 1987: 139). This Conference was attended by the main maritime powers. They agreed to the formation of the International Radiotelegraph Union. The Conference also saw the beginnings of cooperation on technical standards and frequency allocation (frequencies were actually allotted in relation to maritime standards and non-public government stations). All states at the Conference agreed that regular meetings would be needed.

German leadership on radio regulation was crucial. It was Germany which saw the dangers, both military and civilian, of allowing Marconi to continue building a worldwide monopoly and Germany which put a draft convention, complete with regulations, on the table at the Berlin Wireless Conference of 1906.

European states moved quickly to regulate radio after the international conferences. The US, however, allowed its policy of unregulated airwaves to continue. The sinking of *Titanic* ended that. The stories of death and heroism were seared upon the public mind. Radio was both hero and a culprit. Ships that had been within 30 miles of the *Titanic* did not hear her distress calls because radio-operating procedures were not standardized. In the aftermath of the disaster amateur radio was blamed for the confusion of information. The airwaves were full of conflicting accounts of what had happened. The US regulated in the form of the *Radio Act 1912*. The sinking of the *Titanic* also put pressure on countries to cooperate at the London Radio Conference of 1912. The British Postmaster-General opened the conference by saying that the *Titanic* disaster had shown the need to make more effective use of radio in rescue work (Codding 1972: 98). The principle of obligatory intercommunication was put into the Convention, with the Marconi Company agreeing to implement the principle before the new Convention came into force. The *Titanic* disaster galvanized both small and large states into action. New Zealand, for example, in 1913 made it obligatory for New Zealand ships engaged in trade to carry a wireless. It also regulated the use of wireless by foreign ships in its waters, the purpose being to reduce interference in radio transmissions (Wilson 1994: 92).

The cooperation which had begun between states on the international regulation of radio continued after the London Conference, but in a spasmodic fashion. After the First World War the US began to take a much more active role. In 1920 it proposed, at a meeting in Washington, the creation of a 'Universal Electric-communications Union', which did not eventuate. The Washington Radio Conference of 1927 made further inroads on states' capacity to allocate frequencies independently of one another. States had allowed radio stations to spring up in large numbers, resulting in high levels of interference. At Washington, for the first time, states agreed that the Radio Regulations had to place restrictions on certain kinds of practices, like the use of wide-space frequency waves. States agreed to a detailed table which allocated frequencies to various services and a rule that dealt with priority and first use of frequency (Codding 1972: 123–6). The Conference also established a committee to recommend on the technical aspects of radio regulation. The Washington Conference firmly established the pillars of international radio regulation. States saw that without such pillars chaos would rule the spectrum.

Most states recognized the need for detailed coordination regarding the use of the spectrum. Without such coordination messages about the *Titanic* sinking would get mixed up with the latest pop jingle. Yet the same states took the view that they had sovereignty over an asset which they had to administer in the interests of their respective publics. Broadcasting, communication and culture were too closely linked to take a different view. At the Atlantic City Administrative Radio Conference of 1947 states agreed to the creation of an International Frequency Registration Board (IFRB), whose structure had to take into account the principle of national sovereignty. The solution was to develop a system of frequency registration that distinguished between the notification of a frequency assignment and the registration of a frequency assignment. Registration went beyond notification to indicate a conformity with ITU rules. The IFRB, however, did not have formal powers to prevent a state from going down the path of notification. In the words of the Chairman who helped draw up its working procedures, it was to function as 'a verification Board, such as Lloyd's of London' (Codding & Rutkowski 1982: 119).

The rules dealing with the means of broadcasting were evolving into a complex international regime. There was no parallel evolution of rules for the content of broadcasts. The worldwide amateur radio movement discovered that short waves offered international communication possibilities at low cost. States began to exploit the global communication possibilities of the technology. On 25 December 1932, King George V began a broadcast to the British empire with the words: 'Through the marvels of modern science, I am enabled this Christmas Day to speak to all my peoples throughout the world' (Wood 1992: 36). International broadcasting was not confined to messages of goodwill. During the 1930s England, Germany, Italy and Russia led the way in propaganda broadcasting. Propaganda broadcasting continued to escalate after the Second World War. The US began to secure overseas locations for its transmitters. There was in effect a two-tier regulatory structure for US broadcasting. The domestic scene was controlled by the FCC and was characterized by liberal rules on ownership of radio stations. International broadcasting by the US was controlled by the US Information Agency, which answered to the State Department. The Voice of America became 'the world's first truly global broadcasting network' (Wood 1992: 108). In the 1950s the CIA entered the radio propaganda game by establishing Radio Free Europe. Although presented to the world as a privately funded radio station, it was actually a CIA operation. Passionate anti-communist intellectuals were hired to send out airwaves of criticism for reception in Russia. Radio Free Europe was followed by Radio Liberty and Radio Free Asia. Naturally, Russia retaliated with its own propaganda broadcasting (Radio Moscow). In radio land the Cold War settled into a 'pattern of US broadcasting and Soviet jamming' with both competing over the airwaves for the loyalties of other states (Warlaumont 1988: 46).

No global regime emerged on the content of broadcasts that crossed state borders. Human rights discourse remained vague and controversial and so could not function as the basis upon which to develop concrete rules for the content of international broadcasting (Kessler 1985).

## Satellite Regulation[1]

Satellite regulation has a short history. The first satellite devoted to civilian purposes was Telstar, which began operations in 1962 (Luard 1977: 37). The international regulation of satellites began with the passage in the US of the *Communication Satellite Act 1962*. The policy behind the

---

1 This section is based on work by Richard Joseph & Peter Drahos 1998, 'Contested Arenas in International Telecommunications: Towards an Integrated Political Perspective' in S. Macdonald & G. Madden (eds), *Telecommunications and Socio-Economic Development*, Elsevier Science, 99–118.

Act was to create a commercial communications satellite system, which would itself be part of an international satellite system. The Act established COMSAT, a public company half-owned by the US government. In 1964 twelve developed nations met in Washington to discuss the possibility of an international satellite system for the world. The outcome of that meeting was the establishment of the International Telecommunications Satellite Organization (INTELSAT). The idea was that each state and its national carrier would participate in INTELSAT. Through this participation INTELSAT would enjoy a monopoly over international satellite services. European states agreed to participate in the system through their PTTs and the US through COMSAT. The expectation was that states would not set up satellite systems outside of INTELSAT. The Preamble to the INTELSAT Agreement stated expressly that states were committed to 'the aim of achieving a single, global commercial telecommunications satellite system'. The US initiative may have been partly a desire to provide a public good (a single global system for the world, beyond the reach of any one nation) or one can agree with Noam (1992: 299): 'Intelsat is a reflection of the US desire to embed its own technical lead in satellites and launchers in an international regime of coordinated monopoly, subject to a weighted voting that benefits industrialized countries'.

INTELSAT never became a UN agency. It was both an international organization and an international corporation operating as a commercial entity (Smith 1990: 29). The US saw it as a commercial arrangement in which flexibility was the key. Flexibility came to mean deregulation.

INTELSAT membership started with eleven signatories and has become the world's largest satellite system, with twenty-five in-orbit satellites and 137 member nations. At the same time its monopoly position has deteriorated. Regional satellite systems have emerged (INMARSAT for maritime needs, EUTELSAT for Europe, ARABSAT for Arab countries and PALAPA for South-East Asian countries). These regional systems were established with the blessing of INTELSAT, which approved them because essentially the regional systems did not deprive it of significant revenue flow. The Soviet Union, with eight other socialist states, created a regional agreement known as INTERSPUTNIK (Smith 1990). This had no impact on INTELSAT's economic viability, and there were cooperative links between the organizations.

The real threat to INTELSAT began in 1983 and 1984 when a number of private US satellite companies (Orion Satellite, International Satellite, Cygnus, Pan American, RCA American Communications and Finansat) sought permission from the FCC to operate international satellite services. The first application was from Orion Satellite, to build and operate a private satellite facility between the US and Europe. The FCC under the deregulatory leadership of Chairman Mark Fowler moved quickly to process the application (Colino 1985: 112). INTELSAT responded with resolutions which expressed deep concern over developments in the US and stated that parties to INTELSAT remained committed to a single global satellite system. A paper by members of an influential Washington communications law firm drew attention to the difficulty of the US unilaterally trying to deregulate the international satellite communications system and suggested that the US proceed in consultation with INTELSAT (Colino 1985: 128). President Reagan issued a Determination on 28 November 1984 which stated that separate international communication satellite systems were required in the national interest and that the FCC had to consult with INTELSAT. On 25 July 1985 the FCC allowed three of the applications, subject to restrictions so as to protect INTELSAT from economic harm.

INTELSAT's gradual moves towards accepting open competition were encouraged in late 1991 by a series of moves from the US. The US Commerce and State Departments reported that their studies showed that the INTELSAT system would not be economically harmed if separate satellite systems were allowed to sell private line services interconnected with public-switched networks (Fujimoto & Berejka 1993: 266). The US Commerce and State Departments also recommended that all restrictions on separate systems' provision of switched services should be eliminated by January 1997. The FCC was quick to accept the recommendations, essentially putting the US firmly behind open competition as far as INTELSAT's future was concerned. Growing private satellite interests such as PanAmSat were also positioning themselves behind the US position, as they stood to benefit from the demise of the INTELSAT monopoly (Daffner 1996).

In line with this pressure from the US, by mid 1991 INTELSAT was moving to recommend 'that full competition be eased in and that significant steps in that direction be taken now' (Fujimoto & Berejka 1993: 266). In late 1994 INTELSAT moved much closer to restructuring on competitive lines by establishing a working party to review the future direction of the organization. US pressure has played a significant part in this:

> Comsat, the largest investor in Intelsat, has aggressively pursued a pro-competitive privatization policy within the Intelsat organization, while simultaneously seeking the support of the US Government for the privatization of Intelsat. Comsat's initial drive towards privatization, combined with the subsequent leadership of the US government resulted in the AP [the INTELSAT Assembly of Parties] decision to seek recommendations to implement a commercial subsidiary (Shea 1996).

Satellites are most effective when they are placed in a geostationary satellite orbit (GSO). During the 1970s the ITU's work in this area proceeded on the assumption that the GSO was a scarce resource (Rothblatt 1980: 413). States took the view that space was a resource that fell under the 'common heritage of mankind' principle (reflected in the Outer Space Treaty of 1967). In a series of conferences in the 1970s the ITU developed a set of principles for satellite communications that complemented the common heritage of humanity principle. These conferences – the World Administrative Radio Conference for Space Telecommunications (1971), ITU Plenipotentiary Conference (1973), World Administrative Radio Conference for Broadcasting Satellites (1977) and the World Administrative Radio Conference (1979) – moved in the direction of ensuring equitable access to GSO. Under the influence of a large Third World membership, led to some extent by India, the ITU moved towards a plan of 'a priori assignment of the spectrum/orbit resource among all ITU members' (Rothblatt 1980: 418). Developing countries supported such a plan because it guaranteed them orbital slots at the point at which they required them. Under the 'first-come, first-served' approach, which had characterized the ITU's approach to frequency and orbit allocation, developing countries believed they would not be given locations suitable to their communication needs.

The US opposed the move towards a priori assignments on the grounds of efficiency (orbital slots could be reserved without being used) and that technology would solve the problem of scarcity. Some US representatives began making noises about leaving the ITU. At the 1977 World Administrative Radio Conference for Broadcasting Satellites, the Chairman of the FCC floated the possibility that in light of Third World politics at the Conference the US might look for an 'alternative forum to resolve the kind of issues that the ITU was once attuned to handle' (Codding 1977: 231).

However, not even the US could simply leave the evolving ITU process for the regulation of the GSO. The US was probably the biggest user of geostationary satellites. The lack of a multilaterally coordinated regime for its many satellites would have affected its interests as much as those of developing countries, particularly when those countries began to develop satellite technology. For these reasons the US participated in the next major conference on satellite regulation, the International Telecommunications Union World Administrative Radio Conference on the Use of the Geostationary-Satellite Orbit and the Planning of Space Services Utilizing It (known as 1985 Space WARC). At the Conference the US suggested a compromise, which involved a multilateral planning mechanism for certain fixed satellite bands and a method of allotting portions of spectrum for satellite use that took into account the interests of developing countries. Space WARC 1985 produced a compromise between the US and developing countries (Waite & Rowan 1986: 363). The US avoided the system of *a priori* assignment that developing countries had been campaigning for, and the developing countries gained recognition for a more multilateral approach to regulating the use of satellite technology.

### Standard-setting in Telecommunications

One meaning of standardization is the making of products that are compatible (Farrell 1989). Generally, standardization issues in telecommunications relate to product and systems compatibility. The benefits of standards as economic institutions include reducing transaction costs, enhancing demand and allowing the competitive process to operate at the level of products rather than systems (Antonelli 1994). The desirability of having standards is beyond question. The difficulty lies in having a reliable decision-making procedure which ensures that the costs of standards are kept down and that standards are introduced at the right time and in the right form. Should markets be left to generate de facto standards? The danger is that if such standards emerge as proprietary ones they may become a source of dominant market power, or they may be premature (the bandwagon effect) and inhibit technological advances (David 1987).

Decision-making procedures for standards can be unilateral or coordinated and public or private. This produces a simple matrix in which there are private unilateral, private coordinated, public unilateral and public coordinated decision procedures for the generation of standards. In practice the four types of decision procedures are not so neatly divided. Firms have realized that standards can be used to protect their business or to increase it. The importance of standard-setting to individual business survival has meant that, over time, private interest in public international standard-setting has grown.

Decision procedures for telecommunication standards began with states acting unilaterally to set standards for their telegraph systems, but this soon ran into incompatibility problems. Sometimes, for a telegraph message to cross a border, the telegraph employee of one country had to walk across the border to hand the message to the telegraph employee of the other so that the transmission of the message could be continued (Codding 1972: 14). One of the main reasons for the creation of the ITgU was the need for a forum in which states could work out technical standards that would allow messages to cross borders without interruption. In other words, the ITgU offered states an internationally coordinated decision procedure.

The first work the ITgU did in the area of standards was, naturally enough, in relation to telegraph standards. We can see in these standards an evolution from specification standards (e.g. specifying the Morse technology) to performance standards. Radio standards, particularly for ships, was another early area of work. Standard-setting in the ITgU evolved into a very complex, slow and cumbersome process. The International Telecommunication Convention is divided into Basic Provisions and General Regulations. The Convention is complemented by the Telegraph Regulations, the Telephone Regulations and the Radio Regulations. Standards of various kinds can be found in all. There were also the recommendations of the two main standard-making bodies of the ITU, the CCITT (now taken over by the Telecommunications Standardization sector) and CCIR (now taken over by the Radiocommunications sector). These recommendations were published in the CCITT Yellow Book and the CCIR Green Book – actually dozens of books amounting to thousands of pages (Codding & Rutkowski 1982: Ch. 10). The CCITT Yellow Book, for example, dealt with tariff principles, telephone switching and signalling, data communication over the telephone network and hundreds of other topics; the Green Book dealt with matters like propagation in ionized and non-ionized media. The sheer cost of purchasing and processing the information in these books meant that the standard-setting game at the ITU was dominated by players from developed countries. This is still true. Developing countries use their energy in getting the ITU to focus on technical assistance.

Despite the bureaucratic complexity that characterized the ITU standard-setting processes, ITU standards were and continue to be influential. The reason for this lies in the fact that states had much to gain from cooperating on the setting of international standards (ease of communication across borders) and so were prepared to meet the costs of an international standard-setting forum. For a while, standard-setting in international telecommunications fitted into the economist's category of the 'pure coordination case' (Besen & Saloner 1989: 180). The stability of the pure coordination system was helped by the fact that telecommunications regulation within the US and Europe took the form of a regulated monopoly. Single suppliers like AT&T had considerable discretion in setting standards for what were essentially local markets. Only comparatively minimal levels of coordination were required at the international level. Telephone usage did not reflect the distance possibilities of the technology. Mueller points out that of the calls placed with the Chicago Telephone Company in 1923, only 0.5 per cent were interstate calls and in 1930 98.6 per cent of the calls dealt with by the Bell system were intrastate (Mueller 1993: 12).

Over time political and business 'impurities' began to enter the standard-setting process, as business actors came to realize the importance of standards to their survival. International standard-making became increasingly politicized (Shurmer & David 1996: 9). Standards not only allow interoperability; they also open product markets to competition. Business actors saw that international coordination on a standard could see them lose markets as well as gain them. These actors, who were usually very strong in their domestic market, saw that a common standard would allow foreign suppliers into their domestic market. Properly designed standards could enliven markets. Standards thus became things to play for, which at times meant resisting rather than cooperating in the standard-setting process (Besen & Farrell 1994).

A good example of this is the development of many incompatible national standards for colour television and the adoption, at the international level, of three different standards (NTSC, PAL and SECAM, with a total of sixteen variations) (Nickelson 1990: 303). This drama has been re-enacted in the case of standards for high-definition television (HDTV). There is little doubt that HDTV standards which would permit a global trade in programs are economically preferable (at least for buyers of television sets). Japan was the first to develop and propose a global standard (known as Hi-Vision). The EU, worried about the future of its industry, formed the Eureka-95 program in 1986 which led to the HD-MAC standard. And the US, led by its broadcasters and with the support of the FCC, opted for a standard (ATV) that was consistent with the interests of its terrestrial broadcasters (Hopkins & Davies 1990). Throughout this the CCIR stuck to its task of trying to develop a common set of standards, in which it did not succeed. Instead of one set of HDTV standards for a global television public three kinds emerged: Hi-Vision (Japan), HD-MAC (Europe) and ATV (US) (Shurmer & David 1996 10). HDTV remains the subject of complex manoeuvrings. In December 1996 the FCC, after an inquiry begun in 1987, made a decision that committed US players to a digital HDTV system. In Europe the HD-MAC standard was dropped in 1993 (presumably since it had done its job against Japan's Hi-Vision). The Digital Video Broadcasting Group (DVBG), comprising European broadcasters, satellite operators, manufacturers and public instrumentalities, was established the same year (Hart 1998:218). This group is working to produce regional standards that ETSI and the European Committee for Electrotechnical Standardization can adopt. The strategy of the DVBG is that these European standard-setting bodies will push for the globalization of the European standard through the ITU (Hart 1998: 218). Japan, somewhat more slowly, is also moving towards all-digital HDTV standards. One thing which is clear from this process is that before the standards of any one region can hope to become the global standards industry, that region must present a united front. Once regional consensus on a standard is achieved the ITU can be used as the gateway to globalization of the standard. The DVBG is a good example of the way in which in an actor can initiate a bottom-up sequence of regulatory globalization, a sequence we theorize in Chapter 23.

Standard-making in telecommunications is more fragmented than in the past. The need for coordinated standard-setting has increased because many states and businesses which are consumers of telecommunications services want globally integrated communication networks. At the same time, some states and business actors see that an international consensus on standards may threaten their economic interests and so have an incentive to block its emergence. The convergence between telecommunications and computing technologies has also expanded dramatically the number of private actors wanting a place at the standard-setting table. These actors want quick action on standards for products that have a short lifecycle. The ITU cannot meet the demands of market players for standards. Its failure to deliver open network standards, coupled with the emergence of an Internet that did not rely on ITU leadership, are examples that support such a view. The future of standards in telecommunications and computing is in the hands of individual entrepreneurs who can lock markets into their standards, or of industry associations pushing a particular standard.

Our fieldwork suggests that it may be too early to pronounce the last rites over standards bureaucracies like the ITU. It is true that the breakdown of private and public monopoly models of telecommunications, combined with the ever-quickening lifecycles of technologies, has placed these bodies under enormous pressure. Their response has been to reorganize. In 1998 a reorganized ITU was able to deliver a V.90 standard for modems, in roughly sixteen months. The Conference on European Posts and Telecoms (CEPT), which was created in 1959, has completely reorganized. It has gone to a flexible committee structure (two committees – the European Radiocommunication Committee and the European Committee for Regulatory Telecommunications Affairs), as well as delegating some of its standards work to ETSI. Within the ITU, ETSI, CEPT and many other standards bodies there are all kinds of study groups, working groups, project teams, coordinating boards and technical committees, all working to be more responsive to the demand for standards.

The heightened complexity of the standards game in telecommunications was nicely out-lined in one of our interviews. A senior executive from Motorola told us, reminiscing about the old days of standard-setting, 'we would set the standards'. A European regulator we interviewed agreed: 'Motorola have a patent in nearly every GSM [Groupe Speciale Mobile] standard at the ITU'. A large company like Motorola or IBM would develop a system, which would become the industry standard. But the same executive pointed out how much the standards game had changed even for large players. This change occurred primarily because of the focus on inter-national markets and the presence of other players in those markets. The object of the game – making one's technology the industry standard – remains the same. Strategic thinking about how to achieve it, however, has changed, at least for some players. The experience of Nippon Hoso Kyokai (NHK) with its Hi-Vision standard revealed to all players in the electronics industry that being first in the market with an innovative technology did not necessarily confer a competitive advantage unless the business also had influence over the politics of standard-setting. Both Europe and the US realized that NHK might achieve another consumer-based technological tri-umph with its Hi-Vision system if the ITU agreed to Japan's proposal in 1986 that it become the global production standard (Seel 1998: 210). Their response was to play a blocking game by set-ting up processes to develop alternative standards.

Standards battles may increasingly feature complex mixes of private and public actors. China, for instance, has hinted that it is prepared to embrace the mobile telephony standard known as CDMA (code division multiple access), thereby giving US manufacturers like Motorola and Lucent Technologies a powerful grip on its market. The losers would be companies such as Ericsson, which have developed the European GSM standard. For China, the telecom standard issue is part of a bigger trade game it is playing with the US.

The apparently chaotic detail of standard-setting reveals a standards game that has become much more pluralistic. Standard-setting continues to develop new sources. No public or private organization now has a natural monopoly over the setting of standards. In one of the paradoxes of globalization, standard-setting has become a more democratic affair. The ITU can no longer pronounce from Olympian heights what the standard shall be. Motorola, IBM and other players cannot just sit back and set standards as they did in the good old days. They have to guard against standards that can rob them of international markets, they have to attend the meetings of stan-dards bodies because their competitors do, they have to watch the activities of regional standards bodies because those bodies have globalist aspirations – as shown on ETSI's webpage: 'ETSI pro-motes the worldwide standardization process whenever possible' (http://www.etsi.org).

There is a networked complexity about standard-setting in telecommunications (as well as standard-setting more generally) to which it is hard to do justice. ISO and the International Elec-trochemical Commission (IEC) collaborate. They have, for example, a joint committee (JTC1: Joint Technical Committee – Information Technology) working on matters like data-compression standards. This committee is one of the ways in which both ISO and the IEC link to the ITU. The general regional standard-setting bodies like the European Committee for Standardization (CEN) and the European Committee for Electrochemical Standardization (CENLEC) are linked to ETSI (the telecommunications specialist). CEN is linked by a formal agreement (the Vienna Agree-ment 1991) to ISO and CENLEC by formal agreement to IEC (the Dresden Agreement 1996). ETSI's work program is coordinated with the ITU. ETSI is linked to CEPT and the EC. The ITU is linked to the WTO and the ISO, and IEC helps the WTO to monitor the operation of the Code of Good Practice on standards in the Agreement on Technical Barriers to Trade.

### International Accounting Rates[2]

When regional cooperation on the telegraph first began to develop in the form of the Austro-German Telegraph Union in 1850, one of the main aims was to settle the issue of how revenues for international telegraphs would be divided between participating states. A telegraph (and later a telephone call) originates in one country and ends in another. Two networks are involved. Working out a system for revenue-sharing and payment between states which took into account such matters as sudden currency devaluations became one of the ITgU's most important areas of work. Devising such a system was made easier by the fact that it had to accommodate the interests of a monopoly carrier in each country. The system which emerged (regulated under the International Telecommunication Regulations) required that the monopoly carrier of one country negotiate an agreement with the monopoly carrier of another country to cover the costs of terminating a call in the second country. For example, a monopoly carrier such as the former Australian Telecom would have an agreement with AT&T which set the price that AT&T would charge to Telecom for terminating a call in the US which started in Australia. Telecom would charge a price to its customer (the collection charge) and would also agree to pay a price (the accounting rate) to AT&T for the service of terminating the call in the US. Imbalances between the number of incoming and outgoing calls were settled by the originating carrier with the greater traffic agreeing to pay a settlement rate to the other carrier (International Telecommunication Union 1994: 27). So if AT&T sent more calls to Australia than Telecom did to the US, AT&T would pay Telecom a settlement fee.

This system meant that countries which sent more calls than they received became net importers of a service and countries which received more calls than they originated became net exporters of a service. The accounting rates system devised for a world of monopoly carriers proved useful in a quiet world with comparatively low traffic volumes. But in 1992 the estimated volume of traffic between carriers was put at 40 billion minutes (International Telecommunication Union 1994). Marshall McLuhan's global electronic village had turned into a 24-hour information metropolis.

The US became increasingly dissatisfied with the ITU accounting rates system. As we have seen, it had been deregulating domestic telecommunications since the 1950s. But the fact that it had a deregulated domestic system did not help much with international tariffs, since US carriers had to negotiate with monopoly public carriers in other countries. Since those monopoly carriers were in effect exporters of a service they had an incentive to keep accounting rates high, thereby generating a trade surplus in telecommunications. There was no incentive for those carriers to lower prices and they could pass on their higher prices to US consumers. Further, a foreign monopoly carrier could play off competing US carriers (AT&T, MCI) wishing to obtain termination services in that country (known as 'whipsawing'). Since US citizens tend to make more calls than they receive the accounting rates system began to produce large deficits for the US (in 1990 nearly $US3 billion: Noam 1992: 339). The prize for deregulation under this system seemed to be profits for others.

The US was not alone in expressing dissatisfaction with the ITU accounting rates system. Other countries like Australia, New Zealand, Sweden and the UK, which had begun to travel the

---

2  This section is based on work by Richard Joseph & Peter Drahos 1998, 'Contested Arenas in International Telecommunications: Towards an Integrated Political Perspective' in S. Macdonald & G. Madden (eds), *Telecommunications and Socio-Economic Development*, Elsevier Science, 99–118.

deregulatory path, saw their deficits increase because by lowering costs for termination they were in effect lowering the price for an export. Developing countries favoured the accounting rates regime because they saw it as a means of raising revenue for the purpose of modernizing their telecommunications infrastructures. And Western countries that were net exporters were not about to campaign for a change.

With some support from countries like Australia, the UK and Canada, the US began to take steps to dismantle the accounting rates regime. In August 1991, FCC Chairman Sikes indicated that unless progress was made in lowering accounting rates, the issue was likely to become part of the highly political arena of trade policy (Aamoth 1993). US pressure within the ITU at about this time (and pressure from the UK and Canada) led to a greater awareness of the need to reform account-ing rates. Consequently, ITU–CCITT Recommendation D.140 sought to redress the problem of the growing divergence between accounting rates and collection charges by emphasising that both should be cost-oriented. In 1992 the FCC introduced a system of accounting rate benchmarks. The strategy was to encourage non-US carriers to agree to accounting rates within two to five years. Inspiring this move was US interpretation of the CCITT Recommendation D.140, which requires accounting rates to be cost-oriented and non-discriminatory (Aamoth 1993).

The US began to employ other tactics to rock the system. For example, in line with an FCC order, 'AT&T along with other US carriers filed progress reports on accounting rate negotiations with foreign carriers on January 1 1993' (Aamoth 1994: 101). In its report, AT&T identified prob-lem accounting-rate countries in two lists – a 'problematic' list and an 'egregious' list. The lists comprised mainly developing countries and AT&T's aim was apparently to put pressure on those countries to lower accounting rates. By being listed, offending countries were presumably meant to be vulnerable to possible unilateral punitive action by the FCC or AT&T (Aamoth 1994: 102). In common with US strategies revealed in other chapters of this book, an interviewee from the OECD explained: 'The US wanted to set the agenda by expanding bilateral agreements until its agenda is a *fait accompli*'.

Despite these manoeuvrings, the trade-deficit argument has been overtaken by an emphasis on building a cost-based accounting rate. The US position is clearly reflected in comments from AT&T Chairman Robert Allen: 'AT&T continues to deliver the message that it's time for monopoly carriers to base accounting rates on actual costs, to reflect the true efficiencies for customers' (Allen 1995b).

However, the FCC has had difficulty in establishing convincing data that its cost-based approach can be developed and applied internationally. On the contrary, the ITU has produced figures which suggest that developing countries face costs that are on average 2.08 times greater than those faced by carriers such as AT&T (Aamoth 1994: 101). The result has been that progress toward a regime of cost-based accounting rates within the ITU has been slower than the US might have liked. However, developing countries have not been able to totally resist pressures for change. At present, the ITU is seriously considering a number of options for changing the tradi-tional regime.

The pattern is like the one in Chapter 7 in relation to intellectual property. An international regime no longer favours the US (US business) in trade terms. The US (through the FCC in close cooperation with US carriers) embarks on what others see as aggressive unilateralism (e.g. the FCC issued a Benchmarks Order in August 1997 establishing the rates that US carriers may pay their for-eign counterparts for terminating calls originating in the US, the purpose being to lower those rates). The US (the FCC) says that it is interested in a multilateral solution but in the meantime must take action to bring competitiveness and efficiency to the existing telecommunications order. The ITU bravely struggles on, knowing its fate depends on finding a solution.

This recent history also reveals the tactic of forum-shifting (the theory of forum-shifting is developed in Chapter 24). The limited success of the US in the ITU forum may have prompted it to seek opportunities in other fora, specifically the World Trade Organization (WTO). Forum-shifting is a tactic the US used to great effect in intellectual property when it took sole responsibility for intellectual property standards away from the World Intellectual Property Organization (WIPO) and gave the WTO a role. It is interesting to note that recent negotiations on telecommunications in the WTO have placed emphasis on technical details concerning costs and interconnection. This development has alarmed the ITU to the extent that it does not wish to be sidelined by the WTO in setting the policy agenda for telecommunications. To this end the ITU has sought a closer working relationship with the WTO (in much the same way that WIPO has sought a closer relationship with the WTO).

### Recent History: Trade and Telecommunications

The history of telecommunications has largely been a history of the ITU and the monopoly providers of telecommunications within states. On 15 April 1994 this history took a dramatic turn. Telecommunications and the many services it underpins were brought into the trading regime of the Final Act of the Uruguay Round of trade negotiations. The Final Act contains the General Agreement on Trade in Services (GATS), which contains an Annex on Telecommunications and an Annex on Negotiations on Basic Telecommunications. The Final Act also contains a Decision of Ministers to establish a Negotiating Group on Basic Telecommunications (NGBT), the object of the Group being to move towards the 'liberalization of trade in telecommunications transport networks and services' within the GATS framework. Other parts of the Final Act also affect telecommunications. The GATT schedules on tariff concessions, the Agreement on Technical Barriers to Trade and the Government Procurement Code are all relevant to telecommunications, particularly the equipment market. TRIPS is relevant to telecommunications services. The various agreements which constitute the Final Act, when put together, cover most of telecommunications.

The connection between trade and telecommunications is significant at a number of levels. An inept policy move by the ITU can lead to its abandonment by a powerful actor like the US. The shift to the WTO is also significant, because it has a dispute-settlement procedure to settle arguments between states concerning GATS provisions. GATS also represents a multilateral commitment by states to the process of liberalizing their telecommunications sectors. Under the ITU system which had prevailed for more than a hundred years, states and their monopolies coordinated on the development of telecommunications policy and regulation. Under GATS, states have committed themselves to a process of trade in telecommunication-based services and the progressive liberalization of basic telecommunications. The establishment of the NGBT can be seen as a means of ensuring that concrete action follows the expectations that GATS recognizes.

The recent history of telecommunications has been dominated by the US and various services industries such as finance, travel, insurance and data-processing. The lead corporate actors in the trade in services initiative were the 'American International Group (an insurance company), American Express, Citicorp, Merrill Lynch, and Sea-Land (a shipping firm)' (Office of Technology Assessment 1993: 139). These actors had realized what economists had begun to talk about – the importance of trade in services in the international economy. They also saw that services were constituted by law at a national level in a way that goods were not. Constituting a global trading regime in services would mean an incursion into states' capacity to determine who could provide what services. Persuading states to do something about trade in telecommunications services in the context of the ITU would have been impossible. The European PTTs would have seen nothing but danger in such an initiative. US corporate actors in the services industries saw opportunities. Even US telecommunications manufacturers began to realize that a global trading regime in services which included telecommunications would be in their best interests. Domestically they were faced by the FCC, which was continuing to open the US telecommunications market. After divestiture, it became apparent to AT&T that a possible scenario was a deregulated US domestic market and closed foreign markets. Siemens would be able to sell switching equipment in the US but AT&T would be wasting its time trying to sell to Deutsche Telekom. The balance-of-payment implications were not lost on US politicians.

The history of the push to link telecommunications and trade is bound up with the general push by the US to place services into the GATT (see Chapter 10). The conceptual work for incorporating services within the trading regime was at first carried out within the OECD. Particularly important was the work of the OECD Trade Committee which, under Chairman Geza Feketekuty, produced the thinking and the piles of paper necessary to show that linking the trade regime to services was both feasible and desirable (Feketekuty 1986). Feketekuty was also a senior policy adviser in the Office of the United States Trade Representative (USTR), which was an important supporter of the idea of trade in services. Trade in telecommunications became one of the priority areas listed by Congress in its *Omnibus Trade Act 1988* (Part 4 of that Act is entitled the *Telecommunications Trade Act 1988*). Once the US had clarified its position it set about building an international consensus and, as in the case of intellectual property, it targeted Europe and Japan. Some countries with a comparative advantage in services were quick to support the US; others were more cautious. Developing countries led by India remained suspicious, but to some extent were mollified by the promise of special treatment in any agreement on services.

GATS and the agreements on telecommunication which emerged at the end of the Uruguay Round were, in terms of their drafting, akin to slippery slopes. Rather than requiring countries to liberalize fully and immediately, GATS establishes a process in which countries are channelled in the direction of liberalizing trade in services. GATS itself functions like a framework agreement. It defines trade in services (Article 1) and prescribes the principles that are relevant to that trade. The crucial principles are Most Favoured Nation (MFN) (Article 2), market access (Article 16), national treatment (Article 17) and transparency. GATS allows states to modify the application of these principles. Each member state has to begin the process of trade in services by submitting, in the form of schedules of commitments, offers of services or service sectors in which it is prepared to grant market access to other members. The application of core GATS principles to these offers can be modified. States may list a particular sector or subsector in a schedule of commitments, but place limitations on the operation of the principles of national treatment and market access to those sectors. For instance, a state may decide to limit the operation of the market access principle by restricting the number of service providers in a particular subsector, such as circuit-switched data transmission services. Similarly, it may limit the application of the national treatment principle by not granting foreigners tax breaks it grants to nationals. States can also impose measures that are inconsistent with the MFN principle provided that they are listed by that state as an MFN exemption.

The schedules of commitments which states submit become legally binding upon them. In effect, they become treaty obligations.

The structure of GATS was designed to entice sovereign states to the negotiating table. They could, by limiting the application of the principles in GATS, hedge their bets. In the case of the NGBT discussions this clever drafting has had the desired effect. The NGBT started with a group of twenty countries with the three main players in telecommunications (the US, Japan and Europe) all participating. The negotiations stalled at various points, with Europe and the US accusing each other of not offering enough in the way of market access. The NGBT negotiations had an official deadline of 30 April 1996. At the initiative of WTO Director-General Ruggiero, states agreed to plan for further negotiations in February 1997. A new body, the Group on Basic Telecommunications, assumed responsibility for the negotiations. On 15 February 1997 these negotiations closed. Sixty-nine states representing most of the world's telecommunications revenues tabled hundreds of pages of commitments on basic telecommunications that, on 1 January 1998, formally became a part of GATS. In most newspapers this trade-based regulatory revolution in telecommunications barely rated a few paragraphs.

### More Recent History: Telecommunications, the NII and the GII

In September 1993, the Clinton administration released the *National Information Infrastructure: Agenda for Action* (NII). The NII was described as a 'seamless web of communication networks, computers, databases, and consumer electronics that will put vast amounts of information at users' fingertips' (NII 1993: 3). Had this remained a national regulatory event it would not form part of this history of telecommunications globalization. But in a remarkably short space of time the NII went global. Under the sponsorship of Al Gore, the NII became the Global Information Infrastructure (GII). In February 1995 it became an agenda item for a G-7 meeting. Countries everywhere began to establish their own version of the NII. The EU responded by establishing a group of prominent persons to report on information infrastructure in Europe. The result was a report to the European Council, called *Europe and the Global Information Society* (Bangemann Report) (1994), followed by *Towards the Information Society* (1995). Individual European states followed the US lead and produced their own versions of the future and its highways (e.g. *Optical Fibre Networks*, Report by the Trade and Industry Committee of the House of Commons 1994; *Les Autoroutes de l'information*, Théry Report, France 1994; *Information Superhighway: From Metaphor to Action*, Netherlands 1994). Smaller players like Australia also responded with their vision of the information society (*Networking Australia's Future* 1994). Important individual actors like Bill Gates went on proselytizing missions gladhanding prime ministers on behalf of the GII.

The NII's importance to telecommunications came in the form of the policy recommendations that accompanied the various reports and the US actions under the NII initiative. The Bangemann Report recommended that member states 'accelerate' the process of telecommunications liberalization. The US NII made telecommunications one of the cornerstones of an information society. A Telecommunications Policy Committee was set up as part of the NII initiative. Clinton underscored his commitment to telecommunications restructuring by approving legislation requiring the transfer of 200 MHz of spectrum from federal agencies to the private sector.

The importance of the NII and GII lay in the fact that, by adopting the ideas contained in the initiatives, states could achieve a broad consensus on the kind of regulatory framework that would be necessary for the information society. Roughly, this involved the liberalization of telecommunications sectors around the world, market access so that trade in services and information could take place, strong intellectual property rights protection and privacy protection. The

NII and the GII pushed states toward regulatory convergence in the direction of telecommunications reform. To maintain this regulatory impetus the US continues to release policy papers that articulate a global market access model for telecommunications, a recent example being the policy paper released by President Clinton and Vice-President Gore entitled *A Framework for Global Electronic Commerce* (1997).

## Actors

### Companies

Telecommunications is a field in which the business consumers of telecommunications services have been important agents of change. Businesses of all kinds, from car manufacturing and oil exploration to insurance and banking, began from the 1950s to disperse their enterprises, both nationally and globally. They developed an 'acute corporate dependence on telecommunications' (Schiller 1982: 88). As a result, business users became interested in a cheaper and more flexible telecommunications system. International accounting firms, stock exchanges, large banks, airlines, insurance companies and credit card providers are examples of actors that have much to gain from cheaper and more open telecommunications markets. These industries are characterized by the presence of large corporate service providers operating, like CNN, internationally and on a 24-hour basis. As an FCC officer said during interview, France takes notice of Citibank as a player when they say 'we can do this for X in the US, why for X plus 20 in France?'

Other actors have also seen opportunities in the removal of the monopoly system. What Eli Noam has termed the '"second" electronic industry', comprising members of the US computer industry (led primarily by IBM and supported by other computer firms), has allied itself with the user service coalition (American Express, Time-Warner and Citicorp) (Noam 1992: 47). Companies like American Express are multidimensional businesses providing services in insurance, travel and banking in most countries. These companies are tireless workers for telecommunications deregulation. For example, American Express was active in supporting US legislation that would give the USTR a mandate for the incorporation of services into GATT. These companies advise the US government on the principles that the US should negotiate for and those it should avoid in devising rules for the services and information sector. The following quote from a Senior Vice-President of American Express illustrates the point:

> Bilateral agreements with our communications partners can be a first step. But for the long-range future, information flows should be subject to multilateral rules. Strict bilateral, sectoral reciprocity in communications, which is now a very limited and little-used tool of the Federal Communications Commission in the US, would be a significant and dangerous departure from the unconditional, most-favoured-nation principle which the US has followed in the GATT (Freeman 1984: 202).

To a considerable extent states are agents of corporate actors in the telecommunications field. During interviews we asked one senior official of an international organization: 'Is it the IBMs and AT&Ts pushing the US government or the US government pulling its companies into international competition?' His reply was: 'Companies push always. They even write the papers sometimes. That is, the papers relating to preparations for bilateral agreements are written by the private firms'.

Companies have also been central in international standardization activities. At the ITU, for instance, in 1992 there were approximately three hundred companies participating in the work of the CCIR and the CCITT. These companies included manufacturers of telecommunications equipment and users of such equipment. And as we have seen, US companies have been key players in loosening INTELSAT's monopoly on international satellite services.

Within this category of actors the work of international consultancy firms that have experience in the markets where liberalization occurred first, such as McKinsey, PricewaterhouseCoopers, PA Consulting, Peat Marwick Mitchell and Touche-Ross, should not be overlooked. These companies have been important in diffusing deregulatory models of telecommunications regulation. For example, three of the above-mentioned prepared consultancy reports that helped to steer New Zealand telecommunications down the path of total deregulation and privatization (Wilson 1994: 147, 179, 183).

## Business Organizations

The International Telecommunications Users' Group (INTUG) has twenty-three national TUGs as members (which were generally catalyzed by INTUG), fifty TNC members which are major users of telecom services (like American Express) and about twenty academic and individual members. Two-thirds of the funds come directly from the TNC members. TNCs have also became members of national business organizations in order to keep up the user pressure on governments. The Bank of America, for instance, became a member of the Telecommunications Managers Association, the British Bankers Association and the British National Committee of the ICC (McKendrick 1984: 215). Within the UK the Telecommunications Managers Association and the Post Office Users National Council were particularly important (Duch 1991: 236). No organizations representing residential consumers belong, as part of INTUG's agenda is to eliminate cross-subsidies of residential users by business users.

INTUG was formed in Europe in 1974 by members of the Telecommunications Managers Association from large users, with American Express and Bank of America playing strong leadership roles. Its agenda was not privatization but deregulation, though INTUG was happy to support, influence and legitimate the privatization policies Margaret Thatcher developed in the late 1970s and early 1980s. INTUG is what we describe in Chapter 25 as a model monger. It 'looks for opening doors then pushes on them'. When there are prospects of liberalization in a market that matters to its TNC members, INTUG helps set up a national TUG through local telecom managers: 'You wait to see where opportunities develop, then you cash in on that. INTUG can't do the lobbying [itself]. They don't want foreigners coming in' (INTUG Executive Director interview). Examples of national TUGS include the Australian Telecom Users Group, the Deutsche Telecom eV and the Association Française des Utilisateurs du Téléphone et des Télécommunications. In the US an alliance between national business organizations on telecommunications regulation had all the makings of an irresistible force. It included the Automobile Manufacturers Association, the National Retail and Dry Goods Association, the American Newspaper Publishers Association, the National Association of Manufacturers and the Central Committee on Radio Facilities of the American Petroleum Institute (Horwitz 1989: 225). Also important was the Corporate Committee of Telecommunication Users, which represented an alliance of forty-five of the largest corporate users of telecommunications in the US (Schiller 1982: 93). National TUGs have not been established in any developing countries. In Eastern Europe INTUG sees doors to deregulation opening in Hungary, Poland and the Czech Republic but not in Russia, Bulgaria or Albania: 'So we work with the good ones and hope they will influence the bad ones'. We will see in Chapter 25 that in a world with limited resources to open or close doors, this model mongering strategy can be effective.

Even though INTUG was established in Europe to influence European debates on liberalization, its leadership was dominated by US companies and US ideas. In response to this, the EC reached the conclusion that INTUG was too pro-US and pro-Japanese, encouraging and even initiating the formation of the European Committee of Telecom Users Associations (ECTUA). INTUG has not resisted this strongly, allowing ECTUA to represent its members' interests in EC policy debates.

More important than INTUG in the liberalization of leased lines has been SWIFT (Society for Worldwide Interbank Funds Transfer) and SITA (SWIFT's equivalent for airline seat reservations). SWIFT and SITA also broaden the lobbying for liberalization since their membership is not limited to big business users in big countries (as in the case of INTUG). The tourist and hotel industries add their voice to calls for liberalization even in developing countries.

The words of the INTUG Chairman in 1984 vividly capture the strategy that has been employed by organizations which represent telecommunication users. After outlining the principles that INTUG stands for (user-oriented regulation, use of networks on a non-discriminatory basis, freedom of equipment choice and cooperation), Ernst Weiss states:

> we are working in the corridors of power to gain acceptance for these points and to press their practical interpretation with the appropriate bodies involved with these issues. Specifically on the question of regulatory controls and monopoly authorities we are pressing our views with the OECD on non-discriminatory access to networks. We have a work group to carry out lobbying activity in the EEC. On maximum freedom of user choice of equipment, we have representatives working in a joint committee with the ICC.
>
> In addition INTUG is taking an increasingly active role in CCITT study group discussions where we have our own experienced delegation. All this is long-term work. It requires faith and stamina and perseverance (Weiss 1984: 151–2).

It is a classic example of Olson's logic of collective action in action. A comparatively small group of business users have borne the costs of organizing in order to secure benefits for themselves, benefits which in effect become a public good for other users. Business actors have had a sense of urgency about the need to reform the telecommunications sector. In the words of a representative from Unilever, 'they [business] cannot simply stand by like members of some lost tribe whilst the anthropologists interpret their behaviour and decide what is best for them' (Austin 1984: 180). The members of INTUG have set about organising for telecommunications policy at the national and international levels. INTUG and other business organizations, such as the ICC and the Business and Industry Advisory Committee to the OECD, have pushed the issue of telecommunications reform before international organizations like the OECD and the ITU. INTUG has acquired observer status at the ITU's CCITT and CCIR, the ISO and ETSI and works closely with other influential international business organizations like the ICC. INTUG's Executive Director believes that 'User pressure has been important', that the current degree of globalization of deregulation would not have happened without the pressure of business users.

The ICC has established a specific working party on telecommunication issues, which is developing a Global Action Plan on e-commerce. The ICC claims that eighteen international organizations are working on e-commerce. It wants to reduce and rationalize this involvement to leave space for the ICC to develop a global business self-regulatory approach: 'It's hard to orga-nize worldwide self-regulation. But that's what we're interested in' (1998 ICC interview). This ambitious ICC attempt at forum-shifting seeks to follow up on its more modest victory of scut-tling the development of an ISO standard on privacy then, a year later, moving to coordinate an ICC self-regulatory standard on privacy marks.

The strategy of telecommunication users has been a mutually reinforcing one. International business organizations have pressured national governments to liberalize telecommunications. Governments have looked to international organizations like the OECD to do policy work in this area. And these international organizations, when they have set up committees to study the issues, have found themselves being shadowed by working parties on telecommunications that have been set up within international business organizations. During interviews we found that certain individuals had, by virtue of their expertise, become key flywheels within several business organizations. For instance, one IBM executive we spoke to was the Program Director of Telecom-munications at IBM, Chair of the International Telecommunications Program of the US Council for International Business and on the ICC Committee for Telecommunications. In these roles he had provided papers, comments and advice from a telecommunications user's perspective to the USTR, the EC and the OECD.

## States

Telecommunications does not contain the stark single-state hegemonies which have been found in some of the other regulatory domains discussed in this book. Instead it has been a regulatory arena dominated by Western states, with different states at different times taking a leadership role. France, realizing the importance of a unified telegraph system in Europe, in 1864 took the initia-tive which led to the creation of the ITgU. It was Germany in 1903 which, worried by the effects of Marconi's monopoly, called a meeting in Berlin which led to the Berlin Radio Convention and Radio Regulations of 1906. It is probably true to say that after the First World War the US slowly became the single most important and influential player in telecommunications. Before the First World War the US took the view that government regulation of radio, telegraph and telephony should be kept to a minimum, so it took little interest in international regulatory developments. This was consistent with its position that communications systems were best developed under rules of private ownership. For various reasons the US began to realize that it would have to take a more active role in the development of international rules for telecommunications. For instance, the first Radiotelegraph Union Conference after the First World War was held in Wash-ington in 1927, with the US playing a major role in reshaping the Radiotelegraph Convention and Regulations (Codding 1972: 116–30). More importantly, it was a US initiative in 1947 that led to three conferences in Atlantic City; the Administrative Radio Conference, the Telecommuni-cation Conference and the Administrative High Frequency Broadcasting Conference. These Con-ferences, at which the US made many proposals and did much of the organizational work, resulted in the regulatory structure for telecommunications which is still largely in place today.

Among state actors the US, since the Second World War, has been a leader in telecommuni-cations deregulation. The US led both the globalization of the regulation of satellite orbits in the 1960s and its global deregulation in the 1980s. But it has been assisted by other states, notably the UK. When the FCC signalled its changed thinking on private satellites INTELSAT and the established carriers attempted to prevent new carriers from linking to national networks within

Europe. This failed because the UK was prepared to act as an international transmissions haven (Noam 1992: 336–7). The UK and Japan have been key supporters of the US in the deregulatory shifts in recent years. However, Japan has not been a leader. As one FCC official overstated it: 'Whenever the Japanese are asked to support the US in international communications forums, they always have'.

Telecommunications policy in the US has many bureaucratic nodes. There are more than twenty agencies with responsibilities for telecommunications (McGivern 1983:1298). This has given user coalitions within the US many points of access to the process of policy formation. Among the bureaucracies, the FCC and recently the USTR have been the most important players in pushing a telecommunications reform agenda beyond US shores. Through its domestic decisions and the sheer size of the US communications market, the FCC can destabilize existing international regulatory arrangements. Its decision on satellite regulation is an example. Very few other state agencies have this capacity. Through its various decisions and rule-making procedures, the FCC attempted 'to introduce competition into the international telecommunications market' (Chiron & Rehberg 1986–87: 55). It should be said that in the beginning the FCC was to some extent led along a deregulatory path by US courts responding to cases taken by the Antitrust Division of the Department of Justice. It was a US Federal Court that reversed the FCC's decision not to allow an individual to market a device, called Hush-A-Phone, for attachment to phones (the FCC's decision thereby supporting AT&T's hold on the equipment market).[3] The FCC was similarly led when its decision not to allow MCI into the switched long-distance telephone market was reversed.[4] It was Department of Justice litigation that catalyzed the breakup of AT&T.

US courts continue to be key players in telecommunications liberalization because antitrust law has become the principal means by which the policy of encouraging market entry is being secured (Scott 1996b: 389).[5] The emphasis on antitrust as a tool of telecommunications regulation means that the Department of Justice retains an important role – a global role, in the case of its supervision of mergers among telecommunication and media giants.

In summary, the US moved from a posture of *laissez-faire* (which enabled European hegemony) to hegemonic supporter of centralized global regulatory regimes for satellites and other matters, to hegemonic forcer of global deregulation.

## Organizations of States

The OECD, as in other domains discussed in this book, has exerted an important influence upon the cognition and perception of other actors in the telecommunications domain since 1985. Through its many working parties and committees (e.g. the Committee on Information, Computer and Communications Policies) the OECD cranks out hundreds of policy reports, studies and bulletins in the telecommunications/computing/information services area (e.g. OECD 1988, 1989, 1990, 1991). Its agenda has been 'doing studies to put intellectual pressure on market opening' (OECD interview). These reports often frame issues such as telecommunications costs

---

3  Hush-A-Phone, 20 FCC 2d 391 (1955), rev'd 238 F2d 266 (DC Cir. 1956).
4  MCI Telecommunication Corp., 60 FCC 2d (13 July 1976), rev'd 561 F2d (DC Cir. 1977).
5  Scott (1996b: 393) observes that a single judge (Judge Greene) of the District Court for the District of Columbia has used his continuing jurisdiction obtained under the consent decree in relation to the breakup of AT&T 'to an unprecedented degree, creating a self-standing regulatory régime based on structural separation'.

and rates restructuring in terms of North American debates, sometimes because no other country has yet had the debate (OECD 1991: 16). This literature, like many ripples in a pond, spreads out and touches different shores. The biennial OECD *Communications Outlook* in 1993 produced data showing that countries which had done most to liberalize their telecommunications regime had also experienced the highest growth in telecommunications services as a proportion of GDP. This kind of data is noted by organizational actors in other countries. At a telecommunications conference in 1996, the Group Vice-President of Nippon Telegraph & Telephone (NTT), after outlining the OECD data, observed that NTT could no longer stay a 'plain old telephone company'. It would have to transform itself into a multimedia company (Hayashi 1996). The OECD has also been an active supporter of the principle of transparency in relation to telecommunications (OECD 1989: 84).

The World Bank has become involved in the telecommunications sector through its support for privatization. Beginning in the early 1980s, and mainly in developing countries, the World Bank's lending operations have supported the privatization of many state-owned enterprises, telecommunications being the most important (Kikeri, Nellis & Shirley 1992). For example, the World Bank helped to identify Argentina's telephone company (Entel) as suitable for privatization and aided the process with structural adjustment loans and specific assistance loans.

Within Europe, the single most important player in telecommunications deregulation has been the EC. Much as in the case of the US, competition law has been an important tool of liberalization (meaning that within the EC, DG IV, the competition directorate, has been an important player: Scott 1996b: 398). It has been something of a deregulatory policy entrepreneur. The publication of its Green Paper on Telecommunications in 1987 outlined a common policy framework for European telecommunications. Influenced by developments within the US and the UK, it placed pressure on leadership states such as Germany in an effort to institutionalize market access principles with respect to their telecommunications sectors. Its interest in telecommunications reform has been spurred by its fundamental belief that a protected and divided telecommunications market would not help Europe to compete against Japan and the US. During the 1980s and the 1990s it intensified its efforts to develop an integrated and open European telecommunications system. Its strategy has been to say to its member states: 'Look, competition is coming, be ready, don't be last'.

The EC has also been assisted by decisions of the European Court of Justice. The Court interpreted Article 90 of the Treaty of Rome in a way that allowed the EC, through the vehicle of Directives, to apply Treaty competition rules to national telecommunications monopolies (see the Commission's Guidelines on the Application of EEC Competition Rules in the Telecommunications Sector, 92/C 233/02, OJ C233, 6.9.91). It is principally through Directives that the EC has moved towards its plan of a pan-European telecommunications system. The EC was instrumental in the 1988 creation of ETSI, an important initiative. It is the regional equivalent of an ITU, developing standards for states in the EU and some neighbouring states. With 647 members from forty-nine countries, the standards it produces are 'true voluntary standards although some of these may go on to be adopted by the EC as the technical base for Directives or Regulations' (see http://www.etsi.org).

In an interview at the EC on telecommunications, one of us said: 'So your resources are small compared to member countries. You are deregulatory reformers with intellectual and legal resources and central power, but not implementation power'. The interviewee replied, 'We concentrate on framework legislation rather than nitty-gritty regulation. Internal consensus is easier when you are small. Reformers need this'.

In terms of gaining practical outcomes the WTO has proven to be crucial. The successful resolution of the negotiations on basic telecommunications, in which participating states made significant market access concessions to other states, is evidence of this. Through its GATS regime the WTO is likely to continue to be the single most important organization in telecommunications liberalization. There are two reasons for making this claim. GATS applies the principles of MFN, transparency and national treatment to telecommunications. The Agreement Establishing the WTO itself contains an enforcement mechanism in the form of a dispute resolution procedure.

In the longer sweep of the past 150 years the ITU has been the most important organization of states. Since the Second World War, after a century of European domination, it became a US-dominated UN agency: 'The ITU is largely dominated by the US. Nearly every Chairman and Vice-Chairman [on technical committees] is American' (German telecommunications regulator). Later in the same interview the regulator said: 'You can only be successful at the ITU if you send good experts. The Chairman is responsible for organizing large meetings. The costs are high. So only well-resourced companies can do it. It's almost a full-time job...Often the best corporate PR and political operators get their technology enshrined in a standard'. At the ITU itself we were told a similar story. The costs of participating and developing standards have increased as the standards have become more technically advanced. Fewer nations are genuine participants and industry interests have become more organized and more influential to the point where 'it's practically all industry experts doing the work' (ITU interview). More correctly, US domination of the ITU is domination by a set of specific US firms.

The risk of forum-shifting to the WTO in the 1990s has been an important factor in shifting the ITU from an anti-liberalization carriers' club to a club more captured by private transnational technical suppliers and the epistemic community of liberal market economics. In the late 1980s and early 1990s, shifting of the intellectual agenda to the OECD was another risk the ITU faced. As one OECD deregulatory entrepreneur said, it was in effect put to the ITU: 'Unless you reform the OECD is going to buy into this. This actually works a little bit. [Developing countries start to think it better to consider reform] within the existing structure of the ITU, otherwise, the OECD will take over. So while we don't have power, we can be used as a lever' (OECD interview).

### NGOs and Mass Publics

International NGOs have been particularly important in the area of standard-setting. The most important have been ISO, the International Electrochemical Commission, the International Federation of Information Processing and the International Union of Radio Science (Codding & Rutkowski 1982: 225). ETSI, CEN and CENLEC have been important in Europe. These organizations participate in the standards work of the ITU and also act independently of it in areas where ITU standards have been slow to emerge or not much work has been done. While many national consumer groups have been significant players in shaping national telecommunication policies, neither national nor international consumer groups have been important players at the ITU, the GATS negotiations, the OECD and other global fora. 'There is no barrier to entry [onto ITU study groups] for the IOCU. Consumer groups are occasionally seen, but quickly get bored' (ITU interview). Unlike the Codex, the ISO and some other standard-setting bodies, the ITU does not see itself as having a constitutionalizing mission to ensure balance or countervailing power in its deliberations. Trade unions have offered formidable national resistance to telecommunications deregulation in states such as Germany and Australia. However, unions have not been significant players in the global debates on either economic liberalization or technical standards.[6]

Mass publics have not been important in telecommunications as they have in other areas examined in this book. The sinking of the *Titanic* is an exception to this claim. Public reaction to the sinking helped galvanize states into cooperating on radio safety at sea. Hate speech and pornography on the Internet have caused varying degrees of concern among the publics of different states. But the level of this concern, for the time being at least, has not led to an international regime. Regulation of the on-line world remains a state matter. Similarly, the content of television broadcasts has been a concern of mass publics, but not a concern that has translated into global or even regional regulatory initiatives. For example, the concern of the Canadian public over US television domination caused media products to be explicitly excluded from NAFTA. US fears of Mexican television grabbing a big slice of the US Hispanic market was also a factor.

## Epistemic Communities of Actors

The epistemic communities that congregate around telecommunications regulation consist of economists, bureaucrats, lawyers including trade lawyers, engineers and individuals representing the business users of telecommunications services. At the level of macro policy it is the deregulatory voice of economists that dominates. The result has been an economically technical approach to major issues. Postmodern soliloquies at telecommunication conferences are likely to elicit the silent groan and a hasty departure to the parallel session on the latest demand-side studies for telecommunication services. The selections of what are to count as major issues have reflected the central assumptions and theoretical preoccupations of economics. Pricing theory and its regulatory implementation has become a major area of scholarship in the economics of telecommunication. It is economists who have generated various rate-of-return regulatory models and evaluated their success. Once economists establish a consensus, or even a persuasive case for a given regulatory model, it can spread quickly through the telecommunications community. This seems to have happened with price-cap regulation.[7] The key power-bases of this epistemic community have been the ministries and universities in the UK and US, the EC telecommunications policy groups, the OECD and the WTO. Increasingly, as states have turned to competition law to achieve their market access objectives in telecommunications, the competition policy epistemic community (described in Chapter 10) is becoming important. It is this community, particularly its US and EU members, which will have to deal with the global regulatory issues raised by mergers and strategic alliances between TNCs operating in the telecommunications market.

The other important epistemic community within telecommunications consists of the engineers, technicians and business players who sit on standards committees. Economists can write about the importance of standards, but it is the engineers who know what is technically feasible

---

6  Even at the national level of states in which unions are influential, they find telecommunications technical standards work too complex and too far removed from their core concerns: 'If trade unions wanted to take part, they could, but they don't' (German regulator).

7  Price-cap schemes set the limits of price increases in telecommunications services by reference to the increases in inflation minus a set amount known as the X factor (Xavier 1995: 599).

and the business players who do the pushing for their chosen standards. It was the experts from various national telegraphic systems who drafted the Regulations which accompanied the Paris Telegraph Convention of 1865 (Codding 1972: 21). Technical specialists probably had the standards field to themselves when international telecommunications was run by a club of monopoly operators. These days standard-setting is as much affected by political feasibility as technical feasibility. Engineers now have to take into account the microdynamics of company interest.

Within the epistemic communities of telecommunications the entrepreneurship of individual bureaucrats seems to have been pivotal in the development of regulation, as the following quote from Frederick Tipson, the International Public Affairs Vice-President of AT&T, illustrates (1997: 257–8):

> the quality, empowerment and continuity of individual decision-makers becomes a key factor in the quality of a country's responses to changes in the global industry. We learn to appreciate those governments which give appropriate authority to capable people and then keep them in place long enough to execute some consistent approaches. I would not want to seem to be 'buttering up' Professor Ehlermann by placing him in that category, but he is an example from DGIV of the European Commission of just such continuity of talent, and he was able to engineer some further continuity after his retirement by seeing to the appointment to DGIV of Herbert Ungerer from DGXIII to oversee the further development and implementation of telecommunications competition policy. Dr Ungerer has been able, largely through the strength of his intellect and continuity, to exercise enormous impact on the quality of the Commission's approach to telecommunications regulation in Europe. But there are other individuals around the world of comparable impact, such as Alex Arena in Australia and then Hong Kong, Stuart McPherson in Canada, Neil MacMillan in the UK, and Rafael del Villar in Mexico, to cite just a few.

## Contest of Principles

### Deregulation, Harmonization, Market Access v. National Sovereignty

The opening words of the International Telecommunication Convention recognize the sovereign right of each country to regulate its communications. In the past states have insisted on this principle because of fears about their national security. The spectrum and the technologies that utilized it were thought to be an important military asset. S. Douglas (1987), in her study of the origins of US broadcasting, describes a meeting in New York on 8 April 1919 in which members of the US Navy met with officials of GE. In Douglas' words, they 'emphasized what they considered to be the essential feature of any postwar wireless communications network: it had to be controlled by Americans' (p. 285). This meeting was the beginning of the end for Marconi of the US. It was taken over by a company expressly incorporated to do just that, the Radio Corporation of America.

States still remain committed to the principle of national sovereignty in the area of telecommunications, but the commitment has become more symbolic than real. The shift to a market access model of telecommunications around the world means that national telecommunications markets will become subject to much higher levels of foreign investment and ownership (Drahos & Joseph 1995). GATS entrenches a principle of market access for telecommunication markets that were largely state-based monopolies. The standard-setting process at the ITU is another example of the way in which states have subcontracted their national sovereignty. To be able to send a fax from one part of the world to another, harmonized standards are needed. The ITU is an organization of states, but its standard-setting processes represents a complex form of private ordering. Hundreds of experts from companies representing manufacturers, service providers and business users participate in working groups and meet in Geneva in order to settle on the harmonized standards needed to make global interconnectivity a reality. Put another way, the principle of harmonization has progressively triumphed over the principle of deregulation with technical standards and economic regulation, however, it is the principle of deregulation that has triumphed during the past two decades.

The principle of deregulation has become important in the international accounting rates area, because the ITU system for settling the cost of international phone-calls favours exporters (mainly developing countries) at the expense of importers (usually developed countries with a deregulated telecommunications sector). This contest is in its infancy. The US wants to shift to a more market-responsive system.

### Harmonization v. Strategic Trade

Telecommunications deregulation has been linked to claims about jobs growth and economic growth, even though the corporatization and privatization of national carriers typically has resulted in job losses. It is also clear that some states see trade gains for themselves in a globally deregulated telecommunications market. The possibility of these trade gains has ushered into telecommunications practice the principle of strategic trade. The best example is to be found in the standard-setting process. We have already seen in our discussion of HDTV standards how standard-setting matters strategically to players wishing to capture a market or stop other players from doing so. When international standard-setting was carried out in the regulatory context of monopoly carriers and a few equipment suppliers, the principle of harmonization was likely to receive strong support. Players going to standards meetings in Geneva were not principally interested in each other's markets. With liberalized telecommunications markets, a standard-setting process which is essentially run by private actors offers somewhat weaker support for the principle of harmonization. Motorola is not likely to sit by and watch a European standard for paging systems globalize. It will attempt to block it or try to replace it. The contests between the principle of harmonization and the principle of strategic trade are likely to prove among the most complex in the telecommunications arena. The ITU has itself articulated a fear that it may be overtaken by other national or regional standardization fora. Users of telecommunications equipment will support the principle of harmonization in standard-setting because it will encourage competition in the direction of cheaper equipment. Some states will follow the principle of strategic trade because they will want to secure the promised jobs of telecommunications reform for their nationals. Manufacturers will support the principle of harmonization if it is their standard which is tied to the principle or if they believe they can compete under the standard.

### MFN, National Treatment, Deregulation v. Reciprocity

The principle of reciprocity has played an important role in bargaining over market issues in telecommunications. The US, because it has been a leader in telecommunications deregulation, has been the main supporter of reciprocity. Some private actors like AT&T have taken the view that the US should insist on reciprocity rather than opening its telecommunications market to foreign entrants on a unilateral basis (Globerman 1995: 25). The UK is another key supporter of reciprocity. In practice, the US and UK have been reluctant to view each other as reciprocally open, thereby denying each other's carriers the right to lease lines. Australia, in contrast, allows the principle of deregulation to trump the principle of reciprocity – anyone can lease a line for international telecommunications purposes.

The principle of national treatment has become important in telecommunications regulation through GATS. The principle is really, in the telecommunications context, an alternative to the principle of reciprocity. We saw in Chapter 7, on property, that the principle of national treatment was supported by the US only where it could influence the regulatory standards to which the principle attaches. This is also true in the domain of trade in telecommunications. Since the principle of national treatment assimilates foreigners and citizens, a country like the US only gains significant market opportunities in a country that is already liberalizing its telecommunications regime. A state which chooses to retain a monopoly model of telecommunications, thereby denying citizens and non-citizens market access to the sector, acts consistently with the principle of national treatment. The principle of national treatment does not create opportunities, it merely equalizes them. In other words, it must be complemented by other principles, like those of deregulation and market access (OECD 1990: 30). Where this complementarity of principles does not obtain, an actor like the US, which already has a liberalized telecommunications regime, is likely to do better by relying on the principle of reciprocity in negotiations with a country that has not deregulated its telecommunications sector.

The interaction between reciprocity and the principles of Most Favoured Nation, national treatment and deregulation came to the fore in the NGBT (Negotiating Group on Basic Telecommunications) negotiations. GATS allows states to make use of conditional MFN. States could and did exempt telecommunications sectors from unconditional MFN. States could also qualify the application of the principle of national treatment in GATS by not listing a particular sector or listing but qualifying the application of the principle. The upshot of GATS and the NGBT negotiations was that one state could qualify its offers on telecommunications until another state responded with what the first state regarded as a suitable offer. During the NGBT negotiations the US made various threats, including withdrawing from the negotiations and denying MFN to those states which did not make satisfactory offers on telecommunications liberalization. It was using access to its lucrative market as a means of obtaining reciprocity from its trading partners. This particular contest of principles is in many respects perhaps the most crucial in recent telecommunications history. The states which participated in the NGBT represented, in terms of revenue, 90 per cent of the total world telecommunications market (International Telecommunication Union 1997: 3). Had the NGBT negotiations failed, bilateral reciprocity would have remained the dominant pattern of trade in telecommunications. The successful resolution of the NGBT negotiations means that all states with major telecommunications markets have become subject to the disciplining effects of MFN and national treatment in telecommunications trade.

## Transparency

During most of the history we have examined, the principle of transparency has neither been sought nor wanted. Transparency is not a principle favoured by cartelists. Under the European PTT system or the private monopoly system in the US it was very difficult for anyone outside the club to get information on matters like market entry, price and interconnection. Monopoly carriers could come to international agreements on tariffs and the division of those tariffs, and charge their business users accordingly. The actual cost of making an overseas call was not advertised. These agreements were bilateral and often kept secret from other monopoly carriers. The principle of transparency has been formally recognized in GATS. Its application to telecommunications is progressively strengthening.

### Free Flow of Information v. National Sovereignty

The US has been a consistent supporter of the principle of free flow of information. US corporations whose livelihood depends on transborder data flows are keen supporters of the free-flow principle (McKendrick 1984: 213). In areas such as television broadcasting and the use of satellites, the US has argued for unrestricted flows of information. The US has also been the strongest supporter of the principle within the UN and UNESCO (Hasse 1990: 110). Most other states have countered the US articulation of the free-flow principle with the principle of national sovereignty. In the name of cultural sovereignty (an aspect of national sovereignty) the EC adopted the Directive Concerning the Pursuit of Television Broadcasting Activities (1989). The Directive required member states to ensure that a majority of broadcast time was used for European works. For this the EC earned itself, in 1991, a place on the priority watch-list under the US Section 301 process. The US was worried about its trade surplus in TV programming with Europe.

At the level of international law the principle of national sovereignty over information remains inchoate. When it is recognized in international regulation, as in the UN Resolution on Principles Relating to Remote Sensing of the Earth from Space (1987), it is in a vague and ambiguous form (DeSaussure 1989). At the same time, detailed regimes that deal with information technologies that create global information flows (e.g. ITU standards) do not prevent the US from acting on the basis of the free-flow principle. The WTO trading regime may also help the US cause, since national prohibitions on the flow of information may be seen as a trade barrier.

### Common Heritage of Mankind v. First-come, First-served

This clash of principles has been important in the context of satellite regulation and the allocation of geostationary orbits. Developing countries have used the common heritage principle to argue for regulatory schemes based on the idea of substantive equality (each state having an *a priori* right to some number of orbits). Developed states have in the past been happy to accede to a regulatory regime based on the first-come, first-served principle. It is a principle of formal equality (no state is denied the opportunity to apply for an orbit) that favours them because of their capabilities in satellite technology.

### World's Best Practice

In Chapter 12, on environment, we drew on the work of Michael Porter to argue that states, through the adoption of higher regulatory standards, could construct a competitive advantage for themselves. By shifting to higher standards of environmental regulation, states bind themselves to achieving higher levels of innovation. The strategy of engineering competitive advantage through adopting world's best practice is also manifest in telecommunications. The UK and US, by shifting to market access models of regulation for telecommunications, have begun to satisfy the demands of sophisticated business users for a greater variety of services and the equipment needed to carry out those services.

## *Mechanisms*

### Military Coercion

Military coercion has played almost no direct role in the spread of telecommunications regulation. After the First World War Germany, under the Treaty of Versailles, was obliged to implement any new radio treaty that was settled in the following five-year period (Codding 1972: 110). Military coercion is, however, fundamental to the creation of empires and from the late nineteenth century telecommunications integration was seen as important to the military effectiveness of the British empire. The hegemony of the British empire proved important in the spread of cable links between Britain, Canada, Australia and New Zealand. An Imperial Cable Committee had been established in 1896 to plan the building of such a cable, and the cable came into operation in 1902. Built by a London company, supported by politicians, the UK Chamber of Commerce and administered under the UK *Pacific Cable Act 1901*, it was the concrete expression of a desire to maintain and integrate the empire (Wilson 1994: 97-104). The empire link was responsible for international cooperation on telecommunications between former empire members in other ways. Cable & Wireless (Imperial & International Communications Ltd) had been incorporated in England in 1929. This new company incorporated the Marconi Wireless Telegraph Co., the Eastern Extension Co., the Pacific Cable Board and other smaller companies. Company policy was determined by an Imperial Communications Advisory Committee (Wilson 1994: 116).

### Economic Coercion

Economic coercion has not played a dominant role in the spread of telecommunications regulation. Nevertheless, there are examples of the US listing a state under its 301 process in relation to a telecommunication matter, for example listing Europe for its Directive on televison programming. This kind of formal coercion has not been widespread. The FCC has also used the threat of denying access to the US market as lever to enable US carriers to gain concessions in European markets (Chiron & Rehberg 1986–87: 51). FCC thinking on the use of the domestic market is revealed in the following quote from Chairman Hundt of the FCC: 'what we are doing is using the lure of lucrative, lovely American telecommunications markets to leverage open foreign markets' (Warren 1998: 87).

Economic coercion has not been a dominant force in globalization of telecommunications simply because the main markets in telecommunications exist in the US–Europe–Japan triangle. There are limits on the extent to which any one can successfully coerce the other two.

### Modelling

The modelling mechanism has been very important in the spread of regulatory policies for telecommunications. It, and the mechanism of reciprocal adjustment, explains the proliferation of bilateral and regional agreements on telegraphic communications between Central and Western European states in the first half of the nineteenth century. Modelling explains not only the diffusion of a regulatory scheme, but also its maintenance and stability. One of the reasons why the monopoly model of telecommunications regulation lasted so long was that individual actors saw no reason to question the model as long as others did not. In the US, the *Radio Act 1927* was based on the assumption that the spectrum belonged to the people and that the government had to manage the asset in the public interest (G. Douglas 1987: 95–6). The same assumptions under-pinned the regulation of broadcasting in Canada, the UK and the US until the 1970s (Armstrong 1982: 15–17).

From the 1950s various technological innovations (microwave radio, fibre-optic cable and satellites) made it increasingly difficult to defend existing telecommunications regulation on the basis that it was a natural monopoly. It was in the US that the first serious discussions and experiments with regulatory alternatives took place. The model of 'no property rights in the electromagnetic spectrum' also fell victim to this discussion, as auctions of licences were considered then implemented. The modelling mechanism worked through established cultural pathways. Not surprisingly, Canadian telecommunications policy and regulation has followed US developments 'more closely...than is the case anywhere else in the world' (Kaiser 1986: 174). In interviews at the US FCC we were told one reason their approaches were being partially modelled by so many post-communist societies was the rich informational resource of the Federal Register: 'They pick the US because we have more paper. Rules coming out of our ears. If you go to OFTEL, they've got a copy of a statute. British administrative practice is more fluid' (FCC interview).

The history of the modelling mechanism for telecommunications in any country is more complicated than we can describe here. In Japan, for instance, MITI in the 1970s and 1980s became an advocate of aspects of the US system (it argued for a distinction between basic and enhanced services) while other parts of the Japanese bureaucracy took opposing lines (Ito 1986: 217). In the 1960s Japan explicitly copied the industrial policies of the US and Europe as part of a catch-up game, but in the 1970s it began to devise its own models. Within telecommunications the policy of 'informationalization' (*johoka*) proved particularly important (Ito 1986: 215). The UK looked to the US experience in devising a new telecommunications system based on a specialized regulatory agency (OFTEL) and a privatized public network (Majone 1991: 93). Holland watched the UK experiment with great interest and its regulatory reforms became a source of institutional learning for the rest of Europe:

> The Dutch reorganization was particularly significant because it served as a model of corporatization for other European countries. The extensive competitiveness in the US made its system institutionally too distant to be directly applicable. The UK policy, favouring privatization and the establishment of a competitive carrier, was also too radical for the continental countries. The Japanese model suffers from the lack of transparency of Japanese governmental and economic processes. Holland, on the other hand, is a close and respected neighbour, and its policies cannot be easily dismissed as attempts at hegemony (Noam 1992: 169).

In its 1987 Green Paper the EC drew on US, UK and Dutch regulatory developments in formulating a telecommunications strategy for Europe. The reforms in Western Europe have provided Eastern European states with privatization models for telecommunications. The Czech Republic, Hungary and Latvia have privatized their telephone companies. In many developing countries telecommunications reform has come as part of broader economic reforms. These countries faced economic and financial crisis during the 1980s. They were desperate for solutions. Selling their national telecommunications carrier was part of the deregulatory kit of remedies sold to them by global financial institutions like the IMF and the World Bank.

Policy entrepreneurs at the OECD see themselves explicitly fostering modelling: 'With our papers we're trying to show the ones that are fairly backward by holding up those that are breaking new ground to them' (OECD interview).

The US NII initiative is also a striking example of the way in which the modelling mechanism can have an almost cascading effect, once a particular model takes hold. We have seen how quickly other states followed the US lead in proposing their own versions of the NII.

Telecommunications is an area of regulation which is characterized by technical complexity and uncertainty. This, combined with the fact that state actors are anxious to secure the promised benefits of reform, makes it an area ripe for modelling. Somewhat paradoxically, the very complexity of telecommunications creates modelling opportunities for smaller actors. A state like Nebraska which experiments by essentially abolishing rate-of-return regulation is watched closely by others. A good example of how quickly regulation can be diffused through modelling is price-cap regulation. It was first applied to British Telecom in 1984, and to AT&T in the US and Telecom in Australia in 1989. France, the Netherlands, Mexico, Germany, Sweden and Denmark have followed with their own versions of price-cap schemes (Xavier 1995: 599). Similarly, the changes in telecommunications regulation described by Scott (1998), which are taking place in a number of OECD countries, such as the greater emphasis on procedural rules and the greater reliance on competition authorities, are best explained, we would contend, in terms of the mechanism of modelling.

## Reciprocal Adjustment, Non-reciprocal Coordination

The mechanism of reciprocal adjustment has proven to be the other major mechanism in the globalization of telecommunications regulation. It was the mechanism which constituted the early international regulatory order for telecommunications, in the form of the International Telegraphic Union. Countries realized early that they had to cooperate on the assignment of frequencies so as to maximize communication possibilities and minimize problems of interference. The 1906 Berlin Radio Conference's choice of a common distress signal (SOS), its commitment to obligatory communication between ship and shore and its adoption of standards for the operation of radio are examples of the mechanism in action. Another example is the formation of the Union Internationale de Radiotéléphonie (UIR) in 1925. European states had allowed voice broadcasters within their borders to grab the frequencies most suitable for their purpose. The lack of coordination between states produced interference for all. At England's initiative the UIR was formed, and it managed to settle frequencies amongst European broadcasters on a voluntary basis (Codding 1972: 113).

Much of the early part of international telecommunications regulation is characterized by the presence of positive reciprocal adjustment (states agreeing to cooperate on the formation of a set of rules). But negative reciprocal adjustment (the refusal to cooperate on a set of rules or withdrawing support for a set of rules) has been important in bringing change to international telecommunication regimes. A good example was the progressive withdrawal of support by the US from the INTELSAT regime of coordinated monopoly for the provision of satellite communications. The result has been a significant destabilization of that international system. Another example of where negative reciprocal adjustment has been important is in the area of standard-setting. We have seen, for instance, that neither the US nor Europe wanted to see the Japanese standard for HDTV globalize, so they blocked the emergence of that standard.

Reciprocal adjustment has been and is likely to remain a dominant driver of telecommunications regulation simply because there are few alternative mechanisms. Military and economic coercion are not really viable options. Almost the only way in which states can achieve a set of harmonized rules on frequency management, satellite orbits and standards that allow for inter-connection and interoperability, is through cooperation.

Non-reciprocal coordination has been a crucial mechanism only in recent years in GATT negotiations that trade telecommunications liberalization against other trade policy concessions.

### Capacity-building

The ITU began to be involved in development assistance programs in 1952. As more and more developing countries joined the ITU they began to push for a greater focus on development assistance, a push which has been resisted by the US in particular. Despite this, the role of the ITU in training and technical assistance has grown into one of its major functions.For example, the ITU in Africa helped with the creation of frequency management facilities in Malawi and rural radio services in Ethiopia. It also helped to start the Pan-African Telecommunication Network (Codding & Rutkowski 1982: 288–90). The World Bank has been important in providing financial and technical assistance to Eastern European countries to help them restructure telecommunications regulation (Holcer 1995: 280).

## Conclusion

Telecommunications is a domain where regulation globalized early. States found that if they did not agree on matters like technical standards and frequency allocation their citizens found it difficult to communicate and international transport safety would be compromised. No one wants a world in which there is only one radio operator on a ship – who is asleep when the nearby *Titanic* sinks. Diverting some of their sovereignty to the many ITU study groups so that harmonized standards can be produced is something that states accept as a practical necessity. It is also consistent with the interests and safety of their citizens.

Beginning with the US in the 1950s, the evolution of national telecommunications systems has come to be dominated by the principle of deregulation. The giant public and private telecommunication monopolies that existed in Europe and the US for most of the twentieth century have fallen or soon will. Deregulation of telecommunications is occurring in regions like South America and Asia. The shift to competitive markets in telecommunications is an example of global regulatory convergence rather than harmonization, because the details of regulation of matters like equipment, basic and enhanced services still vary greatly. The sovereignty effect of this convergence varies according to the type of sovereignty we are talking about. At the level of national sovereignty, the choices for states relate to the pace of deregulatory reform rather than the principle. No state wants to be seen as a regulatory island, in the matter of telecommunications. The fear is that multinational corporations will simply bypass such a state in terms of location and investment decisions if, for example, there are too many restrictions placed on their capacity to build private networks. A deregulatory telecommunications policy has become one of the flags that a state hoists when it wishes to attract investment. It is a flag for cities as much as for states. Telecommunications deregulation was one way in which London in the 1980s, for example, could maintain and further its status as a major financial and banking centre.

The capacity of states to leave the competitive loop of telecommunications deregulation is limited. What would be the effects on the sovereignty of their citizens? There have been some clear gains. Telecommunications more than any other technology has changed what sociologists term 'functional distance'. Technologies like the telephone, fax and e-mail mean that groups can form and sustain themselves across borders that previously divided. The opportunity to have a richer group life is a positive gain. It would also be nice to be able to say that telecommunications deregulation represents a win for consumer sovereignty in terms of cheaper prices. But the deregulatory experiment in telecommunications has a way to go before we can be completely confident about that claim. National competition in telecommunications can hardly be said to follow the model of perfect competition. In the UK, BT still commands a 90 per cent share of the market and in the US recent work suggests that long-distance is 'price-umbrella oligopoly, led by AT&T' (D. Allen 1995: 14) – and this is in two leading deregulatory states. Under the former monopoly system cross-subsidization of rural and domestic users at the expense of business users was a common practice in many states. One of the reasons that business users set about reforming the system was to rid themselves of exactly that. As telecommunication carriers move to service the business value chain, citizens in rural areas may find that overcoming distance costs them more. So perhaps the globalization of telecommunications deregulation will be a mixed benefit for individual consumers. Multinational users of telecommunications are clear beneficiaries of telecommunications deregulation. A genuinely global company like American Express can only benefit from the explosion in value-added networks and value-added services that has characterized deregulation. But as one member of the ITU commented to us in passing, not many companies need or have a presence in 200 countries.

There is also more to citizen sovereignty than just consumer sovereignty. Telecommunications deregulation holds the promise of a world linked by broadband, interactive networks. These pipelines are not ends in themselves, but a means to deliver and receive content. The prospect of content being able to flow freely throughout the world raises the issue of cultural sovereignty. And the sovereignty effect varies for citizens and states. The US, because of its commitment to and experience with free-speech principles, is well-adjusted to handling the waves of information that will wash through states with the spread of telecommunication networks. The US is also the world's major supplier of cultural information. While theorists of culture elevate difference, an extraordinary number of people are at any given moment glued to episodes of *Baywatch* and *The X Files*, to mention only two US cultural flagships. US cultural models are seen and imitated in many places. The success of US culture abroad means that US concerns about culture are not, unlike those of other countries, preservationist concerns. Under such circumstances the principles of sovereignty and deregulation do not seem to be in opposition. The US becomes the natural ally of actors that support a market access model of telecommunications. Other states see a conflict between these principles. Developing countries have long complained that the emerging communications order will erode their sovereignty. Some Western states, notably France, have articulated a similar fear.

Standard-setting in telecommunications is an example of a global regime which seems to be differentiating. In the days when the ITU was dominated by an epistemic community of technocrats, engineers and monopoly operators, there were reasonably strong prospects of getting an agreement on a technical standard between states. The more that control over standards has come to be seen as determining marketplace success, the readier leading states in telecommunications have been to lend their companies a hand in fighting for the relevant standards. But the reassertion of national sovereignty over standard-setting, or the growth of regional standard-setting, does not necessarily increase consumer sovereignty. Consumers globally would probably have been better off if the Japanese HDTV standards had been allowed to globalize, but Europe and the US had different ideas. In the long run, however, cooperation rather than competition may dominate the international standard-setting process. At best, states and major companies can only play a spoiling game when it comes to standards. Europe can stop a standard from spreading, but it would find it almost impossible to globalize unilaterally its own standards. Pressure to cooperate on standard-setting will also come from business consumers. They attend standards meetings like those held at the ITU in Geneva and while, as one ITU official remarked to us, 'they get bored' listening to the technical discussions, their presence at the negotiating table constitutes a force for standards that allow for global interconnectivity and interoperability.

At first, many parts of international telecommunications regulation appear to be a case of US hegemony. It is the US which is responsible for the emergence of a satellite regime and it is the US which is bringing change to it. The US is also the main initiator of reform to the international accounting rates system. And the US, by establishing a link between trade and telecommunications, has significantly opened up European and Japanese telecommunication markets. There are also striking parallels between US strategic behaviour in telecommunications and in some of the other areas we have described. We saw in Chapter 7 on the globalization of property that one reason why the US successfully campaigned to give jurisdiction over intellectual property to the GATT was that in that forum it believed it had a good chance of bargaining its way to an agreement that suited its interests. This was something it could never have hoped to achieve in the context of its membership of WIPO and the traditional intellectual property conventions. A similar kind of analysis applies in the context of the ITU. The ITU started as a Western club. Over time more developing nations have joined, and they have engaged in strategic behaviour on rights to frequency and its management (Codding & Rutkowski 1982: 49–50). This kind of behaviour has contributed to a changed US perception of the ITU. Just as in the case of intellectual property, the WTO has been given some competence over telecommunications matters.

But this US hegemony is not really a hegemony that can operate too far beyond the limits of cooperation with other states. The US still has to reach an agreement with states, developing states included, on the division and use of geostationary orbits. Likewise, states have to have an agreement on international accounting rates. The levels of investment which are required to make the information superhighway a reality are too great for there not to be cooperation on its infrastructure. The vision of a world linked by a web of interactive networks and trade in services and products taking place via those networks implies a giant coordination task. Somewhat paradoxically, the US desire to turn its NII initiative into a GII makes it more dependent upon the cooperation of other key players. If the US were concerned only with its own telecommunication markets the costs to it of non-cooperation would be lower. But the GII signals a desire that telecommunications markets around the world be open markets. It is possible for a key state to destabilize an existing telecommunications regime by withdrawing its cooperation, as the US has done in relation to the INTELSAT regime. But this still leaves a coordination problem. Keohane (1984) argues that cooperation between states in the form of international institutions can continue even in the absence of a hegemonic power to police those institutions, because those institutions help to reduce transaction costs and the costs of uncertainty for individual states. Telecommunications is an example of where one state, the US, disrupts a traditional pattern of cooperation in the hope that it will secure a better outcome for itself by doing so. That better outcome can only, in the case of telecommunications, come in the form of agreed rules between key states. The US is not in a position to impose a new regime on other key states. It may, of course, secure the better outcome it seeks through superior negotiating and organizational capabilities. But the US and other states will have to develop new telecommunications regimes through a process of reciprocal adjustment. The extent to which this mechanism will be allowed to work will be affected by the deeper role that telecommunications is playing in the transformation of developed economies and the opportunities actors in telecommunications see in that transformation. The failure of this mechanism to operate will see regionalization become the future of telecommunications.

*History of Globalization*

### Five Regimes

The history of the pharmaceutical industry is the history of its regulation. It is a history that, as we will show, leads to the creation of five totally separate regulatory regimes for different types of drugs:

1   an illicit drugs regime (heroin, cocaine, cannabis, ecstasy, LSD etc.) subject to totally globalized prohibition;

2   a prescription drugs regime which was globalizing slowly under US/WHO leadership until 1980 and somewhat faster under EC leadership since then;

3   national non-prescription drugs regimes which are not globalizing;

4   national alcohol regulation regimes which are not globalizing (prohibition here, regulation here, deregulation there);

5   national tobacco regulation regimes, elements of which are progressively globalizing due to global social movement politics and globalizing enforcement of tort law.

In the nineteenth and early twentieth century in the West pharmacy was a family business, progressively subject to regulation by Pharmaceutical Societies. Pharmacists would mix their own medicines. Patent-medicine peddlers travelled the countryside with their wares or used local grocers as retail outlets. Some of these family businesses saw the opportunities in internationalizing. They created new products by learning from indigenous medicine in exotic places. Most of the large companies imported opium and coca leaves from places like India or Java. The new international companies found the tropics particularly rich sources of new biological materials in much the same way as they now find them sources of genetic materials.

Regulation favoured these international companies, crushing their small business competitors. Pharmacopoeias started more as recipe-books than as instruments of regulation as long ago as the fifth century BC in Greece (McCoy 1992: 239). Pharmacists, like cooks, could experiment with the basic recipes and market their innovations. It was the medical profession which crushed pharmacist control over advice to consumers on drugs (Willis 1983). In most Western countries, before the twentieth century was very old, the medical profession had successfully lobbied for laws to require potent drugs to be sold only on the prescription of a licensed medical practitioner. At the end of the twentieth century, developing countries are on the same trajectory, though for most of the world's poor the local pharmacist remains a more important source of therapeutic power and advice than the doctor or the transnational pharmaceutical company. The first global regulatory divide was the accomplishment of a globalizing medical profession in separating the second from the third regimes on the list of five regimes.

An objective of the medical profession was, and is, to stop pharmacists from acting as the source of advice on which drug to take for an ailment (or whether to take one at all), to prevent pharmacists from giving patients the drugs they could formulate most profitably, to monopolize medical advice and to be paid as gatekeepers to desired drugs. The American Medical Association supported alcohol prohibition from 1917 and by 1928 its members were making $US40 million a year writing prescriptions for whisky. This was an ultimately unsuccessful attempt to absorb regime 4 on the list into regime 2. Though the objective was to shift power from pharmacists to doctors, the prescription regulations also shifted power to the emerging international pharmaceutical companies, away from pharmacists and patent-medicine producers who sold direct to the public or through grocers. The drugs that doctors would prescribe followed exactly the specifications in pharmacopoeias, favouring systematic manufacturing operations with satisfactory quality control. Later they would prescribe only the products of companies who could afford to fund extensive research on the safety and efficacy of their products. After the thalidomide disaster of 1961, the medical profession lobbied states to require safety-testing and then to provide evidence of efficacy before a product was allowed to be marketed. In the 1970s, manufacturers were also required in Western nations, then progressively in developing countries, to comply with Good Manufacturing Practices regulations, written by the US Food and Drug Administration (FDA) then promulgated by the World Health Organization (WHO).

By 1990 no pharmacist or 'bathtub' manufacturer could afford the average $US231 million[1] for the research health regulators require before allowing doctors to prescribe a new drug (D'Arcy & Harron 1991). Thus regulation has favoured the strong – the doctors and the TNCs – over the pharmacists and patent-medicine peddlers. In the poorest countries, where regulation is harder to enforce and where consumers do not have enough money for the pharmaceutical industry or the medical profession to be overly worried about chasing business, the global shift of power to them from the local pharmacists and sellers of traditional medicines is yet to occur.

### The New Regulatory Divide at Versailles

Early in the twentieth century, another kind of regulation removed an important segment of the drug market from the pharmaceutical giants, effectively giving it back to small business. The drugs at issue were first opium and heroin, then cocaine, then cannabis. These drugs were subject to prohibition and criminalization rather than regulation. Prior to prohibition, it was the big European manufacturers – the largest German chemical corporations and Swiss companies like Hoffman-La Roche – who imported opium in large quantities to the West. The German company E. Merck & Co first learnt how to manufacture morphine commercially from opium in 1827. The same company

---

1   In its comment on a draft of this chapter, the IFPMA contended that this figure was out of date even when quoted, the cost today being in excess of $US500 million.

in 1862 first commercially manufactured cocaine (McCoy 1980: 15). It was the German company Bayer which first marketed heroin (a bonding of morphine and acetic acid to form a more concentrated form of opiate), in 1898. This is one reason why it was not Europe, but the US, which led the prohibition campaign. It has recently been revealed that the greatest political leader of that era, Otto von Bismarck, was a morphine addict (Davies 1997: 841). There was a much more modest and short-lived domestic US crusade for the prohibition of tobacco, where US manufacturers and agricultural producers dominated world markets. Another geopolitical reason was that at the Shanghai Conference of 1909 to discuss the British opium trade, it was good foreign policy for the US to support the Chinese against the British (who still opposed prohibition) in order to strengthen its trading and political relationship with China.

But the reasons for US leadership toward prohibiting drugs of addiction were not only economic and geopolitical. There was a vigorous US social movement politics for prohibition of drugs of addiction, the most important target of which was not opium, but alcohol. This social movement, led by Protestant churches and women who were also leaders in the women's suffrage campaign – pre-eminently the Women's Christian Temperance Union (WCTU) – successfully lobbied for the prohibition of alcohol in the US in 1918 after opium and cocaine prohibition came into effect in 1915. In Australia also it was women and the Church who led the anti-opium crusade (McCoy 1980: 79). Similarly in the UK, the Church and (increasingly) women were major forces in the Society for the Suppression of the Opium Trade, which was founded in 1874 and the Woman's Anti-Opium Urgency Committee, established in 1891. While alcohol prohibitionists in the US were also narcotic prohibitionists, among the narcotic-law reformers there was division on support for alcohol prohibition (Musto 1973: 68). In India, in contrast, prohibitionists after the First World War simultaneously picketed liquor shops and opium dens as integral to the social movement against drugs (Gandhi 1952). From 1893, Mahatma Gandhi had been a campaigner working with the WCTU and other Christian and women's groups not only in India and South Africa, but also in other parts of Asia, such as Burma, against both the opium and alcohol trades (Gandhi 1952).

As an enforcement operation, prohibition of narcotics and of alcohol effectively got underway in the US at the same time (1920). During the 1920s in the US, the Narcotic Division was part of the Prohibition Unit in the Bureau of Internal Revenue that was responsible for both alcohol and narcotic prohibition. Prohibition of alcohol ultimately failed because it posed too much of a challenge to entrenched producer interests and because of the Depression-induced state interest in taxing those interests and for the same reason that the women's movement stalled between the world wars – there were just too many respectable white drinking men who resented being moralized at by a new women's movement. So the US prohibition of alcohol did not spread internationally and collapsed internally. But by the time the WCTU missionaries had returned to Chicago from the far-flung lands where they had been sent to proselytize against drug use, the US crusade for the prohibition of opium, heroin and cocaine was globalizing very effectively.

Whereas the US elite backed away from a politically and economically unpalatable prohibitionist cause on alcohol, with opium and cocaine (prohibited except by prescription in the US under the *Harrison Act 1914*) and cannabis (prohibited in 1937), the US not only embraced the missionary work, it all but completely took it over. While the US eventually shied away from upsetting male drinkers and campaign contributors, the moral crusade against opium was a crusade against a 'degenerate minority', the Chinese. This race dimension continued even into the 1960s, with the Federal Bureau of Narcotics' Harry Anslinger and the FBI's J. Edgar Hoover construing heroin trafficking as a deliberate communist Chinese strategy to morally degrade the West (Manderson 1993: 123). Similarly, cocaine was seen as a vice of prostitutes and blacks. The *New York Times* of 8 February 1914 reports Dr Christopher Kochs as concluding that 'Most of the attacks upon white women of the South are the result of the cocaine-crazed Negro brain'. Marijuana, one of the few Mexican words to become part of the English language, was seen as a threat from Mexican immigration in the 1920s and 1930s (McCoy 1980: 71). In the first half of the twentieth century, there were no big campaign contributors against the prohibition of heroin, cocaine and marijuana; there was no mass electoral backlash from white users; it was all populist white-supremacist politics. In the second half of the twentieth century, the 'war on drugs' held firm to its origins in the politics of race. By 1990 almost one in four young black men in America (in the twenty to twenty-nine age-group) on any given day was under the supervision of the criminal justice system – either in prison, on probation or on parole. The numbers continued to rise during the 1990s, despite a falling crime rate. The war on drugs has been the single biggest contributor to this outcome (McCoy & Block 1992: 8).

Conscious attempts to forge international institutions of civil society against the narcotics threat from a US base continued as support for alcohol prohibition crumbled (except in the Islamic countries which had prohibited it a thousand years earlier). The leading propagandist of the International Narcotic Education Association (1923), the World Conference on Narcotic Education (1926) and the World Narcotic Defense Association (1927), Richmond P. Hobson, had also been the highest-paid of the Anti-Saloon League's 'special speakers' (Musto 1973: 190). While the WCTU continued to proselytize about the importance of spreading and enforcing narcotics prohibition during the 1920s and 1930s (extending it to marijuana), Hobson and his supporters built a middle-class white male momentum of disgust for narcotics abuse through that emergent new force in US civil society of the 1920s – lodges and service clubs (Musto 1973: 192, 214).

The British had a different view. They had fought two Opium Wars in 1842 and 1858 to force a China reeling from the first (and the worst) experience in history of mass narcotics addiction to legalize the importation of opium by the British East India Company. Managing a culturally plural empire gave them a cultural sensitivity that had never been a political expedient for the more insular US. Britain did not want to foment unrest on the Indian subcontinent by cracking down on the traditional use of opium and the smoking of Indian hemp, for example. There was fiscal as well as cultural sensitivity; 53 per cent of the taxes collected by the colonial government of British Malaya came from opium sales (McCoy 1992: 247). There was a British social movement against opium, but it focused on shutting down exports from British India to China; the social movement folded when this objective was accomplished. Britain and its dominions (led by India), plus Germany, Japan, Turkey, Persia and the Dutch (in support of their coca-growing colony in Java and the huge Dutch East India Company opium-trading business), initially resisted total prohibition in international fora, while generally supporting progressive regulation and restrictions on trade (Musto 1973: 198). With the rise of US hegemony during the twentieth century, international support for US prohibitionism and criminalization gradually built. The last domino to fall was the Netherlands, which had held out with an anti-prohibitionist policy until the mid 1990s. The lingering UK attachment to a medical rather than a criminal model of dealing with heroin addicts effectively fell in the 1960s (Manderson 1993). Until the 1960s, the UK supported prescribed supply of heroin to addicts on a fairly substantial scale.

The biggest shift in support to the US prohibitionist model came with the defeat of Japan in 1945. As the US occupied the Asian territories that had been conquered by the Japanese, it dismantled the state opium monopolies that supplied addicts, forcibly installing instead its prohibitionist policy. The 1945 shift was not just about military coercion. It was also about hegemony. Manderson (1993) has shown how Australia, which realized from the Pacific war that it was now the US rather than the UK which could defend it, from 1945 ceased to support the UK position on the international control of narcotics, instead following US thinking (Manderson 1993).

From the 1912 Opium Convention in the Hague, as incorporated into the Versailles Peace Treaty of 1919, the European TNCs, such as Bayer, Merck and Hoffman-La Roche, got out of the opium, heroin and cocaine trades[2] as US companies had begun to do after the *Pure Food and Drugs Act 1906*. Similarly, the successful US-led efforts to internationalize the prohibition then criminalization of the distribution and use of marijuana took the transnational 'ethical pharmaceutical companies' (as they liked to call themselves) out of this market. From this point, there was a new divide in drug regulation – one regime for illicit drugs and another for 'ethical pharmaceuticals' or prescription drugs.

## From Disorganized Crime to Global Crime

The first divide in drug regulation created opportunities for small business to strengthen its position in the heroin, cocaine and cannabis markets that until the First World War were progressively being taken over by big business. After the First World War, decades of aggressive marketing by patent-medicine manufacturers had created demand through advertising in the new mass-circulation newspapers for products that would 'pick you up' (cocaine) or 'sooth worn nerves' (opiates), even 'give you joy' (as with the widely advertised cannabis 'Cigales de Joy'). That demand was partially filled by new illicit drug distributors who were generally ethnic minority businesspeople already suffering under WASP (white Anglo-Saxon Protestant) stigmatization, of which the US crusade against narcotics was a part. The most important of these were Chinese and Sicilian. In the late twentieth century, others such as Colombians, became important. Denied a respected place in the Western business world, limited in the opportunities they could seize through legitimate business, the very racism that enabled global prohibition of heroin, cocaine and marijuana created stupendous opportunities for ethnic minority businesses who were willing to operate outside the law.

---

2   The first meeting of the International Opium Commission in 1909 in Shanghai achieved the barest minimum of a framework agreement when thirteen key nations agreed on little more than that 'the use of opium and its alkaloids for non-medical purposes was evil, was spreading, and ought to be restrained both domestically and through international consultation' (Scott 1969: 131). But the Hague International Opium Convention that followed was a conference of commitments, or at least it was by its reconvened meeting in 1914. Thirty-four powers signed a convention agreeing to bring opium and cocaine under 'gradual and effective' state regulation 'with due regard for the varying circumstances of each country concerned'. The League of Nations took over after the Versailles Treaty included a commitment to abide by the Hague Convention. In 1924 the League's Advisory Committee on the Traffic in Opium and other Dangerous Drugs issued a list of sixty-two countries which had signed the Hague Convention, almost all the nation-states of the time, with only a handful still to ratify. The Geneva Conferences of 1924–25 then led to a system of import certificates to certify that the imported narcotics were for medical use only; signatories agreed to pass 'effective laws or regulations to limit exclusively to medical and scientific purposes the manufacture, import, sale, distribution, export and use' of all narcotic drugs. A Permanent Central Opium Board was set up to collect statistics for monitoring progress in reducing global consumption of narcotics. The 1931 Geneva Convention required signatories to notify quantities of narcotics needed for medicine and science and were prohibited from manufacturing more than was needed to fulfil that need. The 1936 Geneva Convention for the Suppression of the Illicit Traffic in Dangerous Drugs required signatories to punish, by imprisonment, possession as well as sale; it also provided for extradition.

As the US, and later other Western states, escalated public investment in brutal criminal justice reactions against the illicit drug trade, it shifted from being a domain of small business to one of bigger business, from disorganized crime to more organized crime. While growing the illicit crops and street-selling continued to be done by expendable marginal people, trafficking became increasingly oligopolized by organized crime. Hong Kong- and Taiwan-based triads facilitated Chinese involvement in the narcotics trade in most of the world's Chinese communities. The triads are not primarily drug-trafficking organizations today; they are TNCs with massive legitimate investments of much greater contemporary significance than their historical connections to an opiate trade they once dominated from Shanghai.

The organizations that became most important to the international illicit drug trade were criminal organizations with experience of enforcing total discipline on their members, a strict code of silence under interrogation, willingness to use violence ruthlessly and knowhow in corrupting criminal justice officials and politicians. Pre-eminent among these were the Sicilian and US mafia and Chinese triads from quite early in the twentieth century, the Colombian cocaine cartels from the 1980s and the Russian mafia from the 1990s. While terms like 'mafia' and 'cartels' exaggerate in the public mind the level of monopoly and central control of these networks, there is no doubt many of them grew phenomenally and have become much more organized.

Outcast Anglo-Saxon groups with strong discipline and credibility in the issuance of threats, such as certain motorcycle gangs, also became important in some markets, but not to the control of international trafficking. They do not seem to have the capacity to buy banks, politicians, police chiefs and judges (or kill them if necessary) in the way that the Russian, Colombian and Sicilian syndicates seem to. Shona Morrison of the Australian Office of Strategic Crime Assessments has concluded, from her research into what makes drug-trafficking groups successful, that the environment has changed from one where capacity to mobilize violence was important to one where the requisite skills are rather those of a competent corporate criminal:

> Indeed, it was their high level of violence which finally prompted the Colombian government to do something about the Medellin cocaine traffickers (leading to their downfall). The more subtle tactic of corruption employed by the Cali groups was successful for longer. My work in this area forecasts that to take advantage of current economic policies (such as privatization and trade agreements), the skill requirements for successful trafficking will shift closer to those required in successful legitimate business and will probably lead to widespread investment by crime groups in licit structures and services.

As 'bad' as American gang-leaders take pride in being, the disciplined pride of Russian organized criminals in 'dying like a thief', according to Sterling (1994: 31) gives them a competitive advantage over other criminal organizations whose members buckle under threat of torture by other gangs or the police. In international organization, the Russians moved as early as 1950 to bring together senior thieves from many nations for a Europe-wide All-Thieves Congress 'to hammer out some kind of general rule on questions of ethics' (Sterling 1994: 32). While the Congress failed to persuade the disorganized thieves of other lands to adhere to the Russian code of ethics, it indicated a certain seriousness of international intent. The Iron Curtain made it difficult for Russian criminals to gain the mobility they needed to push this very far until 1989. Since the opening of the former Soviet Union in 1989 as a free-trade zone for organized crime, 'liberalization in Russia is not leading to the old-style black market evolving into legitimate business, but to the new, legitimate businesses being sucked into the old black market' (Shelley 1995: 175), leading, for example, to organized crime control of banks and perhaps 'half the commercial real estate in central Moscow' (Shelley 1995: 176). Corruption of the political process has enabled the Russian mafia to corrupt the privatization process to the point where alliances of former Communist Party officials and organized crime groups, not new capitalist entrepreneurs, control, according to Louise Shelley (1995: 170), 'the preponderance of capital in post-Soviet states'. This seems to describe the situation in some and to be important to understanding the destabilization of Boris Yeltsin and of the world economy at the time of writing.

The vast new drug, money-laundering and arms markets in and out of the former Soviet empire seems to have allowed the most organized criminal groups – the Sicilian and US mafias, Chinese organized crime groups, Japanese yakuza and the Colombian cocaine networks – to increase their international cooperation to respect each other's partial regional monopolies, while cooperating to crush or coopt less organized competitors. While the Colombians manufacture most of North America's cocaine, Sterling (1994) contends that Chinese groups ship most of the heroin imported into North America, a market separation which prevents them wiping each other out. There is enough international cooperation to ensure that 'For all the killing on the turf of each, there is no killing where their paths cross' (Sterling 1994: 22) (or at least only a regulated amount of killing). Boronia Halstead of the Australian Office of Strategic Crime Assessments contests this market-separation thesis, pointing out that about half the heroin seized in the US is of South American origin. Halstead is also 'wary of seeing the Russian *mafiya* as a monolithic phenomenon, since there are many ethnically diverse criminal groups subsumed within the Russian *mafiya* tag, which have been involved in bitter and bloody struggles with one another. In this context, one has to wonder about the real long-term impact of the much vaunted "summits" or the "Congress"' (see also Rosner 1995).

The illicit drug market today is almost certainly worth more (around $US400 billion, or 8 per cent of world trade in 1996 according to the UN International Drug Control Program) than the 'ethical pharmaceuticals' market ($US175 billion in 1991). While early in the twentieth century big pharmaceutical companies left illicit drug markets to small-time disorganized criminals, as demand for narcotics rebounded and globalized international trafficking came increasingly under the control of more organized criminals, not hierarchically organized like the early cocaine and heroin corporations or in the popular image of *The Godfather*, but organized in resilient networks. Just as the ethical pharmaceutical transnationals do not pay much attention to working with the medical profession for the kind of regulation that will secure their domination in Third World markets until their citizens become wealthy enough to pay monopoly prices for patented drugs, organized criminal networks do not bother to foster demand (by organizing convenient networks of street-dealers) for the drugs in which they enjoy partial regional export monopolies until people are wealthy enough to pay their prices. Both kinds of partial oligopoly are products of global regulatory regimes forged by US hegemony: the patent monopolies of the ethical manufacturers are enabled by the US-led global intellectual property regimes discussed in Chapter 7, the domination of organized crime in illicit drug trafficking by the global regimes of US-initiated prohibition that awards the biggest prizes to the most ruthless criminals in some contexts and to the most sophisticated in others. These regimes cross in unexpected ways. Monopolies depend on order. In the case of intellectual property this order depends on the rule of law, but in states where this rule is only partly present (e.g. Russia) multinationals and criminals form shadowy alliances. For example, the Georgian mafia are hired to protect the trademarks of multinationals because the state's enforcement apparatus is too weak to do the job reliably.

## The Globalization of Narcotics Regulation

The first period of globalization in the regulation of opiates and cocaine that was coordinated by the League of Nations (under external pressure from the US and a global social movement for prohibition) was something of a success. Most of the world, including nations such as Japan, which was deriving considerable economic benefit from export of heroin to China and other parts of Asia, agreed to control promotion and usage of narcotics, then to prohibit exports, and eventually to restrict medically supervised supply to addicts. Using League and UN figures, McCoy (1992: 268) concludes that global opium production fell from a peak of 41 600 tons in 1906 to 7600 in 1934, continuing to fall to 1000 tons by 1970 after which (according to the US Drug Enforcement Agency) it rose to 4200 tons by 1989. While the earlier figures can be questioned because they reflect generally licit production voluntarily reported by governments, the 1989 US government estimate includes estimated illicit production, suggesting that while the drop in opium consumption was not as sharp as the League of Nations figures suggest, it almost certainly was substantial. The International Narcotics Control Board in 1969 estimated illicit production of opium at around 1200 tons a year (Bruun, Pan & Rexed 1975: 24).

After the 1925 Geneva Accord tightened controls and the League's Limitation Convention of 1931, legal heroin production dropped from 9000 kg in 1926 to 1000 kg five years later (McCoy 1992: 268). Again, we do not know to what extent this must be counterbalanced by a rise in illegal heroin production in the years before the Depression. We must be especially careful because rising regulation increased the comparative attraction of illicit demand for heroin over opium, because heroin is more concentrated and less bulky. Seizures of raw opium internationally peaked in 1936 at 124 497 kg, falling to a low of 35 970 kg in 1960. Between 1936 and 1960, prepared opium seizures fell from 18 063 to 672 kg, heroin from 867 to 390 kg and cocaine from 70 to 10 kg, notwithstanding improved international enforcement capabilities. This improved capability is reflected in the massive growth in cannabis seizures from 16 283 kg in 1936 (before cannabis prohibition in most countries) to 875 849 kg in 1960 (Bruun, Pan & Rexed 1975: 229). In the US, as in China, it seems that the peak of opiate addiction occurred 'about the turn of the century, when the number [of addicts] probably was close to 250 000 in a population of 76 million, a rate so far never equalled or exceeded' (Musto 1996: 2).

With cocaine as well as opiates, there is no doubt that getting big business to stop indiscriminate use in its products reduced addiction and demand, with cocaine trafficking almost disappearing by the 1950s before rebounding in the 1970s and 1980s. But the period of decline in opiate and cocaine trafficking lasted only as long as the new illicit trade remained a totally disorganized small-business activity. That period of disorganized marketing lasted for only two or three decades mid-century, especially when we bear in mind that big pharmaceutical companies, such as Hoffman-La Roche, covertly supplied the illicit opium trade through the 1920s before it finally left the illicit opiate and cocaine trade in response to international shaming after the Canton Road Smuggling Case of 1925 (Bruun, Pan & Rexed 1975: 223-4). Fifty years later we saw the same phenomenon, with 20 per cent of US amphetamine manufactures diverted to the illicit traffic (Bruun, Pan & Rexed 1975: 236).

In the 1960s, the possibility of drug trafficking becoming an organized activity that generated new demand was barely recognized, as reflected in the quaint optimism of a 1966 review of 'Twenty Years of Narcotic Control Under the United Nations': 'By now the problems have been clearly defined and some of them have been solved, or the instruments of their solution have been created: non-medical consumption of opium, coca leaf, cannabis, and of the drugs manu-factured from them is outlawed in principle and is bound to disappear after transitional periods of adaptation' (Bruun, Pan & Rexed 1975: 33). Closure of shipping lanes during the Second World War greatly disrupted the organizing of drug trafficking, with merchant seamen important in the limited and disorganized trafficking in opiates that occurred during the 1940s.

### The CIA, the KGB and the Globalizing of Protection Rackets

Unfortunately, as we have seen, US-led global enforcement policies increased the competitive advantages of more organized (networked) and politically protected drug traffickers by crushing their less organized opposition. An additional important factor was the way anti-communist insurgency movements learnt that they could combine their capacity for systematic violence, dis-cipline, experience in money-laundering and ability to call on the political protection of the US CIA (and other intelligence agencies, such as that of Taiwan) to fund their military activities through the drug trade.

Scholars such as McCoy (1972, 1980) have documented how the CIA supported a variety of anti-communist forces who relied on drug trafficking: Kuomintang insurgents against the People's Republic of China from bases in the Golden Triangle, Burmese and Laotian druglords during the period of Indo-Chinese instability from the 1950s to the 1970s (Lintner 1992; McCoy 1992), the Contras in Nicaragua (Block 1992; Scott 1992), Miami and Tijuana Cubans (Kruger 1980; Marshall 1992; Scott 1992) the Mujaheddin in Afghanistan, elements in the Pakistani mili-tary (Lifschultz 1992) and Noriega in Panama (Scott 1992). In Asia the result was that 'By attack-ing heroin trafficking in the separate sectors of Asia's extended opium zone in isolation, the [US] Drug Enforcement Administration inadvertently diverted heroin exports from America to Europe and shifted opium production from South-West Asia to South-East Asia and back again – raising both global consumption and production with each move' (McCoy 1992: 267). For example, shutting down the export of Turkish production through Marseilles expanded opportunities for Golden Triangle traffickers protected by the CIA. When the post-Vietnam US turned its war on drugs against the Golden Triangle producers, they responded by shifting their supply to Europe and Australia, which were then flooded with heroin dealers.

What the CIA did was protect new narcotic entrepreneurs from regulation for long enough for new production areas to be linked into the world market and new trafficking organizations to be established. Drug organizations are most vulnerable while these links are being established. Once they were organized, they continued to flourish after CIA protection was withdrawn, just as the Russian organized crime groups continued to flourish after KGB protection evaporated. The pattern of states helping to create, through their foreign policies, a global problem which brings forth a later global regulatory response is a pattern that we find with piracy on the high seas (see Chapter 17).

While the intellectual property regime that strengthened the transnational pharmaceuti-cal companies (Chapter 7) and the narcotics regime that strengthened the drug mafias are stories of globalization under the sway of US hegemony, the globalization of the regulation of the safety and efficacy of prescription drugs is rather a story of European hegemony. To that story, we now turn.

## Global Pharmaceuticals Regulation

Detailed regulation of pharmaceuticals has a long history in most developed countries, starting in the second half of the nineteenth century with laws to license and monitor the standards of pharmacists, laws supported by pharmacists who wanted to restrict competition by professionalizing. Six thousand years earlier, priests in Egypt had done the same, asserting religious grounds for monopolizing the dispensing of potent drugs such as opium (Scott 1969: 5). Because of this long history, international harmonization of regulation has proved more difficult than with pesticides and other toxic chemicals, where most regulations have been written since 1970. The OECD (see Chapter 12) could coordinate impressive harmonization in that domain because most countries did not have sunk investments and scientific commitments to a long-standing way of regulating.

The WHO made little progress in securing convergence of regulatory standards for pharmaceuticals during the same period when it, in collaboration with the Food and Agriculture Organization (FAO), achieved quite impressive convergence of food standards globally (Chapter 16). The reason for this difference is that the US and a small number of European countries (and more recently Japan) account for nearly all the world's pharmaceutical exports. At the WHO, it has therefore always been tempting for developing countries supported by consumer groups to use their numbers to call for regulatory standards that the US and other exporting countries would never accept. Indeed, demands for increased international pharmaceuticals regulatory activities by WHO caused the US to scale down and threaten to withdraw financial support during the 1980s and Japan to allegedly buy votes to put its own Director-General in charge of WHO during the 1990s. With food, most countries are both big exporters and big importers. Some of the poorest nations are major food exporters, and so are the US and Europe. This has rendered agreement on food standards under the auspices of the UN easier than agreement on pharmaceuticals. With food, externalities tend to be reciprocal and therefore more negotiable; with drugs, externalities are non-reciprocal.

As we have said, pharmacopoeias date from at least the fifth century BC. They were given self-regulatory status by the health-care professions (particularly pharmacy and medicine) and later by the state in all nations and supranationally by the EU. The influence of the pharmacopoeias predates US hegemony. The biggest shapers were probably the British pharmacopoeia, an influence strongest during the British hegemony until the First World War, and later the European pharmacopoeia, though in Latin America the US pharmacopoeia is more influential. The Nordic and International pharmacopoeias also had important internationalizing influences on norms. Corporate dominance of the industry was also overwhelmingly European until the Second World War, with German and Swiss companies particularly important. The I.G. Farben conglomerate, which the US broke up into Hoechst, BASF and Bayer after the war, was particularly dominant, building considerably on its wealth from the use of slave labour such as at its massive Auschwitz plant.

European drug regulators were also more outward-looking than insular FDA bureaucrats, partly because the pharmaceuticals trade internationalized so early in Europe. International Medical Congresses, the first of which was held in Paris in 1867, early established Europe as the centre of epistemic communities on pharmaceutical regulation. The Council for International Organizations of Medical Sciences (1992) is still based in Geneva, along with WHO. The most important factor in European leadership of the globalization of pharmaceuticals regulation has been regulatory entrepreneurship from Brussels. This started with a 1965 EC Directive on Medicinal Products, which defined common criteria on quality, safety and efficacy for EU national regulatory authorities to apply before they could approve a drug for marketing.

A 1975 Directive harmonized the national authorization procedure and established a Committee for Proprietary Medicinal Products (CPMP) in Brussels to manage the paper warfare of the thousands of pages of scientific data required pursuant to each standardized marketing application. Amendment of this Directive in 1983 established a multilateral procedure and a mutual recognition scheme whereby a drug manufactured and sold in one member state could be authorized in another member state except for special cases which were submitted to the CPMP. Mutual recognition, however, was not obligatory for member states under the 1983 regime and basically it did not work: only a small proportion of applications were considered under the multistate procedure and when they did the assessments by one state were almost always challenged by other states. German firms boycotted the multistate procedure. More time was needed for a workable level of trust and convergence.

The next step toward a pan-European regime was the 1987 'concertation procedure', limited to biotechnology and high-technology products whereby a recommendation on safety, quality and efficacy would be made centrally by the CPMP before any national decision could be made. In 1995 a new European Agency for the Evaluation of Medicinal Products (EMEA) was established in London. From 1995 to 1998 the EMEA coordinated a centralized procedure reserved for biotechnology and other innovative products and a decentralized procedure based on mutual recognition of national marketing authorizations for most products, with provision for member states to opt out and run their own national authorization procedure. Under the centralized procedure EC decisions are binding; opting out was only possible under the decentralized procedure. In 1998 opting out ended; there is compulsory arbitration by the EMEA whenever the authorization of the first member state to apply the authorization procedure to a new product is not accepted by another. In EU law, the post-1995 regime is one of regulations rather than directives or recommendations. From 1965 to 1998 Europe moved toward a system of binding regulation that applies uniformly throughout the EU. One can overstate the unification. There is no 'grandfathering' of former national authorizations into the pan-European regime. Even under the post-1998 regime, only on biotechnology products will the centralized authorization procedure be compulsory (it will also be available on request by companies, but only for innovative products); the majority of new applications for authorization will be handled at the national level (by what will effectively be a lead state whose regulatory decisions will be either subject to mutual recognition or contested at arbitration by other member states). The regulatory resources of national agencies will continue to be many times greater than those in the EMEA (100 staff in 1996 compared to 3000 in the national agencies). Hence, even the centralized procedure is not centralized in the style of an FDA bureaucracy of experts; there are 1650 experts on 'the European experts list' – most of them from the civil societies of member states.

The EMEA delegates assessment of a particular drug to a national agency that acts as a rapporteur. A second national agency acts as a co-rapporteur to provide a double-check. Industry resistance to the EMEA has been partly based on its loss of the right to choose the rapporteur country, although it is invited to make suggestions, which are generally followed.[3] To date rap-

---

3  In no case under the centralized procedure up to August 1996 had the person suggested by the company not been appointed as rapporteur or co-rapporteur. In 1996 the EMEA began to ask the company to nominate three alternatives for rapporteur.

porteurships and co-rapporteurships have been disproportionately allocated to the states with the most sophisticated evaluation capabilities – the UK, Germany and France. Most recently, the practice has been to bracket a more sophisticated and a less sophisticated authority as rapporteur and co-rapporteur so that the latter will learn from the former.

Consumer groups have been most worried about the decentralized parts of the new centralized–decentralized mix of European regulation. BEUC (the European consumer movement peak council) lobbied with some success for the EMEA having centralized regulatory power (Burstall 1991: 163). The European Federation of Pharmaceutical Manufacturers Associations, in contrast, lobbied for the decentralized part of the mix. In particular, it prevailed in the design of the 1983 multistate procedure with the policy that the applicant company has the right to choose the member state where it will apply for marketing authorization (which would then be subject to mutual recognition). This industry victory fuelled fears of lowest-common-denominator standards in Europe which, given European domination of global regulation, could mean lowest-common-denominator global regulation.

We are not so sure that lowest-common-denominator regulation will be the result, even though it is far too early to reach a judgment based on empirical experience. Our expectation, from interviews with industry insiders is that we will not see a flood of Portuguese applications, while the tougher French, UK and Germans get none. There are two reasons. One is that the Portuguese regulators would not have the resources to process a flood of pan-European applications; a backlog would quickly develop and make applicants lose money while they wait to get their new product processed. Second, the superior resources and expertise focused on a German, UK or French marketing approval would have more credibility. This increases the likelihood of other EU nations refraining from appeal to compulsory arbitration. This is a telling point, since more than one European informant expressed the concern that 'Member states are reluctant to accept each other's assessments'.[4] For example, a German approval is more likely to result in Canada or Australia following Europe than a Portuguese approval.

There will doubtless be some products where clever corporate operators secure pan-European marketing for products that under the old national regimes would have been declined approval in some or most European nations. They will accomplish this by targeting regulators who are slack, corrupt or scientifically overcommitted to a view favourable to a particular product. Although that may happen, we think it will be more common for European standards to rise to those of the most credible European regulators. If this is wrong, the credibility of European regulation will fall in the eyes of regulators elsewhere, an outcome the European pharmaceutical industry would regret and one which national regulators with higher standards would probably choose to challenge through arbitration.

Provision was made for members of the European Economic Area (EEA, who were not members of the EU) to participate in the EU regime, but the extent to which that will happen remains to be seen. What is already clear is that non-European OECD members such as Australia, Canada and New Zealand look to the EU for regulatory modelling more than to the US or Japan, which one might expect to be the more natural models because of regionalism (e.g. APEC) and the fact that the US is modelled more than Europe in most of the domains considered in this book. Similarly, the post-communist states, although they are influenced by technical assistance from the FDA, clearly look to EC regulations for their models. So we have seen the dominant

---

4  By August 1996 this situation seemed to be changing, with only three of the first forty mutual-recognition cases under the new decentralized procedure requiring arbitration between states.

regulatory regimes in Europe – Germany, France and the UK – slowly converge then dominate the EU through mutual recognition, harmonization and partial centralization. Their regulatory models now begin to attract EEA members, former communist societies and OECD members who are independent of the big three. With these additions, and with Europe being the biggest internal market in the world (and accounting for two-thirds of the world's exports), EU leadership in pharmaceuticals is now formidable.

### European Leadership and the International Conference on Harmonization

From this position of growing strength, the EC initiated contact with the other big two players – Japan and the US – on a major global harmonization initiative from the mid 1980s. The US was initially reluctant to participate, fearing any compromise to European standards that its Congress, consumer movement and professions would not broach. Bilateral meetings on harmonization between the EC and Japan started in 1981 and between the EC and US in the mid 1980s, and trilateral meetings in 1991. Given European dominance in the industry and Japanese agreement to cooperate, the US had little choice but to agree. Even then it hesitated. But after the US Pharmaceutical Manufacturers Association (PMA) commenced active collaboration, emphasizing the dangers of exporting the US drug lag to the rest of the world, the FDA had to join the process to defend its position. The world had changed to the point where, as a senior FDA official expressed it during interview: 'We've only recently stopped the expectation that we'll write our standards and the rest of the world can follow', or, as the Executive Vice-President of the International Federation of Pharmaceutical Manufacturers Associations (IFPMA) put it during his interview, a former FDA Commissioner expressed the attitude that 'harmonization is fine so long as the world harmonizes to us'.

The International Conference on Harmonization of Technical Requirements for Registration of Pharmaceuticals for Human Use (ICH) started with six principals – the EC and the European Federation of Pharmaceutical Industry Associations, the Japanese Ministry of Health and Welfare and the Japanese Pharmaceutical Manufacturers Association, the US FDA and the US PMA. The IFPMA was asked to provide the secretariat. Panels of experts met in parallel technical symposia on a variety of topics concerned with harmonizing quality, safety and efficacy requirements. Preparatory committee work by experts for ICH meetings was extensive. Twelve hundred people attended the first ICH meeting (twice that number attended the third meeting, in 1995). As ICH architect Fernand Sauer of the EMEA said to us in 1994, the ICH is a 'fragile construction' that 'could collapse at any time': 'It's promising, but we haven't delivered yet'. Perhaps this is still true, but it is also true that the range of fundamental issues of non-uniform regulation among the big three that have been tackled by the ICH, in some of which consensus has already been accomplished, is encouraging. And when the big three actually implement a new consensus, the rest of the world have little choice but to follow. Already, however, there have been cases where the FDA has agreed to an ICH consensus then retreated from it when faced with a backlash from the US pharmacological research community. Equally, however, ICH moved the US FDA for the first time to a willingness to approve drugs on the basis of foreign data. This has helped to make drugs more available to US consumers. By the Yokohama ICH conference of 1995 nineteen trilateral guidelines had been finalized, with another nineteen scheduled to be finalized for the 1997 Conference in Brussels. Vogel (1998) reports that implementation of the ICH guidelines by states and leading firms has been impressive: 'The world's twenty-five largest firms have adopted nearly all' of the first set of guidelines.

The European leadership of the 1990s was built on the ashes of a failure of US and WHO leadership, both of which were more important than European leadership until the Reagan presidency. The decline of US and WHO leadership was partly a tale of mutual destruction. WHO's accomplishments in globalizing pharmaceuticals regulation have been modest. The most important have been the Action Program on Essential Drugs (really a technical assistance program to help developing countries secure affordable access to essential drugs) and the 1975 Certification Scheme on the Quality of Pharmaceutical Products Moving in International Commerce (whereby exporting countries certify drugs as authorized for domestic sale – as a countermeasure to dumping of banned products – and certify that the plant where the drugs were manufactured has been regularly inspected to ensure compliance with the WHO Good Manufacturing Practices Act).

In WHO, it has always been possible to create a veto coalition against any major move toward international regulatory convergence. The US would veto initiatives pushed by developing countries and the international consumer movement; the latter would veto US leadership of the exporting countries. Fed up, the US reduced its commitment to WHO. Until the mutual delegitimation of WHO and US leadership occurred during the 1980s, further enfeebled by US protest over a corrupt Japanese takeover of WHO leadership in the 1990s, there had been considerable US leadership that was usefully followed up by WHO. For example, US leadership in establishing Good Manufacturing Practice and Good Laboratory Practice Regulations in the 1970s was effectively globalized through WHO. US leadership in the regulation of marketing claims was picked up by the WHO through WHO Ethical Criteria for Medicinal Drug Promotion. The IFPMA successfully lobbied to render this toothless, a low WHO priority, yet part of its lobbying campaign involved writing its own self-regulatory marketing code, which led to some extremely modest globalization of regulatory standards in the promotional domain (Hardon 1992: 50–2).

## Global Regulation and Industry Structure

There is no area where the globalization of regulation has had more dramatic effects on industry structure than drugs. The globalizing of higher and higher standards for prescription drugs has made this a domain dominated by more globalized TNCs than any sector of business. In developing economies and with non-prescription drugs in developed economies, where regulatory standards are not globalized and much less costly, small business remains central. When global prohibition caused big business to quit the markets for heroin, cocaine and cannabis, production of those drugs shifted from big legitimate business to small illegitimate business. But repressive policies most affected the smallest, least corrupt and least ruthless of the small businesses, creating a natural selection where bigger, better organized and more sophisticated drug traffickers became more dominant.

The most widely used legal drugs, alcohol and tobacco, were regulated as drugs only very soon after the introduction of tobacco to certain countries, such as Russia, the Ottoman empire, China and some parts of Germany in the seventeenth century (all of whose rulers found the new product so offensive that they prescribed death for smoking) and in some US states which banned tobacco as well as alcohol during the 1920s. Because their use was so widespread, their supply on prescription by a doctor was not part of the debate (except with tobacco in Louis XIII's France and alcohol during prohibition in the US), as it has been continuously with narcotics since the nineteenth century.

In Islamic countries, prohibition applies to alcohol under a regime similar to narcotics prohibition; in the rest of the world, alcohol production is regulated under a food standards regime rather than a drug regime, though for at least five hundred years its retailing has been controlled by idiosyncratic local licensing laws subject to not the slightest semblance of globalization (Webb & Webb 1903). This is also true of the retailing of cigarettes, where in most parts of the world only retailing to minors is regulated. Everywhere in the world, small businesses such as boutique breweries continue to flourish, manufacturing the comparatively unregulated drug of alcohol. This is also true of tobacco in some parts of the world. But in the US, which dominates the tobacco industry, by 1890 one massive trust controlled 80 per cent of the market (Corina 1975). This was broken up in a landmark US antitrust case of 1911. But concentration in the hands of the big four US tobacco companies increased later in the century, partly driven by the way high-spending television advertising was critical for market growth (Rogers 1982).

The tobacco industry is under threat from private rather than public law and more from civil society than the state, though recently in the US governments have modelled NGO litigation tactics using private law, with enormous impact. Public-interest groups concerned with the health risks of tobacco launch salvo after salvo of lawsuits against tobacco companies. These groups are well-organized internationally through networks such as GASP, ASH and Consumers International and have strong connections to powerful associations of health professionals. Since 1980 they have succeeded in changing tobacco from a virtually unregulated drug to one whose advertising is banned, whose labelling must include dire health warnings and whose consumption in public places and sale to minors is increasingly regulated throughout the world. Insurance companies are also increasingly part of this private regulation, as some withdraw insurance coverage from smokers and from companies that fail to protect workers and the public from passive smoking. As a result, it is inconceivable that a small new cigarette manufacturer could start in the US today. The WHO, under the more aggressive new leadership of former Norwegian prime minister Brundtland, is now building consensus for a framework convention on tobacco regulation. So, with drugs we have seen a progressive splitting of the domain into five separate regulatory regimes:

1   an illicit drugs regime (heroin, cocaine, cannabis, ecstasy, LSD etc.) subject to totally globalized prohibition;

2   a prescription drugs regime which globalized slowly under US/WHO leadership until 1980 and somewhat faster under EU leadership since then;

3   national non-prescription drugs regimes which are not globalizing;

4   national alcohol regulation regimes which are not globalizing (prohibition here, regulation here, deregulation there);

5   national tobacco regulation regimes, elements of which are progressively globalizing under global social movement politics and globalizing enforcement of private law.

Even this five-way classification of regimes is simplistic. For example, in many countries Chinese traditional medicines are regulated as foods, avoiding the need for pre-marketing clearance based on randomized trials to demonstrate therapeutic efficacy, as long as the Chinese exporters make no therapeutic claims on the outside of the packet. They get around this restriction by making the therapeutic claims inside!

With all these product markets, with alcohol, tobacco and pharmaceuticals, most countries have conscious regulatory policies to influence the price of drugs. For alcohol and tobacco, these are normally high-tax policies to dampen demand and deal with the externalities of drug abuse.

With pharmaceuticals there are typically price controls to keep national pharmaceutical benefits schemes affordable, policies to enable generic substitution for products whose patents have expired, and in some cases provision for compulsory licensing of competitors for drugs that are life-saving but unaffordable because of patent monopolies. AIDS groups have performed international arbitrage with national pricing schemes, buying expensive AIDS drugs in cheap markets for resale in expensive markets. With the exception of the global effect of WTO obligations, regulation of the price of drugs has not globalized in any important ways, remaining part of nationally specific health, welfare and tax regimes. This said, WTO obligations may turn out to have a significant effect on national sovereignty over drug prices. One reason why India has been able to deliver cheap pharmaceuticals to its citizens and the citizens of neighbouring countries is that its patent law does not allow product patents for pharmaceuticals. Under TRIPS it and other developing countries will have to grant such product patents. In Pakistan, which already allows the patenting of drug products, prices are much higher than in India (Keayla 1996).

The WHO Action Program on Essential Drugs has seen limited tangible action in terms of financial aid for developing countries' health systems. At least it has provided a model of which essential drugs a state should ensure are affordable. It has motivated modest shifting of public resources from non-essential to essential drugs in some sixty countries participating in the program. However, Bangladesh, the country that has done most to implement the policy, has buckled under pressure from the pharmaceutical industry and the World Bank to reverse the policy, in particular by lifting pricing controls on drugs. Even within the EU there has been no harmonization of pharmaceuticals pricing regulation, only a directive requiring transparency of rules and procedures under non-uniform pricing regimes.

## Actors

### States and Organizations of States

The US has been the most important actor in the globalization of drug regulation. Its leadership was primarily responsible for the great regulatory divide between the demedicalization and criminalization of the regulation of opium, heroin, cocaine, cannabis and LSD. With regulation of ethical pharmaceuticals, US leadership was pre-eminent from the Pure Food and Drugs Act to the election of President Reagan in 1981. Today the EU is more hegemonic, or perhaps there is a tregemony of the EU, the US and Japan. Within global narcotics regimes, systematic empirical work by Bruun, Pan and Rexed (1975: 117) has shown the US, the UK, France and India to be the most centrally involved states.

Many have argued and many more hoped that WHO would become an international pharmaceuticals regulatory agency. Until the 1980s, this seemed a possibility. It was sponsoring International Conferences of Drug Regulatory Agencies every few years and accomplished some harmonization of nomenclature through its International Nonproprietary Names for Pharmaceutical Substances program. In the 1970s WHO followed the model of so many UN agencies discussed in this book. The US as hegemon would introduce a new kind of regulation following domestic regulatory crises, such as Good Manufacturing Practices in the early 1970s (Braithwaite 1984); WHO would globalize these through mechanisms such as certification of GMP implementation through the 1975 Certification Scheme on the Quality of Pharmaceutical Products

Moving in International Commerce (a scheme with 138 national signatories, albeit with major problems of implementation: WHO/DAP 1994). However, the anti-UN Reagan and Bush administrations undermined this mechanism of US influence by limiting its interest in (and funding support to) WHO. The EU pharmaceutical manufacturing countries were pleased to go along with the disempowering of WHO because the forum that secured pre-eminence in the post-WHO era was the EC and the ICH that it brokered.

The thing that frightened the drug-exporting countries was the way WHO was captured by global consumer movement politics with the 1981 adoption of the International Code of Marketing of Breast-milk Substitutes. This was a response to well-documented health problems, particularly among the poorest people in the world, as a result of mothers abandoning breast-feeding in favour of breast-milk substitutes (Chetley 1979). Many of the breast-milk substitute manufacturers were pharmaceutical companies. This Code was the first WHO attempt to deal with a public health problem by regulating the marketing practices of TNCs. The Code restricts direct advertising of breast-milk substitutes, prohibits provision of free samples to the general public (a key strategy for getting consumers hooked) and regulates the information to be provided to health professionals. Sixty countries have at least partially implemented the Code as a result of the WHO initiative. This success frightened the pharmaceutical industry, particularly when the international consumer movement, flushed with the success of the breast-milk substitute Code, started to build international support for a WHO pharmaceuticals marketing code. The US had had enough; the WHO trajectory toward increasing internationalization of regulation under its auspices was thrown into reverse.

But the US did not switch the global discussion to a new forum such as the OECD, in which it might have dominated. Instead, it arrogantly assumed that other nations would continue to follow its leadership, as they had until their retreat from multilateralism. The mechanism it relied upon was bilateral negotiation of Memoranda of Understanding. An MOU, it assumed, would ensure that smaller countries would continue to take US exports on US regulatory terms and export to the US in compliance with the standards of the US market. But once European regulation unified, the US was no longer the biggest player; smaller countries followed Europe more than the US. Through the 1990s the US complained of the new international regulatory order of pharmaceuticals as 'Fortress Europe', showing the lack of coherent US international strategy that was evident in Chapter 7 on intellectual property (ironically led, among others, by the CEO of pharmaceutical company Pfizer). There, the US shifted the forum from the World Intellectual Property Organization to GATT; here it shifted the forum from WHO to a US-dominated bilateralism that the rest of the world spurned in favour of following a newly unifying Europe.

WHO's role on pharmaceuticals is still very important to the less developed regions of the world. After 1989 there were valuable efforts at technical assistance to post-communist societies whose laws and inspection were insufficiently credible to get their products widely accepted in Western markets. WHO assisted developing countries with computerizing drug registration systems. WHO software has induced a degree of international regulatory convergence. It also fosters regulatory growth internationally because, in the words of one WHO officer: 'When you have an efficient system, you can ask for money from the company for registration; so it can pay for itself'. Since the early 1990s CD-ROMs have been updated monthly with information on which products are approved for marketing in a number of countries and under what conditions (approved dosage levels, label warnings, indications, contraindications, etc.). These have been an invaluable resource to registration authorities who want up-to-date information on the thinking of registration authorities with more sophisticated assessment capabilities than their own. One might say that these days WHO evinces a discourse-driven harmonization via standardization of nomencla-ture, standard questions asked in a computer discourse directed at registration authorities: What indications have been approved by other authorities? Now what do you approve? If, as Dryzek (1996) suggests, discourses are the software of institutions and rules are the hardware, at least WHO has made some progress on software.

The idea of a WHO code for pharmaceuticals promotion was not completely forgotten. The 1988 World Health Assembly approved a set of Ethical Criteria for Medicinal Drug Promo-tion, but evaluations have considered it to be a failure (CIOMS/WHO 1993; Harvey & Caran-dang 1992), lacking performance indicators, not systematically monitored by WHO, with no capacity-building provided to developing countries by a WHO now timid about upsetting the pharmaceutical industry.

Some of WHO's limited harmonization successes have been complemented by other inter-national organizations. Pre-eminently, the European Free Trade Association (EFTA) commenced a Pharmaceutical Inspection Convention (PIC) in 1970. Members reciprocally recognize inspec-tions of pharmaceutical manufacturing plants based on exchange of inspection reports to ensure credibility, which includes compliance with the WHO Good Manufacturing Practices Regula-tions. Non-EFTA members can and do accede to PIC. There are some twenty members of PIC, and the number is growing. PIC matters because many countries are reluctant to import from non-PIC members.

This kind of international cooperation and harmonization is important because of the propensity of pharmaceutical companies to play international law evasion games. There are cruder and more sophisticated versions. An example of a cruder form of evasion is an impure or understrength product that is banned from sale in one country being dumped in another nation with looser laws (Bryan 1981). With products where there is reason to believe that risks could be high during the experimental stage, initial testing can be done on developing country popula-tions who do not have a practical capacity to sue or to stir up public opinion in the firm's home country (Braithwaite 1984: 266). This strategy has been an element of a much more sophisticated international law evasion strategy whereby a firm develops an integrated plan of where it will do the early testing and where it will do its final testing; where it will seek marketing approval first, second, third, penultimately and ultimately; and where it will locate manufacturing of the new product. While a remote jungle clinic may be ideal for initial testing, sophisticated final testing has to be done by internationally reputable clinicians in the First World if the FDA is to be impressed. As far as marketing is concerned, after the initial testing in a Third World market, an OECD country with permissive standards for approval might be the next choice; Belgium was such a country at the time of Braithwaite's research in the 1980s. Belgian approval might then be used to justify entry to a number of large Third World markets such as Brazil. The first manufac-turing plant could be located in Belgium, so that Belgium could issue the certificate of free sale required by most developing nations – a certificate indicating that the product is approved for marketing in the country of manufacture (Wall 1984). Then the firm might work its way up through First World markets with progressively more demanding registration requirements, using evidence from the safe and efficacious use of the products in the less sophisticated markets to gain entry to more sophisticated markets.

Using people in the Third World as guinea pigs is part of a complex whole. It is a complex-ity that shows the rationality of a TNC in finding the line of least resistance to early marketing through the complex jungle of the international regulatory nonsystem. TNCs use system against nonsystem. While the TNC's worldwide goals are coherent, the goals of the regulatory agencies of the world conflict. So TNCs play one off against the others. Corporations exploit the fact that regulatory goals have coherence only at a national level while corporate coherence is transnational. TNCs also sometimes use – or turn a blind eye to – intermediaries who smuggle a product into countries where marketing approval has not been obtained. But such blatant law-breaking was never the main game. In fact, it is a rather unimportant one for a transnational pharmaceutical corporation. The main game is the more subtle business of computer-assisted strategizing to find the path of least legal resistance through the international regulatory thicket. Instead of one nation's laws being viewed as an obstacle to be overcome by law violation, compliance becomes a resource for getting around the spirit of another nation's laws.

This international law evasion game became progressively more significant as the pharmaceutical industry globalized rapidly during the 1950s, 1960s and 1970s. Products that had previously been tested first in domestic US and European markets for predominantly domestic consumption would, like the contraceptive pill, be tested first on black women in South Africa or somewhere else on peoples beyond the reach of protective private and public law. By the 1990s, we had come full circle to the situation in the first half of the century: 40 per cent of new drugs were approved in the US first and most of the rest in Europe. Global convergence in regulatory standards, willingness of states to accept foreign evaluation data and the dramatic reduction in the drug lag have mostly eliminated incentives to play the international law evasion game just described. Firms today go after (much quickened) approval in the big markets first and conduct their clinical trials in markets where the quality and credibility of the science is highest. The globalizing of social movement scrutiny of the pharmaceutical industry and of the reach of mass tort litigation were also factors in change.

But in fact, Braithwaite's (1984) research showed that national governments never had to harmonize their laws perfectly to prevent TNCs from playing one country's set of laws off against another's. Indeed, the practical economic constraints of law evasion are often such that a country that sets higher regulatory standards can effectively impose its higher standards on all other countries in a region. This is particularly so when the country is large and powerful, such as the US. But strategic government intervention even by small countries can change lowest-common-denominator regulation into highest-common-factor regulation. For example, a Central American regional director for a transnational pharmaceutical company explained to Braithwaite (1984) that when Costa Rica banned a suspected carcinogenic additive in one of its products, the company took the additive from all products being distributed in all Central American countries, since the cost of special production runs for the Costa Rican market was prohibitive. Similarly, Costa Rica has long ruled that all disclosures and warnings made on packages and inserts in the country of origin should also be made in Costa Rica. The executive explained, 'From our point of view, that means they all have to say what we say in [our home country] because the cost of having different packaging for the different Central American countries is too great'.

However, because of the TNC's capacity to shift its activities around the world, there are limits to how high Costa Rica can raise all Central American standards. The same executive noted:

> Let me put it this way. It would not be in our interests to locate more of our manufacturing in the United States. For [one of the company's main products], our literature in Europe, Africa, Australia, South America, and so on claims some 10 indications for the product. In the US, the FDA approves only 3. We don't want to be forced by Costa Rica and others to suggest only three indications worldwide when we believe in 10.

Even though Costa Rica did not push this European company's standards up to those of the US, the interesting thing is that it could push them up to some degree across all Central America. Where international conventions failed, little Costa Rica succeeded in harmonizing minimum standards upward.

## Regional Actors

The Costa Rican situation illustrates the fact that within a region, harmonization is possible. There are costs for TNCs in playing the international law evasion game – shuffling operations, product and money around the world is never frictionless. A progressive nation does not always have to use the whole world to defeat international law evasion in its region. The EU and EFTA provide various examples of this, though they also provide examples of nations with higher regulatory standards being pegged back to a regional norm (Wall 1984: 334). The Benelux countries (Belgium, the Netherlands, Luxembourg), NAFTA (US, Canada, Mexico), the five Nordic countries, and the Andean Pact (Peru, Ecuador, Bolivia, Colombia, Venezuela) have made some progress toward establishing a degree of uniformity in drug regulation within their regions. Sweden, Canada and Australia, which have rather comparable systems, have a trilateral understanding on exchange of data. Canada, a pivotal state on matters of pharmaceutical regulation, is part of a third tripartite meeting group – the US, the UK and Canada. The US, like many other nations, has signed a number of bilateral MOUs. These bind the FDA and the foreign regulator to common standards for good laboratory practices and pre-clinical testing (Wall 1984: 335).

Overall, the regional harmonization game can be a win–win game for industry and consumers. While harmonization lessens possibilities for international law evasion by industry, a uniform set of regulatory requirements also reduces costs. Even if consumers in some countries some of the time get products meeting lower standards under harmonized rules, they also get improved protection against products designed to meet far lower standards. And as we have seen, consumers in a lot of countries a lot of the time will get products that meet higher standards. This is because in regional regulatory fora, a captured or corrupt bureaucrat who wants to set standards well below the international average tends to be less persuasive than a crusading bureaucrat from a country that, because of a history of special problems with the product, wants to set standards well above the international average.

## Social Movement Actors

It is clear that social movement politics has been not an unimportant force in the global politics of drugs. At WHO, Health Action International has had moments of influence, though it has never been any match for industry. Domestically, consumer groups have not been influential in a way that has shaped the position of lead national players, such as the US, in global fora. Sid Wolfe's Health Research Group in Washington and BEUC in Brussels, among others, have had significant influence on the domestic policies of the big players. Since the late 1980s AIDS groups have had some significant countervailing deregulatory influence on drug safety and efficacy testing because of their desire to get speculative new therapies available to AIDS patients more quickly. They have lobbied against US efforts to bully poor countries into repealing laws that allow compulsory licensing of AIDS drugs. Consumer group influence on the ICH has hardly been major. Progressively, as Mintzes and Hodgkin (1996) point out, NGOs have moved from the 'shifting sand' of campaigns directed against specific pharmaceutical products to the 'solid ground' of long-term reform of national and global regulatory regimes.

Social movement politics has been very influential in globalizing the regulation and prohibition of drugs of addiction through the agency of groups such as the WCTU, the Women's Anti-Opium Urgency Committee, the International Narcotic Education Association, Action Against Smoking and Health, GASP and Consumers International. The temperance movement of the nineteenth century rivalled the environmental and women's movements of the twentieth century in grassroots involvement. Following themes from the Societies for the Reformation of Manners established in England from 1691 and the Society for the Suppression of Vice and the Encouragement of Religion and Virtue Throughout the United Kingdom from 1802 (Webb & Webb 1903: 137–51), the first US temperance society was formed by 1789. By the 1830s there were 6000 local societies in the US with a membership of a million (Bruun, Pan & Rexed 1975: 8). According to another estimate, by 1835 1.5 million of 13 million citizens had pledged to refrain from distilled spirits, resulting in a dramatic drop in spirits consumption, accomplished essentially by citizen self-regulation combined with minor licensing reforms (National Clearinghouse for Alcohol and Drug Information 1996).

## Individual Actors

Some individuals prominent in social movements came to hold the reins of state power, the most important example being the opium and alcohol prohibitionist Mahatma Gandhi. When Gladstone's Liberals won in 1892, three members of the Society for the Suppression of the Opium Trade were elevated to Cabinet (Johnson 1975: 311).

Certain individuals have been extremely important in social movement politics, for example, Andy Chetley with the globalization of pharmaceuticals regulation. When people mention the influence of the UK group Social Audit in this domain, they are really speaking of the influence of one person, Charles Medawar. The leadership of the US state in the globalization of narcotics prohibition was largely due to the leadership of Harry Anslinger, head of the Federal Bureau of Narcotics from 1930 to 1961 (Bruun, Pan & Rexed 1975: 124). Criminalization of use (rather than sale) was an Anslinger idea from the days when he sought to rejuvenate the enforcement of alcohol prohibition during the 1920s (Musto 1973: 212). However, it is important not to adopt an excessively individualistic theory of why Anslinger's Federal Bureau of Narcotics crusaded for prohibition. The Bureau was distinguished from narcotics regulators in other parts of the world which also performed medical, policing and customs duties; narcotics was the Bureau's sole duty, 'so if "drugs" ceased to matter, so too did FBN' (Manderson 1993: 66).

With the globalization of pharmaceuticals regulation during the 1990s, Fernand Sauer of the EC, the architect of the ICH, stands out as an individual who could inspire others. In his first interview with us in 1993, he said: 'Participants [in the ICH process] are more enthusiastic, innovative, they work more on weekends than they do in their normal jobs because it's a big-picture challenge, something new and interesting and out of the ordinary'. In the shift of global power from the US to the EU, the difference between Sauer's approach and that of the FDA leadership has been described as the difference between a diplomat and a policeman, a description which Sauer did not reject during our interview. As one European regulatory official put it: 'In dealings with and within the FDA, there is an FDA chief who dominates. People are silenced by him. At the EC, there is no boss at the decision-making table. It is more a discussion among equals'. We would agree with Goodman and Moravcsik (1993: 1) when they conclude that policy initiation with ICH 'stemmed neither from industry pressure, nor from a transnational "epistemic community" of regulators, but from the leadership (or political entrepreneurship) exercised by the Commission'. As with Anslinger, however, it is important to recognize the institutional opportunity Sauer seized, being able to bring a unified EC to a trilateral bargaining table. With a reduction in the number of actors, there is a reduction in the transaction costs of leadership. Moreover, with Japan wanting to harmonize below the more demanding US standards on some matters, Europe was well positioned to be a middle ground that most nations might reluctantly follow.

### Professions as Actors

Professional associations have also been of crucial importance, particularly medical associations, from sponsoring prescription laws in the battle with pharmacists to supporting prohibition so doctors could make money out of prescribing alcohol, to insisting on laws to require testing of the safety and efficacy of drugs. An interesting group has been the Medical Lobby for Appropriate Marketing. Dr Peter Mansfield, the inspiration behind MaLAM, sends a large number of medical members around the world (about 6000) information about a product that is being marketed inappropriately by a particular company in a particular country. These doctors then write to the company – generally at its world headquarters, in the country where the conduct occurred or in their own country – demanding an explanation of the alleged inappropriate marketing practice. A naive strategy, hard-bitten advocates of state deterrence might say. But it works often enough to make it an extremely cost-efficient method of social control for activists with scarce resources. Writing letters is cheap. It is also a decent method of social control based on a reasoned appeal to corporate and medical responsibility. Sometimes MaLAM decides that it wrongly assessed a situation and writes to the company with an apology. Pharmaceutical executives, even some of the very worst, do have a better side, a responsible side, to which appeals to professional and corporate responsibility can be made. They have multiple selves that make it worth considering a strategy that encourages them to put their best self forward. When that does not work, there are other strategies available to advocacy groups – muck-raking in the media and calls for state enforcement, for example, and in extreme cases, threats of consumer or professional boycotts.

In addition to corporate executives having a socially responsible self that can be brought to the fore surprisingly often, pharmaceutical companies have self-interested reasons to listen and respond seriously to rising groundswells of professional concern about their marketing practices. Pharmaceutical companies survive in the marketplace by persuading physicians to prescribe their products. In other words, they depend for success on convincing health-care professionals that they are trustworthy. Sometimes they make the judgment that the best way to promote their long-term success is to actually be trustworthy, to admit a mistake and put it right. Five of seventeen MaLAM letters between January 1988 and June 1989 resulted in an agreement by the targeted company to alter claims or withdraw the product in question (Wade, Mansfield & McDonald 1989: 1261–4). This strike rate increased to five of nine between July 1989 and June 1990 (Mansfield 1991).

In pharmaceuticals, there are many kindred professional networks to MaLAM, such as the International Society of Drug Bulletins, the Network for Rational Use of Medication in Pakistan, the International Network for Rational Use of Drugs, the International Network for Pharma-cotherapy Teaching (INDEPTH) and the Alliance for the Prudent Use of Antibiotics, which in some way are a check on the irresponsible promotion of drugs.

## Business Actors

The centrality of business organizations in globalization is well-proven by the fact that the IFPMA (formed in 1968) has acted as the secretariat for the ICH. At the same time, the industry has tended to be divided on many of the big regulatory questions. Some of the established firms have created obstacles to European harmonization, for example, because they calculate that they know how to work the European regulatory maze; this gives them a competitive advantage over newer and smaller players of the drug innovation game. Some of the idiosyncratic traditions of Japanese toxi-cology combined with legitimate concerns about racial difference in therapeutic effect have given Japanese companies an unassailable advantage in the large Japanese market. Consequently, indus-try association executives often 'beat the drum' for global harmonization only to see member com-panies marching to the beat of many different drums (Orzack, Kaitin & Lasagna 1992).

The centre of world power in Europe has always been characterized by a corporatist style of regulatory decision-making (Greenwood & Ronit 1991). For example, the setting up of the origi-nal EC regulatory regime in the 1960s was negotiated with representatives of the International Pharmaceutical Industry Group for the EEC Countries (GHP), the Union of Industries of the European Community (UNICE), the Consumers Contact Committee in the Common Market, the Permanent Medical Committee of the European Economic Community, the Trade Union Sec-retariat of the Six within the International Confederation of Free Trade Unions, and the European Organization of the International Federation of Christian Trade Unions. The greatest source of contention was that a drug must have proven 'therapeutic potency' before it was authorized. The representatives of doctors, pharmacists, consumers and trade unions all viewed this requirement as indispensable, while the industry representatives (GHP and UNICE), supported by the German government, were opposed. Industry lost (Orzack, Kaitin & Lasagna 1992: 853).

Major disasters were a cause of defeats for business (for example, thalidomide) and an important resource for professional and reformist groups wanting to strengthen regulatory laws. The US assumed a position of international leadership in drug regulation after the elixir sulfanil-amide disaster caused the agonising death of 107 in 1938 (Braithwaite 1984: 113–14). The 1938 US standards (requiring safety- and efficacy-testing of drugs before they could be marketed) globalized following the thalidomide disaster, involving a German product that caused 8000 deformed chil-dren to be born across forty-six countries, and about twice that number to die, in the early 1960s. It was after the thalidomide disaster that the EC entered pharmaceuticals regulation and that most states set up credible regulation for the first time.

These and other disasters (Braithwaite 1984) have also been a resource for reformers within TNCs. Individuals within TNCs often have professional and even consumer activist iden-tities that rival in importance the identity they share with other employees of the corporation. The 131 interviews Braithwaite conducted with pharmaceutical industry executives between 1978 and 1981 revealed how they have plural identities and multiple loyalties to multiple orga-nizations. For example, a Lilly research executive may have a loyalty to her research team that is stronger than her more remote loyalty to Lilly as a corporation. She may have a loyalty to her profession, to her patients if she is a doctor, and so on. The identity 'Lilly executive' is only one of many identities.

An important conclusion was that consumers receive more protection from the high standards that these competing identities bring into a firm than from enforcement of the law. This is particularly true with regard to developing countries. As many have demonstrated, drug companies have double and triple standards when it comes to marketing drugs in the Third World (Medawar 1979; Dukes & Swartz 1988; Silverman, Lee & Lydecker 1982). It is also true, however, that most, if not all, transnational pharmaceutical companies set much higher standards in the least-regulated developing markets than they are required to meet by the laws of those countries. They set higher standards because it would be intolerable to the professional standards of their employees to stoop to the levels allowed by lax laws. There are other reasons, that we will discuss later. But in Braithwaite's fieldwork, and in his work as a consumer advocate, he has encountered many instances of responsible professionals within TNCs exposing the unethical conduct of their own executives to the professional disapproval of their peers within the firm. This occurs even in firms that are among the worst law-breakers in an industry with an unusually bad record for lawbreaking (Clinard & Yeager 1980: pp. 119–22).

Those in the best position to know about corporate wrongdoing are within the corporation. Those in the best position to understand whether organizationally and technologically complex corporate conduct actually amounts to wrongdoing are those who have an understanding of the organization, its technology and the potential effects of that technology. The actors in the best position to mobilize informal sanctioning and disapproval that wrongdoers will care about are the peers with whom they share daily professional life. These are reasons why intracorporate self-regulation by employees with consciences is the form of regulation that probably saves the greatest number of lives. If transnational pharmaceutical companies really did meet the minimum standards in the law of all the countries in which they operated, and never performed above those legal standards, the death toll from prescription drugs would be horrific. This observation shows the fundamental limitation of state law enforcement as a control strategy.

In all firms, there are constituencies that support the intent of regulatory laws. In pharmaceutical companies, the office of medical director and the quality assurance group are often such constituencies, and in some cases the general counsel's office also pushes for compliance with the law. Effective self-regulation largely depends on strengthening the hand of such offices. An example is the strategy, now widespread throughout the industry, of allowing decisions of quality control on batches of drugs to be overruled only by the signature of the chief executive. This eliminates much of the day-to-day nullifying of quality control by production managers who insist on meeting production targets when they deem attainment of specifications as good enough. Such a management policy enormously strengthens a pro-regulation internal constituency.

A phenomenon quite unlike that in any of the other industries studied is the Regulatory Affairs Professionals Society (RAPS), with over 4000 members from the global pharmaceutical industry and national regulators. Through this epistemic community a shared identity between state and corporate regulators is constituted. In addition, ideas for global convergence are worked up within RAPS.

Interfirm regulation is one of the things that can constitute the intrafirm self-regulation that Braithwaite concluded was so important (Braithwaite 1984) – but it can also be constituted by state regulation, such as a law requiring the signature of the chief executive when quality control is overruled, or by consumer activism. Interfirm regulation can occur at a number of levels. National industry associations can write and enforce self-regulatory codes, as can international industry associations. Single firms can seek to upgrade the standards of corporate peers. Each level of interfirm regulation will now be illustrated.

An example of national industry association self-regulation is the Australian Pharmaceutical Manufacturers Association Code of Conduct (1990), which relates primarily to the promotion of prescription drugs. Throughout the 1980s, John Braithwaite, with other leaders of the Australian consumer movement, believed that self-regulation was not appropriate for controlling pharmaceutical advertising, that tougher government regulation was needed. Braithwaite still believes that in principle this is an area in which government regulation ought to be more effective and efficient than self-regulation. After the total failure of such regulation during the 1970s and 1980s, however, the government decided to give a rejuvenated self-regulation scheme a three-year trial, beginning in 1988. Self-regulation during that period was more effective at improving the integrity of pharmaceuticals promotion than the limp government regulation of the previous decade had been (Trade Practices Commission 1992). Although Australian consumer activists who have been involved first-hand with this issue do not doubt the finding that self-regulation worked better than the feeble government regulation that it replaced, they still believe that inappropriate marketing practices are widespread and unremedied. Nevertheless, improvement is improvement, and it warrants the concession that historical circumstances may result in self-regulation working better than government regulation even in an area where in principle the reverse should be true. The reasons for the success of this scheme were contingent; they included a substantial industry investment in prepublication monitoring of advertisements for compliance with the code, repeated post-publication surveys of the percentage of advertisements that complied (conducted independently by the Australian Society of Clinical and Experimental Pharmacologists: Moulds & Wing 1989; Carandang & Moulds 1994) and the knowledge that the self-regulation scheme would be evaluated by the Trade Practices Commission to determine whether it should be replaced by government regulation.

IFPMA has also been in the business of self-regulation. Indeed, the Australian Pharmaceutical Manufacturers Association code, discussed above, received part of its impetus from pressure for increased self-regulation from IFPMA (IFPMA 1987). In turn, the fear of de facto international and national regulation by WHO in conjunction with Third World governments in order to implement the WHO list of essential drugs – that is, to eliminate non-essential drugs from the market so that health budgets could be concentrated on life-saving products – prompted IFPMA in 1982 to start supplying essential drugs to a few pilot countries (Cohn 1983: 352). In countries such as The Gambia and Sierra Leone, the initiative seems to have been responsible for some improvement in primary health-care and in the availability of life-saving drugs (Chetley 1990: 133–4). On the whole, however, one would have to say that IFPMA efforts at self-regulation have been token (Lexchin 1992) and that only in a few countries such as Australia have they been taken seriously because of extra pressure from professional and consumer constituencies.

An interesting development in interfirm regulation has been at the level of a single firm – the Swiss giant Ciba-Geigy (now Novatis, after its merger with Sandoz) – that sought to persuade its corporate peers to upgrade self-regulatory standards voluntarily. Ciba-Geigy was a pariah firm until the late 1980s as far as the international consumer movement was concerned (Hansson 1989). It had done terrible things in product-testing, such as spraying Third World agricultural workers with experimental chemicals without their consent and aggressively marketing products such as clioquinol that had disastrous side effects, which were then covered up. Ciba-Geigy also persisted in marketing products in the Third World after they had been demonstrated to be unsafe and had been withdrawn from First World markets. Cynics will say that it was the public relations setbacks associated with the consumer movement perception of Ciba-Geigy as a killer corporation, combined with the threat of an international consumer boycott, that caused the corporation to change its spots. Greater cynics will say that Ciba-Geigy has not altered its spots at all. Our view is that Ciba-Geigy did change.

At the end of 1986, the company initiated a program called the Risk Assessment of Drugs – Analysis and Response (RAD-AR). RAD-AR's goal was to get leading companies to be more open about the risk factors associated with their products and to foment a more constructive dialogue about the risks and benefits of particular pharmaceuticals, a dialogue in which industry critics take part. RAD-AR's success was extremely limited and patchy, varying from one part of the world to another. Representatives of many companies attended RAD-AR seminars, but not many acted to make their safety and efficacy data more genuinely open to competitors and critics. The US company G.D. Searle, formerly a prominent practitioner of research during which rats died when exposed to a drug but managed to be alive by the end of the study, is one organization that has moved significantly in the direction of greater openness about its products (Chetley 1990: 139). It is both interesting and theoretically significant that the companies that have taken the most determined steps toward greater openness and dialogue about the risks of an industry that markets tamed poisons, have been those such as Ciba-Geigy[5] and Searle which have been subjected to some of the strongest consumer vilification.

A more minor business actor that should be retrieved from our narrative of the history of drug regulation is the insurance company. Insurers have been a source of pressure to implement globalizing tobacco regulation on questions like smoking in the workplace. The emergence of global law firms with some ability to pursue TNCs anywhere, combined with the wider horizons of insurers (Grabosky 1994), mean that it is now seen as risky to test drugs on developing nation guinea pigs who formerly never sued. In the illicit drug trade, part of the regulation that organized crime groups exercise over disorganized local distributors and farmers is that in many circumstances they insure the product. Farmers are guaranteed payment even if crops are sprayed with defoliant, distributors get paid even for missions where couriers are lost. While this is not as important as fear of execution, or addiction, in keeping the fungible players working in the trade, it is not unimportant.

## An Epistemic Community of Many Actors

The story of the impact of different types of actors on the globalization of regulation is one of modest impacts on the regulation of prescription pharmaceuticals, virtually no impact on the regulation of over-the-counter drugs, alcohol and (except until very recently) tobacco, and sweeping impact on the global regulation of illicit drugs. While each type of actor in the prescription drugs domain has had weak effects – insurers, WHO, ICH, EFTA, the EU, the European Pharmacopoeia Convention, the FDA, regional, trilateral and bilateral collaborations, industry associations and consumer groups, RAPS, the professions of medicine and pharmacy, the MaLAM and the likes of the Society of Clinical and Experimental Pharmacologists – their combined effect has brought

---

5  In a letter of 2 June 1992 from Ciba-Geigy to MaLAM, it was stated: 'Another dimension of our policies is that neither safety nor efficacy data of marketed products are considered as confidential. Therefore, anyone can obtain a copy of a CIBA-GEIGY BDI [Basic Drug Information] or the documents referenced in the BDI for a marketed product. This allows medical professionals, the media, and the public to monitor Ciba-Geigy's compliance with our information and communications policies for marketed products.' We have doubts, however, that this commitment to openness has survived the merger to form Novatis.

substantial global regulatory convergence. Similarly, while the effects of each actor in levering compliance with global standards is weak, their combined effect can be strong. Quite unlike the situation with nuclear regulation, actors meet regularly at events such as RAPS conferences and share a globalized regulatory language. They have forged an epistemic community of some vitality wherein the principles discussed below are debated.

## Contest of Principles

Increasingly, rule compliance is not a principle pursued simply through enforcement by state regulatory authorities. TNCs are not subject only to national regulatory control; they are subject to a whole web of controls – the national regulators of other states to whom they export, insurers, mass tort litigation, MaLAM, WHO, EMEA, industry self-regulation schemes, the ethical codes of the professionals who work for them and fear of exposure by the consumer movement and the media. Every strand of that web is weak, including the national regulator. But interrelationships among the strands create a web of controls that must be taken more seriously than any single strand. A social movement like the consumer movement might be disorganized and weak, but when it can mobilize media assaults, sow seeds of professional distrust of the industry, foment consumer cynicism about industry products, heighten the threat of government regulation, put the credibility of self-regulation under pressure and initiate mass tort litigation, the entire web of influences can and does change industry conduct.

As a result of this web of controls, the global-law evasion game that Braithwaite documented as the reality of pharmaceuticals globalization in the 1970s (Braithwaite 1984) is mostly not accurate today. There is still competition to attract pharmaceutical investment through low regulatory standards. Through following a principle of rule compliance rather than one of continuous improvement, firms still seek to find the line of least legal resistance through the international regulatory nonsystem. But there is more system and less nonsystem in the world today. The principle of lowest-cost location still flourishes. However, the principle of world's best practice is a more important principle now than it was in the 1970s, the principle of lowest-cost location less so.

Pharmaceutical companies can see it as a competitive disadvantage to locate pharmaceutical manufacturing in an Eastern European country that might have low labour costs and minimal regulation. Today they tend to see it as a competitive disadvantage to return to drug-testing on Third World guinea pigs in jungle clinics where lawsuits might be unheard of, but where science and the conditions for rigorous experimental control are also bad. The absence of demanding regulators, demanding professional standards, demanding science, demanding law firms and demanding consumer groups means that companies from these countries are totally unprepared for competition in sophisticated markets. The corporate pursuit of the principle of deregulation was more muted in the 1990s than in the 1970s and 1980s. Firms located in states that fall behind in regulatory standards are seen to suffer a trade disadvantage. There is seen to be an advantage in having standards high enough to be one of the twenty countries invited into PIC, for example. On the other hand, the principle of deregulation still has rhetorical power. Moreover, shortening the drug lag between development and approval of new drugs remains important to the competitiveness of pharmaceutical companies. Obviously, the principle of deregulation has very little support within the global narcotics regime.

The principle of deregulation has had no support in the prescription drugs regime in relation to intellectual property issues. We saw in Chapter 7 that pharmaceutical companies were at the forefront of the push for global, harmonized patent laws. Higher levels of intellectual property regulation will bring increased costs, costs that will be borne by citizens and states as part of health-care budgets (e.g. extending a patent term means a longer period of monopoly profit for drug companies). In this particular contest of principles, the principles of deregulation and national sovereignty both lose to harmonization.

With the mixed centralized–decentralized system of pharmaceuticals approval in Europe, some of the people interviewed spoke of the virtues of 'competition between the centre and nations' and regulatory competition between nations. To the extent that this is competition in the efficiency of the drug-evaluation process and gets the job done well and quickly, no one could argue with the virtues of regulatory competition. What most commentators hope is that this competition in efficiency will be complemented by competition for credibility rather than competition to be more captured, corrupt or negligent than other states. Whether this hope is misplaced remains to be seen.

At one level, the story is similar to the one we saw with environmental regulation – a contest between the principles of lowest-cost location and deregulation versus world's best practice and regulation. But there is a third model with drugs – a principle of mega-regulation, destruction of markets, prohibition or criminalization with drugs that are called narcotics (misleadingly, in the case of cannabis). In its simplicity, this principle has proven easier to globalize as a principle than the other set of paired principles. Yet globalization of corporate compliance with the principle has totally failed, also because its analysis of markets is so simplistic.

Within the EU, NAFTA and the ICH, battles rage between the principles of national sovereignty and national treatment (identical treatment for imports and similar domestic products). For Japan, national sovereignty in pharmaceuticals has meant distinctive toxicological principles that have erected non-tariff barriers, rendering national treatment a practical impossibility. But this is breaking down and Japan is an extreme case; within Europe national treatment has prevailed over national sovereignty as a matter of law and gradually as a matter of practice. Within Europe the Most Favoured Nation principle applies to pharmaceuticals. Globally this is not the case: foreign investors who build local plants and invest in local R&D tend to get a better deal from state pharmaceutical benefit schemes. The principle of reciprocity (we'll let your product in if you let ours on your market) has less effect on pharmaceutical markets than others because states take absolutist stances on standards affecting human life (afraid of vilification by consumer and professional groups if such trading were to lead to a major disaster). Equally, the moral absolutism of debates over illicit drugs has not been conducive to the principle of reciprocity.

Transparency is a principle that RAD-AR, and a few TNCs such as Ciba-Geigy and Searle, have largely failed in persuading the industry to follow. It is a principle with limited application in EC price regulation for drugs. In general, whether with narcotics or pharmaceuticals, regulation of drugs is secretive. With institutions like the ICH, there is a paradox of sovereignty, part of which is that the ICH is negotiated more transparently than traditional state regulation. As one EC official explained, certain kinds of international reciprocal adjustment require a level of transparency that may be unnecessary under national regulation: 'Documents have to be simple and transparent to be capable of persuading twelve countries. Parliamentarians were never involved in drug-marketing decisions. If the EC increases transparency, the parliamentarians might engage more'. Indeed, the advent of the EMEA has seen an increase in the transparency of regulation to citizens. For the first time for most of Europe, the public has been given some (though not total)[6] access to the scientific data on which drug-marketing decisions are made through the European Public Assessment Report. It is available on the Internet (http://www. eudra.orgl.emea.html) in a way the data for most national decisions are not. This possibility of a paradox of sovereignty is an intriguing one.

National consumer groups outside the US and a few other developed countries have virtually no capacity to monitor the highly technical deliberations of their national authorities on the matter of pharmaceuticals regulation. Even when they have the capacity, a 1997 international survey (Bardelay 1997) found that 78 per cent of expert informants found obtaining 'access to unpublished data on drug efficacy and safety' from their drug regulatory authority 'difficult'. An international NGO like Health Action International still has only a very limited capacity to monitor the international deliberations of the ICH. While it gets to listen, it rarely gets to speak, and has little influence in the ICH. But national consumer groups may gain more influence by pooling their resources and their best and most expert people through HAI to focus monitoring on global fora like the ICH, than they can have through national regulators. In a world of increasingly internationalized regulation, focusing weak glimmers of scrutiny from 100 national consumer groups onto one international forum of decision-making may increase popular sovereignty from nothing to something. An irony of the ICH process for citizen groups is that it occurs much more in the open than national regulatory negotiations. Why? Not to allow citizen sovereignty over the regulatory process, not as a concession to consumer groups demanding accountability. It has been open and well-documented as a concession to governments which have been complaining because of their exclusion from the process. No claim is made here that NGO networking to wire international fora like the ICH back to the people can create a Jeffersonian sovereignty for the modern world. Perhaps it can create a little more sovereignty than the delusion of popular and parliamentary sovereignty that is the status quo of the technically and quantitatively demanding domains of business regulation. The paradox of sovereignty is that an institution like ICH, that reduces national sovereignty, may increase citizen sovereignty. National sovereignty is certainly a principle we need to problematize.

Regional and global harmonization through the ICH, the EU, EFTA and other groupings has been a fundamental principle. Mutual recognition has been, at least in Europe, not a principle that has competed with harmonization, but one that has been enabled by it. That is, the achievement of partial harmonization through the mechanism of reciprocal adjustment discussed below makes mutual recognition a more acceptable approach. Has harmonization and mutual recognition contributed to deregulation (a race-to-the-bottom) or world's best practice (a race-to-the-top)? Perhaps in the 1990s there was a productive stalemate among these principles, as Vogel (1998) has concluded: 'the result of increased coordination has been neither a strengthening nor a weakening of national standards; rather it has helped make national government regulation more efficient and effective'.

Harmonization has been an absolute non-starter with over-the-counter drugs. Even members of the EU cannot agree on product summaries for aspirin. But because OTC regulation does not matter as much as prescription drug regulation, despite the lack of interest in harmonization EU members are generally happy to allow mutual recognition to work on OTC products that flow freely across European borders.

---

6 Information judged to be commercial-in-confidence is excised.

Strategic trade has not been an important principle, as Vogel (1998) has explained: 'international coordination of nations' drug approval standards has generally taken place outside the framework of trade negotiations, largely because distinctive national regulatory requirements have not functioned as trade barriers'. Tough regulatory standards in the US disadvantage European firms in the US market, and vice versa. At times, there has been a suggestion that Japan has used distinctive toxicological standards to advantage Japanese firms in their home market.

## Mechanisms

### Military Coercion or Hegemony?

Military hegemony has been shown to be quite an important mechanism of globalization. In the nineteenth century, the British enforced a policy of tolerance of drug use that suited the British East India Company and Britain's pharmaceuticals and tobacco-manufacturing interests. When China defied the policy of tolerance and free trade in drugs, Britain fought two opium wars to force China to legalize opium use. The result was that the Chinese opium problem, by the turn of the twentieth century, had become the most massive plague of drug addiction the world has seen. Between the First and Second World Wars Japanese occupying armies also enforced the right of Japanese pharmacists to install a chain of North Asian pharmacies selling Japanese-manufactured heroin. The US occupying armies of 1945 shut down the state opium monopolies that were ubiquitous throughout Asia, just as they had done in the Philippines following the US military defeat of the Spanish in 1898.

Germany, which monopolized cocaine manufacturing prior to the First World War, used effective stalling tactics to prevent cocaine from being included in the implementation of the Hague Convention of 1912 (Bruun, Pan & Rexed 1975: 12). By stalling until 1914, Germany hoped winning the First World War might crush the global regulation of cocaine. At Versailles the UK enforced compliance with the Hague Convention, which encompassed cocaine. While there was an initial diffusion of cocaine abuse globally as a result of troops returning from the war and spreading the habit among prostitutes, the peace settlement had the effect of massively reducing cocaine use; by mid-century it had almost disappeared as a problem.

After the Second World War, the US had inchoate fears about the I.G. Farben chemicals cartel which had first synthesized heroin, had been important in cocaine manufacture and had conducted murderous psychotropic drug experiments on Jews during the war. I.G. Farben ranks with the Standard Oil Trust as one of the two greatest industrial cartels in history. The Allied occupation broke up the cartel into companies now known as Bayer, BASF and Hoechst (the latter rebuilt by the 1970s to be the biggest drug company in the world). Twelve of I.G. Farben's top management were sentenced at Nuremberg to terms of imprisonment as war criminals.

Manderson shows that after the Second World War established US hegemony, Australia ceased allowing the UK to dictate Australian drug policy. The UK was no longer able to instruct its former dominion how to vote at Hague Conventions, as it had done between the wars. From 1945 Australia turned away from the UK medical model of narcotics policy (Manderson 1993: 106), following the US to a criminalization policy. Manderson's analysis of how, during the twentieth century, Australia fitted in to the global regimes forged in the image of US policy, is a perceptive account of how in domains like drugs, which are not of high foreign-policy importance, international regimes can piece by piece put together a jigsaw of domestic policy. The global regime influence occurs in a way that is perceived neither by foreign-policy strategists (who are too occupied with the big questions of war, peace and strategic balance to worry about drug policy) nor by domestic drug-policy specialists (for whom this month's policy debate is a domestic one where international obligations are rarely considered).

> Paradoxically, the inexorable development of drug policy was driven by its relative unimportance, the absence of domestic or political controversy and the consequent influence of international and bureaucratic factors. As the structure of modern drug laws took shape, each brick depending on those below for support and validity, few remembered or even thought to question why the bricks had ever been laid. So effective had the gradual process of entrenchment been that alternative processes soon became unthinkable (Manderson 1993: 75).

The bricks that neither the prime ministers who supported the criminalization model nor the drug policy specialists in Australian bureaucracies could see were the Shanghai Commission of 1909, the Hague Conventions of 1912 and 1914 and the Geneva Conventions of 1924, 1925, 1931 and 1936. This indeed is hegemony in the classic Gramscian sense – bricks that were put in place hegemonically, but bricks that are not noticed by those they wall in. The sequence of narcotics conventions foreshadowed the strategy of green groups later in the century – a framework convention (Shanghai in 1909, see footnote 1) into which growing global consensus gradually pours content and national commitments.

The Nixon and Reagan–Bush Wars on Drugs were in some senses literally so. Over time they were increasingly funded from the military rather than from the health or criminal justice budgets. Assassination of key drug distributors became part of the strategy (Epstein 1990). The US military was not only heavily deployed in drug interdiction in the Caribbean, but US military technology such as helicopters was supplied for moving the war from US streets to controlling crops and factories in developing countries. In Colombia a virtual state of war has prevailed between the government and the cocaine cartels which control most cocaine imported into the US. A consequence of the militarization of the war on drugs was that drug interdiction was a subordinate foreign policy goal to the defeat of communism. Consequently, we have seen how CIA protection of Noriega in Panama, Kuomintang insurgents, Burmese and Laotian druglords, Nicaraguan Contras, the Mujaheddin in Afghanistan and their ilk (followed by crackdowns when they were no longer needed) actually created bigger and more ruthless controllers of drug trafficking and linked organized trafficking into new markets.

### Economic Coercion

Economic coercion is less important than military coercion in the globalization of drug regulation, the only domain, except for nuclear regulation, where this is true. The US certainly led both licit and illicit drug regulation for most of the twentieth century; before the twentieth century there had been little globalization of regulation apart from the globalization of free trade in drugs enforced primarily by British hegemony and supported by Germany. With illicit drugs, US hegemony rose throughout the century; with licit drugs it was replaced by an EU hegemony in the 1980s, or perhaps by a tripolar hegemony of the EU, the US and Japan.

The decline of US hegemony was due to its deeply defective drug diplomacy. The US enfeebled WHO as a forum, allowing the G-77 and Japan to become unusually influential players in the resulting leadership vacuum. Instead of shifting to a new forum that the US could dominate, it allowed the EC to do that. The US evinced an insular commitment to the principle of national sovereignty, against its own interests. It assumed that, as had happened until the 1970s, the rest of the world would follow its lead on matters of pharmaceuticals regulation. This didn't happen. Even its closest ally, Canada, follows European regulatory leadership on pharmaceuticals more than US leadership.

With narco-diplomacy, the globalization of the US 'criminalization and destruction of markets' policy has been dramatic. To some extent, the policy's globalization has been bought by increasing foreign aid to states who comply, cutting aid off to states that defy the US line (most recently, Colombia in 1996) and providing political support to election candidates in front-line states such as Colombia who toe the US line (Walker 1993–94). Massive foreign aid to Turkey was involved in the successful diplomacy to shut down heroin supply, cutting the 'French connection' that supplied Turkish heroin to the US through Marseilles in the early 1970s. But at the same time the CIA was protecting anti-communist insurgents and leaders in various parts of the world, who in time used this protection to replace the Turkey–Marseilles supply route. US hegemony therefore has only an appearance of success. Nations dutifully sign US-sponsored conventions – they have no strong interest against signing them – but they do not effectively implement them, because they are unimplementable. The markets cannot be destroyed; the rest of the world resents the fact that one of the reasons they have not been destroyed is that new traffickers grow powerful under CIA protection. The realist edge is that the US state gets domestic political kudos by painting the drug problem as a foreign conspiracy to corrupt the US that must be fought as a war (e.g. by extraditing Colombian kingpins and General Noriega to face US justice). For most other states, drugs is an easy domain in which to comply with US wishes, building goodwill that can be used on questions that are strategically important. Most of the world's leaders know that US drug policy will fail, but given that they do not have a strong idea of an alternative that will succeed and that beating the drum for the war on drugs looks good at home, realists let the US have its way. The hegemonic accomplishment is perhaps fragile, however. When global epistemic communities coalesce around an alternative narcotics control policy that is shown empirically to succeed better than the US war on drugs, the shallow US hegemony will be at risk.

That fragility is well illustrated by the limited success of copying the highly successful watch-list innovation from US trade policy. Annually, the State Department certifies its allies in the war on drugs. In 1997, economic sanctions were threatened against Colombia, Nigeria, Afghanistan, Syria, Iran and Burma for failing to cooperate fully with the US in the fight against drugs. Three others – Belize, Lebanon and Pakistan – were also deemed not to be fully cooperating, but economic sanctions against them were suspended on national-interest grounds. States unbeloved by the CIA tend to figure prominently on these lists. While blacklisting does tend to worry the states named, what was interesting about the 1997 listing was that Colombia responded to its blacklisting by suspending its drug-crop eradication program. When front-line officers in the program were regularly killed, there was Colombian resentment at US failure to accomplish demand-reduction. Coercion, as we will discuss in Chapter 23, can be counterproductive.

The US Trade Representative persistently and with considerable success used the threat of Section 301 sanctions under its Trade Act in the 1980s and early 1990s to overturn policies in a number of Asian countries that regulated national monopoly in tobacco sales. This included demands to lift proposed advertising bans (e.g. in Taiwan) on grounds that US market entrants would have no prospect of fair competition against entrenched domestic monopolies unless they could advertise. According to a Gallup poll cited by a US General Accounting Office Report, after South Korean import restrictions were lifted in 1988, smoking rates increased from 18 per cent to 30 per cent among male Korean teenagers in one year and from 2 per cent to 9 per cent among female teenagers between 1988 and 1989 (*Multinational Monitor*, February 1992, p. 5).

### Systems of Reward

US hegemony in the illicit drugs arena has therefore been delivered by the mechanism of systems of reward, in the form of economic and military aid for programs such as crop substitution and protection for drug pushers the CIA chooses to support. But because aid for crop substitution has sometimes clashed with the bigger political objective of subsidies to US farmers producing the same licit crops (Block 1992), because rewarding effective drug enforcement with aid and political support has clashed with the need to protect drug trafficking by powerful anti-communists, systems of reward has been a mechanism that has backfired in its practical effects on the globalization of US narcotic prohibitionism.

### Modelling

We have seen that until 1980 quite a lot of globalization of drug regulation occurred by the US instituting a regulatory initiative and the rest of the world progressively following that initiative. Good Manufacturing Practices and Good Laboratory Practices Regulations for pharmaceuticals are examples, where WHO fostered the modelling by putting GMPs in the Certification Scheme on the Quality of Pharmaceutical Products Moving in International Commerce. WHO also fosters modelling by publishing Guiding Principles for Small Drug Regulatory Authorities and (with the Pan-American Health Organization) a Model Software Package for Drug Registration. Since the early 1990s, getting updated decisions of major regulatory authorities to smaller ones on CD-ROM has facilitated the modelling of these European authorities. Digital promulgation of the *UN Consolidated List of Products Whose Consumption and/or Sale have been Banned, Withdrawn, Severely Restricted or Not Approved by Governments* was also important. Through its computer software, WHO also promulgates a shared regulatory discourse, as it does through its International Non-proprietary Names for Pharmaceutical Substances program. The WHO monthly Pharmaceutical Newsletter is a form of communication that also fosters international modelling, though it is less influential than the private for-profit publication *Scrip* or the European or US pharmacopoeias. WHO's most important work in fostering modelling is through supporting NGOs that promote rational drug use in developing countries. Under the banner of the Action Program on Essential Drugs and Vaccines, this has had a subtle but major influence on drug policy.

The most fundamental globalization of a single regulatory strategy with pharmaceuticals did not occur as a result of military or economic coercion, nor pursuant to any cooperative international agreement. It occurred through modelling, primarily of US leadership. The most distinctive feature of pharmaceuticals regulation, compared with the regulation of food or of the safety of other consumer products, is that pharmaceuticals are subject to a pre-marketing clearance regime. A food or a toy can be sold until evidence appears that it is dangerous; then it must be banned and subject to a recall order to remove it from the market. Pharmaceuticals cannot be sold until evidence is produced that they are safe and efficacious. The requirement of evidence of efficacy as well as safety is also distinctive: manufacturers do not have to prove that toys are fun before they are allowed to market them. The globalization of a pre-marketing clearance regime based on both safety and efficacy has been total. We know of no country that does not have it. Nearly all nations have modelled the 1938 US adoption of this model only since the thalidomide disaster of the 1960s. Modelling the US was greatly facilitated by the fact that the FDA prevented thalidomide from being marketed in the US. The US in turn had modelled much of its post-1938 pre-marketing approval regulations on the Seal of Acceptance Program that the American Medical Association operated from 1905 to 1955. Under this program drugs would be refused advertising space in AMA journals unless manufacturers satisfied its Council on Pharmacy and Chemistry that the drug was fully identified, met standards of efficacy and toxicity and that claims in relation to it were truthful (Dowling 1970).

The other central regulatory idea that has accomplished amazing globalization through modelling rather than coercion or international agreement is that once a pharmaceutical has been approved for marketing, it can only be sold on the prescription of a doctor (usually to be dispensed by a licensed pharmacist, though in some countries doctors dispense as well). The model was adopted from the requirement in Louis XIII's France that tobacco be supplied only on prescription by a doctor. While developing countries have extremely low levels of compliance with prescription laws, most have them on their books. The widespread proliferation of these models is due to the monopoly interests of the professions of medicine and pharmacy, which pushed the model. Even when drugs were criminalized, doctors tended to prevail in sustaining their professional prerogative to prescribe the prohibited drug, as they did in the US during alcohol prohibition and for many decades after the introduction of narcotics prohibition.

An important stage in the globalization of the US vision of a prohibitionist regime for narcotics was using Japan as a model. In this domain, it has never been attractive for the US to hold itself up as a model! But when the Philippines Commission on Opium, established in 1903 after the US takeover of the Philippines from Spain, scoured Asia looking for attractive models of opium management, the US investigators found the model they liked in Japan. The Japanese model at that time was Asia's most effective law enforcement against the opium trade. Japan claimed to have experienced international learning: 'China's curse has been Japan's warning' (Owen 1968: 327).

Corporation-to-corporation modelling is also important. Braithwaite (1984) found that when some leading companies adopted the policy of forbidding the overruling of quality-control decisions except on the CEO's signature, many others copied this, and later national governments began to require it as a matter of law. Corporate practice modelled on leading corporations; law modelled on corporate practice.

### Reciprocal Adjustment, Non-reciprocal Coordination and Capacity-building

Reciprocal adjustment through deliberative fora such as WHO, the ICH and other trilateral and bilateral fora has (until the 1990s) had limited impact on global convergence of law. The bigger impact has been through reciprocal adjustment within the EU, followed by modelling of Europe in other parts of the world. The significant progress of the 1990s follows a century of abject failure in securing reciprocal adjustment by WHO, the League of Nations and International Conferences on Pharmacy which failed to standardize pharmaceutical formulae in a series of meetings between 1865 and 1910.

The limits and recency of harmonization efforts through WHO and ICH at one level are surprising. Harmonization of drug-testing standards can save enormous costs through duplicative testing that unnecessarily exposes human subjects to placebos and animals to dosage levels that cause painful death. Most importantly, it is now clear that harmonization is delivering on its promise of making products available to consumers faster. Vogel (1998), noting the contribution of international harmonization to shortening the average approval time in the US for a new drug from thirty-three months in 1987 to nineteen in 1995 (six months for 'major therapeutic advances'), has in our view correctly concluded that 'the undermining of national regulatory sovereignty has improved both the effectiveness and efficiency of government regulation'. By eliminating duplicative research, harmonization saves money for creative research and better husbands the scarce talent available to undertake high-quality research. Fernand Sauer of the EC claims that the right mix of harmonization can simultaneously reduce regulatory costs and 'raise the level of public health in all countries'. However, harmonization and mutual recognition are a threat to national sovereignty, uniformity can stultify innovation in research protocols and, most importantly, some old hands at particular regulatory games lose their competitive advantage over novices if the global regulatory system is simplified. These have been sufficient reasons for many actors to sabotage harmonization and mutual recognition.

Since WHO has been rendered a less-than-credible forum for reciprocal adjustment toward harmonization, capacity-building for the regulatory systems of developing countries has been its preoccupation. We have seen that its accomplishments in capacity-building have been considerable. The Guiding Principles for Small Drug Regulatory Authorities illustrates this work. The FDA also provides considerable technical assistance to developing nation regulatory authorities, particularly in Latin America.

Reciprocal adjustment and capacity-building across borders have not happened with national alcohol, tobacco and OTC drug regulatory regimes. Both have been important to the illicit drugs regime, however. Non-reciprocal coordination has also been important to the illicit drugs regime but unimportant to the other four (including pharmaceuticals). For example, the US has been willing to adjust its policies in trade, aid and defence support when other states have adjusted their drug policies in compliance with US wishes.

## Modernity, Globalized Regulatory Protection of Strong States, Mass Addiction

Now that we have considered the key actors, the contests of principles and the mechanisms of globalization, it is possible to reinterpret the globalization of drug regulation, a history which is much more segmented than any of the other histories in this book. Prior to the great regulatory divides of the twentieth century that established radically different kinds of regulatory regimes for prescription drugs, OTC drugs, tobacco, alcohol and illicit drugs, all had been therapeutic drugs. The opiates or 'a tot of brandy' were the most widely used therapeutic substances of the nineteenth century, usage in both cases dating from thousands of years BC. Tobacco was more recent in Europe and Asia, an import from the New World where it was used in religious rituals from at least the first century BC by the Mayans. Jean Nicot (whence 'nicotine'), the French ambassador to Portugal, brought the product to Paris, the emergent model of Western civilization, in 1556. Yet until the end of the sixteenth century, physicians prescribed tobacco for medicinal use, 'frowning on its use for personal pleasure and relaxation' (Corina 1975: 43). In 1665 Eton boys were required to smoke daily as protection against the Great Plague, 'under penalty of a housemaster's whip for non-compliance' (Corina 1975: 40). In fact, nicotine did not become a drug of mass consumption until 1890, when the Imperial Tobacco Company was on its way to becoming the biggest corporation in the British empire and Buck Duke set up the American Tobacco Trust. They used new technologies and sold the drug through the medium of the compact cigarette, which was portrayed as avant-garde via modern mass-marketing techniques. Trade names such as Vanity Fair, Napoleons, Opera Puffs and High Life tapped romance and appealed to different sorts of personal identities.

Cocaine did not become a drug of mass addiction until its mass marketing via patent-medicine advertisements in the newly popular newspapers and in addictive consumer products such as Coca-Cola (regulation forced Coca-Cola to replace cocaine with caffeine in 1903). Opium did not become a drug of mass addiction until the modern drug trafficking of the British East India Company created a Chinese market by adapting the product to Chinese taste, combining tobacco and opium in a pipe for smoking (to replace opium-eating). Here the trick was an early version of market research more than marketing, though the latter was also important. It took at least 6000 years of the poppy being known to be a 'plant of joy' and at least 4000 years of international trade in opium (starting with the Cyprus–Egypt trade) before mass addiction occurred in China.

Alcohol, which can be brewed even in a prison cell, is an exception in becoming a drug of mass addiction centuries before modernity. With tobacco, opium, heroin, cocaine, LSD, barbiturates and amphetamines, we do not see mass addiction until modernity enables efficient production and distribution by transnationally deployed organizations like the British and Dutch East India Companies, the American Tobacco Trust, the I.G. Farben Chemicals Cartel, the Coca-Cola Corporation, Hoffman-La Roche and the mafia. Not until such organizations use modern market research and modern marketing to create demand do we see a therapeutic drug become the fashionable drug of mass consumption. Indeed, even with alcohol, the majority of the world's population who live in villages away from the urban centres of developing countries do not have the problem of mass alcohol addiction: they still await the arrival of transnational peddlers of alcohol with sophisticated manufacturing, distribution and marketing capabilities.

Drugs of mass addiction in the twentieth century became much bigger markets than therapeutic drugs, though prescription drugs also grew after the Second World War faster than any other product market. Mass addiction is a product of modernity and the globalizing qualities of modernity. Global regulation is implicated in constituting the mass addiction. Mass addiction requires that strong states offer protection to drug pushers for long enough to link organized production with distribution and marketing systems in new consumer markets. Britain was a strong state that protected the British East India Company while organized opium production was linked into the Chinese, Australian and other Asian markets. Germany protected its cocaine manufacturers as they were linked into new markets everywhere. Japan protected its heroin manufacturers and pharmacy chains as they penetrated North Asian markets between the wars. Sicilian elites and the Italian state protected the mafia. The Russian and Soviet states protected the networks of Russian mafia and earlier organized criminal groups. The CIA protected Kuomintang insurgents involved in trafficking, Burmese and Laotian druglords in the Golden Triangle, the Mujaheddin in Afghan drug trafficking, and many others like them.

European states and the US protected TNCs like Hoffman-La Roche which pushed the new postwar psychotropic drugs of addiction such as Valium. This protection was of a different kind. It protected legitimate aggressive marketing of the product within the medical prescription regulatory framework, allowing aggressive marketing because consumers were safeguarded by the need for a prescription. Protection by hegemonic states involved supporting their TNCs against other states which sought to keep new psychotropic drugs off their market, which sought to 'unreasonably' restrict the indications for which they could be prescribed, which sought to mandate warnings to doctors and patients which were 'unreasonably alarming', which sought to 'unreasonably' regulate marketing practices by pharmaceutical TNCs (Braithwaite 1984).

It tended not to matter if state protection of the drug pushers were lifted, as it eventually was in most of the cases listed above. McCoy shows how a sequence of protecting X against its enemies, then withdrawing X's protection, followed by protecting Y, then withdrawing Y's protection, then Z and withdrawal, can leave the world with an X, a Y and a Z all protected for long enough to become much more organized than other producers. The strong linkages into new markets are already secure by the time the state protection is lifted. Patent protection of ethical pharmaceuticals operates in much the same way. The state gives the patent-holder a monopoly protected by the state. When it withdraws the protection upon expiry of the patent, the evidence is that brand loyalty to the old monopoly remains a barrier to competition (Slatter 1977; Whitten 1979; Bond & Lean 1977). The key difference is that the street-level pushing is done by sales representatives in suits who give out free samples and opera tickets to doctors, not by addicts who are given free drugs and money as long as they find friends to sell to. The common element is protection under the regulatory umbrella of a strong state for long enough to organize the linkages from local demand creation to transnational supply.

The conditions for mass addiction are conditions of modernity: protection by a state that is sufficiently powerful for that protection to have transnational reach; efficient mass manufacture in a form of chemical delivery that market research shows to have mass appeal; sophisticated, organized and disciplined international distribution networks; marketing that portrays consumption as fashionable or identity-enhancing; and a large number of (usually disorganized and replaceable) street-level sellers who are corrupted by their own addiction, bribes or fraudulent claims about the safety and virtue of use.

The final connection of mass addiction to modernity is through the desire to regulate bodies to comply with the industrial rhythms of modernity:

> Bound to an industrial regimen which required a uniform level of performance throughout the twelve-hour working day, the nineteenth-century factory worker was pressed to use stimulants which could tune his body's rhythms to the pace of industry. After a half-century of unchanging dietary habits, the average Englishman's consumption of sugar (a quick energy source) jumped fourfold from 20 pounds per person in 1850 to 80 pounds in 1900, while average per capita consumption of tea increased threefold…The simple eighteenth-century English diet of milled grains had given way by 1900 to one spiced with large quantities of beef (protein), coffee (stimulant), sugar (energy rush) and tea (stimulant). If an energized diet of proteins, glucose and caffeines could be used to stimulate the body artificially and make it maintain a constant level of performance through a long working day, then patent medicines could be used to sooth and relax it during the hours of rest. Patent medicine manufacturers produced drugs to assist every bodily function and to induce any desired state of mind. There were cocaine-based drugs to overcome fatigue, morphine remedies to soothe worn nerves, and heroin medications to calm the agitated mind or respiratory system (McCoy 1980: 16).

A fact of modernity is the rationalized and ritualized use of drugs to regulate our bodies. States which during modernity, as Weber (1967) noted, seek to rationalize thus regulate our bodily regulation. We have seen that the attraction to global harmonization and rationalization results in regulation by global regimes of national regulation of the ways we regulate our bodies with drugs. Regulation of regulation of regulation in pursuit of control/countercontrol, discipline/counterdiscipline, fitting in with the modern at a personal, national and global level.

## Conclusion

What is most distinctive about this case study is the way the drug domain has subdivided into a number of very different regulatory regimes, with these regulatory divides dramatically shaping the nature of the industry. With OTC drugs and alcohol, there has been absolutely minimal globalization, total commitment to national sovereignty. With tobacco, social movement and healthcare politics have delivered some globalization of litigation, package warnings and restrictions on smoking in public places, but commitment to national sovereignty is otherwise overwhelming.

Compared with OTC drugs, alcohol and tobacco and the other domains in this book, commitment to the principle of national sovereignty has been weak for both prescription drugs (since 1991) and narcotics (since 1919). Surrender of national sovereignty to US illicit drugs policy was hegemonic in a classic Gramscian sense (Murphy 1994). As Manderson (1993) put it, the narcotics treaties did not seem the most important foreign policy issues at Versailles or after; yet brick by brick they walled in a framework convention unnoticed by actors with short time-horizons. The cases of the ICH and the EMEA show, however, how there can be a paradox of sovereignty; loss of national sovereignty can be accompanied by an increase in citizen sovereignty and in transparency to those affected by regulatory decisions.

The US is an exception where national sovereignty over drug policy, licit and illicit, has remained a profound commitment. The US has sustained national sovereignty with illicit drugs by dominating the rest of the world to do things the US way, hegemonically, with unusually heavy use of military coercion and reward as mechanisms. With legal drugs, it has clung to national sovereignty at the cost of losing its hegemony to Europe. Young and Osherenko (1993) found empirically with regulatory models for the environment that simplicity is a key feature for influence. Narcotics prohibitionism swept the world because the media communicated it as a model deadly simple in its appeal to the imagination of mass publics. It constituted drug trafficking as a crime under customary international law (Murphy 1998) at a time when there was no such thing as international criminal law (Schwarzenberger 1950), paving the way for the subsequent international criminal law of terrorism, genocide and the like. Pharmaceuticals regulation, in contrast, is complex, a mystery to mass publics who entrust the regime to epistemic communities of experts, which include a few experts (like Andrew Herxheimer and Ken Harvey of HAI) from consumer groups. Until recently, Japan was another exception, with its strong commitment to national sovereignty over a system of regulation for pharmaceuticals that was a non-tariff barrier to trade.

Reciprocity has also been an unusually weak principle for all nations, and national treatment a strong one, in a domain infused with the pretence of principle that cannot be traded. Bilateral negotiations between the US and Japan under the Market-Oriented, Sector-Specific talks in the early 1990s (on issues such as requirements that testing on humans be done in Japan) were an exception, where reciprocity was an important principle. While reciprocal adjustment has been important as a mechanism, modelling has been much more important. Disasters such as thalidomide have accomplished remarkable globalization of the unusually interventionist practice of pre-marketing clearance of drugs based on safety, quality and efficacy. Reciprocal adjustment within the EU followed by modelling of the EU by the rest of the world is an increasingly important hybrid mechanism toward globalization of pharmaceutical standards. Earlier in the twentieth century state regulation was partly modelled on principles worked out in self-regulation by Pharmaceutical Societies (dating from the nineteenth century) and the American Medical Association's Seal of Acceptance Program (from 1905).

For all these differences, with drugs we can see clashes between the principles of lowest-cost location and world's best practice, between rule compliance and continuous improvement, that are very similar to the clashes of environmental regulation. During the 1990s, attempts at deregulation have aimed at harmonized deregulation, not attempts by single states to attract investment via low regulatory standards. There is growing acceptance of the idea that there is a strategic trade disadvantage from location in a state notorious for low standards.

Epistemic communities are particularly central in importance. In the domain of health, we have the highwater-mark of professionalism. The health-care professions have constituted strong epistemic communities that have included participants from government, business and NGOs. In no other domain do we see a phenomenon like the 4000-strong RAPS, a new global NGO drawing on business and government people in a way that helps constitute global epistemic community. Much of the most important action with the globalization of standards is internal to TNCs, whereby leaders committed to continuous improvement and transparency diffuse their regulatory innovations through epistemic communities such as RAPS and RAD-AR. Globalized corporation-to-corporation modelling is even more important than nations modelling the regulations of other nations. Pharmacopoeias, WHO computer software, capacity-building for regulators and codification of non-proprietary names have been important in constituting a global regulatory discourse to frame the globalizing dialogues within these epistemic communities.

Individuals use drugs to regulate their bodies alongside other bodily regimes – exercise, diet, meditation, therapy, contraception, marriage, education. Drugs are part of a web of influences we consciously impose on our bodies. At the next level, this bodily regulation is itself regulated by a web of national controls, which in turn are regulated by a web of global controls. We have seen that each strand in these layers of webs may be weak, yet the entire fabric of controls can work to transform the human condition in major ways. Once-charming corners of great US cities can become desperate places where people live in fear of armed thugs who market drugs. Opium wars can change the history of the most important of nations. Cocaine addiction can be regulated practically out of existence by an effective web of controls over pharmaceutical companies, only decades later to be brought back as a mass addiction by new sets of controls manipulated by national intelligence agencies and globalizing criminal networks.

CHAPTER **16** | Food

## History of Globalization

### The Rise of Victorian Central State Regulation

The laws of Moses include proscriptions on food similar to some features of modern food laws (see Leviticus 17: 24; Deuteronomy 25: 13–15), features whose globalization was doubtless assisted by the widespread influence of the Bible. The most systematic ancient treatment of food law is found in the Roman civil law, which had a particularly strong emphasis on weights and measures, labelling, economic loss and fraud (Hutt & Hutt 1984: 6–7). This had an early influence across the Roman empire into the laws of future European imperial powers. In England, the Magna Carta (1215) laid the most important foundation for the law of weights and measures in common-law countries. Private law such as in England's common law has encompassed cases of food adulteration (e.g. putrid cheese) as well as false claims about weights and measures since the thirteenth century (Hutt & Hutt 1984: 22). From at least 1200 in Europe guilds sought to regulate food in the interests of consumers and honest traders, and doubtless at times in ways that protected monopolies for guild members, at least in some cities (Fallows 1988: 29; London Food Commission 1988: xi; Thompson 1996: 1).

State regulation of food adulteration blossomed surprisingly late, though in England the Assize of Bread nationally regulated the amount of flour per pound of bread from 1266, with administration in the hands of local justices of the peace (Guyer 1993: 802). Scarce and costly foods were subject to some regulation in England during the eighteenth century by laws such as the *Adulteration of Tea and Coffee Act 1724*. An important event in England was the publication of F.C. Accum's (1820) *Treatise on Adulteration of Food and Culinary Poisons*, which for the first time demonstrated the adulteration problem through chemical analysis and called for state regulation. That took forty years. The Lancet Analytical and Sanitary Commission of 1851–54 was important in building professional and public concern, as was the Parliamentary Select Committee of Inquiry into Adulteration of 1855–56 (Paulus 1974). A Bill introduced in 1857 was withdrawn in response to industry opposition. However, anti-adulteration pressure groups such as the Social Science Association in Birmingham kept up pressure until an 1858 outbreak of food poisoning in Bradford afflicted 200 people, seventeen fatally, thereby prompting legislative change (Burke 1980: 26).

Another popular book, *The Jungle*, Upton Sinclair's (1906) fictitious account of unhealthy practices in a Chicago meat-packing plant, made a decisive contribution to the demands of mass

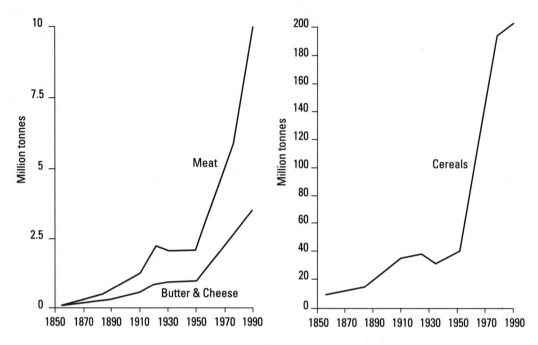

**FIGURE 16.1** World exports of meat, butter, cheese and temperate cereals, 1850–1990
Sources: Grigg (1993: 237); Stern (1960: 44–64); Trade Yearbooks, Rome, various dates

publics for what quickly became the US *Pure Food and Drug Act 1906* and the *Meat Inspection Act 1906*. The era of regulation dominated by central states lasted only a century.

### Codex

Most food is still consumed in the country it was produced. Until the 1970s this was true of 90 per cent of the world's food (Grigg 1993: 236). Stagnating during the 1930s and 1940s, exports of foods did not become of real economic significance until the 1950s, as illustrated for meat, butter, cheese and cereals in Figure 16.1. It was only then that interest in international harmonization of food standards began in earnest. From 1903 the International Dairy Federation developed international standards, but only for milk and milk products (Randell 1995: 36). During the Second World War, Eleanor Roosevelt had become persuaded that food was a key to long-term peace and postwar reconstruction. She persuaded FDR to convene a 1943 conference on food and agriculture, which built momentum for postwar institutional development (notably FAO).

In 1958 the Council of Europe established the Codex Alimentarius Europaeus 'to publish definitions, methods of testing and principles for judging foodstuffs' (Leive 1976: 377). The leadership of the Austrian Minister for Agriculture was important in Europe. The Codex Alimentarius Austriacus had been established in the 1890s to regulate the considerable movement of food across the diverse Austro-Hungarian empire. Between 1958 and 1963 fifteen to twenty-one European states attended meetings of the European Codex. The US and some other non-participating states became nervous about the trade implications of this European agenda-setting. The US pushed for a worldwide Codex Alimentarius Commission in Rome in 1962, something Europe was keen to support because the thin infrastructure of the European Codex was proving inadequate. Both the US and Europe pushed for Codex because they saw themselves as having high standards toward which they wanted to pull the rest of the world.

As one US Food and Drug Administration (FDA) official explained, the impetus was not just fear of food standards being used as non-tariff barriers by Europe: 'So many developing countries can get export income by selling food and there was so much fear by developed countries that they would poison someone'.

The Codex was established as a subsidiary body of the Food and Agriculture Organization (FAO) and the World Health Organization (WHO). The biggest funder of the establishment of the Codex Alimentarius Commission was not the US state but the US food industry. The US food industry money was 'laundered through states', as one informant put it. Indeed, the Codex has become one of the more industry-dominated international organizations. More corporations have members of delegations to Codex committees (140) than nations (105) (Renouf 1993: 22). The UK's National Food Alliance (1993: 1) found that there were 445 industry representatives on Codex committees compared with eight representatives of public interest groups. Forty-nine per cent of the members of US delegations to the Codex were representatives of the food industry, as were 61 per cent of the Swiss delegations. These US and Swiss industry representatives were greater in number than all the members from all the nations of Africa (Avery, Drake & Lang 1993: 5). The facts therefore sustain the thrust of McMichael and Myhre's (1991: 85) (nevertheless overstated) claim that 'Whereas the nineteenth-century movement of political liberalism culminated in nationally regulated capitalism, the current movement of liberalism substitutes global economism for national regulation'. Although large states still have a lot of clout, their central sway over local markets succumbed after only one century; there is now considerable sway over them by global markets, and global regulation wherein agendas are set by global companies. However, we can assign too much significance to the raw numbers of industry participants in the Codex process. Typically, the most strategic bargaining on Codex expert committees is done by government representatives of the key states.

The standard-setting accomplishments of the Codex Commission since 1962 have been impressive. The Codex Alimentarius now runs to twenty-five volumes in three languages. It includes over 200 standards, forty codes and guidelines for food production and processing, maximum levels for about 500 food additives, and 2700 maximum-residue limits for pesticide residues in foods and food crops. In 1979 US leadership was important in the development of a Codex Code of Ethics for International Trade. This Code is aimed at preventing dumping of unsafe food in developing countries by requiring nations to alert one another when they refuse entry to unsafe products (Sachs 1990: 29). As one national regulator commented on the sweep of the standards: 'Codex has developed standards for all major products traded internationally and probably most minor ones. Now the territory has been covered, Codex is going back over the standards, removing non-essential components (those that are not necessary for public health) to simplify them. Simplification makes international consensus easier. The detail can be put in an advisory text, for example, a Code of Practice'.

Global convergence of food standards therefore occurred much earlier than with pharmaceuticals, where, as we saw in the last chapter, serious global harmonization had to await the 1990s. According to a senior US FDA official, consensus-building has been much easier at the Codex on food than it has been on harmonizing standards for drugs:

As with pharmaceuticals, if you take contaminants or pesticide residues in food, the importing countries want low levels and the exporting countries want more reasonable levels. With drugs, only a few countries do most of the exporting and developing countries are just importers. But with food, lots of countries do both (a lot of importing and exporting) including developing countries. So the North–South divide is more complicated [North–South consensus is easier].

Many developing countries adopt Codex standards widely but have great difficulties finding the resources to enforce them in any meaningful way. The US, in contrast, has achieved equivalence for only about a third of Codex standards, but takes them very seriously when it does adopt them. Most other developed economies fall between the US and developing-country situations on acceptance and enforcement.

## The Rise and Rise of EC Influence

The EU's approach to standards for all consumer products, not only food, changed in 1985 when it was decided that from then the EC would provide only general standards, relying on member states to fill in the detailed specifications, and requiring members to recognize the specifications of other states as long as the general standard was met (Treveline 1993). This followed the momentous decision of the European Court of Justice in the *Cassis de Dijon* case (Case 120/78, *Rewe-Zentral AG v. Bundesmonopolverwaltung fur Branntwein* [1979] 26 CMLR 494), which struck down a German ban on the import of a French liqueur on the grounds of insufficient alcohol content. Gray (1990: 111) sees the European food sector, the biggest manufacturing industry in Europe with 2.5 million factory workers (Codex 1987: 4), as the 'trailblazer of policy-making in creating the internal market'.

It was not always so. Between 1962 and 1979 the EC adopted only nine food directives, confronting much resistance to standardization efforts that were seen as risking 'Eurobland' food (Vogel 1995: 27–8). Some nations had a positive list of additives (additives could not be used unless permitted), others a negative list (any additive could be used unless it was prohibited). The progress after 1985 in consensus-building on general standards combined with mutual recognition on specifics took a further major step in 1992. In that year the scope of *Cassis* was expanded by a decision granting the EU's Council of Ministers an option to declare by qualified majority that 'all national laws, regulations, and administrative practices not harmonized by the end of 1992 must be recognized as equivalent' (Vogel 1995: 36). Vogel's (1995: 52) study found that 'few EU standards are laxer than those of the "average" member state: in most cases they are comparable, and in a few cases they are stricter'. His analysis is that food has shown how massive regulatory convergence can be accomplished: 'there may not be a European welfare state, but there certainly is a European regulatory state' (Vogel 1995: 54). 'Each successive revision of the Treaty of Rome has expanded and strengthened the competencies of the Community in social regulation' (Majone 1993: 63). 'Harmonization without mutual recognition would have been administratively impossible, while mutual recognition without harmonization was politically infeasible' (Vogel 1995: 55).

## WTO–Codex Linkage

In 1985 the EU Council of Ministers, responding to lobbying from consumer groups and small European beef farmers, banned growth-promoting hormones in beef. A decade after the ban, by some estimates 30 per cent of European beef production used illegal beef hormones, some of them dangerous ones that would not be used under conditions of regulated use. The US viewed this as a blatant non-tariff barrier against US imports; indeed, US beef exports to Europe fell by 80 per cent in the year following the ban (Vogel 1995: 159). This and other disputes which the US viewed as the application of non-tariff barriers against US agricultural exports by Europe and Japan caused the US to lobby successfully for an Agreement on the Application of Sanitary and Phytosanitary Measures (SPS) to expand the reach of the Tokyo Round agreement of GATT on Technical Barriers to Trade.

> My explanations of the driving forces behind the negotiations also include reference to the South American interest in changing the ban on meat from foot-and-mouth disease infected countries, and the EC concern (part way into the negotiations) when the US banned imports of some EC wines because of residues of the fungicide procymidone (which was not registered for use in the USA) (comments on an earlier draft by Gretchen Stanton, WTO).

The Agreement on Sanitary and Phytosanitary Measures, which was included in the 1993 Final Act of the GATT Uruguay Round, set Codex standards as a reference in trade disputes. This was the biggest single step in the history of the globalization of food standards. Signatories to the Uruguay Round agreement of GATT are allowed to set higher food standards than the Codex. But if they do, they must be able to show they are 'necessary', 'not maintained without sufficient scientific evidence' and grounded in risk assessment (Vogel 1995: 188). A kind of inertial influence of Codex standards is established by placing a burden of proof on nations that wish to depart from them.

In addition to Codex standards being an agreed yardstick for international food trade disputes, guidelines or recommendations set by the International Office of Epizootics were agreed to set the inertial position for sanitary requirements for the import and export of animals and zoonoses (animal diseases such as rabies that can be spread to humans) and International Plant Protection Convention standards for plant health protection and quarantine.

The effect of the Uruguay Round agreement has been significant. Some nations have since conducted reviews of their national food standards for compliance with the Codex and some have made sweeping changes as a result. As with EU food harmonization, there is hot debate over whether the threat of WTO enforcement of Codex standards will render the Codex a floor or a ceiling. There is no doubt that some developed countries have lowered standards to the Codex level, while the Codex has caused a much greater number of developing economies (and some developed economies) to raise their standards. In 1997, the catalytic EC ban on growth-promoting hormones in beef was found GATT-illegal by a WTO dispute settlement panel.

The WTO–Codex linkage has increased hesitancy about supporting new Codex standards. States which feel their trade interests might be threatened by a new standard put together a veto coalition 'to prevent work from even starting' (UN official). The same official pointed out that Codex had become 'more political, less technical' as a result of the trade linkage, with votes at Codex plenaries becoming common whereas previously they were almost non-existent (though the overwhelming majority of matters are still settled by consensus). NGOs are more active and more aggressive. The negative side of linkage, from a Codex secretariat perspective, has been erosion of consensus decision-making, vetoing of discussions that ought to occur and politicizing of the epistemic community. The positive side is that the standards that do get through are taken more seriously and are subject to trade-enforceable review for compliance.

The NAFTA agreement of 1993 among the US, Canada and Mexico contained provisions on convergence of food standards and technical assistance for Mexico regarding enforcement.

However, NAFTA, unlike GATT, does not require the signatories to achieve their desired standard of consumer protection by the least trade-restrictive means possible. Indeed, the main effect has not been to change the standards in the laws of the three countries, which are all fairly high, but to pressure Mexico into improving the effective enforcement of its theoretically applicable standards.

## Other Linkages

Without access to genetic resources, food and agricultural production stops. The production of food and agriculture increasingly relies on genetic engineering; for example, modified soya is present in about 60 per cent of the processed foods that we eat. Genetically modified foods (labelled by opponents as 'Frankenstein foods') have triggered food adulteration crises in Europe. The global regimes that are developing for the regulation of genetic resources for food and agriculture are turning food production into an object of global multiplex regulation. TRIPS (which deals with intellecual property protection for plants, animals and microorganisms), the Convention on Biological Diversity (CBD) and the FAO Global System all play a role in the regulation of food.

Much of the world's genetic material that is important to crop production is held in gene banks. Some of the most important of these form part of what is known as the Consultative Group for International Agricultural Research (CGIAR) system. CGIAR is made up of key international agricultural research centres, about thirty-eight donor governments and some private foundations (e.g. the Rockefeller Foundation and the Ford Foundation) and development banks. The UN Development Program, the UN Environment Program, the World Bank and the FAO are all centrally involved in the CGIAR system. A World Bank official, Ismaeil Scrageldin, chairs CGIAR. The CGIAR system, which began in 1971, owes its origins to the Rockefeller, Kellogg and Ford Foundations. The US, UK, Australia and Canada were also involved early (Mooney 1996: 48). The genetic resources that CGIAR controls are not covered by the CBD. The CBD recognizes the sovereignty of states over their genetic resources, but it does not apply to genetic resources collected and held in gene banks before the CBD came into force.

Access to the genetic holdings of the various centres that are part of the CGIAR system is governed by a contract that the Chair of the CGIAR system signed, on behalf of the centres, with the FAO in 1994. Under the terms of the contract, each CGIAR centre agrees to hold its plant genetic resources in trust for the international community. The transfer of plant material from a CGIAR centre to an outside research body is governed by what are termed 'material transfer agreements'. In effect, the CGIAR system recognizes the principle of the common heritage of mankind in regard to ownership of plant genetic resources. The exact role of intellectual property rights in this system has yet to be worked out, but generally there is an understanding that intellectual property rights should not be sought over material that can be said to be clearly part of the international commons. The diffusion of useful plant material ('getting the stuff out there'), especially in poorer countries is the overriding goal of the system, we were told in an interview (1999 interview). Regulation of the system depends to a remarkable extent on dialogue between the parties – the individual CGIAR centres (which are autonomous), the donors and the international organizations that chair the meetings, as well as the NGOs that have gained rights of participation at meetings. The system has become more robust – more than five hundred actors now participate in meetings. Higher levels of transparency have accompanied this growth (1999 interview). It is easier for NGOs to monitor what is happening to the transfer of germplasm, easier for them to know what is going on. Responding to a question about whether NGOs now play a greater role in exercising vigilance over the system, a member of one of the CGIAR centres agreed that this was probably so. He cited the work that an NGO, the Rural Advancement Foundation International (RAFI), had carried out in exposing attempts by Australian researchers to gain intellectual property rights over chickpea varieties, contrary to the spirit of understanding that governed the use of that material.

The FAO is responsible for what is known as the Global System for the Conservation and Utilization of Plant Genetic Resources for Food and Agriculture (the Global System). The system originated in the FAO's formation of an intergovernmental forum called the Commission on Plant Genetic Resources (CPGR) in 1983 (renamed the Commission on Genetic Resources for Food and Agriculture) and the adoption of a framework agreement known as the International Undertaking on Plant Genetic Resources (IUPGR). Both CPGR and the IUPGR were initiatives of the South, in this case led by Mexico. The Global System has become a complex regime comprising codes of conduct (the International Code of Conduct for Plant Germplasm Collecting and Transfer 1993), new principles (Farmers' Rights),[1] model agreements (CGIAR–FAO gene bank agreements) and monitoring and reporting of the world's plant genetic resources. The Global System is predominantly voluntary and non-legal, yet 171 countries participate in it. In this system the North–South divide is sharp. The South takes the view that Northern food and agricultural systems of production are rooted in a biodiversity that the South holds and has built up over the centuries. Access to plant genetic material and sharing the benefits of the exploitation of that material are the key issues that occupy states in the Global System. The US (with the occasional assistance of Canada and Australia) has been the most consistent opponent of the system. The US, for example, made an attempt to persuade Northern countries to boycott the first meeting of CPGR. This failed, with the US ending up participating as an observer (Mooney 1996: 22). With so many countries participating in the FAO forum, the US has had to take its seat at the table when parts of the system, like the IUPGR in 1994, have come up for revision. In the matter of exchanging plant material, probably no state wants to take its chances in an exclusively bilateral world. A multilateral framework on the exchange of plant genetic material offers states more certainty of access and a greater level of transparency than does bilateral dealing.

## Actors

### Organizations of States

The Codex Alimentarius Commission, which today has 154 states as members, is the most important international organization in the globalization of food standards. It is a joint establishment of the FAO and WHO, headquartered at the FAO in Rome. It has achieved much more

---

1 Farmers' rights is a principle put forward by RAFI in an attempt to secure benefits for farmers as a group. FAO Resolution 5/89 describes these rights as 'rights arising from past, present and future contributions of farmers in conserving, improving and making available plant genetic resources, particularly those in the centres of origin/diversity. These rights are vested in the International Community as trustee for present and future generations of farmers in order to ensure full benefits for farmers, and supporting the continuation of their contributions as well as the attainment of the overall purposes of the International Undertaking'.

rapid and sweeping success in globalizing standards than either of its parent organizations. Codex's accomplishments with food-standard harmonization have been formidable compared to WHO's failures with pharmaceuticals standards. Its success has been achieved by a dynamic secretariat of only six professionals working to maintain a unity to the Codex corpus of standards.

Codex has acquired enhanced clout since the signing of the Uruguay Round of GATT made its standards the benchmark in trade disputes. It was the US who pushed this move: 'Some people at Codex saw the GATT as an opportunity. But Codex basically neither pushed nor resisted the GATT move' (WTO official). The third critical organization of states, the EU, was responsible for the Codex–WTO linkage through instituting the beef hormone ban that triggered US demands for the linkage. Since the 1940s the UN Economic Commission for Europe has also played a role in standard-setting (largely for quality) on perishable products, mainly fruit and vegetables.

## States

There are three powerful groups of states. The first is the Quadrilateral Group of countries – the US, Canada, Australia and New Zealand – all grain- and animal-exporting countries. The UK used to be a member of this group on food standards issues, but increasingly it identifies with European interests rather than those of the US group. On the crucial WTO–Codex linkage campaign, the Latin American states were US allies 'once foot-and-mouth disease was perceived as having caused an out-of-date outright ban on meat from countries with a history of foot-and-mouth' (WTO official). Australia and Canada led the Cairns Group of agricultural-exporting states into the US camp on this issue. US domination of the trade–food-standards linkage was via the US Department of Agriculture (USDA), which ran the SPS negotiations at GATT 'until the Environmental Protection Agency and Food and Drug Administration woke up [that something important was going on] for the last two sessions of the negotiations' (UN official). In comparison with the EPA and FDA, the USDA was more 'outward looking, seeking to shape global regimes'.

The second group of states is dominated by Tokyo. Japan is a more prominent player at the Codex than it is in most international organizations: 'The Japanese more or less represent Asia, though they would be reluctant to say so' (senior US official). Even so, Tokyo's leadership is much weaker than that of Washington and Brussels: 'The US must get at least the EC for a minimum to be able to move something forward, and then some. But really, given that Japan does not play hardball, that means get the EC and you have the game' (WTO official). A Codex insider described the limited Japanese influence in the following terms: 'The Japanese Ministries of Health and Agriculture talk to each other little domestically. Then the cultural need for consensus means they cannot speak at an international forum. The Koreans are more hard-nosed than the Japanese and are becoming more influential players'.

The third group is the EU. The Nordics are a related influential group, overlapping with the EU but often acting independently of it: 'If it comes to a vote at Codex, the US is weak and the Europeans can prevail. They have more in their group and many wanting to join the EU. Those countries want to prove how supportive they can be to the EU countries. For example, the Europeans won the hormone ban vote in 1991. Fortunately, decisions are not often made by vote. Usually it is consensus' (senior US official). In summary, it might be said that while the US has the strongest leadership and on many issues the strongest and largest scientific presence, Europe often has the strongest numbers when these are relevant. Decision-making by consensus among the major players is still the norm, however.

As one WTO insider put it: 'smaller states do not have a clue what is going on. They have not comprehended what the SPS agreement means'. Another informant was less negative, saying 'Some do, some don't'. Our own impression is that most smaller states have almost non-existent engagement with and understanding of the Codex–WTO linkage.

The attitude of the US Congress, the EPA (on pesticides) and the FDA in the past has been: 'No bureaucrat in Rome is going to tell us what to do' (senior US official). Slowly, however, the US attitude of 'guard the borders and don't pay much attention to international issues' is changing. Its leadership toward Codex standards being recognized by the WTO, following the beef hormone ban, marked a turning-point in attitude. The USDA was the key bureaucratic actor in linking the Codex and GATT regimes. Different fractions of the US state embody quite different emphases in the interests they pursue: 'The FDA is interested in safe imports, in restricting *imports*. The US Trade Representative is interested in open *exports*' (FDA official).

Another way of grouping the key actors is the US and its supporters; the EC; and the G-77. Australia's establishment of the Cairns Group was 'a brilliant move' according to one senior informant, because it broke up the old pattern of things being settled by the US, the EC and leaders of the G-77: 'The Cairns Group could play one off against the other'.

States vary enormously in the stringency and vigilance they apply to inspecting food produced domestically for domestic consumption, food produced domestically for export, and imports. In Australia, exported meat is subject to more rigorous inspection than meat for domestic consumption. The US, in contrast, has much less rigorous inspection of various exported foods than of the same food for domestic consumption. The US makes strong demands on Australia concerning the rigour of the inspection it requires for exports to the US, while Australia generally makes minimal demands on the US, considering it is Australia's job to check at the point of importation. These differences are based on market power. Australia cares more about the value of the US export market than it does about the health of its own consumers. The US would consider it impertinent for a small market like Australia to demand anything special for US exports to its shores.

The tendency for states with market power to demand other states comply with their standards, while states with less power do not, is important (see Vogel 1995). This is because the states with market power – the US, the EU and Japan –have considerably higher standards than the world average. China is not one of the major players in the Codex regime, unable to coordinate its own food standards infrastructure. In the US, the EU and Japan, NGOs are more vigilant about food standards, as are the epistemic community of food experts; reputations can be built by championing new regulatory technologies to make food safer. In the future China may be similar, however, although a consumer movement has started there and is indeed one of the few social movements tolerated by the government, China has a long way to go to produce a Ralph Nader or Consumers Union. China's policy, though it is not yet a member of the WTO, is to adopt Codex standards directly into its domestic food law.

## Business Organizations

The Swiss company Nestlé had thirty-eight representatives on national delegations to Codex committees between 1989 and 1991, more than any other company. Next in importance were Coca-Cola, Unilever and the US agrochemical corporation Monsanto (Avery, Drake & Lang 1993: 17–18). Colonial records reveal that in British Africa, the United Africa Company, a division of today's Unilever, was a key player in the development of African food product standards (Guyer 1993: 804).

Many of the biggest food manufacturers in Europe today are US companies so, at the business level, there is not a sharp divide between US and European industry associations. The big companies lobby directly at key fora such as Codex; small companies work through industry associations. National Grocery Manufacturers Associations and national Food Processors Associations, particularly the US GMA, are prominent players at Codex, as is the International Council of Grocery Manufacturers Associations and the European food industry association CIAA. National farmers' organizations are not. The Canners League of California was an early influential player in setting up the Codex.

The International Federation of National Associations of Pesticide Manufacturers sent no fewer than twenty-eight representatives to the 1990 Codex Committee on Pesticide Residues meeting and twenty-nine to the 1991 meeting (most such meetings attracted one or no consumer or environmental group representatives).

In short, although farmers and small business do most of the value-adding to food, it is the transnational food manufacturers and agrochemical corporations which dominate regulatory fora and set regulatory agendas, partly through their influence over the most influential state, the US, but more through shaping early drafts on Codex technical committees that set the framework for later debates. As one insider put it:

> With US chairing of the Codex Committee on Processed Fruits and Vegetables you can see the hand of the National Canners Association [now National Association of Food Processors]. With the UK chairing of the Committee on Fats and Oils, Unilever is behind it. With the UK chairing of Sugars, Tate and Lisle. With the Netherlands chairing of the Pesticides Residues Committee, you can see Shell in there. And you can see why Norway chose to chair Fish and Fishery Products (1996 interview).

Corporate capture is institutionalized by systems like this where governments choose which committees they will host, assuming financial responsibility and chairing them. States do not choose to chair on the basis of concern for the diffuse interests of consumers, but on the basis of concern for the concentrated interests of producers. This kind of institutionalization pushes global regulation to be more captured than balanced national regulation.

In commenting on a draft of this chapter, Ruth Lovisolo, Food Standards Policy Manager of the Australian Quarantine and Inspection Service, qualified the above analysis by arguing a perspective with which other state officials agree: 'government officials at Codex Committees...are not overly managed by the industry representatives that have observer status on the respective country delegations to Codex committees, although industry may have a prominence in the corridors to meetings'.

### NGOs and Mass Publics

The objective basis for mass public response to exposés such as Sinclair's *The Jungle* remains strong. A recent Canadian study estimated that the country had 2.6 million victims of food-borne diseases annually, including 3862 deaths (FAO 1990: 7).

An anti-adulteration social movement in England during the nineteenth century led by organizations such as the Social Science Association and the Anti-Adulteration Society (Paulus 1974) forged the most influential model of food standards as a central state responsibility. More recently, the National Food Alliance in the UK has been an influential NGO through direct lobbying, NGO networking and publications like *Cracking the Codex: An Analysis of Who Sets World Food Standards* (Avery, Drake & Lang 1993; see also Lang 1992). In the US, the Consumers Union, the Centre for Science and the Public Interest and Public Citizen (the Nader group) have been vocal, though only recently have they become engaged with international, as well as domestic, aspects of food regulation. A coalition of consumer groups led by Consumers Union supported signing GATT and NAFTA, while Nader and Lori Wallach led an opposition coalition. The latter groups formed new alliances with environmental groups and trade unions opposed to NAFTA and GATT.

The divide was on whether Codex standards would operate as a floor or ceiling and whether more concern was placed on developing countries' standards being raised or developed standards being eroded. Consumers Union and Consumers International, although critical, also saw opportunities for the WTO linkage to increase the transparency of the food regulatory process in many countries.

The Bureau of European Consumer Unions (BEUC) played an active role in Europe in ensuring that mutual recognition arising from *Cassis* would not be a regulatory race-to-the-bottom (Vogel 1995: 32–3). The history of US response to the European beef hormone ban, with the WTO–Codex linkage, begins with BEUC working with farmers for the ban. This is pre-dated by the activism of national consumer groups; for example, the French consumer groups organizing a boycott of hormone-treated veal that resulted in a 70 per cent decline in veal purchases (Vogel 1995: 154) and ultimately an EC hormone ban that was declared to be inconsistent with the SPS by a WTO panel in 1997 (Wynter 1997). Genuinely influential consumer-group power has been exerted on only a tiny number of sensational issues capable of capturing the imagination of mass publics, such as hormones in beef, irradiation and genetic modification of food. Even there the influence has been very partial and prone to heavy-handed response by industry – as with the WTO–Codex linkage in response to hormones in beef. Consumer-group influence on the main body of the twenty-five volumes of the Codex has been slight.

Notwithstanding the Nader–Consumers International divide, all consumer groups agree that to overcome the gross overrepresentation of industry interests at Codex, 'Every country should establish a National Codex Committee, with equal representation from industry, consumers and government' and that 'If national delegations include representatives of industry, there should be an equal number of consumer representatives' (Renouf 1993: 21).

The relationship between Codex and the International Organization for Standardization (ISO) is an important one, with many food processors now adopting ISO 9000 standards.

### Epistemic Communities of Actors

Codex documents continually characterize Codex decision-making as done by 'experts', notwithstanding the massive presence of industry representatives on expert committees and the growing presence of NGO representatives. For example the document *Introducing Codex Alimentarius* (Codex 1987) says 'At all times the need for objectivity has influenced the development of these procedures' (p. 12) and 'The discussions take place in an objective and scientific atmosphere from which emotional considerations can be eliminated' (p. 16). The FDA's Decoding Codex (Sachs 1990: 29) repeats the same icons of expertise, objectivity, independence and science:

Documents must 'pass muster' in two ways before they are adopted as Codex standards. First, independent scientific experts from around the world review the scientific validity and soundness of proposed Codex standards and codes or limits. Second, committees of regulators (who are very often subject-matter experts themselves) reach a consensus on the practicality and enforceability of the standards or limits.

'Codex provides a forum for the world's leading experts to discuss, debate, and reach scientific consensus on the food safety issues that affect trade', said Lester M. Crawford (US coordinator for Codex).

'Access to Codex is access to the world's most current and most complete body of scientific information on food safety issues', according to Fred Shank, PhD, director of FDA's Center for Food Safety and Applied Nutrition.

Industry experts have very effectively infiltrated these epistemic communities; consumer group experts have not. If the latter want to be effective in more than a sensational issue that has a moment of attention from mass publics, they must join the epistemic communities. Running media campaigns on 'Frankenstein foods' is effective for several days, but the media's attention rapidly wanders.

A key industry instrument of influence in epistemic communities has been the International Life Sciences Institute (ILSI). Coca-Cola initiated the establishment of ILSI after a Codex committee recommended an effective ban on caramel colour additives after evidence they suppressed white bloodcell formation. Coca-Cola also established the International Technical Caramel Association. These organizations conducted research to identify exactly what in caramel colour additives was causing the problem. Then they led the re-specification of standards to remove the problem elements from the additives, seemingly to the satisfaction of all. After this success, ILSI tackled the safety problems of aspartame, cyclamates and caffeine (all Coke ingredients), using the same strategy. This strategy can be summarized as follows: fund an arm's-length technical association to do the needed science; use the results to lobby for new Codex standards; in the process, engage all national epistemic communities with the need for change in their national laws.

This strategy has also been used by Ajinimoto, the Japanese company that dominates global markets for MSG. Again, ILSI was the research vehicle used to change the views of epistemic communities on MSG. When there was a problem of cholera spread by food in Latin America, ILSI organized a seminar there to educate health authorities that the risk could be controlled by appropriate policies. Referring to that case, a Codex official explained that 'ILSI defuses hysterical situations in the interests of food trade. That is pretty much what we are interested in so we work with them'. Note that ILSI does not seek to 'defuse hysterical situations' by vacuous public relations – it uses good science and good public health education that brings epistemic communities with it.

## Contest of Principles

### National Sovereignty v. Harmonization, Mutual Recognition

As in so many domains of business regulation, the US has been the last state to substantially retreat from the principle of national sovereignty. In the 1990s the US retreat was dramatic, becoming a US-led charge toward global harmonization at the Codex. Harmonization and mutual recognition have been complementary principles since the *Cassis de Dijon* conflict between France and Germany. Without a minimum level of harmonization, state regulations would have been too different to make mutual recognition possible. In turn, mutual recognition has encouraged openness to the regulatory thinking of other states, fostering further convergence through the mechanism of modelling.

The WTO principle of equivalency corresponds to mutual recognition. Equivalency requires signatories to permit imports that do not meet their own safety standards as long as they 'meet the importing country's appropriate level of health protection' (Article 4 of SPS). In other words, as long as an exporting country can show that its product, although not produced in the manner prescribed by the importing country, is equally safe, it should be allowed to sell that product.

In Europe, and increasingly elsewhere, the movement has been toward harmonization over matters that genuinely affect health and safety and deregulation of standards that do not (Vogel 1995: 33). For example, standards defining what ingredients are needed for a beverage to be described as beer are subject to global mutual recognition, allowing global brewers to trade their products freely.

Early attempts by the EC to harmonize on the composition of foodstuffs engendered a revival of the principle of national sovereignty. The UK wanted its horrible bangers, not the Brussels sausage, to be the eurosausage standard; no one wanted eurobread or eurobeer (Vogel 1995: 35). The European Court in *Cassis* was a key actor, catalyzing a new model of safety harmonization and compositional liberalization that ultimately set the agenda at the Codex. It was a truce based on unity of safety standards within culinary diversity. Increasing effort is being directed to harmonizing labelling requirements so that consumers everywhere can understand the composition of what they are buying.

## Deregulation v. Strategic Trade and Food Security

The last section pointed out that deregulation has strengthened as a principle in domains of regulation not affecting health, safety or intellectual property rights (or the environment, with agrochemicals). While there is lively debate about whether the Codex is lowering or raising more health and safety standards, the principle of health and safety deregulation is rarely advocated on either side of the debate. Rather, the debate is articulated in terms of the effects of the principle of harmonization.

European farmers joined forces with consumer groups on the beef hormone ban on the basis of strategic trade thinking – they benefited from keeping out US beef. Similarly, the Europe-based coalition in which the UK's National Food Alliance has been a key player brought together an anti-WTO–Codex-linkage coalition that combined consumer fears about a race-to-the-bottom on safety standards and producer concerns to defend non-tariff barriers to competition from foreign food. 'Food security' became an important principle for this coalition, the principle that a nation should avoid being overly dependent on other nations for its food imports. This principle had a strong resonance in European states and Japan, that had suffered hunger during war. But this coalition lost the GATT campaign, as the similar Nader-led coalition lost the NAFTA campaign in North America.

To date there has been neither a race-to-the-bottom nor a resurgence of the principle of strategic trade. Health and safety standards may have harmonized up more than down (Vogel 1995). The pandemic use of compositional and identity standards as a non-tariff barrier to the food trade has largely retreated before the principle of mutual recognition. Food security continues to capture the imagination of policy-makers and mass publics alike, even in the major agricultural-exporting states. Food security, along with the principles of common heritage of mankind, farmers' rights, access and benefit-sharing are important in the FAO Global System.

## Reciprocity v. National Treatment, Most Favoured Nation

Reciprocity, national treatment and the Most Favoured Nation principles have all been supplanted by a new principle in SPS that one commentator has called 'international treatment' (Charnovitz 1994: 89). Under this agreement nations are required to do more than base their standards reciprocally on the basis of the recognition by other states of their standards, to grant more than national treatment, more than treatment equal to the best given to any other nation. Nations are required to regulate according to 'international standards, guidelines and recommendations, where they exist' (Charnovitz 1994: 90). We see the national treatment and Most Favoured Nation principles as weakening, in favour of the principle of international treatment. In some ways this is misleading because the principle of non-discrimination, normally manifest as national treatment or the Most Favoured Nation principle, is strengthening under the principle of international treatment.

## Lowest-cost Location v. World's Best Practice

Food production is an industry with comparatively firm roots! Unlike the situation with drugs or motor vehicles, in most nations most food is produced domestically for domestic consumption. The nations that host the most efficient producers of food of a particular type tend to export their surpluses, and regulatory standards are not a major determinant of production costs (Vogel 1995). These are circumstances where patterns of production are not driven by decisions by corporate producers to locate where regulatory costs are lowest – the principle of lowest-cost location is extremely weak.

However, when food adulteration scandals are attributed to the insufficiently strong regulation of the exporting country, the market penalties can be gigantic, as happened to Australian meat exports in the early 1980s (Woodward Royal Commission 1982) and to US meat exports with the hormone scare a few years later (Vogel 1995). Consequently, sometimes a state seeks to secure its international competitiveness; for example, during the 1980s Australia strengthened its Export Inspection Service with 2000 inspectors (Grabosky & Braithwaite 1986: 99). This intensive inspection sustained international confidence in Australian food exports. In fact, one of Australia's first priorities after it became a federated nation in 1901 was the *Commerce (Trade Descriptions) Act 1905*. This Act prohibited exports unless the Australian government approved the export. It followed earlier colonial legislation such as Queensland's *Livestock and Meat Export Act 1895*, which required that all meat for export be inspected, and Victoria's Exported Products Act which, in the case of butter, required all consignments to be inspected and stamped 'Approved for Export' (Hammer 1969: 40).[2] The idea was to create a brand image of quality for Australian

---

2  The *Commerce (Trade Descriptions) Act 1905* was based on the British *Merchandise Marks Act 1862*. Both were introduced in response to scandals over substandard exports undermining the reputation of Australian and British exports. However, the Australian law went far beyond the 1862 British intellectual property solution of sanctions against false use of trademarks. It also provided for the compulsory use of prescribed trade descriptions and the establishment of mandatory standards of quality for export (Hammer 1969: 38).

agriculture. In many areas higher standards were required of exports than of produce for local consumers, hence the Australian marketing device for domestic beer of labelling it 'export quality'. Not many agricultural exporters followed the Australian approach to constituting competitiveness through high standards. Perhaps it had an influence on India when, in the early 1960s India established Export Inspection Agencies administered by the Ministry of Commerce rather than the Ministry of Health or Agriculture. The Australian best-practice principle had a more partial influence on other exporters, New Zealand, South Africa and Canada at times seeking to create a brand image of quality for specific commodities through high standards.

This is not to say that the principle of world's best practice extends to TNCs' decisions to shift location to states with stronger food standards that they think anticipate the direction of Codex standards. The comparative immobility of food production means that shifting location to pursue either laxer or tighter regulation holds limited charm.

### Rule Compliance v. Continuous Improvement

Rule compliance has certainly been a more dominant principle in the food industry than continuous improvement, in terms of food health and safety. The 1996 Codex Draft Guidelines for the Taking Into Account of ISO Standards of the 9000 Series by Official Systems for Food Import and Export Inspection and Certification were, however, an attempted step toward a global regulatory regime that requires producers to continuously improve the safety and quality of food. However, the draft has not received sufficient support to continue work on it. According to some, 'ISO 9000–9004 is quickly becoming the industry standard' (FAO 1994: 28). Among other things, the standard implies 'rigorous selection of suppliers, including on-site inspections, examination of samples, and a thorough critical review of the supplier's history and reputation' (FAO 1994: 28). Others believe that the Hazard Analysis Critical Control Points (HACCP) approach to food safety is becoming the more influential self-regulatory model. Although not incompatible with ISO 9000–9004, HACCP does not require continuous improvement (Parker 1998a).

### Transparency

The importance of Rome as a global forum for interpreting the new principle of international treatment has led to demands for more open deliberation on Codex committees, with more observers from a plurality of perspectives. One positive response to this demand came at the Twenty-first Session of the Codex Commission in July 1995, when one of the agreed Principles for Food Import and Export Inspection and Certification (CAC/GL 20-1995) was: 'Transparency: While respecting legitimate concerns to preserve confidentiality, the principles and operations of food inspection and certification systems should be open to scrutiny by consumers and their representative organizations, and other interested parties'.

We have seen that part of Consumers Union and Consumers International support for SPS in the Uruguay Round was the hope that it would open a more transparent regulatory arena to the many national consumer movements that had struggled for decades against regulatory secrecy. When a trade dispute arises over a food standard, GATT now requires the state which set the standard to give reasons to the international community, which also increases transparency intranationally. More importantly, Certification Agreements and Equivalence Agreements under the Codex require states to provide other nations with a great deal of information about their food inspection systems to facilitate equivalence and certification judgments (Codex 1996). One country often places its own inspectors in foreign plants, with its inspection reports being sometimes more publicly available than inspection reports in the host country. The US, EC and Japan in particular have permanent off-shore inspectors that can provide a limited window of accountability into many nations. They also have bilateral memoranda of understanding with most states that export to them, which have the effect of global regulatory consensus being fostered by a process of inspectors inspecting other inspectors across the world.

## Mechanisms

### Military Coercion

Military coercion does not seem to have played a part in the history of the globalization of food standards beyond the transfer of British food standards to colonies conquered by Britain after 1870 and the similar transfer of their food standards to the South by other European colonial powers.

### Economic Coercion

The decisive step toward the strengthening of the Codex was achieved by US leadership partly because the US was feeling the economic impact of the beef hormone ban. This meets our definition of economic coercion as a mechanism of globalization even though in this case the ban was not imposed with the intention of persuading the US toward globalization of standards. A more widespread threat of economic coercion motivating national cooperation with Codex standards today is the fear of trade sanctions, against which a state can be protected by complying with Codex standards.

### Systems of Reward

Systems of reward do not seem to have been used to raise the expected value of compliance with the global food order.

### Modelling

We have seen that the key forum, the Codex, is heavily influenced by business actors, vastly outnumbering the combined presence of farmers' organizations, consumer groups, other NGOs and delegates from developing countries. The dominant models are increasingly set in Rome and TNCs early shape the parameters for the models via Codex technical committees. Model mongering by the powerless is hard to detect. Rather, the consumer movement, for example, has been reactive to agendas set by global business. While British food law provided a leading model in the nineteenth century and US law for most of the twentieth century, since the 1980s EC harmonization has increasingly been modelled beyond Europe. In the twenty-first century, we can expect that the models shaped at the Codex Alimentarius Commission will be the most imitated. For the moment, however, modelling of the standards of the leading states remains crucial: 'The FDA canning defects chart is posted on the wall of virtually every regulatory laboratory in the People's Republic of China' (Sachs 1990: 29). The HACCP model in food regulation was originally developed by NASA hazard analysis, to ensure the safety of food for its astronauts. The US firm Pillsbury took the model into the food industry in the 1960s. With its emphasis on in-process diagnosis, control and documentation rather than end-product testing, HACCP is increasingly appealing to governments who want to cut their inspection function to simply audit documentation of in-process controls.

Guyer (1993) has an interesting analysis, based on the case of Nigerian modelling of British food law, of the eclectic way models from the centre arrive at the periphery:

> The history of food regulation suggests that administrative models have succeeded one another in the metropolitan repertoire over the past century but without the outmoded models disappearing from the cultural repertoire of modernity. They remain available, to be invoked and partially applied according to judgments about the match between the attributes of the populations or nations concerned and the attributes of past and present metropolitan populations (Guyer 1993: 809).

Reminiscent in some respects of Manderson's (1993) analysis of the brick-by-brick construction of a narcotics regime (Chapter 15) and MacDonagh's (1961) analysis of the British administrative state (Chapter 17), Guyer finds that 'British policy on issues defined as technical was extraordinarily, and perhaps uniquely, empiricist in explicit philosophy. It could take decades to construct a regulatory agency piece by piece, and no measure – once put in place – was eliminated from the books' (Guyer 1993: 799). This accretion of elements, structured multiplicity within and across models, made it possible for Nigerian regulatory rubrics to be selected 'from the model immediately previous to the one currently developing or fully operating in the metropolitan world' (Guyer 1993: 802).

### Reciprocal Adjustment

Reciprocal adjustment has usually operated surprisingly smoothly in the Codex food standard-setting process. Nations with high standards are forever concerned about downward harmonization; those with low standards are, usually more covertly, concerned with upwards harmonization. Yet mutual adjustment has occurred to a remarkable degree, partly because the structural basis for reciprocity is strong. Most countries, rich or poor, are both substantial exporters and substantial importers of food. This structural situation creates a favourable climate for give-and-take in the international forum. As a result, most global standards are forged without great political pain and mostly through the mechanism of reciprocal adjustment.

Even in the case of genetic resources where, broadly speaking, the South exports and the North imports, reciprocal adjustment has worked to deliver a multilateral system for the exchange of genetic resources. The fact that these genetic resources are linked to food and seeds, and therefore the export and import interests of all countries, accounts for the strength of the mechanism in this area.

The issue of genetically modified foods is likely to test the workings of this mechanism, as the reciprocity of interests begins to break down. The US enjoys a great comparative advantage in the production of such foods (Monsanto, for example, has the bulk of the market in genetically modified soya), whereas other countries (including many European countries) have not committed to genetic engineering in their agricultural systems to anything like the same extent. The very real consumer resistance to such genetically modified foods may lead states with the capacity to deliver genetically unadulterated foods to supermarket shelves commit to a principle of strategic trade. In such a case we would expect economic coercion and non-reciprocal coordination to become more important.

### Non-reciprocal Coordination

Opposition to the WTO–Codex linkage came from substantial fractions of the consumer and farm lobbies in many countries, but it did not set states in fierce opposition. Hence there was no major need to offer veto states a benefit in order to bring them to the table on WTO–Codex linkage. As one food standards insider explained: 'At the WTO, the chair says "any objection?" If a hand goes up the chair says there is no consensus on that and moves on to the next agenda item. Later the big players and the secretariat beat up on the state who put their hand up'. A contrasting view from another insider was that disputing by raising complaints in the SPS committee is much more common than disputing through formal trade disputes: 'Jumping up at a meeting and saying "we have a problem" takes very little political capital. A trade dispute takes a lot'. Nevertheless, most countries remain too intimidated or too disorganized to raise complaints to the SPS committee; most complaints are raised by the US and most of the rest by the EC: 'There are so many abuses of food standards as non-tariff barriers out there, so few that we are aware of [that have been raised formally with the WTO]' (WTO official).

Within the Codex itself issue linkage is limited, because different experts from different countries and, perhaps more critically, from different companies, participate in the work of different committees. This means that trading a loss in one place for a win in another is not the way the game is played.

### Capacity-building

The Codex Alimentarius Commission does not provide assistance to developing countries, except to the extent that participating in the standard-setting dialogue is a learning experience. However, its parent organizations, the FAO and WHO, do provide assistance to developing countries to improve their food control systems. Inspectors that major states such as the US send to developing countries to check the safety of food destined for their country also play a useful role in transferring regulatory technology. Indeed, the home state has an interest in such transfers, so that regulatory costs can be externalized over time. Some capacity-building is linked to the solution of trade disputes. For example, when Russia banned salmonella-infected chicken from the US during the 1990s, the USDA funded Russians to attend Codex meetings and funded training programs for Russian regulators in the belief that regulatory incompetence was part of the reason for the trade dispute.

## Conclusion

The story of the globalization of food regulation is less complex than the globalizations of most domains discussed in this book. The postwar growth in the international trade in food was not like pharmaceuticals or motor vehicles, where most nations were only importers. Most nations both import and export economically significant quantities of food (FAO 1994: 9–17). We have argued that the structural fact of such trade growth is conducive to reciprocal adjustment, which is the most important mechanism of globalization in this case. This is not to say that the globalization of food regulation is a story of brute structural determinism. The strategic action of the European Court of Justice in *Cassis* clearly shows the importance of actors.[3] Across a wide front, standards are increasingly being set in Rome. At the same time, Geneva is driving a substantial global deregulation of identity and compositional standards that are irrelevant to health.

In terms of the conclusions we reach in Chapter 26 about what consumers want, there are grounds for guarded optimism that globalization in this arena might in the long run lower food prices while raising health and safety standards more often than lowering them. Whether the latter occurs will depend on how well-organized, how expert and how well-resourced consumer representatives become in the corridors of Codex meetings and how effectively domestic consumer groups in major states push them to demand higher standards at the Codex. If pressure is not strong, given the history of industry influence at the Codex since its inception, this optimism will prove misplaced. Instead there will be the spectre articulated by Ralph Nader, Lori Wallach, Tim Lang, Jeremy Rifkin and other leaders of the NGO resistance to the WTO – standards driven down internationally by continued corporate capture of the Codex. The irony is that if their pessimistic prediction fails to come true, it will be because of the vigilance of their organizations.

In broad terms, the history of the regulation of the global food trade began with a mercantile model based on contract and *caveat emptor* until 1862. The British *Merchandise Marks Act 1862* begins an era of defending the reputation of food exports against false use of trademarks and British efforts to globalize this intellectual property regime. Early in the twentieth century some major agricultural exporters such as Australia sought to secure a national brand image of quality by regulating for export standards. By the time of the creation of the Codex in 1962, the export-standards era was over. Codex was a regime for harmonizing standards set by importing countries. It built substantially on European regional accomplishments in harmonization, with the mechanism of reciprocal adjustment proving powerful and in most cases comparatively politically painless. However, reciprocal adjustment is unlikely to work so smoothly with the contemporary debates on genetically modified food.

---

3 The court's strategic action would not have catalyzed a major transformation had the EC not responded with a major rethink of how to blend harmonization and mutual recognition in regulatory policy. We must qualify any conclusion that this is a case that refutes Rosenberg's claim that courts do not effect major social change (Rosenberg 1991).

## History of Globalization

### Rhodes to Rome to Hamburg

Although ships are less important than motor vehicles or planes for moving people, they move 95 per cent of international trade (Mankabady 1984: 177). The regulation of shipping acquired a global character earlier than most of the regimes discussed in this book. The industry always had an international character and risks were and still are high. Almost every year more than two hundred large ships (over 500 tons) sink (Lloyd's Register of Shipping a; Lloyd's Register of Shipping b). Since Roman times, when Pompey the Great was authorized in 68 BC to lead an expedition against the pirates of the eastern Mediterranean, countless ships have been lost to piracy (Rubin 1988: 7). These days piracy is much less of a problem.

The Sea Law of Rhodes, which is thought to have dated from about 300 BC, was important in the customary law of commerce of the Roman empire (Berman 1983: 340). For example, the 'law of general average' in Rhodian Law provided that 'it is lawful to throw over as much of the loading as might put the ship in a position to resist the storm. And because it seldom happens that the whole loading belongs to one merchant, it is justly provided that the person whose goods are cast overboard shall not be the only loser, but that the others shall contribute towards the loss of those that were thrown overboard proportionately and not according to bulk but to value' (Astle 1981: 1). The *Digest of Justinian* (Justinian 1985: 419–22) explicitly incorporates the Rhodian Law of general average into Roman law. After the rediscovery of Justinian's *Digest* at the end of the eleventh century, considerable refinement of Roman maritime law occurred through codifying the trading practices of the Italian city-states. These Mediterranean foundations have given the law of bills of lading, for example, 'remarkable likenesses in all countries' (Astle 1981: 1).

Even though by the nineteenth century a millennium of globalization had created a situation where all nations subscribed to the law of general average, the law was applied in different legal systems in different ways. Therefore, a Glasgow conference in 1860 adopted a number of resolutions on general average, and a conference at York in 1864 saw the formulation of eleven York rules (Mankabady 1987: 283). These were elaborated further at Antwerp thirteen years later, to become the York–Antwerp Rules. An attempt at further refinement was the Hamburg Rules, developed in 1974 under the auspices of the UN Commission on Trade and Development (UNCTAD) with assistance from UNCITRAL (the UN Commission on International Trade Law).

**Regulating the Jolly Roger**

Piracy has been a serious problem throughout most of history. The Barbary pirates at one time so dominated shipping in the Mediterranean that even the US paid tribute between 1785 and 1799 to the Dey of Algiers so its shipping could go unmolested (Gosse 1932: 63). Yet, remarkably, it was not until 1926 that a committee of the League of Nations produced eight draft articles on the suppression of piracy (Rubin 1988: 306). Many states took the view that the problem was no longer significant enough to merit an international conference. It was also clear that there was no real agreement among states on what constituted piracy, so agreement on a convention would be unlikely. The draft remained a draft. The same controversy over the definition and codification of piracy characterized the inclusion of articles dealing with piracy in the UN Convention on the Law of the Sea 1982 (Rubin 1988: 319–37).

Why had it taken so long for states to attempt international coordination on the problem of piracy? The explanation echoes the explanation we gave in Chapter 15 for the promotion of global drug trafficking. There we saw that the state (the US via the CIA) forged alliances with anti-communist forces that relied on drug trafficking. Drug trafficking grew as a result. In the case of piracy, states tolerated and even encouraged it because piracy became an instrument of their imperial ambitions. The story of Henry Morgan (Gosse 1932: 154–60), the famous seventeenth-century buccaneer, reveals a macro truth about the 'need' of states for pirates. Morgan operated out of Port Royal, Jamaica. The Governor of Jamaica, Sir Thomas Modyford, gave Morgan various commissions to move against Spanish shipping and towns. From time to time Morgan was ticked off about exceeding the terms of his commissions (he slaughtered the Spanish cruelly and in excessive numbers), but he always came back laden with booty and all was forgiven. His next commission was issued. When Morgan sacked Panama he was taken back to England to be tried for piracy, because England and Spain had concluded a treaty and England had to show that it was serious about stopping attacks on Spanish shipping. But things worked out well for Morgan – he was knighted and sent back as the Deputy Governor of Jamaica. England was not the only state to use pirates. Piracy in the Mediterranean increased in the sixteenth and seventeenth centuries as shipping increased and the expelled Moors of Spain had reason to organize against the Spanish. The early successes of the Barbarossa brothers, Arouji and Kheyr-ed-in, against the Spanish led to them acquiring many followers. The Barbary pirates became the Barbary communities of Tunis, Tripoli, Algiers and Salee. They were, in effect, recognized as states, for Western powers like France concluded alliances with them. Nor were the Barbary pirates the only ones raiding ships in the Mediterranean. In the sixteenth and seventeenth centuries the nationals of one country routinely preyed upon the shipping of other countries (Gosse 1932). Thus the English preyed on the Spanish, the Dutch on the English, the French on the Spanish, the English on the French and the Barbary states on everyone, except those who happened to be their temporary allies. Everyone accused everyone else of piracy.

The regulation of piracy remained a matter of state municipal law. When international cooperation of a kind did emerge late in the twentieth century, piracy had ceased to be a global problem. Piracy is only a niche market activity today, at locales such as the Thai coast where lucrative bounties of heroin from the Golden Triangle might fall to those brave enough to be post-modern swashbucklers. Behind the failure of states to develop a common code for the problem of piracy lay the sovereign self-interest of each in maintaining its colonies and robbing others of the profits of their colonial holdings. The major powers allowed piracy to flourish because it was militarily and economically useful. States turned pirates into privateers. In Britain in the eighteenth century a sophisticated system of regulation developed, with the High Court of Admiralty issuing licences to 'privateers'. The purpose of this regulation was to maximize the efficiency of privateering 'as a tool of war' (Starkey 1993: 40). Pirates were those who made their living outside state-regulated systems of privateering. Piracy on a large scale was eventually stamped out, with the UK (and to a lesser extent the US) being the key actor: 'Corpses [of pirates] dangled in chains in British ports around the world' (Rediker 1987: 283). Rubin puts it well (1988: 341):

> Britain's expanding and aggressive mercantile interest, overwhelming naval dominance, and self-perception as a law-abiding race bringing justice to benighted parts of the globe from the time of the end of the Napo[l]eonic Wars to the World War of 1914–1918, brought together a combination of factors making universal 'standing' under the law, with Great Britain the only country likely to be able to exercise it, seem a compelling legal rationale for police actions.

Britain's navy thus put paid to a problem in the interests of an empire that depended on safe shipping lanes.[1] Britain functioned as a global regulator, neither needing nor really wanting the benefit of a multilateral regime on piracy. To the extent that it needed to justify its actions, it drew on an imperial law of piracy that had been constructed by its courts and parliament. The key difference between regulating piracy on the high seas and the 'piracy' of intellectual property (see Chapter 7) is that in the case of intellectual property the US has put in place a multilateral regime (Agreement on Trade Related Aspects of Intellectual Property Rights, TRIPS) and insists that other states bear the costs of enforcement.

### Britannia Rules the Waves

Disastrous outbreaks of cholera and plague in the late nineteenth century created a new climate of international cooperation to enforce quarantine, ship inspection, disinfecting and notification of plague on ships (Silverstein 1978: 12). The first attempt to form an international organization for maritime regulation occurred in 1889 at a Washington conference that discussed regulations for preventing collisions, safety of life, shipwreck salvage and lanes for steamers, among other topics. In 1897, the International Maritime Committee was established to deal with legal aspects of merchant shipping, and played a leading role in all subsequent globalization of maritime law. Following the loss of more than 1500 lives in the *Titanic* disaster the International Maritime Committee showed leadership in the 1914 Convention for the Safety of Life at Sea. War and the Depression intervened to prevent the Convention from coming into force until 1933. This Convention, its elaboration and global enforcement, eventually became the core work of the International Maritime Organization (IMO, IMCO initially). The Convention for the Safety of Life at Sea specifies minimum standards for the construction, equipment and operation of ships. After having waited nearly twenty years (1914 to 1933) before coming into force, commercial rivalries then frustrated the creation of an IMO to implement it from 1933 until 1948, when the UN decided to set up the IMO, and then until 1959 when it actually came into existence in London. What opponents feared was IMO jurisdiction over maritime trading regulation, a function IMO

---

1 In the period 1850–1914 UK shipping companies operated close to 50 per cent of the world's sea-going cargo capacity. World trade and world shipping revolved around a British axis (Hope 1990: 331).

therefore did not take on but which was picked up in a modest way in the 1970s by UNCTAD. The UNCTAD Liner Code allows two countries connected by a shipping route to reserve 80 per cent of the freight between them (40/40) for their own merchant fleets. This system is likely to be targeted for deregulation in the Millennium Round of GATT.

It would be a major mistake to conclude that because there was no IMO until the later twentieth century, ship safety regulation globalized little and late. We saw in Chapter 14 that ship safety was a major issue in the international regulation of radio. The Berlin Radio Conference of 1903 and the Berlin Radiotelegraph Convention of 1906 were primarily concerned with flexibility and obligatory communication between ship and shore. Such communication had been made difficult by the Marconi Company's practice of not communicating with stations that did not use Marconi equipment. From 1920, with the International Seafarers Code, the International Labour Organization (ILO) gave early priority to the health, safety and other employment conditions of workers at sea (Mankabady 1986: 22–5). But the more important reason why it would be wrong to conclude that ship safety globalized little and late is that the globalization of private regulation has been much more important than agreements among nations to globalize public regulation.

The key actors in the 'spontaneous ordering' have been the classification societies and insurance companies. Pre-eminent was the spontaneous ordering that began in Edward Lloyd's coffee-house in London from 1691. Lloyd was the founder of the now totally separate commercial entities of the Lloyd's of London reinsurance market and Lloyd's Register of Shipping. Edward Lloyd 'created a sort of club, to which every man of consequence in the shipping business found it prudent to belong' (Blake, undated: 2). Lists of ships sailing from England were posted in the coffee-house, auctions were conducted, insurance brokered and all manner of shipping intelligence announced from a pulpit (still in limited use today).

Insurers and investors at Lloyd's needed assurance that ships were safely constructed for the purposes for which they were deployed. Underwriters employed their own surveyors of ships and kept registers of the surveys that were published through the Register Book Society at Lloyd's. Hulls were rated in five categories according to their appropriateness for the type of service intended, while equipment was rated 'good, middling or bad'. The Underwriters Register – the Green Book – lost subscribers during the eighteenth century to a rival shipowners' register, the Red Book. These were amalgamated in 1823 as Lloyd's Register of Shipping, under the control of a General Committee of both underwriters and shipowners and builders. The Committee of Inquiry which established Lloyd's Register envisaged that it would receive public funding. This never happened. MacDonagh's (1961) classic study of the British *Passenger Acts 1803–55* sees them as heralding the growth of the central state as a regulatory authority. While growth of the regulating central state there certainly was in Victorian England, including the Passenger Act inspectorates, this state regulatory function withered with the decline of British and Irish emigration to North America, and the private regulation of seagoing by classification societies and insurers grew and globalized. Between the two World Wars, Lloyd's Register controlled 80 per cent of the market for ship classification.

An interesting case is the important innovation of the plimsoll line painted on hulls to clearly show overloading. On one reading, this was a triumph of the central regulation of the Victorian state. Samuel Plimsoll was a member of the British parliament who sponsored freeboard tables which, largely as a result of his pleading in parliament, were adopted by the Board of Trade in 1876. These UK rules were the foundation for the 1930 International Load Line Convention. But the freeboard tables sponsored by Plimsoll were an improved version of the long-standing

Lloyd's Rule (from 1835), the improvements having been developed by Lloyd's Register's chief ship surveyor, Benjamin Martell. The British underwriters of the world's shipping who gathered at Lloyd's were not only interested in visibly self-enforcing load limits on British-flag ships but on all ships of all nations they insured. Hence, private regulation by classification societies had spread the innovation of a loading line among British shipping while Samuel Plimsoll was a small boy. Moreover, it had done so globally for a century before the International Load Line Convention. The central state regulation and international convention ensured that the regulation was enforceable against the minority of unclassified ships. Today no significant port anywhere will allow in an unclassified ship without a plimsoll line.

Lloyd's Register, which today competes with some fifty classification societies, two of them rivalling Lloyd's in size, has 3900 technical and administrative staff, including marine engineers, naval architects and other specialists. The large classification societies have more regulatory personnel than the large states. Indeed, most states actively contract some of their regulatory activities to the classification societies. Lloyd's Register is formally recognized by 130 states as an inspection authority to undertake statutory surveys on their behalf. This is neither recent nor restricted to small states. That is, the phenomenon is not a manifestation of the 'new regulatory state' (Loughlin & Scott 1997; Majone 1994b) – the new regulatory state which considers it best for states to delegate and steer rather than row (Osborne & Gaebler 1992). In 1895 the German imperial government, for example, delegated to the Hamburg classification society Germanischer Lloyd, responsibility for surveying and licensing ships on behalf of the German state, a function it still performs today. Germanischer Lloyd experts also advise the German Minister for Transport on marine safety laws and represent Germany on IMO working groups, exerting a major influence on global rule-making. In turn, the German government has representatives on the management bodies of Germanischer Lloyd.

Only eleven of the fifty-plus classification societies are members of the International Association of Classification Societies (IACS). IACS members class 92 per cent of the world's fleet by tonnage, but only about half the ships (O'Neil 1993: IX). IACS conducts quality assurance audits of members. The six major classification societies are the American Bureau of Shipping, Bureau Veritas, Det Norske Veritas, Germanischer Lloyd, Nippon Kaiji Kyokai and Lloyd's Register of Shipping. These societies compete for reputational capital from the insurance industry by insisting on stringent standards. In 1992 it was reported that Det Norske Veritas and the American Bureau of Shipping refused to class 600–700 ships because they were substandard or unprepared to upgrade (Parliament of Commonwealth of Australia 1992: 69). On the other hand, Cheit (1990a) reports that the Tanker Advisory Center found that Bureau Veritas of France had twice the loss record of other IACS members during the 1980s.

## Britannia Waives the Rules

Many of the fringe classification societies compete by providing cheap and permissive classification. Nations with higher standards, like the UK, recognize their classification pursuant to treaty obligations. Panama authorizes twelve non-IACS societies to issue on its behalf certificates of compliance with ship safety conventions. A ship that cannot secure insurance or classification in Germany by Germanischer Lloyd can thus still trade in German ports under a Panamanian flag. This is why, in one year, thirty-four ships from the small state of Panama sank, compared with only four from the much larger economy of the Federal Republic of Germany (Mankabady 1987:

28). Many of these shipowners compete on price and evade their liabilities through bankrupting their 'brass-plate' companies when ships sink, and starting again with another company. They avoid prosecution by residing outside the jurisdiction of the flag state and refusing to testify at inquiries established by that state.

One area where central state regulation was important, a century before the growth of other aspects of the regulatory state, was limitation of liability of shipowners for cargo. Early in the eighteenth century, European states wished to encourage their national fleets to expand by shielding shipowners from the fear that they might lose more than the capital they had invested in high-risk maritime ventures. England was a follower rather than a leader, imitating its maritime competitors by introducing the concept of limitation of shipowners' liability into English law in 1733 after a shipowner was held liable without limit for the loss of a cargo of bullion (Mankabady 1984: 236). The law and its successors on limitation of shipowners' liability were explicitly motivated by feared loss of international competitiveness, an early appearance of the principle of lowest-cost location.

A new approach to limitation of liability was adopted at the London Conference of 1976 in response to the reality of globalized insurance and reinsurance of the risks of twentieth-century seagoing. This new approach is well-captured by the summary of discussions within the IMO Legal Committee provided to the London conference: 'The earlier concept of limitation held that a shipowner should be able to free himself from liabilities which exceeded his total interest in a venture subject to marine perils. The more modern view is that the shipowner should be able to free himself from liabilities which exceed amounts coverable by insurance at reasonable costs' (Mankabady 1984: 239).

The 1976 Convention on Limitation of Liability for Maritime Claims globalized liability limitations that created incentives for marine insurance without making insurance compulsory. However, the IMO-sponsored Oil Pollution Convention and Hazardous and Noxious Substances Convention did require compulsory insurance or evidence of financial capability to meet liability claims. Hence, late twentieth-century state and interstate regulation has strengthened the grip of insurers' regulation over shipping, a grip that was always stronger than that of state and UN regulation.

## Ships of Shame

For bulk carriers that do not trade in noxious substances or oil, the regulatory emphasis on ships that do opened up opportunities for ruthless uninsured operators to compete on price by effectively evading international standards. Following the sinking of six bulk carriers in close succession off the Western Australian coast between early 1990 and mid 1991, an Australian parliamentary committee produced an internationally influential report exposing this problem, entitled *Ships of Shame* (Parliament of the Commonwealth of Australia 1992). The Committee reported:
- the operation of unseaworthy ships;
- the use of poorly trained crews, crews with false qualification papers or crews unable to communicate with each other or Australian pilots;
- ships' papers carrying false information;
- classification societies providing inaccurate information on certificates;
- flag states failing to carry out their responsibilities under international maritime conventions;
- careless commercial practices by maritime insurers;

- inadequate, deficient and poorly maintained safety and rescue equipment;
- classification societies that readily classed ships rejected by more reputable societies;
- beatings of sailors by ships' officers;
- sexual abuse of young sailors;
- crews being starved of food;
- crew members being forced to sign dummy paybooks indicating they had been paid much more than they actually received;
- sailors being forced to work long overtime for which pay was refused;
- crew members being denied telephone contact with home when family members have died;
- sailors not being paid for several months and/or remittances not being made to their families at home;
- sailors being denied medical attention;
- officers regarding crew members as dispensable;
- crew being denied basic toilet and laundry materials (Parliament of the Commonwealth of Australia 1992: ix).

These practices benefit not only the low-cost shipowners and operators, but also the cut-rate classification societies and the flag states that accept ship registration fees while paying lip-service to international obligations. According to the Australian report, IMO standards are not the problem. Nor is their level of international acceptance. The problem is their non-enforcement by states and classification societies which supposedly subscribe to them. It is not a leading-down of global standards. Rather, it is a problem of a market niche that allows a minority of the industry – albeit a substantial minority – to profit by evading enforcement of global standards and falling back on limited liability and bankruptcy whenever loss-bearers attempt litigation to internalize the externalities they inflict on the world.

As the Australian report points out, this situation is not inevitable in the way the world economy works. It recommends that the IMO set performance criteria for classification societies and introduce a 'seal of approval' program for classification societies that meet its set criteria, among other national and international measures that could improve the performance of classification societies. One standard tactic of operators of substandard ships has been to swap classification societies to avoid or delay inspections and surveys. To counter this, the IACS set up a database of all transferring ships, depriving hundreds of substandard ships of that loophole.

The biggest incentive for shipowners to use flags of convenience, such as the Liberian flag, is avoiding tax – not avoiding safety requirements. In fact, it was US shipowners who initiated the problem through flagging out to Panama in 1917 in order to avoid US taxes. Obviously, therefore, strategic global harmonization of tax rates, as discussed in Chapter 8, is another possible path to changing the situation where half the ships that sink are from flags-of-convenience states that regulate safety inadequately. Even without this, the network of interconnected regulatory influences outlined in this chapter can and does prevent widespread global law evasion from degenerating into a fully fledged race-to-the-bottom. Fewer ships sink today than sank in decades past. There are fewer serious casualties at sea (O'Neil 1993). Only a third of the amount of oil spilt in 1981 was being spilt in 1989 (IMO 1993).

The most important recent development in the history of maritime regulation has been the regulation of pollution from ships, a topic covered in Chapter 12, which will not be repeated here.

## *Actors*

### States

The UK has been the most important state in the history of the globalization of maritime regulation, because so many of the important globalizing changes occurred during the nineteenth century when the British fleet accounted for half the world's tonnage. Britain would legislate, often following private regulatory custom worked out at Lloyd's in the City of London, and other nations would follow. Mid-century, rules to prevent collisions at sea were developed under British–French cooperation, as was the Brussels Salvage Convention half a century later, in 1910. The fact that the IMO was located in London in 1959 indicates that UK leadership remained important well into the twentieth century. Silverstein's (1978) systematic study of the first two decades of the IMO (IMCO as it then was) found that more than a sixth of the secretariat was British, no nation served on IMCO more than the UK, no nation scored higher on an acceptance index of IMO conventions and no nation contributed as many person-months of technical assistance to the regime (Silverstein 1978: 84, 160, 171). The EU is only an observer at the IMO and a much less important player than the UK or Germany. The US and Japan are the other major national players today at the IMO; Canada also leads to some extent.

The Soviet bloc nations were never leading players at the IMO, nor was Cold War rivalry ever a major feature of contestation within the agency. As in so many international regimes, the minority of nations with the technical capability to lead do so by chairing or writing drafts for committees that prepare the regulations to go to the IMO Council. National sovereignty regained in this way is limited but non-trivial, since states volunteer to take the lead on the matters most important to them.

Notwithstanding the general domination by British regulatory ideas since the opening of Lloyd's coffee-house, it would be wrong to think that the common-law tradition has dominated maritime law. Rather the law of Admiralty has been forced to adapt in the common-law countries to the domination of the civil-law tradition traced above from Rhodes to Rome, to the law of the northern Italian republics shaped during the Renaissance. 'This branch of English Law [mercantile and maritime law] has undoubtedly drunk deep out of the well of old Roman law, as well as the living waters of mercantile custom' (Potter, quoted in Zweigert & Kotz 1987: 201). One might say that the deep structure of maritime law was laid down on the Continent before the British state had become a practical reality.

Historically, Britain has been the most important global regulator of piracy. The law of piracy that it enforced was a complex intermingling of English and international law principles. With the international law of piracy, British hegemony made it very difficult to distinguish between propositions of British law and international law (Rubin 1988: 201).

### Organizations of States

While UNCTAD, UNCITRAL and the ILO have had significant roles in the globalization of maritime regulation, as we saw above, by far the most important organization of states has been the IMO. Within Europe the EU fills many of the gaps left by the minimum-standards approach of the IMO. Another way the EU has played a complementary role to the IMO has been through the EEC Memorandum on Port Control 1982. This requires port authorities in fifteen signatory countries to inspect 25 per cent of foreign vessels for compliance with international conventions. The memorandum has provided a model for similar regional agreements to increase enforcement across ports in Latin America (a 15 per cent inspection target) and Asia and the Pacific (25 per cent).

During its comparatively short life the IMO has been an active international rule-maker, approving more than forty conventions and protocols, adopting more than seven hundred resolutions and formulating a number of codes. It has 155 member states and a budget contributed by member states primarily on the basis of the tonnage of their merchant fleet. This results in a very different configuration of funding from that of any other UN agency, with Panama and Liberia far ahead as the top two contributors. Notwithstanding their budgetary significance, these states do not enjoy the influence within the IMO that the European and North American maritime states do. Silverstein (1978: 84) found that until the late 1970s Liberia and Panama had no representatives in the IMO secretariat and had never been elected to the Council: 'This is not surprising given the infrequent appearance of native Liberians even on its own national delegation which is dominated by an industry group based in New York' (Silverstein 1978: 84). Since then, however, both Panama and Liberia have served on the Council.

In its early years, the IMO moved slowly in introducing amendments to conventions in response to changing technology. This was because amendments came into force only after a percentage of member states, usually two-thirds, accepted them. IMO responded with a 'tacit acceptance' procedure whereby amendments enter into force by a specified date unless objections are received from a specified percentage of contracting states, usually a third. Lethargy and inertia are therefore the foe rather than the friend of veto coalitions.

Tacit acceptance is certainly a blow to national sovereignty. However, the major threat to national sovereignty has come not from the IMO but from the various flags of convenience or open registries (predating the IMO) which take about a third of the world's fleet outside the control of any nation they visit. Having a voice in the IMO is the most practical way of reasserting sovereignty; the tacit acceptance procedure a practical way of responding to the obstructionism of flags-of-convenience states to IMO attempts to make them accountable for the ships from which they take registration fees.

### Insurers and Classification Societies

We have already argued that insurers and classification societies have been the key players in the history of maritime regulation, and IMO moves to mandate classification, and progressively to make insurance compulsory (or to restrict limitation of liability to losses not coverable by insurance) have further strengthened their hand. We can see how the key players in the global web of controls are intertwined. The major maritime states hand over a national sovereignty frayed by flags of convenience, to the IMO. States then enforce the rule of IMO law in their ports and foster it regionally through agreements such as the Paris (EEC), Latin American and Asia-Pacific memoranda on port-level enforcement of IMO conventions. The IMO globalizes mandatory classification and, for some contexts, mandatory insurance. Most states also strengthen the hand of the classification societies who compete on integrity more than on price by approving only them for purposes of national registration. The most solvent insurers protect their solvency by declining to

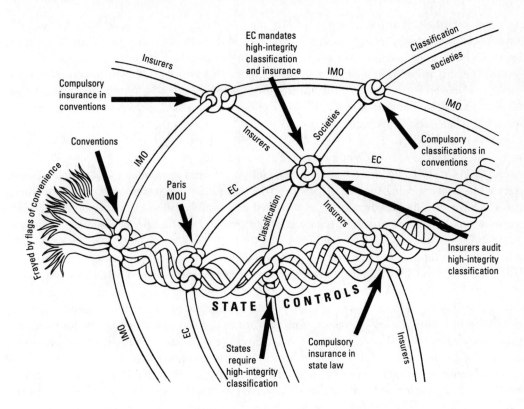

**FIGURE 17.1    Part of the web of maritime regulatory controls**

insure ships classified by low-cost–low-integrity classification societies. This section of the global web of shipping controls is represented pictorially in Figure 17.1.

This web is beginning to be strengthened further by the IACS, whose members classify 92 per cent of world merchant tonnage. IACS has achieved substantial global uniformity of standards for its members and been a force for mandating those standards for all shipping through the IMO. In 1992 IACS introduced a quality assurance program which members must satisfy as a condition of membership, and it has increased audit intensity under the program since then. The central objectives are to ensure that members have their own internal quality systems that work, and that they meet standards and procedures set down by the IACS. The system is based on applicable parts of ISO Standard 9001: 1994 as adopted and applied in ISO 9004, which mandates continuous improvement in the quality of classification. This ties the ISO to the web of controls. France has tied the ISO to its national control, mandating ISO 9000 for all transporters of dangerous goods into France, a policy it has not been able to persuade other EU members to share.

The International Chamber of Shipping successfully proposed in the early 1990s that the IMO adopt Guidelines on Management for the Safe Operation of Ships and for Pollution Prevention. This is now the International Safety Management Code, which became mandatory under the International Convention for the Safety of Life at Sea for high-risk vessels in 1998 and will extend to other vessels in 2002. The International Safety Management Code for maritime standards joins the trend toward global management standards that we see with ISO 9000 (product quality), ISO 14000 (environmental management) (Chapter 12) and the Hazard Analysis Critical Control Points on the management of food safety (Chapter 16).

In 1992 London insurance underwriters introduced a policy under which ships that were considered doubtful after a new structural condition survey, had to be surveyed by the Salvage Association. In the first year of this policy, 84 per cent of the 133 ships surveyed by the Salvage Association failed the first attempt (O'Neil 1993: IX). The group – the London Market Joint Hull Committee – has indicated that it might drop the requirement for special Salvage Association surveys if classification societies continue to raise their standards.

The UK P & I Club (Protection and Indemnity Club) has responded to a dramatic rise in claims against it by doing its own inspections to check those undertaken by classification societies. This has also increased pressure on the integrity of classification society work. As a result, some owners have faced premium increases of 400 per cent, tighter policy wording, increased deductibles and scrapping of loyalty bonuses (Ion 1992: 15, 34).

Certain London-based underwriters and P & I Clubs (of shipowners) have agreed to lift pollution cover by more than 40 per cent on tankers over twenty-five years old, while holding down premiums for tankers less than six years old. Although this increases incentives for those who insure to transport oil in newer tankers which have been mandated to include superior oil-spill prevention technology, it also increases incentives not to insure, an option taken by hundreds of ships operated by brass-plate companies. P & I Clubs have an interest in protecting their revenue as a club by encouraging the maintenance of insurance. As a collectivity of shipowners, they also have an interest in protecting the reputation of the industry and their own competitive positions by keeping everyone insured. Yet shipowners also have an interest in requiring higher-risk operators to pay their share of the cost of insurance proportionate to the risk they create. Hence, P & I Clubs may, given enough information, do a reasonable job of optimizing on these self-regulatory choices through the insurance price mechanism.

One can make a good case that single strands in this web of controls, even critical ones like classification societies (Cheit 1990a), are weak. But the strength is in their ties to other weak strands, ties that have bound more strands into the web of controls over time.[2]

## Other Industry Actors

Already we have referred to the important role of industry associations, to associations of shipowners and insurers that created the Red and Green Books, to the P & I Clubs that constituted the classification and insurance institutions which are the key strands of the global web of controls, and how they have acted to reinforce these strands when they frayed. We have seen how the International Chamber of Shipping proposed IMO involvement in continuous improvement of safety and pollution control management. At the IMO, the IACS, the International Association of Producers of Insurance and Reinsurance, the International Group of Protection and Indemnity Associations, the ICC and the International Chamber of Shipping are all key organizations with consultative status. The IACS played a particularly important role in maintaining the quality of

---

2 Cheit (1990a: 37) recognizes this when he says: 'That is why the IMO is so important to the success of classification societies: it provides an external and universal regulatory force'.

the information on which regulation is based by establishing a procedure for transferring ships from one member classification society to another. This gives the new classification society access to the previous classification society's records, so all previous surveys may be accepted.

Shipping regulation is so globalized that no national industry association we know of is a particularly dominant player. It is the international associations that go straight to the IMO to debate new regimes, unlike the commoner process in other domains, where national industry associations shape the law in a dominant state and that law becomes the model for less-powerful states and for global regimes.

Individual firms which are major users of shipping can also add an important strand to the web of controls. For example, the *Ships of Shame* report concludes that the major oil companies, particularly Shell, maintain extensive ship information systems for the purpose of ship-vetting (Parliament of the Commonwealth of Australia 1992: 91). The report also found instances of exemplary performance in the vetting of ships by bulk-loading terminals and charterers, Australian examples being Port Waratah Coal Services and the Queensland Sugar Corporation (Parliament of the Commonwealth of Australia 1992: 72).

The ICC plays a distinctive role in this domain, running an International Maritime Bureau which deals with all types of maritime crime, including fraud, cargo theft and piracy – acting as a global private security consultant to its members.

## NGOs

The most important NGOs associated with the maritime regime have been professional associations and unions. Passenger safety has not occupied the attention of contemporary consumer groups. Despite the suffering of nineteenth-century emigrants that resulted in the Passenger Acts 'no League or Association was dedicated to its amelioration' (MacDonagh 1961: 7).

As we saw in the environment chapter (Chapter 12), Friends of the Earth International has been a significant player with respect to IMO's environmental protection work. Greenpeace, the International Union for Conservation of Nature and Natural Resources, and the World Wide Fund for Nature also have consultative status at IMO. This is a recent development. Silverstein's (1978: 119) systematic research into the period 1958–72 found 'zero representation of any international private ecological, oceanographic, conservation or pollution control organization at every level of IMCO decision-making'. ISO representation in key fora was more regular, however, and voluntary standards organizations have been independently important in the way they have set standards that have been followed globally and picked up in IMO deliberations.

Unions representing seafarers have concentrated more of their energies on ILO than on IMO. The International Transport Workers Federation is active in encouraging members to report unsafe ships to flag-state and port administrations. Missions to Seamen have been the NGOs that have been longest active in articulating public concern about the appalling safety record of sea transport, but there is little evidence of them crafting strategic regulatory interventions.

The International Association of Ship Managers has been a promoter of the introduction of quality management systems into ship management. Professional associations with consultative status at IMO include the International Institutes of Navigation, the International Federation of Shipmasters Associations, the International Bar Association and the International Maritime Committee.

These NGOs play significant roles but have much less significance in shaping the globalization of maritime regulation than do the insurance and classification societies, key nation-states or IMO. National (as opposed to international) NGOs are quite unimportant, for the same reasons that national industry associations are less important than in more state-centric regimes.

## Mass Publics

For the first two thousand years of the globalization of maritime regulation, mass publics were quite unimportant, regulatory patterns being laid down through the custom and institution-building of collectively organized commercial interests. As MacDonagh's (1961) classic study of the Passenger Acts shows, in the nineteenth century the central state became a key player for the first time (and non-industry NGOs also assumed some (lesser) significance for the first time). It was not until the twentieth century, when newspaper-reading became widespread, that mass publics loomed as significant. But when they did it was in a big way, after the *Titanic* sank (unclassified because it was believed to be unsinkable!). The disaster led to the 1914 Convention for the Safety of Life at Sea, which led to the IMO. It also stimulated cooperation at the London Radio Conference of 1912 on rules to improve the effectiveness of radio in sea rescue. Public reaction to the *Torrey Canyon* oil-spill disaster of 1967 led to a new generation of oil pollution prevention conventions and changed the shape of IMO by creating a Legal Committee, initially to consider the legal problems caused by the disaster. Mass outrage over the *Herald of Free Enterprise* ferry capsize in the English Channel brought into effect a slate of new IMO safety standards for roll-on–roll-off passenger ships in 1989.

## Epistemic Communities of Actors

Edward Lloyd's coffee-house constituted an epistemic community of actors concerned with shipping at the centre of maritime power during the formative eighteenth and nineteenth centuries. As they sipped their coffee and stronger beverages, shipowners, builders, charterers and insurers forged a common regulatory language, innovated through self-regulatory institutions that helped consolidate London as the place where one could invest in the intrinsically hazardous activity of shipping with greater security than elsewhere.

On the opposite side of the Thames today, the IMO continues to refine this language and these institutions. It provides technical assistance to developing countries which want to learn how to make them work. It opened the World Maritime University in 1983 to assist with technical assistance, particularly by training African students to be trainers at the nautical schools of their own countries.

Another IMO activity explicitly directed at nurturing shared regulatory discourse across the maritime epistemic community has been the development of a 'Standard Marine Vocabulary' (Mankabady 1984: 146–8). It has not gone as far as mandating English as the navigational language, as has happened with the air transport epistemic community.

The two Lloyd's (the insurance market and the classification society) were the crucibles of the distinctiveness of the London commercial arbitration epistemic community. Its global niche, connected to the English Commercial Court, has been based in related maritime and insurance disputes (Dezalay & Garth 1996: 129–31). The Commercial Court sits above an expert lay (non-lawyer) arbitration community of the London Maritime Arbitration Association.

## Contest of Principles

### Lowest-cost Location v. World's Best Practice

Panama's and Liberia's success in capturing more than 20 per cent of the world's merchant shipping tonnage is a triumph of the principle of lowest-cost location (even if it is more related to tax than to shipping regulation). The growing dominance of British shipping during the eighteenth and nineteenth centuries was a triumph of the principle of world's best practice, grounded in credible regulatory standards generating secure investment. The twentieth-century success, built on that British foundation, of IACS member classification societies classifying over 90 per cent of world tonnage is also a triumph of the principle of world's best practice.

There is a market niche for both principles. The principle of world's best practice grounded in credible regulatory standards defines the dominant market opportunities. Even most ships registered in Panama and Liberia are classified by IACS members so they can better guarantee the security and prudence that most big and small investors want. But there is also a market niche for lowest-cost transport in unsafe ships crewed by undertrained, underpaid (and often abused) sailors. The contest of principles by the end of the twentieth century has become a no-contest at the level of ideas. Even at the level of practice, the fact is that the small market attracted to lowest-cost standards is shrinking. We have seen that there are extra strands that can be tied into the global web of regulatory controls illustrated in Figure 17.1, enabling prospects for a further decline in the proportion of ships that are ships of shame.

Yet it is hard to conceive of a world where there will not be shady operators who register under flags of convenience, cut costs by failing to meet obligations, and manipulate shelf companies using clever bankruptcy practitioners to escape the large legal liabilities that can befall them.[3] Our world is not one where these operators are leading global standards down. It is one where a partial triumph of the principle of world's best practice based on credible regulation has led standards up, increased the detectability of ships of shame and thereby reduced the demand for their services. Yet it is also a world where the cost of the regulations and insurance premiums that can be evaded are higher and therefore where there remains a market niche for ships of shame.

### National Sovereignty v. Harmonization v. Mutual Recognition, Reciprocity

Even if flags of convenience are used only to avoid tax, their effect has been to deflate any illusion of national sovereignty. Today no investor would buy or build a ship that did not comply with IMO standards. Nor in any major maritime nation would operators think of lobbying their national government to stand alone with standards that diverge significantly from IMO requirements. In short, there has been a decisive triumph of global harmonization of standards over national sovereignty.[4] The place of mutual recognition in this is restricted. Although the standards are harmonized, there is mutual recognition of the classification procedures used to ascertain

---

3  Justice Frank Callaway qualified this sentence appropriately in commenting on a draft of this chapter: 'There is not much that one can do about one-ship companies but modern admiralty law does cater for sister ships or surrogate ships. You can arrest a ship to enforce a claim against her sister ship. See s. 19 of the *Admiralty Act 1988*'.

4  At the same time, we must concur with Hindell's (1996: 371) judgment: 'When the member states of the IMO put on their rule-making hats they are at their most benign and most constructive. It is when they go home to exercise their "national sovereignty" by applying these international regulations that the facts of day appear'.

compliance with them. Even here, though, there is an effort through IMO to promulgate guidelines to enhance the uniformity of the classification work subject to mutual recognition. There is little place for reciprocity in such a system of global regulation.

## Deregulation, Strategic Trade, World's Best Practice

The principles of deregulation and strategic trade are weak in most of the world. Although the principle of deregulation rules supreme on the waterfront and, to some degree, with the weakening of economic regulation by shipping conferences, with the operation of the ships themselves the international impetus is to increase regulatory standards, except in a few flag-of-convenience states which exploit an exceptionalist commitment to a principle of deregulation. The commitment to strengthening regulation – moving to world's best practice – is not based on states seeking to secure a strategic trade advantage by being slightly ahead of the pack on higher standards. Being ahead of the pack might mean that a state could lose ship registrations to flag-of-convenience states. Instead, most states see themselves as having an interest in foreign shippers imposing fewer externalities on their citizens via oil spills, costly search-and-rescue operations, collisions and the like. The IMO is the vehicle for forcing all states to upgrade to more prudential standards for ships that bear their flag.

## Rule Compliance v. Continuous Improvement

We have seen that IMO, IACS and France have recently put in place guidelines or mandatory requirements for continuous improvement of safety and environmental management of shipping. These management changes are imposed on a foundation of a rule compliance regime of minimum structural standards for hulls, segregated ballast tanks and the like. Hence there is not really a contest between continuous improvement and rule compliance. Rather, we have a situation where continuous improvement is gaining momentum as a principle on the management side and rule compliance remains the regulatory philosophy on the structural side.

## Transparency

The plimsoll line and the posting of data on the safety of ships at Lloyd's coffee-house illustrate the historical leadership that maritime regulation has shown on the question of transparency. IACS members swapping survey reports when ships change class is an interesting recent step toward increased transparency. On the downside, the safety and environmental management auditing programs currently being put in place tend not to mandate public disclosure of audit results. Transparency of data known to classification societies has always been limited (Cheit 1990a). The important point is that insurers, classification societies, potential buyers or charterers and even major corporate users of ships can effectively demand the results of safety and environmental surveys. If there is reluctance to hand them over, a potential buyer may walk away from the purchase unless it can have Lloyd's Register or a competitor do a condition survey of the ship. As pointed out in Chapter 12, one reason for the 98 per cent compliance rate with the MARPOL regime for prevention of pollution from ships has been the improved transparency of the new equipment subregime over that of the former discharge subregime (Mitchell 1994a: 445). It is easy to check that a tanker has segregated ballast tanks, but hard to detect discharges at sea. There is actually a long tradition of the MARPOL strategy in global maritime regulation. Under British anti-slavery treaties with the Netherlands, Sweden, Norway, Brazil, Spain, Portugal, the US, Argentina, Uruguay, Bolivia, Chile and Ecuador between 1822 and 1862, ships observed to be carrying certain equipment could be condemned and broken up. Forbidden equipment included a slave deck in the form of a spare plank, excess bulkheads, hatches with gratings, and shackles – any of these could lead to condemnation of a ship even if no slaves were on board (Eltis 1987: 86).

### National Treatment and Most Favoured Nation

National treatment and Most Favoured Nation are principles that carry no real weight in maritime regulation. We have seen that the commitment to global harmonization of standards is strong. Although port states grant mutual recognition to the implementation efforts of the flag states whose ships sail into their ports, they also selectively exercise their right to inspect those ships while they are in port. Port state inspection is not about national treatment or Most Favoured Nation treatment. It is about supporting the principle of harmonized standards. Most port states are openly committed to fighting the lax standards of flags-of-convenience states by prioritizing their ships for port inspections (Hindell 1996: 373). Canada has been explicit in publishing the fact that it is targeting bulk carriers more than ten years old and between 40 000 and 100 000 tons flying the flag of Cyprus, Panama, Liberia, Iran, Croatia, Malta, the Bahamas or the Philippines (Parliament of the Commonwealth of Australia 1992: 50). Norway is an example of a traditional maritime country which has responded to flags-of-convenience states by developing a separate register for ships involved in international trade. Norwegian ships plying national trade only are required to meet costlier standards – inverting the normal breach of national treatment (which means imposing less-costly demands on nationals).

## Mechanisms

### Military Coercion

Military coercion has certainly been (and continues to be) important in ending piracy and smuggling in ships which are exempt from international regulation through operating in a black market. At the same time, military coercion was the reason why piracy was tolerated by states for so long. Pirates made useful recruits for a navy or as privateers to raid rivals' shipping, for *imperium*. Piracy was at times part of the mechanism of military coercion and at others the object of regulation. During war, states deprive merchant vessels of use of shipping lanes that is their right under international maritime law. Ports are sometimes blockaded in violation of such law. These are temporary aberrations, however, and the global maritime regulatory order is restored as soon as hostilities cease. Military conquest, while unimportant today, did play a small role in proliferating the maritime law of Justinian's Code to lands as distant as England. However, most proliferation of Roman law occurred through modelling within the epistemic community that spread from Bologna in the Renaissance. Military coercion by Roman legions played a part in setting the ancient framework, if not the modern content, of maritime regulation.

## Economic Coercion

The economic hegemony of the British empire during the nineteenth and early twentieth centuries saw it more than simply impose its maritime regulation on its many colonies. Ships entering and leaving the great trading ports of the British empire were progressively required to comply with the standards expected of British ships in those ports; for example, by displaying a plimsoll line. More important than national British coercion, however, was the hegemony of British economic institutions, most critically the insurance and reinsurance market of the City of London.

## Systems of Reward

The major example of the role of systems of reward in proliferating the global order for the regulation of shipping, is a very consequential one – the systematic and long-standing practice of international insurers granting lower premiums to ships found to be structurally safer for a given purpose in regular surveys. Another interesting system of reward arises from the creation of a new watchdog to evaluate marine training by IMO members under the revised Convention on Standards of Training, Certification and Watchkeeping for Seafarers: 'The watchdog will create a "white-list" of safety-conscious flags...At present a black-list...would be rather long' (Hindell 1996: 379).

## Modelling

While military conquest may have accounted for the partial spread of Justinian's Code throughout the Roman empire, the proliferation of maritime regulation beyond the Roman empire depended on modelling of the developments in Roman law by the successful trading states of the Italian Renaissance. States with whom those city-states traded learnt that the successful framework of their maritime law enabled sea trading to be more secure than the more anarchic conditions of other forms of trade with other parts of the world. From 1300 Italian merchants were trading into India and China, spreading ideas about how to use credit, banking, bills of lading, bookkeeping and risk-spreading to manage long-distance sea trade. Florentine firms assumed the historically critical ascendancy in England in the fourteenth century, financing Edward II's wars against Scotland and Edward III's moves against France at the beginning of the Hundred Years' War and muscling aside Jewish money-lenders to control the international trade in English wool (Braudel 1979: 392–3).

The modelling of the partially codified, partially customary law of long-distance sea trade occurred through the agency of successive waves of money-lending diasporas – Armenian, Jewish, Hanseatic, Florentine, Venetian, Genoan (Braudel 1979) and later Chinese (Lever-Tracy, Ip & Tracy 1996). The models of incipient mercantile capitalism were imitated because they worked, at least until a major creditor (such as a Spanish king) defaulted. Repeated modelling in different parts of the world insinuated a global regulatory order:

> in a varied universe, forms and performances can be similar: there are towns, routes, states, patterns of trade which in spite of everything resemble each other. We are indeed told that there are as many 'means of exchange as there are means of production'. But in any case these means are limited in number, since they are directed to solving elementary problems, the same the whole world over (Braudel 1979: 133).

Elementary problems like ships sinking.

Obviously, the most important modelling has been of the idea of a classification society that began in Edward Lloyd's coffee-house. Germanischer Lloyd is a prominent example of successful adoption of the model in a country that was extremely good at modelling in the late nineteenth century.

### Reciprocal Adjustment and Non-reciprocal Coordination

The level of reciprocal adjustment with maritime regulation has been historically remarkable. The UK did not use its hegemony in the nineteenth century to overwhelm the Roman-law traditions of maritime regulation with common-law principles. Rather, Admiralty adjusted to continental realities. Neither the Soviet Union nor the US deployed their new-found power after the Second World War to seek to dominate the IMO, as the US did in so many other domains of globalizing regulation since the Second World War. Cold War politics always seemed to succumb to reciprocal adjustment. No doubt there was a pragmatic desire to get on with the business of transporting 95 per cent of world trade in ships, with minimum friction and maximum comity.

For the part of the industry effectively untouched by the cooperative spirit of reciprocal adjustment – the users of flags of convenience – one might expect to find the principle of non-reciprocal coordination. One might expect Panama to be offered improved access to northern markets for its tropical fruits, for example, in return for shipping regulatory reform. We have not, however, found serious evidence of such non-reciprocal coordination.

### Capacity-building

Neither the British state nor the classification societies nor the insurance companies – the key actors in our story – have been particularly strong on technical assistance to developing countries on maritime regulation. We have seen, however, that this is one of the gaps that IMO has begun to fill, mainly through the World Maritime University. Of course, the professionalization of seafaring predates the IMO by many centuries. Naval training, nautical schools, guilds, apprenticeships before the mast, the International Association of Ship Managers, the International Institutes of Navigation, the International Federation of Shipmasters Associations and their national constituent members have all played important roles in building capacity for safety at sea through the professionalization of seafaring.

## Conclusion

International trade by sea is older than capitalism and older than the nation-state because it was important in constituting them. MacDonagh (1961) argues rightly that, from the mid nineteenth century in England and from somewhat later in most other states, there was enormous growth in the regulatory institutions of the nation-state. Public maritime regulatory laws burgeoned from the mid nineteenth to the mid twentieth centuries – the golden era of nation-state regulation. We have attempted to show what a brief interlude this was, however, in the much larger pattern of global regulatory development. The nineteenth-century public laws of the great maritime states were founded on more than two millennia of private law. This private law traced from Rhodes to Rome to Florence to London. Modelling was the key mechanism of globalization – diasporas of

Armenian, Jewish, Florentine, Genoan and Chinese trading families helped spread customs that rendered the shipping of produce by sea an activity that investors could risk without facing bankruptcy if a big cargo sank.

What drove global regulatory improvements in the safety of sea transport until the rise of the regulatory nation-state was not concern for the lives of sailors, slaves or emigrants, but concern for the security of maritime investment. Fundamentally, though, this concern also improved seafarers' safety. Loss of life at sea did decline.

As we saw in the environment chapter (Chapter 12), the IMO learnt from the history of the progressive success of maritime regulation in its efforts to render workable the International Convention for the Prevention of Pollution from Ships (MARPOL). The IMO's discharge subregime, based on obliging states to prosecute dischargers at sea, was an utter failure, never enforced, desultory in impact on the level of oil spills. In contrast, the equipment subregime that succeeded it engendered 98 per cent compliance (Mitchell 1994a) and by 1989 had reduced oil spillage from ships to one-third the amount in 1981 (IMO 1993). Compliance with the treaties banning the slave trade in the nineteenth century must have approached the same high level, given the seeming demise of the industry by century's end. The empirically documented MARPOL result was achieved by IMO, insurers and states requiring classification societies to insist on segregated ballast tanks and crude oil washing before ships could be classified. Many IMO standards have a self-enforcing quality since 'insurance certificates are needed to enter most ports of the world, and because of the competitive nature of the shipping business, insurance rates are often too high to operate economically if IMCO standards are not met' (Plano 1972: 19).

Our history is of two millennia of development of private regulatory institutions – private maritime law, underwriters, classification societies and the professionalization of seafaring – that were the key strands in a web of controls that made sea transport more secure for people and for investors. Regulation by the nation-state assumed such importance from the mid nineteenth century, that it should be added to this list as another key strand of regulation. Yet before we were far into the twentieth century, most nation-states were delegating large swathes of their regulatory functions back to classification societies, and the growth of flags of convenience rendered national sovereignty obsolete. The ILO became a significant new strand in the first half of the twentieth century, while in the second half the IMO became a new strand of truly major import.

We have attempted to show how changes in state law and in international conventions have rendered it more necessary for ships to be classified and insured, further strengthening these key strands in the web of controls. Figure 17.1 illustrates a number of nodes where this web of controls is tied together, each strand joined to others in a way that strengthens the capacity of the web as a whole to lessen the risks of sea transport to people, capital and the environment. The text around Figure 17.1 documents how various other strands – IACS, the International Chamber of Shipping, the Salvage Association, maritime schools, ILO, the London Market Joint Hull Committee, seafarers' unions and the International Confederation of Free Trade Unions – are interwoven into this web. We find the web metaphor a useful one, particularly in the way it enables us to construct a usable normative analysis (in Chapters 23 to 26) of how to manage the globalization of regulation in a way that might enhance the sovereignty of citizens. However, it has analytic limitations.

This chapter shows those analytic limitations well. The institutions that grew out of Lloyd's coffee-house do not simply mutually reinforce the power of the British regulatory state. They were not just tied to state maritime regulation; they constituted it and continue to transform it. Obversely, state policies such as compulsory insurance (or limiting liability to losses up to what could reasonably be insured) transformed the private prudential institutions of shipping. The nineteenth-century British state had a major hand in deciding that Lloyd's Register of Shipping and the Lloyd's of London reinsurance exchange should be separate institutions and should remain private, neither funded nor managed by the state. A model that treats actors as discrete, pre-given but interconnected, does not capture the reality we describe as well as does a theory of structuration.

According to Giddens' (1984) theory of structuration, the form of agency that actors practise is constituted by social structures. Obversely, those structures are constituted and continually reproduced by the practices of those actors. Actors and structures are therefore in a recursive relationship, mutually constituting and reconstituting each other. This produces not static structures but unfolding structuration, not static actors but actors whose make-up is constantly remade. Hence, the practices of individuals like Edward Lloyd and his shipowning customers structurated an insurance market, which in turn reconstituted Lloyd's from a coffee-house to a gentlemen's club and institutionalized information exchange for shippers, then to a Register Book Society and a reinsurance auction and brokerage house. Edward Lloyd, doubly institutionalized as reinsurance exchange and classification society, then acted to constitute the British maritime regulatory state, which in turn acted to reconstitute the Lloyd's institutions and the people who reproduce them. This structurates the embedded but constantly adjusting state–market ordering of maritime capitalism.

We do not have to choose between the structuration account of the patterns described in this and other chapters, and the webs of control account. The moving feast of the structuration account is more descriptively rich and analytically accurate. Yet to make suggestions on how to engage politically with the world, we must simplify it in a way that renders it momentarily static, that defines a type of actor we can examine in a slice of time. Then we can consider how we might want it to be different at some future time and what strategic policy we might advocate to bring about the change. Even though the British state or the British Department of Transport is a static reification, it can make policy sense to argue that Britain ought to support convention X at IMO and that Greenpeace ought to lobby Britain to amend its law to give effect to the provisions of convention X. To say that the British state once never existed and is constantly transformed in processes of structuration is not a decisive objection to such normative work. What the structuration account does is help us see that at some points in the process of its structuration, the static category 'British state' is analytically useless; at other points and for other purposes it will be less useful than, for example, 'the British Cabinet' or 'the British delegation to IMO'. This is an important point because the dominant modes of scholarship for considering the globalization of regulation have seen it as a matter of international relations or international law traditions which grant priority to the actions of nation-states.

The most interesting questions for the future of the regulation of sea transport are how far the hitherto-modest moves toward continuous improvement in safety and environmental protection will go, and whether international pressure can force flag-of-convenience states to hold all ships carrying their flag more accountable.

## History of Globalization

Road transport is regulated in three main ways. First by the layout of roads and traffic signs. Since international agreements (notably the 1931 Convention on the Unification of Road Signals) mostly do not regulate business to accomplish this, it is outside the scope of our study. That is to say, it was individuals who were mainly regulated by the famous roadsign in Baden of the German Reichstaat ('state ordered by law'): 'It is permitted to travel on this road' (Davies 1997: 438). Second, drivers are regulated through licensing and police enforcement of compliance with road rules. Since these drivers are mostly private citizens, we have also decided to exclude this domain of regulation from the scope of the study. The third domain is regulations concerning how motor vehicles should be manufactured, which is the subject of our analysis.

The history of the globalization of this regulation is recent. Motor vehicles only appeared on the world's roads in the 1890s. The first national regulation appeared in that decade. The only design requirement in the British *Locomotives on Highways Act 1896* was that cars should carry lights at night and have a 'bell or other instrument capable of giving audible and sufficient warning' (Plowden 1971: 22). Sixteen European states concluded the first Convention on Road Traffic in 1909. It contained motor vehicle design provisions to exclude risks of explosion, limit nuisance from noise and vapours, mandate two separate braking systems, and regulate lighting and steering. The 1926 International Convention Relating to Road Traffic and the 1926 International Convention Relating to Motor Traffic established more detailed rules covering exhaust silencers, rear-view mirrors, pneumatic tyres, lights and licence plates. The Convention on Road Traffic concluded in 1949 was the framework for postwar globalization of vehicle manufacturing standards. The Economic Commission for Europe (ECE) set up a Working Party on the Construction of Vehicles (Working Party 29) in 1953 and agreed upon its first regulation in 1958. This became the pre-eminent global forum for motor vehicle standards. Yet the first seventy years of the motor vehicle's existence saw only limited globalization of its regulation, and quite limited national regulation as well.

### Nader Raids the Rules

An explosion of regulatory activity occurred in the US as a result of the publication of Ralph Nader's *Unsafe at Any Speed* in 1966. Because General Motors, the target of Nader's attack, sold vehicles in most parts of the world, the impact of Nader's exposé of inadequate regulatory assurance of car safety was felt everywhere. The US Congress responded with the National Traffic and Motor Vehicle Safety Act and the Nixon administration set up the National Highway Traffic Safety Administration (NHTSA) in 1970 as a new agency to oversee motor vehicle safety standards. Because of the scale of that organization and the greater concentration of expertise it recruited, NHTSA acquired a position of considerable international leadership and mostly, though not invariably, set higher safety and fuel efficiency standards than the rest of the world.

While US regulatory expertise and stringency was unassailably ahead of the world during the 1970s, it was not in a good position to coordinate safety and environmental standards globally. Europe had already assumed that role in the 1950s by establishing the Working Party on the Construction of Vehicles (Working Party 29) of the UN ECE (henceforth WP29). WP29 was established more out of a concern to liberalize European trade in motor vehicles than because of safety concerns. From 1958 WP29 set out to lay the foundations for mutual recognition of 'type approvals' which each European state would grant to manufacturers to sell a vehicle of a specified type. The scheme was that a German factory would get approval from the German government to manufacture vehicles of a design it would submit to its government. As with the new pharmaceuticals regulation of the 1960s, this was pre-marketing approval of product specifications. Once the vehicle type had been approved, other European states would grant mutual recognition to the type approval. The job of WP29 was to ensure that the grounds for type approvals in different states converged sufficiently to make mutual recognition acceptable. From 1958, WP29 began to write regulations that member states were asked to 'apply'. Application means that they would not grant a type approval to any vehicle design that failed to meet the regulation.

Twenty-eight European states are parties to the ECE's Agreement Concerning the Adoption of Uniform Conditions of Approval and Reciprocal Recognition of Approval for Motor Vehicle Equipment and Parts. These states formally indicate whether they will apply each regulation agreed by WP29. But all fifty-five member countries of the ECE can take part in the WP29 work. This is the basis on which all the major non-European motor vehicle manufacturing states participate – the US, Japan, South Korea, Canada, Australia, etc. – without being contracting parties. These states decided to participate in the Working Party for two reasons. If Europe was going to set standards so as to remove barriers to trade within Europe, non-European manufacturers wanted to put their case on how it might be done so that they could also benefit from the liberalization of trade. Second, WP29 became the pre-eminent forum for exchange of information between states on new regulatory challenges as motor vehicle technology changed. They attended WP29 meetings to learn from each other, to be part of the Geneva epistemic community.

### The US Rules Alone

When the US introduced its new regulatory order for motor vehicle safety in response to the Nader exposé, it went its own way. The US Congress and administration wanted the best motor vehicle safety regulation in the world and it decided that European type approval was not the way to achieve that. Instead of firms submitting design information to the government for the state to decide whether the design met its safety and environmental requirements, the US opted for self-certification. The government would set safety and emission standards (basically performance standards), then the manufacturer (domestic or foreign), not the government, would self-certify that it met the standards. The manufacturer is free to use whatever product-testing or quality assurance methods it deems appropriate to ensure the vehicle meets the standards. The NHTSA periodically checks compliance with its standards by buying new cars or new parts and testing them. If they fail to comply, a recall is likely to be ordered. The recall has international effect; the Pope's Cadillac was affected by a recall. In addition, the manufacturer may be fined for failing to meet the standard. An effect is that self-certification relies more on recalls than type approval and makes no assumption that the vehicles that are actually produced meet the specifications in the pre-marketing designs submitted for type approvals.

The overwhelming majority of nations have followed the WP29 path of type approval rather than the US model of self-certification. The divergent models do not preclude substantial global harmonization, which has indeed happened. If the WP29 regulations that must be satisfied by the type approvals of party states are the same as NHTSA standards, as they sometimes are, then the standards are harmonized in content, if not in enforcement. The ECE 1958 Agreement Contracting Parties' 28-nation market constitutes the biggest market, so most other countries follow the WP29 regulations more than any other, though occasionally they will follow the second major alternative, the NHTSA standards. An Australian government statement illustrates this common scenario:

> It is the Australian government's policy to harmonize, wherever possible, with international standards unless there are significant safety grounds to do otherwise. At present, over 60 per cent of the ADRs [Australian Design Rules] are aligned with international standards, predominantly the European ECE Regulations. The remainder, especially in the vehicle exhaust emissions area, mirror the US regulations (ECE 1997: 32).

Given that US–ECE dialogue and reciprocal adjustment is considerable whenever standards diverge, policies such as the Australian one deliver quite a high degree of effective global harmonization. There has to be, given the level of global integration of the industry. While talk of the new 'world car' was a little overblown during the 1980s, Figure 18.1 shows how the first clearcut world car, General Motors' J-car of the early 1980s, had production locations in the US, Canada, Germany, Belgium, the UK, Japan, South Africa, Australia and Brazil.

The harmonization to accommodate such global assembly has been facilitated by both the ECE and the NHTSA moving toward performance standards and away from specification standards, and adopting a Best Available Technology (BAT) philosophy. A specification standard for car lighting, for example, would specify how many lights there should be, how powerful they should be and where they should be located. A performance standard simply requires the manufacturer to be able to illuminate certain objects at various points on the road without blinding drivers coming the other way, allowing manufacturers to locate lights wherever they think most efficient for achieving the performance required.

Much of the European regulation of the 1960s and 1970s was specification standards (e.g. in Germany), and the UK did not have a type approval system until it joined the EU. So WP29, in collaboration with NHTSA, has been at the heart of a considerable global convergence on a philosophy of performance standards and BAT. This combination means that BAT does not mandate the new and better technology; it mandates the level of performance achieved by the best technology that is economically feasible.

## Brussels Rules the Roads

In an important sense, the way the ECE rather than the US has achieved world domination is anomalous. ECE decisions are made by meetings of experts from member states. The WP29

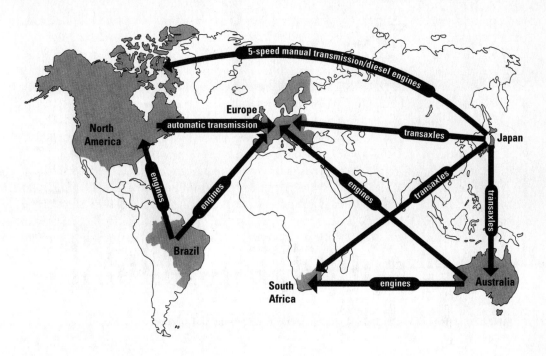

FIGURE 18.1    General Motors putting the world car together[1]

secretariat in Geneva since 1990 has consisted of one professional, sometimes supplemented by a second, supported by two secretarial staff. It is all very well to say that safety professionals are on the six standing meetings of experts and the WP29 secretariat are only administrators, but in political reality this creates a vacuum when there is a competing US regulatory model controlling almost as big a market with a staff of eight hundred.

That vacuum has been filled by Directorate-General III of the EC. Not that DG-III has a large cadre of in-house motor vehicle safety professionals. There are only three; but they use consultants extensively, and experts from the major states. Early in its history, the EC let WP29 set motor vehicle standards. In fact all the initial EC motor vehicle standard directives were simply taken from the WP29 work. Progressively, however, the EC helped to develop new standards. As one insider put it during our interviews, between WP29 and the EC, 'Informally, it was a matter of you do this, we do that'. For over a decade, however, both industry and insiders suggest the reality has become that the EC calls the shots. DG-III decides on a standard that can be agreed among the experts in its member states, then one EU member state is delegated to take the agreed standard to WP29. In effect, the EC now uses WP29 to attempt to globalize a direction for standards it has settled for the EU. Of course, many times such machinations fail because the standards are politically sensitive outside the EU inner circle. But as one insider qualified this description: 'This is how it works on politically sensible [as opposed to sensitive!] subjects'.

The European motor vehicle industry, which is concentrated in the largest EU states, mostly supports the partial shift in the effective centre of power from Geneva to Brussels. At the time of

---

1    Graph from Sinclair, Stuart 1983, *The World Car: The Future of the Automobile Industry*. New York: Facts on File, p.
   73. Reproduced with approval.

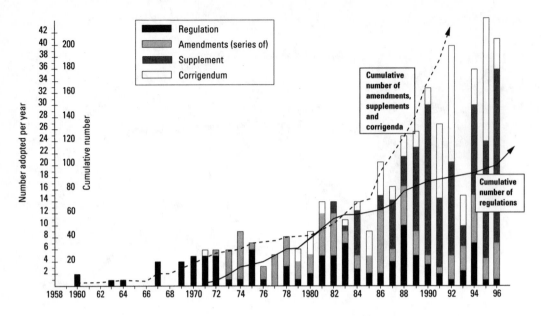

FIGURE 18.2    Activity of WP29, 1958–1996: numbers of regulations and amendments adopted[2]

our interviews in the mid 1990s the EC was pushing a reform proposal for WP29 that would see it become a more global committee with the EC, the US and Japan as full parties rather than just participating observers. Under such a reform, the EU would still have fifteen of the votes of the twenty-four to twenty-eight states that participate regularly in WP29 meetings, so that it could block any standard that did not suit it. At the time of writing, the US was pushing the idea of a 'multinational proposal for a global agreement' (ECE 1996, 1997), in effect to parallel the 1958 ECE agreement in a way that allows non-European states to be contracting parties.

In some ways this case study is like pharmaceuticals (Chapter 15) in the way Brussels strategists have seized the historical initiative from Washington. A difference is that with motor vehicles it is more clearly a strategic trade move. Ultimately, it is not so much Brussels technocrats who call the shots as the industry leaders from the large European states. As the head of one European motor vehicle regulatory authority put it: 'Often on these committees the representative from Germany is really the representative from DaimlerBenz and the representative from France is really the representative from Peugeot'.

### Nader's Global Legacy

Figure 18.2 shows that globalization of regulation through the agency of WP29 only began seriously after *Unsafe at Any Speed* in 1966 and only accelerated in a really major way after 1980.

Has the global growth in regulation since *Unsafe at Any Speed* succeeded in saving lives? For the US, where the regulation was stringent earliest (at least of safety, if not of quality), fatalities

---

2  Graph from TRANS/SC.1/WP29/R.628, p. 16. Reproduced with the approval of the Economic Commission for Europe.

have fallen to 1.9 per 100 million miles driven from a high of 5.8 in the 1960s. In the most care-ful and detailed study undertaken on the topic, the Brookings Institution has concluded that reg-ulation may have been responsible for reducing fatalities by 40 per cent between 1966 and 1981, saving as many as 23 000 lives a year in that country (Crandall et al. 1986; see also Friedland, Trebilcock & Roach 1990). In Japan, where regulation has not been as tough (Otake 1982), fatal-ities per million miles have risen since 1971. But the nature of Japan's problem is very different from that of the US. In Japan, 40 per cent of fatalities are pedestrians and cyclists, a problem exac-erbated as traffic density grows and one that is difficult to ameliorate through vehicle redesign. In the US people walk less and when they do, they are more effectively separated from traffic.

Although Ralph Nader was the catalyst for the process of global regulatory growth, since the 1970s consumer groups have not been especially important influences. Rather, it has been strate-gic trade positioning in a context of demand for safety from mass publics that has ratcheted-up standards, saving lives. At times, however, those same strategic trade imperatives have held back regulatory innovations that might have spread globally. Hence, although there has been progress in building safer cars, and it has had a global character, it has certainly not gone as far or as fast as it might have in meeting the public demand for safety. A more recent kind of public demand is for higher anti-theft standards in cars. The process of globalizing these standards is now begin-ning at WP29.

## Actors

### States

Clearly, the NHTSA is the most influential state actor, but in a context where Brussels has more clout than Washington. Within the EU, Germany, France and the UK, with their substantial indus-tries, overwhelmingly dominate decision-making. Germany exercises considerable clout in requir-ing Eastern Europe to succumb more quickly to the European regulatory order than it otherwise might. For example, it signs bilateral agreements mandating that trucks from Eastern Europe trav-elling through Germany must meet EU standards. Italy has a very substantial industry, but govern-mentally does not seem as technically organized to exert influence in Brussels as the big three.

Japan is the world's largest exporter of motor vehicles (accounting for 30 per cent of all exports) though Germany is the biggest exporter of components and the second-largest exporter of complete cars (23 per cent). Japan takes seriously deliberations at WP29, having a technical expert office in Geneva for WP29 liaison. While it is clearly the most influential player after the EU states and the US, its influence is a pale reflection of its significance in this industry. As a key insider put it: 'The Japanese cooperate very actively but do not propose new standards'. Part of the explanation for this may be history. Japan entered the motor vehicle safety regulatory game later than Europe and the US, a kind of path-dependency argument that also explains why Europe enjoys some ascendancy over the US. But there is more to it than that. As a senior EC official put it, the Japanese attitude is: 'Let us know what you want and we'll meet it. The Japanese have never asked to intervene in a Commission experts committee on the ground that the EC standard must be changed or compromised so that it can become a basis for consensus later at WP29'.

The Nordic countries are the final group that have been significant. Sweden has a substan-tial industry, and its manufacturers have tended to lead on safety innovation. This gives Sweden a strategic trade interest in higher global standards that force Sweden's competitors to meet the cost of safety catch-up. Sweden is now a forceful articulator of the case for tough standards in Brussels and Geneva (after a period when it pulled out of WP29 in disgust at feeble standard-setting). The Nordics also historically have imposed higher environmental standards on cars, but with integration into the EU regulatory order they are now pulling back to European norms. The Netherlands is another active state at WP29. South Korea and China are becoming progressively more prominent. Even at the height of its power, the Soviet Union was never an influential player at WP29. It never significantly blocked anything and never brought Cold War rivalry into the forum.

## Organizations of States

Motor vehicle standard-setting is unusual in the way that standards have become so effectively global without there being an international organization in which all states can participate fully or a convention that all states can ratify. Instead, a couple of administrative staff in Geneva serve as a secretariat for a European group in which most non-European states are effectively no more than observers. This has suited the preference of the major European manufacturing interests to shift effective power to the Industry Directorate-General of the EC, where Euro-industry leverage is at its maximum.

## Business Actors

Motor vehicle manufacturers are among the largest TNCs in the world. Their chief executives have easy direct access to the most powerful heads of state, as the Watergate tapes inside President Nixon's office vividly illustrated. Consequently they do not need to lobby through industry associations. The situation is a little different with lobbying governments other than their home state. In some states in which they have more modest manufacturing interests or joint ventures, they may work through the industry association in that host state; in countries where they have no manufacturing, they may work through the participation of their dealer networks in trade associations. But the CEOs of Ford in Australia or the UK can get direct access to the prime ministers of those countries if need be. DaimlerBenz does not rely on representation through industry associations in Brussels. It has a delegate from its Board of Management there in Brussels calling the shots.

A reason for manufacturers' preference to represent themselves is that the motor vehicle standards game is a strategic trade game. Safety innovation is more a cause than an effect of regulation. Since manufacturers witnessed the reaction of mass publics to *Unsafe at Any Speed*, they have been convinced that consumers want more design safety. Contemporary advertising reflects this, a realization brought home during our fieldwork in the early 1990s when we saw a Chrysler Plymouth 'ahead of its time' advertisement in the US: 'includes all 1998 safety standards now' and an advertisement urging European consumers to buy a Saab that 'meets American safety and environmental standards'. Manufacturers increased their investment in safety R&D from 1970 (for General Motors, see Fisse & Braithwaite 1983: 33–40).

Safety innovations come from this private investment by single companies. When a company designs a safety improvement, the company may go to NHTSA and DG-III to persuade them that they have improved on BAT with respect to a certain standard. Many, perhaps most, safety breakthroughs also come from component manufacturers like Bosch. Bosch may also go to NHTSA and DG-III with the claim that it has the basis of a new BAT. A component manufacturer's interest is in NHTSA and DG-III writing a new standard or amending an old one to mandate the new BAT, bringing all manufacturers knocking at their door to buy or license the new technology. Car manufacturers' interest is in mandating the new technology so that competitors are forced into expensive catch-up redesign, or into joint ventures or licensing of the technology.

DaimlerBenz does not want to lobby jointly with other German manufacturers when it does this, because it wants to score a strategic trade advantage against them. However, the German state is likely to vigorously support DaimlerBenz at DG-III because all the strategic trade advantage flows to Germany and most of the strategic trade disadvantage (with the exception of the other German manufacturers) is foreign. DG-III may then ask Germany to prepare a proposal for a new EU standard. DaimlerBenz will then drive the German proposal, sitting at the table as an adviser at all the meetings of experts. As one key insider put it: 'It is a government that proposes, but the work is usually done by the company'. If there is sufficient EU consensus then Germany will take the proposal to WP29, or Germany might move simultaneously in Brussels and Geneva. A seasoned participant at WP29 meetings explained how things work in Geneva:

> In practice, it usually starts with one country preparing a proposal. If only three or four support it, we'll keep it on the backburner and discuss it with the US. Take the example of plastic lenses for head-lamps. A European company proposed these. There was opposition that they would not last. So a regulation was drafted on durability standards. But there still was opposition for ten to twelve years. Then the US and Japan introduced them, so it was taken off the backburner here.

Of course not all states in the EU and WP29 are major automotive manufacturing states. These other states tend to be cynical about the industry domination of delegations from states such as Germany and France. They see their responsibility as protecting the interests of their consumers against what they perceive to be the industry capture of the manufacturing states. Hence, when a cost-effective new safety technology might become available to their consumers, they will tend to support Germany if it is seeking to get a strategic trade advantage for DaimlerBenz against opposition from France, the UK, Japan and the US (who do not want to suffer the concomitant trade disadvantage). They will oppose Germany if they see the new BAT as exorbitantly costly for consumers or if they see the German proposal as locking the regulatory framework into specification (as opposed to performance) standards that will disadvantage other safety technologies that might emerge from competing manufacturers. The states of Europe not involved in the type of manufacture at issue (e.g. most states with motorcycle or truck manufacture) are the most important bulwarks against industry capture in the world system.

Influential European informants claim that in this strategic trade game, the US uses waivers to further increase its national advantage:

> The US regulates on the new technology leader immediately. The technology leader has an interest in forcing higher technical standards that they have enabled on all their competitors. But if Ford can't do it after GM invents it, Ford will successfully lobby for a waiver. Foreign companies won't get the waiver. Europe has less flexibility. We can't postpone or grant waivers as in the US. Its impossible in a multinational context. As soon as a technology is available to every European manufacturer and is economically feasible, the new BAT comes in.

Actually, there are sources of regulatory inflexibility on both sides of the Atlantic. At WP29, the requirement for unanimous agreement from all states that have applied a regulation before it can be amended is an impediment to regulatory change. In the US, the requirements of the

Administrative Procedure Act for regulatory impact analyses is, perhaps ironically, often a source of major delay in implementing regulatory change desired by both US manufacturers and consumers.

Another European informant pursued this line:

> The advantage for GM of getting their new technology into US regs is not just that they make Ford get it. Foreign manufacturers will have to use it locally even if they don't at home at first and then it is more likely to become feasible globally. The US are champions in using technical standards for trade policy.

Only the US (with Canada almost always following it) has a large enough domestic market, and a significant market for imports, to play a national strategic trade game of this sort. Japan and Korea cannot. Germany can only play it by capturing the EC. While Japan is not proactive in playing the strategic trade game, it can be an effective resister of the proposals of other states when its manufacturers advise their government that they will have difficulty meeting a new BAT: 'The Japanese often don't want to align with Europe for trade barrier reasons. So the EC and Japan have bilaterals'.

Industry associations tend to become involved in lobbying on generic problems for the industry, often shying away from issues that cut across efforts by specific members to introduce or resist new standards. However, they tend to be a voice against a higher regulatory standard being imposed on the industry as a result of one of their members creating a new BAT, unless the technology can be purchased by all their members. They also tend to be a voice for performance standards rather than specification standards that pose greater dangers as non-tariff barriers. National associations, such as the US Motor Vehicle Manufacturers Association, belong to the OICA in Paris (the International Organization of Motor Vehicle Manufacturers). The OICA 'has furnished studies and draft proposals for new or amended UN/ECE Regulations, e.g. pollution and noise, braking and steering, buses and coaches, lighting and light-signalling, frontal and lateral collision. OICA has also given editorial support to the ECE secretariat by preparing complete texts of extensive draft Regulations or their revision' (ECE 1993: 47). OICA has nine groups of experts which mirror the ECE meetings of experts. These OICA groups prepare comments on all agenda items for ECE meetings.

The International Motorcycle Manufacturers Association (IMMA) 'has furnished contributions to most of the 27 ECE Regulations which currently apply to motor cycles and mopeds or their components' (ECE 1993: 47). The international industry association for component manufacturers – CLEPA (Liaison Committee for the Manufacture of Automobile Equipment and Spare Parts) – is also active in international standard-setting. In more specialized areas, it is European peak bodies, not global ones, which liaise with the ECE. Key specialist peaks have been the European Tire and Rim Technical Organization and the Federation of European Manufacturers of Friction Materials (which have been concerned with eliminating asbestos in brake linings). The ACEA (Association des Constructeurs Européens d'Automobiles) is an important European umbrella body with consultative status to the EC.

The insurance industry is nowhere near as important a player with motor vehicle safety regulation as it is with ship safety, even though motor vehicle insurance losses are greater than ship losses and compulsory insurance began in states such as New Zealand in the 1920s (Plowden 1971: 245). The key difference is that ship insurance is 'lumpier'. It is worthwhile for insurers to insist on improved self-regulatory performance from large, high-risk ships. The transaction costs of doing so cannot be justified for the relatively modest loss-risk of even the most expensive motor vehicle. Most insurers have adopted a purely actuarial approach to motor vehicle insurance – let the costs fall as they may and set premiums to cover them. An important exception has been a group of US insurers forming the National Insurance Institute for Highway Safety. Ralph Nader had a hand in encouraging insurers to set up this group. It played a particularly important role working with Nader in the successful campaign for compulsory airbag installation in motor vehicles.

## NGOs

The most important NGOs are the voluntary standards organizations, particularly the International Organization for Standardization (ISO). ISO standards serve as a basis for many WP29 standards or as a reference for them. The NHTSA incorporates standards from the American Society for Testing and Materials (ASTM) and the National Institute of Standards and Technology into US regulations. Regulators on both sides of the Atlantic adopt the attitude that if sound engineering deliberation on voluntary standards organizations has come up with a standard acceptable to the industry, 'why should we waste taxpayers' money reinventing the wheel' with a new standard 'especially if a proliferation of standards will add to confusion'.

Consumer groups have built rather feebly on the initial early impact of *Unsafe at Any Speed*. In the US, the Center for Auto Safety, the Institute for Injury Prevention and Public Citizen are important influences on NHTSA. Indeed, one chief executive of Public Citizen, Joan Claybrook, became the administrator of NHTSA. Only in the 1990s did Consumers International start attending WP29 meetings, sending a representative who seems to command respect, some influence and a lot of opposition. Consumers International has concentrated on the issue of passive safety – frontal and lateral crash-testing, child restraints, safety-belts and helmets for motorcycles. As one insider put it: 'The [Consumers International] representative at WP29 is quite influential. He can get publicity, so they listen to him. In a certain respect the consumer movement is dangerous to manufacturers and governments. But they are not seen as irresponsible. [Consumers International] changed outcomes on some restraint issues'. Similarly, BEUC (the peak body of European consumer organizations) is a respected participant in formulating motor vehicle directives at Brussels.

The International Automobile Federation (FIA) represents eighty million families of motorists who are organized into automobile clubs in 105 countries. In most smaller nations the automobile clubs are more energetic participants in standard-setting than the generalist consumer groups. At WP29, the FIA puts positions on a wider range of safety and environmental protection issues than Consumers International. Its representatives enjoy superior technical backup compared to Consumers International representatives. The FIA tends to see itself as a partner with the industry and is therefore reluctant to engage in media assaults on the industry.

The Society of Automotive Engineers is an important professional force in US standard-setting and has developed a number of significant voluntary standards.

## Epistemic Communities, Mass Publics

WP29 is clearly the most important site of a global epistemic community of automotive standards, though ISO is also important. While engineers from the major manufacturers are commanding players, we have seen that there are many types of significant participants in the epistemic community, including technically competent consumer representatives. Beyond this epistemic community, not only have mass publics been more important than the organized consumer movement, there are important senses in which the modern consumer movement was actually created by the response of the mass public to *Unsafe at Any Speed*.

## Contest of Principles

### Deregulation v. Strategic Trade

At an abstract level, the automotive industry complains regularly and loudly about the cost of regulation and the need for deregulation. Firms urge their industry associations to march under the banner of deregulation or reducing regulatory costs. However, whenever a firm can secure a competitive advantage by strengthening a standard it can meet more easily than its competitors, that firm is likely to persuade its home state to pursue the strategic trade advantage of the new standard. When it does so, it is likely to find support from the public and from non-manufacturing states which respond to public demand. It is also likely to encounter opposition from competitors which invoke the principle of the cost of regulation, with support from the states in which they are located. This means that industry support for the principle of deregulation is equivocal; the principle is continually weakened because the strongest firms repeatedly undermine it. The historical outcome is overall regulatory growth rather than deregulation. Even so, the contest between the principle of deregulation and the principle of strategic trade is the key contest for shaping the motor vehicle regime.

### Lowest-cost Location v. World's Best Practice

There is no point in firms locating in states where standards for domestic sales are lower than elsewhere. Vehicles manufactured in such a place would be unexportable to the big markets in North America, Europe and North Asia. All major firms opt for credible regulatory standards over the principle of lowest-cost location with respect to regulatory demands (and labour costs). They invest in R&D in the hope that it will develop innovations that put their firm ahead of the pack in terms of cost-effective safety and fuel efficiency. They aim for a world's best practice that is hard for their competitors to match, while resisting world's best practice when regulation tries to force them to live up to a competitor's new benchmark. Mostly, they do not as individual firms plan to lag behind on safety and environmental challenges, though collectively they seek to hold the pack back. What manufacturers will do is produce cheaper production runs for markets with less stringent safety standards, when doing so does not involve costly retooling. Hence, Japanese exporters produce cars with weaker, lighter, more fuel-efficient bodies for the Asian market than for the US market. Indeed, in the 1970s when Californian laws on vehicle emissions were much tougher than in the rest of the US, General Motors sold cleaner cars there and dirtier cars throughout the rest of the US (Nader & Taylor 1986: 75). Double standards certainly, but not locating in the states where standards are lowest.

### Rule Compliance v. Continuous Improvement

We have seen that major manufacturers invest in R&D in an attempt to continuously improve on safety and emissions, yet the commitment to continuous improvement is partial. If an improvement in safety or fuel efficiency is not one they developed and can sell – this means most improvements – they resist it vigorously. If their resistance fails and a new standard is introduced to reflect a new BAT, they follow the principle of rule compliance, doing the minimum possible to meet the legal standard. Sometimes they will not even satisfy rule compliance, seeking a waiver until they think that the new standard has become economically feasible.

## National Sovereignty v. Harmonization, Mutual Recognition

National sovereignty is a strong principle in the US, as shown in its decision to go it alone with self-certification. But even in the US it is a weakened principle. In neighbouring Canada there is little semblance of national sovereignty in this domain. As a practical matter, it is not an option for Canada to diverge widely from the approach set by the US. Similarly, as much as Sweden might want to set higher standards than the rest of Europe, being part of the European market imposes severe limits on how far Sweden can diverge from WP29 expectations. As much as Russia might want to set less demanding standards, if it wants to be a serious car manufacturer it has to make good-faith efforts to apply WP29 norms. From 1996, national sovereignty disappeared in Europe for motor vehicle safety, with fifty mandatory EU directives replacing national requirements throughout the EU.

The WP29 accomplishment has been to move away from national sovereignty in favour of mutual recognition of type approvals, based on increasingly internationally harmonized performance standards. There is considerable harmonization of the performance standards that underpin both US self-certification and type approval. Global harmonization on test protocols and test equipment is an important part of this. European regulators frequently visit the US, for example, to witness crash-testing of vehicles so that these tests can be granted recognition in Europe.

## National Treatment, Most Favoured Nation, Reciprocity

Nations seem to do their best to respect the Most Favoured Nation principle – extending a regulatory privilege to one importing nation creates enormous pressure to extend the same privilege to others. Formally, national treatment is a strong principle in motor vehicle safety regulation. If Australia audits test facilities for fitness to test to Australian Design Rules it, like most nations, will impose the same requirements on other countries either by sending Australian inspectors overseas to do the audits or by reaching bilateral arrangements with agents (such as local regulatory authorities) in those countries. There is reciprocity in using each other's auditing capabilities. But the principle of reciprocity is not extended to the approval of arrangements where one nation imposes more lax safety requirements on imports from another in return for similar treatment of its exports.

National treatment is widely honoured in the breach, however. If not in theory, in practice the NHTSA is more likely to grant a waiver to Chrysler than to Saab. Japan and the US 'manage' trade in motor vehicles, applying reciprocal agreements to meet targets with respect to each other's automotive imports and exports. In part these targets are accomplished by manipulating non-tariff barriers on trade with other nations. The EU, like the US, sometimes sets its standards in a way that favours local manufacturers. On neither side of the Atlantic, however, is this as blatant or as easy to do as it was in the past when specification standards were more common.

## Transparency

Many nations have not been at all transparent in their motor vehicle regulatory decision-making, largely concealing captured relationships between industry and government and excluding consumer and motoring organizations from participation in decision-making. Fear that motor vehicle safety regulation is being used as a non-tariff barrier has created pressure for transparency. WP29 has played a valuable role in imposing expectations on participants that their regulatory practices be transparent, as has the WTO's Trade Policy Review Process. In response, WP29 receives submissions, such as the following by Japan:

> the Ministry of Transport prepares the draft for enactment or amendment of a motor vehicle standard, while maintaining the transparency of drafting process, for example, offering opportunities for allowing foreign parties concerned to express their views. After following those steps, the Ministry of Transport notifies GATT of the planned enactment or amendment, finally leading to promulgation of the standard concerned (ECE 1993: 57).

In a world in which the EC, WP29, the WTO, foreign governments and foreign manufacturers all demand greater transparency in national regulatory deliberation, citizens also benefit from the publication and public discussion of draft standards. The fact that global fora nurture transparency (often against the resistance of national regimes) was well-illustrated during our research when the secretariat of WP29 granted us permission to sit in on a meeting of the working party, but the Australian delegation successfully objected to our admission.

## Mechanisms

### Military Coercion

We know of no semblance of military coercion being used in the process of globalizing the regulation of motor vehicle standards.

### Economic Coercion

Economic coercion has been minimal in bringing about the globalization of regulation. The EU has used the lever of denying the economic benefit of admission to the EU to Eastern Europe until there is strong evidence of compliance with EU directives, including motor vehicle standards directives. Germany has threatened to close Eastern European truck access to its road transport corridors until bilateral agreements are signed committing Eastern Europe to EU standards.

The US seems to have applied economic coercion remarkably little in this domain. There is little point in attempting to economically coerce states into following US standards in a world where ECE standards are dominant. And Europe is too big for the US to dominate. The main game is one of mutual influence between the US and Europe, a negotiation game between more or less economic equals.

### Systems of Reward

For the same reason that coercion has been unimportant, systematic rewards for nations or firms to comply with either ECE or US standards do not seem to have been applied.

## Modelling

The ECE is a forum that facilitates regulatory modelling. Nations table their proposed regulatory innovations at this forum. When a nation proposes a draft regulation, the innovation goes on the backburner unless there are other nations interested in modelling the idea. Many countries are like Australia, modelling WP29 (EC) standards most of the time, but sometimes modelling US regulations. Dialogue at WP29 discusses how such states weigh the merits of each kind of modelling. Strengthening the principle of transparency has greatly facilitated this modelling.

Individual firms cope with new BATs by forming joint ventures with firms which are ahead in the relevant technology. This is a form of modelling. When modelling of a particular safety innovation within the industry becomes sufficiently widespread, this lays the basis for a new global standard requiring all firms to adopt the innovation. The modelling of seatbelt installation reflects this pattern; perhaps the current voluntary modelling of airbag installation is laying the foundations for airbags to be an example of the same innovation–modelling–regulation sequence.

## Reciprocal Adjustment and Non-reciprocal Coordination

We have seen that reciprocal adjustment is substantial between the two big players, the US and Europe. A good example was provided by the Director of International Harmonization at NHTSA:

> Harmonization does not have to mean identical standards. It can mean a window of compliance. For example, on the intensity of rear yellow [amber] lights [direction indicators], the European maximum and the US minimum were the same. So there was only one level that was right for both. They changed their maximum and we changed our minimum to create a window, based on mutually acceptable research.

Non-reciprocal coordination does not seem to be an important mechanism. While motor vehicle standards have been discussed in US–Japan trade talks, we cannot identify any historic bargains to trade motor vehicle standards for some other trade benefit.

## Capacity-building

Technical assistance is quite limited in this domain of regulation. Perhaps this is because the manufacturing states want developing countries simply to accept their standards and their type approvals of vehicle models without dabbling in new standards. Indeed, this is what most developing countries do, having no effective regulation of vehicle standards of their own. The NHTSA is unusual among major US regulatory agencies in having no technical assistance program, though regulators from developing countries do visit the NHTSA on a regular basis. Nor does the German Ministry of Transport have a significant program. Both WP29 and the EC have tiny secretariats with no capability for giving technical assistance.

## *Conclusion*

Globalization of standards has been substantial and recent with motor vehicles. While there is a contest between European type approval and US self-certification combined with an active recall program, underlying the two models is growing convergence on performance standards. Under the two converging umbrellas, safety and environmental standards have been slowly led up rather than down, with a little reciprocal adjustment down by states such as Sweden. There is little doubt that standards in Eastern Europe, Asia and Australia have been raised by the North Atlantic powers, with tens of thousands of lives saved annually as a result.

Nader's *Unsafe at Any Speed* was a catalyst of rising mass concern over safety that motorists' associations, consumer groups, governments and finally the industry itself took up. The industry is now persuaded that safety sells, and invests in R&D accordingly. When manufacturers develop a safety improvement, they and their host state seek to persuade the EC, WP29 and NHTSA (and sometimes ISO) to give them the strategic trade advantage of a new or higher standard to reflect the new BAT they have developed. Because regulators have responded to the demand for greater safety from mass publics and their political leaders, on both sides of the Atlantic they are committed to continually upgrading standards in response to new BATs, so they are responsive to a proposal for a new standard from the innovating state. Non-manufacturing states tend to be particularly supportive as long as the innovation will not cause a substantial rise in the price of a car. But all the other firms which lag on the new BAT are likely to resist the standard, as are regulatory bureaucrats from their home states who are captives of industry.

A drawn-out struggle is likely, with most of the auto industry and most of the manufacturing states on one side and, on the other, the innovating manufacturer and its state, mass publics, consumer and motorists' groups and non-manufacturing states sympathetic to their mass publics. It is unclear who will win any such struggle. Professional engineering opinions on the magnitude of the likely safety benefits and the likely costs often carry the balance of power within the epistemic community. What is almost certain is that whichever side prevails, will not do so quickly. Even the most obviously cost-effective innovations, like seatbelts, experienced a tortuously slow path to global adoption. However, globalization has occurred. And the design of this particular regulatory ratchet as a competition between two BAT regimes is of a slow ratchet-up.

The fact that the long-term direction of the global ratchet is up rather than down increases firms' incentive to invest in safety R&D to get the kind of strategic trade advantage that Porter (1990: 648) describes in *The Competitive Advantage of Nations*: 'Particularly beneficial are stringent regulations [or self-regulation] that *anticipate* standards that will spread internationally'.

This paints too cynical a picture of the global epistemic community we discovered during our research. Although it is the hard-edged realities of strategic trade and the responsiveness of vote-maximizing governments to the demands of mass publics that drive the direction of the ratchet, at another level the epistemic community is driven by a dispassionate scientific discourse of automotive engineering. The epistemic community is populated by regulatory bureaucrats who might be from the home state of manufacturers fiercely opposed to a new standard, but who read the research and conclude that the standard should be supported because of the evidence that lives can be saved at low engineering cost. It is populated by corporate automotive engineers who indicate at the relevant tables that their company is opposed to the standard, but tell their firm how easy it would be to make the engineering changes to make the standard work.

The strategic trade game is not the conspiracy against the public interest that it once might have been, for two main reasons. One is the shift from specification to performance standards. In a world where Renault could prevail on France to ensure that all cars had headlights of a certain lurid yellow incandescence, French consumers were deprived of competition in price and safety. But in a world where any car can be registered in France that meets EU performance standards on lights, the French public has better prospects of cheaper and safer cars. A new BAT that moves the required performance upwards is only a strategic advantage to the owner of the BAT until its competitors invent their own technologies to meet or surpass the BAT, or until it sells the technology to competitors on licence during negotiation of the new standard.

The second reason why the strategic trade game is not the conspiracy against the public interest that it once was, is that the new global regulation is more transparent and more deliberative than most of the old state regulation. States are required to make their case for new regulations in international fora in the presence of consumer representatives, motorists' associations and hostile manufacturers from rival manufacturing states. These parties produce written analyses of draft regulatory proposals, which are widely disseminated. The standards of disclosure and reason-giving do not match those of the US Administrative Procedure Act, but they surpass the traditional practices of most states. Indeed, the work of WP29 disseminates globally the regulatory deliberation that does occur pursuant to the US Administrative Procedure Act and adds many expert voices to it. At WP29, proposing states must give reasons for their draft standards. These reasons are dissected in the meetings of experts that the EC, WP29, industry associations like OICA and consumer interests like FIA set up in advance of full deliberation at ECE. All this committee work generates a great deal of written analysis that is widely available to interested parties.

Under the old regulation of national sovereignty, it would be common for South Korea, for example, to do the regulatory bidding of Hyundai in a smoke-filled room when Hyundai wanted a new non-tariff barrier. The national sovereign would not be required to provide good reasons; there was no risk that its reasoning might become known to consumer groups, let alone excoriated by their critiques. The post-1980 global regulatory order no longer works this way. South Korea will have to give reasons for the regulation, in Geneva. These reasons will be exposed to critique by hostile foreign firms, by independent professionals from non-manufacturing states or from the Society of Automotive Engineers, and by consumer advocates. If the standard is a spurious one, the South Korean public will find out by Consumers International passing the information to Korean consumer groups. South Korea will risk a WTO complaint and panel hearing over the non-tariff barrier and it may jeopardize type approval of its vehicles in states that have performance standards which are deliberatively defensible.

While democracies have lost national sovereignty, the new global regulatory order in this domain has strengthened the republican virtues of transparency and public-regarding deliberation. It also institutionalizes a new kind of separation of powers among states, business elites, professionals, international organizations and representatives of mass publics. This novel separation of powers delivers a contestation that protects against the worst excesses of domination by a state–industrial complex. It would be romantic to see this as republican contestation displacing the iron triangle of private lobbyists, corrupt legislators and captured bureaucrats, just as it is a mistake to reduce the strategic trade manoeuvres of car-makers to no more than self-interested profiteering. Much of the contestation is private interest masquerading as public concern; much of the strategic trade manoeuvring represents the dedicated work of engineers at Hyundai who really want to make cars safer for people.

CHAPTER **19** Air Transport

Air transport regulation is different from that of sea and road transport in that economic regulation (explicitly excluded from the domain of the IMO and WP29) looms as large as safety regulation. The reason for this is that the air transport industry is structurally much more like telecommunications than are sea or road transport. Just as almost every nation has its own telecommunications carrier (and rarely more than one), almost every nation has a flagship airline (and rarely more than one). The state controls landing rights (just as it tends to control the telecommunications infrastructure) and rations those rights, usually in ways that favour the national flag-carrier. In comparison, the delivery of sea and road travel is much more decentralized, access to the sea and the roads less rationable.

## History of Globalization

### ICAN–IATA

The First World War developed the recent invention of the aeroplane into a vehicle that could be used for commercial transport. So at the Versailles Peace Conference of 1919, the International Convention for Air Navigation was signed and the International Commission for Air Navigation (ICAN) created. ICAN was concerned with technical coordination on matters such as the rules for the safe operation of airports, radio communications and the like (what later came to be known as flight standards). The year 1919 also saw the first incarnation of the International Air Transport Association (IATA), an association of European airlines that admitted its first US member in 1938. Before the Second World War IATA was not involved in the regulation of fares, being preoccupied with reaching agreement on the procedures for handling air traffic.

As with shipping, regulation of the design safety of aircraft was initiated by insurers. In the US, Underwriters Laboratories, at the request of the National Aircraft Underwriters' Association, formed an aviation department in 1920 to certify the airworthiness of aircraft and develop airworthiness standards (Cheit 1990b: 79), a function ultimately taken over by the Federal Aviation Administration (FAA).

## ICAO–IATA

The degree of globalization of regulation was quite limited until the Second World War because air travel was mainly regional. After the Second World War trans-Atlantic flight became common-place in the wake of the huge technical leap in aviation delivered by the war. US President Roosevelt saw this coming and convened the International Civil Aviation Conference in Chicago in 1944. The Chicago Convention on International Civil Aviation was a framework convention, setting out general rules under which international air transport could be operated and establish-ing the International Civil Aviation Organization (ICAO) to take over the functions of ICAN. ICAO would harmonize the licensing of pilots and mechanics, navigational aids, maintenance schedules for aircraft, and other technical matters, interline arrangements for fare transfers, cus-toms arrangements, freedom to enter the airspace of sovereign nations and the like. Roosevelt used late-war US hegemony to decisively shift the prewar international coordinating institutions – ICAN and IATA – from their European domination, to engender a freedom of the skies that US industry could dominate. The postwar ICAO and IATA were located in Montreal and thenceforth the US did dominate the globalization of the divergent systems of regulation that had evolved on opposite sides of the Atlantic. FAA continued to provide the full-time services of US staff mem-bers for the ICAO into the 1960s. The Soviet Union pulled out of the Chicago Conference at the last moment and decided to deny other nations the right to overfly the skies it controlled, setting up a separate regulatory system for the Eastern bloc (Gidwitz 1980: 46).

The postwar IATA had two functions. First, it was the industry association for airlines that represented their interests at ICAO as ICAO began globalizing flight standards and airworthiness regulations for aircraft. Second, IATA became a kind of global economic regulator after the war. It established the machinery for agreeing fares and rates among international air transport com-panies. An important part of this machinery was Traffic Conferences, based on geographic areas, for reaching agreement on pricing arrangements. A critical bilateral agreement on flights between the two major civil aviation powers, the US and UK (the Bermuda Agreement), became a model for 4000 subsequent bilateral agreements (Brancker 1977: 37). Bilateralism was complemented by the IATA Traffic Conferences because fares into the Netherlands, for example, could not be set-tled in a vacuum that did not consider fares into Belgium. IATA therefore coordinated the setting of mutually acceptable prices for the same traffic corridors, in effect coordinating a series of geo-graphic cartels.

The postwar reality was ICAO being responsible for technical regulation and IATA for eco-nomic regulation. IATA, an association of airlines, became the most significant private inter-national economic regulator the world has seen. At the height of its power, the secret economic regulation of IATA reached extraordinary levels. It had a Compliance Office to check for 'malprac-tices' such as illegal discounting and to levy heavy fines. The extent of its regulatory intervention-ism is illustrated by the 'sandwich war': 'the "sandwich war" erupted when SAS began serving a sandwich described by its competitors as more than a sandwich and therefore improper under existing regulations. SAS countered that its sandwiches were of the larger Scandinavian variety and that surely airlines should be permitted to serve food according to national tradition' (Gid-witz 1980: 95).

### Global Economic Deregulation

The US was never an enthusiastic participant in IATA-orchestrated cartelization, considering it contrary to the philosophy of US antitrust law. At the 1944 Chicago Conference, the US wanted free skies and a free market for air travel. All other countries resisted this, fearing 'the specter of the American colossus, untouched by war devastation and well-supplied with aircraft, dominating international civil aviation' (Gidwitz 1980: 48). So the IATA system of economic regulation had widespread support from sovereign nations as well as the industry. But there were corporate dissenters driving in wedges to destabilize the regional cartels. Singapore Airlines and several other Asian airlines stayed out of arrangements that they saw as entrenching the interests of the older Western airlines. The US carriers, Northwest and Delta, withdrew from IATA in the 1970s.

In the US the 1970s saw a resurgence in commitment to competition as opposed to economic regulation. Airline deregulation was a high priority, attracting a seemingly implausible coalition of support from consumerist liberals, notably Ralph Nader, and pro-business economic rationalists, such as Alfred Kahn (Chairman of the Civil Aeronautics Board in the late 1970s). President Carter became a strong supporter of airline deregulation. In 1977 a new bilateral agreement between the US and UK, Bermuda II, was negotiated. Its tariff clause downgraded the role of IATA, ushering a new bilateralism in fare-setting that destabilized IATA cartelization. Then came domestic US economic deregulation of airlines in 1978. In the same year, the US Civil Aeronautics Board issued a show-cause order, an interim finding that IATA Traffic Conference procedures were not in the public interest. This set in train the eventual revocation of antitrust immunity for US and foreign airlines who fixed prices into the US air services market. Both the US and the UK then set about reshaping their bilateral agreements toward more liberal policies. For example, France has been the most vigorous opponent of liberalization, so the US worked at isolating France by negotiating open-skies agreements with Belgium and other countries around France.

The 'open sky' bilaterals negotiated between the US and more than a dozen other states replaced the US–UK Bermuda Agreements as the influential new model. The two states party to an open-skies agreement allow their airlines to fly any route as often as they like between the two countries and beyond (in slot-constrained airports, as often as they can secure a slot in non-discriminatory competition with other carriers).

A group of nations became supporters of the US-led liberalization, the UK, the Netherlands, Australia, New Zealand, Singapore and Canada being the most committed. 'Perhaps a maximum of only twenty states support open skies. But these might account for 70 per cent of international flights', was the opinion of one insider. France and Japan were the most powerful resisters of the push toward liberalization. They enjoyed enormous numerical support at IATA, with virtually universal support from Africa and South America. IATA cartelization remains strong on the latter two continents, with IATA fighting a rearguard action against liberalization everywhere else, slowly losing its hold on rate-setting. The IATA interlining price continues to be some sort of benchmark in many markets.

In short, the process in the 1990s is US-led liberalization that is seeing the world become gradually and chaotically more competitive. The process is chaotic because even the most liberal states, such as the US and UK, in the words of one of our informants are 'liberal mercantilists': 'The British lecture everyone in Europe about open skies while being mercantilist in the extreme in their own practices'. Another chaotic element is that many European, African, and South American states support liberalization within their continents but want protection from competition outside the continent (especially from the US). A semblance of a trading bloc in air services – internally deregulated, externally protected – is emerging, particularly in Africa and South America.

The mercantilist elements in the bilateralism of all states holds back the process of liberalization, as does the explicit resistance of Japan, France, developing countries with national airlines and IATA. Arrayed against these forces on the liberalizing side are the manoeuvres of the liberal states led by the US, the European open-skies policy emerging from the European Court of Justice (LiCalzi 1987), the EC and an ICAO that knows it will lose regime authority to a WTO takeover unless it fosters some progress toward liberalization.

The WTO's General Agreement on Trade in Services (GATS) is only nibbling at the deregulation of air transport through an annex on the repair and maintenance of aircraft, sale and marketing of air transportation and computer reservation systems: 'IATA rules and air transport rules are swept under the carpet for the moment [at the WTO]' (1995 USTR interview).

But the ICAO is haunted by the WIPO–WTO spectre of the TRIPs agreement (Chapter 7) – that the US might succeed in shifting much of the content of its specialist regime to the generalist trade regime of the WTO. While this spectre remains unrealized, states have an interest in holding back on airline deregulation. It can then be something they trade in a basket of trade reforms at the WTO. Once they have deregulated, they have thrown away that chip. Still, trade offers at the WTO are not the only chips to be swapped. Iceland wanted a US military base, and traded airline deregulation for it.

## Global Regulatory Growth on Flight Standards and Airworthiness

ICAO continued the work of ICAN after the Second World War in substantially harmonizing flight standards concerns from pilot and mechanic training, to standardization on English communication protocols, separation rules for flight paths and so on. ICAO mounted substantial technical assistance programs to developing countries on flight standards and ultimately responded to US demands to audit national compliance with ICAO standards. When ICAO implementation teams find persistent failure to meet ICAO obligations, other states are advised of their right to deny aircraft of the non-complying state access to their territory.

The US FAA has always had global reach of regulatory influence because it regulates the flight standards performance of US operators throughout the world, and has had regional FAA offices across the globe for this purpose since the war. Repair stations everywhere have been continuously inspected by FAA and many other national authorities. Joint ventures of US operators with foreign airlines, for example KLM and Northwest's seamless approach to travel where personnel are shared and maintenance practices are jointly approved, have long given the FAA leverage off-shore.

In 1993 the FAA introduced an International Aviation Safety Assessment Program. This program began to audit the compliance of over a hundred national civil aviation agencies with ICAO annexes concerning aviation safety. Assessments are made of targeted foreign airlines. When it finds inadequate standards, the US adopts a 'softly, softly' approach, in the words of FAA's Flight Standards Director, because it 'fears retaliatory measures by just pulling the plug on them'. Nevertheless, the International Aviation Safety Assessment Program is explicit in threatening cessation of flying rights to the US for countries and airlines that do not satisfy

ICAO standards. The FAA displays publicly at US airports lists of foreign airports that have failed its safety assessment.

US domination of airworthiness regulation since the Second World War has been even greater. Since then, over 80 per cent of commercial planes (excluding those from communist countries) were manufactured in the US. FAA certifies each aircraft individually as airworthy before it can go into service. Because new aircraft reach the US market first, they get their first regulatory approval from the US even though they will be ultimately destined for many countries. Cheit (1990b: 67) points out that the FAA:

> functions by leaving much to the discretionary judgment of the airlines and airframe manufacturers. Aviation technology is so complicated that the FAA realized years ago it did not have the resources or expertise to pass judgment independently on all new airframe designs. Instead, 'designated engineering representatives', engineers employed by the airframe manufacturers, certify new airplanes for the agency.

The FAA is in a game of technological catch-up with industry leaders who have a more holistic view of what is required to make a new design configuration safe. So in some important senses firms like Boeing set the new rules for large aircraft in the US, which then become the design rules for large aircraft for the world. In various respects the airworthiness standards for small aircraft follow those for large aircraft. The only airworthiness regimes substantially different from the US regime surrendered to conformity with FAA norms – France, the UK, then the Soviet Union in 1990.

Once Boeing has received FAA certification for its first production run of a new aircraft, other national regulators will send teams to Seattle for the purpose of granting type certification for their market. Most will send a team of three to twenty experts for a period of one to three weeks. 'Everybody sending a team over to rubberstamp it to their rules is expensive', in the words of one Boeing executive we interviewed, especially when the capacity to make regulatory decisions different from the US is circumscribed.

The Joint Aviation Authorities (JAA) started to coordinate European safety regulation in a modest way in 1970 (as the Joint Airworthiness Authorities). This coordination has since extended to twenty-three countries and all areas of regulation affecting safety except air traffic control (a responsibility of Eurocontrol) and airport standards (a national responsibility to conform with ICAO standards). Today a single joint certification team, working on behalf of all JAA countries, certifies new aircraft and engines, allowing the simultaneous issue of type certificates by all JAA states. The original set of JAA standards for large aircraft were the FAA standards. In 1998, EU transport ministers agreed to establish a European Aviation Safety Authority over the next three years with the aspiration of matching the FAA as a regulatory player.

The world airplane has not developed as far as the world car. However, Boeing airliners are made from components manufactured in a number of countries. This generates part of the imperative for globalized regulation. The fact that most of the large aircraft are finally assembled in the US generates the imperative for US domination of regulation.

Fatalities per 100 million passengers have fallen significantly since the 1980s (ICAO 1993: 10), though not as dramatically as motor vehicle fatalities. A raging debate proceeds over whether globalizing economic deregulation has globalized a precariousness in airline profitability that has resulted in widespread corner-cutting on safety. FAA targets special safety inspections on financially troubled carriers at risk of bankruptcy to protect against this happening. In less-regulated parts of the world, it is hard to believe that loss-making airlines would not seek to survive liberalization by cutting safety costs. At the time of writing, however, both safety and airline profitability seem to be slowly improving.

## Actors

### States

The US has clearly been and continues to be a hegemonic influence on the globalization of the regulation of air transport. This arises from its domination of production and strategic action to create international agencies in its own image and threaten to abandon them when they do not conform to that image. In the section on harmonization below we will see that another reason for the US domination of this arena, compared to its failure to dominate the other pre-marketing clearance regimes for products – drugs, ships and cars – has been the FAA's rather sophisticated cultural sensitivity that always eluded agencies like the FDA. The US needs the goodwill that FAA eschewal of aggressive parochialism has wrought. There is some distrust of satellite-landing capability for automatic landing of aircraft, for example. States worry about handing the capacity to switch off such a capability to a US-controlled satellite – a worry they do not have with a terrestrial facility under national control.

Historically the US has operated by setting standards in response to the new technologies that have almost invariably arisen in the US first, then proceeded to seek to persuade the ICAO and the JAA to adopt those US standards. In recent years, however, the US has put in place a variety of consultative mechanisms with the JAA and foreign governments in advance of US rule-making so that it can take US standards to the ICAO with some international support.

In Europe, the UK has been a leader both on safety regulation and economic deregulation, as has been Germany, particularly on safety. France has been a laggard on both safety regulation and economic liberalization. Japan has been pushed by developing countries with national flag-carriers to lead the international resistance to liberalization, although with safety standards it has been quiescent in following US leadership.

The Soviet Union was an obstacle to globalization until 1990. It had a rather different set of standards from the rest of the world, which it enforced throughout Eastern Europe. However, now the FAA and Russia have a bilateral agreement which brings Russia into line with US standards, with some exceptions. One is that Russia has tougher standards concerning operation in very cold conditions, doubtless for good climatic reasons. The US has become less prescriptive in this area, requiring operators to develop de-icing plans appropriate to the environmental context where they operate. These tailor-made plans are then approved in climatic context by local FAA staff.

On the economic regulation of airlines, the simplifying assumption that states act is shown to be flawed. In many of the states that oppose liberalization, the Ministry of Trade supports liberalization. Even for France, the most potent national opponent of economic deregulation, French trade negotiators at WTO have been quite supportive of liberalization. In virtually every state, trade ministries are more powerful than transport ministries. Hence, if trade ministries decide that air transport deregulation is important enough, they may muscle aside transport ministries that are captives of their carriers. When it is the trade ministry doing the negotiations, as it increasingly is, national opponents may suddenly become national champions of liberalization.

More crucially, long-term prospects for the US to prevail over France, Japan and most of the rest of the world are bright because of the credibility with which it can threaten forum-shifting from ICAO to WTO and the strong likelihood that the trade ministries of many of its opponents will be effective in supporting the move.

## Organizations of States

The ICAO effectively covers the world, with 183 members. Proactive compliance auditing supported by a large staff (800 in total for ICAO) distinguishes ICAO from the IMO and the ECE, indeed almost all the UN agencies in this study. The ICAO is at some risk of declining as a motor of globalization unless it also becomes a facilitater of liberalization. For the US, there is some appeal in forum-shifting from the hands of transport ministries at ICAO to trade ministries at WTO, particularly given the large number of ICAO votes held by developing countries opposed to liberalization, votes that count for little at the WTO. Another attraction of the WTO as a forum for considering the economic regulation of air transport is that the EC (that is, not France), did the air services negotiations for the Uruguay Round of GATT on behalf of EC members.

The JAA has been an important actor, though it has hardly approached the importance of FAA or ICAO. In addition to the reasons we have already articulated for why it has followed rather than led, there is the sheer question of resources. Its budget in the mid 1990s was less than $US4 million compared to an FAA budget in excess of $US10 billion. 'It is a club, not really a single authority', in the words of one insider. Unlike FAA which certifies individual aircraft, JAA does only type certifications for new models on behalf of member states. On the other hand, JAA has been motivated to prove to the EU that it is a substantial command organization, an authority capable of making a lot of rules that member states and the industry follow. Its hope was that the EU might increase the recognition granted to it and vote it extra resources. Instead the EU has decided to establish the European Aviation Safety Authority. The EC has tended to incorporate JAA standards into European law without reconsideration or revision.

With more resources, the JAA could upgrade its modest program of multinational standardization teams that spend a week auditing the performance of national authorities against JAA standards. Standardization team reports identifying problems that require remedy from the national authority have been useful to European epistemic community building and have attracted constructive responses from member states.

An important regional organization is the African Civil Aviation Commission, a specialized agency of the Organization of African Unity, with forty-two African member states. It covers the setting of fares and cargo-pricing as well as flight standards and airworthiness. The Latin American Civil Aviation Commission fulfils similar functions.

The European Court of Justice has been an important actor in striking out cartelization in the European skies (LiCalzi 1987). Its decisions have created the climate for open-skies deregulation across both the EU and EFTA areas; even domestic routes are now open to foreign national carriers across Europe.

## Business Actors

Boeing is a particularly dominant business actor, especially since it merged with McDonnell-Douglas. It is exaggerating only a little to say that Boeing sets regulatory standards for the world.

Like ICAO, IATA enjoys wide coverage of its constituency, members accounting for over 90 per cent of scheduled international air services. It is perhaps the most lavishly staffed international business organization in the world, with 550 employees, a thousand if one includes bank settlement staff. Yet in the face of the US assault against it, IATA is declining in influence. Divisions among members run deep and will be hard to reconcile.

National and regional industry associations have not been key players in the globalization of air transport regulation. Airlines and major manufacturers like Boeing tend to represent themselves directly in international fora. Most airlines are part of their state, so some of the people who represent airlines at IATA represent states at ICAO. Of course, this was somewhat less true during the 1990s, with the spate of airline privatizations.

The US Chamber of Commerce was a critical supporter of the deregulatory shifts of the US government. It was also a strong advocate of cost–benefit analyses of new regulations. 'Down there at the Chamber of Commerce they realize they've shot themselves in the foot on that because it holds up getting aircraft into the market. Europeans don't do cost–benefit on new standards and that can be a benefit for them in being able to bring in economically competitive standards more quickly', in the words of one FAA observer of US Chamber of Commerce involvement.

## NGOs and Mass Publics

In many countries the organized consumer movement has provided the only NGOs that have consistently lobbied for economic deregulation of air transport. Business consumers of air services have been less vigorously represented by industry associations, who have either regarded it as a low priority or feared antagonizing their own members from the aviation industry. On air safety, Ralph Nader and his organization have been sporadically active in the US for twenty years (Nader & Smith 1993). More consistently active, and more respected by regulators for their depth of knowledge, is the International Airline Passengers Association (IAPA), which has over 100 000 members from 160 countries, who usually join by filling in a membership application advertised in airline magazines.

IAPA is often networked on safety issues with the International Federation of Airline Pilots Associations (IFALPA). IFALPA has its own corps of accredited accident investigators. Another player is the Council of International Aircraft Owner and Pilot Associations. In its literature the IAOPA says it 'was founded in 1964 in order to gain official observer status at ICAO…as a counterweight against airline domination of this organization' (http://www.canit.se/aopa_spaf/www-inte.htm). It is thus an example of the structuration point made in the conclusion to the sea transport chapter (Chapter 17). The IAOPA is not only an actor that stands independent of the international institutions as it seeks to shape them; international institutions created it. Other active NGOs with observer status at the ICAO are the International Transport Workers Federation and Consumers International. Pilot and union groups have been active at the JAA, participating on JAA committees, but not the consumer groups. Cabin workers' unions have been particularly active on cabin safety issues nationally and internationally, for example with the successful campaign in the US to prevent the Boeing 747 with ten-door exits being converted to an eight-door aircraft. The regulators we interviewed were awed by the power of NGOs when they could get their safety critiques aired on networked television programs, risking a panic from mass publics that can make the life of regulators very uncomfortable.

As Cheit's (1990b: 65–88) work shows, a variety of voluntary standard-setting organizations are also important to setting standards for smaller parts of aircraft.

### Epistemic Communities of Actors

The epistemic community for the economic regulation of aviation that has been organized around IATA since the Second World War is falling apart. For three decades from 1945 that epistemic community developed a shared regulatory discourse in Traffic Conferences and bilaterals. That shared discourse was shattered by the discourse of competition policy and free trade in services. Now there are two epistemic communities – the epistemic community of liberalizers and the epistemic community of regulators.

The safety epistemic community is more unified under US and ICAO leadership and fostered in Europe by the European Civil Aviation Conference and its associated body the JAA (ICAO 1993: 46–7). Some critics, such as Nader, stand apart from it. But the IAPA, together with key union and pilot representatives, are very much part of it. ICAO's TRAINAIR networking initiative for civil aviation training centres is an important contribution to epistemic community building.

The safety epistemic community is essentially a scientific epistemic community: 'Aerodynamics is aerodynamics. We were always able to talk to the Russians in the old communist days because science is science. Good scientific analyses are the same everywhere and that's the language we talk' (FAA official). The epistemic community separates itself from the world of mass media scaremongering about safety and political response to mass publics.

> **JB:** 'If one country has a disaster that leads to higher standards in that country as a result of a political backlash, do those higher standards spread throughout the world?'
>
> **FAA official:** 'Not necessarily. Sometimes you have political pressure that takes over safety decisions. But when the political decisions are not supported by the experts in the country, the professionals in other countries know and understand this and the higher standard does not spread internationally. An unusual accident somewhere that causes a country to have a tighter standard, well we all understand that authority's political predicament. Their standards on this are recognized for what they are. It is very rare for these outliers to become global standards.'

Politicians have only national power; technocrats have international power. Politicians play at the symbolic power of diverting taxpayers' resources to issues that agitate mass publics through their media profile. Technocrats networked in the global epistemic community have deep and wide power to structure the international regulatory agenda in the ways that really count for safety, cost and competitiveness.

Reputational capital in the epistemic community rests on independence from politics and industry:

> If political interference occurs on a regular basis, an authority can find it loses international respect. But we all understand that it will happen to everyone occasionally. You evaluate an authority by asking the question: 'Is the authority independent of the rest of the government? Is it able to make judgments without constant political pressure…or industry pressure? (FAA official).

An ideal way for industry engineers to enhance their reputational capital within the epistemic community is through diplomatic demonstrations of independence from the economic interests of their own firm, by showing a greater attachment to objective scientific analysis than to self-interest. Given the interest of their firms in having them respected within the epistemic community, the position of industry engineers is therefore paradoxical, thriving on astute hypocrisy of commitment to both loyalties.

## Contest of Principles

### National Sovereignty v. Harmonization, Mutual Recognition

The surrender of national sovereignty in the safety regime has been substantial. It is not excessively rhetorical to say that the sovereignty of Boeing exceeds and considerably supplants that of nation-states in this regime. Certainly no nation-state apart from the US can compete with Boeing as a shaper of the global airworthiness regime.

Global harmonization, much more than mutual recognition, has been the principle to which national sovereignty has succumbed. There is mutual recognition of type certifications, maintenance inspections and flight standards among countries, albeit only to the extent that they accomplish an adequate level of compliance with harmonized ICAO standards.

The tenacity of the principle of harmonization is reflected in the extremeness of the language regulators use in this regime. For example, the Deputy Director of the FAA's Aircraft Certification Service said: 'Harmonization absolute and complete is the goal. We may never get to 100 per cent, but the closer we get the better for everybody'. The manufacturer is seen as the main beneficiary of moving away from a world of 'performance-testing to different standards' and from a world where the manufacturer is required to 'design to an envelope of standards'.

There has been some shift to harmonization on performance standards rather than harmonization on specifications. 'Required navigational performance' can be complemented by a menu of acceptable means of attaining the required performance, leaving the operator to find other means should it wish. Plural acceptable means reduces harmonization of specifications, as it accomplishes harmonization of performance standards – a kind of harmonized diversity.

FAA leadership is critical to harmonization efforts. This leadership has been more culturally sensitive than in other regulatory domains. One senior FAA official put it this way: 'The problem is culture in harmonization. Cultural differences get wrapped up in our minds and affect what we do'. He pointed out that 'US regulators have to learn to be less aggressive' given that harmonization is 'done by relationships between people, for example by sharing perspectives on joint teams to approve foreign repair stations'. One might add that Japanese regulators need to learn to be more assertive if they are to have more productive input of their engineering perspectives. In the interests of harmonization, the FAA gives its staff cultural training.

ICAO has a procedure rather similar to IMO's tacit acceptance to force the pace of harmonization. The ICAO Commission on Air Navigation, with a membership of only twelve, in effect drafts the standards, which are passed by the council of thirty-three without reference to the full assembly of members. Yet these standards are binding for all members unless an objection is raised within a specified period. Luard (1977: 71–2) summarizes the sweep of the harmonization and the seemingly willing sacrifice of national sovereignty that has transpired:

> The 'standards' and 'practices' laid down in the Annexes to the Convention are revised periodically. The former are obligations on the members; and with the latter they must endeavour to conform as soon as possible. There are sixteen separate sets of these international standards and recommended

practices, each contained in a separate Annex. In addition there are 'procedures' (PANS) which are recommended only, but often later become standards or practices. There are also regional supplementary procedures peculiar to particular regions. Taken together, they represent a very large body of rules, established by an international authority and accepted by governments with virtually no resistance: here, therefore, international government is seen at work in its most painless form.

With economic regulation of air transport, commitment to both national sovereignty and harmonization of prices has weakened, slowly surrendering to the principle of consumer sovereignty in the marketplace.

## Deregulation v. Strategic Trade

Air transport has been an area where the principle of mercantilism and, more recently, strategic trade have been strong. The principle of strategic trade is manifest in agreements which give national airlines monopolies of preferential treatment on flight routes. Strategic trade drove European subsidization of the Airbus and technical standard-setting accommodating to it.

With economic regulation, we have seen a substantial strengthening of the principle of deregulation, led by the US. With safety regulation, the US has led a strengthening of regulation globally. US informants we interviewed were not reticent about confessing that US domination of global regulatory systems, followed with technical assistance on the systems, does confer a trade advantage on firms like Boeing: 'If Arabs are trained in US policies and procedures, they are more likely to buy the US product with systems geared to those standards. Also they learn to trust and ask: "Which do you think is better, John, the Boeing or the Airbus?"' Such strategic trade advantages must be kept in perspective, however. They have not been central to constituting Boeing's international success, which has been based on the quality and reliability of its products.

Flight standards do affect international competitiveness. State regulators can set low standards that allow their national airline to carry heavier loads, more passengers at lower cost, than competitors who fly in from nations with higher flight standards. Foreign competitors might be allowed in but on the basis of maintenance schedules that are costly, and so on. Local standards on stopping distances might be easy to meet for local aircraft designed to meet them, but commit foreign competitors to very frequent brake replacement as wear occurs, lengthening stopping distances.

At times global regulatory contests have been vociferously fought as strategic trade contests. For example, in the late 1970s ICAO considered several microwave landing systems as a world standard. The UK, France, Germany, the US and Australia were shameless in touting for votes for technologies their firms had developed, the operative national motivations clearly based on the principle of strategic trade rather than any more public-regarding principle like world's best practice (see Gidwitz 1980: 84–6).

## Reciprocity v. National Treatment, Most Favoured Nation

Today bilateralism rules – 'reciprocity is everything', in the words of one informant – with the economic regulation of airlines. No nation has opted for a full commitment to free trade in air services. Even the leading liberalizing states liberalize reciprocally, not unconditionally. Recent bilateral agreements between liberalizing states have sought to strengthen the principle of national treatment. However, most states continue to be shameless in systematically favouring their own national carriers in their air transport policies.

A Most Favoured Nation approach has currency in the discourse of bilateral negotiation of route exchange. In this context it means that one nation considers itself equivalent to a second nation and therefore requests the same route access the other country enjoys with third countries. It is a qualified notion of the Most Favoured Nation principle because of dispute over what constitutes equivalence: 'Although two countries may be approximately equal in size and population, they may differ substantially in criteria of importance to air transportation, such as geographic situation (relation to other countries), tourism potential, or number of possible destinations' (Gidwitz 1980: 152).

With safety, the national treatment and Most Favoured Nation principles are usually respected, though distortions to favour local carriers and disadvantage the most-feared foreign competitors are common. Reciprocal recognition of inspections is highly elaborated, though complemented by off-shore inspecting and auditing of other nations' inspections.

### Lowest-cost Location v. World's Best Practice

Airlines usually locate where their customer bases are found. Exotic and creative exceptions occur, however, pursuant to the principle of lowest-cost location. Some countries have no regulatory infrastructure at all, so aircraft are never checked by independent state inspectors. The tiny South American country of Belize is one. A Miami-based US airline cut regulatory costs for a while by registering in Belize and operating as Belize Air.

Pursuit of lowest-cost location is not an important factor in driving standards down, however, in an industry where states are more concerned to keep competitors out than to attract them. As one European regulator put it: 'It is more often a matter of corruption when countries have low standards than of the desire to attract business'.

For manufacturers also, while components can be made in locations like China or Russia where skilled, cheap workforces exist and regulatory standards are low, the highest-cost location where regulatory standards are high and most intensively scrutinized – the US – is the most attractive location for assembling the final product. The manufacturer wants the quickest possible approval from the toughest regulator who guards the largest market, and hopes this satisfies all other regulators. Manufacturers pursue a principle of world's best practice through investing in new technologies that will make planes safer. Boeing has an interest in doing this when it knows the mission statement of the FAA Flight Standards Service says: 'To provide the public with accident-free aircraft operations through the highest standards in the world'. The FAA is committed to continuous improvement in its delivery of safety, as are many regulators, for example the Danish civil aviation authority which has a performance contract with its government to achieve better safety outcomes than Germany and the other Scandinavian countries. This makes the FAA loosely a best available technology (BAT) regulator, though the slowness of its standards adjustment means that it consistently lags behind the cutting-edge of safety in the industry. Boeing and its suppliers – the main inventors of new safety technology – may ask FAA for a higher performance standard when an aircraft reaches new standards of safety performance. They do this to make it harder for competitors to catch them or to undercut them on price with inferior safety performance.

**Rule Compliance v. Continuous Improvement**

Even though safety standards are relatively demanding and expensive for air transport compared with sea or road transport, both the leading airlines and the leading manufacturers tend to seek continuous improvement with safety performance. They are not satisfied with simply meeting the rules. This is because airlines fear the safety reputation that Continental acquired before its bankruptcy and manufacturers fear the safety reputation the DC-10 acquired in the 1980s. Many of the struggling airlines, however, particularly in developing countries, seek to stay solvent by doing the minimum possible in terms of safety standards. Possibly this philosophy is part of what keeps them as struggling airlines, but the fact of life is that there are many such airlines subscribing to a principle of minimum rule compliance. Both continuous improvement and rule compliance are strongly supported principles, to different sectors of the aviation industry.

**Transparency**

The economic regulation of air transport globally has been the antithesis of transparency. IATA Traffic Conferences are closed to the public, conducted in total secrecy. ICAO recently improved transparency by making a computerized databank on the main provisions of bilateral air transport agreements available for public access (ICAO 1994: 36).

While ICAO meetings are open to plural observers, an important contest over transparency has concerned ICAO's safety oversight work in reporting on member states' compliance with the Annexes to the Chicago Convention. The US has argued unsuccessfully that these reports should be published. However, the US itself publishes only some of its audits under the FAA's assessment program of foreign air carriers and foreign regulators. This is because it uses threat of publication as a lever for improvement.

The FAA rule-making that dominates the world on the safety side is comparatively transparent. Proposed rules have long been published and public comment invited before they become final. Transparency concerning draft rules is obviously inferior, however, to transparency of the deliberation within the FAA leading up to the draft rules. To improve deliberative transparency, FAA has established official advisory committees for rule-making (ARACs) that will give stakeholders – manufacturers, airlines, foreign regulators, airline employees and consumers – a window of accountability at the front end of rule-making.

## Mechanisms

### Military Coercion

Military coercion after the Second World War kept countries like Czechoslovakia, Poland and Yugoslavia, which participated in the Chicago Civil Aviation Conference of 1944, within the Soviet-dominated regulatory order for air travel rather than the Western-dominated order that they would have preferred. Although Soviet hegemony fostered a period of regional harmonization in Eastern Europe, ultimately this was an impediment to globalization rather than a cause of it, however, because it was displaced by the Western regime after 1990. We could only say that military coercion has contributed to globalization if we consider it military coercion that the hegemony of the US in late 1944 was won on Europe's battlefields.

## Economic Coercion

The US dominates air transportation, for economic reasons. It dominates because it is responsible for most of the manufactures, because it is the biggest market for air services, the biggest importer and the biggest exporter of air services and the source of most new technology. Because US economic supremacy is so clear in this domain, the US does not often need to threaten economic consequences to get its way. Its domination is hegemonic. However, it does threaten economic consequences when it feels it needs to, for example threatening to withdraw US landing rights to states that fail to measure up to ICAO safety standards. The FAA has publicized lists of countries and foreign operators it finds less than satisfactory in terms of safety. Even without withdrawal of landing rights, this adverse publicity can have a devastating effect on operators into as big a market as the US. US bilateral airworthiness agreements routinely require all aircraft components to meet US quality standards (Zacher & Sutton 1996: 96).

## Systems of Reward

The US rewarded Iceland with a military base in return for liberalizing its international air transport policy. This may not seem systematic, but it is in fact part of a systematic approach to negotiate bilaterally in a way that rewards liberalizing countries, usually with landing rights in the US, in this case with a military base.

Critics of the FAA suggest that it should systematically reward high safety performers among the airlines and systematically punish poor performers by publishing safety ratings of airlines based on accidents, near misses and inspections (Nader & Smith 1993: 326–7). Alternatively, it could fund consumer groups to do this and allow access to all the data they need to do the job. This kind of proposal for systems of reward has not found favour with any national regulator, however, in an era where regulators fear being blamed for airline bankruptcies.

## Modelling

US economic hegemony in air transport mostly has effect through states simply choosing to imitate US standards and certifications of aircraft types. Some globalization of new safety standards occurs through airlines modelling the self-regulatory practices of other airlines, as opposed to states modelling laws. A US-based network of NGOs, the Campaign for Smoke-Free Skies Worldwide (White & Douglas 1992: 21–2) has run an unsuccessful campaign for an ICAO ban on smoking on all international aircraft. Although a global regulatory prohibition seems unlikely, airlines have modelled major airlines which adopted the practice of providing smoke-free flights; by 1995 sixty airlines had taken action to limit or abolish smoking on their flights (IATA 1995) and flights that allow smoking are difficult to find.

With economic regulation, the Bermuda I and Bermuda II bilateral agreements between the US and UK became models for subsequent bilaterals among other nations that transformed the shape of economic regulation globally. The new bilateral model is the open-skies deal negotiated between the US and more than a dozen other states.

### Reciprocal Adjustment and Non-reciprocal Coordination

Until recently, reciprocal adjustment had limited application on the safety side of air transport regulation. The adjusting was not very cooperative, with everyone adjusting to the US and the US not offering much reciprocal accommodation. Even then, however, there was reciprocal adjustment on ICAO technical committees and its Council. Today FAA engages in considerable dialogue with foreign regulators, particularly the JAA, before standards are settled. Similarly, Boeing sometimes discusses its design ideas earlier rather than later with foreign regulators so that any new standards implicit in its design proposals can be cooperatively adjusted to foreign requirements before designs are finalized.

Reciprocal adjustment worked to create conventions on the problem of aircraft hijacking. Although the first recorded hijack of a plane occurred on 21 February 1931 in Peru, it was not until the late 1950s and early 1960s that the problem of aircraft piracy became an international problem with both US aircraft and non-US aircraft being hijacked (see the data in Mickolous 1980). A comparative consensus on the problem was achieved in the form of three conventions: the Tokyo Convention on Offences and Certain Other Acts Committed on Board Aircraft 1963, the Hague Convention for the Suppression of Unlawful Seizure of Aircraft 1970 and the Montreal Convention for the Suppression of Unlawful Acts Against the Safety of Civil Aviation 1971 (Williams & Williams 1996: 37). We saw that in the case of piracy on the high seas (Chapter 17) and piracy of intellectual property (Chapter 7), reciprocal adjustment was not an important mechanism in bringing about global regulation. In the case of aircraft piracy there was a genuine reciprocity of interest to do something about the problem, with the result that reciprocal adjustment worked quickly.

Non-reciprocal coordination is also an important mechanism, with states granting all manner of trade-offs (e.g. military bases and licences for landing slots) to other states which cooperate with their regulatory objectives.

### Capacity-building

There could not be a greater contrast with road transport than with the mechanism of capacity-building. Between 1988 and 1992, the ICAO spent nearly $US250 million on technical assistance to developing countries (ICAO 1994: 48). TRAINAIR has been a cooperative venture between ICAO and the UN Development Program to coordinate civil aviation training centres into a cooperative network, particularly for providing standardized training packages and other curriculum materials.

FAA's substantial technical assistance program began in 1949 under the then CAA. In the early years it consisted of rather direct supervision of airport construction, installation of air navigation aids, communications installation and putting flight standards procedures in place (Burkhardt 1967: 181–4). Today it is more remedial, a new priority being to offer assistance to national authorities or airlines that perform poorly under the FAA's International Aviation Safety Assessment Program.

## Conclusion

Writing as Australians, we can read this case study as the most extreme assault on our national sovereignty in any domain to date, the clearest case of US hegemony over a global regulatory system. We can recoil with horror at the revelation that employees of the Boeing Corporation have more influence over the shape of our airworthiness standards than does our elected government. Or we can react more positively. What Australians want is safe, cheap air travel; it is obvious that this is what citizens would want to exert their sovereignty to get. Their elected Australian government would deliver less safe, more expensive air travel if it opted out of the US-hegemonic order of the skies.

Boeing engineers contribute more to making Australian skies safer than anyone in Australia. We don't have to buy the planes they sell or recognize the standards they shape, but we would be foolish to exercise our sovereignty to make that choice. US hegemony is contestable: if we want cheaper, less safe planes, we can place orders elsewhere, for example in Russia or China. While constrained within the general configuration of US standards, we can buy Boeing and ask Boeing to add extra safety features for the aircraft it builds for the Australian market, as nations sometimes do. Flight standards regulation allows much more leeway for local sovereignty than airworthiness standards, and indeed there have been vigorous debates in Australia recently about the sort of flight standards regime we want. Australia's sovereign choice is for a more liberalized economic regulation of air transport. While Australia could not have moved on its own to foster the kind of liberalization chaotically unfolding, it could have chosen to follow Japan and France in this contest rather than to follow the US. If the US seeks to accelerate the shift of forum for air services regulatory negotiation from IATA and ICAO to WTO, Australia can choose whether to count as one of the supporters or the opponents of the forum-shifting.

So sovereign Australian citizens like ourselves might make the judgment, as we do, that US hegemony in this particular domain has been comparatively benign (that is, compared to the alternatives, and compared to US hegemony in other domains) in delivering cheaper, safer air travel out of Australia.

The global international air transport regulatory system has many serious flaws. Yet its aggregate effect is to ratchet safety standards (and noise and environmental standards) up. Air Belize is an exotic case; there is no race-to-the-bottom overall. So how does it ratchet standards up?

Most of the technological innovation occurs in the US. The FAA is committed to continuous improvement in safety regulation. In an effectively BAT regime, innovations by Boeing, by its suppliers or competitors or by a US innovator in navigational aids that improve safety will (with considerable lag) ratchet-up US standards. US regulatory hegemony then may deliver the new US standard as the new global standard. The major site of contestation of the US standard has been the JAA (in future the European Aviation Safety Authority). However, the JAA track record has never been to undercut the US standard. It occasionally demands more, perhaps because it is less captured by US industry than is the FAA, certainly because it fears public exposure by cabin workers' unions, the IAPA and other watchdogs if it undercuts US standards: 'JAA generally starts with FAA regulations as a basis, then either leaves it as is or makes it stricter. They never go the other way' (FAA official). So in effect the JAA has been a second little upward ratchet attached to the big US ratchet (see Ashford 1996). Moreover, 'It is often cheaper to build to the stricter of two standards than to have two production lines. In any case, your US buyer may want the option of being able to sell the aircraft on to Europe at a later date' (FAA official). Within Europe there are other even tinier ratchets, again which go up rather than down, such as the Danish civil aviation authority having a performance contract to be safer than Germany and elsewhere in Scandinavia. Some qualification is required about European upward ratchets, however. Some European states have had to lower some standards to the level in JAA standards; these instances, however, are small in number compared to nations raising their standards to JAA requirements.

Collective international deliberation results in another kind of upwards global ratchet that the small group psychological theories of social comparison and self-categorization both predict well (see Turner 1987: 147, 155):

> In meetings of national experts, given the nature of government people, it is much easier to come to compromise by going for the stricter of the two rules. You assemble experts on flaps from many countries in one room and say 'Any problems with existing standards?', then someone will come up with a pet problem. Just the process of getting the specialists together encourages them to outdo each other by coming up with problems. The way to make a name for yourself as the world's prime authority on ailerons is to have the strictest rule on ailerons (FAA official).

In short, the micro process of professional reputation-building in a small subgroup of a global epistemic community can engender a highest-common-factor (rather than a lowest-common-denominator) macro dynamic.

Finally, the entire global airworthiness regime is contestable by the underwriting industry which, between the World Wars, ran the regime. It has pulled out because it trusts the state regulatory regimes. If that trust were eroded, the underwriting industry could be counted upon to re-enter the game with a classification-based regulation of the riskworthiness of aircraft comparable to the scheme for the underwriting of ships. Contestability that is not actually contested at a particular moment is still an important strand that binds resilience into a web of controls. Underwriters have no reason to intervene to lower safety standards, only to lift them. The quiescent contestability of state regulation by underwriters is a ratchet set to move only one way – up.

The US has a more transparent and participatory regulatory order than, say, Australia. If Australia were dominating the world system, Australian consumers in IAPA would have less of a window into the rule-making than in the circumstance where the US dominates. The rise of JAA as a second major force has led to the institutionalization of annual FAA–JAA conferences open to public participation by all stakeholders, at which emerging regulatory issues are discussed. ICAO debate has also become more open to participation by consumer constituencies such as the IAPA, and opens up fora where FAA domination can be contested dialogically.

Within the US, the FAA has responded to concern for greater up-front participation of foreign regulators, unions and the IAPA in rule-making by establishing rule-making advisory committees with broad stakeholder participation. In the past, foreign regulators who objected to an FAA standard could only object when draft standards were published for comment in the Federal Register, a point at which the Boeing production juggernaut was so far advanced on the assumption of the new standard that the FAA was not likely to budge. As one Boeing executive put it: 'In the old days, twenty years ago, we knew the FAA didn't pay much attention to foreign countries in writing rules'.

Boeing has also changed its attitude, away from one of keeping regulators in the dark over technological innovations until it has all the problems sorted out in a tightly wrapped design package. Now, our interviews in Seattle revealed, Boeing's philosophy is to talk to FAA and foreign regulators at 'go-ahead' – four or five years before the first passenger service is scheduled – to share their concerns so that by the time a new aircraft is ready to roll on the production line there is a global consensus on how to deal with any concerns: 'We have to do this with JAA and FAA looking over each other's shoulders, often racing each other to be strictest' (Boeing executive). Dialogue starts between FAA and Boeing after Boeing provides an initial design and fault tree to the FAA systems engineering and structural engineering groups. Later there will be a sharing of perspectives with FAA test pilots.

Part of FAA reciprocal adjustment to the concerns of foreign regulators has been to shift to writing performance standards, rather than specification standards, for a new BAT. This means that Airbus is not required to use Boeing's technology for the new BAT; Airbus can find its own design path to the new BAT without necessarily buying the same technology from Boeing's supplier. This form of harmonized diversity as the world ratchets-up to higher performance standards fuels further innovation and protects against US-dominated BATs being used as a non-tariff barrier. It is far from true that specification standards are no longer used to deliver a competitive advantage to the US aviation industry. However, the structural shifts successfully demanded by foreign regulators are pro-competitive and pro-innovation.

Having worked the world system in a way that both ratchets-up safety and entrenches the market domination of US technological leadership, the US is now further entrenching that domination and further ratcheting-up safety through its International Aviation Safety Assessment Program. This helps make the skies safer for US citizens. It also induces states which are making do with inferior technologies of navigation, allowing stopping distances that aircraft with worn brakes can meet, to invest in upgrading. This upgrading will frequently mean the purchase of replacement US technology.

Again, Australian citizens benefit when the International Aviation Safety Assessment Program of the FAA succeeds in improving the enforcement of ICAO standards worldwide, a benefit the Australian state could never provide. The benefit would be much greater if the FAA, following Nader's suggestion, were more systematic in releasing to the public (of Australia as well as the US) its safety assessments of both foreign and US carriers. Even as many national regulatory authorities continue to have appalling or non-existent air safety regulation, if consumers could exercise their sovereignty to choose an airline they trust will not take them into airports or traffic corridors whose safety they cannot guarantee on the basis of their access to the results of ICAO and FAA audits, then the market could further ratchet-up safety. For that to happen, we need a much more transparent global regulatory system, where safety audits are more public, dialogue about their meaning more robust and their results laid out in a way that can be more readily digested by the readers of *Consumer Reports* in the US or *Choice* in Australia.

Air transport regulation is not as competitive, as safe, as harmonized, as transparent, as open to contest by stakeholders as it could be. Yet our conclusion is that it has become more price-competitive, safer, more effectively harmonized, more transparent and more inclusive of dialogue with stakeholders. The dynamic of upward-ratcheting is due to the domination of a US committed to continuous improvement at both the corporate and state levels. It occurs in a world where the US can no longer rule alone, a world in which its view of what makes for continuous improvement is increasingly contested by European regulators, the IAPA and the many other strands we have documented within an increasingly elaborate web. There are worse worlds that sovereign Australian citizens might choose.

# Part III
## ANALYSIS

CHAPTER **20** | Contests of Actors

## States

### Realist Power

Our data have demonstrated the unsurprising conclusion that many different kinds of actors have played important roles in the globalization of business regulation. Some might read the data selectively as demonstrating the death of the nation-state. This would be an erroneous reading of the facts we have assembled. Notwithstanding the complex plurality of actors we have shown to be involved in global regulatory games, if we ask the crude question, 'which is the type of actor that has had the greatest influence?', the answer is fairly clearly the nation-state. If we ask which single actor has had the greatest influence, that answer is even clearer – the US state.

What has changed is the nature of state power. As Stopford and Strange (1991: 1) put it: 'states are now competing more for the means to create wealth within their territory than for power over more territory. Where they used to compete for power as a means to wealth, they now compete more for wealth as a means to power'. At the same time, we have shown that in the era of information capitalism and the new regulatory state, control from the nation's territory of abstract objects like patents is crucial to building the nation's wealth, as is embedding global principles of regulation that suit the wealth-creators from the state's territory. The resilience of a US power that many had expected to wane in the 1990s can be understood in terms of the masterful work of the Clinton administration in these arenas.

Table 20.1 shows that in every chapter the US state is one of the most important actors. The UK is clearly the second most important state actor, with twelve entries in Table 20.1, followed by Germany with four, France and Japan with three, and Sweden and the Soviet Union with two. The Nordic countries are state players with an influence beyond their size across a number of domains. This is particularly so in the many arenas, like the OECD chemicals regime (Chapter 12), which have instituted a lead-country approach, where states take it in turns to lead technical committees on specific regulatory problems. Canada, Australia and India are among the weaker states that frequently chair technical committees on which so much of the real work of the globalization of regulation is done.

US influence ranges from nuclear safety, where US hegemony has been supreme, to much weaker US influence over sea transport and labour standards. Labour is the only domain where other states, notably the UK, were more influential in shaping the regime. Even in the labour

**TABLE 20.1**   Some of the most influential actors in the globalization of regulation

| KEY ACTORS | CONTRACT AND PROPERTY RIGHTS | FINANCE | CORPORATIONS AND SECURITIES | TRADE AND COMPETITION | LABOUR | ENVIRONMENT |
|---|---|---|---|---|---|---|
| **Organizations of states** | WTO, WIPO, EU, UNCITRAL, UNIDROIT, Hague Conference of International Private Law | League of Nations, OECD, IMF, World Bank, Basle Committee, BIS, Financial Action Task Force, EU, G-5, G-3, G-10 | International Organization of Securities Commissions, EU | OECD, GATT/WTO, EU, Quad, Cairns Group | ILO, Council of Europe | OECD, EU, G-7, IMO, UNEP, CSD, World Bank, treaty secretariats |
| **States** | US | Roman and Persian empires, Italian city states, US, UK, Germany | US, UK | US, UK | UK, France, Germany, Soviet Union | US, Germany, Sweden, Norway, Netherlands |
| **International business organizations** | IPC, IIPA, BSA, ICC, Keidandren, UNICE, Lombardian Guild, ICC, merchant families | ICC, Business and Industry Advisory Committee to the OECD | None | ICC | International Organization of Employers | UNICE, Industry Cooperative for Ozone Layer Protection, Responsible Care, Business Council on Sustainable Devt |
| **National business organizations** | Motion Picture Association of America | None | Amsterdam, London, New York Stock Exchanges | American Bar Association, Motion Picture Association of America | US Council for International Business | US Chemical Manufacturers Association, Japanese Whaling Association |
| **Corporations** | IBM, DuPont, Pfizer | CitiCorp, American Express, Big Five accounting firms, Lloyd's of London | Italian and Jewish diasporas (Rothschilds), JP Morgan, Standard & Poor's, Moody's, Peat Marwick, Price-waterhouseCoopers | Pfizer, IBM, American Express | Levi-Strauss, Reebok, Starbucks Coffee | DuPont, ICI, SGS, Lloyd's Register of Shipping, classification societies, insurers |
| **International NGOs** | International Law Assn, Int. Assn of Legal Science, Institute of Int. Law, AIPPI, Licensing Executives Society International | International Accounting Standards Committee | International Accounting Standards Committee | Consumers International, International Confederation of Free Trade Unions | International Confederation of Free Trade Unions | ISO, Greenpeace, International Union for the Conservation of Nature, PAN, Climate Action Network, World Rainforest Network |
| **National NGOs** | American Law Institute | None | American Institute of Accountants | Public Citizen | Anti-slavery groups, AFL-CIO, TUC, Women's groups | Environmental Defense Fund and other US NGOs, British Standards Institute |
| **Mass publics** | Starting to become important in intellectual property | Yes, middle-class investing public catalyzed by banking and stock market crashes from 1719 onwards | Yes, middle-class investing publics catalyzed by crashes in 1719, 1929, 1987 | Yes, increasingly | Yes, catalyzed by outrageous abuses of labour rights | Yes, catalyzed by *Silent Spring*, Bhopal, *Torrey Canyon* |
| **Individuals** | Gaius, Justinian, Irnerius, Mansfield Chalmers, Ed Pratt, Jacques Gorlin, Jack Valenti, Eric Smith | Merchant families e.g. Bardi, Medici; merchant financiers; e.g. Barings, Brandts, Rothschilds, Raphaels, Seligmans, Morgans; JM Keynes, HD White, V Giscard d'Estaing, H Schmidt, G Shultz, J Delors | Lorenzo Ponti, Franklin Roosevelt, James Landis | Ed Pratt, Jacques Gorlin, Eric Smith, Franklin Roosevelt, Sir Eric Wyndham White | Edward Phelan, William Wilberforce, Eleanor Roosevelt, Karl Marx | Rachel Carson, Mostafa Tolba, Maurice Strong |
| **Epistemic communities of actors** | Strong | Strong | Strong | Strong | Strong | Strong |

| NUCLEAR SAFETY | TELECOMMUNI-CATIONS | DRUGS | FOOD | SEA TRANSPORT | ROAD TRANSPORT | AIR TRANSPORT |
|---|---|---|---|---|---|---|
| IAEA, EURATOM, OECD, G-7 | ITU, OECD, World Bank, WTO | WHO, EU, EFTA, International Conference on Harmonization | Codex, WTO, EU | International Maritime Organization, EU | EU, Economic Commission for Europe | International Civil Aviation Organization, WTO |
| US, France, UK, Soviet Union | US, UK | US, UK, Germany, Japan, France, India | US, UK, Japan | UK, US, Japan | US, Germany, Sweden | US, UK |
| World Association of Nuclear Operators | INTUG, SWIFT, SITA, ICC | IFPMA, EFPIA | International Federation of National Associations of Pesticide Manufacturers | IACS, ICS, ICC | OICA, IMMA, CLEPA, ACEA | International Air Transport Association |
| Institute of Nuclear Power Operations | Telecommunications Managers (UK) Association, Corporate Committee of Telecommunication Users (US) | Pharmaceutical Manufacturers Association | Grocery Manufacturers Association (US) | None | MVMA (US), National Insurance Institute for Highway Safety (US) | US Chamber of Commerce |
| Insurers, banks Electricité de France Duke Power | IBM, Time-Warner, CitiCorp, American Express, Bank of America, accounting firms | Ciba-Geigy (Novartis), global law firms, East Indies Companies | Nestlé, Coca-Cola, Unilever, Monsanto | Lloyd's Register of Shipping, classification societies, insurers | DaimlerBenz, General Motors, Ford | Boeing |
| Greenpeace | ISO, Int. Electrochemical Commission, Int. Federation of Information Processing, Int. Union of Radio Science | HAI, MaLAM, BEUC, ASH, GASP, WCTU, RAPS | Consumers International | International Maritime Organization, Friends of the Earth International, International Confederation of Free Trade Unions | ISO, FIA, Consumers International, BEUC | IFALPA, IAPA, International Transport Workers Union |
| Union of Concerned Scientists, Critical Mass Energy Project | National Telecoms Users Groups | Health Research Group, Society for Suppression of Opium Trade, AIDS groups, health professions | National Food Alliance (UK), Public Citizen, Consumers Union | None | ASTM, Public Citizen, Society of Automotive Engineers | Cabin Workers Unions |
| Yes, catalyzed by Three Mile Island, Chernobyl | Radio regulation safety methods catalyzed by sinking of *Titanic* | Yes, catalyzed by elixir sulfanilamide, thalidomide disasters | Yes, catalyzed by beef hormone scare, adulteration outbreaks | Yes, catalyzed by the *Titanic, Torrey Canyon* and *Herald of Free Enterprise* disasters | Yes, catalyzed by *Unsafe at Any Speed* | Yes, catalyzed regularly by major crashes |
| Dwight Eisenhower, Mikhail Gorbachev, Three Wise Men, Lord Marshall, Ralph Nader | None | Fernand Sauer, Andrew Chetley, Charles Medawar, Peter Mansfield, Harry Anslinger | Tim Lang, F.C. Accum | Edward Lloyd, Justinian | Ralph Nader, Joan Claybrook | Alfred Kahn, Ralph Nader, Franklin Roosevelt |
| Strong | Strong | Strong | Strong | Strong | Strong | Strong (safety) Fracturing (economic) |

standards domain, where France and Germany have, in addition to the UK, been more influential than the US, the Clinton administration was during the 1990s the most aggressive state in using and threatening bilateral sanctions for inadequate labour standards and the most forceful national advocate of linking labour standards to the GATT.

In finance, the US is today more important than the UK though the reverse was true until the First World War. With prescription drugs (since 1980), road transport and possibly food standards, the EU has become more influential than the US, though the US remains the most significant single state in that domain also. At the GATT, where one can see the most systematic quantitative evidence of US hegemony, we saw in Chapter 10 that the US launches more disputes than any other state, wins more often than any other and, if it loses, is more likely than other states to thumb its nose at the ruling. In the trade regime and beyond, the US is the biggest demander of new regulatory agreements as well as the strongest resister of regimes other states want. When it does not get the agreement it wants, a strategy evident in most chapters is to leave the negotiating table and use its muscle bilaterally for the terms it seeks. Once the bilateral agreements sew up all the key states, the rest of the world often signs the US terms, out of fear of exclusion from the benefits of the international cooperation. In short, most of the obituaries for the death of US hegemony have been exaggerated.

Considering which are the most influential actors gives some insight in correcting more extreme accounts of Japan and China overtaking the US as a great power, of the central significance of the rise of the Asian Tigers. China and the Asian Tigers do not rate a mention in Table 20.1. Europe is the only actor which has toppled US hegemony, and only in a few domains. But these really are crude questions.

Our data do confirm the basic tenet of realist international relations theory – that states are the major actors in world affairs (Morgenthau 1978). Just as surely, they show that the realist model of the global, as bigger- and smaller-state billiard balls using their weight to push one another around a table, is a poor one.[1] If it were a good model, Japan, the second-biggest billiard ball, would appear in more than three columns in Table 20.1.

In no domain is Japan a more significant player than are the US and Europe. Even in the auto safety regime, where it is the world's largest exporter with the world's most powerful manufacturers, its influence is far surpassed by the EU and the US (Chapter 18). There are a plethora of resolutions to this puzzle that connect to the great variety of actor types we show to be important in the globalization of regulation. In the auto safety regime, for example, we showed that Ralph Nader was important, and he is not Japanese. The most ironic feature of Japan's consistent comparative impotence across these regimes is that it is a quintessentially unitary realist state actor. In most of the domains where we conducted interviews, insiders told us that the Japanese would not come to the negotiating table with a clearly articulated position until they had a domestic consensus. Domestic consensus is hard to secure for any state. In regard to an emissions standard for motor vehicles, a transport ministry, an environment ministry and a consumer affairs ministry are almost bound to have different views, and industry and trade ministries may have broader trade-offs in mind that give them different perspectives again.

US influence, in contrast, is often grounded in one national agency, usually the one with the most powerful corporate clients, getting a mandate to ride roughshod over the views of state

---

1 This is increasingly true of armed conflict as well as business regulation: in recent decades there have been more intrastate than interstate armed conflicts and more people have lost their lives in internal than in international conflicts (March & Olsen 1998: 10).

governments and other federal agencies. US state influence in companies and securities is actually the influence of the Securities and Exchange Commission (SEC) and in air safety it is the influence of the Federal Aviation Administration (FAA). Although it is focused executive branch influence, we will see that the influence is enhanced by the possibility that the legislature and judiciary might unravel the deals done. Unitary US state power, in other words, is best understood in terms of the separation of powers which underwrites it.

SEC or FAA clout is not only about realist state power, it is also about expertise. We will see that epistemic communities of actors that facilitate modelling as a mechanism of globalization are very important. There is simply no greater repository of technical expertise on securities regulation than the SEC, on air safety than the FAA. Technocrats from these agencies thus become dominant in epistemic communities. Their dominance is not mediated by flexing of US muscle, but by the fact that colleagues from other nations respect their expertise and respect the SEC or the FAA as the kind of competent regulator they would like to be. The comparative transparency of US governance helps render this competence accessible. Foreign regulators have long been able to read about the reasoning and the technical analyses underlying US regulation in the Federal Register (now available on the Internet).

In the next section, we will consider a variety of reasons why realist international relations theory is of limited value in understanding the globalization of business regulation. We will argue that state power is best viewed not as statically structural but as emerging from a process of structuration (Giddens 1984). The state is constituted by and helps constitute a web of regulatory controls that is continually rewoven to remake the regulatory state. States act as agents for other actors such as business corporations and other actors act as agents for states. This reflexive agency reconstitutes both agents and principals continually. It follows that we cannot be satisfied with Slaughter's (1997: 195) compromise of networked 'transgovernmentalism' where 'networks of [state] institutions perform the functions of world government – legislation, administration, and adjudication – without the form'.[2]

### The Decentring of the State

Most of the institutional foundations for the international regimes in this book were laid between 1944 and 1974. These decades happen to have been the highwater-mark of the Keynesian state and of US hegemony. At the same time, we have seen that many of the foundations for many of the globalizations we have documented were laid centuries earlier. It was the Treaty of Westphalia in 1648 at the end of the Thirty Years War that solidified a European state system which did not become a fully global one until well into the twentieth century. It did not incorporate non-Christian states until the Ottoman empire was admitted to the Concert of Europe after the Crimean War, or Asian states until the admission of China, Japan and Siam toward the end of the nineteenth century. Until the two centuries of state-making that preceded Westphalia, the world was not organized into one system: 'There were several. There was the empire of Arab-Islam. There was that of the Indians, of the Mongol-Tartars, and of the Chinese. There were the New

---

2 We cannot conclude in favour of the transgovernmentalism compromise, not only because of the evidence in our data of enrolment of states by non-state actors and mutual constitution of states and non-states within networks of action. There is also the more straightforward fact that in the arena of global financial regulation, actors like the Big Five accounting firms, Citibank, Moody's, Standard & Poors, the New York Stock Exchange and Lloyd's of London are more important players than the finance ministries or the judiciaries of developing countries.

World empires of the Incas and the Aztecs, and those of West and East Africa. All these empires had a centre, surrounded by zones of diminishing control' (Pettman 1991: 47).

Much that we have shown to be constitutive of European regulatory states and their economic power originated in these other empires: coins and paper money, paper itself that enabled and transformed complex state regulatory bureaucracies and legal systems that could carry its commands across long distances (China), monetary policy, commercial credit (China–Arab), tariffs and the Arabic system of numeration (modelled from the Hindu number system) that enabled double-entry bookkeeping, maritime trading regulations, the *commenda* that was the foundation of the limited liability corporation, bills of exchange (India–Arab–Islam), systems for efficiently regulating slave labour (Africa–Arab–US) and perhaps the regulatory institutions of guilds and trade standardization such as by weights and measures (India–Pakistan). The Roman empire was an earlier European system whose laws mediated the entry of the regulatory concepts of these other empires into the Westphalian state system.

Even after states became sovereign, pre-state regulatory institutions often continued to dominate. Guilds continued to enforce trading standards in late medieval and early modern European states. Canon law legitimated by the Church persisted for centuries, commanding a competing authority with new laws of states. The *Lex Mercatoria* forged among merchant guilds faded, but only after state law incorporated many of its precepts. The Bank of England dominated monetary policy and prudential regulation as a private bank before it was brought under national control in the mid eighteenth century and fully nationalized in 1946. Lloyd's of London and Lloyd's Register dominated the regulation of insurance and shipping until the mid twentieth century. Even today Lloyd's of London's regulatory staff of 500 and Lloyd's Register's 3900 administrative and technical staff dwarf most UK regulatory inspectorates.

Maritime regulation has the longest history as a sophisticated globalizing regulatory regime because it became important around the Mediterranean in the ancient world (Rhodes, the Phoenicians, Alexandria) and was central to the rise of late medieval city-states such as Venice and Genoa and to early modern national powers – Spain, Portugal, Holland, France and England. The history we told in Chapter 17 was of two millennia of development of non-state regulatory institutions – where private maritime law, underwriters, classification societies and the professionalization of seafaring were key strands in a web of controls that made seafaring more secure for both people and investors. Only from the mid nineteenth century did regulation by the nation-state become important enough to be added to this list, as another crucial strand of regulation. Yet in the twentieth century, most nation-states delegated large swathes of their regulatory functions back to classification societies, and the growth of flags of convenience for shipping rendered national sovereignty obsolete. The International Maritime Organization (IMO) is a more important actor than any state actor. State supremacy occupies only one century in a 2000-year history.

Maritime regulation is the extreme case of national supremacy as a short-lived phenomenon of the immediate past. This is both because of the longer pre-history of non-state regulation and (as a result of existing vibrant non-state institutions such as Lloyd's) the unusually early emergence of the 'new regulatory state' (Osborne & Gaebler 1992: Majone 1994; Loughlin & Scott 1997; Parker forthcoming; Braithwaite 2000; Hood et al. 1999) that rows more than steers,[3] that delegates service delivery and some regulatory functions to non-state actors. In most regulatory

---

3 With apologies to Osborne and Gaebler's (1992) maritime metaphor!

domains we have studied, the rise of the Victorian central regulatory state documented by MacDonagh (1961, 1977) has a new lease of life from the Keynesian regulatory state which grew unassailably from 1933 until the Carter and Reagan administrations and the Thatcher government in the English-speaking world. The demise of the Keynesian state occurred a little later elsewhere. Regulation did not decline from the 1980s, but state regulation was significantly supplanted by self-regulation and private regulation of a kind exemplified by classification society inspections of ship safety. As a consequence, self-regulatory organizations frequently become more influential than states in the epistemic communities that frame debates over regulatory design.

State regulatory policies are just as much constituted by as constitutive of private regulation. To take a simple example, the nineteenth-century British maritime hegemon enacted a law requiring the plimsoll line on ships, which assured the globalization of that requirement. It was only possible for Britain to accomplish this because the private regulation of Lloyd's of London had constituted the requirement as a widespread industry practice. Once the legal mandate of the hegemonic state further globalized the plimsoll line, because it was a self-enforcing measure constituted by private regulation, the state law further strengthened self-regulation. Insurers who looked out their window could see overloaded ships in the harbour. Mutually constituting state and private regulatory power is the main story here. We told (in Chapter 9) a more complex story of how the self-regulatory practices of the Amsterdam, London and New York stock exchanges were constitutive of the regulatory mandates of the US SEC that were then substantially modelled by other states. In all the chapters, state regulation follows industry self-regulatory practice more than the reverse, though the reverse is also very important. This has always been so, and as we have moved from the era of the indicative planning state (Robertson 1984) to the new regulatory state, it has become even more true. It is why it can be more strategic for an environmental NGO to shape the internal compliance rules of the cutting-edge corporation that sets world's best practice than it is to influence the laws of the most powerful state.

The recursive quality of global regulation means that there are many possible points of entry to influence the direction of change. Some actors, however, are major motors of transformation and others are not. KPMG is; a suburban accountant is not. The US is; Gabon is not. The London Stock Exchange is; the Port Moresby Exchange is not. The question is which major motors of state power move major motors of corporate power, and vice versa. This is very different from the realist international relations theory question of which is the most powerful state. For an actor interested in influencing labour standards, at the height of US hegemony there was limited leverage from transforming US labour law because the US was not a player in the ILO; it had the weakest trade union movement in the developed world and as a result its labour law was too idiosyncratic to be a widely attractive model. Ironically, for the same reasons, there would have been limited short-term influence and no long-term influence in shaping Soviet labour law. There are other reasons why the realist strategy is wrong in the Soviet case, the most important one being that the Soviet motor of public power was not hooked up to the most powerful motors of corporate power.

It does not follow that actors are destined to irrelevance unless they are cogs in either a powerful state or a powerful corporation. There can be strength in a large set of comparatively weak ties to powerful motors that drive other powerful motors in a recursive system. The genius of Australia, a fairly weak state, in setting up the Cairns Group of agricultural-exporting nations, was that Canada delivered a weak tie to the powerful motors of the Quad (US, Canada, EC, Japan) and the G-7, Thailand to ASEAN, Brazil and others to the G-77, others to APEC, and so on.

The most powerful states are often captives of concentrated corporate interests which care enough about an issue to be willing to hurt their state's political leaders unless they do what they're told. If an interest group has large corporations in its coalition, as the environment movement did with its extremely weak tie to DuPont concerning ozone diplomacy, enough strength to transform the world can follow from the weak tie (Chapter 12).

This way of seeing the limits of realist analysis is akin to Rose and Miller's development of Foucault's conception of power (Miller & Rose 1990; Rose 1996; Rose & Miller 1992). Power is conceived in terms of networks and alliances whereby 'centres of calculation' exercise 'government at a distance':

> Power is not a matter of imposing a sovereign will, but instead a process of enlisting the cooperation of chains of actors who 'translate' power from one locale to another. This process always entails activity on the part of the 'subjects of power' and it therefore has built into it the probability that outcomes will be shaped by the resistance or private objectives of those acting 'down the line' (Garland 1997: 182).

This in turn draws on Latour's (1986, 1987) notions of power as translation or enrolment. We exercise power by enrolling the capacities of others to our purposes. Power depends on a linkage of locales where action occurs (like a national patent office granting a patent) to loci of calculation where knowledge can be accumulated (like the World Intellectual Property Organization in Geneva and the epistemic community of intellectual property lawyers which depends on it). Power is diffused by the actions of chains of agents, each of whom 'translates' it according to their own projects. The fact that power is translated means that in some senses power is out of the control of the powerful.[4] No translation is ever perfect. Reichman, in an unpublished CONGLAS e-mail list contribution, makes the point eloquently about her research on the globalization of regulation: 'In my own research, it often seems power is the ability to "grab hold of", to "bundle" circulating resources, to tap into the flows of images, information, commodities to create new frameworks (spaces?) of action'.

That was precisely our empirical experience when we encountered, for example, a university professor who at different times had represented France, Monaco and the European Banking Federation at the UN Commission on International Trade Law; Greenpeace activists who managed to get themselves appointed as state delegates to international meetings; academics at the Centre for International Environmental Law presiding over the formation of an Association of Small Island States as a key player in the global-warming debate (Chayes & Chayes 1995: 260–2); and Hermann Muntingh, a Dutch member of the European Parliament, organizing 'Globe', a trilateral initiative to bring together environmentally concerned members of the European, Japanese and US legislatures (Al Gore was also active in it). We thought of Reichman's conclusion when a former official of the US Office of the Management of the Budget said to us: 'When Congress or the Executive

---

4 While we regard Latour's model as the most productive way to view power as we see it exercised in contests over global business regulation, we do not go so far as to support Latour's (1986: 264) claim that 'power is not something one can possess' or accumulate. We do conceive of business actors who accumulate more wealth also accumulating power, of princes who accumulate control over more territory as accumulating power, and judges and ministers who have decision-making authority as possessing power. This does not affect our empirical agreement with Latour on the basis of the data analyzed in this book, that effectiveness at enrolling others to one's projects is a more important determinant of the effective exercise of power than resources possessed. Those who exercise the greatest power are those who enrol many others with more resources and authority than themselves, and, more importantly, those who enrol others who are even better at enrolling others than themselves.

knocks back a regulation, the bureaucrats go to an international forum and come back saying there's an international agreement requiring them to implement the rejected regulation'.

Enrolling public sources of power is also central to the difficulties globalizing regulation must combat, as is evident from the history of some who cast votes at the IMO:

> St Vincent and the Grenadines...sublets its shipping register to a shipowner. Besides his official duties, the Commissioner for Maritime Affairs not only registers his own ships but has turned the organization into a family business by appointing his son to run one office and his daughter to run another. He is not only a proud father but also a shipowner, a regulator, and a profitmaker. This 'family firm as flag state' arrangement is accorded full status at the IMO without public criticism even though St Vincent is not a small insignificant register. In 1995 it claimed 1300 vessels totalling 6.5 million gross tons. It also had one of the worst casualty rates in the business: twenty-four total losses in the last four years (Hindell 1996: 372).

Because states are not unitary in the way realist theory supposes, it is possible for weak actors to enrol the power of embattled minority fractions of powerful states in ways that can be transformative. Putnam and his colleagues, in one of the classic studies of political science, has demonstrated how this can happen even at the most commanding heights of economic policy-making in the world system. Their study was of the Bonn Economic Summit of 1978, which secured agreement on crucial elements of the Tokyo Round of the GATT (substantial tariff reductions and a subsidies and countervailing duties code) particularly from a reluctant France, and negotiating for commitments by the trade-surplus states of Germany and Japan and oil-price deregulation by the US (Putnam & Bayne 1987; Putnam 1988; Putnam & Henning 1989). According to the Putnam analysis, the summit accord was only possible because all key states were internally divided. Influential minority factions within the economic policy epistemic communities of the key states forged a winning global coalition of minority factions. A coalition of President Carter's international and economic advisers favoured oil-price decontrol, but this was opposed by the President's domestic policy advisers and a strong majority in Congress. German pump-priming was favoured only by a small minority of officials in the Economics Ministry and the Chancellery, leaders of labour unions and the left wing of the Social Democrats; it was opposed by the Free Democrats, the Bundesbank, most of the business and banking community and most government economic officials. Expansionism by Japan was supported by a coalition of business interests and LDP politicians of modest power, but implacably opposed by the Ministry of Finance, the most powerful actor in Japanese government. In each key state, 'advocates of the internationally desired policy acted (in the words of one of the Americans) as a kind of benevolent "conspiracy", and in each case they signalled to their foreign counterparts that additional international pressure would be welcome' (Putnam & Henning 1989: 107). Other empirical research suggests that at least half the time during international crises, top national decision-makers are not unified (Snyder & Diesing 1977). Minority factions of divided states frequently conspire to solicit international pressure from the Trade Policy Review Mechanism of the WTO (as we saw in Chapter 10) and the World Bank or IMF. A documented instance was conservative Italian Christian Democrats mobilizing IMF pressure in 1977 for unpalatable domestic reforms (Putnam & Henning 1989: 109).

Putnam's (1988) theoretical conclusion from the successful Bonn Summit is that the politics of global negotiation is best viewed as a two-level game – a game of domestic interest-group politics and another of international deal-making to avert threats to national interests.

> Each national political leader appears at both game boards. Across the international table sit his for-
> eign counterparts, and at his elbows sit diplomats and other international advisers. Around the
> domestic table behind him sit party and parliamentary figures, spokespersons for domestic agencies,
> representatives of key interest groups, and the leader's own political advisers. The unusual complexity
> of this two-level game is that moves that are rational for a player at one board (such as raising energy
> prices, conceding territory or limiting auto imports) may be impolitic for that same player at the other
> board…On occasion, however, clever players will spot a move on one board that will trigger realign-
> ments on other boards, enabling them to achieve otherwise unattainable objectives. This 'two-table'
> metaphor captures the dynamics of the 1978 negotiations better than any model based on unitary
> national actors (Putnam 1988: 434).

The fact that national division can deliver national strength in international bargaining was
well-illustrated in Chapter 10 by the way the US Trade Representative (USTR) drives a hard bargain
for the kinds of liberalizing WTO agreements they want by invoking the spectre of a protectionist
Congress voting down an entire GATT round. It is a perfect analogy to the interrogation
philosophy of hard-cop and soft-cop as a way of strengthening police effectiveness. India is
another state which has effectively used the spectre and the reality of its parliament refusing to
ratify GATT agreements during negotiations, and the EC sometimes invokes intervention by the
European Parliament.

We must qualify this with the observation that in many international negotiations the state
does become unitary in the person who occupies the one seat available to that state during the
final negotiation. As we saw in Chapter 10, in a trade and environment negotiation, a national
negotiator from the trade ministry will normally push the environment ministry official out of the
seat. However, the ghosts of environment ministers float above the negotiations, invoked regularly
as disrupters who could spook an unpalatable trade-off with domestic environmental concerns.

Divisions within national executives and between national executives and legislatures are
more important sources of negotiating clout than divisions between the executive and the judiciary. The EC sometimes brings member states into line by invoking the prospect of a *Cassis de
Dijon*-style decision of the European Court of Justice (see Chapter 16). When we designed this
study we had not thought it likely that courts would be important actors in the globalization of
regulation. They turned out to play significant roles in the globalization of contract and property
rights (Chapter 7), trade and competition (Chapter 10), food standards (Chapter 16), telecommunications (Chapter 14) and air transport (Chapter 19). Ikenberry (1988: 51) concluded from
his study of US oil policies that 'The American state is a continually transformed, internally differentiated area of conflict rather than an integrated institution'. A neglected feature of that differentiation in the research of international relations scholars is the (less outspoken, largely
invisible) hand of the judiciary.

In summary, we have five major qualifications to the seeming centrality of states in our
data. First, it is a contingent fact that much of the framework of global regulation was laid during
the heyday of the Keynesian state. Second, the regulatory power of Keynesian states was constituted from private and self-regulatory power. Third, the post-Keynesian new regulatory state delegates much of its regulatory power back to self-regulatory structures similar to those from whence
came its power. Fourth, states are often best conceived as agents of other actors, particularly private corporations. Fifth, when states seem to prevail it is sometimes, as in the Bonn Summit or the
Montreal Protocol, actually an embattled minority constituency within the state that is prevailing.
None of this denies that states still matter more than any other kind of actor in games of regulatory diplomacy. It does deny that realist international relations theory is the best framework for
understanding how they matter.

As Hirst and Thompson (1996) point out, a special virtue of states is that they are still part of a state system that territorially covers the entire population of the world, even if it does not cover the seas and space. Corporations might make more and bigger economic decisions than states, but they do not cover in terms of membership much of the world's population. Nor does the membership of NGOs. Informal self-regulatory law might change economic behaviour more than state law, but only state law can claim universal application to a population. In democratic states, only state law is constitutionalized by the sovereignty of a people and ultimately democratically accountable. Legitimacy and universality of coverage are therefore what makes state regulatory law peculiarly significant. The state not only reaches down to whole populations, under the conditions of the present state system where only states vote in UN bodies (the ILO aside), the state has a reach up which is also distinctive. This is what Hirst and Thompson mean when they describe the state as a crucial locus of governance in a galaxy of increasingly interlinked institutions of governance above and below it.

## International Organizations of States

The EU has already been introduced in this chapter as an organization of states that plays an important role in all the domains of regulation studied in this book. By 1994 it had issued 1600 directives concerning business regulation and 22 000 regulations (Jacobs 1994). Other regional organizations of states such as NAFTA, OAS, OAU, ASEAN and APEC are of minor importance in comparison. In domains discussed in other chapters, other European bodies such as the Council for Europe, the European Free Trade Association, the UN Economic Commission for Europe and EURATOM play special roles. The EC is more important because of the way it dominates the US in agenda-setting in a few arenas – prescription drugs, food, automobile safety – and is nearly an equal partner to the US in agenda-setting for other regimes. Its influence also extends beyond its membership, as it dictates the regulatory improvements it expects from more than a dozen states which aspire to become EU members.

The US hegemony of Bretton Woods is being replaced with a tripolarity of the US, the EC and Japan. Japan, we have seen, is never an equal partner. Most global regulatory agendas are set by the US; if the EC vetos those agendas, they go nowhere. Whaling (Chapter 12) is a rare example of Japanese aggression in leading a veto coalition.

Beyond the EC, the diversity of international organizations which have played important roles in the globalization of business regulation is staggering. The most broadly powerful ones are GATT/WTO, which affects the regulation of all business activity that is traded, and the IMF which, under the banner of a conditionality that demands 'good governance', increasingly affects the conduct of all domains of national regulation. The World Bank and other development banks are also important in spreading Western regulatory models to developing countries. What they spread is the dominant Washington orthodoxy – Keynesian economics in their first decades, deregulation and privatization through the 1980s and into the 1990s, then a reinventing government (Osborne & Gaebler 1992) philosophy for the 1990s which took the good governance of regulatory institutions more seriously as steering mechanisms that could facilitate the private sector to do the rowing.

International organizations are least influential in some of the most foundational domains of our study – companies and securities (Chapter 9), where the International Organization of Securities Commissions is not a dominant force, and the contract part of property and contract

(Chapter 7). Some international organizations, like the International Labour Organization (ILO), have declined in influence; others like the WTO have increased their authority. While the WTO is a contracting organization where the big players (the Quad) call the shots, the ILO has always been more secretariat-driven. Some tiny secretariats for specialized environment treaties wield enormous agenda-setting influence in their little corner of business regulation (Sandford 1992, 1994). Within most international organizations, specialist technical committees are a way of settling a consensus on specific aspects of the regulatory regime. Often these are secretariat-driven, though often they are driven by a chair from a particular state (or a particular corporation which has enrolled a state).

The more important point, however, is that collectively international organizations have expanded their influence over the globalization of regulation through sheer growth in the numbers that are serious players, administering treaties of widening scope. From the mid nineteenth century the first intergovernmental organizations gradually increased in number. By 1914, there were about fifty and by 1939 there were about eighty. After Bretton Woods they exploded, to over 600 by 1980 (Picciotto 1991: 53).

Across the spectrum of regulatory activity, the OECD plays a distinctively important role. There are a few areas, such as chemicals, where it actually settles what become global regulatory standards. But mostly its influence is intellectual. Talk-shops like the OECD seem, to practical people, to be a waste of time when they are engaged in them. Yet standing back, they can see that many of the regulatory transformations aggressively prosecuted in other international organizations have been conceived and refined in OECD talk-fests. In the late 1990s this happened, for example, in the OECD discussions on trade and environment and on the need for a Multilateral Agreement on Investment. Later, we will discuss the importance of epistemic communities of actors. No international organization plays a more significant role in regulatory epistemic community formation than the OECD.

With the end of the Cold War, international organizations where the G-77 had greatest influence – such as the UN Centre on Transnational Corporations and UNCTAD – have declined in importance. Developing countries no longer have the capacity to play off the West against the Soviet bloc by calling on Soviet support to strengthen fora that embed principles inhospitable to the US. Obversely, the G-7 has grown in influence. G-7 summits during the 1990s have discussed all the global regimes in this book except (to our knowledge) corporations and securities. Once the G-7 decides on something – or brings Russia in to form the G-8 in the case of nuclear regulation – regulatory change will happen.

Other non-regional groups of states play more modest roles. The G-10 of leading banking states calls the shots at Basle (Chapter 8). The G-24 of essentially OECD countries has played an important role in transferring regulatory technology, such as nuclear safety technology, to former communist states. In addition, more institution-specific ad hoc groups of states such as the Cairns Group, the Group of 10 developing countries and other less influential coalitions at the WTO (Chapter 10) have a place as significant international groupings.

The secretariats of some international organizations, such as the ILO, International Atomic Energy Agency (IAEA), UNCTAD and WHO, have had more than a thousand staff. Many others, like the International Civil Aviation Organization (ICAO, 800 staff), approach that size. Working Party 29 of the Economic Commission for Europe (ECE), which is the pre-eminent organization for setting safety and environmental standards for automobiles, has a secretariat of three. The size of a secretariat does not predict its clout. UNCTAD has a huge secretariat which wields limited influence, WTO a much smaller one which, notwithstanding the Quad-driven nature of WTO, wields infinitely more influence than UNCTAD (see Chapter 10). Chapter 12 reviewed empirical studies showing how influential environmental treaty secretariats can be with so few staff they can be counted on one's fingers. Some of the secretariat leaders we interviewed emphasized the virtues of an aggressive, tight-knit group focused on shared policy objectives. Secretariats with a modus operandi that requires a large staff are also more vulnerable to states which make the largest contributions to the agency. However, vulnerability to the US seems to have been the only recurrent vulnerability of this sort. The flag-of-convenience states of Panama and Liberia are by far the largest financial supports of the IMO's large staff, yet the organization does not seem vulnerable to them.

Voting rules are much more important to state domination. At the IMO, contributions but not votes are weighted by shipping tonnage. The US has dominated the UN Security Council since the end of the Cold War because most states do not get to vote. The US dominates the IMF because votes are weighted according to the size of financial contributions to the Fund. The most common one-nation–one-vote rule suits veto coalitions. Consensus decision-making, where votes are rarely taken, is the way the big players deal informally with the formal obstacles one-nation–one-vote might pose. The crucial feature of consensus as a decision rule is that abstention counts as an affirmative rather than a negative vote. States which do not agree with the dominant coalition can abstain without bearing the diplomatic cost of blocking the agreement, and states that emphatically oppose can be left out as long as their number does not become significant. Hence, at the WTO, a Quad consensus will often be tabled at meetings. The Chair reads aloud the elements of the proposed agreement, calling for objections. No objection means that there is consensus agreement. An objection leads to the Chair announcing that there is no consensus; US and EC negotiators make the appropriate threats or offers to the dissenter(s) outside the formal meeting until they can come back with a proposal to which no state will dare object. Even so, the one-nation–one-vote rule at the WTO does leave some power in the hands of weak states. A weak state can cause embarrassment by calling for a vote on a domestically unpopular measure that states would rather portray as a product of hard bargaining to forge a consensus. To be seen to cast an open vote for it can cause domestic political grief (see Putnam's (1996) two-level game model).

The tripartite voting rules of the ILO – each member with one government, one employer and one employee vote – transforms the culture of deliberation in that body, making dishonest posturing by governmental delegates about domestic practice more vulnerable to refutation by business or union delegates (Chapter 11). As we will discuss in Chapter 24, it has also made forum-shifting away from the ILO by key states an impractical option. How the votes are counted is also important.

Voting rules also affect the clout of the international organization. In Chapter 15 we saw that the WHO has been a weak shaper of the prescription drugs regime because veto coalitions have been easy to assemble in Geneva when delegates gather there to vote. In stark contrast, the IMO regime in London has been an extremely active regulation-writer since it moved to a 'tacit acceptance' procedure whereby amendments to standards proposed by technical committees enter into force by a specified date unless objections are received from a specified percentage of contracting states, usually one-third (Chapter 17). Under tacit acceptance, lethargy and inertia become the foe rather than the friend of veto coalitions. The ICAO has a procedure rather similar to IMO's tacit acceptance. Recommendations from, in effect, a technical executive, become binding on members without reference to the ICAO General Assembly unless objections are lodged within a specified period (Chapter 19). Again, this has made ICAO a prodigious international law-maker. The Understanding on Rules and Procedures Governing the Settlement of Disputes of the 1994 Final Act of the Uruguay Round of GATT demolished the former capacity of states to block GATT Dispute Resolution Panel reports by adopting a 'reverse consensus' rule. A consensus is required *not* to adopt a decision (McEwin 1998: 5): 'A consensus will occur if no member lodges a formal objection to the decision within sixty days. Appellate Body decisions are also binding on states unless all members vote unanimously to overrule them' (Evans 1998: 12). Tacit acceptance and reverse consensus are principles that can and do greatly accelerate the globalization of regulation. The move from unanimous to weighted majority decision-making at the EU has been an important factor in the dramatic increase in the number of business regulation directives issued by the EU during the 1990s. Obversely, the fact that some taxation directives require a unanimous vote ensures that there will be limited pan-European tax coordination (see Chapter 8).

The upshot of the activities of international organizations is that today most citizens greatly underestimate the extent to which most nations' shipping laws are written at the IMO in London, air safety laws at ICAO in Montreal, food standards at the FAO in Rome, intellectual property laws in Geneva at the WTO/WIPO, banking laws by the G-10 in Basle, chemicals regulations by the OECD in Paris, nuclear safety standards by IAEA in Vienna, telecommunications laws by the ITU in Geneva and motor vehicle standards by the ECE in Geneva.

## Business

Business actors are listed in Table 20.1 according to whether they are international business organizations, national business organizations or individual companies. We can also consider the role of business in the globalization of regulation according to whether they are business actors who shape the actions of states and international organizations, whether they are actors who globalize business regulation directly through their own action in implementing new regulatory norms, through regulating other business actors or through regulating states. These are the headings we will use to consider the influence of business actors.

### Shaping the Behaviour of States and International Organizations

Table 20.1 shows the diversity of international business organizations that have played important roles in the globalization process. The International Chamber of Commerce (ICC) has been the most important of these since it started in 1905. It lobbies on behalf of business interests across the whole gamut of UN organizations. As one informant put it: 'The ICC looks for key loci of decision-making in the globe and builds a poultice of influence around them'. The International Organization of Employers since 1920 has specialized in industrial relations matters, particularly at the ILO. The Business and Industry Advisory Committee (BIAC) is not important enough in any specialized field of regulation to rate a listing in Table 20.1, but it plays a significant role across all domains in filtering business views to the OECD. In a similar way, the US Industry Coordinating Group and UNICE (the European Employers Federation) play across-the-board roles in coordinating business views before the EC. More specialized international business organizations often position themselves to decisively capture the global regulatory agenda, however, as in the case of the International Federation of Pharmaceutical Manufacturers Association acting as the secretariat for the International Conference on Harmonization, which rivalled WHO as a forum for harmonization during the 1990s (Chapter 15).

The most important national business organizations are the US Chamber of Commerce and the Japanese *Keidandren*. A different kind of influence is wielded by the Global Business Forum in New York. Through a formidable structure of specialist committees it undertakes lobbying before international organizations on behalf of the 300 TNCs, law firms and business associations that are its members. It led lobbying through BIAC for a Multilateral Agreement on Investment to be negotiated at the OECD, which would be open to non-OECD members to sign. It also prepares analytic papers on a wide range of global regulatory questions being digested at the OECD and in other influential fora. Equally important, it runs dozens of conferences and lunch-time meetings in New York that allow strategic players of international regulatory games to meet US business leaders:

> a two-way dialogue in a totally non-threatening environment designed to open up questions rather than settle them. For example, the Chairman of the Commission on Sustainable Development asking their support and their opinion on how to transfer environmental technology. The top Japanese pharmaceuticals regulator meeting with American industry. What's happening from a Japanese perspective? People like it because they're not under pressure (interview at Global Business Forum).

A newer kind of national business organization is the corporate front group which presents itself to the community as an NGO rather than a business organization. Consumers for World Trade (a pro-GATT industry coalition), Citizens for Sensible Control of Acid Rain (a coal and electricity industry front), and the National Wetlands Coalition (US oil company and real estate developers) are examples. These 'astroturf' (as distinct from grass-roots) NGOs, of which there are dozens in the US, are the most sincere form of flattery the business community pays to the efficacy of social movement politics.

In some arenas national business associations matter little. For example, in the case of the highly globalized maritime regulatory regime, international business associations do the lobbying directly at IMO meetings. This is quite a different dynamic from the more common one of national industry associations shaping the law in a dominant state then that law becoming the model for less-powerful states and for global regimes.

The lobbying of European business is more corporatist in style – mostly mediated through national, pan-European and global business organizations. US companies do much more direct lobbying on their own account. On the other hand, smaller US firms have little choice but to wield their influence through business associations, and there are many exceptions where European firms do direct lobbying. Industry sectors vary according to the degree of unity or division in the interests of member firms. The nuclear industry is an extreme case of a community of shared fate, where the knowledge that another Chernobyl could wipe out the entire industry results in a solidaristic approach to global regulatory questions (Chapter 13). It can also be the case that firms that are ruthless competitors in some respects are a community of shared fate in others; for example, they can cooperate on fictitious trades to inflate transfer prices on an agreed day in order to avoid national tax laws (Chapter 8). In a systematic empirical way, Kruglak (1989: 183) was able to show how the International Organization of Employers was able to sustain 81 per cent cohesion of employer votes at the ILO. Motor vehicle standards are at the other extreme (Chapter 18). Industry associations are minor players in a strategic trade game where the big auto manufacturers and the major parts manufacturers lobby for standards that force their competitors to catch up with new technologies they have developed. The following quote gives an influential European informant's view on how the US plays the automotive game: 'The US regulates on the new technology leader immediately. The technology leader has an interest in forcing higher technical standards that they have enabled on all their competitors. But if Ford can't do it after GM invents it, Ford will successfully lobby for a waiver. Foreign companies won't get the waiver'. Here is the view of a US State Department Official on how the Europeans play the game: 'On the frontal- and side-impact standard, the US, Japan and Australia wrote a standard. The EC opposed it at WP29 and then wrote their own lower standard. This was to protect small European cars. If we want to play dirty we can work with European NGOs. But we won't accuse them openly of a non-tariff barrier'.

The State Department considers it part of its job to cool down such mutual recriminations in a world of complex interdependency where states must continue dealing on many issues.

Some of the most direct forms of capture of international regulatory processes are to be found at the International Telecommunication Union (ITU), where US companies in particular use the support of their government to gain the chairmanship of technical committees, which they use to write their own patents into global technical standards (Chapter 14). Three hundred companies have succeeded in placing their employees on ITU committees. The earlier conclusion – that the US state has been the most influential actor in the globalization of regulation – needs to be qualified in the light of these data. A German telecoms regulator can say to us: 'The ITU is largely dominated by the US. Nearly every Chairman and Vice-Chairman [on technical committees] is American'. But that domination is actually by specific US corporations. In later interviews at Motorola, we were told of the good old days when 'we would set the standards' in Geneva. A European regulator complained that 'Motorola have a patent in nearly every GSM [Groupe Speciale Mobile] standard at the ITU'.

Global food standard-setting is less blatant. As we saw in Chapter 16, however, the Swiss company Nestlé had thirty-eight representatives on Codex committees between 1989 and 1991, followed closely by Coca-Cola, Unilever and Monsanto.

US corporations exert more power in the world system than corporations of other states because they can enrol the support of the most powerful state in the world, which is prepared to deal directly with the corporations (partly due to the fund-raising methods of US political campaigns). When we talked with the CEO of Australia's largest company, a larger firm than most of those listed in Table 20.1, he complained at how little clout he had in global regulatory debates compared to smaller US companies. His cog could certainly gear up the Australian state, but Australia supplies minimal leverage in the world system. The other advantage of US companies is that the Washington political environment (as opposed to the Brussels or Tokyo environment) is hospitable to ad hoc groupings of like-minded companies setting up a Washington lobbying office and gaining political access at the highest levels. There are more large corporations with common interests in the US that can increase one another's political capacities than in any other nation. IBM, Pfizer, American Express and large accounting firms such as KPMG and PriceWaterhouse-Coopers have been particularly adept at this. American Express was a key player in globalizing the International Telecommunications Users Group, for example, which Chapter 14 shows has been the most influential force in the deregulation of telecommunications since the 1980s. It formed the AMEX Coalition of CEOs that led services, specifically financial services, onto the GATT agenda in the 1980s.

Hybrids – direct lobbying by TNCs on their own behalf and through trade associations – are common. DuPont worked at ozone diplomacy both directly and through the Chemical Man-ufacturers Association. Layered networking – vertical and horizontal integration – is common. Firms network members of a national sectoral association (e.g. for chemicals), network national sectoral associations within an international sectoral association, network national sectoral asso-ciations within a national peak association (e.g. the US Chamber of Commerce), and network national peak associations within an international peak association (e.g. the ICC).

Single individuals can be the pivot of such pyramids of networking. An individual such as Jack Valenti of the Motion Picture Association of America can be so successful in enlisting the power of many business organizations that trade negotiators from major foreign governments will visit his office to negotiate personally with him (Chapter 7). The intellectual property regime also shows how Washington policy entrepreneurs such as Eric Smith or Jacques Gorlin can sell their regulatory ideas to a few powerful CEOs such as Edmund Pratt of Pfizer, then network more and more widely until they draw UNICE and the *Keidandren* into their web. When the level of Japanese imports created serious political difficulties for the Nixon administration, Washington trade lawyers transformed the game by inventing the voluntary restraint agreement, whereby Japan undertook to persuade private companies to limit their US exports (Chayes & Chayes 1995: 13). Latour's (1986) translation theory of power as enrolment again provides a relevant under-standing of this process. One IBM executive told us he was Director of Telecommunications at IBM, Chair of the International Telecommunications Program of the US Council for International Business, Chair of the International Telecommunications Committee of the Global Business Forum, on the ICC Committee for Telecommunications and a sometime consultant to the USTR, the EC and the OECD.

## Shaping Regulation Directly

One of the major findings of this study is that global regulatory norms follow globalizing self-regulatory practice. For example, while the International Accounting Standards Committee's har-monized international standards were enforced as IOSCO listing requirements by all major stock exchanges in 1999, in 1990 a Touche Ross survey of 278 major multinational companies found that two-thirds already substantially complied with them (*Journal of Accountancy*, April 1990, pp. 15–16). Modelling is the key mechanism of globalization that lays the foundation of global norms. Long before the nineteenth-century invention of the international organization that sets business regulatory standards, globalization of regulation proceeded through modelling of busi-ness practice across national borders. Banking regulatory norms crystallized during the fourteenth century, by which time it is estimated there were 150 Italian banking companies operating multi-nationally (Dunning 1993: 97–8). After the Italians, there was the German banking dominance of the Welsers and the Fuggers of Augsberg, who spread double-entry bookkeeping throughout Germany and across a business empire that traversed Europe from the western Mediterranean to Dubrovnik in the east, further east still to India and west to Chile: 'the empire of this huge firm was vaster than the mighty empire of Charles V and Philip II, on which as we know the sun never set' (Braudel 1979: 187). In fact, the Fuggers were the main financiers of Charles V's sixteenth-century empire. Charles was under their thumb as he got deeper into debt. The Amsterdam fami-lies of finance became the next vehicles for modelling the regulatory institutions of capitalism.

Securities regulation was largely forged from the practices of the Amsterdam, London and New York Stock Exchanges over four centuries (Chapter 9).

National commercial law was formed in similar ways across many states under the influence of the *Lex Mercatoria* that evolved from medieval trade fairs. A new *Lex Mercatoria*, a private international judiciary of commercial arbitrators, grew in the twentieth century: ICC arbitration consisted of 3000 cases between 1923 and 1976, but the next 3000 cases took just eleven years (Dezalay & Garth 1994: 6). In 1997 it took on a record 452 new disputes; a small number perhaps, but behind these lie millions of contracts with ICC arbitration clauses that are settled before they become a dispute – settled in the shadow of ICC law. A key crucible of both insurance and maritime law was the exchange which became more ordered over time in Edward Lloyd's coffeehouse in London.

Global technical standardization is not only accomplished as a result of internal corporate standards being adopted as international standards: 'IBM was setting standards before they were writing standards. Their dominance set standards by dint of demand for product compatibility' (Standards Australia interview). As Chapter 19 shows, it is only a small exaggeration to say that global air safety standards are written by the Boeing Corporation in Seattle when it negotiates specifications for its next generation of passenger aircraft with the FAA. It is possible that the future road-rules of the information superhighway will also be written in Seattle, by the Microsoft Corporation.

A deep mistake is to see standard-setting at an international organization as the decisive moment in the history of the globalization of a form of regulation. That standard-writing may be only formalizing or legitimating what is a deeply embedded and consistently practised informal regulatory reality in the life of dominant corporations. In a world where, in the mid 1990s, for the first time the majority of the hundred largest economies in the world were corporations rather than states, it is foolish to see harmonization of state standards as invariably more consequential than harmonization of private corporate standards. This is a different world from that of Max Weber; in 1910 Krupp was the largest firm in Europe, with 64 000 employees – a pygmy compared to the Prussian–Hessian state railway that employed 560 000 and the Prussian Ministry of Public Works, with 680 000 (Mann 1993: 494).

## Shaping Regulation by Regulating other Businesses or States

IATA, with its army of 550 employees, has actually run the economic regulation of the air transport industry for decades (Chapter 19). The World Association of Nuclear Operators (WANO) is a global self-regulatory association that is increasing its influence in regulating nuclear safety worldwide (Chapter 13). The New York Stock Exchange regulates not only the US securities market, but sets the pace for global transparency capitalism by acting as the gatekeeper of foreign securities listings (as does the London Stock Exchange) (Chapter 9). In Chapter 9, we also saw that the Big Five accounting firms play a crucial role in regulating their clients toward the requirements of US transparency capitalism. As one TNC executive put it: 'The key effective regulatory presence in Third World financial markets are these international accounting firms. Firms are reliant on a clean bill of health from them to get foreign capital, not on national regulators'.

The most fascinating story of regulation by a private corporation is of the Swiss company Société Générale de Surveillance (SGS). SGS provides environmental inspection services in many countries and has taken over the customs service of Indonesia and other developing countries.

SGS 'sells trust' (SGS interviews) by persuading nations to sell large parts of their customs work to SGS because of its reputation for incorruptibility; it then delivers huge savings to governments. A 1991 press statement of the Indonesian Minister for Finance claimed SGS had saved Indonesia $US4.5 billion of foreign exchange between 1985 and 1990 and earned it $US1 billion in extra duties and taxes. SGS cuts average customs clearance times from weeks to one or two days as well as reducing losses from corruption. Because such testimonials bring SGS business, it has a financial incentive to catch cheats and weed out corruption in its own ranks. A major corruption scandal that might seem quite normal in the case of a developing country customs authority might wipe out SGS. SGS sets up its inspection gates in the country of export (where superior intelligence on over- or under-invoicing is available) rather than in the importing country. It accomplishes this by having a thousand heavily audited offices at all the world's major exporting sites. SGS does not engage in any manufacturing or financial activity that would threaten its independence.

Selling trust and selling competent regulation is profitable, so operatives are well-paid. The company's Senior Vice-President conceded to us that slip-ups had sometimes been detected by its internal security; not surprising, in an organization with 27 000 employees. But in all major ways it had been possible to maintain a company with an incentive structure to reward trust. Among its other regulatory activities, SGS certifies compliance with the conditions for use of Japan's consumer product safety guarantee mark. It also audits ISO 9000 (product quality), 14000 (environmental stewardship) and other ISO series and does shipping, motor vehicle safety and environmental inspections and occupational health and safety and hazardous export compliance audits. Major accounting firms such as KPMG are important competitors for the last-mentioned regulatory business.

We discussed the way the ICC lobbies in international fora on behalf of business. In Chapter 7, however, we saw that the ICC has a private-ordering strategy as well as this interest-group strategy for shaping regulation. The ICC private-ordering strategy is based on recording its members' customary practices and releasing them in the form of model rules and agreements. ICC dominance in the international commercial arbitration market – the ICC as a private business court (the ICC International Court of Arbitration) – has helped gain it the authority and knowledge for this task. One result of the private-ordering strategy is that ICC Incoterms, the ICC Uniform Rules on Letters of Credit and its Rules of Conduct to Combat Extortion and Bribery in International Business Transactions enjoy widespread recognition around the world. The mission of the ICC Institute of World Business Law 'is to strengthen links between international business practitioners and the legal profession' (ICC, World Business Organization in 1998).

In some industry sectors, though not most, insurers can be powerful business regulators. In Chapter 13 we saw how the insurance industry would never have allowed the nuclear power industry to emerge without the state underwriting potential losses with taxpayer funds and limiting nuclear liabilities at common law. Before the FAA took it over in the US, insurers using Underwriters Laboratories set aircraft safety standards. With both maritime safety (Chapter 17) and the regulation of oil pollution at sea (Chapter 12), we saw that insurers would not insure ships that failed to meet the standards of classification society surveyors and inspectors. The insurer–classification–society nexus has been the most potent regulatory force in these domains. Protecting citizens from passive smoking by banning smoking in workplaces and other enclosed public places is something that is globalizing because of insurers' unwillingness to pay up when firms do not meet their obligations to limit those risks (Chapter 15). In the US, insurers in the late 1970s and 1980s supported Ralph Nader's campaign for mandatory fitting of airbags in automobiles, indeed

they took it over. Underwriters Laboratories, the premier product-testing lab in the US, was originally affiliated with the insurance industry, but became independent of it in 1936 (Cheit 1990b:
94–5). Greenpeace successfully persuaded insurers and re-insurers to become a major force at
Kyoto for a strong protocol to regulate greenhouse-gas emissions globally (Chapter 12).

The major credit ratings agencies, Standard & Poors and Moody's in the US and Fitch IBCA
in Europe in effect are corporations that regulate states in ways not dissimilar to the way the IMF,
the EC and the World Bank regulate states (Chapters 8 and 9). They also regulate other private
regulators: Standard & Poors gives Lloyd's of London a security rating. When Moody's reduces the
creditworthiness of a government's bonds, that government has little choice but to adjust its
monetary or fiscal policy in a way that is seen to be responsive to the ratings agency sanction, or
at least it must be seen to do so. For example, Moody's explicitly says that its ratings are influenced by the 'degree of independence on critical monetary policies that the central bank has over
the treasury' (Sinclair 1994: 458). Positive sanctions are equally important: when Moody's
upgraded Argentina's credit rating in 1992, it cited 'significant steps in dismantling administrative
and regulatory controls' (Sinclair 1994: 457). The ratings agencies similarly regulate corporations
that issue bonds. Mara Bún of the Australian Consumers Association raised in discussions with us
the possibility that NGOs might seek in future to regulate corporations directly by making submissions to ratings agencies on specific corporations that are marketing unsafe products (an
option with many tobacco, asbestos, pharmaceutical, breast implant and other medical device
corporations) or that have irresponsible environmental practices (e.g. BHP's exposure to the Ok
Tedi environmental disaster in New Guinea). Environmental activists are already promoting to
ratings firms the notion of an 'environmental risk rating', not as a measure of the 'greenness' of a
company, 'but the likelihood that it might lose money for environment-related reasons' (Andrew
Hilton, Director of the Centre for the Study of Financial Innovation, quoted in Schmidheiny &
Zorraquin 1996: 153). It is not clear that environmental impacts will be taken seriously enough
to affect ratings, though one chemical company has reported that a banking institution gave it
reduced loan rates because it joined the Responsible Care program (and was thereby regarded as
a lesser credit risk) (McChesney 1996: 17).

## Individuals

> In Washington Lord Halifax
> Once whispered to Lord Keynes
> It's true *they* have all the money bags
> But *we* have all the brains (cited in Murphy 1994: 239).

In the above sections on states and business actors, we cited a number of cases where individuals enrolled the power of states and major business actors to their projects. Jack Valenti, Jacques
Gorlin and Eric Smith are cited as examples in both Chapter 7 and Chapter 10, Mostafa Tolba
and Maurice Strong are good examples of enrolment of institutional power on behalf of the
environment in Chapter 12, and Fernand Sauer with the prescription drugs regime in Chapter
15. In companies and securities, trade and tax, individual legal entrepreneurs have been significant in selling transformative ideas to corporate clients (Cain & Harrington 1994; McBarnet
1994; Powell 1993).

Latour's (1986) translation theory of power as enrolment of other actors supplies a useful understanding of this process. The image of individuals as passive puppets of inexorable global forces, corporate and state, is not the self-image held by many of our informants listed in the Acknowledgments. Many see themselves as deft puppeteers, capable of pulling strings and moving big players that remain passive until activated by someone who can show them where their interests lie. Then they help link principles to those interests. Their view is that large corporate and state bureaucracies tend to dither, paralyzed by the complexity of world regulatory networks, craving guidance by someone who can see a clear path of interest-enhancing action through the complexity.

Of course, the capture of institutional power by individuals is not as profound as it was in feudal and early modern times, when a family like the Habsburgs long commanded the most powerful institutions on earth. The early chambers of commerce that sprang up across Europe in the eighteenth century continued this tradition: 'All the chambers of commerce…are good for nothing but ruining general trade by making five or six individuals the absolute masters of shipping and commerce wherever they have been established' (Dunkerque merchant 1710, quoted in Braudel 1979: 81). While individual control of institutions in the twentieth century was much more temporary and hedged, we must still be wary of an institutional analysis of TNCs, states, NGOs and business organizations that treat them as institutional actors, writing their enrolment by individuals out of the script.

Young and Osherenko's (1993) study of polar regimes is the most systematic empirical demonstration of the importance of the leadership of entrepreneurial individuals in regime formation. Sir Eric Wyndham White (Chapter 10) did not exercise leadership by enrolling the capacities of a major institution. Rather, he saw the potential in the GATT, utterly hamstrung non-organization that it was, and transformed it into the most potent institution in the global regulatory arena. Edward Phelan used the debt of the Allied powers to the trade union movement to build the ILO as the most successful and enduring League of Nations institution. Marx and Keynes had influence as intellectuals, but as unusually activist intellectuals in practical affairs.

Justinian (two entries in Table 20.1) and Franklin Roosevelt (three entries) became two of the three most important individuals in the history of the globalization of business regulation, without having to enrol the power of any institution beyond the hegemon they headed.[5] Justinian ordered the systematizing of Roman law that laid the foundations of most global regulatory regimes today. FDR and Eleanor Roosevelt (who has her own entry under the labour standards regime in Table 20.1, was influential in establishing the FAO and was an early leader of the global human rights regime) showed remarkable leadership in building a new form of transparency capitalism checked by independent regulatory agencies, that the US exported to the world. The Bretton Woods institutions that FDR also nurtured were agents of that export. As James Landis wrote to FDR when he resigned as SEC Chairman: 'Our Commission and our work sprang from your mind, your utterances, your ideals' (Seligman 1982: 155).

The third of the three most influential individuals listed in Table 20.1 is Ralph Nader. He is listed as a key individual in the nuclear safety regime, road transport and air transport but might

---

5  There are many ways our data show the importance of this simple kind of individual influence that did not have enough global impact to justify mention in the text; for example, the energy Helmut Kohl, the German Chancellor, showed on tropical forests because of his personal interest and concern. He also played a leading role in the 1980s and 1990s in transforming the EU into a formidable transnational regulator. Kohl is thus a good example of a notable omission.

well have been listed in a number of others, since he has had some involvement in every domain cited in Table 20.1, with the possible exception of sea transport. He has been a major figure in the campaign against the new intellectual property order (Chapter 7), exposed Delaware as the company-state in fomenting a race-to-the-bottom in US corporations law (Chapter 9), exposed 'corporate welfare' to TNCs who pay little or no tax, led campaigns for tighter prudential regulation of banks and protection of consumer rights in the face of financial deregulation (Chapter 8), was an important leader of the virtual coalition against the Multilateral Agreement on Investment (Chapter 9), provided the base for and led the anti-GATT and anti-NAFTA coalitions in the US (Chapter 10), exposed abusive labour practices of US firms abroad (Chapter 11), played a key role in the establishment of the EPA, the most influential national environmental agency (Chapter 12), and established highly influential US public interest centres on pharmaceuticals regulation (Chapter 15) and food standards (Chapter 16). Nader is one of the great historical figures of the twentieth century because he did not get things done by heading a powerful actor (like FDR) nor by enrolling powerful states and corporations to his projects. What Nader enrolled to his projects were NGOs and mass publics. In this, he followed in the tradition of William Wilberforce and the first-wave feminists (Chapter 11). Remarkable individuals all.

Individual action is also important to understanding the unfolding of global regimes in much more unremarkable ways. As one US trade negotiator said to us: 'What I want to know if I negotiate with someone is: what ministry are you from and what it takes for you to get promoted'. As a former WIPO official explained to us, one way in which many developing countries from Africa and the Pacific were persuaded to sign WIPO intellectual property treaties was that WIPO officials told individual bureaucrats from those countries that membership of the treaties would entitle them to WIPO-funded trips to Geneva (with allowances). Seemingly irrational state action can often be understood this way (and by more criminal forms of bribery). Realism often fails as a theory because other states cleverly orchestrate incentives for individual trade negotiators to betray the interests of the state they represent. If you are the only individual from your state in a room in Geneva when the deal is done, as you typically will be, often you can get away with betrayal without the principals in your capital learning that you have actually 'reinterpreted' to them what you said in that room.

Individual betrayal of the institutions they represent in global negotiations is often more noble and more complex than in the picture just painted. Our discussion of epistemic communities' hold on safety engineering over corporate actors in Chapter 19 illustrates this:

> An ideal way for industry engineers to enhance their reputational capital within the epistemic community is through diplomatic demonstrations of independence from the economic interests of their own firm, by showing a greater attachment to 'objective scientific analysis' than to self-interest. Given the interest of their firms in having them respected within the epistemic community, the position of industry engineers is therefore paradoxical, thriving on astute hypocrisy of commitment to both loyalties.

Confident individuals from conflicting states invited to chair negotiation sessions often wield great power. In Chapter 10, we saw that the Swedish Chair of the TRIPS negotiating group wielded enormous influence in the way he manoeuvred a hundred states to sign an agreement that would leave them poorer. The Director-General of GATT has repeatedly exerted strategic power as the drafter of final texts. We have seen that this individual drafting power is greatest when parties agree that the text must be settled, but the US and EC have opposed views of how it should be settled. In the final drafting of the Rio Declaration of 1992, the Chair of the main negotiating committee defined 350 bracketed statements as in dispute, defined all other text as settled, ruled out-of-order repeated attempts at further discussion on them and refused to allow any delegation to add a new proposal if it met with a single objection (Koh 1994: 169). In the context of such rulings, the Chair is more powerful than the most powerful of states. Of course states can move a vote of no-confidence in the Chair, but this is difficult when, as is typical, a deadline for finalizing the text is looming.

## NGOs and Mass Publics

The Internet has greatly assisted low-cost networking and coalition-forming among NGOs wishing to mobilize jointly against a common concern. Some, like the Pesticides Action Network (bridging environmental and consumer groups) and Health Action International (bridging consumer groups and health professionals), have had considerable lobbying success. Keck and Sikkink (1998) suggest that these developments mean that transnational advocacy networks are a more important object of study than NGOs or social movements. They see motivation by values or principled ideas (rather than by material interests or professional norms) as giving these disparate networks a sense of direction and a genuine record of accomplishment.

It is precisely the non-hierarchical nature of these networks, according to Keck and Sikkink (1998), that allows them to move around obstacles to achieve their objectives. For example, if state A blocks the agenda of its domestic NGOs in the transnational network, those NGOs will provide information to NGOs in state B, which will pressure state B to apply pressure to state A. The transnational advocacy network will also mobilize pressure on state A through intergovernmental organizations. Our data support the view that transnational advocacy networks can thus outflank powerful resistance. Shared values are often enough to accomplish objectives because the change methodology is simple: 'promoting change by reporting facts' (Keck & Sikkink 1998: 19). The important thing is that the facts are credible – detail is documented – and communicated with 'drama', which usually means stories of effects on human lives.

We have seen that a prior task to 'promoting change by reporting facts' is to define or name the facts. Hence, sexual harassment did not become a regulatory fact of Japanese law until the 1990s because there was no expression for it in the Japanese language. It was feminist advocacy networks that brought *sekushuaru harasumento* or *seku hara* into the discourse (Wolff 1996: 517), winning the 1989 Gold Award for the 'Best New Word' in the Japanese language! While our data suggest Keck and Sikkink (1998) are right that transnational advocacy networks have become increasingly important motors of value-driven change, the data also suggest that NGOs with paid staff are the important nodes of those networks. Hierarchical NGOs like trade unions, professions and churches have also played critical roles in the history of globalization, and continue to do so.

The first NGOs to have a major influence on business regulation were in the temperance movement (Chapter 15)[6]. In England, their pedigree started with the Societies for the Reformation of Manners from 1691. In the US, by the 1830s there were 6000 local temperance societies with a membership of a million in a population of 13 million citizens. It became a remarkably globalized social movement before it collapsed after the failure of the US experiment in prohibition.

---

6 Strictly speaking, following Durkheim, we should say the Christian church was the first great NGO to supply a set of norms which regulated business practice transnationally: 'Not anarchy or anomie but normative regulation was provided by Christendom. Political and class struggles, economic life and even wars were, to a degree, regulated by an unseen hand, not Adam Smith's but Jesus Christ's' (Mann 1986: 398).

The anti-opium trade social movement in the late nineteenth and early twentieth centuries also globalized to some degree.

The anti-slavery movement was the second great social movement and a much more successful one than the temperance movement. In the eighteenth century in Britain and North America, it pioneered use of a petition signed by thousands of citizens, consumer boycotts and NGO use of the courts to sanction exploitative business practices. Growth in literacy enabled campaigning through pamphlets and newspaper coverage of protests.

The victories of the early social movements in abolishing slavery, and prohibition and the abolition of the legal opium trade by pharmaceutical corporations are perhaps more visible because of the passage of time, than Nader's impact in transforming the regulation of motor vehicle safety. Perhaps we also need more time to appreciate the impact of two other major nineteenth-century global social movements, the labour movement and the women's movement. From humble beginnings in the platform of the First International (1864–76), principally drafted by Marx, the labour movement in the twentieth century fomented revolutions and Communist Party dictatorships over a large proportion of the world's population. Like prohibition, this was not sustained, but the more meliorative social democratic regulatory changes promulgated by the ILO were sustained to a significant extent, notwithstanding post-Keynesian labour market deregulation. The most sustained accomplishment of the women's movement – universal suffrage – was not a business regulation reform. But ultimately, the women's movement did use the ILO and progressive TNCs, among other vehicles, to globalize the idea of equal employment opportunities for women. Later social movements for the disabled, gays and lesbians and ethnic minorities followed the women's movement model in making limited headway against discrimination in employment.

No two social movements could be more different than the labour movement – hierarchical and highly structured into federations of unions nationally and internationally – and the women's movement, non-hierarchically committed to nurturing plurality in the women's voices that are heard.[7] The women's movement model has been much more influential upon subsequent major social movements – the environment movement, the civil rights movement, the anti-nuclear and peace movements, the consumer movement, the gay and lesbian rights movement. The way hierarchical trade unions so frequently fell under the control of corrupt oligarchs made their model of organization unattractive to social movements. Yet that organization gave the trade union movement something that no other social movement has ever achieved – voting rights at the forum where international standards are set. It also gave the International Confederation of Free Trade Unions the secretariat resources to audit whether the ILO is pursuing the worst abuses of labour standards in all nations (not just Western ones) through its *Annual Survey of Violations of Trade Union Rights*. No other social movement has been able to be so globally systematic in its monitoring of regulatory standards. O'Brien et al. (1999) also find that while the IMF has actively courted organized labour, it has not done so with other social movements such as the environment and women's movement.[8]

---

7  The women's movement also illustrates that effective leadership without entrenched hierarchy is possible. NGO participants at the Rio Earth Summit of 1992, when surveyed, rated the women's groups as the most effective lobbyists at the summit, closely followed by the business groups then the environment groups. Respondents to the survey attributed this success to the strong leadership of Bella Abzug of the Women's Environment and Development Organization. The Women's Caucus at Rio was a well-organized group at Summit PrepComs which accomplished many textual changes (Doherty 1994: 209-10).

8  On the other hand, O'Brien et al. (1999) do find some increase in the influence of the environment and women's movement at the World Bank and WTO.

A good contrast is the anti-nuclear movement, which has succeeded totally in almost every Western state in preventing the construction of new nuclear power plants since the 1980s (Chapter 13). But the movement has not had the organization to extend its reach to stopping the substantial proliferation of nuclear plants outside the West during the same period.

The best-resourced and most organized of the new twentieth-century social movements has been the environment movement. By 1982, there were 2230 environmental NGOs in developing countries and 13 000 in developed economies (Caldwell 1988: 19). The 120 national-level environmental organizations that comprise the European Environmental Bureau have a combined membership of 20 million (Porter & Brown 1991: 57). Keohane, Haas and Levy (1993: 14) concluded from their study, *Institutions of the Earth*, that 'If there is one key variable accounting for policy change, it is the degree of domestic environmentalist pressure in major industrialized democracies, not the decision-making rules of the relevant international institution'. New regulatory ideas for international regimes usually come not from states (Caldwell 1988: 17) but from NGOs and the scientific community.

In this, the environmental movement is atypical of NGOs working in the other domains of regulation discussed in this book. NGOs can have a major impact on symbolic issues that attract a lot of media concern, but not on the plethora of technical regulatory details that are the substance of regimes. The anti-nuclear NGOs are the extreme manifestation of this – totally successful at stopping the building of new Western plants through being able to mobilize not-in-my-backyard (NIMBY) sentiment, but barely relevant to the regulatory changes that have made existing plants safer (Chapter 13).

The consumer movement is a less extreme case. But if we look at the food regime, we see much effectiveness in securing regulatory reticence on issues like food irradiation and genetic modification of food, a decisive French consumer boycott that reduces consumption of hormone-treated veal by 70 per cent, but a consumer movement utterly outgunned by industry on the constant grinding-out of global food standards at the Codex in Rome (Chapter 16). This is the situation with most of the regimes studied, where consumer interests are vitally affected; indeed at some, such as the ITU where a consumer voice on technical standards is virtually never heard, the situation is worse.

The basic problem is that the consumer movement has not had the resources to employ staff to sit on the countless technical committees of global regulatory regimes and has not had the energy to mobilize and monitor networks of technically competent volunteers to do so. Energy and resources are more likely to arrive after the horse has bolted. Mass rallies attracted as many as 500 000 people into Indian streets in 1993 after the implications of the TRIPS agreement of the GATT became clear, but during the many years that this intellectual property agreement was being negotiated, there was no involvement from the Indian consumer movement, indeed no serious involvement from any national or international consumer movement. There were simply too few consumer movement antennae, already busy detecting too many other things.

This critique is true even of the best-resourced NGOs of the environment movement, particularly during its early decades. For example, Silverstein (1978: 119) showed systematically that between 1958 and 1972 representation of any kind of environmental NGO at any level of IMO decision-making was zero. In more recent years, Friends of the Earth, with Greenpeace and a few other NGOs, have had some involvement, but the coverage has been extremely patchy.

The good news for democratic engagement is that NGOs internationalized prodigiously during the twentieth century. In 1909 there were 176 international NGOs; by 1993, there were 28 500 if we define international as requiring operation in at least three countries. The work of the Commission on Global Governance (1995: 32) shows that more than 90 per cent of this growth has occurred since 1970. Since 1970, the former European domination of international NGOs has been tempered by strong growth in the proportion of participation accounted for by African and Asian NGOs (Commission on Global Governance 1995: 33). NGOs continue to be quite nationalist in their outlook, however, giving only modest proportions of their resources to their international arm.

Professional bodies are other important NGOs (e.g. the International Accounting Standards Committee) and voluntary standards organizations, most notably the ISO. We will have more to say about the ambiguous nature of these organizations in the next section, on epistemic communities.

Much of the impact of ordinary citizens on global regulatory change is not mediated through NGOs. We have found that in all the regimes we studied, during the twentieth century anxiety among mass publics, triggered mostly by reading stories of disasters in the mass media, had substantial effects in globalizing new forms of regulation. In addition to the catalogue of catalytic disasters listed in Table 20.1, such as the *Titanic*, Chernobyl, Bhopal, the *Torrey Canyon* and major stock market crashes, *Silent Spring* and *Unsafe at Any Speed* were books that constructed a pattern of perceived disaster not from a single incident but from an accumulation of regulatory neglect. Upton Sinclair's (1906) *The Jungle* and F.C. Accum's (1820) *Treatise on Adulteration of Food and Culinary Poisons* had similar effects on the early development of the food standards regime, as did Harriet Beecher Stowe's *Uncle Tom's Cabin* (1852) during the later stages of the anti-slavery movement, when it sold a million copies in England in its first eight months on the market.

In *Between Facts and Norms*, Habermas (1996) sees these mass reactions not as something to be cynical about , but as profoundly enriching democracy:

> in general, one can say that even in more or less power-ridden public spheres, the power relations shift as soon as the perception of the relevant social problems evoke a *crisis consciousness* at the periphery. If actors from civil society then join together, formulate the relevant issue, and promote it in the public sphere, their efforts can be successful, because the endogenous mobilization of the public sphere activates an otherwise latent dependency built into the internal structure of every public sphere, a dependency also present in the normative self-understanding of the mass media: the players in the arena owe their influence to the approval of those in the gallery (p. 382).
>
> In the proceduralist paradigm, the public sphere is not conceived simply as the back room of the parliamentary complex, but as the impulse-generating periphery that *surrounds* the political centre: in cultivating normative reasons, it affects all parts of the political system without intending to conquer it (p. 442).

The promotion by Maurice Strong and others of an NGO summit to parallel the Rio Earth Summit in 1992 and the adoption of the same approach at the Beijing World Conference on Women in 1995 were literal attempts in global politics to 'surround the political centre with an impulse-generating periphery'. For all its limitations, this was accomplished in a way that was more dialogic than media waves of mass concern about disasters.

Sometimes NGOs do use the periodic outpourings of mass concern associated with disasters to pull reform agendas out of their top drawer and get them implemented. At other times, mass concern has hurt NGOs. For example, the US Congress responded to public outcry over an ECOSOC decision to grant consultative status to the International Lesbian and Gay Association by threatening to withhold $US129 million from the UN if it implemented the decision. ECOSOC responded by expelling the International Lesbian and Gay Association from consultative status in 1994 (Otto 1996: 116–17).

NGOs do not have to be representative or to have huge budgets to be effective. They do have to be able to convince regulatory policy-makers that they might, if push comes to shove, be able to mobilize mass publics around their concerns. When mass publics are actually stirred, major regulatory change often occurs in a short space of time. NGO influence is weak, however, in the face of industry domination of week-in, week-out technical standard-setting and domination of daily decisions not to enforce the standards which do make it into existence.

## Epistemic Communities

Keohane and Nye's (1974) notion of 'transgovernmental elite networks' is too narrow a concept, limited as it is to governmental actors, for the regulatory communities uncovered by our empirical research. Epistemic communities are loose collections of knowledge-based experts who share certain attitudes and values and substantive knowledge, as well as ways of thinking about how to use that knowledge (Haas 1989). While this means that science is bound to be central in many epistemic communities, we do not assume that the shared discourse and expertise must be scientific. The discourse and expertise of Wall Street is about how to trade on financial markets. We have found that there is community on Wall Street, which includes a lot of care, trust, mutual respect and shared values, though we would not say that Wall Street was a cohesive political force or a collective actor. If regulations and procedural rules are the hardware of international regimes, the knowledge and discourses of epistemic communities of actors are its software (Dryzek 1996). Sometimes the software of epistemic communities hijacks the hardware of the institutional order. This is one way of reading the French revolution: 'Versailles lost cultural pre-eminence to Parisian salons' (Mann 1993: 176).

Regulatory epistemic communities, we have found, bring together adversaries (see Meidenger 1987; Hancher & Moran 1989; Black 1997; Parker 1998b, 1999; Picciotto & Mayne 1999). We observed knowledgeable advocates associated with Health Action International, the Medical Lobby for Appropriate Marketing and Consumers International attend meetings of the 4000 strong Regulatory Affairs Professionals Society, dominated by pharmaceutical company executives and regulators. While they disagree on a lot, it is also remarkable how much they can agree upon – they have a basis in shared values for dealing with one another. They certainly speak the same regulatory language. They have learnt a transnational regulatory discourse so they can all engage in constructing global institutions. One is trying to tighten a screw while another seeks to loosen it, but they work on the same scaffolding and make decisive compromises from time to time on how many turns of the screw there should be before they leave it for a period.

Sometimes NGOs are pretty much excluded from the epistemic community, as in the nuclear regulatory case, and speak another language, for example about pushing over the entire rotten scaffolding, as they see it.

Most epistemic communities start with professions. Venice's Luca Pacioli's *Summa de Arithmetica* (1494) earned him the accolade 'Father of Accounting'. There were many fathers of law in China, the Middle East, Rome and Bologna. Hugo Grotius is the seminal theorist in discovering the importance of what we now call transnational epistemic communities (Buzan 1993). In the Grotian tradition, international law is seen as constituting a community of participants in the international legal order. Lawyers still have their own epistemic communities, including epistemic communities of ICC commercial arbitration, for example, that continue to develop a kind of *Lex Mercatoria* important to the regimes discussed in the early chapters of this book.[9] But we find that these epistemic communities are rather subsidiary to the core epistemic communities that forge the regulatory customs that are taken into the *Lex Mercatoria*. The community of international lawyers that Grotius forged was less important than the diasporas of Jews, Armenians, Venetians and Genoese who used their shared language, religion, kinship and culture to reduce uncertainty in international trade by forging customs for the extension of credit, contracting, defining property rights and merchantable quality (Curtin 1984). The law was forged in the shadow of their custom (to paraphrase Dezalay (1996), paraphrasing Galanter).

The minority of lawyers who are present in the core epistemic communities that grip our attention in this book are the really interesting lawyers. These are the legal entrepreneurs (McBarnet 1994, Powell 1993, Cain & Harrington 1994) of whom Grotius himself may have been the most brilliant, not the more standard kind of lawyer who takes instructions from the big end of town and delivers on them. Lawyers were important in the International Association for Labour Legislation which laid the foundations for the ILO from the end of the nineteenth century (Chapter 11). It is the legal entrepreneurs who devise the idea of linking the intellectual property and trade regimes, a strategy for a hostile takeover or a poison pill to defend against a takeover (Powell 1993), and sell it to clients who they believe should have an interest in acting on it. As Young (1993) has shown, leadership is crucial to framing ideas for regime formation. So we must be wary of methods such as survey research, which bury the leaders in a thicket of data dominated by followers. While law has not produced an institutional entrepreneur of the significance of a Keynes, James Landis, Lord Mansfield and Louis Brandeis are not insignificant figures in this sense, and Ralph Nader is an extremely significant one, if we count him as a lawyer. To understand why the Code Civil was so important to the globalization of law, it helps to know that 72 per cent of the French revolution's elected representatives, and a majority of the 'Twelve Who Ruled', including Robespierre, were trained as lawyers (Mann 1993: 187–92). This was the epistemic community of governance that Napoleon succeeded.

Scientists are much more dominant than lawyers in the epistemic communities that are centrally important in eight of the thirteen domains discussed this book. Yet science is like law in the way it supplies discourses that can unify, in common projects, interest groups that are otherwise divided: 'Aerodynamics is aerodynamics. We were always able to talk to the Russians in the old communist days because science is science. Good scientific analyses are the same everywhere and that's the language we talk' (US FAA official).

When you are negotiating a regime with an actor representing diametrically opposed interests, science is bound to be a more productive discourse than self-interest. Science is actually not a bad foundation for a public-regarding discourse. At the end of the day it must be put in the service of the economic concerns of business on one side and the environmental concerns of a green group on the other side, for example. Yet new scientific findings or ways of framing a debate are often found, in our case studies, to dissolve divisions, though at other times they exacerbate them. Shared scientific endeavours within epistemic communities can supply what Young and Osherenko (1993) found in their studies of polar regimes to be 'salient solutions' – formulae that discover a new simplicity to break a deadlock in how the parties view the conflict, 'a formula that is easy for policy-makers to grasp and that is intuitively appealing to the general public' (Young & Osherenko 1993: 236).

---

9  The emergence of these epistemic communities is richly documented in Dezalay and Garth (1996).

Remarkably, perhaps, Table 20.1 shows that we found a strong epistemic community in every domain with the exception of the weakening epistemic community hanging off IATA for discussing the economic regulation of air transport. This old epistemic community is irrevocably dividing into an epistemic community of liberalizers who want to push over the scaffolding on which the old community toils, and an epistemic community of orderly regulators.

Business strategists have been the most sensitive to the significance of epistemic communities. They realize that 'Dreary bureaucratic meetings are the key to an exciting agenda' (IAEA interview), that regime formation is 'talk, talk and more talk' (Sandford 1994). The Industry Cooperative for Ozone Layer Protection, Responsible Care and the Business Council for Sustainable Development (Chapter 12) are examples of business engagement with epistemic communities explicitly committed to expanding a needed global regulatory regime. Coca-Cola's initiation of the International Life Sciences Institute (ILSI) and the International Technical Caramel Association (Chapter 16) are more ambiguous cases. These were fair-minded efforts to support quality science, but selectively funded in domains where Coca-Cola and other companies thought the good science would support their interests. We summarized their strategy as follows: fund an arm's-length technical association to do the needed science; use the results to lobby for new Codex standards; in the process, engage all national epistemic communities with the need for change in their national laws.

ILSI has been most influential in food standards epistemic communities. NGOs cannot match this kind of strategy, nor the industry dominance of epistemic communities generally. Yet to be effective NGOs must be part of, rather than separate from, the epistemic community. One option discussed in Chapter 26 is to shift the way they use their limited resources for recruitment of advocates, away from young employed activists with BAs in politics toward staff to service a larger cadre of grey-haired volunteers with experience and qualifications in science and, yes, in business – many respected semi-retired NGO fish swimming in the water of epistemic community, rather than activists repulsed by the water because fish fornicate in it.[10]

A weakness of this book is that in chapter after chapter it fails to communicate the importance of what goes on in countless little technical committees at international organizations and more so in voluntary standard-setting bodies like the ISO, the British Standards Institute, Underwriters Laboratories, the American National Standards Institute, the International Commission on the Rules for the Approval of Electrical Equipment, the International Electro-Technical Commission and the European standardization bodies (CEN and CENELEC). These are crucial sites of epistemic community-building. They are neglected in our discussion because each little decision they make is so small in the overall scheme of things as not to justify a mention. Collectively, however, their importance is in both the incremental construction of regimes and epistemic communities of the regime-builders. Their importance to trade and economic growth has seen the inclusion in the WTO of a Code of Good Practice for the Preparation, Adoption and Application of Standards (see Annex 3 of the Agreement on Technical Barriers to Trade). As Cheit (1990: 30) points out: 'In most areas involving the environment, health or safety, there are far more private standards than public ones'. Since he wrote that, the number of ISO standards has doubled. They increased from fifty-seven in 1957 to 721 in 1967, to 11 258 in 1997 (1997 ISO Annual Report). The voluntary standards organizations that sustain over 30 000 standards in the US alone are utterly industry-dominated (much more so than in Europe). Yet Cheit finds that many of these

---

10 Apologies to W.C. Fields.

industry representatives are 'unrecognized advocates' of health and safety, sometimes because they represent insurers or safety equipment suppliers. Cheit also reported that representatives on these committees surprisingly often go against the interests of their employers when the engineering analyses do not commend those interests. What follows for us, if not for Cheit, is that it is far from pointless for NGO advocates to participate in these fora; it is far from pointless to engage with industry-dominated private standard-setting, because NGO allies are readily found there. One of the more interesting epistemic communities in this regard is the community of competition regulators. States are increasingly relying on competition law to help them meet their market-access objectives in areas such as trade, telecommunications and financial services. It is a community that is quietly and informally increasing its levels of international coordination. Its links with business actors and consumers, as well as its low barriers to entry (e.g. compared to the community that surrounds central banking) make it, we argue, centrally important in developing a program for citizen sovereignty over global regulation. We return to this theme in the final chapter.

Some epistemic communities that hang off environmental treaties are already close to being dominated more by environmentalists than by business. The ILO is the only major business regulatory epistemic community which has been decisively less dominated by business than by NGOs. Bill Dee and Allan Asher's entrepreneurship in establishing the Society of Consumer Affairs Professionals in Business in Australia in 1992 (which previously existed in the US and now exists in several other countries also) was a fascinating exercise in creating an epistemic community dominated by business people with strong sympathies for the consumer movement. SOCAP even organized a temporary funding rescue mission for Australia's peak consumer body, the Consumers Federation of Australia, when a conservative government cut its funding in 1996! Consumer movement purists were right to see this as capture, for mutual capture of opposed interest is at the heart of the idea of epistemic communities of regulation.

## Conclusion

All the types of actors listed in Table 20.1 have been shown to play important roles in the globalization of business regulation. Useful research on globalization can be done at the level of specific types of actors. For example, counting votes of nations in international organizations can be revealing. Yet if the Japanese voting delegate is the President of the Japanese Whaling Association and the delegate from a Pacific island state is a Greenpeace operative, if some of the others are from environment ministries, some from fisheries ministries and others are diplomats with no knowledge of or interest in the issues being voted, then we must realize that we are counting apples and oranges. International relations theory realism is not attractive for the phenomena we have investigated, because the size of the apples and the oranges is not the crucial variable.

What we find to be crucial is how state and non-state actors are linked. Entrepreneurship to interlink chains of actors explains the globalization of business regulation. Not billiard balls of differing weights bouncing around a table, but activist cells reaching out to chain other cells into complex molecular structures that reproduce to enmesh the billiard table in a web of new life-forms.

One could respond to our data by adding a realist corporate economics to realist international relations theory: add the size of the corporate billiard balls in a coalition as another term in the regression equation, alongside the size of the states. We have seen why this would generate theories of extremely limited explanatory power. Japan and China are among the three most 'powerful' national economies in the world and Mitsubishi, Mitsui, Itochu, Sumitomo and Marubeni are among the half-dozen most 'powerful' corporations (in revenues).[11] In 1995, Japan hosted twenty-four of the largest fifty TNCs, all of them with sales greater than the GNPs of most states (Anderson & Cavanagh 1996). Given the weight they have to throw around, these actors have proved remarkably uninfluential in our stories. This is because they have been only weakly linked to chains of actors across the world system. They are part of networks and yet manage neither to capture those networks nor even to be integrated into them. Each of the corporations might have many thousand times more revenue than Greenpeace, but it has had less influence on the globalization of business regulation because Greenpeace has had a superior capacity to enrol others (including, but not limited to, mass publics), to its projects. This in turn is connected to Greenpeace's superior competence at the entrepreneurship of linkage. In this chapter we illustrated the impotence of unlinked corporate power using the example of Australia's largest corporation for most of its history, BHP. Yet we might contrast this case with Rupert Murdoch's News Ltd, which is emerging as a major future shaper of regulatory institutions in the communications field because of the way Murdoch has linked himself to the Chinese and US states (in the latter case, to the point of relinquishing Australian in favour of US citizenship).

US power has not declined in proportion to its declining share of world trade. The question is whether US power has declined at all. US influence has survived because the US state is still enrolled by many of the most powerful corporations in the world, as well as by the strongest environmental movement, by Ralph Nader and so on. Paradoxically, the weakest trade union movement in the West can enrol its state to be the most forceful voice for the linkage of labour standards to the WTO, for example. The even deeper paradox is that this persistent enrolment of US global activism results from the way the separation of powers in the US polity gives special vitality to Putnam's analysis of global politics as a two-level game played simultaneously at a domestic game-board and an international one.

In contrast, European states have been weakened (as state actors) in the world system by the choices of the most powerful European business organizations to enrol the EC (rather than nation-states) as the prime champion of their causes. While Britain could once enrol an empire and its businesses, now it is enrolled by the EC (and its businesses seek to enrol Brussels). We have seen that the cumulative effect of this enrolment is that since 1980 the EC has actually become more influential than the US in several regulatory regimes. The EC and US are sufficiently equally matched that the outbreak of regulatory conflict between them produces a stalemate akin to the US–Soviet strategic stalemate during the Cold War. The difference is that most important matters proceed by the US and EC enrolling each other after negotiating a mutually beneficial compromise. If Japan used its economic muscle to resist the US–EC position, it would be a major setback that could foment widespread Asian resistance, but Japan almost never does so. Typically, Japan follows, basking in the fiction that it is an equal partner with the US and EC when the joint position comes out of the Quad or the G-7. However adverse that joint position is to the majority of the world's people, it is the position that is likely to prevail.

Resistance is less possible than it was when the G-77 could parley for an allegiance of the Soviet bloc against the West. Empowerment of the Third World through institutions like

---

11 'Fortune's Global 500: The World's Largest Corporations', *Fortune*, 5 August 1996, F-1.

UNCTAD crumbled in the absence of a Second World. Creative resistance is possible – such as Australia's initiative in establishing the Cairns Group of agricultural-exporting nations. However, this influence works by seeking to enrol the US and EC, not by defeating them. In the end, the innovative links among the weak are more enrolled than enrolling. The Cairns Group gets an agricultural agreement (with which the US and EU do not comply) in return for a new world information and intellectual property order with which the Cairns Group is forced to comply. International coalitions of the weak prevail only when the coalition includes domestic players from the US or Europe (even if they are comparatively weak ones, like the US labour movement or Ralph Nader). A combination of Latour's theory of power as enrolment and Putnam's theory of global politics as a two-level game does reveal, nevertheless, the possibility of the weak prevailing.

## CHAPTER 21

Contests of Principles

Principles have played no role in the globalization of business regulation. Had this been our hypothesis it would have turned out to be false. In every domain we have investigated we have found that actors have supported some principles and opposed others, using principles to do so. Contests of principles are a key phenomenon in the process of the globalization of business regulation. This finding requires an analysis of their role, the purpose of this chapter.

The chapter is written in two parts. The first identifies those principles that have been entrenched in business regulation and those that have not. The second part looks at principles more abstractly. Drawing on the findings of the first part, it identifies the characteristics of principles in aggregate (e.g. they can be active or passive) and explores relations between principles (e.g. principles can be co-active or oppositional). This analysis of principles sets the stage for a processual theory of forum-shifting to enact contests of principles over how regulation should globalize, presented in Chapters 23 and 24.

## Contests

### Triumph of Transparency

Of all the principles we have surveyed, transparency has been the one which has most consistently strengthened in importance. The only domain in which we found it weakly present was air transport and even there it is strengthening somewhat (see Table 21.1) In nuclear regulation, although strengthening, transparency has a somewhat restricted operation. Transparency is at its strongest in the domains of finance, corporations and securities, so much so that we depicted one shift in capitalism as being a shift from an insider network capitalism to a global transparency capitalism. Within finance, transparency has a sister principle, that of consolidation. Consolidation requires the total supervisory coverage of a firm's financial affairs, which a transparency of financial affairs enables. Transparency is also a principle which has become entrenched in some regulatory domains by means of law. It is, for example, a general obligation in the General Agreement on Trade in Services (GATS) and the Agreement on Trade-Related Aspects of Intellectual Property Rights (TRIPS). Transparency obligations are dotted throughout the Final Act Embodying the Results of the Uruguay Round of Multilateral Trade Negotiations (Final Act) and they also feature in regional agreements like the North American Free Trade Agreement (NAFTA).

**TABLE 21.1** The contest of principles

| CONTEST OF PRINCIPLES | CONTRACT AND PROPERTY RIGHTS | FINANCE | CORPORATIONS AND SECURITIES | TRADE AND COMPETITION | LABOUR | ENVIRONMENT |
|---|---|---|---|---|---|---|
| Lowest-cost location | Weak | Weakening | Weakening | Strong | Strong | Strong |
| World's best practice | Weak | Strengthening | Strong | Strong | Weak | Strengthening |
| Deregulation | Weakening | Strengthening | Weakening | Strengthening | Strengthening | Strong |
| Strategic trade | Weak | Weak | Weak | Strengthening | Weak | Strengthening |
| Rule compliance | Strong | Strong | Strong | Weak | Weakening | Strong |
| Continuous improvement | Weak | Strengthening | Weak | Weak | Strengthening | Strengthening |
| National sovereignty | Weakening (intellectual property) Strong (contract) | Weakening | Strong | Weakening | Weakening | Weakening |
| Harmonization | Strengthening | Strengthening | Strengthening | Strengthening | Strong | Strengthening |
| Mutual recognition | Weak | Strengthening | Strong | Strengthening | Weak | Weak |
| Transparency | Strengthening | Strong | Strong | Strengthening | Strong | Strengthening |
| National treatment | Strong | Strengthening | Weak | Strong | Weak | Weak |
| Most Favoured Nation | Strong | Strengthening | Weak | Strong | Weak | Weak |
| Reciprocity | Weakening | Weakening | Weak | Strong | Weak | Strong |
| Other principles | Free flow of information, common heritage of mankind | Conditionality, consolidation | Nil | Mercantilism | Tripartism, labour not a commodity | Best available technology, world's best practice, sustainability, precautionary principle |

Aside from the existence of formal transparency obligations in the Final Act, transparency is entrenched there as a process. A good example is to be found in the Agreement on Agriculture, which obliges states to convert their non-tariff barriers (e.g. quantitative import restrictions, variable import levies, minimum import prices) into 'ordinary customs duties'. Requiring non-tariff barriers to be turned into tariff barriers is an example of transparency, since tariff barriers are easier to identify and quantify.

Transparency is the most striking emergent principle of globalization. In those regimes that have globalized early, transparency has also emerged. A good example of this is the regulation of shipping, which globalized early. There we saw that maritime regulation has exercised a historical leadership on transparency through initiatives like the plimsoll line and the posting of data on the safety of ships at Lloyd's coffee-house. An even better example of transparency as an emergent property of globalization is in the regulation of drugs. At the national level of drug regulation, consumer groups have had to struggle to acquire information from national regulatory authorities. When the European Commission (EC), the European Federation of Pharmaceutical Industry Associations, the Japanese Ministry of Health and Welfare, the Japanese Pharmaceutical Manufacturers Association, the US Food and Drug Administration (FDA) and the US Pharmaceutical Manufacturers Association met at the International Conference on Harmonization of Technical

| NUCLEAR SAFETY | TELECOMMUNI-CATIONS | DRUGS | FOOD | SEA TRANSPORT | ROAD TRANSPORT | AIR TRANSPORT |
|---|---|---|---|---|---|---|
| Weak | Weak | Weakening | Weak | Strong | Weak | Weak |
| Fairly weak | Strong | Strengthening | Weak | Strong | Strong | Strong |
| Weak | Strong | Strong (licit) Weak (illicit) | Strong | Weak | Weakening | Strengthening (economic) Weakening (safety) |
| Weak | Strong | Weak | Weakening | Weak | Strong | Strong |
| Weakening | Weak | Weakening | Strong | Strong | Strong | Strong |
| Strong | Weak | Strengthening | Strengthening | Strengthening | Strengthening | Strong |
| Weak | Weak | Weak (prescription) Strong (alcohol, tobacco, OTCs) | Weakening | Weak | Weak | Weak |
| Strong | Strong | Strengthening | Strengthening | Strong | Strong | Strong |
| Weak | Weak | Strengthening | Strengthening | Weak | Strong | Weak |
| Restricted yet strengthening | Strengthening | Strengthening | Strengthening | Strong | Strengthening | Weak |
| Weak | Strengthening | Strong | Weakening | Weak | Strengthening | Strengthening |
| Weak | Strengthening | Weakening | Weakening | Weak | Strengthening | Weak |
| Weak | Strong | Weak | Weakening | Weak | Weak | Strong |
| Nonproliferation | Market access, free flow of information, common heritage of mankind, first-come, first-served | Prohibition, regulatory competition | Food security, farmers' rights, common heritage of mankind | None | Best available technology | Best available technology |

Requirements for Registration of Pharmaceuticals for Human Use, transparency became a necessary byproduct of this international initiative. Each actor had to provide the others with information about their respective technical standards and regulatory systems. Harmonization is a form of coordination and coordination is an information-intensive activity. When global harmonization is the goal, the information demands of the actors involved in the process, as well as the demands of those outside who are watching it, wondering whether to join, are very high.

This phenomenon of transparency appearing more at the international level than at the national level can also be seen in food regulation. Under the Agreement on the Application of Sanitary and Phytosanitary Measures (SPS) states have a general transparency obligation. In addition they must explain the reasons for their sanitary or phytosanitary measures if those measures are likely to constrain the exports of other states. Again, this is a better level of transparency than consumer movements have been able to obtain within many national systems of food regulation. Similarly, with labour standards the International Labour Organization (ILO) has been able to open, to a degree, some windows of transparency on the labour practices of totalitarian regimes (Kent 1997). Transparency has also increased its hold in motor vehicle regulatory decision-making as the EC, the Economic Commission for Europe (ECE) and the World Trade Organization (WTO) have moved to prevent motor vehicle standards from being used as non-tariff trade barriers by insisting on transparency in the setting of national motor vehicle safety standards.

Air transport regulation, we observed, has been the antithesis of transparency. Transparency is not a principle favoured by cartelists. Despite the US-led push for free skies and free markets for air travel, the International Air Transport Association (IATA, initially dominated by European airlines) remains a powerful leader and coordinator of geographic cartels for parts of the airline industry. There is a parallel here with telecommunications. Under the European PTT (Post, Telephone and Telegraph) system or the private monopoly system of AT&T in the US, it was impossible for those not in the club to get information on matters of market entry, price and interconnection. It was an area rife with secret bilateral deals (and remains so in the area of international accounting rates, although even here transparency is increasing as a result of efforts by the International Telecommunication Union (ITU) and the Federal Communications Commission (FCC) to change the system). Telecommunications has been deregulated to a greater extent than has air travel. With deregulation the principle of transparency has assumed a stronger and stronger presence. Telecommunications has been one of the key sectoral negotiations within the GATS framework, an agreement on basic telecommunications (taking the form of a protocol to GATS) being concluded by members in February 1997. Article 4 of the Annex on Telecommunications (the Annex is part of GATS) requires members to make publicly available information on matters like tariffs and technical interfaces for public telecommunications transport networks. GATS also contains an Annex on Air Transport Services. It applies to aircraft repair and maintenance, selling and marketing of air transport services and computer reservation system services, but not the traffic rights that lie at the heart of the industry.

Even in those areas where secrecy has been a dominant norm, selective forms of transparency are developing. Trade negotiations take place in secret between trade officials, as do the negotiations between key business organizations that shape the outcome of trade negotiations. The culture of trade negotiators remains one of private negotiations, private deals and private bullying. NGOs do not have the formal observer status at WTO that NGOs have at the World Intellectual Property Organization (WIPO) or the ITU. However, transparency has made some inroads on even this culture. The WTO pushes for transparency of trade restrictions (primarily through its Trade Policy Review Mechanism) and transparency of outcome (the availability of its documentation is improving). Transparency of the negotiating process is reserved for those who are in the trade negotiators' club. Within the club of nuclear power plant operators, the individual responsibility of each member of the club for the fate of all means that transparency within the group is becoming progressively dominant. This is clearly the case in the US, where plant CEOs meet annually to discuss why their plants finished where they did on the basis of indicators put out by the Institute of Nuclear Power Operations.

Transparency helps to facilitate information flows between actors. Actors have at least three reasons to encourage the flow of information between them, and therefore three reasons to support transparency. These are reasons of economic calculation, coordination and trust. In the days when AT&T played primarily in the US market there was no need to go to the ITU and insist on information about the pricing of services in Australia. Similarly, transparency in the setting of motor vehicle standards was less of an issue when car manufacturers focused on domestic markets, and in any case the real problem about overseas markets was high tariffs. Nowadays many market actors push for transparency because it enables them to make better strategic calculations concerning market entry. One factor, for instance, affecting Pfizer's decision to invest in India's pharmaceuticals industry is the transparency of India's legal system, particularly the way in which that system protects and enforces intellectual property rights. Governments of economically powerful states support transparency because it is likely to benefit some of their industries. Transparency also helps actors to coordinate their actions to a desired end, the global harmonization of pharmaceuticals regulation being an example. Finally, transparency helps to build trust. The act of exchanging information or making information available is often the first step in building a relationship of trust. Nuclear regulation, we have seen, is an example of where a limited form of transparency has helped to constitute trust among the community of nuclear power plant operators.

### Recognizing and Harmonizing the Decline of National Sovereignty

The principle which has most consistently declined in the strength of its operation has been the principle of national sovereignty. A glance at Table 21.1 confirms this. With the exceptions of the regulation of contract, corporations and securities, and alcohol, tobacco and over-the-counter (OTC) drugs, the principle of national sovereignty is weak or weakening. Even so, it remains a vibrant principle in many of the domains where it is weakening. National sovereignty has most regularly been opposed to the principle of harmonization. This particular contest has been played out:
- in contract, where there have been largely unsuccessful attempts to harmonize national systems of contract law through international conventions;
- in property, where harmonization under the auspices of WTO has been remarkably successful in the case of intellectual property;
- in environment, where harmonization has had some pockets of success (e.g. the chemicals regime developed by the OECD);
- in telecommunications, where harmonization has been important in the area of technical standards;
- in motor vehicle regulation, where ECE standards have had a harmonizing effect globally;
- in the regulation of food standards, where harmonization has acquired more clout through linking standards to the determination of WTO disputes concerning technical barriers to trade;
- in sea transport, where the International Maritime Organization's (IMO) standards dominate;
- in air transport, where the air safety regime is to a considerable degree globally led by the FAA and Boeing;
- in the labour standards domain, where the ILO, the EC and the US Occupational Safety and Health Administration (OSHA) have been active harmonizers;
- in nuclear regulation, where the International Atomic Energy Agency's (IAEA) safeguards regime and to a lesser extent its safety regime operate under the principle of harmonization;
- in trade, where states by signing the Final Act have opened themselves up to the harmonizing influences contained in the various agreements in that Final Act.

In contests with national sovereignty, the principle of harmonization has a close ally in the form of mutual recognition. The two principles are often co-active in opposition to national sovereignty. This simply means that they operate together to produce the same result (the loss of national sovereignty). Where harmonization has been largely successful there is little need for mutual recognition. Examples where mutual recognition has only restricted operation because of the success of harmonization are sea transport, air transport and nuclear regulation. The more successful harmonization has been the easier it is for state actors to accept the principle of mutual recognition, since the different rule or standard sets are more likely to approximate each other (our discussion of the principle in food standards, drugs and road transport provide examples).

A degree of harmonization can enable mutual recognition. Mutual recognition can operate to allow regulatory standards not made uniform by harmonization to cross national borders. Harmonization is also sometimes co-active with national treatment in a contest against sovereignty. Harmonization requires that states move to the same set of standards or rules. The principle of national treatment obliges a state to pass on the benefits of the harmonized standards to foreigners. Intellectual property is an example of where the co-activity of harmonization and national treatment have removed state sovereignty over the adjustment of property rights in information.

Mutual recognition is consistent with diverse regulatory standards, the operation of the principle in the corporate and securities area being an example. The principle of mutual recognition can have a harmonizing effect under certain circumstances. For instance, where individual states recognize the standards of the same international standard-setting body or bodies, they will move to the same set of standards. There is no necessary connection between the principle of mutual recognition and a harmonizing outcome, since there may be more than one standard-setting body that states can choose to recognize. The Toys and Children's Products Safety Ordinance of Hong Kong shows the way in which the principle of mutual recognition can cause a link between national regulatory systems and different standard-setting bodies.

> 3. Requirement to meet safety standards for toys
>
> (1) No person shall manufacture, import or supply a toy unless the toy, including its packaging, complies with each and every applicable requirement contained in one of the following sets of safety standards for toys:
>> (a) International Voluntary Toy Safety Standard established by the International Committee of Toy Industries;
>> (b) European Standard EN71 established by the European Committee for Standardization;
>> (c) ASTM F963 established by the American Society for Testing and Materials.

To summarize the co-activity of harmonization and mutual recognition: harmonization may enable mutual recognition (and therefore mutual recognition can carry on a process of convergence begun by harmonization), and mutual recognition may have a harmonizing effect.

### Trade Principles: Most Favoured Nation, Reciprocity, National Treatment, Mercantilism, Strategic Trade

Historically, the dominant contest in trade has been between reciprocity on the one side and Most Favoured Nation (MFN) and national treatment on the other. At a more abstract level it has also been between liberalization/deregulation and mercantilism/strategic trade. MFN and national treatment have their roots in non-discrimination. Actors which accept these two principles find themselves in the position of opening market opportunities and guaranteeing rights for citizens of foreign states. Unless those foreign states also accept the principles, a state may find that it has not secured market opportunities or rights for its citizens in those other states. The principle of reciprocity allows a state to pursue an equality of outcome, an equivalence of exchange with other states. The contest between these principles is a complex one in which it is difficult to find a clear victor. For example, on the face of it MFN emerges the victor in GATS, for it is enshrined in Article II as a general obligation for all members. However, Article II also allows members to gain an exemption from MFN under the conditions set down in the Annex on Article II exemptions. States could, under the exemption, extend favourable treatment on services to one state without being obliged to extend that same treatment to other states. The sectoral negotiations under GATS have often seen the principle of reciprocity in action. The US, for instance, threatened to withdraw from the financial services negotiations unless other states improved their offers. Before GATS many states would operate in the financial services sector on the basis of reciprocity. They would extend favourable terms to foreign banks if their own banks could get such favourable treatment in return. A similar kind of tussle between reciprocity and MFN/national treatment has featured in negotiations carried on by the Negotiating Group on Basic Telecommunications. In both financial services and telecommunications services reciprocity was used by the US to nudge states towards making increasingly better offers so that national treatment and MFN could work to maximal effect.

National treatment and MFN are inching towards a formal juridical triumph through their entrenchment in trade agreements of the Uruguay Round. National treatment has always been one of the pillars of intellectual property conventions since its entrenchment in the Paris and Berne Conventions at the end of the nineteenth century. Reciprocity still remains a powerful and practical principle in intellectual property. We saw, for example, that the principle of reciprocity lay behind the US extending protection for semiconductor chips to other states. In some of the areas left largely outside the ambit of the Final Act, reciprocity rules. Bilateral arrangements based on the principle of reciprocity dominate the trade in air traffic arrangements between states. Modern tax treaties remain driven by the principle, much as they were in the thirteenth century.

There are some areas where trade principles have played no real role, corporations and securities and labour standards being two examples. The principles have not been important in nuclear regulation because the trading of nuclear energy has been limited. Where states have committed themselves to the principle of harmonization, trade principles may cease to matter much, as in the case of maritime regulation. The silence of these principles in the labour standards area is in strong contrast to their dominance in intellectual property and financial regulation (capital, in other words). Using trade principles in the labour standards area would mean that developing countries could compete to send teams of labourers to build skyscrapers in the US, and that the US would have to give the same rights, privileges and protections to those foreign workers as it gives to its own. Non-discrimination, once institutionalized, can work in powerful ways, which no doubt is why national treatment and MFN have not been allowed to become contestants in the labour standards arena. Their presence in GATS in relation to the movement of natural persons has been carefully contained both through the drafting of the Annex on the movement of natural persons and through the structuring of negotiations under GATS (see Chapter 11).

The principle of strategic trade has proven to be one of the more difficult principles to map, primarily because actors do not particularly want to be seen publicly supporting the principle.[1] Strategic trade is more a principle of regulatory praxis, less a principle of public rhetoric and

---

1 The principle of strategic trade owes its name to that body of 'new trade theory' that models strategic interventions by governments in trade under conditions of imperfect competition (Krugman 1994). Strategic trade policy was being practised by governments before economists gave it that label (the use of tariffs and subsidies is an obvious example, as is the practice of many states in the nineteenth century of recognizing only the copyright of their citizens). Critics of the new trade theory simply see it as neo-mercantilism or a new form of protectionism. It is ultimately an empirical question as to whether the theories and models being developed within the strategic trade paradigm deliver welfare benefits to states. In summarizing the empirical work in new trade theory, Krugman says: 'It is also true that the research generally provides little support for a drastic rethinking of trade policy. Nobody has yet provided empirical evidence that would suggest large gains from protection or export subsidy. This is itself a useful result, but it does not excite as much attention as would a striking pro-interventionist result' (Krugman 1994: 7).

dialogue. As we observed in our discussion of the principle in the trade chapter, trade negotiators want to advance the practice of strategic trade while mouthing the principles of liberal trade. Strategic trade, one might conclude, is the most dominant principle of those identified since at one level strategic trade occurs in most international business regulation. When the US, for example, pushed for the non-discriminatory principles of national treatment and MFN in the context of TRIPS it did so because its trade negotiators knew that US firms gave the US state an enormous comparative advantage in the trade of intellectual property rights. These principles promised much in the way of trade gains for the US, in the case of intellectual property. A similar kind of analysis could be made of world's best practice or best available technology (BAT). Firms support these principles when they mandate others' purchase of their technology. Similarly in telecommunications, the US and the UK have been strong supporters of the principle of deregulation because AT&T and BT are companies that can take advantage of that principle in the international telecommunications market. Strategic trade on this reductive analysis might turn out to be a principle of meta-regulation, one that underlies many of the others that we have discussed. This, however, is not an analytically strategic move because it throws out the distinction between principles and mechanisms.

Clearly, actors have different motives for supporting the entrenchment of a given principle. Perhaps it was not the only motive, but DuPont did see economic pay-offs in helping other actors to globalize the regulatory demands for CFC substitutes – it was ahead of the pack on the development of substitutes. The motives of environmental NGOs in supporting CFC reduction were clearly different. But DuPont and environmental NGOs supported the same principle of world's best practice when it came to CFC reduction. Importantly for us, the fact that DuPont's motive may have been economic does not turn the principle of word's best practice into the principle of strategic trade. Strategic trade is not defined, for us, in terms of what motivates actors. Nor do we seek to link the definition to the presence or absence of welfare gains. Whether or not the principle is welfare-enhancing is a matter of empirical economics. Instead, principles are defined in terms of what they normatively prescribe. So when an actor pushes for practices or standards that substantially exceed the requirements set by present regulation it is supporting the principle of world's best practice. This is true even if it has strategic economic considerations, as Germany did in the late 1980s when it supported substantial nitrogen oxide reductions as part of the acid rain regime within Europe. German car manufacturers had the best technologies for helping to achieve the necessary reductions. When an actor argues for reducing the number of rules, it is arguing for the principle of deregulation and not strategic trade, even if it is thinking of economic gains. If a government decides to advantage its firms in an export market by giving them a subsidy, thereby deterring foreign firms from entering that export market, that government is following the principle of strategic trade. It is formally designing regulation in a way that advantages its nationals over foreigners.

Within trade, we have described strategic trade as strengthening. The long-term fate of the principle of strategic trade is in the hands of the economist members of the epistemic community that provides the cognitive maps for governments in trade and competition policy. If history is our guide, the principle of strategic trade may join forces with a cluster of older principles – mercantilism, protectionism and intervention – existing as a permanent resource, awaiting the historical moments when it is deployed by members of the epistemic community wishing to reform policies driven by principles of liberalization, deregulation and free trade – liberal trade theory, in other words.

Outside trade, strategic trade is basically a weak or weakening principle. This is partly because some areas of regulation, corporations being an example, have not entered the trade arena in any significant way. In other areas, the principle of strategic trade, though strongly present, is declining in the face of principles of deregulation, MFN and national treatment. Telecommunications regulation is an example where states formerly favoured national carriers over foreign carriers, but the principle is retreating as national monopolies are deregulated and telecommunications services are opened to foreign entrants. The international accounting rates regime is one area where the principle may experience a resurgence, as the US pushes for reforms that favour importers rather than exporters (which are mainly developing countries). Air transport has been an area of regulation where the principle has been strong. States put in place regulatory arrangements for airline routes that favour national carriers. At the level of aircraft production, the Airbus was the product of heavy subsidization by European governments (Klepper 1994: 101). There is, however, a vigorous contest between strategic trade and deregulation in the economic regulation of the airline industry. The US helped to create this contest when it deregulated its airline industry in 1978. The struggle between strategic trade and deregulation is repeated in motor vehicle regulation. Manufacturers push for standards that disadvantage their competitors; their competitors counter by invoking the costs of regulation and the virtues of deregulation.

## Deregulation

Deregulation dwells deep in liberalism's heartland. *Perestroika* moved it beyond that heartland. Our simple definition of it as reducing the number, stringency or enforcement of rules connects it to the classical liberal conception of freedom as freedom from restrictions. How has this key principle fared in global regulatory contests? It has had mixed fortunes. Table 21.1 shows that in seven areas it is weak or weakening and in eight areas it is strong or strengthening. In the case of air transport economic deregulation is strengthening, but not the deregulation of safety standards. Globalization has certainly not entrenched deregulation as a master principle.

Where regulated communities have realized that the fate of one can determine the fate of all, the principle of deregulation has sometimes dropped out of the regulatory discourse altogether. In other words, where shared concerns about the safety of systems have occurred the principle of deregulation has been largely bypassed by actors as a prescription for conduct. We saw this in the case of nuclear regulation, where actors like the World Association of Nuclear Operators have led standards of nuclear safety up rather than down. Concern about the safety of the world's banking system led to the formation of the Basle Committee on Banking Supervision, which through its standard-setting work provides an increasingly global regime of prudential oversight for the world's banking system. The regulation of airworthiness has been led by the US where, under the leadership of the US Federal Aviation Administration and Boeing, aircraft safety standards have progressively risen and globalized. Concerns by insurers and investors about the safety of ships have seen the regulatory principles of world's best practice and continuous improvement grow at the expense of deregulation. We saw that drugs regulation is complex because it involves five distinct regimes, only some of which have globalized. Deregulation has been a big loser in the globalized illicit drugs regime, since the dominant norm is regulation in the form of prohibition. Likewise, national tobacco regimes are increasing rather than decreasing their regulatory content. There is so much variety in national alcohol regimes that it is difficult to conclude much about deregulation beyond the demise of prohibition as a principle other than in the Islamic world. Nor is the principle of deregulation strongly present in the prescription drugs regime. The large players in this global industry, like Novartis and Roche, when faced with the regulatory costs of getting their drugs to national markets, have mostly not invoked the principle of deregulation. Instead they have argued for and received in most jurisdictions an extension to the patent term to compensate them for the time they have lost in seeking marketing approval from authorities like the FDA. Getting more favourable regulation elsewhere has been their response, rather than relying on deregulation to lessen the time it takes to pass standards for safety, quality and efficacy.

Safety is such a core concern in drugs regulation that deregulation has to be very carefully deployed by pharmaceutical manufacturers. Deregulation which brings efficiency in the processing of marketing approvals is fine. Deregulation that compromises safety turns manufacturers into targets for consumer groups, health professionals and the media. Moreover, in the sophisticated consumer markets of Europe, the US and Japan there are potential trade effects that limit the use of the principle of deregulation. Meeting the cost of high standard pharmaceutical regulation buys credibility in those marketplaces. The high-standard regulator's stamp of approval functions almost like a trademark in this respect. It allows a pharmaceutical manufacturer to capture what might be termed 'regulatory goodwill'. So if manufacturers are to push the principle of deregulation they must do so in concert, otherwise they risk conferring a trade advantage on those who comply with the higher regulatory standards. There is no prospect that the principle of deregulation can be used by pharmaceutical companies to engender a regulatory race-to-the-bottom among Western nation-states. Deregulation, to whatever extent it happens, will be harmonized deregulation. The International Conference on Harmonization has set in train a process of convergence and harmonization at the global level between the big players and regulators from the US, Japan and Europe. It has contributed to speeding up new drug approvals.

Food regulation is another case where issues of safety and health have set limits on the operation of the principle of deregulation. Most states are both importers and exporters of food. This double interest means that harmonization is the best long-term principle for states to support. We saw in Chapter 16, on food, that harmonization and mutual recognition were the key principles underpinning food regulation in Europe. More globally, members of the WTO have, in the Agreement on the Application of Sanitary and Phytosanitary Measures entrenched the principle of harmonization as a goal (Article 3) and agreed to base their food standards on the international standards developed by the Codex Alimentarius Commission (Codex). Deviations have to be scientifically justified. Where a single body like the Codex is given the task of harmonizing standards, the principle of deregulation cannot be used to trigger a race among many actors. Deregulatory races occur because participants can keep changing their standards. Harmonization requires that participants agree on a standard. The conclusion, however, is not that harmonization can cage the deregulatory tiger. Harmonization and deregulation can work in tandem to produce a downward pressure on regulatory standards, not a race but a shift. We saw that this was the fear of consumer activists about the Codex–WTO linkage, that corporate capture of the standard-setting process at the Codex would lower food standards globally. One fear is that in an era of genetically engineered food products the giant food firms will globalize standards before the dangers of a food technology are properly evaluated. Deregulation (in combination with harmonization) can still produce shifts in standards – global shifts, if those standards are set globally. The answer to these kinds of fears lies in ensuring that principles do not go uncontested. This in turn means that international fora must be constituted in ways that allow for the possibility of contests. We return to this argument in Chapter 24.

Deregulation (liberalization) has become the dominant principle in trade, certainly at the rhetorical level. At the level of implementation it faces opposition from strategic trade. Financial regulation has also come to be driven by deregulation. The regulated exchange rates regime agreed to at Bretton Woods has been replaced by a floating rates regime based on cooperation. Deregulation in financial services has allowed organizational actors to cross boundaries – banks into securities and insurance, securities companies into banking and so on. Megafirms and financial conglomerates like Citibank and American Express have been the result. Prudential financial regulation, however, has not been captured by this principle. Constant crises in international financial markets have seen a prudential regulation slowly globalize, based on principles of transparency and consolidation and led by G-10 nations. Around the world governments have moved to a market access model for telecommunications. The dominance of the economic deregulation of telecommunications looks as if it will be total. The principle of deregulation dominates the US labour market and is increasingly setting the direction of reform for other states, such as the UK, Australia and New Zealand.

Environmental regulation is also a complex case when it comes to the principle of deregulation. We noted in Chapter 12 that there may be five hundred international agreements that affect national environmental regulation. On the basis of this number, environmental regulation would seem to be flourishing. However, many of these treaties are essentially framework treaties. Such treaties recognize problems, express desires for change, and articulate principles. At the level of symbolism, rhetoric and discourse these treaties represent an important victory. They help to create among international actors a common language which the well-intentioned and less well-intentioned must use publicly. The problem, however, is the familiar one of the commitment of language not being matched by a commitment to action. Faced with the very real prospect of a mass extinction of species (Swanson 1994: 77), states continue to move slowly in creating new international institutions to deal with the problem.

The widespread use of environmental regulatory language does not correspond with the regulatory practices of actors. The principle of deregulation has an important influence at the practical level, with the result that environmental regulation breaks up into a complex mix of successes and failures of the principle. Where health and safety concerns link directly to environmental regulation, as they do in the production and use of chemicals, the principle of deregulation does not drive regulatory development either nationally or globally. The US and the OECD lead a global regime on chemicals testing. Deregulation was also a loser in the regulation of CFC production. The Montreal Protocol is perhaps a rare example of where deeds lived up to the expectations created by the words of a treaty. The environmental management standards developed by the International Organization for Standardization (ISO) and the Responsible Care Program followed by many chemical manufacturers are examples where business actors have replaced deregulatory impulses with a commitment to higher self-regulatory standards. There are also many examples in the area of environment where regulatory action is slow in coming (meaning that the principle of deregulation is strong), for example biodiversity, desertification and the preservation of wetlands.

The principle of deregulation is invoked by business actors to draw attention to the costs of environmental regulation. Where environmental regulation imposes high short-term costs and its omission long-term costs, deregulation tends to prevail as a short-run principle. The successful implementation of deregulation means that actors can escape the cost of the negative externalities they are generating. It is comparatively easy in international negotiations on environmental matters to get a veto coalition to form around the principle. Someone will always stand up for the right to produce a negative externality (unless those externalities are reciprocally linked). It is much harder to get a consensus among all states in favour of regulation. Within environmental regulation the principle of deregulation usually takes the form of a prescription not to act (rather than dismantling existing regulation, as in the case of telecommunications). Not acting to build an international institution has, of course, some immediate cost advantages that institution-building does not. One effect of all this is that the principle of deregulation acts as something of a drag on the rate at which we build institutions for the earth.

### Ratchets and Races: Lowest-cost Location, Rule Compliance, World's Best Practice, Continuous Improvement, Best Available Technology, Best Available Practice

The interactions in this group of principles have been some of the most important we have observed. We begin with some abstract observations. These principles can set regulatory systems in motion. Firms subscribing to the principle of lowest-cost location help to foster regulatory races-to-the-bottom. World's best practice can push regulatory standards upwards. When some of these principles are made co-active they prevent a reversal of the race's direction – standards can only travel in one direction.

When lowest-cost location is an active and dominant principle, regulation comes under downward pressure or remains static. Labour standards in developing countries tend to be driven by this principle. The Prime Minister of Malaysia, Dr Mahathir, captures its importance for developing countries:

> Cheaper labour cost is a form of competitive advantage that most developing countries rely upon out of necessity, but this has now been labelled as an unfair advantage. 'Social clauses' have been promoted to govern international trade, which may sound like concern for the welfare of the workers in the developing countries but which will effectively negate any competitive advantage that we may have.[2]

Within developed countries the debate over labour standards is generally not driven by a principle of world's best practice, but by better practice or good practice. The principle has had a major effect in tax regulation, where it underpins competition on tax incentives between states. It has a lesser role in banking and insurance, although even there companies have made use of banking and insurance havens (Bermuda is one of the world's biggest insurance centres). Within environment there is a genuine contest between lowest-cost location and world's best practice, something we shall come back to in a moment. The same is true of pharmaceuticals regulation, where pharmaceutical companies in the 1960s and 1970s searched out low-cost regulatory systems as part of their strategy for getting products onto world markets in the quickest way possible. Increasingly, lowest-cost location in this industry faces competition from world's best practice and continuous improvement. Sea transport provides an interesting example of an equilibrium of principles, in which lowest-cost location has allowed Panama and Liberia to capture 20 per cent of the world's merchant shipping tonnage while much of the world has progressively moved towards the

---

2 Speech by the Prime Minister of Malaysia, the Honourable Dato Seri Dr Mahatir Bin Mohamad at the Inaugural Plenary of the Sixth G-15 Summit on Behalf of Asian Members of G-15 at Harare, Zimbabwe, on Sunday, 3 November 1996, p. 3.

best practice standards required by the members of the International Association of Classification Societies. There is no danger that Panama and Liberia, through their support for lowest-cost location, will trigger a globally encompassing race-to-the-bottom, the kind of race we see in other areas such as tax. The reason lies in the fact that in the case of shipping there is no contest at the level of ideas between lowest-cost location and world's best practice. When a principle becomes a tenet within an epistemic community, its oppositional counterpart is confined to niche markets (albeit a large one, in the case of shipping), surviving more in practice than in belief. All the important actors support world's best practice in shipping (compare the role of business NGOs in shipping (discussed in Chapter 17) with the role of the ICC in tax (discussed in Chapter 8)). Under these circumstances the principle of lowest-cost location allows a small group of actors to position themselves to fulfil a market demand, but not to engender a regulatory race.

World's best practice is a principle which imposes costs on actors, costs of monitoring what the best practice is, costs of implementation and compliance and so on. Lowest-cost location is by definition a cost-reducing principle. One might predict therefore that world's best practice would rarely triumph over lowest-cost location. Yet, as Table 21.1 shows, world's best practice is either strong or strengthening in more areas than we might expect, given its costs for actors. In financial regulation, fear of systemic failure increasingly inclines actors like the Basle Committee towards adopting the principle. Other actors, such as the New York Stock Exchange, favour it because they see that it serves their economic interests. Companies know that if they list in New York it says something to global markets that a Shanghai listing does not. In the transport sectors, sea, air and motor vehicles, the principle of world's best practice is becoming stronger. Car manufacturers competing in the lucrative markets of the US, Europe and Japan cannot afford to substantially undercut best practice principles. Boeing is also a supporter of the principle; by doing so it makes life harder for its competitors. Although world's best practice is a costly principle for actors to follow, it is also an asset-building principle. It helps to create the asset of reputation. Where world's best practice is weak, it is because the driver of reputation matters less and immediate costs determine all. Environment and drugs regulation are both examples where the reputational capital of world's best practice has become more important to firms. Likewise, the reputational value of world's best practice is becoming increasingly important to states and regions in the area of financial regulation, as they seek to divert global investment flows into their economies.

Our discussion of environmental, drug and nuclear regulation mentioned the ratcheting-up of regulatory standards. We use the term 'ratchet' to capture the idea that regulatory standards can be made to travel in one direction, and one direction only. Ratchets can be of two kinds, positive and negative. Positive ratchets drive regulatory standards up. Negative ratchets drive them down. Negative ratchets are not necessarily undesirable since they may promote efficiency gains. Regulatory competition can deliver allocative efficiency gains. Where safety is a major issue, positive ratchets may be preferred over negative ones. For a ratchet effect to come into existence, three conditions have to be satisfied:

1   a minimum standard of some kind has to be entrenched;

2   a principle which encourages innovation has to be put in place;

3   a feedback loop has to be created between each new innovation and the minimum standard so that with each new innovation the minimum standard goes up (positive ratchet) or down (negative ratchet).

An example of a minimum standard in environmental regulation would be the ISO 14001 standard on environmental management, not the best practicable standard possible, for the reasons that Gunningham (1996) gives, but a decent minimum nevertheless. Examples of principles that can prescribe innovation as a way of doing things for the relevant actors are continuous improvement, best available technology (BAT), best available practice and, in the case of negative ratchets, lowest-cost location. Condition 2 also requires that the relevant principle selects for innovative performance rather than for compliance with a specific technology or a particular practice. We saw, for instance, that in German law the principle of BAT does not require the adoption of a specific technology; it requires firms to perform to the level of the new technology. The performance version of BAT allows firms to innovate around another firm's technology which for the time being sets the standard. This version of BAT is also being used by the US Federal Aviation Administration (FAA) to allow foreign aircraft manufacturers to choose between adopting Boeing technology and finding an alternative technology. A global ratchet based on the BAT principle is also present in the car industry, although there it operates slowly as manufacturers and others within that epistemic community argue over just what is the technology that constitutes the BAT. The crucial point is that for condition 2 to be satisfied, the relevant principle must fix an outcome as the standard, not a specific way of doing something. The effect of the latter is usually to turn a minimum standard into an industry faith.

Condition 3 requires institutional rules and practices that secure innovations as a new minimum standard. Accreditation and certification bodies monitoring for continuous improvement are one way in which a feedback loop between a principle of innovation and a minimum standard can be created. It is the existence of a loop which ensures that the institutionalized standard continues being raised or lowered. The quote in Chapter 12 from a nuclear plant quality control manager is worth repeating here: 'INPO's [Institute of Nuclear Power Operators] standards continue to improve each year so that if you get an outstanding grade from INPO this year, and you don't make improvements in your processes or your programs, then you won't get that same high score from INPO because their standards have gone up in the meantime' (quoted in Rees 1994: 83). Without an INPO-like circuit, conditions 1 and 2 are not sufficient to bring about the ratchet effect.

More than one principle may be involved in a regulatory ratchet. In abstract, when world's best practice, continuous improvement and harmonization combine, the effect is to pressure all actors into regulatory dynamism. When lowest-cost location and rule compliance combine, the result is a move towards regulatory stasis. Principles do not bring these ratchets into existence in some mechanically simple fashion. Ratchets are part of a complex evolutionary reality in the process of globalization. As we saw, they are an emerging phenomenon in the interactions between actors and regulatory systems that are part of environmental regulation. The business philosophy of total quality management has continuous improvement as a core principle. Standard-setting bodies like ISO have taken this principle and linked it to environmental standards. Key corporate actors like IBM, realizing the strategic importance of a standard-setting process tied to a widely accepted business philosophy, threw their weight behind the process and helped it to globalize. Transaction cost analysis helps to explain the desire of TNCs for one global standard rather than many different national ones.

Before leaving the topic of ratchets, it is worth noting that treaties can formally embed a regulatory ratchet. The provisions of TRIPS are drafted so as to oblige members to enact minimum standards of protection for intellectual property. Article 1 of TRIPS leaves it open to members to implement more extensive protection. Article 71(2) allows for the possibility that higher standards of intellectual property protection achieved in other multilateral agreements and 'accepted under those agreements by all members of the WTO' may be adopted by the Ministerial Conference of the WTO 'without further formal acceptance process' (see Article X(6) of the Agreement Establishing the WTO). Under TRIPS, therefore, intellectual property standards can travel in only one direction. Moreover, an increase in the standards of protection achieved in another forum (such as WIPO) can be folded into TRIPS. When we suggested this possibility to a member of the WTO secretariat (1998 interview) he said that it was unlikely that all WTO members would agree to an increase in standards in a multilateral negotiation that took place outside the context of the WTO. Nevertheless the possibility of this particular ratchet remains on the books. Entrenching a positive ratchet of this kind was clearly part of US business strategizing during the negotiations over TRIPS. Thus in a 1992 interview at the US Chamber of Commerce one of us was told that on the issue of the TRIPS negotiations and standards of intellectual property protection 'we hope they don't define a ceiling but a floor'.

Some business actors also argued for a treaty ratchet in the proposed Multilateral Agreement on Investment. Here they want states to accept a standstill clause with respect to restrictions on investment and a rollback clause allowing for existing restrictions to be lifted over time. In the case of investment, states are being asked to entrench a ratchet that restricts their capacity to impose regulatory standards, whereas in the case of TRIPS the ratchet pushes them in the direction of increasing standards of protection for intellectual property.

Continuous improvement, like world's best practice, imposes costs on actors. Despite this, and for probably the same reasons we gave for world's best practice, it has strengthened in a number of regulatory domains. Many employers have embraced the principle in employment and training opportunities for women and occupational health and safety (firms have often integrated the latter standards into their ISO 9000 Quality Assurance Systems). In sea transport, improving the safety and environmental management of shipping is not contested as a matter of principle. The principle is strong in aircraft safety standards because airlines fear acquiring the reputation of a Continental. Nuclear power plant operators do not want to be a Three Mile Island. Car manufacturers support the principle where it relates to a technology they have developed. With the innovations of others they practise rule compliance.

Rule compliance is the oppositional principle to continuous improvement. They can and do coexist in different parts of a given regulatory domain. So in the case of shipping regulation, continuous improvement is part of a management philosophy that rests on top of a rule compliance regime of minimum structural standards for hulls, segregated ballast tanks and so on. In other cases both principles remain strong contestants because actors switch their support from one to the other depending on circumstance. An example is the regulation of motor vehicles, where manufacturers switch to rule compliance when somebody else's technology becomes the basis of a standard. Airlines that worry less about reputation and focus on cost of travel stick to a principle of minimum rule compliance. With labour standards it is easy to take the view that the only kind of competitive advantage labour can deliver is cost-based. At the micro level many employers take just that view. The macro argument going the other way, that high labour standards can be a source of global competitiveness, is a hard argument to sell. The upshot is that rule compliance is a resilient principle in the regulation of labour. Food regulation is an example where there is growing contest between the two principles, both strongly entrenched. In some cases continuous improvement has provided no opposition to rule compliance, the regulation of contract, trade, competition and companies being examples.

We embarked upon this study expecting that an analysis of mechanisms would explain when ratchets-up and races-down occurred. In fact the contest of principles turned out to be of greater importance, for it is principles that set the direction of regulatory change. It is in the interplay of principles and mechanisms that the most rounded understanding lies. For most domains, we have identified elements of both competition in laxity and upward ratchets. However, there is a strong generalization we can make about these data. For the last quarter of the twentieth century, the ratchets driving the regulation of environment, safety and financial security have predominantly been upwards ratchets; with other domains of economic regulation the principle of deregulation has driven predominantly downwards ratchets.

'Social regulatory ratchets-up, economic regulatory ratchets-down' would not be quite right as a description of this generalization because prudential regulation, regulation of intellectual property, of accounting standards, of corruption, securities and money-laundering have been moved more by upwards than downwards ratchets and e-commerce will almost certainly move that way. The core domains of globalizing deregulatory movement have been in licensing restrictions on financial institutions, exchange rate controls, tax competition driving rates down and eliminating taxes, some (limited) driving-down of corporate law standards through corporate law havens and competition toward limited liability (with little countervailing upwards harmonization), reduction and elimination of tariffs, technical barriers to trade, restrictions on the free movement of investment, breaking up of cartels and restrictive business practices, licensing of telecommunications, and the economic regulation of air transport. There have also been some preliminary skirmishes in the direction of deregulating the globalized 'conference system' for the economic regulation of shipping. Labour standards fit our analysis that basic safety and financial security standards have been ratcheted-up (across two centuries, with labour) in occupational health and safety, discrimination in employment, slavery, child labour and freedom of association. Yet during the last quarter of the twentieth century there has simultaneously been some globalization of labour market deregulation outside these core safety and security domains, and the beginnings of deregulation of professional services.

It may be that the increased regulation of property, specifically intellectual property, and the contractualization of the world (Chapter 7) are the key exceptions to this generalization. Perhaps this is not so for conservatives, who view security of property and contract as core financial security values. Indeed, perhaps it is partly the fact that laws of property and contract can be viewed as sanctified that those with an interest in doing so have been able to ratchet-up their regulatory sway. Another irony of our generalization that financial security regulation has ratcheted-up while other domains of economic regulation have ratcheted-down is that the ratcheting-down has been achieved by ratcheting-up regulation designed to achieve deregulation. Competition law, which has slowly begun to globalize and gain clout, is the classic case of a regulatory instrument designed to achieve a deregulatory purpose. The WTO, EC and IMF are regulatory institutions whose expanded clout has been used to effect economic deregulation. A business objective of the Multilateral Agreement on Investment is a regulatory process to achieve standstill and roll-back of regulatory restraints on investment.

We trust it is clear from Chapters 7, 8, 11 and 12 that the race-to-the-bottom to pollution havens has been a less powerful dynamic than ratcheting-up framework conventions. This is not to say that the ratcheting-up has gone very far, that environmental treaties hold much sway over most of the planet. It is to say that during the last quarter of the century ratchets up have caused more movement than races down. We would say the same about nuclear safety, occupational health and safety, agricultural chemicals, the regulation of prescription drugs, illicit drugs, tobacco (but not alcohol), food standards, safety at sea, road safety and air safety. Air safety unequivocally fits our analysis: air safety regulation has become progressively more demanding and more global in reach. A US airline setting itself up as Air Belize in a safety regulation haven is only a minor move in the other direction. Flags of convenience with shipping is a more significant countercurrent, but still only a market niche created by the main current of IMO-orchestrated ratcheting-up of the web of controls. Food is a more controversial case, where many consumer advocates would disagree with Vogel's (1995) conclusion, and ours, of EU- and Codex-driven movement that on balance is more upwards than downwards.

Some might hypothesize that where economic deregulation has occurred, it has been because of regulatory competition driving the costs of regulation down; where ratcheting-up has occurred, it has resulted from command and control. But this is not right. Protectionism has been ratcheted-down by a ratcheting-up of WTO controls in successive GATT rounds. Chapter 15 shows that regulatory competition in pharmaceuticals has been a competition in credibility rather than competition in laxity. We cannot understand the indeterminacy in the direction of both ratchets and regulatory competition (and whether they will promote economic efficiency or inefficiency) without understanding how the contest of principles plays out.

There is room for argument about where our generalization is wrong that environment, safety and financial security have been characterized by more ratcheting up than down, while globalizing ratcheting-down characterizes other areas of economic regulation. The more important point is that we can understand where the generalization is right and wrong, by deploying an analysis of the contest of principles. We can analyze, for example, where world's best practice, continuous improvement and harmonization combine to drive a regulatory ratchet.

## Dedicated Principles

Some principles we have identified are domain-specific or have less general application than principles such as reciprocity or deregulation. Food security and sustainable development are examples of domain-specific principles, while the free flow of information is an example of less general application. The abstract nature of principles means that principles are not necessarily confined to the one or two domains in which they exist at the moment. They may in the future have an application outside those domains.

The free flow of information is an interesting case because it reveals how liberal interpretations of principles have prevailed in regulatory contests. The free flow of information is a principle which the US has used to ground arguments for allowing unrestricted transborder data flows and the removal by nation-states of restrictions on the acquisition of foreign programming and broadcasting (see Chapter 14). As Jack Valenti, the CEO of the Motion Picture Association of America explained in an interview, 'ideas and art ought to be able to flow freely in the world' (1994 interview). In conjunction with the principle of the common heritage of mankind, the free flow principle has been used by developing countries to argue that technological information which is locked up by means of intellectual property rights should be made freely available to all (see Chapter 7). TRIPS has put paid to the common heritage/free flow principles for technological information. Through the trade regime, the US is progressively achieving the goal of a free flow of information throughout the world. The difference between the two versions of the free flow principle comes to this. In the context of telecommunications and broadcasting the free flow principle relates to the free flow of commodified information. The principle is made co-active with private property rights. In the context of intellectual property the principle was, under the agenda of the New International Economic Order, given a collectivist interpretation by developing states – technological information should flow to all since it is jointly owned by all as part of common heritage. This principle has no place in TRIPS, whose preamble states that 'intellectual property rights are private rights'. One place where the principle of common heritage might lay claim to some practical application is in environmental regulation. Even here, though, the extent to which the principle has grounded regulatory solutions is questionable. The regulation of the seabed, which has been declared by the UN to be part of common heritage, might be an example. The status in law of the common heritage principle remains juristically complex (Schachter 1991: 291–6). In many ways the principle of common heritage is seen more as part of the problem of environmental degradation than as driving regulatory solutions. Common heritage is linked to the idea of the commons. The unregulated common, as Hardin has pointed out, leads to tragedy (1968). In the absence of private property rights the commoners have an incentive to exploit and no incentive to conserve. Ironically, the principle of the common heritage of humanity, once used in an attempt to dismantle Western intellectual property regimes, is itself giving way to arguments that intellectual property style regimes can be used to foster biodiversity conservation (see, e.g., Swanson 1994: 245–6). At the same time the principle of common heritage illustrates that principles have a basic resiliency. The principle remains an important one in the context of negotiations over access to genetic resources at the FAO (Chapter 16).

The fate of the common heritage/free flow principles also reveals the way in which the operation of principles can be affected through an interpretive ordering. These principles have the potential to ground a destabilizing critique of a private property rights regime in abstract objects. Yet the interpretation of these principles which has prevailed in the fora that matter in the globalization of regulation sees important relations being established between them and property rights. The free flow principle is made consistent with property rights in abstract objects by being reassigned to the task of promoting the free flow of commodified abstract objects. The common heritage principle which might be used to prioritize the intellectual commons over monopoly privileges in abstract objects is simply not recognized as relevant in that forum (the WTO) which is driving the globalization of these monopoly privileges. The crucial relation established through this process of interpretive ordering is that property rights in abstract objects, which lie at the heart of information capitalism, are given a lexical priority over those principles that might threaten their operation. For us, this outcome is not the necessary result of some abstract dialectic of history. As we have shown, acts of individual entrepreneurship were central to the globalization of intellectual property. If there is a dialectic at work here it is a messy, indeterminate one in which actors, restricted by structures but also using them, carry on contests using mechanisms and principles, and sometimes secure great victories and sometimes suffer defeats.

Zacher and Sutton (1996) identify 'technical interconnection' as an important principle in a number of regimes (e.g. telecommunications, shipping – as in container size) in enabling not only the free flow of information, but free flow of goods and services. We saw that freedom of the skies was an important issue in the air transport regime, as is free movement in outer space in the emerging *Lex Spatialis* (Steinhardt 1998: 337). Freedom of the seas is arguably the oldest principle of international law, being a central theme in the writing of Grotius. Britain fought the Opium

Wars for the principle of free trade in drugs. Free flow of information can thus been seen as information capitalism's analogue to industrial capitalism's free movement of goods.

Conditionality is a principle which is entrenched in the IMF's articles of agreement (see Chapter 8). Although this principle is only listed under finance in Table 21.1, its reach is much greater. We have described it as an enabling principle. One of the effects of IMF or World Bank conditionality is that the states which are subject to it have to accept and insitutionalize other principles, such as deregulation, liberalization, market access, national treatment and MFN, in a range of regulatory domains including trade, labour and telecommunications. Conditionality helps, in other words, to make these principles active in the world, promoting globalization through promoting the operation of these principles.

The principle of tripartism structures the ILO as an organization. Its formal effect is to involve representatives of government, employers and workers in the decision-making processes of the ILO. By entrenching those three groups in the organizational life of the ILO, the principle might be said to produce a degree of substantive equality in the form of more balanced deliberation. We can contrast this kind of equality outcome with the first-come, first-served principle of telecommunications regulation. That principle does not deny any state the right to seek a satellite orbit, but clearly favours states that have satellite technology or that acquired it first.

The principle of sustainable development and the precautionary principle were invented comparatively recently. 'Sustainable development' was popularized by the Brundtland Report, *Our Common Future*, in 1987; the precautionary principle acquired currency only in the 1990s. Compared to principles with a long history, such as deregulation or reciprocity, these environmental principles have exercised a diffuse influence rather than grounding actual regulatory victories. In environmental regulation the principle of BAT is primarily responsible for concrete victories. One reason for the diffuse influence of these two principles is that they are perhaps the most abstract of the principles we have discussed. Sustainable development is interpretively open in a way that MFN, national treatment and rule compliance are not. Sustainable development is mainly a penumbra of doubt without a core of fixed meaning. This openness gives the principle maximum flexibility and therefore widens its appeal among green factions, but it also makes it harder to link the principle to specific rules. The rule implications of a principle such as national treatment or harmonization are clear. What are the rule implications of the principle of sustainable development – as many as there are visions of an environmentally sustainable way of life? These two environmental principles are nevertheless vitally important. They motivate sensibilities rather than specific rules. The idea of sustainable growth drives critiques of neo-classical economic growth models. The principles help to unify green thinking and policies. They can also operate as tools of capture. Once they are accepted into organizations like the World Bank they serve as a peg on which future environmental policies might hang. The fact that the principle of sustainable development appears in the preamble of the Agreement Establishing the World Trade Organization is an important symbolic victory. With a symbolic victory achieved, the longer-run game for environmentalists becomes the development of WTO rules on matters like countervailing environmental subsidies aimed at countries with low environmental standards, or trade rules that recognize the role of environmentally harmful process and production methods in the WTO – rules, in other words, that give life to the principle of sustainable development (Wynter 1998).

Two principles of prohibition have been successfully globalized in two different domains, both by the US. They are the principle of non-proliferation in nuclear regulation in the form of the Nuclear Non-Proliferation Treaty and what we called in Chapter 15 a principle of mega-regulation

– the destruction of markets, prohibition or criminalization, in the case of narcotic drugs. If compliance is a criterion of success then at least in the case of narcotics the globalization of prohibition can hardly be called a success.

Food security is the ability of a state to meet the consumption needs of its population (Chisholm & Tyers 1982: 5). As a regulatory principle it prescribes that states enact rules consistent with achieving their consumption targets. This principle aligns with national sovereignty over food resources, for all states consider it vital to independently guarantee food security for their populations. We have seen that the regulation of food standards has harmonized considerably through the Codex, with a consequent loss of national sovereignty. Despite the Agreement on Agriculture which was concluded as part of the Uruguay Round, national sovereignty over food production remains strong. That Agreement did bring agriculture into the world trading regime for the first time, but made only comparatively minor inroads into agricultural protectionism.

During the Uruguay negotiations on agriculture and food standards the principle of food security was called upon by a number of actors. Consumer and farmer groups in Europe and the US unsuccessfully invoked the principle in trying to stop Codex standards entering the WTO trading regime. In India a broad-based coalition of jurists, scientists, farmers, consumers and others, led by the National Working Group on Patent Laws, also used the principle of food security, arguing that the Agreement on Agriculture endangered the capacity of developing states to offer food subsidies to their populations.[3] (The Agreement does recognize the right of governments to stockhold products as part of a food security program: see Article 3 of Annex 2.) Indian NGOs have raised the principle of food security in drawing attention to the cross-regulatory implications of TRIPS and the Agreement on Agriculture. Put simply, their fear is that the WTO regimes will bring about liberalized markets in agriculture which will be totally dominated by TNCs like Monsanto and Continental Grain, because those corporations will own most of the intellectual property rights in the world's seeds and genes – they will own the world's crucial agricultural resources (Iyer et al. 1996: 80). For developing countries, globalization is in some respects less about complex interdependencies and more about establishing (or re-establishing) simple dependencies. The US, for example, during the 1960s restricted wheat shipments to India on a weekly basis for political purposes. The supply of food and food aid has in the past been used by surplus states as a tool of coercion (Johnson 1982; Provost 1992). For these kinds of reasons it seems likely that food security will feature strongly in those regulatory domains related to food (agriculture, intellectual property, sanitary and phytosanitary standards, environment).

## Properties of Principles

Table 21.1 lists thirty-three principles. Given the number of regulatory domains (thirteen) we have covered and the fact that we have identified the principles empirically, this is not a large number. What this reveals is that a comparatively small number of principles are recurrently important in the globalization of business regulation. The table also shows that some principles are common to

---

3  See 'Report on International Convention on People's Approach to GATT Negotiations Organized by National Working Group on Patent Laws', 18–20 February 1993, New Delhi, unpublished, p. 7.

a number of different regulatory systems. Analytically it might be possible to make the number even smaller, by reducing principles to meta-principles. The easiest example of such a reductive move is to decompose national treatment, MFN and mutual recognition into a principle of non-discrimination. Following this line of thought gives us these additional reductions:

- BAT, best available practice, world's best practice, continuous improvement and lowest-cost location become 'principles of innovation';
- deregulation, liberalization, market access and free flow of information become the 'principle of freedom of movement';
- non-proliferation and criminalization become the 'principle of prohibition';
- strategic trade and mercantilism become the 'principle of protectionism'.

The problem with reducing principles to meta-principles is that the different effects of related principles can get lost. For example, if state A is under a national treatment obligation towards state B it has to equalize the way it treats its citizens and the citizens of state B. It has no such obligations towards the citizens of state C unless all three states are members of a treaty that imposes MFN obligations on all of them. Meta-principles, along with the remaining principles, reveal even more strongly how the contests in global business regulation are driven by a few key principles.

Keeping our principles as listed in Table 21.1, we can now set about the task of identifying some of their general characteristics. Our purpose is not to place the principles into a logical scheme of some kind (although clearly logical relations hold between some of the principles), but rather to identify the characteristics of principles that emerge from their role in regulatory contests.

### Principles as Oppositional

Throughout our case studies we have seen that actors, through their submissions, reports, position papers, negotiations and backroom lobbying, argue for some principles and oppose others. They oppose principles with other principles. This is crucial. Actors come to the negotiating table armed with principles. The US argued for national treatment and harmonization of standards in the case of intellectual property. Developing countries argued for national treatment without harmonization. The American Express coalition in the US on trade in services began by arguing for market access in the contest of trade in services, but when it realized that this would be tied to MFN in a multilateral trading regime it fell back on the principle of reciprocity.

One reason why business regulatory contests are fought at the level of principles is that the informational demands of rule systems would make any contest at this level intolerably complex. Trade negotiators cannot, for example, walk into rooms in Geneva with their respective Telecommunications Acts under their arms and say to their counterparts, 'this is what we want'. Often they will have very little idea about the details of their domestic systems. (One US trade negotiator told us that US trade people were 'ignorant' of intellectual property law. The US overcame this by sending several intellectual property specialists as part of its negotiating team on TRIPS.) Moreover, they know that in rapidly changing areas like finance and telecommunications, rules cannot but principles might keep up with the pace of change. Trade negotiators can walk into those Geneva rooms and argue about principles of market access, MFN, liberalization and national sovereignty in telecommunications knowing that the issues of rule complexity will be sorted out by the specialist telecommunications epistemic community once the principles are in place, knowing (if they represent the US or Europe) that their domestic models may well become global blueprints for other states, that their consultants acting as model missionaries will spread their domestic rulebooks, that the principles can be enforced at the level of rules in bilateral negotiations.

Our claim that principles are oppositional is a modest empirical claim. It simply says that actors support principles in regulatory contests because those principles lead to effects desired by actors. The claim that principles are oppositional does not lead, as far as we are concerned, into an argument that principles are part of a process of dialectical contradiction or that they can be structured into necessary binary opposites. The opposition between principles is essentially a contingent matter. It arises through circumstance and chance. No one thirty years ago would have thought that the principle of food security would come to feature in regulatory contests in the intellectual property domain. Whether or not a given contest between principles occurs in a given domain is partly driven by the inventiveness of individuals. By creating principles like the common heritage of mankind, individuals give the weaker collectivities they represent a principle for which to fight.

### Principles as Rhetorical, Symbolic and Instrumental

Rhetoric, 'the art of persuasive communication' (Vickers 1988: 1), has a place in international negotiations and lobbying affecting business regulation. When US business NGOs lobby Congress they do not simply rely on the 'numbers' (economic costs and benefits), as one informant put it. They also attempt to sway judgment through techniques that Aristotle and Cicero would recognize and call rhetorical. Arousing passion and emotion lies at the heart of the rhetorician's art. Thus when it came to intellectual property Asian states were not merely copyists but 'pirates', 'bootleggers' and 'counterfeiters'. Corporations like Pfizer would arrange for 'editorial opinion' pieces to appear in the *New York Times* with titles like 'Stealing from the Mind'.[4] It is, as Aristotle observes in the *Rhetoric*, a matter of putting one's 'hearers, who are to decide, into the right frame of mind' (1377b 24).

Business and NGO rhetorics were not part of our study, yet they are clearly important phenomena in international business regulation. It does seem clear that principles are rhetorically deployed by actors. The appeal to the principle of national sovereignty is potentially a strong element in a rhetorical strategy, as is the appeal to reciprocity in a trade context. It is not too great a jump to conclude that principles have a rhetorical use.

The idea that regulation by government can be primarily a symbolic act in which meaning is generated without significant changes in behaviour or resource allocation has been the subject of some classic explorations (Gusfield 1963; Edelman 1964). Edelman, for instance, argues that government regulation on a topic often produces 'political quiescence' among mass publics even though the regulation does little to channel resources into the problem (1964: 22–3). This kind of regulation is essentially symbolic. This theory of regulation is relevant to parts of international regulation. We saw, for example, that international environmental regulation is dotted with framework agreements. The core principles in that kind of treaty function symbolically.

---

4  MacTaggart, Barry 1982, 'Stealing from the Mind', *New York Times*, 9 July, p. 23.

They do not require states to engage in much direct action, but they help to unify perceptions about the importance of an issue. They provide a common framework of principles within which states can give further consideration to the problems. Principles, we shall say, can function symbolically.

By far the most important use of principles is an instrumental use. As the summaries of principles and mechanisms have showed, both have effects in the world. For instance, when principles form part of a regulatory ratchet they can drive standards up or down. Actors use principles to fulfil desires. Desires, Pettit argues, 'dispose the agent to try to bring about a certain state of the world – the goal at which they point – in demanding to be satisfied' (1993: 19). In the case of business regulation actors use principles and mechanisms to fulfil their desires and bring about their goals. The instrumental use of principles requires actors to use them to bring about certain desired effects. It is a use in which actors bring their regulatory world into line with their desires. It follows that the creation and use of principles is an important mode of action. We take up the significance of this in our discussion of forum-shifting.

### Principles as Active or Passive

Principles can be active or passive within a given regulatory domain. They are active when they are used by agents either rhetorically (as in the case of a treaty negotiation) or instrumentally (when they bring about desired effects). Principles are passive when they are not being used within a domain or when they are used symbolically. An objection to classifying the symbolic use of principles as passive might be that on our own definition the symbolic use of principles still serves a purpose. Such principles help to unify attitudes towards a particular matter of concern. A compromise might be to say that a symbolic principle is only weakly active in the world. We prefer to say passive, since we want to drive home the point that for real change to occur symbolic principles must be made active in the world. Generally, to have operational effect the principles we have discussed have to be tied to rules. By itself a principle such as national treatment prescribes little unless it is linked to a body of rules which define the rights, advantages and powers that a state bound by the principle must extend to foreigners. Similarly, the principle of mutual recognition entails the recognition of another state's system of rules. The symbolic effects of principles are mostly weak effects and to highlight this we describe such principles as passive. Principles are at their most active when they become institutionalized in a regime which functions to bring about desired effects, or at least some desired effects.

We have also seen that principles can be co-active, for example the principles of consolidation and transparency or the principles of harmonization and mutual recognition. Regulatory ratchets may also be constituted through the co-activity of principles. The co-activity of principles simply refers to the fact that principles may operate together in mutually reinforcing ways to bring about particular effects.

Principles can change their use and their status within a given domain. They can go from being used rhetorically and symbolically to an instrumental destiny. Similarly, a principle can be an active and dominant one and over time become passive. There was a time when reciprocity would have been the dominant norm of international treaty-making. It has largely given way to principles of national treatment and MFN. As Table 21.1 shows, a principle can be simultaneously active in one area and passive in another. Finally, the principles in Table 21.1 are those which over time have been the most consistently active in the globalization of business regulation.

## Conclusion

Actors desiring certain goals set out to remake their regulatory worlds. They do so using mechanisms and principles. We find that actors achieve effects or bring change to business regulation through mechanisms and principles. The result is that regulation either globalizes or does not. The macro-causal sequence which is shown in the domains we have examined is that actors use mechanisms to entrench particular principles rather than others. Those principles then pattern regulatory development. The creation of a positive ratchet based on the principles of BAT and continuous improvement means, for instance, that regulatory standards are driven up.

Can actors use mechanisms without principles? Since the connection between principles and mechanisms is contingent, the answer is yes. It is conceivable, for example, that a state could economically coerce another state each time the latter acted inconsistently with the former's interests on a regulatory issue. But that would be a costly strategy for even a well-resourced state. Not even the US could afford to keep using economic coercion to achieve its agenda even on a matter as crucial as intellectual property. Both economic and military coercion are cost-intensive, short-run mechanisms. Ultimately, what the US requires on intellectual property is a global regime like TRIPS, compliance with which has been faithfully internalized by other states. Without TRIPS, the US would have had to fight continual costly (both reputationally and economically) bilateral battles with other states. The reason why we find mechanisms linked to contests of principles in regulation is that principles, with their attendant rule complexity, bring about a long-term convergence of expectations among actors. Mechanisms need principles to guide action effectively. Principles need mechanisms to be made concrete in a regulatory domain.

Actors, we have seen, can have different motives for supporting the same principle. One reason why this is possible is that the same principle can accommodate different goals. World's best practice can simultaneously serve the environmental goals of NGOs and the profit goals of firms. The principle of deregulation, in telecommunications, can serve consumer interests by bringing down the price of telephone calls and can help firms enter a previously closed market. Because the same principle can serve different interests and goals, strategic alliances between different types of actors to support the institutionalization of a given principle become possible. The globalization of regulation has brought a politics of principles. In part this politics consists, as we have seen, of some actors setting out to build a consensus or alliance around a particular principle or principles. Intellectual property is a case in point. There, individuals connected with US business built an alliance between the US, Europe and Japan and the business communities of those states around the key principles of national treatment, MFN and harmonization in intellectual property. TRIPS was the creation of that alliance. Financial regulation is another example where strategically linked players play the politics of principles, articulating principles, often at moments of crisis when others are likely to be listening, building alliance networks around those principles, pushing them into other fora and encouraging their absorption into legal systems where those principles become deeply institutionalized through rule complexity. The Basle Committee is doing this with the principle of consolidation, the International Accounting Standards Committee with the principle of harmonization. Sometimes the consensus around principles is so overwhelming that there is no contest of principles. The victorious principles become part of regulatory ideology. No one demurs from them. Compliance becomes the only issue. With other principles there is a real contest. In other cases the clash of principles has a long history, a history in which oppositional principles have become akin to dialectical partners and one principle always plays a role contrary to the other.

The clash in trade regulation between liberalization/deregulation and mercantilism/strategic trade is an example of a long traditional struggle between principles.

There is one last aspect to our conclusion about principles. Our analysis shows that the globalization of regulation has ushered in the rule of principles. The rule of principles needs to be distinguished from the rule of law. The rule of law is a prescriptive, institutional ideal. The rule of principles (meaning that regulatory contests are fought at the level of principles) is, as we have demonstrated, the empirical reality of global business regulation. Liberal versions of the rule of law develop the idea that autonomous individuals should be left to pursue their interests within a framework of rules enacted by a neutral state. The international rule of law amounts to a similar kind of neutral legalism, in which international law administered and enforced by international organizations and courts provides a framework in which sovereign states can pursue their individual interests.[5] The state, because of its monopoly over legal norms, features strongly in both the rule of law and the international rule of law. This liberal ideal of the rule of law is some way from the reality that we have termed the rule of principles. Principles do not provide a neutral framework in which autonomous actors pursue their interests. Rather, they are oppositional tools that serve to entrench or defend the goals of actors. Principles need not be enacted by states, they need not be recognized by law in order to be part of a regulatory contest and to influence conduct. The self-regulatory impact of the meta-principles of innovation illustrates this point. So far all we have is a disjunction between what ought to be (the rule of law) and what is (the rule of principles as we have described it).

This disjunction gives rise to an important question about whether one ought to continue to advocate the rule of law as part of a prescriptive solution to the problems of globalization (the possible loss of citizen sovereignty, for example). Liberals and republicans can both advance cogent reasons for supporting the rule of law, since rules can be used to prevent interference in the liberty of others (the liberal version of freedom) as well as to create the conditions for preventing the arbitrary exercise of power, thus serving the republican conception of freedom as non-domination (Pettit 1997: 172). There are arguments the other way about the rule of law, however. To those working within critical theory, rules are indeterminate (Drahos & Parker 1992). This indeterminacy opens up the possibility of manipulations, manipulations that both mystify and serve the power-interests of elites. Under this analysis, the rule of law becomes part of the problem.

Our response to this issue is to avoid opening up a long line of abstract argument on the merits and demerits of the rule of law. The rule of law is an ideal, but it is also an instrumental ideal – it is pressed into service on behalf of deeper theories of freedom. For republicans at least, the defence of the rule of law is not just a philosophical exercise, but a task that has to be undertaken in the light of empirical realities (Pettit 1997: 173). It is at the level of non-ideal theory that we are seeking to make a contribution, when we develop our processual theories of the globalization of regulation (Chapters 23 and 24). Our point of departure is the global rule of principles. We ask how might we achieve greater consonance between the processes that constitute the transjudicial rule of principles and the republican aim of freedom as non-domination.

---

5 See, for example, the 1995 report by the Section of International Law and Practice of the American Bar Association entitled 'Report on Improving the Effectiveness of the United Nations in Advancing the Rule of Law in the World', *International Lawyer* 29: 293–334.

Mechanisms of the globalization of business regulation are social, economic or political processes that increase the extent to which patterns of regulation in one state are similar to or linked to patterns of regulation in other states. As such, we can call processes at very different levels of abstraction 'mechanisms'. Speech is a higher-order mechanism of globalization under this definition. We have chosen to define our mechanisms at a level of abstraction that inductively our histories of globalization show to be illuminating (see Chapter 4). This causes us to opt for the more recurrently concrete mechanisms of military coercion, economic coercion, systems of reward, reciprocal adjustment, non-reciprocal coordination, modelling and capacity-building.

## Military Coercion

Under this mechanism, globalization of regulation is achieved by the threat, fear or use of military force. Table 22.1 shows that it is far from the most consistently important mechanism of globalization. In some domains where almost all the globalization has occurred since the Second World War, such as environment and motor vehicle standards, there are no specific globalizations of regulatory standards that can be attributed to military coercion. Nevertheless, military coercion turned out to be much more important than we expected at the commencement of this study.

**TABLE 22.1** Mechanisms of Globalization

| MECHANISMS | CONTRACT AND PROPERTY RIGHTS | FINANCE | CORPORATIONS AND SECURITIES | TRADE AND COMPETITION | LABOUR | ENVIRONMENT |
|---|---|---|---|---|---|---|
| **Military coercion** | Important | Important | Minor | Important | Important | None |
| **Economic coercion** | Important | Important | Minor | Important | Important | Minor |
| **Systems of reward** | Minor | Minor | Minor | Important | Strengthening | Minor |
| **Modelling** | Important | Important | Important | Important | Important | Important |
| **Reciprocal adjustment** | Important | Important | Important | Important | Important | Important |
| **Non-reciprocal coordination** | Minor | Minor | Minor | Important | Minor | Important |
| **Capacity-building** | Important | Important | Of some importance | Minor | Important | Important |

Even with regimes where almost all the globalization occurred after the Second World War, one might say there is an indirect effect of the war. This chapter shows that by far the most important single actor during this period in the range of domains we have studied is the US state, a hegemony that was considerably secured on the battlefields of Europe and the Pacific.

Military coercion is least important with less foundational forms of regulation such as motor vehicle standards, and most important with the forms of regulation which have been constitutive of the very possibility of global capitalism. While the institutions of property diffused first through the mechanisms of modelling, their further diffusion was coerced and solidified when empires that conquered expanding territories stood behind them. The most important of these was the Roman empire. But before then Persian and Greek armies, among others, spread as far as India the idea that a single currency should be legal tender across vast expanses of territory ruled by a centralized monetary policy and, later, a unified tax administration.

The project of globalizing the business regulatory precepts codified by Justinian lay dormant for a millennium until the colonial armies of Spain and Portugal spread them across all South and Central America and parts of North America, Asia and Africa. The Dutch were next to impose Justinian's order, mainly in what we call today Indonesia and South Africa. As we saw in Chapter 7, Napoleon's armies played an important role in globalizing the principles of the Code Civil. Later French, Belgian and German colonizers globalized their Roman law inheritance through military conquest. The British empire's imposition of common law through military invasion is only slightly surpassed in importance by Roman and Spanish conquest. Wood's (1997) survey of financial law shows that 33 per cent of the world's population is squarely under the common law. Another third have had a Roman legal tradition of some form imposed upon them and 5 per cent have a mixed Roman and common law framework. The 30 per cent of the world's population that Wood classifies as 'emerging' or as unclassified jurisdictions, mostly former communist states and China, are moving toward either Roman or common law dominated hybrids. Only the 1 per cent of the world's population Wood classifies as having an Islamic financial law are subject to a non-European framework.

Much of the colonial conquest that blanketed the world with European business regulatory precepts was undertaken by private rather than state armies and navies, such as those of the East Indies companies based in different states, and the Massachusetts, Virginia and Hudson's Bay Companies (see Chapter 9). Not all the regulatory law imposed at the point of a musket was

| NUCLEAR SAFETY | TELECOMMUNI-CATIONS | DRUGS | FOOD | SEA TRANSPORT | ROAD TRANSPORT | AIR TRANSPORT |
|---|---|---|---|---|---|---|
| Important | Minor | Important | Minor | Important | None | Minor |
| Important | Minor | Important | Important | Important | Minor | Important |
| Minor | Minor | Important | None | Important | None | Important |
| Important | Important | Important | Important | Important | Important | Important |
| Important | Important | Important | Important | Important | Important | Important |
| Important | Minor | Important | Minor | Minor | Minor | Important |
| Important | Of some importance | Important | Important | Important | Minor | Important |

globalizing in effect. Some was glocalizing. For example, while the conquistadores and the colonial trading companies of the sixteenth, seventeenth and eighteenth centuries imposed slave systems based on the precepts of Roman slave law (even in predominantly common-law North America), they also coopted existing local customary law for the regulation of slavery when that smoothed the way for profitable plantation economies (see Chapter 11). After the ban on slavery globalized in the nineteenth century, until well into the twentieth century colonial administrations maintained plantation workforces in conditions of near-slavery through adapting European master and servant law to the purpose. This move meant that, structurally, colonialism pushed the labour law of the South back to pre-capitalist forms that were out of harmony with the labour laws won by trade unions in the North (see Chapter 11). Colonial imposition of law through military conquest therefore had a complex mix of globalizing and counter-globalizing effects. Slavery is a particularly interesting case because it was so substantially imposed by military conquest and, in the biggest slave-owning states of Brazil and the US, the abolition of slavery was enforced militarily.

The same point about simultaneous globalizing and counter-globalizing effects might apply, in a somewhat different way, to the impact of the military conquest of most of Eastern and Central Europe by the Soviet Union in 1945. This unified business regulatory principles over vast tracts of the globe. There were two competing globalizing projects in everything from labour law to air transport law – a capitalist and a communist one. The Soviet Union really did erect an Iron Curtain to separate the two models. While the US promulgated the principle of freedom of the skies, the USSR opposed this principle, essentially requiring passengers to fly in communist aircraft operating under Soviet rules if they wanted to traverse communist space. The USSR prevented Czechoslovakia, Poland and Yugoslavia from continuing their participation in the US-dominated postwar air transport regime that they had begun with their participation in the 1944 Chicago Civil Aviation Conference (Chapter 19). Until *glasnost* in the 1980s, rather than permit reciprocal adjustment of communist and capitalist law when trade across the Iron Curtain was mutually beneficial, the USSR preferred contracts that provided for commercial arbitration in non-aligned Stockholm. Hence, Soviet conquest of Eastern and Central Europe both integrated disparate legal systems under the hegemony of Soviet regulatory law and delayed the wider integration of the East under globalizing Western regulatory law.

US regulatory hegemony after the Second World War was often connected to its military domination. During the occupation the US insisted on competition laws that broke up Germany's cartels and the Japanese *zaibatsu* (Chapter 10). During the Cold War, insiders we interviewed said that US negotiators would invoke with West Germany its military commitment to 'defend Berlin' when haggling over the trade regime. One does not need access to interviews with senior trade insiders to see the evidence of newspaper stories like the following, leaked to soften up adversaries during trade negotiations:

### 'US Defence Warning Keeps Heat on Japan'

The US kept up the heat on Japan yesterday with a senior official warning that relations between the two economic giants, including their defence and political ties, could become 'poisonous' if nothing was done to address US complaints about Japan's closed car markets (*Australian*, 21 May 1995).

This linkage is even more explicit in the nuclear safeguards regime. For example, we saw in Chapter 13 how South Korea only signed the Nuclear Non-Proliferation Treaty because it was threatened with the withdrawal of US military support. The safeguards regime of the International Atomic Energy Agency is also unlike that of any other business regulatory organization in that it is underwritten by the authority of the UN Security Council to react to non-compliance with the Non-Proliferation Treaty as it sees fit, including militarily.

The Treaty of Versailles had less profound effects on the globalization of business regulation than the Second World War. Germany was required by the Treaty of Versailles to implement any new radio treaty settled in the next five years (Chapter 14). While the ILO was established as part of that Treaty, no vanquished power was forced to sign, indeed the German labour movement was prominent and successful in pushing German and international support for it. The most significant impact of the Versailles Treaty was that Germany was forced to ban cocaine in compliance with the Hague Convention of 1912 (Chapter 15). German pharmaceutical companies had monopolized cocaine manufacture prior to the war and prevented its inclusion in the implementation of the Hague Convention in the hope of winning the war. Among all the regimes discussed in this book, military coercion is most important as a mechanism in the drugs domain. In the nineteenth century, Britain fought two opium wars with China to assert its policy of free trade in drugs. Japanese occupying armies between the two world wars enforced the right of Japanese pharmacists to install a chain of North Asian pharmacies selling Japanese-manufactured heroin. Conversely, the US occupying armies in 1945 shut down the state opium monopolies that had been ubiquitous throughout Asia, as they had done in the Philippines in 1898 following US military defeat of the Spanish. While the replacement of the British medical model of drug regulation with the utter global hegemony of the US criminalization model was also about economic coercion and soft hegemony in a Gramscian sense, much of the history is dominated by military imperatives. As recently as the 1980s, there was a profound US militarization of the war on drugs, waged by the assassination of key drug distributors and supply of helicopters and other military technology to front-line states in the war on drugs, such as Colombia, where a virtual state of war prevailed between the state and the cocaine cartels (see Chapter 15).

## Economic Coercion and Systems of Reward

Economic coercion is generally a more important mechanism of globalization than military coercion; the only two domains where the reverse is true are nuclear regulation and the regulation of drugs. Economic coercion is most effectively applied by the IMF and the World Bank. Beyond that, as with military coercion, most economic coercion deployed to globalize business regulation is deployed by dominant states, mainly the US, though private corporations are also sometimes the actors who wield coercive threats. Many environmental treaties provide for economic sanctions for non-compliance, but these are virtually never applied bilaterally or multilaterally. The US occasionally threatens to impose a trade sanction, as it did with Taiwan over ozone-depleting substances, but has never actually done so. Environmental NGOs from one state occasionally attempt to enforce compliance with treaty obligations in the courts of other states.

The area where economic sanctions are sometimes imposed is in the trade regime. These are not multilateral, but bilateral. The US has been the most aggressive user of bilateral trade sanctions, its campaign of the 1990s to globalize US intellectual property rules being perhaps the most aggressive domain of application, with South African anti-apartheid sanctions (which were not mainly about business regulation, though partially about non-discriminatory labour standards). Even here, however, threat and watch-listing have been far more common than the actual application of sanctions. In summary, the rest of the world virtually never imposes trade sanctions for non-compliance with international business regulatory standards, and rarely threatens their use; the US quite frequently threatens their use in domains ranging from labour standards to food standards to telecommunications to agricultural trade and intellectual property, but very rarely applies them.

Trade threats by the US are not restricted to denial of access to its markets. They can also involve denial of supply of technology, as when Japan was motivated to adhere to the Nuclear Non-Proliferation Treaty out of fear the US might cut off nuclear fuel supplies, crippling the Japanese nuclear industry (see Chapter 13). Even though experience is that states rarely impose trade sanctions, linking other business regulatory regimes to the trade regime (as the international union movement would like to accomplish with labour standards and as the unions, environment and consumer groups sought to do with the Multilateral Agreement on Investment) is a means of strengthening the regime at issue. The truth of this has been graphically illustrated by the increased potency of both intellectual property norms (Chapter 7) and the global food standards of the Codex (Chapter 16) after they were made GATT-enforceable in the Uruguay Round.

The form of threat that a wider group of states sometimes applies is cutting off or cutting back foreign aid or withdrawing preferential tariff rates for developing country exporters. As both tariff levels and foreign aid budgets have declined, so has the power of these mechanisms of economic coercion.

The more profound the hegemony of a state, the less it has to resort to the threat or use of economic sanctions, yet the more the compliance it secures is grounded in the fear of that possibility. The extreme case of US regulatory hegemony is the air transport regime. The reasons are clear: the US dominates manufactures (through Boeing), is the biggest market for air services, the biggest importer of air services, the biggest exporter and the source of most new technology, and it has the greatest concentration of expertise in regulatory technology. For all that, its hegemony often fails, so from time to time it does bring a state or an airline to heel when it fails to measure up against ICAO safety standards; for example, it threatens withdrawal of US landing rights.

Economic coercion is more frequently imposed as a matter of conditionality by the IMF, the World Bank and other development banks. As we saw in Chapter 8, these institutions regularly require business regulatory reforms, such as introducing competition laws, implementing the Most Favoured Nation principle in trade regulation or meeting the G-10's capital adequacy standards for banks, as a condition for lending money. When states are desperate to be bailed out or to get funds for development projects, these institutions can accomplish formidable compliance with their demands. This is a two-way street, however. Because the World Bank is a disciplinary lender, it can raise and lend money at lower interest rates than private banks without the institutional capacity to discipline creditor states.

The insurance industry has been important in its capacity to impose economic sanctions in some industries. In the nineteenth century, when Britannia ruled the waves, Lloyds of London was in the driver's seat in setting the sort of standards for ship safety that private classification societies like Lloyd's Register ought to impose. If it could not get insurance in the Lloyd's insurance market, a classification society would not want to let a ship through classification. Ships risked being turned away from British ports unless they had met the standards enforced by the classification (see Chapter 17). Similarly, Mitchell's (1994a) work on the IMO oil-pollution regime shows the insurance industry sanction of withdrawing willingness to insure is the ultimate guarantor of a high level of compliance (Chapter 12).

Systems of reward globalize regulation by systematic means of raising the expected value of compliance with a globalizing order (as opposed to coercion, which reduces the expected value of non-compliance). Like economic coercion, systems of reward are talked about much more than implemented. Carbon taxes, globalization of environmental off-sets and environmentally adjusted national accounts that would systematically reward environmentally compliant states through their creditworthiness are much discussed but are years away from implementation. On the other hand, we have seen debt-for-environment swaps negotiated at the Paris Club of creditor states, debts generously forgiven by states like Germany and credibly responded to with environmental investment by states like Poland (see Chapter 12). The most substantial investment in carrots has been the Global Environmental Facility (GEF), funded by the rich nations pursuant to Agenda 21 of the Rio Summit and administered under the auspices of the World Bank. The cost of this to the rich nations explains why systematic reward for environmental initiatives or any other kind of regulatory initiative is not a widely used mechanism.

The Atoms for Peace program of the Eisenhower administration was perhaps the most impressive investment in reward. States which signed the nuclear safety and safeguards regimes sponsored by the US were rewarded with free access to a swathe of US nuclear technology and transfer of knowhow on its use. More recently, North Korea has been able to negotiate a package valued at $US5 billion for undertakings on compliance with the regime (see Chapter 13).

The EU in 1998 implemented a social incentive clause into its General System of Preferences to grant preferential trade access to Europe for developing countries. Supplementary duty preferences are given to states that comply with specified ILO core standards, standards on adequate control of drug movements and money-laundering, and compliance with Uruguay Round market access objectives.

National treatment and Most Favoured Nation treatment can be read as systematic rewards for states that comply with the business regulatory standards which are membership conditions of the most consequential clubs in the world, the EU and the WTO (and potentially NAFTA, if it expands to become the American Free Trade Agreement). The tortuous process of negotiating the entry of Eastern European states to the EU and China to the WTO for more than a decade reveals how valuable these rewards are considered to be. Once states are admitted to these clubs, the leverage of other states declines markedly. This is why there are such demanding business regulatory (and deregulatory) hurdles for admission.

Insurers also deploy systematic rewards in global regulatory regimes to some degree. For example, insurers offer lower premiums for ships that attain higher performance standards against the tests set by the IMO and international voluntary standards associations.

The actual application of economic sanctions and systems of reward is rare because they are expensive. The main cost of the latter is paying for the rewards. Economic sanctions may have a lower up-front dollar cost of imposition. Certainly the threat of economic sanctions is low-cost in dollar terms. But the diplomatic costs in a world of complex interdependency (Keohane 1984) from disrupted relationships with actors who can sanction a nation in return, during the long sequence of diplomatic games that they play together, are seen by our informants as the greater anxiety. Even the US moves carefully in the final stages of a section 301 process. Decisions relating to the use of 301 have to go through an inter-agency process that includes the State Department, among others.

The big difference in the effectiveness of these two mechanisms, however, is that economic coercion can deliver results time after time by threatened use which is not imposed. This cannot be done with rewards. Promising rewards time after time and never delivering not only does not work; it is counterproductive. Even if change would have occurred without the promised reward, if the reward does not arrive resentment at the broken promise can undo change until the promise is kept. In the case of change occurring without a sanction being applied, the credibility of the non-applied sanction is enhanced; it is said that the threat of the sanction worked in motivating the change. The unkept promise is a plus for the credibility of the mechanism in the sanction case, a minus in the reward case.

'Ah', one might say, 'but in cases where the targeted actor fails to implement the desired change, broken promises to sanction are just as damaging to credibility as broken promises to reward'. This is not the experience of the regulatory diplomats we interviewed. There are various ways to hold back on a sanction in a way that will have the restraint interpreted as a gift or generous gesture, or a negotiated settlement in which both sides make concessions. The last is always a possibility even with an utterly intransigent adversary, because of the option of playing the non-reciprocal coordination game we discuss later in this chapter. A player that does not want to pay the cost of delivering on a threat can widen the negotiating agenda to ask for a concession in another arena that it suspects the targeted actor is already willing to concede; the supposed concession accomplished by issue linkage can then be presented to assure both domestic and international audiences that no weakness has been demonstrated. This diplomatic game can be played in a way that builds goodwill from the adversary, through the adversary perceiving the backdown as a generous gesture from a foe who could easily have been bloody-minded; to audiences external to the negotiation, it is read as a negotiated settlement in which both sides made concessions. None of these tactics is available when the adversary is waiting for the promised cheque (reward) to arrive in the mail.

The pattern of regulatory diplomacy we observe is consistent with this interpretation offered by our informants. Apart from the granting of admission to valued clubs such as the WTO and the EU, both the promising and giving of systematic rewards is rare. Actually, promising admission to the EU on agreed terms is also a rare (one-off) historical event. Imposing economic coercion is also rare but threatening it is quite common, at least by the US, and not uncommon on the part of the EC and other more moderately powerful states such as France, China and Russia. US section 301 trade diplomacy is explicitly designed to regularly deliver threats without often having to pay the cost of delivering them. The US displays a trade sanction regulatory pyramid to the world (Ayres & Braithwaite 1992: Ch. 2). First it discusses bilaterally policies it cannot abide – be they about intellectual property, labour standards or dumping – that are 301-vulnerable. If progress does not occur in those discussions it might encourage domestic actors to lodge formal complaints urging the imposition of section 301 sanctions. If that does not induce concessions, it launches a formal investigation into the behaviour of the targeted state, various results of which may be reported to the Congress and the people. If that does not work, the state may be watch-listed and put on notice of what it must do, and by when, to avert sanctions. If there is still no movement, modest sanctions may be imposed that do not hurt anyone in the US. If there is still no movement, more formidable sanctions with a higher domestic cost may be imposed. What is displayed to the targeted actor is an image of US invincibility. The US trade negotiators explain that the target is on a slippery slope that will lead to a sticky end (see generally Hawkins 1984). Most adversaries make sufficient concessions to the US before it gets to delivering on threats that involve a serious cost. Occasionally, but only very occasionally, the US is forced to carry out trade sanctions that involve a serious domestic political and economic cost. Having to do so occasionally is a good investment in underwriting the credibility of US economic coercion.

Hence, this empirical pattern of a high ratio of threat to delivery of economic coercion that cannot be replicated in the case of systems of reward, is what makes economic coercion the more potent mechanism. Economic coercion is usually only a mechanism of minor importance to the globalization of regulation in domains such as corporations and securities, where the US does not consider it has an especially profound national interest in the globalization of regulatory standards. Of course, both economic coercion and systems of reward are mechanisms that cannot be resourced by the majority of the world's states which are weak states, the majority of the world's corporations and NGOs (which can rarely threaten a consumer boycott with credibility).

## Modelling

In contrast to the first three mechanisms, modelling, as we will discuss in Chapter 25, is a potent weapon the weak can use. As Table 22.1 shows, the substantive chapters have proven modelling to be an important mechanism of globalization in every domain; in fact, it is more often than any other the most important of all our mechanisms At the same time, modelling can be a weapon of the weak that the strong choose to crush by economic coercion if the interests at stake are large enough. For example, in Chapter 7 we saw that developing countries at BIRPI (the World Intellectual Property Organization's predecessor) developed a draft model law on patents that met their economic interests as technology-importing countries. African states in the 1960s developed a copyright law to protect folklore. Much of the modelling by weak states of these initiatives was swept aside by the 1994 TRIPS agreement which coerced compliance with the threat of lost access to US and European markets.

Modelling achieves globalization of regulation by observational learning with a symbolic content, learning based on conceptions of action with cognitive content that makes modelling more than mere imitation. The theory of modelling is developed in Chapter 25. Global modelling was enabled early as a mechanism because by 200 AD Asia, the Middle East and the Mediterranean were linked by trade routes which were conduits for the spread of ideas. Later globalizations of business regulation which we interpret as exemplars of modelling may be interpreted by others as products of military or economic coercion. The more ancient the history, the less plausible is organized global coercion as an explanation of globalization. It is hard to explain the adoption of the technological innovation of the plough across Europe, North Africa, the Middle East, India and China by 2000 BC (Barraclough 1997: 6–7) via a mechanism other than modelling. Before the concentration of power inherent in the rise and spread of cities, it would be hard to attribute the spread of agriculture among hunter-gatherer peoples from a narrow agricultural base in the Middle East, Crete and Thessaly by 6000 BC and across most of Europe and a strip of North Africa by 4000 BC, to the use of coercion (Barraclough 1997: 14–15). With the early history of business regulation as well, modelling is the basic mechanism of globalization.

By the time of the spread of principles of property, tort and contract from the Laws of Eshunna on the Tigris (from at least the eighteenth century BC), the Babylonian Code of Hammurabi (perhaps a century later) and the book of Exodus (some centuries later again) (Watson 1974: 22–23), it is less possible to judge how much diffusion occurs by the mechanism of modelling and how much by military conquest. Watson (1974: 24) can plausibly argue that:

'The nature of the similarities of style and substance is such that they exclude the possibility of parallel legal development'. Stronger evidence, though only suggestive, exists that Roman law was considerably and consciously modelled on the laws of various Greek cities, with a Roman tradition suggesting that legal study groups travelled to Greece (Watson 1974: 25). Perhaps even in ancient Rome there was 'an impetus to globalization from a desire to travel!' (US FDA interview). Roman modelling of Greece includes early modelling of labour law in the form of laws regulating relationships between masters and slaves.

As we have seen, military conquest seems to have been fundamental to the later spread of Roman law. But modelling spread Roman law further than military conquest ever did. The spread of the *Corpus Iuris* from eleventh-century Bologna throughout Europe and later the colonies of Europe, giving rise to the Roman family of legal systems, is an example of enduring conquest by modelling that no state could ever match militarily. In the less hegemonic world of Europe a millennium after the Roman empire, we can be equally sure that the *Lex Mercatoria* was modelled through the agency of merchants because only later did states incorporate it into their law (see Chapter 7). So we can agree with Watson's (1974: 22) approving quotation of Roscoe Pound: 'History of a system of law is largely a history of borrowings of legal materials from other legal systems and of assimilation of materials from outside the law'. Watson (1974: 95) concludes that legal transplants are not only 'extremely common' from the ancient Near East to the present day, but that transplanting is 'the most fertile source of development':

> Most changes in most systems are the result of borrowing. This is so both for individual rules and for systematics as can be seen in the overwhelming importance for the Western world's private law of Roman civil law and English common law. Of his own country's system G. Tedeschi writes: 'In the Law of the State of Israel the foreign elements predominate, and their foreign origin is obvious and unmistakable. This is the case to such an extent that in most spheres it is difficult to point to any significant contribution of our own'.

The latter may be an exaggeration or an extreme case but, as we will argue in Chapter 25, the more peripheral states are, the more their law is modelled from the centre: Australian law, for example, is clearly overwhelmingly modelled from the Northern hemisphere, which is not to say that the transplants have not budded in distinctively Australian ways. A contract of sale everywhere in the Western world and beyond 'is fundamentally that which existed at Rome in the later second century AD' (Watson 1974: 95). This spread cannot be accounted for only, or even mainly, by Roman military expansion.

Contemporary discussions of globalization of law through modelling tend to be excessively obsessed with the new *Lex Mercatoria* controversy: to what extent do arbitration clauses or decisions of international commercial arbitrators at the ICC and elsewhere concerning disputes among foreign contractors or investors and states shape commercial law? This is just one of many influences documented in this book, hardly as important as the combined effect of the early modern *Lex Mercatoria*, global modelling of accounting standards starting with double-entry bookkeeping, modelling of the institution of the stock exchange and its self-regulatory norms from Amsterdam to London to New York to the rest of the world, modelling of the new twentieth-century separation of powers (a central bank responsible for the regulation of money independent of political influence from the legislature and executive), the emergence of a transnational judicial discourse of human rights, New Deal lawyers drafting competition laws for postwar European states, influencing those of the European Coal and Steel Community and fomenting anti-monopoly thinking among British Keynesians like Beveridge and Gaitskell (Picciotto 1991: 52), modelling by international voluntary standards organizations not only of technical standards but of environmental management systems, quality assurance systems and complaints-handling and compliance systems, NGOs pressuring at least thirty national governments to model a notion such as the environmental impact assessment procedure first introduced by the US *National Environmental Policy Act 1969*, the impetus to an international common law (Cooke 1995) from reciprocal cross-national citing of opinions and judges such as Sir Anthony Mason and Sir Robin Cooke, former Chief Justices of Australia and New Zealand sitting together on the Hong Kong Court of Final Appeal and the Fiji Supreme Court, and between them sitting in the British House of Lords, the Court of Appeal of the Solomon Islands and the Samoan Court of Appeal.

We have seen in chapter after chapter that even when efforts to build consensus on an international treaty fails, as it did on environmental impact statements (Chapter 12), modelling can still succeed in globalizing the regulatory innovation. The ILO can effectively foster global modelling in domains where voting for a treaty might be difficult because 'When the ILO issues codes of practice, some countries virtually copy them into their mandatory national laws' (ILO interview). The ILO cannot secure consensus for a convention on positive or affirmative action, but it does disseminate and promote in training modules corporate and state positive action programs. The EC sets up networks to foster positive action for women. The US Department of Labor issues 'trendsetter' lists of firms which monitor and improve the labour standards performance of their subcontractors globally.

One reason the US has not felt moved to deploy our first three mechanisms in pursuit of a global harmonization of corporations and securities laws is that the rest of the world has substantially modelled the regulatory standards of the SEC and the New York Stock Exchange, although not entirely, leaving New York unassailed as the most transparent and credible securities market. We saw in Chapter 9 the importance of the Big Five accounting firms as global model mercenaries for regulatory innovations such as the Board Audit Committee first mandated by the New York Stock Exchange.

Global modelling often proceeds by piggy-backing on a bilateral agreement initially settled on the basis of a significant dose of economic coercion. For example, Chapter 10 shows how the bilateral agreement between the US and South Korea on intellectual property caused other states to make a beeline for Seoul to negotiate the same deal and to follow the same principles in a proliferation of bilaterals involving neither South Korea nor the US. Without the element of economic coercion, those subsequent agreements may not have been as strong as the agreement the US secured from South Korea, but there is a partial globalization of the terms of the seminal bilateral. International treaties are often modelled on seminal bilaterals negotiated by a hegemon (the US, and earlier the UK). For example, the EURATOM and IAEA safeguards regimes were modelled on US bilaterals and the terms of the US *Atomic Energy Act 1954*. And as we saw in Chapter 7, the tax treaty negotiated between the US and the UK in 1945 became the basis of the postwar international system of tax.

Economic coercion can also sometimes piggy-back on modelling. One Taiwanese regulator commenting on the use of trade coercion by the US said: 'US pushes [on matters like telecommunications, services, intellectual property] are blessings in disguise' (1995 interview). Some Taiwanese regulators, already convinced by the efficacy of foreign models, use the fact of US trade coercion as a means of promoting models in which they already believe.

Where a process is modelled, the process of modelling is reinforced. Thus when Taiwan models the process of regulatory competition through adopting a plan to turn Taiwan into an Asia-Pacific Regional Operations Centre (Council for Economic Planning and Development 1995) that process commits Taiwan to more modelling. Under the plan, Taiwan will match or better the regulatory standards affecting investment set by Hong Kong and Singapore. It is, as one Taiwanese regulator explained, 'a benchmarking concept' (1995 interview).

The fact that US and EU law are modelled more than others is not only because of their economic hegemony and the fact that weaker economies want to meet their terms for admission to the clubs they dominate. In the case of the US in particular, modelling is underwritten by the sheer depth of regulatory expertise Washington agencies can offer and the detailed analyses of regulatory reasoning that are available in the Federal Register. Regulations backed by an explicit and public technical case are more likely to be modelled. Systems of rules that are detailed, comprehensive and provide answers to problems are more likely to be modelled. One Taiwanese regulator, in explaining the influence of multinational companies on regulation in Taiwan, said: 'They [TNCs] have collected experience in-house…Their attorneys provide you with nitty-gritty details' (1995 interview). This kind of knowhow modelling is a powerful shaper of regulation. Access to other states' regulations and regulatory analyses on the Internet is further fostering modelling.

Depth of expertise is one of the keys to successful modelling in areas of great technical complexity. This is illustrated by the following:

> the success of the Association's [International Swaps and Derivatives Association] documentation for derivatives can be attributed in no small part to a broad-based effort to achieve a 'collective' wisdom about relevant issues. Literally hundreds of legal experts from around the globe have contributed to ISDA's documentation – it serves as an industry standard in the international market – and the Association's committees and working groups have systematically studied the risks referred to in the joint statement of the regulators. Thus, the belief that regulator and regulated can reach a common view may not be so far-fetched, there being tremendous mutuality of interest, namely, reduction of risk and tremendous opportunity to build on a considerable collective wisdom that already exists (Golden 1994: 295).

We note that this quote illustrates our conclusion that the globalization of regulation is never the product of one mechanism. In the financial community of shared fate, reciprocal concerns over the use of derivatives (reciprocal adjustment) triggers a search for a common set of regulatory norms. Since this process of private ordering is led by those with expert practical knowledge, the guidelines produced become authoritative in financial circles. Modelling ensures the international spread of what becomes an industry standard. This sequence of events is an example of the way mechanisms can work to deliver bottom-up globalization.

Sometimes US leadership of new regulatory ideas has not been modelled by the rest of the world until a major disaster mobilizes mass publics. The leading instance is the total globalization of the 1938 US innovation of making pharmaceuticals subject to pre-marketing clearance for safety, product by product. This did not spread much beyond the US until the thalidomide disaster hit so many countries in the 1960s. Interestingly, the US pre-marketing approval laws of 1938 had themselves been modelled on the Seal of Acceptance Program operated by the American Medical Association from 1905. The sequence is leading self-regulatory practice modelled by lead state law that globalizes after disasters that affect many countries.

Global modelling is sometimes institutionalized firm-to-firm (bypassing states) by the kind of peer review and plant-pairing programs that we saw the World Association of Nuclear Operators implement (Chapter 13). We saw in Chapter 21 the importance of epistemic communities of actors in fostering direct modelling of regulatory practice from corporation to corporation. TNCs play a vital role in modelling self-regulatory innovations that later become law, from one sub-sidiary to another, from subsidiaries to subcontractors in the periphery. Chapter 18, on motor vehicle regulation, is a good illustration of the importance of a sequence of corporate innova-tion–corporate modelling–state regulation. If one kind of innovation-modelling-regulation sequence has occurred in Europe and another in the US, at the global regulatory forum in Geneva we saw that both models are likely to be tabled. Decisions by a number of independent states, like Australia, to choose the European or the US regulatory model may tip the balance in favour of one or the other privately generated standard. TNC modelling is the least visible but the most vital kind of modelling because of the propensity of regulatory law to follow commercial custom. Its influence has been impressively transcontinental since 1300, when Italian firms begin trading as far as India and China, spreading models of how to manage credit, banking, bookkeeping and risk-spreading through dispersed corporate ownership.

## Reciprocal Adjustment and Non-reciprocal Coordination

Reciprocal adjustment arises where each of two or more actors moves their regulatory policy in response to a move by the other. When states mutually adjust satellite orbits so that they do not coincide with the orbit slots approved under the regulations of other states, this is a classic case of reciprocal adjustment. No military or economic coercion is required to accomplish it, because all states have an interest in preventing their satellites crashing into satellites from another state. It is the most uncomplicated of all the mechanisms.

Table 22.1 shows that reciprocal adjustment shares with modelling the distinction of being important in every regime. Moreover, in domains such as food standards and telecommu-nications, reciprocal adjustment sits alongside modelling as a fundamentally important mecha-nism in globalization of business regulation. These two mechanisms often work in mutually reinforcing ways. In the prescription drugs regime, for example, reciprocal adjustment persis-tently failed to occur at WHO. However, it did occur in the EU. Globalization proceeded by rec-iprocal adjustment in Europe, followed by modelling of the European compromise by most of the rest of the world.

Reciprocal adjustment to a shared principle – such as Most Favoured Nation or mutual recognition – often implies non-adjustment of rules; a multiplicity of rules is accorded mutual recognition. On the other hand, in Chapter 7 we saw that the foundations of property and con-tract were laid (through the Law Merchant) as mutual adjustment of principles, which later became a convergence of rules. In the late twentieth century this process continued at inter-national fora like UNCITRAL, the ICC's court of arbitration and its commissions on harmoniza-tion progressively elaborating rules of a new *Lex Mercatoria*. Most reciprocal adjustment we have discussed is positive – agreement to form a set of rules. But some is negative – mutual adjustment away from an existing set of rules. This means reciprocal adjustment away from globalized regu-lation, toward globalized deregulation. We saw this with positive reciprocal adjustment led by the US toward the INTELSAT regime in the 1960s for coordinated monopoly in the provision of satel-lite services; then negative reciprocal adjustment led by the US in the 1980s to deregulate INTEL-SAT, opening space to private competition (see Chapter 14).

Deliberation at international fora frequently fosters reciprocal adjustment by enabling actors to discover previously unknown interests in cooperation. Pacific island states learn, through participation in international environmental fora, that they have an interest in working with other states to combat greenhouse-gas emissions, lest their islands be covered by a rising ocean. Arrangements like the WTO Trade Policy Review Mechanism are designed with the idea of helping states recognize new interests in trade liberalization. Bargaining forums like the World Intellectual Property Organization reduce the transaction costs of states meeting to discover where there might be mutual benefit from reciprocal adjustment. This is one of the things Haas, Keohane and Levy (1993) mean when they say that regimes can enhance the contractual environment. They also found that regimes foster reciprocal adjustment by increasing governmental concern and building national capacity (see below). Like Chayes and Chayes (1995), from their empirical work on global environmental regimes they conclude that regimes accomplish quite a lot in these three ways; their effectiveness is rarely based on applying sanctions. The data from the wider array of regimes discussed in this book confirms that conclusion, though we have found that military and economic coercion are also important.

It follows that framework conventions that initially seem to have little substance are a good strategy for those wanting to make global regulatory regimes effective by enhancing the contractual environment, increasing governmental concern and building national capacity. An initial negotiating text that is more procedural than substantive, more about principles than rules, can be a framework that acquires formidable content over time. Framework conventions are also a good strategy for actors who would prefer internationally institutionalized rules of fair play in arenas of bilateral conflict where outcomes from future contests are uncertain. As Young (1989: 362) explains, citing Brennan and Buchanan's *The Reason of Rules*:

> And to use the formulation of Geoffrey Brennan and James Buchanan, 'As both the generality and the permanence of rules are increased, the individual who faces choice alternatives becomes more uncertain about the effects of alternatives on his own position'. This uncertainty actually facilitates efforts to reach agreement on the substantive provisions of international regimes. As Brennan and Buchanan observe, in a discussion directed toward municipal institutions, 'to the extent that a person faced with constitutional choice remains uncertain as to what his position will be under separate choice options, he will tend to agree on arrangements that might be called "fair" in the sense that patterns of outcomes generated under such arrangements will be broadly acceptable, regardless of where the participant might be located in such outcomes'.

Majone (1994a) has pointed out that reciprocal adjustment is most likely when externalities are reciprocal. Externalities occur when one actor imposes uncompensated costs on another. International externalities are reciprocal in the case of Italians and Greeks both pouring pollutants into the Mediterranean and both suffering the consequences. They are non-reciprocal when prevailing winds blow Italian air-pollution into Greece but Greek pollution is not blown into Italy. Italy has no incentive to be cooperative because of the non-reciprocal nature of the externality. We found that in a domain like food standards, the structural basis for reciprocal adjustment is strong because most states are both major importers and major exporters of food. In regimes such as prescription drugs, where only a few states are exporters, there is a higher likelihood that non-reciprocal externalities will motivate the formation of veto coalitions, as they have done at the WHO.

Reciprocal adjustment is strongest when states recognize that there is a problem and have no doubts of their reciprocal interests in dealing with the problem. We saw that in the cases of piracy on the high seas (Chapter 17), piracy of aircraft (Chapter 19) and piracy of intellectual property (Chapter 7) the mechanism worked with varying degrees of strength. In the case of intellectual property, economic coercion has been the dominant mechanism because states have not had and still do not have reciprocal economic interests in globalizing property rights in information. Even more fundamentally, there is a question of whether all states believe that there is a problem. 'Piracy' of intellectual property remains a highly contested concept. The US version of piracy, for example, in which developing countries steal high-technology products from individual corporate patent-holders, is not the version of piracy that India, for example, uses when it accuses US corporations of stealing traditional medicinal knowledge that exists as a collective asset for its people. What is and what is not in the public domain, and conceptions of rights, are constructed in very different ways in these disputes. As Indian feminist Vandana Shiva asks, 'who are the real pirates?' For the postmodernist there is no objective answer to this question; there are only language games to deconstruct. But as this book has shown, global regulation is not just about language games. Mechanisms of coercion take over where reciprocal adjustment has failed to produce a common language, a perception of a common problem. Piracy on the high seas is slightly different in that states seem to have been readier to recognize the problem. But the economic and military usefulness of pirates to individual states at various times prevented the recognition of reciprocal interests in dealing with the problem. By the time the first signs of reciprocal adjustment appeared (when states began discussing in the League of Nations the possibility of a convention on piracy), the problem had ceased to be a global one. British policing of the high seas had turned piracy into a niche market activity. Coercion, it seems, abhors the vacuum left by the failure of cooperation. Aircraft piracy, discussed briefly in Chapter 19, shows the speed at which reciprocal adjustment can work if both conditions are met. Hijacking of aircraft started around 1960, and a convention was on the books in 1963.

Non-reciprocal coordination rather than reciprocal adjustment becomes the more important mechanism in circumstances of non-reciprocal externalities. Where there is no contract zone that allows both negotiating parties to be winners, creative bargaining to link issues can constitute a contract zone. We saw in Chapter 10 that the WTO is designed as an institution to broaden the agenda when a negotiation breaks down, because the benefits one state gets by adjusting its rules are a cost to another state that makes the adjustment. The proposition becomes: 'if you take a loss here by adjusting your rules to this global norm, we'll let you take a big gain over there by wearing a loss ourselves in adjusting to that global norm'. For example, the Quad said to the Cairns Group: 'We'll give you agriculture if you give us intellectual property'. The WTO works by transforming dozens of separate negotiations which are mostly win–lose for any pairing of states, into a package of linked negotiations that allows win–win outcomes for the overwhelming majority of pairings of significant states. The agenda-broadening by the end of a GATT round also has the effect of making it too big to fail. The fact that all states are given a win on one or more issues means that they all have an incentive not to allow the negotiations to fail – the negotiations become too important to be allowed to fail. That is why we are headed for a 'Millennium Round' extravaganza of globalization.

But the trade regime is by no means the only one where contract zones are expanded through non-reciprocal coordination. Atoms for Peace was a grand bargain of non-reciprocal coordination: the US offered the rest of the world access to fissionable material and nuclear technology for peaceful purposes in return for signing non-proliferation and safety regimes. Encompassing institutions like G-7 summits, the EU and the WTO are the key to enabling non-reciprocal coordination. However, most international agreements are negotiated not at encompassing institutions but in specialist ones – like the World Intellectual Property Organization, the Food and Agriculture Organization or the International Civil Aviation Organization – dominated by specialist epistemic communities. It is this fact that makes reciprocal adjustment a more widely important mechanism than non-reciprocal coordination, as is clear from Table 22.1. On the other hand, shifts of forum from a specialist one to an encompassing one, as we will see in Chapter 24, is an important factor we must understand if we are to understand how the globalization of business regulation proceeds.

## Capacity-building

Capacity-building means globalization of regulation achieved by helping actors get the technical assistance to implement global standards. We saw, in Part II, that the three major contributors of technical assistance in regulatory matters are US and European regulatory agencies and international organizations. Some degree of capacity-building exists in all the regimes we have studied. Even when we say in Table 22.1 that the importance of capacity-building is minor, those involved in the regime still think it is important to do and it does go on. For example, capacity-building is said to be of only minor importance compared to other mechanisms in achieving globalization of trade and competition rules. While this is true, in the competition regime the US, EU and UNCTAD all gave significant technical assistance, particularly to post-communist societies during the 1990s, to set up competition authorities.

At the other extreme, where capacity-building is important as a mechanism of globalization, even at international organizations like the ILO with regulatory technical assistance budgets over $US100 million (which is rare), the resources available are modest compared to the magnitude of the task. To build national capacities to implement global standards for, say, the regulation of pharmaceuticals would take enormous technical assistance budgets that the rich nations are simply not willing to fund. Their willingness is higher in an arena like the safety of air transport, where rich nations are worried about the safety of their nationals flying into poorer nations. Another example of shared fate motivating substantial spending on technical assistance is the willingness of nuclear plants in more sophisticated economies to pair with nuclear plants in poorer nations under the auspices of the World Association of Nuclear Operators.

In a number of the international organizations we studied there is a kind of non-reciprocal coordination which sees developing countries focus on chasing the crumbs available in the technical assistance budget, while the wealthy nations concentrate on cutting the standard-setting cake.

## Conclusion

This study has found that military coercion, economic coercion, systems of reward, modelling, reciprocal adjustment, non-reciprocal coordination and capacity-building all have some significant importance across these regimes. There is no master mechanism of globalization. We found that the most consistently important mechanism was modelling, but it was not always the most important and its importance is always less than the combined importance of the other mechanisms. Chapter 25 recognizes the special significance of modelling, a significance neglected in the regulatory and international relations literatures. We will see that this neglect is a pity, because modelling works with a subtlety that is intriguing, and intriguingly connected to normative theories of global politics.

The mechanism we found to be second in importance is reciprocal adjustment. It is such a simple mechanism that we do not need to dedicate a special chapter to it. For example, A, B and C are helped by international deliberation to recognize that there is a contract zone where if they all agree to adjust their rules they would be better off – so reciprocal adjustment occurs in that domain of regulation. We must not underrate its significance just because it is prosaic in operation. In comparison, since the Second World War much less globalization of regulation has been accomplished by military coercion (which was more important in the early histories of globalization), economic coercion and systems of reward. It turns out to be wrong that substantial globalization cannot be achieved without a world state or a hegemon that can administer rewards and sanctions. Yet it would be equally wrong to deny the historical significance of hegemony in our histories or to fail to see the contemporary 'tregemony' of the US, EU and Japan in so many regimes.

It is also a mistake to adopt a mode of analysis that only asks which have been the most important mechanisms. Table 22.1 is guilty of this simplicity. Chapters 7 to 19 show that mechanisms are connected in interesting ways. The ILO connects its offers of capacity-building to attempts to enforce compliance – it never attempts to be a hard cop without at the same time offering help to meet international obligations (Chapter 11). The linkage of IMF and World Bank conditionality (economic coercion) to offers of help is a related though different kind of connection. When mutual adjustment is not possible, non-reciprocal coordination can be accomplished by institutionalizing systems of reward. Atoms for Peace was a non-reciprocal coordination where compliance with nuclear safeguards was linked to systematic reward through the flow of nuclear materials and knowhow (Chapter 13). The EU established a Cohesion Fund to benefit the poorer regions of Europe, that gain least and suffer the most damaging competition from opening Europe's borders to freer trade (Chapter 10). The strengthening linkage of environment and development since the Rio Summit and through specific funds, such as the Global Environment Facility and funds made available to developing countries under the Montreal Protocol on Ozone-Depleting Substances, have become quite a significant linkage of capacity-building and systems of reward to reciprocal upwards adjustment of environmental standards. Chapter 25 can be read as an extended treatment of the linkages of one mechanism – modelling – to all the others.

Chapters 7 to 19 also show that the mechanisms are activated by the range of different types of actors discussed in Chapter 20 through appeal to the various principles discussed in Chapter 21. These observations about interconnectedness set up Chapter 23, which considers the implications of conceiving globalization as arising from a web of principles and mechanisms woven by a plurality of actors. Some will want to read the conclusions to this chapter within a parsimonious rational-actor framework. Reciprocal adjustment occurs when the pay-offs to the parties allow it. When they don't, issue linkage can create a contract zone. When that cannot be accomplished, military or economic coercion or rewards are needed to change pay-offs.

That reading is limiting in several ways. First, we have found that pay-offs in a world of changing regulatory technologies are not given but discovered. For example, we saw in Chapter 20 the importance to the process of discovery of epistemic communities and international institutions that enhance the contractual environment. Once discovered, there is perplexing incommensurability in the pay-offs pursued. Some actors are pursuing profits, others sovereignty, military conquest, reputation in professional communities, a safer world, the precautionary principle, sustainable development, development without regard to sustainability, tax revenues or compliance with the law. The difficulty we had in narrowing the range of recurrently important principles in Chapter 21 shows the severe limits of any parsimonious rational-choice account. The multiplicity of important players demonstrated in Chapter 20, at different levels of aggregation with different levels of knowledge of the moves being made by other players, evinces a level of complexity beyond the grasp of extant game-theory paradigms.

A recurrent theme, for example, has been that realist international relations theory that privileges nations as actors with a single kind of value-maximizing motivation ignores the fragmentation of national action and motivation (the environment ministry with a different agenda from the trade ministry or the judiciary) and the fact that other actors such as corporations can be more important than states and even regulators of states (Moody's). We find state power not to be statically structural but as emerging from a process of structuration (Giddens 1984). The state is constituted by and helps constitute a web of regulatory controls that is continually rewoven to remake the regulatory state. States act as agents for other actors such as business corporations and other actors act as agents for states; this reflexive agency reconstitutes both agents and principals continually (see Chapter 20). States are part of actor networks; far from rising above these actor networks, state action has little impact without them.

As we saw in Chapter 9, rational-choice theorists can light on a fact such as the globalization of the institution of the stock exchange and quite sensibly say that it has globalized because it satisfied the economic interests of certain kinds of actors. At the same time, institutionalists can point out that at most points in history and in most cities today it was and would be impossible to organize market-makers to forge a stock exchange: 'Our account is that to understand the corporatization and securitization of the world by the modelling of London and New York we need to understand the way specific entrepreneurial actors kept innovating, building one institution on another' (Chapter 9). Even when actors have discovered what their commensurable interests are, often they cannot realize them because they lack the knowhow to run drug registration laboratories, or an air traffic or satellite navigation system. A theory of the globalization of interest which is not linked to a theory of the globalization of capacity will not explain much.

Histories of globalization have a complexity of networked action which means that few if any actors have the synoptic capacity to be rational in the way rational-choice theory would have it. They dither in confusion at a complexity they cannot grasp, which is why they can be led with such remarkable ease by entrepreneurs with the policy imagination to show them a plausibly interest-enhancing path. For the majority who persist in dithering without effective leadership, globalization, like shit, happens, as Manderson (1993: 75) explained the development of global illicit drug policy:

> drug policy was driven by its relative unimportance, the absence of domestic or political controversy and the consequent influence of international and bureaucratic factors. As the structure of modern drug laws thus took shape, each brick depending on those beneath it for support and validity, few remembered or even thought to question why they had ever been laid. So effective had the gradual process of entrenchment been that alternative processes soon became unthinkable.

This does not make it impossible for researchers to go back and reconstruct how each brick was laid, by which actors pursuing which principles, as we have attempted to do in this book. While most actors may lack any synoptic grasp of their interests, we can understand how concern gets mobilized among a limited range of actors with a capacity to lay some bricks. We find that once such concern is catalyzed, the bricks most likely to be laid first are principles in a framework agreement or convention. A second generation of actors refines these principles into rules. In a minority of the regimes we have studied, rules have then been refined into enforceable rules. Concern, principles, rules, enforceable rules – the recurrent path from framework to substance that we have uncovered. When rules are enforced the enforcement is rarely or only partially done by an international organization. Normally, it is states, private corporations or industry associations that are enrolled to enforce the rules, with the key actors applying pressure for rule enforcement being NGOs, mass publics mobilized by disasters and international organizations asking for reports on national compliance. Yet the sequence of concern, principles and rules without further movement to enforceable rules can engender impressive globalization, as we will see in the more extended and normative analysis of the principle of modelling in Chapter 25.

| Regulatory Webs and
Globalization Sequences

Having, in Chapters 20 to 22, summarized our empirical findings about the actors, mechanisms and contests of principles involved in the globalization of business regulation, in this chapter we take our inductive approach to theory formulation to a higher level of abstraction. The first part builds on the conclusion that globalization of regulation is never due to the operation of any single mechanism of globalization nor because of the agency of any one or two types of actors invoking only one or two principles. It follows that realist international relations theory, which studies the actions of one type of actor (states) in terms of a single abstract mechanism (pursuit of interest) fails to offer a useful explanatory framework. To understand how an accomplishment as difficult as the globalization of regulation is institutionalized, we need to understand the operation of a whole web of influences. Strategic wisdom involves actors understanding which strand(s) to seek to tighten at which moment in order to tauten a web that floats in time and space.

In Chapter 17 and Chapter 15, there is a more extended treatment than in the other substantive chapters of how most single strands in global webs of regulatory controls are weak. Weak strands are shown to acquire strength through being tied to other weak strands. In Chapter 13, the Institute of Nuclear Power Operations (INPO) is shown to have weak coercive powers and the US Nuclear Regulatory Commission is shown to have weak capacities for dialogue and persuasion. Yet these two weak strands are tied together in such a way that the weaknesses of each are reinforced by some strengths of the other. In fact, one of INPO's principal architects recalled an aspiration for other ties to reinforce INPO's weaknesses: 'We intended to tie together the INPO evaluations and insurance as an enforcement tool' (Rees 1994: 94). INPO created a mutual insurance organization – Nuclear Electric Insurers – with the idea that it would give INPO the clout to revoke the insurance of a recalcitrant utility. In the end it was decided this tie would be overkill: 'what the withdrawal of insurance would do to any utility, it would immediately affect their bond rating, their Wall Street situation. It could very well be financially catastrophic. It would be kind of like having a nuclear bomb in your arsenal' (Rees 1994: 94). The web of controls worked to reduce SCRAMS from seven per unit in 1980 to one per unit in 1993 without that extra strand.

The web of influences analysis has implications for regulatory management that we do not explore in this book. If there is no central locus of control, regulatory policy becomes a matter of managing a network rather than managing a hierarchy. All organizations in the network must do their strategic planning in a way that takes into account the way other organizations do theirs (Metcalfe 1994). Sovereign 'good government' is a different matter from non-hierarchical 'good governance' through global networks.

The second part of the chapter formalizes two sequential micro–macro theories of processes of globalization. In the first, individuals entrepreneurially enrol resource-based power to mould the shape of global regulation. The second is a more reactive, disaster-driven sequence where individuals can only seek to steer in the face of an overwhelming momentum of events. In both processes, modelling emerges as a pivotal mechanism. In Chapter 25, we therefore explore more fully the modelling mechanism and its implications for a politics of empowerment. In the chapter which follows this one we formalize a third process of globalization, a macro–macro sequence which involves the use of forum-shifting.

The bad news for the sovereignty of ordinary citizens is that most of them do not belong to states that can activate most of the mechanisms discussed in this chapter and the next. Only powerful states can play the forum-shifting game, can weave webs of reward and coercion with any success. The qualified good news for sovereignty is that webs of reward and coercion are usually less influential than dialogic webs. Weak states and NGOs can effectively tug at many of the strands of dialogic webs of influences. The qualification is that dialogic webs of control still tend to be dominated by major states and big business. Hegemony means that within dialogic webs there is more reason to hear the voices of those with a capacity to escalate to webs of reward and coercion.

## Webs of Influence

We have found that globalization of business regulation sometimes occurs through globalization of rules followed by globalization of compliance to bring business practice into compliance with those rules. Conversely, globalization often occurs first through globalization of business practice via the mechanism of modelling, that then becomes codified and solidified as globalized rules. Our data show that webs of control are relevant to understanding how both kinds of globalization of regulation occur, though the webs relevant in the case of practice preceding rules are more informal; they are more formal in the case of rules preceding practice.[1]

Sometimes practice remains solidly globalized without any formal rules. We will illustrate with an extended analysis of a form of globalized regulation most readers will have experienced during air travel. As we check in at every airport in the world, we encounter a line for first- and business-class. We cannot join that line if we have an economy ticket. Then we must choose one of several lines to wait for a chance to check in. It is against the rules to go to the front of the line. It is against the rules to jump ahead of someone who arrived twenty minutes after us but who was lucky enough to join a line that moves faster than ours. The same rules apply to lining up to pass through customs and immigration. These practices are utterly globalized without, to our knowledge, anywhere being formalized into rules.

---

1 Metaphors akin to the web of controls are commonplace in the globalization literature, for example McGrew's (1992: 13) 'cobweb image of global politics'.

Totally informal webs of control secure this order. We are steered into it by the Foucaultian architecture (Shearing & Stenning 1985) of the airport from our first intimidating encounter as a neophyte traveller, keen to follow the logic of appropriateness (March & Olsen 1998) manifest in the cues of the more sophisticated travellers we model. Of course, for those infatuated with rational choice logics, the near-perfection of the globalization of this ordering at thousands of decentralized sites around the world is a mystery. It matters to people to check in without undue waiting. There is an incentive to cheat in conditions that, from a formal rational-choice perspective, make coordination difficult. Airline passengers rarely know one another, so have no experience of their propensity to reciprocate compliance with compliance. There is no basis for stable expectations, not even a common culture that delivers identical socialization experiences, and no written rules. Second, 'interactions of this type are fleeting, and non-iterative, so that the discipline of time cannot be expected to work effectively' (Young 1979: 31) (if I give him his turn this time, he will give me my turn next time).[2] Third, membership of the group will fluctuate as people move from one queue to the end of a shorter one, as we move from the check-in queue to the customs queue, to the security queue to the boarding queue. Fourth, mechanisms for the coordination of expectations are weak, as it is difficult for individuals to show leadership. Fifth, the group is too large and time is too short for explicit processes of bargaining and negotiation to develop, though if we are at dire risk of missing our plane it is not inappropriate to appeal for an act of grace. Sixth, the rewards from taking enforcement action against a cheat are limited. If deterrence succeeds, the expected gain is the average time for one check-in divided by the number of operators at the end of the queue, the confrontation may be unpleasant, even dangerous, it may require dealing with language differences and it will hardly seem worth abandoning our place in the queue if we are required to move to censure an individual several places ahead of us. Still, our resentful scowling when someone cheats has some power and the scowling of the person at the check-in counter has even more power in the web of controls that operates here. In fact, many of the understandings that deliver regulatory consistency have globalized under the influence of regulatory webs that work without formal rules.

The most important distinction we wish to make is between different types of webs – dialogic webs and webs of reward and coercion. These webs are very often intertwined. However, one reason the distinction is worth making is because, while all cases of webs of rewards and coercion in our data are connected to dialogic webs, dialogic webs often exist without any web of reward and coercion. Dialogue can work quite well in globalizing compliance without any sanctions. We show that, strategically, most actors in the world system prefer to work through dialogue before they resort to laying strands of reward and coercion. We will argue that this strategy is sound, if the objective is to globalize compliance with an agreed set of rules. We will also show that while dialogic webs can be woven by all the actor types in our study, webs of rewards and punishment are accessible only to some actor types – those with concentrated and liquid resources. Yet we will show that this leaves resource-poor actors less disadvantaged than might be assumed, because dialogic webs are generally more influential and more common than webs of reward and coercion. Mechanisms such as modelling will be shown to be extremely influential in the hands of social movement actors with a strategic sense of world system.

---

2  Some of the points in this list are taken from Young's (1979: 30–1) list of obstacles to decentralized social ordering to secure compliance with appropriate behaviour in a crowded train carriage.

## Webs of Dialogue

Dialogic webs are more fundamentally webs of persuasion than webs of control. They include dialogue in professional associations, self-regulatory dialogue in industry associations, auditors from one subsidiary of a TNC auditing the compliance with regulatory standards of auditors from another subsidiary, naming and shaming of irresponsible corporate practices by NGOs, discussions in intergovernmental organizations at the regional and international levels, plus any number of idiosyncratic strands of deliberation that occur within and across epistemic communities. In dialogic webs actors convene with each other officially and unofficially, formally and informally. Dialogue helps actors to define their interests, thereby giving scope for the operation of mechanisms of reciprocal adjustment and non-reciprocal coordination. Mechanisms form part of dialogic webs. Dialogic webs include more than the concrete, lower-order mechanisms we have detailed in our case studies. Higher-order mechanisms like language mix with lower-order mechanisms, all connecting to form an intricate reality of persuasion and engagement.

Issue definition is the first form of persuasion delivered by dialogic webs that is a prerequisite for a global regime. Before there can be a global-warming regime, global warming needs to be defined as a problem that requires action, by key actors in the world system. Then dialogue is needed to redefine the interests of those actors as an interest in solving the problem. That is, global warming is not only an important problem, it is a problem that each actor has an interest in helping to solve.

Because there are so many issues that states and other major actors in global business can only resolve cooperatively (through reciprocal adjustment), these actors are in relationships that Keohane and Nye (1989) describe as 'complex interdependency'. A consequence is that they do not defect from cooperation with a regime to solve what they have defined as a problem, even in the absence of sanctions for cheating. The reason is that they fear, in a world of complex interdependency, that other players will not cooperate in solving other agreed problems (Keohane 1984). Hence, dialogue that enables an issue to be defined as a problem constitutes incentives to subscribe to a global regime. Self-regulated cooperation without enforcement by a leviathan is possible, according to Ostrom's (1990: 186) research on domestic cooperation when there is a commitment 'to follow the rules so long as (1) most similarly situated individuals adopt the same commitment and (2) the long-term expected net benefits to be achieved by this strategy are greater than the long-term expected net benefits for individuals following short-term dominant strategies'. Dialogue is the key condition of the contracting environment that enables the commitment and mutual understanding of shared interests to be sustained. Dialogue can also enable the more complex accomplishment of non-reciprocal coordination where actor A is persuaded to comply with rules that are persistently against its interests as long as others continue to comply with other rules which are in A's interests but not theirs.

However, dialogue also constitutes normative commitments, persuasion that compliance is morally right. One key player, for example a social movement, may be persuaded to a normative commitment to a global warming regime, while another, for example a state, is not so persuaded. Then the social movement may create political incentives in the form of domestic electoral support to persuade the state to comply with the regime – Putnam's two-level game swings into play.

Dialogue often builds concern and normative commitment first; when there is shared concern, a regime can move on to agreement on principles, then to agreement on rules, then to com-

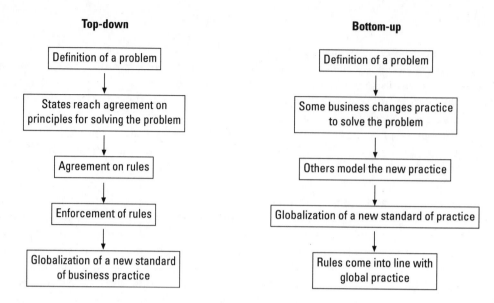

**FIGURE 23.1    Top-down and bottom-up globalization of regulation**

mitment to enforce rules (see Figure 23.1). The conclusion to Chapter 12 demonstrates this nicely. Yet often enforcement of rules is not necessary to compliance (Chayes & Chayes 1995) because dialogue that redefines interests, delivers the discipline of complex interdependency and persuades to normative commitments is enough. This is especially true when the interest redefinition, complex interdependency and normative commitments generate habits of compliance that are institutionalized into bureaucratic routines or standard operating procedures (Young 1979: 39–41).

Moreover, as we saw above, rather than business practice following from norms and rules, often the mechanism of modelling delivers globalization of practice which is subsequently codified in the rules. Hence, before we need even consider whether the power of rule enforcement is required, we must consider whether the *persuasive* power of redefined interests, complex interdependency, normative commitments to principles, modelling and the habits of compliance that are ingrained by all three are sufficient to bring about a workable global regime without any credible global enforcement. For the majority of regimes in this book they are, important exceptions being the intellectual property, trade, labour, nuclear safety, drugs and air transport regimes.

At the micro level, habit is probably an underestimated mechanism in our case studies. Habits are efficient for human beings most of the time. If they are habits engendered of normative commitment, they save us the anxiety of agonizing moral deliberation over every little dilemma. If they are habits born of rational calculation that the habit will generally pay off, they economize on calculation costs. The efficiencies of habits of compliance have even more force with states and TNCs which have policy-deliberative processes that are constantly backlogged, because states and TNCs must efficiently settle policies in a much wider range of domains than individual actors. This is why habits of compliance get institutionalized into bureaucratic routines (Young 1979: 39–41).

> There is a kind of economy in the decision to comply with a treaty as a matter of standard operating procedure, rather than weight the costs and benefits each time an issue of compliance arises. Gathering information, generating options, predicting pay-offs, securing interagency agreement and the other elements of rational decision-making are high-cost activities and can be performed only with respect to relatively important decisions. When a state participates in treaty negotiations and decides to adhere, it makes the cost–benefit calculus on a wholesale basis. In the absence of a convincing change of circumstances, it is hard to muster the resources of time and energy necessary to repeat the process in full with respect to discrete and more or less routine decisions and actions under the treaty (Chayes & Chayes 1991: 325).

A further strand of uncoerced compliance beyond institutionalized habit, modelling, redefining of interests, complex interdependency and normative commitments delivered by dialogic webs is capacity-building. States may be persuaded to the normative commitments which would deliver habits of compliance if only they had the capacity to cultivate them. For a viable global-warming regime, many states, firms and industry associations need help, especially in developing countries, to develop their capacity to monitor emissions. In every single regime in this book, capacity-building was an important strand in the web of influences. In every case study, epistemic communities of actors of varied types – from academics to UN bureaucrats – were important to the dialogic nurture of capacity-building.

Where the dialogue in epistemic communities made important contributions to the globalization of business regulation in this book, informal praise and shame were often found to be important. We concluded that it matters to labour ministries appearing before the Freedom of Association Committee or the Committee of Experts of the ILO (Chapter 11). It matters in the nuclear industry self-regulatory processes under INPO and the World Association of Nuclear Operators (WANO) (Chapter 13). Even in the most hard-edged regime of all, the trade regime, the WTO's Trade Policy Review Mechanism relies in interesting ways on pride and shame. Indeed, the Council on TRIPS relies on a fairly similar dialogic mechanism as its first recourse in multilateral enforcement of intellectual property norms. During the late 1940s and early 1950s, the OEEC, the predecessor to the OECD, 'established a sophisticated system of organized cross-examination, by which members were gradually badgered and bullied towards greater liberalization of trade and currency controls. This was a highly successful operation by which the policies of member governments were very substantially influenced' (Luard 1977: 299). Finance ministers of debtor countries are sometimes called before the Executive Board of the IMF to give an account of their actions and are more routinely cross-examined by IMF staff in conferences that lead to pledges to control fiscal and monetary imbalances, called 'declarations of intent'. Empirically, we found that informal shame and praise of pharmaceutical companies by the Medical Lobby for Appropriate Marketing for alleged non-compliance with International Federation of Pharmaceuticals Manufacturing Association standards completely failed 62 per cent of the time. However, possibly having influence 38 per cent of the time is enough to show that informal shame and praise is important to the web of controls in the pharmaceuticals regime.

In the most developed dialogic webs, praise and shame are institutionalized. The commonest way of seeking to enforce international agreements is not the imposition of international sanctions; it is simply to require states to report on compliance: 'There is competition between ministers. Who is the best at implementing? They compare each other's implementation record and brag about it if theirs is good. It's a matter of honour' (EC interview). The most dialogic international institutions – the ILO, WTO, INPO/WANO, the Financial Action Task Force (money-laundering) – institutionalize special fora for discussing cases of poor or exemplary compliance in the presence of the states responsible and their diplomatic peers. The OECD does this through peer reviews of members' environment, economic, agricultural, fisheries and energy policies (Chayes & Chayes 1995: 243–4). Moravcsik (1995) has studied the European human rights regime as a success story of shame and a story of the failure of external sanction and reciprocity. The success, however, has not been in the transformation of undemocratic regimes but in the improvement of democratic ones. If independent domestic judiciaries and NGOs do not exist to be coopted to the shaming of non-compliant states, then systems of individual petition and supranational judicial review might have little leverage. On the other hand, Ron (1997: 281) shows that stories containing the words 'human rights' increased 1000 per cent in China's Xinhua news agency between 1982 and 1994, about twice the increase evident in Reuters World Service and on the BBC Summary of World Broadcasts.

In some regimes shaming is more sporadic and more public: for example, the US Federal Aviation Administration (FAA) produces systematic 'assessments' of the safety performance of foreign airlines and regulatory authorities, which it sometimes chooses to make public (Chapter 19). At the systematic extreme in the institutionalizing of praise and shame is the ILO. Members must submit all ILO conventions and recommendations to their legislatures and, if they do not ratify them, governments must submit reasons for the non-ratification to the ILO. Moreover:

> they must continue to report regularly on the reasons for non-ratification, and must submit to cross-questioning and challenge on them: first by an independent 'committee of experts', and subsequently by a tripartite committee at the annual conference. Finally, and most important of all, once they have ratified, they must also report regularly on the measures taken to implement the convention; and, here again, must submit to even more searching questioning, by the same or similar bodies, on the effectiveness and adequacy of those measures. Both the committee of experts and tripartite committees issue reports on the results of their examination, and if these show there are insufficient grounds for non-ratification, or that a convention that has been ratified is not being adequately applied, the government concerned suffers considerable adverse publicity and loss of face among the membership as a whole (Luard 1977: 298–9).

In summary, webs of dialogue regularly deliver the goods in globalizing forms of regulation that are complied with moderately well. They do this because the dialogue: (1) defines issues as a problem; (2) enhances the contracting environment so that complex interdependency and issue linkage can motivate agreement and compliance; (3) constitutes normative commitments; (4) institutionalizes habits of compliance; and (5) institutionalizes informal praise and shame for defection from the regime. Webs of dialogue can use these means to deliver both globalization of business practice habits that precedes globalization of formal rules, and globalization of rules that precedes globalization of practice.

Chayes and Chayes (1991, 1995) conducted a program of research in which they examined more than a hundred multilateral treaties to which the US was a party, encompassing national security as well as business regulatory matters. They found heavy reliance on the above means to secure compliance, but very little resort to sanctions. Indeed, few treaty texts even embodied the possibility of formal enforcement of compliance. Chayes and Chayes pose the puzzle of why, in fifty years of UN organizations, for example, the sanctions of expulsion and suspension were applied in only one case – South Africa. A large part of their answer is that webs of dialogue and persuasion generally work fairly effectively without such sanctions. Conversely, the empirical evidence is that international economic sanctions have any success in only about a third of the cases when they are deployed (Hufbauer, Schott & Elliott 1990), though US use of section 301 trade sanctions has a significantly higher success rate (Bayard & Elliott 1992). Although finding some exceptions, such as South Africa and apartheid, their research supports the thrust of Henkin's (1979: 47) dictum that 'almost all nations observe almost all principles of international law and almost all of their obligations almost all of the time'. We would qualify Henkin's rather extravagant dictum, on the basis of our data, to say that states mostly honour their agreements when other major actors are willing to make their obligations a serious issue in negotiations.

## Webs of Reward and Coercion

While all the regimes in this book rely on dialogic webs of control to some degree, they rely much more selectively on webs of reward and coercion. Indeed, some regimes barely rely on them at all. Wealthy nations, particularly the US, together with the IMF and World Bank, are the primary dispensers of rewards to other actors who are reluctant to join enthusiastically into a regime simply on the basis of normative commitment or persuasion that doing so is in their interests. Foreign aid is often increased in return for compliance with global business regulatory regimes, as is defence cooperation or transfer of valuable technology.

Regimes with actual systems of reward are more rare, though some of the most sweeping proposals for the future, such as the global carbon tax as a solution to global warming, come under the systems of reward mechanism of globalization. To date, however, as we saw in Chapter 22, there are few regulatory regimes where even moderately systemic rewards are widely used.

While rewards are about raising the expected value of compliance, coercion is about reducing the expected value of non-compliance. Reward, we saw in Chapter 22, is used less frequently than coercion. Most of the uses of systems of reward, military coercion and economic coercion summarized in Chapter 22 were by a single actor – the US. It follows that much of the use of reward and coercion has been hegemonic. Coercion is a mechanism that weaker states and other non-state actors generally feel it is risky to deploy.

A surprising empirical finding of this study is that military coercion was an important mechanism of globalization in seven of the thirteen case studies. Notwithstanding the significance of military coercion, economic coercion was a more important mechanism across the regimes in this book (Chapter 22). Military and economic coercion cover most of the negative sanctions that are applied in pursuit of the globalization of regulatory regimes. There have been cases of reduced freedom of movement to the US, such as the cancellation of Colombian President Samper's US visa in a 1996 attempt to induce him to succumb to the global regime for the prohibition of narcotics distribution (Chapter 15), downgrading diplomatic representation and the like, but these are relatively unimportant in all cases compared to military and economic coercion.

## Why Webs of Reward and Coercion are Less Important than Webs of Dialogue

Almost all five hundred actors interviewed for this study had a strong preference for playing games of global regulation through dialogue rather than through rewards and sanctions. Rewards and sanctions were considered only when dialogue failed, and this was a very general rule. The reasons are simple. Paying rewards is expensive. Why do that unless there is no alternative? Coercion, even the threat of coercion, often backfires in diplomacy. Managing the backlash created (such as reciprocal trade sanctions) and implementing the coercive measure can approach the expense of paying rewards. Economic and military coercion were used often enough in our cases, but we cannot locate any instance where they were hastily resorted to. In the case of intellectual property the US had had years of bilateral discussion with South Korea. It persevered with the discussions even though they were, in the words of one US trade negotiator, 'slow and painful' (1993 interview). Moreover, as one Korean trade negotiator explained to us, when US negotiators began to threaten Korea with trade sanctions they pointed out to their Korean counterparts that they had to make the threats because of domestic pressure (1995 interview). The game of coercion is played out at Putnam's two levels, with one eye on preserving dialogue. Actors like the IMF which have a maximum capacity to wield potent economic coercion prefer to work through epistemic communities to weave webs of dialogue: 'The idea is to develop a club spirit among neighbours through which they can encourage one another to pursue sound policies. A healthy dose of peer pressure could be a most valuable contribution to stability' (IMF Managing Director Camdessus on the 1997 Asian crisis).

In terms of the webs of influence model, precipitate resort to coercion can unravel the entire web (Craig & George 1990: 192–200). A wealth of psychological research evidence on reactance shows how threat tends to cause individuals to redefine their interests in the direction of resisting the threat (Brehm & Brehm 1981). Nations, no less than individuals, react against attempts to control them. Astute politicians, like a Hitler, are able to use the psychological reactance of a German people against the coercive terms of the Versailles Treaty to foment a will to resist and attack national adversaries (Scheff 1994). Reactance was well-illustrated in Chapter 15 by the decision of the Colombian government in 1997 to suspend drug crop eradication in response to US decertification of its anti-narcotics effort. Another concept from the discipline of psychology that applies here is that extrinsic incentives (rewards or punishments) undermine intrinsic motivation to comply (Ayres & Braithwaite 1992: 49). The psychological research evidence showing that rewards and punishments routinely accomplish short-term compliance by undermining long-term commitment is now overwhelming – documented and elaborated in over a hundred studies, research studiously ignored by rational-choice theorists.

One way of summarizing these studies is to use an example: if I or my organization comply over a period without any attempt to force me to do so, we persuade ourselves that we comply because we find it intrinsically valuable to do so (Kohn 1995). Hence, threat not only undermines definition of interests favourable to compliance, it erodes normative commitments that support compliance. Threats can put on hold habits of compliance that have a life of their own even in situations where compliance is not in the actor's interests. Threats can cause actors to question the bureaucratic routines to which habits of compliance give rise (Young 1979: 39–41). In fact, all of the dialogue-based strands of control can be weakened by threats. They are especially likely to unravel when threat is the measure of first recourse. Threats have greater acceptability when reasoned dialogue has been tried first, and failed. There is a strong foundation for this claim in micro data that ground a micro–macro analysis of why cooperation is likelier when webs of dialogue are tried before webs of reward and coercion are even considered (Ayres & Braithwaite 1992; Braithwaite 1997). Equally, as we have found, there is a strong foundation for the claim in the experience of global regulatory diplomacy among our five hundred informants.

In practical terms, only the US now has the capacity to mobilize military and economic coercion on a wide front to secure regulatory globalization, though economic coercion can be mobilized in a limited range of contexts by a few other big players such as China and Europe. But even the US cannot afford the collateral damage from playing the global-cop role in all but exceptional circumstances. On the other hand, coercion works better for the US with global regulation than it does with domestic regulation. The reason is the greater multiplexity of global regulatory games.

For example, if the US Environmental Protection Agency (EPA) unreasonably deploys enforcement against the US chemical industry, the failure to treat individual and corporate citizens as responsible can engender such a hostile relationship that all subsequent attempts at change through dialogue between the EPA and the chemical industry will be poisoned. In the international arena, non-US players do not expect to be treated by the US with the respect worthy of responsible citizens, because they are not citizens of the US. They expect international negotiation to involve US pursuit of self-interests. Even so, backlash against the heavy-handed use of coercion in international regulatory negotiations by the US is common enough. When backlash occurs, the US has options that it does not have in the domestic case of poisoned dialogue. In the multilateral game, the US can persuade other states with whom it has a good relationship to do the interest-redefining, commitment-building and habit-building work with the players with whom the US now has a poisoned relationship.

This book has documented many cases where coercion has been used successfully in pursuit of US interests, though remarkably few cases where coercion has been used successfully by other states. Coercion is therefore an inherently inequitable mechanism that is effectively available only to the very strong in the world system. NGOs who urge the US to impose sanctions in pursuit of objectives such as human rights are therefore in the position of defending an inherently inequitable means to an equitable end. Even for the US, however, the many Americans we interviewed for this study were virtually unanimous in seeing coercion as a last resort that should not be rushed into. This is why former US Trade Representative Clayton Yeutter is leading a campaign by thirty US companies to persuade Congress to greater restraint in providing for trade sanctions as a remedy for states' refusal to comply with US wishes. Hence, for the US, as for every other actor in this study, a web of dialogue is always created before webs of reward and coercion.

## A Processual Micro–Macro Theory

Our work has shown empirically that key individuals matter a great deal in shaping world systems. All of us as individuals come into a world dominated by institutionalized structures of global power that constrain most of our actions. Yet constituting those very structures of domination starts with strategic action by certain individuals. Rarely are those individuals the most powerful people in the world, though the globalization of nuclear regulation has been shown to be one arena where US presidents have counted as strategic individual actors. Ralph Nader is the individual who comes across as an influential player in the widest range of cases in this book (Chapter 20).

Nader epitomizes how individual power tends to work here – entrepreneurially rather than by commanding large organizations or armies. In Chapter 25, we see how actors like Nader can be conceived as model mongers. On the business side, the way Washington lawyers and economists triggered major globalization of the intellectual property regime through brokering the simple idea of linking intellectual property rules to the trade regime illustrates the entrepreneurial nature of individual power. In that case, the organizations ultimately enrolled by the entrepreneurs had massive resource bases – first fifteen major US TNCs, then the US Trade Representative's Office, then European industry associations, then the EC and ultimately 111 states which signed the Agreement on Trade-Related Aspects of Intellectual Property Rights (TRIPS). Yet as we sat in the Washington offices of the key entrepreneurs of the TRIPS accord, they were little operations, with staffing levels we could count on our fingers.

Individual power in global regulatory systems arises from enrolling organizational power (see Latour 1986), rarely from commanding it. The enrolling occurs through webs of dialogue and persuasion, not through webs of reward and punishment. Treaty secretariats often provide the organizational site that allows powerful individuals to enrol the power of many business, state and NGO actors. Again, treaty secretariats tend to be tiny organizations but, like the offices of Washington legal entrepreneurs or Nader's Washington office, they are sited strategically in the relevant metropole where many enrollable heads of power come together. The power of some key individuals, such as Mustafa Tolba with environmental regimes, comes from their capacity to move in and out of a number of treaty secretariats at key moments of enrolment.

Given the universal importance to globalization of epistemic communities of actors, we must consider intellectuals as sometime key individuals. Few are listed in Table 20.1[3] because their power is even more indirect than that of the Naders and Tolbas.

Consider Michael Porter's influence, disseminated through such books as *The Competitive Advantage of Nations*. Of course, his influence is partly mediated by his enrolment of the prestige of his employer, the Harvard Business School. More importantly, an intellectual like Porter acquires power because of a capacity to synthesize more clearly than others the direction where much thinking and innovative practice is going. Yet that clarifying role is crucial in enrolling many additional heads of power to a new direction of global change. We will trace micro–macro linkages from Porter to illustrate the theory we wish to develop.

Porter explains why it is best for TNCs to be leaders rather than laggards in a variety of areas of regulatory standards, such as anti-pollution standards (see Chapter 12). Significant numbers of business leaders and business strategists are convinced by Porter that this is right. They implement continuous improvement in environmental management within major corporations to capture the savings on waste, the early-mover advantages and the other competitive benefits Porter explicates. The mechanism is dialogue that redefines interests. Some industry associations are captured by environmental progressives among their corporate members and are enrolled to bring entire national industries up to a higher standard. Sometimes national industry associations from other countries model the early-moving national industry associations and sometimes a point is reached where a global self-regulatory scheme is adopted. A simple illustration is Responsible Care, starting with the Canadian Chemical Producers Association in the mid 1980s, then modelled by the US industry, then globalized for the large-firm end of the chemical industry (Gunningham 1995). As continuous improvement at the big end of town drives up standards of practice, the large firms seek to secure their early-mover advantage against late-moving smaller firms by lobbying states to upgrade standards to the new benchmark of large-firm practice. The states that succumb to this ratcheting-up of standards then have an interest in ensuring that their firms do not suffer a competitive disadvantage from the costs of the higher standards, and indeed gain Porter's early-mover

---

3  Keynes is of course the pre-eminent intellectual on the list. James Landis and Alfred Kahn had distinguished careers as intellectuals before and after their careers as heads of regulatory agencies. A Frankfurt economist, J. von Herrfeldt, in two articles in 1841 and 1842 was the entrepreneur of the idea of an international organization to coordinate postal services globally (Codding 1964: 18).

advantage, by lobbying for regional (e.g. EU) and global standards at the new benchmark. Naturally, upgraded environmental standards are attractive to green NGOs. Whether independently or collaboratively with lead states and lead TNCs, they join the lobbying for the higher standards.

Meanwhile, national voluntary standards organizations see what is going on. Individual environmental entrepreneurs see both an opportunity to ratchet-up environmental standards and an opportunity to make money by selling new standards that have wide appeal to the corporate clients who purchase standards. The British National Standards Institute has noticed that the continuous improvement intellectual current is so strong now that its standard on continuous improvement in product quality brought in half its revenue and two-thirds of its surplus in 1992/93 (Shurmer & David 1996: 11). So it writes a continuous improvement standard for environmental management. The EU writes a directive which Europeanizes this standard and then lobbies for its approach to a global environmental management standard within the International Organization for Standardization (ISO).

The detail of this story and its linkage to other ratcheting-up mechanisms such as best available technology (BAT) and world's best practice standards need not detain us here, as it is set out in Chapter 26. The point is to retell this story as an example of a micro–macro theory that starts with strategic actions by individuals such as Porter with minimal resource-based power. Moreover, we see that there are strategic roles from individual entrepreneurs who can enrol a British Standards Institute – a good example of a modest secretariat, a nodal site where dialogue occurs among major players who wield direct power. The story also illustrates the primacy of webs of dialogue over webs of reward and coercion, including the primacy of dialogue for activating the entrepreneurs of ideas like Porter and the model mongers like Nader. While Porter's environmental influence is a global regulatory growth story, this book cites cases of globalizing deregulation which fit this basic sequence, for example air transport deregulation and telecommunications deregulation.

The theoretical sequence is individual entrepreneurship, enrolment of organizational power, modelling and then globalization of standards. The outcome is a web of controls – many actors, many mechanisms to enforce many principles.

Another explanatory sequence is represented in Figure 23.2, however, in which strategic individual action is much less important. In this sequence a disaster occurs which captures the imagination of mass publics after media organizations dramatize the incident. A list of such disasters is provided in Table 20.1. Without any particularly strategic action by individual regulatory entrepreneurs from business or NGOs, states see a clear need to act to placate mass publics and the media. Moreover, if the problem has global repercussions – the collapse of an international bank, an international outbreak of plague or cholera spread by shipping, a major oil-spill that affects the coastlines of more than one country – states may see that international regulatory coordination is required to placate each of their domestic mass publics. In this sequence, individual entrepreneurship, enrolment and modelling are comparatively unimportant. The key players are not brokers who enrol the power of others but actors who have direct organizational control of states' capacity to respond to a crisis that threatens a state's legitimacy among its citizens.

There is a qualification, however. It is that individual entrepreneurs who understand the disaster-driven dynamic of globalizing regulatory change are sometimes strategic model mongers. They have a number of regulatory models on the backburner waiting for a disaster to which one of their models is the remedy. They know that at a time of disaster that scandalizes the media, those who control state power and power in international organizations are thrown into panic. In such a crisis, power can pass to the cool head who can pull from their desk a sophisticated and persuasive plan of action to remedy the problem and prevent recurrence. Even if the plan is too

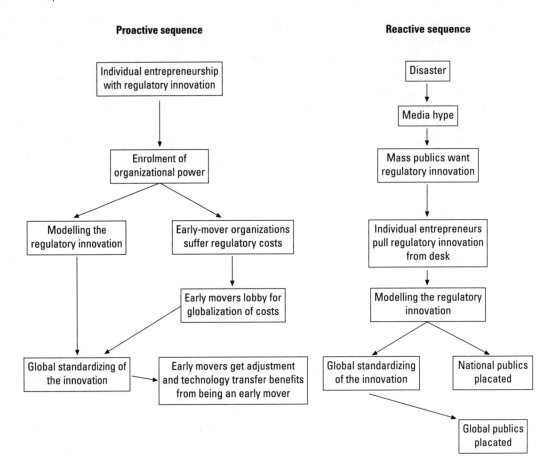

**Proactive sequence**

**Reactive sequence**

FIGURE 23.2    Two theoretical sequences of strategic micro action to secure global regulatory change

radical to prevail against vested interests that would be disadvantaged by it, our analysis of modelling in Chapter 25 shows that the model that is first put on the table at least exerts considerable power in shaping the parameters of the debate, eliminating some issues from the political agenda and elevating others. Hence, in the entrepreneurship–enrolment sequence, individual power is proactive, while in the disaster-model sequence individual power is reactive – clever model mongers are proactive about their readiness to be reactive. They react to harness the diffuse discontent of mass publics instead of enrolling the redefined interests of major centres of power.

## Conclusion

Through dialogic webs actors discover the state of their relations with others, as well as information about relations between others. Under conditions of uncertainty actors can never be sure which relations will be costly to forgo, which will be costly to maintain and which will bring the most benefit. Webs of dialogue are the key way in which actors deal with the uncertainties of the world. One reason that actors prefer dialogic webs to webs of coercion is that coercion disrupts relations, thereby causing a net gain in uncertainty even if some concrete short-term objective is achieved. The hunger for information and consequent reduction of uncertainty is so great by actors caught up in global regulatory processes that the leaders of even powerful states do their utmost to maintain dialogic webs. Thus, when confronted by a Congress pushing him down the path of coercion, President Clinton said: 'What always happens if you have automatic sanctions legislation is it puts enormous pressure on whoever is in the executive branch to fudge an evaluation of the facts of what is going on…And that's not what you want. What you want is to leave the president some flexibility' (*International Herald Tribune*, Friday, 15 May 1998).

Dialogic webs reduce uncertainty in another way. They are one means by which actors create and globalize regimes. The norms which constitute regimes bring a further reduction in uncertainty. Dialogic webs also heighten the probability that the norms established by means of the web will be internalized by actors who are part of the web. Dialogic commitments to a regime bring a fidelity to norms that webs of coercion do not. Obtaining fidelity to norms means that compliance with the norms is more likely to be robust. Using and complying with the rules over time cultivates habits of rule-following that further entrench a regime, reducing the need for enforcement measures. Dialogic webs are also, at least to some extent, hierarchically neutral. Very few actors, as our case studies have shown, can effectively use military and economic coercion to globalize a regime. The use of coercion is part of a top-down process reserved for the very few. But as Figure 23.1 illustrates, dialogue allows actors to globalize regulation from the bottom up by persuading each other to follow a practice which is then spread throughout the relevant community by a mechanism like modelling.

Webs of coercion and reward are closely intertwined with dialogic webs in regulatory negotiations. An actor like the US which can achieve some of its goals through webs of coercion knows that it must not utilize those webs in displays of excessive strength, or it will unravel the dialogic webs upon which it also depends. It must avoid throwing its weight around, but it knows that its capacity to use webs of coercion and reward allow it to appear authoritative to other actors. It must tread a careful path between appearing not to be excessively dominant and appearing not to be weak. It does this by utilizing dialogic webs first, letting coercive webs float in the background. For other actors, knowing that they are dealing with an actor capable of entangling them in webs of coercion provides another reason for preferring to resolve issues through dialogic webs.

In a world where even dominant actors prefer dialogic webs over webs of reward and coercion, the opportunities for individuals to act in strategic and influential ways increase. The habit of dialogue among actors involved in global business regulation means that individuals can enter existing webs as purveyors of new regulatory ideas and models. Dialogic webs offer such individuals a way into inner decision-making circles. By conversing with those in inner circles, individuals create opportunities to enrol and aggregate the organizational power that belongs to members of inner circles. Through micro action some individuals can, as our case studies and the two sequences in Figure 23.2 show, remake macro regulatory worlds. Obviously the possibility of micro-action–macro-change cannot be implemented in an easy-to-follow recipe-book fashion. But in a world where actors prefer to rely on dialogic webs to resolve contests of principles, the possibility of micro action to secure global regulatory change is real.

Finally, our finding that webs of dialogue are more important than webs of reward and coercion recalls an insightful comment by Avineri on Hegel's theory of the state: 'the modern state, based on self-consciousness and the citizens' readiness to cooperate with each other, calls for increasingly less and less coercion. Coercion is the mark of undeveloped, undifferentiated structures. Where self-consciousness comes into its own, coercion becomes superfluous' (Avineri 1972: 193).

## CHAPTER 24

Forum-shifting and Contests
of Principles

Forum-shopping, in the words of one US judge, is a 'national legal pas-time' in the US (Wright 1967: 333). Plaintiffs spend a lot of time shopping around for a jurisdiction that they believe will give their case the best chance. The growth of international commercial arbitration allowed TNCs a more global smorgasbord of sites, of rules of the game – some more common-law, some more civil-law, some more informal, some enclaves of Western law within communist states (Dezalay & Garth 1996).

International forum-shifting was not an important strategy prior to the Second World War, when the number of international fora was so small as to afford little choice. It became an important strategy for the first time during the era of US hegemony. The US state in fact translated its 'national legal pastime' of forum-shifting into the realm of international regulatory contests. When it is staring at defeat on a given regulatory agenda in a given international forum it shifts that agenda to another forum, or simply abandons that forum. Part of its thinking behind abandonment is that the abandoned international organization will be shocked into a more compliant mode of behaviour, endeavouring to woo back the world's most powerful state (and its financial contributions) with more favourable policies and attitudes. This fate, we shall see, befell the UN Educational, Scientific and Cultural Organization (UNESCO). On other occasions forum-shifting is used to run a parallel agenda in two international fora. Here the strategy is to cast both fora in the role of warring suitors, making each strive to do better than the other in terms of fulfilling the regulatory desires of the US. The World Intellectual Property Organization (WIPO) found itself competing in this way with the WTO when the latter was also given jurisdiction over intellectual property.

Forum-shifting thus encompasses three kinds of strategies – moving an agenda from one organization to another, abandoning an organization and pursuing the same agenda in more than one organization. For the sake of completeness we should also mention a strategy that might be termed a 'forum-blocking' strategy. This is where the powerful state ensures that an international organization does not become a forum for an agenda that threatens its interests. In our fieldwork we came across one clear example. Copyright is not, as one UNESCO official told us, a priority area in the organization. On the face of it this presents a puzzle since copyright plays a basic role in the constitution of the intellectual commons and one of the basic tasks of UNESCO is 'to create the conditions for the widest possible diffusion of works of the human mind'.[1] When one of us asked

---

1 Unpublished and undated document received by us from UNESCO, entitled 'UNESCO'S Mandate in the Field of Copyright and So-called Neighbouring Rights', p. 1.

why, he was told that when the member states of UNESCO meet they decide that 'copyright is not a priority area for UNESCO'. The result is that the Director-General does not allocate funds to it (1993 interview). This, the official said, has led the UNESCO copyright unit 'into a vicious circle'. Without funds it can do little of significance, and since it does little of significance in the area there is no reason to support it. Its fate is that of being constantly scaled down. As we shall see a little later in this section, this allocation of priorities has everything to do with UNESCO's history as a forum in which authors (as opposed to copyright owners) and users of copyright (especially users from developing states) had a voice. Lack of resources have turned UNESCO, as far as copyright is concerned, into an observer organization.

The reason for forum-shifting is that it increases the possibility of a victory over one's opponents or prevents one's opponents from gaining victory. Borrowing the vocabulary of game theory for a moment (but not its methods) we can say that the rules and modes of operation of an organization (particularly its formal and informal norms on voting) constitute the pay-offs that a state might expect to receive if it plays in that particular forum. The pay-offs it actually receives depend on the decisions it and other players make. Pay-offs are thus collectively determined. Forum-shifting is a way of constituting a new game. Each international organization has different rules by which it operates and so offers different games and different pay-offs. Forum-shifting is a form of optimizing behaviour. An actor avoids a suboptimal outcome by shifting to a new game in which it has a better shot at an optimal outcome.

Clearly, very few actors in the context of global regulation have the capacity to run strategies of forum-shifting. In fact, as we shall see, only the US has used this strategy with any frequency. An environmental NGO has no more capacity to cause an agenda to shift from one international organization to another than the two authors of this book have to pursue a tort claim in Japanese courts for an injury sustained in Australia using a Japanese product. Forum-shifting is a strategy that only the powerful and well-resourced can use. From the point of view of weaker actors in the regulatory systems we have described, it might seem desirable to consider ways to limit the possibility of forum-shifting. Since it is a strategy available only to powerful actors, it follows that a weaker opponent may be robbed of victory by it but can never use it to obtain an advantage. Actor rationality would seem to dictate that weaker actors oppose forum-shifting.

There are two things to say about this. First, attempting to limit the capacity of a powerful state to forum-shift seems infeasible. Why would a state which was capable of forum-shifting ever compromise its strategic powers by signing a convention which limited its capacity to do so? Second, forum-shifting may create opportunities for weaker actors. In a given forum an issue may be deadlocked, in the way that the US and developing countries were deadlocked over revisions to the Paris Convention for the Protection of Industrial Property (1883) (the Paris Convention) within WIPO (Sell 1998: Ch. 4). Shifting to another forum may give weak actors as well as strong actors an opportunity to progress the same or different agendas, particularly where that forum, as in the case of WTO, allows actors to trade deals over a range of different subject-matters.

A related point is that in some ways weaker players are better off in a world where there are multiple fora capable of dealing with similar agendas. We see fora as entry-points into global regulatory dialogues. International organizations are sites at which weak actors can begin to weave parts of the dialogic webs discussed in Chapter 23. Before we develop this point, which will lead us into a processual theory of the contests of principles, we need to draw together the examples of forum-shifting in previous chapters.

## Financial Regulation

After the suspension of dollar convertibility by the US in 1971 it shifted discussions about the resulting monetary crisis from the G-10 (the other members of which it had alienated by its action) to an informal committee within the IMF called the C-20 (see Chapter 8).

## Intellectual Property

Probably no organization other than the UN Conference on Trade and Development (UNCTAD) would have had a greater claim to develop a trade-related agreement for intellectual property. As the very title of UNCTAD suggests, its economic mission was to examine the connections between trade and development. Through its work on the Code of Conduct on Transfer of Technology it had done more analytical work on the trade implications of intellectual property rights than any other UN organization. When UNCTAD moved to gain organizational competence over intellectual property, 'exasperated disputes were the result' (Joos & Moufang 1989: 30). The turf of intellectual property belonged to WIPO, said developed states. The same kind of technical arguments over organizational competence were used by developing states to try to prevent the GATT (General Agreement on Tariffs and Trade) from moving in on intellectual property. They failed. The US was successful in its push to give GATT jurisdiction over the trade-related aspects of intellectual property, thereby robbing UNCTAD of any influence on the issue. Voting rules played an important role. UNCTAD was the first international organization to institutionalize bloc voting by developing states (the G-77) (Zamora 1980: 580). Bloc voting combined with the one-state–one-vote rule meant that the US would always lose on the intellectual property issue to developing states. The price that UNCTAD paid for this domination by developing states was a loss of legitimacy (in the eyes of developed states) and ultimately a de facto loss of norm-making power on intellectual property. That was granted to GATT. WIPO was also a victim of forum-shifting. Like UNCTAD, it operated on a one-state–one-vote rule and so the US could never expect to get its way on intellectual property issues through a voting contest. On the eve of GATT gaining jurisdiction over intellectual property, the then head of WIPO, Arpad Bogsch, suggested in somewhat querulous tones that when this happened it would produce a 'duplication of WIPO's activities', 'a phenomenon that most governments rigorously condemn' (Bogsch 1992: 21). More importantly, though, WIPO began to compete to regain US affection. One of the US complaints about WIPO was that it had a poor record on the enforcement of intellectual property. In 1990 a discussion on a possible treaty on dispute resolution began in a WIPO Committee of Experts (Bogsch 1992: 38), inspired at least partly by the GATT draft on dispute resolution.

## Telecommunications

The International Telecommunication Union (ITU), like the national telecommunication operators that attended its meetings, ran an organizational monopoly. When the US began to support the principle of deregulation for telecommunications it also pushed telecommunications into the WTO through the General Agreement on Trade in Services (GATS). The ITU, like WIPO now has a competitor. If, for example, it does not make satisfactory progress on the reform of matters like the international accounting rates system it can expect that issue to go to WTO (see Chapter 14).

## Labour Standards

We saw in Chapter 11 that the US withdrew from the International Labour Organization (ILO) from 1977 to 1980. This is the only example in our case-study chapters where the US did not gain a clear advantage through forum-shifting. The reason, we have suggested, lies in the tripartite constitution of the ILO. This gave the ILO a bedrock legitimacy in the politics of international organizations, a legitimacy that enabled it to withstand the effects of forum-shifting in a way that UNCTAD could not. More recently, the resilience of the ILO as a forum was illustrated in the decision by member states in June 1998 to adopt the ILO Declaration on Fundamental Principles and Rights at Work. The Declaration obliges members to promote the basic rights which are enshrined in ILO conventions (freedom of association, elimination of compulsory labour and child labour, and the elimination of discrimination in respect of employment and occupation) even if they have not ratified those conventions. Developing states, despite their traditional opposition to the globalization of labour standards, probably agreed to the adoption of the Declaration because by doing so they give the US and Europe less reason to push for the inclusion of labour standards in WTO – to some extent they avert the threat of forum-shifting. We also conjecture that the US is happy with the outcome at ILO, since it can point to progress on labour standards without having to embark on a complicated domestic political game (overcoming the opposition of US business) to collect support for a proposal to make labour standards enforceable under the WTO regime – it is using the threat of forum-shifting to get limited action on labour standards at ILO.

## Competition

We saw in Chapter 10 that the development of a competition code of some kind for TNCs, a key agenda item for UNCTAD and the UN Centre on Transnational Corporations, has been reinterpreted to fit the general frameworks of competition policy and investment. With US support, the WTO and the OECD are the two key fora doing work on the globalization of competition regulation and investment. The UN Centre on Transnational Corporations was abolished under US pressure, the most extreme example of forum-shifting we have seen in our case studies.

## Air Transport

In Chapter 19 we saw the beginnings of a strategy of forum-shifting being developed by the US for the economic deregulation of national air transport regimes. The International Air Transport Association is already a diminished forum. Similarly, the International Civil Aviation Organization may find that the WTO will take over significant parts of its standard-setting role.

## Sea Transport

After UNCTAD negotiated the Liner Code in the mid 1970s, which permitted two states to reserve 80 per cent of freight for their two merchant fleets, the US led most of the developed countries into a new agreement in a new forum, the Consultative Shipping Group.

## Nuclear Safeguards

In Chapter 13 we saw that the US wanted an alternative forum to the International Atomic Energy Agency, where it could introduce more demanding safeguards for suppliers of nuclear technology. It established the Nuclear Suppliers Group.

## Privacy

The ICC successfully lobbied in the mid 1990s to prevent the International Organization for Standardization (ISO) from establishing a privacy standard against which international business could be audited, following the lead of a Canadian standard. At the time of writing the ICC is moving to establish itself as the forum where an international standard on privacy marks acceptable to business will be written.

## Food Standards

Chapter 16 showed that it was the US that was primarily responsible for pushing the standards of the Codex Alimentarius Commission (Codex) into WTO. The outcome was the Agreement on the Application of Sanitary and Phytosanitary Measures. Forum-shifting in this case has made the Codex more important, not less, since the Sanitary and Phytosanitary Agreement incorporates Codex standards by reference. Forum-shifting in this case has given the Codex a partner rather than a competitor. We also saw that the US attempted to prevent the Commission on Plant Genetic Resources from emerging as a forum for the regulation of access to genetic resources. The US remains engaged in the present FAO Commission on Genetic Resources for Food and Agriculture, but WTO and the Agreement on Trade Related Aspects of Intellectual Property Rights (TRIPS) may serve as a trumping forum on the issue that matters most to the US and its life sciences industry – ensuring that there are no exceptions to the patentability of genetic and biological material.

## Drugs

Chapter 15 provides another example of forum-shifting, this time involving two players, the US and Europe. In the context of the regulation of pharmaceutical drugs the US attempted to shift standard-setting from the WHO to itself through a process of bilateralism. It failed to globalize US standards by this means. More successful was the EC initiative of establishing the International Conference on Harmonization as an alternative forum to WHO. The International Conference on Harmonization became the key forum in the globalization of pharmaceuticals regulation for a time after this shift, because the big players in the world market – the US, the EC and Japan – supported it.

These examples of forum-shifting do not constitute an exhaustive list. Another example, which we did not discuss, was the withdrawal by the US from UNESCO in 1984. The Reagan administration over a period of eighteen months reviewed its participation in nineteen international organizations and concluded that six of those organizations had 'serious problems of politicization' (Hoffer 1986: 162, fn 6). The six were the Internation Atomic Energy Agency, the Food and Agriculture Organization (FAO), the ILO, the UN Environment Program, the ITU and UNESCO. Why did the US pull out of UNESCO? One commentator suggested that the US chose to make an example of UNESCO because it was 'the smallest, weakest international organization...the Grenada of the UN' (Charles W. Maynes, quoted in Hoffer 1986: 167, fn 26). The case of UNESCO also fits with our broader theory of regulatory globalization as a contest of principles. One of the reasons why the US was critical of UNESCO was that it had become a forum for developing countries to oppose the US version of the free flow principles that we described in Chapter 21 (Hoffer 1986: 184–7). Developing countries supported the principle of free flow of information as it related to technological information, but not as it related to cultural and media information. A UNESCO official told us that the organization tended to consider the issue of copyright from the perspective of users. As far as US intellectual property owners were concerned this was the wrong perspective. UNESCO began to push for the principle of balanced information flows through a program called the 'New World Information Order'. This principle required the world's media 'to balance the traditional media concern and fascination with crises, famines and disasters with more news about economic and social development' (Aggarwala, cited in Hoffer 1986: 186). In our terms, this principle was an oppositional principle to the free flow of information. UNESCO was making concrete a regulatory principle that threatened US media interests. This principle also cut deeply across US First Amendment jurisprudence. By abandoning UNESCO as a forum, the US rendered passive the principle of balanced information.

The presence of forum-shifting further supports our claim in Chapter 23 that most actors, including powerful ones like the US, prefer to work through dialogue. International fora are important sites for global regulatory dialogues. The fact that an actor like the US is prepared to move from site to site in order to secure its goals rather than resort to the blunter tools of economic and military coercion is revealing. The US willingness to persist with dialogue is reinforced because dialogue has brought success. It has done so because US actors understand and utilize dialogic webs better than most other actors in the regulatory systems we have described. Forum-shifting also enhances the appeal of dialogue for the US because it knows that it has a reasonable chance of moving the regulatory dialogue into a forum, the organizational rules of which give it a reasonable prospect of being able to dominate the outcome.

Crucial to US dominance of dialogic outcomes has been the fact that international organizations have moved to taking decisions by consensus (M'Bow 1978). Under the League of Nations system states operated under a unanimity rule – decisions required the agreement of all states. The effect was to give every state a veto. The resulting paralysis in decision-making led to systems of majority rule being adopted by the UN and other international organizations (Zamora 1980: 574; Osieke 1984: 381–2). These systems are based on the one-state–one-vote rule, itself the product of the idea dating back to the Treaty of Westphalia (1648) that states are sovereign equals. But the majority rule, like the unanimity rule, produced deadlocks in international organizations. The US or a US-led coalition, for example, could never hope under a majority rule to outvote developing states at UNCTAD or WIPO. The sheer number of developing states invalidated that strategy. The result was that treaty projects such as a code on technology transfer, the revisions to the Paris Convention or programs like the New International Economic Order stalled or made little progress. Voting power for developing states, however, did not and has not brought them real power. Without US support for the Code of Conduct on Transfer of Technology, for instance, the code was largely meaningless. The US simply followed the path of self-help – bilateralism, in other words.

The evolution of consensus as a practical norm of decision-making in international organizations has been important to the US. In the words of a former Director-General of UNESCO,

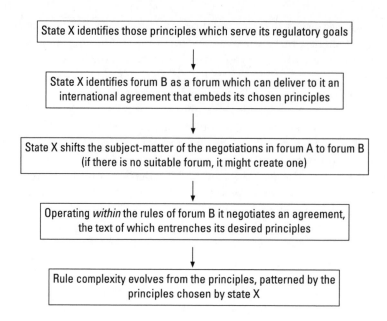

FIGURE 24.1    A forum-shifting sequence

consensus refers to a 'practice designed to achieve the elaboration of a text by means of negotiation, and its adoption without taking a vote' (M'Bow 1978: 893). Decision-making under consensus means that a decision is made when no state objects to the decision. In practice, as we pointed out in our summary of actors in Chapter 20, consensus does not require an affirmative act, merely the absence of objection. We also saw there the problem with consensus decision-making. A powerful state no longer needs to obtain positive majorities; it needs to obtain only the support of other powerful states and the silence of others. One reason why the US has been prepared to shift its agenda into WTO is that consensus offers it a tool of domination. We saw that GATT negotiations did not move forward without the support of the four states of the Quad (with Canada and Japan likely to follow once the US and Europe agreed on a matter). A Quad consensus was a precondition for a general consensus among GATT members. The fact of Quad consensus made general consensus more likely. The practice of consensus continues in WTO. Article IX(1) of the Agreement Establishing the World Trade Organization obliges members to practise consensus: 'The WTO shall continue the practice of decision-making by consensus followed under the GATT 1947'.

Bearing in mind this discussion of voting rules and forum-shifting we can outline a contest of principles sequence which features forum-shifting. The sequence assumes a treaty negotiation among states in forum A which has come to a standstill and cannot be progressed. State X is present in that forum. It has the power to forum-shift. Our case studies suggest that something like the sequence in Figure 24.1 will develop.

Our case studies fill in the detail of this particular global regulatory sequence. Usually the powerful state engineers a crisis over the credibility of forum A, as we have seen the US do with WHO (Chapter 15), IATA (Chapter 19), UNCTAD (Chapter 10) and UNESCO and the UN Centre on Transnational Corporations a little earlier in this chapter. The process of forum-shifting will involve the strong state in tugging at webs of reward and coercion. The US used economic coercion in order to sign bilateral treaties on intellectual property. Developing states in the end agreed to intellectual property being part of the Uruguay Round because they believed it would bring them relief from US bilateral trade pressure.

This particular globalization sequence seems to bespeak structuralism. Unlike the two micro–macro sequences in Chapter 23, it is a macro–macro sequence. It is a game only the powerful can play, collectivities in the form of powerful states playing for national interests or powerful industries persuading states to play for industry's interests. When weak players do attempt to forum-shift it is likely to fail. We saw, for instance, in Chapter 11 a failed attempt to create a forum of interlinked international trade secretariats to drive up labour standards globally. The structuralism at work here, however, is not one of impersonal forces in which individuals are only subjects and never agents. As we saw in Chapters 7 and 10, collectivities can be mobilized as part of this regulatory sequence through acts of individual entrepreneurship. Entrepreneurs of ideas such as Eric Smith and Jacques Gorlin helped to propel the US into the forum-shifting game in the case of intellectual property. Naturally, the capacity of individuals to trigger forum-shifting games is very limited. Individuals have to be members of the right epistemic community in order to be listened to. Their ideas have to occur during fertile,circumstances. In the case of the US and intellectual property fears over the loss of US hegemony, trade imbalances and worries about falling US competitiveness combined to make the idea of linking trade and intellectual property sound like a good one (Drahos 1995).

## A Processual Theory of the Contests of Principles

So far we have outlined three basic sequences of regulatory globalization. The two discussed in Chapter 23 are micro–macro, the third is macro–macro. They can be read both prescriptively and descriptively. Our case studies inductively support the existence of these theoretical sequences. They are processes that are constitutive of creation or change in global regulatory regimes. They can also be read as prescriptions for strategic micro or macro action for agents who wish to bring about global regulatory change. The two micro sequences leave space for individual strategic action. What makes the third sequence macro–macro is the fact that it leaves limited space for individual actors to use it as a means of bringing about global regulatory change.

All three regulatory sequences involve actors following or entrenching principles. Our case studies show the way in which the shape of global regulatory regimes emerges from a contest of principles. Principles serve as anchor-points for regulatory change and innovation. The webs of influence we described in Chapter 23 – dialogic webs and webs of reward and coercion – are ways in which actors in a regulatory domain activate and support their chosen principles. A state like the US can support the principle of national treatment in intellectual property with the mechanism of economic coercion; an environmental NGO can, through dialogue, support the principle of sustainable development in the countless public conversations of states and international organizations about the environment and economic growth. The environmental NGO may be able to engage in one of the two sequences of strategic micro action outlined in Figure 23.1, but the macro–macro sequence is not available to it.

How might this macro–macro sequence be made more open so that the environmental NGO becomes at least a participant in a regulatory sequence rather than a hapless subject of a globalization process? Our answer comes in the form of a group of propositions. These propositions constitute, in a simplified way, an argument for how regulation should best globalize if we are concerned about democratic citizenship – in other words, the processual theory of the contests of principles alluded to at the beginning of this chapter.

Our first proposition is a preference that the contests in the globalization of regulation be conducted at the level of principles rather than at the level of systems of rules. Conflicts at the level of principles are sharper, clearer and more accessible than at the level of systems of rules. The principles catalogued in Table 21.1 are simple and readily understandable. Rule complexity can mask the basic issues and generates high transaction costs in the context of negotiations. It favours those with high levels of organizational capital and thus tends to disadvantage non-business NGOs. At the level of principle the well-resourced actor has to work harder in dialogic terms to persuade. The advantage of superior resources is, to some extent, diminished. Principles and purpose also enjoy a close nexus. This is not to imply that rules cannot be understood in terms of purpose, but rather that the purpose of rule systems can be harder to discern. The closeness of purpose and principles is an aid to transparency. Finally, principles encourage the tendency among actors to utilize webs of dialogue rather than webs of reward and sanction.

Our second proposition is that principles must not go uncontested. This means that actors must utilize oppositional principles, and where such principles do not exist they must invent them. A good example of principle-creation is the formulation in 1985 of the principle of farmers' rights by a small NGO called the Rural Advancement Foundation International (RAFI). In the words of Pat Mooney, one of the co-founders of RAFI, the principle was introduced into the then UN Food and Agricultural Organization Commission on Plant Genetic Resources 'as a counter to Plant Breeders' Rights', a regime heavily tilted in favour of agrochemical TNCs (Mooney 1996: 25). The principle has since found its way into the FAO's International Undertaking on Plant Genetic Resources, Agenda 21 and the Biodiversity Convention (Mooney 1996: 182).

Our case studies suggest that principles rarely go uncontested for any length of time. The principles we have identified function as a common language for actors. But our case studies also reveal that actors do not have voices of equal power. We saw, for instance, that in the case of intellectual property developing states did contest the principles of national treatment and harmonization, relying on the principles of common heritage and national sovereignty. The contest was in many ways an unequal one. Clearly, developing states did not have at their disposal the webs of coercion which the US did. We were also told during our interviews at GATT that consumer NGOs were not players in the negotiations over TRIPS, although that agreement contained provisions that deeply affected their interests. The patents part of TRIPS, for instance, will raise the cost of pharmaceutical drugs, especially in developing states (Faunce & Drahos 1999). Business NGOs, led by key players like Jack Valenti, did have a powerful albeit informal presence in those negotiations. GATT did not grant observer status to NGOs, but the Director-General, we were told, would have informal consultations with influential NGOs concerning the parts of negotiations that mattered to them. Another example of an unequal contest is in the domain of tax, so dominated by large business that it has affected the capacity of states to provide public goods for their citizens.

The existence of unequal contests leads to our third proposition – that barriers to the contestability of principles have to be lowered. One path to lowering these barriers was shown in Chapter 11, where we saw that the tripartite constitution of the ILO made it difficult for the US or the Soviet Union to shift the game over labour standards to another forum. Although the US may have been able to drag most states and employer associations to another forum, it would have been unable to shift labour unions. Consequently, the new forum would have much less legitimacy than a tripartite ILO. There is no doubt that tripartism is 'the real strength of the ILO' (Bartolomei de la Cruz, von Potobsky & Swepston 1996: 10). This tripartism permeates the whole organization, including its voting rules. Under the ILO constitution each member state can send four delegates to meetings of the International Labour Conference, two from government, one from employers and the other from workers. Each has one vote. Employer and worker delegates from the same member state can and do vote against their own government delegates as well as against each other (Osieke 1984: 383–4). The tripartite structure also applies in the committees of the International Labour Conference, where most of the work is done. Again, voting rules are drafted in such a way that each group has the same number of votes even if they do not have the same number of representatives on the relevant committee (Osieke 1984: 390).

The case of ILO suggests that perhaps tripartism ought to become a constitutionalizing principle for international organizations. There are game-theoretic reasons for thinking that a tripartism which empowers public interest groups may overcome the problems of corruption and capture in national regulatory systems (Ayres & Braithwaite 1992: Ch. 3). Perhaps a tripartism of structure and voting rules for international organizations might act as a partial check on the use of forum-shifting by a hegemonic power to achieve its ends. The American Bar Association, in the context of human rights development, has made suggestions for increasing the role of NGOs in the UN system that help to flesh out the kind of institutional reform that would be consistent with a tripartite spirit of structure. After commenting that 'NGO participation in international institutions is hampered by inadequate status, anachronistic procedures, and insufficient accommodations' the report proposes that NGOs ought to be granted 'Enhanced rights of participation in standard-setting institutions…Streamlined procedures for participating in international fact-finding and compliance regimes…Efforts to ensure protection of NGOs operating at the local level'.[2]

Our attraction to tripartism should not be read as suggesting that all other international organizations should be modelled on ILO. Tripartism is for us a broader principle that can drive regulatory and organizational praxis. There are probably many organizational models that are consistent with the principle. What is crucial to the use of the principle in the case of international fora is that the interest groups of international civil society be given some degree of formal power in international fora. The present UN system is heavily dependent upon the thousands of NGO actors within it. In the case of human rights, for example, 'human rights NGOs are the engine for virtually every advance made by the United Nations' (Gaer 1996: 51). Our case studies reveal the disproportionate influence that business NGOs like the ICC have exercised on the course of global business regulation. Representatives of business have invaded international corridors of power notionally reserved for states. During our interviews we saw and were told of key business leaders who would travel with US trade negotiators and hang about in corridors ready to offer advice, if need be, during an important negotiation. On technical committees, such as those at the ITU, the business representatives do not have to wait in the corridors; they chair the meetings. Non-business NGOs do not have this kind of access. Most non-business NGOs remain basically a consultative resource within the UN system. Their accession to consultative

---

2  See the Report by the Section of International Law and Practice of the American Bar Association 1995, 'Report on Improving the Effectiveness of the United Nations in Advancing the Rule of Law in the World', *International Lawyer* 29, p. 311.

status in the UN system is carefully regulated by the Economic and Social Council of the UN (Weiss & Gordenker 1996: 22). Observer status within an international organization is usually granted to an NGO by member states of the organization. Both within the UN system and outside it the role of NGOs in global governance is being rethought (Weiss & Gordenker 1996). The principle of tripartism we support requires something more than consultative status for NGOs. Ultimately it points in the direction of NGO representation on those key enclave committees in international fora whose decisions shape the globalization of regulation, thereby affecting the interests of citizens everywhere.

There are some examples where NGOs have become actively involved in international decision-making processes that were once the exclusive province of states. NGOs have, for example, played an important role in the enforcement of the Convention on International Trade in Endangered Species, even participating in a working group to develop new listing criteria (Cameron & MacKenzie 1996: 143–4). NGOs are sometimes willing to bear the monitoring costs of treaty enforcement. Often they have better information about compliance and enforcement than do states and international organizations. Naturally this information is valuable to states and international organizations. One reason why actors keep webs of dialogue open is that the webs allow them to gain valuable information about the world from other actors. The openness of dialogic webs offers opportunities to NGOs to insinuate themselves into decision-making processes. Dialogue and the desire to reduce uncertainty about the world are the natural allies of tripartism. Perhaps the situation described by Penny Wensley, the Australian Ambassador for the Environment, may one day no longer seem anomalous:

> The role of NGOs in the negotiation and implementation of agreements (which has increased dramatically during and since the UNCED process) will continue to grow. Two weeks ago, in Geneva, I was startled to find the Chairman of a meeting of the *ad hoc* Committee on [sic] Parties to the Basel Convention giving the floor to the representative of Greenpeace to negotiate as an equal with governments on drafting language – something which I have never before witnessed in twenty years of involvement with multilateralism (cited in Cameron & MacKenzie 1996:149).

Our case studies also suggest that the principle of tripartism should shape voting rules in some way. A tripartism of voting may provide less reason for a powerful state to forum-shift. The case of WIPO illustrates the point. WIPO has over the years granted observer status to hundreds of international and national NGOs and consults with those NGOs regularly. However, those NGOs do not have the right to vote on treaty revisions. That is a right of states. Had the voting rules of WIPO been defined differently (e.g. requiring each national delegation to have an owner representative, an intellectual property user representative and a governmental head of delegation) the US might have remained engaged in the WIPO process of standard-setting a little longer lest it upset the intellectual property user delegates. Significantly, as GATT standard-making in intellectual property loomed closer to reality WIPO strove harder to involve NGOs, including national NGOs in its activities. But it could not, of course, give them a vote.

Our fourth and final proposition is that principles ought to be used to create 'nested games'. The theory of nested games was developed by Tsebelis to explain why an apparently rational actor chooses a suboptimal action. Is it that the actor is not acting rationally? The answer is no. Rather, the intuitive idea is that in such cases actors are 'involved in a whole network of games' (Tsebelis 1990: 7). Deliberately taking a loss in one arena is part of a networked strategy. What appears to observers to be a suboptimal choice is actually the product of an optimal strategy across a number of arenas, beyond the one arena the observer is watching. This analysis is powerful because in politics, where Tsebelis derives his case studies, actors are much more likely to be involved in nested games. This game theory, in other words, does a much better job of modelling the dynamics of politics than a game theory which conceptualizes the problem as one independent game. It also partly captures the complex interdependencies of global regulation. The approach is not dissimilar to Putnam's two-level game which we discussed in Chapter 20, the principal difference being that the Putnam analysis operates sequentially, whereas the theory of nested games operates simultaneously (Tsebelis 1990: 244). Our purpose, however, is not to compare the modes of analysis but to explore the implications of nested games for a processual theory of conflicts of principles.

On the face of it our prescription that principles be used to create nested games would seem to work against weaker states. For example, in the last GATT round many developing states simply did not have the experts in the various committees during the negotiations – they did not have intellectual property experts or telecommunications experts. If they sent anyone at all it was diplomats who happened to be based in Geneva, who at best could only deliver a speech rather than negotiate with experts from developed states. Playing in the networks of games at the level of a multilateral trade round involves capacities at horizontal and vertical levels. At the vertical level state actors are involved in Putnam's two-level game because they have to keep a weather eye out for the activities and interests of domestic constituencies. At the horizontal level they have to pursue their interests across very different sectors (intellectual property, services, food standards and so on), forming different alliances for different sectors. There are very few states with the capacity to keep abreast of this two-level nested-game complexity. How, then, does it help weaker states to increase complexity by using principles to create yet more nested games?

The key lies in weaker actors using principles not to create more complexity for themselves, but for their more powerful opponents. One of the reasons why the US was able to secure victories in the form of TRIPS and GATS was that in those two sub-arenas it did not have to, at the negotiating stage, deal with vertical nested-game complexity. US business had more or less instructed the US state that agreements on intellectual property and services were required outcomes of the Uruguay Round. There was consensus at the highest level of US business about the need for that. Strategic CEOs secured the president's seal of approval for their agenda. Non-business NGOs remained largely ignorant of the implications of these agreements. After the negotiations were over and the US was moving to enact legislation approving the Final Act of the Uruguay Round, an anti-GATT coalition led by actors like Ralph Nader came close to derailing approval by Congress. But the game over approval was independent of the concluded trade negotiations.

How might principles have been used to increase the complexity of the task facing the US in the negotiations over intellectual property? Since TRIPS, Nader and his colleague James Love[3] have been campaigning against the parts of TRIPS that will have an adverse effect on public health-care, especially the cost of pharmaceutical drugs. In a letter written to the then US Trade Representative, Michael Kantor, they point out that in the case of intellectual property:

> the administration is advancing positions which are too narrowly focused on the interests of the international pharmaceutical companies, while ignoring important public health and development issues…Many physicians have criticized the PTO's [US Patent and Trademark Office] decision to grant patents for surgical procedures. Pharmaceutical companies and patients have raised objections to the

3  James Love is the Director of Economic Research in the Center for Study of Responsive Law, Washington DC.

patenting of gene sequences. Some members of the US Congress have expressed an interest in compulsory licensing as a tool to lower the price of pharmaceutical drugs...In short, there are many controversies in the US regarding the appropriate national policies for intellectual property rights and there is no consensus that 'more is better'.[4]

In terms of our theory of principles, Nader and Love are seeking to make the principle of health-care an oppositional principle to the principles contained in TRIPS. Their problem, of course, is that the ink has dried on the TRIPS agreement. But their choice of oppositional principle remains a good one. As we know all too well, it is hard to get students excited about patent law! But people do get excited about the standard of public health-care and its costs. The reaction of mass publics is an important factor in public health policy-making. Interestingly, a former US trade negotiator involved in TRIPS told us that generic pharmaceutical manufacturers in developing states had a powerful public health argument on their side. 'Pharmaceutical pirates' in developing countries, he said, had a 'wonderful public policy argument on their side – they provided cheap health-care' (1994 interview). However, it was an argument that went nowhere in the negotiations over TRIPS because it did nothing to increase the nested-game complexity facing US trade negotiators. They knew that the US was committed to securing a high-standard intellectual property agreement and that it had Quad support on the matter. They also knew that the US could achieve its goal under the consensus endgame that would finally determine the outcomes of the negotiations. They could, therefore, ignore the public health argument.

Things might have been different if they also had to deal with a vertical-game complexity. Had TRIPS been framed as a public health issue, the anxiety of mass publics in the US and other Western states might have become a factor in destabilizing the consensus that US business elites had built around TRIPS. Those supporting and negotiating TRIPS would have had to find ways to steer through vertical-game complexity. US negotiators would have had to face simultaneous vertical and horizontal games. Even under conditions of increased game complexity TRIPS might still have come to pass – as we said at the beginning of this chapter, hegemony means that those who speak the language of principles with mechanisms of coercion and rewards by their side have the greater capacity to influence. But perhaps weaker states and consumers might have been able to wring more concessions from US trade negotiators. TRIPS might have ended up a weaker agreement. It might not have achieved the status of a multilateral trade agreement 'binding on all members' (see Article II(2) of the Agreement Establishing the World Trade Organization), finishing instead as a plurilateral agreement binding only on those members which accepted its obligations. The pay-off of the forum-shifting strategy might not have been so great. For nested complexity to erode capabilities for forum-shifting in this way, a set of reforms (discussed in Chapter 26) to enhance the sovereignty of citizens would help. For example, Nader would have been able to invoke the public health principle earlier had there been a better window of transparency into the framing of the Uruguay Round agenda.

---

4 Letter of 9 October 1995 by Ralph Nader and James Love to Michael Kantor, USTR, expressing concern about positions taken by the Clinton administration with respect to intellectual property rights and health care. Circulated in Background Documents on Health Care and Intellectual Property Rights, by James P Love, Center for Study of Responsive Law at the International Conference on TRIPS, MAI and Spread of Global Dominance of MNCs, New Delhi, India, 14–15 November 1996.

## Conclusion

The processual theory being offered here in summary form comes to this. Regulatory globalization proceeds under conditions of the rule of principles. One way in which to contest regulatory outcomes or change existing regulatory structures is to engender a contest of principles. Contests should first be fought at this level. Principles should be debated first, allowing rule complexity to follow. Contests of principle are facilitated by lowering the barriers to contestability. One way of doing this is to use the principle of tripartism as a constitutionalizing principle in international fora. Tripartism is one way in which to combat the effects of forum-shifting. Finally, principles should be used strategically by weaker actors to increase levels of nested complexity for stronger actors. Like tripartism, increasing levels of nested complexity for strong actors may reduce the pay-offs they obtain from initiating a sequence of forum-shifting.

Naturally, the application of this processual theory is no guarantee of success or of increased levels of citizen sovereignty. The saccharine-sweet triumphs of individuals that feature so regularly in Hollywood scripts do not occur with anything like the same frequency in a world where international business and powerful states ally to dominate global regulatory agendas. All too often individuals and weak organizational actors are left to carry on an interstitial struggle within structures and parameters defined by those powerful actors using their webs of influence. The mechanism of modelling is, we shall see in the next chapter, one mechanism by which the weak can carry on that struggle.

## CHAPTER 25

Modelling, Globalization and the
Politics of Empowerment

In Chapter 22, we saw that modelling was an important mechanism with all the regimes that we have found to have globalized.[1] Indeed, without modelling it is hard to make sense of many of the globalizations in our data. Global diplomacy itself is a product of modelling of the fourteenth-century Venetian innovation of a systematized diplomatic service (Craig & George 1990: 11). We do not need modelling to explain why many countries simultaneously recognize that there is a hole in the ozone layer and simultaneously adopt similar countermeasures against ozone-depleting substances. We do not need modelling to explain why almost every country has established an environment ministry. But we do need modelling to explain why most of the world's developed nations and many developing ones established national environmental agencies between 1971 and 1972 (Janicke 1991: 19), even though they were experiencing very different levels of environmental collapse. In the same way, it is hard to explain without modelling why all the communist societies except North Korea and Cuba experienced mass public outpourings against communism in 1989, even though these nations were experiencing dramatically different structural conditions, such as economic growth in 1989 (Braithwaite 1994: 445–6). The contention of this chapter is that there is a worldwide patterning of regulatory institutions and a recurrent dynamic of institutional change that can be understood by modelling the process of modelling. What we will find interesting about modelling is its connection to emancipatory politics, a theme we will take a step further in the next chapter. The sociology of modelling shows that structural explanation will often be wrong because the world can also be understood through the dynamics of modelling. But the important thing is that it shows how strategic use of processes of modelling can be an important source of hope for the structurally weak to defeat the strong.

Marx had an explanation of the world that motivated an emancipatory politics. Unfortunately, the historical explanation turned out to be flawed and the emancipatory politics enslaved citizens with a new set of structures. This disaster motivates an attempt to forge an explanation–emancipation interface that starts with micro-process rather than macro-structure. Along the way, using the tools of modelling to effect change from below comes to grips with the brute force of structures of power. Yet in the end, there is no new set of structures to be got right. There is only continuous struggle, because new structures enable new dominations. The

---

1  Much of this chapter is taken from John Braithwaite 1994, 'A Sociology of Modelling and the Politics of Empowerment,' *British Journal of Sociology* 45: 443–79.

most useful sort of emancipatory politics is therefore not myopically structural; it illuminates the processes of struggle available to whoever are the losers from the structures prevailing at any point in history. Conceptual tools to analyze processes of modelling become crucial resources for emancipation.

A social science that explains why those with the guns and the money win most of the time is hardly an accomplishment. Explaining their defeats is the challenge. Marx was on a fruitful track with the idea of contradiction. Where he took a wrong turn was with a conception of contradiction that was structurally determinate. We will attempt to show that a fertile conception of contradiction is one that is processual and imagined rather than structural and determinate. The following ten propositions will be advanced toward an explanation of when the weak defeat the strong.

1   A consequence of domination is reactance. Those imputed low status by a dominant power can choose to solve their status problem by creating new status systems that invert the hegemonic status system. An inverted status system guarantees success to those who are failures under the hegemonic status system (e.g. inversion of the housewifely virtues by 1960s women's liberationists with career aspirations).

2   Model missionaries popularize the oppositional models that are the product of such reaction formation (e.g. 1970s feminist writers such as Greer, Millett and Oakley).

3   When model missionaries get a toehold, in the world capitalist market there are model mercenaries whose market niche is specializing in turning such toeholds into footholds (e.g. publishers promote women's magazines with a feminist orientation).

4   The work of model missionaries and model mercenaries does little more than give oppositional groups a start. The crucial step to empowerment is moving into institutional politics by model mongering. Model mongers experimentally float many oppositional models, rather than commit resources to a single preferred model (e.g. the work of Australian femocrats, hawking feminist models at international meetings such as the 1995 Beijing Congress on Women and around various branches of the Australian bureaucracy: Yeatman 1990). Dominant groups generally find it unwise to model monger. Rather, they commit their resources to defending the extant models that confer their privilege. In doing this, the dominant group gives its opposition the capacity to set the framework for debates. Because the model has a power that is independent of the interests that advocate it, a weak interest group with a strong model can defeat a strong interest group.

5   Model mongering is a key to the powerless acquiring a strategic advantage over the powerful because persistent application of the strategy eventually draws out contradictions in the identities propagated by dominant models (e.g. contradictions between the position of women and a national identity valuing equality of opportunity).

6   Because modelling is not only about pursuing interests but also about sustaining identities, model mongers prevail by precipitating identity crises that prise open cracks in hegemonic structures (e.g. identity crises among nations that claim to be democracies cause a succession of nations to give women the vote).

7   Model mongers often prevail when they find a model miser or a model modernizer who needs a pre-packaged quick-fix to an institutional problem (e.g. a political candidate, lagging

with female voters, in the market for a 'bold policy' to project an image of commitment to women's rights).

8    Model mongers succeed when they experiment with insurgent models until they strike one that poses an insoluble collective-action problem for the dominant group. Every actor in the dominant group may have an interest in defeating the insurgent model, but each actor may also have an interest in free-riding on the resistance of others while parlaying support from the opposition group, privately succumbing to their demands (e.g. the businessman urges others to resist affirmative action laws, but takes the heat off his firm by succumbing to demands for in-house reforms).

9    Guns, money and institutional control constitute the self-efficacy of the powerful. For the powerless, the self-efficacy that enables continued struggle against overwhelming odds comes from the inspiration of models of successful struggle from other places and times (e.g. the suffragettes).

10   Self-efficacy that sustains strategic global model mongering over an extended period of history is more important than the capacity and resources available to the weak in their struggles against the strong.

These propositions serve to signpost where we are headed. But because our aspiration is for processual understanding, they only illuminate when they can be linked together into a processual explanation. Figure 25.1 and the accompanying text are an illustration of how this might be done. Before we can imagine processes of social change, however, we must lay some foundations for a sociology of modelling. In the next section we discuss what modelling is, and a provocative modelling formulation is advanced. This is modified to produce a more conciliatory formulation that incorporates structural explanation. The final section summarizes what we know about the patterning of diffusion in the world system.

On these foundations, the third part of the chapter seeks to explain the diffusion of models using new tools for diagnosing the process. The key conceptual tool for comprehending the possibility of a politics of empowerment is the process of model mongering. The fourth part illustrates how the micro-process tools of the previous section can be combined to explain a transformation of the world system that involves weaker actors prevailing over stronger ones.

## Foundations for a Theory of Modelling

### Conceptualizing Modelling

Modelling is conceptualized here as more than mere imitation – where imitation means one actor matching the actions of another, usually close in time. For Bandura (1986), the leading psychological theorist of the subject, modelling means observational learning with a symbolic content, not just the simple response mimicry implied by the term 'imitation'. Modelling is based on conceptions of action portrayed in words and images.

The nice thing about modelling is that it lends itself to a generality of abstraction that makes it a useful concept for psychologists, sociologists and political scientists who study international relations. It has analytical multiplexity that facilitates micro–macro synthesis. When the fashion model parades we say she is modelling, and when the observer copies her we say she is modelling the model, and we call the whole pattern of fashion diffusion of which this is a part, modelling. This is good usage because the fact of the process is that the woman who goes to fashion parades herself becomes a model for others. Modelling is therefore defined as action(s) that constitute a process of displaying, symbolically interpreting and copying conceptions of action (and this process itself). A model is a conception of action that is put on display during such a process of modelling. A model is that which is displayed, symbolically interpreted and copied.

Models as symbolically interpreted by those who 'invent', 'adapt' and 'copy' them are foundational to our analysis. However, it is not our purpose to make a contribution to the understanding of these foundations, but to build on them. Those interested already have access to rich literatures on these micro foundations from both psychological work in the social cognitive tradition (Bandura 1986) and sociological literature in the symbolic interaction tradition (Mead 1950; Burke 1945; Duncan 1969; Turner 1974). That foundation is of a world of humanly articulated futures formulated from reflection on the past enactments of others.

## A Provocative Formulation

A structural problem of social science is that, as in most other important institutions, there is a hegemony of thinkers from countries that see themselves as model-builders rather than model-copiers. How could that be other than a good sort of hegemony? The problem is that the model-builder bias drives our scholarship toward a narrow focus on social change as fashioned from tests of strength between constituencies who struggle to build particular institutions and opposing constituencies who seek to tear them down or build other institutions. We have a social science of wheel-invention fashioned in cultures with inventive identities and an impoverished science of wheel-copying. It is therefore a science particularly poorly adapted to social explanation outside the North Atlantic powers. But we will also argue that there are limitations even within the North Atlantic nations, because the identity that social scientists share as citizens of countries which are creators of institutions is based on a certain degree of delusion.

A provocative statement of the modelling thesis is that more of the variance in culture and institutional structure is explained by patterns of modelling than by configurations of actor interests and their relative power. The clash of interests is not only quantitatively less important as an explanation, it is causally secondary: the interests of actors are constituted in response to received models; they do not pre-exist institutions that they shape *ab initio*. The idea of the working class and its organization through unions and socialist parties, the idea of women as an interest and of feminist politics, have been crucial in Australian history. Yet these were not ways of thinking about interest politics that were structurally inevitable in Australia; they were interest group concepts modelled from the North Atlantic powers at the points in history when these models became influential there, not at some later point when Australia's structural conditions reached alignment with those in the North. The received models that are embedded in tradition and history set the framework for the debate more often than creative institutional design forged by existing interests.

Hence, in Australia we have laws criminalizing rape not because of any titanic struggle between a women's movement (or some other actor) which demanded rape laws and others who resisted them; rather, we acquired them without debate from British criminal law. Having occurred, it is now nearly impossible for any actors with any amount of political power to argue for a way of dealing with rape that disposes of the criminal-law model in favour of a radically different strategy. It is hard for interest groups to break free of the frameworks imposed by received models.

It follows from this formulation that relatively powerless actors can have influence disproportionate to their resources if they are skilled at putting models on the political agenda, to which more powerful actors are forced to react. Indeed, we will argue that a way for politically weak actors to be powerful is to model monger, and that when they do it well they can be quite powerful.

## A Conciliatory Formulation

To say that we have the rape laws we do because we modelled them is to say something rather banal, unless we can also say something about why modelling occurs and how it is patterned. This is a challenge we begin to meet in the next section. The modelling perspective causes social scientists to look for different kinds of explanations from those within the framework of structural explanation.

Consider the explanation of the rise of the welfare state in Britain or Australia. Traditionally in sociology, one would analyze outbreaks of worker unrest; the threat to the legitimacy of the capitalist system posed by unbridled exploitation of workers; the rise of the trade union movement, then social democratic parties, then the International Labour Organization (ILO); threats to the peaceful reproduction of labour on the demand side for the welfare state; and rising affluence as making the welfare state fiscally possible on the supply side. The modelling perspective broadens our focus away from these structural variables and toward the process of adapting models. So we will attend to data like the speeches of Churchill, Lloyd George and Campbell-Bannerman when they argued in favour of the welfare state as a program to replicate Bismarck's strategy of defeating socialism in the nation which was emerging as the great power of the time (see Jones 1951; Semmel 1960).[2]

It should be clear from this example, however, that the modelling explanation and structural explanation can be complementary rather than contradictory. They direct our attention to different aspects of an integrated understanding. Indeed, in this conciliatory formulation it becomes possible for a structural problem to precede a model which is sought for solving it, or for a successful model to be grasped first (with structural forces subsequently aligning around different parameters of the model). Our critique of sociology is that the quest for structural explanations for the forging of romantic new institutions tends to suppress consideration of whether what is going on is perhaps a more mundane copying of old institutions. In short, the conciliatory formulation of the modelling perspective is advanced as a corrective, as a particular form of action-oriented complement to structural explanation.

## The Patterning of Modelling

A politics of empowerment grounded in a sociology of modelling must begin with a sensitivity to the strong tendencies for structures of power to be both constituted by modelling and constitutive of modelling (see generally Giddens 1984). In this section, we conclude that the periphery

---

2 'It is not enough for the social thinker in this country to meet the socialist with a negative. The English progressive will be wise if in this at any rate, he takes a leaf from the book of Bismarck who dealt the heaviest blow against German socialism not by his laws of oppression…but by the great system of state insurance which now safeguards the German workman at almost every point in his industrial career' (H. Spencer, Lloyd George's publicity agent in 1902, quoted in Gilbert 1966: 257).

models the centre in the world system more than the centre models the periphery. This is the most important special case of a general tendency for powerful actors to be modelled more than less-powerful ones. The upshot is that modelling constitutes a world system dominated from the core and a tendency toward international homogenization.

Both the psychological literature on modelling and the sociological work on diffusion of innovation, as well as the data on the modelling of US and UK regulation in this book, overwhelmingly support the hypothesis that modelling is patterned according to configurations of power. This abstract truth was brought home to us in microcosm in an interview with a Korean lobbyist working for a Korean business organization (itself modelled on US business organizations) when he said: 'Whatever the US do, if you follow the US you cannot be a loser' (1995 interview). Modelling is gendered (Bandura 1986: 92–8). Children model adults more than adults model children. Less-powerful people model powerful adults more than the reverse (Lefcowitz, Blake & Mouton 1955; Bussey & Bandura 1984; Rogers & Shoemaker 1971: 354–7, 377). Advertisers exploit these facts by projecting their models as economically successful men, or wives and girlfriends of economically successful men. It is likely that we can build on this solid microfoundation by showing also that struggling organizations model economically successful organizations, more than the reverse.

Modelling is patterned in many other respects. Actors are modelled more when they are attractive in ways independent of their wealth or power. When Marilyn Monroe committed suicide, many others followed (Phillips 1974). Modelling is stronger between homophilous actors (Rogers & Shoemaker 1971: 376; Rogers 1983), actors who share similar attributes. A common world-view is important here, especially a common political or religious ideology. Islamic states model other Islamic states frequently; communist states used to model other communist states; Australian Catholics send priests to Rome, so that when in Australia they can do as the Romans do.

Spatial proximity facilitates modelling (see Walker 1969 for US states; Poel 1976 for Canadian provinces). Korea looked to Japan for models of family conglomerates. Papua New Guinea is more likely to model Australia and Indonesia than Canada and Mexico. Modelling is stronger within common-language communities: Anglophones model Anglophones; Francophones model Francophones. China looks to Taiwan for models of commercial law. Important as these other patterns of modelling are, they are becoming progressively less important because of the growth in communications technology,[3] in the increasing use of English and the growing power of other constitutive features of the world system. For example, Korean and Taiwanese policymakers closely study New Zealand's models of regulatory liberalization. Regional and global modelling work to create complex regulatory lineages. Taiwan's *Fair Trade Law 1991* follows German and EU models of competition law, but some of its anti-monopolization provisions are 'copied from the Fair Trade Law of Korea' (Liu 1995:331).

If we seek to find creativity in its most developed form, we look to New York, Paris and London, because even within the First World modelling is mostly from centre to periphery (Walker 1969: 883; Gray 1973: 1184), and at the micro level earlier adopters of new models have more cosmopolite characteristics than late-adopters (Rogers & Shoemaker 1971: 369). So after London claimed to have invented the idea of a professional police force in 1829, it spread

---

3 This includes telecommunications, desktop publishing of customized printed communications and air travel. At a level between the micro and the world system, we also know that the degree of communication integration in a social system is positively related to the rate of adoption of innovation (see the studies reviewed in Rogers & Shoemaker 1971: 352 and Rogers 1983).

throughout England, and then to every city in the world, an utterly globalized regulatory model. Ideas people in the pre-eminent world cities become extremely powerful in the world system. But in fact these creative power-brokers at the core are not so creative; they are scavengers and adapters of models – models they find in an interaction they see in the street or in a Shakespearean play. While it is true that Louisiana models New York more than the reverse (Walker 1969; Gray 1973), this is partly because New York sucks up the ideas of Louisiana and defines them as its own. Model developers, however, mostly have an interest in obscuring their limited originality. They must cultivate a creative mystique, the romantic idea of the individual and original author. An artistic genius in Greenwich Village will not usually disclose, nor want to admit even to herself, that her genius is the art of modelling through the ideas of peripheral figures, such as songs of black women from Louisiana. Creative geniuses tend to be plagiarists, clever at appearing not to be so and deluding themselves that they are not so. The ancients, who appear the most original of all scholars, may only appear so because the work of those they imitated has been destroyed (Weinsheimer 1984: 57).

Managing the impression of originality is differentially important between centre and periphery. In Taiwan, it will often be strategic to market a model with 'This is how they do it in the US', even if that is a misrepresentation. The US will be less willing to use or believe the fact that it received a certain idea from Taiwan; it is generally not a selling-point to say 'Made in Taiwan'. The creative genius who poached the idea from Taiwan will usually have a career interest in cooperating with the delusion that it is a US idea.[4]

This is not to deny that reactions in the periphery assert and cultivate local values that are distinctive from those of the centre. Debate over broadcasting and film industry policy in Australia is continually infused with pleas to counter the Americanization of Australian television. Yet the Americanization has already happened in an overwhelming way. The very existence of centrifugal forces as oppositional movements confirms the empirical claim that what are being railed against are dominant paradigms from the centre.

Much of the patterning of modelling is sustained as much by fidelity to identities as by economic interests. Sustaining identities – as an Islamic people, a US citizen, the Catholic Church – is a central impetus to modelling at the macro, micro and meso levels. Hence, patterns of modelling that superficially seem driven by economic interests may be more profoundly identitive. A wealthy person may wish to model other wealthy people so that her identity is clear as a wealthy person. She drives a luxury car not because she needs a car so big and exquisitely engineered, but to draw on the signification of its model type.

Human actors seize models that help them to display and discover who they are. The centrality of this struggle for identity becomes clearest when we observe the insecurity or confusion of identity that typifies the immiseration of many we call mentally ill or adolescent (Erikson 1968). Politics is not simply a sequence of power-plays to compete for scarce resources; it is also a 'contest over who we are to become' (Bowles & Gintis 1986: 8), a contest in which identities are both starting-points and outcomes of political struggles. In organizational life, identitive power (power derived from symbols of identity or belonging) is often greater than Etzioni's (1965)

---

4 We do not want to deny that there will be occasions when it will be chic for First World creators to explicitly recognize the African input into their music, or indeed occasions when they acknowledge it openly as a matter of principle and pride. We will argue that there is a dynamic to how counterhegemonic models can come to acquire appeal.

other two fundamental forms of organizational power – coercive and utilitarian power. The reason is that identitive power is superior at generating commitment, while utilitarian and (particularly) coercive power risks greater resistance (Etzioni 1965: 651). Hence, at the levels of individual action, organizational action and political action, we are identity-seeking and identity-projecting animals. This is why modelling at all three levels is about sustaining and adjusting identities.

## Explaining the Diffusion of Models

In the above section we showed how models tend to become the property of the centre. Empirically, we can see this in the patent ownership of technology.[5] Actors in the periphery who crave money or influence for their ideas often do best to hand them over to the centre; and the centre will often have good reason to claim these as ideas of the centre. The result is a concentration of models at the centre. How do these models get adopted throughout the periphery? What is the dynamic process that accounts for the static pattern?

In the discussion that follows, we will illustrate diffusion with the dominant case, core–periphery diffusion. But similar processes are at work when diffusion is core–core or periphery–core. To understand these processes, we consider five types of actors: model missionaries, model mercenaries, model mongers, model misers and model modernizers. The first two, missionaries and mercenaries, play their most important role on the side of the model source; the remainder on the side of the emulator. Just as in the psychological theory of modelling (Bandura 1986), modelling is likely to persist when both she who models and she who is modelled are motivated to support modelling. When a child models the eating habits of the family both the child and the family enjoy more pleasant meal-times, devoid of flying food and interruption. With modelling of the major institutions in the world system, we will argue that modelling is likely to persist when actors on both sides of the process are motivated to model by economic, political and identitive concerns.

Let us now define the five types of actors involved in the diffusion of models and then consider how each operates.

- Model missionaries are promoters of models who, motivated by belief in a model sourced in their part of the world, travel abroad to spread the word about the model.
- Model mercenaries are promoters of models in the world system who commercially exploit models.
- Model mongers are agents who pursue their political agenda by experimental floats of large numbers of (mostly foreign) models.
- Model misers are adopters of models who prefer copying to innovating, to economize on model debugging and to economize on marshalling political support for the idea.
- Model modernizers are actors who adopt models from the centre for reasons of legitimacy, in order to harness the identitive power of being perceived as modern, civilized or progressive.

---

5 Thirty-nine per cent of the patents issued in Australia in 1990 were issued to US owners, 30 per cent to EU owners, 16 per cent to Japanese, 8 per cent to Australian and 7 per cent to owners from the rest of the world (data supplied by the Australian Patents, Trademarks and Designs Office).

It is possible, particularly for organizational actors, to satisfy the requirements of more than one type at once, for example, for missionaries to be mercenaries and modernizers as well.

## Model Missionaries

In the next section, we emphasize the role of model mercenaries who make money by promoting models. In this section, we emphasize that promoting models is not only about money, it is also about power and affirming a sense of identity. When a student of regulation models a regulatory scholar's way of thinking, the scholar enjoys savouring her intellectual power and enjoys the affirmation that her way of thinking must have value – it has been voluntarily embraced by others. And because the scholar becomes so persuaded, she is motivated by the belief that she is doing good by passing on her models.

Christian missionaries have for centuries travelled to distant lands to spread the gospel, including, as we saw in Chapter 15, the gospel of alcohol and narcotics prohibition. Missionaries sincerely believe that models dominant in their homeland are superior to those of the lands where they go to spread the word. For true believers in the home country it is an affirmation of the superiority of their ways to see well-motivated people devote their lives to spreading those ways in less-fortunate lands. Tithing to support missionary work is a potent self-vindication of the superiority of that to which we adhere. More generally, it may be that part of what a power needs to remain a great power is the ability to persuade its citizens that what is good for the great power is good for the world. For example, when Iraq is invaded, political support from citizens can be sustained if the citizens believe that the invasion is not only good for the superpower, but also good for those invaded, and good for the peace and stability of the world (partly because, in this case, of the enforcement of compliance with the Nuclear Non-Proliferation Treaty).

The model missionaries push not only religious and philosophical models. The Regulatory Affairs Professionals Society is a missionary organization for convergence in pharmaceuticals regulation. The Medical Lobby for Appropriate Marketing is a missionary society for ethical promotional practices with pharmaceuticals. WHO has missionaries who promote regulatory practices to improve the availability of essential drugs. The World Intellectual Property Organization (WIPO) sends intellectual property experts from elite centres like the Max Planck Institute to Africa where they preach the virtues of intellectual property rights for the economic development of states.

Why is it more usual for model missionaries to succeed when they travel from core to periphery than when they migrate from the periphery to the core? A simple answer is the concentration of power at the centre. The Christian missionaries spread Christianity so successfully throughout Latin America because of the military might of the conquistadors. Soviet *glasnost* in the 1980s had an influence that exceeded the Hungarian equivalent of the 1950s or the Czechoslovakian equivalent of the 1960s because the Soviet version was backed by the authority of the centre, while the other two were challenging that authority.

## Model Mercenaries

Model mercenaries make money out of the proliferation of the model. The difference between missionaries and mercenaries is not simply a motivational one – the difference between identitive and utilitarian motivation (Etzioni 1965) is commonly muddied by a mixture of motivations. However interpenetrated, this motivational divide has a structural basis in the location of mercenaries in capitalist market institutions. Missionaries tend to have their base in pre-capitalist institutions such as churches, universities and states.

Often there is a sequence where the periphery is softened up for the new model by missionary endeavours, then model mercenaries move in to do the hard sell and execute model implementation. Missionaries of privatization first came to Australia in the 1980s from the Thatcherist and Reaganite faiths. They told Australia that many of its state functions should be privatized – telecommunications, airlines, banks, railroads, hospitals, even prisons could and should be privatized. Then came the Prisons Corporation of America – model mercenaries – to consummate the setting-up of Australia's first private prison. Worldwide capitalist markets amplify modelling effects; whenever missionaries get a toehold, there are mercenaries to be found who have discovered a specialized market niche in turning such toeholds into footholds.

Sometimes the modelling sequence begins with model mercenaries. In the case of intellectual property the US softened up the periphery through its section 301 watch-list process (Chapters 7 and 10). Trade coercion paved the way for model mercenaries like the Business Software Alliance, which regularly sends its experts from Washington to places like Canberra to deliver talks to Australian bureaucrats on the evils of Internet piracy and what to do about it.

The model mercenaries and missionaries we have discussed so far move from the centre to the periphery. But local missionaries and local mercenaries are soon recruited – the education system bestows careers on locals hired to teach the models, the Prisons Corporation of America employs local executives (and may later encourage local investors with the local political contacts to lobby for further proliferation of the model). Foreign educated locals return to their countries to spread a regulatory gospel. They become senior bureaucrats, pushing at home, for example, US models of competition law as well as in their regional fora like the Asia-Pacific Economic Cooperation Forum (APEC). Partners in local law firms and accounting firms, realizing the opportunities that foreign models may bring, become experts in foreign regulatory models. Local mercenaries band together with foreign mercenaries. A local law firm in Taiwan develops a close working relationship with the American Chamber of Commerce (ACC) in Taiwan and helps the ACC write its position papers on Taiwan's regulatory system. When the Taiwanese government needs to rewrite its commercial laws, partners from the local firm are hired to do the job. Thus the models of the centre are diffused through the pathways of individual careers.

The seduction of the periphery with models from the centre is not simply mediated by particular firms with an interest in such seduction. At a more aggregated level, First World nations have a collective interest in promoting generalized dependency and reverence from the periphery. It is in US interests, when it decides to go to war in Vietnam or Iraq, that Australia should be in the habit of modelling US strategic thinking and therefore decide to join the fight. Collectively, it is in the interests of US economic growth that things are viewed as good in the periphery just because they are American. To the extent that this generalized prejudice holds, all US exporters are advantaged. And by 'things', we do not mean only consumer durables. When Australian hospital administration follows US models, there are US architectural firms, management consultants, educational institutions and hospital supply corporations poised to take advantage of it. The model brings an entire business infrastructure. When Australian voluntary standards organizations adopt US standards, US companies who had a hand in shaping those standards to accommodate their interests, are beneficiaries. The First World has an economic and strategic interest in encouraging a general propensity to model it in the periphery. Thus, the US Information Agency is one of the best investments US taxpayers make.

## Model Mongers

Modern democracies and, to a lesser extent, contemporary totalitarian societies are densely populated with reformist NGOs. The US manifests this tendency in its most developed form.[6] It is a fair generalization that in the US reform groups are more impressive in their number, resources, lobbying and the quality of their policy research than in other countries. Yet, to be effective, in a sense they need these superior qualities because they operate in a different way from reform groups in other countries. To some extent, they are victims of their own parochialism. Many US consumer groups, for example, are poorly informed about what the consumer movement is accomplishing in other parts of the world. This is especially ironical because these foreign groups are in important ways US offspring. The 'Consumers Union' model and the Nader model have been the leading trendsetters in the international consumer movement.

US reformers work harder because so often they tend to operate by devising reform proposals from first principles. In contrast, reform groups in much of the rest of the world operate more as model mongers. Because their resources are so thin, the best way for them to be effective is to eschew the detailed work their US counterparts do (such as in actually producing draft legislation). Instead, they scan the international horizon for pre-packaged models. The US enacts a Freedom of Information law, so an Australian group gets hold of it and the lobbying materials produced for it, modifying them only slightly in its own campaign. The Australian bureaucracy ends up changing the US model substantially, but it is the US package that sets the framework for the debate.

For consumer groups in the periphery there are many worthy models. Consumers International facilitates communication about new models. A rational strategy for an organization with meagre resources is to run many campaigns with half-baked off-shore models. Models, because they are information, can be distributed quickly and at little cost. Those that gather serious support, such as by being incorporated into the election platforms of major parties, then become the subject of more rigorous development and lobbying. This is what we mean by model mongering.

The models which do not attract serious political support are not forgotten under this political strategy. They are left on the backburner, continuing to appear in consumer movement policy documents as needed reforms. In later years, other model mongering national consumer movements may have more success with reform. Eventually, the point may be reached where a campaign can be put on the front-burner under the banner that 'Ours is the only country in the region that has failed to introduce this reform'. The International Telecommunications Users Group (Chapter 14) exemplified the model monger strategy. Most national doors were closed to telecommunications deregulation; its stategy was 'not to push on a door until it began to open'.

Politics from the modelling perspective is not about problems looking for solutions. It is about solutions waiting for the right problem (to justify their implementation) and the right moment. We can see this with agenda-setting by activist senators, lobbyists and crusading journalists in the US Senate:[7]

---

6  This is perhaps a manifestation of McCarthy and Zald's (1977: 1224) hypothesis: 'As the amount of discretionary resources of mass and elite publics increases, the absolute and relative amount of resources available to the social movement sector increases'.

7  Mayer's (1991) study of agenda-setting on consumer issues begins with the conventional presumption of three stages in the emergence of an issue: (1) publicity in the mass media; (2) arousal of public opinion; and (3) address by policy-makers. Mayer found (with US consumer protection from 1960 to 1987) more often that the process was more or less reversed, with policy-makers seeking to seize the agenda, thereby arousing media publicity and public opinion.

> Often solutions may become known before problems can be found to which they can be applied, or before a convincing case can be made for the seriousness of the problems that they are meant to address. Activist senators or interest groups dedicated to the value of a given solution – such as income grants in lieu of services, or administrative decentralization – are frequently out looking for social problems to which their nostrum can be applied, or are anxious to define problems in such a way that their pet solutions will be applicable (Walker 1973: 431).

While conservative politics involves reluctantly scratching when the electorate gets an itch, entrepreneurial politics involves scratching all over until a spot is found that makes the electorate itchy.

Pre-packaged models have enormous appeal to actors in both the legislative and executive branches of the state, for a simple reason. The state has limited time and energy and a limitless range of issues on which it would like to be seen to be making progress. So Simon's (1957) satisficing model of decision-making applies rather well. A state does not – cannot – search for the best solution to the problems it would like to do something about. Solutions that are good enough will do. Hence, when someone offers a pre-packaged model that is good enough, it is often an efficient use of the state's time to buy it instead of initiating a search for the best solution. This is how it is possible for twenty US states to copy almost verbatim a Californian law, ten of them even copying two serious typographical errors (Walker 1969: 881–2).

The more powerless, disorganized and poorly resourced a group is, the more likely that model mongering will be its best strategy. It is a strategy that produces political victories for powerless groups. At the same time, it is a strategy that does not refute the proposition that powerful groups generally prevail over powerless ones. Most of the model monger's models are put on the backburner for precisely this reason. Yet the strategy means that resources are not wasted on the detailed development of losing campaigns. Model mongering minimizes development costs and maximizes reform opportunities by transmitting many models through political networks. An effective model monger puts in significant resources only when she can smell victory.

A sociological theory of modelling, by taking the model mongering of powerless groups seriously, should cause us to take a different, less pessimistic view of the way power is exercised in the modern world system. In addition to the reasons already adduced, this source of power for the powerless arises from the fact that persuasiveness depends less on the power of the promoter than on the power of the model. The power of a model that is taken seriously is that, by being taken seriously, it sets the framework of debate. The model monger has succeeded in putting on the table the terms of debate – the terms in the model. Moreover, she can insist that they are not terms of her creation – they have an existence and authority that are independent of her constituency.[8] The model is the product of a cross-constituency consensus in another polity, or so it is said by the skilful model monger. As we saw in Chapter 20, NGOs that can pull the right model from their top drawer are particularly likely to enrol the support of mass publics and the media for the model when they can also draw on the power of a major disaster.

Such claims can be disingenuous. The most gifted model mongers will be strategic model misrepresenters: 'When they tried this in country A, they found that feature X was essential for the

---

8 'The very activity of institution-building, if visible as such, could thus easily end up in the hyper-rationality trap' (Elster) of 'willing what cannot be willed'. It cannot be willed because if it is seen as being willed rather than 'inherited' or 'replicated', it will be more controversial and less binding than if it is seen as a legacy or imitation (Offe 1992: 25).

program to work'. The model misrepresenter gambles on no one bothering to check that feature X was even a part of the program in faraway country A. Model misrepresentation occurs unintentionally as well. One nation models another's food safety laws when they are not food safety laws at all but non-tariff barriers to competitive foods from other nations (disguised as food safety laws). Modellers routinely misunderstand and misrepresent what they are modelling.

There is power in the choice within the model of the central issues, in what is left off the agenda by the model (Lukes 1974) and in the terms of its discourse (Clegg 1989). There is power in what is said, what is unsaid and how the saying is framed. There is power in framing whether rape is a problem of penal law, of sex education, of family counselling, of oppression of women, or of protecting women as the property of men (Smart 1989; Naffine 1985). The model can seduce wider audiences than the reformers can capture without the model, because of properties of the model. These wider audiences are the model misers and the model modernizers who we will now discuss. We will see that model misers and modernizers are persuaded not by the imperatives of solving the problems addressed by the model, but by the virtues of the modelling as modelling.

## Model Misers

Thinking through new ways of doing things is costly in time, money, mental effort and conflict. It is inefficient to reinvent the wheel. This is especially true in less-affluent (or affluent but small) societies where the pool of research resources is tiny. The centre has a comparative advantage over the periphery in developing new models; the periphery a comparative advantage in adapting existing models to local conditions. It may therefore be that periphery businesses in a competitive world economy, just like NGOs in the periphery, will do best to perfect the art of model mongering. While the US and Europe have an interest in enforcing the international intellectual property order of patents, designs, copyright and trademarks (because they own most of them), the periphery has an interest in subverting that order. It is an ironic testimony to the power of modelling that so many developing countries model First World intellectual property law in preference to subverting it.

Model misers are actors who can see that the resources are not available for a research effort to solve a problem from first principles. We might say that model misers are those who are happy to satisfice by rummaging through a rubbish bin full of models that have been known to have been applied to similar problems elsewhere (Cohen et al. 1972). But this characterization paints too negative a picture of the advantages of modelling. Model-following balances the advantage of debugging against the disadvantage of less-than-perfect fit to local conditions. Some solutions to a problem will entail defects so glaring once implementation begins that the solution will be abandoned as soon as these glaring problems are brought to light. While in retrospect the defects are agreed by everyone to be glaring, they were not so in prospect. Such solutions rarely survive as models, and the modeller has the advantage of avoiding them. For the creator, they are unavoidable. Any solution to a problem is likely to entail some defects that are universally agreed to be defects but that can be readily debugged with a little experience. Received models have the advantage of having been cleared of these obvious bugs. This does not mean that they will not contain features that are bugs to one constituency but things of beauty to others. Nevertheless, an undoubted advantage of buying rather than writing a computer program is that it is debugged, independent of the judgment of how well-designed the program is for any given purpose. Model misers are not only miserly on the costs of creation but on the costs of debugging (or the costs of falling into the traps hidden in a program that has not been debugged).

Modelling is efficient in many contexts. But model misers risk becoming model morons when they attempt transplantation without local adaptation. Debugging removes the glaring bugs that are uncontroversially bad in any context. But new contexts breed new bugs. For organizations or nations to be efficient they do not have to invest in research to build new models, but they must invest both in model search and in model development to make sure their models are adapted in the light of local understanding.

In the modern world system, the rewards of being a model miser are increasing. In previous centuries, an emulator could scan only a limited horizon for ideas. Twentieth-century communications have expanded those horizons. The possibilities for efficient search for good ideas to copy have increased enormously, especially with the advent of the Internet. It follows that the advantage of inventive societies over imitative societies is shrinking. Indeed, societies that spend most of their R&D on R of their own ideas may do poorly in comparison to societies that spend a high proportion on the D of others' ideas.

Good public policy analysis and good strategic decision-making in business is not the art of muddling through, as Braybrooke and Lindblom (1970) would have us believe. It is the art of modelling through. The effective policy-maker does not allow herself to be surrounded by a muddle; she is surrounded by an information system about the problem and about models that have been applied elsewhere to analyzing and solving such problems.[9]

It is true that model morons are common. The ubiquity of model morons is explained by the seductive exaggerations of model missionaries who are insensitive to cultural difference, and the dollar appeal of model mercenaries. Furthermore, we will see in the next section that the identitive appeal (Etzioni 1965) which grips model modernizers can also readily account for the adoption of patently ineffective models.

## Model Modernizers

Models are adopted when they appeal to identities that we hold dear. An identity that is particularly crucial in this regard is that of being successful, modern, civilized, advanced. The periphery models the centre in the world system partly because of this pursuit of modernity in identity (or postmodernity, for the truly avant-garde). However grudgingly, and often very grudgingly, the centre is recognized as more 'advanced' or 'sophisticated' than the periphery, and so the periphery seeks to model the symbols of progress. Modernity in these cases leads modernization rather than being its byproduct.

This process is not simply a matter of model envy. It is more fundamentally a matter of legitimacy. Meyer and Rowan (1977) have argued that the formal structures of many organizations in the modern world reflect the myths of their institutional environments instead of the demands of their work activities. For example, part of the institutional environment of many organizations has involved the rise of professionalized economics. This has made it useful for organizations (including public organizations) to employ groups of economists even though no one reads, understands or believes their analyses. What the econometrician delivers is not

---

9 Hugh Stretton has been a prominent advocate of this strategy in Australia. He suggests a National Research Bureau to assemble exemplary policy solutions to critical problems from around the globe.

efficiency but legitimation of the organization's plans in the eyes of investors, customers and even insiders. Thus, Meyer and Rowan (1977: 352) hypothesize: 'Organizations that incorporate societally legitimated rationalized elements in their formal structures maximize their legitimacy and increase their resources and survival capacities'. We are asserting here that in the periphery, much of this legitimation is more colonial than societal; organizations in the periphery (including states) maximize their legitimacy by demonstrating that they have incorporated the most advanced First World models into their regulatory structures.

Meyer and Rowan (1977: 356) further suggest that, to thrive, organizations must not only conform to myths that are crucial to legitimacy but must also maintain the appearance that the myths actually work. Hence, the perceived efficacy of the modelling is reproduced even when it is not in fact efficacious. Modelling connected to sustaining organizational legitimacy is especially pervasive and tenacious. If modelling Japanese quality circles and ISO 9000 standards on continuous improvement of quality were only a matter of attempting to improve efficiency by seeking out efficient organizations and learning from them, then we would still have a lot of modelling of Japan. But we have much more modelling than this, because modelling legitimates management as committed to quality and as up-to-date, even if the Japanese quality circles do not work. If they don't work, there are reasons to pretend that they do, thereby encouraging other quality-conscious, up-to-date but unfortunate organizations into the ranks of the model morons.

One of the things the modelling of these bases of legitimacy does is to tie actors together, effecting mutual reinforcement, in global regulatory webs. As Boli (1999: 292) puts it:

> IGOs [international governmental organizations] gain legitimacy by incorporating INGO [international non-government organization] knowledge and views in their reports and policy proposals, because INGOs represent informed 'world public opinion' and are buttressed by the ultimate sovereignty that inheres in their individual members as world citizens. INGOs enhance their prestige by collaborating with the IGOs that are formally responsible for the domains in question, thereby improving their chances of exercising greater influence in future policy debates.

In a federal system, reform lobbyists will identify some states, or some legislators within some states, as attached to the identity of being 'progressive' or a pace-setter. For such targets, the lobbying pitch might be: 'Sweden has been the first state in Europe to enact this model; you should be the one to take the lead here'. Other states will be conservative but nevertheless will be concerned to avoid the stigma of being backward. For these targets, model mongers will concentrate scarce resources on models mostly adopted elsewhere: 'Most governments in the Western world are moving toward this reform; within a decade we expect all will be doing so'. In short, model mongers see the domino theory not as a matter of structural explanation, but as an effect they seek to cause through purposive lobbying action. In seeking to make the dominos fall, the appeal of legitimacy and modernity are among model mongers' most powerful weapons.

After an interview with Tunisia's chief trade negotiator, we were struggling to understand why she was so enthusiastic about getting her country to comply with TRIPS when it seemed to involve greater costs than benefits to the Tunisian economy. Then it became clear she was a model modernizer. She wanted Tunisia to be a legitimate player of the liberalization game. At all points in history there is a kind of national identity, the cultivation of which maximizes the global conferral of legitimacy – in 1999 a neo-liberal identity. We can understand the following comment of Davies (1997: 429) about a fourteenth-century royal marriage to form a union of Poland and Lithuania in the same model modernizer terms we applied to contemporary Tunisia: 'Lithuania, still ruled by a pagan elite and anxious about the rise of neighbouring Moscow, was looking for an entrée into the mainstream of Christendom'.

## The Dynamics of Oppositional Models

While there have been tendencies for North Atlantic, particularly Anglophone, models to progressively increase their sway, important countercurrents exist. To understand how this is possible, consider the school as a system that dispenses extremely potent rewards for modelling. Yet the school is also a competitive institution, and in a competitive institution there will be those who are defined as failures. Cohen (1955) pointed out that those who fail in the status system of the school have a status problem and are in the market for a solution. One solution is what Cohen calls 'reaction formation', wherein a delinquent subculture creates a status system with values which are the exact opposite of those of the school – immediate impulse gratification instead of impulse control, contempt instead of respect for property and authority, violence instead of control of aggression. For children who fail in the status system of the school, the inverted status system of the delinquent subculture supplies them with status criteria on which they are guaranteed success. Their status problem is solved, at least for a time.

In centre–periphery modelling in the world system we can see many examples of reaction formation, or what psychological theorists call reactance (Brehm & Brehm 1981). Iran is a clear example, with a sharp anti-US turn after the fall of the Shah and the associated resurgence of Islamic regulatory models internationally (such as alcohol prohibitionism). More important cases were the turn of Protestant nations away from Rome with the Reformation and the reaction of Eastern Europe against communism. It follows that a dialectical imagination is required to understand the patterning of modelling. We must abandon linear thinking about A causing B, in favour of finding the seeds of the future inside the contradictions that shape the present (Morgan 1986: 233–72). The modelling of Eastern European subservience accomplished by Moscow in Hungary (1956) and Czechoslovakia (1968) contained the seeds of the reactive modelling of the 1989 revolutions and the subsequent scramble to adopt Western business regulatory models.

Consider the application of the dialectics of modelling to the oppression of women. Before considering reactive modelling, we will diagnose patriarchal models. These are reproduced by modelling, literally so, in the case of fashion magazines. Women who spurn the models will not be rewarded by male suitors or by the admiration of female peers who are slaves to fashion. They may even jeopardize conventional careers in business and the professions. These micro-processes of modelling reproduce the structures of cosmetic, fashion, film and advertising industries that appeal to success against the yardsticks of patriarchal models. The economic interests of model mercenaries in these industries are important to understanding the reproduction of patriarchy, as are those of model misers in periphery industries who find it efficient to mimic Paris and New York. But so are model missionaries (e.g. Women Who Want to be Women, the US Catholic women at the 1995 Beijing Conference on Women). Moreover, model mongers among writers for women's magazines continually speculate in the market for reconstructing new models of an enduring female identity.

All this makes reaction formation difficult to sustain. Yet one of the blessings of urban life is that it can sustain communities of oppositional influence. This is also one of the blessings of universities, which have been incubators of reaction formation against patriarchal models in so many countries. Furthermore, institutions which seek to segregate those who subscribe to oppositional models – prisons, mental institutions, reformatories for wayward children, streaming in schools, ghettos, interdisciplinary departments within universities – can actually enhance the subcultural vitality of reaction formation (Scheff 1966). Epistemic communities of the excluded are the incubus of regulatory models for asserting the claims of the excluded: feminist epistemic communities develop affirmative action and equal employment opportunity models and lobby for them through ILO, the WTO and the World Bank.

Once oppositional models have currency, they become a resource for drawing out contradictions in the identities propagated by majoritarian models. Hence, even though a feminist identity may have very circumscribed support in a society, the national identity that 'we are a society that values equality of opportunity' might have wide support. Feminists can then create openings for model mongering by highlighting contradictions between patriarchy and equality of opportunity. Interstices within patriarchy can be prised open. Feminists can put powerful actors on the spot and force them to choose between their egalitarian and patriarchal identities. And they can mobilize disapproval first against shocking instances of denying the ideal of equality of opportunity, and later against more subtle manifestations of patriarchy.

Since modelling is not only about the pursuit of interests but also about the sustaining of identities, weaker interests can prevail against domination by bringing on an identity crisis. Ideas are important when new models are synthesized to resolve the identity crisis. Intellectuals can be influential not only as model mongers but also as synthesizers who, observing the reactions to a range of models advanced by others, reconcile the contradictions among acceptable and unacceptable identities.

### Capacity and Outcome

Once structurally weak model mongers succeed in creating an identity crisis against the hegemony of majoritarian models, they create a minority constituency for their oppositional model. When this minority constituency passes a critical threshold, model mercenaries can put substantial marketing resources behind expanding that minority. For example, Rupert Murdoch, never the model missionary but ever the model mercenary, will invest in the international feminist magazine *New Woman*. Similarly, the Australian Fairfax group bought the American magazine *Ms*.

Thus, while it is true that models emanating from and serving the interests of the powerful are most likely to be copied, modelling can be effectively harnessed by the powerless. Because the powerful often see their interests as simply maintaining the status quo their power has shaped, they are vulnerable to model mongering in the political system (even when their own success is based on model mongering in the economic system). If a conservative elite does not want to put new models on the table, and if the strategic advantage rests with the actor who chooses the model that sets the terms of a reform debate (especially in the wake of a disaster or crisis), then powerless model mongers can reverse the disadvantage which would otherwise be their lot. This is especially true when the powerless realize that battles over models are not just battles won and lost in terms of economic interests (if this were true, the stronger interests would always prevail), but are also battles over identities. The mass media are a resource, since identities that appeal to mass publics generally sell more advertising than identities that appeal to elites. The most economically powerful TNC can find it difficult to compete with a weaker public interest group in a contest for the high moral ground of the identitive power of the 'national interest'. In such a battle for models that satisfy cherished identities, the very visibility of the international fiscal power of the TNC can be a drawback in media messages to a disempowered demos. Moreover, we have seen that weak actors can play a game of ju-jitsu, using against the power structure the identitive power of extant models supported by the power structure. This is the game of prising open interstices within social structures by drawing out contradictions between the identities sustained by different majoritarian models.

Here we have a concrete illustration of why what Hindess (1982) calls 'capacity-outcome' approaches to understanding struggles are misguided. A capacity-outcome approach assumes that all one need do to determine the likely outcome of struggles is identify the resources or capacities available to the conflicting interests; the outcome of the struggle can then be read in an *a priori* fashion. We have seen that the effectiveness of the model monger depends less on the power of the promoter than on the power of the model. Moreover, we have seen that the model monger can use scarce resources efficiently by mongering among many (losing) models until a model is selected that uses identitive power to catch the powerful adversary off-balance. Then all the limited resources of the model monger are momentarily thrown into a feat of political ju-jitsu that flips the off-balance adversary.

Models, we have seen, are empowering. Although the data in this book show that economically powerful actors have a greater capacity to make models work for them, they do not need to model through, and they are typically too conservative to gamble with the risks that political model mongering poses to a status quo that suits them. A conservative elite installs politicians who refrain from scratching with new models of state intervention until popular itches become unbearable. Though the disenfranchised have less capacity to get their models accepted, model mongering (scratching everywhere until an unbearable itch is inflamed) can be their most efficient path to empowerment.

The powerless also desperately need models to nurture self-efficacy. Powerlessness begets hopelessness and political paralysis. What the powerless need to conquer the psychology of defeatism is models of other powerless actors in similar circumstances in other places prevailing against powerful odds. This, we suspect, is an important part of the answer to why there was a revolution in Rumania in December 1989. At that historical moment, citizens who had been paralyzed in the face of a brutal, seemingly all-powerful regime, threw off their paralysis and found new belief in their self-efficacy inspired by models of the successful struggles waged in other communist countries throughout 1989. The powerful do not need models to convince them of their self-efficacy; the powerless do. Stalin did not need a model; but African-Americans needed Martin Luther King and Rumania needed Poland, China, Hungary, East Germany, Czechoslovakia and Bulgaria.

## Using the Concepts for Micro–Macro Synthesis

A case has been made for why a number of world system structural variables and processual modelling variables are crucial to understanding how the world acquired its present institutional shape. How do we put all these variables together in an integrated explanation? Useful tools should be used in different ways to solve different problems. In our conclusion, we will argue that sustained world-system empirical work is crucial to elaborate different integrated theories appropriate to each crucial aspect of the system. In this section, we illustrate integrated explanation with a phenomenon for which we have already laid explanatory foundations – the impact of the emergence of an international consumer movement. Figure 25.1 summarizes this endeavour.

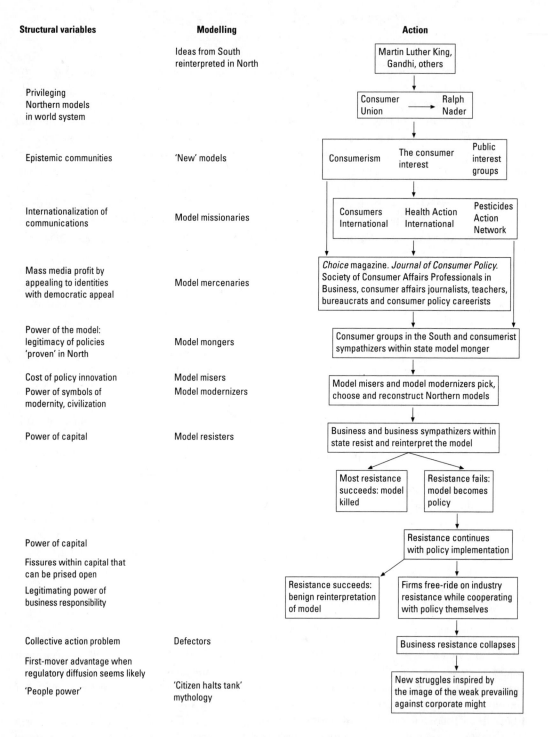

**FIGURE 25.1**  Integrated explanation of the importance of modelling to consumer protection regulation in an emerging world system

On the left side of Figure 25.1 are structural variables that enable the political action on the right side. The modelling variables in the centre conceptualize this action. The following paragraphs put some flesh on the bones of the explanation in Figure 25.1.

The explanation is processually integrated in that it starts with initiatives of model missionaries that are exploited by mercenaries, brokered by model mongers, then adopted by misers and modernizers as contradictions fracture the collective strength of business resistance.

The explanation begins with individual actors and ends with a transformed world system. First, a number of individuals in the US – the most important being Ralph Nader and the founders of Consumers Union – apply extraordinary energy and flair to the construction of a new interest group model. The consumer movement was born with the founding of Consumers Union in 1936 but acquired significant political power only in the late 1960s after drawing inspiration from civil rights struggles in the South. Both the Consumers Union model (based on product-testing and a mass-circulation magazine), and the Nader model (cells of crusaders producing exposés commending regulatory reforms) were quickly imitated in every country in the developed world. By the 1970s, these national consumer organizations had formed international networks in collaboration with existing organizations with bases in developing countries, such as churches and environmental groups. Specific campaign networks, such as the Nestlé boycott and the breast-milk substitute campaign generally, were crucial to building consumer groups in developing countries. Most crucial, however, was Consumers International, which opened regional offices in the South. These are the model missionaries. But there are model mercenaries as well.

The crucial model mongers are to be found within consumer organizations and regulatory agencies. Some of the model mongers within the state have backgrounds in the consumer movement; most are just fellow-travellers. The emphasis is on statutory models for regulating business. Ideas for new regulatory agencies are continually floated. Most are quashed by model resisters in the business community, but some succeed. A flood of new regulatory agencies was created in the Nixon era in the US, generally later in other developed nations, and only in recent years has the process of establishing such agencies begun in most developing countries. Though continually punctuated by setbacks, their growth is internationally cumulative.

Support for consumer rights has become a necessary ingredient to securing an identity as a progressive political leader. The staffers of even conservative politicians seek to polish the progressiveness of their masters' images by having them sponsor consumer protection reforms. But because these are not 'important' issues – unlike the economy, defence, foreign policy and law and order – the staffers are miserly in the time they devote to consumer affairs. They scan the horizon for pre-packaged models, which the consumerist model mongers enthusiastically supply.

All of this politicizing and media lauding of consumerism does not leave business executives untouched. The Society of Consumer Affairs Professionals in Business, a US organization modelled in other countries such as Australia, is a kind of model monger epistemic community, building bridges from the business sector to consumerists. Certainly business successfully resists most reforms initiated by the consumer movement. But everyone in business realizes that an improved sense of corporate responsibility is the price they must pay to sustain legitimacy (Snider 1987). Defection from resistance to consumerist models also occurs in a more insidious way. Once the consumer movement has prised open a fissure in business resistance to regulation by creating a cadre of capitalists with a serious commitment to business responsibility, having that commitment turns out to be a good way of keeping the consumerists, and more importantly the regulators, off one's back. Now business confronts a classic collective-action problem. When the regulators knock on your factory door, the best strategy is to welcome them with open arms: 'These new regulations don't worry our company. Our corporate standards have exceeded these requirements for years because we have always been a company with a responsible...'[10] Executives believe, sometimes wrongly but usually correctly, that these tactics are the best way to divert regulatory and consumerist scrutiny away from themselves to their competitors. The incentive structure facing an individual firm may be to encourage other firms to resist new regulations, to pay industry associations to do so on its behalf, but to refrain from resisting regulation itself. The business temptation to free-ride on the resistance of others is unspoken but profound.

In an empirical project on nursing-home regulation in four nations, Valerie Braithwaite, Diane Gibson, Toni Makkai, David Ermann and John Braithwaite interviewed a number of industry executives who have spoken frankly about this incentive structure. Moreover, we have directly observed its effects: there are individuals observed to speak vigorously against the evils of the regulators and regulations at industry association meetings who welcome them enthusiastically during their firm's regulatory encounters; new regulatory models opposed by the industry association at enactment are supported by over 90 per cent of chief executives in the industry within two years. Aggregated free-riding on industry resistance can cause business resistance to collapse totally in a short space of time.

Moreover, Porter's (1990: 585–8, 647–9) massive study *The Competitive Advantage of Nations* concludes that firms that are early movers in meeting higher regulatory standards gain a competitive advantage in the world system. Similarly, nations that move first to set new standards that will eventually spread internationally give their firms a competitive advantage. Porter gives various examples – Swedish companies dominating technology for the handicapped as a result of early Swedish regulation in that area, US firms gaining markets for anti-pollution technology as a result of the US being a first mover on certain environmental regulations during the 1970s. The lobbying opportunity implied in this analysis has not been lost on the model mongers of the consumer movement (Australian Consumers Association 1991). When the international consumer movement can signal that it is likely to campaign effectively throughout the world for a new standard, a sympathetic national government or firm can be targeted for a campaign of persuasion to seize the first-mover advantage. The consumer movement's tacit appeal to the first-mover is: 'We'll be the model missionaries that will make you a rich model mercenary'. The data in this book show there is more than a grain of empirical validity in Porter's conclusions; strategic modelling by NGOs can make Porter's analysis become more widely true. Strategic NGO support for early movers can help transform a grain of truth into a beachhead for global regulatory transformation. This is particularly so where the model monger captures a powerful actor in a core state, for example a DuPont or a GM.

It is common, however, for an industry to at least partially solve the collective-action problems that risk a tightening regulatory ratchet. A new and interesting strategy is for business to form its own 'public interest' organizations, such as 'Consumers for World Trade' (a coalition of TNCs seeking to use GATT to lower health, safety and environmental standards) and 'Citizens for Sensible Control of Acid Rain' (a front for coal and utility corporations) (Corporate Crime Reporter 1992). Another is to coopt existing citizen groups, such as the international pharmaceu-

---

10 In Braithwaite's various empirical studies on regulatory inspection (e.g. Braithwaite 1984, 1985), he has repeatedly observed that this is a common response of business executives to inspectors and a common way for business to actually think.

tical industry's successful harnessing of gay rights groups to lobby for fewer regulatory hurdles to the marketing of new drugs. Business can also partially solve its collective-action problem even after it has lost a battle over a new regulation at the legislative stage. It can wage an effective war of resistance at the implementation stage. This is a common outcome because, although model mongering consumerists may have the tactical advantage of setting the terms of a legislative debate, they never have the resources to adequately monitor industry capture at the implementation stage. Hence, we get the result first identified by Edelman (1964): diffuse interests get symbolic rewards at the legislative stage, while concentrated interests protect their tangible rewards at the implementation stage.

Even the symbolic victories are important, however, in sustaining an international momentum for citizen empowerment. When a citizen appears to stop a tank in view of television cameras, it is an inspirational victory for people-power. In truth, it probably involves a mythological construction of people-power in one of two ways: either the tank stopped because there were other ways of crushing the citizen without being seen to do so on television, or it stopped because its commander was already a defector to the citizen's cause. Models of empowerment are the crucial ingredient for continuing the cycle of struggle for people-power, whether the slaying of the corporate dragon by the plucky consumerist is symbolic or real.[11]

Figure 25.1 is therefore a model of how to bring together (1) an analysis of structures – the internationalization of communications, the power and legitimacy of First World models, the power of capital and the structure of collective action problems in competitive markets; (2) an analysis of strategic modelling; (3) a view of how cumulative changes of major import can spread rapidly throughout the world, thereby constituting a world system; and (4) a view of how effective political action can constitute weak individuals as an interest that can wage struggles with some degree of success. Figure 25.1 is a more concrete specification of Figure 23.2, which encompasses an understanding of why the institutional form of the world is the way it is and informs the practice of emancipatory politics from below in such a world. In Chapter 26 we build further in the direction of a political program for citizen sovereignty over global regulation.

## Conclusion

Figure 25.1 is still an unsatisfactorily sketchy illustration of how a modelling analysis can accomplish a sweep of micro–macro synthesis from individual to world system. Other preliminary work suggests that transnational modelling has some significance in the rise of many of our most fundamental institutions – the institutions of education (Benavot et al. 1991; Meyer 1980; Meyer et al. 1977), the welfare state (Collier & Messick 1975)[12] and indeed the model of a centralized state

---

11 Boulding's (1973: 122, 126) is the seminal work on the importance of an optimistic image of a better future to any successful struggle for progress (see also Duncan 1968: 48, 236). The theme is picked up by social cogitative psychologists under the rubric of perceived self-efficacy (Bandura 1986: 390–453).

12 Collier and Messick (1975) juxtapose against a diffusion explanation the structural explanation that adoption of social security is a function of modernization. According to the structural analysis, social security policies should not be implemented until certain levels of modernization are reached: 'If a pattern of diffusion is present in which countries tend to imitate other countries that are at higher levels of modernization, this should be reflected in a tendency for each successive adopter to adopt at a progressively lower level of modernization' (1975: 1308). This indeed is what is found – a fairly strong tendency for later adopters to be less modernized at the time of adoption.

itself as a monopolist of force enabling commerce to flourish within pacified spaces (Trevelyan 1985; Garraty & Gay 1981), not to mention the spread of the world's major religions. Modelling seems important in the most significant political changes that have occurred in our lifetime, such as the falling communist dominos, as well as the most important economic changes of our lifetime, such as the new regulatory agencies of the 1970s, the deregulatory shifts of the 1980s, OPEC as an outcome of the modelling of the Algerian and Libyan oil nationalizations in the early 1970s by 'virtually every other producer in the mid East, Africa, Asia and Latin America' (Kobrin 1985: 26) and the privatizations of the 1990s.

Unfortunately, the wide empirical sweep of this study provides no more than the kind of starting sketch in Figure 25.1 and an articulation of such sketches to the micro–macro explanatory frameworks of Chapter 23 and the normative frameworks for global politics of the next. What is also needed is more detailed empiricism to elaborate (Vaughan 1992) starting sketches like Figure 25.1. Unfortunately, few social scientists are interested in understanding our rapidly changing world system as something shaped by human imaginings. Rather, economists understand it as shaped by demand and supply, sociologists look backward to a 'US society' or a 'Thai society' structurally determined by the push of a mute past. Yet only the pull of a humanly articulated future enables the possibility of emancipatory politics. Only the futures once formulated in forgotten models can allow us to understand our present. This means attending to model-making voices from the past that have been rendered mute by our science.

Voices belong to actors, individual and collective. The disciplinary abstractions of sociology and economics tend to be non-actors – US society, the ruling class, women as a group, the market, new technology (Hindess 1987). The trade union model monger is a more useful abstraction than the working class, first because it acts and second because its action is not dependent on a circumscribed type of institutional oxygen, such as social movement politics. Model mongers act in political parties, professions, courts, bureaucracies, the military and the Church.

We have attempted to show that modelling can link structural analysis to both a processual account of the constitution of a world system and to a practical politics of empowerment within that emerging system. Models of successful struggle help the structurally weak to imagine and believe in the possibility of emancipatory collective action. Model missionaries are the actors who inspire this self-efficacy. Model mercenaries cash in on it. But the key players in transformative politics are the model mongers – pragmatic, empirical practitioners of experimental politics. When the structural reality is that the odds of the weak defeating the strong are a hundred to one, the weak need advocates with a hundred agendas.

Those with little to lose can take the risks of setting a hundred agendas running. For those who have entrenched power, it is foolish (or brave, in the case of a model monger like Gorbachev) to start a hundred agendas, any one of which could unseat them if it ran out of control. The vaster the organizational empires controlled by the powerful, the more profound their collective-action problems, the more fissures that can be prised open to turn part of the empire against itself. Strength engenders specific weaknesses that can be exploited by the strategy of model mongering. This is a modelling account of how and why the world is regularly transformed.

In the increasingly networked world of the new information order, the rate and international pervasiveness of these regular transformations will increase. The powerful may be less able to control the future of the world when the future they want is the present. Model mongers hold the future in their hands, though they have a hundred different views of what that future might be.

If change is dialectical rather than linear and if agenda-setting roulette is a key to that change, then we cannot predict or plan the future. But by modelling the process of modelling, we might understand it, steer it and imagine means of purposive struggle to bring the future under more democratic control. One way of constituting the regulatory orders of the future is through choosing principles, principles that carry forward our ideas and identities, clothing those principles in rules and diffusing all this through modelling. This is a choice that we have, perhaps the only one, in the face of the hegemonic structures that exist in the domains we have discussed.

A social science of modelling supplies some conceptual tools to meet these challenges. Modelling turned out to be more consistently important than we expected in our empirical findings on the globalization of regulation, as did military and economic hegemony of an old-fashioned sort. The intellectual property story in Chapter 7, for example, fits moderately well a crude instrumentalist Marxist explanation. Indeed, in many of our case studies, political power does come from the barrel of a gun or the vault of a bank.

What our micro–macro method reveals little support for is a supposedly more sophisticated structuralist Marxist explanation which subordinates purposive action to the reproduction of a systemic inevitability. Nor does our analysis find appeal in postmodernism, because we find the gun and the bank to be forces of domination that refer to a concrete external reality, not just words that point to other words in the construction of a social reality. Like Adam Smith (1776), our empirical findings are that purposive conspiracies by business actors with the resources to enact change are common in shaping regulatory change globally. Equally, we find that purposive model mongering by NGOs to exploit fissures between powerful states and corporations can also shape global change, but against the odds. In chapter after chapter we find dramatic regulatory change during the last half-century in which neither the Bretton-Woods capitalism nor the state socialism that dominated the world mid-century are reproduced or survive. How can ordinary citizens engage democratically with a world of real conspiracies against them by powerful states and TNCs, real resistance and real global change? That is the challenge we take up in the next chapter.

## CHAPTER 26

# A Political Program for Sovereignty over Global Regulation

## *The Three Sovereignties*

National sovereignty is a sixteenth-century idea whose invention is normally attributed to Jean Bodin (1576). It was consolidated as a reality at the Treaty of Westphalia of 1648 that ended the Thirty Years War. A state system was created at the expense of weakening the power of the Holy Roman empire and the house of Habsburg. Westphalia marked the most decisive shift in the locus of control over citizens from the domination by the Church and empires to domination by nation-states. The diffuseness of the Habsburg empire and the limited territorial concentration of city-states could no longer survive artillery warfare that required larger professionalized armies and navies, capital-intensive supply that demanded centralized, orderly administration, capital accounting and ultimately a rolling national debt (see Chapter 9; Mann 1986: 440–55).

At Westphalia, national sovereignty became not only crucial to surviving war, but the key idea for preventing war. National sovereignty became the cornerstone of international law. Nations being sovereign meant that other states were forbidden to make war against them in order to interfere in their internal affairs, especially their religion. Initially, however, this was only a European state system which applied only to Christian states.

A new conception of sovereignty appeared soon after the Peace of Westphalia with calls during England's Puritan Revolution for parliamentary sovereignty. Oliver Cromwell did not deliver this, but it became an incipient reality of the Restoration. From the late seventeenth century, the sovereignty of the crown was progressively eroded in favour of parliamentary sovereignty. It was not until the nineteenth century that parliamentary sovereignty had much international currency beyond England and its colonies. Dicey (1959), following the lead of Blackstone's *Commentaries* (1978), was the pre-eminent articulator of the English model of the sovereignty of an elected legislature, that spread to more and more former kingdoms, chiefdoms and other despotic regimes from the late nineteenth century. The number of states under the sovereignty of an elected legislature rose in three surges – before the First World War (an increase from eight in 1850 to nineteen in 1914: Mann 1993: 766–7), after the Second World War (Japan, Germany, Italy and some of the states they had conquered) and after 1980 (increasing from twenty-eight in 1981 to fifty-three in 1995) (LeDuc, Niemi & Norris 1996: 9).

The new states of Africa no sooner secured national sovereignty against colonial domination, then parliamentary sovereignty, before they began to lose it to globalization – to the sovereignty of other states' markets and other actors' regulatory standards. In none of the processes of globalization of regulation we have described have African states been among the central actors, not at least since Ancient Egypt and Carthage. Less integrated into the world economy, African states are at the same time less influential in it and less influenced by it. Yet many of the global regimes, such as that on food standards, vitally affect their interests and remove sovereignty from, for example, a parliament in Tunis to a committee dominated by agribusiness in Rome. When Rome sacks Carthage's granaries today, its weapon is a committee that could not be halted at the Mediterranean by the might of a million militarized elephants. While the decline of national sovereignty and the sovereignty of national parliaments is inevitable in the face of the processes of globalization documented in this book, this is not inevitable in respect of our third conception of sovereignty, the sovereignty of the people.

Like the other two sovereignties, the expression 'the sovereignty of the people' became influential through the republican writings of the seventeenth century. Rousseau (1968) was the most forceful articulator of the view that sovereignty resides in the people and ought to stay there. John Locke (1963: 413, 477) was the most influential articulator of the view that 'the *Community* perpetually retains a SupreAm Power' over its prince or legislature. Of course, the underlying ideal is as old as the republican tradition itself, with origins in Ancient Greece and Rome, revitalized by northern Italian states during the Renaissance (e.g. Marsillio of Padua in *Defensor Pacis* (Procacci 1970: 42), spreading to the Dutch provinces (Grotius, Spinoza) and throughout the West until the ideal of a sovereign people reached its practical zenith under Jefferson and for a few more decades in the US, the world described by Tocqueville (1835/1969). By the late nineteenth century throughout the West, however, democratic movements were articulated less in terms of the sovereignty of the people, and more in terms of influencing parliamentary sovereignty by enfranchising the propertyless and women.

The compromise of national sovereignty and parliamentary sovereignty that progressively enfranchised the propertyless had the support of *haute finance* – notably the Rothschilds and J.P. Morgan – which accumulated an awesome sway in the last third of the nineteenth and the first third of the twentieth centuries (Chapters 3, 4; Polanyi 1957: 10). The European democratic constitutional transformations of the mid nineteenth century had the support of *haute finance*. The Rothschilds were a Jewish diaspora subject to no nation's sovereignty, more powerful than nations in most important senses. Their wealth depended on peaceful trade between great economic powers that were not racked by internal revolution. They were happy to fund localized wars to crush states of minor trading significance while they underwrote a peace among the Great Powers that endured for a century, from Napoleon to 1914: 'The Pax Britannia held its sway sometimes by the ominous poise of heavy ship's cannon, but more frequently it prevailed by the timely pull of a thread in the international monetary network' (Polanyi 1957: 14). National sovereignty and parliamentary sovereignty were purchased at the price of republican sovereignty of the people, which became progressively more subservient to finance capital.

Still, parliamentary sovereignty with peace and prosperity was not such a bad deal. The further accomplishment of *haute finance* for humanity during its nineteenth-century reign was to secure a limited rule of international law. The objectives of *haute finance* were not humanitarian; they were to guarantee the peaceful continuance of business during war. The most remarkable accomplishment was to secure, from 1815 until the decimation of the Rothschilds in Hitler's gas chambers,[1] an end

---

1 Actually, most continental Rothschilds managed to flee the gas chambers while leaving much of their wealth behind (and by one eyewitness account a Rothschild who was caught was spared the gas chamber, being singled out for the special treatment of being thrown alive into the oven).

to the confiscation of the private property of enemy subjects (Polanyi 1957: 16). The way all the major powers would allow enemy ships laden with valuable cargo to leave ports from the Crimean War to the First World War is historically astounding. States came to see it as unthinkable to renege on loans to banks domiciled in enemy territory. The habits of taking international law seriously had many side benefits in protecting soldiers, civilians and prisoners with more humane rules of war which states regularly honoured to their immediate disadvantage.

At the same time as they were securing the sovereignty of states and a parliamentary sovereignty of peaceful, tolerant, democratic great powers, *haute finance* was laying the foundations for the progressive destruction of the sovereignty of citizens by the securitization and corporatization of the world (Chapter 9) and by its contractualization (Chapter 7). The domination of princes was replaced by the chains of oppressive contracts which citizens had no choice but to sign on terms dictated by corporate power.

Organizing labour into a force within parliaments and as a countervailing force to business in negotiating contracts in the labour market became the central democratic imperative. After the Russian revolution, socialist political practice did not take the ideal of the sovereignty of the people seriously, and crushed parliamentary sovereignty in favour of the sovereignty of one party. The social democratic wing of the labour movement, for its part, settled for corporatism under an impoverished parliamentary sovereignty that discounted sovereignty of the people. As long as social democratic parties sometimes won elections and trade unions were granted privileged status alongside business at economic policy negotiating tables, the corporatist social democrats were satisfied. Like the liberal parliamentary sovereignty guaranteed by *haute finance*, the welfare state parliamentary sovereignty of social democratic politics was not such a bad deal, especially at its zenith in Scandinavia. The comfort, health and security of ordinary people were greatly improved.

The key idea of the sovereignty of the people is that organized power must be subservient to the power of individual citizens. What the status of being a citizen means is enjoyment of assurance against domination of the free choices of individuals by others, including agents of the state, combined with an opportunity for individuals to have a say in the arrangements that deliver this assurance against their domination. The biggest debates within republicanism, as within socialism, were about how to secure this opportunity for citizens to have a say. Marxists believed a revolutionary workers' party could oversee the withering of the state and the handing of power to citizens who would control the conditions of their own productive activity. Republican thinking took the very different path of considering that assurance against domination was best guaranteed under a rule of law that could not be dominated by any party, however democratic its intentions (Pettit 1997). An entrenched constitution was needed to separate and balance the powers of parliaments, executives and judiciaries in systems that may be federal rather than unitary so as to maximize the assurance of citizens against domination (Braithwaite 1997). This was a long way from the romantic visions of many early democrats (such as the US anti-federalists: Ketcham 1986) and later anarchists of decision-making by town meetings and village courts.

The phenomena discussed in this book – regulatory rules for telecommunications systems that are inherently global, indeed extraterrestrial – are of course utterly beyond the romance of control by town meeting. They are not, however, beyond the republican aspiration of a set of institutional arrangements that provides improved assurance against domination of citizens by concentrations of power, combined with the best feasible mechanisms to give all citizens channels through which they can participate in deliberations over the shape of those arrangements. Under the republican ideal of the sovereignty of the people, national sovereignty and parliamentary sovereignty are best conceived as subordinate sovereignties. They are good things only inso-far as they promote the republican ideal of the freedom as non-domination of citizens (Pettit 1997). National sovereignty as negotiated at the Peace of Westphalia was a good thing from this perspective because of the increase in security of religious freedom it enabled, together with increased security from domination by invading armies. Similarly, the rise of parliamentary sov-ereignty was a good thing from a republican perspective; it gave propertied males the opportunity to influence, through their vote, the voices that would prevail in parliamentary deliberation, which was partly about how to curb the domination of an unelected king.

Yet the national and parliamentary sovereignties delivered by liberalism and social democ-racy were impoverished in terms of the sovereignty of the people. The party sovereignty of com-munism was utterly destructive of it. While communists saw that the greatest threat to the sovereignty of citizens in a corporatized world was no longer the nation-state, their remedy – of a corporatized world controlled by one party – was the greatest tyranny possible.

Those who saw most clearly where the gravest threats to the sovereignty of citizens lay in the twentieth century were the fomenters of the great social movements, actors away from the centre stage of national parliamentary politics, such as Esther Petersen, one of our informants, whom we selected in our dedication of this book. The women's movement and the environment movement have been the most significant in keeping alive the republican ideal of the sovereignty of the people by eschewing the corporatist path of the labour movement. They achieved a high degree of organization while directly engaging ordinary citizens in pluralistic internal debates about how to wage campaigns which were as much against abuse of corporate power as against abuse of state power. They eschewed the chauvinism of national sovereignty in favour of citizen sovereignty by 'thinking globally and acting locally'. The consumer movement has had much less grassroots momentum, but has nevertheless been historically significant. At the time of writing, the con-sumer movement, like the environment movement, has stalled. Yet we will argue that in the con-ditions of a corporatized, contractualized globe, it has a uniquely important role for the future.

Old republicans always wanted to restrain parliamentary sovereignty through Constitu-tional Conventions of elected citizens that would limit parliamentary power to interfere in certain aspects of citizens' lives, that would empower courts to bring the parliament to heel when it defied the constitution so framed. The new republicanism of Ralph Nader's 'public citizens' simi-larly saw representative democracy under conditions of either interest group liberalism or social democratic corporatism as feeble democracy. Their attempts to recover the republican virtues of active citizenship were not oriented to the direct democracy of small-scale communal life, but to active citizenship in Washington, New Delhi and Geneva and to the lobbies of large corporations in New York.

The reality of globalization means that republicans are considering new Constitutional Conventions to discuss how to reassert the sovereignty of citizens in the face of the global erosion of national and parliamentary sovereignty in domains as fundamental as the business regulatory regimes discussed herein. Just as parliamentary sovereignty can reduce freedom as non-domina-tion of the people when it tramples on the people's constitution, so national sovereignty can reduce republican freedom when a global regime would actually be less dominating of most of the world's people than a patchwork of national regimes. For example, one reason why nations gave up their sovereignty over intellectual property law by signing the Trade Related Intellectual Property Rights Agreement (TRIPS) of the GATT Final Act was that they thought that the prospect of a national sovereignty subject to the bilateral domination of US trade sanctions might be a worse form of US domination for their citizens than a multilateral agreement (still dominated by US interests) that was open to some influence by their parliament and incorporated some protection against bilateral trade retaliation. In some cases they may have been wrong, in other cases right. But the principle is clear: if a nation's objective is to secure its citizens against domination, it can sometimes be better to give up national sovereignty in favour of a global regime with superior assurances of impartial dispute resolution.

## Paradoxes of Sovereignty

If one's view is that national and parliamentary sovereignty ought to be subservient to the sovereignty of the people, there are bound to be paradoxes of sovereignty. In pharmaceuticals regulation, the advent of the European Agency for the Evaluation of Medicinal Products (EMEA) has seen an increase in the transparency of pharmeuticals regulation to European citizens (Chapter 15). The International Conference on Harmonization (ICH) discussed in Chapter 15 is a good example. of the paradox of sovereignty, which is worth repeating at length:

> National consumer groups outside the US and a few other developed countries have virtually no capacity to monitor the highly technical deliberations of their national authorities as they go about the business of pharmaceuticals regulation. An international NGO like Health Action International still has only a very limited capacity to monitor the international deliberations of the ICH. While it gets to listen, it rarely gets to speak and has little influence in the ICH. But national consumer groups actually may have more influence by pooling their resources and their best and most expert people through Health Action International to focus on global fora like the ICH than they can have through national regulators. In a world of increasingly internationalized regulation, focusing weak glimmers of scrutiny from a hundred national consumer groups onto one international forum of decision-making may increase popular sovereignty from nothing to something. An irony for citizen groups of the ICH process is that it occurs much more in the open than national regulatory negotiations. Why? Not to allow citizen sovereignty over the regulatory process, not as a concession to consumer groups demanding accountability. It has been so open and well-documented as a concession to governments who have been complaining because of their exclusion from the process. No claim is made here that NGO networking to link international fora like the ICH back to the people can create a Jeffersonian sovereignty for the modern world. Perhaps it can create a little more sovereignty than the delusion of popular and parliamentary sovereignty that is the status quo of the technically and quantitatively demanding domain of business regulation. Thus, the paradox of sovereignty is that an institution like ICH, that reduces national sovereignty, may increase citizen sovereignty. National sovereignty is certainly a principle we need to problematize.

Many global regimes do increase transparency to citizens. Our case studies demonstrate that transparency is an emergent property of globalization (Chapter 21). Even the institutions which are (rightly) most vilified by NGOs for the inadequacy of their transparency, such as the WTO, have actually enhanced transparency to citizens in important ways. National governments regularly do corrupt, foolish or politically expedient deals with powerful business groups over industry protection that disadvantage consumers in ways the governments manage to keep secret from those adversely affected. The WTO's Trade Policy Review Process reports publicly on such industry protection in a manner that makes it transparent to consumer groups who watch what is going on at the WTO (see Chapter 10). Chinese workers are more likely to find out what is going on with government policies toward abuse of their rights in hearings before the ILO's Freedom of Association Committee in Geneva, than they are in Beijing (Kent 1997). Reporting under various environmental treaties achieves a similar result. The International Organization for Standardization (ISO), through COPOLCO (the ISO Committee on Consumer Policy), has better mechanisms for allowing consumer organizations to contest producer domination of private standard-setting than do most national standard-setting bodies.

Majone (1993: 24) has articulated the paradox of sovereignty in a different way:[2]

> The comparative advantage of EC (and international) regulation lies in large measure in the relative insulation of supranational regulators from the political considerations and pressures which tend to dominate national policy-making. For example, the fact that the EC Commission regulates a large number of firms throughout the Community makes it less likely to be captured by a particular firm or industry than a national regulator.

This observation seems to us correct; it was certainly oft repeated to us by supranational regulators in Brussels and Geneva. Indeed, it was vividly illustrated through the research process itself when the head of one supranational regulator agreed to allow us to attend an international regulatory negotiation in Geneva – until the head of the Australian delegation objected. The governmental founders of GATT believed that governments could not trust themselves with trade policy; they believed that inevitably governments would sell out the sovereignty of their consumers to organized producer interests unless there was globally institutionalized regulation of protectionism. The paradox of sovereignty of GATT, we would agree, is that by nations tying their hands against exercising their sovereign right to buckle under protectionist demands, they enhance the sovereignty of their citizens as consumers. An important qualification arose with the Codex regime for food standards and the ITU regime for telecommunications, where various nations opted to capture chairmanship of the technical committee most relevant to their export industries. Structurally, this means that many committees can be more dominated by export than by consumer protection concerns than would be the case with national regulation.

## Recapturing the Sovereignty of the People

Some leading social theorists (e.g. Habermas 1996: 456) and many sovereign citizens of our time see a world government – the demise of national sovereignty – as the solution to the inevitable globalization of phenomena such as business regulation. The problem with such proposals is more than utter utopianism in the face of the capacity of states with mighty armies and treasuries to defend their sovereign powers. Even if we were to imagine that a world government could be elected with a responsibility for harmonizing policy on vital issues like banking, monetary policy, tax policy and investment, how would the US and other major powers react? They would react as they did when UNCTAD became a more genuinely democratic force for a New International Economic Order (where developing nations could use their superior numbers to win votes). They set up the G-7 to make the major coordinating decisions on the international economic order, shift trade policy to GATT and investment, tax and competition policy to the OECD, and consolidated the G-10 as the dominant forum on banking policy. Meanwhile UNCTAD languished as a talk-shop with dwindling budget and clout. This is the lesson of Chapter 24 on forum-shifting as a fundamental strategy of potent players.

A more promising approach than a new, more democratic decision-making forum is a forum which is a check and balance on all other decision-making fora. This may be a productive

2  The point was made in a slightly different way again in a 1993 Bank of England interview: 'We can't let you, not because we say but because other countries insist. That is, international obligations can give you political backbone to do what you believe you should do anyhow'.

way of thinking about the idea of a Second Assembly of the UN, directly elected by the people of the world (Segall 1990; Held 1995). As a Second Assembly, this proposal lacks the unreality of supplanting the votes of undemocratic states in the existing General Assembly. What it might do is expose undemocratic states to the empowered voices of their people, their oppressed minorities, on the floor of the Second Assembly. A fundamental role of a Second Assembly could be to establish international committees of parliamentarians elected by the people to oversee the work of international organizations like WTO, IMF and ITU and to hear complaints against them by citizen groups. Parliamentary committees could be a window of accountability into the work of global regulatory organizations in the way the European Parliament is an increasingly significant window of accountability into the EC. Committees of the Second Assembly might also have standing to take cases to the International Court of Justice or the proposed International Criminal Court, on behalf of aggrieved individual citizens. These are the kinds of ways it might, instead of supplanting decision-making in the fora of the current state system, be a check and balance on those decisions. A reconfigured republican separation of powers writ globally.

Fundamentally, however, democracy is too fragile to be guaranteed by any single or second global forum. The fabric of a rich globalizing democracy, as we saw in Chapter 23, is a plural web of dialogic influences. A sensible way to view a Second Assembly is as a useful extra strand in a web of dialogue designed for robustness in the face of the reality that strands snap regularly when pressured by corporate or state power. A Second Assembly could never be as important as having a network of assertive and competent social movements – a women's movement, an environment movement, a human rights movement and so on.

For a variety of reasons, we therefore concur with Mann's (1993: 293) conclusion: 'Just as history has disconfirmed Hobbes' belief that domestic peace and order required a single powerful sovereign, so it disconfirms the notion that international peace and benign order need an imperial hegemon. Rather, it needs shared norms and careful multistate diplomacy'.

In monetary regulation, for example, Chapter 8 showed that the imperium of the US dollar that the world experienced for much of the twentieth century was in fact financially dangerous. A world with a strong dollar, a strong euro and a strong yen would be less precarious because of the possibility for two other strong currencies to be a check against beggar-thy-neighbour management of one currency by those who control it. Hobbesian thinking has indeed been a grave threat to humanity. In the end, the efforts of *haute finance* were not enough to sustain the long peace among the great powers from 1815; once the balance of power shifted from being tripolar to bipolar, the resumption of Great Power warfare in 1914 was assured (Polanyi 1957: 19). And in the aftermath 'Neither the League of Nations nor international *haute finance* outlasted the gold standard; with its disappearance both the organized peace interests of the League and its chief instruments of enforcement – the Rothschilds and Morgans – vanished from politics. The snapping of the golden thread was the signal for world revolution' (Polanyi 1957: 27).

Our data show that military coercion is an important mechanism of the globalization of business regulation and should not be discounted just because we are temporarily in a time when military coercion is declining. While nations control military machines, the hegemony of a single power is dangerous because of the interest subordinated nations have in uniting to counter the hegemon. A bipolar world poses an even more immediate danger; a tripolar or multipolar world, where any unified force can be contested by the threat of a coalition of the combined greater force of other poles, is safer. Mikhail Gorbachev was right to fear a UN whose strings were pulled by a US that alone controlled a kind of Star Wars military capability that others could never counter.

Another politically infeasible idea for the moment, but in this case a desirable one, would be that one day we might see all the citizens of the world elect delegates to a convention to redraft the Charter of the UN. Agenda items could include the creation of a Second Assembly of the UN elected directly by the people of the world. The convention might debate whether treaties negotiated by a majority of states could be void unless ratified by a majority vote of the elected representatives of the Second Assembly. This would increase the assurance that treaties might be in the interests of the majority of the world's people rather than the interests of superpowers and TNCs. It might supplant the sham of national parliaments voting to ratify treaties when they have no prospect of influencing its content (especially once it is at the ratification stage) and no practical way of excluding their people from the effects of the regime. Yet it would respect the reality that only executive governments can make treaties work, so it should be executive governments (democratic and undemocratic) that negotiate their contents.

A global peoples' convention might constitutionalize the treaty-writing process in other ways as well, for example a treaty on treaties that required the kind of tripartism in meetings on the enforcement and revision of treaties discussed in Chapters 11 and 24. This was one response we proposed to the forum-shifting problem. Another might be a constitution for the UN that tied members' hands to negotiate treaties of a certain type under the auspices of a specific UN agency and other types of treaties under the auspices of other specific agencies. If it were an environmental treaty, for example, a new UN constitution might require that a secretariat would have to be set up within the UN Environment Program. Under such a proposal there would be no delay due to argument over whether the secretariat should be located there or somewhere else, or as a result of a key player pulling out to start a new process under other auspices. The parties would be required to argue it out at the UNEP until they reached an accommodation, or failed to do so. Of course, it is precisely such a prospect – a threat to US and European domination of the fora where each treaty will be framed – which might cause the US and Europe to thwart a more accountably republican world order.

## What Citizens Want and What Citizens Get

In most of the domains of regulation discussed in this book, ordinary citizens want higher standards of regulatory protection than they get. They want a level of assurance of the quality and purity of their food and drugs that extant regulation does not deliver, especially if they live in a developing country. They want tougher protection of the environment (Papadakis 1993) and stronger consumer protection standards (Braithwaite 1988). International Social Survey Program (ISSP) surveys on the role of government for the US, the UK, Australia, Ireland and Germany show that many more people want their governments to spend more rather than less on the environment. In all these states there is more than ten times the citizen support for legal regulation of the environment than for industry self-regulation. In many countries, citizens want better security against a nuclear accident (Chapter 13; see also 1993 ISSP Environment Survey). This is not to deny that ordinary citizens also see merit in eliminating unncecessary regulation, though support for this fell somewhat in ISSP polls between 1985 and 1990 in the US, the UK, Australia, Ireland and Germany. Except in the US, citizen perceptions that business and industry had too much power increased during these years (ISSP). Citizens, especially women, are particularly likely to overwhelmingly agree with opinion statements like 'There should be stronger government control over the activities of multinational companies' and 'Multinational corporations have too much power in Australia' (M. Evans 1995).

When people are not getting the level of regulatory protection they would like, it is commonly because concentrations of power in business and government benefit from withholding it – they benefit from reduced business costs or political pay-offs from others with power and resources. When domination and corruption crushes the regulatory sovereignty of citizens to get the level of security they want, public interest groups are needed to lead campaigns to raise global standards. So the normative argument we want to use is not a simple democratarian one: citizens should get what they want. It is a republican one: citizens should be free from domination and have at their disposal the means to resist domination (Braithwaite & Pettit 1990; Pettit 1997).

Sometimes regulatory standards are lower than citizens want not because of corruption or capture of government by industry, but because economic analysis has persuaded governments that their firms would become less economically competitive to the point where the public interest in saving jobs is greater than the interest in stronger consumer or environmental protection. When this is the case, what is still needed (from a republican perspective) is NGO campaigning to lift regulatory standards globally rather than country by country – so businesses in all economies internalize their externalities, and none increases its market share by making others pay for cleaning up the environment or taking care of injured consumers.

Our view is therefore that because of capture or corruption of states by business, sometimes reinforced by races-to-the-bottom in the world system motivated by the desire to lower regulatory costs, regulatory standards are very often lower than required for the sovereignty of citizens to secure maximum freedom. We are therefore interested to use our data to illuminate how NGOs might activate webs of global influence to transform races-to-the-bottom to global ratcheting-up of standards. This is not a utopian agenda; our data show that, at least with respect to regulation of the environment, safety and financial security, ratcheting-up of standards from a low base is a more dominant dynamic of the late twentieth century than driving them further down (Chapter 21).

None of this is to deny that citizens often misunderstand their own interests – they want higher regulatory protection when they would be better off with less regulation and lower prices. It is simply to say that often we need to make our democracy work better so that citizens have the information to make well-informed trade-offs between the regulatory security they want and the lower prices they want. NGOs are the key to this, because NGOs have better information-gathering and analytic capacities than do individual citizens. Deregulatory economists in business and government underestimate the capacities of consumer organizations to make sophisticated trade-offs between regulatory and economic benefits to citizens. They misread the history as showing that sophisticated economists have been responsible for the major deregulatory accomplishments that have benefited consumers, when Ralph Nader may have been the more influential advocate for globalizing airline deregulation, when it has been NGOs which have led campaigns for most national antitrust laws used in the 1990s to deregulate telecommunications to the benefit of consumers, as they are now campaigning for competition laws in China.

Nor does any of this deny that sometimes higher global regulatory standards are touted by industry and its hired economists and are opposed by NGOs. TRIPS is an example where consumer groups too late and too ineffectively opposed the higher and more costly regulatory standards in TRIPS (see Chapters 7 and 10). The consumer movement was campaigning against the expansion of legal monopoly and in favour of competition. As we saw in the conclusion to Chapter 10, however, TRIPS achieved a positive linkage to the trade regime of an upwards regulatory ratchet, something that has never been accomplished before (Picciotto 1998). The irony is that NGOs seek a positive linkage to the trade regime of an upwards ratchet of environment, labour and consumer protection standards. They defeated the Multilateral Agreement on Investment when demands for positive linkage of such standards were denied. A right to freedom of investment in return for an obligation to meet a continuous improvement code of conduct for TNCs remains a political possibility.

By now it should be clear that there are two major conceptual planks to the consumer movement's global campaigning. One is to ratchet-up regulatory standards where concentrated corporate power has kept those standards lower than undominated analysis and dialogue among citizens reveals to be warranted. The second is to lower prices and increase economic efficiency by championing competition, dismantling monopoly sustained by concentrated corporate power. Together, they offer a regulatory thrust and a deregulatory thrust grounded in a common republican philosophy of the sovereignty of citizens over domination by corporate and state power.

Our normative judgment, grounded in a republican concern for freedom as the non-domination of a sovereign people, is that when NGOs campaign to ratchet-up global regulatory standards, they are very often acting in the public interest defined in this republican way. When NGOs campaign against monopoly, our normative judgment is also that they very often are campaigning to advance freedom as non-domination. Libertarians, although holding with a different view of liberty, might also read NGO activity against monopolies as freedom-advancing. Monopolies, after all, are not just a form of economic inefficiency. As Hayek argues in *The Road to Serfdom*, those who have control over the use of economic resources also control our liberty. Partly because NGOs matter, but also because NGOs quite often succumb to flawed analyses that defeat the discovery and attainment of the public interest, it is important for intellectuals to direct their scholarship at improving NGO analytic capacity. This is one of our objectives.

Crucial to republican democracy is a rich public dialogue about the political choices made by NGOs, critique of their actions and economic analyses, contestability by other NGOs of the right of one NGO to a place at a negotiating table (Ayres & Braithwaite 1992: Ch. 3) and democratic contestability of elected office in NGOs. Many NGOs do not have deep democratic roots, their membership bases being tiny. But even in these cases, their campaigning will get nowhere if they fail to advance policies that enjoy popular support. NGOs which advance causes that most citizens reject tend not to accomplish policy victories; they lose membership and financial viability, and die. A large part of the basis for business power is that business controls the money; a large part of the basis for government power is that government controls the law and the guns; judicial power comes from a professional constituency that demands security of tenure. The only political power NGOs control comes directly from the sovereignty of citizens, thus rendering their power more democratically vulnerable than the power of any other. Occasionally republican romance with the democratic significance of a flourishing civil society occurs, to the neglect of business responsibility and state responsibility. From a republican perspective, however, the deeper malaise is that scholarly endeavour is overwhelmingly directed at informing government policy choices and business choices.

Against this background of justification on why it is important to illuminate how NGOs can campaign to ratchet-up global regulation and how they can campaign to enhance competition globally, let us inquire of our data in these terms. In the next section we consider strategies for intervening in global webs of regulation to ratchet-up standards; in the final section we consider strategies to enhance competition globally.

## Five Strategies for Intervening in Global Webs of Regulation to Ratchet-up Standards in the World System

We have found NGOs to be among the weakest elements in the web of influences that shape business behaviour in global markets. At the same time, we have found that no single player (not even the US or the EC) and no single mechanism ever brings about global regulatory change alone. For success, many players employing many mechanisms must be enrolled. While weak players like NGOs have less resource-based power than other actors, and no military power, at times they can be more resourceful at enrolling many big players than can big players themselves. Skill in enrolling the mass media, as we have seen throughout the book, is common among NGOs because they survive through appealing to citizen identities with mass appeal in the same way that the media must. When NGOs can enrol a credible web of controls through learning how to pull the right strands of that web at the right moment, they can trigger global change – and have done so, as we have seen in cases like Nader's impact on motor vehicle safety regulatory standards or the impact of Greenpeace and other NGOs on whaling. As John Braithwaite said in an address to the Annual Meeting of the Australian Consumers Association in 1996:

> There is a world system dynamic that creates lowest-common-denominator regulation. But there is another kind of world system dynamic that enables highest-common-factor regulation. The intellectual challenge for social movements is to understand the difference between the lowest-common-denominator dynamic and the highest-common-factor dynamic. To learn how to intervene strategically through our lobbying to encourage the latter dynamic and discourage the former.

In this section, we consider five strategies for NGOs to intervene in webs of regulation to ratchet-up standards in the world system:

1   exploiting strategic trade thinking to divide and conquer business;

2   harnessing the management philosophy of continuous improvement;

3   linking Porter's *Competitive Advantage of Nations* analysis to best available technology (BAT) and best available practice (BAP) standards;

4   targeting enforcement on 'gatekeepers' within a web of controls – actors with limited self-interest in rule-breaking, but on whom rule-breakers are dependent;

5   taking framework agreements seriously.

### 1 Exploiting Strategic Trade Thinking to Divide and Conquer Business

The social movement against the slave trade was an instance of the success of this stategy (Chapter 11). Once the social movement had succeeded in getting Britain out of the slave trade, the British state prosecuted a strategic trade interest in coercing other states from supplying slave labour to compete with the British empire's plantation economy. Our most instructive case study is ozone diplomacy, documented in Chapter 12. The strategic trade game involved getting the US to pass legislation that favoured US manufacturers of chlorofluorocarbon (CFC) substitutes. The key victory of the environment movement was in 1977, when a stratospheric ozone amendment was passed to the US *Clean Air Act*. US production of CFCs for aerosols quickly fell by 95 per cent and substitutes were soon on the market. The reason why the US moved on CFCs so many years before the rest of the world was that business opposition was divided. The biggest player, DuPont, was ready to make large profits from cornering the market for CFC substitutes. Once the Reagan administration got over its early hang-ups about environmental deregulation and Anne Gorsuch Burford had been replaced as Administrator of the EPA, green NGOs globally had the US state and US business as allies (along with the UN Environment Program, Canada, the Nordics and Switzerland) in a campaign to convert the EU and then the rest of the world to what became in 1987 the Montreal Protocol.

The Montreal Protocol became one of the most potent and effective global environmental agreements we have seen, because of what Americans call a 'Baptists and bootleggers' coalition (De Sombre 1995; Vogel 1995). Ronald Reagan, leading the pro-regulatory charge at the G-7 summit in Venice, was not the Baptist but the bootlegger, and scruffy green activists were the implausible Baptists. We prefer to use the language of strategic trade: bootleggers can secure a strategic trade advantage in prohibition as a regulatory move, so they join with Baptists who see a public interest in alcohol regulation.

As a more general claim about the way we have found the world system to work, a coalition of NGOs can almost never defeat a coalition of the US, the EC and US and European business. But a coalition of NGOs strong enough to capture the world's media, supported by US business and the US president, can roll European business and the EC. Given that a consensus between North America (Canada usually follows the US) and the EC on business regulation almost always leads to global implementation of that consensus, the key move is to model monger (Chapter 25) on whichever side of the Atlantic is likely to grasp the strategic trade advantage. Of course, the story is more complex than this. Infiltrating the model into a treaty secretariat is important. Capturing non-EC states (like Switzerland and the Nordics in the ozone case), which might see an early-mover advantage in intra-European trade by pre-empting the EC, is also important.

Just as an alliance of a unified social movement and US business can defeat European business, so an alliance of a social movement and European business can defeat US business. Chapter 12 discussed the green victory in Europeanizing the UK environmental management standard as EMAS, and then, with only partial success, seeking to take EMAS principles, against US resistance, into global ISO environmental management standards. This titanic struggle followed the much less painful globalizing of UK quality management standards (as the ISO 9000 series of standards) with support from the consumer movement and ultimately from business, which came to see the advantage of transparency in suppliers' quality management systems. Indeed, the push within ISO to globalize EMAS started with the ISO Committee where the consumer movement is strongly represented, COPOLCO, arguing that ISO 9000 had been good for business and global competitiveness and was one of the most widely influential standards in the history of international standardization. Today, the Canadian consumer movement is cultivating European support within COPOLCO for a global privacy standard, against ferocious opposition from US business and the ICC, which currently seem to be prevailing. Australia is cultivating European support against initial US opposition for both an ISO complaints-handling standard that it argues has increased the competitiveness of Australian business (the strategic trade advantage)[3] and (with Norway) an occupational health and safety management standard.

---

3  One of the authors led the Australian delegation to the 1998 meeting of COPOLCO in Tunis which supported the continuation of a Working Group on Consumer Protection in the Global Market on this matter chaired by Standards Australia.

The prediction of our theory is that not all these campaigns will fail, notwithstanding US opposition. They will not all fail, at least not totally, because the international strategic trade advantages at issue can to a certain degree be exploited within large national markets. For example, one reason why US business has more reason than European business to resist a global complaints-handling standard is that its failure to meet such a standard would be used against it in mass tort litigation which poses greater threats to business survival in the US than in European courts. At the same time, the fact that US business is divisible on this issue is evident in the fact that the greatest business influence within Australia in motivating the Standards Australia Complaints Handling Standard was a US company, American Express. Research commissioned by the Society of Consumer Affairs Professionals in Business, funded by American Express, showed that 90 per cent of consumers who were not satisfied with the way their complaint was handled said they would not deal with that company again. This was hardly a surprise. The more surprising result that alerted Australian business to the prospect of seizing a competitive advantage through this standard was the finding that 83 per cent of complainants who felt the company had done more to fix the complaint than they had expected said that they would buy from the company again (TARP 1995). The strategic trade analysis therefore leads to the prediction that US firms such as American Express, which already meet the standard (indeed in this case have already assisted in the campaign for its introduction in Australia), will be defectors from US business resistance to it.

The environment chapter (Chapter 12) also illustrates the internal divide-and-conquer dynamic within Europe. On acid rain, Germany led the substantial European nitrogen oxide emission reductions of the late 1980s because of 1983 legislation which required German cars to have catalytic converters and because Germany was leading in other emission-reduction technologies. A different kind of strategic trade move was the way Greenpeace obtained German government support for a near-bankrupt East German fridge manufacturer to make its 'green fridge', a technology that then globalized with support from the World Bank to developing-country manufacturers. Yet another was the enactment of the *Foreign Corrupt Practices Act 1977* in the US, followed by two decades of lobbying by US business supported by NGOs (especially Transparency International) and the Big Five accounting firms to get non-US TNCs to play by the same rules. In 1997 an OECD agreement required signatories to enact laws of rather similar effect to the *Foreign Corrupt Practices Act* (Chapter 10).

When we talk to audiences of green activists about the ozone and like cases, they say 'There was no sense in which we were genuinely strategic in securing victory in the US first and then dividing and conquering business in a strategic trade game. We did not trust companies like DuPont. Collaboration with them, let alone Ronald Reagan, was not great'. One of us was involved in a minor way with Friends of the Earth in the early 1980s on the ozone campaign, and can certainly confirm that he had no sense at that time of the strategy articulated here. The point is that NGOs can learn from successful strategies they stumble into. Part of that learning involves contemplating whether, in light of this retrospective understanding, the ozone hole might have been closed earlier had the social movement been more explicitly collaborative with the Reagan administration and the US chemical industry. In the green fridge case, Greenpeace had a more explicit strategy of global and business collaboration.

Strategic trade games do not need to be the conspiracy against consumers that they once were. This was well illustrated in Chapter 18, where we found that the higher vehicle safety standards manufacturers get written into standards when they engineer a safety improvement increasingly tend to be written as a higher performance standard than as a standard that specifies the firm's new technology. This allows competing manufacturers to engineer their own, potentially cheaper, way of meeting the higher safety (or pollution or theft-prevention) standard.

## 2 Harnessing the Management Philosophy of Continuous Improvement

A standard view among consumer and environmental activists (and indeed civil liberties activists on matters like privacy standards) is that voluntary standards are toothless and therefore unimportant. First, they are not toothless, because they are sometimes used in tort cases against business (and business worries more about tort litigation than criminal prosecutions – which are more infrequent and incur lower costs). There has been a degree of competition with some US jurisdictions in effect saying 'come to us to sue foreign corporations because our courts are fast and our juries generous'. Second, toothlessness misses the point of Chapter 23, that compliance globalizes more through webs of dialogue than through webs of coercion, and the lesson of Chapter 25, that it globalizes more through modelling than by legal enforcement. Third, as sketched in Figure 23.1, it is more common for globalization of law (with teeth) to follow globalization of a new standard of business practice than for globalization of a new standard of business practice to follow after a new law demands it. The lead firm that pulls up standards is a more important upward dynamic than a (largely unenforceable) minimum standard to push up the laggards. As we saw with pharmaceuticals in Chapter 15, the level of standards in firms is determined less by the stringency of the local laws where they are operating, than by the stringency of the expectations set by corporate headquarters. Or as Levinson (1996: 435) found: 'In general, differences across plants in their environmental practices seem to be affected more by home-country regulations than host-country regulations'.

Hence, the premise of this second NGO strategy is that working directly with business to change their practices matters. It can matter enormously if we can not only persuade an innovator to lead the pack (like the German green fridge manufacturer) but also persuade the pack that continuous improvement is a good thing (so it has to catch up with the leader).

US business certainly thinks it matters. We note the gigantic effort it mobilized (with partial success) to oppose translating into ISO 14000 standards the continuous improvement philosophy of EMAS. There are no fewer than a thousand people (mostly from business) working on fifty ISO committees concerned with environmental management standards, at the time of writing. Business actors are not so naive as to fail to grasp that an ISO voluntary standard can lead global standards up or down, with major cost implications for them.

Voluntary standards in the ISO 9000 tradition institutionalize the managerial principle of continuous improvement – the idea that product quality, workplace safety or privacy should have better measurable outcomes this year than last year and better outcomes again next year and every subsequent year. Much of the extraordinary power of ISO 9000 in global business arose from the fact that large purchasers (like major corporations or defence departments) could instruct their purchasing divisions to buy only from firms who could guarantee quality through an independent ISO 9000 certification. To the extent that management practice, global voluntary standards, governmental standards and intergovernmental agreements explicitly incorporate the principle of continuous improvement, the global system structurally induces upward rather than downward movement in the global norm.

Chapter 12, in its discussion of the way the NGO–retailer coalition, the Forest Stewardship Council, was beginning to work, considered a peculiar power that could arise from arranging ratchets in series, especially if one is a continuous improvement ratchet:

Local law sets a platform; ISO 14001 requires the honouring and exceeding of that platform; plural coalitions like the Forest Stewardship Council require honouring and improving upon the ISO 14001 platform. The effect of ratchets in series is that whenever the demands of either state law or ISO 14001 or the Forest Stewardship Council or local agreements pursuant to FSC audits go up, the standards for sustainable foresting are driven up. Any one of these four ratchets can drive the system up; all four define a platform which protects regulation from being driven down. It would be fanciful to see such smoothly working ratchets as a reality, but it would be unperceptive to fail to see them as one emerging possibility.

## 3 Linking Porter's Competitive Advantage of Nations Analysis to BAT and BAP

Porter's influential book, *The Competitive Advantage of Nations*, argues that it is not necessarily good business for firms to locate where regulatory costs are lowest. He concludes the contrary, as shown in the following advice based on a considerable amount of empirical analysis of what makes firms internationally competitive:

> Establish norms exceeding the toughest regulatory hurdles or product standards. Some localities (or user industries) will lead in terms of the stringency of product standards, pollution limits, noise guidelines, and the like. Tough regulatory standards are not a hindrance but an opportunity to move early to upgrade products and processes.
>
> Find the localities whose regulations foreshadow those elsewhere. Some regions and cities will typically lead others in terms of their concern with social problems such as safety, environmental quality, and the like. Instead of avoiding such areas, as some companies do, they should be sought out. A firm should define its internal goals as meeting, or exceeding, their standards. An advantage will result as other regions, and ultimately other nations, modify regulations to follow suit.
>
> Firms, like governments, are often prone to see the short-term cost of dealing with tough standards and not their longer-term benefits in terms of innovation. Firms point to foreign rivals without such standards as having a cost advantage. Such thinking is based on an incomplete view of how competitive advantage is created and sustained. Selling poorly performing, unsafe, or environmentally damaging products is not a route to real competitive advantage in sophisticated industry and industry segments, especially in a world where environmental sensitivity and concern for social welfare are rising in all advanced nations. Sophisticated buyers will usually appreciate safer, cleaner, quieter products before governments do. Firms with the skills to produce such products will have an important lever to enter foreign markets, and can often accelerate the process by which foreign regulations are toughened.

Chapter 12 summarizes the considerable evidence that location in states with tougher environmental standards does confer a long-run competitive advantage. Of greater interest to NGO activists is that firms that have upgraded their standards early because they are located in a state that is an early mover to higher standards have an interest in making Porter's prediction come true. They will not get the predicted early-mover advantage unless other states follow the lead of their home state. So the NGO analysis is to model monger among nations that might be attracted to their reformist regulatory model until they find one so convinced of the attractions of the model that it and its firms believe they may get a strategic trade advantage through being first to require it. The NGO should then work with those firms to help them reap that strategic trade advantage by lobbying together for a global standard.

On a Consumers Federation of Australia platform with Ralph Nader, John Braithwaite summarized the strategic advice to NGOs by turning to Nader in the following terms:

How might a sophisticated international consumer movement have responded when Ralph's campaign for compulsory airbags in cars faltered with the election of Ronald Reagan in 1980? Consumers International might have convened a meeting to consider which would be the country best able to marshall political and business support for a compulsory airbags law. International lobbying resources would be put into that country. Imagine that country was Australia. The job of the Australian consumer movement would then have been to go to the manufacturer which had been globally targeted as likely to be sympathetic to their approach. Our job would be to persuade them, following Porter's logic, that 'We are going to help make money for you by campaigning in Australia, and then globally, for mandatory airbag laws'. This multinational would then become an ally in that campaign, in a similar way to that in which the US insurance industry was an ally in Ralph's campaign. Australian consumers would have had to put up with higher prices for a time, but that would have been worth the lives saved, the increased long-term competitiveness of the Australian auto industry and the huge national benefit of the sale of airbag technology to the rest of the world. All of this, it seems to me, would have been true because we knew in the consumer movement that consumers were becoming more safety-conscious and in the medium term would be demanding airbags. Moreover, the auto industry has known the truth of Porter's analysis for some time, witness a Chrysler Plymouth television advertisement I saw in the US in March [1994] which announced that Chrysler was 'ahead of our time' because of 'including all 1998 safety standards now'.

The best way for a globalized NGO to reap a strategic trade advantage for the most innovative firms in a state that collaborates with a Porteresque competitiveness strategy would be to link the strategy to a BAT or BAP form of standard in the German tradition. In Chapter 12 we pointed out that Germany has a very different way of thinking about BAT than does the US (to which BAT means forcing a specific technology in a way that stultifies technological innovation). The German approach to BAT does the reverse, refusing to mandate any specific technology. It fosters innovation by using the BAT to set an outcome standard that the BAT (but not inferior technologies) can meet, and then challenging German industry to come up with a cheaper or better technology for achieving that outcome. When a better technology is invented in another country, German industry is given time to either come up with a more cost-effective technology for matching or beating the outcome it can deliver, or to buy that technology. Usually, German innovation being what it is, industry can manage the former rather than have to accept someone else's technology. Moreover, German clout being what it is, it has been able to convince Europe and much of the rest of the world to adopt its approach to BAT in environmental regulation.

To the extent that other countries take this approach to BAT seriously rather than simply paying lip-service to it, we have a powerful strategy for ratcheting standards up but never down. Whenever any one of the BAT countries invents a better way of achieving a regulatory outcome, a competition is triggered among BAT countries to outperform that technology or buy it from the innovator. The same argument applies to BAP. Following Porter's analysis, this will cause involved states to leave the rest of the world behind, with declining long-run competitiveness when non-BAT states remain committed to static-outcome standards or (worse) standards that force (yesterday's) specific technology.

As attractive as this strategy is for NGOs wanting to ratchet-up standards in a particular area, it is only likely to work when appeal can be made to a nation (such as Germany with the environment regime) confident enough that its firms can match foreign BATs and powerful enough to persuade other states to adopt BAT. But California (Vogel 1995) and Japan can, and to a considerable extent do, play the same game as Germany within North America and Asia respectively. What North America and Asia have not done is commit to BAT and BAP as a continually rising target, settling instead for periodic lifting of fixed-outcome standards. As a result, when they do lift their outcomes, they buy much of their technology from a Europe that has already ratcheted-up to a higher standard.

Note the connections among our first three strategies. Strategic trade divides and conquers by enticing some global business actors into supporting hurdles that others will find difficult to jump. Continuous improvement is the business philosophy which can be used to persuade the rest of the pack to attempt the jump. The more strategic trade and continuous improvement are used, the more it makes sense for business actors to build competitive advantage (or regain competitive advantage lost to strategic trade manoeuvrings) by searching out higher standards of regulation. That is, more upward momentum means more incentive to race ahead of the pack even faster. To the extent this happens, the truer Porter's predictions become and the more benefit a state like Germany can gain from a German-style approach to BAT or BAP. For some kinds of problems, ratcheting-up standards achieves little without ratcheting-up enforcement, which takes us to our fourth strategy.

## 4 Targeting Enforcement on 'Gatekeepers' within a Web of Controls

In any complex web of controls there are many gatekeepers. There are firms that certify other firms as complying with an ISO standard. Then there are accreditation organizations that accredit the certifiers. One nation's accreditation organization will often audit another nation's accreditation organization as part of a process of mutual recognition. Within a TNC there are financial auditors, and auditors from one part of the company who audit auditors from another part, external auditors who audit internal auditors, a board audit committee which oversees their work, governmental companies and securities regulators who monitor both the external auditors and the board, with IOSCO and the Basle Committee on Banking Supervision monitoring governments. An attractive feature of many of these gatekeepers is that they are soft targets for enforcement because, while they have the capacity to prevent rule-breaking, they do not benefit from rule-breaking in the way that those who run the organization do.

Our strategy was well-illustrated by Mitchell's (1994a, 1994b, 1994c) work on the prevention of oil spills at sea (Chapter 12). Treaty obligations on states to prosecute ships that spilt oil were utterly ineffective. What worked was shifting the enforcement target from the ships which benefited from the pollution to builders, insurers and classification societies which did not. Insurers would not insure ships that were not classified, classification societies would not classify ships without segregated ballast tanks and crude oil washing to prevent oil spills, and builders would not be silly enough to build ships which could not be classified or insured. Globally, 98 per cent compliance with IMO requirements to install technologies which dramatically reduced oil discharges at sea, was obtained. The interesting feature in this success story is that enforcement targeting was shifted from ships, which had an economic interest in cheating, to builders, classification societies and insurers whose interest, if any, was in more expensive ships. So compliance was improved by shifting enforcement onto gatekeepers on whom principals were dependent but who had a limited interest in rule-breaking. Where mighty states could not succeed in reducing oil spills at sea, Lloyd's of London could. Another example was the way corruption in the Indonesian customs service was reduced by contracting the customs services to Société Générale de Surveillance (Chapter 20), which operates by setting up thousands of audited gatekeepers across all exporting countries instead of having one corruptible national gateway at the point of import.

NGO imagination about how they can achieve the enforcement end of global regimes tends to be limited to traditional state enforcement. In the global arena, this leads to despair when NGOs realize that many state regulatory authorities are corrupt, uninterested, underresourced, captured or incompetent. The commonest remedy, as we have seen, is to design into the regime a requirement that regulated actors pay for gatekeepers to audit their compliance, and those gatekeepers are monitored in a way that ensures that competence, integrity and diligence are the best way for them to flourish.

## 5 Taking Framework Agreements Seriously

The 1909 Shanghai framework agreement of the International Opium Commission is an example of a vague and platitudinous agreement that, brick by brick over the decades, became an utterly globalized, highly specific, fiercely punitive criminal regime for narcotics (Chapter 15, fn 2). Every chapter of this book has an example.

Most NGO activists are colourful and charming people with limited tolerance for spending long hours, days and years in Geneva sitting around large tables surrounded by punctilious bureaucrats in grey suits. When all the fraught drafting of principles and proposals finishes with a vague and platitudinous agreement, they have been known to go berserk, creating rare spectacles of interest in the dreary cityscape of Geneva. What NGO activists had hoped for was enforceable rules, specific credible commitments from states, well-resourced monitoring mechanisms, trade sanctions for non-compliance. What they got was ever so vague – principles, just principles. Our prescription is for social movement activists to become more tedious, disciplined people who learn to value poring over every word in the Chairman's non-draft of principles.

Our message has been that principles are in fact very important. The globalization of regulation is played out as a contest of principles. Agreements would rarely be made if they started as enforceable bodies of rules. Any precision in the rules would immediately create a veto coalition disadvantaged by that way of framing the rules. The uncertainty implicit in principles concerning a problem (that everyone agrees is a problem) allows everyone to sign on. All hope the regime will not become more specific over time in a way that will hurt their future interests. But since they may not be sure of what those future interests will be (e.g. whether they will more frequently end up as complainants or defendants under the rules), they sign. Indeed, a virtue of a thicker veil of uncertainty is that it 'increases incentives to formulate provisions that are fair or equitable' (Young & Osherenko 1993: 13). Sometimes this causes parties to intentionally thicken the veil of uncertainty initially (e.g. by lengthening the time or the range of issues to which a regime will apply) to ensure that all parties can lock in to mutually acceptable and just foundational principles for a new regime.

In most of our chapters we have given examples of framework conventions being beefed up in the wake of major disasters that stir the conscience and feeling of mass publics that something must be done. Table 20.1 summarizes a number of these disasters and Figure 23.2 summarizes the mechanism whereby disasters mobilize mass publics to agitate for change. Levy, Keohane and Haas (1993: 412–13) show in their systematic study of consequential environmental regulatory regimes that most started as 'deep disappointments' to those who worked to create them. Moreover, most of the positive effects of *Institutions of the Earth* were not a result of enforcement, but of enhancing the contractual environment (a site where mass concern can later be channelled into action, where model mongers can ply their trade), increasing governmental concern and building national capacity. Under the umbrella of broad shared principles, Sand (1991a: 94) shows that there is often 'a club within a club', a group of states that work together to set higher standards than the rest. The club within the club sets higher targets, as we saw with the acid rain regime in Chapter 12, or individual states simply make voluntary commitments to higher standards in meetings of the club (as at the Beijing Women's Conference – Chapter 11). The Financial Action Task Force's strategy for money-laundering (Chapter 8) – expanding the size and deepening the commitments of a white-list of states, as an alternative to creating a black-list – is one of the most sophisticated examples.

As Carlson (1985: 1205) put it in respect of soft law as an alternative to hard law: 'When firm rules cannot be generated, soft law is said to provide an "alternative to anarchy" that over time may produce an "accretion of firm law" through an international analogue of the common law process'. Some regimes have accomplished remarkable specificity over time by allowing 'technical annexes' or 'regulations' which are kept up-to-date by intergovernmental expert committees without any need for ratification. We have seen this with the ITU, WHO, IMO and ICAO. The ICAO innovation of technical standards that are binding unless a group of states launches a successful campaign to vote them down is another interesting illustration of how what started as a vague framework agreement has acquired formidable specificity. Increasingly, NGOs are securing access to technical committees where considerable power is exercised.

What we lauded as the ILO's accomplishments in dragging recalcitrant nations such as China before its Committee on Freedom of Association to give an account of itself (Kent 1997) have taken many decades of progressing from starting principles. Over time – mostly a long time, as we saw in Figure 23.1 – there is progression from agreeing on principles, to rules, then to enforcement of rules.

This fifth strategy, of getting framework agreements in place where possible, is the most basic. It enables the clever NGO strategist to keep in her desk the models she wants to run under our first four strategies, ready for the morning she wakes up to a Chernobyl, a thalidomide or a Barings. When that day dawns, the framework agreement will have created a global forum, a contracting space, where she can table her model and demand popular support for action.

## Strategies for Intervening in Global Webs of Regulation to Increase Competition

The argument of this section will be that a radically reorganized consumer movement, funded by a visionary foundation, would be best placed to play the most crucial roles in four strategies for intervening in global webs of regulation to increase competition:

1   using competition policy to divide and conquer business;

2   harnessing continuous improvement in competition law compliance;

3   building global epistemic community in competition enforcement;

4   transforming the consumer movement into a pro-competition constituency.

These are strategies of deregulation needed when regulation is used to help monopolists dominate consumers. They complement the regulatory strategies needed when consumers are dominated by the unregulated externalities of market power.

## 1 Using Competition Policy to Divide and Conquer Business

Antitrust or competition laws are the most generally useful tool in the armoury of consumer groups. Yet most countries still do not have them and in most that do, the laws are not very credible. It follows that the trade and competition policy development agenda at WTO, OECD and UNCTAD (Chapter 10) are important lobbying sites for the consumer movement.

A great attraction of competition law is that it recruits business to do the consumer movement's work. In the US, private actions by injured business competitors have been encouraged by the prospect of obtaining enormous damages; for example, there were dozens of private actions against AT&T before it was dismantled (Scott 1996b: 396). Anti-competitive practices usually have business as well as consumer victims; the business victims normally have more resources and incentive to launch court cases against monopolistic practices. When business players unite to check the predatory practices of one or more of their own kind they create positive externalities for citizens. Sometimes these externalities have a global reach. Competition law is a way of constituting these externalities. For example, the best chance of checking Microsoft's domination of the rules for the electronic superhighway is antitrust suits funded by other computing industry firms. At the level of lobbying for structural change, a good framework of competition law, as existed in the Anglo-Saxon countries during the 1980s, allowed the International Telecommunications Users Group to challenge the monopoly of the major telecommunications provider in one country after another. The result is that consumers in many nations now have much cheaper telephone services. INTUG was not a consumer group in the sense of a group of household consumers; it was a coalition of big business users of telecommunications services led by companies like American Express.

On the down side, INTUG has had considerable success in lobbying for restructuring of telecommunications in ways that benefit large business users to the detriment of ordinary consumers, especially rural consumers. It is too late now for the consumer movement to join INTUG. INTUG does not need its support. Two decades ago, however, when the liberalization agenda was no more than a twinkle in an economist's eye, a globally forward-looking consumer movement might have captured that agenda by working with companies like American Express to organize an INTUG still mostly funded by business users, but in coalition with household users. Such opportunities will recur in other arenas, electronic commerce on the Internet being the latest example of a consumer movement reacting too late, allowing the ICC to be the model monger.

One of the criticisms of this approach is that it would shift the resources of the global consumer movement to First World campaigns in the metropoles where liberalizing agendas begin. Yet it seems to us that the *realpolitik* of a better deal for developing-country telecommunications consumers is for global social movements to give them a voice in harnessing neo-liberal agendas. Social movements like the consumer movement can be, and should be, more assertive in demanding Wealth Redistribution Impact Statements for the policies of the ITU, IMF, WTO and other agents of global neo-liberalism. Voluntary transfer of technology (and subsidies for developing country adjustment, as in the Montreal Protocol) are likely to be structured into competition agendas only if the consumer movement works with developing states to include them in reform models that they frame.

## 2 Harnessing Continuous Improvement in Competition Law Compliance

Strategic victories for the consumer interest in the courts of countries like Australia and Canada have delivered a case law that says firms can expect higher antitrust penalties unless they have credible internal compliance systems to prevent anti-competitive practices. The US Sentencing Guidelines provide for large discounts on sentence when corporations have exemplary internal compliance systems that failed to work in a particular case (Gruner 1994). These provisions, combined with large penalties for competition law violations, have provided an incentive for considerable growth in investment in competition law compliance systems. The Association of Compliance Professionals of Australia was established with encouragement from the Australian Competition and Consumer Commission to foster excellence in compliance systems (Parker 1998b, 1999).

The next step is to harness the philosophy of continuous improvement to competition law compliance so as to ratchet-up standards nationally and globally. Australia has taken the lead on this by writing an Australian Standard on Compliance Programs that requires continuous improvement. The Australian hope is that courts will take note of this requirement and ask for documented evidence of the pursuit and accomplishment of continuous improvement by companies that get into trouble with the law, and that the idea of a continuous improvement compliance standard will globalize through the ISO.

In Chapter 10 we argued for the application of the continuous improvement principle at the level of states as well as firms. The idea was for a Competition Policy Review Process something like the WTO's Trade Policy Review Process. Performance indicators of state competition policies would be developed and state outcomes reviewed on a regular cycle. Naming and shaming of states that fail to allow competition, with monopolies controlled by princelings or the army, could be tempered with technical assistance to put credible competition policies in place, in the manner so astutely pioneered by the ILO (Chapter 11). As at the ILO, there would be virtue in having both national consumer NGO and business representatives present at a public discussion of the review report on their state.

## 3 Building Global Epistemic Community in Competition Enforcement

Bill Dee's work in establishing the Association of Compliance Professionals of Australia, as with his earlier work in catalyzing the Society of Consumer Affairs Professionals in Business Australia, is a good example of epistemic community building. The Regulatory Affairs Professionals Society (RAPS), with 4000 members across the international pharmaceutical industry, is another example. The consumer movement has been actively engaged with these epistemic communities of compliance professionalism and has been a voice for competition and against monopoly within them. Engaging the legal profession with preventive law approaches to improved compliance with competition law is also important (Parker, forthcoming). In the domain of compliance with Australian affirmative action laws, Braithwaite (1992) has shown that equal employment opportunity officers in organizations are more likely to be effective in improving compliance if they have professional links to EEO officers in other firms. Professional community nurtures regulatory effectiveness.

There has been limited globalization of the above compliance-oriented epistemic communities. Assisting their globalization is an important activity. Until 1998, there was not even a society of competition law government officials. Again, the Australian Competition and Consumer Commission took the lead in getting government officials together at the Consumers International Congress in Santiago, to establish an International Society of Consumer and Competition Law Officials. The intention is that this will be an epistemic community which will link consumer affairs officials to both competition regulators and the consumer movement, as signified by the site of its creation.

## 4 Transforming the Consumer Movement as a Pro-competition Constituency

Our interviews with lead players at the scenes of the decisive battles in shaping the competitiveness of the world economy – the WTO, ITU, OECD, Basle Committee, IMF etc. – fairly consistently elicited the response that the international consumer movement has not been a significant contributor to the debates. The consumer movement influence has been felt more in domains such as health and motor vehicle safety than in economic policy.

Notwithstanding this record of impotence, we see a possibility for the consumer movement to be a uniquely strategic social movement in the twenty-first century. We certainly see it as having a special opportunity in the world we now occupy. And we hope, for the sake of the sovereignty of citizens, that it seizes it. First, we have that hope because we see dangers in a social movement politics that seizes opportunities to ratchet-up standards exploiting strategic trade thinking, as discussed in the last section, without a balancing commitment to a more competitive and efficient economy. This is more than a normative point about preferring a safer world with declining unemployment to a safer and poorer world. It is also a political point about the long-run infeasibility of global ratcheting-up of regulatory standards transacted in an anti-competitive fashion. That is a prescription for the return of a global politics of Reaganism/Thatcherism, that would see more examples of the crushing of the UN Centre on Transnational Corporations, of crippling UNCTAD.

The consumer movement has credentials in competition law and policy that no other social movement has. It therefore is uniquely placed to lead an agenda of jointly ratcheting-up standards that enhance the welfare of citizens and ratcheting-up the competitiveness of the world economy. This does not mean that we envisage the consumer movement emerging as some kind of master social movement. On the contrary, there can be little doubt that the women's, human rights and environment movements will continue to be vital social movements that engage greater swathes of the populace and that the trade union movement will continue to have a superior resource base.

What the consumer movement might deliver, however, is a trained vigilance for regulatory transformation that diminishes monopolization and enhances economic efficiency. One advantage it has in this respect is that it is more engaged than other social movements in public policy discourse that features competition, markets and efficiency. To pull it off, the consumer movement must accomplish a wide coverage of key sites of regulation that would be folly for other social movements. This distinctive form of organization, we will argue, would give the consumer movement a special capacity to coordinate networks of NGOs to attack specific lobbying problems. Working in its competition mode, the goal of the consumer movement would be to ensure that the demand for global regulatory standards is not exclusively constituted through the push and pull of business group activity. On this view, the consumer movement would become a strategic social movement of the twenty-first century because it would enable other social movements to ratchet-up regulation in coalition with an 'economically responsible' consumer movement which was a watchdog of competition; it would have a breadth of competence and involvement in all regulatory arenas that would make it pivotal for coordinating networking.

How could such a presently weak social movement accomplish that? Before tackling this question, let us underline just how big a question it is. Where the analysis of this book leads is that the regulatory change that matters in our contemporary world is transacted not in hundreds but in thousands of highly specialized global epistemic communities. Social movements cannot effect change in the contemporary world unless they connect the political momentum delivered to them by the anxieties of mass publics, with knowhow about working the epistemic communities where regulatory policies are settled. Epistemic communities on pesticide residues in food standards, on quality assurance in the pharmaceutical industry, on trade in various services, on complaint-handling, on standards for car batteries – all such communities are important. Regulatory progress also occurs by insinuating continuous improvement into the self-regulatory practices of BAT and BAP-oriented lead companies and industry associations. By now we are concerned not with thousands, but with tens of thousands of key sites globally. And we are suggesting that consumer advocates should not only engage with technical progress in the regulatory debates at these sites, but should also be watchdogs for monopolistic practices at all the sites! All this in a world where our empirical work has documented that the shape of trade-related regulation is dictated by the 'negotiating fatigue' and 'disputing fatigue' of comparatively richly resourced states (Chapter 10). 'Treaty fatigue' in the environment sector is almost equally palpable (Chapter 12).

Yet the magnitude of the problem is precisely why there is a problem. Industry can utterly dominate so many little epistemic communities which meet at the Codex in Rome or the ITU in Geneva because no one else has the energy to do so. Real power accrues through the capacity and competence of the individuals at the thousands of tedious meetings that ultimately shape global regulation. Obversely, there is opportunity. We know, for example from Working Party 29 of the Economic Commission for Europe, that when Consumers International puts a competent delegate on a committee making crucial decisions on global motor vehicle safety, he can achieve quite a lot (Chapter 18).

And in another of the paradoxes that globalization brings, the standards game may be made easier for outsiders by the WTO Code of Good Practice (the Code) for standardizing bodies, in the Agreement on Technical Barriers to Trade. The Code, in effect, sets standards for the making of standards. For example, the Code requires that standards bodies must use international standards where they exist, they must specify performance standards rather than standards based on specific description, they must allow at least sixty days for submission of comments on the draft standard, they must take those comments into account and they must explain why a deviation from international standards is necessary (see Annex 3 of the Agreement on Technical Barriers to Trade). This creates more opportunities for winning plays for NGOs than ever before. Each international standard they secure can be improved through linkage to the principles of continuous improvement, BAT and BAP (see strategies 2 and 3 of the strategies for intervening to ratchet-up regulatory standards). Once secured, the international standard potentially becomes the standard for other standard-setting bodies. Why? Because under the Code, converging on international standards becomes one of the standards by which good standard-making will be increasingly judged.

But there is a structural reality to be faced. The ISO has some 2800 committees working on standards, and it is only one of the standards organizations whose work affects the interests of citizens. IBM can afford to send senior executives to the meetings of committees that are important to it, meetings that take place in different parts of the world, meetings at which those senior executives are listened to by virtue of the kudos, reputation and knowhow attached to the IBM name. It is for reasons like this that many NGOs are pessimistic about outcomes in the standards game. What can the consumer movement do?

To control the problem and seize the opportunity, the consumer movement would have to radically reorganize. The only way it could do that would involve high risks and breaking with its traditions. Those traditions focus on lobbying activity to get national governments to enact laws. In the recent past much of that activism has been misdirected; for example, activism over the form of national green labelling laws which will soon be superseded by global standards for environmental labelling enforced by WTO panels.

The accomplishment of globalization, we have seen, requires actors to form alliances, it requires epistemic communities to develop ideas, principles and models and finally it requires thousands of committees working in many organizational sites to make these things concrete in the world through the creation of workable norms. Campaigning by all the major social movements, including the consumer movement, is much more networked than it once was, and more global. Some of it is also oriented to steering a process rather than tackling a corporate opponent or stopping a policy change. Networked, global, process-steering changes are where the largest returns to the public interest are likely to be secured, according to our analysis. Well-organized national consumer movements will find they can do more for local consumers by using a significant proportion of their resources to support bit parts in global dramas than by taking lead roles in national productions.

The most consequential roles in global dramas are driven by an intelligence of the process of globalization, and intelligence based on active participation in that process. Roughly, the organizational transformation we have in mind is to turn the consumer movement into a distributed network of powerful information workers. The purpose of the network would be to overlap the work of those epistemic community networks that enable the process of globalization. Consumer information workers would become part of the information flows and tacit workings of technical committees, drafting committees and standards committees, so that when a business representative on such a committee proposes a draft, a guideline, a standard or a rule that advantages his company, a consumer information worker would be there to begin evaluating whether the proposal simply amounts to, in Adam Smith's (1776) words, 'a conspiracy against the public' or a 'contrivance to raise prices'. Regulatory globalization is delivering increasing levels of transparency, levels that make feasible the kind of organizational capability we have in mind for the consumer movement. What, then, is the further detail of the organizational transformation needed to turn the consumer movement into a distributed network of information workers who are competition watchdogs?

First, national consumer organizations would take special responsibility for monitoring the activities of major TNCs headquartered on their soil. They would have at least one consummate activist whose special responsibility was to get to know management of that company, to network with other NGOs involved in campaigns concerning it, with union representatives at its major plants and with NGOs in other countries when they ought to know about things the company is planning, and to launch complaints against the company when it breaches the obligations of agreements and laws by which it is bound.

Second, the national consumer organizations would have at least one moderately competent activist participating in the national epistemic communities that mirror important global epistemic communities, for example the national committee that deals with an area of food standards that is the subject of an important Codex committee. The work of national epistemic communities would not be unimportant but neither would it be vitally important from a global perspective, because what, for example, Australia thinks in Rome usually does not count for much. The significance of work in the national subsidiary of global epistemic communities is that it is a training ground for two more important tasks: graduating to becoming responsible for monitoring the global activities of a major TNC, and being selected by Consumers International to become the coordinator of all national representatives of an epistemic community and to go to the meetings in Rome. The key job of the full-time professional campaigning manager at a national consumer organization becomes to look for volunteers who show exemplary political skills and strategic thinking, who understand that one has to rub shoulders with the epistemic community at conferences (and socially), who draft pithy press releases.

We say 'volunteers' because this strategy would require hundreds of consumer representatives and only a few consumer organizations have hundreds of paid staff. Using hundreds of volunteers guarantees that some will do disastrously incompetent things and occasionally bring the association's name into disrepute. Paid staff do this as well, but volunteers will be subject to fewer checks and balances. On the other hand, recruiting volunteers can be a sophisticated and proactive process of getting the best person in the country for a job. If a consumer organization seeks to position a representative in an air safety epistemic community, in addition to advertising the vacancy to its membership and beyond, the campaign manager might ask around to find a recently retired airline pilot, highly respected for being outspoken on safety issues. In John Braithwaite's experience of the consumer movement, such people are mostly flattered to be approached out of the blue and asked to be the national representative of a respected consumer organization. In short, although volunteers are less subject to scrutiny and discipline than are paid staff, the former airline pilot is more knowledgeable and respected in that specialist community than the best person on a paid staff is likely to be and can spend more of his time dedicated to that particular epistemic community. These days, early retirees aged fifty-five to seventy are plentiful in many countries and can bring the wisdom of years to lobbying tasks that benefit from maturity.

Volunteers under this model would have a campaigning role, but they would have to seek approval before giving media interviews and have press releases cleared by the professional campaign manager. This would impoverish the role of the campaign manager from its current proactive one to a reactive one. But it would increase her effectiveness in campaigning, according to our analysis. When the consumer movement selects a few topics, from among a plethora of possibles, that it can resource effectively with paid staff, it battles away on them against more powerful adversaries that normally defeat it. In contrast, when it is organized at a modest level on hundreds of topics through trained volunteers, it can wait until a disaster occurs affecting one of those topics and then mobilize its best paid staff to exploit the disaster. It can model monger (Chapter 25).

To use a hypothetical example: we will say that, for the first time in its history, the Australian airline Qantas has a crash that kills hundreds. Our retired pilot is ready with a new model for air safety, pulled from his top drawer, to submit for the consideration of the paid campaigning staff. He already has a seat on the relevant decision-making committee. He already knows which key regulators might be likely to support reform. Contrast this with a situation where air safety has been totally ignored because staff are dedicated to three (more important) campaigns. The model mongering opportunity of the theory developed in Chapter 25 must be passed over when the plane crashes. Our analysis is that readiness for model mongering is the decisive weapon of the weak; strategic planning to select the highest-priority topic for campaigning is the weapon of the strong. At a single point in time, the highest-priority topic will be one where its very priority will ensure that more potent players organize to prevail. But at some point in time the clever model monger will get her chance to prevail over big business on every priority topic.

While it might seem that this leaves campaign staff with a less interesting job than the proactive setting of their own agenda, we actually do not think so. Campaigning jobs are most interesting when you win and are really not much fun when the kites you fly are repeatedly shot down, however important the strategic plan says the kites are. The consumer movement will get more financial support from the community when it wins more often, when supporters see it is active on a wide range of issues, and particularly when it arrives on the scene immediately (and with answers) when mass publics get agitated. This extra support would help fund the staff resources needed to recruit, train and monitor the campaigning of volunteers. Note also that the volunteers would play a role in invigorating the grassroots of the consumer movement. Instead of a handful of paid staff recruiting grassroots engagement in campaigning, hundreds of new volunteers would be doing so on the Internet, again a strategy for rejuvenating the relevance and ultimately the community funding of the social movement. This strategy would require more than community funding, however. To work globally, it would require a major foundation to see the opportunity for a safer, more equitable and more efficient world economy – and fund it. It could implement such a vision through funding networks of citizen NGOs independent of the existing international consumer movement, though that would be a more expensive way of doing it.

We now return to the consumer movement's special competence in competition law and policy. It would be critical to train all consumer representatives in this area. Hence, for example, a technical specialist sitting on a humble National Standards Committee on the safety of car batteries that can blind consumers when they explode would have enough training to know when to blow the whistle on a group of manufacturers who are controlling a standard-writing process to advantage them over competitors or suppliers who are not represented on the committee. It is hard to overestimate how important this simple watchdog role will be in the world of the twenty-first century where, as Porter (1990) argues, higher standards demanded by sophisticated purchasers will be critical to the constitution of competitive advantage. Some of the more sophisticated TNCs already have a 'Vice-President, Strategic Standardization'. As one informant from the US Chamber of Commerce evocatively put it: 'The computer industry sets standards to get a lock on the market'. A competition watchdog role, across all the key sites of regulatory decision-making nationally and internationally, is a role that consumer movement volunteers would be better placed to fill than government officials would be. It is a role of such vital importance to our economic future that it justifies government funding of the training and resourcing of those consumer representatives. Therefore, part of a foundation funding strategy would be to leverage matching funding from governments and international organizations, such as ISO.

The diaspora of consumer representatives/competition watchdogs we advocate would give the consumer movement a capability no social movement has ever accomplished, a capability attuned to how global regulatory change occurs. We concluded it occurs by mobilizing a whole web of influences, where any single strand of the web is weak. The diaspora of consumer representatives would give the consumer movement at least one hand on every organizational strand of the webs that matter. Putting this in place could never make sense for the environment movement, for example. But when the environment movement wanted to run a campaign on the environmental implications of paper used in publishing, it could plug into the distributed network of consumer information workers. A national consumer organization would have a representative who monitored the corporate practices of the largest publishing and newspaper conglomerates, and many would have representatives on relevant technical committees of national standards bodies, linked to relevant ISO committees, on governmental Trade Policy Advisory Committees linked to relevant WTO committees and so on, who could network with the environment movement in cases approved by national consumer organizations.

Many of the best-run national consumer organizations are already part-way toward the model we advocate: they have more than a hundred representatives on national technical and policy committees, they train them and remind them of competition policy concerns, they monitor their home-base TNCs with a sense of global responsibility, they mix model mongering and strategic planning and they have shifted significant proportions of national budgets to global campaigning. But these shifts would have to be multiplied several times among the wealthy consumer associations, and globalize to consumer organizations in developing countries, if the consumer movement were to become an NGO powerhouse of the next century. And this would require the funding leverage of a visionary foundation.

## Conclusion

Contemporary institutions of global business regulation are certainly eroding national and parliamentary sovereignty. If we cared enough for the ideal of parliamentary sovereignty, it would be possible to retrieve some of it by having a Second Assembly of the UN directly elected by the peoples of the world, empowered to oversee global regulatory institutions and even to veto treaties. Failing that, there is at least a need to enable the sovereignty of citizens by increasing the transparency of institutions like the WTO and IMF and giving citizen groups effective opportunities to make their voices heard at their meetings. Better still, tripartite constitutions of representatives of states, business and organizations representing public beneficiaries of the regime, as argued in Chapter 24, would both enhance the sovereignty of citizens and thwart domination by forum-shifting.

Although another ILO constitution is unlikely, at the time of writing President Clinton, Prime Minister Blair, President Mandela and others among the world's most respected leaders have shown their appreciation of the need to give a greater voice to NGOs if vital institutions like the WTO, IMF and World Bank are not to be destabilized by anti-liberal populism of the Ross Perots, Le Pens and Pauline Hansons of national polities. The liberalizing populism of the kind of consumer movement we advocate could be a stabilizing force against another beggar-thy-neighbour threat to peace. Globalization of competition policy that accommodates just and efficient regulation is a formidable challenge: it requires the engagement of many other NGOs, and the enrolment of many states, professions and international organizations.

One reason why we think that liberalizing populism can secure victories over both the anti-liberal populism of a Ross Perot and the anti-regulation elitism shown in Reagan's Office of the Management of the Budget is Vogel's (1995: 263) finding that the trade treaties that have done most to reduce the use of regulation as a trade barrier have also done most to ratchet-up the stringency of regulation (e.g. the *Single European Act*). Moreover, with the pharmaceuticals, chemicals and environmental regimes, Vogel (1998: 22) concludes that 'the increase in international regulatory cooperation and the corresponding reduction of national regulatory sovereignty has strengthened the ability of national regulatory officials to achieve their policy objectives'. Because electors have good reasons to want these regulatory objectives (safer drugs, a shorter drug lag) and to want a more efficient economy, empirical demonstration that international cooperation can simultaneously enhance both shows a path to a social movement politics of mass appeal. Even against the mass appeal of the chauvinism of a Perot or Reagan.

On the other hand, our story of the globalization of regulation is a story of domination. The global law-makers today are the men who run the largest corporations, the US and the EC. Women, excluded national minorities and citizens of developing countries are the law-takers. The domination of North Atlantic business has given us, as Chomsky (1993: 163) put it: 'the rule of law for the weak, the rule of force for the strong; neo-liberalism for the weak, state power and intervention for the strong'. When the strong have wanted regulation, very often it has been to protect their monopoly; when they have wanted deregulation it has been to save them paying for the burdens they inflict on ordinary citizens. Consequently, most citizens of the world – men and women, black and white – rightly want the opposite: deregulation of monopoly privilege and strengthened regulation to protect the community from the abuse of corporate power. The struggle for the sovereignty of citizens is an uphill battle to effect that reversal.

However successful the strategies in this chapter are in ratcheting-up protective regulation and deregulation of monopoly power, the sovereignty of big business over globalizing regulation will continue to dominate. Our purpose has not been to deny this, but to affirm that limitation of the sovereignty of big business is possible. We have shown that the weapons of the weak are replete with paradox: strategic trade theory and competition law; enrolling the power of American Express and Margaret Thatcher to tackle telecommunications monopoly; of DuPont and Ronald Reagan to close the ozone hole; loss of national sovereignty to international institutions that give citizen groups a stronger voice; transfer of power from secretive, captured national regulators to transparent, less-captured global regulators; model mongering that can put the future in the hands of the weak, although there are a hundred different guesses on what that future might be. There are threads we can grasp to tighten the knots of these paradoxes. Those with a gift for grasping them will be the champions of the people's sovereignty in this new century.

# Acknowledgments

We thank our families for their support and tolerance of our absences to conduct this research, and we especially thank Val and Julie for their wise counsel on the manuscript itself. Chris Treadwell, Anne Robinson, Mary Hapel, Jean Norman, Anne Tatalovich, Joanne Martin, Alison Pilger, Stephen Free, Tonia Vincent, Declan Roche and James Morauta gave us dedicated administrative and research support. We are grateful to the US National Science Foundation, American Bar Foundation and Australian Research Council for financial support. The wonderful collegiality of the Australian National University, the American Bar Foundation and the wider community of regulatory scholars have nurtured our ideas. Finally, thanks to anonymous reviewers and to Phillipa McGuinness and her colleagues at Cambridge University Press, who were all a joy to work with. There are so many people we cannot begin to list who have contributed in small and not-so-small ways by supplying us with information and contributions to our thinking.

So we restrict ourselves to acknowledging by name 512 people who, since we started in 1990, have made a major identifiable contribution to the facts and ideas in this work. More than four hundred of them are or were significant players in global regulatory regimes who were kind enough to give us interviews for an hour or more; some gave us several. Other key insiders were generous enough to read draft chapters, in some cases sending us many pages of comments and wads of additional documentation. Some were colleagues who gave us an insight during relaxed conversations in the Coombs tea-room or in an office of the Canberra bureaucracy. We also thank the people we interviewed who prefer not to be acknowledged; they include some of our most valuable and senior informants in sensitive industries such as the nuclear industry. The positions of people we interviewed are generally given as at the date of our meeting with them.

Mr Richard Abnett, European Patent Agent, Reddie & Grose

Mr Thomas C. Accardi, Director, Flight Standards Service, US Federal Aviation Administration

Mr Rudolf Adlung, Trade and Environment Division, World Trade Organization

Professor Phillip Alston, European Universities Institute, Consultant to the World Conference on Human Rights

Dr Glen Anderson, Polish Environmental Project, Harvard Institute for International Development

Ms Halina Antoszyk, Ministry of Privatization, Poland

Dr Richard B. Arnold, Executive Vice-President, International Federation of Pharmaceutical Manufacturers Associations

Ambassador Lars Arnell, Chair, TRIPS Negotiating Committee

Mr John Arrowsmith, Senior Adviser (European Monetary Union), Bank of England

Dr Chris Arup, La Trobe University

Mr Allan Asher, Deputy Chairman, Trade Practices Commission, Australia; Chairman, OECD, Consumer Policy Committee

Mr Tobias Asser, Assistant General Counsel, International Monetary Fund

Ms Julie Ayling, Department of Communications and the Arts, Canberra

Mr William Bach, First Secretary for Cultural Affairs, US Embassy, Canberra

Dr K. Balasubramaniam, Pharmaceutical Adviser, Consumers International, Regional Office for Asia and the Pacific, Malaysia

Prof. Leszek Balcerowicz, Former Deputy Prime Minister and Minister of Finance, Poland

Dr Harvey Bale, Director-General, International
Federation of Pharmaceutical Manufacturers
Association

Ms Michelle Balfour, International Division, US Federal
Trade Commission

Dr John Ballard, Australian National University

Mr Peter Banki, Partner, Phillips Fox; Chair, Australian
Copyright Council

Dr Taeho Bark, Vice-President, Korea Institute for
International Economic Policy

Dr Dietrich Barth, Head of Division, Ministry of
Finance, Germany

Ms Libby Baulch, Executive Director, Australian
Copyright Council

Professor Bob Baxt, Partner, Robinson Hedderwicks,
Melbourne; former Chairman, Trade Practices
Commission

Ms Lisa Beard, US Internal Revenue Service

Ms Cynthia Beerbower, Deputy Assistant Secretary (Tax
Policy), US Department of Treasury

Mr Kerry Bell, Chief Executive, Australian
Pharmaceutical Manufacturers Association

Prof. George Berman, Columbia University, Consultant
to Federal Aviation Administration

Mr Geo. R. Besse, International Air Transport
Association, Montreal

Mr Knut Beyer, Federal Ministry for the Environment,
Nature Protection and Nuclear Safety, Germany

Mr Lech Biegunski, Director, Anti-monopoly Policy
Department, Anti-monopoly Office, Poland

Mr Jaroslaw Biernacki, Deputy Director, Banking and
Financial Institutions Department, Ministry of
Finance, Poland

Mr Michael Blakeney, Dunhills, London, formerly
World Intellectual Property Organization

Mr Jenö Bobrovszky, Head, Central and Eastern Europe
Section, World Intellectual Property Organization

Mr Bernie Bond, International Affairs Department,
AFL-CIO, Washington DC

Mr Ian Bond, Senior Adviser (Financial Economics),
Bank of England

Mr Brett Bonfield, National Crime Authority, Melbourne

Prof. Michael Joachim Bonnel, Legal Consultant of
UNIDROIT, Representative of Italy to UN
Commission for International Trade Law

Dr Agostino Borra, Division of Drug Management and
Policies, World Health Organization

Mr Malcolm Bosworth, Counsellor, Trade Policies
Review Division, World Trade Organization

Prof. Steve Bottomley, Australian National University

Mr Vladimir Boulanenkov, International Atomic Energy
Agency

Ms J. Bouravel, Ministry for Women and Youth,
Germany

Ms Megan Bowman, Federal Affairs Manager,
Microsoft

Mr Paul Bradstreet, Industry Commission, Australia

Dr Valerie Braithwaite, Australian National University

Dr Ursula Braubach, Ministry of Posts and
Telecommunications, Germany

Mr Cornelis Brekelmans, Head of Standardization
Sector, European Commission

Mr Jonathan Brown, Director, Bankwatch, Washington,
DC

Mr Robin Brown, International Society of Consumer
and Competition Law Officials

Mr Philippe R. Brusick, Chief, Restrictive Business
Practices Unit, UNCTAD

Dr Wolf Brueckmann, Director, International
Investment Policy, International Division, US
Chamber of Commerce

Mr Karl Buhl, Senior Policy Manager, Microsoft

Ms Mara Bùn, Public Affairs Director, Australian
Consumers Association

Ms Yvonne Burckhardt, General Secretary, International
Federation of Musicians

Ms Chris Burnham, Business Council of Australia

Mr Ross Burns, International Trade Law and
Intellectual Property Branch, Attorney-General's
Department, Canberra

Justice Frank H. Callaway, Court of Appeals, Melbourne

Mr Paul Carlson, International Division, US Federal
Trade Commission

Mr Michael Carney, Trade Negotiations and
Organisations Division, Department of Foreign
Affairs and Trade, Australia

Mr David Carr, Financial Institutions and Company
Law Directorate-General, European Commission

Mr Joe Cascio, Program Director, IBM; Chairman of the
US Technical Advisory Group to ISO Technical
Committee 207 on Environmental Management

Mr Richard A. Cawley, Telecommunications and
Information Industries Division, European
Commission

Mr Francois-Gabriel Ceyrac, International Chamber of
Commerce, Paris

Mrs Pamela Chan Wong Shui, Chief Executive,
Consumer Council, Hong Kong, President
Consumers International

Prof. Hilary Charlesworth, Australian National
University

Mr Stuart M. Chemtob, Special Counsel for
International Trade, Antitrust Division, US
Department of Justice

Mr Doug Chester, Director, Intellectual Property
Section, Department of Foreign Affairs and Trade,
Australia

Mr Bala Chettur, Department of Foreign Affairs and
Trade, Australia

Mr Yu-Lan Chien, Chung-Hua Institution for Economic
Research, Center for Energy and Environmental
Studies, Taiwan

Mr Ke-Young Chu, International Monetary Fund

Mr Li-Hui Chu, Economic Research Department, Council for Economic Planning and Development, Taiwan

Ms Hsu Chun-Fang, Deputy Director, Board of Foreign Trade, Ministry of Economic Affairs, Taiwan

Mr Christophe Churlet, Banque Nationale de Paris, Paris

Mr Peter Clark, Head of International Relations, Australian Securities Commission

Mr Paul Clements-Hunt, Policy Manager, Environment and Energy Affairs, International Chamber of Commerce, Paris

Mr Harrison Cohen, Legislation Counsel, Joint Committee on Taxation Staff, Washington DC

Mr John Cohrssen, Office of the US Vice-President's Council on Competitiveness

Mr Stephen Collins, Head, Industrial World Division, Bank of England

Ms Margaret Cone, Vice-President for Scientific Affairs, International Federation of Pharmaceutical Manufacturers Associations, Geneva

Ms Lloyce M. Constant, Head, Implementation Division, Trinidad and Tobago Bureau of Standards

Mr Charles Constantinou, Chief, Energy and Natural Resources Branch, Division for Sustainable Development, DPCSD, New York

Mr Anthony Cook, Manager, Regulatory Services Group, Lloyd's of London

Mr Charles W. (Bill) Cooper, Assistant Director, Center for Food Safety and Public Nutrition, US Food and Drug Administration

Mr Karl Cordewener, Basle Committee on Banking Supervision

Mr Lee Cordiner, Chief Executive, Société Générale de Surveillance, Australia

Mr Chris Creswell, Assistant Secretary, International Trade Law and Intellectual Property Section, Attorney General's Department, Australia

Mr Jean-Pierre Cristel, International Organization of Securities Commissions, Montreal

Dr Alexander Cristofaro, Director Air and Energy Policy Division, Environmental Protection Agency, Washington DC

Mr Allen Cullen, Executive Director, Australian Bankers Association

Mr Richard Cunnane, Head of Sector, External Relations, European Commission

Mr David Curtis, General Counsel, Microsoft

Ms Bridget Czarnota, Internal Market and Financial Services, European Commission

Mr Philip Datwiler, Global Markets, Deutsche Morgan Grenfell, Frankfurt

Dr Peter Dauvergne, Australian National University

Mr Richard Dawson, Chief, Food Quality and Standards Service, UN Food and Agriculture Organization, Rome

Ms Genevieve de Bauw, Union des Confederations de L'Industrie et des Employeurs D'Europe

Mr Chris Decure, Trade Negotiations and Organisations Division, Department of Foreign Affairs and Trade, Australia

Mr Bill Dee, Australian Consumer and Competition Commission

Mr Dennis de Freitas, Consultant, International Federation of the Phonographic Industry

Mr Bill DeJong, Minister (Special Labour Adviser), Permanent Mission of Australia to the UN, Geneva; Chair, Committee on Multinational Enterprises, International Labour Organization

Ms Julie Delahunty, North–South Institute

Dr Kilian Delbruck, Federal Ministry for the Environment, Nature Protection and Nuclear Safety, Germany

Mr Paul de Lusignan, Internal Market and Industrial Affairs, European Commission

Dr David de Souza, Minister (Health), Australian High Commission, UK

Mr Alban de Villepin, Chief of Sector, Environment, European Commission

Mr Rajan Dhanjee, Technology Program, UNCTAD, Geneva

Dr Adolf Dietz, Max Planck Institute, Germany

Prof. Julian Disney, Chair, International Council on Social Welfare Global Working Group on Social Development Summit

Mr George S. Dragnich, Labour Attaché, US Embassy, Canberra

Dr Thomas Drier, Max Planck Institute, Germany

Ms Teresa Drozdowska, Director Legal Department, Ministry of Culture and Art, Poland

Mrs Maria Ducci, Special Adviser for Women Workers' Questions, International Labour Office, Geneva

Mr John Duffield, World Association of Nuclear Operators, London

Mr Mark Dunstan, Telecommunications and Trade Director, Department of Communications, Australia

Mme Frederique Dupy, Trade Union Advisory Committee to the OECD, Brussels

Mr Andrzej Dziekonski, Chief Adviser, Ministry of Foreign Economic Relations, Poland

Dr Robyn Eckersley, Monash University

Mr Colin Edgell, International Trade Law and Intellectual Property Branch, Attorney-General's Department, Australia

Mr Richard Eglin, Director, Technical Barriers to Trade and Trade and Environment Division, World Trade Organization

Dr Dieter Eisele, Global Head of Compliance, Deutsche Bank, Frankfurt

Dr Andrew Elek, Chairman, Trade Policy Subcommittee, Asia-Pacific Economic Cooperation Forum

Mr William T. Ellis, Washington Counsel, Intellectual Property Law, IBM

Dr Maria Estor, Ministry for Women and Youth, Germany

Mr Alistair Evans, International Department, Lloyd's of London

Mr Phillip Evans, Consumers International, London

Mr Anwar Faisal, UNDP Kuala Lumpur, formerly President, International Organization of Consumers Unions

Mr R.H. Farrant, Deputy Head, Banking Supervision Division, Bank of England

Mr Geza Feketekuty, Senior Policy Adviser to the US Trade Representative; Chair OECD Trade Committee

Prof. Allan Fels, Chairman, Trade Practices Commission, Australia

Mr Jock Ferguson, Political Reporter, *Globe and Mail*, Toronto

Mr Jacques Feuillan, International Division, US Federal Trade Commission

Ms Jean Ffrench, International Labour Office; Department of Education, Employment and Youth Affairs, Canberra

Mr Krzysztof Filinski, Anti-monopoly Office, Poland

Mr Brent Fisse, Gilbert & Tobin, Sydney

Mr Derek Fittler, International Trade Law and Intellectual Property Section, Attorney General's Department, Australia

Mr Ortlieb Fliedner, Assistant Secretary, Ministry of the Interior, Germany

Mr Scott Forseth, Attorney, Dewey Ballantine

Mr Richard Foster, Chairman, British Standards Institute Consumer Coordination Committee on Personal Protection, Systems and Services

Mr Alain Frank, Director, External Relations Division, General Agreement on Tariffs and Trade

Mr Allen Frankel, Chief, International Banking, Board of Governors, US Federal Reserve System

Mr Wolfgang Fritsch, Head of International Monetary and Economic Developments Division, Deutsche Bundesbank

Mr Toshihiko Fujii, Ministry of International Trade and Industry, Tokyo

Mr Irving L. Fuller Jr, Counselor for International Affairs, Environmental Protection Agency, Washington DC

Mr Geoffrey Gamble, Associate General Counsel, DuPont

Dr Bryant Garth, Director, American Bar Foundation

Mr Digby Gascoine, AQIS, Vice-Chairman, Codex Expert Committee on Food Inspection and Certification Systems

Mr Fabien Gelinas, International Chamber of Commerce International Court of Arbitration

Mr Matthijs Geuze, Legal Affairs Officer, Group of Negotiations on Goods and Policy Affairs Division, General Agreement on Tariffs and Trade

Mr James Gillman, Senior Vice-President and Motorola Director of Patents, Trademarks and Licensing, Motorola

Mr Hans Glatz, Delegate of the Board of Management, Corporate Representation Brussels, DaimlerBenz

Mr Padmanabh Gopinath, Director, Institute for Labour Studies, International Labour Office

Ms Gojová, Ministry for Economic Competition of Czech Republic

Dr Jacques Gorlin, The Gorlin Group, Consulting Economist to the Intellectual Property Committee

Ms Katharine Gourle, Director Consumer Products, Canadian Bureau of Consumer Affairs

Dr Peter Grabosky, Australian Institute of Criminology

Dr David Graham, Therapeutic Goods Administration, Australia

Ms Alix Grice, Law and Corporate Affairs Corporate Attorney, Microsoft

Mr Hugh Griffiths, Internal Market and Industrial Affairs, European Commission

Dr Alberto Grignolo, President, Regulatory Affairs Professionals Society

Mr Bjoerne Grimsrud, International Confederation of Free Trade Unions

Dr Nicholas Gruen, Business Council of Australia

Mr Jorge Guardia, International Monetary Fund; formerly Governor, Central Bank of Costa Rica

Mr Evgueni Guerassimov, Acting Chief, Copyright Section, United Nations Educational, Scientific and Cultural Organization

Mr Pierre Guislain, Senior Private Sector Development Specialist, World Bank

Mr Manuel Guitan, Associate Director, Monetary and Exchange Affairs Department, International Monetary Fund

Prof. Neil Gunningham, Australian National University

Mr John D. Gunther, Chief Economic Policy Section, International Civil Aviation Organization, Montreal

Dr Wolf Gunther, Head of Division, Ministry of Finance, Germany

Dr Francis Gurry, Director-Adviser, World Intellectual Property Organization, Geneva

Mr Paul Guy, Secretary-General, International Organization of Securities Commissions

Mr Greg Hall, Certification Project Manager, Federal Aviation Administration, Seattle

Dr Rod Hall, Medical Director, Merck, Sharp & Dohme, Australia

Dr Hans Peter Kunz Hallstein, Lawyer, Germany

Ms Boronia Halstead, Commonwealth Law Enforcement Board, Canberra

Dr Martin Ten Ham, Chief, Drug Safety Unit, World Health Organization

Mr Kent Hamlin, Deputy Director, World Association of Nuclear Operators, London

Mr W.C.K. Hammer, Former Australian Agricultural Attaché, Washington, DC

Mr Edward Hand, Antitrust Division, US Justice Department

Mr John Hannoush, Trade Negotiations and Organisations Division, Department of Foreign Affairs and Trade, Australia

Mr Tony Hartnell, Chairman, Australian Securities Commission

Mr David Hartridge, Director, Group of Negotiations on Services Division, General Agreement on Tariffs and Trade

Mr Todd Harper, International Affairs Office, US Occupational Safety and Health Administration

Mr Martin Harvey, European Agency for the Evaluation of Medicinal Products

Mrs Nancy Harvey Steorts, Chairman, ANSI Consumer Interest Council; former Chair US Consumer Product Safety Commission

Mr Ronald Hauber, US Nuclear Regulatory Commission

Prof. Carol Heimer, American Bar Foundation

Mr Doug Hellinger, The Development Gap, Washington DC

Mr John Henry, Standards Australia

Mr Herbert Henssler, Head of Section, Regulatory Aspects, Motor Vehicles, European Commission

Ms Ann Herbert, Salaried Employees and Professional Workers Branch, International Labour Office

Mr Christopher Herman, Division of International Activities, Environmental Protection Agency, Washington DC

Mr Henning Hesse, Federal Ministry of Transport, Germany

Prof. Barry Higman, Australian National University

Mrs Jenny Hillard, Vice-President, Policy Issues, Consumers Association of Canada

Ms Jane Hodges, Equality and Human Rights Coordination Branch, International Labour Office

Ms Catherine Hodgkin, Health Action International, Amsterdam

Dr Michael W. Hodin, Vice-President Public Affairs, Pfizer Inc.

Ms Ellen Hoen, Médecins sans Frontières

Mr Stephen Hoffman, Division of Banking Supervision and Regulation, Board of Governors, US Federal Reserve System

Dr Ulrike Hoffmann, Ministry of Posts and Telecommunications, Germany

Mr Paul Hohnen, Policy Director, International Treaties and Conventions, Greenpeace International

Mr William E. Holder, Deputy General Counsel, International Monetary Fund

Mr Robert W. Holleyman II, President, Business Software Alliance

Professor Robert Holton, Flinders University

Mrs Sadie Homer, Standards Officer, Consumers International

Mr James Howard, International Confederation of Free Trade Unions

Mr Robert Hull, Adviser to the Director-General, Environmental Policy, European Commission

Ms Maria Elema Hurtado, Consumers International, London

Mr Gene Hutchinson, Director of Trinidad and Tobago Bureau of Standards; DEVCO Chairman of the International Organization for Standardization

Dr Iur Li Hwang, National Chengchi University, Taiwan

Mr Peter Ingleton, Technical Director, International Air Transport Association, Montreal

Mr Atsushi Iwai, Ministry of International Trade and Industry, Tokyo

Mr Thomas R. Jacob, Senior Analyst, DuPont

Mr Scott Jacobs, Public Management Service, OECD, Paris

Mr Neil Jaggers, Senior Adviser (Central and Eastern Europe), Bank of England

Mr Jin-Ho Jeong, Korea Economic Research Institute

Mr Chul-Ho Ji, Deputy Director, International Affairs Division I, Fair Trade Commission, Korea

Dr Frank Joshua, Development Finance, UNCTAD, Geneva

Dr Soon Sik Ju, Director, International Affairs Division I, Fair Trade Commission, Korea

Mr Bernard Kaczmarek, Ministry of Environmental Protection, France

Dr Susanne Karstedt, University of Bielefeld, Germany

Mr Abraham Katz, President, US Council for International Business

Ms Sally Kaufman, Environmental and Consumer Activist

Mr Ken-Ichi Kawamoto, Ministry of International Trade and Industry, Tokyo

Mr B.K. Keayla, National Working Group on Patent Laws, New Delhi

Ms Margaret Kelly, Deputy Director, External Relations Department, International Monetary Fund

Dr Tim Kelly, Strategic Planning Unit, International Telecommunication Union

Mr Tom Kelly, Director, Regulatory Management Evaluation Office, US Environmental Protection Agency

Mr David F. Kenmir, Enforcement Division, Securities and Futures Authority, London

Dr Ann Kent, Australian National University

Mr Colin Kent, Deputy Banking Ombudsman, Australia

Mr Michael Keplinger, US Department of Commerce, Patents and Trademarks Office

Ms Chahloul Khadija, Chief World Trade Organization Negotiator for Tunisia, Ministry of Commerce, Tunis

Mr Jong-An Kim, Deputy Director, Appellate Trial Board, Korean Industrial Property Office

Mr Jong Kap Kim, Director, International Trade Policy Division, Ministry of Trade, Industry and Energy, Korea

Mr Jobst von Kirchmann, Internal Market and Financial Services, European Commission

Mr Roger Kohn, International Maritime Organization, London

Mr Gert Kolle, Director, International Legal Affairs, European Patent Office, Munich

Mr Jaroslav Koneny, Department of International Economic Organizations, Ministry of Foreign Affairs, Czech Republic

Dr Konig, Head of Economics Department, Deutsche Bundesbank, Frankfurt

Dr Sabine Kopp-Kubel, Drug Regulatory Support Unit, World Health Organization

Mr Juhani Korhonen, Public Management Department, Ministry of Finance, Finland

Dr Wieslaw Kotarba, President, Polish Patent Office

Mr Michael Kourteff, Assistant Director, International Competitiveness Branch, Foreign Affairs and Trade, Australia

Mr Jerzy Kowalczyk, Director, International Economic Relations, Ministry of Foreign Affairs, Poland

Mr Piotr Kozerski, Director, OECD Countries, Ministry of Foreign Economic Relations, Poland

Mr Peter Krisor, Ministry of Posts and Telecommunications, Germany

Mr Pawel Krzeczunowicz, Ministry of Privatization, Poland

Dr Jacek Kurczewski, Deputy Speaker, Polish Parliament

Mr Jeffrey P. Kushan, US Department of Commerce, Patents and Trademarks Office

Mr Edward Kwalasser, Executive Vice-President, Regulatory Group, New York Stock Exchange

Ms Elsa Kwan, Hong Kong Customs and Excise Department

Ms Yong Sook Kwok, Health Action International

Mr Hyuk-Jung Kwon, Deputy Director, Trademark Division, Korean Industrial Property Office

Mr David R. Kyd, International Atomic Energy Agency

Mr Eric F. Lacey, Principal Administrator, Competition Policy, OECD

Ms Grazyna Lachowicz, Senior Expert, Polish Patent Office

Mr Sam Laird, World Trade Organization, Geneva

Prof. Don Lamberton, Consultant to the Prices Surveillance Authority; Former Member, Industrial Property Advisory Committee, Australia

Mr Reino Lampinen, Ministry of Transport, Finland

Mr John Langmore MP, Chair, Trade Subcommittee, Joint Standing Committee on Foreign Affairs, Defence and Trade, Australian Parliament

Mr Paul A. Leder, Assistant Director, Office of International Affairs, US Securities and Exchange Commission

Mr Gyehyng Lee, Director, World Trade Organization Affairs Division, Ministry of Trade, Industry and Energy, Korea

Mr Joseph S. Lee, Vice-President, Chung-Hua Institution for Economic Research, Taipei

Mr Kenneth Leeson, Program Director of Telecommunications, IBM

Mr Richard Lehmann, IBM Director of Public Affairs, Governmental Programs

Mr George Lemonidis, External Relations, European Commission

Mr Michel Lesage, Occupational Health and Safety Branch, International Labour Office

Mr Brian Levy, World Bank

Mr Wlodzimierz Lewandowski, Economist, Anti-monopoly Office, Poland

Mr John Ley, National Road Transport Commission, Melbourne

Mr Nigel N.T. Li, Attorney-at-Law, Taipei, Taiwan

Mr Shin-Pyng Liao, National Chengchi University, Taipei, Taiwan

Mr David Lieberman, Legal Counsel, IBM

Ms Therese de Liedekerhne, Union des Confederations de L'Industrie et des Employeurs D'Europe

Mr Kurt Lietzmann, Federal Ministry for the Environment, Nature Protection and Nuclear Safety, Germany

Mr Ake Linden, Special Adviser to the Director-General, General Agreement on Tariffs and Trade

Mr Erick Linke, Consumer Policy, OECD, Paris

Ms Eija-Leena Linkola, Ministry of Finance, Finland

Mr Lawrence Shao-Liang Liu, Asia-Pacific Regional Operations Center, Taipei, Taiwan

Mr Stephen Locke, Consumers Association, UK

Mr William P. Looney, Deputy Executive Director, Global Business Forum

Ms Helen L'Orange, General Manager, Worksafe Australia

Mr Brian Loton, former Chief Executive Officer BHP, Deputy Chairman, National Australia Bank

Ms Ruth Lovisolo, Manager, Food Standards Policy, Australian Quarantine and Inspection Service

Prof. William W. Lowrence, Executive Director, International Medical Benefit/Risk Foundation, Geneva

Mr Edward L. Lowry, Executive Director, Bell Atlantic Corporation

Mr Bernard Lynch, Intellectual Property Section, Multilateral Trade Division, Department of Foreign Affairs and Trade, Australia

Mr Daryl Maddern, Chair, OECD Working Party on Consumers and Banking

Mr Joao Magalhaes, Agriculture and Commodities Division, General Agreement on Tariffs and Trade

Prof. Giandomenico Majone, European Universities Institute, Florence

Mr Paul Malric-Smith, Directorate-General for Competition, European Commission

Dr Peter Mansfield, Medical Lobby for Appropriate Marketing

Mr Fernando Mansito, Deputy Director-General, Agriculture, European Commission

Mr Christos Mantziaris, Australian National University

Mr Phil Marchionni, Manager, Policy and Media, Australian Consumers Association

Mrs Fiona Mareq, Union des Confederations de L'Industrie et des Employeurs D'Europe

Dr Ray Marshall, former US Secretary of Labor

Mr Ian Martin, Telecommunications Policy Division, Department of Transport and Communications, Australia

Mr James K. Martin, Director, Regulatory Affairs, Treasury Board of Canada

Dr Gabriel Martinez, Head of Deregulation Program, Ministry of Trade and Industry, Mexico

Sir Anthony Mason, former Chief Justice of Australia

Dr Additya Mattoo, Economic Research and Analysis Unit, General Agreement on Tariffs and Trade

Mr Gerald Mauch, US Nuclear Regulatory Commission

Mr Petros C. Mavroidis, Legal Affairs Officer, General Agreement on Tariffs and Trade

Dr John McEwan, Medical Director, Commonwealth Serum Laboratories, Australia

Mr George McKendrick, Executive Director, International Telecommunications Users Group, London

Mr Bob McMullan, Minister for Trade, Australia

Mr Thomas McSweeny, Deputy Director, Aircraft Certification Service, US Federal Aviation Administration

Mr Patrick Meaney, Australian Securities Commission

Mr Rob Melvin, Supervising Examiner of Patents, Australian Industrial Property Organization

Mr Roland Michelitsch, World Bank, Washington DC

Ms Julie Misner, Bureau of International Labor Affairs, US Department of Labor

Prof. Ronald Mitchell, University of Oregon

Mr Russell Mokhiber, NGO Activist; Editor, *Corporate Crime Reporter*

Mr Oreste Monalto, Administrator Principal, Internal Market and Industrial Affairs, European Commission

Mr Franklin Moore, Division of International Activities, Environmental Protection Agency, Washington DC

Mr Vic Morgenroth, Chemicals Division, OECD, Paris

Mr Robert Morris, Senior Vice-President, US Council for International Business

Dr Shona Morrison, Commonwealth Law Enforcement Board, Canberra

Mr Paul Mortimer-Lee, Financial Markets and Institutions Division, Bank of England

Mr Peter Mozet, Federal Ministry of Labour and Social Affairs, Germany

Dr Robert Mroziewicz, Under-Secretary of State, Foreign Affairs, Poland

Dr Agasha Mugasha, Australian National University

Ms Janine Murphy, International and Investment Division, Department of Treasury, Australia

Mr Joseph Murphy, Senior Attorney, Bell Atlantic

Mr Frederik C. Musch, Secretary-General, Basle Committee on Banking Supervision, Bank for International Settlements

Mr Ralph Nader

Mr S. Narasimhan, former UNCTAD Official, New Delhi

Ms Lenore Neal, Executive Officer, Intellectual Property and Investment Section, Foreign Affairs and Trade, Australia

Mr Roland Niggestich, Federal Ministry of Transport, Germany

Mr Osamu Nishiwaki, Ministry of International Trade and Industry, Tokyo

Ms Marjorie Nordlinger, US Nuclear Regulatory Commission

Mr G. Oberreuter, Federal Ministry of Transport, Germany

Ms Kathleen M. O'Day, Associate General Counsel, Board of Governors, Federal Reserve System, Washington DC

Mr Max Ogden, Australian Council of Trade Unions

Dr Assad Omer, Technology Program, UNCTAD, Geneva

Mr Magnus Orrell, Basle Committee on Banking Supervision

Mr Derry Ormond, Head Public Management Service, OECD, Paris

Mr Wojciech Ostrowski, Ministry of Foreign Affairs, Poland

Mr Adrian Otten, Director, Policy Affairs Division, General Agreement on Tariffs and Trade

Mr Richard Owens, Copyright Department, World Intellectual Property Organization

Mr Tommaso Padoa-Schioppa, Director, European Central Bank, Frankfurt

Mr Peter Fei Pan, Attorney-at-Law, Taipei, Taiwan

Mr John Parisi, International Division, US Federal Trade Commission

Mr Aurelio Parisotto, Multinational Enterprises Branch, International Labour Office

Dr Christine Parker, University of New South Wales

Mr Barry B. Paul, Vice-President, South African Bureau of Standards

Ms Jacqui Pearce, Australian Competition and Consumer Commission

Mr Trevor Pearcy, Finance Director, International Federation of the Phonographic Industry

Mr Rinaldo Pecchtoli, Financial Regulation, OECD, Paris

Prof. Jacques Pelkmans, Centre for European Policy Studies

Mr Jorge Perez-Lopez, Director, Office of International Economic Analysis, US Department of Labor

Mr Michael Pertschuk, Director, Advocacy Institute, Washington DC

Mrs Esther Peterson, Consumers International; former White House Adviser

Prof. Philip Pettit, Australian National University

Dr Peter Pflaum, Therapeutic Goods Administration, Australia

Mr Vladimifr Pftra, Deputy, Czech Industrial Property Office

Prof. Sol Picciotto, University of Warwick

Ms Gae Pincus, Chief Executive Officer, National Food Authority, Australia

Dr Chandra Pinnagoda, Chief, Occupational Safety and Health Branch, International Labour Office

Mr Jacek Pitatkowski, Multilateral Treaties Department, Ministry of Foreign Economic Relations, Poland

Mr Michael D. Platzer, Director, West European Affairs, International Division, US Chamber of Commerce

Dr Jacek Postupdski, National Institute of Hygiene, Poland

Mr Peter Prendergast, Director, Consumer Policy Service, European Commission

Mr Larry Promisel, Division of International Finance, Board of Governors, US Federal Reserve System

Ms Anne Rafferty, Office of Special Trade Activities, US State Department

Dr Raimund Raith, Head, Intellectual Property and Investment Section, European Commission

Mr Alan W. Randell, Food and Agriculture Organization/World Health Organization Food Standards Program, Rome

Prof. Joseph Rees, Virginia Tech

Ms Carole Renouf, International Organization of Consumer Organizations Representative to the Codex Alimentarius Commission

Prof. Peter Reuter, University of Maryland

Mr John Richard, Executive Assistant to Mr Ralph Nader

Ms Bonnie Richardson, Attorney, Motion Picture Association of America

Ms Palm Risse, Federal Ministry for the Environment, Nature Protection and Nuclear Safety, Germany

Mr Kenneth Robinson, Senior Legal Adviser to the Chairman, US Federal Communications Commission

Mr Roberto Rodriguez, International Monetary Fund, Washington DC

Mr Hans Volker Rohmann, Deutsche Bundesbank, Frankfurt

Mr Morris Rosen, Director of Nuclear Safety, International Atomic Energy Agency, Vienna

Mr David Rosenbloom, Attorney, Caplin & Drysdale

Ms Edna Ross, Australian Council for Overseas Aid

Mr Richard P. Roulier, Financial Sector Development Department, World Bank

Mr Serguei Routchkine, World Association of Nuclear Operations

Mr Jeffrey Rozwadowski, US Internal Revenue Service

Dr Wojciech Ruduichi, Legal Department, Ministry of Health and Social Welfare, Poland

Ms Ruhl, Federal Ministry for the Environment, Nature Protection and Nuclear Safety, Germany

Ms Virginia Russell, President's Office, American Bar Association, Chicago

Mr Des Ryan, former International President, Licensing Executives Society; former Member, International Executive, International Association for the Protection of Intellectual Property

Mr Gary P. Sampson, Director, Regional and Preferential Trade and Trade and Finance Division, World Trade Organization

Mr Luis Fina Sanglas, Head, Employment and Labour Market Directorate, European Commission

Mr Ricardo Sateler, Assistant Legal Counsel, World Intellectual Property Organization

Mr Fernand Sauer, Head of Service, Pharmaceuticals, European Commission

Mr J. Freidrich Sauerlander, Senior Vice-President, Société Générale de Surveillance, Geneva

Dr Marion Sawer, Australian National University

Mr Josef Schiller, Aviation and Space Division, Federal Ministry of Transport, Germany

Prof. Karl Schiller, former Finance Minister, Federal Republic of Germany

Ambassador John Schmidt, US Ambassador to the General Agreement on Tariffs and Trade

Mr Greg Schoepfle, Director, Foreign Economic Research Office of International Economic Affairs, US Department of Labor

Mr Helmut Schol, International Transport Relations, Federal Ministry of Transport, Germany

Mr Ralph Seccombe, former Field Adviser of the UN International Drug Control Program

Mrs Irene Seiferling, Director, Standards Commission of Canada

Dr W. Sengeberger, Head, New Industrial Organization Program, International Labour Office

Ms Deidre E. Shanahan, International Division, US Federal Trade Commission

Ms Nina Shawarshon, Ministry of Health and Social Welfare, Poland

Justice Ian Sheppard, Chairman, Copyright Law Review Committee, Australia

Ms Jennifer Silk, International Affairs Office, US Occupational Safety and Health Administration

Mr Emery Simon, Washington Policy Entrepreneur; former Deputy Assistant US Trade Representative

Mr Tony Simpson, International Adviser, Australian Conservation Foundation

Mr Eric H. Smith, Executive Director and General Counsel, International Intellectual Property Alliance, Washington DC

Mr J.R.G. Smith, International Association of Classification Societies Permanent Representative to the International Maritime Organization

Dr Merton V. Smith, International Harmonization and Trade Affairs, US Food and Drug Administration

Mr Thomas E. Smith, Chair, American Bar Association Section of Intellectual Property Law, Chicago

Dr Michal Sobolewski, Deputy Director, Ministry of Health and Social Welfare, Poland

Mr Byung-Doo Sohn, Vice-President/Chief Executive Officer, Korea Economic Research Institute

Prof. Song Sang Hyun, Seoul National University; President of the Korean International Trade Law Association

Mr Renaud Sorieul, UN Commission on International Trade Law, Vienna

Dr David Soskice, Wissenschaftszentrum Berlin, Adviser to Prime Minister Blair, UK

Pavel Soukal, First Deputy Minister, Ministry for Economic Competition of Czech Republic

Mr Hank Spier, Chief Executive, Trade Practices Commission, Australia

Mr Charles Spring, Bureau of International Labor Affairs, US Department of Labor

Ms Gretchen Stanton, Counsellor, Agriculture and Commodities Division, World Trade Organization

Mr Charles C. Stark, Chief, Foreign Commerce Section, Antitrust Division, US Justice Department

Dr Stefan Stefanski, Minister's Adviser, Ministry of Foreign Affairs, Poland

Mr Ross Stevens III, Manager, Corporate Issues, DuPont

Prof. Art Stinchcombe, Northwestern University

Mr E. Stohr, International Legal Affairs, European Patent Office

Dr Jan Strásky, Minister of Transport, Czech Republic

Dr Pawet Strucinski, National Institute of Hygiene, Poland

Mr Yeong-Chin Su, National Chengchi University, Taipei, Taiwan

Ms Maria Suchowiak, Ministry of Health and Social Welfare, Poland

Mr Norman Sullivan, Manager, Standardization Branch, Federal Aviation Administration, Seattle

Mr Timothy Sullivan, International Banking and Finance, US Comptroller of the Currency

Mr Jakob Suppli, Contract Governance Unit, Ministry of Finance, Denmark

Ms Johanna Sutherland, Australian National University

Mr Alastair Sutton, Forrester, Norall & Sutton, Brussels

Mr Lee Swepston, Chief, Equality and Human Rights Coordination Branch, International Labour Office

Ms Louise Sylvan, Chief Executive Officer, Australian Consumers Association; Vice-President, Consumers International

Ms Ewa Szymanska, Adviser to the President, Antimonopoly Office, Poland

Mr Thayre Talcott, Dow Chemical, Chair, Chemical Manufacturers Association Task Force on Harmonization

Dr John Tamblyn, First Assistant Commissioner, Trade Practices Commission, Australia

Mr Vito Tanzi, Director, Fiscal Affairs, International Monetary Fund

Mr Leon S. Tarrant, International Banking and Finance, US Comptroller of the Currency

Ms Elizabeth Thornton, Associate Legal Counsel, US Equal Employment Opportunity Commission

Mr Victor Thuronyi, Counsel (Taxation), International Monetary Fund

Mr Eric J. Toder, Deputy Assistant Secretary (Tax Analysis), US Department of Treasury

Dr Ing-Wen Tsai, Commissioner, Fair Trade Commission, Taiwan

Mr Geoffrey Turner, Senior Director, Public Affairs, Securities and Futures Authority, London

Mr Frank Turpin, Director, International Harmonization, US National Highway Traffic Safety Administration

Mr Joe Tymczyszyn, Manager International Airworthiness, Boeing Commercial Airplane Group, Seattle

Prof. Dr Hans Ullrich, Max Planck Institute, Germany

Mr Martin Ullrich, Head Program Evaluation Branch, Office of the Comptroller-General, Canada

Mr Uranek, Czech Republic Services Negotiator, General Agreement on Tariffs and Trade

Mr Jack Valenti, President and Chief Executive Officer, Motion Picture Association of America

Mr Vandergheynst, Industrial Property Division, European Commission

Mr Christiaan van der Valk, Policy Manager, International Chamber of Commerce, Paris

Mr Raymond van Ermen, Director, European Environmental Bureau

Mr Mark Van Fleet, Director, Asia-Pacific Affairs, International Division, US Chamber of Commerce

Prof. Richard Vann, Consultant, OECD

Dr S. Vedaraman, Controller-General of Patents, Designs and Trade Marks, Government of India, Bombay

Ing. Stanislav Vesely, Foreign Trade Section, Ministry for Business Affairs, Czech Republic

Prof. David Vines, Oxford University

Prof. David Vogel, University of California, Berkeley

Mr Richard Vollmer, US Nuclear Regulatory Commission

Mr Rene Vosenaar, Trade and Environment Section, UNCTAD

Mr Hendrik Vygen, Federal Ministry for the Environment, Nature Protection and Nuclear Safety, Germany

Mr Philippe Wacker, Lobbyist, Bates & Wacker, Brussels

Dr Stanislaw Wajda, Ministry of Environmental Protection, Poland

Ms Lori Wallach, Coordinator, Public Citizen Tradewatch Campaign

Mr David J.P. Wang, Section Chief, Board of Foreign Trade, Ministry of Economic Affairs, Taiwan

Dr Grant Wardlaw, Commonwealth Law Enforcement Board, Australia

Mr Paul Waterschoot, Director, Approximation of Laws, Internal Market and Industrial Affairs, European Commission

Mr Roger Watson, Department of Trade and Industry, UK

Mr Douglas A. Webb, Principal Counsel, Private Sector Developer, Legal Department, World Bank

Mr Tony Webb, Food Policy Alliance

Mr Ludwig Weber, Senior Legal Counsel, International Air Transport Association, Montreal

Ms Václava Weignerová, Director, Ministry for Economic Competition of Czech Republic

Mr Luc Werring, Director of Safety, Technology and Road Transport Environment, European Commission

Prof. Ted Wheelright, Council Member, Australian Consumers Association, Transnational Corporations Research Project

Mr Darwin Wika, Manager, Safety, Health and Environmental Affairs Program, DuPont

Mr Ian Wilkinson, Head of Division, Financial Institutions and Company Law, European Commission

Mr Dietrich Willers, Federal Ministry of Labour and Social Affairs, Germany

Mr Ed Willett, Director Business Law, Office of Regulation Review, Department of Treasury, Australia

Ms Kelly Winegardener, US Internal Revenue Service

Mr Johannes Witt, Head of Maritime Technology Section, Federal Ministry of Transport, Germany

Dr Manfred Witte, Ministry of Posts and Telecommunications, Germany

Ms Zofia Wlodarczyk, Economist, Anti-monopoly Office, Poland

Mr Thomas Wolf, International Monetary Fund, Washington DC

Mr Alan Wolff, Attorney, Dewey Ballantine

Ms Diane Wood, Deputy Assistant Attorney-General, Antitrust Division, US Justice Department

Mr John Wood, Director, Federal Bureau of Consumer Affairs, Australia

Ms Marie Wynter, Department of Foreign Affairs and Trade, Australia

Mr Richard Yates, Operations Director, Joint Aviation Authorities, Amsterdam

Mr Dimitri Ypsilanti, Telecommunications Policy, OECD, Paris

Mr Geoffrey Yu, Director-Counsellor, Office of the Director-General, World Intellectual Property Organization

Ms Simonetta Zarrilli, Trade and Environment Section, UNCTAD

Mr Chinlong Zheng, Chung Hua Institution for Economic Research, National Taiwan University

# Bibliography

Aalders, Marius V.C. 1991 'Regulation and Internal Company Environment Management in the Netherlands', Paper to Law and Society Association, Metting, Amsterdam.

Aamoth, Robert 1993 'The Dynamics and Impact of US Telecom Policy on Accounting Rates and International Simple Resale', in J. Savage & D. Wedemeyer (eds) *Proceedings of the Fifteenth Annual Conference of the Pacific Telecommunications Council*. Hawaii: Pacific Telecommunications Council.

Aamoth, Robert 1994 'The Impact of Accounting Rate Policy upon Telecommunications Carriers in Developing Countries', in J. Savage & D. Wedemeyer (eds) *Proceedings of the Sixteenth Annual Conference of the Pacific Telecommunications Council*. Hawaii: Pacific Telecommunications Council.

Abbot, Frederick M. 1997 'The WTO TRIPS Agreement and Global Economic Development', in Frederick M. Abbot & David J. Gerber (eds) *Public Policy and Global Technological Integration*. London: Kluwer Law International.

Abu-Lughod, Janet L. 1989 *Before European Hegemony*. New York: Oxford University Press.

Albrow, Martin 1970 *Bureaucracy*. London: Pall Mall Press.

Allen, David 1995 'Beyond Competition: Where are we in the Dialog about Policy for Telecommunications?', in D.M. Lamberton (ed.) *Beyond Competition: The Future of Telecommunications*. Amsterdam: Elsevier.

Allen, Robert 1995 'Toward Competition and Choice', *IEEE Communications Magazine* 33: 48–9.

Alston, Philip & Simma Bruno 1987 'First Session of the UN Committee on Economic, Social and Cultural Rights', *American Journal of International Law* 81: 747–56.

Anderfelt, Ulf 1971 *International Patent-Legislation and Developing Countries*. The Hague: Martinus Nijhoff.

Anderson, S. & J. Cavanagh 1996 *The Top 200: The Rise of Global Corporate Power*. Washington DC: Institute for Policy Studies.

Anstey, Roger 1975 *The Atlantic Slave Trade and British Abolition 1760–1810*. London: Macmillan.

Antonelli, C. 1994 'Localized Technological Change and the Evolution of Standards as Economic Institutions', *Information Economics and Policy* 6: 195–216.

Archibugi, Daniele & David Held (eds) 1995 *Cosmopolitan Democracy: An Agenda for a New World Order*. London: Polity Press.

Armstrong, Mark 1982 *Broadcasting Law and Policy in Australia*. Sydney: Butterworths.

Asher, Bernard 1996 'The Development of a Global Securities Market', in F. Oditah (ed.) *The Future of the Global Securities Market*. Oxford: Clarendon Press.

Ashford, Ronald 1996 'A Single Authority: The Needs and the Problems', Paper to the Royal Aeronautical Society Air Law Group Conference on the Future of Aviation Safety Regulation from a European Perspective (http://www.iapa.com/gorind/problems.htm).

Astle, W.E. 1981 *The Hamburg Rules*. Norwich: Fairplay Publications.

Atiyah, Patrick S. 1979 *The Rise And Fall of Freedom of Contract*. Oxford: Clarendon Press.

Austin, Ray 1984 'A View from Industry', in J.F. Rada & G.R. Pipe (eds) *Communication Regulation and International Business*. North Holland: Elsevier Science.

Australian Accounting Research Foundation 1995 'The Audit Profession and the Environment', Discussion paper prepared by the International Auditing Practices Committee. Auditing Standards Board of the Australian Accounting Research Foundation.

Australian Consumers Association 1991 'Submission to the Economic Planning Advisory Council', Canberra.

Australian Pharmaceutical Manufacturers Association 1990 *Code of Conduct of the Australian Pharmaceutical Manufacturers Association Inc*. Sydney: APMA.

Avery, Natalie, Martine Drake & Tim Lang 1993 *Cracking the Codex: An Analysis of Who Sets World Food Standards*. London: National Food Alliance.

Avineri, Shlomo 1972 *Hegel's Theory of the Modern State*. London: Cambridge University Press.

Axelrod, Robert 1984 *The Evolution of Cooperation*. New York: Basic Books.

Ayling, Julie 1997 'Serving Many Voices: Progressing Calls for an International Environmental Organization', *Journal of Environmental Law* 9: 243–69.

Ayres, Ian & John Braithwaite 1992 *Responsive Regulation: Transcending the Deregulation Debate*. New York: Oxford University Press.

Baldwin, Summerfield 1968 *Business in the Middle Ages*. New York: Cooper Square Publishers.

Band, Jonathan & Masanobu Katoh 1995 *Interfaces on Trial: Intellectual Property and Interoperability in the Global Software Industry*. San Francisco: Westview Press.

Bandura, A. 1986 *Social Foundations of Thought and Action: A Social Cognitive Theory.* Englewood Cliffs: Prentice-Hall.

Barak, Aharon 1968 'The Uniform Commercial Code: Commercial Paper: An Outsider's View', *Israel Law Review* 3: 7–49.

Barak, Aharon 1983 'The Nature of the Negotiable Instrument', *Israel Law Review* 18: 49–75.

Bardelay, Danielle 1997 'ISDB Assesses the Transparency of Drug Regulatory Agencies', *Essential Drugs Monitor* 24: 21–2.

Barraclough, Geoffrey (ed.) 1997 *The Times Atlas of World History*, 6th concise edn. London: Times Books.

Bartolomei de la Cruz, Héctor G., Geraldo von Potobsky & Lee Swepston 1996 *The International Labor Organization: The International Standards System and Basic Human Rights*. Boulder, Colorado: Westview Press.

Basle Committee (Committee on Banking Regulations and Supervisory Practices) May 1983 'Principles for the Supervision of Banks, Foreign Establishments', Basle, 1–9.

Basle Committee, April 1990 'Supplement to the Concordat: The Ensuring of Adequate Information Flows between Banking Supervisory Authorities', Basle, 1–6.

Basle Committee, June 1992 'Minimum Standards for the Supervision of International Banking Groups and their Cross-Border Establishments', Basle, 1–7.

Baughcum, Alan 1986 'Deregulation, Divestiture, and Competition in US Telecommunications: Lessons for Other Countries', in Marcellus S. Snow (ed.) *Telecommunications Regulation and Deregulation in Industrialized Democracies*. North Holland: Elsevier Science.

Baumol, William J., Sue Anne Batey Blackman & Edward N. Wolff 1991 *Productivity and American Leadership: The Long View*. Cambridge, Mass.: MIT Press.

Bayard, Thomas O. & Kimberly A. Elliott 1992 '"Aggressive Unilateralism" and Section 301: Market Opening or Market Closing?', *The World Economy* 15: 695.

Baylis, Craig 1994 *Food Safety: Law and Practice*. London: Sweet & Maxwell.

Beck, Ulrich 1992 *Risk Society: Towards a New Modernity*. Newbury Park: Sage.

Becker, Brandon 1988 'Global Securities Markets', *International Tax and Business Lawyer* 6: 243–61.

Beckles, Hilary 1995 'The Concept of "White Slavery" in the English Caribbean During the Early Seventeenth Century', in John Brewer & Susan Staves (eds) *Early Modern Conceptions of Property*. London: Routledge.

Beier, Friedrich-Karl 1984 'One Hundred Years of International Cooperation: The Role of the Paris Convention in the Past, Present and Future', *International Review of Industrial Property and Copyright Law* 15: 1–20.

Benavot, A., C. Yun-Kyung, D. Kamens, J.W. Meyer & W. Suk-Ying 1991 'Knowledge for the Masses: World Models and National Curricula, 1920–1986', *American Sociological Review* 56: 85–100.

Bendiner, Burton 1987 *International Labour Affairs: The World Trade Unions and the Multinational Companies*. Oxford: Clarendon Press.

Bendix, Reinhard 1977 *Max Weber: An Intellectual Portrait*. Berkeley: University of California Press.

Benedick, Richard Elliot 1991 *Ozone Diplomacy: New Directions in Safeguarding the Planet*. Cambridge, Mass.: Harvard University Press.

Berman, Harold J. 1983 *Law and Revolution: The Formation of the Western Legal Tradition*. Cambridge, Mass: Harvard University Press.

Berman, Harold J. & George L. Bustin 1975 'The Soviet System of Foreign Trade', *Law and Policy in International Business* 7: 987–1056.

Berman, Harold J. & Colin Kaufman 1978 'The Law of International Commercial Transactions (*Lex Mercatoria*)', *Harvard International Law Journal* 19: 221–77.

Besen, Stanley M. & Joseph Farrell 1994 'Choosing How to Compete: Strategies and Tactics in Standardization', *Journal of Economic Perspectives* 8: 117–31.

Besen, Stanley M. & Garth Saloner 1989 'The Economics of Telecommunications Standards', in Robert W. Crandall & Kenneth Flamm (eds) *Changing the Rules*. Washington DC: Brookings Institution.

Bethell, Leslie (ed.) 1987 *Colonial Spanish America*. Cambridge: Cambridge University Press.

Bhagwati, Jagdish N. 1988 'Trade in Services: Developing Country Concerns', *Economic Impact* 62: 58–64.

Bhagwati, J. 1990 'Aggressive Unilateralism: An Overview', in J. Bhagwati & H.T. Patrick (eds) *Aggressive Unilateralism: America's 301 Trade Policy and the World Trading System*. Ann Arbor: University of Michigan Press.

Bhagwati, J. & H.T. Patrick (eds) 1990 *Aggressive Unilateralism: America's 301 Trade Policy and the World Trading System*. Ann Arbor: University of Michigan Press.

Birdsall, Nancy & David Wheeler 1992 'Trade Policy and Industrial Pollution in Latin America: Where Are the Pollution Havens?', in Patrick Low (ed.) *International Trade and the Environment*. Washington DC: World Bank.

Birks, P. & G. McLeod 1987 'Introduction', *Justinian's Institutes*. London: Duckworth.

Black, Julia 1997 *Rules and Regulators*. Oxford: Clarendon Press.

Blackstone, William 1978 *Commentaries on the Law of England*. London: Garland Publishing.

Blake, G. undated *Lloyd's Register of Shipping 1760–1960*. London: Lloyd's Register of Shipping.

Blakeney, M. 1998 'The Role of Intellectual Property Law in Regional Commercial Unions in Europe and Asia', *Prometheus* 16: 341–50.

Blazejczak, Jurgen & Klaus Lubbe 1993 *Environmental Protection and Industrial Location: The Influence of Environmental Location-Specific Factors on Investment Decisions: Statements and Summary in English*. Berlin: Erich Schmidt Verlag.

Bloch, Henry S. & Heilemann, Cyril E. 1946 'International Tax Relations', *Yale Law Journal* 55: 1158–73.

Block, Alan A. 1992 'Failures at Home and Abroad: Studies in the Implementation of US Drug Policy', in A. McCoy & A. Block (eds) *War on Drugs: Studies in the Failure of US Narcotic Policy*. Boulder, Colorado: Westview Press.

Bloomfield, Arthur I. 1968 'Rules of the Game of International Adjustment?', in C.R. Whittlesey & J.S.G. Wilson (eds) *Essays in Money and Banking in Honour of R.S. Sayers*. Oxford: Clarendon Press.

Blumberg, Phillip I. 1993 'The American Law of Corporate Groups', in Joseph McCahery, Sol Picciotto & Colin Scott (eds) *Corporate Control and Accountability*. Oxford: Clarendon Press.

Bodin, Jean 1576 *On Sovereignty: Four Chapters from Six Books of the Commonwealth* (edited and translated by Julian H. Franklin), 1992 edn. Cambridge: Cambridge University Press.

Boer, Ben 1995 'The Globalisation of Environmental Law: The Role of the United Nations', *Melbourne University Law Review* 20: 101–25.

Bogsch, Arpad 1992 *Brief History of the First 25 Years of the World Intellectual Property Organization*. Geneva: World Intellectual Property Organization.

Boli, John 1999 'Conclusion: World Authority Structures and Legitimations', in John Boli & George M. Thomas (eds) *Constructing World Culture: International Nongovernmental Organizations since 1875*. Stanford, CA: Stanford University Press.

Boli, John, Thomas A. Loya & Teresa Loftin 1999 'National Participation in World-Polity Organization', in John Boli & George M. Thomas (eds) *Constructing World Culture: International Nongovernmental Organizations since 1875*. Stanford, CA: Stanford University Press.

Bond, Ronald S. & David F. Lean 1977 *Sales, Promotion and Product Differentiation in Two Prescription Drug Markets: Staff Report to the Federal Trade Commission*. Washington DC: US Government Printing Office.

Bonell, M.J. 1992 'Unification of Law by Non-Legislative Means: The UNIDROIT Draft Principles for International Commercial Contracts', *American Journal of Comparative Law* 40: 617–33.

Bonell, Michael Joachim 1994 *An International Restatement of Contract Law: The UNIDROIT Principles of International Commercial Contracts*. Irvington, New York: Transnational Juris Publications.

Bonnassie, Pierre 1991 *From Slavery to Feudalism in South-Western Europe* (translated by Jean Birrell). Cambridge: Cambridge University Press.

Bordeaux-Groult, Robert 1987 'Problems of Enforcement and Cooperation in the Multinational Securities Market: A French Perspective', *University of Pennsylvania Journal of International Business Law* 9: 453–65.

Borg, Parker W. & Fredric A. Emmert 1989 'Telecommunications: A Bridge to Better East–West Relations', *North Carolina Journal of International Law and Commercial Regulation* 14: 279–86.

Bortolotti, Fabio (ed.) 1993 *The ICC Agency Model Contracts: A Commentary*. Boston: Kluwer Law & Taxation Publishers.

Boulding, Kenneth 1953 *The Organizational Revolution*. New York: Harper.

Boulding, K. 1973 *The Image*. Ann Arbor: University of Michigan Press.

Bowles, S. & H. Gintis 1986 *Democracy and Capitalism*. London: Routledge & Kegan Paul.

Braithwaite, John 1980 'Inegalitarian Consequences of Egalitarian Reforms to Control Corporate Crime', *Temple Law Quarterly* 53: 1127–46.

Braithwaite, John 1984 *Corporate Crime in the Pharmaceutical Industry*. London: Routledge & Kegan Paul.

Braithwaite, John 1985 'Corporate Crime Research: Why Two Interviewers are Needed', *Sociology* 19: 136–8.

Braithwaite, John 1988 'Economic Policy: What the Electorate Thinks', in J. Kelley & C. Bean (eds) *Australian Attitudes: Social and Political Analyses from the National Social Science Survey*. Sydney: Allen & Unwin.

Braithwaite, John 1989 *Crime, Shame and Reintegration*. Cambridge: Cambridge University Press.

Braithwaite, John 1994 'A Sociology of Modelling and the Politics of Empowerment', *British Journal of Sociology* 45: 443–79.

Braithwaite, John 1997 'On Speaking Softly and Carrying Big Sticks: Neglected Dimensions of a Republican Separation of Powers', *University of Toronto Law Journal* 47: 305–61.

Braithwaite, John 1998 'Institutionalizing Distrust, Enculturating Trust', in V. Braithwaite & M. Levi (eds) *Trust and Governance*. New York : Russell Sage Foundation.

Braithwaite, John 2000 'The New Regulatory State and the Coming Decline of Criminology', *British Journal of Criminology*.

Braithwaite, John & Philip Pettit 1990 *Not Just Deserts: A Republican Theory of Criminal Justice*. Oxford: Oxford University Press.

Braithwaite, Valerie 1992 *First Steps: Business Reaction to Implementing the Affirmative Action Act. Report to the Affirmative Action Agency*. Canberra: Research School of Social Sciences, Australian National University.

Brancker, J.W.S. 1977 *IATA and What It Does*. Leyden: A.W. Sijthoff.

Braudel, F. 1975 *Capitalism and Material Life: 1400–1800*. New York: Harper & Row.

Braudel, Fernand 1979 *The Wheels of Commerce: Civilization and Capitalism 15th–18th Century*, vol. 2. New York: Harper & Row.

Braudel, Fernand 1984 *The Perspective of the World: Civilization and Capitalism 15th–18th Century*, vol. 3. New York: Harper & Row.

Braybrooke, D. & C.E. Lindblom 1970 *A Strategy of Decision*. New York: Free Press.

Brehm, Sharon S. & Jack W. Brehm 1981 *Psychological Reactance: A Theory of Freedom and Control*. New York: Academic Press.

Brenton, Tony 1994 *The Greening of Machiavelli*. London: Earthscan Publications.

Briggs, William 1906 *The Law of International Copyright*. London: Stevens & Haynes.

Brown, Ronald H., H. O'Leary & C. Browner 1993 *Environmental Technologies Exports: Strategic Framework for US Leadership*. Washington DC: US Department of Commerce.

Brundtland, G.H. 1987 *Our Common Future*. Melbourne: Oxford University Press.

Bruun, Kettil, Lynn Pan & Ingemar Rexed 1975 *The Gentlemen's Club: International Control of Drugs and Alcohol*. Chicago: University of Chicago Press.

Bryan, David A. 1981 'Consumer Safety Abroad: Dumping of Dangerous American Products Overseas', *Texas Tech Law Review* 12: 435–58.

Buckland, W.W. 1963 *A Text-Book of Roman Law from Augustus to Justinian*, 3rd edn (revised by Peter Stein). London: Cambridge University Press.

Burke, Carole S. 1980 'International Legislation', in R.H. Tilbury (ed.) *Developments in Food Preservatives*. London: Applied Publishers.

Burke, K. 1945 *A Grammar of Motives*. New York: Prentice-Hall.

Burkhardt, Robert 1967 *The Federal Aviation Administration*. New York: Praeger.

Burley, Anne-Marie Slaughter 1993 'Law Among Liberal States: Liberal Internationalism and the Act of State Doctrine', *Columbia Law Journal* 92: 190–6.

Burns, A.R. 1965 *Money and Monetary Policy in Early Times* (reprint of original 1927 edition). New York: Augustus M. Kelley, Bookseller.

Burrough, Bryan & John Helyar 1991 *Barbarians at the Gate: The Fall of RJR Nabisco*. New York: Harper.

Burstall, M.L. 1991 'Europe After 1992: Implication for Pharmaceuticals', *Health Affairs* 10: 157–71.

Bussey, K. & A. Bandura 1984 'Gender Constancy, Social Power and Sex-Linked Modelling', *Journal of Personality and Social Psychology* 47: 1292–302.

Buzan, Barry 1993 'From International System to International Society: Structural Realism and Regime Theory Meet the English School', *International Organization* 47: 327–52.

Caccamise, C. William Jr 1988 'US Countermeasures Against Tax Haven Countries', *Columbia Journal of Transnational Law* 26: 553–71.

Cain, Maureen 1994 'The Symbol Traders', in M. Cain & C.B. Harrington (eds) *Lawyers in a Postmodern World: Translation and Transgression*. Buckingham: Open University Press.

Cain, Maureen & Christine B. Harrington 1994 'Introduction', in M. Cain & C.B. Harrington (eds) *Lawyers in a Postmodern World: Translation and Transgression*. Buckingham: Open University Press.

Cairns, David, H. 1996 'The Role of International Accounting Standards in Improving and Harmonising Financial Reporting', *Corporate Governance* 4: 48–59.

Caldwell, Lynton K. 1988 'Beyond Environmental Diplomacy: The Changing Institutional Structure of International Cooperation', in John E. Carroll (ed.) *International Environmental Diplomacy: The Management and Resolution of Transfrontier Environmental Problems*. Cambridge: Cambridge University Press.

Calmfors, Lars & John Driffill 1988 'Bargaining Structure, Corporatism and Economic Performance', *Economic Policy* 6: 14–61.

Cambridge, Charles 1984 'Emerging Trends in the Industrial Relations Systems of Former British Colonies: The Ratification of International Labor Conventions', *Journal of African Studies* 11: 129–34.

Cameron, James & Ruth MacKenzie 1996 'Access to Environmental Justice and Procedural Rights in International Institutions' in A.E. Boyle & M.R. Anderson (eds) *Human Rights Approaches to Environmental Protection*. New York: Oxford University Press.

Cameron, Rondo 1967 'England 1750–1844', in Rondo Cameron, Olga Crisp, Hugh T. Patrick & Richard Tilly *Banking in the Early Stages of Industrialization*. New York: Oxford University Press.

Cameron, Rondo 1989 *A Concise Economic History of the World: From Paleolithic Times to the Present*. New York: Oxford University Press.

Campbell, John L. 1988 'Collective Organization, Corporations, and the State: Industry Response to the Accident at Three Mile Island', Paper to Society for the Study of Social Problems.

Canan, Penelope & Nancy Reichman 1993 'Ozone Partnerships, the Construction of Regulatory Communities, and the Future of Global Regulatory Power', *Law and Policy* 15: 61–74.

Carandang, E.D. & R.F.W. Moulds 1994 'Pharmaceutical Advertisements in Australian Medical Publications: Have They Improved?' *Medical Journal of Australia* 161: 671–2.

Carlson, Jonathan 1985 'Hunger, Agricultural Trade Liberalization, and Soft International Law: Addressing the Legal Dimensions of a Political Problem', *Iowa Law Review* 70: 1187–277.

Carroll, John E. (ed.) 1988 *International Environmental Diplomacy: The Management and Resolution of Transfrontier Environmental Problems*. Cambridge: Cambridge University Press.

Carruthers, Bruce & Wendy Nelson Espeland 1991 'Accounting for Rationality: Double-Entry Bookkeeping and the Rhetoric of Economic Rationality', *American Journal of Sociology* 97: 31–69.

Carter, April 1992 *Peace Movements: International Protest and World Politics Since 1945*. London: Longman.

Cascio, Joe 1994 'International Environmental Management Standards: ISO 9000's Less Tractable Siblings', *ASTM Standardization News* April: 44–9.

Cassis, Youssef 1991 'Financial Elites in Three European Centres: London, Paris, Berlin, 1880s–1930s', in Geoffrey Jones (ed.) *Banks and Money: International and Comparative Finance in History*. London: Frank Cass.

Castleman, Barry I. 1979 'The Export of Hazardous Factories to Developing Nations', *International Journal of Health Services* 9: 569–606.

Castleman, Barry I. 1981 'More on the International Asbestos Business', *International Journal of Health Services* 11: 339–40.

Chalmers, M.D. 1886 'An Experiment in Codification', *Law Quarterly Review* 2: 126–34.

Chalmers, M.D. 1903 'Codification of Mercantile Law', *Law Quarterly Review* 19: 10–18.

Chandler, Alfred D. Jr 1977 *The Visible Hand: The Managerial Revolution in American Business*. Cambridge, Mass.: Belknap Press.

Chandler, Alfred D. Jr 1990 *Scale and Scope: The Dynamics of Industrial Capitalism*. Cambridge, Mass.: Belknap Press.

Channon, Derek F. 1988 *Global Banking Strategy*. New York: John Wiley & Sons.

Charlesworth, Hilary 1996 'Women as Sherpas: Are Global Summits Useful for Women?', *Feminist Studies* 22: 537–47.

Charnovitz, Steve 1987 'The Influence of International Labour Standards on the World Trading Regime: A Historical Overview', *International Labour Review* 126: 565–84.

Charnovitz, Steve 1994 'The World Trade Organization and Environmental Supervision', *International Trade Reporter* 26: 89–90.

Chase-Dunn, C. 1989 *Global Formation: Structures of the World Economy*. Oxford: Blackwell.

Chayes, Abram & Antonia Handler Chayes 1991 'Compliance Without Enforcement: State Behavior Under Regulatory Treaties', *Negotiation Journal* 7: 311–30.

Chayes, Abram & Antonia Handler Chayes 1995 *The New Sovereignty: Compliance with International Regulatory Agreements*. Cambridge, Mass.: Harvard University Press.

Cheek, James H. III 1996 'Approaches to Market Regulation', in F. Oditah (ed.) *The Future of the Global Securities Market*. Oxford: Clarendon Press.

Cheit, Ross E. 1990a 'Reducing Risk Through Insurance: An Institutional Analysis of Loss Prevention', Paper to the Annual Research Conference of the Association for Public Policy Analysis and Management, San Francisco.

Cheit, Ross E. 1990b *Setting Safety Standards: Regulation in the Public and Private Sectors*. Berkeley: University of California Press.

Chernow, Ron 1990 *The House of Morgan: An American Banking Dynasty and the Rise of Modern Finance*. New York: Atlantic Monthly Press.

Chetley, Andrew 1979 *The Baby Killer Scandal: A War on Want Investigation into the Promotion and Sale of Powdered Baby Milks in the Third World*. London: War on Want.

Chetley, Andrew 1990 *A Healthy Business? World Health and the Pharmaceutical Industry*. London: Zed Books.

Chiron, Stuart Z. & Lise A. Rehberg 1986–87 'Fostering Competition in International Telecommunications', *Federal Communications Law Journal* 38: 1–57.

Chisholm, Anthony H. & Rodney Tyers 1982 'Food Security: An Introduction and Overview', in Anthony H. Chisholm & Rodney Tyers (eds) *Food Security: Theory, Policy, and Perspectives from Asia and the Pacific Rim*. Lexington, Mass: D.C. Heath & Co.

Chomsky, Noam 1993 'World Order and Its Rules: Variations on Some Themes', *Journal of Law and Society* 20: 145–65.

Chung, John 1993 'Case Study of Korea', in OECD, *Public Participation in Nuclear Decision-Making*. Paris: OECD.

CIOMS/WHO 1993 *Consultation on WHO's Ethical Criteria for Medicinal Drug Promotion*. Geneva: Council for International Organizations of Medical Sciences.

Clarence-Smith, W.G. 1993 'Labour Conditions in the Plantations of Sao Tomé and Principe, 1875–1914', *Slavery and Abolition* 14: 149–67.

Clarke, Michael 1986 *Regulating the City: Competition, Scandal and Reform*. Milton Keynes: Open University Press.

Clarke, Stephen, V.O. 1977 'Exchange-Rate Stabilization in the Mid-1930s: Negotiating the Tripartite Agreement', *Princeton Studies in International Finance* 41. Princeton, New Jersey: Princeton University.

Clegg, S. 1989 *Frameworks of Power*. London: Sage.

Clifford, Mark 1994 'Social Engineers', *Far Eastern Economic Review* 157: 56–60.

Clinard, Marshall & Peter Yeager 1980 *Corporate Crime*. New York: Free Press.

Coase, R.H. 1960 'The Problem of Social Cost', *Journal of Law and Economics* 3: 1–44.

Codding, George A. 1964 *The Universal Postal Union: Coordinator of the International Mails*. New York: New York University Press.

Codding, George Arthur Jr 1972 *The International Telecommunication Union: An Experiment in International Cooperation* (reprint edition). Arno Press, New York.

Codding, George A. 1977 'The United States and the ITU in a Changing World' *Telecommunications Journal* 44: 231.

Codding, George A. Jr 1995 'The International Telecommunication Union: 130 Years of Telecommunications Regulation', *Denver Journal of International Law and Policy* 23: 501.

Codding, George A. Jr & Anthony M. Rutkowski 1982 *The International Telecommunication Union in a Changing World*. Dedham, Mass.: Artech House.

Codex Alimentarius Commission 1987 *Introducing Codex Alimentarius*. Rome: Codex Alimentarius Commission.

Codex Alimentarius Commission 1996 *Joint FAO/WHO Food Standards Programme Codex Committee on Import and Export Food Inspection and Certification Systems, Fourth Session, Sydney*. CX/FICS 96/7. Rome: Codex Alimentarius Commission.

Cohen, A. 1955 *Delinquent Boys: The Culture of the Gang*. Glencoe, Ill.: Free Press.

Cohen, Benjamin J. (ed.) 1993 *The International Political Economy of Monetary Relations*. Brookfield, Vt: Edward Elgar.

Cohen, M.D., J.G. March & J.P. Olsen 1972 'A Garbage Can Model of Organisational Choice', *Administrative Science Quarterly* 17: 1–25.

Cohn, E. & D.P. Farrington 1992 'Who are the Most Influential Criminologists in the English-Speaking World?', Unpublished manuscript, Institute of Criminology, Cambridge University.

Cohn, Ellen N. 1983 'International Regulation of Pharmaceuticals: The Role of the World Health Organization', *Virginia Journal of Transnational Law* 23: 331–61.

Coleman, James S. 1982 *The Asymmetric Society*. Syracuse, New York: Syracuse University Press.

Coleman, James S. 1990 *Foundations of Social Theory*. Cambridge, Mass.: Harvard University Press.

Colino, Richard, R. 1985 'A Chronicle of Policy and Procedure: The Formulation of the Reagan Administration Policy on International Satellite Telecommunications', *Journal of Space Law* 13: 103–56.

Colley, Peter 1994 'Trade and Environment: Relationship to International Labour Standards'. Sydney: Mining and Energy Division of the Construction, Forestry, Mining and Energy Union.

Collier, D. & R.E. Messick 1975 'Prerequisites versus Diffusion: Testing Alternative Explanations of Social Security Adoption', *American Political Science Review* 69: 1299–315.

Commission on Global Governance 1995 *Our Global Neighbourhood: The Report of the Commission on Global Governance*. Oxford: Oxford University Press.

Committee of Experts on the Application of Conventions and Recommendations 1988 *Equality in Employment and Occupation*. Geneva: International Labour Office.

Commonwealth Attorney-General's Department 1996 '10 July, Copy of Answers to Questions from the US concerning TRIPS', Canberra.

Commonwealth of Australia, 1995 *Networking Australia's Future. The Final Report of the Broadband Service Expert Group, December 1994*. Canberra: Australian Government Publishing Service.

Compa, Lance & Tashia Hinchcliffe-Darricarrere 1995 'Enforcing International Labour Rights through Corporate Codes of Conduct', *Columbia Journal of Transnational Law* 33: 663–89.

Conference on Transfer Pricing 1993 *Canadian Tax Journal* 41: 901–21.

Cooke, C.A. 1950 *Corporation, Trust and Company: An Essay in Legal History*. Manchester: Manchester University Press.

Cooke, Sir Robin 1995 'The Dream of an International Common Law', Melbourne Conference: The Mason Court and Beyond.

Cooper, Frederick (ed.) 1983 *Struggle for the City: Migrant Labor, Capital, and the State in Urban Africa*. California: Sage.

Cooper, Frederick 1996 *Decolonization and African Society: The Labor Question in French and British Africa*. Cambridge: Cambridge University Press.

Cooper, Kerry S. & Donald R. Fraser 1993 *The Financial Marketplace*, 4th edn. Reading, Mass.: Addison-Wesley.

Cooter, Robert D. 1996 'Decentralized Law for a Complex Economy: The Structural Approach to Adjudicating the New Law Merchant', *University of Pennsylvania Law Review* 144: 1643–96.

Copyright Law Review Committee 1988 *Report on Moral Rights*. Canberra: Australian Government Publishing Service.

Corina, Maurice 1975 *Trust in Tobacco*. London: Michael Joseph.

Corporate Crime Reporter 1992 'Corporate Front Groups Proliferate, Are Used to Deceive and Confuse the Public, Report Finds. 36 Groups Identified and Profiled', *Corporate Crime Reporter* 6: 1–3.

Correa, Carlos M. 1990 'Legal Protection of the Layout Designs of Integrated Circuits: The WIPO Treaty' *European Intellectual Property Review* 12: 196–203.

Council for Economic Planning and Development 1995 *The Plan for Developing Taiwan as an Asia-Pacific Regional Operations Center*. Republic of China: Executive Yuan.

Council of the European Communities, Commission of the European Communities 1992 'Agreement on the European Economic Area'. Brussels: European Commission.

Cowen, Denis V. & Leonard Gering 1966 *Cowen on the Law of Negotiable Instruments in South Africa*, 4th edn. Cape Town, Wynberg, Johannesburg: Juta & Co.

Craig, Gordon A. & Alexander L. George 1990 *Force and Statecraft*, 2nd edn. New York: Oxford University Press.

Crandall, R.W., H.K. Gruenspecht, T.E. Keeler & L.B. Lave 1986 *Regulating the Automobile*. Washington DC: Brookings Institution.

Craven, Paul & Douglas Hay 1994 'The Criminalization of "Free" Labour: Master and Servant in Comparative Perspective', *Slavery and Abolition* 15: 71–101.

Creighton, Breen 1993 'Occupational Health and Safety Regulation: The Role of ILO Standards', in Michael Quinlan (ed.) *Work and Health: The Origins, Management and Regulation of Occupational Illness*. Melbourne: Macmillan.

Creighton, W.B. & A.J. Stewart 1994 *Labour Law: An Introduction*, 2nd edn. Sydney: Federation Press.

Cunliffe, Barry 1988 *Greeks, Romans and Barbarians*. London: B.T. Batsford.

Curtin, Philip D. 1984 *Cross-Cultural Trade in World History*. Cambridge: Cambridge University Press.

Cushing, Luther S. 1854 *An Introduction to the Study of Roman Law*. Boston: Little, Brown.

Daffner, Gregg 1996 'Intelsat Restructuring: How Can the Public Interest be Served?', in Dan Wedemeyer & Richard Nickelson (eds) *Proceedings of the 18th Annual Conference of the Pacific Telecommunications Council*. Hawaii: Pacific Telecommunications Council.

Dahl, Karl Nandrup 1968 'The Role of ILO Standards in the Global Integration Process', *Journal of Peace Research* 5: 309–51.

Dale, Richard 1984 *The Regulation of International Banking*. Cambridge: Woodhead-Faulkner.

Dale, Richard 1996 *Risk and Regulation in Global Securities Markets*. New York: Wiley.

Daly, Hermann & Robert Goodland 1994 'An Ecological–Economic Assessment of Deregulation of International Commerce under GATT', *Ecological Economics* 9: 73–92.

Danzig, R. 1975 'A Comment on the Jurisprudence of the Code', *Stanford Law Review* 27: 621–35.

D'Arcy, P.F. & D.W.G. Harron (eds) 1991 *Proceedings of the First International Conference on Harmonization.* Belfast: Queen's University of Belfast.

Dauvergne, Peter 1996 'Globalization and Unsustainable Logging in Southeast Asia and Melanesia'. Canberra: Department of International Relations, Australian National University.

David, P.A. 1987 'Some New Standards for the Economics of Standardization in the Information Age', in P. Dasgupta & P. Stoneman (eds) *Economic Policy and Technological Performance.* Cambridge: Cambridge University Press.

David, Wilfred L. 1985 *The IMF Policy Paradigm.* New York: Praeger.

Davidow, Joel 1990 'The Worldwide Influence of US Antitrust', *Antitrust Bulletin* 35: 603–30.

Davidson, Scott J. 1994 'The International Organizations of Securities Commissions', in G. Walker & B. Fisse (eds) *Securities Regulation in Australia and New Zealand.* Auckland: Oxford University Press.

Davies, Andrew 1994 *Telecommunications and Politics: The Decentralised Alternative.* London: Pinter.

Davies, Glyn 1994 *A History of Money.* Cardiff: University of Wales Press.

Davies, Norman 1997 *Europe: A History.* London: Pimlico.

Davis, John P. 1961 *Corporations: A Study of the Origin and Development of Great Business Combinations and their Relation to the Authority of the State.* New York: Capricorn Books.

Degan, A. Stephen 1998 'Macro View of US R&D Licensing', *Les Nouvelles* 33: 144–7.

Dell, Sidney 1983 'Stabilization: The Political Economy of Overkill', in John Williamson (ed.) *IMF Conditionality.* Washington DC: Institute for International Economics.

Deming, W.E. 1986 *Out of the Crisis.* Cambridge, Mass.: Cambridge University Press.

Demsetz, H. 1967 'Toward a Theory of Property Rights' *American Economic Review* 57: 347–59.

Department of Industrial Relations 1994 'Status of ILO Conventions in Australia: 1994'. Canberra: Department of Industrial Relations.

de Rooy, Frans P. 1984 *Documentary Credits.* Deventer, Netherlands: Kluwer Law & Taxation.

de Saint Phalle, Thibaut 1985 *The Federal Reserve: An Intentional Mystery.* New York: Praeger.

DeSaussure, Hamilton 1989 'Remote Sensing Satellite Regulation by National and International Law' *Rutgers Computer and Technology Law Journal* 15: 351–81.

De Sombre, Elizabeth R. 1995 'Baptists and Bootleggers for the Environment: The Origins of United States Unilateral Sanctions', *Journal of Environment and Development* 4: 53–75.

Dezalay, Yves 1991 'Les Professionnels des Affaires et la Regulation Internationale du Marche des entreprises', *Revue Politiques et Management Public* 3 (translated by Brian Cleeve in Y. Dezalay & D. Sugarman (eds) *Professional Competition and the Social Construction of Markets.* London: Routledge).

Dezalay, Yves 1994 'The Forum Should Fit the Fuss: The Economics and Politics of Negotiated Justice', in M. Cain & C.B. Harrington (eds) *Lawyers in a Postmodern World: Translation and Transgression.* Buckingham: Open University Press.

Dezalay, Yves 1996 'Between the State and the Market: The Social and Professional Stakes in the Construction and Definition of a Regulatory Arena', in W. Bratton, J. McCahery, S. Picciotto & C. Scott (eds) *International Regulatory Competition and Coordination: Perspectives on Economic Regulation in Europe and the United States.* Oxford: Clarendon Press.

Dezalay, Yves & Bryant G. Garth 1994 *Grand Old Men vs Multinationals: The Routinization of Charismatic Arbitration into Off-Shore Litigation.* Chicago: American Bar Foundation.

Dezalay, Yves & Bryant G. Garth 1996 *Dealing in Virtue: International Commercial Arbitration and the Construction of a Transnational Legal Order.* Chicago: University of Chicago Press.

Dicey, A.V. 1959 *Introduction to the Study of the Law of the Constitution,* 10th edn. London: Macmillan.

Dickson, P.G.M. 1993 *The Financial Revolution in England: A Study in the Development of Public Credit, 1688–1756.* Brookfield, Vt: Gregg Revivals.

Dinnen, Sinclair 1996 'Challenges of Order in a Weak State', Unpublished PhD dissertation, Law Program, Research School of Social Sciences, Australian National University.

Doherty, Ann 1994 'The Role of Nongovernmental Organizations in UNCED', in Bertram I. Spector, G. Sjostedt & I.W. Zartman (eds) *Negotiating International Regimes: Lessons Learned from the United Nations Conference on Environment and Development (UNCED).* London: Graham & Trotman.

Douglas, George H. 1987 *The Early Days of Radio Broadcasting.* Jefferson, NC: McFarland & Co.

Douglas, Susan J. 1987 *Inventing American Broadcasting 1899–1922.* Baltimore: Johns Hopkins University Press.

Dowling, Harry F. 1970 'The American Medical Association's Policy on Drugs in Recent Decades', in John B. Blake (ed.) *Safeguarding the Public: Historical Aspects of Medicinal Drug Control*. Baltimore: Johns Hopkins University Press.

Downs, Anthony 1972 'Up and Down with Ecology: The "Issue-Attention Cycle"', *Public Interest* 28: 38–50.

Downs, George W., David M. Rocke & Peter N. Barsoom 1996 'Is the Good News about Compliance Good News about Cooperation?', *International Organization* 50: 379–406.

Drahos, Peter 1995 'Global Property Rights in Information: The Story of TRIPS at the GATT', *Prometheus* 13: 6–19.

Drahos, Peter 1996 *A Philosophy of Intellectual Property*. Dartmouth: Aldershot.

Drahos, P. & Richard A. Joseph 1995 'Telecommunications and Investment in the Great Supranational Regulatory Game', *Telecommunications Policy* 19: 619–35.

Drahos, Peter & Stephen Parker 1992 'Rule Following, Rule Scepticism and Indeterminacy in Law: A Conventional Account', *Ratio Juris* 5: 109–19.

Drucker, P.F. 1993 *Post-Capitalist Society*. New York: Harper Business.

Dryzek, John 1996 'The Informal Logic of Institutional Design', in Robert E. Goodin (ed.) *The Theory of Institutional Design*. Cambridge: Cambridge University Press.

Duch, Raymond M. 1991 *Privatizing the Economy: Telecommunications Policy in Comparative Perspective*. Ann Arbor: University of Michigan Press.

Dudley, Leonard M. 1991 *The Word and the Sword*. Cambridge, Mass.: Blackwell.

Dukes, M.N.G. & B. Swartz 1988 *Responsibility for Drug-Induced Injury*. Amsterdam: Elsevier.

Duncan, H.D. 1968 *Symbols in Society*. New York: Oxford University Press.

Duncan, H.D. 1969 *Symbols and Social Theory*. New York: Oxford University Press.

Dunning, J.H. 1993 *Multinational Enterprises and the Global Economy*. London: Addison-Wesley.

Dussol, Robert J. 1990 'The European Nuclear Industry and the French Nuclear Industry', *Papers in Nuclear Science and Technology 1990/91*. Sutherland, NSW: Australian Nuclear Association.

Dworkin, R. 1967 'The Model of Rules', *University of Chicago Law Review* 35: 14, 25.

Economic Commission for Europe 1993a *Working Party on the Construction of Vehicles: Its Role in the International Perspective, Note by the Secretariat*. Trans/SC1/WP29/ R.628, 24 May 1993, Geneva.

Economic Commission for Europe 1993b *Working Party on the Construction of Vehicles: Report of the Working Party on its One-Hundred-and-Eleventh Session*. TRANS/WP29/534, 24 March 1997, Geneva.

Economic Commission for Europe 1996 *Working Party on the Construction of Vehicles: Proposal for a Draft Agreement Concerning the Establishing of Global Technical Regulations for Vehicles, Engines and Components*. TRANS/WP29/R796, 18 December 1996, Geneva.

Edelman, Murray 1964 *The Symbolic Uses Of Politics*. Urbana: University of Illinois Press.

Edmunds, John C. 1996 'Securities: The New World Wealth Machine', *Foreign Policy* 104: 118–38.

Einaudi, L. 1928 'La Co-opération International en Matière Fiscale', Académie de Droit International, La Haye, *Receuil des Cours* 25: 1–123.

Einzig, Paul, 1949 *Primitive Money*. London: Eyre & Spottiswoode.

Einzig, Paul 1970 *The History of Foreign Exchange*, 2nd edn. London: Macmillan.

Elster, Jon 1989 *Nuts and Bolts for the Social Sciences*. Cambridge: Cambridge University Press.

Eltis, David 1987 *Economic Growth and the Ending of the Transatlantic Slave Trade*. New York: Oxford University Press.

Eltis, David 1993 'Labour and Coercion in the English Atlantic World from the Seventeenth to the Early Twentieth Century', *Slavery and Abolition* 14: 207–26.

Emmer, P.C. 1993 'Capitalism After Slavery? The French Slave Trade and Slavery in the Atlantic, 1500–1900', *Itinerario* 17: 103–16.

Epstein, Edward Jay 1980 *Agency of Fear: Opiates and Political Power in America*. London: Verso.

Erikson, E.H. 1968 *Identity, Youth and Crisis*. New York: Norton.

Esty, Daniel C. 1994 *Greening the GATT: Trade, Environment and the Future*. Washington DC: Institute for International Economics.

Etzioni, A. 1965 'Organisational Control Structure', in James G. March (ed.) *Handbook of Organisations*. Chicago: Rand McNally.

Euromoney Publications 1992 *International Securities Law*. London: Euromoney Publications.

*Europe and the Global Information Society: Recommendations to the European Council* (Bangemann Report) Brussels, 26 May 1994.

European Commission 1992 *Treatment Accorded in Third Countries to Community Credit Institutions and Insurance Companies*, Working Document of the Commission Services, XV/4004/92-EN.

Evans, G.E. 1998 'Issues of Legitimacy and the Resolution of Intellectual Property Disputes in the Supercourt of the World Trade Organization', Unpublished manuscript, Southern Cross University.

Evans, M.D.R. 1995 'Public Opinion on Multinational Corporations', *Worldwide Attitudes Electronic Journal* 1995 0814. http://coombs.anu.edu.au/Depts/RSSS/NSSS/WWA.html http

Evans, Phillip 1995 'The Internationalisation of Competition Policy: A Way Forward for Consumers?' London: Consumers International Discussion Paper.

Falk, Jim 1982 *Global Fission: The Battle over Nuclear Power*. Melbourne: Oxford University Press.

Fallows, Stephen J. 1988 *Food Legislative System of the UK*. London: Butterworths.

Farnsworth Allan E. 1992 'Closing Remarks' *American Journal of Comparative Law* 40: 699–702.

Farrell, J. 1989 'Standardization and Intellectual Property', *Jurimetrics Journal* 30: 35.

Faunce, T.A. & P. Drahos 1998 'Trade Related Aspects of Intellectual Property Rights (TRIPS) and the Threat to Patients: A Plea for Doctors to Respond Internationally', *Journal of Law and Medicine* 17: 299–310.

Featherstone, M. (ed.) 1990 *Global Culture: Nationalism, Globalisation and Modernity*. London: Sage.

Feitshans, Ilise Levy 1995 *Human Rights to Healthy Workplaces: A Global Perspective on Implementation and Compliance*. New York: School of Law, Columbia University.

Feketekuty, Geza 1986 *International Trade in Services*. Washington DC: American Enterprise Institute.

Feketekuty, Geza 1990 'US Policy on 301 and Super 301', in J. Bhagwati & H.T. Patrick (eds) *Aggressive Unilateralism: America's 301 Trade Policy and the World Trading System*. Ann Arbor: University of Michigan Press.

Feketekuty, Geza 1993 'The Link between Trade and Environmental Policy', *Minnesota Journal of Global Trade* 2: 171–205.

Feketekuty, Geza 1996 'US Trade Policy and the Public Discourse: A Postscript' in D. Perkins, A. MacIntyre & G. Feketekuty 'Trade, Security, and National Strategy in the Asia Pacific', *Analysis* 7: 35–9.

Financial Action Task Force on Money Laundering 1990 *Report*. Paris: Financial Action Task Force on Money Laundering.

Finkelman, Paul 1985 *Slavery in the Courtroom: An Annotated Bibliography of American Cases*. Washington: Library of Congress.

Finkelman, Paul 1986 *The Law of Freedom and Bondage: A Casebook*. New York: Oceana.

Finley, M.I. 1980 *Ancient Slavery and Modern Ideology*. London: Chatto & Windus.

Fisse, Brent & John Braithwaite 1983 *The Impact of Publicity on Corporate Offenders*. Albany: State University of New York Press.

Fisse, Brent & John Braithwaite 1993 *Corporations, Crime and Accountability*. Melbourne: Cambridge University Press.

Fitzpatrick, Peter 1984 'Law, Plurality and Underdevelopment', in D. Sugarman (ed.) *Legality, Ideology and the State*. London: Academic Press.

Flam, Helena (ed.) 1994 *States and Anti-Nuclear Movements*. Edinburgh: Edinburgh University Press.

Flavin, C. 1986 *Reassessing Nuclear Power: The Fallout from Chernobyl*. Paper 75. Washington DC: Worldwatch Institute.

Fletcher, George P. 1976 'The Metamorphosis of Larceny', *Harvard Law Review* 89: 469–530.

Fogel, Robert William & Stanley L. Engerman 1974 *Time on the Cross: The Economics of American Negro Slavery*. Boston, Toronto: Little, Brown.

Food and Agriculture Organization 1990 *FAO/WHO Conference on Food Standards, Chemicals in Food and Food Trade*. Rome: FAO.

Food and Agriculture Organization 1994 *FAO Yearbook*. Rome: FAO.

Ford, Daniel 1982 *The Cult of the Atom*. New York: Simon & Schuster.

Foss, Nicole 1999 *Nuclear Safety and the Internationalisation of Governance in the Nuclear Power Industry: An Assessment of the Strategies Developing in Eastern Europe*. Oxford University: Oxford Institute of Energy Studies.

Freedeman, Charles E. 1993 *The Triumph of Corporate Capitalism in France 1867–1914*. Rochester, New York: University of Rochester Press.

Freeman, Harry L. 1984 'A User's View of International Communications', in J.F. Rada & G.R. Pipe (eds) *Communication Regulation and International Business*. North Holland: Elsevier Science.

Freyer, Tony 1992 *Regulating Big Business Antitrust in Great Britain and America, 1880–1990*. Cambridge: Cambridge University Press.

Friedland, Martin, Michael Trebilcock & Kent Roach 1990 *Regulating Traffic Safety*. Toronto: University of Toronto Press.

Frings, K. Viviane 1995 'The Turbulent but Commercially Valuable Chinese', *Itinerario* 19: 48–68.

Fujimoto, Shirley & Berejka, Marc 1993 'The Rise of Competing Satellite Systems and the Fall of the Intelsat Monopoly', in J Savage & D Wedemeyer (eds) *Proceedings of the Fifteenth Annual Conference of the Pacific Telecommunications Council*. Hawaii: Pacific Telecommunications Council.

Fukuyama, Francis 1995 *Trust: The Social Virtues and the Creation of Prosperity*. New York: Free Press.

Furmston, M.P. 1996 'UNIDROIT General Principles for International Commercial Contracts', *Journal of Contract Law* 10: 11–20.

Gaer, Felice D. 1996 'Reality Check: Human Rights NGOs Confront Governments at the UN', in Thomas G. Weiss & Leon Gordenker (eds) *NGOs, the UN and Global Governance*. Boulder, Colorado: Lynne Rienner.

Galligan, B. 1987 *Politics of the High Court*. Brisbane: University of Queensland Press.

Gandhi, M.K. 1952 *Drink, Drugs and Gambling*. Ahmedabad: Navajivan Publishing House.

Garland, David 1997 '"Governmentality" and the Problem of Crime: Foucault, Criminology, Sociology', *Theoretical Criminology* 1: 173–214.

Garraty, J.A. & P. Gay 1981 *The Columbia History of the World*. New York: Harper & Row.

Garro, A.M. 1992 'Unification and Harmonization of Private Law in Latin America', *American Journal of Comparative Law* 40: 587–616.

General Accounting Office 1991 *Money Laundering: The US Government is Responding to the Problem*. Washington DC: General Accounting Office, GAO/NSIAD-91-130.

Gerber, David J. 1992 'The Origins of European Competition Law in Fin-de-Siècle Austria', *American Journal of Legal History* 36: 405–40.

Germain, Randall D. 1997 *The International Organization of Credit*. Cambridge: Cambridge University Press.

Gerth, H.H. & C. Wright Mills (trans. and ed.) 1967 *From Max Weber: Essays in Sociology*. London: Routledge & Kegan Paul.

Getlan, Myles 1995 'TRIPS and Future of Section 301: A Comparative Study in Trade Dispute Resolution', *Columbia Journal of Transnational Law* 34: 173–218.

Geva, Benjamin 1987 'From Commodity to Currency in Ancient History: On Commerce, Tyranny, and the Modern Law of Money', *Osgoode Hall Law Journal* 25: 115–57.

Ghai, Dharam (ed.) 1991 *The IMF and the South: The Social Impact of Crisis and Adjustment*, London: Zed Books.

Ghebali, Victor-Yves 1989 *The International Labour Organization: A Case Study on the Evolution of UN Specialised Agencies*. Dordrecht, Netherlands: Martinus Nijhoff.

Giddens, Anthony 1984 *The Constitution of Society: Outline of a Theory of Structuration*. Berkeley: University of California Press.

Gidwitz, Betsy 1980 *The Politics of International Air Transport*. Lexington, Mass.: Lexington Books.

Gilbert, B.B. 1966 *The Evolution of National Insurance in Great Britain: The Origins of the Welfare State*. London: Joseph.

Glaser, B. & A. Strauss 1967 *The Discovery of Grounded Theory*. Chicago: Aldine.

Gledhill, A. 1954 'The Influence of Common Law and Equity on Hindu Law since 1800', *International and Comparative Law Quarterly* 3: 576–603.

Globerman, Steven 1995 'Foreign Ownership in Telecommunications', *Telecommunications Policy* 19: 21–8.

Godek, Paul E. 1991 'Antitrust Will Stifle, Not Spur Eastern Growth', *Wall Street Journal Europe* July: 26–7.

Golden, Jeffrey B. 1994 'Regulating Derivatives: The Importance of Asking the Right Questions and Listening to the Answers', *Journal of International Banking Law* 8: 295.

Goldsmith, Andrew & Colleen Lewis (eds) 2000 *Civilian Oversight of Policing: Governance, Democracy and Human Rights*. Oxford: Hart.

Goode, Roy 1995 *Commercial Law*, 2nd edn. Harmondsworth: Penguin.

Goodman, John & Andrew Moravcsik 1993 'Negotiating between Regional Blocs: Interests, Ideas and Bureaucratic Incentives in the Mutual Recognition of Pharmaceuticals', Paper to Annual Meeting of American Political Science Association, Washington DC.

Gosse, Philip 1932 *The History of Piracy*. London: Longmans, Green.

Grabosky, Peter 1994 'Green Markets: Environmental Regulation by the Private Sector', *Law and Policy* 16: 419–48.

Grabosky, Peter 1995a 'Using Non-Governmental Resources to Foster Regulatory Compliance', *Governance* 8: 527–50.

Grabosky, Peter 1995b 'Regulation by Reward: On the Use of Incentives as Regulatory Instruments', *Law and Policy* 17: 256–81.

Grabosky, Peter & John Braithwaite 1986 *Of Manners Gentle: Enforcement Strategies of Australian Business Regulatory Agencies*. Melbourne: Oxford University Press.

Granovetter, Mark S. 1974 'The Strength of Weak Ties', *American Journal of Sociology* 78: 1360–80.

Gray, Paul 1990 'Food Law and the Internal Market', *Food Policy* April: 111.

Gray, R. with J. Bebbington & D. Walters 1993 *Accounting for the Environment*. London: Paul Chapman.

Gray, V. 1973 'Innovation in the States: A Diffusion Study', *American Political Science Review* 67: 1175–85.

Green Paper on the Development of the Common Market for Telecommunications Services and Equipment, COM (87) 290 final.

Green, Cynthia et al. (eds) c. 1994 *A Business Week Guide: The Quality Imperative*. New York: McGraw Hill.

Greenwood, Justin & Karsten Ronit 1991 'Pharmaceutical Regulation in Denmark and the UK: Reformulating Interest Representation to the Transnational Level', *European Journal of Political Research* 19: 327–59.

Grieg, D.W. 1994 'Reciprocity, Proportionality, and the Law of Treaties', *Virginia Journal of International Law* 34: 295–403.

Grigg, David 1993 *The World Food Problem*, 2nd edn. Oxford: Blackwell.

Groenewoud, Margo 1995 'Towards the Abolition of Penal Sanctions in Dutch Colonial Labour Legislation: An International Perspective', *Itinerario* 19: 72–90.

Gruen, Nicholas, Ian Bruce & Gerard Prior 1996 *Extending Patent Life: Is it in Australia's Economic Interests?* Staff Information Paper. Canberra: Industry Commission.

Gruner, Richard 1994 *Corporate Crime and Sentencing*. Charlottesville, VA: Michie Co.

Guitián, Manuel 1992 *The Unique Nature of the Responsibilities of the International Monetary Fund*. Washington DC: International Monetary Fund.

Gunningham, Neil 1990 'Moving the Goalposts: Financial Market Regulation and the Crash of October 1987', *Law and Social Inquiry* 15: 1–48.

Gunningham, Neil 1993 'Thinking about Regulatory Mix: Regulating Occupational Health and Safety, Futures Markets and Environmental Law', in P. Grabosky & J. Braithwaite (eds) *Business Regulation and Australia's Future*. Canberra: Australian Institute of Criminology.

Gunningham, Neil 1995 'Environment, Self-Regulation and the Chemical Industry: Assessing Responsible Care', *Law and Policy* 17: 57–109.

Gunningham, Neil 1996 'From Adversarialism to Partnership?: ISO 14000 and Regulation', Paper to the Conference *ISO 14000: Regulatory and Trade Challenges*, Canberra, Australia.

Gunningham, Neil 1998 'Environmental Management Systems and Community Participation: Rethinking Chemical Industry Regulation'. Canberra: Mimeo, Australian Centre for Environmental Law, Faculty of Law, Australian National University.

Gunningham, Neil & Peter Grabosky with Darren Sinclair 1998 *Smart Regulation: Designing Environmental Policy*. Oxford: Clarendon Press.

Gunter, Bernhard, G. 1996 'Reforming the International Monetary System Towards a World Central Bank: A Summary of Proposals and Fallacies', in J.M. Griesgraber & B.G. Gunter (eds) *The World's Monetary System*. London: Pluto Press.

Gusfield, Joseph R. 1963 *Symbolic Crusade: Status Politics and the American Temperance Movement*. Urbana: University of Illinois Press.

Gutterman, Alan S. & Robert Brown (eds) 1997 *Intellectual Property Law of East Asia*. Hong Kong and Singapore: Sweet & Maxwell Asia.

Guyer, Jane 1993 '"Toiling Ingenuity": Food Regulation in Britain and Nigeria', *American Ethnologist* 20: 797–817.

Guzzini, Stephano 1993 'Structural Power: The Limits of Neorealist Power Analysis', *International Organization* 47: 443–78.

Haas, Ernst B. 1964 *Beyond the Nation State: Functionalism and International Organization*. Stanford, CA: Stanford University Press.

Haas, Peter M. 1989 'Do Regimes Matter? Epistemic Communities and Mediterranean Pollution Control', *International Organization* 43: 377–403.

Haas, Peter M. 1993 'Protecting the Baltic and North Seas', in Peter M. Haas, Robert O. Keohane & Marc A. Levy (eds) *Institutions for the Earth: Sources of Effective International Environmental Protection*. Cambridge, Mass.: MIT Press.

Haas, Peter M., Robert O. Keohane & Marc A. Levy (eds) 1993 *Institutions for the Earth: Sources of Effective International Environmental Protection*. Cambridge, Mass.: MIT Press.

Habermas, Jurgen 1996 *Between Facts and Norms: Contributions to a Discourse Theory of Law and Democracy* (translated by William Rehg). London: Polity Press.

Hackney, James V. & Kim Shafer 1986 'The Regulation of International Banking: An Assessment of International Institutions', *North Carolina Journal of International Law and Commercial Regulation* 11: 475–96.

Hammer, W.C.K. 1969 'The Commerce (Trade Descriptions) Act of 1905: Its Enactment, Origins and Application with Particular Reference to the Export of Primary Products', Unpublished thesis, Australian National University, Canberra.

Hancher, L. & M. Moran 1989 'Organizing Regulatory Space', in L. Hancher & M. Moran (eds) *Capitalism, Culture and Economic Regulation*. Oxford: Clarendon Press.

Hannah, Leslie 1991 'Mergers, Cartels and Concentration: Legal Factors in the US and European Experience', in Giles H. Burgess Jr *Antitrust and Regulation*. Aldershot: Edward Elgar.

Hansson, Olle 1989 *Inside Ciba-Geigy*. Penang: International Organization of Consumers Unions.

Haq-ul, Mahbub, Inge Kaul & Isabelle Grunberg (eds) 1996a *The Tobin Tax: Coping with Financial Volatility*. New York: Oxford University Press.

Haq-ul, Mahbub, Inge Kaul & Isabelle Grunberg 1996b 'Overview', in Mahbub Haq-ul, Inge Kaul & Isabelle Grunberg (eds) *The Tobin Tax: Coping with Financial Volatility*. New York: Oxford University Press.

Hardin, Garrett 1968 'The Tragedy of the Commons', *Science* 162: 1243–8.

Hardon, Anita 1992 'Consumers versus Producers: Power Play behind the Scenes', in Najmi Kanji, Anita Hardon, Jan Harnmeijer, Masuma Mamdani & Gill Walt (eds) *Drugs Policy in Developing Countries*. London: Zed Books.

Harriss, G.L. 1975 *King, Parliament, and Public Finance in Medieval England to 1369*. Oxford: Clarendon Press.

Harry, R. Jörn S. 1995 'IAEA Safeguards and Non-Proliferation', in Marianne van Leeuwen (ed.) *The Future of the International Nuclear Non-Proliferation Regime*. Dordrecht: Martinus Nijhoff.

Hart, Jeffrey A. 1998 'Digital Television in Europe and Japan', *Prometheus* 16: 217–37.

Harvey, Ken & D. Carandang 1992 *The Impact of WHO Ethical Criteria for Medicinal Drug Promotion: A Study by Health Action International*. Amsterdam: Health Action International.

Hasse, Lizbeth 1990 'Finding a Basis for International Communications Law: The Satellite Broadcast Example', *Case Western Journal of International Law*, 22: 97–116.

Hatch, Michael T. 1986 *Politics and Nuclear Power: Energy Policy in Western Europe*. Lexington: University of Kentucky Press.

Hawkins, David 1983 *Project Y: The Los Alamos Story, Part I: Toward Trinity*. San Francisco: Tomash Publishers.

Hawkins, Keith 1984 *Environment and Enforcement: Regulation and the Social Definition of Pollution*. Oxford: Clarendon Press.

Hay, Douglas & Paul Craven 1993 'Master and Servant in England and the Empire: A Comparative Study', *Labour/Le Travail* 31: 175–84.

Hayashi, Koichiro 1996 'From One to the PTOs to a Unique Multimedia Company: How NTT Plans to Transform Itself', Paper at the 11th Biennial Conference of the International Telecommunication Society, Seville, Spain.

Hayward, Peter C. 1991 'Prospects for International Co-Operation by Bank Supervisors', in Joseph J. Norton (ed.) *Bank Regulation and Supervision in the 1990s*. London: Lloyd's of London Press.

Hazeltine, H.D. 1926 'The Renaissance and the Laws of Europe', in P.H. Winfield & A.D. McNair (eds) *Cambridge Legal Essays*. Cambridge: Heffer & Sons.

Health Action International 1994 *WHO Ethical Criteria for Medicinal Drug Promotion: Off the Shelf and Into the Legislatures*. Amsterdam: HAI Europe.

Heimer, Carol 1985 *Reactive Risk and Rational Action*. Berkeley: University of California Press.

Held, David 1995 *Democracy and the Global Order: From the Modern State to Cosmopolitan Governance*. Stanford, CA: Stanford University Press.

Held, David, Anthony McGrew, David Goldblatt & Jonathon Perraton 1999 *Global Transformations*. Cambridge: Polity Press.

Henkin, Louis 1979 *How Nations Behave*, 2nd edn. New York: Columbia University Press.

Henn, Harry G. 1953 'The Quest for International Copyright Protection', *Cornell Law Quarterly* 39: 43–73.

Herold, J. Christopher 1987 *The Age of Napoleon*. Boston: Houghton Mifflin.

Herring, Richard J. & Robert E. Litan 1995 *Financial Regulation in the Global Economy*. Washington DC: Brookings Institution.

Higgott, R.A. & A.F. Cooper 1990 'Middle Power Leadership and Coalition Building: Australia, the Cairns Group and the Uruguayan Round of Trade Negotiations', *International Organization* 44: 589–632.

Hindell, Keith 1996 'Strengthening the Ship Regulating Regime', *Maritime Policy and Management* 23: 371–80.

Hindess, B. 1982 'Power, Interests and the Outcomes of Struggles', *Sociology* 16: 498–511.

Hindess, B. 1987 *Politics and Class Analysis*. Oxford: Blackwell.

Hirst, Paul & Grahame Thompson 1996 *Globalization in Question: The International Economy and the Possibilities of Governance*. London: Polity Press.

Hoffer, Perri A. 1986 'Upheaval in the United Nations System: United States' Withdrawal from UNESCO', *Brooklyn Journal of International Law* 12: 161–207.

Hoffmaster, Barry 1988 'The Ethics of Patenting Higher Life Forms', *Intellectual Property Journal* 4: 1–24.

Holcer, Nikola 1995 'The Changing Telecommunications Environment in CEE', in D.M. Lamberton (ed.) *Beyond Competition: The Future of Telecommunications*. North Holland: Elsevier.

Holden, Milnes J. 1955 *The History of Negotiable Instruments in English Law*. London: Athlone Press.

Holdsworth, William 1937 *A History of English Law*, vol. 8, 2nd edn. London: Methuen.

Holm, Hans-Henrik & Georg Sorensen 1995 'Introduction: What has Changed?', in Hans-Henrik Holm & Georg Sorensen (eds) *Whose World Order: Uneven Globalization and the End of the Cold War*. Boulder, Colorado: Westview Press.

Holtfrerich, Carl-Ludwig 1987 'The Modernisation of the Tax System in the First World War and the Great Inflation, 1914–23', in Peter-Christian Witt (ed.) *Wealth and Taxation in Central Europe*. New York: Berg.

Holtzman, Abraham 1966 *Interest Groups and Lobbying*. New York: Macmillan.

Homer-Dixon, Thomas F. 1994 'Environmental Scarcities and Violent Conflict: Evidence from Cases', *International Security* 19: 5–40.

Honoré, A.M. 1961 'Ownership', in A.G. Guest (ed.) *Oxford Essays in Jurisprudence*. Oxford: Oxford University Press.

Hood, Christopher, Colin Scott, Oliver James, George Jones & Tony Travers 1999 *Regulation Inside Government: Waste Watchers, Quality Police and Sleaze-busters*. New York : Oxford University Press

Hope, Ronald 1990 *A New History of British Shipping*. London: John Murray.

Hopkins, R. & K.P. Davies 1990 'HDTV Emission Systems Approach in North America', *Telecommunication Journal* 57: 330–4.

Horwitz, Robert Britt 1989 *The Irony of Regulatory Reform: The Deregulation of American Telecommunications*. New York: Oxford University Press.

Housman, Robert F. & Durwood J. Zaelke 1993 'Making Trade and Environmental Policies Mutually Reinforcing: Forging Competitive Sustainability', *Environmental Law* 23: 545–73.

Howell, Kristin 1993 'The Role of the Bank for International Settlements in Central Bank Cooperation' *Journal of European Economic History* 22: 367–80.

Howlett, Darryl A. 1990 *EURATOM and Nuclear Safeguards*. London: Macmillan.

Hoya, Thomas W. 1970 'The COMECON General Conditions: A Socialist Unification of International Trade Law', *Columbia Law Review* 70: 253–305.

Hsu, Paul S.P. & Lawrence S. Liu 1988 'The Transformation of the Securities Market in Taiwan, the Republic of China', *Columbia Journal of Transnational Law* 27: 167–94.

Hudec, R.E. 1990 'Dispute Settlement', in J.J. Schott (ed.) *Completing the Uruguay Round*. Washington DC: Institute for International Economics.

Hudec, Robert E., Daniel L.M. Kennedy & Mark Sgarbossa 1993 'A Statistical Profile of GATT Dispute Settlement Cases: 1948–1989', *Minnesota Journal of Global Trade* 2: 1–113.

Hu-Dehart, Evelyn 1993 'Chinese Coolie Labour in Cuba in the Nineteenth Century: Free Labour or Neo-Slavery?', *Slavery and Abolition* 14: 67–86.

Hudson, Manley O. & A.H. Feller 1931 'The International Unification of Laws Concerning Bills of Exchange', *Harvard Law Review* 44: 333–74.

Hufbauer, C.C., J.J. Schott & K.A. Elliott 1990 *Economic Sanctions Reconsidered*. Washington DC: Institute for International Economics.

Hughes, Steve & Rorden Wilkinson 1998 'International Labour Standards and World Trade: No Role for the World Trade Organization?', *New Political Economy* 3: 375–89.

Hulbert, John 1996 'Regulation, Trade and Environment: Environmental Management Systems International Trade and Regional Issues', Paper to the Conference *ISO 14000: Regulatory and Trade Challenges*, Canberra, Australia.

Hurrell, Andrew & Benedict Kingsbury (eds) 1992 *The International Politics of the Environment: Actors, Interests and Institutions*. Oxford: Clarendon Press.

Hutt, Peter Barton & Peter Barton Hutt II 1984 'A History of Government Regulation of Adulteration and Misbranding of Food', *Food, Drug and Cosmetic Law Journal* 39: 2–73.

Ikenberry, John 1988 *Reasons of State: Oil Politics and the Capacities of American Government*. New York: Cornell University Press.

*IMF Survey* 1997, vol. 26.

*IMF Survey* 1998, vol. 27.

IMF 1993 *International Capital Markets: Part II: Systemic Issues in International Finance*. Washington DC: IMF.

Information Infrastructure Task Force 1993 *National Information Infrastructure Agenda for Action*. September. IITF.

Intellectual Property Committee, Keidanren, UNICE 1988 (June) *Basic Framework of GATT Provisions on Intellectual Property: Statement of Views of the European, Japanese and United States Business Communities*. Brussels: UNICE.

International Air Transport Association 1995 *Annual Report*. Geneva: IATA.

International Chamber of Commerce 1986 *ICC Statement on Extraterritorial Application of National Laws and Policies*. Committee on Extraterritorial Application of National Laws. Geneva: ICC.

International Chamber of Commerce 1998 'E-commerce Roles, Rules and Responsibilities: A Roadmap', 4 June 1998, 11.

International Civil Aviation Organization 1993 *Annual Report of the Council*. Geneva: ICAO.

International Civil Aviation Organization 1994 *Memorandum on ICAO*. Geneva: ICAO.

International Confederation of Free Trade Unions 1992 *Environment and Development: The Trade Union Agenda*. Brussels: ICFTU.

International Federation of Pharmaceutical Manufacturers Association 1987 *IFPMA Code of Pharmaceutical Marketing Practices*. Geneva: IFPMA.

International Fiscal Association, *Yearbook 1994*.

International Labour Conference 1988 *Equality in Employment and Occupation: General Survey by the Committee of Experts on the Application of Conventions and Recommendations*. Geneva: ILO.

International Labour Organization 1994 'NAFTA Comes Into Force: With a Glimmer of a Social Clause', *International Labour Review* 133: 113–19.

International Maritime Organization 1993 'Oil Pollution Declines as Shipping Measures Take Effect', *IMO News* 3: 1–2.

International Organization of Securities Commissions 1993 *Annual Report*. Montreal: IOSCO.

International Telecommunication Union 1994 *World Development Report*. Geneva: ITU.

International Telecommunication Union, Press Release, ITU/97–2, 14 February 1997.

Ion, E. 1992 'Hull Rates, Too Cheap for Too Long', *European Gateways*, September.

Ishikawa, K. 1985 *What is Total Quality Control? The Japanese Way*. Englewood Cliffs, NJ: Prentice-Hall.

Ito, Youichi 1986 'Telecommunications and Industrial Policies in Japan: Recent Developments', in Marcellus S. Snow (ed.) *Telecommunications: Regulation and Deregulation in Industrialized Democracies*. North Holland: Elsevier Science.

Iyer, Krishna V.R., Chinnapa O. Reddy, D.A. Desai & Rajinder Sachar 1996 *People's Commission on GATT: On the Constitutional Implications of the Final Act Embodying the Results of the Uruguay Round of Multilateral Trade Negotiations*. Sarita Vihar, New Delhi: Centre for Study of Global Trade System and Development.

Jackson, John H. 1989 *The World Trading System: Law and Policy of International Economic Relations*. Cambridge, Mass.: MIT Press.

Jackson, John H. 1990 *Restructuring the GATT System*. London: Pinter.

Jackson, John H. 1993 'Managing Economic Interdependence: An Overview', *Law and Policy in International Business* 24: 1025–33.

Jackson, John H., Jean-Victor Louis & Mitsuo Matsushita 1982 'Implementing the Tokyo Round: Legal Aspects of Changing International Economic Rules', *Michigan Law Review* 81: 267–397.

Jacobs, Scott 1994 'Regulatory Co-Operation for an Interdependent World: Issues for Government', in Organisation for Economic Co-operation and Development *Regulatory Co-Operation in an Interdependent World*. Paris: OECD.

Jacobson, H.K. 1984 *Networks of Interdependence: International Organizations and the Global Political System*. New York: Knopf.

Jaffe, Adam B., Steven R. Peterson, Paul R. Portney & Robert N. Stavins 1995 'Environmental Regulation and the Competitiveness of US Manufacturing: What Does the Evidence Tell Us?', *Journal of Economic Literature* 33: 132–63.

Jain, Prakash C. 1988 'Exploitation and Reproduction of Migrant Indian Labour in Colonial Guyana and Malaysia', *Journal of Contemporary Asia* 18: 189–206.

Janicke, Martin 1991 'Institutional and Other Framework Conditions for Environmental Policy Success', Paper to Meeting of Law and Society Association, Amsterdam.

Jimenez, Jacinto D. 1997 'Philippines', in Alan S. Gutterman & Robert Brown (eds) *Intellectual Property Laws of East Asia*. Hong Kong: Sweet & Maxwell Asia.

Johnson, B. 1975 'Righteousness before Revenue: The Forgotten Moral Crusade against the Indo-Chinese Opium Trade', *Journal of Drug Issues* 5: 304.

Johnson, Harry G. 1968 'Problems of Balance-of-Payments Adjustment in the Modern World', in C.R. Whittlesey & J.S.G. Wilson (eds) *Essays in Money and Banking in Honour of R.S. Sayers*. Oxford: Clarendon Press.

Johnson, Roger T. 1982 'US Grain Trade Policy towards the USSR and China', *Wisconsin International Law Journal* 1: 1–15.

Johnston, Douglas M. 1988 'Marine Pollution Agreements: Successes and Problems', in John E. Carroll (ed.)
*International Environmental Diplomacy: The Management and Resolution of Transfrontier Environmental Problems.*
Cambridge: Cambridge University Press.

Jones, Rodney W., Cesare Merlini, Joseph H. Pilat & William C. Potter (eds) 1985 *The Nuclear Suppliers and Non-
Proliferation: International Policy Choices.* Lexington, Mass.: Lexington Books.

Jones, T. 1951 *Lloyd George.* Cambridge, Mass.: Harvard University Press.

Joos, Ulrich & Rainer Moufang 1989 'A Report on the Second Ringberg-Symposium', in Friedrich-Karl Beier &
Gerhard Schricker (eds) *GATT or WIPO? New Ways in the International Protection of Intellectual Property.*
Cambridge: VCH.

Joppke, Christian 1993 *Mobilizing against Nuclear Energy: A Comparison of Germany and the United States.* Berkeley:
University of California Press.

Jordan, Cally 1996 'Review of the Hong Kong Companies Ordinance', Asia Pacific Economic Law Forum 2nd
Conference, Canberra.

Joseph, Richard & Peter Drahos 1998 'Contested Arenas in International Telecommunications: Towards an
Integrated Political Perspective', in S. Macdonald & G. Madden (eds) *Telecommunications and Socio-Economic
Development.* North Holland: Elsevier Science.

Juran, J. 1988 *Juran on Planning for Quality.* New York: Free Press.

Justinian 1985 'The Rhodian Law of Jettison', in Theodor Mommsen, Paul Krueger & Alan Watson (eds) *The Digest
of Justinian,* vol. I. Philadelphia: University of Pennsylvania Press.

*Justinian's Institutes* (533 AD) 1987 (translated by Peter Birks & Grant McLeod). London: Duckworth.

Kahler, Miles 1995 *International Institutions and the Political Economy of Integration.* Washington DC: Brookings
Institution.

Kaiser, Gordon E. 1986 'Developments in Canadian Telecommunications Regulation', in Marcellus S. Snow (ed.)
*Telecommunications Regulation and Deregulation in Industrialized Democracies.* North Holland: Elsevier Science.

Kampelman, Max M. 1947 'The United States and International Copyright', *American Journal of International Law*
41: 406–29.

Kapstein, Ethan B. 1989 'Resolving the Regulator's Dilemma: International Coordination of Banking Regulations',
*International Organization* 43: 323–47.

Kardono, Supriyani A. & Darrell R. Johnson 1997 'Indonesia', in Alan S. Gutterman & Robert Brown (eds)
*Intellectual Property Laws of East Asia.* Hong Kong: Sweet & Maxwell Asia.

Kaser, Max 1965 *Roman Private Law* (translated by Rolf Dannenbring). Durban: Butterworths.

Keayla, B.K. 1996 *New Patent Regime: Implications for Domestic Industry, Research & Development and Consumers.* New
Delhi: National Working Group on Patent Laws.

Keck, Margaret E. & Kathryn Sikkink 1998 *Activists beyond Borders: Advocacy Networks in International Politics.* Ithaca
and London: Cornell University Press.

Keesing, Donald B. 1997 *Trade Practices Laid Bare: Further Improving the WTO's Trade Policy Review Mechanism.*
Geneva: WTO.

Keller, Morton 1991 'Regulation of Large Enterprise: The United States Experience in Comparative Perspective', in
Giles H. Burgess Jr (ed.) *Antitrust and Regulation.* Aldershot: Edward Elgar.

Kemeny, John G. et al. 1979 *Report of the President's Commission on the Accident at Three Mile Island.* New York:
Pergamon.

Kenny, Paul 1993 *Worldwide Guide to Offshore Companies.* London: IBC Publishing.

Kent, Ann 1997 'China, International Organizations and Regimes: The ILO as a Case Study in Organizational
Learning', *Pacific Affairs* 70: 517–32.

Keohane, Robert 1984 *After Hegemony: Cooperation and Discord in World Politics.* Princeton, NJ: Princeton University
Press.

Keohane, Robert 1986 'Reciprocity in International Relations', *International Organization* 40: 1–28.

Keohane, Robert O., Peter Haas & Marc A. Levy 1993 'The Effectiveness of International Environmental
Institutions', in Peter M. Haas, Robert O. Keohane & Marc A. Levy (eds) 1993 *Institutions for the Earth:
Sources of Effective International Environmental Protection.* Cambridge, Mass.: MIT Press.

Keohane, Robert O. & Joseph S. Nye 1974 'Transgovernmental Relations and International Organizations', *World
Politics* 27: 45–6.

Keohane, Robert O. & Joseph S. Nye 1989 *Power and Interdependence,* 2nd edn. Glenview, Ill.: Scott Foresman.

Kessler, Bruce S. 1985 'Politics among the Airwaves: An Analysis of Soviet and Western Perspectives on
International Broadcasting and the Right to Exchange Ideas and Information Regardless of Frontiers',
*Houston Journal of International Law* 7: 237–69.

Ketcham, Ralph 1986 *The Anti-Federalist Papers and the Constitutional Debates*. New York: Mentor Books.

Keynes, John Maynard 1980 *The Collected Writings of John Maynard Keynes* (Donald Moggridge ed.), vol. 26. *Activities 1941–1946: Shaping the Post-War World: Bretton Woods and Reparations*. London: Macmillan.

Kikeri, S., J. Nellis & M. Shirley 1992 *Privatization: The Lessons of Experience*. Washington DC: World Bank.

Kim, Chulsu 1990 'Super 301 and the World Trading System: A Korean View', in J. Bhagwati & H.T. Patrick (eds) *Aggressive Unilateralism: America's 301 Trade Policy and the World Trading System*. Ann Arbor: University of Michigan Press.

Kindleberger, Charles 1973 *The World in Depression, 1929–1939*. Berkeley: University of California Press.

Kindleberger, Charles P. 1978 *Manias, Panics, and Crashes*. New York: Basic Books.

Kindleberger, Charles P. 1984 *A Financial History of Western Europe*. London: George Allen & Unwin.

King, Wilfred 1936 *History of the London Discount Market*. London: Routledge.

Klepper, Gernot 1994 'Industrial Policy in the Transport Aircraft Industry', in Paul Krugman (ed.) *Empirical Studies of Strategic Trade Policy*. Chicago: University of Chicago Press.

Kline, John M. 1985 *International Codes and Multinational Business. Setting Guidelines for International Business Operations*. Connecticut: Quorum Books.

Knight, Jeff 1996 'Strength and Opportunities: Integrating Safety, Health and Environment Issues', Paper to the Conference *ISO 14000: Regulatory and Trade Challenges*, Canberra.

Knorr, K. 1956 *EURATOM and American Policy: A Conference Report*. Princeton University: Princeton Center for International Studies.

Kobrin, S.J. 1985 'Diffusion as an Explanation of Oil Nationalisation: Or the Domino Effect Rides Again', *Journal of Conflict Resolution* 29: 3–32.

Koh, Tommy Thong-Bee 1994 'UNCED Leadership: A Personal Perspective', in Bertram I. Spector, G. Sjostedt & I.W. Zartman (eds) *Negotiating International Regimes: Lessons Learned from the United Nations Conference on Environment and Development (UNCED)*. London: Graham & Trotman.

Kohn, Alfie 1995 *Punished by Rewards*. Boston: Houghton Mifflin.

Krasner, Stephen D. 1982a 'Regimes and the Limits of Realism: Regimes as Autonomous Variables', *International Organization* 36: 497–510.

Krasner, Stephen D. 1982b 'Structural Causes and Regime Consequences: Regimes as Intervening Variables', *International Organization* 36: 185–205.

Kruger, Henrik 1980 *The Great Heroin Coup: Drugs, Intelligence and International Fascism*. Boston: South End Press.

Kruglak, Gregory 1989 'Tripartism and the ILO', in David P. Forsythe (ed.) *The United Nations and the World Political Economy: Essays in Honour of Leon Gordenker*. New York: St Martin's Press.

Krugman, Paul 1994 'Introduction', in Paul Krugman & Alasdair Smith (eds) *Empirical Studies of Strategic Trade Policy*. Chicago: University of Chicago Press.

Krygier, Martin 1990 'Marxism and the Rule of Law: Reflections after the Collapse of Communism', *Law and Social Inquiry* 15: 633–63.

Krygier, Martin 1997 *Between Fear and Hope: Hybrid Thoughts on Public Values*. Sydney: ABC Books.

Kuhn, T.S. 1970 *The Structure of Scientific Revolutions*, 2nd edn. Chicago: University of Chicago Press.

Kumarasivam, K. 1996 'Implementation of EMS in Malaysia', Paper to the Conference *ISO 14000: Regulatory and Trade Challenges*, Canberra.

Kuroda, Makoto 1990 'Super 301 and Japan', in J. Bhagwati & H.T. Patrick (eds) *Aggressive Unilateralism: America's 301 Trade Policy and the World Trading System*. Ann Arbor: University of Michigan Press.

Ladas, Stephen P. 1930 *The International Protection of Industrial Property*. Cambridge: Harvard University Press.

Ladas, Stephen P. 1975a *Patents, Trademarks, and Related Rights: National and International Protection*, vol. 1. Cambridge: Harvard University Press.

Ladas, Stephen P. 1975b *Patents, Trademarks, and Related Rights: National and International Protection*, vol. 3. Cambridge: Harvard University Press.

Landis, James 1931 'The Study of Legislation in Law Schools: An Imaginary Inaugural Lecture', *Harvard Graduates Magazine* 39: 433–42.

Landis, James 1938 *The Administrative Process*. New Haven: Yale University Press.

Lando, Ole 1992 'Principles of European Contract Law: An Alternative to or a Precursor of European Legislation', *American Journal of Comparative Law* 40: 573–85.

Landy, E.A. 1966 *The Effectiveness of International Supervision: Thirty Years of ILO Experience*. London: Oceana.

Lang, Tim 1992 *Food Fit for the World? How the GATT Food Trade Talks Challenge Public Health, the Environment and the Citizen*. London: SAFE Alliance.

Latek, Stanislaw 1993 'Difficulties in Achieving Public Acceptance of Nuclear Energy in Poland', in OECD, *Public Participation in Nuclear Decision-Making*. Paris: OECD.

Latour, Bruno 1986 'The Powers of Association', in John Law (ed.) *Power, Action and Belief: A New Sociology of Knowledge?* Sociological Review Monograph 32. London and Boston: Routledge & Kegan Paul.

Latour, Bruno 1987 *Science in Action*. Buckingham: Open University Press.

Law, R.C.C. 1990 'North Africa in the Period of Phoenician and Greek Colonization, c. 800 to 323 BC', in *Cambridge History of Africa. Vol. 2. c.500 BC–AD 1050*. Cambridge: Cambridge University Press.

LeDuc, Lawrence, Richard G. Niemi & Pippa Norris 1996 'Introduction: The Present and Future of Democratic Elections', in L. LeDuc, R.G. Niemi & P. Norris (eds) *Comparing Democracies; Elections and Voting in Global Perspective*. Thousand Oaks, CA: Sage.

Lee, R.W. 1961 *An Introduction to Roman-Dutch Law*, 5th edn. Oxford: Clarendon Press.

Lefcowitz, M., R.R. Blake & J.S. Mouton 1955 'Status Factors in Pedestrian Violation of Traffic Signals', *Journal of Abnormal and Social Psychology* 51: 704–5.

Leibfried, Stephan & Elmar Rieger 1995 'Conflicts over Germany's Competitiveness ('Standort Deutschland'): Exiting from the Global Economy?' Occasional Paper, Centre for German and European Studies, Berkeley, University of California.

Leive, David M. c. 1976 *International Regulatory Regimes*. Lexington, Mass.: Lexington Books.

Lenhoff, Arthur 1954–55 'Reciprocity: The Legal Aspect of a Perennial Idea', *Northwestern University Law Review* 49: 619–41, 752–79.

Leonard, H. Jeffrey 1988 *Pollution and the Struggle for World Product*. Cambridge: Cambridge University Press.

Lever-Tracy, C., D. Ip & N. Tracy 1996 *The Chinese Diaspora and Mainland China*. London: Macmillan.

Levi, Margaret 1988 *Of Rule and Revenue*. Berkeley: University of California Press.

Levinson, Arik 1996 'Environmental Regulations and Industry Location: International and Domestic Evidence', in Jagdish Bhagwati & Robert E. Hudec (eds) *Fair Trade and Harmonization, Vol. I, Economic Analysis*. Cambridge, Mass.: MIT Press.

Levy, Marc A. 1993 'European Acid Rain: The Power of Tote-Board Diplomacy', in Peter M. Haas, Robert O. Keohane & Marc A. Levy (eds) *Institutions for the Earth: Sources of Effective International Environmental Protection*. Cambridge, Mass.: MIT Press.

Levy, Marc A. 1995 'Is the Environment a National Security Issue?' *International Security* 20: 35–62.

Levy, Marc A., Robert O. Keohane & Peter M. Haas 1992 'Institutions for the Earth: Promoting International Environmental Protection', *Environment* 34: 12–17, 29–36.

Levy, Marc A., Robert O. Keohane & Peter M. Haas 1993 'Improving the Effectiveness of International Environmental Institutions', in Peter M. Haas, Robert O. Keohane & Marc A. Levy (eds) 1993 *Institutions for the Earth: Sources of Effective International Environmental Protection*. Cambridge, Mass.: MIT Press.

Lewis, Michael 1989 *Liar's Poker: Rising Through the Wreckage on Wall Street*. New York: W.W. Norton.

Lexchin, Joel 1992 'Pharmaceutical Promotion in the Third World', *Journal of Drug Issues* 22: 417–53.

LiCalzi, Jacqueline O. 1987 'Comment: Competition and Deregulation: Nouvelles Frontières for the EEC Air Transport Industry?', *Fordham International Law Journal* 10: 808–41.

Lifschultz, Lawrence 1992 'Pakistan: The Empire of Heroin', in A. McCoy & A. Block (eds) *War on Drugs: Studies in the Failure of US Narcotic Policy*. Boulder, Colorado: Westview Press.

Lindsay, Samuel McCune 1934 'The Problem of American Cooperation', in James Brown Scott (ed.) *The Origins of the International Labor Organization*, vol. 1. New York: Columbia University Press.

Lintner, Bertil 1992 'Heroin and Highland Insurgency in the Golden Triangle', in A. McCoy & A. Block (eds) *War on Drugs: Studies in the Failure of US Narcotic Policy*. Boulder, Colorado: Westview Press.

Lis, Catharina & Hugo Soly 1994 '"An Irresistible Phalanx": Journeymen Associations in Western Europe, 1300–1800', *International Review of Social History* Supplement 39: 11–52.

Liu, Lawrence S. 1995 'Efficiency, Fairness, Adversary and Moral Suasion: A Tale of Two Chinese Competition Laws', in Chih-Kang Wang, Chia-Jui Cheng & Lawrence S. Liu (eds) *International Harmonization of Competition Laws*. Dordrecht: Martinus Nijhoff.

*Lloyd's Register of Shipping* a (published annually) Casualty Returns. London: Lloyd's Register of Shipping.

*Lloyd's Register of Shipping* b (published annually) Statistical Tables. London: Lloyd's Register of Shipping.

Locke, John 1963 *Two Treatises on Government*. Cambridge: Cambridge University Press.

London Food Commission 1988 *Food Adulteration and How to Beat It*. London: Unwin.

Long, Olivier 1987 *Law and its Limitations in the GATT Multilateral Trade System*. London: Graham & Trotman/Martinus Nijhoff.

Longstreth, Bevis 1988 'Global Securities Markets and the SEC', *University of Pennsylvania Journal of International Business Law* 10: 183–93.

Lonngren, Rune 1992 *International Approaches to Chemicals Control: An Historical Overview*. Stockholm: National Chemicals Inspectorate, Sweden.

Loughlin, M. & C. Scott 1997 'The Regulatory State', in P. Dunlevy, I. Holliday & G. Peele (eds) *Developments in British Politics 5*. London: Macmillan.

Lovell, W. George 1983 'To Submit and to Serve: Forced Native Labour in the Cuchumatán Highlands of Guatemala, 1525–1821', *Journal of Historical Geography* 9: 127–44.

Luard, Evan 1977 *International Agencies: The Emerging Framework of Interdependence*. Dobbs Ferry, New York: Oceana.

Lukes, S. 1974 *Power: A Radical View*. London: Macmillan.

Lyons, B. 1987 'International Trade and Technology Policy' in P. Dasgupta & P. Stoneman (eds) *Economic Policy and Technological Performance*. Cambridge: Cambridge University Press.

MacDonagh, Oliver 1961 *A Pattern of Government Growth 1800–1860*. London: MacGibbon & Kee.

MacDonagh, Oliver 1977 *Early Victorian Government*. London: Weidenfeld & Nicolson.

Macdonald, Stuart 1990 *Technology and the Tyranny of Export Controls: Whisper Who Dares*. London: Macmillan.

Machlup, Fritz 1962 *The Production and Distribution of Knowledge in the United States*. Princeton, NJ: Princeton University Press.

Machlup, Fritz & Edith Penrose 1950 'The Patent Controversy in the Nineteenth Century', *Journal of Economic History* 10: 1–29.

Magwood, John M. 1981 *Competition Law of Canada. Development of Common Law, Statutory and Voluntary Combines Remedies, Constitutional Proposals and American Comparisons*. Toronto: Carswell.

Maine, Henry 1861 *Ancient Law* (introduction and notes by Frederick Pollock, new edn, 1930). London: John Murray.

Majone, Giandomenico 1991 'Cross-National Sources of Regulatory Policymaking in Europe and the United States', *Journal of Public Policy* 11: 79–106.

Majone, Giandomenico 1993 'The European Community Between Social Policy and Social Regulation', *Journal of Common Market Studies* 31: 63.

Majone, Giandomenico 1994a 'Comparing Strategies of Regulatory Rapprochement', in OECD, *Regulatory Co-Operation for an Interdependent World*. Paris: OECD.

Majone, Giandomenico 1994b 'The Rise of the Regulatory State in Europe', *West European Politics* 17: 77–101.

Manderson, Desmond 1993 *From Mr Sin to Mr Big*. Melbourne: Oxford University Press.

Mankabady, Samir (ed.) 1984 *The International Maritime Organization*. London: Croom Helm.

Mankabady, Samir 1986 *The International Maritime Organization, Vol. 1: International Shipping Rules*. London: Croom Helm.

Mankabady, Samir 1987 *The International Maritime Organization, Vol. 2: Accidents at Sea*. London: Croom Helm.

Mann, Michael 1986 *The Sources of Social Power, Vol. 1: A History of Power from the Beginning to AD 1760*. Cambridge: Cambridge University Press.

Mann, Michael 1993 *The Sources of Social Power, Vol. II: The Rise of Classes and Nation-States, 1760–1914*. Cambridge: Cambridge University Press.

Mansfield, Peter R. 1991 'Classifying Improvements to Drug Marketing and Justification for Claims of Efficacy', *International Journal of Risk and Safety in Medicine* 2: 171–84.

Marceau, Gabrielle 1994 *Anti-Dumping and Anti-Trust Issues in Free-Trade Areas*. Oxford: Clarendon Press.

March, James G. & Johan P. Olsen 1998 'The Institutional Dynamics of International Political Orders', Working Paper No. 5, ARENA program, Research Council of Norway.

Marsh, David 1993 *The Bundesbank: The Bank that Rules Europe*. London: Mandarin.

Marshall, Jonathan 1992 'CIA Assets and the Rise of the Guadalajara Connection', in A. McCoy & A. Block (eds) *War on Drugs: Studies in the Failure of US Narcotic Policy*. Boulder, Colorado: Westview Press.

Martens, G.F. 1985 'Nouveau Recueil, General', in E.J. Osmanczyk (ed.) *The Encyclopedia of the United Nations and International Agreements*. Philadelphia: Taylor & Francis.

Martin, David A. 1987 'The Evolution of Industrial Policies: A World Perspective', in Robert L. Wills, Julie A. Caswell & John D. Culbertson (eds) *Issues after a Century of Federal Competition Policy*. Lexington, Mass.: Lexington Books.

Marx, Karl, & Frederick Engels 1987 *Collected Works* (translated by Emile Burns & Clemens Dutt). London: Lawrence & Wishart.

Mathews, Jessica Tuchman 1991 *Preserving the Global Environment: The Challenge of Shared Leadership*. New York: Norton.

Mayer, R.N. 1991 'Gone Yesterday, Here Today: Consumer Issues in the Agenda-Setting Process', *Journal of Social Issues* 47: 121–39.

M'Bow, Amadou-Mahtar 1978 'The Practice of Consensus in International Organization', *International Social Science Journal* 30: 893–903.

McBarnet, Doreen 1994a 'Legal Creativity: Law, Capital and Legal Avoidance', in M. Cain & C.B. Harrington (eds) *Lawyers in a Postmodern World: Translation and Transgression*. Buckingham: Open University Press.

McBarnet, Doreen 1994b 'Outlining a Theory of Legal Practice', in M. Cain & C.B. Harrington (eds) *Lawyers in a Postmodern World*. Buckingham: Open University Press.

McCaffery, David P. & David W. Hart 1998 *Dancing on a Pin on Wall Street: Law and Compliance in the Securities Industry*. New York: Oxford University Press.

McCarthy, J.D. & M.N. Zald 1977 'Resource Mobilisation and Social Movements: A Partial Theory', *American Journal of Sociology* 82: 1212–41.

McChesney, Allan 1996 'Responsible Care Initiative: Canadian Chemical Producers Association: A Case Study from Canada', *OECD Public Management Occasional Papers No. 18*. Paris: OECD.

McCoy, Alfred W. 1972 *The Politics of Heroin in Southeast Asia*. New York: Harper Torchbooks.

McCoy, Alfred W. 1980 *Drug Traffic: Narcotics and Organized Crime in Australia*. Sydney: Harper & Row.

McCoy, Alfred W. 1992 'Heroin as a Global Commodity: A History of Southeast Asia's Opium Trade', in A. McCoy & A. Block (eds) *War on Drugs: Studies in the Failure of US Narcotic Policy*. Boulder, Colorado: Westview Press.

McCoy, Alfred W. & Alan A. Block 1992 'US Narcotics Policy: An Anatomy of Failure', in A. McCoy & A. Block (eds) *War on Drugs: Studies in the Failure of US Narcotic Policy*. Boulder, Colorado: Westview Press.

McCraw, Thomas K. 1984 *Prophets of Regulation*. Cambridge, Mass.: Harvard University Press.

McEwin, Ian 1998 'Trade and Intellectual Property: Non-Violation Complaints under TRIPS', Unpublished manuscript. Canberra: Australian National University.

McGivern, Joan M. 1983 'US International Telecommunications and Information Policy: Congress Considers Reorganizing Policymaking', *Law and Policy in International Business* 15: 1297–332.

McGrew, Anthony 1992 'Conceptualizing Global Politics', in A.G. McGrew & P.G. Lewis et al. (eds) *Global Politics: Globalization and the Nation-State*. Cambridge, Mass.: Polity Press.

McKendrick, G.C. 1984 'Transborder Data Issues as Seen by a US Bank', in J.F. Rada & G.R. Pipe (eds) *Communication Regulation and International Business*. North Holland: Elsevier Science.

McMichael, Philip & David Myhre 1991 'Global Regulation vs the National-State: Agro-Food Systems and the New Politics of Capital', *Capital and Class* 43: 83–105.

McMillan, John 1990 'Strategic Bargaining and Section 301', in J. Bhagwati & H.T. Patrick (eds) *Aggressive Unilateralism: America's 301 Trade Policy and the World Trading System*. Ann Arbor: University of Michigan Press.

Mead, G.H. 1950 *Mind, Self and Society*. Chicago: University of Chicago Press.

Medawar, Charles 1979 *Insult or Injury?* London: Social Audit.

Meehan, Elizabeth 1992 'European Community Policies on Sex Equality: A Bibliographic Essay', *Women's Studies International Forum* 15: 57–64.

Meek, C.K. 1968 *Land Law and Custom in the Colonies*, 2nd edn. London: Frank Cass.

Mehta, Pradeep & Ann Davison 1993 *Trading Up: The GATT Agreement and Developing Countries*. London: International Organization of Consumers Unions.

Meidinger, Errol 1987 'Regulatory Culture: A Theoretical Outline', *Law and Policy* 9: 365.

Mertens, Hans-Joachim 1997 '*Lex Mercatoria*: A Self-applying System beyond National Law?', in Gunther Teubner (ed.) *Global Law Without a State*. Aldershot: Dartmouth.

Metcalfe, Les 1994 'The Weakest Links: Building Organisational Networks for Multi-Level Regulation', in OECD, *Regulatory Co-Operation for an Interdependent World*. Paris: OECD.

Meyer, J.W. 1980 'The World Polity and the Authority of the Nation-State', in A. Bergesen (ed.) *Studies of the Modern World System*. New York: Academic Press.

Meyer, J.W., F.O. Ramirez, R. Rubinson & J.B. Bennett 1977 'The World Educational Revolution, 1950–1970', *Sociology of Education* 50: 242–58.

Meyer, J.W. & B. Rowan 1977 'Institutionalized Organizations: Formal Structure as Myth and Ceremony', *American Journal of Sociology* 83: 340–63.

Meyer, Rudolf 1994 *Bona Fides und Lex Mercatoria in der Europaischen Rechtstradition*. Gottingen: Wallstein.

Michie, R.C. 1987 *The London and New York Stock Exchanges, 1850–1914*. London: Allen & Unwin.

Michie, Ranald 1988 'Different in Name Only? The London Stock Exchange and Foreign Bourses, c. 1850–1914', in R.P.T. Davenport-Hines & G. Jones (ed.) *The End of Insularity: Essays in Comparative Business History*. London: Frank Cass.

Mickolous, Edward F. 1980 *Transnational Terrorism*. Westport, Connecticut: Greenwood Press.

Miller, Peter & Nikolas Rose 1990 'Governing Economic Life', *Economy and Society* 19: 1–31.

Mintzes, Barbara & Catherine Hodgkin 1996 'The Consumer Movement: From Single-Issue Campaigns to Long-Term Reform', in Peter Davis (ed.) *Contested Ground: Public Purpose and Private Interest in the Regulation of Prescription Drugs*. New York: Oxford University Press.

Mitchell, Deborah 1995 'Women's Incomes', in A. Edwards & S. Margarey (eds) *Women in a Restructuring Australia*. Sydney: Allen & Unwin.

Mitchell, Ronald 1993 'Intentional Oil Pollution of the Oceans', in Peter M.Haas, Robert O. Keohane & Marc A. Levy (eds) *Institutions for the Earth: Sources of Effective International Environmental Protection*. Cambridge, Mass.: MIT Press.

Mitchell, Ronald B. 1994a 'Regime Design Matters: International Oil Pollution and Treaty Compliance', *International Organization* 48: 425–58.

Mitchell, Ronald B. 1994b 'Compliance Theory: A Synthesis', *Receuil* 2: 327–34.

Mitchell, Ronald B. 1994c *Intentional Oil Pollution at Sea: Environmental Policy and Treaty Compliance*. Cambridge, Mass.: MIT Press.

Mitchell, Ronald B. 1995 'Strategies of International Social Control: Beyond Carrots and Sticks', Unpublished manuscript, Department of Political Science, University of Oregon.

Mitrany, David 1948 'The Functional Approach to World Organization', *International Affairs* 24: 350–63.

Montgomery, David 1993 *Citizen Worker: The Experience of Workers in the United States with Democracy and the Free Market during the Nineteenth Century*. New York: Cambridge University Press.

Mooney, Pat Roy 1996 'The Parts of Life', *Development Dialogue*, Special Issue 1–2: 7–183.

Moran, Michael 1986 *The Politics of Banking*, 2nd edn. London: Macmillan.

Moravcsik, Andrew 1995 'Explaining International Human Rights Regimes: Liberal Theory and Western Europe', *European Journal of International Relations* 1: 157–89.

Moreira, Marcilio Marques 1990 'The Point of View of an Emerging Trading Nation: Brazil', in J. Bhagwati & H.T. Patrick (eds) *Aggressive Unilateralism: America's 301 Trade Policy and the World Trading System*. Ann Arbor: University of Michigan Press.

Morgan, E. Victor 1965 *The Theory and Practice of Central Banking 1797–1913*. London: Frank Cass.

Morgan, E. Victor & W.A. Thomas 1962 *The Stock Exchange: Its History and Functions*. London: Elek Books.

Morgan, G. 1986 *Images of Organization*. Beverly Hills: Sage.

Morgenthau, Hans Joachim 1978 *Politics among Nations: The Struggle for Power and Peace*, 5th edn. New York: Alfred A. Knopf.

Moulds, R.F.W. & L.M.H. Wing 1989 'Drug Advertising', *Medical Journal of Australia* 150: 410–11.

Muchlinski, Peter T. 1997 '"Global Bukowina" Examined: Viewing the Multinational Enterprise as a Transnational Law-Making Community', in Gunther Teubner (ed.) *Global Law without a State*. Aldershot: Dartmouth.

Mueller, Milton L. 1993 *Telephone Companies in Paradise: A Case Study in Telecommunications Deregulation*. London: Transaction.

Mugasha, W.W. 1988 'Standby Letters of Credit in International Transactions', Master of Laws thesis, York University, Canada.

Munro, Doug & Stewart Firth 1990 'German Labour Policy and the Partition of the Western Pacific. The View from Samoa', *Journal of Pacific History* 25: 85–102.

Murphy, Craig N. 1994 *International Organization and Industrial Change: Global Governance since 1850*. Cambridge: Polity Press.

Murphy, John F. 1998 'International Crimes', in Christopher C. Joyner (ed.) *The United Nations and International Law*. New York: Cambridge University Press.

Musto, David F. 1973 *The American Disease: Origins of Narcotics Control*. New Haven: Yale University Press.

Musto, David F. 1996 *The History of Legislative Control over Opium, Cocaine, and Their Derivatives*. Internet address: http://www.calyx.com/~Schaffer/HISTORY/ophs.html.

Nader, Ralph 1966 *Unsafe at any Speed: The Designed-In Dangers of the American Automobile*. New York: Grossman.

Nader, Ralph 1994 'Testimony of Ralph Nader on the Uruguay Round of GATT before the Trade Subcommittee of the House Ways and Means Committee', Washington DC, 2 February.

Nader, Ralph & Wesley J. Smith 1993 *Collision Course: The Truth about Airline Safety*. New York: McGraw Hill.

Nader, Ralph & William Taylor 1986 *The Big Boys: Power and Position in American Business*. New York: Pantheon.

Naffine, N. 1985 *An Inquiry into the Substantive Law of Rape*. Adelaide, South Australia: Premier's Department.

Nanda, Ved P. & Sinha Prakash Surya 1996 *Hindu Law and Legal Theory*. Aldershot: Dartmouth.

National Clearinghouse for Alcohol and Drug Information 1996 *A Short History of the Drug Laws*. Internet address: http://www.calyx.com/~Schaffer/LIBRARY/Shrthist.html.

Neal, Larry 1990 *The Rise of Financial Capitalism: International Capital Markets in the Age of Reason*. Cambridge: Cambridge University Press.

Neumann, Franz 1929 *Die Politische und Soziale Bedeutung der Arbeitsgerichtlichen Rechtsprechung*. Berlin.

Nicholas, Barry 1962 *An Introduction to Roman Law*. London: Oxford University Press.

Nicholls, Christopher C. 1998 'Financial Institution Reform: Functional Analysis and an Illustrative Look at Deposit Insurance', *Banking and Finance Law Review* 13: 235–54.

Nickelson, R.L. 1990 'HDTV Standards: Understanding the Issues' *Telecommunication Journal* 57: 302–12.

Nieburg, H.L. 1963 *Nuclear Secrecy and Foreign Policy*. Washington DC: Public Affairs Press.

Noam, Eli 1992 *Telecommunications in Europe*. Oxford: Oxford University Press.

Noonan, John T. Jr 1984 *Bribes*. New York: Macmillan.

Nora, Simon & Minc Alain 1980 *The Computerization of Society: A Report to the President of France*. Cambridge, Mass.: MIT Press.

North, Douglass C. 1990 *Institutions, Institutional Change and Economic Performance*. Cambridge: Cambridge University Press.

Norton, Joseph J. 1991 'Background Note on the Basle Committee', in Joseph J. Norton (ed.) *Bank Regulation and Supervision in the 1990s*. London: Lloyd's of London Press.

Novak, Miroslaw 1993 'Czechoslovak Experience from Large Public Debates on Nuclear Programme after Political Changes in 1989', in OECD, *Public Participation in Nuclear Decision-Making*. Paris: OECD.

Nuclear Energy Agency 1993 *Achieving Nuclear Safety: Improvements in Reactor Safety Design and Operation*. Paris: OECD.

Nuclear Energy Agency 1994 *Liability and Compensation for Nuclear Damage: An International Overview*. Paris: OECD.

Nuclear Regulatory Commission 1993 *Annual Report of the Nuclear Regulatory Commission*. Washington DC: NRC.

O'Brien, Robert, Anne Marie Goetz, Jan Aart Scholte & Marc Williams 1999 *Contesting Global Governance: Multilateral Economic Institutions and Global Social Movements*. Cambridge: Cambridge University Press.

O'Neil, William A. 1993 *World Maritime Day 1993*. London: IMO.

OECD 1985a *Trends in Banking in OECD Countries*. Paris: OECD.

OECD 1985b *Trends in International Taxation*. Paris: OECD.

OECD 1987a *Minimising Conflicting Requirements. Approaches of 'Moderation and Restraint'*. Paris: OECD.

OECD 1987b *Prudential Supervision in Banking*. Paris: OECD.

OECD 1988 *The Telecommunications Industry: The Challenges of Structural Change*. Paris: OECD.

OECD 1989 *Telecommunication Networked-Based Services: Policy Implications*. Paris: OECD.

OECD 1990 *Trade in Information, Computer and Communication Services*. Paris: OECD.

OECD 1991 *Universal Service and Rate Restructuring in Telecommunications*. Paris: OECD.

OECD 1992 *The Periodic Safety Review of Nuclear Power Plants: Practices in OECD Countries*. Paris: OECD.

OECD 1993a *Export Promotion and Environmental Technologies*. Paris: Environment Directorate, OECD.

OECD 1993b *Public Participation in Nuclear Decision-Making*. Paris: OECD.

OECD 1995 *Securities Markets in OECD Countries: Organisation and Regulation*. Paris: OECD.

OECD Committee on Fiscal Affairs 1996 *Model Tax Convention on Income and on Capital*. Paris: OECD.

Oechslin, Jean-Jacques 1982 'Employers' Organizations: Current Trends and Social Responsibilities', *International Labour Review* 121: 503–17.

Offe, C. 1992 'Designing Institutions for East European Transitions', Paper at the Institutional Design Conference, Research School of Social Sciences, Australian National University, Canberra.

Office of Technology Assessment 1993 *US Telecommunications Services in European Markets* OTA-TCT–548. Washington DC: US Government Printing Office.

Okidi, Charles Odidi 1978 *Regional Control of Ocean Pollution: Legal and Institutional Problems and Prospects*. Alphen aan den Rijn, The Netherlands: Sijthoff & Noordhoff.

Orzack, Louis H., Kenneth I. Kaitin & Louis Lasagna 1992 'Pharmaceutical Regulation in the European Community: Barriers to Single Market Integration', *Journal of Health Politics, Policy and Law* 17: 847–68.

Osborne, David & Ted Gaebler 1992 *Reinventing Government: How the Entrepreneurial Spirit is Transforming the Public Sector*. Reading, Mass.: Addison-Wesley.

Osieke, Ebere 1984 'Majority Voting in the ILO and IMF', *International and Comparative Law Quarterly* 33: 381–408.

Ostrom, Elionor 1990 *Governing the Commons: The Evolution of Institutions for Collective Action*. Cambridge: Cambridge University Press.

Otake, Hideo 1982 'Corporate Power in Social Conflict: Vehicle Safety and Japanese Motor Manufacturers', *International Journal of the Sociology of Law* 10: 75–103.

Otto, Diane 1996 'Non-Governmental Organisations in the United Nations System: The Emerging Role of International Civil Society', *Human Rights Quarterly* 18: 107–41.

Owen, David Edward 1968 *British Opium Policy in China and India*. New Haven: Yale University Press.

Owens, Jeffrey 1993 'Globalisation: The Implications for Tax Policies', *Fiscal Studies* 14: 21–44.

Paarlberg, Robert L. 1993 'Managing Pesticide Use in Developing Countries', in Peter M. Haas, Robert O. Keohane & Marc A. Levy (eds) *Institutions for the Earth: Sources of Effective International Environmental Protection*. Cambridge, Mass.: MIT Press.

Palmer, Karen, Wallace E. Oates & Paul R. Portney 1995 'Tightening Environmental Standards: The Benefit–Cost or the No–Cost Paradigm?', *Journal of Economic Perspectives* 9: 119–32.

Panchamukhi, V.R. 1996 'Multilateral Agreement on Investment (MAI): What Should be the Response of the Developing Countries?', Paper issued in conference materials for the International Conference on New Patent System, Foreign Investment and Emerging Issues in WTO, 14–15 November. New Delhi: Parliament House.

Papadakis, Elim 1993 'The Role of Interest Groups, Public Opinion and Political Parties in the Making and Administration of Environmental Policy in Australia', Paper to International Symposium on Environmental Policy in Federal States, Australian National University, Canberra.

Parker, Christine 1998a *Corporate Compliance Programs: Why, When, Where and How?* Sydney: Continuing Legal Education Paper, University of New South Wales Law School.

Parker, Christine 1998b 'Is There a New Compliance Profession', Paper to the Australian Society of Compliance Professionals Conference, Melbourne.

Parker, Christine 1999 'Compliance Professionalism and Regulatory Community: The Australian Trade Practices Regime', *Journal of Law and Society* 26: 215–39.

Parker, Christine forthcoming *Just Lawyers: Regulation and Access to Justice*. Oxford: Oxford University Press.

Parliament of the Commonwealth of Australia 1992 *Ships of Shame: Inquiry into Ship Safety. Report from the House of Representatives Standing Committee on Transport, Communications and Infrastructure*. Canberra: Australian Government Publishing Service.

*Patents, Innovation and Competition in Australia: A Report to the Hon. Barry O. Jones, MP, Minister for Science and Technology, 29 August 1984*. Canberra: Industrial Property Advisory Committee.

Patrick, Hugh T. 1967 'Japan, 1868–1914', in Rondo Cameron, Olga Crisp, Hugh T. Patrick & Richard Tilly *Banking in the Early Stages of Industrialization*. New York: Oxford University Press.

Paulus, Ingeborg 1974 *The Search for Pure Food: A Sociology of Legislation in Britain*. London: Martin Robertson.

Penrose Tilton, Edith 1951 *The Economics of the International Patent System*. Baltimore: Johns Hopkins University Press.

Penvenne, J. 1995 *African Workers and Colonial Racism: Mozambican Strategies and Struggles in Lourenco Marques 1877–1962*. Johannesburg: Witwatersrand University Press.

Perez-Lopez, Jorge F. 1993 'Promoting International Respect for Worker Rights through Business Codes of Conduct', *Fordham International Law Journal* 17: 1–47.

Peters, Aulana L. & Andrew E. Feldman 1988 'The Changing Structure of Securities Markets and the Securities Industry: Implications for International Securities Regulation', *Michigan Yearbook of International Legal Studies* 9: 19–52.

Pettit, Philip 1993 *The Common Mind: An Essay on Psychology, Society, and Politics*. Oxford: Oxford University Press.

Pettit, Philip 1997 *Republicanism: A Theory of Freedom and Government*. Oxford: Oxford University Press.

Pettman, Ralph 1991 *International Politics*. Melbourne: Longman Cheshire.

Phillips, D.P. 1974 'The Influence of Suggestion on Suicide: Substantive and Theoretical Implications of the Werther Effect', *American Sociological Review* 39: 340–54.

Phillips, William D. 1996 'Continuity and Change in Western Slavery: Ancient to Modern Times', in M.L. Bush (ed.) *Serfdom and Slavery: Studies of Legal Bondage*. London: Longman.

Phillips, William D. Jr 1985 *Slavery from Roman Times to the Early Transatlantic Trade*. Minneapolis: University of Minnesota Press.

Picciotto, Sol 1989 'Slicing a Shadow: Business Taxation in an International Framework', in Leigh Hancher & Michael Moran (eds) *Capitalism, Culture, and Economic Regulation*. Oxford: Clarendon Press.

Picciotto, Sol 1991 'The Internationalisation of the State', *Capital and Class* 43: 43–63.

Picciotto, Sol 1992 *International Business Taxation*. London: Weidenfeld & Nicolson.

Picciotto, Sol 1993 'Transfer Pricing and the Antinomies of Corporate Regulation', in Joseph McCahery, Sol Picciotto & Colin Scott (eds) *Corporate Control and Accountability*. Oxford: Clarendon Press.

Picciotto, Sol 1996 'The Regulatory Criss-Cross: Interaction between Jurisdictions and the Construction of Global Regulatory Networks', in W. Bratton, J. McCahery, S. Picciotto & C. Scott (eds) *International Regulatory Competition and Coordination: Perspectives on Economic Regulation in Europe and the United States*. Oxford: Clarendon Press.

Picciotto, Sol 1998 'Linkages in International investment Regulation: The Antinomies of the Draft Multilateral Agreement on Investment', *University of Pennsylvania Journal of International Economic Law* 19: 731–68.

Picciotto, Sol 1999 'Introduction: What Rules for the World Economy?', in S. Picciotto & R. Mayne (eds) *Regulating International Business: Beyond the MAI*. London: Macmillan.

Picciotto, Sol & Ruth Mayne (eds) 1999 *Regulating International Business: Beyond Liberalization*. London: Macmillan.

Pinto, Carlo 1998 'EU & OECD to Fight Harmful Tax Competition: Has the Right Path been Taken?', *International Tax Review* 26: 386–410.

Pirzio-Biroli C. 1990 'A European View of the 1988 US Trade Act and Section 301', in J. Bhagwati & H.T. Patrick (eds) *Aggressive Unilateralism: America's 301 Trade Policy and the World Trading System*. Ann Arbor: University of Michigan Press.

Plano, Jack 1972 *International Approaches to the Problems of Marine Pollution*. Institute for the Study of International Organisation Monograph Series, No. 7. Sussex, England: University of Sussex.

Plowden, William 1971 *The Motor Car and Politics, 1896–1970*. London: Bodley Head.

Poel, D.H. 1976 'The Diffusion of Legislation among the Canadian Provinces', *Canadian Journal of Political Science* 9: 605–26.

Pöhl, Karl Otto 1994 *International Herald Tribune*, 9 May, 9.

Polanyi, Karl 1957 *The Great Transformation: The Political and Economic Origins of Our Time*. Boston: Beacon Hill.

Porter, Gareth & Janet Welsh Brown 1991 *Global Environmental Politics*. Boulder, Colorado: Westview Press.

Porter, Michael 1990 *The Competitive Advantage of Nations*. New York: Macmillan.

Porter, Michael & Claas van der Linde 1995a 'Green *and* Competitive: Ending the Stalemate', *Harvard Business Review* September–October: 120–34.

Porter, Michael & Claas van der Linde 1995b 'Reply to Portney's Critique of Porter and van der Linde (1995) "Green *and* Competitive: Ending the Stalemate"', *Harvard Business Review* November–December: 206–8.

Porter, Michael & Claas van der Linde 1995c 'Toward a New Conception of the Environment–Competitiveness Relationship', *Journal of Economic Perspectives* 9: 98–118.

Portney, Paul R. 1995 'Critique of Porter and van der Linde (1995) "Green *and* Competitive: Ending the Stalemate"', *Harvard Business Review* November–December: 204–6.

Postan, M.M. 1973 *Medieval Trade and Finance*. London: Cambridge University Press.

Potter, William C. 1995 'The Nuclear Proliferation Challenge from the Soviet Successor States: Myths and Realities', in Marianne van Leeuwen (ed.) *The Future of the International Nuclear Non-Proliferation Regime*. Dordrecht: Martinus Nijhoff.

Pounds, N.J.G. 1994 *An Economic History of Medieval Europe*, 2nd edn. London: Longman.

Powell, Louise Jane 1990 '1992: Single European Market Implications for the Insurance Sector', *Boston College International and Comparative Law Review* XIII: 371–89.

Powell, Michael J. 1993 'Professional Innovation: Corporate Lawyers and Private Lawmaking', *Law and Social Inquiry* 18: 423–52.

Price, Jerome 1989 *The Antinuclear Movement*, revised edn. Boston: Twayne.

Procacci, Giuliano 1970 *The History of the Italian People* (translated by Anthony Paul). Harmondsworth: Penguin.

Provost, René 1992 'Starvation as a Weapon: Legal Implications of the United Nations Food Blockade against Iraq and Kuwait', *Columbia Journal of Transnational Law* 30: 577–639.

Putnam, Robert D. 1988 'Diplomacy and Domestic Politics: The Logic of Two-Level Games', *International Organization* 42: 425–60.

Putnam, Robert D. 1993 *Making Democracy Work: Civic Traditions in Modern Italy*. Princeton, NJ: Princeton University Press.

Putnam, Robert D. 1995 'Bowling Alone: America's Declining Social Capital', *Journal of Democracy* 6: 65–78.

Putnam, Robert D. & Nicolas Bayne 1987 *Hanging Together: Cooperation and Conflict in the Seven Power Summits*. Cambridge, Mass.: Harvard University Press.

Putnam, Robert D. & C. Randall Henning 1989 'The Bonn Summit of 1978: A Case Study in Coordination', in Richard N. Cooper, Barry Eichengreen, C. Randall Henning, Gerald Holtham & Robert D. Putnam (eds) *Can Nations Agree? Issues in International Economic Cooperation*. Washington DC: Brookings Institution.

Quinn, Brian 1991 'The Influence of the Banking Acts (1979 and 1987) on the Bank of England's Traditional Style of Banking Supervision', in Joseph J. Norton (ed.) *Bank Regulation and Supervision in the 1990s*. London: Lloyd's of London Press.

Randell, Alan 1995 'Codex Alimentarius: How it all Began', *Journal of Food, Nutrition and Agriculture* 13/14: 35–40.

Ratner, Sidney 1967 *Taxation and Democracy in America*. New York: John Wiley.

Raz, Joseph 1972 'Legal Principles and the Limits of Law', *Yale Law Journal* 81: 823–54.

Rediker, Marcus 1987 *Between the Devil and the Deep Blue Sea*. Cambridge: Cambridge University Press.

Rees, Joseph 1994 *Hostages of Each Other: The Transformation of Nuclear Safety since Three Mile Island*. Chicago: University of Chicago Press.

Rees, Joseph 1997 'Development of Communitarian Regulation in the Chemical Industry', *Law and Policy* 19(4): 477–528.

Reese, Willis L. 1956 'Some Observations on the Eighth Session of the Hague Conference on Private International Law', *American Journal of Comparative Law* 5: 611–16.

Reiss, Mitchell 1988 *Without the Bomb: The Politics of Nuclear Nonproliferation*. New York: Columbia University Press.

Reiss, Mitchell 1995 *Bridled Ambition: Why Countries Constrain their Nuclear Capabilities*. Washington DC: Woodrow Wilson Center Press.

Renouf, Carole 1993 'Cracking the Codex', *Consuming Interest* July: 20–22.

Repetto, Robert 1993 'Trade and Environment Policies: Achieving Complementarities and Avoiding Conflicts', *Issues and Ideas* (July). Washington DC: World Resource Institute.

Repetto, Robert 1995 *Jobs, Competitiveness and Environmental Regulation: What are the Real Issues?* Washington DC: World Resources Institute.

Report from the House of Representatives, Select Committee on the Print Media. 1992 *News and Fair Facts: The Australian Print Media Industry*. Canberra: Australian Government Publishing Service.

Rhodes, Carolyn 1989 'Reciprocity in Trade: The Utility of a Bargaining Strategy', *International Organization* 43: 273–99.

Ricardo, David 1817 *The Principles of Political Economy and Taxation*, 1976 edn. London: J.M. Dent.

Ricketson, S. 1984 *The Law of Intellectual Property*. Sydney: Law Book.

Ricketson, Sam 1987 *The Berne Convention for the Protection of Literary and Artistic Works: 1886–1986*. Kluwer: Centre for Commercial Law Studies, Queen Mary College.

Rihill, Tracey 1996 'The Origin and Establishment of Ancient Greek Slavery', in M.L. Bush (ed.) *Serfdom and Slavery: Studies of Legal Bondage*. London: Longman.

Ringer, A. Barbara 1968 'The Role of the United States in International Copyright: Past, Present, and Future', *Georgetown Law Journal* 56: 1050–79.

Ritchie, Donald A. 1980 *James M. Landis: Dean of the Regulators*. Cambridge, Mass.: Harvard University Press.

Roberts, Brad 1995 'NPT Extension, International Security, and the End of the Cold War', in Marianne van Leeuwen (ed.) *The Future of the International Nuclear Non-Proliferation Regime*. Dordrecht: Martinus Nijhoff.

Robertson, A.F. 1984 *People and the State: An Anthropology of Planned Development*. Cambridge: Cambridge University Press.

Robinson, J. Michael 1985 *International Securities: Law and Practice*. London: Euromoney Publications.

Rogers, Andrew, Justice 1989 'Contemporary Problems in International Commercial Arbitration', *International Business Lawyer* 17: 154–60.

Rogers, E. 1983 *The Diffusion of Innovations*, 3rd edn. New York: Free Press.

Roger, E. & F. Shoemaker 1971 *Communication of Innovations*. New York: Free Press.

Rogers, Richard Theron 1982 'Advertising and Concentration Change in US Food and Tobacco Products, 1954 to 1972', Unpublished PhD dissertation, University of Wisconsin, Madison.

Rogoff, Kenneth 1985 'Can International Monetary Policy Cooperation be Counterproductive?', *Journal of International Economics* 18: 199–217.

Romano, Roberta 1996 'Explaining American Exceptionalism in Corporate Law', in I. McCahery, W. Bratton, S. Picciotto & C. Scott (eds) *International Regulatory Competition and Coordination*. Oxford: Clarendon Press.

Ron, James 1997 'Varying Methods of State Violence', *International Organization* 51: 275–300.

Rose, Nikolas 1996 'Governing "Advanced" Liberal Democracies', in A. Barry, T. Osborne & N. Rose (eds) *Foucault and Political Reason*. Chicago: University of Chicago Press.

Rose, Nikolas & Peter Miller 1992 'Political Power beyond the State: Problematics of Government', *British Journal of Sociology* 43: 173–203.

Rosenberg, Gerald N. 1991 *The Hollow Hope: Can Courts bring about Social Change?* Chicago: University of Chicago Press.

Rosett, A. 1992 'Unification, Harmonization, Restatement, Codification and Reform in International Commercial Law', *American Journal of Comparative Law* 40(1): 683–97.

Rosner, Lydia 1995 'The Sexy Russian Mafia', *Criminal Organisations* 10.

Rothblatt, Martin A. 1980 'International Regulation of Digital Communications Satellite Systems', *Federal Communications Law Journal* 32: 393–436.

Rousseau, Jean-Jacques 1968 *The Social Contract*. Harmondsworth: Penguin.

Rowlands, Ian H. 1995 *The Politics of Global Atmospheric Change*. Manchester: Manchester University Press.

Rubin, Alfred P. 1988 *The Law of Piracy*. Newport, Rhode Island: Naval War College Press.

Rungta, Radhe Shyam 1970 *The Rise of Business Corporations in India 1851–1900*. Cambridge: Cambridge University Press.

Ryan, Alan 1973 'Introduction', in Alan Ryan (ed.) *The Philosophy of Social Explanation*. Oxford: Oxford University Press.

Ryan, K.W. 1962 *An Introduction to the Civil Law*. Sydney: Law Book.

Sabine, B.E.V. 1966 *A History of Income Tax*. London: George Allen & Unwin.

Sachs, Jeffrey D. 1989 'Introduction', in Jeffrey D. Sachs (ed.) *Developing Country Debt and the World Economy*. Chicago: University of Chicago Press.

Sachs, Sharin 1990 'Decoding Codex', *FDA Reporter* February: 28–31.

Sackman, Simon & Margaret Coltman 1996 'Legal Aspects of a Global Securities Market', in F. Oditah (ed.) *The Future for the Global Securities Market: Legal and Regulatory Aspects*. Oxford: Clarendon Press.

Sacks, H. 1969 'Crisis in International Copyright: The Protocol Regarding Developing Countries', *Journal of Business Law* 26–32, 128–34.

Samet, Jack I. & Judy A. Sherman 1984 'The Audit Committee: In Search of a Purpose', *Corporation Law Review* 7: 42–55.

Samson, K.T. 1979 'The Changing Pattern of ILO Supervision', *International Labour Review* 118: 569–87.

Samuels, J.M. & Piper, A.G. 1985 *International Accounting: A Survey*. New York: St Martin's Press.

Sand, Peter H. 1991a 'Institutions for Global Change: Whither Environmental Governance?', *Policy Studies Journal* 19: 93–102.

Sand, Peter H. 1991b 'International Cooperation: The Environmental Experience', in Jessica Tuchman Mathews (ed.) *Preserving the Global Environment: The Challenge of Shared Leadership*. New York: W.W. Norton.

Sandford, Rosemary 1992 'Secretariats and International Environmental Negotiations: Two New Models', in Lawrence E. Susskind, Eric Jay Dolin & J. William Breslin (eds) *International Environmental Treaty Making*. Cambridge, Mass.: Program on Negotiation, Harvard Law School.

Sandford, Rosemary 1994 'International Environmental Treaty Secretariats: Stage-Hands or Actors?', in Helge Ole Bergesen & Georg Parmann (eds) *Green Globe Yearbook of International Co-operation on Environment and Development*. Oxford: Oxford University Press.

Sands, Philippe J. & Albert P. Bedcarre 1990 'Convention on International Trade in Endangered Species: The Role of Public Interest Non-Governmental Organizations in Ensuring the Effective Enforcement of the Ivory Trade Ban', *Environmental Affairs* 17: 799–822.

Sarna, James Adam 1990 'Japan and Insider Trading: Some Problems when there are Different Definitions of Right and Wrong', *ILSA Journal of International Law* 14: 67–81.

Sayers R.S. (ed.) 1952 *Banking in the British Commonwealth*. Oxford: Clarendon Press.

Schachter, Oscar 1991 *International Law in Theory and Practice*. Dordrecht: Martinus Nijhoff.

Schechter, Frank I. 1927 'The Rational Basis of Trademark Protection', *Harvard Law Review* 40: 813–33.

Scheff, T. 1966 *Being Mentally Ill*. Chicago: Aldine.

Scheff, Thomas J. 1994 *Bloody Revenge: Emotions, Nationalism and War*. Boulder, Colorado: Westview Press.

Scheinman, Lawrence 1987 *The International Energy Agency and World Nuclear Order*. Washington DC: Resources for the Future.

Schiller, Dan 1982 'Business Users and the Telecommunications Networks', *Journal of Communication* 32: 84–96.

Schindler, D. & J. Tornau 1985 'The Laws of Armed Conflicts', in E.J. Osmanczyk (ed.) *The Encyclopedia of the United Nations and International Agreements*. Philadelphia: Taylor & Francis.

Schmidheiny, Stephan & Federico Zorraquin 1996 *Financing Change: The Financial Community, Eco-Efficiency, and Sustainable Development*. Cambridge, Mass.: MIT Press.

Schneider, Barry R. 1994 'Nuclear Proliferation and Counter-Proliferation: Policy Issues and Debates', *Mershon International Studies Review* 38: 209–34.

Schneider, Friedrich 1994 'Ecological Objectives in a Market Economy: Three Simple Questions, but no Simple Answers?', in Michael Faure, John Vervaele & Albert Weale (eds) *Environmental Standards in the European Union in an Interdisciplinary Framework*. Antwerp: Bureau JA Vormgevers, Tilburg.

Schulz, Fritz 1946 *History of Roman Legal Science*. London: Oxford University Press.

Schwarzenberger, Georg 1950 'The Problem of International Criminal Law', *Current Legal Problems* 3: 263–95.

Scott, Colin 1996a 'Current Issues in EC Telecommunications Law', in Colin Scott & Olivier Audéoud (eds) *The Future of EC Telecommunications Law*, vol. 19. Trier: Academy of European Law.

Scott, Colin 1996b 'Institutional Competition and Coordination in the Process of Telecommunications Liberalization', in William Bratton, Joseph McCahery, Sol Picciotto & Colin Scott (eds) *International Regulatory Competition and Coordination*. Oxford: Oxford University Press.

Scott, Colin 1998 'The Proceduralization of Telecommunications Law', *Telecommunications Policy* 22: 243–54.

Scott, J.M. 1969 *The White Poppy: A History of Opium*. New York: Funk & Wagnalls.

Scott, Peter Dale 1992 'Honduras, the Contra Support Networks, and Cocaine: How the US Government has Augmented America's Drug Crisis', in A. McCoy & A. Block (eds) *War on Drugs: Studies in the Failure of US Narcotic Policy*. Boulder, Colorado: Westview Press.

Sebenius, James K. 1991 'Designing Negotiations toward a New Regime: The Case of Global Warming', *International Security* 35: 110–48.

Seel, B. Peter 1998 'The Path from Analog HDTV to DTV in Japan', *Prometheus* 16: 209–16.

Segall, J. 1990 'Building World Democracy through the UN', *Medicine and War* 6: 274–84.

Seid, Sherif 1999 Unpublished draft chapters of a PhD thesis expected to be submitted in 2000. Law Program, Research School of Social Sciences, Australian National University.

Seligman, Joel 1982 *The Transformation of Wall Street: A History of the Securities and Exchange Commission and Modern Corporate Finance*. Boston: Houghton Mifflin.

Sell, Susan K. 1995 'Intellectual Property Protection and Antitrust in the Developing World: Crisis, Coercion, and Choice', *International Organization* 49: 315–49.

Sell, Susan K. 1998 *Power and Ideas: North–South Politics of Intellectual Property and Antitrust*. New York: State University of New York Press.

Semmel, B. 1960 *Imperialism and Social Reform: English Social-Imperial Thought 1895–1914*. London: George Allen & Unwin.

Servais, J.M. 1989 'The Social Clause in Trade Agreements: Wishful Thinking or an Instrument of Social Progress?', *International Labour Review* 128: 423–32.

Shah, Atul K. 1996 'The Dynamics of International Bank Regulation', *Journal of Financial Regulation and Compliance* 4: 371–85.

Shapiro, Susan 1984 *Wayward Capitalists: Target of the Securities and Exchange Commission*. New Haven, Connecticut: Yale University Press.

Sharpe, Diana 1989 *Protecting Intellectual Property in Asia-Pacific*, 2nd edn. Melbourne: Longman Professional.

Shaw, Bill & John R. Rowlett 1993 'Reforming the US Banking System: Lessons from Abroad', *North Carolina Journal of International Law and Commercial Regulation* 19: 91–121.

Shea, Timothy 1996 'The Privatization of Intelsat: a User Perspective', in Dan Wedemeyer & Richard Nickelson (eds) *Proceedings of the 18th Annual Conference of the Pacific Telecommunications Council*. Hawaii: Pacific Telecommunications Council.

Shearing, Clifford & Philip Stenning 1985 'From the Panopticon to Disneyworld: The Development of Discipline', in A. Doob & E. Greenspan (eds) *Perspectives in Criminal Law*. Aurora: Canada Law Book.

Shelley, L.I. 1995 'Post-Soviet Organized Crime and the Soviet Successor States', *International Annals of Criminology* 33: 169–90.

Sherman, Brad 1995 'Remembering and Forgetting: The Birth of Modern Copyright Law', *Intellectual Property Journal* 10: 1–34.

Sherman, Lawrence W. 1978 *Scandal and Reform: Controlling Police Corruption*. Berkeley: University of California Press.

Shineberg, Dorothy 1991 '"Noumea no Good. Noumea no Pay": "New Hebridean" Indentured Labour in New Caledonia, 1865–1925', *Journal of Pacific History* 26: 187–205.

Shiva, Vandana 1996 *Protecting Our Biological and Intellectual Heritage in the Age of Biopiracy*. New Delhi: Research Foundation for Science, Technology and Natural Resource Policy.

Shivji, Issa G. 1982 'Semi-Proletarian Labour and the Use of Penal Sanctions in the Labour Law of Colonial Tanganyika (1920–38)', in Colin Summer (ed.) *Crime, Justice and Underdevelopment*. London: Heinemann.

Shurmer, Mark & Paul A. David 1996 'Formal Standards-Setting for Global Telecommunications and Information Services', Background Paper for the ESRC/GEI Programme Workshop held at the London Business School.

Sidell, Scott R. 1988 *The IMF and Third-World Political Instability*. London: Macmillan.

Siegman, Charles J. 1994 'The Bank for International Settlements and the Federal Reserve', *Federal Reserve Bulletin* 80: 900–6.

Silver, Morris 1995 *Economic Structures of Antiquity*. Westport, Connecticut: Greenwood Press.

Silverman, Milton, Philip R. Lee & Mia Lydecker 1982 *Prescriptions for Death*. Berkeley: University of California Press.

Silverstein, Harvey B. 1978 *Superships and Nation-States: The Transnational Politics of the Intergovernmental Maritime Consultative Organization*. Boulder, Colorado: Westview Press.

Simon, H. 1957 *Administrative Behavior*. New York: Macmillan.

Simons, Geoff 1994 *The United Nations: A Chronology of Conflict*. New York: St Martin's Press.

Simpson, F.D. 1925 'How Far Does the Law of England Forbid Monopoly?', *Law Quarterly Review* 41: 393–4.

Simpson, John 1983 *The Independent Nuclear State: The United States, Britain and the Military Atom*. London: Macmillan.

Simpson, William R. 1994 'The ILO and Tripartism: Some Reflections', *Monthly Labor Review* 117: 40–5.

Sinclair, Stuart 1983 *The World Car: The Future of the Automobile Industry*. New York: Facts on File.

Sinclair, Timothy J. 1994 'Between State and Market: Hegemony and Institutions of Collective Action under Conditions of International Capital Mobility', *Policy Sciences* 27: 447–66.

Sinclair, Upton 1906 *The Jungle*. Melbourne: G. Robertson.

Slatter, Stuart St P. 1977 *Competition and Marketing Strategies in the Pharmaceutical Industry*. London: Croom Helm.

Slaughter, Anne-Marie 1997 'The Real New World Order', *Foreign Affairs* 76: 183–97.

Smart, C. 1989 *Feminism and the Power of Law*. London: Routledge & Kegan Paul.

Smith, Adam 1776 *The Wealth of Nations*, vols 1 and 2, 1970 edn. London: J.M. Dent.

Smith, Adam 1776 *The Wealth of Nations*, 1981 edn. Harmondsworth: Penguin.

Smith, Milton L. 1990 *International Regulation of Satellite Communication*. Dordrecht: Martinus Nijhoff.

Snider, L. 1987 'Towards a Political Economy of Reform, Regulation and Corporate Crime', *Law and Policy* 9: 37–68.

Snow, Marcellus S. 1986 'Communications Policy in Seven Developed Countries: Introduction, Background, and Conclusions', in Marcellus S. Snow (ed.) *Telecommunications Regulation and Deregulation in Industrialized Democracies*. North Holland: Elsevier Science.

Snow, Marcellus S. 1995 'The AT&T Divestiture: A 10-Year Retrospective', in D.M. Lamberton (ed.) *Beyond Competition: The Future of Telecommunications*. North Holland: Elsevier.

Snyder, Glenn H. & Paul Diesing 1977 *Politics among Nations: Bargaining, Decision Making and System Structure in International Crises*. Princeton, NJ: Princeton University Press.

Solow, Barbara L. 1987 'Capitalism and Slavery in the Exceedingly Long Run', *Journal of Interdisciplinary History* XVII: 711–37.

Sornarajah, M. 1989 'The UNCITRAL Model Law: A Third World Viewpoint', *Journal of International Arbitration* 6: 7–20.

Soros, George 1994 *The Alchemy of Finance*. New York: Wiley.

Soros, George 1998 *The Crisis of Global Capitalism*. London: Little, Brown.

Soskice, David 1999 'Divergent Production Regimes: Coordinated and Uncoordinated Market Economies in the 1980s and 1990s', in H. Kitschelt, P. Lange, G. Marks & J.D. Stephens (eds) *Continuity and Change in Contemporary Capitalism*. Cambridge: Cambridge University Press.

Spector, Bertram I., G. Sjostedt & I.W. Zartman (eds) 1994 *Negotiating International Regimes: Lessons Learned from the United Nations Conference on Environment and Development (UNCED)*. London: Graham & Trotman.

Springer, Allen L. 1988 'United States Environmental Policy and International Law: Stockholm Principle 21 Revisited', in John E. Carroll (ed.) *International Environmental Diplomacy: The Management and Resolution of Transfrontier Environmental Problems*. Cambridge: Cambridge University Press.

Stairs, Kevin & Peter Taylor 1992 'NGOs and Legal Protection of the Oceans: A Case Study', in Andrew Hurrell & Benedict Kingsbury (eds) *The International Politics of the Environment*. Oxford: Clarendon Press.

Starkey, David J. 1993 'The Origins and Regulation of Eighteenth-Century British Privateering', in Tony Barrow (ed.) *Pressgangs and Privateers*. London: Bewick Press.

Stein, Peter 1988 *The Character and Influence of the Roman Civil Law: Historical Essays*. London: Hambledon Press.

Steinhardt, Ralph G. 1998 'Outer Space', in Christopher C. Joyner (ed.) *The United Nations and International Law*. New York: Cambridge University Press.

Sterling, Claire 1994 *Crime without Frontiers: The Worldwide Expansion of Organised Crime and the Pax Mafiosa*. London: Little, Brown.

Stern, R.M. 1960 'A Century of Food Exports', *Kyklos* 13: 44–64.

Stewart, R. 1985 'Reforming Environmental Law', *Stanford Law Review* 37: 1333.

Stopford, John M. & Susan Strange with John S. Henley 1991 *Rival States, Rival Firms: Competition for World Market Shares*. Cambridge: Cambridge University Press.

Strang, David & Patricia Mei Yin Chang 1993 'The International Labor Organization and the Welfare State: Institutional Effects on National Welfare Spending, 1960–80', *International Organization* 47: 235–62.

Subramanian, A. 1991 'The International Economics of Intellectual Property Right Protection: A Welfare-Theoretic Trade Policy Analysis', *World Development* 19: 45–56.

Sunstein, Cass 1990 *After the Rights Revolution*. Cambridge, Mass.: Harvard University Press.

Sunstein, Cass R. 1996 *Legal Reasoning and Political Conflict*. New York: Oxford University Press.
Sutherland, Johanna 1998 'TRIPS, Cultural Politics and Law Reform', Paper presented to the National Intellectual Property Teachers' Workshop, Australian National University.
Swanson, Timothy M. 1994 *The International Regulation of Extinction*. London: Macmillan.
Swepston, Lee 1994 'The Future of ILO Standards', *Monthly Labor Review* 117: 16–23.
Swire, Peter P. 1996 'The Race to Laxity and the Race to Undesirability: Explaining Failures in Competition among Jurisdictions in Environmental Law', *Yale Law and Policy Review* 14: 67–110.
Sykes, Edward J. 1986 *The Law of Securities*, 4th edn. Sydney: Law Book.
Symposium 1982 'Origins and Evolution: Drafters Reflect upon the Uniform Commercial Code', *Ohio State Law Journal* 43: 535–84.
Talley, Dorsey 1991 *Total Quality Management: Performance and Cost Measures: The Strategy for Economic Survival.* Milwaukee: ASQC Quality Press.
Tanzi, Vito 1990 'The IMF and Tax Reform', IMF Working Paper, Unpublished, April. Washington DC: IMF.
TARP 1995 *American Express-SOCAP Study of Complaint Handling in Australia*. Geelong: Society of Consumer Affairs Professionals in Business.
Tawney, R.H. 1938 *Religion and the Rise of Capitalism*. Harmondsworth: Penguin.
Tellegen-Couperus, Olga 1993 *A Short History of Roman Law.* London: Routledge.
Temperley, Howard 1972 *British Antislavery: 1833–1870*. London: Longman.
Teubner, Gunter 1997 '"Global Bukowina": Legal Pluralism in the World Society', in G. Teubner (ed.) *Global Law without a State*. Aldershot: Dartmouth.
*The National Information Infrastructure: Agenda for Action*. Information Infrastructure Task Force, 15 September 1993.
Thomas, Christopher & Greg A. Tereposky 1993 'The Evolving Relationship between Trade and Environmental Regulation', *Journal of World Trade* 27: 23–46.
Thompson, Edward 1973 'International Protection of Performers' Rights: Some Current Problems', *International Labour Review* 107: 303–14.
Thompson, Katherine 1996 *The Law of Food and Drink*. Crayford, Kent: Shaw.
Tiebout, C. 1956 'A Pure Theory of Local Expenditures' *Journal of Political Economy* 64: 416–24.
Tipson, Frederick 1997 'Global Telecommunications and Local Politics', in Frederick M. Abbot & David J. Gerber (eds) *Public Policy and Global Technological Integration*. London: Kluwer Law International.
Tobin, James 1996 'Prologue', in Mahbub Haq-ul, Inge Kaul & Isabelle Grunberg (eds) *The Tobin Tax: Coping with Financial Volatility*. New York: Oxford University Press.
Tocqueville, Alexis de 1835 *Democracy in America* (translated by George Lawrence 1969). New York: Harper & Row.
Tomasic, Roman & B. Pentony 1989 'Insider Trading and Business Ethics', *Legal Studies Forum* XIII: 151–70.
Tomasic, Roman & B. Pentony 1991 *Casino Capitalism: Insider Trading in Australia*. Canberra: Australian Institute of Criminology.
Tomlins, Christopher L. 1993 *Law, Labor, and Ideology in the Early American Republic*. New York: Cambridge University Press.
Toutain, Jules 1930 *The Economic Life of the Ancient World*. London: Kegan Paul.
Trade Practices Commission 1992 *Report by the Trade Practices Commission on the Self-Regulation of Promotion and Advertising of Therapeutic Goods.* Canberra: Trade Practices Commission.
Traill, Bruce 1994 *New Food Consumption Patterns and Product Quality in Europe and Adaptation of Agricultural Production*. Rome: FAO.
Trakman, Leon E. 1983 *The Law Merchant: The Evolution of Commercial Law*. Littleton, Colorado: Fred B. Rothman.
Trebilcock, M. & R. Howse 1995 *The Regulation of International Trade*. London: Routledge.
Trevelline, Michael J. 1993 'European Communities Standardisation Policy: A New Means to Regulate Foodstuffs', *European Competition Law Review* 2: 46–52.
Trevelyan, G.M. 1985 *A Shortened History of England*. Harmondsworth: Penguin.
Triffin, R. 1960 *Gold and the Dollar Crisis*. New Haven: Yale University Press.
Trimble, R.J. 1948 'The Law Merchant and the Letter of Credit', *Harvard Law Review* 61: 981–1008.
Tripartite Working Party on Labour Standards 1996 *Report on Labour Standards in the Asia-Pacific Region*. Canberra: Australian Government Publishing Service.
Tsebelis, George 1990 *Nested Games: Rational Choice in Comparative Politics*. Los Angeles: University of California Press.
Turner, John C. with Michael Hogg, Penelope J. Oakes, Stephen D. Reicher & Margaret S. Wetherell 1987 *Rediscovering the Social group: A Self-Categorization Theory*. Oxford: Basil Blackwell.

Turner, V. 1974 *Dramas, Fields, and Metaphors*. Ithaca: Cornell University Press.

Tyree, Alan 1997 *Digital Cash*. Sydney: Butterworths.

UNCITRAL 1971 *Yearbook: vol. 1 1968–1970*. New York: UN.

UNCITRAL 1994 *Yearbook: vol. 23 1992*. New York: UN.

UN Department of Economic Affairs 1950 *The Effects of Taxation on Foreign Trade and Investment*. Lake Success, New York: UN.

UNCTAD 1992 Combating Global Warming: Study on a Global System of Tradeable Carbon Emission Entitlements. New York: UN.

UNCTAD 1996 *World Investment Report 1996: Investment, Trade and International Policy Arrangements*. New York and Geneva: UN.

UNCTAD World Investment Report 1998 *Trends and Determinants*, August. Geneva: UNCTAD.

US Council on International Business 1992 *Cooperative Efforts of the US and Mexican Business Communities to Address Labor and Environment Issues in the NAFTA*. New York: US Council on International Business.

US Department of Treasury 1983 *Treasury Bulletin*, Table CM-V-1, CM-V-2, March, 1988. Washington DC: US Department of Treasury.

US Department of Treasury 1988 *Treasury Bulletin*, Table CM-V-1, CM-V-2, March, 1983. Washington DC: US Department of Treasury.

van Bergeijk, Peter A.G. & Dick L. Kabel 1993 'Strategic Trade Theories and Trade Policy', *Journal of World Trade* 27: 175–86.

Vann, Richard J. 1991a 'A Model Tax Treaty for the Asian-Pacific Region?', *Bulletin for International Fiscal Documentation* 45: 99–111.

Vann, Richard J. 1991b 'A Model Tax Treaty for the Asian-Pacific Region?', *Bulletin for International Fiscal Documentation* 45: 151–163.

Vaughan, D. 1992 'Theory Elaboration: The Heuristics of Case Analysis', in Charles C. Ragin & Howard S. Becker (eds) *What is a Case? Issues in the Logic of Social Enquiry*. San Francisco: University of California Press.

Veale, Sarah E., James M. Spiegelman & Ilkka Ronkainen 1988 'Trade in Services: The US Position', *Economic Impact* 62: 53–7.

Veneziani, Bruno 1986 'The Evolution of the Contract of Employment', in Bob Hepple (ed.) *The Making of Labour Law: A Comparative Study of Nine Countries up to 1945*. London: Mansell.

Vickers, Brian 1988 *In Defence of Rhetoric*. Oxford: Clarendon Press.

Vines, D. 1996 'International Economic Institutions', Seminar presentation, Economics, Research School of Pacific and Asian Studies, Australian National University.

Vinogradoff, Paul 1929 *Roman Law in Medieval Europe*, 2nd edn. London: Oxford University Press.

Vogel, David 1995 *Trading Up: Consumer and Environmental Regulation in a Global Economy*. Cambridge, Mass.: Harvard University Press.

Vogel, David 1998 'The Globalization of Pharmaceutical Regulation', *Governance* 11:1–22.

Vogel, Ezra F. 1979 *Japan as No. 1: Lessons for America*. Cambridge, Mass.: Harvard University Press.

Wade, V.A., P.R. Mansfield & P.J. McDonald 1989 'Drug Company Evidence to Justify Advertising', *Lancet* 25 November: 1261–3.

Waite, Barbara L. & Rowan Ford 1986 'International Communications Law, Part II: Satellite Regulation and the Space WARC', *International Lawyer* 20: 341–65.

Walker, J.L. 1969 'The Diffusion of Innovations among the American States', *American Political Science Review* 63: 880–900.

Walker, J.L. 1973 'Setting the Agenda in the US Senate: A Theory of Problem Selection', *British Journal of Political Science* 7: 423–45.

Walker, Jill, 1998 'The Interface between Intellectual Property Rights and Competition Law and Policy: An Australian Perspective', *Prometheus* 16: 383–93.

Walker, William O. 1993–94 'The Foreign Narcotics Policy of the United States since 1980: An End to the War on Drugs?', *International Journal* XLIX: 37–65.

Wall, Rosemary Pierce 1984 'International Trends in New Drug Approval Regulation: The Impact of Pharmaceutical Innovation,' *Rutgers Computer and Technology Law Journal* 10: 129.

Walsh, Edward J. 1988 *Democracy in the Shadows: Citizen Mobilization in the Wake of the Accident at Three Mile Island*. New York: Greenwood Press.

Walter, Andrew 1991 *World Power and World Money*. New York: Harvester Wheatsheaf.

Wang, Yi 1996 'Most-Favoured-Nation Treatment under the General Agreement on Trade in Services: And its Application in Financial Services', *Journal of World Trade* 30: 91–124.

WANO 1995 *World Association of Nuclear Operators: Annual Review 1995*. London: WANO.

Warlaumont, Hazel G. 1988 'Strategies in International Radio Wars: A Comparative Approach', *Journal of Broadcasting and Electronic Media* 32: 43–59.

Warren, Tony 1998 'The Political Economy of Telecommunications Services Trade and Investment Policy: Australia, Japan and the US' in S. Macdonald & G. Madden (eds) *Telecommunications and Socio-Economic Development*. North Holland: Elsevier.

Waters, Malcolm 1995. *Globalisation*. London: Routledge.

Watson, Alan 1974 *Legal Transplants: An Approach to Comparative Law*. Edinburgh: Scottish Academic Press.

Watson, Alan 1987 *Roman Slave Law*. Baltimore and London: Johns Hopkins University Press.

Watson, Alan 1991 *Roman Law & Comparative Law*. Athens and London: University of Georgia Press.

Watson, Alan 1995 *The Spirit of Roman Law*. Athens and London: University of Georgia Press.

Weale, Albert 1992 *The New Politics of Pollution*. Manchester and New York: Manchester University Press.

Webb, Michael, C. 1991 'International Economic Structures, Government Interests, and International Coordination of Macroeconomic Adjustment Policies', *International Organization* 45: 309–42.

Webb, Sidney & Beatrice Webb 1903 *The History of Liquor Licensing in England*. London: Longman.

Weber, Max 1967 *From Max Weber: Essays in Sociology* (edited by H.H. Gerth & C. Wright Mills). London: Routledge & Kegan Paul.

Wechsberg, J. 1966 *The Merchant Bankers*. Boston: Little, Brown.

Weinsheimer, J. 1984 *Imitation*. London: Routledge & Kegan Paul.

Weiss, Ernst 1984 'Telecommunications Policy: The Users Need for Telecommunication Systems. A Review of Trends in Europe', in J.F. Rada & G.R. Pipe (eds) *Communication Regulation and International Business*. North Holland: Elsevier Science.

Weiss, Thomas G. & Leon Gordenker 1996 'Pluralizing Global Governance: Analytical Approaches and Dimensions', in Thomas G. Weiss & Leon Gordenker (eds) *NGOs, The UN, & Global Governance*. London: Lynne Rienner.

Whalan, Douglas J. 1982 *The Torrens System in Australia*. Sydney: Law Book.

Wheeler, David & Ashoka Mody 1992 'International Investment Location Decisions: The Case of US Firms', *Journal of International Economics* August: 57–76.

Wheeler, David & Maria Sillanpää 1997 *The Stakeholder Corporation: A Blueprint for Maximizing Stakeholder Value*. London: Pitman.

White, John D. & Clifford E. Douglas 1992 'Fighting for Smoke-Free Skies', *Multinational Monitor* Jan./Feb.: 21–2.

Whitehouse, G. 1992 'Legislation and Labour Market Gender Inequality: An Analysis of OECD Countries', *Work, Employment and Society* 6: 65–86.

Whitten, Ira Taylor 1979 *Brand Performance in the Cigarette Industry and the Advantage of Early Entry, 1913–1973*. Staff Report to the Federal Trade Commission. Washington DC: US Government Printing Office.

Whittlesey, C.R. 1968 'Rules, Discretion, and Central Bankers', in C.R. Whittlesey & J.S.G. Wilson (eds) *Essays in Money and Banking in Honour of R.S. Sayers*. Oxford: Clarendon Press.

WHO/DAP 1994 *Use of the WHO Certification Scheme on the Quality of Pharmaceutical Products Moving in International Commerce*. Geneva: DAP Research Series No. 16.

Wilentz, Sean 1984 *Chants Democratic: New York City and the Rise of the American Working Class, 1788–1850*. Oxford and New York: Oxford University Press.

Wilkinson, Rorden 1999 'Labour and Trade-Related Regulation: Beyond the Trade–Labour Standards Debate?', *British Journal of Politics and International Relations* 1.

Williams, David 1968 'The Evolution of the Sterling System', in C.R. Whittlesey & J.S.G. Wilson (eds) *Essays in Money and Banking in Honour of R.S. Sayers*. Oxford: Clarendon Press.

Williams, Eric 1944 *Capitalism and Slavery*. Chapel Hill, NC.: University of North Carolina Press.

Williams, Geoffrey Lee & Alan Lee Williams 1996 *Terrorism: The Failed Response*. Occasional Paper 66. London: Institute for European Defence and Strategic Studies.

Williamson, John 1977 *The Failure of World Monetary Reform, 1971–74*. New York: New York University Press.

Williamson, John 1983a 'On Judging the Success of IMF Policy Advice', in John Williamson (ed.) *IMF Conditionality*. Washington DC: Institute for International Economics.

Williamson, John 1983b 'The Lending Policies of the International Monetary Fund', in John Williamson (ed.) *IMF Conditionality*. Washington DC: Institute for International Economics.

Willis, Evan 1983 *Medical Dominance: The Division of Labour in Australian Health*. Sydney: George Allen & Unwin.

Wilson, A.C. 1994 *Wire and Wireless: A History of Telecommunications in New Zealand 1860–1987*. New Zealand: Dunmore Press.

Windcott, Harold 1946 *The Stock Exchange*. London: Sampson Low.

Windmuller, J.P. 1980 *The International Trade Union Movement*. Deventer, Netherlands: Kluwer.

Winham, Gilbert R. 1992 *The Evolution of International Trade Agreements*. Toronto: University of Toronto Press.

Wolff, J.J. 1951 *Roman Law: An Historical Introduction*. Norman: University of Oklahoma Press.

Wolff, Leon 1996 'Eastern Twists on Western Concepts: Equality Jurisprudence and Sexual Harassment in Japan', *Pacific Rim Law and Policy Journal* 5: 509–35.

Wollstonecraft, Mary 1995 *A Vindication of the Rights of Men and a Vindication of the Rights of Woman* (edited by S. Tomaselli). Cambridge: Cambridge University Press.

Wood, James 1992 *History of International Broadcasting*. London: Peter Peregrinus.

Wood, Philip R. 1995 *International Loans, Bonds and Securities Regulation*. London: Sweet & Maxwell.

Wood, Philip R. 1997 *Maps of World Financial Law*. London: Allen & Overy.

Woodward, A. 1982 *Report of the Royal Commission into the Australian Meat Industry*. Canberra: Australian Government Publishing Service.

Wright, J. 1967 'The Federal Courts and the Nature and Quality of State Law', *Wayne Law Review* 13: 317.

Wright, Robert Alderson, Baron, 1939 'Introduction', to Philip Warren Thayer *Cases and Materials in the Law Merchant*. Cambridge, Mass.: Harvard University Press.

Wymeersch, Eddy (ed.) 1994 *Further Perspectives in Financial Integration in Europe*. Berlin: Walter de Gruyter.

Wynter, Marie 1997 'The Agreement on Sanitary and Phytosanitary Measures in Light of the WTO Decisions on EC Measures Concerning Meat and Meat Products (Hormones)', *Report to Hague Academy of International Law*.

Wynter, Marie 1998a 'The Compatibility of Trade and Environmental Concerns: Lessons from the Shrimp–Turtle Dispute', International Conference on International Environmental Law: Market Mechanisms and Environmental Justice, Auckland University.

Wynter, Marie 1998b 'Countervailing Environmental Subsidies in our World Trade Order', in L. Elliott (ed.) *Proceedings of the 10th Ecopolitics Conference*, Canberra, Ecopolitics Association of Australasia. 429–39.

Xavier, Patrick 1995 'Price Cap Regulation for Telecommunications', *Telecommunications Policy* 19: 599–617.

Yarbrough, Beth V. & Robert M. Yarbrough 1992 *Cooperation and Governance in International Trade*. Princeton, NJ: Princeton University Press.

Yeatman, A. 1990 *Bureaucrats, Technocrats and Femocrats*. Sydney: Allen & Unwin.

Yelpaala, Kojo 1984 'The Efficacy of Tax Incentives within the Framework of the Neoclassical Theory of Foreign Direct Investment: A Legislative Policy Analysis', *Texas International Law Journal* 19: 365–414.

Young, Oran 1979 *Compliance and Public Authority: A Theory with International Implications*. Baltimore: Published for Resources for the Future by Johns Hopkins University Press.

Young, Oran R. 1989 'The Politics of International Regime Formation: Managing Natural Resources and the Environment', *International Organization* 43: 349–75.

Young, Oran R. & Gail Osherenko (eds) 1993 *Polar Politics: Creating International Environmental Regimes*. London: Cornell University Press.

Zacher, Mark W. with Brent A. Sutton 1996 *Governing Global Networks: International Regimes for Transportation and Communications*. Cambridge: Cambridge University Press.

Zamora, Stephen 1980 'Voting in International Economic Organizations', *American Journal of International Law* 74: 566–608.

Ziegler, P. 1988 *The Sixth Great Power: Barings 1762–1929*. London: Collins.

Zweigert, Konrad & Hein Kotz 1987 *Introduction to Comparative Law, Vol. I* (translated by Tony Weir). Oxford: Clarendon Press.

# Index